Entertainment Law
and Practice

Entertainment Law and Practice

SECOND EDITION

Jon M. Garon
DEAN AND PROFESSOR OF LAW
NOVA SOUTHEASTERN UNIVERSITY
SHEPARD BROAD LAW CENTER

CAROLINA ACADEMIC PRESS
Durham, North Carolina

ISBN 978-1-61163-464-8
LCCN 2014935108

Carolina Academic Press
700 Kent Street
Durham, North Carolina 27701
Telephone (919) 489-7486
Fax (919) 493-5668
www.cap-press.com

Printed in the United States of America

For my family
Avery, Alec Sasha (z"l), Noah,
and Stacy Blumberg Garon.

Summary of Contents

Contents

Table of Principal Cases

Preface to the Second Edition

Although I have endeavored to update the first edition of *Entertainment Law and Practice* every other year with a supplement, technological change and court decisions required that I publish a new edition of the casebook itself. In industries such as publishing, the central debates challenging the industry a decade ago have been entirely replaced as new economic realities reshape the relationships within the industry. The casebook also has a great many more Supreme Court decisions than the prior edition because the concerns of the entertainment industries have become profound enough to warrant the time of the Court.

From a substantive law perspective, copyright has undergone the greatest transformation in the past decade. Once a primarily commercial body of law involving disputes between creators and distributors of content, or on rare occasion a dispute between copyright industries and commercial industries which utilized copyrighted works, most of the new cases reproduced in the second edition focus on consumers and the public rather than commercial defendants. This change in the role of the law may explain a good deal about how the entertainment industries have been transformed in the past decade.

The transformation is well underway, but still has miles to go. As these changes affect the lives of more and more individuals, the concerns covered in the casebook will increasingly become the focus of public debate. I hope the second edition provides a helpful tool to facilitate that debate in a thoughtful, well-informed manner. Entertainment has always been fun. Today it is more important than ever.

All questions, comments, and inquiries should be directed to me, Jon M. Garon, Dean and Professor of Law, Nova Southeastern University Shepard Broad Law Center, at phone number 954-262-6101 or garon@nova.edu.

Jon M. Garon, editor
Ft. Lauderdale, FL

Preface to the First Edition

In choosing to write, publish, adopt, or study a casebook, the threshold question to be answered is Why this book? The editorial structure of this casebook is an extension of my work attempting to demonstrate that entertainment law is more than a series of generally applicable laws that can be applied to the fun and exciting world of entertainers. Entertainment law has evolved into a discrete body of law whereby other legal doctrines take on unique interpretations. (See Jon M. Garon, *Entertainment Law*, 76 Tulane L. Rev. 559 (2002).) Broad areas of law such as copyright, privacy, and free speech have been transformed by or translated through the entertainment industries. This casebook reflects more of the unified or thematic approach to entertainment law than others previously published.

The unified approach to entertainment, however, does not tell the complete story. There are other areas of entertainment practice that are governed by laws specifically written to regulate these industries. There are also historical practices—some centuries old—that dictate the relationships between parties and the structure of the industry. In many situations, these practices bear no relation to entertainment as a whole, but instead focus on practices highly concentrated on one particular industry, such as professional theatre, music publishing, or commercial film. As a result, the practice of entertainment is an equally important aspect of study for any serious student of entertainment law.

The law and practice sections of the book reflect the broad dichotomy between those areas where entertainment has reshaped general law and those areas where the entertainment practice is specific to a particular industry or industries. Admittedly, this dichotomy may sometimes be subtle or artificial. The organization is my preferred structure, but each subchapter stands as a complete module, so that each instructor may design the course to fit his or her pedagogy and objectives.

The thematic structure of the casebook may help to explain why the topics covered are sometimes quite different than other books on the topic. One example may help illustrate the approach. Every entertainment law casebook has some discussion of trademark principles and how these concepts apply to film titles and professional credits. This book also includes a specific review of trademark analysis and partnership law as it applies to the ownership of a band's name. Although this topic is central to practitioners' texts and arguably the most valuable asset owned by a musical performer, the unique intersection of trademark, publicity, free speech and partnership law has not previously been addressed in any of the commercially available casebooks.

Useful teaching materials are more likely to come from those developed in the classroom than those created in isolation, and I have been very fortunate to have built this casebook over time as my students worked through the materials selected and provided me with feedback and insight. When teaching Entertainment Law or either of my breakout courses, Law of Motion Pictures and the Performing Arts and Music Management &

Licensing, my teaching objectives are to develop the students' problem-solving skills using issues related to the entertainment industry and business planning; to familiarize students with the intellectual property rights and contractual relationships between the media producers, distributors and authors in these industries and to introduce the deal-making aspects of practice in the entertainment industry; and to track the legal and business structure of the entertainment industries.

The included notes, questions, and problems help focus the reading on the problem solving skills of the students. To this end, some materials are included to illustrate tensions in the law and limitations imposed by legal rules, collective bargaining restrictions, or practical consequences. Other materials simply illustrate industry practice. In addition, the range of cases promotes traditional critical reading and reasoning skills.

Depending on the course hours available, many professors may elect to assign less than the entire text. Part I can be considered sufficient to teach an entire survey course. Alternatively, selected sections of Part II can be integrated with Part I to focus on music, film, television, or theatre, depending on the interests of the course and the instructor.

The entertainment industries rely heavily on copyright, trademark, First Amendment, antitrust, labor law, and telecommunications law. The casebook provides introductions to explain the relevant principles in the context of entertainment law. Questions, hypotheticals, notes, statutes, and historical materials provide a robust context in which to explore the entertainment industries and develop a sophisticated understanding of these critically important and highly complex materials.

Each subchapter provides sufficient context that it can be read without regard to the chapter as a whole. Helpful historical cases and materials are typically left to the notes so that the student can identify the current law or practice instead of tracking the growth of a doctrine or custom through voluminous reading.

Each chapter has a bibliography focused on the general themes of the chapter. Most sections have notes and questions that help focus and refine the topics under consideration. In addition, most sections have a problem—always focused on Bryce, the client who comes to students for advice throughout the book. As Bryce's career moves through the various entertainment fields and chapters of the book, Bryce's concerns become more sophisticated, creating an opportunity to integrate the topics being explored. These problems move beyond the materials of the section, often highlighting the intersection of various themes in the book and serving as potential research topics or areas for further study.

To make the student assignments manageable in length, it is necessary to heavily shorten most of the materials. Deletions of textual material are generally noted with ellipses (...), except for footnotes and citations, which are not noted. In addition, some central footnotes have been moved directly into the text where the note would otherwise have been placed. The remaining footnotes are renumbered. Insertions and any editorial changes are placed in brackets ([ ]). Where necessary, paragraph breaks have also been added or deleted without notation.

Finally, I have endeavored to edit the cases in a manner that allows the students to see the interrelation between multiple causes of action. Many cases involve a copyright, trademark, unfair competition, and publicity rights cause of action for the same alleged misconduct. The First Amendment is sometimes invoked as a defense to all of these. As a result, fewer but longer cases may better inform students regarding the relationship between the doctrinal legal boxes taught elsewhere. I have attempted to keep the book capable of longer or shorter reading assignments to provide flexibility for instructors who seek to emphasize some topics, but not others.

Like any casebook, particularly one where the area of law and practice is in such a state of transformation, the book is constantly evolving. I appreciate all feedback and suggestions.

Jon M. Garon, editor
jgaron@hamline.edu
St. Paul, MN 2004

Acknowledgments

This book has been a continual outgrowth of my practice and academic work in the area of entertainment law. I have benefited from the assistance of colleagues at each of the four law schools where parts of this work were developed: Western State University College of Law, Franklin Pierce Law Center (now University of New Hampshire School of Law), Hamline University School of Law, and Northern Kentucky University Salmon P. Chase College of Law. Among my colleagues who assisted, I would like to thank Maryann Jones, Susan Richey, Sophie Sparrow, Tom Field, Larry Bakken, Carol Swanson, Dennis Honabach, and Kevin Kirby. I also appreciate the assistance of attorneys with whom I have worked at the firms of Hawes & Fisher and Gallagher, Callahan, & Gartrell.

My thanks go out to Stacy Blumberg Garon for her editing on this book and many of my articles, Luke (Walter) Bubenzer who has worked on the second edition of the casebook as well as the 2012 Supplement, Matthew Ryan for his work on the second edition, and Jacqueline A. Olson, my research assistant on the 2010 supplement. I also wish to thank Lindsey Jaeger and Laurie Darwish, who have worked extensively with me at the NKU Chase Law + Informatics Institute and who have made it possible for me to complete this edition. Finally, I wish to recognize my research assistant Marissa Duquette at my newest professional home, Nova Southeastern University Shepard Broad Law Center.

I must also acknowledge the reliance I have made on the casebooks I have used throughout my teaching as models and guides for this book. Robert Gorman and Jane Ginsburg, *Copyright Cases and Materials*, and Eugene Volokh, *The First Amendment—Law, Cases, Problems, and Policy Arguments*, both served as models for me in determining what should be included and omitted from this book.

From the first edition, I would like to recognize the assistance provided by Ed Kroening, my old friend and editor at that time; by Carol Swanson, my Associate Dean for Academic Affairs at Hamline; and to Hamline Law Students Shelley Ryan, Corinna Venters, Amanda Leonhardt, Kristin Luckenbill, Chris Viloria, and Chris Rogers, for their assistance with editing, proofing, and adjusting the text. Of course, all responsibility for the content is solely my own.

About the Author

Jon Garon is the dean of Nova Southeastern University Shepard Broad Law Center, serving as chief academic officer for the law school, providing strategic leadership on programming, curriculum, enrollment management, marketing, and finance. He is a nationally recognized authority on technology law and intellectual property, particularly copyright law, entertainment and information privacy. A Minnesota native, he received his bachelor's degree from the University of Minnesota in 1985 and his juris doctor degree from Columbia University School of Law in 1988.

Prior to joining Nova Southeastern University, Dean Garon was the inaugural director of the Northern Kentucky University Salmon P. Chase College of Law, Law + Informatics Institute. Dean Garon served as dean and professor of law at Hamline University School of Law in St. Paul, Minnesota. He was professor of law from 2003–2011, Dean of the Law School from 2003–2008 and Interim Dean of the Graduate School of Management in 2005–06. Before Hamline, Dean Garon taught Entertainment Law and Copyright at Franklin Pierce Law Center in Concord, New Hampshire and Western State University College of Law in Orange County, California.

Among his publications on intellectual property, Dean Garon has written the following books, book chapters and law review articles:

Books

Author, ENTERTAINMENT LAW & PRACTICE (Carolina Academic Press Second Edition 2014).

Author, THE INDEPENDENT FILMMAKER'S LAW & BUSINESS GUIDE — FINANCING, SHOOTING, AND DISTRIBUTING INDEPENDENT AND DIGITAL FILMS (Second Edition, A Cappella Books/Chicago Review Press, June 2009) (First Edition 2002).

Author, OWN IT — THE LAW & BUSINESS GUIDE TO LAUNCHING A NEW BUSINESS THROUGH INNOVATION, EXCLUSIVITY AND RELEVANCE (Carolina Academic Press, September 2007).

Book Chapters

Author, *Copyright at the Crossroads of Commerce, Culture and Creativity*, in ESTUDOS AVANÇADOS EM DIREITO DE AUTOR (*COPYRIGHT ADVANCED STUDIES*) (Leonardo Machado Pontes, ed., Elsevier 2014).

Author, *The Band—Artistic, legal and financial structures which shape modern music*, in MUSIC AND LAW (Mathieu Deflem ed., Emerald Group Publishing 2013).

Author, *Legal Issues for Database Protection in the US and Abroad*, in Bioinformatics Law: Legal Issues for Computational Biology in the Post-Genome Era (Jorge Contreras ed., American Bar Association 2013).

Author, *Copyright, Trademark, Trade Secret and Publicity Rights Concerns*, in Emerging Legal Issues in RFID and Other Contactless Data Exchange Systems: What Lawyers Should Know (Sarah Jane Hughes ed., American Bar Association 2012).

Author, *Localism as a Production Imperative: An Alternative Framework for Promoting, Intangible Cultural Heritage*, in Transnational Culture in the Internet Age (Sean A. Pager & Adam Candeub eds., Elgar Publishing 2012).

Author, *Google, Fairness and the Battle of the Books*, in The 2010 IP Book (Midwest Intellectual Property Institute 2010).

Contributor, Annual Review of Intellectual Property Law Developments 2006–2008 (George Jordan ed., ABA Section of Intellectual Property Law 2009).

Contributor, Theater Law: Cases and Materials (Robert Jarvis, *et al.*, Carolina Academic Press, July 2004) (with Teacher's Manual).

Law Review Articles

Article, *Commercializing the Digital Canvas: Renewing Rights of Attribution for Artists in the Networked Economy*, 1 Tex. A&M Law. Rev. ___ (2014) (forthcoming).

Article, *To Promote the Progress: Incentives, Exclusives, and Values to Build a more Perfect Creative Culture*, 40 Ohio N. L. Rev. ___ (2014) (forthcoming).

Article, *Tidying up the Internet: Take Down of Unauthorized Content under Copyright, Trademark and Defamation Law*, 41 Capital U. L. Rev. 513 (2013).

Article, *Digital Hollywood2.0: Reimagining Film, Music, Television and Publishing Distribution as a Global Artist Collaborative*, 21 Mich. St. Int'l L. Rev. 563 (2013).

Article, *Legal Education in Disruption: The Headwinds and Tailwinds of Technology*, 45 Conn. L. Rev. 1165 (2013).

Article, *Beyond the First Amendment: Shaping the Contours of Commercial Speech in Video Games, Virtual Worlds and Social Media*, 2012 Utah L. Rev. 607 (2012), *reprinted* Entertainment, Publishing and the Arts Handbook (West 2013).

Article, *Mortgaging the Meme: Financing and Managing Disruptive Innovation*, 10 Nw. J. Tech. & Intell. Prop. 441 (2012).

Article, *The Heart of the Deal: Intellectual Property Aspects in the Law & Business of Entertainment*, 17 J. Int. Prop. L. 443 (2012).

Article, *Revolutions and Expatriates: Social Networking, Ubiquitous Media and the Disintermediation of the State*, 11 J. Int. Bus. L. 293 (2012).

Article, *Technology Requires Reboot of Professionalism and Ethics for Practitioners*, 16 J. Internet L. 3 (2012).

Article (Co-authored with Elaine Ziff), *The Work for Hire Doctrine Revisited: Startup and Technology Employees and the Use of Contracts in a Hiring Relationship*, 12 Minn. J.L. Sci. & Tech. 489 (2011) (republished 2012 Intellectual Property Law Review (Thomson Reuters)).

Article, *Content, Control and the Socially Networked Film*, 48 U. LOUISVILLE L. REV. 771 (2010), *reprinted* ENTERTAINMENT, PUBLISHING AND THE ARTS HANDBOOK (West 2011).

Article, *Searching Inside Google: Cases, Controversies and the Future of the World's Most Provocative Company*, 30 LOYOLA L.A. ENT. L. REV. 429 (2010).

Article, *The Implications of Informatics on Data Policy*, 1 MEDIA L. REV. 16 (2010) (NALSAR University of Law, Hyderabad, India).

Article, *Wiki Authorship, Social Media and the Curatorial Audience*, 1 HARV. J. SPORTS & ENT. L. 95 (2010).

Article, *Reintermediation*, 2 INT. J. OF PRIVATE LAW 227 (2009) (republished in SYNERGIES AND CONFLICTS IN CYBERLAW (2008) (Sylvia Kierkegaard, Ed.).

Article, *Playing in the Virtual Arena: Avatars, Publicity and Identity Reconceptualized through Virtual Worlds and Computer Games*, 11 CHAPMAN L. REV. 465 (2008).

Article, *What if DRM Fails?: Seeking Patronage in the iWasteland and the Virtual O*, 2008 MICH. STATE L. REV. 103 (2008).

Article, *To Make a Difference: Dean as Producer*, 39 U. TOL. L. REV. 297 (2008).

Article, *Take Back the Night: Why an Association of Regional Law Schools will Return Core Values to Legal Education and Provide an Alternative to Tiered Rankings*, 38 U. TOL. L. REV. 517 (2007).

Article, *Acquiring and Managing Identity Interests*, 1 FLA. ENT. L. REV. 39 (2006).

Article, *Normative Copyright*: *A Conceptual Framework for Copyright Philosophy & Ethics*, 88 CORNELL L. REV. 101 (2003).

Article, *Entertainment Law*, 76 TULANE L. REV. 559 (2002).

Article, *The Electronic Jungle: The Application of Intellectual Property Law to Distance Education*, 4 VAND. J. ENT. L. & PRAC. 146 (2002).

Article, *Media and Monopoly in the Information Age: Slowing the Convergence at the Marketplace of Ideas*, 17 CARDOZO ARTS & ENT. L.J. 491 (1999).

Article, *Star Wars: Film Permitting, Prior Restraint and Government's Role in the Entertainment Industry*, 17 LOYOLA ENTERTAINMENT L.J. 1 (1996). Reprinted, ROBERT THORNE & JOHN DAVID VIERA, ED., ENTERTAINMENT, PUBLISHING & THE ARTS HANDBOOK, 1997–1998 EDITION (West Group 1997).

Article, *Charity Begins at Home: Alternatives in Nonprofit Regulation*, 2 W. ST. U. CONSUMER L.J. 1 (1993).

Note, *The Director's Choice: The Fine Line Between Interpretation and Infringement of an Author's Work*, 12 COLUM.-VLA J.L. & ARTS 277 (1988).

Part I
Legal Issues in the Entertainment Industries

Chapter I

The Nature of Entertainment Law

A. Overview

Entertainment law covers the legal disciplines of copyright, publicity, privacy, trademark law, antitrust, contracts, First Amendment, and labor law. The creative content industries have trade, custom, usage, and other unique attributes that make the practice of entertainment law unique, even for those who practice within a single doctrinal discipline within a particular industry.

The cases below are designed to introduce the sweep of Supreme Court jurisprudence with regard to Entertainment Law. In 1911, in *Kalem Company v. Harper Brothers*, the Court first recognized the potential for a silent film to infringe the copyright in a written book, carrying forward a line of cases in which each new entertainment medium had been incorporated into the sweep of legal protection. In *Joseph Burstyn, Inc. v. Wilson*, the Court acknowledged for the first time that motion picture licensing has First Amendment implications. Finally, in *Zacchini v. Scripps-Howard Broadcasting Co.*, the Court addressed the right of an entertainer to have a publicity interest in his performance. In each case, the Court articulates its own history of struggling with the role of entertainment against the concepts of copyright, free speech, and privacy law—the areas most systemically changed by the influences of the entertainment industry.

Kalem Company v. Harper Brothers
222 U.S. 55 (1911)

MR. JUSTICE HOLMES delivered the opinion of the court.

This is an appeal from a decree restraining an alleged infringement of the copyright upon the late General Lew Wallace's book 'Ben Hur.' The case was heard on the pleadings and an agreed statement of facts, and the only issue is whether those facts constitute an infringement of the copyright upon the book....

[T]he question that has the most general importance is whether the public exhibition of these moving pictures infringed any rights under the copyright law. As amended by the act of March 3, 1891, authors have the exclusive right to dramatize any of their works. So, if the exhibition was or was founded on a dramatizing of Ben Hur this copyright was infringed. We are of opinion that Ben Hur was dramatized by what was done. Whether we consider the purpose of this clause of the statute, or the etymological history and present usages of language, drama may be achieved by action as well as by speech. Action can tell a story, display all the most vivid relations between men, and depict every kind of human emotion, without the aid of a word. It would be impossible to deny the title of drama to pantomime as played by masters of the art. But if a pantomime of Ben Hur would be a dramatizing of Ben Hur, it would be none the less so that it was exhibited to the audience by reflection from a glass and not by direct vision of the figures—as sometimes has been done in order to produce ghostly or inexplicable effects. The essence of the matter in the case last supposed is not the mechanism employed but that we see the event or story lived. The moving pictures are only less vivid than reflections from a mirror. With the former as with the latter our visual impression—what we see—is caused by the real pantomime of real men through the medium of natural forces, although the machinery is different and more complex. How it would be if the illusion of motion were produced from paintings instead of from photographs of the real thing may be left open until the question shall arise.

It is said that pictures of scenes in a novel may be made and exhibited without infringing the copyright and that they may be copyrighted themselves. Indeed it was conceded by the Circuit Court of Appeals that these films could be copyrighted and, we may assume, could be exhibited as photographs. Whether this concession is correct or not, in view of the fact that they are photographs of an unlawful dramatization of the novel, we need not decide. We will assume that it is. But it does not follow that the use of them in motion does not infringe the author's rights. The most innocent objects, such as the mirror in the other case that we have supposed, may be used for unlawful purposes. And if, as we have tried to show, moving pictures may be used for dramatizing a novel, when the photographs are used in that way they are used to infringe a right which the statute reserves.

But again it is said that the defendant did not produce the representations, but merely sold the films to jobbers, and on that ground ought not to be held. In some cases where an ordinary article of commerce is sold nice questions may arise as to the point at which the seller becomes an accomplice in a subsequent illegal use by the buyer. It has been held that mere indifferent supposition or knowledge on the part of the seller that the buyer of spirituous liquor is contemplating such unlawful use is not enough to connect him with the possible unlawful consequences, was made with a view to the illegal resale the price could not be recovered. But no such niceties are involved here. The defendant not only expected but invoked by advertisement the use of its films for dramatic reproduction of the story. That was the most conspicuous purpose for which they could be used, and the one for which especially they were made. If the defendant did not contribute to the infringement, it is impossible to do so except by taking part in the final act. It is liable on principles recognized in every part of the law.

It is argued that the law construed as we have construed it goes beyond the power conferred upon Congress by the Constitution, to secure to authors for a limited time the exclusive right to their writings. Art. I, § 8, cl. 8. It is suggested that to extend the copyright to a case like this is to extend it to the ideas as distinguished from the words in which those ideas are clothed. But there is no attempt to make a monopoly of the ideas expressed. The law confines itself to a particular, cognate and well known form of reproduction. If to that extent a grant of monopoly is thought a proper way to secure the right to the writings this court cannot say that Congress was wrong. Decree affirmed.

Joseph Burstyn, Inc. v. Wilson

343 U.S. 495 (1952)

MR. JUSTICE CLARK delivered the opinion of the Court.

The issue here is the constitutionality, under the First and Fourteenth Amendments, of a New York statute which permits the banning of motion picture films on the ground that they are "sacrilegious." That statute makes it unlawful "to exhibit, or to sell, lease or lend for exhibition at any place of amusement for pay or in connection with any business in the state of New York, any motion picture film or reel [with specified exceptions not relevant here], unless there is at the time in full force and effect a valid license or permit therefore of the education department...." The statute further provides:

> The director of the [motion picture] division [of the education department] or, when authorized by the regents, the officers of a local office or bureau shall cause to be promptly examined every motion picture film submitted to them as herein required, and unless such film or a part thereof is obscene, indecent, immoral, inhuman, sacrilegious, or is of such a character that its exhibition would tend to corrupt morals or incite to crime, shall issue a license therefore. If such director or, when so authorized, such officer shall not license any film submitted, he shall furnish to the applicant therefore a written report of the reasons for his refusal and a description of each rejected part of a film not rejected in toto.

Appellant is a corporation engaged in the business of distributing motion pictures. It owns the exclusive rights to distribute throughout the United States a film produced in Italy entitled "The Miracle." On November 30, 1950, after having examined the picture, the motion picture division of the New York education department, acting under the statute quoted above, issued to appellant a license authorizing exhibition of "The Miracle," with English subtitles, as one part of a trilogy called "Ways of Love." Thereafter, for a period of approximately eight weeks, "Ways of Love" was exhibited publicly in a motion picture theater in New York City under an agreement between appellant and the owner of the theater whereby appellant received a stated percentage of the admission price.

During this period, the New York State Board of Regents, which by statute is made the head of the education department, received "hundreds of letters, telegrams, post cards, affidavits and other communications" both protesting against and defending the public exhibition of "The Miracle." The Chancellor of the Board of Regents requested three members of the Board to view the picture and to make a report to the entire Board. After viewing the film, this committee reported to the Board that in its opinion there was basis for the claim that the picture was "sacrilegious." Thereafter, on January 19, 1951, the Regents directed appellant to show cause, at a hearing to be held on January 30, why its license to show "The Miracle" should not be rescinded on that ground. Appellant appeared at this hearing, which was conducted by the same three-member committee of the Regents which had previously viewed the picture, and challenged the jurisdiction of the committee and of the Regents to proceed with the case. With the consent of the committee, various interested persons and organizations submitted to it briefs and exhibits bearing upon the merits of the picture and upon the constitutional and statutory questions involved. On February 16, 1951, the Regents, after viewing "The Miracle," determined that it was "sacrilegious" and for that reason ordered the Commissioner of Education to rescind appellant's license to exhibit the picture. The Commissioner did so.

Appellant brought the present action in the New York courts to review the determination of the Regents. Among the claims advanced by appellant were (1) that the statute violates the Fourteenth Amendment as a prior restraint upon freedom of speech and of the press; (2) that it is invalid under the same Amendment as a violation of the guaranty of separate church and state and as a prohibition of the free exercise of religion; and, (3) that the term "sacrilegious" is so vague and indefinite as to offend due process. The Appellate Division rejected all of appellant's contentions and upheld the Regents' determination. On appeal the New York Court of Appeals, two judges dissenting, affirmed the order of the Appellate Division.

As we view the case, we need consider only appellant's contention that the New York statute is an unconstitutional abridgment of free speech and a free press. In *Mutual Film Corp. v. Industrial Comm'n,* 236 U.S. 230 (1915), a distributor of motion pictures sought to enjoin the enforcement of an Ohio statute which required the prior approval of a board of censors before any motion picture could be publicly exhibited in the state, and which directed the board to approve only such films as it adjudged to be "of a moral, educational or amusing and harmless character." The statute was assailed in part as an unconstitutional abridgment of the freedom of the press guaranteed by the First and Fourteenth Amendments. The District Court rejected this contention, stating that the first eight Amendments were not a restriction on state action. On appeal to this Court, plaintiff in its brief abandoned this claim and contended merely that the statute in question violated the freedom of speech and publication guaranteed by the Constitution of Ohio. In affirming the decree of the District Court denying injunctive relief, this Court stated:

> It cannot be put out of view that the exhibition of moving pictures is a business pure and simple, originated and conducted for profit, like other spectacles, not to be regarded, nor intended to be regarded by the Ohio constitution, we think, as part of the press of the country or as organs of public opinion....

It cannot be doubted that motion pictures are a significant medium for the communication of ideas. They may affect public attitudes and behavior in a variety of ways, ranging from direct espousal of a political or social doctrine to the subtle shaping of thought which characterizes all artistic expression. The importance of motion pictures as an organ of public opinion is not lessened by the fact that they are designed to entertain as well as to inform. As was said in *Winters v. New York,* 333 U.S. 507, 510 (1948):

> The line between the informing and the entertaining is too elusive for the protection of that basic right [a free press]. Everyone is familiar with instances of propaganda through fiction. What is one man's amusement, teaches another's doctrine.

It is urged that motion pictures do not fall within the First Amendment's aegis because their production, distribution, and exhibition is a large-scale business conducted for private profit. We cannot agree. That books, newspapers, and magazines are published and sold for profit does not prevent them from being a form of expression whose liberty is safeguarded by the First Amendment. We fail to see why operation for profit should have any different effect in the case of motion pictures.

It is further urged that motion pictures possess a greater capacity for evil, particularly among the youth of a community, than other modes of expression. Even if one were to accept this hypothesis, it does not follow that motion pictures should be disqualified from First Amendment protection. If there be capacity for evil it may be relevant in determining the permissible scope of community control, but it does not authorize substantially unbridled censorship such as we have here. For the foregoing reasons, we conclude that expression by means of motion pictures is included within the free speech and free press guaranty of the First and Fourteenth Amendments. To the extent that language in the opinion in *Mutual Film Corp.* v. *Industrial Comm'n, supra,* is out of harmony with the views here set forth, we no longer adhere to it. To hold that liberty of expression by means of motion pictures is guaranteed by the First and Fourteenth Amendments, however, is not the end of our problem. It does not follow that the Constitution requires absolute freedom to exhibit every motion picture of every kind at all times and all places. That much is evident from the series of decisions of this Court with respect to other media of communication of ideas. Nor does it follow that motion pictures are necessarily subject to the precise rules governing any other particular method of expression. Each method tends to present its own peculiar problems. But the basic principles of freedom of speech and the press, like the First Amendment's command, do not vary. Those principles, as they have frequently been enunciated by this Court, make freedom of expression the rule. There is no justification in this case for making an exception to that rule.

The statute involved here does not seek to punish, as a past offense, speech or writing falling within the permissible scope of subsequent punishment. On the contrary, New York requires that permission to communicate ideas be obtained in advance from state officials who judge the content of the words and pictures sought to be communicated. This Court recognized many years ago that such a previous restraint is a form of infringement upon freedom of expression to be especially condemned. *Near v. Minnesota ex rel. Olson,* 283 U.S. 697 (1931). The Court there recounted the history which indicates that a major purpose of the First Amendment guaranty of a free press was to prevent prior restraints upon publication, although it was carefully pointed out that the liberty of the press is not limited to that protection. It was further stated that "the protection even as to previous restraint is not absolutely unlimited. But the limitation has been recognized only in exceptional cases." In the light of the First Amendment's history and of the *Near* decision, the State has a heavy burden to demonstrate that the limitation challenged here presents such an exceptional case.

New York's highest court says there is "nothing mysterious" about the statutory provision applied in this case: "It is simply this: that no religion, as that word is understood by the ordinary, reasonable person, shall be treated with contempt, mockery, scorn and ridicule...." This is far from the kind of narrow exception to freedom of expression which a state may carve out to satisfy the adverse demands of other interests of society.... Since the term "sacrilegious" is the sole standard under attack here, it is not necessary for us to decide, for example, whether a state may censor motion pictures under a clearly drawn statute designed and applied to prevent the showing of obscene films. That is a very different question from the one now before us. We hold only that under the First and Fourteenth Amendments a state may not ban a film on the basis of a censor's conclusion that it is "sacrilegious."

Reversed.

Zacchini v. Scripps-Howard Broadcasting Co.
433 U.S. 562 (1977)

MR. JUSTICE WHITE delivered the opinion of the Court.

Petitioner, Hugo Zacchini, is an entertainer. He performs a "human cannonball" act in which he is shot from a cannon into a net some 200 feet away. Each performance occupies some 15 seconds. In August and September 1972, petitioner was engaged to perform his act on a regular basis at the Geauga County Fair in Burton, Ohio. He performed in a fenced area, surrounded by grandstands, at the fair grounds. Members of the public attending the fair were not charged a separate admission fee to observe his act.

On August 30, a free-lance reporter for Scripps-Howard Broadcasting Co., the operator of a television broadcasting station and respondent in this case, attended the fair. He carried a small movie camera. Petitioner noticed the reporter and asked him not to film the performance. The reporter did not do so on that day; but on the instructions of the producer of respondent's daily newscast, he returned the following day and videotaped the entire act. This film clip, approximately 15 seconds in length, was shown on the 11 o'clock news program that night, together with favorable commentary.

Petitioner then brought this action for damages, alleging that he is "engaged in the entertainment business," that the act he performs is one "invented by his father and ... performed only by his family for the last fifty years," that respondent "showed and commercialized the film of his act without his consent," and that such conduct was an "unlawful appropriation of plaintiff's professional property." Respondent answered and moved for summary judgment, which was granted by the trial court.

The Court of Appeals of Ohio reversed. The majority held that petitioner's complaint stated a cause of action for conversion and for infringement of a common-law copyright, and one judge concurred in the judgment on the ground that the complaint stated a cause of action for appropriation of petitioner's "right of publicity" in the film of his act. All three judges agreed that the First Amendment did not privilege the press to show the entire performance on a news program without compensating petitioner for any financial injury he could prove at trial.

Like the concurring judge in the Court of Appeals, the Supreme Court of Ohio rested petitioner's cause of action under state law on his "right to publicity value of his performance." The opinion syllabus, to which we are to look for the rule of law used to decide the case, declared first that one may not use for his own benefit the name or likeness of another, whether or not the use or benefit is a commercial one, and second that respondent would be liable for the appropriation, over petitioner's objection and in the absence of license or privilege, of petitioner's right to the publicity value of his performance. The court nevertheless gave judgment for respondent because, in the words of the syllabus:

> A TV station has a privilege to report in its newscasts matters of legitimate public interest which would otherwise be protected by an individual's right of publicity, unless the actual intent of the TV station was to appropriate the benefit of the publicity for some non-privileged private use, or unless the actual intent was to injure the individual.

We granted certiorari to consider an issue unresolved by this Court: whether the First and Fourteenth Amendments immunized respondent from damages for its alleged infringement of petitioner's state-law "right of publicity." Insofar as the Ohio Supreme Court held that the First and Fourteenth Amendments of the United States Constitution required judgment for respondent, we reverse the judgment of that court.

If the judgment below rested on an independent and adequate state ground, the writ of certiorari should be dismissed as improvidently granted, for "[o]ur only power over state judgments is to correct them to the extent that they incorrectly adjudge federal rights.... We are confident, however, that the judgment below did not rest on an adequate and independent state ground and that we have jurisdiction to decide the federal issue presented in this case.

There is no doubt that petitioner's complaint was grounded in state law and that the right of publicity which petitioner was held to possess was a right arising under Ohio law. It is also clear that respondent's claim of constitutional privilege was sustained. The source of this privilege was not identified in the syllabus. It is clear enough from the opinion of the Ohio Supreme Court, which we are permitted to consult for understanding of the syllabus, that in adjudicating the crucial question of whether respondent had a privilege to film and televise petitioner's performance, the court placed principal reliance on *Time, Inc. v. Hill,* 385 U.S. 374 (1967), a case involving First Amendment limitations on state tort actions. It construed the principle of that case, along with that of *New York Times Co. v. Sullivan,* 376 U.S. 254 (1964), to be that "the press has a privilege to report matters of legitimate public interest even though such reports might intrude on matters otherwise private," and concluded, therefore, that the press is also "privileged when an individual seeks to publicly exploit his talents while keeping the benefits private." The privilege thus exists in cases "where appropriation of a right of publicity is claimed." The court's opinion also referred to Draft 21 of the relevant portion of Restatement (Second) of Torts (1975), which was understood to make room for reasonable press appropriations by limiting the reach of the right of privacy rather than by creating a privileged invasion. The court preferred the notion of privilege over the Restatement's formulation, however, reasoning that "since the gravamen of the issue in this case is not whether the degree of intrusion is reasonable, but whether First Amendment principles require that the right of privacy give way to the public right to be informed of matters of public interest and concern, the concept of privilege seems the more useful and appropriate one." ...

The Ohio Supreme Court held that respondent is constitutionally privileged to include in its newscasts matters of public interest that would otherwise be protected by the right of publicity, absent an intent to injure or to appropriate for some non-privileged purpose. If under this standard respondent had merely reported that petitioner was performing at the fair and described or commented on his act, with or without showing his picture on television, we would have a very different case. But petitioner is not contending that his appearance at the fair and his performance could not be reported by the press as newsworthy items. His complaint is that respondent filmed his entire act and displayed that film on television for the public to see and enjoy. This, he claimed, was an appropriation of his professional property. The Ohio Supreme Court agreed that petitioner had "a right of publicity" that gave him "personal control over commercial display and exploitation of his personality and the exercise of his talents." This right of "exclusive control over the publicity given to his performances" was said to be such a "valuable part of the benefit which may be attained by his talents and efforts" that it was entitled to legal protection. It was also observed, or at least expressly assumed, that petitioner had not abandoned his rights by performing under the circumstances present at the Geauga County Fair Grounds.

The Ohio Supreme Court nevertheless held that the challenged invasion was privileged, saying that the press "must be accorded broad latitude in its choice of how much it presents of each story or incident, and of the emphasis to be given to such presentation. No fixed standard which would bar the press from reporting or depicting either an entire occurrence or an entire discrete part of a public performance can be formulated which would not unduly restrict the 'breathing room' in reporting which freedom of the press requires." Under this view, respondent was thus constitutionally free to film and display petitioner's entire act.

The Ohio Supreme Court relied heavily on *Time, Inc. v. Hill,* 385 U.S. 374 (1967), but that case does not mandate a media privilege to televise a performer's entire act without his consent....

The differences between these two torts are important. First, the State's interests in providing a cause of action in each instance are different. "The interest protected" in permitting recovery for placing the plaintiff in a false light "is clearly that of reputation, with the same overtones of mental distress as in defamation." By contrast, the State's interest in permitting a "right of publicity" is in protecting the proprietary interest of the individual in his act in part to encourage such entertainment. As we later note, the State's interest is closely analogous to the goals of patent and copyright law, focusing on the right of the individual to reap the reward of his endeavors and having little to do with protecting feelings or reputation. Second, the two torts differ in the degree to which they intrude on dissemination of information to the public. In "false light" cases the only way to protect the interests involved is to attempt to minimize publication of the damaging matter, while in "right of publicity" cases the only question is who gets to do the publishing. An entertainer such as petitioner usually has no objection to the widespread publication of his act as long as he gets the commercial benefit of such publication. Indeed, in the present case petitioner did not seek to enjoin the broadcast of his act; he simply sought compensation for the broadcast in the form of damages....

It is evident, and there is no claim here to the contrary, that petitioner's state-law right of publicity would not serve to prevent respondent from reporting the newsworthy facts about petitioner's act. Wherever the line in particular situations is to be drawn between media reports that are protected and those that are not, we are quite sure that the First and Fourteenth Amendments do not immunize the media when they broadcast a performer's entire act without his consent. The Constitution no more prevents a State from requiring respondent to compensate petitioner for broadcasting his act on television than it would privilege respondent to film and broadcast a copyrighted dramatic work without liability to the copyright owner, where the promoters or the participants had other plans for publicizing the event. There are ample reasons for reaching this conclusion.

The broadcast of a film of petitioner's entire act poses a substantial threat to the economic value of that performance. As the Ohio court recognized, this act is the product of petitioner's own talents and energy, the end result of much time, effort, and expense. Much of its economic value lies in the "right of exclusive control over the publicity given to his performance"; if the public can see the act free on television, it will be less willing to pay to see it at the fair. The effect of a public broadcast of the performance is similar to preventing petitioner from charging an admission fee. "The rationale for [protecting the right of publicity] is the straight-forward one of preventing unjust enrichment by the theft of good will. No social purpose is served by having the defendant get free some aspect of the plaintiff that would have market value and for which he would normally pay." Moreover, the broadcast of petitioner's entire performance, unlike the unauthorized use of another's name for purposes of trade or the incidental use of a name or picture by the press, goes to the heart of petitioner's ability to earn a living as an entertainer. Thus, in this case, Ohio has recognized what may be the strongest case for a "right of publicity" — involving, not the appropriation of an entertainer's reputation to enhance the attractiveness of a commercial product, but the appropriation of the very activity by which the entertainer acquired his reputation in the first place.

Of course, Ohio's decision to protect petitioner's right of publicity here rests on more than a desire to compensate the performer for the time and effort invested in his act; the protection provides an economic incentive for him to make the investment required to produce a performance of interest to the public.... There is no doubt that entertainment, as well as news, enjoys First Amendment protection. It is also true that entertainment itself can be important news. But it is important to note that neither the public nor respondent will be deprived of the benefit of petitioner's performance as long as his commercial stake in his act is appropriately recognized. Petitioner does not seek to enjoin the broadcast of his performance; he simply wants to be paid for it.... We conclude that although the State of Ohio may as a matter of its own law privilege the press in the circumstances of this case, the First and Fourteenth Amendments do not require it to do so.

Reversed.

Notes and Questions

a. The history of protection for entertainment media has been one of slow but realistic responses to technology and popular culture. Congress added musical compositions to copyright law in 1831. It added photographs in 1865, public performances of plays in 1868, and fine art (including painting, drawing, chromo, and statuary) in 1872. Fine art was ultimately determined to be a form of work rather than an aesthetic standard when the Supreme Court reversed lower court holdings and allowed copyright protection for a circus poster in *Bleistein v. Donaldson Lithographing Co.*, 188 U.S. 239 (1903).

In 1897, Congress added public performances of musical works to those defined as protected performances. This amendment captured the popularity of player pianos and introduction of the phonograph. Player piano rolls, however, received no copyright protection because they had no written notation. Congress extended the protection to the musical composer's work embodied in the phonorecord or piano roll in 1909, when it fundamentally revised the Copyright Act. Sound recordings, the phonorecord equivalents of the piano rolls, were not themselves federally protected by copyright until 1972. Limited protection for the digital performance of a sound recording was added in 1995.

b. Initially not protected by the First Amendment, film and theatrical licensing remained common throughout most of the twentieth century and residual issues remain today. This is true for anti-obscenity licensing schemes, use of public theatrical venues, and the intersection between First Amendment and intellectual property protections. This tension is explored for various media throughout the chapters of the book.

c. Today, the Supreme Court is very protective of First Amendment rights across all forms of entertainment. The most recent example features video games:

> California's effort to regulate violent video games is the latest episode in a long series of failed attempts to censor violent entertainment for minors. While we have pointed out above that some of the evidence brought forward to support the harmfulness of video games is unpersuasive, we do not mean to demean or disparage the concerns that underlie the attempt to regulate them—concerns that may and doubtless do prompt a good deal of parental oversight. We have no business passing judgment on the view of the California Legislature that violent video games (or, for that matter, any other forms of speech) corrupt the young or harm their moral development. Our task is only to say whether or not such works constitute a "well-defined and narrowly limited clas[s] of speech, the prevention and punishment of which have never been thought to raise any Constitutional problem," *Chaplinsky [v. New Hampshire,* 315 U.S. 568, 571–72 (1942)] (the answer plainly is no); and if not, whether the regulation of such works is justified by that high degree of necessity we have described as a compelling state interest (it is not). Even where the protection of children is the object, the constitutional limits on governmental action apply.
>
> California's legislation straddles the fence between (1) addressing a serious social problem and (2) helping concerned parents control their children. Both ends are legitimate, but when they affect First Amendment rights they must be pursued by means that are neither seriously underinclusive nor seriously overinclusive.

Brown v. Ent. Merchants Ass'n, ___ U.S. ___, 131 S. Ct. 2729, 2741–42 (2011).

d. Since 1992, Congress has been a much more active participant in the regulation and balancing of the competing interests in the entertainment industries, enacting more legislation affecting copyright, media, consumer electronics, and international trade than in any prior period in history. At the state level, many regulatory provisions exist that specifically regulate various aspects of the entertainment industry. These include the *New York Theatrical Syndication Financing Act, N.Y. Arts & Cult. Aff. Law 23.01 (McKinney 2006),* which regulates the financing of Broadway productions; family law, such as *Cal. Fam. Code § 6750 (Deering 2003),* protecting child performers from the unscrupulous or wasteful actions of their parents or financial guardians; talent agency licensing statutes, *Cal. Lab. Code §§ 1700–1700.47 (Deering 2003)*; or film permit ordinances, such as *Newport Beach, Cal. Mun. Ordinance ch. 5.46, 10 (2009).*

e. The First Amendment limitations sometimes take on interesting forms. To what extent can anti-counterfeiting laws prohibit the creation of movie-money to serve as real looking props for films? See *Regan v. Time, Inc.,* 468 U.S. 641 (1984).

f. Another of the rapidly changing areas for the entertainment industry is the convergence between commercial speech and marketing of products and services. Expansion of First Amendment protection for commercial speech has led to increasing conflict when names, photographs, or clips are used without the permission of the publicity rights owner, trademark owner, or copyright owner. As the California Supreme Court explained:

> Nor does the fact that expression takes a form of nonverbal, visual representation remove it from the ambit of First Amendment protection. In Bery v. City of New York, 97 F.3d 689 (2d Cir. 1996) the court overturned an ordinance requiring visual artists — painters, printers, photographers, sculptors, etc. — to obtain licenses to sell their work in public places, but exempted the vendors of books, newspapers or other written matter. As the court stated: "Both the [district] court and the City demonstrate an unduly restricted view of the First Amendment and of visual art itself. Such myopic vision not only overlooks case law central to First Amendment jurisprudence but fundamentally misperceives the essence of visual communication and artistic expression. Visual art is as wide ranging in its depiction of ideas, concepts and emotions as any book, treatise, pamphlet or other writing, and is similarly entitled to full First Amendment protection.... One cannot look at Winslow Homer's paintings on the Civil War without seeing, in his depictions of the boredom and hardship of the individual soldier, expressions of anti-war sentiments, the idea that war is not heroic."

Comedy III Prods., Inc. v. Gary Saderup, Inc., 25 Cal. 4th 387, 398–99, 21 P.3d 797, 804 (Cal. 2001).

g. In a new twist on the impact of cyberspace on First Amendment interests, the New Orleans municipal ordinance regulating street artists in the French Quarter limited vendor licenses to those who "manually paint, sketch or draw on plain surfaces only...." Artist Marc Trebert retouches digital photographs with pastels, in violation of the ordinance. With some incredulity, the court explained the New Orleans position: "The City argues that Trebert's digital photographs are not entitled to First Amendment protection because they are not 'art.'... The question is not whether plaintiff's work is art, but whether it is 'speech' within the protection of the First Amendment." Ignoring the "art" question, the court found the photographs to be speech and the ordinance to be inconsistent with the First Amendment. *Trebert v. City of New Orleans,* No. 04-1349, 2005 U.S. Dist. LEXIS 1560 (E.D. La. Feb. 1, 2005) (featured opinion in *infra* Chapter XVII).

B. Transactions in Ideas

1. Overview

Every new work begins with a single idea. The work of writers, directors, artists, musicians, producers, designers, and the many other professionals involved in the entertainment industry may be summarized simply as translating that idea into expression which can be enjoyed by audiences.

The subject matter clause of the Copyright Act of 1976 differentiates those works which have transformed from mere ideas into fully protected expressive works.

17 U.S.C. § 102. Subject matter of copyright: In general

(a) Copyright protection subsists, in accordance with this title, in original works of authorship fixed in any tangible medium of expression, now known or later developed, from which they can be perceived, reproduced, or otherwise communicated, either directly or with the aid of a machine or device. Works of authorship include the following categories:

(1) literary works;

(2) musical works, including any accompanying words;

(3) dramatic works, including any accompanying music;

(4) pantomimes and choreographic works;

(5) pictorial, graphic, and sculptural works;

(6) motion pictures and other audiovisual works;

(7) sound recordings; and

(8) architectural works.

(b) In no case does copyright protection for an original work of authorship extend to any idea, procedure, process, system, method of operation, concept, principle, or discovery, regardless of the form in which it is described, explained, illustrated, or embodied in such work.

In separating out the ideas from the copyrightable expression, copyright policy attempts to encourage multiple authors to explore themes and ideas. "Boy meets girl" plots, "war between the sexes" battles, "coming of age" stories, "spy thrillers," "buddy pictures," and other themes are the ideas that underlie each particular novel, lyric, play, or screenplay.

Nonetheless, while ideas may be too abstract to be protected by copyright, they still have particular economic value. The idea of a shark which terrorizes a local community gave rise to the valuable expression created by Peter Benchley in his novel *Jaws* and in Steven Spielberg's movie of the same name. Even the idea to translate an existing piece of expression from one medium to another may have value to a producer looking for the next hot project. Since copyright is unavailable to protect such interests, however, courts struggle to frame the legal rights available for the sale of such ideas.

2. Source of Ideas

Whether the medium is film, television, theatre, print, video games, or music, the first step for creating a literary work is to begin with the premise and slowly aggregate the necessary legal interests and technical skills essential to complete the work. Only once this is done can the work be exploited in the marketplace.

Most projects start with authorship. Authors include playwrights, novelists, journalists, composers, lyricists, film directors, and music producers, to name just a few. The combination of these skills results in a literary work, the first step in creating entertainment. On occasion, however, identifying the author is somewhat difficult.

> Who, in the absence of contract, can be considered an author of a movie? The word is traditionally used to mean the originator or the person who causes something to come into being, or even the first cause, as when Chaucer refers to the "Author of Nature." For a movie, that might be the producer who raises the money. Eisenstein thought the author of a movie was the editor. The "auteur" theory suggests that it might be the director, at least if the director is able to impose his artistic judgments on the film. Traditionally, by analogy to books, the author was regarded as the person who writes the screenplay, but often a movie reflects the work of many screenwriters. [Richard] Grenier suggests that the person with creative control tends to be the person in whose name the money is raised, perhaps a star, perhaps the director, perhaps the producer, with control gravitating to the star as the financial investment in scenes already shot grows.[1] Where the visual aspect of the movie is especially important, the chief cinematographer might be regarded as the author. And for, say, a Disney animated movie like "The Jungle Book," it might perhaps be the animators and the composers of the music....
>
> The Supreme Court dealt with the problem of defining "author" in new media in *Burrow-Giles Lithographic Co. v. Sarony,* [111 U.S. 53, 61 (1884)]. The question there was, who is the author of a photograph: the person who sets it up and snaps the shutter, or the person who makes the lithograph from it. Oscar Wilde, the person whose picture was at issue, doubtless offered some creative advice as well. The Court decided that the photographer was the author, quoting various English authorities: "the person who has superintended the arrangement, who has actually formed the picture by putting the persons in position, and arranging the place where the people are to be — the man who is the effective cause of that"; "'author' involves originating, making, producing, as the inventive or master mind, the thing which is to be protected"; "the man who really represents, creates, or gives effect to the idea, fancy, or imagination." The Court said that an "author," in the sense that the Founding Fathers used the term in the Constitution, was "'he to whom anything owes its origin; originator; maker; one who completes a work of science or literature.'"

Aalmuhammed v. Lee, 202 F.3d 1227, 1232 (9th Cir. 1999) (quoting *Burrow-Giles Lithographic Co. v. Sarony,* 111 U.S. 53, 61 (1884)).

The key distinction noted by the Ninth Circuit in *Aalmuhammed* is the difference between projects based on an agreement and those based on federal or state law. Contracts, collective bargaining agreements, and other binding arrangements allow the entertainment industries to operate smoothly despite legal doctrines that are often under-developed and stunningly at odds with the industry customs and trade they purport to regulate. Despite a long tradition of handshake agreements, the entertainment industry operates through written, oral, and implied agreements that do far more to regulate the daily business life than any other body of law. The law of the deal, therefore, is as important as any other legal doctrine.

---

1. *See* Richard Grenier, Capturing the Culture, 206–07 (1991).

Blaustein v. Burton

9 Cal. App. 3d 161, 88 Cal. Rptr. 319 (1970)

Plaintiff, on November 14, 1967, filed his complaint against the defendants Richard Burton, Elizabeth Taylor Burton, and Franco Zeffirelli, wherein he sought damages for (1) breach of contract, (2) unjust enrichment, (3) breach of confidential relationship and (4) services rendered and benefits conferred. Answer to the complaint was filed by the Burtons on January 16, 1968, and no other defendant was served or appeared in the action....

The functions of a producer of a motion picture are to (1) generate the enthusiasm of the various creative elements as well as to bring them together: (2) search out viable locations which would be proper for the artistic side of the production and would be proper from the logistic physical production side; (3) create a budget that would be acceptable from the physical point of view as well as satisfactory from the point of view of implementing the requirements of the script; (4) make arrangements with foreign government where the photography would take place; (5) supervise the execution of the script, the implementation of it onto film; (6) supervise the editing of all the production work down through the dubbing process and the release printing process, at least through the answer print process with Technicolor in this case; (7) the obligation of consulting with the United Artists people on advertising and publicity; (8) arrange casting; (9) engage the interests of the kind of star or stars that they (the United Artists' people) would find sufficiently attractive to justify an investment, and (10) develop the interest of a proper director.

During 1964, appellant conceived an idea consisting of a number of constituent elements including the following: (a) the idea of producing a motion picture based upon William Shakespeare's play "the Taming of the Shrew"; (b) the idea of casting respondents Richard Burton and Elizabeth Taylor Burton as the stars of this motion picture; (c) the idea of using as the director of the motion picture Franco Zeffirelli, a stage director, who at that time had never directed a motion picture and who was relatively unknown in the United States; (d) the idea of eliminating from the film version of the play the so-called "frame" (i.e., the play within a play device which Shakespeare employed), and beginning the film with the main body of the story; (e) the idea of including in the film version the two key scenes (i.e., the wedding scene and the wedding night scene) which in Shakespeare's play occur offstage and are merely described by a character on stage; (f) the idea of filming the picture in Italy, in the actual Italian settings described by Shakespeare.

[The Court next discusses a series of meetings and correspondence between Blaustein and various defendants as well as the introduction of the eventual director, Franco Zeffirelli to the project. During those conversations Blaustein's role as producer was called into question. Eventually Columbia Pictures produced a motion picture without Blaustein's participation.] ...

Thereafter, a motion picture based upon William Shakespeare's play "The Taming of the Shrew" was produced and exhibited commencing in or about March 1967. The motion picture stars respondents Richard Burton and Elizabeth Taylor Burton, and is directed by Franco Zeffirelli.... The motion picture as completed utilizes the following ideas disclosed by appellant to respondents: (1) It is based upon the Shakespearean play "The Taming of the Shrew"; (2) it stars Elizabeth Taylor Burton and Richard Burton in the roles of Katherine and Petruchio, respectively; (3) the director is Franco Zeffirelli; (4) it eliminates the "frame," i.e., the play within a play device found in the original Shakespearean play, and begins with the main body of the story; and (5) it includes an enactment of the two key scenes previously referred to by appellant which in Shakespeare's play occur off-stage.

In addition, the film was photographed in Italy, although not in the actual locales in Italy described by Shakespeare. Respondents have paid no monies to appellant, nor have they accorded him any screen or advertising credit.

...

Appellant urges that (1) there are triable issues of fact as to whether a contract was entered into between appellant and respondents pursuant to which appellant is entitled to compensation by reason of respondents' utilization of the idea disclosed to them by appellant; (2) there are triable issues of fact as to whether appellant is entitled to recover from respondents under quasi-contract for services rendered and benefits conferred, and (3) there are triable issues of fact as to whether appellant is entitled to recover from respondents for breach of a confidential relationship.

Respondents urge that ... respondents were not unjustly enriched at appellant's expense, nor did respondents breach any confidential relationship such as to require the law to impose a quasi-contractual obligation upon respondents to pay any sums to appellant....

The rights of an idea discloser to recover damages from an idea recipient under an express or implied contract to pay for the idea in event the idea recipient uses such idea after disclosure is discussed in *Desny v. Wilder*, 46 Cal.2d 715, 731–739 [299 P.2d 257], as follows: "The Law Pertaining to Ideas. Generally speaking, ideas are as free as the air and as speech and the senses, and as potent or weak, interesting or drab, as the experiences, philosophies, vocabularies, and other variables of speaker and listener may combine to produce, to portray, or to comprehend. But there can be circumstances when neither air nor ideas may be acquired without cost. The diver who goes deep in the sea, even as the pilot who ascends high in the troposphere, knows full well that for life itself he, or someone on his behalf, must arrange for air (or its respiration-essential element, oxygen) to be specially provided at the time and place of need. The theatrical producer likewise may be dependent for his business life on the procurement of ideas from other persons as well as the dressing up and portrayal of his self-conceptions; he may not find his own sufficient for survival. As counsel for the Writers Guild aptly say, ideas 'are not freely usable by the entertainment media until the latter are made aware of them.' The producer may think up the idea himself, dress it and portray it; or he may purchase either the conveyance of the idea alone or a manuscript embodying the idea in the author's concept of a literary vehicle giving it form, adaptation and expression. It cannot be doubted that some ideas are of value of a producer.

"An idea is usually not regarded as property, because all sentient beings may conceive and evolve ideas throughout the gamut of their powers of cerebration and because our concept of property implies something which may be owned and possessed to the exclusion of all other persons. We quote as an accurate statement of the law in this respect the following language of Mr. Justice Brandeis, dissenting in *International News Service v. Associated Press*, 248 U.S. 215, 250 (1918), 'An essential element of individual property is the legal right to exclude others from enjoying it. If the property is private, the right of exclusion may be absolute; if the property is affected with a public interest, the right of exclusion is qualified. But the fact that a product of the mind has cost its producer money and labor, and has a value for which others are willing to pay, is not sufficient to ensure to it this legal attribute of property. The general rule of law is, that the noblest of human productions—knowledge, truths ascertained, conceptions, and ideas—become, after voluntary communication to others, free as the air to common use.' Of similar import, but stated negatively: 'The doctrine that an author has a property right in his ideas and is entitled to demand for them the same protection which the law accords to the proprietor of personal property generally finds no recognition either in the common law or in the statutes of any civilized country.'...

"An eminent writer says that 'The elements requisite for an informal contract ... are identical whether they are expressly stated or implied in fact,' ... 'A "contract implied in fact" requires a meeting of the minds, an agreement, just as much as an "express contract"; the difference between the two being largely in the character of the evidence by which they are established.' The same author describes quasi contracts by declaring that 'as quasi contractual obligations are imposed by the law for the purpose of bringing about justice without reference to the intention of the parties, the only apparent restriction upon the power of the law to create such obligations is that they must be of such a sort as would have been appropriately enforced under common-law procedure by a contractual action. Indeed even this limitation is too narrow, for a bill in equity or a libel in admiralty might be the appropriate means of enforcing some quasi contractual obligations. As the law may impose any obligations that justice requires, the only limit in the last analysis to the category of quasi contracts is that the obligation in question more closely resembles those created by contract than those created by tort. On the other hand, a true contract cannot exist, however desirable it might be to have one, unless there is a manifestation of assent to the making of a promise. Furthermore, the measure of damages appropriate to contractual obligations differs from that applicable to quasi contracts ... It is also true that quasi contractual obligations are not so universally based on unjust enrichment or benefit as is sometimes supposed. There are many cases where the law enforces in a contractual action a duty to restore the plaintiff to a former status—not merely to surrender the benefit which the defendant has received.' ..."

From what has been shown respecting the law of ideas and of contracts we conclude that conveyance of an idea can constitute valuable consideration and can be bargained for before it is disclosed to the proposed purchaser, but once it is conveyed, i.e., disclosed to him and he has grasped, it, it is henceforth his own and he may work with it and use it as he sees fit. In the field of entertainment the producer may properly and validly agree that he will pay for the service of conveying to him ideas which are valuable and which he can put to profitable use. Furthermore, where an idea has been conveyed with the expectation by the purveyor that compensation will be paid if the idea is used, there is no reason why the producer who has been the beneficiary of the conveyance of such an idea, and who finds if valuable and is profiting by it, may not then for the first time, although he is not at that time under any legal obligation so to do, promise to pay a reasonable compensation for that idea—that is, for the past service of furnishing it to him—and thus create a valid obligation....

It is held that "... if a producer obligates himself to pay for the disclosure of an idea, whether it is for protectible or unprotectible material, in return for a disclosure thereof he should be compelled to hold to his promise." There is nothing unreasonable in the assumption that a producer would obligate himself to pay for the disclosure of an idea which he would otherwise be legally free to use, but which in fact, he would be unable to use but for the disclosure.

"The producer and the writer should be free to make any contract they desire to make with reference to the buying of the ideas of the writer; the fact that the producer may later determine, with a little thinking, that he could have had the same ideas and could thereby have saved considerable money for himself, is no defense against the claim of the writer. This is so even though the material to be purchased is abstract and unprotected material." An idea which can be the subject matter of a contract need not be novel or concrete.

It may be noted here that the law of the State of New York no longer requires that an idea be "novel" in order to be the subject of contract protection. As stated in *Frederick Chusid & Co. v. Marshall Leeman & Co.*, 279 F. Supp. 913, 917 (S.D.N.Y. 1968): "Under New York law the parties have the right by contract to prevent disclosure of such materials, even though they are not secret or confidential and may indeed be a matter of public knowledge." The court in *Krisel v. Duran*, 258 F. Supp. 845, 860 (S.D.N.Y. 1966) stated: "Under New York law, an idea, if valuable, even though it does not contain novel, secret or confidential material, may be protected by such an agreement. This doctrine applies even when the subject matter of the idea is common or open to public knowledge."

We are of the opinion that appellant's idea of the filming of Shakespeare's play "The Taming of the Shrew" is one which may be protected by contract.

Express or implied contracts both are based upon the intention of the parties and are distinguishable only in the manifestation of assent. The making of an agreement may be inferred by proof of conduct as well as by proof of the use of words. Whether or not the appellant and respondents here, by their oral declarations and conduct, as shown by the depositions and affidavits, entered into a contract whereby respondents agreed to compensate appellant in the event respondents used appellant's idea, is a question of fact which may not be properly resolved in a summary judgment proceeding, but must be resolved upon a trial of the issue. Even where a question of interpretation of contractual provisions is involved on a motion for summary judgment, it is settled that, if the opposing interpretations are both reasonable, a question of fact is raised which precludes summary judgment....

Confidential Relationship. Respondents urge that the record is devoid of any evidence tending to establish the fact that they breached a duty of confidence owed to appellant.

Appellant, in his affidavit, stated: "Because I knew Mr. French to be a highly reputable agent, had had prior dealings with him, had the same firm of attorneys as the Burtons and had been the recipient of an invitation, constantly renewed, to disclose my ideas and render services on the project, I reposed trust and confidence in the Burtons and their representatives and expected that my ideas would be kept in confidence by them. I did not expect or intend that defendants would go forward with production of "Shrew" and make use of my ideas without my participation."

Under the rules governing the granting of a summary judgment, the foregoing declaration on the part of appellant, made in opposition to the motion for summary judgment, is sufficient to raise a triable issue of fact as to whether the disclosure of his idea to respondents was made in confidence, and was accepted by respondents upon the understanding that they would not use it without the consent of appellant. The judgment is reversed.

Faris v. Enberg

97 Cal. App. 3d 309 (Cal. App. 2d 1979)

The developer of an idea for a television sports quiz show (Edgar C. Faris) sued a television sports announcer (Richard Enberg) and others in two separate actions for appropriating his idea and producing a sports quiz show based upon it. This appeal follows the granting of defendants' motion for summary judgment in the trial court. We affirm the judgment....

Faris conceived a sports quiz show idea in 1964, and prepared and registered a format of the idea. A few days before June 4, 1970, Faris called KTLA studios and told a secretary that he had created a sports television show that would interest Mr. Enberg. He left his name and number. The next day Enberg telephoned Faris, who told Enberg that he "… had a sports oriented TV show that I intended to produce and that I desired to talk to him about participating in the show as the master of ceremonies." Faris told Enberg the format of the show and gave Enberg a copy, which Enberg read through at the meeting, and again expressed interest. Enberg asked for a copy, and Faris said it was his "creation" and "literary property." "I discussed with Mr. Enberg his prospects as to both being an MC for the show or, if he desired, actually participating with me in the production of the show and could participate then as a part owner thereof. At all times I discussed my show and Mr. Enberg's participation as a business proposal or offer to Mr. Enberg and I mentioned to him that, if he came with me, we would both make money on the show." Enberg told Faris he was going to talk the next week with some KTLA producers about a sports show. He asked Faris to leave a copy of the format for further review. Faris made these additional statements in his declaration (although the declaration does not say that he told Enberg any of them): that he did not authorize Enberg to discuss the format with anyone or to give it to anyone else; that had Enberg told Faris he planned to show the format to anyone else or discuss the format with anyone else, Faris would not have left a copy with Enberg, and that had Enberg told Faris of his commitment with another sports quiz show, Faris would not have discussed the show with him or let Enberg read or have the format, and would not have "proposed a contractual relationship with him involving either his participation as a owner or acting as MC for my Sports Panel Quiz.…"

Also attached to the response to the motion for summary judgment were portions of Enberg's deposition wherein he testified that he may have revealed to the people that ultimately produced the "Sports Challenge" quiz show, that he had been contacted by someone about a sports quiz show.…

At some time following this meeting, the "Sports Challenge" show appeared on television with Enberg as master of ceremonies, and produced by defendant Gross. There were certain differences and similarities between the show and plaintiff's idea. Although Gross claimed the production of the show was well under way before Faris met Enberg, we cannot in this appeal assume such to be true, nor do we consider any facts in conflict with plaintiff's version of events.…

Turning to consideration of the question of whether there was an implied-in-fact contract, two notable Supreme Court cases have thoroughly dealt with the subject in the area of literary works or ideas. In *Weitzenkorn v. Lesser*, 40 Cal.2d 778 [256 P.2d 947], plaintiff wrote a story about Tarzan and the fountain of youth, and submitted it to producer Sol Lesser. The plaintiff sued on a theory of express contract, defendant's demurrer was granted in the trial court, and reversed by the Supreme Court. The Supreme Court held that regardless of a work's lack of originality, it could be valuable and the subject of contract: "'While the idea disclosed may be common or even open to public knowledge, yet such disclosure if protected by contract, is sufficient consideration for the promise to pay. [Citations.]'" Even if the plaintiff's story and the movie Sol Lesser produced were grossly dissimilar, the court found that plaintiff was entitled to try to prove that defendant agreed to pay for the use of this commonplace idea.

In *Desny v. Wilder*, 46 Cal.2d 715 [299 P.2d 257 (1956)], plaintiff submitted to Billy Wilder's secretary a story based on the life of cave explorer Floyd Collins. The Supreme Court found that there were triable issues of fact, and reversed the lower court's order granting summary judgment to defendant. In doing so, the court carefully explained the subject of implied-in-fact contracts. Plaintiff called Billy Wilder on the telephone, and was told by a secretary that, because Wilder was so busy, plaintiff would have to present a synopsis for Wilder to read. Plaintiff told the secretary that he would have to be paid if they used it. His purpose was to sell the story. Plaintiff prepared the synopsis, read it to the secretary over the phone, and later Wilder produced a film which appeared to be similar to plaintiff's work. The work was not protected on any theory other than a contract express or implied from the facts....

For an implied-in-fact contract one must show: that he or she prepared the work; that he or she disclosed the work to the offeree for sale; under all circumstances attending disclosure it can be concluded that the offeree voluntarily accepted the disclosure knowing the conditions on which it was tendered (i.e., the offeree must have the opportunity to reject the attempted disclosure if the conditions were unacceptable); and the reasonable value of the work.

Applying these elements to the instant case, we find that the trial court correctly determined that there was no triable issue of fact on a cause of action for an implied-in-fact contract. The trial judge correctly concluded that "Enberg ... is entitled to summary judgment, since there is no evidence to support an implied-in-fact contract for the services of revealing plaintiff's format to him. All the evidence is to the contrary. Both participants to the conversation agreed that the format was submitted to Enberg in connection with an inquiry as to whether Enberg would act as master of ceremonies for plaintiff's television show.... There is absolutely no evidence that plaintiff expected, or indicated his expectation of receiving compensation for the service of revealing the format to Enberg. To the contrary, the sole evidence is that plaintiff voluntarily submitted it to Enberg for the sole purpose of enabling Enberg to make a determination of his willingness to enter into a future business relationship with plaintiff."

So far as the record before us reveals, plaintiff never thought of selling his sports quiz show idea to anyone—including Enberg. He appears at all times to have intended to produce it himself, and sought out Enberg, as a master of ceremonies. He obviously hoped to make his idea more marketable by hiring a gifted sports announcer as his master of ceremonies. Not only did Faris seek to induce Enberg to join him by showing him the product, but also sought to entice him by promises of a "piece" of the enterprise for his involvement. Plaintiff never intended to submit the property for sale and did not tell Enberg that he was submitting it for sale. There is no reason to think that Enberg, or anyone else with whom Enberg spoke, would have believed that Faris' submission was an offer to sell something, which if used would oblige the user to pay.

Based on the clear holding of *Desny* an obligation to pay could not be inferred from the mere fact of submission on a theory that everyone knows that the idea man expects to be paid. Nor could it be inferred from the comment by Faris that the format was his "creation" and "literary property." ...

Baer v. Chase
392 F.3d 609 (2004)

Entertainment law covers the legal disciplines of copyright, publicity, privacy, trademark law, antitrust, contracts, First Amendment, and labor law. The creative content industries have trade, custom, usage, and other unique attributes that make practice of entertainment law unique, even for those who practice within a single doctrinal discipline within a particular industry.

This matter comes on before this court on Robert V. Baer's ("Baer") appeal from an order of the district court entered February 20, 2004, granting summary judgment to the defendants, David Chase and DC Enterprises, Inc. (together called "Chase"), pursuant to Federal Rule of Civil Procedure 56(c). This dispute centers on the creation and development of the well-known television series, The Sopranos. Through this action, Baer seeks compensation for what he perceives was his role in the creation and development of the popular and financially successful television series....

Baer predicates his contract claim on this appeal on an implied-in-fact contract rather than on the oral agreement he reached with Chase. The issue with respect to the implied-in-fact contract claim concerns whether Chase and Baer entered into an enforceable contract for services Baer rendered that aided in the creation and production of The Sopranos. In the district court Baer offered two alternative theories in which a purported contract was formed: the "oral agreement/success contingency" and an implied-in-fact contract.

The parties agree for purposes of the summary judgment motion that there was a contingent oral agreement providing for Chase to compensate Baer, depending on Chase's "success," in exchange for the aid Baer provided in the creation and production of The Sopranos. As we noted above, the parties reached the oral agreement in three exchanges in which Baer proposed: "that I would perform the services while assuming the risk that if the show failed [Chase] would owe me nothing. If, however, the show succeeded he would remunerate me in a manner commensurate to the true value of my services." As we have indicated, for purposes of the summary judgment motion only, Chase accepts this version of the events so we will regard the existence of the oral agreement as not in dispute....

The distinction between express and implied contracts rests on alternative methods of contract formation. Contracts are "express" when the parties state their terms and "implied" when the parties do not state their terms. The distinction is based not on the contracts' legal effect but on the way the parties manifest their mutual assent. In other words, the terms "express" and "implied" do not denote different kinds of contracts, but rather reference the evidence by which the parties demonstrate their agreement.

Baer's attempt to find an implied-in-fact contract in his dealings with Chase does not strengthen his claim that Chase breached his contract with him. There is only one contract at issue, Chase's promise to compensate Baer for services he rendered which aided in the creation and production of The Sopranos. Chase's stipulation that there was such a contract has the consequence of making Baer's attempts to label this agreement "implied" rather than "express" to advance a distinction without a difference as the mode of contract formation, as we will explain, is immaterial to the disposition of the breach of contract claim.... Moreover, Baer's claim of an implied-in-fact contract, in the face of an express agreement governing the same subject matter, is legally untenable. There cannot be an implied-in-fact contract if there is an express contract that covers the same subject matter. In other words, express contract and implied-in-fact contract theories are mutually exclusive.

... Baer's alleged implied-in-fact contract, however, rather than being distinct from or unrelated to the express oral contract is identical to it. The stipulated oral agreement included Chase's promise to compensate Baer for the services and ideas that Baer provided Chase. Baer now asks that we find an implied-in-fact contract that subjects Chase to liability for the very same undertaking. Baer provides a litany of facts which indicate that Chase may have used his services or prospered from his ideas. Nevertheless, in light of Chase's stipulation to the existence of an agreement governing this subject matter, this evidence is immaterial to the issues raised by the summary judgment motion with respect to Baer's attempt to establish that there was an implied-in-fact contract between the parties....

In fact there are no distinctions in legal effect, at least in the context of this case, when a promise is implied rather than express.... In fact "[a] contract arises from offer and acceptance, and must be sufficiently definite so 'that the performance to be rendered by each party can be ascertained with reasonable certainty.'" *Weichert Co. Realtors v. Ryan*, 128 N.J. 427, 608 A.2d 280, 284 (1992). Therefore parties create an enforceable contract when they agree on its essential terms and manifest an intent that the terms bind them. If parties to an agreement do not agree on one or more essential terms of the purported agreement courts generally hold it to be unenforceable....

New Jersey law deems the price term, i.e., the amount of compensation, an essential term of any contract. An agreement lacking definiteness of price, however, is not unenforceable if the parties specify a practicable method by which they can determine the amount. However, in the absence of an agreement as to the manner or method of determining compensation the purported agreement is invalid. Additionally, the duration of the contract is deemed an essential term and therefore any agreement must be sufficiently definitive to allow a court to determine the agreed upon length of the contractual relationship.

The New Jersey Supreme Court explicitly has held that an implied-in-fact contract "must be sufficiently definite [so] that the performance to be rendered by each party can be ascertained with reasonable certainty." *Weichert*, 608 A.2d at 284 (citations and internal quotations omitted). If possible, courts will "attach a sufficiently definite meaning to the terms of a bargain to make it enforceable[,]" *Paley v. Barton Sav. and Loan Ass'n, 82 N.J.Super.* 75, 196 A.2d 682, 686 (1964), and in doing so may refer to "commercial practice or other usage or custom." *Lynch v. New Deal Delivery Serv. Inc.*, 974 F. Supp. 441, 458 (D.N.J.1997). But the courts recognize that a contract is "unenforceable for vagueness when its terms are too indefinite to allow a court to determine with reasonable certainty what each party has promised to do." *Id.* at 457.

Baer premises his argument on his view that New Jersey should disregard the well-established requirement of definiteness in its contract law when the subject-matter of the contract is an "idea submission." He cites extensively to a string of cases from various jurisdictions which he urges support his contention. *See, e.g., Wrench L.L.C v. Taco Bell Corp.*, 256 F.3d 446 (6th Cir.2001); *Nadel v. Play-by-Play Toys & Novelties, Inc.*, 208 F.3d 368 (2d Cir.2000); *Duffy* [*v. Charles Schwab & Co.*, 123 F.Supp.2d 802 (2001)]. Baer contends that these cases support the proposition that "[e]very Circuit that has published on the issue, has upheld implied contract claims where price and duration were absent and a price term was implied as the reasonable value of the ideas conveyed."

Baer's argument is inaccurate and misleading. He attempts to transform cases where the issues raised pertain to adequacy of consideration and discrepancies over the use of submitted facts, into the proposition that implied-in-fact contracts involving idea submissions need not be sufficiently definite. For example: *Wrench*, 256 F.3d at 459–63, reversed a summary judgment disposition that held that novelty was required to prove consideration and sustain an implied-in-fact contract claim; *Duffy*, 123 F.Supp.2d at 816–19, held that a plaintiff must prove that an idea disclosed to the defendant was novel in order to find consideration for the alleged contract and denied summary judgment because a material issue existed over novelty and use; *Nadel*, 208 F.3d at 374, reversed a summary judgment granted "only on ground that [the plaintiff's] idea lacked general novelty and thus would not suffice as consideration" and remanded for the district court to determine "whether the other elements necessary to find a valid express or implied-in-fact contract are present here." *Id.* at 382. None of the cases Baer cites holds that there is not a definiteness requirement necessary to create an enforceable contract in idea submission cases. Duffy's holding is helpful in summarizing the actual law to be derived from the above cited cases: "The existence of novelty to the buyer only addresses the element of consideration necessary for the formation of a contract. Thus, apart from consideration, the formation of a contract will depend upon the presence of other elements." *Duffy*, 123 F.Supp.2d at 818 (citing *Nadel*, 208 F.3d at 377 n. 5).

New Jersey precedent does not support Baer's attempt to carve out an exception to traditional principles of contract law for submission-of-idea cases. The New Jersey courts have not provided even the slightest indication that they intend to depart from their well-established requirement that enforceability of a contract requires definiteness with respect to the essential terms of that contract. Accordingly, we will not relax the need for Baer to demonstrate definiteness as to price and duration with respect to the contract he entered into with Chase.

The final question with respect to the Baer's contract claim, therefore, is whether his contract is enforceable in light of the traditional requirement of definitiveness in New Jersey contract law for a contract to be enforceable. A contract may be expressed in writing, or orally, or in acts, or partly in one of these ways and partly in others. In this case, even when all of the parties' verbal and non-verbal actions are aggregated and viewed most favorably to Baer, we cannot find a contract that is distinct and definitive enough to be enforceable.

Nothing in the record indicates that the parties agreed on how, how much, where, or for what period Chase would compensate Baer. The parties did not discuss who would determine the "true value" of Baer's services, when the "true value" would be calculated, or what variables would go into such a calculation. There was no discussion or agreement as to the meaning of "success" of The Sopranos. There was no discussion how "profits" were to be defined. There was no contemplation of dates of commencement or termination of the contract. And again, nothing in Baer's or Chase's conduct, or the surrounding circumstances of the relationship, shed light on, or answers, any of these questions. The district court was correct in its description of the contract between the parties: "The contract as articulated by the Plaintiff lacks essential terms, and is vague, indefinite and uncertain; no version of the alleged agreement contains sufficiently precise terms to constitute an enforceable contract." We therefore will affirm the district court's rejection of Baer's claim to recover under a theory of implied-in-fact contract.

…

[Baer's second cause of action was for payment for his services based on quantum meruit.] The district court therefore erred, at least procedurally, in granting Chase's summary judgment motion based on the statute of limitations with respect to Baer's quantum meruit claim. We therefore will reverse the summary judgment on this point and will remand the question of whether Baer presented a timely and otherwise valid quasi-contract claim to the district court for further consideration.

…

Notes and Questions

a. California has been more explicit about what constitutes a contract for ideas than many other states, likely owing to *Desny v. Wilder,* 46 Cal.2d 715 (1956). In *Klekas v. EMI Films, Inc.,* 150 Cal. App. 3d 1102 (Cal. Ct. App. 1984), the court explained that in order to establish an implied-in-fact contract in the entertainment context, the following was required:

> [Plaintiff must establish] that he or she prepared the work; that he or she disclosed the work to an offeree for sale; that under all circumstances attending disclosure it can be concluded that the offeree voluntarily accepted the disclosure knowing the conditions on which it was tendered (i.e., the offeree must have the opportunity to reject the attempted disclosure if the conditions were unacceptable); and the reasonable value of the work.

b. The issue of novelty and originality continues to be a controversial element of the law pertaining to transactions of ideas. There is a significant amount of confusion between claims for breach of contract and claims for misappropriation of an idea. Over time, it is likely that most misappropriation claims will be preempted by copyright. Properly distinguished, contract claims should survive preemption. See *Orson, Inc. v. Miramax Film Corp.*, 189 F.3d 377, 382 (3d Cir. 1999) (en banc), *cert. denied*, 529 U.S. 1012 (2000) (discussing the various types of preemption in the copyright setting).

c. A screenwriter reads an obituary of a soldier from World War I who recently died. The obituary was written and paid for by the children of the soldier. The sixty-word obituary refers to a particular act of bravery by the soldier when he was stationed in Germany after the war, when he stopped a gang of hooligans from beating and possibly killing a young man named Adolph Hitler. The screenwriter uses the idea to write a screenplay which is made into a successful motion picture. In an action by the family against the screenwriter and the motion picture studio, what is the appropriate result and why? See, for example, *Desny v. Wilder*, 46 Cal.2d 715, 299 P.2d 257 (1956).

d. How can a client develop a work as a producer or in a similar capacity without the risk of that effort being stolen? Are there bodies of law beyond copyright, trademark and contract to provide protection? Should such protection even be available?

e. Was the idea behind *American Idol* stolen? *Star Search* did not sue, and a short court opinion dismissed other claims. See *Keane v. Fox Television Stations, Inc.*, 129 Fed. Appx. 874 (5th Cir. 2005).

f. The general industry practice regarding submission of treatment is to use releases to waive all claims other than copyright infringement. At a minimum, defendants should retain the releases. See *Sims v. Viacom, Inc.*, 2009 U.S. Dist. LEXIS 107938 (E.D. Pa. Nov. 17, 2009).

g. In *Baer v. Chase*, Baer also attempted to claim a breach of confidentiality under New Jersey law.

> The court in *Flemming [v. Ronson Corp.*, 107 N.J. Super. 311, 258 A.2d 153, 156–57 (1969)] articulated the test for determining whether the law will imply an obligation to pay for a confidentially submitted idea: When "a person communicates a novel idea to another with the intention that the latter may use the idea and compensate him for such use, the other party is liable for such use and must pay compensation if ... (1) the idea was novel; (2) it was made in confidence [to the defendant]; and (3) it was adopted and made use of [by the defendant in connection with his own activities]."

Flemming, 258 A.2d at 156–57 (citations omitted). The decisions do not explain what ideas can be novel, merely that "even an otherwise novel idea would lose its novelty if it was 'in the domain of public knowledge' before the defendant used it." *Baer v. Chase*, 392 F.3d 609, 628 (3d Cir. 2004) quoting *Flemming*, 258 A.2d at 157–58.

Problem I-B

Meet Bryce. Bryce is a talented, up-and-coming artist — a hyphenate actor, writer, singer, director, and producer — in other words, a fairly typical young talent. Throughout the course of the textbook, Bryce will engage in transactions involving the development of new ideas into film, music, television, theatre, and computer-game projects.

As a student using this casebook, you are placed in the role of a senior associate in the firm of Story, Marshall & Cardozo, a national law firm with offices in New York, London, Newport Beach, California, and your own home town.

Bryce has met with you for the first time since signing a representation agreement with Story, Marshall & Cardozo[2] as legal counsel. Bryce has the idea to create a multimedia project based on an original story idea. Bryce has already composed songs for the project. What are the steps that Bryce and you must take to protect the work before it is shown to potential investors or producers? Identify the legal mechanisms available to help protect Bryce, as well as the limitations Bryce might face.

C. Written Submission Agreements

Nadel v. Play-By-Play Toys
208 F.3d 368 (2d Cir. 2000)

Plaintiff-appellant Craig P. Nadel ("Nadel") brought this action against defendant-appellee Play-By-Play Toys & Novelties, Inc. ("Play-By-Play") for breach of contract, quasi contract, and unfair competition. The thrust of Nadel's complaint was that Play-By-Play took his idea for an upright, sound-emitting, spinning plush toy and that, contrary to industry custom, Play-By-Play used the idea in its "Tornado Taz" product without paying him compensation. Play-By-Play also filed several counterclaims against Nadel, alleging that Nadel falsely told other members of the toy industry that Play-By-Play had stolen his idea, thereby harming its ability to receive toy concepts from toy industry members.

For the reasons that follow, we vacate that part of the district court's order granting Play-By-Play's motion for summary judgment and dismissing Nadel's complaint and affirm that part of the district court's order dismissing Play-By-Play's counterclaims.

Nadel is a toy idea man. Toy companies regularly do business with independent inventors such as Nadel in order to develop and market new toy concepts as quickly as possible. To facilitate the exchange of ideas, the standard custom and practice in the toy industry calls for companies to treat the submission of an idea as confidential. If the company subsequently uses the disclosed idea, industry custom provides that the company shall compensate the inventor, unless, of course, the disclosed idea was already known to the company.

In 1996, Nadel developed the toy concept at issue in this case. He transplanted the "eccentric mechanism" found in several hanging Halloween toys then on the market — such as "Spooky Skull" and "Shaking Mutant Pumpkin" — and placed the mechanism inside

---

2. *See* Chapter IV regarding the issues of the lawyer's ethical issues. What unique provisions might be needed in the law firm representation (or retainer) agreement?

of a plush toy monkey skin to develop the prototype for a new table-top monkey toy. This plush toy figure sat upright, emitted sound, and spun when placed on a flat surface.

In October 1996, Nadel met with Neil Wasserman, an executive at Play-By-Play who was responsible for the development of its plush toy line. According to Nadel, he showed his prototype monkey toy to Wasserman, who expressed interest in adapting the concept to a non-moving, plush Tazmanian Devil toy that Play-By-Play was already producing under license from Warner Bros. Nadel contends that, consistent with industry custom, any ideas that he disclosed to Wasserman during their October 1996 meeting were subject to an agreement by Play-By-Play to keep such ideas confidential and to compensate Nadel in the event of their use.

Nadel claims that he sent his prototype monkey toy to Wasserman as a sample and awaited the "Taz skin" and voice tape, which Wasserman allegedly said he would send, so that Nadel could make a sample spinning/laughing Tazmanian Devil toy for Play-By-Play. Wasserman never provided Nadel with the Taz skin and voice tape, however, and denies ever having received the prototype monkey toy from Nadel.

Notwithstanding Wasserman's denial, his secretary, Melissa Rodriguez, testified that Nadel's prototype monkey toy remained in Wasserman's office for several months. According to Ms. Rodriguez, the monkey toy was usually kept in a glass cabinet behind Wasserman's desk, but she remembered that on one occasion she had seen it on a table in Wasserman's office. Despite Nadel's multiple requests, Wasserman did not return Nadel's prototype monkey toy until February 1997, after Play-By-Play introduced its "Tornado Taz" product at the New York Toy Fair.

The parties do not dispute that "Tornado Taz" has the same general characteristics as Nadel's prototype monkey toy. Like Nadel's toy, Tornado Taz is a plush toy that emits sounds (including "screaming," "laughing," "snarling," and "grunting"), sits upright, and spins by means of an internal eccentric vibration mechanism.

Nadel claims that, in violation of their alleged agreement, Play-By-Play used his idea without paying him compensation. Play-By-Play contends, however, that it independently developed the Tornado Taz product concept and that Nadel is therefore not entitled to any compensation. Specifically, Play-By-Play maintains that, as early as June or July of 1996, two of its officers — Wasserman and Slattery — met in Hong Kong and began discussing ways to create a spinning or vibrating Tazmanian Devil, including the possible use of an eccentric mechanism. Furthermore, Play-By-Play claims that in late September or early October 1996, it commissioned an outside manufacturing agent — Barter Trading of Hong Kong — to begin developing Tornado Taz.

Play-By-Play also argues that, even if it did use Nadel's idea to develop Tornado Taz, Nadel is not entitled to compensation because Nadel's concept was unoriginal and non-novel to the toy industry in October 1996. In support of this argument, Play-By-Play has submitted evidence of various toys, commercially available prior to October 1996, which used eccentric motors and allegedly contained the same characteristics as Nadel's prototype monkey toy....

Nadel's factual allegations present a familiar submission-of-idea case: (1) the parties enter into a pre-disclosure confidentiality agreement; (2) the idea is subsequently disclosed to the prospective buyer; (3) there is no post-disclosure contract for payment based on use; and (4) plaintiff sues defendant for allegedly using the disclosed idea under either a contract-based or property-based theory. For the reasons that follow, we conclude that a finding of novelty as to Play-By-Play can suffice to provide consideration for Nadel's contract claims against Play-By-Play. Accordingly, because we also find that there exists a genuine issue of material fact as to whether Nadel's idea was novel to Play-By-Play at the time of his October 1996 disclosure, we vacate the district court's grant of summary judgment on Nadel's contract claims. With respect to Nadel's misappropriation claim, we similarly vacate the district court's grant of summary judgment and remand for further proceedings to determine whether Nadel's idea was original or novel generally.

A. Submission-of-Idea Cases under New York Law.

Our analysis begins with the New York Court of Appeals' most recent discussion of the law governing idea submission cases, *Apfel v. Prudential-Bache Securities, Inc.,* 81 N.Y.2d 470 (1993). In *Apfel,* the Court of Appeals discussed the type of novelty an idea must have in order to sustain a contract-based or property-based claim for its uncompensated use. Specifically, *Apfel* clarified an important distinction between the requirement of "novelty to the buyer" for contract claims, on the one hand, and "originality" (or novelty generally) for misappropriation claims, on the other hand.

Under the facts of *Apfel,* the plaintiff disclosed his idea to the defendant pursuant to a confidentiality agreement and, subsequent to disclosure, entered into another agreement wherein the defendant agreed to pay a stipulated price for the idea's use. The defendant used the idea but refused to pay plaintiff pursuant to the post-disclosure agreement on the asserted ground that "no contract existed between the parties because the sale agreement lacked consideration." The defendant argued that an idea could not constitute legally sufficient consideration unless it was original or novel generally and that, because plaintiff's idea was not original or novel generally (it had been in the public domain at the time of the post-disclosure agreement), the idea provided insufficient consideration to support the parties' post-disclosure contract.

In rejecting defendant's argument, the Court of Appeals held that there was sufficient consideration to support plaintiff's contract claim because the idea at issue had value to the defendant at the time the parties concluded their post-disclosure agreement. The *Apfel* court noted that "traditional principles of contract law" provide that parties "are free to make their bargain, even if the consideration exchanged is grossly unequal or of dubious value," and that, so long as the "defendant received something of value" under the contract, the contract would not be void for lack of consideration.

The *Apfel* court explicitly rejected defendant's contention that the court should carve out "an exception to traditional principles of contract law" for submission-of-idea cases by requiring that an idea must also be original or novel generally in order to constitute valid consideration. In essence, the defendant sought to impose a requirement that an idea be novel in absolute terms, as opposed to only the defendant buyer, in order to constitute valid consideration for the bargain. In rejecting this argument, the *Apfel* court clarified the standards for both contract-based and property-based claims in submission-of-idea cases. That analysis guides our decision here.

The *Apfel* court first noted that "novelty as an element of an idea seller's claim" is a distinct element of proof with respect to both (1) "a claim based on a property theory" and (2) "a claim based on a contract theory." The court then proceeded to discuss how the leading submission-of-idea case—*Downey v. General Foods Corp.,* 31 N.Y.2d 56 (1972)—treated novelty with respect to property-based and contract-based claims. First, the Apfel court explained that the plaintiff's property-based claims for misappropriation were dismissed in Downey because "the elements of novelty and originality [were] absent," i.e., the ideas were so common as to be unoriginal and known generally. Second, the *Apfel* court explained that the plaintiff's contract claims in Downey had been dismissed on the separate ground that the "defendant possessed plaintiff's ideas prior to plaintiff's disclosure [and thus], the ideas could have no value to defendant and could not supply consideration for any agreement between the parties."

By distinguishing between the two types of claims addressed in *Downey* and the different bases for rejecting each claim, the New York Court of Appeals clarified that the novelty requirement in submission-of-idea cases is different for misappropriation of property and breach of contract claims. The Court of Appeals underscored this important distinction by citing *Ferber v. Sterndent Corp.,* 51 N.Y.2d 782 (1980), which also refers to the two different types of novelty, i.e., novelty to the buyer and novelty generally....

Thus, the *Apfel* court refused to read *Downey* and "similar decisions" as requiring originality or novelty generally in all cases involving disclosure of ideas. Rather, the *Apfel* court clarified that the longstanding requirement that an idea have originality or general novelty in order to support a misappropriation claim does not apply to contract claims. For contract-based claims in submission-of-idea cases, a showing of novelty to the buyer will supply sufficient consideration to support a contract.

Moreover, *Apfel* made clear that the "novelty to the buyer" standard is not limited to cases involving an express post-disclosure contract for payment based on an idea's use. The *Apfel* court explicitly discussed the pre-disclosure contract scenario present in the instant case, where "the buyer and seller contract for disclosure of the idea with payment based on use, but no separate post-disclosure contract for the use of the idea has been made." In such a scenario, a seller might, as Nadel did here, bring an action against a buyer who allegedly used his ideas without payment, claiming both misappropriation of property and breach of an express or implied-in-fact contract. The *Apfel* court recognized that these cases present courts with the difficult problem of determining "whether the idea the buyer was using was, in fact, the seller's." Specifically, the court noted that, with respect to a misappropriation of property claim, it is difficult to "prove that the buyer obtained the idea from [the seller] and nowhere else." With respect to a breach of contract claim, the court noted that it would be inequitable to enforce a contract if "it turns out upon disclosure that the buyer already possessed the idea." The court then concluded that, with respect to these cases, "[a] showing of novelty, at least novelty as to the buyer" should address these problems.

We note, moreover, that the "novelty to the buyer" standard comports with traditional principles of contract law. While an idea may be unoriginal or non-novel in a general sense, it may have substantial value to a particular buyer who is unaware of it and therefore willing to enter into contract to acquire and exploit it. See *Robert Unikel, Bridging the "Trade Secret" Gap: Protecting "Confidential Information" Not Rising to the Level of Trade Secrets,* 29 Loy. U. Chi. L.J. 841, 877 n. 151 (1998) (noting that, if a valuable idea is already known to an industry but has not yet been acquired by a prospective buyer, one of two circumstances may exist: "(1) the person[ ] ha[s] not identified the potential value of the easily acquired information; or (2) the person[ ] ha[s] not identified the means, however easy or proper, for obtaining the valuable information"). As the *Apfel* court emphasized, "the buyer may reap benefits from such a contract in a number of ways — for instance, by not having to expend resources pursuing the idea through other channels or by having a profit-making idea implemented sooner rather than later."

In fact, the notion that an unoriginal idea may still be novel (and valuable) to a particular buyer is not itself a novel proposition. In *Keller v. American Chain Co.,* 255 N.Y. 94, 174 N.E. 74 (1930) — which is cited by *Apfel* — the parties entered into a verbal pre-disclosure contract whereby the plaintiff allegedly agreed to disclose money-saving information to the defendant in exchange for one-third of the savings realized. The disclosed idea—that the defendant could use a more favorable freight rate classification for his auto chains—was not original or novel to the industry, as several railroads already adhered to the lower rate. Nonetheless, the *Keller* court stated that, where the defendant used and benefited from information otherwise unknown to it, there can be sufficient consideration to enforce the parties' pre-disclosure contract.

In contrast to contract-based claims, a misappropriation claim can only arise from the taking of an idea that is original or novel in absolute terms, because the law of property does not protect against the misappropriation or theft of that which is free and available to all. See *Murray v. National Broad. Co.*, 844 F.2d 988, 993 (2d Cir. 1988) ("Since ... non-novel ideas are not protectible as property, they cannot be stolen.")....

Finally, although the legal requirements for contract-based claims and property-based claims are well-defined, we note that the determination of novelty in a given case is not always clear. The determination of whether an idea is original or novel depends upon several factors, including, inter alia, the idea's specificity or generality (is it a generic concept or one of specific application?), its commonality (how many people know of this idea?), its uniqueness (how different is this idea from generally known ideas?), and its commercial availability (how widespread is the idea's use in the industry?). *Cf. Murray*, 844 F.2d at 993 ("In assessing whether an idea is in the public domain, the central issue is the uniqueness of the creation."). Thus, for example, a once original or novel idea may become so widely disseminated over the course of time that it enters the body of common knowledge. When this occurs, the idea ceases to be novel or original. See *e.g., Murray*, 844 F.2d at 989, 991–92 (affirming district court's finding that plaintiff's idea for a television sitcom "The Cosby Show" about "black American family life" was not novel or original because it "merely combined two ideas which had been circulating in the industry for a number of years—namely, the family situation comedy, which was a standard formula, and the casting of black actors in non-stereotypical roles," even though "the portrayal of a non-stereotypical black family on television was indeed a breakthrough").

Moreover, in assessing the interrelationship between originality and novelty to the buyer, we note that in some cases an idea may be so unoriginal or lacking in novelty that its obviousness bespeaks widespread and public knowledge of the idea, and such knowledge is therefore imputed to the buyer. In such cases, a court may conclude, as a matter of law, that the idea lacks both the originality necessary to support a misappropriation claim and the novelty to the buyer necessary to support a contract claim.

In the first of two post-*Apfel* decisions in New York—*Oasis Music, Inc. v. 900 U.S.A., Inc.*, 614 N.Y.S.2d 878 (1994)—the plaintiff alleged that the defendant misappropriated its ideas for an interactive telephone game in violation of a pre-disclosure confidentiality agreement. The *Oasis Music* court correctly began its contract analysis by reciting *Apfel's* "novelty as to the buyer" standard. But after concluding that the various aspects of plaintiff's ideas already existed in the public domain, the court appeared to dismiss plaintiff's claims for lack of novelty generally. In light of *Apfel*, we read the *Oasis Music* opinion to hold that, because plaintiff's ideas had such a high degree of commonality, the ideas were so unoriginal that, as a matter of law, they were non-novel to the buyer.

In the other post-*Apfel* decision in New York—*Marraccini v. Bertelsmann Music Group, Inc.*, 221 A.D.2d 95 (3d Dep't 1996)—the plaintiff alleged that the defendant breached their pre-disclosure agreement and misappropriated his idea for a "Pop TV" music channel. On appeal from the Supreme Court, New York's Appellate Division reiterated *Downey's* statement that, "[w]hen there is no postdisclosure agreement for the use of an idea, 'no promise to pay for its use may be implied, and no asserted agreement enforced, if the elements of novelty and originality are absent, since the property right in an idea is based upon these two elements.'" We agree with the *Marraccini* court's statement that "*Downey* ... and its progeny remain[ ] intact," insofar as that line of cases was clarified by *Apfel*, but we conclude that the *Marraccini* court's reliance on *Downey's* language for the proposition that the consideration for the contract in contract-based claims must consist of originality or novelty generally—as opposed to just novelty to the buyer—has been foreclosed by *Apfel*. We do not understand *Apfel's* holding to be limited only to situations where there is an express post-disclosure contract between the parties.

In sum, we find that New York law in submission-of-idea cases is governed by the following principles: Contract-based claims require only a showing that the disclosed idea was novel to the buyer in order to find consideration. Such claims involve a fact-specific inquiry that focuses on the perspective of the particular buyer. By contrast, misappropriation claims require that the idea at issue be original and novel in absolute terms. This is so because unoriginal, known ideas have no value as property and the law does not protect against the use of that which is free and available to all. Finally, an idea may be so unoriginal or lacking in novelty generally that, as a matter of law, the buyer is deemed to have knowledge of the idea. In such cases, neither a property-based nor a contract-based claim for uncompensated use of the idea may lie.

[B.] Nadel's Contract Claims.

Mindful that, under New York law, a finding of novelty as to Play-By-Play will provide sufficient consideration to support Nadel's contract claims, we next consider whether the record exhibits a genuine issue of material fact on this point.

Reading the record in a light most favorable to Nadel, we conclude that there exists a genuine issue of material fact as to whether Nadel's idea was, at the time he disclosed it to Wasserman in early October 1996, novel to Play-By-Play. Notably, the timing of Play-By-Play's development and release of Tornado Taz in relation to Nadel's October 1996 disclosure is, taken alone, highly probative. Moreover, although custom in the toy industry provides that a company shall promptly return all samples if it already possesses (or does not want to use) a disclosed idea, Play-By-Play in this case failed to return Nadel's prototype monkey toy for several months, despite Nadel's multiple requests for its return. According to Wasserman's secretary, Melissa Rodriguez, Nadel's sample was not returned until after the unveiling of "Tornado Taz" at the New York Toy Fair in February 1997. Ms. Rodriguez testified that from October 1996 through February 1997, Nadel's sample was usually kept in a glass cabinet behind Wasserman's desk, and on one occasion, she remembered seeing it on a table in Wasserman's office. These facts give rise to the reasonable inference that Play-By-Play may have used Nadel's prototype as a model for the development of Tornado Taz....

We therefore conclude that there exists a genuine issue of material fact as to whether Nadel's idea was, at the time he disclosed it to Wasserman in early October 1996, novel to Play-By-Play. As to whether the other elements necessary to find a valid express or implied-in-fact contract are present here, e.g., mutual assent, legal capacity, legal subject matter, we leave that determination to the district court to address, if necessary, on remand.

FASA Corp. v. Playmates Toys Inc.
892 F. Supp. 1061 (N.D. Ill. 1995)

Plaintiff FASA Corporation ("FASA") is the creator, developer, publisher, promoter and distributor of various fictional universes, including but not limited to BATTLETECH, which form the basis for board games, role-playing games, novels, game systems and other game supplements which it licenses to third parties for the development of location-based interactive entertainment games and centers, disk-based computer games, cartridge-based computer games, models, miniatures, merchandise, movies, television programming, toys and other items. Defendant Playmates Toys, Inc. ("Playmates"), is a distributor of toys supplied by a related company, Playmates Toys (Hong Kong) Ltd. ("Playmates HK"), including TEENAGE MUTANT NINJA TURTLES, STAR TREK, ADDAMS FAMILY and various Disney characters.

The lawsuit centers on Playmates' alleged infringement of FASA's intellectual property and proprietary rights in BATTLETECH by designing and marketing the ExoSquad toy line. In late 1991, Robert Allen, a Cincinnati, Ohio, toy designer, asked FASA for the opportunity to interest toy companies in the BATTLETECH property. Although Allen and FASA never reached agreement on the nature and scope of Allen's role, FASA did permit Allen to make at least three presentations to toy companies regarding a BATTLETECH toy line.

When Allen arrived at Playmates on December 11, 1991, to present BATTLETECH, Playmates presented Allen with an untitled document that Playmates represented as its standard "New Product Submission Form." This New Product Submission Form reads as follows:

> It is the policy of Playmates Toys, Inc. not to review or consider any unsolicited proposals of any kind. You have advised us that you have an "idea" which you believe may be of interest to us. We are prepared to consider your idea only upon the following terms:
>
> 1. You will expressly waive any and all claims of any kind whatsoever, past, present or future, known or unknown against Playmates Toys, Inc. in any way relating to or connected to the "idea".
>
> 2. In consideration for such waiver, Playmates Toys, Inc., will review your "idea" in written form. We will return all materials submitted in connection therewith within two weeks after submission.
>
> 3. At our sole and complete discretion, we may then enter into negotiations with you for a contractual agreement regarding the idea.
>
> 4. Except as to any future agreement entered into under Paragraph 3, we shall have no obligation of any kind toward you in connection with the proposed idea. The disclosed matter relates to: [handwritten] (1) "BATTLETECH" (2) "WENDY & HER WAGON" (3) "SPEEDBALLS".

Allen had signed nondisclosure or new product submission forms before which did not require or include waivers of either copyright or trademark infringement claims or of other future unknown claims by the owner of the property. Playmates knew that Allen was not an employee of FASA. Although Playmates had never dealt with FASA in the past, Playmates made no effort to verify Allen's authority. At no time did Playmates attempt to contact FASA. There was no communication of any type between Playmates and FASA until this lawsuit was filed, and FASA did not explicitly authorize Allen to waive any of its intellectual property rights in BATTLETECH.

While the Court finds that many toy companies use nondisclosure or new product submission forms—the Court finds that such companies do not require, as a standard practice, a waiver of all the intellectual property rights held by the inventor. In this regard, the Court notes that Playmates' own experts testified that it is not typical in the toy industry for a toy company to require an inventor to waive all rights to the invention in order to submit it for review. Moreover, even Playmates' president testified that he did not understand the waiver provision in Playmates' new product submission form to include a waiver of copyright, trademark, or patent claims.

Under the California Civil Code, "[a]n agent has such authority as the principal, actually or ostensibly, confers upon him," Cal. Civil Code § 2315, and "[a]n agent represents his principal for all purposes within the scope of his actual or ostensible authority." Cal. Civ. Code § 2330. Only those liabilities "which would accrue to the agent from transactions within [his actual or ostensible authority], if they had been entered into on his own account, accrue to the principal."

Because FASA did not confer authority on Allen to waive its intellectual property rights in BATTLETECH, and because Allen did not believe that he had authority to waive FASA's intellectual property rights, the Court finds that Allen did not have actual authority to waive FASA's intellectual property rights.

Having determined that FASA cannot be bound by Allen's purported waiver of its intellectual property rights, our inquiry could be at an end. However, we proceed to offer an alternate basis for our holding that FASA is not bound by Allen's purported waiver— namely, that Playmates' waiver form is unenforceable as a matter of law. This issue, as the parties concede, seems to be one of first impression.

As a threshold consideration in assessing the enforceability of the purported waiver, we must address what law governs this issue. Playmates contends that since the underlying claims at issue are federal claims, federal law controls. And, in this limited sense, they are correct....

In the instant case, we find that federal authority, as well as that of Illinois and California converge on the conclusion that Playmates' waiver form is unenforceable because it purports to require the signor to waive unknown future claims. Such a waiver is void as against public policy.

The California Civil Code provides that "A general release does not extend to claims which the creditor does not know or suspect to exist in his favor at the time of executing the release...." Cal. Civ. Code § 1542. Thus, we believe that California recognizes the general proposition that a waiver of future unknown claims is unenforceable. Similarly, under Illinois caselaw, "A general release is inapplicable to an unknown claim." The Court finds no federal authority supporting Playmates' position that waiver of future unknown claims is valid....

In the Securities context a waiver, like the waiver sought to be enforced by Playmates, is explicitly precluded by statute. Similarly, in the antitrust context, Judge Shadur even in the absence of a statutory prohibition has nevertheless refused to enforce a waiver that purported to bar a lawsuit based on anticompetitive events arising after the signing of the waiver.... [S]uch a waiver could itself become a contract in restraint of trade.

In the instant case, we are persuaded that a purported waiver of future, unknown federal intellectual property rights is unenforceable and void as against public policy. Such a waiver would permit a party to violate another's intellectual property rights with impunity in contravention of the clear and long standing public policies underlying the trademark, copyright and patent laws. Giving force to such waivers would invariably stifle creativity and inventiveness and inhibit inventors from presenting their creations to others. Thus, even if we were not to look at state law as a guide we would reach the same conclusion: The waiver of unknown future claims is unenforceable.

Playmates' New Product Form violates public policy because it allows Playmates to violate federal intellectual property law with impunity. Playmates' New Product Form also violates California law to which this Court may look in fashioning federal common law.

Conclusion. For all of the reasons set forth herein the Court finds that Playmates' New Product Form is legally unenforceable under the facts and circumstances of this case. The Court therefore finds that defendant Playmates has not met its burden of establishing its affirmative defense of waiver.

Notes and Questions

a. One of the most significant and potentially misleading cases on the topic of waiver comes from the Second Circuit. In *Murray v. National Broadcasting Company, Inc.,* 844 F.2d 988 (2d Cir. 1988), the court determined that a staff writer's submission describing a modern *Dick Van Dyke Show,* to star Bill Cosby in an upper class African-American household with five children, was not protected against NBC when that network contracted with Carsey-Werner for the creation of *The Cosby Show*. The court found for NBC after determining that the idea had to be novel. Subsequent decisions, however, seem to have rejected this analysis.

Instead of novelty, the New York Court of Appeals explains that in a contract dispute, the idea need merely be unknown to the purchaser. Under this alternative, NBC would still have won the dispute because Bill Cosby himself had first proposed the show two decades earlier. Murray's idea was known to NBC. The Second Circuit recognized this, reporting Cosby's earlier statement that this *Dick Van Dyke*-style show "'will be radically different. Everyone in it will be a Negro.' ... Nearly twenty years later, on September 20, 1984, Cosby's dream for a 'color-blind' family series materialized with the premier of *The Cosby Show*—a situation comedy about a family known as the Huxtables." *Id.* at 989. One final irony of the decision is that Carsey-Werner was paid for the idea rather than Bill Cosby.

b. Every large media company regularly receives thousands of suggestions for new projects, both unsolicited and solicited. What steps would you suggest that a media company take to protect itself from expensive litigation brought by third parties?

c. Given the invalidity of the submission agreement in *FASA*, what terms should be included and excluded in a contractual submission agreement in order to make such an agreement enforceable?

d. As a practical matter, a strongly worded waiver provision may discourage claims against entertainment entities. As an attorney for such an entity, what ethical rules, or rules of professional conduct, limit participation in writing an agreement like that used in *FASA*? As the attorney for an originator of an idea, to what extent can you counsel your client to sign the agreement because it is not likely to be binding?

e. A written submission agreement can take two forms. The first requires the submitting party to waive any rights to the ideas or contract. The submitting party must rely exclusively on copyright protections, as applicable. In the context of unsolicited material, this should be the expectation of both parties. The second form may be used in the context of solicited material, through adoption of a nondisclosure agreement. Heavily utilized in some entertainment industries such as software and videogames, these are far less common in the film, television, and publishing industries. Nonetheless, the purposes and effectiveness are the same. Here are sample provisions of the key provisions:

1. *Confidentiality*. Recipient shall not directly or indirectly disclose, disseminate, publish, or use for its business advantage or for any other purpose, at any time during or after the term of this Agreement, any information received from Creator deemed confidential by the other party ("Confidential Information") without the express written permission of Creator for a period of five (5) years following the date of receipt of the Confidential Information.

a. *Definitions*. For purposes of this Agreement, Confidential Information shall be defined as any information not generally known in the industry about Creator's ideas, concepts, products, designs, intellectual property, trade secrets, services, or any combination thereof, whether or not such information would be recognized as proprietary absent this Agreement, including but not limited to information related to the Property developed by Creator.

b. *Limitations*. Notwithstanding any other provision of this Agreement, Recipient shall not be liable for disclosing, disseminating, publishing or using information which (i) was already known prior to the receipt of the Confidential Information; (ii) is now or becomes public information through no wrongful act of the Recipient; (iii) is independently developed or acquired by Recipient without any use of the Confidential Information in such development; or (iv) is required to be disclosed by law.

2. *Documents and Materials*. The documents and materials of Creator (including but not limited to all scripts, scenarios, treatments, data, reports, projections, records, notes, lists, specifications and designs) are furnished in accordance of this Agreement and shall remain the sole property of Creator. This information (collectively known as "Evaluation Material") shall upon the termination of this Agreement be promptly returned to Creator, including all copies thereof, which are in the possession or control of Recipient, its agents, and its representatives.

Problem I-C

You have spoken with an acquaintance, Angel, an investor, who might be willing to finance a multimedia project for an up-and-coming talent like Bryce. Angel is a classic "angel" investor, someone who is willing to invest in high-risk entertainment projects because the investor believes in developing new talent and enjoys the vicarious thrill of participating. Neither you nor your firm provides legal representation to Angel.

Bryce remains quite concerned that the project's concept will be stolen, if not by Angel directly, then by someone with whom Angel shares the information. Can a contract be drafted that accommodates Bryce's concerns and does not discourage Angel from learning more about the project? Since Angel considers dozens of potential projects for each one that receives any funds, any agreement must be sufficiently narrow that it does not unduly burden Angel. Identify the primary terms of such an agreement and how you would accommodate the needs of both Bryce and Angel. Also consider what issues, if any, are raised by your role in introducing Bryce to Angel.

Entertainment industries must greatly control the access to potential projects in order to avoid claims of access to copyrighted material. Unsolicited materials are returned unread. Only agents or lawyers are permitted to submit materials. Contracts explicitly waiving the right for compensation are sometimes required. These steps are necessary to protect the creators of copyrighted works from claims of copyright infringement, breach of contract, and theft of ideas.

D. Bibliography and Links

Treatises to Be Used throughout the Course:

Alexander Lindey & Michael Landau, Lindey on Entertainment, Publishing and the Arts (West) (looseleaf).

David Nimmer & Melville Nimmer, Nimmer on Copyright (Matthew Bender) (looseleaf).

Melvin Simensky, et al., Entertainment Law, Document Supplement (2d Ed. 1998) (an excellent compendium of relevant collective bargaining agreements and sample contracts).

Law Review Articles for Chapter I:

Samantha Barbas, *How the Movies Became Speech*, 64 Rutgers L. Rev. 665 (2012).

Benjamin R. Barber, *Free Speech and Community: The Market as Censor: Freedom of Expression in a World of Consumer Totalism*, 29 Ariz. St. L.J. 501 (1997) (discussing the contextualized meaning of entertainment media and First Amendment principles).

Clay Calvert & Robert D. Richards, *Mediated Images of Violence and the First Amendment: From Video Games to the Evening News*, 57 Me. L. Rev. 91 (2005).

Michael Coblenz, *Not for Entertainment Only: Fair Use and Fiction as Social Commentary*, 16 UCLA Ent. L. Rev. 265 (2009).

Christine Haight Farley, *Judging Art*, 79 Tul. L. Rev. 805 (2005).

Jon M. Garon, *The Heart of the Deal: Intellectual Property Aspects in the Law & Business of Entertainment*, 17 J. Int. Prop. L. 443 (2012).

William O. Knox, *The Role of Novelty in a California Idea Submission Case*, 11 UCLA Ent. L. Rev. 27 (2004).

Glen L. Kulik, *Copyright Preemption: Is This the End of Desny v. Wilder?*, 21 Loy. L.A. Ent. L.J. 1 (2000).

Joseph P. Liu, *The New Public Domain*, 2013 U. Ill. L. Rev. 1395 (2013).

David Nimmer, *The Moral Imperative Against Academic Plagiarism (Without a Moral Right Against Reverse Passing Off)*, 54 DePaul L. Rev. 1 (2004).

Frederick Schauer, *Harm(s) and the First Amendment*, 2011 S. Ct. Rev. 81 (2011).

Rebecca Tushnet, *Copyright as a Model for Free Speech Law: What Copyright has in Common with Anti-Pornography Laws, Campaign Finance Reform, and Telecommunications Regulation*, 42 B.C. L. Rev. 1 (2000).

Rebecca Tushnet, *Performance Anxiety: Copyright Embodied and Disembodied,* 60 J. Copyright Socy. U.S.A. 209 (2013).

Daniel E. Wanat, *Entertainment Law: An Analysis of Judicial Decision-Making in Cases
where a Celebrity's Publicity Right is in Conflict with a User's First Amendment Right,*
67 Alb. L. Rev. 251 (2003).

Mary W. S. Wong, *Toward an Alternative Normative Framework for Copyright: From Private Property to Human Rights,* 26 Cardozo Arts & Ent. L.J. 775 (2009).

Websites

ABANetwork Forum on Ent. & Sports Ind., www.abanet.org/forums/entsports/home.html

Hollywood Reporter, www.hollywoodreporter.com/

Los Angeles Times—Entertainment Business, www.latimes.com/business/custom/cotown/

Loyola of Los Angeles Entertainment Law Journal, www.law.lmu.edu/student/elj/
eljhome.htm

United States Copyright Office, www.copyright.gov

United States Federal Communications Commission, www.fcc.gov

United States Patent and Trademark Office, www.uspto.gov

Variety, http://variety.com/

Chapter II

International Implications of Entertainment Law and Practice

Although this casebook is drafted from an American perspective, the importance of the broader, international perspective is critical to understanding the economics of the industry. Simply put, the United States dominates the world with English-based content distribution. Except where banned on religious or moral grounds, Bob Dylan's music can be heard in virtually every country on the globe. The commercial record industry, for example, which had been once dominated by companies in Germany and England has largely consolidated into United States companies, led by Universal Music Group and Warner Music Group. Sony Music Entertainment is a U.S.-based company though it is owned by the Japanese conglomerate.

Conversely, the largest entertainment conglomerates are not limited to the United States, but include many multinational companies such as the Japanese manufacturing and content giant Sony Co.; the Australian-based television, satellite, and newspaper producer News Corp. (parent of Twentieth Century Fox); and Liberty Global, the UK company which acquired Virgin Media.

India and Taiwan are representative of local industries that generate tremendous amounts of regional commercial entertainment content. Though those works do not play a significant role in the U.S. market, they influence the global marketplace. Similarly, almost every nation has some indigenous entertainment industry, so often the international concerns focus on promoting the local industry and seeking to participate in the positive aspects of cooperative international trade.

This chapter provides a general framework for the global practice of entertainment law and highlights a few of the current debates.

A. Overview

Any comprehensive review of international entertainment must take into account the importance that the entertainment and copyright industries have as an engine of economic trade and development. In addition to trade and the international treaty regime designed to foster such trade, U.S. entertainment companies are very interested in the debates over the balance between protectionism and localism, and the increasing significance of intellectual property recognition for folklore and indigenous knowledge.

1. Internationalization of Entertainment

In 2012, the core copyright industries contributed $1 trillion dollars to the United States gross domestic product, according to a report by International Intellectual Property Alliance. Foreign sales involving those same core copyright industries exceeded $142 billion dollars, outpacing aerospace exports ($106 billion), agriculture ($70 billion), food ($65 billion), and agriculture ($51 billion).

Worldwide, the results are similar, though perhaps not as dramatic. The World Intellectual Property Organization (WIPO) estimates that the gross domestic product for the entertainment and copyright industries has grown at a rate twice that of the general economies.

Interestingly, the U.S. was a latecomer to the primary copyright treaty, the Berne Convention, as well as to most of the international protection of copyright. The U.S. joined only as of March 1989. The U.S. had been a member of the Universal Copyright Convention beginning in 1955, and had had limited bilateral cooperation with other countries as far back as 1891. Because the primary international framework for the entertainment industries stems from the Berne Convention and a series of international copyright treaties, the international copyright fundamentals and related treaties are outlined in Chapter II-B, below.

2. Economics of Trade Protection and Localism

Both inside and outside the U.S., the political debate around copyright often stems from the issues of copyright piracy and the appropriateness of actions to stop consumers from illegally downloading MP3 and computer files, or from buying unauthorized bootleg copies of films, DVDs, and software.

While this dialogue continues in the developing as well as the developed nations, countries with smaller entertainment markets must also address the issue of trade barriers, governmental support, and protectionism for the industry. In reality, these topics are all part of the same debate over the appropriate economic framework. Each nation must ask what is needed to develop a sustainable entertainment enterprise.

The economics are simple. Pirated goods are sold at a cost vastly lower than authorized goods. For example, the cost to manufacture a motion picture DVD ranges from $0.25–$0.75, which covers the cost of the disk, the case, and the cover. A $19.99 suggested retail price represents the costs associated with the licensing of various rights to the packaging artwork, the novel on which the motion picture was based, the actors, director, technicians, musical score, musicians, production costs and overhead, and an assessment that the selected price will result in highest rate of return.[1] The price has little to do with the cost of manufacturing the disk, case, and cover. As a result, the bootleg or

---

1. The home video market was originally conceived on the economic assumption that most people would choose to rent rather than own a motion picture. The pricing was set generally at $80.00 to $100.00 per copy, a price at which few consumers elected to buy the tape, but which provided the video rental companies a modest return. To generate the same revenue, a producer would have to sell slightly more than four times as many tapes at $20.00 to $25.00 to make the same income (the "slightly more" reflects the packaging and distribution costs). Legend suggests that Steven Spielberg recognized this axiom of pricing and created the "sell-through" market with the release of *E.T.* priced to encourage consumer purchases.

pirated version of the work generates income for the pirate at any price over the cost of materials, but generates no income to the participants who created or financed the work.

Piracy, therefore, has the direct effect of reducing income to the creator of that work. While each piratical sale does not directly equate to a lost sale (since the purchaser willing to pay $1.00 may not be someone willing to pay $10.00 or $20.00), piracy has a direct, negative influence on the sales of copyrighted works.

Piracy has a second, more pernicious, impact on the entertainment industry in smaller markets. The pirated DVD directly replaces the commercially available DVD which sells for $20.00. For those unwilling to pay $20.00, however, there had been a market of $5.00 to $10.00 projects that were produced locally with a lower cost (and possibly a lower quality than the Hollywood product). If Hollywood films are illegally sold in smaller, foreign markets, these sales have the potential to financially cripple the local, more fragile entertainment economies. In Singapore, for example, the Wall Street Journal reported that the number of films produced annually had dropped from 300 to less than 20 in 2002 as a result of piracy.

The U.S. entertainment industries have found ready allies with countries both large and small which are embracing copyright laws to attack piracy. This should not be viewed as any endorsement of the U.S. content, nor as a sign of political weakness. These countries recognize that to foster a local industry, the respect for copyright must apply to all works.

As a result, the primary focus for domestic protectionism takes the form of enforcement of international copyright treaties. Only by cracking down on piracy do the domestic producers have a chance to compete.

Beyond the common goal of copyright enforcement, there is some notable disagreement as to which protectionist measures are appropriate. Some countries compete with the U.S. by funding arts organizations or content producers. Unlike the U.S., many countries have government-owned or wholly-funded entertainment companies. Other countries place content requirements on the entertainment distributors. These regulations may include a requirement that a certain portion of each television station's broadcast be produced locally or is produced in the native language of that country; a certain percentage of motion pictures shown in each theater be domestically produced; include tax incentives for local productions; or include excise taxes on foreign projects.

One of the objectives of the various free trade agreements is to eliminate anti-competitive tariffs. The entertainment industries generally benefit from such treaties. The Berne Convention is not directly tied to these agreements, so countries may provide copyright protection without participating in free trade agreements.

Without copyright protection and enforcement, however, it is quite unlikely that a country can develop a strong entertainment community. Since the costs of developing a music industry and even a film industry are quite high, many nations have come to recognize that copyright protection and enforcement is a rather low cost method to enter the world trade markets.

3. The Folklore Debate and Collective Recognition

The other concern raised in developing countries is the risk of exploitation of indigenous knowledge and folklore traditions. Indigenous knowledge includes the common wisdom of non-industrialized communities; knowledge held by leaders, healers, or elders in such communities; and highly prized knowledge, traditions and practices. A rough translation into U.S. legal parlance would be that indigenous knowledge is akin to trade secrets which are owned by communities rather than corporations, and the secret may range from a highly select group of recognized individuals to a more broadly held trade secret held by the community as a whole. In her paper "The Role of Intellectual Property Rights in the Sharing of Benefits Arising from the Use of Biological Resources and Traditional Knowledge," Anil K. Gupta[2] describes indigenous knowledge as follows:

> When individual knowledge is shared with the community, whilst the general relationship between, for example, a plant and its uses may be known to the community, the more specialized uses associated with the plant may still be restricted to individual experts; for instance, individual healers who know how to calibrate the dose and combination of herbal drugs according to the condition of the patient. Such an expert may, or may not, be free to share their knowledge, according to the rules of the community, since there may be taboos implying that a particular remedy might lose its effectiveness if revealed to others. Such a taboo leads to erosion of knowledge when such a knowledge expert dies without ever sharing the secret.[3]

While the analogy to trade secrets may be helpful, this is not the legal construction historically given to indigenous knowledge. Foreign corporations have been known to identify valuable information — such as the use to which a particular plant may be made for a medical remedy or the efficacy of a rare combination of chemicals — in order to exploit the knowledge. This exploitation has two components. First, European and American companies treat developing regions imperialistically whenever such a company "discovers" a commonly known practice, if the only discovery is to document the indigenous knowledge. If the knowledge is commonly held, then such knowledge should be sufficient to invalidate the patent claim. Second, assuming the discovery is patentable, the revenue should be shared in an appropriate and equitable manner among the holders of the indigenous knowledge. To usurp such knowledge without permission or remuneration is akin to the theft of a trade secret.

The folklore debate takes these same concepts to the issues of copyright. Many local communities have dance, music, craft, and art histories that are collective in nature. Often, these works have never been fixed in a tangible form, so no copyright has ever existed. In some cases, third parties from outside the community observe these works and then adapt them for sale without prior permission. In other situations, members of the communities take personal authority to copyright and publicly exploit these historically communal works. In both cases, difficult issues are faced regarding ownership, exploitation, and the moral or legal right to exploit the works.

With respect to both indigenous knowledge and folklore, WIPO is working closely with member nations and others to identify solutions to provide ownership schemes that balance the competing interests involved in these culturally significant disputes. Nonetheless, as Professor Gupta acknowledges, "[t]he discussions in the WIPO Intergovernmental Committee on Intellectual Property and Genetic Resources, Traditional Knowledge

---

2. Chair Professor of Entrepreneurship, Indian Institute of Management, Ahmedabad and Executive Vice Chair, National Innovation Foundation, Department of Science and Technology, Government of India, Ahmedabad. *See* http://www.sristi.org, http://www.gian.org, http://www.nifindia.org.

3. ANIL K. GUPTA, WIPO-UNEP STUDY IN THE ROLE OF INTELLECTUAL PROPERTY RIGHTS IN THE SHARING OF BENEFITS ARISING FROM THE USE OF BIOLOGICAL RESOURCES AND ASSOCIATED TRADITIONAL KNOWLEDGE 12 (World Intell. Prop. Org. & U.N. Env't. Programme eds., 2001).

and Folklore demonstrate a detailed understanding of the tensions existing among different countries on the issues of IP and access and benefit-sharing. However, the more difficult and challenging issue of providing incentives within a country for different kind of resource regimes and knowledge domains has not been adequately pursued so far."[4] Reconciling the competing demands and interests involving indigenous knowledge and folklore will be an ongoing process for years to come.

B. International Copyright

1. Introduction

Copyright provides one of the earliest modern legal doctrines protecting the intellectual endeavor. In 1710, England adopted the Statute of Anne, which was designed both to create some legal property rights in authorship and to reduce the prior monopolies held by the printers, who had exclusive rights to print. Among the significant terms of the Statute of Anne were limits regarding the scope of protection to English language printing, a term of 14 years, which was renewable if author was living at the end of the term; the power to fine and to destroy infringing works; and the reserved power to limit the price of a seller's books (recognizing the monopoly power granted by the Statute). By the end of the century, copyright protection was extended in both France (1791 and 1793) and the United States (1790) immediately following great political change.

Copyright protection has extended virtually worldwide. In general, each country's law of copyright governs only its own territory. Copyright does not extend extraterritorially. As a result, throughout the nineteenth century, works created in one country could be reproduced without need for a license in other countries. The ease of export for copyrighted works created the need for greater international coordination. Not surprisingly, these arrangements started as bilateral agreements between close, neighboring states, but they grew broader in scope throughout the nineteenth and twentieth centuries.

The Berne Convention

This process culminated with the adoption of the Berne Convention for the Protection of Literary and Artistic Works in 1886. The most important of the international copyright laws, the Berne Convention rests on two primary principles. First, each member state must provide *national treatment* for all authors. National treatment requires that any work originating in a Berne Union country be afforded the same treatment as that state provides for its own nationals. With only a few limited exceptions, national treatment guarantees equality of protection within each Berne Union country. Second, each Berne Union country must provide *minimum rights* regarding the protections. In this way, the Berne Convention serves as an international floor for the scope of copyright protections afforded throughout much of the world. There are presently 148 member states who are members of the Berne Union.

The application of the Berne Convention to domestic law varies. In some countries, it is self-executing, meaning that the text is treated as the law of the land, analogous to any other statute. In other jurisdictions, such as the United States, it has no direct effect

---

4. *Id.* at 14.

on domestic law. Instead, the national laws must be modified to comply with the terms of the convention.

In addition to the Berne Convention itself, there are a number of important related international treaties. These include the Trade Related Aspects of Intellectual Property Rights (the TRIPS Agreement), World Intellectual Property Organization Copyright Treaty (WCT), and the WIPO Performances and Phonograms Treaty (WPPT). Each is dealt with briefly below.

2. Subject Matter of Copyright

Original Works or Authorship

Copyright provides the author or creator of an original work of authorship the exclusive ownership of that work. Although variously defined, authorship generally incorporates literary and artistic works. The enumerated list of the U.S. Copyright act is representative:

> (1) Literary works; (2) musical works, including any accompanying words; (3) dramatic works, including any accompanying music; (4) pantomimes and choreographic works; (5) pictorial, graphic, and sculptural works; (6) motion pictures and other audiovisual works; (7) sound recordings; and (8) architectural works.

The Berne Convention has a similar list of criteria that essentially covers the same broad range of categories, although drafted in a somewhat different manner:

> The expression "literary and artistic works" shall include every production in the literary, scientific and artistic domain, whatever may be the mode or form of its expression, such as books, pamphlets and other writings; lectures, addresses, sermons and other works of the same nature; dramatic or dramatico-musical works; choreographic works and entertainments in dumb show; musical compositions with or without words; cinematographic works to which are assimilated works expressed by a process analogous to cinematography; works of drawing, painting, architecture, sculpture, engraving and lithography; photographic works to which are assimilated works expressed by a process analogous to photography; works of applied art; illustrations, maps, plans, sketches and three-dimensional works relative to geography, topography, architecture or science.

In both categories, the list is broad and inclusive. Although neither specifically includes software, the U.S. and most countries extend copyright to software as well.

Ideas Not Protected

Copyright limits the scope of the ownership afforded to the author of the work. The law protects only the expression of the work, not ideas, procedures, processes, or facts. This protects the creativity of the expression but does not give any author a monopoly on the facts or ideas presented.

Originality and Creativity Necessary

To be afforded copyright protection, an author must have created the work, meaning that the work is original to that author. There is no requirement that the work is novel or unique, merely that the work derives from the person who is the author. Similarly, there must be some creative spark, no matter how minor, that serves to set the work apart.

Fixation Requirements

The copyright ownership initially vests in the author of the work. If the country has a fixation requirement, the copyright will vest upon fixation. In a large number of countries, copyright protection is available only once the work is fixed in a tangible form. Technology has made the fixation requirement increasingly easy to accomplish, so that today, a written copy of a speech, sheet music, or videotape of an improvisational dance will all serve to fix the work.

Despite the growing ease of fixation, it remains a barrier to copyright protection for some works, such as unwritten speeches or improvisational theater. As a result, the Berne Convention and many other countries do not require fixation as a prerequisite to copyright protection. In the U.S., federal law imposes the fixation requirement, but most U.S. states will afford limited copyright protection for unfixed works.

Eligibility for Berne Convention

An author shall be afforded the protections of the Berne Convention if that author is a national of one of the Berne Union countries, or if the work is first published in a Berne Union country. This may be accomplished by simultaneously publishing a work in a Berne Union country, which means that such publication occur within 30 days of any other publication. In addition, authors who are not nationals of one of the countries of the Union but who have their habitual residence in a Union country shall be treated as nationals of that country.

3. Exclusive Rights of Copyright Ownership

Economic Rights

The exclusive property rights of the copyright owner fall into the following broad categories: (1) reproduction or copying; (2) translation, adaptation, modification, or the creation of derivative works; (3) distribution by sale, license or other transfer of ownership, or by rental, lease, or lending; (4) public performance; and (5) public display.

The exact scope of these exclusive rights may vary somewhat from country to country. For example, England provides for a lending right, which guarantees a minimal payment to the copyright holder when a work is transferred from the owner of the copy of the work to any successive owner.

Moral Rights

In addition to the economic rights, article 6bis of the Berne Convention provides that an author shall have the right to claim authorship of the work and to object to any distortion, mutilation or other modification of, or other derogatory action in relation to, the said work which would be prejudicial to his honor or reputation. In the U.S., these rights are extended by section 106A of the Copyright Act only to works of visual arts created in series of no more than 200 copies. As provided in the Berne Convention, moral rights are neither assignable nor waivable and remain fully enforceable by the author of the work, even if that person is no longer the copyright owner. The failure of the United States to fully meet its Berne Convention obligation regarding these rights remains a significant international trade issue.

Term of Ownership

The Berne Convention sets as the minimum copyright duration for most works the life of the author, plus an additional 50 years. Increasingly, however, the European Union and many other countries have extended the term of copyright for the life of the author plus 70 years.

If the work is made as a work for hire, then the term is 95 years from publication or 120 years from creation, whichever is less. In the U.S., this is also the term provided for anonymous and pseudonymous works, but this term varies significantly from country to country.

4. Formalities of Copyright Protection

The Berne Convention prohibits the member country from requiring any formalities as a prerequisite to receiving copyright protection. Nonetheless, there remain a few general formalities that are often encouraged by member countries, although they do not bar copyright protection. In some situations, the copyright holder is given additional remedies from infringement. In addition, registration can also serve as prima facie evidence of the information contained in the registration form, which can be helpful in any legal disputes relating to the use or ownership of the copyright.

The first requirement is notice that the work is protected by copyright, which typically includes the copyright symbol "©" or the word or abbreviation for copyright along with the year of publication and the name of the copyright holder. This should be featured prominently in a place a reader would expect to look, such as the title page of a book.

The second formality is registration, which often requires payment of a filing fee and submission of a copy of the work to the country's copyright office. In the U.S., for example, while registration is no longer required, it does provide some benefits if a legal dispute ever erupts regarding the work, including prima facie evidence of the facts in the copyright application and statutory damages and attorneys' fees if filed in a timely fashion.

The U.S. also requires that the author provide the Library of Congress with two copies of the best edition of every published work made in the United States. This deposit, however, is generally made as part of the registration process. In the situation where a copyright holder of a published work elects not to register the work, he or she is still obligated to submit the copies to the Library of Congress. If the copyright owner refuses to send the copies after receiving a demand letter, then the copyright office can levy substantial fines.

5. Transfers of Copyright

Copyright is often described as a "bundle of rights" that can be separated into any number of exclusive and non-exclusive transfers. Exclusive rights can be granted for a period of time, for a geographic location, or for a particular use. In most countries, the transfer of rights is accomplished either by a license of some portion of the copyright holder's interest or an assignment of the copyright holder's entire interest. In some countries, however, an assignment of copyright is not permitted. Even in these countries, a license of the copyright holder's interest remains valid, so long as the license encompasses something less than the entire copyright holder's interest. As a result, the practical effect can place the licensee in the same position as if it were an assignee of the copyright.

6. Related or Neighboring Rights

When first developed, copyright extended only to books, maps, and fine arts. The expansion of copyright to broadcasters, performers, and sound recordings has evolved slowly in the past century. As a result, the protection for these rights is sometimes incorporated into the copyright laws of a country but are sometimes treated as rights related to copyright. In those countries that do not incorporate these art forms directly into their copyright law, there may be shorter duration for protection than under traditional copyright laws.

Typically, the related rights focus on the rights of (1) performing artists, such as actors and musicians, in their performances, (2) producers of sound recordings, and (3) broadcasting organizations in the broadcast of their programming. In each of these three areas, international treaties require at least a grant of minimal protection from unauthorized exploitation.

For performing artists, such as actors and musicians, the neighboring rights regime codifies mandatory minimal protection, providing that a person's performance cannot be fixed, broadcast or sold without the performer's permission. This right is particularly important where the culture relies heavily on an oral tradition, recognizing the moral and economic interest of the performer in the activity.

For the producers of sound recordings, the neighboring rights regime recognizes the interest in the phonogram (or CD, cassette tape, or other technological format) that embeds a musical composition. The author of the musical composition is often not the author of the phonogram. Instead, modern law acknowledges that there is sufficient artistry and economic interest in the creation of the phonogram so that it should be treated as a separately protected work. This has become particularly important because the phonogram has seen the greatest technological change and stands on the forefront of much of the anti-piracy protection today.

For the broadcast organizations, protection of the broadcast signal requires controls over international rebroadcast of the signal by satellite to jurisdictions around the globe. Protection of the interest of the broadcasters in the control of their transmission serves to protect the interest of the industry and the national interest in regularizing the global telecommunications among countries.

These principles have been made the subject of the International Convention for the Protection of Performers, Producers of Phonograms and Broadcasting Organizations, known as the Rome Convention of October 26, 1961. Under the Rome Convention, the parties are granted the protections of national treatment, and protections in each of the three performance rights identified by the neighboring rights. Many of these same protections have been expanded under the Trade Related Aspects of Intellectual Property Rights (TRIPS Agreement).

Subsequent Treaties and Conventions

Many of the same topics covered by the Rome Agreement have been the subject of expanded protection through a series of additional international agreements. In particular, the areas of sound recordings and broadcast require increasing protection and enforcement authority because of the constant advances in technology, concomitant growth of piracy, and the constant danger of copyright infringement.

TRIPS Agreement

In 1994, significant advances were made in the international protection of copyrighted works with the TRIPS Agreement, which expanded the protection for copyright holders or holders of neighboring rights. The TRIPS Agreement extended the obligations to all members of the World Trade Organization (WTO), rather than just the signatories to the TRIPS Agreement itself. The TRIPS Agreement required all WTO members to protect all recordings released within the past fifty years. In addition, the TRIPS Agreement provided the phonogram copyright holders the ability to control rental of their recordings. The TRIPS Agreement also clarified and expanded the subject matter of copyright protection to specifically include computer programs, compilations of data, cinematographic works, and sound recordings.

The TRIPS Agreement also supplemented and expanded the Rome Convention by extending the protection of neighboring rights to all WTO members and by increasing the term of protection for sound recordings from 20 to 50 years.

It furthered the goal of protecting copyright holders from piracy of the works by requiring that members of the WTO to ensure that effective enforcement procedures are available. Similarly, the TRIPS Agreement includes provisions requiring action by customs authorities against suspected counterfeit or pirated goods.

Finally, the TRIPS Agreement also established that countries can bring an action against other countries for infringement of these rights through the World Trade Organization. While the WTO can't change a country's laws, it can impose tariffs as penalties if a country is found to be in violation of TRIPS.

WIPO Copyright Treaty

After the adoption of the TRIPS Agreement, work continued to address issues not yet resolved through the TRIPS Agreement. This process culminated with the "WIPO Diplomatic Conference on Certain Copyright and Neighboring Rights Questions" which took place in Geneva from December 2 to 20, 1996. The Diplomatic Conference adopted two treaties, the WIPO Copyright Treaty (WCT) and the WIPO Performances and Phonograms Treaty (WPPT).

The WCT expands the protection of the TRIPS Agreement by granting to copyright owners the exclusive right of distribution of the physical copies of their work. It also reflects the growing importance of the Internet by treating on-demand communication of works to individuals as public performances. Finally, like the TRIPS Agreement, it articulated requirements concerning technological measures intended to safeguard copyright through rights management protection that may be digitally embedded within the music, software, and/or hardware. Rights management information is that which identifies the work, the author, the owner of any right of the work, the conditions of use, and any data that represent this information. Increasingly, protection of the copyrighted work is tied to the digital transmission or reproduction of the work.

Countries must prohibit the circumvention of technological measures used by copyright holders to protect their works. Similarly, the nation must provide adequate and effective legal remedies against persons who remove or alter electronic rights management information without authority, or knowingly distribute works that have been stripped of the electronic rights management without authority.

WIPO Performances and Phonograms Treaty

The WPPT expressly granted that producers of phonograms would have the exclusive right of direct or indirect reproduction of their works, in any form. This expanded the control over the neighboring rights first protected by international convention in the Rome Convention. It gave producers and performers the exclusive right to authorize on-demand transmissions, providing an excellent platform for international e-commerce. Finally, the WPPT provided limited rights to both producers and performers regarding remuneration for broadcasting or any communication to the public of their work. As a result, the international sound recording industry has moved to the forefront of legal protection and international treaty in copyright.

7. Enforcement of Copyright Interests

Individual Claims

Copyright claims are enforced in the country where the unauthorized activity or infringement actually took place. Because copyright does not apply extraterritorially, a copyright holder cannot sue in his or her home country for infringements that take place in another country.

Typically, the copyright holder must establish that he or she is the valid owner of the copyright. The copyright holder must also establish that the defendant in the lawsuit copied or otherwise violated one of the exclusive rights reserved to the copyright holder. Typically this is shown by establishing the access the defendant had to the work and the similarity between the two works.

A court can order the seizure and destruction of infringing copies of a work. Depending on the country, fines may be levied, the profits made by the infringement may be paid to the copyright holder, or the damages sustained by the copyright holder may be paid by the infringer. In addition, criminal charges may be brought by the appropriate government prosecutors. Criminal suits generally follow the country's laws regarding criminal procedure and process.

Performing Rights Societies

Since the middle of the nineteenth century, copyright owners have recognized that individual lawsuits are economically inefficient in stopping copyright infringement. A composer simply cannot spend $1,000 to collect $10.00 in copyright royalties. Instead, composers recognized that the only method of effective collection and compensation is through organized societies that collect royalties on behalf of their members.

The performing rights societies typically license their library of music to performance halls, broadcasters, and similar venues. The licensee pays a fee for the right to publicly perform the music to the performing rights society. Organizations generally operate nationally or regionally, including ASCAP (American Society of Composers, Authors, and Publishers), SACEM (Societe Des Auteurs Compositeurs Et Editeurs De Musique) and SIAE (Societa Italiana Degli Autori Ed Editori), to name a few. The revenue received from the sale of licenses is then divided among the members based on the internal formula adopted by the organization. These payments are generally tied to the proportion of public performance attributed to each author in any given period. In some countries, the performing rights society is part of the government itself while in other jurisdictions the societies are separately organized.

With the growth of the Internet, performing rights societies have taken on increasing importance as a method of protecting the rights of holders of various copyright interests. Depending on the country, the rights to publicly perform a song may now require the authorization of the composer, the phonogram copyright holder, and the performers on the recording. Through the use of performing rights societies, the rights can be aggregated, payments collected, and funds distributed.

8. "Making Available" or Communication Right[5]

What Is the "Making Available" Right?

The "making available" right is an exclusive right for authors, performers and "phonogram producers" to authorise or prohibit the dissemination of their works and other protected material through interactive networks such as the internet.

This exclusive right is one of the most important achievements of the WIPO Treaties and constitutes a basic requirement for the development of electronic commerce. The international community, in the 1996 Diplomatic Conference that adopted the treaties, unanimously acknowledged that record producers in particular needed this exclusive right to cover the use of their phonograms in the digital environment.

The reason was not only to fight piracy. The international community also recognised that the dissemination of phonograms in digital networks such as the internet constitutes a primary form of exploitation of music, and therefore should be subject to the control of the rights owner.

The making available right covers both the actual offering of the phonogram or other protected material and its subsequent transmission to members of the public. The exclusive right provides control over the act of "making available" by all means of delivery—by wire or wireless means—and whenever members of the public may access the work or phonogram from a place and at a time individually chosen by them.

This broad formulation is capable of accommodating many different types of exploitation, from services allowing only the listening of music, to services allowing the download of permanent copies of music tracks, to exciting future uses of technology.

9. Defenses and Limitations on Copyright

Public Domain

With few exceptions, copyright does not have a perpetual duration. Instead, copyright holders' exclusive rights to works eventually expire and those works become freely available to the public. Once a work has ceased to be protected by copyright, it is considered to be in the public domain and free for any party to use in any manner.

---

5. International Federation of the Photographic Industry, *The WIPO Treaties: 'Making Available' Right* (2003), http://www.ifpi.org/content/library/wipo-treaties-making-available-right.pdf. This overview of international copyright has been provided by the International Federation of the Phonographic Industry (IFPI). Copyright International Federation of the Phonographic Industry (IFPI), London, www.ifpi.org. Reprinted with permission. Photographs, captions, and some inset text boxes have been removed.

A person may take a public domain work and modify, translate, or adapt that work into something new. The author of this new work receives copyright protection for the new creation, but does not receive any ownership or protection of the source work that has fallen into the public domain. In this way, many different authors can create works based on popular works that have fallen into the public domain.

Fair Use

The Berne Convention and most laws limit the exclusive rights of the copyright holder, at least to the extent necessary to allow for some general criticism, comment, news reporting, scholarship, or research. This protects the public's need to comment on a work, to quote portions in other critical works, and to build upon the works that have gone before. The laws protecting unauthorized use of a work for comment or criticism vary considerably from country to country, but virtually all recognize that the absolute ownership of copyright must be tempered to some degree with the need for public discourse.

10. Conclusion

At its heart, copyright protects the creations of the mind—the literature, art, music, and content that an individual creates. These works serve as the economic and cultural heart for every country in the world. The protection of these works and the promotion of the unique voice of each author and nation has gained increased importance in the world economy as these works take priority in international trade.

Through international agreements such as the Berne Convention, the TRIPS Agreement, and other WTO understandings, the common basis for copyright protection has grown dramatically over the past twenty years. Although there continues to be much work to be done to include all nations, the expansion and growth of copyright protection and international harmony is unparalleled. As a result, copyright will serve as the basis for much of the international trade in the years to come.

C. Territoriality, Trade, and Damages

Subafilms, Ltd. v. MGM-Pathe Communications Co.
24 F.3d 1088 (9th Cir. 1994) (*en banc*)

In this case, we consider the "vexing question" of whether a claim for infringement can be brought under the Copyright Act when the assertedly infringing conduct consists solely of the authorization within the territorial boundaries of the United States of acts that occur entirely abroad. We hold that such allegations do not state a claim for relief under the copyright laws of the United States.

In 1966, the musical group The Beatles, through Subafilms, Ltd., entered into a joint venture with the Hearst Corporation to produce the animated motion picture entitled "Yellow Submarine" (the "Picture"). Over the next year, Hearst, acting on behalf of the joint venture (the "Producer"), negotiated an agreement with United Artists Corporation ("UA") to distribute and finance the film. Separate distribution and financing agreements were entered into in May, 1967. Pursuant to these agreements, UA distributed the Picture in theaters beginning in 1968 and later on television.

In the early 1980s, with the advent of the home video market, UA entered into several licensing agreements to distribute a number of its films on videocassette. Although one company expressed interest in the Picture, UA refused to license "Yellow Submarine" because of uncertainty over whether home video rights had been granted by the 1967 agreements. Subsequently, in 1987, UA's successor company, MGM/UA Communications Co. ("MGM/UA"), over the Producer's objections, authorized its subsidiary MGM/UA Home Video, Inc. to distribute the Picture for the domestic home video market, and, pursuant to an earlier licensing agreement, notified Warner Bros., Inc. ("Warner") that the Picture had been cleared for international videocassette distribution. Warner, through its wholly owned subsidiary, Warner Home Video, Inc., in turn entered into agreements with third parties for distribution of the Picture on videocassette around the world.

In 1988, Subafilms and Hearst ("Appellees") brought suit against MGM/UA, Warner, and their respective subsidiaries (collectively the "Distributors" or "Appellants"), contending that the videocassette distribution of the Picture, both foreign and domestic, constituted copyright infringement and a breach of the 1967 agreements. The case was tried before a retired California Superior Court Judge acting as a special master. The special master found for Appellees on both claims, and against the Distributors on their counterclaim for fraud and reformation. Except for the award of prejudgment interest, which it reversed, the district court adopted all of the special master's factual findings and legal conclusions. Appellees were awarded $2,228,000.00 in compensatory damages, split evenly between the foreign and domestic home video distributions. In addition, Appellees received attorneys' fees and a permanent injunction that prohibited the Distributors from engaging in, or authorizing, any home video use of the Picture....

As the panel in this case correctly concluded, *Peter Starr* [*Prod. Co. v. Twin Continental Films, Inc.,* 783 F.2d 1440 (9th Cir. 1986)] held that the authorization within the United States of entirely extraterritorial acts stated a cause of action under the "plain language" of the Copyright Act. Observing that the Copyright Act grants a copyright owner "the *exclusive rights* to do and *to authorize*" any of the activities listed in *17 U.S.C. § 106*(1)–(5), and that a violation of the "authorization" right constitutes infringement under section 501 of the Act, the *Peter Starr* court reasoned that allegations of an authorization within the United States of extraterritorial conduct that corresponded to the activities listed in section 106 "alleged an act of infringement within the United States." Accordingly, the court determined that the district court erred "in concluding that 'Plaintiff alleged only infringing acts which took place outside of the United States,'" and reversed the district court's dismissal for lack of subject matter jurisdiction.

The *Peter Starr* court accepted, as does this court, that the acts *authorized* from within the United States themselves could not have constituted infringement under the Copyright Act because "in general, United States copyright laws do not have extraterritorial effect," and therefore, "infringing actions that take place entirely outside the United States are not actionable." The central premise of the *Peter Starr* court, then, was that a party could be held liable as an "infringer" under section 501 of the Act merely for authorizing a third party to engage in acts that, had they been committed *within* the United States, would have violated the exclusive rights granted to a copyright holder by section 106.

Since *Peter Starr,* however, we have recognized that, when a party authorizes an activity *not* proscribed by one of the five section 106 clauses, the authorizing party cannot be held liable as an infringer. In *Lewis Galoob,* we rejected the argument that "a party can unlawfully authorize another party to use a copyrighted work even if that party's use of the work would not violate the Copyright Act," *Lewis Galoob,* 964 F.2d at 970, and approved of Professor Nimmer's statement that "'to the extent that an activity does not violate one of the five enumerated rights [found in *17 U.S.C. § 106*], authorizing such activity does not constitute copyright infringement,'" *id.* (quoting 3 David Nimmer & Melville B. Nimmer, *Nimmer on Copyright § 12.04*[A][3][a], at 12–80 n.82 (1991))....

Even assuming *arguendo* that the acts authorized in this case would have been illegal abroad, we do not believe the distinction offered by Appellees is a relevant one. Because the copyright laws do not apply extraterritorially, each of the rights conferred under the five section 106 categories must be read as extending "no farther than the [United States'] borders." 2 Goldstein, *supra,* § 16.0, at 675. In light of our above conclusion that the "authorization" right refers to the doctrine of contributory infringement, which requires that the authorized act *itself* could violate one of the exclusive rights listed in section 106(1)–(5), we believe that "it is simply not possible to draw a principled distinction" between an act that does not violate a copyright because it is not the type of conduct proscribed by section 106, and one that does not violate section 106 because the illicit act occurs overseas. In both cases, the authorized conduct could not violate the exclusive rights guaranteed by section 106. In both cases, therefore, there can be no liability for "authorizing" such conduct.

To hold otherwise would produce the untenable anomaly, inconsistent with the general principles of third party liability, that a party could be held liable as an infringer for violating the "authorization" right when the party that it authorized could not be considered an infringer under the Copyright Act. Put otherwise, we do not think Congress intended to hold a party liable for *merely* "authorizing" conduct that, had the *authorizing* party chosen to engage in itself, would have resulted in no liability under the Act.

Appellees rely heavily on the Second Circuit's doctrine that extraterritorial application of the copyright laws is permissible "when the type of infringement permits further reproduction abroad." *Update Art, Inc. v. Modiin Publishing, Ltd.,* 843 F.2d 67, 73 (2d Cir. 1988). Whatever the merits of the Second Circuit's rule, and we express no opinion on its validity in this circuit, it is premised on the theory that the copyright holder may recover damages that stem from a direct infringement of its exclusive rights that occurs *within* the United States.

[In] *Sheldon v. Metro-Goldwyn Pictures Corp.,* 106 F.2d 45, 52 (2d Cir. 1939) *aff'd,* 309 U.S. 390 (1940) (L. Hand, J.) [the court explained] ... "[t]he negatives were 'records' from which the work could be 'reproduced', and it was a tort to make them in this country. The plaintiffs acquired an equitable interest in them as soon as they were made, which attached to any profits from their exploitation...." Professor Nimmer formulates the doctrine in the following terms: "If and to the extent a part of an 'act' of infringement occurs within the United States, then, although such act is completed in a foreign jurisdiction, those parties who contributed to the act within the United States may be rendered liable under American copyright law." 3 *Nimmer, supra, § 17.02,* at 17–19 (footnotes omitted).

In these cases, liability is not based on contributory infringement, but on the theory that the infringing use would have been actionable *even if* the subsequent foreign distribution that stemmed from that use never took place. These cases, therefore, simply are inapplicable to a theory of liability based merely on the authorization of noninfringing acts.

Accordingly, accepting that wholly extraterritorial acts of infringement cannot support a claim under the Copyright Act, we believe that the *Peter Starr* court, and thus the panel in this case, erred in concluding that the mere authorization of such acts supports a claim for infringement under the Act.

Appellees additionally contend that, if liability for "authorizing" acts of infringement depends on finding that the authorized acts themselves are cognizable under the Copyright Act, this court should find that the United States copyright laws *do extend* to extraterritorial acts of infringement when such acts "result in adverse effects within the United States." Appellees buttress this argument with the contention that failure to apply the copyright laws extraterritorially in this case will have a disastrous effect on the American film industry, and that other remedies, such as suits in foreign jurisdictions or the application of foreign copyright laws by American courts, are not realistic alternatives.

We are not persuaded by Appellees' parade of horribles. More fundamentally, however, we are unwilling to overturn over eighty years of consistent jurisprudence on the extraterritorial reach of the copyright laws without further guidance from Congress.

The Supreme Court recently reminded us that "it is a long-standing principle of American law 'that legislation of Congress, unless a contrary intent appears, is meant to apply only within the territorial jurisdiction of the United States.'" Because courts must "assume that Congress legislates against the backdrop of the presumption against extraterritoriality," unless "there is 'the affirmative intention of the Congress clearly expressed'" congressional enactments must be presumed to be "'primarily concerned with domestic conditions.'"

The "undisputed axiom," that the United States' copyright laws have no application to extraterritorial infringement predates the 1909 Act and, as discussed above, the principle of territoriality consistently has been reaffirmed. There is no clear expression of congressional intent in either the 1976 Act or other relevant enactments to alter the preexisting extraterritoriality doctrine....

Accordingly ... we reaffirm that the United States copyright laws do not reach acts of infringement that take place entirely abroad. It is for Congress, and not the courts, to take the initiative in this field.

National Football League v. PrimeTime 24 Joint Venture
211 F.3d 10 (2d Cir. 2000)

As almost every red-blooded American knows, the National Football League ("NFL") televises most of its weekly football games. Simultaneously with the broadcast, NFL makes videotape recordings of the games, which it registers with the United States Copyright Office.

PrimeTime 24 Joint Venture ("PrimeTime") is a satellite carrier that makes secondary transmissions of copyrighted television network programming to owners and renters of satellite dish antennae. PrimeTime has a statutorily granted license to make satellite transmissions to its subscribers in United States households that do not have adequate over-the-air broadcast reception from primary television stations, i.e., "unserved" households. However, PrimeTime has not limited its retransmissions to unserved households in the United States. Without securing permission from NFL, PrimeTime also makes secondary transmissions of football broadcasts to its satellite subscribers in Canada.

On several occasions in 1997, NFL officials wrote to PrimeTime demanding that this practice stop. The following excerpt from one of PrimeTime's replies explains why PrimeTime believes it has the right to continue this practice:

> Next, I would like to address your assertion that the provision of PrimeTime
> 24's service to subscribers in Canada infringes your copyright in the United States,

notwithstanding the facts that all of the recipients in question are in Canada, and PrimeTime 24's actions in this regard comport with applicable Canadian law. Under United States copyright law, the NFL is entitled to control the "public" display or performance of any audiovisual work for which it holds a valid copyright. Accordingly, there can be no infringement of the NFL's rights unless and until there has been a public display or performance. Because the copyright laws of the United States have no extraterritorial applicability, "public" performances that occur in other countries cannot trigger liability for copyright infringement under the laws of the United States. Instead, the law of the country in which the public performance does take place protects the copyright holder.

Letter from Sid Amira, Chairman and Chief Executive Officer of PrimeTime, to Frank Hawkins, Vice President of NFL (Aug. 8, 1997).

PrimeTime's continued retransmission of NFL programming into Canada resulted in the litigation now before us. By a memorandum and order dated March 23, 1999, the United States District Court for the Southern District of New York denied PrimeTime's motion to dismiss NFL's complaint. By a decision dated September 24, 1999, the district court granted NFL's motion for summary judgment and referred the case to a magistrate judge for calculation of fees and damages. On October 18, 1999, the district court issued an order permanently enjoining PrimeTime from retransmitting telecasts of NFL football games outside the United States. PrimeTime asks us to reverse the final injunction.

Under the Copyright Act, the owner of a copyright has the exclusive right publicly to perform and display the copyrighted material. The Act explains that the right to perform copyrighted material publicly includes the right "to transmit or otherwise communicate a performance ... of the work ... to the public, by means of any device or process, whether the members of the public capable of receiving the performance ... receive it in the same place or in separate places and at the same time or at different times." Congress stated that "each and every method by which [ ] images or sounds comprising a performance or display are picked up and conveyed is a 'transmission,' and if the transmission reaches the public in [any] form, the case comes within the scope of [§ 106(4) or (5)]." H.R. REP. NO. 94-1476, at 64 (1976), reprinted in 1976 U.S.C.C.A.N. 5659, 5678.

The issue in this case is whether PrimeTime publicly performed or displayed NFL's copyrighted material. PrimeTime argues that capturing or uplinking copyrighted material and transmitting it to a satellite does not constitute a public display or performance of that material. PrimeTime argues that any public performance or display occurs during the downlink from the satellite to the home subscriber in Canada, which is in a foreign country where the Copyright Act does not apply. Although this Court has not squarely resolved the issue, several courts have rejected PrimeTime's reasoning.

In *WGN Continental Broad. Co. v. United Video, Inc.*, 693 F.2d 622, 624–25 (7th Cir. 1982), the Seventh Circuit considered whether an intermediate carrier had publicly performed copyrighted television signals by capturing broadcast signals, altering them and transmitting them to cable television systems. The court determined that "the Copyright Act defines 'perform or display ... publicly' broadly enough to encompass indirect transmission to the ultimate public." Consequently, the *WGN* court concluded that an intermediate carrier is not immune from copyright liability simply because it does not retransmit a copyrighted signal to the public directly but instead routes the signal to cable systems, which then retransmit to the public.

Judge Posner, writing for the court in *WGN*, noted that a contrary result would render the passive carrier exemption in the Act superfluous. The passive carrier exemption provides that a secondary transmission is not copyright infringement if the transmitter has no control over the content or selection of the original signal or over the recipients of the secondary transmission and provides only the wires, cables, or communication channels for the use of others. In other words, if a copyrighted signal is publicly performed or displayed only when received by viewers, there would be no need for a passive carrier exemption because these passive intermediate carriers "do not transmit directly to the public." A district court in the Eighth Circuit has reached the same result....

We believe the most logical interpretation of the Copyright Act is to hold that a public performance or display includes "each step in the process by which a protected work wends its way to its audience." Under that analysis, it is clear that PrimeTime's uplink transmission of signals captured in the United States is a step in the process by which NFL's protected work wends its way to a public audience. In short, PrimeTime publicly displayed or performed material in which the NFL owns the copyright. Because PrimeTime did not have authorization to make such a public performance, PrimeTime infringed the NFL's copyright....

Kirtsaeng v. John Wiley & Sons, Inc.
___ U.S. ___, 133 S. Ct. 1351 (2013)

Justice BREYER delivered the opinion of the Court.

Section 106 of the Copyright Act grants "the owner of copyright under this title" certain "exclusive rights," including the right "to distribute copies ... of the copyrighted work to the public by sale or other transfer of ownership." 17 U.S.C. § 106(3). These rights are qualified, however, by the application of various limitations set forth in the next several sections of the Act, §§ 107 through 122. Those sections, typically entitled "Limitations on exclusive rights," include, for example, the principle of "fair use" (§ 107), permission for limited library archival reproduction, (§ 108), and the doctrine at issue here, the "first sale" doctrine (§ 109).

Section 109(a) sets forth the "first sale" doctrine as follows:

> "Notwithstanding the provisions of section 106(3) [the section that grants the owner exclusive distribution rights], the owner of a particular copy or phonorecord *lawfully made under this title* ... is entitled, without the authority of the copyright owner, to sell or otherwise dispose of the possession of that copy or phonorecord" (emphasis added).

Thus, even though § 106(3) forbids distribution of a copy of, say, the copyrighted novel Herzog without the copyright owner's permission, § 109(a) adds that, once a copy of Herzog has been lawfully sold (or its ownership otherwise lawfully transferred), the buyer of that *copy* and subsequent owners are free to dispose of it as they wish. In copyright jargon, the "first sale" has "exhausted" the copyright owner's § 106(3) exclusive distribution right.

What, however, if the copy of Herzog was printed abroad and then initially sold with the copyright owner's permission? Does the "first sale" doctrine still apply? Is the buyer, like the buyer of a domestically manufactured copy, free to bring the copy into the United States and dispose of it as he or she wishes?

To put the matter technically, an "importation" provision, § 602(a)(1), says that

> "[i]mportation into the United States, without the authority of the owner of copyright under this title, of copies ... of a work that have been acquired outside the United States is an infringement of the exclusive right to distribute

copies ... *under section 106....*" 17 U.S.C. §602(a)(1) (2006 ed., Supp. V) (emphasis added).

Thus §602(a)(1) makes clear that importing a copy without permission violates the owner's exclusive distribution right. But in doing so, §602(a)(1) refers explicitly to the *§106(3)* exclusive distribution right. As we have just said, §106 is by its terms "[s]ubject to" the various doctrines and principles contained in §§107 through 122, including §109(a)'s "first sale" limitation. Do those same modifications apply—in particular, does the "first sale" modification apply—when considering whether §602(a)(1) prohibits importing a copy?...

Putting section numbers to the side, we ask whether the "first sale" doctrine applies to protect a buyer or other lawful owner of a copy (of a copyrighted work) lawfully manufactured abroad. Can that buyer bring that copy into the United States (and sell it or give it away) without obtaining permission to do so from the copyright owner? Can, for example, someone who purchases, say at a used bookstore, a book printed abroad subsequently resell it without the copyright owner's permission?

In our view, the answers to these questions are, yes. We hold that the "first sale" doctrine applies to copies of a copyrighted work lawfully made abroad.

Respondent, John Wiley & Sons, Inc., publishes academic textbooks. Wiley obtains from its authors various foreign and domestic copyright assignments, licenses and permissions—to the point that we can, for present purposes, refer to Wiley as the relevant American copyright owner. Wiley often assigns to its wholly owned foreign subsidiary, John Wiley & Sons (Asia) Pte Ltd., rights to publish, print, and sell Wiley's English language textbooks abroad. Each copy of a Wiley Asia foreign edition will likely contain language making clear that the copy is to be sold only in a particular country or geographical region outside the United States....

Petitioner, Supap Kirtsaeng, a citizen of Thailand, moved to the United States in 1997 to study mathematics at Cornell University. He paid for his education with the help of a Thai Government scholarship which required him to teach in Thailand for 10 years on his return. Kirtsaeng successfully completed his undergraduate courses at Cornell, successfully completed a Ph.D. program in mathematics at the University of Southern California, and then, as promised, returned to Thailand to teach. While he was studying in the United States, Kirtsaeng asked his friends and family in Thailand to buy copies of foreign edition English-language textbooks at Thai book shops, where they sold at low prices, and mail them to him in the United States. Kirtsaeng would then sell them, reimburse his family and friends, and keep the profit....

We must decide whether the words "lawfully made under this title" restrict the scope of §109(a)'s "first sale" doctrine geographically. The Second Circuit, the Ninth Circuit, Wiley, and the Solicitor General (as *amicus*) all read those words as imposing a form of *geographical* limitation. The Second Circuit held that they limit the "first sale" doctrine to particular copies "made in territories *in which the Copyright Act is law,*" which (the Circuit says) are copies "manufactured domestically," not "outside of the United States." 654 F.3d, at 221–222 (emphasis added).... Under any of these geographical interpretations, §109(a)'s "first sale" doctrine would not apply to the Wiley Asia books at issue here. And, despite an American copyright owner's permission to *make* copies abroad, one who *buys* a copy of any such book or other copyrighted work—whether at a retail store, over the Internet, or at a library sale—could not resell (or otherwise dispose of) that particular copy without further permission.

Kirtsaeng, however, reads the words "lawfully made under this title" as imposing a *non*-geographical limitation. He says that they mean made "in accordance with" or "in compliance with" the Copyright Act....

In our view, § 109(a)'s language, its context, and the common-law history of the "first sale" doctrine, taken together, favor a *non*-geographical interpretation. We also doubt that Congress would have intended to create the practical copyright-related harms with which a geographical interpretation would threaten ordinary scholarly, artistic, commercial, and consumer activities. We consequently conclude that Kirtsaeng's nongeographical reading is the better reading of the Act.

The language of § 109(a) read literally favors Kirtsaeng's nongeographical interpretation, namely, that "lawfully made under this title" means made "in accordance with" or "in compliance with" the Copyright Act. The language of § 109(a) says nothing about geography. The word "under" can mean "[i]n accordance with." 18 Oxford English Dictionary 950 (2d ed.1989). See also Black's Law Dictionary 1525 (6th ed. 1990) ("according to"). And a nongeographical interpretation provides each word of the five-word phrase with a distinct purpose. The first two words of the phrase, "lawfully made," suggest an effort to distinguish those copies that were made lawfully from those that were not, and the last three words, "under this title," set forth the standard of "lawful[ness]." Thus, the nongeographical reading is simple, it promotes a traditional copyright objective (combatting piracy), and it makes word-by-word linguistic sense.

The geographical interpretation, however, bristles with linguistic difficulties. It gives the word "lawfully" little, if any, linguistic work to do. (How could a book be *un* lawfully "made under this title"?) It imports geography into a statutory provision that says nothing explicitly about it. And it is far more complex than may at first appear....

A far more serious difficulty arises out of the uncertainty and complexity surrounding the second step's effort to read the necessary geographical limitation into the word "applicable" (or the equivalent). Where, precisely, is the Copyright Act "applicable"? The Act does not instantly *protect* an American copyright holder from unauthorized piracy taking place abroad. But that fact does not mean the Act is *inapplicable* to copies made abroad. As a matter of ordinary English, one can say that a statute imposing, say, a tariff upon "any rhododendron grown in Nepal" applies to *all* Nepalese rhododendrons. And, similarly, one can say that the American Copyright Act is *applicable* to *all* pirated copies, including those printed overseas. Indeed, the Act itself makes clear that (in the Solicitor General's language) foreign-printed pirated copies are "subject to" the Act....

The "first sale" doctrine also frees courts from the administrative burden of trying to enforce restrictions upon difficult-to-trace, readily movable goods. And it avoids the selective enforcement inherent in any such effort. Thus, it is not surprising that for at least a century the "first sale" doctrine has played an important role in American copyright law....

Associations of libraries, used-book dealers, technology companies, consumer-goods retailers, and museums point to various ways in which a geographical interpretation would fail to further basic constitutional copyright objectives, in particular "promot[ing] the Progress of Science and useful Arts." U.S. Const., Art. I, § 8, cl. 8.

The American Library Association tells us that library collections contain at least 200 million books published abroad (presumably, many were first published in one of the nearly 180 copyright-treaty nations and enjoy American copyright protection under 17 U.S.C. § 104); that many others were first published in the United States but printed abroad because of lower costs; and that a geographical interpretation will likely require the libraries to obtain permission (or at least create significant uncertainty) before circulating or otherwise distributing these books.

How, the American Library Association asks, are the libraries to obtain permission to distribute these millions of books? How can they find, say, the copyright owner of a foreign book, perhaps written decades ago? They may not know the copyright holder's present address. Brief for American Library Association 15 (many books lack indication of place of manufacture; "no practical way to learn where [a] book was printed"). And, even where addresses can be found, the costs of finding them, contacting owners, and negotiating may be high indeed. Are the libraries to stop circulating or distributing or displaying the millions of books in their collections that were printed abroad?

Used-book dealers tell us that, from the time when Benjamin Franklin and Thomas Jefferson built commercial and personal libraries of foreign books, American readers have bought used books published and printed abroad. The dealers say that they have "operat[ed] ... for centuries" under the assumption that the "first sale" doctrine applies. But under a geographical interpretation a contemporary tourist who buys, say, at Shakespeare and Co. (in Paris), a dozen copies of a foreign book for American friends might find that she had violated the copyright law. The used-book dealers cannot easily predict what the foreign copyright holder may think about a reader's effort to sell a used copy of a novel. And they believe that a geographical interpretation will injure a large portion of the used-book business.

Technology companies tell us that "automobiles, microwaves, calculators, mobile phones, tablets, and personal computers" contain copyrightable software programs or packaging. Many of these items are made abroad with the American copyright holder's permission and then sold and imported (with that permission) to the United States. A geographical interpretation would prevent the resale of, say, a car, without the permission of the holder of each copyright on each piece of copyrighted automobile software. Yet there is no reason to believe that foreign auto manufacturers regularly obtain this kind of permission from their software component suppliers, and Wiley did not indicate to the contrary when asked. Without that permission a foreign car owner could not sell his or her used car.

Retailers tell us that over $2.3 trillion worth of foreign goods were imported in 2011. And, many of these items bear, carry, or contain copyrighted "packaging, logos, labels, and product inserts and instructions for [the use of] everyday packaged goods from floor cleaners and health and beauty products to breakfast cereals." The retailers add that American sales of more traditional copyrighted works, "such as books, recorded music, motion pictures, and magazines" likely amount to over $220 billion. A geographical interpretation would subject many, if not all, of them to the disruptive impact of the threat of infringement suits.

Art museum directors ask us to consider their efforts to display foreign-produced works by, say, Cy Twombly, Rene Magritte, Henri Matisse, Pablo Picasso, and others. A geographical interpretation, they say, would require the museums to obtain permission from the copyright owners before they could display the work—even if the copyright owner has already sold or donated the work to a foreign museum. What are the museums to do, they ask, if the artist retained the copyright, if the artist cannot be found, or if a group of heirs is arguing about who owns which copyright?

These examples, and others previously mentioned, help explain *why* Lord Coke considered the "first sale" doctrine necessary to protect "Trade and Traffi[c], and bargaining and contracting," and they help explain *why* American copyright law has long applied that doctrine.

Neither Wiley nor any of its many *amici* deny that a geographical interpretation could bring about these "horribles"—at least in principle. Rather, Wiley essentially says that the list is artificially invented. It points out that a federal court first adopted a geographical interpretation more than 30 years ago. Yet, it adds, these problems have not occurred. Why not? Because, says Wiley, the problems and threats are purely theoretical; they are unlikely to reflect reality.

We are less sanguine. For one thing, the law has not been settled for long in Wiley's favor. The Second Circuit, in its decision below, is the first Court of Appeals to adopt a purely geographical interpretation. The Third Circuit has favored a nongeographical interpretation. The Ninth Circuit has favored a modified geographical interpretation with a nongeographical (but textually unsustainable) corollary designed to diminish the problem. And other courts have hesitated to adopt, and have cast doubt upon, the validity of the geographical interpretation.

For another thing, reliance upon the "first sale" doctrine is deeply embedded in the practices of those, such as booksellers, libraries, museums, and retailers, who have long relied upon its protection. Museums, for example, are not in the habit of asking their foreign counterparts to check with the heirs of copyright owners before sending, *e.g.*, a Picasso on tour. That inertia means a dramatic change is likely necessary before these institutions, instructed by their counsel, would begin to engage in the complex permission-verifying process that a geographical interpretation would demand. And this Court's adoption of the geographical interpretation could provide that dramatic change. These intolerable consequences (along with the absurd result that the copyright owner can exercise downstream control even when it authorized the import or first sale) have understandably led the Ninth Circuit, the Solicitor General as *amicus,* and the dissent to adopt textual readings of the statute that attempt to mitigate these harms. But those readings are not defensible, for they require too many unprecedented jumps over linguistic and other hurdles that in our view are insurmountable.

Finally, the fact that harm has proved limited so far may simply reflect the reluctance of copyright holders so far to assert geographically based resale rights. They may decide differently if the law is clarified in their favor. Regardless, a copyright law that can work in practice only if unenforced is not a sound copyright law. It is a law that would create uncertainty, would bring about selective enforcement, and, if widely unenforced, would breed disrespect for copyright law itself.

Thus, we believe that the practical problems that petitioner and his *amici* have described are too serious, too extensive, and too likely to come about for us to dismiss them as insignificant — particularly in light of the ever-growing importance of foreign trade to America. The upshot is that copyright-related consequences along with language, context, and interpretive canons argue strongly against a geographical interpretation of § 109(a)....

For these reasons we conclude that the considerations supporting Kirtsaeng's nongeographical interpretation of the words "lawfully made under this title" are the more persuasive. The judgment of the Court of Appeals is reversed, and the case is remanded for further proceedings consistent with this opinion.

It is so ordered.

Justice KAGAN, with whom Justice ALITO joins, concurring.

I concur fully in the Court's opinion. Neither the text nor the history of 17 U.S.C. § 109(a) supports removing first-sale protection from every copy of a protected work manufactured abroad. I recognize, however, that the combination of today's decision and *Quality King Distributors, Inc. v. L'anza Research Int'l, Inc.,* 523 U.S. 135 (1998), constricts the scope of § 602(a)(1)'s ban on unauthorized importation. I write to suggest that any problems associated with that limitation come not from our reading of § 109(a) here, but from *Quality King*'s holding that § 109(a) limits § 602(a)(1).

As the Court explains, the first-sale doctrine has played an integral part in American copyright law for over a century. *Bobbs-Merrill Co. v. Straus,* 210 U.S. 339 (1908). No codification of the doctrine prior to 1976 even arguably limited its application to copies made in the United States. And nothing in the text or history of § 109(a)—the Copyright Act of 1976's first-sale provision—suggests that Congress meant to enact the new, geographical restriction John Wiley proposes, which at once would deprive American consumers of important rights and encourage copyright holders to manufacture abroad.

That said, John Wiley is right that the Court's decision, when combined with *Quality King,* substantially narrows § 602(a)(1)'s ban on unauthorized importation. *Quality King* held that the importation ban does not reach any copies receiving first-sale protection under § 109(a). So notwithstanding § 602(a)(1), an "owner of a particular copy ... lawfully made under this title" can import that copy without the copyright owner's permission. § 109(a). In now holding that copies "lawfully made under this title" include copies manufactured abroad, we unavoidably diminish § 602(a)(1)'s scope—indeed, limit it to a fairly esoteric set of applications.

But if Congress views the shrinking of § 602(a)(1) as a problem, it should recognize *Quality King*—not our decision today—as the culprit. Here, after all, we merely construe § 109(a); *Quality King* is the decision holding that § 109(a) limits § 602(a)(1). Had we come out the opposite way in that case, § 602(a)(1) would allow a copyright owner to restrict the importation of copies irrespective of the first-sale doctrine. That result would enable the copyright owner to divide international markets in the way John Wiley claims Congress intended when enacting § 602(a)(1). But it would do so without imposing downstream liability on those who purchase and resell in the United States copies that happen to have been manufactured abroad. In other words, that outcome would target unauthorized importers alone, and not the "libraries, used-book dealers, technology companies, consumer-goods retailers, and museums" with whom the Court today is rightly concerned. Assuming Congress adopted § 602(a)(1) to permit market segmentation, I suspect that is how Congress thought the provision would work—not by removing first-sale protection from every copy manufactured abroad (as John Wiley urges us to do here), but by enabling the copyright holder to control imports even when the first-sale doctrine applies (as *Quality King* now prevents).

At bottom, John Wiley (together with the dissent) asks us to misconstrue § 109(a) in order to restore § 602(a)(1) to its purportedly rightful function of enabling copyright holders to segment international markets. I think John Wiley may have a point about what § 602(a)(1) was designed to do; that gives me pause about *Quality King*'s holding that the first-sale doctrine limits the importation ban's scope. But the Court today correctly declines the invitation to save § 602(a)(1) from *Quality King* by destroying the first-sale protection that § 109(a) gives to every owner of a copy manufactured abroad. That would swap one (possible) mistake for a much worse one, and make our reading of the statute only less reflective of Congressional intent. If Congress thinks copyright owners need greater power to restrict importation and thus divide markets, a ready solution is at hand—not the one John Wiley offers in this case, but the one the Court rejected in *Quality King.*

Justice GINSBURG, with whom Justice KENNEDY joins, and with whom Justice SCALIA joins [except as to certain sections not reprinted here]....

Because economic conditions and demand for particular goods vary across the globe, copyright owners have a financial incentive to charge different prices for copies of their works in different geographic regions. Their ability to engage in such price discrimination, however, is undermined if arbitrageurs are permitted to import copies from low-price regions and sell them in high-price regions. The question in this case is whether the unauthorized importation of foreign-made copies constitutes copyright infringement under U.S. law....

The text of the Copyright Act demonstrates that Congress intended to provide copyright owners with a potent remedy against the importation of foreign-made copies of their copyrighted works. As the Court recognizes, this case turns on the meaning of the phrase "lawfully made under this title" in § 109(a). In my view, that phrase is most sensibly read as referring to instances in which a copy's creation is governed by, and conducted in compliance with, Title 17 of the U.S. Code. This reading is consistent with the Court's interpretation of similar language in other statutes.

Section 109(a), properly read, affords Kirtsaeng no defense against Wiley's claim of copyright infringement. The Copyright Act, it has been observed time and again, does not apply extraterritorially. The printing of Wiley's foreign-manufactured textbooks therefore was not governed by Title 17. The textbooks thus were not "lawfully made under [Title 17]," the crucial precondition for application of § 109(a). And if § 109(a) does not apply, there is no dispute that Kirtsaeng's conduct constituted copyright infringement under § 602(a)(1).

The Court's point of departure is similar to mine. According to the Court, the phrase "'lawfully made under this title' means made 'in accordance with' or 'in compliance with' the Copyright Act." *Ante,* at 1358. But the Court overlooks that, according to the very dictionaries it cites, the word "under" commonly signals a relationship of subjection, where one thing is governed or regulated by another. Only by disregarding this established meaning of "under" can the Court arrive at the conclusion that Wiley's foreign-manufactured textbooks were "lawfully made under" U.S. copyright law, even though that law did not govern their creation. It is anomalous, however, to speak of particular conduct as "lawful" under an inapplicable law. For example, one might say that driving on the right side of the road in England is "lawful" under U.S. law, but that would be so only because U.S. law has nothing to say about the subject. The governing law is English law, and English law demands that driving be done on the left side of the road.

The logical implication of the Court's definition of the word "under" is that *any* copy manufactured abroad—even a piratical one made without the copyright owner's authorization and in violation of the law of the country where it was created—would fall within the scope of § 109(a). Any such copy would have been made "in accordance with" or "in compliance with" the U.S. Copyright Act, in the sense that manufacturing the copy did not violate the Act (because the Act does not apply extraterritorially).

The Court rightly refuses to accept such an absurd conclusion. Instead, it interprets § 109(a) as applying only to copies whose making actually complied with Title 17, or would have complied with Title 17 had Title 17 been applicable (*i.e.,* had the copies been made in the United States). Not only does the Court adopt an unnatural construction of the § 109(a) phrase "lawfully made under this title." Concomitantly, the Court reduces § 602(a)(1) to insignificance. As the Court appears to acknowledge, the only independent effect § 602(a)(1) has under today's decision is to prohibit unauthorized importations carried out by persons who merely have possession of, but do not own, the imported copies. If this is enough to avoid rendering § 602(a)(1) entirely "superfluous," it hardly suffices to give the owner's importation right the scope Congress intended it to have. Congress used broad language in § 602(a)(1); it did so to achieve a broad objective. Had Congress intended simply to provide a copyright remedy against larcenous lessees, licensees, consignees, and bailees of films and other copyright-protected goods, it likely would have used language tailored to that narrow purpose....

Notes and Questions

a. The axiom that each nation's copyright enforcement must stop at its own borders is consistent with treaty obligations and international trade and custom. Nonetheless, the multinational aspect of piracy and broadcasting makes this rule a safe haven for pirates. Increasingly, courts and legislatures can be expected to stretch the reach of the law to narrow this gap and provide copyright protection.

b. How can a court hear a copyright claim, if the foreign acts which comprise the alleged infringement are not subject to United States law? See *Litecubes, LLC v. N. Light Products, Inc.*, 523 F.3d 1353, 1367–68 (Fed. Cir. 2008).

> GlowProducts assumed without any analysis that the lack of extraterritorial effect of the copyright laws is a question of subject matter jurisdiction rather than a question of whether a claim upon which relief can be granted has been established. But the cases it relies on provide minimal support for such a position. GlowProducts' reliance on *Subafilms*, which it cites as its primary authority, is misplaced. While GlowProducts is correct that *Subafilms* is a leading case on the extraterritorial reach of the Copyright Act, *Subafilms* did not hold that the extraterritorial limitation limited the subject matter jurisdiction of the federal courts. Rather, *Subafilms* held that "the mere authorization of acts of infringement that are not cognizable under the United States copyright laws because they occur entirely outside of the United States does not state a claim for infringement under the Copyright Act." 24 F.3d at 1099. Moreover, *Subafilms* reaffirmed that "the existence of subject matter jurisdiction under 28 U.S.C. §1338(a) is distinct as a general matter from the question of whether a valid cause of action is stated." *Subafilms*, 24 F.3d at 1091 n. 5.... Similarly, none of the Second Circuit cases on which GlowProducts relies hold that the extraterritorial reach of the Copyright Act is a question of subject matter jurisdiction.... There is no indication that Congress intended the extraterritorial limitations on the scope of the Copyright Act to limit the subject matter jurisdiction of the federal courts. Accordingly, we hold that the issue is properly treated as an element of the claim which must be proven before relief can be granted, not a question of subject matter jurisdiction, and we affirm the district court's denial of GlowProduct's motion for dismissal for lack of subject matter jurisdiction over the copyright claims.

c. To what extent does the limit on territoriality affect measures of damages? See *The Robert Stigwood Group Ltd. v. O'Reilly*, 530 F.2d 1096, 1101 (2d Cir.1976).

d. *Los Angeles News Serv. v. Reuters TV Intern., Ltd.*, 149 F.3d 987 (9th Cir. 1998) provides a look at the measure of damages available when a work is infringed both in the United States and abroad. The court looks to earlier precedent in *Sheldon v. Metro-Goldwyn Pictures Corp.*, 106 F.2d 45, 52 (2d Cir.1939), *aff'd*, 309 U.S. 390 (1940). The Ninth Circuit explained the earlier ruling:

> In Sheldon the court held, in an opinion by Judge Learned Hand, that plaintiff could recover the profits from exhibiting a motion picture abroad where the infringing copy had been made in the United States. As Judge Hand explained:

The [copyrighted film] negatives were "records" from which the work could be "reproduced", and it was a tort to make them in this country. The plaintiffs acquired an equitable interest in them as soon as they were made, which attached to any profits from their exploitation, whether in the form of money remitted to the United States, or of increase in the value of shares of foreign companies held by the defendants. We need not decide whether the law of those countries where the negatives were exploited, recognized the plaintiffs' equitable interest; we can assume arguendo that it did not, for, as soon as any of the profits so realized took the form of property whose situs was in the United States, our law seized upon them and impressed them with a constructive trust, whatever their form.

Under the Second Circuit's rule, by contrast, a party becomes liable for extraterritorial damages only when an act of infringement occurs within the United States, subjecting it to liability as an infringer (or a contributory infringer) under the Copyright Act.... We therefore hold that [Plaintiff] is entitled to recover damages flowing from exploitation abroad of the domestic acts of infringement committed by defendants.

e. Where should copyright litigation occur? Should a U.S. court base its jurisdiction on citizenship, locus of the tortious infringement, or location of the parties? Does it affect jurisdiction or merely choice of forum? See *Byrne v. BBC,* 132 F. Supp. 2d 229 (S.D.N.Y. 2001) (BBC denied summary judgment for copying of Northern Irish song in New York).

f. For a discussion of the apportionment of music royalties based on foreign and domestic activity, see *Yount v. Acuff Rose-Opryland,* 103 F.3d 830 (9th Cir. 1996).

Problem II-C

Bryce comes to you with a question. Bryce purchased a copy of a play in Canada which Bryce believes would be a good project to adapt for the American stage. Bryce would like to add world music, including a few songs Bryce has written and a few songs that Bryce has heard on South African recordings.

Bryce would like to produce the play in a workshop format without "going through the hassle of clearing the rights," but if that cannot be done, Bryce needs to know how to acquire the rights needed. Advise Bryce as to the need to acquire rights for the songs and the play, as well as the general steps necessary to do so.

D. Embargos and Domestic Trade Barriers

Kalantari v. NITV, Inc.
352 F.3d 1202 (9th Cir. 2003)

In this copyright infringement case, we are called on to decide whether the Iranian trade embargo, *31 C.F.R. Part 560,* prohibits the commercial importation of movies from Iran, the copyright of such movies, or the assignment to a "United States person" of the exclusive rights to copyright, distribute, and exhibit the movies in North America. We answer "no" to each of those questions and, accordingly, we reverse.

Plaintiff Masood Kalantari is a producer of television programs and a promoter of Iranian cultural events in the United States. He is a "United States person," *31 C.F.R. §560.314*, who is subject to the Iranian trade embargo.

Under a series of agreements, Plaintiff acquired the rights to three Farsi language films — "Snow Man," "Two Women," and "Corrupted Hands" — from their Iranian owners. For each film, Plaintiff's contract consists of an "Assignment," in English, and a "Contract," in Farsi. In relevant part, the agreements provide that, for a specified term: (1) Plaintiff is assigned, exclusively, all rights to the films, including the exclusive rights to copyright, distribute, and exhibit the films within the United States and Canada; (2) Plaintiff agrees to copyright the films in the United States and to use his "utmost efforts" to show and advertise the films; (3) the films' owners agree to send Plaintiff copies of the films and advertising materials; and (4) Plaintiff agrees to pay (a) for "Snow Man" and "Two Women," an initial deposit of $10,000, followed by quarterly payments of 50 percent of the net profit from showing the films, and (b) for "Corrupted Hands," three installment payments amounting to roughly $13,000.

As agreed, Plaintiff has made the contractual payments and displayed the three films in the United States. Plaintiff has also obtained copyright registrations for all three films. Each copyright certificate lists the Iranian owner as the author of the work and indicates that Plaintiff became the owner of the copyright by way of an assignment of rights.

The Berne Convention allows copyright registration in member countries (including the United States) of works from nonmember countries (including Iran) if publication in the member country is simultaneous with first publication in the nonmember country of origin. "Publication," in the case of a motion picture, includes offering to distribute copies for the purpose of public showing in theaters. Plaintiff acquired United States copyrights for the films under this theory of simultaneous first publication.

After Defendants NITV, Inc., d/b/a National Iranian TV, Zia Atabay, and Parvin Atabay allegedly broadcast the three movies on television in the United States without authorization, Plaintiff brought this action against them for copyright infringement. Defendants moved for summary judgment on the sole ground that the Iranian trade embargo prohibited Plaintiff from purchasing the rights that he purports to possess and that, without a valid assignment, he cannot have a valid copyright that could be infringed. The district court granted Defendants' motion. Plaintiff brought this timely appeal....

A. *IEEPA and the Informational Materials Exemption*

The *International Emergency Economic Powers Act* ("IEEPA"), enacted in 1977, gives the President the authority to "investigate, regulate, or prohibit ... any transactions in foreign exchange" upon declaring an emergency based on a foreign threat. However, the President lacks the authority under IEEPA to regulate information and informational materials:

> The authority granted to the President by this section does not include the authority to regulate or prohibit, directly or indirectly....
>
> (3) the importation from any country, ... whether commercial or otherwise, regardless of format or medium of transmission, of any information or informational materials, including but not limited to, publications, films, posters, phonograph records, photographs, microfilms, microfiche, tapes, compact disks, CD ROMs, artworks, and news wire feeds.

IEEPA is a modification of the *Trading With the Enemy Act* ("TWEA"), which was enacted in 1917. In 1977, Congress moved the President's *peacetime* authority from TWEA to the newly created IEEPA. TWEA now delineates the President's authority during wartime, whereas IEEPA powers may be exercised without a declaration of war. However, a grandfather clause in the 1977 amendment allowed for the continuation of peacetime economic measures taken pursuant to TWEA before 1977. Therefore, the embargo against Cuba, which began in 1962, is governed by TWEA.

Congress added the foregoing exemption for informational materials to IEEPA in 1988, in what is known as the "Berman Amendment." The Berman Amendment was designed to prevent the executive branch from restricting the international flow of materials protected by the *First Amendment*. The Berman Amendment has been described as a reaction to several seizures by the United States of shipments of magazines and books from embargoed countries and to the Treasury Department's restrictions on the permissible forms of payment for informational materials purchased from Cuba.

The IEEPA exemption was expanded in a 1994 amendment entitled "Free Trade in Ideas." The 1994 amendment expanded the exemption's nonexclusive list of informational materials to include new media, such as compact discs and CD-ROMs, and it clarified that the exemption applied to importation and exportation in any "format or medium of transmission." The House Conference Report stated:

> The language [of the original 1988 exemption] was explicitly intended, by including the words "directly or indirectly," to have a broad scope. However, the Treasury Department has narrowly and restrictively interpreted the language in ways not originally intended. The present amendment is only intended to address some of those restrictive interpretations, for example limits on the type of information that is protected or on the medium or method of transmitting the information. The committee of conference intends these amendments to facilitate transactions and activities incident to the flow of information and informational materials....

B. The Iranian Trade Embargo

Pursuant to his authority under IEEPA, President Clinton issued Executive Order Nos. 12959 and 13059, in 1995 and 1997 (respectively), to prohibit most trade with Iran. The Iranian trade embargo was intended "to deal with the unusual and extraordinary threat to the national security, foreign policy, and economy of the United States" presented by "the actions and policies of the Government of Iran."... The President's Executive Orders have largely been codified in the Iranian Transactions Regulations, which prohibit, with few exceptions, "the importation into the United States of any goods or services of Iranian origin" and any "transaction or dealing in" such goods or services.

Notwithstanding their broad scope, however, the regulations permit trade in certain items through general and specific licenses, and they reflect the IEEPA exemption for informational materials:

> The importation from any country ... of information and informational materials as defined in§ 560.315, whether commercial or otherwise, regardless of format or medium of transmission, [is] exempt from the prohibitions and regulations of this part.

1. Importation

The first question that we must answer is whether Plaintiff's importation of the three movies ran afoul of the Iranian embargo. It is clear from the text of the statute and regulation that the bare importation of a movie is permitted. But, because Plaintiff paid Iranians for the movies that he imported, to answer our first question, we also must consider whether a commercial transaction that results in importation is likewise permitted.

The regulation provides, as relevant: "The importation from any country … of information and informational materials…, whether commercial or otherwise…, [is] exempt from the prohibitions and regulations of this part." Grammatically, the noun that the clause "whether commercial or otherwise" modifies is "importation." This reading squares, too, with the statutory text from which the regulations drew the modifier. In 50 U.S.C. § 1702(b)(3) — the IEEPA exemption — the phrase "commercial or otherwise" directly follows the importation/exportation clauses, and quite clearly modifies them.

We note that the result would be the same if the phrase "whether commercial or otherwise" modified, instead, "information and informational materials." The importation of commercial materials, similarly, suggests that the materials will continue to have a commercial use after importation.

We pause here to define "commercial." It means, "of, in, or relating to commerce" or "from the point of view of profit[, as,] having profit as the primary aim." Webster's Third New Int'l Dictionary 456 (unabridged ed. 1993). "Commerce," in turn, is defined as, "the exchange or buying and selling of commodities." In short, the importation of a movie for which a United States person paid is permitted.

In summary, the exemption plainly allows a United States person to pay Iranians in exchange for the importation of a movie.

2. Copyright

The applicable regulations grant an express general license for certain transactions related to intellectual property protection in the United States or Iran:

> All of the following transactions in connection with patent, trademark, copyright or other intellectual property protection in the United States or Iran are authorized:
>
> (1) The filing and prosecution of any application to obtain a patent, trademark, copyright or other form of intellectual property protection, including importation of or dealing in Iranian-origin services, payment for such services, and payment to persons in Iran directly connected to such intellectual property protection;
>
> (2) The receipt of a patent, trademark, copyright or other form of intellectual property protection;
>
> (3) The renewal or maintenance of a patent, trademark, copyright or other form of intellectual property protection; and
>
> (4) The filing and prosecution of opposition or infringement proceedings with respect to a patent, trademark, copyright or other form of intellectual property protection, or the entrance of a defense to any such proceedings.

31 C.F.R. § 560.509(a).

Without question, then, an Iranian movie may be copyrighted in the United States. The narrow question here is whether an assignee may copyright a lawfully imported Iranian movie in view of the absence of "assignment" from the foregoing list of authorized copyright transactions.

3. Assignment

In addition to exempting informational materials, the Iranian Transactions Regulations permit trade in some items by way of general licenses. When the regulations license a transaction, they also authorize "any transaction ordinarily incident to [that] licensed transaction and necessary to give effect thereto."

As discussed above, an Iranian author may copyright a film in the United States, pursuant to a general license. Thus, any transaction "ordinarily incident to [the copyright] and necessary to give effect thereto" is permitted, unless specifically prohibited by another regulation. For the following reasons, we hold that a copyright assignment is an incidental transaction authorized by 31 C.F.R. § 560.405 and not prohibited by any other regulation.

Upon obtaining a copyright, an author automatically acquires certain rights that are inherent in the very nature of a copyright. Specifically, the copyright owner obtains the six exclusive rights of copyright, as well as the right to transfer any or all of those rights: "The ownership of a copyright may be transferred in whole or in part by any means of conveyance or by operation of law...." Without question, an assignment qualifies as a transfer by "any means of conveyance."

The basic rights inherent in a copyright do not change simply because a movie's original owner is an Iranian who is expressly authorized to obtain the copyright. With the general license to obtain a copyright, Iranians as well as Americans obtain the right to transfer the copyright freely, by assignment or otherwise. Thus, because the right to assign a copyright is part of the bundle of rights inherent in holding a copyright, an assignment is a transaction "ordinarily incident" to ownership of a copyright and "necessary to give effect" to that ownership.

Nothing in the regulations suggests that this particular incidental transaction is not authorized by 31 C.F.R. § 560.405. It is true that the regulations that grant general licenses sometimes define related transactions that are impermissible notwithstanding § 560.405. The regulation exempting informational materials, too, carves out certain types of related transactions that are impermissible despite the general exemption:

> This section does not exempt from regulation or authorize transactions related [(1)] to information and informational materials not fully created and in existence at the date of the transactions, or [(2)] to the substantive or artistic alteration or enhancement of informational materials, or [(3)] to the provision of marketing and business consulting services.

31 C.F.R. § 560.210(c)(2) (numbering added). The subsection goes on to give a nonexhaustive list of examples of transactions that would fall within this proscription:

> Transactions that are prohibited notwithstanding [the exemption] include, but are not limited to, payment of advances for information and informational materials not yet created and completed (with the exception of prepaid subscriptions for widely circulated magazines and other periodical publications), and provision of services to market, produce or coproduce, create or assist in the creation of information and informational materials.

The assignment of a copyright to a completed movie is not listed there. Moreover, the delineation of certain still-prohibited incidental transactions implies that all *other* incidental transactions under§ 560.405 are permissible under the exemption. The history of the IEEPA exemption and of§ 560.210(c)(2) supports this understanding.

The House Conference Report on the 1994 amendment to the IEEPA exemption explicitly states that Congress intended to permit related transactions:

> The committee of conference further understands that it was not necessary to include any explicit reference in the statutory language to "transactions incident" to the importation or exportation of information or informational materials, *because the conferees believe that such transactions are covered by the statutory language.*

H.R. Conf. Rep. No. 103-482, at 239 (1994), *reprinted in* 1994 U.S.C.C.A.N. 398, 483 (emphasis added).

Furthermore, the history of *§ 560.210(c)(2)* makes sense when viewed against the background of the House Report's understanding of the exemption. After the embargo began in May 1995, but before the Iranian Transactions Regulations were first issued in September 1995, the Office of Foreign Assets Control published its interim general licenses to provide guidance to the public in interpreting the Executive Orders. General License No. 5 permitted the import and export of informational materials, as well as authorizing "*all financial and other transactions related to* the importation or exportation of information and informational materials."

In the final regulations, which were issued one month later, *§ 560.210(c)(2)* described certain types of transactions that the informational materials exemption did not authorize and provided a list of examples of the still impermissible transactions. In April 1999, this list of examples was augmented to prohibit the "payment of royalties to persons in Iran." But in November 1999, the prohibition on "payment of royalties to persons in Iran" was deleted from the list, leaving the regulations in their current form. It thus appears that, with the understanding that most incidental transactions were permitted, the agency identified a limited set of transactions that did not fall within the general rule. As we have noted, a copyright assignment does not fall within this set of prohibited transactions.

Analogous regulations also support our reading of the Iranian regulations. Because the IEEPA exemption for informational materials is a general limitation on the President's authority, it applies to all U.S. trade embargoes. Not surprisingly, then, the text of the informational materials exemption to the Cuban embargo is substantially the same as that in the Iranian regulations. The Cuban regulations provide guidance in interpreting the exemption by giving several examples applying the regulations to common situations. One of these examples shows that the transfer of intellectual property rights is permitted under the exemption:

> Example # 2: A Cuban party exports a single master copy of a Cuban motion picture to a U.S. party and licenses the U.S. party to duplicate, distribute, show and exploit in the United States the Cuban film ... for five years, with the Cuban party receiving 40% of the net income. All transactions relating to the activities described in this example are authorized....

31 C.F.R. § 515.206(a)(4). The payment of a percentage of net profits for the use of intellectual property, as described in the example, is a royalty. This example is thus consistent with the *deletion* of "payment of royalties" from the list of *prohibited* transactions under the Iranian embargo.

In summary, agreements by which Iranians assign intellectual property rights in a movie to a United States person are "ordinarily incident" to the importation and copyright of the film and are "necessary to give effect thereto." These agreements are incidental transactions permitted by *31 C.F.R. § 560.405* and not prohibited by *31 C.F.R. § 560.210(c)(2)*.

The Iranian embargo does not prohibit the commercial importation of an Iranian movie, the copyrighting of the movie, or the assignment to a United States person of rights to obtain and enforce such a copyright. Therefore, the district court erred in holding that Plaintiff lacked a valid assignment or lacked authority to obtain a valid copyright.

REVERSED and REMANDED for further proceedings consistent with this opinion.

U.S. v. Amirnazmi

645 F.3d 564 (3d Cir. 2011)

In pursuit of his stated goal of transforming the Islamic Republic of Iran into a global chemical powerhouse, Ali Amirnazmi, a chemical engineer, marketed a dynamic software program to Iranian actors and entered into agreements with various Iranian entities in which he pledged to provide technology to facilitate the construction of multiple chemical plants. Following a jury trial, Amirnazmi was convicted on ten charges — [including] four counts stemming from violations of the International Emergency Economic Powers Act (IEEPA).... The District Court denied both motions and sentenced him to a four-year prison term. We will affirm....

Amirnazmi argues the government failed to prove beyond a reasonable doubt that ChemPlan does not fall within the scope of IEEPA's informational-materials exemption. He contends that Congress intended to insulate transactions incident to the free flow of information from regulation and that the sale of ChemPlan, which conveys pricing information and scientific information, falls within this category of presumptively exempt activity. He urges us to vacate his convictions on Counts Two and Five of the superseding indictment, which charged him with ChemPlan-related IEEPA violations, because, he argues, OFAC's interpretation of this exemption both flouts congressional intent and is unconstitutionally vague.

Congress proscribes the Executive from regulating, pursuant to IEEPA,

> the importation from any country, or the exportation to any country, whether commercial or otherwise, regardless of format or medium of transmission, of any information or informational materials, including but not limited to, publications, films, posters, phonograph records, photographs, microfilms, microfiche, tapes, compact disks, CD ROMs, artworks, and news wire feeds....

50 U.S.C. § 1702(b)(3). OFAC has incorporated the statutory exemption into the ITR; the regulations provide a general license authorizing transactions involving "information and informational materials." See 31 C.F.R. § 560.210(c)(1). Although not enumerated in the statute, technology and software are capable of qualifying as "informational materials" under the regulations. See *id.* § 560.418 ("The release of technology or software in the United States ... to any person violates the [ITR] if made with knowledge or reason to know the technology is intended for Iran or the Government of Iran, unless that technology or software meets the definition of information and informational materials in § 560.315."). However, under OFAC's interpretation, the general license is not applicable to "transactions related to information and informational materials *not fully created and in existence at the date of the transactions,* or to the substantive or artistic alteration or enhancement of informational materials, or to the provision of marketing and business consulting services." *Id.* § 560.210(c)(2) (emphasis added)....

Prior to 1988, trade sanctions that hampered the exchange of informational materials were routinely justified under TWEA and IEEPA as incidental to the broader commercial purpose of these trade measures. In *Veterans & Reservists for Peace in Vietnam,* we wrote:

> [A] statute is not overly broad and thus violative of the First Amendment merely because it regulates incident to its scheme protected activities or property. It is only where the statute *directly* regulates speech or expression arguably protected by the First Amendment, or where as its mechanism the statute has granted discretion to a delegatee to determine whether particular items of expression may be prohibited on the basis of their content, that the question of overbreadth

> arises. [TWEA] Section 5(b) does not directly regulate First Amendment protected material, rather it controls transactions concerning property in which an enemy has an economic interest. The purport of the statute is clear on its face, and therefore provides guidance to the delegatee with regard to the exercise of his functions.

459 F.2d at 681. Until 1988, this line of reasoning held sway. The regulations "nominally allowed the importation of informational materials ... but in reality banned it by requiring that the importers make payment into blocked U.S. accounts." *Walsh v. Brady,* 927 F.2d 1229, 1230 (D.C.Cir.1991).

Congress amended section 5 of TWEA and section 203(b) of IEEPA in 1988 to exempt the regulation of informational materials from the Executive's congeries of powers. The amendment specifically removed from the Executive's purview the authority to regulate or prohibit such transactions "directly or indirectly." This Berman Amendment was considered "a reaction to several seizures by the United States of shipments of magazines and books from embargoed countries and to the Treasury Department's restrictions on the permissible forms of payment for informational materials purchased from Cuba." *Kalantari v. NITV, Inc.,* 352 F.3d 1202, 1205 (9th Cir.2003) (footnotes omitted).

In the wake of the Berman Amendment, OFAC amended its regulations to conform with the new statutory language. Paralleling the statute, the new regulations exempted informational materials, "whether commercial or otherwise," from prohibition or regulation. Notably, however, OFAC took a narrow view of what constituted "informational materials." From the outset, OFAC reserved the right to regulate transactions related to "informational materials not fully created and in existence at the date of the transaction" and those concerning "the substantive or artistic alteration or enhancement of informational materials." OFAC also excluded "intangible items, such as telecommunications transmissions," from the definition of "informational materials." ...

In 1994, Congress expanded this limitation on executive authority by enacting the Free Trade in Ideas Act. Pub.L. No. 103-236, § 525, 108 Stat. 382, 474 (1994) (codified as amended at 12 U.S.C. § 95a, 50 U.S.C. § 1702(b)). In part, Congress responded to OFAC's exclusion of intangible materials from the definition of "informational materials" by amending IEEPA's exemption to restrict the Executive from regulating transactions concerning informational materials "regardless of format or medium of transmission." *Id.* § 525(c)(1) (amending 50 U.S.C. § 1702(b)(3)). Congress also added "compact disks, CD ROMS, artworks, and news wire feeds" to the nonexclusive litany of enumerated media that could qualify as "informational materials." *Id.* The House Conference Report stated:

> [N]o embargo may prohibit or restrict directly or indirectly the import or export of information that is protected under the First Amendment to the U.S. Constitution. The language was explicitly intended, by including the words "directly or indirectly," to have a broad scope. However, the Treasury Department has narrowly and restrictively interpreted the language in ways not originally intended. The present amendment is only intended to address some of those restrictive interpretations, for example limits on the type of information that is protected or on the medium or method of transmitting the information.

H.R. Conf. Rep. No. 103-482, at 239 (1994), *reprinted in* 1994 U.S.C.C.A.N. 398, 483. Significantly, although Congress overrode OFAC's interpretation to the extent that it excluded intangible materials from the definition of "informational materials," it did not disabuse OFAC of its belief that it could permissibly regulate "informational materials not fully created and in existence at the date of the transaction." That carve-out remained in place and, to date, has not been challenged as *ultra vires*....

With the Berman Amendment and the Free Trade in Ideas Act, Congress sought to ensure the robust exchange of informational materials would not be unduly inhibited by OFAC. When OFAC enacted regulations that Congress considered at odds with this overarching purpose, the legislature intervened and modified the statutory language to rectify OFAC's perceived missteps. Critically, although Congress addressed one facet of OFAC's 1989 interpretation of the informational-materials exemption by stressing in 1994 that the Executive may not regulate informational materials "regardless of format or medium of transmission," it did not counteract the component of that interpretation at issue here. Presumably cognizant of OFAC's narrowing interpretations, Congress could have inserted text stipulating that the Executive may not regulate informational materials regardless of whether fully created and in existence at the date of the transactions....

At trial, the government adduced sufficient evidence to convince a reasonable fact finder beyond a reasonable doubt that ChemPlan was not "fully created and in existence" at the date of the relevant transactions. Amirnazmi trumpeted the software's dynamism. Joseph Mehl, a computer network support technician who provided services to TranTech, testified to his belief that each ChemPlan package was "specifically tailored to the end user, depending on what industry they worked in." In aggressively pursuing commercial ties with NPC, Amirnazmi attempted to stoke his counterparty's interest by proposing several options for calibrating the software to NPC's unique needs. As explained below, the sale of ChemPlan to NPC was the cornerstone of Amirnazmi's conspiracy to bring his technical expertise to Iran for that country's aggrandizement. Consequently, the transfer of ChemPlan to Iranian purchasers does not fit neatly into the paradigm of informational exchange envisioned by Congress. Quite clearly, Amirnazmi envisioned ChemPlan as being of singular functional utility to Iranian users. Since the inception of the informational-materials exemption, OFAC has excepted such transactions from the scope of the general license.

Accordingly, we conclude that 31 C.F.R. § 560.210(c)(2) is a permissible construction of IEEPA's informational-materials exemption and is worthy of deference under *Chevron*. Therefore, a reasonable factfinder could have found the government proved beyond a reasonable doubt that the sale of ChemPlan to Iranian purchasers did not qualify for exemption from IEEPA as a matter of law....

Notes and Questions

a. Notwithstanding the general provisions against trade with certain anti-American countries, Congress has generally attempted to allow and even encourage intellectual property interaction as a form of engagement diplomacy. As can be seen in *Kalantari v. NITV, Inc.*, the works often made available are not those that would be promoted by the government at which the U.S. trade embargos are focused. The release of the Afghanistan-based film *Osama* followed a similar route: the film was made for $100,000 by filmmaker Siddiq Barmak, who had been forced out of filmmaking for ten years because of the Taliban government.

b. To what extent do these cases reflect the trade policies of the U.S. in intellectual property? Does a regime that allows copyrighted works access to U.S. markets, notwithstanding comprehensive embargos, undermine the embargo policy or balance that policy? In contrast, does a safe-harbor provision that allows U.S. manufacturers to continue to exploit a work derivatively undermine the very trade relationship that the treaty was designed to establish?

c. To what extent do the trade tensions suggested above reflect the domestic tension between copyright law and First Amendment jurisprudence?

d. Competition exists on both sides of each border and on both sides of each project. The U.S. and other nations regularly compete for market share of the entertainment content created. Similarly, the countries compete to be the originating country, fighting for the economic investment in jobs, materials, and facilities that are created by temporary and permanent entertainment activities.

Just as tremendous competition exists to lure film, television, and music production into new states, a similar process occurs at the international level. While the filming of *Lord of the Rings* in New Zealand has been the most visible recent example, the most pervasive competitor to Hollywood has been Canada. With Toronto working as a successful stand-in for New York, and with its beneficial exchange rates, Canada has become a natural alternative for some film production.

E. Copyright Restoration under TRIPS

1. Introduction—Excerpted from Copyright Circular 38B: Copyright Restoration Under the URAA

Congress passed the Uruguay Round Agreements Act (URAA) in 1994 to implement U.S. obligations under the Agreement on Trade-Related Aspects of Intellectual Property Rights (TRIPS) of the World Trade Organization (WTO). TRIPS incorporates by reference many obligations under the Berne Convention for the Protection of Literary and Artistic Works.

The United States signed the Berne Convention in 1989, committing itself to grant the same level of copyright protection to works from other Berne countries that it provides to works of U.S. nationals. The United States acceded to TRIPS in 1995 when it joined the WTO. TRIPS independently mandates compliance with most Berne provisions and provides additional obligations regarding enforcement that are subject to dispute resolution at the WTO.

...

The URAA amended section 104a of the copyright law to restore U.S. copyright to certain foreign works that were in the public domain in the United States but protected by copyright in their countries of origin.

Restoration of Copyrights—Ownership of a restored copyright vests initially in the author or initial rightholder, as determined by the law of the restored work's source country or by the owner of an exclusive right in the United States.

Eligibility Requirements—To be eligible, a work must meet all of the following requirements:

1. At the time the work was created, at least one author (or rightholder in the case of a sound recording) must have been a national or domiciliary of an eligible source country. An eligible source country is a country, other than the United States, that is a member of the WTO, a member of the Berne Convention for

the Protection of Literary and Artistic Works, or subject to a presidential proclamation restoring U.S. copyright protection to works of that country on the basis of reciprocal treatment of the works of U.S. nationals or domiciliaries.

2.   The work is not in the public domain in the eligible source country through expiration of the term of protection.

3.   The work is in the public domain in the United States because it did not comply with formalities imposed at any time by U. S. law, lacked subject matter protection in the United States in the case of sound recordings fixed before February 15, 1972, or lacked national eligibility in the United States.

4.   If published, the work must have been first published in an eligible country and not published in the United States during the 30-day period following its first publication in the eligible country.

Effective Date of Restoration—January 1, 1996, was the effective date of restoration of copyright for works from countries that were members of the WTO or the Berne Convention on that date. Subsequently, the effective date of restoration is the date a newly eligible country accedes to the WTO or the Berne Convention or the date of a presidential proclamation restoring U.S. copyright protection to works of that country.

Term of Copyright—The copyright in any work in which copyright is restored will last for the remainder of the term of copyright that the work would have enjoyed if the work had never entered the public domain in the United States.

Generally, the U. S. copyright term for works published before January 1, 1978, lasts for 95 years from the year of first publication. Although sound recordings fixed before 1972 were not then protected by federal copyright, those sound recordings will receive the remainder of the term they would have received had they been protected by such copyright when published. For example, a sound recording published in 1925 will be protected until 2020. For works published on or after January 1, 1978, the term of copyright is the life of the author plus 70 years. For example:

•   A French short story that was first published without copyright notice in 1935 will be treated as if it had both been published with a proper notice and properly renewed, meaning that its restored copyright will expire on December 31, 2030 (95 years after the U. S. copyright would have come into existence).

•   A Chinese play from 1983 will be protected until December 31 of the 70th year after the year in which its author dies.

•   A Mexican sound recording first published in Mexico in 1965 will be protected until December 31, 2060.

...

Automatic Restoration—Eligible copyrights are restored automatically and no further steps need to be taken to make a restored copyright fully enforceable against any party other than a reliance party.

Notice of Intent to Enforce—Although copyright is restored automatically in eligible works, the URAA directs the owner of a restored work to notify reliance parties if the owner of the rights in a restored work plans to enforce those rights.

A reliance party is typically a business or individual who, relying on the public domain status of a work, was using it before the enactment of the URAA on December 8, 1994. For works from any country that was not eligible under the URAA as of December 8, 1994, reliance parties are those using the work before the date on which the country becomes eligible by joining the WTO or the Berne Convention or as a result of a presidential proclamation.

The URAA authorizes the owner of a right in a restored work to either

• provide actual Notice of Intent to Enforce (NIE) a Restored Copyright by contacting a reliance party directly, or

• provide constructive notice by filing an NIE with the Copyright Office.

The URAA further directs the Copyright Office to publish in the Federal Register, the U. S. government's publication for official agency notices, a list identifying restored works and their ownership when NIEs are recorded with the Office. For inspection and copying by the public, the Office maintains a list identifying all NIEs....

Grace Period for Use of Restored Works—A reliance party has a 12-month grace period to sell off previously manufactured stock, perform or display the relevant work publicly, or authorize others to conduct these activities. The grace period begins when the reliance party receives notice that the owner is enforcing the copyright in the restored work. The date runs from either the date of receipt of the actual notice or the date of publication of the Federal Register issue identifying the work. If notice is provided both by Federal Register publication and service on the reliance party, the period runs from whichever date is earlier. Except for certain reliance parties who created derivative works, a reliance party must cease using the restored work when the 12-month grace period expires unless the reliance party reaches a licensing agreement with the copyright owner for continued use of the restored work.

Subsection (d)(3) of the amended section 104a of the Copyright Act contains special rules for certain derivative works created before December 8, 1994, based on underlying restored works. Examples include the translation of a restored work or a motion picture based on a restored book or a play. A reliance party can continue to exploit such derivative works if the reliance party pays the owner of the restored copyright reasonable compensation.

Overview of Section 104A from *Dam Things From Denmark v. Russ Berrie & Co.*

[The restoration of certain copyrighted works from the public domain has been a controversial part of the TRIPS Agreement. The provision is well explained in *Dam Things From Denmark v. Russ Berrie & Co., Inc.*, 290 F.3d 548 (3d Cir. N.J. 2002). The excerpts below are highly reordered to provide a summary of §104A.]

The United States Trade Representative has described the Agreement on Trade-Related Aspects of Intellectual Property Rights ("TRIPs") as "establishing comprehensive standards for the protection of intellectual property and the enforcement of intellectual property rights in WTO member countries. It requires each WTO member country to apply the substantive obligations of the world's most important intellectual property conventions, supplement those conventions with substantial additional protection, and ensures that critical enforcement procedures will be available in each member country to safeguard intellectual property rights." Office of the United States Trade Representative, The Uruguay Round Agreements Act Statement of Administrative Action: Agreement on Trade-Related Aspects of Intellectual Property Rights (1994) [hereinafter USTR Statement].

In this legislation, Congress declared that a wide range of foreign works previously in the public domain in this country, perhaps for many years, are once again afforded copyright protection. The United States took this action in an effort to comply with agreements it had entered into with foreign governments regarding intellectual property rights....

[Under § 104A,] protection results from the United States' promise, in the context of the TRIPs annex to the Agreement Establishing the World Trade Organization ("WTO"), to adhere to the Berne Convention, which the United States had entered in 1989. In order to comply with the Berne Convention's "Rule of Retroactivity" contained in Article 18, Congress enacted the Uruguay Round Agreements Act. The Act supplanted a previous version of § 104A (enacted only one year earlier in an effort to comply with the North American Free Trade Agreement ("NAFTA")), and provided for broad restoration of foreign works. Section 104A of the Copyright Act now provides for automatic restoration of copyright, as of January 1, 1996, for "an original work of authorship" which meets the following requirements:

> (A) is protected under subsection (a) [which provides for a term of protection equal to what the work would have received "if the work had never entered the public domain in the United States," and excepts certain works which were "ever owned or administered by the Alien Property Custodian"];
>
> (B) is not in the public domain in its source country through expiration of term of protection;
>
> (C) is in the public domain in the United States due to —
>
> (i) noncompliance with formalities imposed at any time by United States copyright law, including failure of renewal, lack of proper notice, or failure to comply with any manufacturing requirements;
>
> (ii) lack of subject matter protection in the case of sound recordings fixed before February 15, 1972; or
>
> (iii) lack of national eligibility; and
>
> (D) has at least one author or rightholder who was, at the time the work was created, a national or domiciliary of an eligible country, and if published, was first published in an eligible country and not published in the United States during the 30-day period following publication in such eligible country.

17 U.S.C. § 104A(h)(6)(A)–(D).

If [a work qualifies], then the copyright "shall subsist for the remainder of the term of copyright that the work would have otherwise been granted in the United States if the work never entered the public domain in the United States." 17 U.S.C. § 104A(a) (1)(B).

Section 104A also provides some relief for "reliance parties" — American authors who copied the restored works while they were in the public domain in the United States. 17 U.S.C. § 104A(d)(2)–(3). Section 104A defines "reliance party" in relevant part as "any person who (A) with respect to a particular work, engages in acts, before the source country of that work becomes an eligible country, which would have violated section 106 if the restored work had been subject to copyright protection, and who, after the source country becomes an eligible country, continues to engage in such acts...." 17 U.S.C. § 104A(h)(4)(A). Parties who were in fact copying the restored work are given one year to sell the now infringing works after being given a "notice of intent to enforce" ("NIE") by the author of the restored work. 17 U.S.C. § 104A(d)(2). But, the statute also provides a safe harbor in the form of a mandatory license for authors of "derivative works"; they are allowed to continue manufacturing and selling their work, but must pay the author of the restored work reasonable compensation. 17 U.S.C. § 104A (d)(3).

In its report on the Copyright Technical Amendments Act, the House of Representatives expressed its reason for providing a special provision in § 104A for derivative works:

> In enacting section 104A, Congress considered the fact that restoring copyright in works that are currently in the public domain creates a potential problem: people may have used these works as the basis for new derivative works, such as motion pictures made from novels. At the time the new derivative work was created, the use of the underlying work was completely lawful, since it was in the public domain. Once copyright in the underlying work is restored, however, the continued use of the derivative work without the consent of the owner of the copyright in the underlying work would constitute copyright infringement.

H.R. Rep. No. 105-25, at 12 (1997)....

The parties to this appeal, Dam Things from Denmark, a/k/a Troll Company ApS (together "Dam Things"), and Russ Berrie and Company, Inc. ("Russ"), are purveyors of trolls—short, pudgy, plastic dolls with big grins and wild hair. Dam Things, a Danish company, asserts that its copyright in its original troll design, the "Basic Good Luck Troll," has been restored pursuant to *17 U.S.C. § 104A*. Section 104A is a highly unusual provision which has restored copyright protection in a vast number of foreign works previously in the public domain. Dam Things brought this action against Russ alleging infringement of its restored copyright....

We believe that the District Court properly determined that Dam Things was likely to establish that [the first troll design (P1)] copyright qualified for restoration and that this copyright was not abandoned by Dam Things. We find, however, that the District Court's subsequent analysis was flawed in two ways. First, the District Court conflated the tests for infringement and derivative works, and it therefore did not properly consider the possibility that any of the Russ trolls qualified for § 104A's safe harbor for derivative works. Second, the District Court did not conduct the proper comparison of each of the allegedly infringing Russ trolls against the restored Dam Things troll—P1. As we believe that the District Court based its grant of the injunction on an incomplete factual and legal analysis, we will vacate the injunction and remand for further consideration by the District Court in light of this opinion.

Golan v. Holder
___ U.S. ___, 132 S. Ct. 873 (2012)

Justice GINSBURG delivered the opinion of the Court.

The Berne Convention for the Protection of Literary and Artistic Works (Berne Convention or Berne), which took effect in 1886, is the principal accord governing international copyright relations. Latecomer to the international copyright regime launched by Berne, the United States joined the Convention in 1989. To perfect U.S. implementation of Berne, and as part of our response to the Uruguay Round of multilateral trade negotiations, Congress, in 1994, gave works enjoying copyright protection abroad the same full term of protection available to U.S. works. Congress did so in § 514 of the Uruguay Round Agreements Act (URAA), which grants copyright protection to preexisting works of Berne member countries, protected in their country of origin, but lacking protection in the United States for any of three reasons: The United States did not protect works from the country of origin at the time of publication; the United States did not protect sound recordings fixed before 1972; or the author had failed to comply with U.S. statutory formalities (formalities Congress no longer requires as prerequisites to copyright protection).

The URAA accords no protection to a foreign work after its full copyright term has expired, causing it to fall into the public domain, whether under the laws of the country of origin or of this country. Works encompassed by § 514 are granted the protection they would have enjoyed had the United States maintained copyright relations with the author's country or removed formalities incompatible with Berne. Foreign authors, however, gain no credit for the protection they lacked in years prior to § 514's enactment. They therefore enjoy fewer total years of exclusivity than do their U.S. counterparts. As a consequence of the barriers to U.S. copyright protection prior to the enactment of § 514, foreign works "restored" to protection by the measure had entered the public domain in this country. To cushion the impact of their placement in protected status, Congress included in § 514 ameliorating accommodations for parties who had exploited affected works before the URAA was enacted.

Petitioners include orchestra conductors, musicians, publishers, and others who formerly enjoyed free access to works § 514 removed from the public domain. They maintain that the Constitution's Copyright and Patent Clause, Art. I, § 8, cl. 8, and First Amendment both decree the invalidity of § 514. Under those prescriptions of our highest law, petitioners assert, a work that has entered the public domain, for whatever reason, must forever remain there.

In accord with the judgment of the Tenth Circuit, we conclude that § 514 does not transgress constitutional limitations on Congress' authority. Neither the Copyright and Patent Clause nor the First Amendment, we hold, makes the public domain, in any and all cases, a territory that works may never exit.

Members of the Berne Union agree to treat authors from other member countries as well as they treat their own. Nationals of a member country, as well as any author who publishes in one of Berne's 164 member states, thus enjoy copyright protection in nations across the globe. Each country, moreover, must afford at least the minimum level of protection specified by Berne. The copyright term must span the author's lifetime, plus at least 50 additional years, whether or not the author has complied with a member state's legal formalities. And, as relevant here, a work must be protected abroad unless its copyright term has expired in either the country where protection is claimed or the country of origin.

A different system of transnational copyright protection long prevailed in this country. Until 1891, foreign works were categorically excluded from Copyright Act protection. Throughout most of the 20th century, the only eligible foreign authors were those whose countries granted reciprocal rights to U.S. authors and whose works were printed in the United States. For domestic and foreign authors alike, protection hinged on compliance with notice, registration, and renewal formalities.

The United States became party to Berne's multilateral, formality-free copyright regime in 1989. Initially, Congress adopted a "minimalist approach" to compliance with the Convention. The Berne Convention Implementation Act of 1988 made "only those changes to American copyright law that [were] clearly required under the treaty's provisions," House Report, at 7. Despite Berne's instruction that member countries—including "new accessions to the Union"—protect foreign works under copyright in the country of origin, the BCIA accorded no protection for "any work that is in the public domain in the United States." ... Congress indicated, however, that it had not definitively rejected "retroactive" protection for preexisting foreign works; instead it had punted on this issue of Berne's implementation, deferring consideration until "a more thorough examination of Constitutional, commercial, and consumer considerations is possible." BCIA House Report, at 51, 52.3

The minimalist approach essayed by the United States did not sit well with other Berne members. While negotiations were ongoing over the North American Free Trade Agreement (NAFTA), Mexican authorities complained about the United States' refusal to grant protection, in accord with Article 18, to Mexican works that remained under copyright domestically....

The landscape changed in 1994. The Uruguay round of multilateral trade negotiations produced the World Trade Organization (WTO) and the Agreement on Trade-Related Aspects of Intellectual Property Rights (TRIPS). The United States joined both. TRIPS mandates, on pain of WTO enforcement, implementation of Berne's first 21 articles [except Article 6*bis* protecting moral rights]. The WTO gave teeth to the Convention's requirements: Noncompliance with a WTO ruling could subject member countries to tariffs or cross-sector retaliation. The specter of WTO enforcement proceedings bolstered the credibility of our trading partners' threats to challenge the United States for inadequate compliance with Article 18.

Congress' response to the Uruguay agreements put to rest any questions concerning U.S. compliance with Article 18. Section 514 of the URAA, 108 Stat. 4976 (codified at 17 U.S.C. § 104A, 109(a)),9 extended copyright to works that garnered protection in their countries of origin, but had no right to exclusivity in the United States for any of three reasons: lack of copyright relations between the country of origin and the United States at the time of publication; lack of subject-matter protection for sound recordings fixed before 1972; and failure to comply with U.S. statutory formalities (e.g., failure to provide notice of copyright status, or to register and renew a copyright).

Works that have fallen into the public domain after the expiration of a full copyright term—either in the United States or the country of origin—receive no further protection under § 514. Copyrights "restored" under URAA § 514 "subsist for the remainder of the term of copyright that the work would have otherwise been granted ... if the work never entered the public domain." § 104A(a)(1)(B). Prospectively, restoration places foreign works on an equal footing with their U.S. counterparts; assuming a foreign and domestic author died the same day, their works will enter the public domain simultaneously. Restored works, however, receive no compensatory time for the period of exclusivity they would have enjoyed before § 514's enactment, had they been protected at the outset in the United States. Their total term, therefore, falls short of that available to similarly situated U.S. works.

The URAA's disturbance of the public domain hardly escaped Congress' attention. Section 514 imposed no liability for any use of foreign works occurring before restoration. In addition, anyone remained free to copy and use restored works for one year following § 514's enactment. Concerns about § 514's compatibility with the Fifth Amendment's Takings Clause led Congress to include additional protections for "reliance parties"—those who had, before the URAA's enactment, used or acquired a foreign work then in the public domain. Reliance parties may continue to exploit a restored work until the owner of the restored copyright gives notice of intent to enforce—either by filing with the U.S. Copyright Office within two years of restoration, or by actually notifying the reliance party. After that, reliance parties may continue to exploit existing copies for a grace period of one year. Finally, anyone who, before the URAA's enactment, created a "derivative work" based on a restored work may indefinitely exploit the derivation upon payment to the copyright holder of "reasonable compensation," to be set by a district judge if the parties cannot agree.

In 2001, petitioners filed this lawsuit challenging § 514. They maintain that Congress, when it passed the URAA, exceeded its authority under the Copyright Clause and transgressed First Amendment limitations. The District Court granted the Attorney General's motion for summary judgment. In rejecting petitioners' Copyright Clause argument, the court stated that Congress "has historically demonstrated little compunction about removing copyrightable materials from the public domain." The court next declined to part from "the settled rule that private censorship via copyright enforcement does not implicate First Amendment concerns."

The Court of Appeals for the Tenth Circuit affirmed in part. The public domain, it agreed, was not a "threshold that Congress" was powerless to "traverse in both directions." But §514, as the Court of Appeals read our decision in *Eldred v. Ashcroft*, 537 U.S. 186 (2003), required further First Amendment inspection. The measure "'altered the traditional contours of copyright protection,'" the court said—specifically, the "bedrock principle" that once works enter the public domain, they do not leave. The case was remanded with an instruction to the District Court to address the First Amendment claim in light of the Tenth Circuit's opinion.

On remand, the District Court's starting premise was uncontested: Section 514 does not regulate speech on the basis of its content; therefore the law would be upheld if "narrowly tailored to serve a significant government interest." Summary judgment was due petitioners, the court concluded, because §514's constriction of the public domain was not justified by any of the asserted federal interests: compliance with Berne, securing greater protection for U.S. authors abroad, or remediation of the inequitable treatment suffered by foreign authors whose works lacked protection in the United States. The Tenth Circuit reversed. Deferring to Congress' predictive judgments in matters relating to foreign affairs, the appellate court held that §514 survived First Amendment scrutiny. Specifically, the court determined that the law was narrowly tailored to fit the important government aim of protecting U.S. copyright holders' interests abroad.

We granted certiorari to consider petitioners' challenge to §514 under both the Copyright Clause and the First Amendment, and now affirm.

We first address petitioners' argument that Congress lacked authority, under the Copyright Clause, to enact §514. The Constitution states that "Congress shall have Power ... [t]o promote the Progress of Science ... by securing for limited Times to Authors ... the exclusive Right to their ... Writings." Art. I, §8, cl. 8. Petitioners find in this grant of authority an impenetrable barrier to the extension of copyright protection to authors whose writings, for whatever reason, are in the public domain. We see no such barrier in the text of the Copyright Clause, historical practice, or our precedents.

The text of the Copyright Clause does not exclude application of copyright protection to works in the public domain.... Our decision in *Eldred* is largely dispositive of petitioners' limited-time argument. There we addressed the question whether Congress violated the Copyright Clause when it extended, by 20 years, the terms of existing copyrights. Ruling that Congress acted within constitutional bounds, we declined to infer from the text of the Copyright Clause "the command that a time prescription, once set, becomes forever 'fixed' or 'inalterable.'" "The word 'limited,'" we observed, "does not convey a meaning so constricted." Rather, the term is best understood to mean "confine[d] within certain bounds," "restrain[ed]," or "circumscribed." The construction petitioners tender closely resembles the definition rejected in *Eldred* and is similarly infirm.

The terms afforded works restored by §514 are no less "limited" than those the CTEA lengthened. In light of *Eldred*, petitioners do not here contend that the term Congress has granted U.S. authors—their lifetimes, plus 70 years—is unlimited....

Historical practice corroborates our reading of the Copyright Clause to permit full U.S. compliance with Berne. Undoubtedly, federal copyright legislation generally has not affected works in the public domain. Section 514's disturbance of that domain, petitioners argue, distinguishes their suit from *Eldred*'s. In adopting the CTEA, petitioners note, Congress acted in accord with "an unbroken congressional practice" of granting pre-expiration term extensions. No comparable practice, they maintain, supports § 514.

On occasion, however, Congress has seen fit to protect works once freely available. Notably, the Copyright Act of 1790 granted protection to many works previously in the public domain. Act of May 31, 1790 (1790 Act), § 1, 1 Stat. 124 (covering "any map, chart, book, or books already printed within these United States"). Before the Act launched a uniform national system, three States provided no statutory copyright protection at all. Of those that did afford some protection, seven failed to protect maps; eight did not cover previously published books; and all ten denied protection to works that failed to comply with formalities. The First Congress, it thus appears, did not view the public domain as inviolate. As we have recognized, the "construction placed upon the Constitution by [the drafters of] the first [copyright] act of 1790 and the act of 1802 ... men who were contemporary with [the Constitution's] formation, many of whom were members of the convention which framed it, is of itself entitled to very great weight." *Burrow-Giles Lithographic Co. v. Sarony*, 111 U.S. 53, 57 (1884).

Subsequent actions confirm that Congress has not understood the Copyright Clause to preclude protection for existing works. Several private bills restored the copyrights of works that previously had been in the public domain. These bills were unchallenged in court.

Analogous patent statutes, however, were upheld in litigation.... Congress has also passed generally applicable legislation granting patents and copyrights to inventions and works that had lost protection. An 1832 statute authorized a new patent for any inventor whose failure, "by inadvertence, accident, or mistake," to comply with statutory formalities rendered the original patent "invalid or inoperative." An 1893 measure similarly allowed authors who had not timely deposited their work to receive "all the rights and privileges" the Copyright Act affords, if they made the required deposit by March 1, 1893. And in 1919 and 1941, Congress authorized the President to issue proclamations granting protection to foreign works that had fallen into the public domain during World Wars I and II....

We next explain why the First Amendment does not inhibit the restoration authorized by § 514. To do so, we first recapitulate the relevant part of our pathmarking decision in *Eldred*. The petitioners in *Eldred*, like those here, argued that Congress had violated not only the "limited Times" prescription of the Copyright Clause. In addition, and independently, the *Eldred* petitioners charged, Congress had offended the First Amendment's freedom of expression guarantee. The CTEA's 20-year enlargement of a copyright's duration, we held in *Eldred*, offended neither provision.

Concerning the First Amendment, we recognized that some restriction on expression is the inherent and intended effect of every grant of copyright. Noting that the "Copyright Clause and the First Amendment were adopted close in time," we observed that the Framers regarded copyright protection not simply as a limit on the manner in which expressive works may be used. They also saw copyright as an "engine of free expression[:] By establishing a marketable right to the use of one's expression, copyright supplies the economic incentive to create and disseminate ideas." (*quoting Harper & Row*, 471 U.S., at 558, 105 S.Ct. 2218).

We then described the "traditional contours" of copyright protection, i.e., the "idea/expression dichotomy" and the "fair use" defense. Both are recognized in our jurisprudence as "built-in First Amendment accommodations." The idea/expression dichotomy is codified at 17 U.S.C. § 102(b): "In no case does copyright protec[t] ... any idea, procedure, process, system, method of operation, concept, principle, or discovery ... described, explained, illustrated, or embodied in [the copyrighted] work." "Due to this [idea/expression] distinction, every idea, theory, and fact in a copyrighted work becomes instantly available for public exploitation at the moment of publication"; the author's expression alone gains copyright protection. *Eldred*, 537 U.S., at 219, 123 S.Ct. 769.

The second "traditional contour," the fair use defense, is codified at 17 U.S.C. § 107: "[T]he fair use of a copyrighted work, including such use by reproduction in copies ..., for purposes such as criticism, comment, news reporting, teaching (including multiple copies for classroom use), scholarship, or research, is not an infringement of copyright." This limitation on exclusivity "allows the public to use not only facts and ideas contained in a copyrighted work, but also [the author's] expression itself in certain circumstances." *Eldred*, 537 U.S., at 219.

Given the "speech-protective purposes and safeguards" embraced by copyright law, we concluded in *Eldred* that there was no call for the heightened review petitioners sought in that case. We reach the same conclusion here. Section 514 leaves undisturbed the "idea/expression" distinction and the "fair use" defense. Moreover, Congress adopted measures to ease the transition from a national scheme to an international copyright regime: It deferred the date from which enforcement runs, and it cushioned the impact of restoration on "reliance parties" who exploited foreign works denied protection before § 514 took effect.

Petitioners attempt to distinguish their challenge from the one turned away in *Eldred*. First Amendment interests of a higher order are at stake here, petitioners say, because they—unlike their counterparts in *Eldred*—enjoyed "vested rights" in works that had already entered the public domain.... To copyright lawyers, the "vested rights" formulation might sound exactly backwards: Rights typically vest at the *outset* of copyright protection, in an author or rightholder. Once the term of protection ends, the works do not revest in any rightholder. Instead, the works simply lapse into the public domain Anyone has free access to the public domain, but no one, after the copyright term has expired, acquires ownership rights in the once-protected works....

Congress determined that U.S. interests were best served by our full participation in the dominant system of international copyright protection. Those interests include ensuring exemplary compliance with our international obligations, securing greater protection for U.S. authors abroad, and remedying unequal treatment of foreign authors. The judgment § 514 expresses lies well within the ken of the political branches. It is our obligation, of course, to determine whether the action Congress took, wise or not, encounters any constitutional shoal. For the reasons stated, we are satisfied it does not. The judgment of the Court of Appeals for the Tenth Circuit is therefore

Affirmed.

Justice BREYER, with whom Justice ALITO joins, dissenting.

In order "[t]o promote the Progress of Science" (by which term the Founders meant "learning" or "knowledge"), the Constitution's Copyright Clause grants Congress the power to "secur[e] for limited Times to Authors ... the exclusive Right to their ... Writings." Art. I, § 8, cl. 8. This "exclusive Right" allows its holder to charge a fee to those who wish to use a copyrighted work, and the ability to charge that fee encourages the production of new material. In this sense, a copyright is, in Macaulay's words, a "tax on readers for the purpose of giving a bounty to writers"—a bounty designed to encourage new production.

As the Court said in *Eldred*, "'[t]he economic philosophy behind the [Copyright] [C]lause ... is the conviction that encouragement of individual effort by personal gain is the best way to advance public welfare through the talents of authors and inventors.'"

The statute before us, however, does not encourage anyone to produce a single new work. By definition, it bestows monetary rewards only on owners of old works—works that have already been created and already are in the American public domain. At the same time, the statute inhibits the dissemination of those works, foreign works published abroad after 1923, of which there are many millions, including films, works of art, innumerable photographs, and, of course, books—books that (in the absence of the statute) would assume their rightful places in computer-accessible databases, spreading knowledge throughout the world. In my view, the Copyright Clause does not authorize Congress to enact this statute. And I consequently dissent....

The Act before us says that it "restores" American copyright to a set of works, which, for the most part, did not previously enjoy American copyright protection. These works had fallen into America's public domain, but as of the "restoration" date, they had not yet fallen into the public domain of the foreign country where they originated....

Despite these temporal limitations, the Act covers vast numbers of works. The first category includes works published in countries that had copyright relations with the United States during this time period, such as most of Western Europe and Latin America, Australia, and Japan, whose authors did not satisfy American copyright formalities, perhaps because the author, who may not have sought an American copyright, published the book abroad without proper American notice, or perhaps because the author obtained a valid American copyright but failed to renew it.

The second category (works that entered the public domain due to a lack of copyright relations) includes, among others, all works published in Russia and other countries of the former Soviet Union before May 1973 (when the U.S.S.R. joined the Universal Copyright Convention (UCC)), all works published in the People's Republic of China before March 1992 (when bilateral copyright relations between the People's Republic and the United States were first established), all South Korean works published before October 1987 (when South Korea joined the UCC), and all Egyptian and Turkish works published before March 1989 (when the United States joined Berne)....

I recognize that ordinary copyright protection also comes accompanied with dissemination-restricting royalty charges and administrative costs. But here the restrictions work special harm. For one thing, the foreign location of restored works means higher than ordinary administrative costs. For another, the statute's technical requirements make it very difficult to establish whether a work has had its copyright restored by the statute.

Worst of all, "restored copyright" protection removes material from the public domain. In doing so, it reverses the payment expectations of those who used, or intended to use, works that they thought belonged to them. Were Congress to act similarly with respect to well-established property rights, the problem would be obvious. This statute analogously restricts, and thereby diminishes, Americans' preexisting freedom to use formerly public domain material in their expressive activities.

Thus, while the majority correctly observes that the dissemination-restricting harms of copyright normally present problems appropriate for legislation to resolve, the question is whether the Copyright Clause permits Congress seriously to exacerbate such a problem by taking works out of the public domain without a countervailing benefit. This question *is* appropriate for judicial resolution. Indeed, unlike *Eldred* where the Court had to decide a complicated line-drawing question—when is a copyright term too long?— here an easily administrable standard is available—a standard that would require works that have already fallen into the public domain to stay there.

Notes and Questions

a. *Dam Things From Denmark v. Russ Berrie & Co., Inc.* reflects the other tension in international copyright—the right to remove formerly copyrighted works from the public domain. Prior to the Uruguay round of TRIPS, it was understood that a work which fell into the public domain was irretrievably lost to ownership. Were the safe-harbor provisions of § 104A necessary to protect the statute from constitutional attack? Do the safe-harbor provisions render § 104A largely ineffectual to achieve the restoration sought under the statute?

b. Challenges to the legitimacy of § 104A of the Copyright Act continue, as companies find themselves barred from exploiting public domain works that have been reclaimed by foreign authors and owners. American publishers have challenged the constitutionality of the copyright restoration provisions. *Luck's Music Library, Inc. v. Gonzales*, 407 F.3d 1262 (D.C. Cir. 2005).

> Plaintiffs challenge the constitutionality of § 514 of the Uruguay Round Agreements Act ("URAA"), codified at 17 U.S.C. §§ 104A, 109, which implements Article 18 of the Berne Convention for the Protection of Literary and Artistic Works.... Section 514 of the URAA establishes copyrights of foreign holders whose works, though protected under the law where initially published, fell into the public domain in the United States for a variety of reasons—the U.S. failed to recognize copyrights of a particular nation, the copyright owner failed to comply with formalities of U.S. copyright law, or, in the case of sound recordings "fixed" before February 15, 1972, federal copyright protection had been unavailable.

Id. at 1262–63.

The court rejected arguments that Congress lacked the power to pull these restored works from the public domain. Ironically, it used *Eldred v. Ashcroft*, 537 U.S. 186 (2003), to bolster the proposition that there needs to be a direct incentive or *quid pro quo* to the author.

> It is by no means clear that *Eldred* requires a direct incentive at all. The majority expressly relied on its understanding that adoption of the 20-year term extension enhanced the United States's position in negotiating with European Union countries for benefits for American authors. Here, similarly, the Senate argued in support of § 514 that its adoption helped secure better foreign protection for US intellectual property and was "a significant opportunity to reduce the impact of copyright piracy on our world trade position." S. Rep. No. 100-352, at 2 (1988).

Id. at 1264 (citation omitted).

c. In 1984, Alexey Pajitnov created *Tetris*, one of the world's most popular computer games. He transferred the rights to Computer Center of the Academy of Sciences of the U.S.S.R. since he was unable to exploit the rights himself. To what extent can the former Soviet computer scientist reclaim those rights? See *Blue Planet Software, Inc. v. Games Int'l, LLC*, 334 F. Supp. 2d 425 (S.D.N.Y. 2004).

Problem II-E

While in Canada negotiating for the rights to produce a new play, Bryce listens to an album from Brazil which is copyrighted in Canada. Upon returning to the United States, Bryce discovers that the album had been marketed in the U.S. since 1965, but because of failure to follow the statutory requirements of notice and registration, the work is now in the public domain.

Bryce comes to you to find out whether a person can distribute the CD version of the album in the United States legally without the permission of the copyright owner. Advise Bryce of the legality of distributing such a CD.

F. Choice of Law

Itar-Tass Russian News Agency v. Russian Kurier, Inc.
153 F.3d 82 (2d Cir. 1998)

This appeal primarily presents issues concerning the choice of law in international copyright cases and the substantive meaning of Russian copyright law as to the respective rights of newspaper reporters and newspaper publishers. The conflicts issue is which country's law applies to issues of copyright ownership and to issues of infringement. The primary substantive issue under Russian copyright law is whether a newspaper publishing company has an interest sufficient to give it standing to sue for copying the text of individual articles appearing in its newspapers, or whether complaints about such copying may be made only by the reporters who authored the articles. Defendants-appellants Russian Kurier, Inc. ("Kurier") and Oleg Pogrebnoy (collectively "the Kurier defendants") appeal from the March 25, 1997, judgment of the District Court for the Southern District of New York (John G. Koeltl, Judge) enjoining them from copying articles that have appeared or will appear in publications of the plaintiffs-appellees, mainly Russian newspapers and a Russian news agency, and awarding the appellees substantial damages for copyright infringement.

On the conflicts issue, we conclude that, with respect to the Russian plaintiffs, Russian law determines the ownership and essential nature of the copyrights alleged to have been infringed and that United States law determines whether those copyrights have been infringed in the United States and, if so, what remedies are available. We also conclude that Russian law, which explicitly excludes newspapers from a work-for-hire doctrine, vests exclusive ownership interests in newspaper articles in the journalists who wrote the articles, not in the newspaper employers who compile their writings. We further conclude that to the extent that Russian law accords newspaper publishers an interest distinct from the copyright of the newspaper reporters, the publishers' interest, like the usual ownership interest in a compilation, extends to the publishers' original selection and arrangement of the articles, and does not entitle the publishers to damages for copying the texts of articles contained in a newspaper compilation. We therefore reverse the judgment to the extent that it granted the newspapers relief for copying the texts of the articles. However, because one non-newspaper plaintiff-appellee is entitled to some injunctive relief and damages and other plaintiffs-appellees may be entitled to some, perhaps considerable, relief, we also remand for further consideration of this lawsuit.

The lawsuit concerns Kurier, a Russian language weekly newspaper with a circulation in the New York area of about 20,000. It is published in New York City by defendant Kurier. Defendant Pogrebnoy is president and sole shareholder of Kurier and editor-in-chief of Kurier. The plaintiffs include corporations that publish, daily or weekly, major Russian language newspapers in Russia and Russian language magazines in Russia or Israel; Itar-Tass Russian News Agency ("Itar-Tass"), formerly known as the Telegraph Agency of the Soviet Union (TASS), a wire service and news gathering company centered in Moscow, functioning similarly to the Associated Press; and the Union of Journalists of Russia ("UJR"), the professional writers union of accredited print and broadcast journalists of the Russian Federation.

The Kurier defendants do not dispute that Kurier has copied about 500 articles that first appeared in the plaintiffs' publications or were distributed by Itar-Tass. The copied material, though extensive, was a small percentage of the total number of articles published in Kurier. The Kurier defendants also do not dispute how the copying occurred: articles from the plaintiffs' publications, sometimes containing headlines, pictures, bylines, and graphics, in addition to text, were cut out, pasted on layout sheets, and sent to Kurier's printer for photographic reproduction and printing in the pages of Kurier.

Most significantly, the Kurier defendants also do not dispute that, with one exception, they had not obtained permission from any of the plaintiffs to copy the articles that appeared in Kurier. Pogrebnoy claimed at trial to have received permission from the publisher of one newspaper, but his claim was rejected by the District Court at trial. Pogrebnoy also claimed that he had obtained permission from the authors of six of the copied articles. The District Court made no finding as to whether this testimony was credible, since authors' permission was not pertinent to the District Court's view of the legal issues....

I. Choice of Law

The threshold issue concerns the choice of law for resolution of this dispute. That issue was not initially considered by the parties, all of whom turned directly to Russian law for resolution of the case. Believing that the conflicts issue merited consideration, we requested supplemental briefs from the parties and appointed Professor William F. Patry as Amicus Curiae. Prof. Patry has submitted an extremely helpful brief on the choice of law issue.

Choice of law issues in international copyright cases have been largely ignored in the reported decisions and dealt with rather cursorily by most commentators. Examples pertinent to the pending appeal are those decisions involving a work created by the employee of a foreign corporation. Several courts have applied the United States work-for-hire doctrine, see 17 U.S.C. § 201(b), without explicit consideration of the conflicts issue.

The Nimmer treatise briefly (and perhaps optimistically) suggests that conflicts issues "have rarely proved troublesome in the law of copyright." See Nimmer on Copyright § 17.05 (1998) ("Nimmer") (footnote omitted). Relying on the "national treatment" principle of the Berne Convention and the Universal Copyright Convention ("U.C.C."), Nimmer asserts, correctly in our view, that "an author who is a national of one of the member states of either Berne or the U.C.C., or one who first publishes his work in any such member state, is entitled to the same copyright protection in each other member state as such other state accords to its own nationals."

Nimmer then somewhat overstates the national treatment principle: "The applicable law is the copyright law of the state in which the infringement occurred, not that of the state of which the author is a national, or in which the work is first published." The difficulty with this broad statement is that it subsumes under the phrase "applicable law" the law concerning two distinct issues—ownership and substantive rights, i.e., scope of protection. Another commentator has also broadly stated the principle of national treatment, but described its application in a way that does not necessarily cover issues of ownership. "The principle of national treatment also means that both the question of whether the right exists and the question of the scope of the right are to be answered in accordance with the law of the country where the protection is claimed." S.M. Stewart, *International Copyright and Neighboring Rights* § 3.17 (2d ed. 1989).

Prof. Patry's brief, as Amicus Curiae, helpfully points out that the principle of national treatment is really not a conflicts rule at all; it does not direct application of the law of any country. It simply requires that the country in which protection is claimed must treat foreign and domestic authors alike. Whether U.S. copyright law directs U.S. courts to look to foreign or domestic law as to certain issues is irrelevant to national treatment, so long as the scope of protection would be extended equally to foreign and domestic authors.

We agree with the view of the Amicus that the Convention's principle of national treatment simply assures that if the law of the country of infringement applies to the scope of substantive copyright protection, that law will be applied uniformly to foreign and domestic authors.

Source of conflicts rules. Our analysis of the conflicts issue begins with consideration of the source of law for selecting a conflicts rule. Though Nimmer turns directly to the Berne Convention and the U.C.C., we think that step moves too quickly past the Berne Convention Implementation Act of 1988. Section 4(a)(3) of the Act amends Title 17 to provide: "No right or interest in a work eligible for protection under this title may be claimed by virtue of ... the provisions of the Berne Convention.... Any rights in a work eligible for protection under this title that derive from this title ... shall not be expanded or reduced by virtue of ... the provisions of the Berne Convention."

We start our analysis with the Copyrights Act itself, which contains no provision relevant to the pending case concerning conflicts issues. We therefore fill the interstices of the Act by developing federal common law on the conflicts issue. In doing so, we are entitled to consider and apply principles of private international law, which are "'part of our law.'"

The choice of law applicable to the pending case is not necessarily the same for all issues. See *Restatement (Second) of Conflict of Laws § 222* ("The courts have long recognized that they are not bound to decide all issues under the local law of a single state."). We consider first the law applicable to the issue of copyright ownership.

Conflicts rule for issues of ownership. Copyright is a form of property, and the usual rule is that the interests of the parties in property are determined by the law of the state with "the most significant relationship" to the property and the parties. The Restatement recognizes the applicability of this principle to intangibles such as "a literary idea." Since the works at issue were created by Russian nationals and first published in Russia, Russian law is the appropriate source of law to determine issues of ownership of rights. That is the well-reasoned conclusion of the Amicus Curiae, Prof. Patry, and the parties in their supplemental briefs are in agreement on this point. In terms of the United States Copyrights Act and its reference to the Berne Convention, Russia is the "country of origin" of these works, see *17 U.S.C. § 101* (definition of "country of origin" of Berne Convention work); Berne Convention, Art. 5(4), although "country of origin" might not always be the appropriate country for purposes of choice of law concerning ownership....

Selection of Russian law to determine copyright ownership is, however, subject to one procedural qualification. Under United States law, an owner (including one determined according to foreign law) may sue for infringement in a United States court only if it meets the standing test of *17 U.S.C. § 501*(b), which accords standing only to the legal or beneficial owner of an "exclusive right."

Conflicts rule for infringement issues. On infringement issues, the governing conflicts principle is usually *lex loci delicti*, the doctrine generally applicable to torts. We have implicitly adopted that approach to infringement claims, applying United States copyright law to a work that was unprotected in its country of origin. In the pending case, the place of the tort is plainly the United States. To whatever extent *lex loci delicti* is to be considered only one part of a broader "interest" approach, United States law would still apply to infringement issues, since not only is this country the place of the tort, but also the defendant is a United States corporation.

The division of issues, for conflicts purposes, between ownership and infringement issues will not always be as easily made as the above discussion implies. If the issue is the relatively straightforward one of which of two contending parties owns a copyright, the issue is unquestionably an ownership issue, and the law of the country with the closest relationship to the work will apply to settle the ownership dispute. But in some cases, including the pending one, the issue is not simply who owns the copyright but also what is the nature of the ownership interest. Yet as a court considers the nature of an ownership interest, there is some risk that it will too readily shift the inquiry over to the issue of whether an alleged copy has infringed the asserted copyright. Whether a copy infringes depends in part on the scope of the interest of the copyright owner. Nevertheless, though the issues are related, the nature of a copyright interest is an issue distinct from the issue of whether the copyright has been infringed. The pending case is one that requires consideration not simply of who owns an interest, but, as to the newspapers, the nature of the interest that is owned.

II. Determination of Ownership Rights Under Russian Law

Since United States law permits suit only by owners of "an exclusive right under a copyright," *17 U.S.C. § 501*(b), we must first determine whether any of the plaintiffs own an exclusive right. That issue of ownership, as we have indicated, is to be determined by Russian law....

Under Article 14 of the Russian Copyright Law, Itar-Tass is the owner of the copyright interests in the articles written by its employees. However, Article 14(4) excludes newspapers from the Russian version of the work-for-hire doctrine. The newspaper plaintiffs, therefore, must locate their ownership rights, if any, in some other source of law. They rely on Article 11. The District Court upheld their position, apparently recognizing in the newspaper publishers "exclusive" rights to the articles, even though, by virtue of Article 11(2), the reporters also retained "exclusive" rights to these articles.

Having considered all of the views presented by the expert witnesses, we conclude that the defendants' experts are far more persuasive as to the meaning of Article 11. In the first place, once Article 14 of the Russian Copyright Law explicitly denies newspapers the benefit of a work-for-hire doctrine, which, if available, would accord them rights to individual articles written by their employees, it is highly unlikely that Article 11 would confer on newspapers the very right that Article 14 has denied them. Moreover, Article 11 has an entirely reasonable scope if confined, as its caption suggests, to defining the "Copyright of Compilers of Collections and Other Works." That article accords compilers copyright "in the selection and arrangement of subject matter that he has made insofar as that selection or arrangement is the result of a creative effort of compilation." Russian Copyright Law, Art. 11(1).

Article 11(2) accords publishers of compilations the right to exploit such works, including the right to insist on having its name mentioned, while expressly reserving to "authors of the works included" in compilations the "exclusive rights to exploit their works independently of the publication of the whole work." *Id.* Art. 11(2). As the defendants' experts testified, Article 11 lets authors of newspaper articles sue for infringement of their rights in the text of their articles, and lets newspaper publishers sue for wholesale copying of all of the newspaper or for copying any portions of the newspaper that embody their selection, arrangement, and presentation of articles (including headlines) — copying that infringes their ownership interest in the compilation....

Nor can the District Court's conclusion be supported by its observation that extensive copying of newspapers will ensue unless newspapers are permitted to secure redress for the copying of individual articles. In the first place, copying of articles may always be prevented at the behest of the authors of the articles or their assignees. Second, the newspapers may well be entitled to prevent copying of the protectable elements of their compilations. Lastly, even if authors lack sufficient economic incentive to bring individual suits, as the District Court apprehended, Russian copyright law authorizes the creation of organizations "for the collective administration of the economic rights of authors ... in cases where the individual exercise thereof is hampered by difficulties of a practical nature." Russian Copyright Law, Art. 44(1). Indeed, UJR, the reporters' organization, may well be able in this litigation to protect the rights of the reporters whose articles were copied by Kurier.

Relief. Our disagreement with the District Court's interpretation of Article 11 does not mean, however, that the defendants may continue copying with impunity. In the first place, Itar-Tass, as a press agency, is within the scope of Article 14, and, unlike the excluded newspapers, enjoys the benefit of the Russian version of the work-for-hire doctrine. Itar-Tass is therefore entitled to injunctive relief to prevent unauthorized copying of its articles and to damages for such copying, and the judgment is affirmed as to this plaintiff.

Furthermore, the newspaper plaintiffs, though not entitled to relief for the copying of the text of the articles they published, may well be entitled to injunctive relief and damages if they can show that Kurier infringed the publishers' ownership interests in the newspaper compilations. Because the District Court upheld the newspapers' right to relief for copying the text of the articles, it had no occasion to consider what relief the newspapers might be entitled to by reason of Kurier's copying of the newspapers' creative efforts in the selection, arrangement, or display of the articles. Since Kurier's photocopying reproduced not only the text of articles but also headlines and graphic materials as they originally appeared in the plaintiffs' publication, it is likely that on remand the newspaper plaintiffs will be able to obtain some form of injunctive relief and some damages. On these infringement issues, as we have indicated, United States law will apply.

Finally, there remains for consideration what relief, if any, might be awarded to UJR, acting on behalf of any of its members whose articles have been copied. In its opinion granting the newspapers a preliminary injunction, the District Court noted that the plaintiffs had not "established the union's organizational standing to sue to enforce the rights of its members," an issue the Court expected would be considered later in the lawsuit. In its ruling on the merits, the District Court ruled that the UJR had standing to sue on behalf of its members. However, the Court noted that UJR sought only injunctive relief and then ruled that since UJR declined to furnish a list of its members, the Court was unable to frame an injunction that would be narrowly tailored and sufficient to give the defendants notice of its scope.

In view of our conclusion that the newspaper plaintiffs may not secure relief for the copying of the text of any articles as such, it will now become appropriate for the District Court on remand to revisit the issue of whether relief might be fashioned in favor of UJR on behalf of the authors. Despite UJR's unwillingness to disclose its entire membership list, it might be possible to frame some form of injunctive relief that affords protection for those author-members that UJR is willing to identify. And UJR should now be given an opportunity to amend its prayer for relief to state whatever claim it might have to collect damages for the benefit of its member-authors whose rights have been infringed. Finally, the District Court should consider the appropriateness and feasibility of giving some form of notice (perhaps at the defendants' expense) that is calculated to alert the authors of the infringed articles to their right to intervene in this lawsuit. Such notice might, for example, be addressed generally to the group of reporters currently employed at each of the plaintiff newspapers.

In view of the reckless conduct of the defendants in the flagrant copying that infringed the rights of Itar-Tass, the rights of the authors, and very likely some aspects of the limited protectable rights of the newspapers, we will leave the injunction in force until such time as the District Court has had an opportunity, on remand, to modify the injunction consistent with this opinion and with such further rulings as the District Court may make in light of this opinion.

Accordingly, we affirm the judgment to the extent that it granted relief to Itar-Tass, we reverse to the extent that the judgment granted relief to the other plaintiffs, and we remand for further proceedings. No costs.

Alameda Films S A De C V v. Authors Rights Restoration Corp.
331 F.3d 472 (5th Cir. 2003)

Plaintiffs-Appellees-Cross-Appellants Alameda Films, S.A., et al. (collectively, "the Plaintiffs") are 24 Mexican film production companies that sued Defendants-Appellants-Cross-Appellees Authors Rights Restoration Corp., Inc., Media Resources International, Television International Syndicators, Inc., and H. Jackson Shirley, III (collectively, "the Defendants"), claiming copyright violations in 88 Mexican films that the Defendants distributed in the United States ("U.S.").... The jury returned a verdict for the Plaintiffs on all claims.

On appeal, the Defendants proffer myriad issues, but their principal complaints implicate the district court's [ ] determining that production companies, such as the Plaintiffs, can hold copyrights under Mexican law....

In the mid-1980s, the Defendants began distributing a variety of Mexican films in the U.S. This activity included 88 films that had been produced and released by the Plaintiffs in Mexico during that country's "golden age" of cinema, between the late-1930s and the mid-1950s. The Plaintiffs acknowledge that, at the time the Defendants began distributing these 88 films in the U.S., 69 of them had lost their copyrights here for failure of the authors to comply with U.S. copyright formalities, such as registering and renewing copyrights. According to the Plaintiffs, however, the legal status of these films changed in 1994 when the U.S. adopted the Uruguay Round Agreement Act ("URAA"), thereby amending the 1976 Copyright Act. The URAA eliminated many of the formalities previously required for copyrighting foreign works in the U.S, including registration and notice. The URAA also provided, effective January 1, 1996, for the automatic restoration of copyrights in various foreign works that had fallen into the public domain in the U.S. as a result of their foreign authors' failure to follow U.S. copyright formalities.

Following Congress's 1994 adoption of the URAA, the Defendants began to obtain assignments of "rights" to the films from some individual "contributors," such as screenwriters and music composers. The Defendants did not, however, contact any of the Plaintiffs to obtain assignments or licenses to these films. The Defendants continued to distribute Mexican films in the U.S. after January 1, 1996, the date on which the U.S. copyrights were automatically restored in those films that were eligible for copyright restoration under the URAA.

In June 1998, the Plaintiffs filed suit in the U.S. District Court for the District of Columbia, alleging that the Defendants violated the Plaintiffs' (restored) U.S. copyrights in the 88 films here at issue.... The Defendants filed a counter-claim, and, a few months later, the case was transferred to the Southern District of Texas....

A. Can film production companies hold copyrights under Mexican law?

The URAA provides that a "copyright subsists ... in restored works, and vests automatically on the date of restoration." The copyright in a restored work "vests initially in the author or initial rightholder of the work as determined by the law of the source country of the work." The URAA thus establishes two categories for foreign copyright owners whose U.S. copyrights can be restored: (1) authors, and (2) initial rightholders. The class of "initial rightholders" includes only owners of a copyright in a "sound recording," e.g., music composers; whereas, the class of "authors" includes all other creators of works originally copyrighted in foreign jurisdictions. Accordingly, the Plaintiffs can claim restored copyrights in their films under the URAA only if the Plaintiffs are considered "authors" under Mexican copyright law — the law of the source country of the work.

The Defendants' principal contention on appeal is that the Plaintiffs, as film production companies, cannot be "authors" under the Mexican Civil Code. The Defendants maintain that the Mexican Civil Code permits only individuals, i.e., natural persons, to be "authors"; that the law does not permit corporations or other legal entities to be "authors" for purposes of claiming copyright entitlements. In contending that only natural persons can hold copyrights under Mexican law, the Defendants argue that we should never reach the restoration analysis under the URAA, because the Plaintiffs fail this threshold determination of qualification to hold copyrights under the "law of the source country of the work."

In response, the Plaintiffs — and the Government of Mexico, as amicus curiae — urge that the Defendants' failure even to mention the Collaboration Doctrine of the Mexican Civil Code is telling. They note that in Mexican law, the Collaboration Doctrine covers various provisions regarding copyrights claimed by corporations, which necessarily create copyrighted works only through the collaboration of individuals, viz., their agents and employees. Thus, Article 1,198 of the 1928 Mexican Civil Code provides:

> The person or corporation that imprints or publishes a work made by various individuals with the consent of such individuals will have the property in the entire work, except each individual will retain the right to publish anew their own composition, independently, or in a collection.

Subsequent amendments and re-enactments of Mexico's copyright laws in 1947 and 1956 specify that "whoever" creates a work with the "collaboration" of one or more other authors is entitled to the "author's right" (derecho de autor) in the entire work, as long as the contributors are mentioned in the work and are paid for their respective contributions. Finally, the 1963 amendment of the Mexican copyright laws provides explicitly that "physical persons and legal entities who produce a work with the special and remunerated collaboration of one or more persons shall enjoy with respect to that work the author's right therein...."

The Defendants devote a substantial portion of their briefs to discussing the role of Collective Bargaining Agreements ("CBA") in Mexico. The Defendants appear to believe that the Plaintiffs maintained before the district court (and continue to maintain on appeal) that they have copyrights in the films by virtue of having obtained assignments of the copyrights via the CBAs of the "natural persons" who worked for the production companies. If the Defendants harbor such a belief, they are mistaken. The CBAs that the Plaintiffs submitted into evidence were meant to prove only that the Plaintiffs' employees had been paid, thereby satisfying one of the requirements under the Collaboration Doctrine for the Plaintiffs, as production companies, to claim copyrights in the films that they produced.

The Defendants' insistence that an "author's right" under Mexican law vests only in a "natural person" is simply wrong. As amicus, the Government of Mexico explains that "throughout every iteration of its intellectual property laws, [Mexico] has recognized the producer as the rightful owner of the copyright of any film in its entirety." Provisions of the Mexican Civil Code identified by the Plaintiffs clearly support this position. Thus, the district court correctly determined that the Plaintiffs can be and are "authors" under Mexican law, and thus can hold Mexican copyrights (derecho de autor) in the films that they have produced....

The district court conducted this complex case commendably, particularly given the difficulties inherent in interpreting and applying foreign law and the extensive motion practice of these vigorous litigants. We affirm....

Notes and Questions

a. Among the many difficulties of interpreting international aspects of copyright are issues of whether the parties before the court are the correct rights holders, the interpretation of foreign law, and the interesting question of whether works created during communist rule allow for sufficient property ownership in the copyright to be recognized as exclusive or beneficial ownership for purposes of copyright. See *Films by Jove, Inc. v. Berov,* 154 F. Supp. 2d 432 (E.D.N.Y. 2001).

b. The Second Circuit recognized that issues of international interpretation of copyright have not historically been given the respect they deserve. The Second Circuit points to the following as examples of this laxity:

> *Aldon Accessories Ltd. v. Spiegel, Inc.,* 738 F.2d 548, 551–53 (2d Cir. 1984) (U.S. law applied to determine if statuettes crafted abroad were works for hire); *Dae Han Video Productions, Inc. v. Kuk Dong Oriental Food, Inc.,* 1990 U.S. Dist. LEXIS 18329, 19 U.S.P.Q.2D (BNA) 1294 (D. Md. 1990) (U.S. law applied to determine if scripts written abroad were works for hire); *P & D International v. Halsey Publishing Co.,* 672 F. Supp. 1429, 1435–36 (S.D. Fla. 1987) (U.S. work for hire law assumed to apply). Other courts have applied foreign law. See *Frink America, Inc. v. Champion Road Machinery Ltd.,* 961 F. Supp. 398 (N.D.N.Y. 1997) (Canadian copyright law applied on issue of ownership); *Greenwich Film Productions v. DRG Records Inc.,* 1992 U.S. Dist. LEXIS 14770, 1992 WL 279 (S.D.N.Y. 1992) (French law applied to determine ownership of right to musical work commissioned in France for French film); *Dae Han Video Production Inc. v. Dong San Chun,* 1990 U.S. Dist. LEXIS 18496, 17 U.S.P.Q.2D (BNA) 1306, 1310 n.6 (E.D. Va. 1990) (foreign law relied on to determine that alleged licensor lacks rights); *Autoskill, Inc. v. National Educational Support Systems, Inc.,* 994

F.2d 1476, 1489 n.16 (10th Cir. 1993) (U.S. work for hire law applied where claim that contrary Canadian law should apply was belatedly raised and for that reason not considered); *Pepe (U.K.) Ltd. v. Grupo Pepe Ltda.,* 1992 U.S. Dist. LEXIS 17144, 24 U.S.P.Q.2D (BNA) 1354, 1356 (S.D. Fla. 1992) (congruent foreign and U.S. law both applied).

Itar-Tass Russian News Agency v. Russian Kurier, Inc., 153 F.3d 82, 88–89 (2d Cir. 1998). In other cases, the courts tend to finesse the international issues or determine that they need not be reached. See *Greenwich Film Productions S.A. v. D.R.G. Records, Inc.,* 1992 U.S. Dist. LEXIS 14770, 25 U.S.P.Q.2D (BNA) 1435, 1437–38 (S.D.N.Y. 1992).

c. Courts and parties must be particularly diligent when dealing with international interpretation to assure that the interpretation of law provided is accurate. The disdain held by the court in *Alameda Films S. A. De C. V. v. Authors Rights Restoration Corp.* is well placed: parties that misrepresent foreign law will find their position before the court quite untenable, whether that misrepresentation is by explicit statement or by omission of other relevant portions of the law.

d. Choice of law questions continue to challenge U.S. courts in both traditional copyright and in more modern Internet related cases. Consider the U.S. action related to the French ban on Yahoo!'s facilitation of the sale of Nazi paraphernalia. The conflict provides a useful discussion of the First Amendment, comity, and the interplay between multiple courts. The tensions between U.S. and foreign courts also highlight the differing national interests at stake involving the intersection of cyberspace on territorial law. See *Yahoo!, Inc. v. La Ligue Contre Le Racisme et L'Antisemitisme,* 169 F. Supp. 2d 1181 (N.D. Cal. 2001).

> The French Court found that approximately 1,000 Nazi and Third Reich related objects, including Adolf Hitler's *Mein Kampf, The Protocol of the Elders of Zion* (an infamous anti-Semitic report produced by the Czarist secret police in the early 1900's), and purported "evidence" that the gas chambers of the Holocaust did not exist were being offered for sale on Yahoo.com's auction site. Because any French citizen is able to access these materials on Yahoo.com directly or through a link on Yahoo.fr, the French Court concluded that the Yahoo.com auction site violates Section R645-1 of the French Criminal Code, which prohibits exhibition of Nazi propaganda and artifacts for sale. On May 20, 2000, the French Court entered an order requiring Yahoo! to (1) eliminate French citizens' access to any material on the Yahoo.com auction site that offers for sale any Nazi objects, relics, insignia, emblems, and flags; (2) eliminate French citizens' access to web pages on Yahoo.com displaying text, extracts, or quotations from *Mein Kampf* and *Protocol of the Elders of Zion*; (3) post a warning to French citizens on Yahoo.fr that any search through Yahoo.com may lead to sites containing material prohibited by Section R645-1 of the French Criminal Code, and that such viewing of the prohibited material may result in legal action against the Internet user; (4) remove from all browser directories accessible in the French Republic index headings entitled "negationists" and from all hypertext links the equation of "negationists" under the heading "Holocaust." The order subjects Yahoo! to a penalty of 100,000 Euros for each day that it fails to comply with the order....
>
> [T]he purpose of the present action is to determine whether a United States court may enforce the French order without running afoul of the First Amendment....

Id. at 1184–85, 1191–92. The district court and subsequent Ninth Circuit opinions have each been reversed. In an *en banc* rehearing, the Ninth Circuit entered a judgment reversing and remanding the district court decision, with instructions to dismiss the action, holding that "if Yahoo! violates the speech laws of another nation, it must wait for the foreign litigants to come to the United States to enforce the judgment before its First Amendment claim may be heard by a U.S. court." *Yahoo! Inc. v. La Ligue Contre Le Racisme Et L'Antisemitisme*, 433 F.3d 1199 (9th Cir. 2006).

Problem II-F

Bryce elected to negotiate for the rights to the Canadian play (see Problem II-C). When negotiating for those rights, Bryce entered into discussions about jointly creating the American version of the play. Bryce began working with Stewart, the Canadian playwright. Using email, the two writers traded drafts of the play, each editing the other's work and adding new scenes. As the process progressed, Bryce and Stewart began having disagreements over the play, and Bryce has come to you for advice. Bryce now wishes to produce the new play without Stewart in the U.S.

The emails have many statements that make it clear to you that at the time each author was contributing, they both expected to create one play that they would each partially own and that together they would manage. Bryce would like to know whether Canadian or U.S. law will govern the ownership of the play. (See Chapter IX for a discussion of ownership under U.S. law).

G. Bibliography and Links

Treatises and Reports

Lucinda A. Low, Patrick M. Norton, & Daniel M. Drory, International Lawyer's Deskbook (2d Ed. 2004).

Stephen E. Siwek, Copyright Industries in the U.S. Economy: The 2013 Report, International Intellectual Property Alliance, November 2013 (available at www.iipa.com).

Law Review Articles for Chapter II

Graeme W. Austin, *Domestic Laws and Foreign Rights: Choice of Law in Transnational Copyright Infringement Litigation*, 23 Colum.-VLA J.L. & Arts 1 (1999).

Troy L Harris FCIArb, *Ethics in International Arbitration: They're Not Just for Lawyers*, 8 Construction L. Int'l 37 (2013).

William Gable, *Restoration of Copyrights: Dueling Trolls and Other Oddities Under Section 104A of the Copyright Act*, 29 Colum. J.L. & Arts 181 (2005).

Daniel J. Gervais, *Transmissions of Music on the Internet: An Analysis of the Copyright Laws of Canada, France, Germany, Japan, the United Kingdom, and the United States*, 34 Vand. J. Transnat'l L. 1363 (2001).

Jane C. Ginsburg, *The Concept of Authorship in Comparative Copyright Law*, 52 DePaul L. Rev. 1063 (2003).

Reto M. Hilty & Alexander Peukert, *"Equitable Remuneration" in Copyright Law: The Amended German Copyright Act as a Trap for the Entertainment Industry in the U.S.?*, 22 Cardozo Arts & Ent L.J. 401 (2004).

Brent C. Johnson, *The Making Available Argument: Is Actual Distribution Required to Find Infringement Upon the Copyright Holder's Distribution Right*, 85 N. Dak. L. Rev. 371 (2008).

Amy Lai, *Sailing Toward A Truly Globalized World: Wto, Media Piracy in China, and Transnational Capital Flows*, 18 UCLA Ent. L. Rev. 75, 76 (2011).

Edward Lee, *The New Canon: Using or Misusing Foreign Law To Decide Domestic Intellectual Property Claims*, 46 Harv. Int'l L.J. 1 (2005).

P. Sean Morris, *Beyond Trade: Global Digital Exhaustion in International Economic Regulation*, 36 Campbell L. Rev. 107 (2013).

William Patry, *Choice of Law and International Copyright*, 48 Am. J. Comp. L. 383 (2000).

Hannibal Travis, *Wipo and the American Constitution: Thoughts on A New Treaty Relating to Actors and Musicians*, 16 Vand. J. Ent. & Tech. L. 45 (2013).

Kristy Wiehe, *Dollars, Downloads and Digital Distribution: Is "Making Available" a Copyrighted Work or a Violation of the Author's Distribution Right?*, 15 UCLA Ent. L. Rev. 117 (2008).

WIPO Secretariat, *Consolidated Analysis of the Legal Protection of Traditional Cultural Expressions*, (WIPO/GRTKF/IC/5/3) (*available at* www.wipo.net).

WIPO Secretariat, *Comparative Summary of Sui Generis Legislation for the Protection of Traditional Cultural Expressions*, (WIPO/GRTKF/IC/5/INF 3) (*available at* www.wipo.net).

Websites

Guide on Surveying the Economic Contribution of the Copyright-Based Industries, http://www.wipo.int/copyright/en/publications/pdf/copyright_pub_893.pdf

T. Janke, Minding Culture—Case Studies on Intellectual Property and Traditional Cultural Expressions, prepared for WIPO (WIPO/GRTKF/Study/2) (*available at* www.wipo.net)

Voice of America, http://www.voa.gov/index.cfm?sectionTitle=Internet

World Intellectual Property Organization, http://www.wipo.int/

WIPO, Traditional Knowledge and Cultural Expressions, http://www.wipo.int/tk/en/index.html

Chapter III

Copyright for Entertainment Law

A. Overview

Jon M. Garon, *The Electronic Jungle:*
The Application of Intellectual Property Law to
Distance Education[1]

A. Copyright Background

Copyright provides the author of an original work the sole power to sell or transfer the rights to the work. Subject to certain limitations, such as fair use, the copyright holder retains a monopoly over the work. The subject matter of copyright is the expression of ideas, rather than the ideas themselves. Copyright protection subsists in original works of authorship fixed in any tangible medium of expression. Works of authorship include the following categories: (1) literary works; (2) musical works, including any accompanying words; (3) dramatic works, including any accompanying music; (4) pantomimes and choreographic works; (5) pictorial, graphic and sculptural works; (6) motion pictures and other audiovisual works; (7) sound recordings; and (8) architectural works.

Copyright protects only the expression of the work (e.g., the writing style and detailed plot of the story), not its ideas, procedures, processes or facts. In other words, copyright protects the creativity of the expression, but does not give any author a monopoly on the facts or ideas presented. No copyright in course materials, therefore, can preclude another faculty member from creating her own materials to teach the same subject matter.

The exclusive rights of the copyright holder are categorized into seven distinct rights. Generally, these rights provide the copyright owner with exclusive power of (1) reproduction or copying; (2) adaptation or the creation of derivative works; (3) distribution by sale or other transfer of ownership, or by rental, lease or lending; (4) public performance of literary, musical, dramatic and choreographic works, pantomimes, and motion pictures and other audiovisual works; and (5) public display. In addition, two categories of protection are specific to certain works. In the case of sound recordings, the copyright owner (typically a record label) has the right to perform the copyrighted work

---

1. 4 VAND. J. ENT. L. & PRAC. 146 (2002) (reprinted with permission).

publicly by means of a digital audio transmission. In the case of a work of visual art (made in a series of fewer than 200 copies), the creator receives the additional rights to receive credit for creating the work and to ensure that the work is not mutilated or destroyed by the owners of each copy of the work.

B. Copyright Mechanics

For works created after January 1, 1978, the term of copyright lasts for the life of the author, plus 70 years. If the work is made as a work for hire, then the term is 95 years from publication or 120 years from creation, whichever is less. This is also the term provided for anonymous and pseudonymous works.

For works created prior to January 1, 1978, the copyright term is more difficult to calculate. United States works published prior to January 1, 1923 are in the public domain, and thus receive no copyright protection. Works published between January 1, 1964 and December 31, 1977 have a copyright term of 95 years. Works published between January 1, 1923 and December 31, 1963 had an original copyright term of 28 years which could be extended by an additional 67 years if the copyright owner renewed the copyright. Because many works were not renewed, the copyright in those works lapsed and the materials are now in the public domain. For works published during this period, however, no assumption can be made that a given work is in the public domain, so each work must be researched to determine its copyright status.

In addition to the requirements that works published in the United States prior to January 1, 1963 be properly renewed, there are other rules that continue to apply from former law. The most important of these is the statutory formalities of copyright. There are three steps for formally protecting a published work. Under current law, however, none of these serves as a condition of receiving copyright, and the importance of the formalities has lessened considerably during the past twenty years. The first requirement is notice, which includes the copyright symbol "©" (or the word or abbreviation for copyright) along with the year of publication and the name of the copyright holder. This should be featured prominently in a place a viewer would expect to look (e.g., the title page of a book).

The second formality is registration, which requires that a filing fee (presently $30.00), the appropriate form and a copy of the work be submitted to the Copyright Office. While this is no longer required, it does provide some benefits if a legal dispute ever arises regarding the work, including prima facie evidence of the facts in the copyright application and statutory damages and attorneys' fees if the suit is filed in a timely fashion.

Although the registration of current works is no longer mandatory, this has only been the case since February 28, 1989 when the Copyright Act was amended to provide for adherence by the United States to the Berne Convention. For works published between January 1, 1923 and February 28, 1989, the work must have been properly registered within three months of its publication to receive copyright protection. [If it was not properly registered when published, the work will fall into the public domain.]

The third and final formality remains mandatory even under the present statute. The Library of Congress is entitled under the Copyright Act to receive two copies of the best edition of every published work made in the United States. This deposit is generally made as part of the registration process. In the situation where a copyright holder of a published work elects not to register the work, the copyright owner is still obligated to submit copies to the Library of Congress. If the copyright owner refuses to send copies after receiving a demand letter, then the copyright office can levy substantial fines.

Copyright Transfers
Circular 1, U.S. Copyright Office (2011)

Transfer of Copyright

Any or all of the copyright owner's exclusive rights or any subdivision of those rights may be transferred, however, the transfer of exclusive rights is not valid unless that transfer is in writing and signed by the owner of the rights conveyed or such owner's duly authorized agent. Transfer of a right on a nonexclusive basis does not require a written agreement.

A copyright may also be conveyed by operation of law and may be bequeathed by will or pass as personal property by the applicable laws of in testate succession.

Copyright is a personal property right, and it is subject to the various state laws and regulations that govern the ownership, inheritance, or transfer of personal property as well as terms of contracts or conduct of business....

Transfers of copyright are normally made by contract. The Copyright Office does not have any forms for such transfers. The law does provide for the recordation in the Copyright Office of transfers of copyright ownership. Although recordation is not required to make a valid transfer between the parties, it does provide certain legal advantages and may be required to validate the transfer as against third parties....

Termination of Transfers

Under the previous law, the copyright in a work reverted to the author, if living, or if the author was not living, to other specified beneficiaries, provided a renewal claim was registered in the 28th year of the original term.[2] The present law drops the renewal feature except for works already in the first term of statutory protection when the present law took effect. Instead, the present law permits termination of a grant of rights after 35 years under certain conditions by serving written notice on the transferee within specified time limits.

For works already under statutory copyright protection before 1978, the present law provides a similar right of termination covering the newly added years that extended the former maximum term of the copyright from 56 to 95 years....

Works Made for Hire under the 1976 Copyright Act
Circular 9, U.S. Copyright Office (2010)

INTRODUCTION. Under the 1976 Copyright Act as amended (title 17 of the United States Code), a work is protected by copyright from the time it is created in a fixed form. In other words, when a work is written down or otherwise set into tangible form, the copyright immediately becomes the property of the author who created it. Only the author or those deriving their rights from the author can rightfully claim copyright. Although the general rule is that the person who creates a work is the author of that work, there is an exception to that principle: the copyright law defines a category of works called "works made for hire." If a work is "made for hire," the employer, and not the employee, is considered the author. The employer may be a firm, an organization, or an individual.

---

2. The copyright in works eligible for renewal on or after June 26, 1992, will vest in the name of the renewal claimant on the effective date of any renewal registration made during the 28th year of the original term. Otherwise, the renewal copyright will vest in the party entitled to claim renewal as of December 31st of the 28th year.

To understand the complex concept of a work made for hire, it is necessary to refer not only to the statutory definition but also to its interpretation in cases decided by courts.

STATUTORY DEFINITION. Section 101 of the copyright law defines a "work made for hire" as:

(1) a work prepared by an employee within the scope of his or her employment; *or*

(2) a work specially ordered or commissioned for use as a contribution to a collective work, as a part of a motion picture or other audiovisual work, as a translation, as a supplementary work, as a compilation, as an instructional text, as a test, as answer material for a test, or as an atlas, if the parties expressly agree in a written instrument signed by them that the work shall be considered a work made for hire. For the purpose of the foregoing sentence, a "supplementary work" is a work prepared for a publication as a secondary adjunct to a work by another author for the purpose of introducing, concluding, illustrating, explaining, revising, commenting upon, or assisting in the use of the other work, such as forewords, afterwords, pictorial illustrations, maps, charts, tables, editorial notes, musical arrangements, answer material for tests, bibliographies, appendixes, and indexes; and an "instructional text" is a literary, pictorial, or graphic work prepared for publication and with the purpose of use in systematic instructional activities.

DETERMINING WHETHER A WORK IS MADE FOR HIRE. Whether or not a particular work is made for hire is determined by the relationship between the parties. This determination may be difficult, because the statutory definition of a work made for hire is complex and not always easily applied. That definition was the focus of a 1989 Supreme Court decision (*Community for Creative Non-Violence v. Reid,* 490 U.S. 730 [1989]). The court held that to determine whether a work is made for hire, one must first ascertain whether the work was prepared by (1) an employee or (2) an independent contractor.

If a work is created by an employee, part 1 of the statutory definition applies, and generally the work would be considered a work made for hire. *IMPORTANT:* The term "employee" here is not really the same as the common understanding of the term; for copyright purposes, it means an employee under the general common law of agency. This is explained in further detail below.

If a work is created by an independent contractor (that is, someone who is not an employee under the general common law of agency), then the work is a specially ordered or commissioned work, and part 2 of the statutory definition applies. Such a work can be a work made for hire only if both of the following conditions are met: (1) it comes within one of the nine categories of works listed in part 2 of the definition and (2) there is a written agreement between the parties specifying that the work is a work made for hire.

Employer-Employee Relationship Under Agency Law

If a work is created by an employee, part 1 of the copyright code's definition of a work made for hire applies. To help determine who is an employee, the Supreme Court in *CCNV v. Reid* identified certain factors that characterize an "employer-employee" relationship as defined by agency law:

1) *Control by the employer over the work (e.g.,* the employer may determine how the work is done, has the work done at the employer's location, and provides equipment or other means to create work).

2) *Control by employer over the employee (e.g.,* the employer controls the employee's schedule in creating work, has the right to have the employee perform other as-

signments, determines the method of payment, and/or has the right to hire the employee's assistants).

3) *Status and conduct of employer (e.g.*, the employer is in business to produce such works, provides the employee with benefits, and/or withholds tax from the employee's payment).

These factors are not exhaustive. The court left unclear which of these factors must be present to establish the employment relationship under the work for hire definition, but held that supervision or control over creation of the work alone is not controlling.

All or most of these factors characterize a regular, salaried employment relationship, and it is clear that a work created within the scope of such employment is a work made for hire (unless the parties involved agree otherwise).

Examples of works for hire created in an employment relationship are:

- A software program created within the scope of his or her duties by a staff programmer for Creative Computer Corporation.
- A newspaper article written by a staff journalist for publication in the newspaper that employs him.
- A musical arrangement written for XYZ Music Company by a salaried arranger on its staff.
- A sound recording created by the salaried staff engineers of ABC Record Company.

The closer an employment relationship comes to regular, salaried employment, the more likely it is that a work created within the scope of that employment would be a work made for hire. However, since there is no precise standard for determining whether or not a work is made for hire under the first part of the definition, consultation with an attorney for legal advice may be advisable.

WHO IS THE AUTHOR OF A WORK MADE FOR HIRE? If a work is a work made for hire, the employer or other person for whom the work was prepared is the author and should be named as the author in Space 2 of the application for copyright registration. The box marked "work made-for-hire" should be checked "yes."

WHO IS THE OWNER OF THE COPYRIGHT IN A WORK MADE FOR HIRE? If a work is a work made for hire, the employer or other person for whom the work was prepared is the initial owner of the copyright unless there has been a written agreement to the contrary signed by both parties.

EFFECT ON TERM OF COPYRIGHT PROTECTION. The term of copyright protection of a work made for hire is 95 years from the date of publication or 120 years from the date of creation, whichever expires first. (A work not made for hire is ordinarily protected by copyright for the life of the author plus 70 years.) For additional information concerning the terms of copyright protection, request Circular 15a "Duration of Copyright."

EFFECT ON TERMINATION RIGHTS. The copyright code provides that certain grants of the rights in a work that were made by the author may be terminated 35 to 40 years after the grant was made or after publication, depending on the circumstances. The termination provisions of the law do not apply to works made for hire.

Notes and Questions

a. Treatment of work for hire reflects general United States agency concepts that work done for an employer belongs to that employer, making the employer the statutory author of the work. The status of authorship is higher than that of mere owner. Ownership under copyright as a work for hire changes the term of the copyright and eliminates the reversionary rights otherwise incorporated into assignments of copyright as a matter of law. Where the employer is a corporation (or other non-natural person), this makes complete sense. The life-plus-seventy term of copyright is inapplicable to a corporation which has a perpetual existence, and since the corporation can only act through its employee-agents, its assertion of copyright can only exist through either an assignment of copyright by its employees or a legal assumption that a transfer has occurred.

b. Although there are two different categories of work for hire, the use of the same term for both species of work for hire often leads to undue confusion. To be considered work for hire in the traditional employment setting, the employee must be within the employ of the employer and providing services within the general scope of that employee's employment. While the Supreme Court in *Community for Creative Non-Violence v. Reid,* 490 U.S. 730 (1989), required that traditional agency factors be reviewed, most cases turn on more narrow employment criteria such as the tax and benefit status of the person. A corporate employer is hard-pressed to treat a person as an independent contractor for tax purposes while claiming employment status for copyright purposes. See *Aymes v. Bonelli,* 980 F.2d 857, 863 (2d Cir. 1992) ("[E]very case since *Reid* that has applied the test has found the hired party to be an independent contractor where the hiring party failed to extend benefits or pay social security taxes."). See also *Hi-Tech Video Prods. v. Capital Cities/ABC,* 58 F.3d 1093 (6th Cir. 1995) (invalidating the copyright in the plaintiff's video because the registration as a work for hire was incorrect and invalid). In addition to the creator of the work being an employee based on restatement of agency principles, the employee's work must fall within the scope of the person's employment. Under this requirement, all the reports, brochures, or other written material a person normally creates a work will be covered under the work for hire doctrine, vesting the copyright in the employer. A novel written after hours was not made within the scope of the person's employment and not owned by the employer.

Questions arise if the expressive works are created in unique situations. Would photographs taken on behalf of the company be work for hire, if the photographer had never been asked to take pictures at any other time and the subject matter of the photographs was unrelated to the employee's normal duties?

Academic employees creating syllabi, tests, and teaching materials fit within the general definition of work for hire, while scholarly writings and creative projects relevant to faculty tenure but not under economic control of their home institutions may be outside the scope of an academic employee's work product. To what extent is this distinction consistent with *Reid* and the definition in § 101? Regardless of the answer, the default rule provided by the work for hire doctrine can be varied by the parties, so academic employees generally look to faculty handbook and collective bargaining agreements for the particular terms of their employment.

c. The second category of work for hire regards specially commissioned works. For this category, the work must both fall within one of the nine categories listed in the statute[3] and be evidenced by a writing signed by both parties. This writing requirement is the most stringent required under copyright law.

---

3. 17 U.S.C. § 101 provides that a work for hire includes "a work specially ordered or commissioned for use as a contribution to a collective work, as a part of a motion picture or other audiovisual work, as a translation, as a supplementary work, as a compilation, as an instructional text, as a test, as answer material for a test, or as an atlas, if the parties expressly agree in a written instrument signed by them that the work shall be considered a work made for hire."

The nine enumerated categories are also significant in the context of the music industry. Sound recordings were briefly added to the enumerated categories as a technical amendment, but when the musicians' unions and others learned of the change, Congress not only retreated from the position, but also eliminated the amendment retroactively. This is a strong indication that sound recordings should not be treated as falling within the work for hire subject matter for specially commissioned works. Nonetheless, since audiovisual works are within the nine categories, some sound recordings still fall within the definition.

d. Regardless of the work for hire definition, other problems remain — particularly for specially commissioned works. Outside the United States, the concept of works for hire is generally rejected. As a result, contractual provisions providing for such results may be declared void. To avoid this result, contracting parties should incorporate assignment of copyright language as an alternative to work for hire language as a matter of course. This may also avoid many of the interpretative problems by further evidencing the intent of the parties.

e. In recent years, the rights of authors to terminate prior licenses and grants have taken on financial significance as these rights begin to vest. Section 203 of the Copyright Act governs transfers made on or after January 1, 1978, while § 304(c) governs those transfers made prior to that date. In addition, § 304(d) governs grants made of a copyright's final twenty year lifespan in cases where other termination provisions were not exercised. The implications of these sections is only now being explored by the courts. Compare *Penguin Group (USA) Inc. v. Steinbeck*, 537 F.3d 193 (2d Cir. N.Y. 2008) (termination notice ineffective because a 1994 license replaced the 1938 grant of copyright by John Steinbeck) with *Marvel Characters, Inc. v. Simon*, 310 F.3d 280 (2d Cir. 2002) (settlement agreement which acceded to work for hire status for Simon, author of Captain America Comics, "constitutes an 'agreement to the contrary' which can be disavowed pursuant to [§ 304(c)].") Estate planning may also be impacted if gifts made in lieu of copyright interests are affected by termination rights. See *Ray Charles Found. v. Robinson*, 919 F. Supp. 2d 1054, 1059 (C.D. Cal. 2013).

f. For works transferred after Jan. 1, 1978, § 203 of the Copyright Act governs. "Termination of the grant may be effected at any time during a period of five years beginning at the end of thirty-five years from the date of execution of the grant; or, if the grant covers the right of publication of the work, the period begins at the end of thirty-five years from the date of publication of the work under the grant or at the end of forty years from the date of execution of the grant, whichever term ends earlier." 17 U.S.C. § 203(a)(3). The party terminating the grant must provide at least two years (nor more than ten years) notice. For example, the rights to publish a novel sold in 1978 may be terminated beginning in 2013. Notices successfully terminating such grants are now being enforced.

Problem III-A

Bryce has been approached by St. James Corporation, a privately owned insurance company, to produce a training program (known in the business as an "industrial") to introduce corporate employees to the issues dealing with client privacy. The industrial is to be used in a variety of media, primarily through video tutorials and self-run computer-based simulations. St. James is interested in producing an industrial video of approximately twenty minutes in length, a computer simulation using text and streaming video content, and a written manual. St. James will provide the primary manual content and the most important talking points for the industrial video and computer simulation.

Bryce has been asked to write a script, produce and direct the video, produce the computer simulation, and incorporate music already written by Bryce for the opening and ending credits.

You are assigned the task of writing the deal memorandum and agreement between Bryce and St. James. St. James insists that the work be treated as a work for hire to the "greatest extent allowed by law," and that it "retain the rights to modify the material or update it from time to time, as needed." Bryce is willing to part with ownership and control, but insists on "credit in all the materials, the right to use copies as examples of prior work, and the retention of copyright in all music used in the work."

Outline the key terms of the understanding (leaving blanks for delivery date and payment details). Identify other possible provisions that might be needed in such an agreement.

B. Comparison between Works — Ideas & Abstractions

Nichols v. Universal Pictures Co.
45 F.2d 119 (2d Cir. 1930)

L. HAND, Circuit Judge. The plaintiff is the author of a play, "Abie's Irish Rose," which it may be assumed was properly copyrighted under section five, subdivision (d), of the Copyright Act, 17 USCA § 5(d). The defendant produced publicly a motion picture play, "The Cohens and The Kellys," which the plaintiff alleges was taken from it. As we think the defendant's play too unlike the plaintiff's to be an infringement, we may assume, arguendo, that in some details the defendant used the plaintiff's play, as will subsequently appear, though we do not so decide. It therefore becomes necessary to give an outline of the two plays.

"Abie's Irish Rose" presents a Jewish family living in prosperous circumstances in New York. The father, a widower, is in business as a merchant, in which his son and only child helps him. The boy has philandered with young women, who to his father's great disgust have always been Gentiles, for he is obsessed with a passion that his daughter-in-law shall be an orthodox Jewess. When the play opens the son, who has been courting a young Irish Catholic girl, has already married her secretly before a Protestant minister, and is concerned to soften the blow for his father, by securing a favorable impression of his bride, while concealing her faith and race. To accomplish this he introduces her to his father at his home as a Jewess, and lets it appear that he is interested in her, though he conceals the marriage. The girl somewhat reluctantly falls in with the plan; the father takes the bait, becomes infatuated with the girl, concludes that they must marry, and assumes that of course they will, if he so decides. He calls in a rabbi, and prepares for the wedding according to the Jewish rite.

Meanwhile the girl's father, also a widower, who lives in California, and is as intense in his own religious antagonism as the Jew, has been called to New York, supposing that his daughter is to marry an Irishman and a Catholic. Accompanied by a priest, he arrives at the house at the moment when the marriage is being celebrated, but too late to prevent it, and the two fathers, each infuriated by the proposed union of his child to a heretic, fall into unseemly and grotesque antics. The priest and the rabbi become friendly, exchange trite sentiments about religion, and agree that the match is good. Apparently out of abundant caution, the priest celebrates the marriage for a third time, while the girl's father is inveigled away. The second act closes with each father, still outraged, seeking to find some way by which the union, thus trebly insured, may be dissolved.

The last act takes place about a year later, the young couple having meanwhile been abjured by each father, and left to their own resources. They have had twins, a boy and a girl, but their fathers know no more than that a child has been born. At Christmas each, led by his craving to see his grandchild, goes separately to the young folks' home, where they encounter each other, each laden with gifts, one for a boy, the other for a girl. After some slapstick comedy, depending upon the insistence of each that he is right about the sex of the grandchild, they become reconciled when they learn the truth, and that each child is to bear the given name of a grandparent. The curtain falls as the fathers are exchanging amenities, and the Jew giving evidence of an abatement in the strictness of his orthodoxy.

"The Cohens and The Kellys" presents two families, Jewish and Irish, living side by side in the poorer quarters of New York in a state of perpetual enmity. The wives in both cases are still living, and share in the mutual animosity, as do two small sons, and even the respective dogs. The Jews have a daughter, the Irish a son; the Jewish father is in the clothing business; the Irishman is a policeman. The children are in love with each other, and secretly marry, apparently after the play opens. The Jew, being in great financial straits, learns from a lawyer that he has fallen heir to a large fortune from a great-aunt, and moves into a great house, fitted luxuriously. Here he and his family live in vulgar ostentation, and here the Irish boy seeks out his Jewish bride, and is chased away by the angry father. The Jew then abuses the Irishman over the telephone, and both become hysterically excited. The extremity of his feelings makes the Jew sick, so that he must go to Florida for a rest, just before which the daughter discloses her marriage to her mother.

On his return the Jew finds that his daughter has borne a child; at first he suspects the lawyer, but eventually learns the truth and is overcome with anger at such a low alliance. Meanwhile, the Irish family who have been forbidden to see the grandchild, go to the Jew's house, and after a violent scene between the two fathers in which the Jew disowns his daughter, who decides to go back with her husband, the Irishman takes her back with her baby to his own poor lodgings. The lawyer, who had hoped to marry the Jew's daughter, seeing his plan foiled, tells the Jew that his fortune really belongs to the Irishman, who was also related to the dead woman, but offers to conceal his knowledge, if the Jew will share the loot. This the Jew repudiates, and, leaving the astonished lawyer, walks through the rain to his enemy's house to surrender the property. He arrives in great dejection, tells the truth, and abjectly turns to leave. A reconciliation ensues, the Irishman agreeing to share with him equally. The Jew shows some interest in his grandchild, though this is at most a minor motive in the reconciliation, and the curtain falls while the two are in their cups, the Jew insisting that in the firm name for the business, which they are to carry on jointly, his name shall stand first.

It is of course essential to any protection of literary property, whether at common-law or under the statute, that the right cannot be limited literally to the text, else a plagiarist would escape by immaterial variations. That has never been the law, but, as soon as literal appropriation ceases to be the test, the whole matter is necessarily at large, so that, as was recently well said by a distinguished judge, the decisions cannot help much in a new case. When plays are concerned, the plagiarist may excise a separate scene Then the question is whether the part so taken is "substantial," and therefore not a "fair use" of the copyrighted work; it is the same question as arises in the case of any other copyrighted work. But when the plagiarist does not take out a block in situ, but an abstract of the whole, decision is more troublesome. Upon any work, and especially upon a play, a great number of patterns of increasing generality will fit equally well, as more and more of the incident is left out. The last may perhaps be no more than the most general statement of what the play is about, and at times might consist only of its title; but there is a point in this series of abstractions where they are no longer protected, since otherwise the playwright could prevent the use of his "ideas," to which, apart from their expression, his property is never extended. Nobody has ever been able to fix that boundary, and nobody ever can. In some cases the question has been treated as though it were analogous to lifting a portion out of the copyrighted work; but the analogy is not a good one, because, though the skeleton is a part of the body, it pervades and supports the whole. In such cases we are rather concerned with the line between expression and what is expressed. As respects plays, the controversy chiefly centers upon the characters and sequence of incident, these being the substance.

We did not in *Dymow v. Bolton,* 11 F.(2d) 690, hold that a plagiarist was never liable for stealing a plot; that would have been flatly against our rulings in *Dam v. Kirk La Shelle Co.,* 175 F. 902, 41 L.R.A. (N.S.) 1002, 20 Ann. Cas. 1173, and *Stodart v. Mutual Film Co.,* 249 F. 513, affirming my decision in (D.C.) 249 F. 507; neither of which we meant to overrule. We found the plot of the second play was too different to infringe, because the most detailed pattern, common to both, eliminated so much from each that its content went into the public domain; and for this reason we said, "this mere subsection of a plot was not susceptible of copyright." But we do not doubt that two plays may correspond in plot closely enough for infringement. How far that correspondence must go is another matter. Nor need we hold that the same may not be true as to the characters, quite independently of the "plot" proper, though, as far as we know, such a case has never arisen. If Twelfth Night were copyrighted, it is quite possible that a second comer might so closely imitate Sir Toby Belch or Malvolio as to infringe, but it would not be enough that for one of his characters he cast a riotous knight who kept wassail to the discomfort of the household, or a vain and foppish steward who became amorous of his mistress. These would be no more than Shakespeare's "ideas" in the play, as little capable of monopoly as Einstein's Doctrine of Relativity, or Darwin's theory of the Origin of Species. It follows that the less developed the characters, the less they can be copyrighted; that is the penalty an author must bear for marking them too indistinctly.

In the two plays at bar we think both as to incident and character, the defendant took no more assuming that it took anything at all than the law allowed. The stories are quite different. One is of a religious zealot who insists upon his child's marrying no one outside his faith; opposed by another who is in this respect just like him, and is his foil. Their difference in race is merely an obbligato to the main theme, religion. They sink their differences through grandparental pride and affection. In the other, zealotry is wholly absent; religion does not even appear. It is true that the parents are hostile to each other in part because they differ in race; but the marriage of their son to a Jew does not apparently offend the Irish family at all, and it exacerbates the existing animosity of the Jew, principally because he has become rich, when he learns it. They are reconciled through the honesty of the Jew and the generosity of the Irishman; the grandchild has nothing whatever to do with it. The only matter common to the two is a quarrel between a Jewish and an Irish father, the marriage of their children, the birth of grandchildren and a reconciliation.

If the defendant took so much from the plaintiff, it may well have been because her amazing success seemed to prove that this was a subject of enduring popularity. Even so, granting that the plaintiff's play was wholly original, and assuming that novelty is not essential to a copyright, there is no monopoly in such a background. Though the plaintiff discovered the vein, she could not keep it to herself; so defined, the theme was too generalized an abstraction from what she wrote. It was only a part of her "ideas."

Nor does she fare better as to her characters. It is indeed scarcely credible that she should not have been aware of those stock figures, the low comedy Jew and Irishman. The defendant has not taken from her more than their prototypes have contained for many decades. If so, obviously so to generalize her copyright, would allow her to cover what was not original with her. But we need not hold this as matter of fact, much as we might be justified. Even though we take it that she devised her figures out of her brain de novo, still the defendant was within its rights.

There are but four characters common to both plays, the lovers and the fathers. The lovers are so faintly indicated as to be no more than stage properties. They are loving and fertile; that is really all that can be said of them, and anyone else is quite within his rights if he puts loving and fertile lovers in a play of his own, wherever he gets the cue. The plaintiff's Jew is quite unlike the defendant's. His obsession is his religion, on which depends such racial animosity as he has. He is affectionate, warm and patriarchal. None of these fit the defendant's Jew, who shows affection for his daughter only once, and who has none but the most superficial interest in his grandchild. He is tricky, ostentatious and vulgar, only by misfortune redeemed into honesty. Both are grotesque, extravagant and quarrelsome; both are fond of display; but these common qualities make up only a small part of their simple pictures, no more than any one might lift if he chose. The Irish fathers are even more unlike; the plaintiff's a mere symbol for religious fanaticism and patriarchal pride, scarcely a character at all. Neither quality appears in the defendant's, for while he goes to get his grandchild, it is rather out of a truculent determination not to be forbidden, than from pride in his progeny. For the rest he is only a grotesque hobbledehoy, used for low comedy of the most conventional sort, which any one might borrow, if he chanced not to know the exemplar.

The defendant argues that the case is controlled by my decision in *Fisher v. Dillingham (D.C.)* 298 F. 145. Neither my brothers nor I wish to throw doubt upon the doctrine of that case, but it is not applicable here. We assume that the plaintiff's play is altogether original, even to an extent that in fact it is hard to believe. We assume further that, so far as it has been anticipated by earlier plays of which she knew nothing, that fact is immaterial. Still, as we have already said, her copyright did not cover everything that might be drawn from her play; its content went to some extent into the public domain. We have to decide how much, and while we are as aware as any one that the line, wherever it is drawn, will seem arbitrary, that is no excuse for not drawing it; it is a question such as courts must answer in nearly all cases. Whatever may be the difficulties a priori, we have no question on which side of the line this case falls. A comedy based upon conflicts between Irish and Jews, into which the marriage of their children enters, is no more susceptible of copyright than the outline of Romeo and Juliet.

The plaintiff has prepared an elaborate analysis of the two plays, showing a "quadrangle" of the common characters, in which each is represented by the emotions which he discovers. She presents the resulting parallelism as proof of infringement, but the adjectives employed are so general as to be quite useless. Take for example the attribute of "love" ascribed to both Jews. The plaintiff has depicted her father as deeply attached to his son, who is his hope and joy; not so, the defendant, whose father's conduct is throughout not actuated by any affection for his daughter, and who is merely once overcome for the moment by her distress when he has violently dismissed her lover. "Anger" covers emotions aroused by quite different occasions in each case; so do "anxiety," "despondency" and "disgust." It is unnecessary to go through the catalogue for emotions are too much colored by their causes to be a test when used so broadly. This is not the proper approach to a solution; it must be more ingenuous, more like that of a spectator, who would rely upon the complex of his impressions of each character....

[T]he case confined to the actual issues; that is, whether the copyrighted work was original, and whether the defendant copied it, so far as the supposed infringement is identical.

The defendant, "the prevailing party," was entitled to a reasonable attorney's fee.

Decree affirmed.

Sheldon v. Metro-Goldwyn Pictures Corp.
81 F.2d 49 (2d Cir. 1936)

L. HAND, Circuit Judge.

The suit is to enjoin the performance of the picture play, "Letty Lynton," as an infringement of the plaintiffs' copyrighted play, "Dishonored Lady." The plaintiffs' title is conceded, so too the validity of the copyright; the only issue is infringement. The defendants say that they did not use the play in any way to produce the picture; the plaintiffs discredit this denial because of the negotiations between the parties for the purchase of rights in the play, and because the similarities between the two are too specific and detailed to have resulted from chance. The judge thought that, so far as the defendants had used the play, they had taken only what the law allowed, that is, those general themes, motives, or ideas in which there could be no copyright. Therefore he dismissed the bill.

[The detailed comparison between the public trial on which the play and novel were based and each of these works is better summarized in a later proceeding before the Supreme Court:

Petitioners' complaint charged infringement of their play 'Dishonored Lady' by respondents' motion picture 'Letty Lynton', and sought an injunction and an accounting of profits. The Circuit Court of Appeals, reversing the District Court, found and enjoined the infringement and directed an accounting.... Petitioners' play 'Dishonored Lady' was based upon the trial in Scotland, in 1857, of Madeleine Smith for the murder of her lover,—a *cause celebre* included in the series of 'Notable British Trials' which was published in 1927. The play was copyrighted as an unpublished work in 1930, and was produced here and abroad. Respondents took the title of their motion picture 'Letty Lynton' from a novel of that name written by an English author, Mrs. Belloc Lowndes, and published in 1930. That novel was also based upon the story of Madeleine Smith and the motion picture rights were bought by respondents. There had been negotiations for the motion picture rights in petitioners' play, and the price had been fixed at $30,000, but these negotiations fell through.

As the Court of Appeals found, respondents in producing the motion picture in question worked over old material; 'the general skeleton was already in the public demesne. A wanton girl kills her lover to free herself for a better match; she is brought to trial for the murder and escapes'. But not content with the mere use of that basic plot, respondents resorted to petitioners' copyrighted play. They were not innocent offenders. From comparison and analysis, the Court of Appeals concluded that they had 'deliberately lifted the play'; their 'borrowing was a deliberate plagiarism'....

Sheldon v. Metro-Goldwyn Pictures Corp., 309 U.S. 390, 396–97 (1940).] ...

The defendants, who are engaged in producing speaking films on a very large scale in Hollywood, California, had seen the play and wished to get the rights. They found, however, an obstacle in an association of motion picture producers presided over by Mr. Will Hays, who thought the play obscene; not being able to overcome his objections, they returned the copy of the manuscript which they had had. That was in the spring of 1930, but in the autumn they induced the plaintiffs to get up a scenario, which they hoped might pass moral muster. Although this did not suit them after the plaintiffs prepared it, they must still have thought in the spring of 1931 that they could satisfy Mr. Hays, for they then procured an offer from the plaintiffs to sell their rights for $30,000. These negotiations also proved abortive because the play continued to be objectionable, and eventually they cried off on the bargain. Mrs. Lowndes' novel was suggested to Thalberg, one of the vice-presidents of the Metro-Goldwyn Company, in July, 1931, and again in the following November, and he bought the rights to it in December....

We are to remember that it makes no difference how far the play was anticipated by works in the public demesne which the plaintiffs did not use.... At times, in discussing how much of the substance of a play the copyright protects, courts have indeed used language which seems to give countenance to the notion that, if a plot were old, it could not be copyrighted. But we understand by this no more than that in its broader outline a plot is never copyrightable, for it is plain beyond peradventure that anticipation as such cannot invalidate a copyright. Borrowed the work must indeed not be, for a plagiarist is not himself *pro tanto* an "author"; but if by some magic a man who had never known it were to compose anew Keats's Ode on a Grecian Urn, he would be an "author," and, if he copyrighted it, others might not copy that poem, though they might of course copy Keats's. But though a copyright is for this reason less vulnerable than a patent, the owner's protection is more limited, for just as he is no less an "author" because others have preceded him, so another who follows him, is not a tort-feasor unless he pirates his work. If the copyrighted work is therefore original, the public demesne is important only on the issue of infringement; that is, so far as it may break the force of the inference to be drawn from likenesses between the work and the putative piracy. If the defendant has had access to other material which would have served him as well, his disclaimer becomes more plausible.

In the case at bar there are then two questions: First, whether the defendants actually used the play; second, if so, whether theirs was a "fair use." The judge did not make any finding upon the first question, as we said at the outset, because he thought the defendants were in any case justified; in this following our decision in *Nichols v. Universal Pictures Corporation*, 45 F.2d 119 (2d Cir. 1930). The plaintiffs challenge that opinion because we said that "copying" might at times be a "fair use"; but it is convenient to define such a use by saying that others may "copy" the "theme," or "ideas," or the like, of a work, though not its "expression." At any rate so long as it is clear what is meant, no harm is done. In the case at bar the distinction is not so important as usual, because so much of the play was borrowed from the story of Madeleine Smith, and the plaintiffs' originality is necessarily limited to the variants they introduced. Nevertheless, it is still true that their whole contribution may not be protected; for the defendants were entitled to use, not only all that had gone before, but even the plaintiffs' contribution itself, if they drew from it only the more general patterns; that is, if they kept clear of its "expression." We must therefore state in detail those similarities which seem to us to pass the limits of "fair use."...

We have often decided that a play may be pirated without using the dialogue.... Were it not so, there could be no piracy of a pantomime, where there cannot be any dialogue; yet nobody would deny to pantomime the name of drama. Speech is only a small part of a dramatist's means of expression; he draws on all the arts and compounds his play from words and gestures and scenery and costume and from the very looks of the actors themselves. Again and again a play may lapse into pantomime at its most poignant and significant moments; a nod, a movement of the hand, a pause, may tell the audience more than words could tell. To be sure, not all this is always copyrighted, though there is no reason why it may not be, for those decisions do not forbid which hold that mere scenic tricks will not be protected. The play is the sequence of the confluents of all these means, bound together in an inseparable unity; it may often be most effectively pirated by leaving out the speech, for which a substitute can be found, which keeps the whole dramatic meaning. That as it appears to us is exactly what the defendants have done here; the dramatic significance of the scenes we have recited is the same, almost to the letter. True, much of the picture owes nothing to the play; some of it is plainly drawn from the novel; but that is entirely immaterial; it is enough that substantial parts were lifted; no plagiarist can excuse the wrong by showing how much of his work he did not pirate. We cannot avoid the conviction that, if the picture was not an infringement of the play, there can be none short of taking the dialogue.

The decree will be reversed and an injunction will go against the picture together with a decree for damages and an accounting. The plaintiffs will be awarded an attorney's fee in this court and in the court below, both to be fixed by the District Court upon the final decree.

Decree reversed.

Zambito v. Paramount Pictures Corp.
613 F. Supp. 1107 (E.D.N.Y. 1985)

This is an action for copyright infringement under Title 17 of the United States Code. Plaintiff Zambito, an archaeologist-screenwriter, asserts that defendants' movie, "Raiders of the Lost Ark" ("Raiders"), infringes copyrightable material contained in his screenplay, "Black Rainbow" ("Rainbow"). Both sides have moved for summary judgment on the issue of substantial similarity. For the reasons set forth below, defendants' motion for summary judgment is granted and plaintiff's motion is denied.

For the purpose of this motion only, defendant concedes the validity of plaintiff's copyright and defendants' access to the plaintiff's copyrighted work. Thus, the only task facing the Court is to determine whether the two works are sufficiently similar to raise a genuine issue of copyright infringement; if such an issue exists a trial is, of course, required.

"Rainbow"

Plaintiff's screenplay, "Black Rainbow," is the story of archaeologist Zeke Banarro's ("Zeke") expedition to the Andes of Peru in search of pre-Columbian gold artifacts. In the preamble to "Rainbow," Zeke is introduced as "a legitimate archaeologist who became a renegade treasure hunter or *huaquero*."

In the opening scene, Zeke is informed by his former lover, Michael Colby, a female museum curator, that Zeke has been replaced as head of an expedition to Peru. Undaunted, Zeke finances his own "bootleg" expedition with the help of a cocaine dealer who fronts Zeke the money in exchange for Zeke's promise to smuggle cocaine from Peru.

Upon arrival in Peru, Zeke and his sidekick, Justo, a Peruvian Indian native, pause to taste the pleasures of cocaine and prostitutes. After assembling an entourage of Indian natives and taking as a partner, Alvarado, who supplied horses and pack animals, the party then proceeds on the expedition.

Along the way, Tumba, Alvarado's servant/mistress, gives birth to a son. Shortly thereafter, Alvarado offers Tumba's services as a prostitute in return for the other Indians' share of the treasure. Zeke seeks to prevent this exploitation by pacifying the natives with cocaine. Ironically, Tumba, who is understandably grateful for this act of humanity, rewards Zeke with sexual favors.

Later, an old Indian mystic tells Zeke that he can locate the cave with the great anaconda snakes, and hopefully the treasure, by observing the reflection of the sun off the side of the cliffs. Upon locating the cave, the party rappels down the side of the cliff, fights off the anacondas with molotov cocktails, and uncovers the treasure in a burial site inside the cave.

As they are about to begin their trek back from the clifftop, the expedition is confronted by the script's principal antagonist, Von Stroessner, and his band of thieves. As it turns out, Von Stroessner was hired by Michael Colby and the museum to follow Zeke and liberate him of his new-found treasure. A fight ensues, in which Zeke and Von Stroessner are wounded and several Indians are killed. Zeke ultimately shoots Von Stroessner in cold blood.

The expedition party continues the journey back, only to be confronted by the Peruvian National Guard. In the ensuing gunfire, Justo is mortally wounded, the remaining Indians are killed, and Zeke and Alvarado are forced to flee through the dense jungle carrying what little gold they can carry. Zeke ultimately shoots Alvarado in a quarrel over the remaining treasure, and the story ends with Zeke hiking back to civilization.

"Raiders"

"Raiders of the Lost Ark," by now familiar to movie-goers everywhere, is the swashbuckling adventure story of archaeologist Indiana Jones ("Indy"). After a brief introductory expedition to South America in 1936, which is foiled by Indy's arch-rival, Belloq, a French mercenary archaeologist, Indy returns home only to find that his services are required by the United States Army. It seems that army intelligence has revealed that Hitler is digging outside of Cairo for the lost Ark of the Covenant. Hitler, we are told, seeks to take advantage of the Ark's vast supernatural powers. Indy's mission, should he choose to accept it, is to beat Hitler to the Ark.

Indy flies to Nepal where he locates Marion Ravenwood, his former lover and the daughter of his mentor. Marion has the headpiece to the Staff of Ra, which is the key to locating the Ark. When attached to a staff and placed in a miniature map room in the ancient city outside Cairo, the headpiece will direct the sun's rays to the location of the Well of Souls, in which the Ark is hidden. After Indy saves Marion from several ruthless Nazis, who are also after the headpiece, the pair heads for Cairo.

There, Indy discovers that Hitler has hired his old rival, Belloq, to direct the excavation. Belloq takes great interest in Marion, who has since been abducted by the Nazis.

Meanwhile, Indy and Sallah, an Egyptian friend, manage to sneak into the excavation and descend into the map room, where they discover the location of the Well of Souls. As they are about to descend into the Well, they discover that its floor is covered with tiny asps. Indy fends off the snakes by dousing them with fuel oil and setting them afire.

Indy and Sallah place the Ark in a crate and hoist it to their helpers waiting above. Once Sallah has ascended, the Nazis, who have observed Indy's discovery, thrust Marion into the well with Indy and seal it up. The two manage to escape through the wall, however, to a neighboring catacomb.

After blowing up a Nazi airplane, Indy realizes that the Ark is now aboard a truck headed for Cairo. In a famous "chase" scene, Indy, riding a white steed, catches up with the Nazi caravan, gains control of the truck, fends off the Nazis, and escapes into the maze of the streets of Cairo.

Indy and Marion depart Cairo with the Ark aboard a ship, only to be overtaken by a Nazi U-boat. Indy, who managed to elude capture, follows the Nazis to an unidentified Mediterranean Island only to be taken captive once again. With Indy and Marion tied up nearby, Belloq and the Nazis open the Ark in a ritualistic ceremony. The grotesque spirits released therefrom converge upon the Nazis in a bizarre swoop of destruction. Only Indy and Marion, who in Old Testament fashion have kept their eyes closed throughout, are spared.

Back in Washington, D.C., as the film closes, we see the crated Ark being transported to an army warehouse where, among thousands of other identical crates, it will lie forever forgotten.

Discussion

Although the question whether two works are substantially similar usually presents a factual issue that does not lend itself to summary judgment, the Second Circuit has recognized the appropriateness of summary judgment in copyright actions, "permitting courts to put 'a swift end to meritless litigation' and to avoid lengthy and costly trials." Clearly, summary judgment is appropriate where, after reviewing the competing works, the Court concludes either that any similarity between the works concerns only noncopyrightable elements or that no reasonable jury, properly instructed, could find the works substantially similar.

The test for substantial similarity has been succinctly described as "whether an average lay observer would recognize the alleged copy as having been appropriated from the copyrighted work." In assessing whether a properly instructed jury may find two works substantially similar, it is helpful to review a few basic principles delineating the scope of copyright protection.

It is, of course, well-settled that a copyright protects only an author's original expression of an idea, not the idea itself. As the Second Circuit has noted:

> While the demarcation between idea and expression may not be susceptible to overly helpful generalization, it has been emphasized repeatedly that the essence of infringement lies in taking not a general theme but its particular expression through similarities of treatment, details, scenes, events and characterizations. In addition, a copyright affords no protection to so-called "scenes a faire," i.e., characters, settings or events which necessarily follow from a certain theme or plot situation.

Plaintiff concedes, as he must, that the basic idea of an archaeologist searching for artifacts is unprotectible. He argues, however, that actionable similarities lie in the characters, devices and action employed in expressing that idea. Defendant, of course, argues that any similarities existing between the two works are, in fact, unprotectible *scenes a faire*. I agree.

It is unnecessary to discuss every alleged similarity in the two works; a brief discussion of the salient portions of plaintiff's argument is illustrative.[4]

---

4. The Court is, of course, mindful of Chief Judge Kaufman's admonition that "in distinguishing between themes, facts and *scenes a faire* on the one hand, and copyrightable expression on the other, courts may lose sight of the forest for the trees." *Hoehling*, 618 F.2d at 979.

First, it is noted that the mood and "feel" of the two works are completely different. "Rainbow" is, for the most part, a somber, vulgar script replete with overt sexual scenes, cocaine smuggling and cold-blooded killing. "Raiders," on the other hand, is a tongue-in-cheek, action-packed, Jack Armstrong, all-American adventure story.

Nor is there substantial similarity in the settings of the two works. "Rainbow" is set almost entirely in a Peruvian jungle. Although "Raiders" begins with a very brief expedition to a booby-trapped cave in a South-American jungle, most of the story is set in and around Cairo. Thus, any similarity of locale is simply too insignificant to warrant protection.

Plaintiff fares no better in his claim of character infringement. As the Second Circuit has stated, "stirring one's memory of a copyrighted character is not the same as appearing to be substantially similar to that character, and only the latter is infringement." A review of plaintiff's claims of character infringement indicates that no jury could reasonably find the characters substantially similar.

Plaintiff argues, initially, that actionable similarity lies between the two protagonists, Zeke Banarro and Indiana Jones. Any similarity ends, however, with the fact that both are male and both are archaeologists. Zeke is basically a serious, self-interested, individual who betrays both the museum for which he works and his illegitimate "backer," strikes out on his own, and ends up shooting his adversaries in cold-blood. Indy, on the other hand, is a larger-than-life adventurer who, in matinee-idol fashion, remains loyal to truth, justice and the American way.

Nor does actionable similarity exist regarding the principal antagonists, Belloq in "Raiders" and Von Stroessner in "Rainbow." Belloq is an articulate, cultured French archaeologist who is Indy's established rival. Although not a Nazi himself, Belloq has been hired by Hitler to find the lost Ark.

Von Stroessner, whose full name is Juan Jose de Maria Lopez y Von Stroessner, is described as a mestizo thief who preys upon archaeologists. Plaintiff claims that the name Von Stroessner was chosen to depict the character as a post-war Nazi. Nothing in the script, however, indicates that Von Stroessner is, in fact, a Nazi. Indeed, it is ultimately revealed that Von Stroessner was hired, not by the Nazis, but by the museum where Zeke formerly was employed.

Plaintiff's assertion that he intended the Von Stroessner character to depict a Nazi does not present an actionable claim. The law of copyright protects the author's actual expression of an idea, and not the idea as it existed in the author's imagination. Clearly, "no character infringement claim can succeed unless plaintiff's original conception sufficiently developed the character, and defendants have copied this development and not merely the broader outlines."

In any event, even if the distorted inference that Von Stroessner is a Nazi could be drawn, no actionable similarity would lie. It is significant that "Raiders" is set in the late-1930s, the Nazi era. "Rainbow," on the other hand, obviously takes place in a contemporary setting, as is evident from various references to the World Trade Center, the King Tut exhibit at the Metropolitan Museum of Art, Laurance Rockefeller, and the cocaine trade. Thus, any similarity caused by a remote reference to Nazism is, to say the least, superficial.

Finally, and incredibly, plaintiff asserts a similarity between Marion Ravenwood of "Raiders" and a combination of Tumba, the pregnant Indian mistress, and Michael Colby, the ambitious museum curator, of "Rainbow." The only similarities between these characters, however, are that they are female and that they share the common experience of a sexual encounter with the respective protagonists.

Upon close inspection, plaintiff's remaining claims of actionable similarity fall within the category of unprotectible scenes a faire. That treasure might be hidden in a cave inhabited by snakes, that fire might be used to repel the snakes, that birds might frighten an intruder in the jungle, and that a weary traveler might seek solace in a tavern, all are indispensable elements to the treatment of "Raiders" theme, and are, as a matter of law, simply too general to be protectible.

Moreover, these scenes were given dissimilar treatment in the respective works. For instance, in "Rainbow," the party's access to the cave was hindered by giant anaconda snakes that ultimately were frightened away by molotov cocktails. In "Raiders," the floor of the Well of Souls was covered by hundreds of tiny asps and a cobra, that were fended off by burning them with fuel oil.

Likewise, an examination of plaintiff's claim that both scripts utilize sunlight to locate the treasure reveals a similarity too general to afford protection. In "Rainbow," the treasure-filled cave is located by observing the reflection of the sun off a crystallized rock formation on the side of a cliff. In "Raiders," however, the location of the Well of Souls is determined in a map room by observing the reflection of the sun through the headpiece of the Staff of Ra.

Finally, plaintiff's claim of dialogue infringement involves generalized insignificant pieces of dialogue which also necessarily flow from a common theme.

In short, having thoroughly reviewed all the plaintiff's claims (and having thoroughly enjoyed both scripts), I am led ineluctably to the conclusion that a "comparison of the two works reveals that their similarity exists only at a level of abstractions too basic to permit any inference that defendants wrongfully appropriated any 'expression' of plaintiff's ideas."

Accordingly, defendants' motion for summary judgment is granted and plaintiff's motion is denied. Defendants' request for attorney's fees is denied. The complaint is hereby dismissed.

Twentieth Century-Fox Film Corp. v. MCA, Inc.
715 F.2d 1327 (9th Cir. 1983)

Appellants claim that their copyrighted production of the book and motion picture "Star Wars" was infringed by appellees' production "Battlestar: Galactica." The district court granted appellees' motion for partial summary judgment. We reverse and remand.

In 1977, Twentieth Century-Fox produced and distributed the motion picture "Star Wars." The commercial success of that venture did not go unnoticed. The following year "Battlestar: Galactica" was released as both a motion picture and television series. Universal Studios, Inc., a subsidiary of MCA, Inc., produced and owned the rights to Battlestar, and ABC televised the Battlestar space saga.

In June 1978, Fox commenced this action against MCA, Universal, and ABC, alleging copyright infringement. Subsequently, Fox's amended complaint joined Lucasfilm, Ltd. as co-plaintiff, and alleged that defendants had also infringed Lucasfilm's copyright in its 1976 Star Wars book.

Defendants moved for partial summary judgment on the copyright claims. In connection with that motion, the trial judge reviewed a videotape montage of prior science fiction works, the Star Wars film and book, and a videotape of the first television episode of Battlestar. Defendants did not contest the validity of plaintiffs' Star Wars copyrights. Further, for purposes of the motion, defendants admitted access to plaintiffs' works.

The only issue raised in the motion was whether defendants' Battlestar: Galactica production was so dissimilar to plaintiffs' Star Wars works, as to both ideas and expression of those ideas, that no material issue of fact existed on the question of substantial similarity, and the question could be decided as a matter of law. The trial court granted defendants' motion for partial summary judgment. This appeal ensued.

The law relating to a grant of summary judgment is clear. Only if no genuine issue of material fact exists will the moving party be entitled to prevail as a matter of law.

On appeal, the question whether summary judgment was properly granted below is one of law. That is, this court must view the evidence and inferences therefrom in the light most favorable to the nonmoving party, herein plaintiffs-appellants Fox and Lucasfilm (collectively referred to as "Fox"). Defendants-appellees MCA, Universal and ABC (collectively referred to as "MCA") may prevail only if no genuine issue of material fact exists on the questions of substantial similarity of idea and idea expression.

After viewing the Star Wars and Battlestar motion pictures, we conclude that the films do in fact raise genuine issues of material fact as to whether only the Star Wars idea or the expression of that idea was copied. At a minimum, it is a close enough question that it should be resolved by way of a trial. We intimate no opinion whether the films are substantially similar as to either idea or expression, but state only that reasonable minds could differ on those key factual issues. Thus, a grant of summary judgment was improvident.

Appellant Fox argued in its brief that a comparison of the two works discloses at least 34 similarities. For illustrative purposes only, we list 13 of the alleged similarities:

(1) The central conflict of each story is a war between the galaxy's democratic and totalitarian forces.

(2) In Star Wars the young hero's father had been a leader of the democratic forces, and the present leader of the democratic forces is a father figure to the young hero. In Battlestar the young hero's father is a leader of the democratic forces.

(3) The leader of the democratic forces is an older man, displaying great wisdom, and symbolizing goodness and leadership, with a mysterious mystical ability to dominate a leader of the totalitarian forces.

(4) An entire planet, central to the existence of the democratic forces, is destroyed.

(5) The heroine is imprisoned by the totalitarian forces.

(6) A leading character returns to the family home to find it destroyed.

(7) The search by the totalitarians and the liberation attempt by the democratic forces are depicted in alternating sequences between the totalitarian and democratic camps.

(8) There is a romance between the hero's friend (the cynical fighter pilot) and the daughter of one of the leaders of the democratic forces.

(9) A friendly robot, who aids the democratic forces is severely injured (Star Wars) or destroyed (Battlestar) by the totalitarian forces.

(10) There is a scene in a cantina (Star Wars) or casino (Battlestar), in which musical entertainment is offered by bizarre, non-human creatures.

(11) Space vehicles, although futuristic, are made to look used and old, contrary to the stereo-typical sleek, new appearance of space age equipment.

(12) The climax consists of an attack by the democratic fighter pilots on the totalitarian headquarters.

(13) Each work ends with an awards ceremony in honor of the democratic heroes.

Since substantial similarity is usually an extremely close question of fact, summary judgment has traditionally been disfavored in copyright litigation. While that may be, we emphasize that summary judgment determinations result from close factual analyses, and are inherently peculiar to each case. Further, if Rule 56 is to be of any effect, summary judgment must be granted in certain situations.

REVERSED and REMANDED.

Notes and Questions

a. For a review of the use of parody as a defense to both literal copying, and arguably copying the total concept and feel of a work, see *Warner Bros. v. American Broadcasting Cos.*, 720 F.2d 231 (2d Cir. 1983) (*infra* at Section XIV-B).

b. It is very difficult to find reported victories over the Hollywood studios regarding theft of screenplays, yet the fear of having a screenplay remains a prominent aspect of the screenwriter's profession. It may be that the plots, ideas, and occasionally protected expression embodied in screenplays are taken, but never with express corporate authority. When a credible claim of copyright infringement occurs, the studios are likely to enter into an agreement to satisfy the parties and to insist on confidentiality regarding that settlement.

c. In the television context, complaints that a television premise has been stolen will come either from the general public or from insiders who regularly work on television projects. Outsiders have a challenge in establishing studio access to their work, so they typically do not fare well with their copyright infringement claims. The more important cases are those brought by television insiders—writers or other production staff who claim that a project originally developed has been credited to someone else. These cases, in turn, fall into two categories: those claims brought under a signed, express contract, and those brought under copyright infringement and an implied contract. In both cases, the issue often flows from whether the television series which ultimately airs is "based upon" the plaintiff's work or whether such work is substantially similar. If the two works are substantially similar under copyright law, then the plaintiff will win in either situation. If the work is based upon the plaintiff's work, but not similar enough to meet the substantial similarity test of copyright, then the written contract claim may survive while the copyright claim and implied contract claim will fail.

d. In *Metcalf v. Bochco*, 294 F.3d 1069 (9th Cir. 2002), Jerome and Laurie Metcalf ("the Metcalfs") sued television producer Steven Bochco over the series "City of Angels." Access was conceded because the Metcalfs had pitched the show three times to Bochco and other defendants. The Ninth Circuit allowed the plaintiffs to avoid summary judgment by analyzing the copyright claim in the sequence, order, and arrangement of the material submitted, including the *scenes a faire* and other unprotectable elements. As a result, Judge Kozinski was reluctant to ignore the similarities:

> Bochco correctly argues that copyright law protects a writer's expression of ideas, but not the ideas themselves. General plot ideas are not protected by copyright law; they remain forever the common property of artistic mankind. Nor does copyright law protect "scenes a faire," or scenes that flow naturally from unprotectable basic plot premises. Instead, protectable expression includes the specific details of an author's rendering of ideas, or the actual concrete elements that make up the total sequence of events and the relationships between the major characters. Here, the similarities proffered by the Metcalfs are not protectable when considered individually; they are either too generic or constitute "scenes a faire."

One cannot copyright the idea of an idealistic young professional choosing between financial and emotional reward, or of love triangles among young professionals that eventually become strained, or of political forces interfering with private action.

However, the presence of so many generic similarities and the common patterns in which they arise do help the Metcalfs satisfy the extrinsic test. The particular sequence in which an author strings a significant number of unprotectable elements can itself be a protectable element. Each note in a scale, for example, is not protectable, but a pattern of notes in a tune may earn copyright protection. A common "pattern [that] is sufficiently concrete ... warrants a finding of substantial similarity."

Id. at 1074 (citations omitted).

Against this backdrop, the decision in *Murray Hill Publns, Inc. v. Twentieth Century Fox Film Corp.*, 361 F.3d 312 (6th Cir. 2003), providing for judgment as a matter of law, becomes more significant. Fox was able to convince the appellate court that it was entitled to judgment as a matter of law, denying any copyright infringement between its film *Jingle All the Way* and the screenplay entitled *Could This be Christmas.* Although Fox had the treatments to both films at the same time, the *Jingle* treatment had been completed and submitted to Fox prior to its receiving the Christmas screenplay.

The Sixth Circuit reviewed the various abstraction-filtration-comparison schemes used by the Second, Ninth and D.C. Circuits to explain why even copyrightable elements may be filtered out for comparison between the works. The Court explained that "elements of a copyright defendant's work that were created prior to access to a plaintiff's work are to be filtered out at the first stage of substantial-similarity analysis," which eliminated all the common elements between *Jingle* and *Christmas.* Of the twenty-four similarities between the two scripts, eighteen were found in the *Jingle All the Way* treatment that the court determined had been completed before access to the plaintiff's script could have occurred. In what the Sixth Circuit said was an issue of first impression, it determined it should filter out those occurrences before determining substantial similarity, and it found the remaining six similarities superficial.

The necessity of filtering out a defendant's own prior material appears self-evident. Access is irrelevant for portions of a plaintiff's work that could not have been drawn from the plaintiff. The interesting question is whether any such material had existed in *Metcalf v. Bochco*, or whether all the development had occurred by plaintiffs, rather than independently but at the same time as Bocho's own production activities. As a legal standard, the Sixth Circuit's gloss that copyrightable elements of a defendant's work will be filtered out if it predates the plaintiff's work helps separate copying from common elements, and will likely seep into the jurisprudence of the other circuits.

Problem III-B

Bryce is struggling to finish the industrial video for St. James Corporation (see Problem III-A, above). The concept of the project is to parallel a famous film featuring privacy issues and work that theme into the corporate setting. Bryce considered *All the President's Men,* by having an employee use corporate records to ferret out political misconduct, *Fatal Attraction,* by showing how an employee could illegally 'stalk' another through the misuse of corporate records, and even *Alien,* by having the corporate records searched to prove that a client was really an android working for the company.

The executives at the St. James Corporation have raised concerns that the parallels between Bryce's suggestions and commercial films could give rise to adverse claims against the company. Bryce has called you for legal and practical advice. Specifically, St. James will allow Bryce to use such a script idea (i) if you can provide a legal opinion letter that the work is not an infringement of copyright for the motion pictures described; and (ii) if Bryce agrees to indemnify the St. James Corporation for all costs, including attorneys' fees, in the event that any third party objects to the use of the plots, characters, dialogue or ideas from any of these commercial films.

Consult with the partners in your firm to confirm whether you can provide such an opinion letter and what advice you would give to Bryce.

C. Other Uses of Copyrighted Works

Ringgold v. Black Entertainment Television, Inc.
126 F.3d 70 (2d Cir. 1997)

This appeal primarily concerns the scope of copyright protection for a poster of an artistic work that was used as set decoration for a television program. Faith Ringgold appeals from the September 24, 1996, judgment of the District Court for the Southern District of New York dismissing, on motion for summary judgment, her copyright infringement suit against Black Entertainment Television, Inc. ("BET") and Home Box Office, Inc. ("HBO"). The District Court sustained defendants' defense of fair use. We conclude that summary judgment was not warranted, and we therefore reverse and remand for further consideration of plaintiff's claim.

Faith Ringgold is a successful contemporary artist who created, and owns the copyright in, a work of art entitled "Church Picnic Story Quilt" (sometimes hereafter called "Church Picnic" or "the story quilt"). "Church Picnic" is an example of a new form of artistic expression that Ringgold has created. She calls the form a "story quilt design." These designs consist of a painting, a handwritten text, and quilting fabric, all three of which Ringgold unites to communicate parables.... Since 1988 the High Museum has held a non-exclusive license to reproduce "Church Picnic" as a poster ("'Church Picnic' poster" or "the poster"), and to sell those reproductions. The "Church Picnic" poster sells for $20.00 a copy and was not produced as a limited edition. Thousands of copies of the poster have been sold since 1988. Although the license to reproduce poster copies of "Church Picnic" has terminated, copies of the poster remain available for sale.

Below the portion of the poster that displays "Church Picnic" are several identifying words. "High Museum of Art" appears in letters 1 1/4 inches high. Below these words is the phrase "Faith Ringgold, Church Picnic Story Quilt, 1988, gift of Don and Jill Childress" in letters 1/8 inch high. Below this line, in smaller type, appears "Courtesy Bernice Steinbaum Galley, New York City. Poster 1988 High Museum of Art, Atlanta."

2. The alleged infringing use.

HBO Independent Productions, a division of HBO, produced "ROC," a television "sitcom" series concerning a middle-class African-American family living in Baltimore. Some time prior to 1992, HBO Independent Productions produced an episode of ROC in which a "Church Picnic" poster, presumably sold by the High Museum, was used as part of the set decoration.... The "Church Picnic" poster was used as a wall-hanging in the church hall....

In the scene, at least a portion of the poster is shown a total of nine times. In some of those instances, the poster is at the center of the screen, although nothing in the dialogue, action, or camera work particularly calls the viewer's attention to the poster. The nine sequences in which a portion of the poster is visible range in duration from 1.86 to 4.16 seconds. The aggregate duration of all nine sequences is 26.75 seconds....

The copy of the poster used in the episode was framed without the identifying wording that appears beneath the artwork. As framed, the poster includes a notice of copyright, but the type is too small to be discernible to a television viewer.

A broadcast television network first televised the episode in 1992, and in October 1994 BET aired the episode for the first time on cable television. In January 1995, Ringgold happened to watch the episode on BET (apparently a repeat showing), and at that time became aware of the defendants' use of the poster as part of the set decoration.

Ringgold sued the defendants, alleging infringement of her copyright in "Church Picnic Story Quilt," in violation of 17 U.S.C. § 106 (1994), because of the unauthorized use of the poster as part of the set decoration for the episode of "ROC." ... Prior to discovery, the defendants moved for summary judgment, contending (i) that they were not liable for copyright infringement, because their use of the story quilt was either *de minimis* or a fair use....

The Copyright Act grants certain exclusive rights to the owner of a copyright, including the right to make and distribute copies and derivative works based on the copyrighted work, and the right to display the copyrighted work publicly. In the absence of defenses, these exclusive rights normally give a copyright owner the right to seek royalties from others who wish to use the copyrighted work. Ringgold contends that the defendants violated this licensing right by using the "Church Picnic" poster to decorate the set of their sitcom without her authorization.

The caselaw provides little illumination concerning claims that copyright in a visual work has been infringed by including it within another visual work. The Nimmer treatise posits the problem of a motion picture in which an actor is reading a magazine of which the cover picture is observable, and acknowledges that "the answer is by no means certain." The treatise observes, with uncharacteristic ambivalence, that a fair use defense might be supported on the ground that "the entire work does not supplant the function of the plaintiff's work," yet also points out that "ordinarily" the copying of a magazine cover into another medium "will constitute infringement, and not fair use."

HBO and BET defend their use of the poster on two separate, though related grounds: (a) that their use of the poster was *de minimis*, and (b) that, as Judge Martin ruled, their use of the poster was a permissible "fair use."

I. De minimis

The *de minimis* Concept in Copyright Law.

The legal maxim "*de minimis non curat lex*" (sometimes rendered, "the law does not concern itself with trifles") insulates from liability those who cause insignificant violations of the rights of others. In the context of copyright law, the concept of *de minimis* has significance in three respects, which, though related, should be considered separately.

First, *de minimis* in the copyright context can mean what it means in most legal contexts: a technical violation of a right so trivial that the law will not impose legal consequences. Understandably, fact patterns are rarely litigated illustrating this use of the phrase, for, as Judge Leval has observed, such circumstances would usually involve "questions that never need to be answered." He offers the example of a New Yorker cartoon put up on a refrigerator.[5] In *Knickerbocker Toy Co. v. Azrak-Hamway International, Inc.,* 668 F.2d 699, 703 (2d Cir. 1982), we relied on the *de minimis* doctrine to reject a toy manufacturer's claim based on a photograph of its product in an office copy of a display card of a competitor's product where the display card was never used.

Second, *de minimis* can mean that copying has occurred to such a trivial extent as to fall below the quantitative threshold of substantial similarity, which is always a required element of actionable copying. In applying the maxim for this purpose, care must be taken to recognize that the concept of "substantial similarity" itself has unfortunately been used to mean two different things. On the one hand, it has been used as the threshold to determine the degree of similarity that suffices, once access has been shown, as indirect proof of copying; on the other hand, "substantial similarity" is more properly used, after the fact of copying has been established, as the threshold for determining that the degree of similarity suffices to demonstrate actionable infringement. Professor Latman helpfully suggested that when "substantial similarity" is used to mean the threshold for copying as a factual matter, the better term is "probative similarity," and that "substantial similarity" should mean only the threshold for actionable copying. See Alan Latman, *"Probative Similarity" as Proof of Copying: Toward Dispelling Some Myths in Copyright Infringement,* 90 Colum. L. Rev. 1187, 1204 (1990). The Nimmer treatise endorses and has implemented the Latman taxonomy, as has this Court.

In the pending case, there is no dispute about copying as a factual matter: the "Church Picnic" poster itself, not some poster that was similar in some respects to it, was displayed on the set of defendants' television program. What defendants dispute when they assert that their use of the poster was *de minimis* is whether the admitted copying occurred to an extent sufficient to constitute actionable copying, i.e., infringement. That requires "substantial similarity" in the sense of actionable copying, and it is that sense of the phrase to which the concept of *de minimis* is relevant.

At first glance, it might seem odd to pursue an inquiry as to "substantial similarity" even after copying as a factual matter has been established. However, the superficial anomaly reflects only a lack of appreciation of the difference between factual copying and actionable copying. The former (probative similarity) requires only the fact that the infringing work copies something from the copyrighted work; the latter (substantial similarity) requires that the copying is quantitatively and qualitatively sufficient to support the legal conclusion that infringement (actionable copying) has occurred. The qualitative component concerns the copying of expression, rather than ideas, a distinction that often turns on the level of abstraction at which the works are compared. The quantitative component generally concerns the amount of the copyrighted work that is copied, a consideration that is especially pertinent to exact copying.[6] In cases involving visual works, like the pending one, the quantitative component of substantial similarity also concerns the

---

5. Presumably, Judge Leval has in mind the posting of a photocopy of the cartoon; photocopying the cartoon, if not insulated by the doctrine *of de minimis,* or subject to some recognized defense, might violate the copyright proprietor's right to reproduce a copy of the work, *see* 17 U.S.C. § 106(1), though if the original page of the magazine was posted, the work would not have been "displayed … publicly," *id.* § 106(5).

6. The Nimmer treatise helpfully refers to exact copying of a portion of a work as "fragmented literal similarity," *see Nimmer,* § 13.03[A][2], in contrast to "comprehensive nonliteral similarity," which refers to an alleged copy that is qualitatively but not exactly similar to a copyrighted work, id. § 13.03[A][1]. We have endorsed that taxonomy. *See Twin Peaks Productions, Inc. v. Publications International, Ltd.,* 996 F.2d 1366, 1372 n.1 (2d Cir. 1993); *Arica Institute, Inc. v. Palmer,* 970 F.2d 1067, 1073 (2d Cir. 1992).

observability of the copied work—the length of time the copied work is observable in the allegedly infringing work and such factors as focus, lighting, camera angles, and prominence. Thus, as in this case, a copyrighted work might be copied as a factual matter, yet a serious dispute might remain as to whether the copying that occurred was actionable. Since "substantial similarity," properly understood, includes a quantitative component, it becomes apparent why the concept of *de minimis* is relevant to a defendant's contention that an indisputably copied work has not been infringed.

Third, *de minimis* might be considered relevant to the defense of fair use. One of the statutory factors to be assessed in making the fair use determination is "the amount and substantiality of the portion used in relation to the copyrighted work as a whole." A defendant might contend, as the District Court concluded in this case, that the portion used was minimal and the use was so brief and indistinct as to tip the third fair use factor decisively against the plaintiff.[7]

Though the concept of *de minimis* is useful in insulating trivial types of copying from liability (the photocopied cartoon on the refrigerator) and in marking the quantitative threshold for actionable copying, the concept is an inappropriate one to be enlisted in fair use analysis. The third fair use factor concerns a quantitative continuum. Like all the fair use factors, it has no precise threshold below which the factor is accorded decisive significance. If the amount copied is very slight in relation to the work as a whole, the third factor might strongly favor the alleged infringer, but that will not always be the case. More important, the fair use defense involves a careful examination of many factors, often confronting courts with a perplexing task. If the allegedly infringing work makes such a quantitatively insubstantial use of the copyrighted work as to fall below the threshold required for actionable copying, it makes more sense to reject the claim on that basis and find no infringement, rather than undertake an elaborate fair use analysis in order to uphold a defense.

B. The *de minimis* Concept Applied to Defendants' Copying.

Defendants contend that the nine instances in their television program in which portions of the poster were visible, individually and in the aggregate, were *de minimis*, in the sense that the quantity of copying (or at least the quantity of observable copying) was below the threshold of actionable copying. The parties appear to agree on the durational aspects of the copying. The segments of the program in which the poster was visible to any degree lasted between 1.86 and 4.16 seconds. The aggregate duration of all nine segments was 26.75 seconds....

A helpful analogy in determining whether the purpose and duration of the segments should be regarded as de minimis is the regulation issued by the Librarian of Congress providing for royalties to be paid by public broadcasting entities for the use of published pictorial and visual works. The Librarian appoints the Register of Copyrights, who serves as the director of the Copyright Office. The Librarian's regulation distinguishes between a "featured" and a "background" display, setting a higher royalty rate for the former. Obviously the Librarian has concluded that use of a copyrighted visual work even as "background" in a television program normally requires payment of a li-

---

7. Whether a use of a copyrighted work that surpasses the de minimis threshold of "substantial similarity" for purposes of actionable copying can nevertheless be de minimis for purposes of the third fair use factor is an inquiry in the class of angelic terpsichore on heads of pins. Perhaps that is why the Supreme Court has quoted approvingly Professor Latman's reference to "the partial marriage between the doctrine of fair use and the legal maxim de minimis non curat lex." *See Sony Corp. of America v. Universal Studios, Inc.,* 464 U.S. 417, 451 n.34, 78 L. Ed. 2d 574, 104 S. Ct. 774 (1984).

cense fee. Moreover, the Librarian has defined a "featured" display as "a full-screen or substantially full screen display for more than three seconds," and a "background" display as "any display less than full-screen or substantially full-screen, or full-screen for three seconds or less," If defendants' program were to be shown on public television, plaintiff would appear to be entitled to a "background" license fee for a "less than full-screen" display.

From the standpoint of a quantitative assessment of the segments, the principal four-to-five-second segment in which almost all of the poster is clearly visible, albeit in less than perfect focus, reenforced by the briefer segments in which smaller portions are visible, all totaling 26 to 27 seconds, are not *de minimis* copying.

Defendants further contend that the segments showing any portion of the poster are *de minimis* from the standpoint of qualitative sufficiency and therefore not actionable copying because no protectable aspects of plaintiff's expression are discernible. In defendants' view, the television viewer sees no more than "some vague stylized [sic] painting that includes black people," and can discern none of Ringgold's particular expression of her subjects. That is about like saying that a videotape of the Mona Lisa shows only a painting of a woman with a wry smile. Indeed, it seems disingenuous for the defendant HBO, whose production staff evidently thought that the poster was well suited as a set decoration for the African-American church scene of a ROC episode, now to contend that no visually significant aspect of the poster is discernible. In some circumstances, a visual work, though selected by production staff for thematic relevance, or at least for its decorative value, might ultimately be filmed at such a distance and so out of focus that a typical program viewer would not discern any decorative effect that the work of art contributes to the set. But that is not this case. The painting component of the poster is recognizable as a painting, and with sufficient observable detail for the "average lay observer," to discern African-Americans in Ringgold's colorful, virtually two-dimensional style. The *de minimis* threshold for actionable copying of protected expression has been crossed.

II. Fair Use

The District Court upheld the defendants' fair use defense after considering the four non-exclusive factors identified in 17 U.S.C. § 107. Concerning the first factor—purpose and character of the use—the Court acknowledged that defendants' use was commercial, but thought this circumstance was "undercut" by the fact that the defendants did not use the poster to encourage viewers to watch the ROC episode and did not try to "exploit" Ringgold's work. The Court acknowledged that the second factor—nature of the copyrighted work—favored Ringgold in view of the imaginative nature of her artwork.

The Court considered the third factor—amount and substantiality of the portion used in relation to the entire work—to favor the defendants because the segments of the program in which the poster is visible are brief, in some only a portion is seen, and in those showing nearly all the poster, it is not in exact focus.

The Court considered the fourth factor—effect of the use upon the potential market for the work—also to favor the defendants. Noting that the television episode cannot be considered a substitute for the poster, Judge Martin predicted "little likelihood" of any adverse impact on poster sales. In addition, he observed that Ringgold did not claim that her ability to license the poster "has been negatively impacted by the defendants' use in the four years" since the episode was aired. Concluding that defendants' use "had little or no effect on Ringgold's potential market for her work," he granted summary judgment in their favor, sustaining their fair use defense.

In reviewing the grant of summary judgment, we note preliminarily that the District Court gave no explicit consideration to whether the defendants' use was within any of the categories that the preamble to section 107 identifies as illustrative of a fair use, or even whether it was similar to such categories. Though the listed categories—criticism, comment, news reporting, teaching, scholarship, and research,—have an "'illustrative and not limitative'" function, and the four factors should be considered even if a challenged use is not within any of these categories, the illustrative nature of the categories should not be ignored. As the Supreme Court's recent and significant fair use opinion in *Campbell* [*v. Acuff-Rose Music, Inc.,* 510 U.S. 569 (1994),] observes, "The enquiry [concerning the first fair use factor] may be guided by the examples given in the preamble to § 107, looking to whether the use is for criticism, or comment, or news reporting, and the like...."

First factor.

Considering the first fair use factor with the preamble illustrations as a "guide[ ]," we observe that the defendants' use of Ringgold's work to decorate the set for their television episode is not remotely similar to any of the listed categories. In no sense is the defendants' use "'transformative.'" In *Campbell*, Justice Souter explained a "transformative" use that would tip the first factor toward a defendant:

> The central purpose of this investigation is to see, in Justice Story's words, whether the new work merely "supersedes the objects" of the original creation, or instead adds something new, with a further purpose or different character, altering the first with new expression, meaning, or message....

The defendants have used Ringgold's work for precisely a central purpose for which it was created—to be decorative. Even if the thematic significance of the poster and its relevance to the ROC episode are not discernible, the decorative effect is plainly evident. Indeed, the poster is the only decorative artwork visible in the church hall scene. Nothing that the defendants have done with the poster "supplants" the original or "adds something new." The defendants have used the poster to decorate their set to make it more attractive to television viewers precisely as a poster purchaser would use it to decorate a home.

In considering whether a visual work has been "supplanted" by its use in a movie or a television program, care must be taken not to draw too close an analogy to copying of written works. When all or a substantial portion of text that contains protectable expression is included in another work, solely to convey the original text to the reader without adding any comment or criticism, the second work may be said to have supplanted the original because a reader of the second work has little reason to buy a copy of the original. Although some books and other writings are profitably reread, their basic market is the one-time reader. By contrast, visual works are created, and sold or licensed, usually for repetitive viewing. Thus, the fact that the episode of ROC does not supplant the need or desire of a television viewer to see and appreciate the poster (or the original) again and again does not mean that the defendants' use is of a "purpose and character" that favors fair use. Indeed, unauthorized displays of a visual work might often increase viewers' desire to see the work again. Nevertheless, where, as here, the purpose of the challenged use is, at a minimum, the same decorative purpose for which the poster is sold, the defendants' use has indeed "superseded the objects" of the original, and does not favor fair use. Of course, no one would buy a videotape of the ROC episode as a substitute for the poster, but the challenged use need not supplant the original itself, only, as Justice Story said, the "objects" of the original.

It is not difficult to imagine a television program that uses a copyrighted visual work for a purpose that heavily favors fair use. If a TV news program produced a feature on

Faith Ringgold and included camera shots of her story quilts, the case for a fair use defense would be extremely strong.[8] The same would be true of a news feature on the High Museum that included a shot of "Church Picnic." However, it must be recognized that visual works are created, in significant part, for their decorative value, and, just as members of the public expect to pay to obtain a painting or a poster to decorate their homes, producers of plays, films, and television programs should generally expect to pay a license fee when they conclude that a particular work of copyrighted art is an appropriate component of the decoration of a set.

The District Court's consideration of the first fair use factor was legally flawed in its failure to assess the decorative purpose for which defendants used the plaintiff's work. Instead, the Court tipped the first factor against the plaintiff because the presence of the poster was "incidental" to the scene and the defendants did not use the poster to encourage viewers to watch the ROC episode. The first point could be said of virtually all set decorations, thereby expanding fair use to permit wholesale appropriation of copyrighted art for movies and television. The second point uses a test that makes it far too easy for a defendant to invoke the fair use defense.

Second factor.

The District Court accepted the plaintiff's contention that the second fair use factor weighs in her favor because of the creative nature of her work.

Third factor.

Though we have earlier noted that the *de minimis* concept is inappropriate for a fair use analysis, since a copying that is *de minimis* incurs no liability, without the need for an elaborate fair use inquiry, the third fair use factor obliges a court to consider the amount and substantiality of the portion used, whenever that portion crosses the *de minimis* threshold for actionable copying. The District Court properly considered the brevity of the intervals in which the poster was observable and the fact that in some segments only a portion of the poster and the nearly full view was not in precise focus. Our own viewing of the episode would incline us to weight the third factor less strongly toward the defendants than did Judge Martin, but we are not the fact-finders, and the fact-finding pertinent to each fair use factor, under proper legal standards, is for the District Court, although the ultimate conclusion is a mixed question of law and fact.

Even if the third factor favors the defendants, courts considering the fair use defense in the context of visual works copied or displayed in other visual works must be careful not to permit this factor too easily to tip the aggregate fair use assessment in favor of those whom the other three factors do not favor. Otherwise, a defendant who uses a creative work in a way that does not serve any of the purposes for which the fair use defense is normally invoked and that impairs the market for licensing the work will escape liability simply by claiming only a small infringement.

Fourth factor.

The fourth fair use factor is "the effect of the use upon the potential market for or value of the copyrighted work." "It requires courts to consider not only the extent of mar-

---

8. We hesitate to say "conclusive" because even existing technological advances, much less those in the future, create extraordinary possibilities. For example, if the news program included a direct shot of an entire story quilt (whether original or poster reproduction), well lit and in clear focus, a viewer so inclined could tape the newscast at home, scan the tape, and with digital photographic technology, produce a full size copy of the original, thereby securing an attractive "poster"-like wall-hanging without paying the $20 poster fee. A news program that recommended this technique would be a weak candidate for fair use.

ket harm caused by the alleged infringer, but also 'whether unrestricted and widespread conduct of the sort engaged in by the defendant ... would result in substantially adverse impact on the potential market for the original.'" Ringgold contends that there is a potential market for licensing her story quilts, and stated in an affidavit that in 1995 she earned $31,500 from licensing her various artworks and that she is often asked to license her work for films and television. Specifically, she avers that in 1992 she was asked to license use of the "Church Picnic" poster by the producers of another TV sitcom and declined because of an inadequate price and inadequate artist's credit.

We have recognized the danger of circularity in considering whether the loss of potential licensing revenue should weight the fourth factor in favor of a plaintiff. Since the issue is whether the copying should be compensable, the failure to receive licensing revenue cannot be determinative in the plaintiff's favor. We have endeavored to avoid the vice of circularity by considering "only traditional, reasonable, or likely to be developed markets" when considering a challenged use upon a potential market. Ringgold's affidavit clearly raises a triable issue of fact concerning a market for licensing her work as set decoration. She is not alleging simply loss of the revenue she would have earned from a compensated copying; she is alleging an "exploitation of the copyrighted material without paying the customary price."[9]

The District Court's assessment of the fourth factor in favor of the defendants was legally flawed. The Court relied primarily on the fact that the ROC episode had little likelihood of adversely affecting poster sales and that Ringgold had not claimed that her ability to license the poster had been "negatively impacted." The first consideration deserves little weight against a plaintiff alleging appropriation without payment of a customary licensing fee. The second consideration confuses lack of one item of specific damages with lack of adverse impact on a potential market. Ringgold is not required to show a decline in the number of licensing requests for the "Church Picnic" poster since the ROC episode was aired. The fourth factor will favor her if she can show a "traditional, reasonable, or likely to be developed" market for licensing her work as set decoration. Certainly "unrestricted and widespread conduct of the sort engaged in by the defendants ... would result in substantially adverse impact on the potential market for [licensing of] the original." Particularly in view of what Ringgold has averred and is prepared to prove, the record on the fourth fair use factor is inadequate to permit summary judgment for the defendants.

Conclusion

For all of these reasons, plaintiff's copyright infringement claim must be returned to the District Court to afford an opportunity for further development of the record and a sensitive aggregate assessment by the fact-finder of the fair use factors in light of the applicable legal principles....

The judgment of the District Court is reversed, and the case is remanded.

---

9. The amicus curiae brief for the Artists Rights Society, Inc. and the Picasso Administration strongly indicates evidence of licensing of artistic works for film and television set decoration, evidence that plaintiff is entitled to present at trial.

Leigh v. Warner Bros., Inc.
212 F.3d 1210 (11th Cir. 2000)

This appeal concerns the scope of a photographer's copyright and trademark rights in his work, the role of the court in determining whether images are "substantially similar" for purposes of copyright, and the power of the court to rule on dispositive motions without first allowing broad discovery. Jack Leigh took the now-famous photograph of the Bird Girl statue in Savannah's Bonaventure Cemetery that appears on the cover of the best-selling novel *Midnight in the Garden of Good and Evil*. Warner Brothers made a film version of the novel and used images of the Bird Girl both in promotional materials and in the movie itself. Leigh sued Warner Brothers, asserting that it infringed his copyright and trademark rights in the Bird Girl photograph. The district court granted summary judgment for Warner Brothers on all claims, except one that the parties now have settled, and Leigh appeals.

The district court correctly ascertained the elements of Leigh's photograph protected by copyright and determined that the Warner Brothers film sequences are not substantially similar to those protected elements. Copyright infringement is generally a question of fact for the jury to decide, however, and the court erred in holding as a matter of law that no reasonable jury could find that the Warner Brothers promotional single-frame images were substantially similar to the aspects of Leigh's work protected by copyright....

In 1993, Random House commissioned Jack Leigh to take a photograph for the cover of *Midnight in the Garden of Good and Evil* ("*Midnight*"), a novel by John Berendt. After reading a manuscript of the novel, Leigh explored appropriate settings in Savannah and ultimately selected a photograph of a sculpture in the Bonaventure Cemetery known as the Bird Girl. Sylvia Shaw Judson had sculpted the Bird Girl in 1938, and she produced three copies of the statue. The Trosdal family had purchased one of the statues and placed it in their plot at Bonaventure Cemetery. The novel does not mention the Bird Girl statue. Leigh granted Random House permission to use the photo, but retained ownership and registered his claim of copyright.

In 1997, Warner Brothers produced a movie based on *Midnight* and decided to use the Bird Girl statue on promotional materials and at the beginning and end of the movie. Because the Trosdals had removed the statue from their cemetery plot after the book's publication, Warner Brothers made a replica of the Bird Girl with the permission of Sylvia Shaw Judson's heir. The company then took photographs and film footage of the replica in a new location in Bonaventure Cemetery. Those images are the subject of this lawsuit.

Three segments of film footage depict the Bird Girl statue. One is a promotional clip, and the others appear at the beginning and end of the Warner Brothers movie. Six still images feature the Bird Girl: a promotional photograph and nearly identical picture on the "goodandevil" web site, a movie poster, a newspaper advertisement, the cover for the movie's soundtrack, and an internet icon. Leigh alleges that these images infringed his copyright and trademark rights in his Bird Girl photograph. The district court granted Warner Brothers' motion to stay all discovery, and later granted summary judgment for Warner Brothers on all claims except a copyright claim pertaining to the internet icon. The parties subsequently settled all claims pertaining to that Internet icon.

We review the district court's grant of summary judgment *de novo*, construing all evidence in the light most favorable to the non-moving party. Summary judgment is only proper when there are no genuine issues of material fact. We review the court's decision to rule on the summary judgment motion without allowing the plaintiff to complete desired discovery for abuse of discretion.

To establish a claim of copyright infringement, a plaintiff must prove, first, that he owns a valid copyright in a work and, second, that the defendant copied original elements of that work. The plaintiff can prove copying either directly or indirectly, by establishing that the defendant had access, and produced something "substantially similar," to the copyrighted work. Substantial similarity, in this sense, "exists where an average lay observer would recognize the alleged copy as having been appropriated from the copyrighted work."

"Substantial similarity" also is important in a second, more focused way. No matter how the copying is proved, the plaintiff also must establish specifically that the allegedly infringing work is substantially similar to the plaintiff's work *with regard to its protected elements.* Even in the rare case of a plaintiff with direct evidence that a defendant attempted to appropriate his original expression, there is no infringement unless the defendant succeeded to a meaningful degree.

For the purposes of its motion for summary judgment and this appeal, Warner Brothers does not contest Leigh's ownership of a valid copyright in the Bird Girl photograph. Leigh, on the other hand, takes issue both with the district court's view of the scope of his copyright and with the court's analysis of the similarities between the Bird Girl images.

Leigh's copyright does not cover the appearance of the statue itself or of Bonaventure Cemetery, for Leigh has no rights in the statue or its setting. Nor does the copyright protect the association of the statue with the *Midnight* story. Leigh may have been the first to think of the statue as evocative of the novel's mood and as an appropriate symbol of the book's themes, but copyright law protects only original expression, not ideas.

Thus, the district court correctly identified the elements of artistic craft protected by Leigh's copyright as the selection of lighting, shading, timing, angle, and film. Leigh suggests that the court also should have considered the overall combination of these protected elements as well as the mood they convey. The court determined that the "eerie," "spiritual" mood was *scenes faire,* expression commonly associated with the subject matter (cemeteries) and thus non-original and unprotectable. Leigh contests the notion that cemeteries are typically portrayed in an eerie, spiritual manner, but there is no need to determine whether *scenes faire* applies in this case.

Analyzing relatively amorphous characteristics of the picture as a whole (such as the "mood" or "combination of elements") creates a danger of unwittingly extending copyright protection to unoriginal aspects of the work. This danger is especially acute in a case such as this, in which the unprotected elements of the plaintiff's work—the haunting pose and expression of the Bird Girl and the cemetery setting—are so significant.

Although some cases have evaluated the "mood" of a work independently, in this case it is safest to focus on the more concrete elements of the photographer's craft. Even as Leigh describes it, the mood is not so much an independent aspect of his photograph protected by copyright, as the effect created by the lighting, shading, timing, angle, and film. The same holds true for the overall combination of elements in the photograph. As long as the analysis is not overly detached and technical, it can adequately address both the effect of the protected, original elements of Leigh's photograph on the viewer and the contribution of those elements to the work as a whole.

In its order granting summary judgment, the court methodically and accurately details a number of differences in the compositional elements between Leigh's photograph and the Warner Brothers images. This circuit has noted, however, that lists of similarities between works are inherently subjective and unreliable, and the same can be true of lists of distinguishing characteristics.

The court was correct to hold as a matter of law that the film sequences featuring the Bird Girl statue are not substantially similar to the protected elements of Leigh's photograph. In one sequence, the cemetery is shrouded in fog, revealing only the Bird Girl and a Celtic cross, a decoration absent from Leigh's photograph. The camera frame also crops the head of the Bird Girl statue. A second sequence is shot at least partly in color and in broad daylight. The statue's plinth is never shown, and as the camera pans up it shows only the upper portions of the statue on the left side of the screen. In the final sequence, the camera rotates around the statue, beginning with a side shot, and captures only the head and shoulders before panning back to show the Bird Girl's torso. Again, the statue is on the left side of the screen and the sequence is shot in daylight. The film sequences were not shot in the same section of the Bonaventure Cemetery as Leigh's photograph, so the surrounding gravestones and greenery are different. These film sequences have nothing substantial in common with Leigh's photograph except the statue itself.

The same cannot be said for Warner Brothers' photographic images. There are, undeniably, significant differences between the pictures. The statue is smaller and more distant in most of the Warner Brothers pictures than in Leigh's photograph, and as a result the vegetation and headstones in the foreground are more prominent. The Bird Girl is approximately the same size only on the soundtrack cover. Although both the Leigh photograph and the soundtrack cover have diffuse light that "glows" about the statue, the lighting contrast is more extreme in most of the Warner Brothers pictures, with beams of light piercing the tree canopy like spotlights. The shafts of light and surrounding shadows obscure details of the statue and the cemetery setting. Finally, Warner Brothers has added elements to some of its images that are absent from Leigh's photo: some have a green or orange tint; some prominently feature a Celtic cross and tree; and the movie poster includes pictures of the cast along its left side.

Although it may be easy to identify differences between the Warner Brothers still shots and Leigh's photograph, however, the Warner Brothers images also have much in common with the elements protected by Leigh's copyright. All of the photographs are taken from a low position, angled up slightly at the Bird Girl so that the contents of the bowls in her hands remain hidden. Hanging Spanish moss borders the tops of all the photographs except the soundtrack cover. The statue is close to centered in all of the pictures except one newspaper advertisement for the movie, which places the Bird Girl in the left third of the frame. Light shines down and envelopes the statue in all of the images, leaving the surrounding cemetery in relative darkness. All of the photographs are monochromatic.

These expressive elements all make the pictures more effective. The Spanish moss provides a top border to the images. The location of the statue and the lighting in the pictures together draw the viewer's attention. The lighting also lends a spiritual air to the Bird Girl. Finally, by keeping the contents of the Bird Girl's bowls hidden, the angle contributes to the mystery and symbolic meaning of the images.

A jury ultimately may conclude that the similarities between the protected elements of the Leigh photograph and the Warner Brothers still shots are not "substantial." The similarities are significant enough, however, to preclude summary judgment. "Substantial similarity" is a question of fact, and summary judgment is only appropriate if no reasonable jury could differ in weighing the evidence....

We AFFIRM the grant of summary judgment for the Defendant on Leigh's trademark claims and the copyright claim as it relates to the film sequences. We REVERSE the grant of summary judgment for the Defendant on Leigh's copyright claim as it relates to Warner

Brothers' single-frame images, and we REMAND for proceedings consistent with this decision.

Notes and Questions

a. One of the most significant factors of fair use is the effect unauthorized use has on the marketplace for the plaintiff's work. The more the use supplants or replaces the existing or potential market for plaintiff's work, the more likely the court is to find the defendant's activities objectionable. A fine example of this is *Campbell v. Acuff-Rose Music, Inc.,* 510 U.S. 569 (1994), where 2 Live Crew not only generated significant mechanical royalties for Roy Orbison, but put those royalties in trust so that Orbison could have dropped his objection and earned the market rate for his songs. By putting the funds in trust, the band moved itself from the category of marketplace infringers to that of First Amendment champions, taking the ethical high ground in the dispute. Applying this to *Ringgold*, to what extent did the preexisting system of compensating the copyright holders of television decorations weigh on the court in determining that the use of the poster was not a fair use based on the nature of the broadcast?

b. Copyrighted works often appear in many public arenas that we take for granted. Does a motion picture producer need a license if a character wears a tee-shirt with copyrighted artwork on the front or back? Does a television entertainment program have the same obligation? Does a network news program have the same obligation? If not, where under copyright law can one defend different results based on the nature of the broadcast?

c. The use of another's copyright can interfere with that work's economic value in two very different ways. As recognized by § 107, the use can replace the original work in the marketplace — stealing the economic opportunity. The second form of economic interference occurs when the defendant's work destroys the perceived value of the plaintiff's work. A vicious but accurate review of a book may quote the plaintiff's work extensively for the purpose of criticizing every aspect of it. The result may be to reduce sales substantially, but this economic destruction does not supplant the original work in the marketplace and, therefore, should not be considered when weighing the fair use factors. In fact, the more the criticism impacts the market, the more likely the criticism is a fair use, as provided by the Section 107 preamble and the history of fair use litigation.

d. Architectural works pose unique problems. Architectural designs for building designs enjoy limited copyright protection under § 106 but limited under § 120. Under the limitation, "[t]he copyright in an architectural work that has been constructed does not include the right to prevent the making, distributing, or public display of pictures, paintings, photographs, or other pictorial representations of the work...." Despite the limitation, building owners and copyright holders sometimes try to extend their property interests into the copyright of the building or the building's silhouette as a trademark for goods or services. See *Leicester v. Warner Bros.,* 232 F.3d 1212 (9th Cir. 2000).

e. Although not an absolute barrier to copyright infringement, authors of factual works have a much narrower interest in their writings than those of fictional writers. Filmmakers, television producers, musicians, and others may freely research the ideas published by other authors. One interesting conflict arises when creative theories are published as fact: do these speculative works receive the broader protection of fiction or the narrower protection of fact? See *Nash v. CBS, Inc.,* 899 F.2d 1537 (7th Cir. 1990).

f. Filmmakers are often challenged to "clear" or obtain copyright releases for all objects that might be filmed in the background of a scene. Such copyrighted materials include not only artwork on walls, but also more useful objects, such as tee-shirts, product labels, and objects with copyrighted images or graphics incorporated into their design. In *Gottlieb Dev. LLC v. Paramount Pictures Corp.*, 590 F. Supp. 2d 625 (S.D.N.Y. 2008), the court found brief glimpses of copyrighted designs in a pinball machine to be *de minimis* as a matter of law.

g. Clearance continues to be a challenge for content producers, particularly those making documentary projects. It is also a significant issue for those involved in online video production and collaborative authorship. The Center for Social Media, a project of American University's School of Communication (http://www.centerforsocialmedia.org), has provided a wealth of best practices materials to assist both lawyers and creative artists.

h. Other decisions challenge the notion that every use of an image must be licensed outside of a non-documentary context, though the risks of litigation are present even if the use is *de minimis* or fair use. See *Sofa Entm't, Inc. v. Dodger Prods.*, 709 F.3d 1273 (9th Cir. 2013), regarding a short television clip from the Ed Sullivan show in a theatrical production and *Seltzer v. Green Day, Inc.*, F.3d 1170 (9th Cir. 2013), regarding the use of an image on a music concert video screen.

Problem III-C

In preparing the St. James Corporation industrial and computer program, Bryce planned to do a great deal of filming of the exterior and interior of the St. James corporate headquarters. The St. James headquarters was designed and constructed in 1995; a commissioned statue stands in the front of the building; and a number of famous modern and classical paintings adorn the halls.

Bryce needs information on the type of location permission required. While St. James intends to use the industrial video and computer simulation exclusively for its own employees, a provision of the production agreement states that Bryce has "obtained all necessary copyright and other clearances to complete the work." St. James has not granted any copyright permission to Bryce, nor does it claim copyright in any of the artwork or sculptures. Advise Bryce on how to proceed. If additional permission is needed to film some or all of the art, identify from whom such permission should be obtained and what should be included in the written release.

D. Scope of Contractually Acquired Rights

Boosey & Hawkes Music Publrs., Ltd. v. Walt Disney Co.
145 F.3d 481 (2d Cir. 1998)

Boosey & Hawkes Music Publishers Ltd., an English corporation and the assignee of Igor Stravinsky's copyrights for "The Rite of Spring," brought this action alleging that the Walt Disney Company's foreign distribution in video cassette and laser disc format ("video format") of the film "Fantasia," featuring Stravinsky's work, infringed Boosey's rights. In 1939 Stravinsky licensed Disney's distribution of The Rite of Spring in the motion picture. Boosey, which acquired Stravinsky's copyright in 1947, contends that the license does not authorize distribution in video format....

We hold that summary judgment was properly granted to Disney with respect to Boosey's Lanham Act claims, but that material issues of fact barred the other grants of summary judgment.... Accordingly, we remand all but the Lanham Act claim for trial.

During 1938, Disney sought Stravinsky's authorization to use The Rite of Spring (sometimes referred to as the "work" or the "composition") throughout the world in a motion picture. Because under United States law the work was in the public domain, Disney needed no authorization to record or distribute it in this country, but permission was required for distribution in countries where Stravinsky enjoyed copyright protection. In January 1939 the parties executed an agreement (the "1939 Agreement") giving Disney rights to use the work in a motion picture in consideration of a fee to Stravinsky of $6000.

The 1939 Agreement provided that

> In consideration of the sum of Six Thousand ($6,000.) Dollars, receipt of which is hereby acknowledged, [Stravinsky] does hereby give and grant unto Walt Disney Enterprises, a California corporation ... the nonexclusive, irrevocable right, license, privilege and authority to record in any manner, medium or form, and to license the performance of, the musical composition herein below set out.

Under "type of use" in Paragraph 3, the Agreement specified that

> The music of said musical composition may be used in one motion picture throughout the length thereof or through such portion or portions thereof as the Purchaser shall desire. The said music may be used in whole or in part and may be adapted, changed, added to or subtracted from, all as shall appear desirable to the Purchaser in its uncontrolled discretion.... The title "Rites of Spring" or "Le Sacre de Printemps", or any other title, may be used as the title of said motion picture and the name of [Stravinsky] may be announced in or in connection with said motion picture.

The Agreement went on to specify in paragraph 4 that Disney's license to the work "is limited to the use of the musical composition in synchronism or timed-relation with the motion picture."

Paragraph Five of the Agreement provided that

> The right to record the musical composition as covered by this agreement is conditioned upon the performance of the musical work in theatres having valid licenses from the American Society of Composers, Authors and Publishers, or any other performing rights society having jurisdiction in the territory in which the said musical composition is performed.

We refer to this clause, which is of importance to the litigation, as "the ASCAP Condition."

Finally, paragraph 7 of the Agreement provided that "the licensor reserves to himself all rights and uses in and to the said musical composition not herein specifically granted" (the "reservation clause").

Disney released Fantasia, starring Mickey Mouse, in 1940. The film contains no dialogue. It matches a pantomime of animated beasts and fantastic creatures to passages of great classical music, creating what critics celebrated as a "partnership between fine music and animated film." The soundtrack uses compositions of Bach, Beethoven, Dukas, Schubert, Tchaikovsky, and Stravinsky, all performed by the Philadelphia Orchestra under the direction of Leopold Stokowski. As it appears in the film soundtrack, The Rite of Spring was shortened from its original 34 minutes to about 22.5; sections of the score were cut, while other sections were reordered. For more than five decades Disney exhibited The Rite of Spring in Fantasia under the 1939 license. The film has been re-released for theatrical distribution at least seven times since 1940, and although Fantasia has never appeared on television in its entirety, excerpts including portions of The Rite of Spring have been televised occasionally over the years. Neither Stravinsky nor Boosey has ever previously objected to any of the distributions.

In 1991 Disney first released Fantasia in video format. The video has been sold in foreign countries, as well as in the United States. To date, the Fantasia video release has generated more than $360 million in gross revenue for Disney.

Boosey brought this action in February 1993. The complaint sought (1) a declaration that the 1939 Agreement did not include a grant of rights to Disney to use the Stravinsky work in video format; (2) damages for copyright infringement in at least 18 foreign countries; (3) damages under the Lanham Act for false designation of origin and misrepresentation by reason of Disney's alteration of Stravinsky's work;(4) damages for breach of contract, alleging that the video format release breached the 1939 Agreement; and (5) damages for unjust enrichment.

On cross-motions for summary judgment the district court made the rulings described above. In determining that the license did not cover the distribution of a video format, the district court found that while the broad language of the license gave Disney "the right to record [the work] on video tape and laser disc," the ASCAP Condition "prevents Disney from distributing video tapes or laser discs directly to consumers." The court therefore concluded that Disney's video format sales exceeded the scope of the license....

We confront four questions on appeal. Disney challenges the summary judgment which declared that the 1939 Agreement does not authorize video distribution of The Rite of Spring. Boosey appeals three other rulings: the dismissal for *forum non conveniens*, and the grants of summary judgment on the claims for damages for violation of the Lanham Act and breach of contract.

A. Declaratory Judgment on the Scope of the License.

Boosey's request for declaratory judgment raises two issues of contract interpretation: whether the general grant of permission under the 1939 Agreement licensed Disney to use The Rite of Spring in the video format version of Fantasia (on which the district court found in Disney's favor); and, if so, whether the ASCAP Condition barred Disney from exploiting the work through video format (on which the district court found for Boosey).

1. Whether the "motion picture" license covers video format.

Boosey contends that the license to use Stravinsky's work in a "motion picture" did not authorize distribution of the motion picture in video format, especially in view of the absence of an express provision for "future technologies" and Stravinsky's reservation of all rights not granted in the Agreement. Disputes about whether licensees may exploit licensed works through new marketing channels made possible by technologies developed after the licensing contract—often called "new-use" problems—have vexed courts since at least the advent of the motion picture. In *Bartsch v. Metro-Goldwyn-Mayer, Inc.*, we held that "licensees may properly pursue any uses which may reasonably be said to fall within the medium as described in the license." 391 F.2d 150, 155 (2d Cir.1968). We held in *Bartsch* that a license of motion picture rights to a play included the right to telecast the motion picture. We observed that "if the words are broad enough to cover the new use, it seems fairer that the burden of framing and negotiating an exception should fall on the grantor," at least when the new medium is not completely unknown at the time of contracting.

The 1939 Agreement conveys the right "to record [the composition] in any manner, medium or form" for use "in [a] motion picture." We believe this language is broad enough to include distribution of the motion picture in video format. At a minimum, *Bartsch* holds that when a license includes a grant of rights that is reasonably read to cover a new use (at least where the new use was foreseeable at the time of contracting), the burden of excluding the right to the new use will rest on the grantor. The license "to record in any manner, medium or form" doubtless extends to videocassette recording and we can see no reason why the grant of "motion picture" reproduction rights should not include the video format, absent any indication in the Agreement to the contrary. If a new-use license hinges on the foreseeability of the new channels of distribution at the time of contracting—a question left open in *Bartsch*—Disney has proffered unrefuted evidence that a nascent market for home viewing of feature films existed by 1939. The *Bartsch* analysis thus compels the conclusion that the license for motion picture rights extends to video format distribution.

We recognize that courts and scholars are not in complete accord on the capacity of a broad license to cover future developed markets resulting from new technologies. The Nimmer treatise describes two principal approaches to the problem. According to the first view, advocated here by Boosey, "a license of rights in a given medium (*e.g.*, 'motion picture rights') includes only such uses as fall within the unambiguous core meaning of the term (*e.g.*, exhibition of motion picture film in motion picture theaters) and exclude any uses that lie within the ambiguous penumbra (*e.g.*, exhibition of motion picture on television)." Under this approach, a license given in 1939 to "motion picture" rights would include only the core uses of "motion picture" as understood in 1939—presumably theatrical distribution—and would not include subsequently developed methods of distribution of a motion picture such as television videocassettes or laser discs. *See* Nimmer, § 10.10[B] at 10–90.

The second position described by Nimmer is "that the licensee may properly pursue any uses that may reasonably be said to fall within the medium as described in the license." Nimmer expresses clear preferences for the latter approach on the ground that it is "less likely to prove unjust." As Judge Friendly noted in *Bartsch*, "So do we."

We acknowledge that a result which deprives the author-licensor of participation in the profits of new unforeseen channels of distribution is not an altogether happy solution. Nonetheless, we think it more fair and sensible than a result that would deprive a contracting party of the rights reasonably found in the terms of the contract it negotiates. This issue is too often, and improperly, framed as one of favoritism as between licensors and licensees. Because licensors are often authors—whose creativity the copyright laws intend to nurture—and are often impecunious, while licensees are often large business organizations, there is sometimes a tendency in copyright scholarship and adjudication to seek solutions that favor licensors over licensees. Thus in *Cohen*[*v. Paramount Pictures Corp.,*] the Ninth Circuit wrote that a "license must be construed in accordance with the purpose underlying federal copyright law," which the court construed as the granting of valuable, enforceable rights to authors and the encouragement of the production of literary works. Asserting that copyright law "is enacted for the benefit of the composer," the court concluded that it would "frustrate the purposes of the [copyright] Act" to construe the license as encompassing video technology, which did not exist when the license was granted.

In our view, new-use analysis should rely on neutral principles of contract interpretation rather than solicitude for either party. Although *Bartsch* speaks of placing the "burden of framing and negotiating an exception … on the grantor," it should not be understood to adopt a default rule in favor of copyright licensees or any default rule whatsoever.[10] What governs under *Bartsch* is the language of the contract. If the contract is more reasonably read to convey one meaning, the party benefited by that reading should be able to rely on it; the party seeking exception or deviation from the meaning reasonably conveyed by the words of the contract should bear the burden of negotiating for language that would express the limitation or deviation. This principle favors neither licensors nor licensees. It follows simply from the words of the contract. The words of Disney's license are more reasonably read to include than to exclude a motion picture distributed in video format. Thus, we conclude that the burden fell on Stravinsky, if he wished to exclude new markets arising from subsequently developed motion picture technology, to insert such language of limitation in the license, rather than on Disney to add language that reiterated what the license already stated.

Other significant jurisprudential and policy considerations confirm our approach to new-use problems. We think that our view is more consistent with the law of contract than the view that would exclude new technologies even when they reasonably fall within the description of what is licensed. Although contract interpretation normally requires inquiry into the intent of the contracting parties, intent is not likely to be helpful when the subject of the inquiry is something the parties were not thinking about. Nor is extrinsic evidence such as past dealings or industry custom likely to illuminate the intent of the parties, because the use in question was, by hypothesis, new, and could not have been the subject of prior negotiations or established practice. Moreover, many years after formation of the contract, it may well be impossible to consult the principals or retrieve documentary evidence to ascertain the parties' intent, if any, with respect to new uses. On the other hand, the parties or assignees of the contract should be entitled to rely on the words of the contract. Especially where, as here, evidence probative of intent is likely to be both scant and unreliable, the burden of justifying a departure from the most reasonable reading of the contract should fall on the party advocating the departure.

We note also that an approach to new-use problems that tilts against licensees gives rise to anti-progressive incentives. Motion picture producers would be reluctant to explore and utilize innovative technologies for the exhibition of movies if the consequence would be that they would lose the right to exhibit pictures containing licensed works....

Neither the plain terms of the 1939 Agreement nor the sparse and contradictory extrinsic evidence require the conclusion that Disney's license is limited to theatrical performance of the composition. Summary judgment is therefore inappropriate. We vacate the summary grant of declaratory judgment in Boosey's favor and remand for a trial....

---

10. We note that commentators and courts have misinterpreted *Bartsch* in just this way. *See, e.g., Film Video Releasing Corp. v. Hastings,* 426 F. Supp. 690, 695 (S.D.N.Y. 1976) (interpreting *Bartsch* to mean that "the words of the grant are to be construed against the grantor"); James W. Dabney, *Licenses and New Technology: Apportioning and Benefits,* C674 ALI-ABA 85, 89, 96 (characterizing Bartsch as a "pro-licensee" decision that articulates a rule of contract construction favoring licensees in new-use cases). We emphasize that Bartsch favors neither party and announces no special rule of contract interpretation for the new-use context. Rather, it instructs courts to rely on the language of the license contract and basic principles of interpretation.

Random House, Inc. v. Rosetta Books LLC
283 F.3d 490 (2d Cir. 2002)

Random House, Inc. appeals from the denial of a preliminary injunction that sought to enjoin appellee Rosetta Books LLC ("Rosetta") from continuing to sell as "ebooks" certain novels whose authors had granted Random House the exclusive right to publish, print, and sell their copyrighted works "in book form." The denial of a preliminary injunction is generally reviewed for abuse of discretion.

A party seeking a preliminary injunction in this Circuit must show: (1) irreparable harm in the absence of the injunction and (2) either (a) a likelihood of success on the merits or (b) sufficiently serious questions going to the merits to make them a fair ground for litigation and a balance of hardships tipping decidedly in the movant's favor. Because, however, an exclusive licensee can, as here, sue for copyright infringement, and because a prima facie case of copyright infringement gives rise to a presumption of irreparable harm, the requirement of proof of irreparable harm can in such a case effectively be met by proof of a likelihood of success on the merits.

Here, however, the district court did not abuse its discretion in concluding that appellant had not established the likelihood of its success on the merits. To be sure, there is some appeal to appellant's argument that an "ebook"—a digital book that can be read on a computer screen or electronic device,—is simply a "form" of a book, and therefore within the coverage of appellant's licenses. But the law of New York, which determines the scope of Random House's contracts, has arguably adopted a restrictive view of the kinds of "new uses" to which an exclusive license may apply when the contracting parties do not expressly provide for coverage of such future forms. In any case, determining whether the licenses here in issue extend to ebooks depends on fact-finding regarding, inter alia, the "evolving" technical processes and uses of an ebook, and the reasonable expectations of the contracting parties "cognizant of the customs, practices, usages and terminology as generally understood in the ... trade or business" at the time of contracting. Without the benefit of the full record to be developed over the course of the litigation, we cannot say the district court abused its discretion in the preliminary way it resolved these mixed questions of law and fact.

As to the alternative way of satisfying at least the second requirement for a preliminary injunction, i.e., showing sufficiently serious questions going to the merits to make them a fair ground for litigation and a balance of hardships tipping decidedly in the movant's favor, here the balance of hardships tips, if anything, in appellees' favor. For while Random House expresses fears about harm to its goodwill if Rosetta is allowed to proceed with its sale of ebooks, Rosetta, whose entire business is based on the sale of ebooks, raises a reasonable concern that the proposed preliminary injunction will put it out of business or at least eliminate its business as to all authors who have executed similar contracts. As the district court found, such legitimate concerns outweigh any potential hardships to Random House which, if it ultimately prevails on the merits, can recover money damages for any lost sales.

Thus, without expressing any view as to the ultimate merits of the case, the Court concludes that the district court did not abuse its discretion in denying Random House's motion for a preliminary injunction, and consequently the judgment is affirmed.

Notes and Questions

a. The New York courts continue to struggle and refine the interpretation of contracts application to new technologies even as the scope of new media distribution methods continues to expand. In *Popovich v. Sony Music Ent., Inc.*, 508 F.3d 348, 357–58 (6th Cir. 2007), the court analyzed whether Sony owed a contractual duty to include the logo of a music producer on works it released for the artist Meatloaf, including "Bat Out of Hell," on Internet downloads.

Popovich appeals the district court's decision on summary judgment finding that the 1998 Agreement unambiguously did not cover internet downloads. The district court held that the language "manufactured by Sony Music after September 1, 1998" precludes items not "manufactured" by Sony. In the words of the district court, "while Sony 'manufactures' albums, CDs, and cassettes, asserting that Sony 'manufactures' Internet downloads or streaming audio requires a liberal interpretation of 'manufacture.' Such an interpretation is simply too great a stretch for this court to conclude that there is ambiguity in the language."

Popovich contends that the "all forms and configurations" language was intended to cover future music formats such as internet downloads, and the "manufactured by Sony Music after September 1, 1998" language merely provides Sony a grace period to comply with its obligations.

The relevant question for this Court is whether the sentence "all forms and configurations ... manufactured by Sony" includes internet downloads. Neither party has cited to, nor have we been able to find, a case holding that internet downloads may be "manufactured." As the district court noted, had the parties included the words "distributed by," the agreement would have lent itself to the interpretation that internet downloads were meant to be included in the logo obligation. As a result, we do not believe the district court erred in its holding that it is an unreasonable interpretation of the language of the agreement to conclude it covers internet downloads.

Popovich raises the doctrine of "new use" in his appeal. According to Popovich, New York courts have held that where one party wants contractual language governing a work's distribution to be broadly construed to govern use in a new medium, and the other party attempts to limit the application of the agreement, the burden of excluding the right to the new use will rest with the party attempting to limit the application, in his case, Sony. The Second Circuit applied the new-use doctrine in *Boosey & Hawkes Music Publishers, Ltd. v. Walt Disney Co.*, 145 F.3d 481, 486–87 (2d Cir.1998). In doing so, the court stated that the words of the contract govern, and a court should not favor one party over the other. "If the contract is more reasonably read to convey one meaning, the party benefitted by that reading should be able to rely on it; the party seeking exception or deviation from the meaning reasonably conveyed by the words of the contract should bear the burden of negotiating for language that would express the limitation or deviation. This principle favors neither licensors nor licensees. It follows simply from the words of the contract." The New York Court of Appeals affirmed the Second Circuit's reasoning in *Greenfield v. Philles Records, Inc.*, 98 N.Y.2d 562, 750 N.Y.S.2d 565, 780 N.E.2d 166, 171–72 (2002). The New York court held that the reasonable interpretation of the contract governs.

It is important to remember that the new-use doctrine has only been applied in the licensing arena and has not been applied to the factual situation in the present case. Regardless, taking into account the new-use doctrine's requirement that the language of the contract must be more reasonably read to include the new-use being proposed—here, internet downloads—the language "all forms and configurations ... manufactured by Sony" is not more reasonably read to include internet downloads than to exclude internet downloads.

Popovich v. Sony Music Ent., Inc., 508 F.3d 348, 357–58 (6th Cir. 2007).

Contrast this outcome with a similar situation involving the film classic *Citizen Kane* brought by the daughter of Orson Welles.

> To display publicly or distribute *Citizen Kane,* the defendants need two rights: First, the defendants need the right to display the motion picture. Second, because a motion picture is derived from its underlying screenplay, the defendants need the right to exploit the screenplay.
>
> In this case, the first paragraph of Section 13 [of the relevant agreement between RKO and Mercury Productions, Inc. which was owned by Welles] deals with the first right the defendants need to distribute *Citizen Kane* on home video— the right to display the motion picture. Section 13 gives RKO "all rights of every kind and nature ... including, but not being limited to, the exclusive rights of distribution, exploitation, manufacture, recordation ... and reproduction by any art or method" in the motion pictures produced under the Production Agreement. This tells us that, as a general matter, the defendants, as successors to RKO, have the right to exploit in any manner the motion pictures produced pursuant to the Production Agreement, including *Citizen Kane.*
>
> However, to distribute *Citizen Kane* on home video, the defendants still need the right to exploit the screenplay from which the *Citizen Kane* motion picture was derived. The original story provision deals with this issue. As noted above, the provision states that Mercury retained the rights to any screenplay written by Mercury or its employees. So, in order to allow RKO to display motion pictures derived from those screenplays, the Production Agreement provided RKO with certain rights in the "original stories" on which those motion pictures were based. Specifically, RKO acquired "the motion picture and television rights in such stor[ies] for such Picture[s] only," and Mercury reserved ownership of "the publication, radio, dramatic and other rights" in those original stories.
>
> Thus, the question before us is whether the defendants' "motion picture and television" rights in the *Citizen Kane* screenplay encompass the right to distribute the *Citizen Kane* screenplay on home video. On one hand, a reasonable argument can be made that distributing a motion picture on home video is simply an exploitation of the defendants' "motion picture" rights in the *Citizen Kane* screenplay. On the other hand, such a broad interpretation would render the additional grant of "television rights" to the defendants superfluous because if "motion picture" rights encompassed home video rights, "motion picture" rights could also be argued to encompass the right to display *Citizen Kane* on television. Thus, it seems to us unclear whether the parties would have intended RKO's motion picture and television rights in the *Citizen Kane* screenplay to include the right to exploit the *Citizen Kane* screenplay in home video form.... We hold that the contract is ambiguous regarding which party owns the right to exploit the Citizen Kane screenplay on home video.[11]

---

11. In so holding, we do not adopt a presumption against applying a grant of rights in "motion pictures" to new technologies. Instead, we simply interpret the written contract of the parties in this case, as our precedent instructs.... [I]n this case, the Production Agreement, in addition to having no future technologies clause, granted RKO only motion picture and television rights in the Citizen

Welles v. Turner Ent. Co., 503 F.3d 728, 735–36 (9th Cir. 2007).

b. In *Boosey & Hawkes Music Publrs., Ltd. v. Walt Disney Co.*, the Second Circuit dismisses the importance of two specific clauses, a "future technologies clause" and a "reservation clause." Notwithstanding the court's comment, these clauses can have an important impact. First, an express grant for "all uses now known or hereafter created" leaves no ambiguity that nothing was retained by the grantor and can readily be enforced. See *Platinum Record Co. v. Lucasfilm, Ltd.*, 566 F. Supp. 226 (D.N.J. 1983). In the alternative, a statement that licenses only expressly listed uses similarly eliminates any ambiguities.

c. Given today's rapid technological changes, the parties could also agree to limit the exploitation of a work to those media from which revenues of not less than $10,000 were generated during the first five years of the license. This rather awkward concept essentially provides that from the date of the license, a set time period will begin to run during which either the grantee will exploit the work in that market or lose that market. Markets not yet existing and markets existing but not exploited would both lapse and those rights would vest in the licensor.

d. There are actually two discrete grant clauses in each agreement for the use of an underlying work. The first right needed is the right to exploit the work, meaning the right to adapt, derive, and modify the licensed material. The second is the right to reproduce, distribute, display, and perform the work in various media. For example, a novel may be licensed to be adapted into a motion picture. A license which provides that the motion picture may be performed in any media may fail to provide the rights to adapt the novel into a stage play, television production, or video game. See *Goodis v. United Artists Television, Inc.*, 425 F.2d 397, 403 (2d Cir. 1970). Occasionally this may be the intent of the parties; more often it is the failure to anticipate the sheer length of time and change of circumstance that the license agreements must regulate.

e. What is the meaning of the following Lucasfilm music synchronization clause for the film *American Graffiti*?

> Subject to our performance of the terms and conditions herein contained, you agree that we have the right to record, dub and synchronize the above mentioned master recordings, or portions thereof, into and with our motion picture and trailers therefor, and to exhibit, distribute, exploit, market and perform said motion picture, its air, screen and television trailers, perpetually throughout the world by any means or methods now or hereafter known.

Platinum Record Co. v. Lucasfilm, Ltd., 566 F. Supp. 226, 227 (D.N.J. 1983). Does the scope of the license apply to the use of the songs in any media, the exploitation of the motion picture—including the songs—in any media, both, or neither? In what way could the language be improved?

f. At other times, the problem of licensing translates into enforcement of the simplest of contract provisions—payment for services rendered. Courts require copyright provisions to be enforced, however, and will not rely on informal industry practice to modify the statute. See *Effects Assoc., Inc. v. Cohen*, 908 F.2d 555 (9th Cir. 1990) (interpreting the transfer of a special effect for the motion picture *The Stuff*).

g. As the technology for publishing continues to change, the struggle to control reprints and print-on-demand continues. When publishing giant Simon & Schuster attempted to

---

Kane screenplay while granting Mercury broad, residual rights in the screenplay. It is thus not clear to us to whom the parties would have intended to grant the right to exploit the screenplay in new mediums.

sweep the board by retaining all rights in their published works regardless of level of prints sold, the Authors Guild stepped in to fight a public relations war so the authors could continue the practice of retaining their out-of-print or out-of-mind works. See Motoko Rich, *Publisher and Authors Parse a Term: Out of Print*, N.Y. Times, May 18, 2007, at C3.[12]

h. The Supreme Court decision in *eBay, Inc. v. MercExchange, L.L.C.*, 547 U.S. 388 (2006), has been extended to copyright decisions, requiring that irreparable injury may not be presumed for copyright infringement actions. In *Salinger v. Colting*, 2010 U.S. App. LEXIS 8956 (2d Cir. N.Y. Apr. 30, 2010), the Second Circuit reversed and remanded the grant of a preliminary injunction involving the unauthorized sequel to J.D. Salinger's *Catcher in the Rye*.

> [P]laintiffs must show that, on the facts of their case, the failure to issue an injunction would actually cause irreparable harm.... But as the Supreme Court has suggested, a copyright holder might also have a First Amendment interest in not speaking. The defendant to a copyright suit likewise has a property interest in his or her work to the extent that work does not infringe the plaintiff's copyright. And a defendant also has a core First Amendment interest in the freedom to express him- or herself, so long as that expression does not infringe the plaintiff's copyright.... Harm might be irremediable, or irreparable, for many reasons, including that a loss is difficult to replace or difficult to measure, or that it is a loss that one should not be expected to suffer.... After *eBay*, however, courts must not simply presume irreparable harm.

Id.

Problem III-D

As author of the musical compositions and sound recordings that will be incorporated into the industrial film and computer program being completed for the St. James Corporation, Bryce has learned to carefully document all transactions. Bryce has asked you to draft a non-exclusive license agreement that provides St. James with the rights needed for the completion of the project, but which will insure Bryce retains as much ownership and control of the musical compositions and sound recordings as possible. On the expectation that St. James will demand a much broader grant of rights, also prepare a much more inclusive license from Bryce to St. James that will still allow Bryce to retain ownership of the musical works and sound recordings, while limiting St. James' use of the music to that of the project.

E. Bibliography and Links

Gregory Duhl, Old Lyrics, *Knock-Offs Videos, and Copycat Comic Books: The Fourth Fair Use Factor in U.S. Copyright Law*, 54 Syracuse L. Rev. 665 (2004).

Barbara Friedman, *From Deontology to Dialogue: The Cultural Consequences of Copyright*, 13 Cardozo Arts & Ent. L.J. 157 (1994).

Jon M. Garon, *Reintermediation*, 2 Int. J. of Private Law 227 (2009).

---

12. *Available at* http://query.nytimes.com/gst/fullpage.html?res=9C03E7DE1131F93BA25756C0 A9619C8B63.

Jane C. Ginsburg, *A Tale of Two Copyrights: Literary Property in Revolutionary France and America*, 64 Tul. L. Rev. 991 (1990).

Peter Jaszi, *Fixing Copyright: Copyright, Fair Use and Motion Pictures*, 2007 Utah L. Rev. 715 (2007).

Jon O. Newman, *New Lyrics for an Old Melody: The Idea/Expression Dichotomy in the Computer Age*, 17 Cardozo Arts & Ent. L.J. 691 (1999).

David Nimmer, *Codifying Copyright Comprehensibly*, 51 UCLA L. Rev. 1233 (2004).

William F. Patry & Richard A. Posner, *Fair Use and Statutory Reform in the Wake of Eldred*, 92 Cal. L. Rev. 1639 (2004).

R. Anthony Reese, *What Copyright Owes the Future*, 50 Hous. L. Rev. 287 (2012).

Darren M. Richard, *Music Licensing 101 A Nuts and Bolts Guide for Filmmakers, Television Producers, Music Publishers, and Songwriters*, 29 Ent. & Sports Law. 12 (2012).

Douglas L. Rogers, *Increasing Access to Knowledge Through Fair Use—Analyzing the Google Litigation To Unleash Developing Countries*, 10 Tul. J. Tech. & Intell. Prop. 1 (2007).

Russ VerSteeg, *Defining "Author" for Purposes of Copyright*, 45 Am. U.L. Rev. 1323 (1996).

Chapter IV

Ethical Issues

A. Agent Regulation

Statutory Regulations

a. Cal. Lab. Code § 1700.5. Necessity and posting of license. No person shall engage in or carry on the occupation of a talent agency without first procuring a license therefor from the Labor Commissioner.

b. N.Y. Gen. Bus. Law § 172. License required. No person shall open, keep, maintain, own, operate or carry on any employment agency unless such person shall have first procured a license therefor as provided in this article.... [Section 171 provides:] "Theatrical employment agency" means any person ... who procures or attempts to procure employment or engagements for circus, vaudeville, the variety field, the legitimate theater, motion pictures, radio, television, phonograph recordings, transcriptions, opera, concert, ballet, modeling or other entertainments or exhibitions or performances, but such term does not include the business of managing such entertainments, exhibitions or performances, or the artists or attractions constituting the same, where such business only incidentally involves the seeking of employment therefor. "Theatrical engagement" means any engagement or employment of a person as an actor, performer or entertainer in employment described in ... this section.

Wachs v. Curry
13 Cal. App. 4th 616 (2nd Dist. 1993)

The Talent Agencies Act (Lab. Code, §§ 1700–1700.47) requires persons who procure employment for artists in entertainment fields, such as motion pictures, television and radio, to be licensed as talent agents by the labor commissioner. The Act exempts from licensing those persons who procure only recording contracts.[1] Plaintiffs, who are not li-

---

1. Cal. Lab. Code § 1700.4 (2003)

    (a) "Talent agency" means a person or corporation who engages in the occupation of procuring, offering, promising, or attempting to procure employment or engagements for an artist or artists, except that the activities of procuring, offering, or promising to procure recording contracts for an artist or artists shall not of itself subject a person or corporation to regulation and licensing under this chapter. Talent agencies may, in addition, counsel or direct artists in the development of their professional careers.

    (b) "Artists" means actors and actresses rendering services on the legitimate stage and in the production of motion pictures, radio artists, musical artists, musical organizations, directors of legitimate stage, motion picture and radio productions, musical directors, writers, cinematographers, composers, lyricists, arrangers, models, and other artists and persons

censed talent agents, challenge the licensing requirement on the grounds it violates their rights to due process and equal protection of the laws.

The trial court held the licensing requirement is constitutional and granted the labor commissioner's motion for summary judgment. The court subsequently entered judgment against plaintiffs. We affirm.

Plaintiffs Wachs and X Management, Inc., provide personal management services to artists and entertainers. Plaintiffs entered into a written contract to provide personal management to entertainer Arsenio Hall in return for 15 percent of Hall's earnings from his activities in the entertainment industry during the term of the contract. The contract recites "You [Hall] have not retained our personal management firm under this agreement as an employment agent or a talent agent. This firm has not offered or attempted or promised to obtain employment or engagement for you and this firm is not obligated, authorized or expected to do so."

Subsequently, Hall filed a petition to determine controversy under section 1700.44 of the Act alleging Wachs had acted as an unlicensed talent agent in procuring and attempting to procure employment for him and requesting the labor commissioner order Wachs to return all moneys collected from Hall or Hall's employers in connection with any of Hall's activities in the entertainment industry. Wachs filed an answer to the petition generally denying Hall's allegations.

While Hall's petition was pending before the labor commissioner, Wachs and X Management filed the present action against the commissioner and other state officials charged with enforcing the Act. The complaint alleges the licensing provisions of the Act are unconstitutional on their face and as applied because no rational basis exists for providing an exemption from the licensing requirement to those who procure recording contracts but not for those who procure other contracts in the entertainment industry and because it cannot be determined from the language of the Act which activities require licensing as a talent agent. Wachs seeks a judgment declaring the licensing provisions of the Act unconstitutional for the reasons stated and enjoining defendants from enforcing those provisions.

On the state's motion for summary judgment the trial court determined there were no triable issues of material fact and the licensing provisions were constitutional. The court granted the motion and subsequently entered judgment for defendants....

We will proceed therefore to rule only on the claims section 1700.4 is unconstitutional on its face because the licensing exemption has no rational basis and the terms of the licensing requirement are so patently vague they provide no standard at all....

III. A Rational Basis Exists for Exempting Those Who Procure Recording Contracts From the Licensing Requirements of the Act.

As we noted above, the state enjoys a wide latitude in economic and social legislation. The conventional "rational relationship" test applies in cases involving occupational licensing. The Act provides, "No person shall engage in or carry on the occupation of a talent agency without first procuring a license therefor from the Labor Commissioner." The Act defines "talent agency" as a "person or corporation who engages in the occupation of procuring, offering, promising, or attempting to procure employment or engagements for an artist...." The Act, however, contains an exemption from its licensing

---

rendering professional services in motion picture, theatrical, radio, television and other entertainment enterprises.

requirement for those who procure employment in the form of recording contracts. This provision states: "the activities of procuring, offering, or promising to procure recording contracts for an artist or artists shall not of itself subject a person or corporation to regulation and licensing under this chapter."

Plaintiffs, who are not licensed talent agents, contend the licensing provisions of the Act are unconstitutional because there is no rational basis for exempting from the licensing requirement those who engage in procuring recording contracts but not other kinds of contracts.

The provision exempting the procurement of recording contracts was added to the Act in 1982 with a sunset provision of January 1, 1986. At the same time, the Legislature created the California Entertainment Commission to study and recommend revisions to the Act. The commission, after two years of study, submitted its recommendations to the Legislature which adopted them with minor language changes. One of the issues the commission studied was whether any changes should be made to the provision exempting persons who procure recording contracts for an artist. The majority of the commission recommended this exemption should be retained in the Act. The commission gave the following reasons for its recommendation.

> A recording contract is an employment contract of a different nature from those in common usage in the industry involving personal services. The purpose of the contract is to produce a permanent and repayable showcase of the talents of the artist. In the recording industry, many successful artists retain personal managers to act as their intermediaries, and negotiations for a recording contract are commonly conducted by a personal manager, not a talent agent. Personal managers frequently contribute financial support for the living and business expenses of entertainers. They may act as a conduit between the artist and the recording company, offering suggestions about the use of the artist or the level of effort which the recording company is expending on behalf of the artist.... However, the problems of attempting to license or otherwise regulate this activity arise from the ambiguities, intangibles and imprecisions of the activity. The majority of the Commission concluded that the industry would be best served by resolving these ambiguities on the side of preserving the exemption of this activity from the requirements of licensure.

On the commission's recommendation, the exemption for those who procure recording contracts became permanent. We believe the report from the Legislature's own commission of experts provides a sufficiently rational basis for the exemption from the licensing requirement. Numerous decisions support the proposition persons in the same general type of business may be classified differently where their methods of operation are not identical.

IV. The Licensing Requirements of the Act Are Not Void for Vagueness.

Plaintiffs contend the term "occupation of procuring [employment]" as used in section 1700.4, subdivision (a) does not sufficiently define the conduct which requires a license. Thus, persons such as plaintiffs, who provide a variety of services to artists and entertainers, cannot determine in advance what conduct they may lawfully engage in without a license. As a result, plaintiffs operate at great financial risk because a subsequent finding by the labor commissioner they "procured" employment without a license may relieve the client of any obligation to repay funds advanced to promote the client's career and entitle the client to restitution of all fees paid the agent.

Although the Act contains no criminal penalty for the unlicensed procuring of employment, the financial penalties to which the unlicensed agent is exposed are clearly sufficient to raise due process concerns. "Statutes, regardless whether criminal or civil in nature, must be sufficiently clear as to provide adequate notice of the prohibited conduct as well as to establish a standard of conduct which can be uniformly interpreted by the judiciary and administrative agencies."

In *Hall v. Bureau of Employment Agencies, supra,* 64 Cal. App. 3d at 494, the court summarized the test a statute must pass to satisfy due process: "'[I]f the words used may be made reasonably certain by reference to the common law, to the legislative history of the statute involved, or to the purpose of that statute, the legislation will be sustained ...; and a standard fixed by language which is reasonably certain, judged by the foregoing rules, meets the test of due process "notwithstanding an element of degree in the definition as to which estimates might differ." Further, even though all statutes regardless of nature must be sufficiently clear to provide fair notice of prohibited conduct: "'"Reasonable certainty is all that is required. A statute will not be held void for uncertainty if any reasonable and practical construction can be given its language.' It will be upheld if its terms may be made reasonably certain by reference to other definable sources."

Resort to the dictionary definitions of the words at issue and the legislative purpose and history of the Act convinces us the statute has an objective content from which ascertainable standards of conduct can be fashioned.

The relevant dictionary definition of "occupation" is "the principal business of one's life: a craft, trade, profession or other means of earning a living."

The history of the Act further illuminates the legislative intent with respect to activities requiring a talent agent's license.

Regulation of what we now refer to as talent agencies originated with the Artists' Managers Act of 1943. The Artists' Managers Act defined an artist's manager as "a person, who engages in the occupation of advising, counseling, or directing artists in the development or advancement of their professional careers and who procures, offers, promises or attempts to procure employment or engagements for an artist only in connection with and as a part of the duties and obligations of such person under a contract with such artist by which such person contracts to render services of the nature above mentioned to such artist."

With the adoption of the Act, the Legislature made a significant change in the definition of the covered activities. The Act provided, "A talent agency is hereby defined to be a person or corporation who engages in the occupation of procuring, offering, promising, or attempting to procure employment or engagements for an artist or artists. Talent agencies may, in addition, counsel or direct artists in the development of their professional careers."

Comparison of the activities regulated in the two acts shows a marked change of emphasis from the counseling function to the employment procurement function. Under the Artists' Managers Act the focus was on persons who engaged in "the occupation of advising, counseling or directing artists" in the "development or advancement" of their careers and who engaged in procuring employment "only in connection with and as a part of" their duties as advisor and counselor. Under the Act, the focus is on persons engaged "in the occupation of procuring ... employment or engagements for an artist...." These persons "may, in addition, counsel or direct artists in the development of their professional careers."

We conclude from the Act's obvious purpose to protect artists seeking employment and from its legislative history, the "occupation" of procuring employment was intended to be determined according to a standard that measures the significance of the agent's employment procurement function compared to the agent's counseling function taken as a whole. If the agent's employment procurement function constitutes a significant part of the agent's business as a whole then he or she is subject to the licensing requirement of the Act even if, with respect to a particular client, procurement of employment was only an incidental part of the agent's overall duties. On the other hand, if counseling and directing the clients' careers constitutes the significant part of the agent's business then he or she is not subject to the licensing requirement of the Act, even if, with respect to a particular client, counseling and directing the client's career was only an incidental part of the agent's overall duties. What constitutes a "significant part" of the agent's business is an element of degree we need not decide in this case.

Plaintiffs' concentrate their attack on the alleged vagueness of the word "procure." They posit numerous examples of conduct which they claim have little if any relationship to the purpose of the Act but which the labor commissioner has held, or might hold, constitutes "procuring" employment. However, as we noted above, the only question before us is whether the word "procure" in the context of the Act is so lacking in objective content that it provides no standard at all by which to measure an agent's conduct. To "procure" means "to get possession of: obtain, acquire, to cause to happen or be done; bring about."

The term "procure" in connection with employment is used in numerous California statutes. The fact none of these statutes has ever been challenged is some evidence the term is well understood.

We recognize the Legislature's failure to define the term "procure" for purposes of section 1700.4 has been criticized by several commentators. None of these commentators have suggested, however, the term "procure" is so lacking in objective content as to render the Act facially unconstitutional.

We conclude the term "occupation of procuring [employment]" is not "so patently vague and so wholly devoid of objective meaning that it provides no standard at all." Whether the Act is unconstitutional as applied to plaintiffs is a question for another day. The judgment is affirmed.

Yoo v. Robi

126 Cal. App. 4th 1089 (Cal. Ct. App. 2005)

Howard Wolf brought this action to recover a commission allegedly due him under a personal management contract with Paul Robi, one of the original members of the legendary singing group The Platters. The trial court awarded judgment to Robi. Wolf and Robi both filed timely appeals. The principal issues in Wolf's appeal are whether Wolf violated the Talent Agencies Act (Cal. Lab. Code § 1700 *et seq.*) by procuring performance engagements for Robi without being licensed as a talent agency and, if so, whether such violation of the Act bars Wolf's recovery of a commission for procuring a recording engagement for Robi—an activity which the Act specifically exempts from the license requirement....

We conclude substantial evidence supports the trial court's finding Wolf procured performance engagements for Robi in violation of the Act thus rendering his contracts with Robi void and barring his recovery of a commission for procuring a recording contract for Robi. We further conclude an appeal from a determination by the Labor Commissioner of a controversy arising under the Act may be filed either in a pending action between the parties to the controversy or in a separate, independent action.

In April 1986 Robi entered into a contract with Jango Records to record a Platters record album in exchange for consideration including royalties based on the number of albums sold. The Platters recorded the album in June and July of 1986 but Jango never released it.

At the time Robi and The Platters recorded the album for Jango, Robi also had a contract with Wolf under which Wolf was to perform certain services for Robi. This contract covered the period November 1985 to November 1986 and was one of a series of one-year contracts with identical terms spanning the period November 1983 to February 1988.

Under these contracts Wolf agreed to: "[A]dvise and counsel in the selection of literary and artistic material; advise and counsel in any and all matters pertaining to public relations; advise and counsel with relation to the adoption of proper formats for presentation of [Robi's] artistic talents [and] in the determination of proper style, mood, setting, business and characterization in keeping with [Robi's] talents; advise and counsel the selection of artistic talent to assist, accompany or embellish [Robi's] artistic presentation; and advise and counsel with regard to general practices in the entertainment industry and with respect to such matters of which [Wolf] may have knowledge concerning compensation and privileges extended for similar artistic values."

As compensation for his services Wolf was to receive "a sum equal to 10% of any and all gross monies or other considerations which [Robi] may receive as a result of [his] activities in and throughout the entertainment, amusement and publishing industries...." Paragraph 8 of the contracts further provided Robi would pay Wolf "a similar sum following the expiration of the term [of the contract] upon and with respect to any and all engagements, contracts and agreements entered into or substantially negotiated during the term hereof relating to any of the foregoing...."

In entering into the contracts with Wolf, Robi acknowledged: "You [i.e., Wolf] have specifically advised me [i.e., Robi] that you are not a 'talent agent' but active [*sic*] solely as a personal manager, and that you are not licensed as a 'talent agent' under the Labor Code of the State of California; you have at all times advised me that you are not licensed to seek or obtain employment or engagements for me and that you do not agree to do so, and you have made no representations to me, either oral or written, to the contrary."

Following Robi's death Martha Robi, his widow and successor in interest, licensed the manufacture of two record albums utilizing the recordings Robi and the Platters made for Jango Records.

Wolf filed this action alleging Paragraph 8 of his contract, quoted above, entitled him to a commission of 10 percent of the gross amount Robi earned from the sale of those albums. Robi filed a demurrer to the complaint which the trial court sustained and we overruled. Robi then answered the complaint raising numerous affirmative defenses. Robi's answer, however, did not include as an affirmative defense a claim Wolf's contract with Robi was void and invalid because Wolf acted under the contract to procure employment or engagements for Robi without a license to do so in violation of the Act.[2]

Although Robi did not raise the invalidity of the contract as an affirmative defense, while this action was pending in the superior court Robi did raise the invalidity issue in

---

2. Labor Code section 1700.4, subdivision (a) defines a talent agency as "a person or corporation who engages in the occupation of procuring, offering, promising, or attempting to procure employment or engagements for an artist...." Labor Code section 1700.5 states: "No person shall engage in or carry on the occupation of a talent agency without first procuring a license therefore from the Labor Commissioner." (All future statutory references are to the Labor Code unless otherwise noted.)

a Petition to Determine Controversy filed with the California Labor Commissioner pursuant to Labor Code, section 1700.44....

[T]he trial court found during each of the years 1983 through 1988 Wolf, acting without a talent agency license, procured and attempted to procure employment and engagements for Robi as an artist in violation of Labor Code, section 1700.5. Wolf contends these findings are not supported by substantial evidence....

Leaving aside Wolf's admission in his opening brief he "work[ed] through regional agents all over America to procure work for [Robi]," the record is replete with illustrations of Wolf's procurement activities on Robi's behalf.

Robi's widow, Martha, testified Robi had no contracts with talent agents in 1986 and that Wolf handled the negotiations for Robi's appearances. She recalled, for example, Wolf obtained an engagement for Robi at the Santa Clara County fair in August 1986. Donnie Brooks, a talent agent, testified he represented Santa Clara in negotiating with Wolf over Robi's appearance at the fair. Brooks also testified he negotiated with Wolf to have Robi perform for one of Brooks' clients in Bristol Connecticut in April 1986. The evidence showed other occasions in 1986 in which Wolf procured or attempted to procure performance engagements for Robi. In addition, Wolf testified he sent out promotional packages "in order to solicit" engagements for Robi and negotiated the details of potential performance contracts offered to him as Robi's agent by other talent agents.

The evidence also showed Wolf negotiated the Jango Records contract on behalf of Robi.

Wolf contends sending out promotional packages and negotiating performance contracts do not constitute "procuring" or "attempting to procure" employment within the meaning of Labor Code, section 1700.4, subdivision (a). If promoting an artist requires a talent agency license, Wolf argues, then public relations firms, publicists and advertising agencies all would have to be licensed as talent agencies. Wolf further maintains when personal managers negotiate performance contracts on behalf of their artist clients they are merely acting as spokespersons for the artists so the artists can concentrate on their artistry and not have to spend their time conversing with booking agents.

We need not decide in this case whether public relations firms, publicists and advertising agencies should be required to register as talent agencies because Wolf does not contend he is any of these. We note, however, a rational distinction can be drawn between promoting an artist to the public generally and "[t]he talent agent's primary function [of marketing] the artist's talent to buyers within the entertainment industry." ...

There is also a distinction between being the spokesperson for a client on a contract and being the negotiator for a client on a contract. The spokesperson merely passes on the client's desires or demands to the person who is contemplating engaging the client....

California courts have uniformly held a contract under which an unlicensed party procures or attempts to procure employment for an artist in violation of the Act is void *ab initio* and the party procuring the employment is barred from recovering commissions for *any* activities under the contract. This rule applies even if, as in the present case, the contract does not call for the procuring of employment or contains an affirmative statement the party seeking compensation has not agreed to obtain employment for the artist....

If negotiating the recording contract with Jango Records in 1986 was the only employment procurement Wolf engaged in on behalf of Robi this case would have to be decided differently because, as Wolf correctly points out, procuring recording contracts does not require a talent agency license. But the evidence shows Wolf engaged in numerous other employment procurement activities on behalf of Robi during the term of the 1986 contract. The fact procuring recording contracts without a license does not in itself violate public policy is not determinative. The same thing could be said about numerous other activities personal managers engage in which do not require a license such as counseling artists in the development of their professional careers, selecting material for their performances, managing their money, and the like. Engaging in those activities without a talent agency license does not violate public policy but those activities are nevertheless noncompensable if they are mixed in with activities which do require a license because of the overriding public policy of deterring unlicensed activities....

Marathon Entertainment, Inc. v. Blasi
42 Cal.4th 974 (2008)

In Hollywood, talent—the actors, directors, and writers, the Jimmy Stewarts, Frank Capras, and Billy Wilders who enrich our daily cultural lives—is represented by two groups of people: agents and managers. Agents procure roles; they put artists on the screen, on the stage, behind the camera; indeed, by law, only they may do so. Managers coordinate everything else; they counsel and advise, take care of business arrangements, and chart the course of an artist's career.

This division largely exists only in theory. The reality is not nearly so neat. The line dividing the functions of agents, who must be licensed, and of managers, who need not be, is often blurred and sometimes crossed. Agents sometimes counsel and advise; managers sometimes procure work. Indeed, the occasional procurement of employment opportunities may be standard operating procedure for many managers and an understood goal when not-yet-established talents, lacking access to the few licensed agents in Hollywood, hire managers to promote their careers.

We must decide what legal consequences befall a manager who steps across the line and solicits or procures employment without a talent agency license. We hold that (1) contrary to the arguments of personal manager Marathon Entertainment, Inc. (Marathon), the strictures of the Talent Agencies Act (Lab. Code, § 1700 et seq.) (Act) apply to managers as well as agents; (2) contrary to the arguments of actress Rosa Blasi (Blasi), while the Labor Commissioner has the authority to void manager-talent contracts *ab initio* for unlawful procurement, she also has discretion to apply the doctrine of severability to partially enforce these contracts; and (3) in this case, a genuine dispute of material fact exists over whether severability might apply to allow partial enforcement of the parties' contract. Accordingly, we affirm the Court of Appeal.

FACTUAL AND PROCEDURAL BACKGROUND

In 1998, Marathon and Blasi entered into an oral contract for Marathon to serve as Blasi's personal manager. Marathon was to counsel Blasi and promote her career; in exchange, Blasi was to pay Marathon 15 percent of her earnings from entertainment employment obtained during the course of the contract. During the ensuing three years, Blasi's professional appearances included a role in a film, *Noriega: God's Favorite*, and a lead role as Dr. Luisa Delgado on the television series *Strong Medicine*.

According to Marathon, Blasi reneged on her agreement to pay Marathon its 15 percent commission from her *Strong Medicine* employment contract. In the summer of 2001, she unilaterally reduced payments to 10 percent. Later that year, she ceased payment altogether and terminated her Marathon contract, stating that her licensed talent agent, John Kelly, who had served as her agent throughout the term of the management contract with Marathon, was going to become her new personal manager.

Marathon sued Blasi for breach of oral contract, quantum meruit, false promise, and unfair business practices, seeking to recover unpaid *Strong Medicine* commissions. Marathon alleged that it had provided Blasi with lawful personal manager services by providing the down payment on her home, paying the salary of her business manager, providing her with professional and personal advice, and paying her travel expenses.

After obtaining a stay of the action, Blasi filed a petition with the Labor Commissioner alleging that Marathon had violated the Act by soliciting and procuring employment for Blasi without a talent agency license. The Labor Commissioner agreed. The commissioner found Marathon had procured various engagements for Blasi, including a role in the television series *Strong Medicine*. Concluding that one or more acts of solicitation and procurement by Marathon violated the Act, the commissioner voided the parties' contract *ab initio* and barred Marathon from recovery.

Marathon appealed the Labor Commissioner's ruling to the superior court for a trial *de novo*.... The trial court granted Blasi's motion for summary judgment and invalidated Marathon's personal management contract as an illegal contract for unlicensed talent agency services in violation of the Act....

The Court of Appeal reversed in part. It agreed with the trial court that the Act applied to personal managers. However, it concluded that under the law of severability of contracts (Civ. Code, § 1599), because the parties' agreement had the lawful purpose of providing personal management services that are unregulated by the Act, and because Blasi had not established that her *Strong Medicine* employment contract was procured illegally, the possibility existed that Blasi's obligation to pay Marathon a commission on that contract could be severed from any unlawful parts of the parties' management agreement....

We granted review to address the applicability of the Act to personal managers and the availability of severance under the Act.

Discussion

I. *Background*

A. *Agents and Managers*

In Hollywood, talent agents act as intermediaries between the buyers and sellers of talent. While formally artists are agents' clients, in practice a talent agent's livelihood depends on cultivating valuable connections on both sides of the artistic labor market. Generally speaking, an agent's focus is on the deal: on negotiating numerous short-term, project-specific engagements between buyers and sellers.

Agents are effectively subject to regulation by the various guilds that cover most of the talent available in the industry: most notably, the Screen Actors Guild, American Federation of Television and Radio Artists, Directors Guild of America, Writers Guild of America, and American Federation of Musicians. Artists may informally agree to use only agents who have been "franchised" by their respective guilds; in turn, as a condition of franchising, the guilds may require agents to agree to a code of conduct and restrictions on terms included in agent-talent contracts. Most significantly, those restrictions typically include a cap on the commission charged (generally 10 percent), a cap on contract duration, and a bar on producing one's client's work and obtaining a producer's fee. These restrictions create incentives to establish a high volume clientele, offer more limited services, and focus on those lower risk artists with established track records who can more readily be marketed to talent buyers.

Personal managers, in contrast, are not franchised by the guilds. They typically accept a higher risk clientele and offer a much broader range of services, focusing on advising and counseling each artist with an eye to making the artist as marketable and attractive to talent buyers as possible, as well as managing the artist's personal and professional life in a way that allows the artist to focus on creative productivity. Given this greater degree of involvement and risk, managers typically have a smaller client base and charge higher commissions than agents (as they may, in the absence of guild price caps); managers may also produce their clients' work and thus receive compensation in that fashion.

B. *The Talent Agencies Act*

Aside from guild regulation, the representation of artists is principally governed by the Act. (§§ 1700–1700.47.) ... In its present incarnation, the Act requires anyone who solicits or procures artistic employment or engagements for artists[3] to obtain a talent agency license. (§§ 1700.4, 1700.5.) In turn, the Act establishes detailed requirements for how licensed talent agencies conduct their business, including a code of conduct, submission of contracts and fee schedules to the state, maintenance of a client trust account, posting of a bond, and prohibitions against discrimination, kickbacks, and certain conflicts of interest. (§§ 1700.23–1700.47.) No separate analogous licensing or regulatory scheme extends to personal managers.

With this background in mind, we turn to two questions not previously addressed by this court: whether the Act in fact applies to personal managers, as the Courts of Appeal and Labor Commissioner have long assumed, and if so, how.

II. *The Scope of the Talent Agencies Act: Application to Managers*

...

We begin with the language of the Act. Section 1700.5 provides in relevant part: "No *person* shall engage in or carry on the occupation of a *talent agency* without first procuring a license therefor from the Labor Commissioner." (Italics added.) In turn, "person" is expressly defined to include "any individual, company, society, firm, partnership, association, corporation, limited liability company, *manager*, or their agents or employees" (§ 1700, italics added), and "'[t]alent agency' means a person or corporation who engages in the occupation of procuring, offering, promising, or attempting to procure employment or engagements for an artist or artists ..." other than recording contracts. (§ 1700.4, subd. (a).)

The Act establishes its scope through a functional, not a titular, definition. It regulates *conduct*, not labels; it is the act of procuring (or soliciting), not the title of one's business, that qualifies one as a talent agency and subjects one to the Act's licensure and related requirements. (§ 1700.4, subd. (a).) Any person who procures employment—any individual, any corporation, any manager—is a talent agency subject to regulation. (§§ 1700, 1700.4, subd. (a).) Consequently, as the Courts of Appeal have unanimously held, a personal manager who solicits or procures employment for his artist-client is subject to and must abide by the Act.

As to the further question whether even a single act of procurement suffices to bring a manager under the Act, we note that the Act references the "occupation" of procuring employment and serving as a talent agency. (§§ 1700.4, subd. (a), 1700.5.) Considering

---

3. 'Artists' means actors and actresses rendering services on the legitimate stage and in the production of motion pictures, radio artists, musical artists, musical organizations, directors of legitimate stage, motion picture and radio productions, musical directors, writers, cinematographers, composers, lyricists, arrangers, models, and other artists and persons rendering professional services in motion picture, theatrical, radio, television and other entertainment enterprises (§ 1700.4, subd. (b).)

this in isolation, one might interpret the statute as applying only to those who regularly, and not merely occasionally, procure employment. However, as we have previously acknowledged in dicta, "[t]he weight of authority is that even the incidental or occasional provision of such services requires licensure." (*Styne v. Stevens*, [26 Cal.4th 42, 51 (2001)].) In agreement with these decisions, the Labor Commissioner has uniformly interpreted the Act as extending to incidental procurement. The Labor Commissioner's views are entitled to substantial weight if not clearly erroneous; accordingly, we likewise conclude the Act extends to individual incidents of procurement....

III. *Sanctions for Solicitation and Procurement Under the Act*

A. *Marathon's Procurement*

We note we are not called on to decide, and do not decide, what precisely constitutes "procurement" under the Act. The Act contains no definition, and the Labor Commissioner has struggled over time to better delineate which actions involve mere general assistance to an artist's career and which stray across the line to illicit procurement. Here, however, the Labor Commissioner concluded Marathon had engaged in various instances of procurement, the trial court concluded there was no material dispute that Marathon had done so, and Marathon has not further challenged that conclusion. We thus take it as a given that Marathon has engaged in one or more acts of procurement and that (as the parties also agree) Marathon has no talent agency license to do so.

We also take as a given, at least at this stage, that Marathon's unlicensed procurement did not include the procurement specifically of Blasi's *Strong Medicine* role....

B. *The Applicability of the Doctrine of Severability to Manager-talent Contracts*

We turn to the key question in Blasi's appeal: What is the artist's remedy for a violation of the Act? In particular, when a manager has engaged in unlawful procurement, is the manager always barred from any recovery of outstanding fees from the artist or may the court or Labor Commissioner apply the doctrine of severability (Civ. Code, § 1599) to allow partial recovery of fees owed for legally provided services?

Again, we begin with the language of the Act. On this question, it offers no assistance. The Act is silent—completely silent—on the subject of the proper remedy for illegal procurement.

On the other hand, the text of Civil Code section 1599 is clear. Adopted in 1872, it codifies the common law doctrine of severability of contracts: "Where a contract has several distinct objects, of which one at least is lawful, and one at least is unlawful, in whole or in part, the contract is void as to the latter and valid as to the rest." (*Ibid.*) By its terms, it applies even—indeed, only—when the parties have contracted, in part, for something illegal. Notwithstanding any such illegality, it preserves and enforces any lawful portion of a parties' contract that feasibly may be severed.

Under ordinary rules of interpretation, we must read Civil Code section 1599 and the Act so as to, to the extent possible, give effect to both. The two are not in conflict. The Act defines conduct, and hence contractual arrangements, that are illegal: An unlicensed talent agency may not contract with talent to provide procurement services. The Act provides no remedy for its violation, but neither does it repudiate the generally applicable and long-standing rule of severability. Hence, that rule applies absent other persuasive evidence that the Legislature intended to reject the rule in disputes under the Act.

The conclusion that the rule applies is consistent with those Labor Commissioner decisions that recognize severability principles may apply to disputes under the Act. In *Almendarez v. Unico Talent Management, Inc.* (Cal. Lab. Com., Aug. 26, 1999) TAC No.

55-97, a radio personality sought a determination that his personal manager had acted as an unlicensed talent agency. The Labor Commissioner concluded the manager had engaged in unlawful procurement—indeed, that procuring employment was the manager's primary role—but stopped short of voiding all agreements between the parties in their entirety....

Until two years ago, Court of Appeal decisions under the Act had neither accepted nor repudiated the general applicability of the severability doctrine. In 2005, in *Yoo v. Robi, supra*, 126 Cal. App. 4th 1089 [(Cal. Ct. App. 2005),] however, the Court of Appeal considered whether to apply Civil Code section 1599 to allow a personal manager to seek commissions for lawfully provided services. It noted, correctly, that severance is not mandatory and its application in an individual case must be informed by equitable considerations. Civil Code section 1599 grants courts the power, not the duty, to sever contracts in order to avoid an inequitable windfall or preserve a contractual relationship where doing so would not condone illegality. The *Yoo* Court of Appeal concluded the windfall for the artist, Robi, was not so great as to warrant severance.

In *Chiba v. Greenwald* 156 Cal. App. 4th 71 [(2007)], the Court of Appeal also considered whether severance was available for an unlicensed manager/agent who in that case alleged she had had a *Marvin* agreement[4] with her deceased musician client/partner. Acknowledging she had acted without a license, the manager relinquished any claim to commissions, and the Court of Appeal thus was not presented with the question whether severance might apply to any management services that required no license. In light of the facts as pleaded, the Court of Appeal concluded equity did not require severance of any lawful portions of the *Marvin* agreement from the unlawful agreement to provide unlicensed talent agency services.

Neither *Chiba* nor *Yoo v. Robi*, stands for the proposition that severance is never available under the Act. In contrast, the Court of Appeal here expressly concluded, as we do, that it is available....

[T]he Legislature has not seen fit to specify the remedy for violations of the Act. Ordinary rules of interpretation suggest Civil Code section 1599 applies fully to disputes under the Act; nothing in the Act's text, its history, or the decisions interpreting it justifies the opposite conclusion. We conclude the full voiding of the parties' contract is available, but not mandatory; likewise, severance is available, but not mandatory.

C. *Application of the Severability Doctrine*

Finally, we turn to application of the severability doctrine to the facts of this case, insofar as those facts are established by the summary judgment record. Given the procedural posture, our inquiry is narrow: On this record, has Blasi established as a matter of law that there is no basis for severance?...

Blasi argues that once a personal manager solicits or procures employment, all his services—advice, counseling, and the like—become those of an unlicensed talent agency and are thus uncompensable. We are not persuaded. In this regard, the conduct-driven definitions of the Act cut both ways. A personal manager who spends 99 percent of his time engaged in counseling a client and organizing the client's affairs is not insulated from the Act's strictures if he spends 1 percent of his time procuring or soliciting; conversely, however, the 1 percent of the time he spends soliciting and procuring does not thereby render illegal the 99 percent of the time spent in conduct that requires no license

---

4. Marvin v. Marvin 18 Cal.3d 660 [134 Cal. Rptr. 815, 557 P.2d 106] (1976).

and that may involve a level of personal service and attention far beyond what a talent agency might have time to provide. Courts are empowered under the severability doctrine to consider the central purposes of a contract; if they determine in a given instance that the parties intended for the representative to function as an unlicensed talent agency or that the representative engaged in substantial procurement activities that are inseparable from managerial services, they may void the entire contract. For the personal manager who truly acts as a personal manager, however, an isolated instance of procurement does not automatically bar recovery for services that could lawfully be provided without a license.

Inevitably, no verbal formulation can precisely capture the full contours of the range of cases in which severability properly should be applied, or rejected. The doctrine is equitable and fact specific, and its application is appropriately directed to the sound discretion of the Labor Commissioner and trial courts in the first instance. As the Legislature has not seen fit to preclude categorically this case-by-case consideration of the doctrine in disputes under the Act, we may not do so either.

...

For the foregoing reasons, we affirm the Court of Appeal's judgment and remand this case for further proceedings consistent with this opinion.

Wil-Helm Agency v. Lynn

618 S.W.2d 748 (Tenn. Ct. App. 1981)

[This 1981 case from Tennessee involving Loretta Lynn provides an unfortunately common story of bad representation, weak statutory safeguards, and years of abuse and neglect. It does not develop additional case law on managers and agents, but should serve to remind lawyers that they need to protect their clients from the fiduciaries who surround them.]

The Wil-Helm Agency sues for damages due to the breach of a theatrical agency contract entered into between the agency and Loretta Lynn, an artist. Loretta Lynn filed a counterclaim wherein she avers that the agency breached the contract and, therefore, owes her damages and she further alleges that the agency released her from the contract. The chancellor found that the agency had breached the contract and, in addition, had released Loretta Lynn from the contract. The chancellor further held that the amounts due each party offset each other and allowed no monetary award to either party.

The agency appeals insisting that the chancellor erred in finding: (1) that the agency breached the contract; (2) that the agency released Loretta Lynn from the contract; and (3) that the damages due the parties offset each other....

Loretta Lynn was born in the area of Van Leer, Kentucky, and at the age of fourteen years married O. V. Lynn of that same area. A few months after the marriage, O. V. Lynn went to the state of Washington and obtained employment as an agricultural laborer. Later Loretta joined him at Custer, Washington. Loretta began singing at local gatherings and formed a band which soon became fully booked in the area at various local places of entertainment. She appeared on the Buck Owens show and entered into a recording contract under the Zero label. Loretta wrote and recorded the song "I'm a Honky Tonk Girl," appeared on various radio shows, appeared as a guest performer on the Grand Ole Opry, and was becoming recognized as a budding young artist.

In 1961 she and her husband moved to Nashville, Tennessee. In that year she entered into her first two-year contract with the Wil-Helm Agency. Thereafter, she entered into another five-year contract with that agency. On April 12, 1966, she and the agency entered into the contract now under consideration. This contract provides in pertinent part as follows:

WITNESSETH

1. The Artist hereby engages the Agent as his sole and exclusive personal representative and adviser in the radio, television, recording and personal appearances field of entertainment throughout the world and in outer space for a period of Twenty years (20 years)

2. The Agent's duties hereunder shall be as follows: To use all reasonable efforts to procure employment for the artist in any branch of the field of entertainment in which the Artist notifies the Agent that his services are or will be available. In addition, at the Artist's request to:

(a) Assist the Artist in negotiating with respect to all forms of advertising and commercial tie-ups in all fields, wherever the Artist's name, business likeness or voice may be used, including but not limited to the radio, television, recording and personal appearances field of entertainment.

(b) Counsel and advise the Artist in matters which concern his professional interest in the radio, television, recording and personal appearances field of entertainment.

3. The Agent hereby accepts this engagement and agrees to perform the services specified herein. The Agent shall have the right to render his services to other persons, either in a capacity in which he is hereby engaged or otherwise. However, the Artist agrees not to engage any other person to act for him in the capacity for which the Agent has been engaged. The Artist hereby represents and warrants that he is wholly free to enter into this agreement and has no contract or obligations which will conflict with it.

An Amendment of the same date was attached to the contract which provides in part as follows:

(3) This Amendment and the Agreement shall be null and void in the event there is a change of ownership in the Agency. It being the Artist (demands) that she be associated only with current management.

The contract and the amendment were signed by Smiley Wilson for the agency and by Loretta Lynn.

The Wil-Helm Agency apparently was a partnership composed of the four Wilburn brothers: Doyle, Teddy, Leslie and Lester. As we view the lawsuit, it is immaterial whether there was a change in the ownership of the agency, and the amendment to the contract will not be further considered.

The parties enjoyed several years of successful association. Loretta's popularity grew, and she is now recognized as an outstanding star in the field of country music. From 1961 through the latter part of the 1960s, the agency assisted Loretta and played an important part in her rise to stardom. Teddy Wilburn worked closely with Loretta. When the 1966 contract was signed, he was spending several hours almost daily with Loretta. He assisted her in rewriting her songs and advised her on costumes, mannerisms, and lines. Loretta was very fond of Teddy Wilburn; she sought his counsel and followed his advice. She appeared as the only female artist on the Wilburn Brothers Show. The agency obtained a recording contract for Loretta with Decca Records. She made appearances on national television and followed a hard-working road show schedule.

In about 1967, Doyle Wilburn began to drink alcohol in excessive amounts. When drinking or drunk, he was extremely abusive and boorish. This conduct by Doyle resulted in Teddy Wilburn leaving the show in 1968. Teddy moved to California and returned to Nashville only to do certain television work. It appears that Smiley Wilson then became the member of the agency upon whom Loretta depended. Wilson did his job and aided the artist; however, she missed the expertise and experience of Teddy Wilburn. It seems that Teddy did relent and return to the show, only to leave again in 1971 for the same reason as previously stated.

With Teddy gone, it appears that Doyle Wilburn took it upon himself to be more closely identified with Loretta and her work. The record is replete with instances which reveal almost constant misconduct on the part of Doyle Wilburn acting as the agent of Loretta. Some of the more glaring instances of misconduct are: (1) insulting the producer of the Johnny Carson Show while there to close a deal for Loretta to appear on that show; (2) drunkenness on the part of Doyle Wilburn while on the stage acting as master of ceremonies; (3) actually disturbing Loretta during performances; (4) the telling of sacrilegious jokes on Loretta's show in Boston, Massachusetts; (5) drunken vomiting on the dinner table at a post-performance party given for patrons, promoters, disc jockeys and their wives; (6) drunkenness throughout most of a tour in England; (7) drunkenness during the time Loretta was preparing jingles for the Coca Cola ads; (8) getting drunk and passing out during the signing of the Glo-coat contract; (9) being so drunk while emceeing Loretta's performance at a rodeo that he fell off the stage; (10) drunkenness when taping Loretta on the Ed Sullivan Show; (11) insulting the black musicians while on the David Frost Show; (12) being drunk on practically every road trip, interfering with Loretta's need for rest on the bus, ignoring instructions of airline personnel while on flights, and generally being an obnoxious drunk in the presence of people upon whom the success of the artist depended. This conduct was carried on while Doyle Wilburn was acting as the representative of the agency with whom Loretta had contracted. This conduct was known to all members of the agency; some effort was made to reason with Doyle, but to no avail.

In about October 1970 Smiley Wilson left the agency. He was replaced by Mr. Brumley who was then replaced by Leslie Hart. Hart advised Loretta that she was being woefully mismanaged and recommended that she see an attorney. Up to this time Loretta had not received independent advice on anything. The agency kept her books, handled her financing, and referred her to the agency's lawyer for any personal legal advice. Upon the advice of Hart, Loretta employed an attorney. Upon investigating the situation, the attorney wrote a letter dated April 1, 1971, to the agency saying the agency had breached the contract, and Loretta would not further abide by it. Further negotiations between the lawyers resulted in certain letters which the chancellor found constitute a release of the contract by the agency. As we view the situation, it is of no import whether the agency released Loretta from the contract; we hold that the contract was breached by the agency.

We agree with the chancellor that the conduct of Doyle Wilburn as the representative of the agency was entirely inconsistent with the duty owed the artist under the contract. The agreement is a bilateral contract wherein each party was obligated to the other to render certain performances, the carrying out of which by each party was essential to the realization of benefits under the contract. Each party to the contract was under an implied obligation to restrain from doing any act that would delay or prevent the other party's performance of the contract. Each party had the right to proceed free of hinderance by the other party, and if such other party interfered, hindered, or prevented the performance to such an extent as to render the performance difficult and diminish the benefits to be received, the first party could treat the contract as broken and was not bound to proceed under the added burdens.

There is ample material evidence that the agency, by the conduct of its representative, committed a substantial breach of its contract with Loretta Lynn. The chancellor is affirmed in this respect.

Damages.

The chancellor referred the question of damages to the clerk and master, but, after the taking of considerable proof, that official passed the issue back to the chancellor without making a finding of any kind. Thereupon, the chancellor found as follows:

> After sifting through the proof and after reviewing the previous Memorandum and the orders based on it, the Court concludes that the claims of the parties off-set each other and should be dismissed. The plaintiff Agency claims $178,556.72 due on the contract up until the date of termination with allowances for dates already booked to November of 1971. The defendant counter-claimed for damages for breach of the management agreement. The proof shows that the defendant was being booked at a fee of $2,500.00 to $4,000.00 per appearance up until the date of termination of the agreement while an artist of her stature should have commanded a much higher figure.
>
> A simple calculation based on the number of dates she worked in a few years prior to 1971 shows how much of a loss that was. In addition, the failure to expose her to national television and the stress of the conditions under which she worked result in damages that are reasonably certain and should off-set the plaintiff's claim. The Court declines to speculate on the amount of damages the plaintiff would be entitled to if the decision had been otherwise.

We accept the figure of $178,556.72 as the amount due the agency under the contract up until the date of termination with allowances for dates already booked to November 1971. The artist claims that this amount can not be awarded to the plaintiff agency because the plaintiff breached the contract and is not entitled to any amount thereunder. We disagree with the artist in this respect.

The record reveals that the plaintiff agency committed a substantial breach of the contract. The defendant artist did not commit any breach of the contract. Therefore, if the plaintiff is to recover at all, it must do so upon the theory that it has rendered a part performance of value, that it has done more good than harm to the artist, and that the artist will be unjustly enriched and the plaintiff unjustly penalized if the artist is allowed to retain the beneficial part performance without paying anything in return. By the same token, the plaintiff is the wrongdoer, and it must not be allowed to profit from its own wrong. Therefore, allowance must be made to the defendant artist in damages for the full extent of the injury that the plaintiff's breach has caused her. Under the facts of this bilateral contract, whereby each party agreed to carry out certain performances in return for performances by the other party, we conclude that the plaintiff agency is entitled to its commissions based upon its part performance less the amount of the injury to the artist caused by the breach. Having accepted the figure of $178,556.72 as the amount due the agency for its part performance, it must now be determined in what amount, if any, the artist was damaged by the breach.

The defendant artist averred by counterclaim that due to the conduct of Doyle Wilburn, she had been deprived of engagements as an artist, that she had suffered physical and emotional distress and had been rendered unable to perform to her capacity, and that subsequent to the breach and the termination of the contract, the agency had held itself out as the sole and exclusive agent of the artist thereby depriving her of engagements and the resulting revenues therefrom. By amendment to the counterclaim, the artist averred that over the years the agency had booked her for engagements at a price below that to which she was entitled and had entered into a recording contract for her at a rate substantially less than her professional ability demanded, all to her financial detriment and in breach of the agency's duties under the contract.

As noted, the chancellor found (1) that the artist was booked at a fee below that which an artist of her stature should have commanded, and (2) that the stress of the conditions under which she was forced to work resulted in damages that are reasonably certain.

There is competent and material evidence that Loretta Lynn won more awards, had a larger following, and was more sought after than any other artist in her field of entertainment. There is competent and material evidence that artists of less ability, following, and demand were drawing from $5,000 to $7,500 for a performance during the late 1960s and up to 1971. There is ample proof that Loretta Lynn should have been drawing those amounts instead of the $2,500 to $4,000 range in which she was booked. The plaintiff agency presented proof (Exhibit 53) which purported to list every performance of Loretta Lynn for which the agency claimed a commission. From a review of the number of those performances and an application of a reasonable average fee at which the artist should have been booked, the chancellor concluded that the damage she suffered from having been "underbooked" for several years more than offset the amount proved by the agency as owing to it.

The chancellor properly held that strain and stress unnecessarily suffered by the actress due to the conduct of the agency representatives resulted in damages for which the artist could recover. There is ample material evidence to sustain the finding that the conditions under which she had to work, rendered the artist nervous, uncertain, dismayed, and embarrassed, all to her professional detriment through no fault of her own.

Although not ruled on by the chancellor, we find another element of damage to the artist based upon the recording contract it entered into for the artist with Decca Records. It seems that in the early years of the recording industry a recording company suffered substantial losses due to records being broken while in transit to the buyers. As a result, a custom built up that when contracting with an artist the recording company would deduct 10% from the sales figures to take care of this breakage, and the artist was paid a royalty based upon 90% of the sales figure. Later records were made of plastic or some other material not subject to the breakage previously sustained. The proof establishes that as of 1966, when Decca contracted to record Loretta, all recording contracts being renewed and all new contracts being entered into provided for a royalty based upon the 100% figure. This was done at the mere request of the artist or agent. However, the plaintiff agency booked Loretta at a royalty based upon the 90% figure. In 1972, after the parties had gone their separate ways, Decca voluntarily changed the contract so as to pay royalties on the 100% figure. There is material evidence that the loss suffered by the artist because of this breach of duty on the part of the agency amounted to approximately $200,000 during the period from 1966 to 1971.

We, therefore, agree with the chancellor that the damages suffered by the artist more than offset those amounts claimed by the agency for its part performance of the contract. Admittedly, neither the chancellor nor this court fix the actual amount of damages to which the artist is entitled due to the breach of the contract by the agency. We have, however, fully satisfied ourselves that the damages thus suffered exceed the amount due the plaintiff agency. The artist did not appeal. We conclude that under all the circumstances of this lawsuit, the chancellor's decree is supported by a preponderance of the evidence, and that decree is affirmed.

The cost in this court is adjudged against the appellant, Wil-Helm Agency, for which execution may issue, if necessary.

Notes and Questions

a. Because agreements to pay unlicensed talent agents are void, the risk is that the manager or unlicensed talent agent will lose all income that might have resulted from the arrangement—even if the relationship goes sour well after the time of the procurement. In *Park v. Deftones,* 71 Cal. App. 4th 1465 (Cal. App. 2d Dist. 1999), Park, the band manager, was fired after arranging for the recording agreement. Because his activity was void and illegal, he has no basis to complain for any mistreatment.

b. In addition to licensing talent agencies, states such as New York and California also regulate the terms of the talent agency agreement. These regulations do not automatically set the fees a talent agency may charge, but they do tend to disapprove of excessive fees. The New York regulations are representative:

§ 37.03. Theatrical employment; contracts

Every licensed person who shall procure for or offer to an applicant a theatrical engagement shall have executed in duplicate a contract or deliver to the parties as herein set forth a statement containing the name and address of the applicant; the name and address of the employer of the applicant and of the person acting for such employer in employing such applicant; the time and duration of such engagement; the amount to be paid to such applicant; the character of entertainment to be given or services to be rendered; the number of performances per day or per week that are to be given by said applicant; if a vaudeville engagement, the name of the person by whom the transportation is to be paid, and if by the applicant, either the cost of transportation between the places where said entertainment or services are to be given or rendered, or the average cost of transportation between the places where such services are to be given or rendered; and if a dramatic engagement, the cost of transportation to the place where the services begin, if paid by the applicant; and the gross commission or fees to be paid by said applicant and to whom. Such contracts or statements shall contain no other conditions and provisions except such as are equitable between the parties thereto and do not constitute an unreasonable restriction of business. Forms of such contract and statement in blank shall be first approved by the commissioner and his determination shall be reviewable by certiorari. One of such duplicate contracts or of such statements shall be delivered to the person engaging the applicant and the other shall be retained by the applicant. The licensed person procuring such engagement for such applicant shall keep on file or enter in a book provided for that purpose a copy of such contract or statement.

N.Y. Art & Cult. Aff. § 37.03 (2013).

c. In addition to the regulation provided by statute, the fees for various industry talent agencies often are controlled under the regulatory auspices of collective bargaining agreements and the trade unions which negotiate them. For example, it is the Screen Actors Guild which prohibits talent agents from charging more than ten percent of their client's salaries as the talent agent fee. Members must limit themselves to licensed agencies that have submitted themselves to the union's review and approval. This serves as the primary regulatory mechanism for the market.

d. One of the ongoing ethical issues involved in entertainment licensing arises from the scale of the corporate organizations. In 1999, David Duchovny, co-star of "The X-Files" television series, sued 20th Century Fox for licensing the series to Fox outlets and subsidiary cable network FX at a price far below market rates, giving rise to claims for breach of contract, breach of good faith, and conspiracy. While that claim was ultimately settled, a similar claim is proceeding. See *Scholastic Entm't, Inc. v. Fox Entm't Group, Inc.*, 336 F.3d 982 (9th Cir. 2003). To what extent does the attorney involved in the subsequent licensing transaction have an ethical duty not to create an intentionally ambiguous contract or to proceed with a transaction knowing it is based on a breach of good faith in another proceeding? Does a third party have a claim for tortious interference of contract against the attorneys if they are aware of the pre-existing agreements?

e. Does the agent representing a film producer owe any fiduciary duty to the screenwriter submitting a script? See *A Slice of Pie Prods. v. Wayans Bros. Entm't*, 392 F. Supp. 2d 297 (D. Conn. 2005).

Problem IV-A

Bryce's talent is starting to be noticed. Bryce has received an offer for representation from Diablo Jones, who styles himself a local film and music agent/manager. Jones provided Bryce a form contract which specifies a fifteen percent fee for management services and a fifteen percent fee for procuring employment "in any entertainment field or media." The term of the proposed form agreement was three years. Jones retained the power to assign the agreement. Jones told Bryce "all his clients signed the agreement in this form because it was standard in the industry."

Thankfully, Bryce has come to you for advice prior to signing the form agreement. Explain to Bryce what terms are reasonable for a talent agent agreement and for a management agreement, describing the difference(s) between the two roles.

B. Regulation of Attorneys

Croce v. Kurnit

565 F. Supp. 884 (D.C.N.Y., 1982)

This diversity action, a portion of which was tried to the court, presented facts which evoked memories of "A Star Is Born," except that the star in this case, James Croce, died all too soon after his ascendancy. The complaint filed by Ingrid Croce, his widow and heir ("Mrs. Croce"), a California resident, sought to obtain certain damages from the defendants, citizens of states other than California, arising out of an alleged breach of certain contracts as well as rescission of the contracts on the ground of fraud, and breach of fiduciary duty. On the findings and conclusions set forth below, judgment will be granted to the defendants dismissing the claims of unconscionability and breach of fiduciary duty against Cashman and West and granting Croce's breach of fiduciary claim against Kurnit. The defendants' motion for judgment notwithstanding the verdict is denied.

This action was filed by Mrs. Croce on July 21, 1978 against Philip Kurnit ("Kurnit"), a New Jersey resident and a member of the bars of New York, New Jersey and California, Thomas R. Picardo, a New York resident, also known as Tommy West ("West"), Dennis

Minogue, also known as Terry Cashman ("Cashman"), a New Jersey resident, Cashman, Pistilli & West ("CP&W"), a New York partnership, Blendingwell Music, Inc. ("Blendingwell"), a New York Corporation, Cashwest Productions, Inc. ("Cashwest"), a New York corporation and Lifesong Records, Inc. ("Lifesong"), a New York corporation and a subsidiary of Blendingwell. Kurnit, West and Cashman are officers of Blendingwell, Cashwest and Lifesong. The complaint set forth nine counts containing causes of action for breach of fiduciary duty (Count 1), fraud (Count 2), unconscionability (Count 3), breach of contracts (Counts 4, 5 and 6), replevin (Count 7), conversion (Count 8) and breach of fiduciary duty (Count 9)....

James Joseph Croce ("Jim Croce") was born in 1943 and in the course of his schooling attended Villanova University. There he met Ingrid, who subsequently became his wife, and also Tommy West, who became both his friend and, as it developed, a business associate. During the college years Jim Croce sang, played guitar and wrote songs, as did West.

After graduation from college, Jim Croce sought to shape a career out of his interest in music, played and sang in coffee houses, and developed both his own style and his own music. He managed to produce a record album entitled *Facets* containing certain of his songs which he performed. He sent the album to Tommy and sought to interest the latter in his work.

West in the meantime also developed a career in music, producing, singing and playing for commercials. He had met Cashman with whom he collaborated as well as Kurnit, an attorney who had been working at ABC Records, Inc. By 1968 all three, West, Cashman and Kurnit were at CBS, Cashman, West in the music department and Kurnit serving in the legal department. The two musicians together with Eugene Pistilli ("Pistilli") decided to enter the record business on their own and set up CP&W for that purpose. Kurnit was also a participant in the enterprise.

In the summer of 1968, while Kurnit was still at CBS, Jim and Ingrid Croce arrived in New York, stayed with West, and met Kurnit, who was introduced to them as "the lawyer." West and the Croces discussed the possibility of CP&W producing a record by Jim Croce. The outlines of the contractual arrangements were discussed, the Croces returned to Pennsylvania and according to West, proposed contracts were taken to them after their trip to New York and before their return to New York on September 17, 1968. Whether or not that occurred (Mrs. Croce maintains it did not), the Croces did not conduct any meaningful review of the contract until September 17, 1968.

On that date the Croces were in New York again, staying with the Wests. They met Kurnit for the second time. He outlined the contract terms to them in a two to three hour meeting. According to Kurnit, there was no negotiation although a minor change in the proposed contract was made. The Croces signed three agreements, a recording contract with CP&W, a publishing contract with Blendingwell and a personal management contract also with Blendingwell ("the contracts"). The Croces were unrepresented, and they were not advised to obtain counsel by Kurnit who signed the contracts on behalf of the corporate entities. Kurnit was known to the Croces to be a participant with Cashman, Pistilli and West in their enterprises. The Croces did not enter into any retainer agreement with Kurnit, were never billed by him in connection with the contracts, and aside from the meeting of September 17, received no advice from him concerning the contracts.

The contracts that were executed on September 17, 1968 provided that Croce would perform and record exclusively for CP&W, as well as the terms under which all the Croce's songs would be published and managerial services would be provided for the Croces. The contracts placed no affirmative requirements on the defendants other than to pay each of the Croces approximately $600 a year and to make certain royalty payments in the event that music or records were sold. The duration of the contracts was seven years if options to extend were exercised by the defendants. All rights to the Croces' musical performances and writings were granted to the defendants. The management contract was assignable.

The expert testimony offered by Mrs. Croce focused on the effect of the assignability of the management contract, the lack of any objective threshold to be achieved before the exercise of options, and the interrelationship of the three contracts. In addition other significant provisions were cited as being unfavorable to the Croces which would have been the subject of negotiation had the Croces in September, 1968 been represented by the expert retained in 1982. These included the term of the contracts, the royalty rate and its escalation, a revision of the copyrights, a minimum recording sides obligation, and the time for making objections to royalty statements.

However, certain of the provisions which were under attack were also contained in the forms published by various organizations involved in the entertainment industry, and there was no evidence presented in this action, meticulously prepared by able counsel on both sides, which established that the terms of these contracts differed significantly from others prepared by Kurnit on behalf of the defendants. These contracts include many terms of art and are customarily the subject of hard bargaining in the event that the artist and the producer both have established economic power. Here, however, no significant changes were made in the contracts as initially proposed by Kurnit on behalf of the other defendants.

After the contracts were executed, the parties undertook their performance. In the summer of 1969 the recording contract was assigned to Interrobang Productions, Inc. ("Interrobang"), as was the management contract a year later. Cashwest is the successor in interest to Interrobang. The management contract was assigned to Showcase Management, a company in which CP&W had an interest, a demonstration record was prepared (a "demo") and thereafter Capital Records undertook to produce a Croce recording under the direction of Nick Vanet. This recording was published in the spring of 1969 and after its publication, Jim Croce worked hard to promote it. By the winter of 1969–70 it was apparent the album was a failure, and Jim turned to other pursuits.

In the fall of 1968 Kurnit represented the Croces in connection with a lease. In April, 1969 Kurnit listed his firm as the party to whom all ASCAP correspondence for Croce should be sent. In January, 1970 Kurnit executed a document as attorney in fact for the Croces and also was involved in the dispute between the Croces and their then manager.

Notwithstanding, on March 19, 1970 Jim and Ingrid, unhappy with the management with which they had been provided, sought legal advice with respect to breaking the contracts. They retained Robert Cushman ("Cushman") of Pepper, Hamilton & Schatz in Philadelphia. On June 9, 1970 Croce wrote to Kurnit seeking to terminate the contracts and advising him that "Ingrid and I are getting out of music." In the summer of 1970, Cushman met with Kurnit and discussed the grievances which the Croces had expressed to him, supported at one point by a statement of Pistilli which, according to Cushman, established that the Croces had been defrauded. Some revisions and amendments to the contracts were discussed.

In December 1970 Ingrid became pregnant, and Jim returned to songwriting and performing. Thereafter, he sent material to West who expressed interest and delight. Cushman requested a further retainer to pursue the revision or cancellation of the contracts and never heard again from either of the Croces.

In the early part of 1971 West and Cashman worked with Croce and prepared a demo. With Kurnit's help, they sold the idea of its production to ABC, interested an established management agency in Croce with the result that Interrobang delegated its management contract for Croce to BNB Associates, Ltd. ("BNB") in September 1971. Once the relationship with the defendants resumed in 1971, Kurnit represented the Croces on various matters. After the summer of 1971 and the birth of his son in September, Jim's career began to move. His work was well received and in April 1972, ABC records contracted to manufacture, distribute and sell Croce records. Jim was on the road late in 1971 and 1972 promoting and performing. His career skyrocketed and until September 20, 1973 the future appeared halcyon for all concerned. During 1972 Kurnit represented Croce on matters other than the contracts.

On September 20, 1973, after a concert in Louisiana, Croce took off in a private plane. The plane crashed in a thunderstorm, and Croce was killed.

Very shortly thereafter Kurnit visited Mrs. Croce and offered to represent the estate and to take care of the wrongful death action arising from the crash. On September 26, 1973, Kurnit became the attorney for the Estate and Mrs. Croce. In connection with the wrongful death action, Kurnit later stated on the form filed with the Appellate Division on October 4, 1973: "Ingrid Croce, and her deceased husband, James J. Croce, have been my clients since 1968. I have been their personal attorney in a majority of their legal matters."

Kurnit served as counsel to the estate from September 26, 1973 until June 24, 1976. During the spring of 1976 Kurnit, on behalf of the defendants, had consulted Donnenfeld and Brent, a Los Angeles law firm, with respect to a movie proposal. Thereafter, at his request on June 24, 1976 that firm was substituted for him as counsel for the estate.

In 1975, Mrs. Croce remarried and in the company of her husband discussed with Kurnit the use of certain material which had not been the subject of the contracts. These discussions, involving what the parties have termed "the estate sides," were the subject of the contract issues concerning the publication of "The Faces I Have Been" album resolved by the jury's Special Verdict. During these discussions Kurnit represented CP&W and after the initial discussion, Mrs. Croce retained Ivan Hoffman, an attorney, to represent her. Hoffman and Kurnit exchanged correspondence, drafts and telephone calls. There is no evidence that Hoffman was consulted about the contracts or Mrs. Croce's rights which resulted from the contracts.

However, in November 1975 Mrs. Croce retained Howard Thaler to represent her on a number of matters unrelated to the contracts. At his deposition, Thaler invoked the attorney/client privilege when questioned about his discussions with Mrs. Croce about the contracts. Thaler's invocation of the privilege may imply that Thaler has information against Mrs. Croce's interests in this action. However, even assuming that this inference is permitted, Kurnit has failed to establish the date on which Mrs. Croce conferred with Thaler concerning the contracts prior to June 10, 1976.

On that day Thaler met with Donnenfeld and some discussion was had concerning Mrs. Croce's rights under the contracts. Mrs. Croce was advised that since the Estate had been referred to them by Kurnit, a conflict of interest existed which precluded their initiating any claim against Kurnit. It was pointed out, however, that since the Estate was shortly to be terminated, Mrs. Croce would thereafter initiate any action she felt appropriate. Obviously these issues had been discussed between Mrs. Croce and Thaler prior to June 10, 1976 but Kurnit has not sustained his burden of proof to establish an earlier date to end the toll of the statute of limitations as discussed below. The Estate was closed on September 27, 1977 and this action was initiated on July 21, 1978.

During the period from 1968 to date the defendants received approximately $6.9 million as a consequence of the performance of the contracts. The recording and entertainment career of Croce is not atypical, representing as it does, initially a famine, and ultimately a feast. No expert who testified claimed the prescience to determine in advance what records the public will buy or in what amount. Though the returns on a successful record are unbelievably high, the risk of initial failure is also high. Judgment, taste, skill and luck far outweigh the time spent or the capital expended on any particular recording.

It is on these facts that Mrs. Croce's claims of unconscionability and breach of fiduciary duty, must be resolved, as well as the defendants' affirmative defenses of the statute of limitations and election of remedies. The claim of fraud has not been pressed by Mrs. Croce, and indeed there is no proof of misrepresentation, falsity or reliance except in connection with the fiduciary duty claims.

1. Representation by Kurnit

The claims of breach of fiduciary duty and procedural unconscionability are based on the role and actions of Kurnit at the signing and during the performance of the contracts. Indeed, the nature of Kurnit's relationship with the Croces determines whether this action is barred by the statute of limitations. Therefore, this court will assess the September 17, 1968 transaction before proceeding to the merits of each claim.

Mrs. Croce asserts that after Kurnit had been introduced to the Croces on a prior occasion as "the lawyer," Kurnit acted as the Croces' attorney at the signing of the contracts or in such a manner as to lead the Croces to reasonably believe that they could rely on his advice. The Croces were aware of the fact that Kurnit was an officer, director and shareholder of Blendingwell and Cashwest on whose behalf Kurnit signed the contracts.

In light of the facts set forth above, Kurnit did not act as the Croces' attorney at the signing of the contracts. Even in the absence of an express attorney-client relationship, however, a lawyer may owe a fiduciary obligation to persons with whom he deals. In particular, a fiduciary duty arises when a lawyer deals with persons who, although not strictly his clients, he has or should have reason to believe rely on him. Kurnit's introduction as "the lawyer," his explanation to the Croces of the "legal ramifications" of the contracts which contained a number of legal terms and concepts, his interest as a principal in the transactions, his failure to advise the Croces to obtain outside counsel, and the Croces lack of independent representation taken together establish both a fiduciary duty on the part of Kurnit and a breach of that duty....

See Model Code of Professional Responsibility DR 7-104(A) (2) (1979).

During the course of his representation of a client a lawyer shall not: ...

Give advi[c]e to a person who is not represented by a lawyer, other than the advice to secure counsel, if the interests of such person are or have a reasonable possibility of being in conflict with the interests of his client.

See also *Model Rules of Professional Conduct* Rule 4.3 comment at 167 (Proposed Final Draft May 1981):

No misconduct is present where a lawyer provides an accurate statement of the law, or prepares papers for settlement or trial, so long as it is made clear that the lawyer does not act as counsel for the unrepresented person or otherwise purport to advance the latter's interests.

Moreover, the limits of the fiduciary relationship as defined in *Penato v. George,* 52 A.D. 2d 939, 383 N.Y.S.2d 900 (2d Dep't 1976) apply. The court there realized that the exact limits of such a relationship are impossible of statement (see Bogert, Trusts & Trustees [2d ed.], §481). Broadly stated, a fiduciary relationship is one founded upon trust or confidence reposed by one person in the integrity and fidelity of another. It is said that the relationship exists in all cases in which influence has been acquired and abused, in which confidence has been reposed and betrayed. The rule embraces both technical fiduciary relations and those informal relations which exist whenever one man trusts in, and relies upon, another.

383 N.Y.S.2d at 904–95. (citations omitted).

This definition of a fiduciary duty applies not only to Kurnit's relationship but also on the facts of this case to West and Cashman, in whom the Croces placed their trust. Before further addressing Mrs. Croce's breach of fiduciary duty allegations, however, the defendants' statute of limitations defense warrants examination. For these purposes, Kurnit's relationship with the Croces controls.

2. Statute of Limitations

The applicable statute of limitations is six years for fraud and breach of fiduciary duty. To avoid the time bar, Mrs. Croce asserts that Kurnit's continuous representation of the Croces from September 17, 1968 to June 24, 1976 tolls the statute under the "continuous representation" doctrine set forth in *Greene v. Greene,* 56 N.Y.2d 86, 436 N.E.2d 496, 451 N.Y.S.2d 46 (1982). In that case, the New York Court of Appeals held that for statute of limitations purposes a cause of action against an attorney for acts arising out of the attorney's representation of the plaintiff does not accrue during the period of that representation....

Although this court has determined that Kurnit did not act as the Croces' attorney at the signing of the contracts, he did thereafter serve as their attorney in related and unrelated matters. Indeed, in the retainer statement dated October 4, 1973, to the Judicial Conference of the State of New York referred to above, Kurnit himself stated that his representation commenced in 1968, after the execution of the contracts on September 18.

A lawyer's "various activities on [a client's] behalf can be seen as part of a course of continuous representation concerning the same or related problem." Although representing the Croces in a lease dispute is not related to the contracts, the representation of the Croces by Kurnit stems from their relationship arising from the contracts. Moreover, Kurnit's listing on the ASCAP application, his correspondence signed as "attorney-in-fact" regarding the songwriting contract and his assistance in resolving claims with the Croce's then-manager indicate continuous representation concerning the performance of the contracts. Kurnit's representation of the Croces on unrelated matters emphasizes the trust and reliance that the Croces placed in Kurnit as their attorney. Consequently, I conclude that Kurnit's representation to the New York Judicial Conference sets the date for the beginning of the tolling period as September 18, 1968.

Kurnit asserts, however, that Jim Croce's consultation of Cushman on March 19, 1970 ends the toll. The rationale for the continuous treatment doctrine lends credence to this assertion. Because a "relationship between the parties is marked by trust and confidence, ... [because] there is presented an aspect of the relationship not sporadic but developing; ... [and because] the recipient of the service is necessarily at a disadvantage to question the reason for the tactics employed or the manner in which the tactics are executed," the continuous treatment doctrine was extended to continuous representation. However, Jim Croce's retention of Cushman in 1970 to attempt to terminate the contracts also terminated the continuing representation by Kurnit.

Mrs. Croce argues that any interruption of the toll by the retention of Cushman should end by December of 1970 when Jim Croce decided to work pursuant to the contracts and discontinued any relationship with Cushman. However, once Jim Croce consulted Cushman, he was no longer the disadvantaged client unable to question or to pursue remedies for perceived wrongs. He inquired of his rights to terminate the contract and chose not to exercise them. Hence, I conclude that the statute of limitations began to run on March 19, 1970 and continued to run for three and one half years until Kurnit was appointed to represent the Estate of Jim Croce.

Nonetheless, once Jim Croce died, his Estate had the right to pursue whatever causes of action survived his death. By the September 26, 1973 appointment of Kurnit as counsel to the Estate, the relationship between the Estate and Kurnit was marked by confidence and trust, once again placing Kurnit in a fiduciary relationship and making the continuing representation doctrine applicable as to the Estate.

Moreover, in *Pet, Inc. v. Lustig,* 77 A.D.2d 455, 433 N.Y.S.2d 934, 935–36 (4th Dep't 1980), the court held that it "would not permit the statute of limitations to run where the one claiming the benefit of the statute is the one charged in law with the duty of asserting and enforcing the claim before the statute runs." In the instant case, Kurnit asserts the statute of limitations as a bar to Mrs. Croce's claims. However, once he was appointed counsel for the Estate, he had the duty of asserting claims on behalf of the Estate. Although it is understandable that Kurnit did not investigate or pursue claims against his own interest, he may not now claim the benefits of the statute of limitations.

Therefore I conclude that the statute of limitations was tolled for two years and nine months from September 26, 1973 until June, 1976 when Donnenfeld and Brent were substituted as counsel for the Estate, which coincided with the period of Mrs. Croce's consultation of Thaler concerning her rights under the contracts. Mrs. Croce argues that the toll should continue until September 27, 1977, the date on which the Estate was closed because of Donnenfeld and Brent's representation that it would not bring any action against Kurnit because of a conflict of interest. While this argument has some merit, it is immaterial. Whether the statute continues to run to June, 1976 or to September, 1977 is of no consequence, neither date would cause this action to be untimely.

The statute of limitations ran for three and one half years from March, 1970 to September, 1973 and for two years and one month from June, 1976 to July 21, 1978, the date on which this action was filed. Hence I conclude that this action is not barred by the statute of limitations.

3. Unconscionability and Breach of Fiduciary Duty

Mrs. Croce contends that the contracts were unconscionable. An unconscionable contract "affronts the sense of decency," and usually involves gross one-sidedness, lack of meaningful choice and susceptible clientele. A claim of unconscionability "requires some showing of 'an absence of meaningful choice on the part of one of the parties together with contract terms which are unreasonably favorable to the other party.'" Additionally, Mrs. Croce alleges that defendants breached their fiduciary duty to the Croces. A fiduciary relationship is bound by a standard of fairness, good faith and loyalty....

As the facts stated above indicate, the contracts were hard bargains, signed by an artist without bargaining power, and favored the publishers, but as a matter of fact did not contain terms which shock the conscience or differed so grossly from industry norms as to be unconscionable by their terms. The contracts were free from fraud and although complex in nature, the provisions were not formulated so as to obfuscate or confuse the terms. Although Jim Croce might have thought that he retained the right to choose whether to exercise renewal options, this misconception does not establish that the contracts were unfair. Because of the uncertainty involved in the music business and the high risk of failure of new performers, the contracts, though favoring the defendants, were not unfair. Therefore, I conclude that the terms of the contracts were neither unconscionable nor unfair and that Cashman and West did not breach a fiduciary duty....

[The Court denied all claims for recission.] Mrs. Croce is, however, entitled to damages resulting from Kurnit's breach of fiduciary duty in failing to advise the Croces to seek independent counsel. Given the bifurcated nature of this lawsuit, and the fact that, but for Kurnit's breach, the second branch of Mrs. Croce's complaint, claiming fraud, unconscionability, and breach of fiduciary duty, would in all likelihood not have arisen, this court assesses Mrs. Croce's damages to be the costs and attorneys' fees expended in prosecuting those claims, and determines that Kurnit is liable for this amount....

Blanks v. Shaw
171 Cal.App.4th 336 (2009)

In this legal-malpractice based lawsuit, plaintiff and respondent Billy Blanks (Blanks) won a multi-million dollar judgment against his former attorneys, defendants and appellants William H. Lancaster (Lancaster) and Seyfarth Shaw, LLP (Seyfarth Shaw), jointly Seyfarth.

... We are ... called upon to discuss the effect of Seyfarth's failure to file a petition with the Commissioner within the Act's one-year statute of limitation (Lab.Code, § 1700.44, subd. (c)), and the doctrine of severability of contracts applied to the TAA as addressed in *Marathon Entertainment, Inc. v. Blasi* 42 Cal.4th 974 (2008)....

Blanks is a celebrity karate champion. He developed Tae Bo, a fitness routine combining calisthenics, karate, dance, and push-ups. The routine was ideal for weight control, organized exercise classes, and training. Blanks developed an enthusiastic following and established the Billy Blanks World Karate Center where people lined up around the block to take classes. Radio and television programs spotlighted the Tae Bo craze. Blanks was in demand for film projects and public appearances. The first mass marketed Tae Bo videotape was a huge success.

In 1991 or 1992, certified public accountant Jeffrey Greenfield (Greenfield) came into Blanks's studio as a client. Soon thereafter, Greenfield became Blanks's accountant.... In December 1997, Blanks hired licensed talent agent Suzy Unger (Unger) at the William Morris Agency. While Blanks was represented by the William Morris Agency, Greenfield arranged a number of movie and television appearances in 1998 and 1999. However, Greenfield's inept actions also harmed Blanks. For example, Greenfield's negotiations relating to a television action project called "Tae Bo Squad" did not result in an agreement. The project fizzled during the contract stage. In 1999, Greenfield's mishandling of the negotiations for a television series called "Battle Dome" resulted in Blanks being paid only as a consultant and at a sum far below Blanks's worth. Greenfield did not return telephone messages from those seeking to hire Blanks, resulting in lost opportunities....

The TAA requires all agents to be licensed. If an agent procures work for an artist and is unlicensed, the Act permits the Labor Commissioner to void ab initio all contracts between the parties and order the unlicensed agent to disgorge funds earned for those services. Such requests for affirmative relief first must be made by filing a claim with the Labor Commissioner, who has original jurisdiction over TAA claims. The TAA has a one-year statute of limitations, which the parties agree begins to run from the date the payment is made to the unlicensed agent. (Lab. Code, § 1700.44.) Generally, there is no right to conduct discovery in TAA matters before the Commissioner....

[Despite the exclusive jurisdiction of the Labor Commissioner, Seyfarth pursued a civil cause of action without first filing with the Labor Commissioner and failed to file before the TAA statute of limitations expired.]

While Seyfarth was handling Blanks's case against Greenfield, Blanks paid Seyfarth approximately $400,000. According to Seyfarth, Blanks still owed approximately $46,000....

On March 11, 2002, the Labor Commissioner issued a formal determination of controversy finding that Greenfield was operating as an unlicensed talent agent and had violated the TAA at least twice (once for "Tae Bo Squad" and once for "Battle Dome"). The Commissioner further ruled that Blanks's petition was untimely because Blanks had not satisfied the one-year TAA statute of limitations and thus, the Commissioner could not order Greenfield to disgorge monies he had received from Blanks....

In this case premised upon a claim of legal malpractice, Blanks accuses Seyfarth of losing his right to seek redress from Greenfield because Seyfarth failed to timely file a petition with the Labor Commissioner.

"In civil malpractice cases, the elements of a cause of action for professional negligence are: '(1) the duty of the attorney to use such skill, prudence and diligence as members of the profession commonly possess; (2) a breach of that duty; (3) a proximate causal connection between the breach and the resulting injury; and (4) actual loss or damage." (*Wiley v. County of San Diego*, 19 Cal.4th 532, 536 (1998).)

"In addressing breach of duty, 'the crucial inquiry is whether [the attorney's] advice was so legally deficient when it was given that he [or she] may be found to have failed to use "such skill, prudence, and diligence as lawyers of ordinary skill and capacity commonly possess and exercise in the performance of the tasks which they undertake."

With regard to causation and damages, the plaintiff is required to prove that but for the defendant's negligent acts or omissions, "the plaintiff would have obtained a more favorable judgment or settlement in the action in which the malpractice allegedly occurred." (*Viner v. Sweet*, 30 Cal.4th 1232, 1241 (2003).) As such, a determination of the underlying case is required. This method of presenting a legal malpractice lawsuit is commonly called a trial within a trial....

The Labor Commissioner is given exclusive original jurisdiction over controversies colorably arising under the TAA, which must be brought within one year.

Labor Code section 1700.44, subdivision (c) details the TAA limitation period. It provides that "[n]o action or proceeding shall be brought pursuant to [the Act] with respect to any violation which is alleged to have occurred more than one year prior to commencement of the action or proceeding." As we held in *Greenfield v. Superior Court, supra*, 106 Cal.App.4th 743, filing a complaint in the superior court does not satisfy Labor Code section 1700.44's filing requirement as it is not an "action or proceeding[ ]" as envisioned in the Act. Rather, a petition must be filed with the Commissioner....

Generally, there is no due process right to discovery in TAA hearings before the Commissioner. Rather, the scope of discovery is governed by statute and the Commissioner's discretion.

After the issues are first addressed by the Commissioner, both parties have the right to a trial de novo. "De novo" review "means that the appealing party is entitled to a complete new hearing—a complete new trial—in the superior court that is in no way a review of the prior proceeding." (*Buchwald v. Katz* 8 Cal.3d 493, 502 (1972)). If an artist seeking to recover funds paid to an unlicensed agent prematurely files a civil lawsuit prior to filing with the Commissioner, the superior court proceedings are stayed until the remedies before the Commissioner are exhausted....

The civil lawsuit filed by Seyfarth on behalf of Blanks on November 4, 1999, identified 17 causes of action, *all* premised upon the allegation that Greenfield must return the $10.6 million paid to him because Greenfield had acted as an agent without first procuring a license as required by the Labor Code. One cause of action alleged a violation of Business and Professions Code section 17200, the Unfair Competition Law (UCL). It alleged that Greenfield had engaged in an unlawful business practice because he did not have the required licensure under the TAA....

Seyfarth argues that even if it was negligent in allowing the TAA statute to expire prior to filing with the Labor Commissioner, such negligence did not harm Blanks because the statute of limitations for Blanks's UCL cause of action had not expired and that cause of action would have yielded the same recovery as alleged in the first cause of action for violating the TAA. Therefore, Seyfarth argues, as a matter of law, Blanks could not prove causation and damages required by the trial-within-a-trial methodology. We hold that by this argument, Seyfarth unpersuasively seeks to circumvent the comprehensive statutory scheme in which the Legislature has given exclusive original jurisdiction to the Labor Commissioner with regard to TAA claims.

... Unlike other statutes that might be used as the basis for a UCL cause of action, the TAA mandates that cases colorably arising under the TAA *must first* be filed with the Commissioner within the one-year statute of limitation period. This is a procedural predicate-filing requirement that cannot be circumvented by recasting a TAA cause of action as a UCL cause of action. Persons, such as Blanks, seeking affirmative relief under the TAA may not invoke the jurisdiction of the Superior Court until after the Commissioner has issued a ruling. This is not a matter of judicial discretion, but is a fundamental rule of procedure.

There can be no argument here that the essence of the underlying case involves a dispute as to whether the relationship between Blanks and Greenfield was controlled by the TAA. The only possible way to satisfy the broad jurisdictional boundaries of the TAA is to require that this issue first be examined by the Commissioner, who would determine if Greenfield procured employment for Blanks. This, and many other issues involved in the *Blanks v. Greenfield* case, including whether or not severance (discussed *infra*) is appropriate, are the precise types of issues that the TAA demands initially be examined by the Commissioner, who has special competence in rendering such decisions. Seyfarth may not plead around the TAA by stating the requested relief alternatively as a UCL cause of action....

Seyfarth [also] contends that the contract between Blanks and Greenfield was subject to the doctrine of severability. This contention is persuasive and because the instructions did not comport with the law in this regard, reversal of the judgment is required.

Blanks's legal malpractice lawsuit against Seyfarth was based upon the theory that he would have been successful in the underlying case against Greenfield had Seyfarth not placed its interests above Blanks's. Blanks argued that had Seyfarth timely filed a petition with the Labor Commissioner rather than delaying the filing of the TAA petition to inflate attorney's fees, Blanks would have been entitled to recover all sums Blanks paid Greenfield because Greenfield was not a licensed talent agent, *i.e.*, had Seyfarth timely filed with the Commissioner, Blanks would have obtained a disgorgement award from the Commissioner of approximately $10.6 million dollars.

Seyfarth did not concede liability. However, it argued that even *if* the Blanks/Greenfield arrangement was tainted with illegality because Greenfield was not a licensed talent agent, and even *if* a TAA petition had been timely filed, the doctrine of severability of contracts applied and Blanks was not entitled to disgorgement of *all* sums paid. In making this argument, Seyfarth noted that Greenfield rendered many non-agent services. Thus, according to Seyfarth, even *if* it was liable, Greenfield's agent-activities (which would have been illegal) had to be severed from the non-agent-activities (which did not violate the TAA), and any recovery to Blanks in the legal malpractice case was limited to those sums attributable to Greenfield's agent-activities....

Marathon recognized that it is often unclear as to whether a person is acting as an artist's agent or in some other capacity, such as a manager. *Marathon* held, however, that the doctrine of severability of contracts, as codified in Civil Code section 1599, applies to contracts involving such arrangements. Thus, if an unlicensed person renders procurement services that require a license under the TAA and also renders non-procurement services, that person may be entitled to compensation for those acts that did not involve unlawful procurement. In such cases, the Labor Commissioner hearing the dispute "is empowered to void contracts in their entirety," however, she is not "obligated to do so.... [Rather, the Labor Commissioner has] the ability to apply equitable doctrines such as severance to achieve a more measured and appropriate remedy where the facts so warrant." (*Id.* at p. 995.)

"In deciding whether severance is available, [*Marathon* has] explained '[t]he overarching inquiry is whether "'the interests of justice ... would be furthered'" by severance.' 'Courts are to look to the various purposes of the contract. If the central purpose of the contract is tainted with illegality, then the contract as a whole cannot be enforced. If the illegality is collateral to the main purpose of the contract, and the illegal provision can be extirpated from the contract by means of severance or restriction, then such severance and restriction are appropriate.' The analysis is case specific. Further, the doctrine of severability can apply even if the unlicensed person "receives an undifferentiated right to a certain percentage of the client's income stream." (*Id.* at 996–98.) ...

The parties did not fully address whether it was equitable or feasible to sever Greenfield's unlicensed procurement activities from the lawful, non-procurement ones. They did not discuss if the income Greenfield derived was attributable to the central purpose of the Blanks/Greenfield agreement, or if Greenfield's talent agent activities permeated all other services rendered. The parties did not discuss the relevance of the fact that Greenfield was entitled to a percentage of Blanks's total income and how this undifferentiated income affects the severability question.

Lastly, it appears the jury accepted Blanks's all-or-nothing approach because the jury awarded Blanks the exact amount he had paid to Greenfield — $10,634,542 — thereby finding that had Seyfarth timely filed a petition with the Commissioner, the Commissioner would have awarded Blanks that sum.

Thus, the trial court's instructional error relating to the doctrine of severability infected the entire trial and the judgment must be reversed....

Todd W. Musburger, Ltd. v. Meier
394 Ill.App.3d 781 (2009)

A jury returned a verdict in favor of plaintiff Todd W. Musburger, Ltd., a law firm, against defendant Garry Meier, awarding $68,750 in damages on count II of plaintiff's verified complaint for services rendered under a theory of quantum meruit.... We affirm for the reasons set forth below.

According to the complaint in the case at bar, plaintiff "is an entertainment law firm that focuses on negotiating and drafting personal services contracts for broadcasters, writers, performers and directors, as well as negotiating and drafting contracts for entertainment projects in development." Todd Musburger is the president of plaintiff law firm, and has been licensed as an Illinois attorney since 1973. Brian Musburger is Todd Musburger's son and is not an attorney and is employed by plaintiff law firm. Brian develops presentations, prepares industry analyses, keeps abreast of the media industry, and assists with negotiations between clients and their media employers, and has been employed with plaintiff law firm since 1998....

The complaint in the case at bar alleges that on or about sometime in January 1998, defendant orally requested plaintiff to "serve as [defendant's] agent and exclusive legal representative for the negotiating and drafting of [defendant's] multi-million dollar agreements with the entertainment fields of radio and television." On February 6, 1998, plaintiff and defendant entered into a written agreement (1998 Agreement) where plaintiff agreed "to provide its services as [defendant's] exclusive representative for negotiating and drafting of [defendant's] agreements in the entertainment fields of radio and television." The complaint further alleges that plaintiff also agreed to provide advice and counseling "as needed," and to use its best efforts to locate other broadcast outlets that would be interested in defendant's services. Under the 1998 Agreement, defendant agreed to pay "the sum of 5% of the gross amount of the contract negotiated by [p]laintiff on [defendant's] behalf," and all expenses incurred on behalf of defendant....

The complaint then alleges that from September 2002 until September 2003, plaintiff "spent well over [200] hours aggressively and effectively negotiating with WLS and other radio stations for a renewal contract that was satisfactory to [defendant]." ... In particular, WLS offered defendant a 10-year renewal contract whereby defendant would be paid over $12 million.

The complaint alleges that on September 11, 2003, defendant instructed plaintiff to cease all negotiations for a one-week period and to terminate all efforts during that time period. On September 22, 2003, defendant executed a letter addressed to plaintiff terminating plaintiff as defendant's agent and legal representative.

On January 23, 2004, plaintiff executed a letter addressed to defendant including a bill for the work performed by plaintiff on defendant's behalf in 2002 and 2003. The bill provided for 170 hours at a billing rate of $475 per hour for the work performed by Todd Musburger, and 40 hours at a rate of $300 per hour for the work performed by Brian Musburger, for a total of $92,750. The bill was not itemized. Defendant refused to pay any portion of the bill.

Plaintiff filed its verified complaint against defendant on April 1, 2004, which included three counts alleging causes of action for breach of contract, quantum meruit, and unjust enrichment, respectively. Counts I and III of the complaint alleging breach of contract and unjust enrichment, respectively, dismissed by the trial court prior to trial because the counts did not state a cause of action, are not before this court. Only the alleged cause of action for quantum meruit is before this court....

This quantum meruit action was brought by plaintiff to collect fees for services performed for defendant between September 2002 and September 2003. A discharged attorney, in this case more accurately, a law firm, is entitled to recover the reasonable value of services performed.

As the trial court recognized, plaintiff law firm could only pursue an action for quantum meruit (and could not pursue a cause of action for breach of contract) because it was representing defendant on a contingent basis and was discharged in the midst of that representation. A client may discharge her attorney at any time, with or without cause. In quantum meruit recovery, the former client is liable for the reasonable value of the services received during the attorney's employment. Quantum meruit is based on the implied promise of a recipient of services to pay for valuable services because otherwise the recipient would be unjustly enriched. In some cases, it is possible for a client to receive services and yet not be enriched in a tangible way....

An attorney representing a client on a contingent basis who is discharged prior to the consummation of a transaction is entitled to recover the reasonable value of her services rendered. The attorney is not, however, entitled to enforce a contractual fee agreement or collect on the contingency. That would unreasonably interfere with a client's right to discharge her attorney at any time. Based on these principals, plaintiff pursued an action in quantum meruit and the jury returned a verdict in its favor....

Section 1 of the [Employment Agency] Act requires employment agencies to procure a license to operate from the Department of Labor. 225 ILCS 515/1 (West 2006). It requires them to file a schedule of fees with the Department and provides that "[i]t shall be unlawful for any employment agency to collect or attempt to collect any compensation for any service not specified in the schedule of fees filed with the department." 225 ILCS 515/1 (West 2006). The term "employment agency" is defined in section 11 of the Act as follows:

> "Any person engaged for gain or profit in the business of securing or attempting to secure employment for persons seeking employment or employees for employers. However, the term 'employment agency' shall not include any person engaged in the business of consulting or recruiting, and who in the course of such business is compensated solely by any employer to identify, appraise, or recommend an individual or individuals who are at least 18 years of age or who hold a high school diploma for consideration for a position, provided that in no instance is the individual who is identified, appraised, or recommended for consideration for such position charged a fee directly or indirectly in connection with such identification, appraisal, or recommendation, or for preparation of any resume, or on account of any other personal service performed by the person engaged in the business of consulting or recruiting; but this exclusion is not applicable to theatrical employment agencies or domestic service employment agencies." 225 ILCS 515/11 (West 2006).

The Act was enacted to provide regulation for the recruiting and placement industry, which otherwise lacked safeguards to ensure the ethical conduct of businesses and individuals who provided recruiting and placement services. *T.E. C. & Associates, Inc. v. Alberto-Culver Co.,* 131 Ill.App.3d 1085, 1096, 87 Ill. Dec. 220, 476 N.E.2d 1212 (1985). The Act governs the conduct of employment agencies and addresses the ability of an employment agency to recover fees for the placement of a job applicant with an employer.

In *National Talent Associates, Inc. v. Holland,* 76 Ill.App.3d 556, 32 Ill.Dec. 195, 395 N.E.2d 142 (1979), this court examined the scope of the Act. The *National Talent* court found that an agency that photographed children and submitted their photographs to booking agencies for consideration in placing children in advertising commercials was not an "employment agency." The purpose of the Act was central to the *National Talent* court's decision. The court first noted "the general rule that statutes which are regulatory and penal in nature generally require strict construction." *National Talent Associates, Inc.* 76 Ill.App.3d at 562, 32 Ill. Dec. 195, 395 N.E.2d 142. Further the court noted that, "the primary purpose of statutory construction is to ascertain and give effect to the intention of the legislature, and in so doing, courts should consider not only the language used but also the evil to be remedied." *National Talent Associates, Inc.,* 76 Ill.App.3d at 562, 32 Ill.Dec. 195, 395 N.E.2d 142. According to the court:

> "The evils incident to private employment agencies, which statutes such as the [Act] were enacted to correct, were summarized in a report published by the United States Bureau of Labor in October 1912 (United States Bureau of Labor Bulletin, No. 109, p. 36), as quoted in *Adams v. Tanner* [244 U.S. 590, 601–02, (1917)] (Brandeis, J., dissenting), as follows:
>
>> '1. Charging a fee and failing to make any effort to find work for the applicant.
>>
>> 2. Sending applicants where no work exists.
>>
>> 3. Sending applicants to distant points where no work or where unsatisfactory work exists, but whence the applicant will not return on account of the expense involved.
>>
>> 4. Collusion between the agent and employer, whereby the applicant is given a few days' work and then discharged to make way for new workmen, the agent and employer dividing the fee.
>>
>> 5. Charging exorbitant fees, or giving jobs to such applicants as contribute extra fees, presents, etc.
>>
>> 6. Inducing workers, particularly girls, who have been placed, to leave, pay another fee, and get a 'better job.'
>>
>> Other evils charged against employment agents are the congregating of persons for gambling or other evil practices, collusion with keepers of immoral houses, and the sending of women applicants to houses of prostitution; sometimes employment offices are maintained in saloons, with the resulting evils."'
>
> ...
>
> The [Act] ... consists primarily of regulations to remedy such abuses." *National Talent Associates, Inc.,* 76 Ill.App.3d at 563, 32 Ill. Dec. 195, 395 N.E.2d 142.

Defendant's claim that plaintiff's failure to comply with the licensing requirements of the Act bars it action to seek recovery for fees related to its representation of defendant in 2002 and 2003 is not persuasive. Plaintiff was not providing recruiting or placement services for defendant. Rather, plaintiff was engaged in negotiating and drafting the terms of defendant's contracts and providing legal counsel on the contract negotiations. Plaintiff law firm represented defendant as his legal counsel and was not sending defendant out to employers to apply for work. Plaintiff was working on a renewal of an existing contract while exploring the industry for a more lucrative contract from other radio and television stations. The services provided by plaintiff to defendant were vastly different than the recruiting and placement services governed by the Act.

The purpose of the Act is clear when all of the sections of the Act are read together in context. The Act is intended to apply to recruiting and placement agencies. An application of the Act's record-keeping requirements to an attorney-client relationship such as that between plaintiff and defendant does not follow logically. The Act requires every licensed private employment agency:

> "[T]o keep a complete record in the English language of all orders for employees which are received from prospective employers. Upon request of the Department, a licensee shall verify the date when the order was received, the name of the person recording the job order, the name and address of the employer seeking the services of an employee, the name of the person placing the order, the kind of employee requested, the qualifications required in the employee, the salary or wages to be paid if known, and the possible duration of the job. Prior to the placement of any job advertisement, an employment agency must have a current, bona fide job order, and must maintain a copy of both the advertisement and the job order in a register established specially for that purpose." 225 ILCS 515/3 (West 2006).

Plaintiff was not taking orders for jobs from anyone on defendant's behalf. Defendant was not "applying" for work; he was already employed by WLS. Defendant had an existing contract and retained plaintiff to assist in negotiating a more favorable renewal agreement when the contract was set to expire in 2004. Plaintiff was not "placing a job advertisement." It was hired to negotiate the terms of a renewal contract with defendant's then-employer, WLS, or a new contract with others in the same industry.

For the foregoing reasons, we cannot say that the trial court abused its discretion by denying defendant's motion for leave to file a fifth affirmative defense seeking to assert that plaintiff could not receive payment for its 2002 and 2003 services because it was not licensed to act as an employment agency pursuant to the Act....

Solis v. Blancarte

TAC-27089 (Sept. 2013)

... This proceeding arises out of the Petition to Determine Controversy filed by [Petitioner Mario Solis (hereinafter "Petitioner")] with the Labor Commissioner on April 30, 2012. The petition alleges that respondent entered into a representation agreement with petitioner, pursuant to which respondent agreed to act and acted as an unlicensed talent agent in violation of Labor Code section 1700.5, a provision of the Talent Agencies Act (TAA), Labor Code section 1700 et seq. The petition seeks a declaration that the contract is void and unenforceable, and that respondent is therefore barred from seeking any recovery under the terms of the contract....

Petitioner is a sports reporter and news anchor for a Los Angeles television station, KNBC Channel 4. Apart from his talents and activities as a broadcast journalist, petitioner's artistic pursuits include acting, script writing, voice overs, and performing as an entertainer. Respondent is a duly licensed attorney who is admitted by the state bar to practice law in the State of California.

Prior to July, 2002, when the parties entered into the engagement contract described below, respondent had on certain occasions provided legal services to the petitioner. In addition, according to petitioner, respondent had provided management type services to petitioner in connection with petitioner's interest in breaking into network television; specifically, respondent advised petitioner that he would keep his eye open for opportunities for petitioner to work in television. Sometime prior to July 8, 2002, KNBC approached petitioner and expressed an interest in hiring petitioner to work for the station as a sports reporter, news anchor, commentator, and analyst, as well as in other roles related to the entertainment programming offered by the station.

Following this expression of interest by KNBC, petitioner contacted respondent and asked him to represent petitioner in handling the negotiation of the terms of his employment with the station. Respondent was receptive to the proposal, and on July 8, 2002 the parties entered into a written engagement contract set out in the form of an engagement letter from respondent to petitioner. At the outset the letter states: "We appreciate your asking us to represent you in connection with your broadcasting and entertainment career, including without limitation, contract negotiations with KNBC Channel 4."

The engagement contract provided that respondent would be paid a five percent (5%) commission on all net monies paid to petitioner under the contract to be negotiated by respondent with KNBC. According to petitioner, respondent wanted to be paid a commission instead of a one-time fee because of the follow-up work he would do on the contract and because he would be acting as petitioner's representative and agent....

[T]hrough the end of 2007, respondent received his 5% share of petitioner's net monthly income under the employment agreement, representing the commissions due pursuant to the engagement contract. Thereafter, petitioner made no further commission payments to respondent....

On December 30, 2011, respondent filed a civil action against petitioner in the Los Angeles County Superior Court, Central District—Blancarte v. Solis, Case No. BC476169. The complaint sought to recover the commissions due under the engagement contract based on the net monies paid to petitioner between January 1, 2008 and August 31, 2009 pursuant to the employment agreement with KNBC.

After filing an answer to the complaint, which included an affirmative defense based on the TAA, petitioner filed the instant petition with the Labor Commissioner seeking a determination that the engagement contract was entered into is violation of the TAA and was therefore void and unenforceable....

[P]etitioner was a person rendering artistic and professional services in the medium of television for purposes of entertaining the public. Thus, it is clear petitioner was an artist within the meaning of section 1700.4, subdivision (b). The next, and crucial question, is whether respondent was engaged in the occupation of a talent agency, that is to say, whether he was engaged in procuring or in offering, promising, or attempting to procure employment or engagements for petitioner.

The principal and dominant activities that respondent performed on behalf of petitioner pursuant to the engagement contract involved the negotiation of the compensation and other terms of the agreements for the employment of petitioner by KNBC. The Labor Commissioner has long recognized that the acts undertaken in the course of negotiating an agreement for the employment of an artist constitute "procuring ... or attempting to procure employment" within the meaning of section 1700.4, subdivision (a).

> The term "procure," as used in Labor Code§ 1700.4(a), means "to get possession of: obtain, acquire, to cause to happen or be done: bring about." *Wachs v. Curry* 13 Cal.App.4th 616, 628 (1993). Thus, "procuring employment" under the Talent Agencies Act is not limited to initiating discussions with potential purchasers of the artist's professional services or otherwise soliciting employment; rather, "procurement" includes any active participation in a communication with a potential purchaser of the artist's services aimed at obtaining employment for

the artist, regardless of who initiated the communication The Labor Commissioner has long held that "procurement" includes the process of negotiating an agreement for an artist's services. Significantly, the Talent Agencies Act specifically provides that an unlicensed person may nevertheless participate in negotiating an employment contract for an artist, provided he or she does so "in conjunction with, and at the request of a licensed talent agent." Labor Code § 1700.44(d). This limited exception to the licensing requirement would be unnecessary if negotiating an employment contract for an artist did not require a license in the first place.

(Danielewski v. Agon Investment Company (Cal.Lab.Com., October 28, 2005) TAC No. 41 03, pages 15–16.)

The negotiation of petitioner's employment agreements with KNBC represented the bulk of the activities that respondent engaged in on behalf of petitioner under the engagement contract. Indeed, the contract was entered into for the purpose of having respondent conduct such negotiations, and respondent carried out the contract by effectuating and accomplishing that purpose. By negotiating the KNBC agreements on petitioner's behalf, respondent attempted to procure and procured employment for petitioner. As a consequence, respondent engaged in and carried out the occupation of a talent agency; because he did so without having first obtained a talent agency license from the Labor Commissioner, respondent violated the provision of Labor Code section 1700.5.

Respondent contends that because he is a duly licensed attorney, his activities in negotiating the KNBC agreements on behalf of petitioner should be treated as exempt from the licensing requirements of section 1700.5. The provisions of the TAA do not contain or recognize any such exemption. Moreover, respondent has provided no authority that would support the propriety of applying or creating such an exemption.

The applicable scope of the TAA has been delineated by the Supreme Court:

> The Act establishes its scope through a functional, not a titular, definition. It regulates conduct, not labels; it is the act of procuring (or soliciting), not the title of one's business, that qualifies one as a talent agency and subjects one to the Act's licensure and related requirements. (§ 1700.4, subd. (a).) Any person who procures employment—any individual, any corporation, any manager—is a talent agency subject to regulation. (§§ 1700.4, subd. (a).)

(Marathon Entertainment, Inc. v. Blasi 42 Cal.4th 974, 986 (2008).) As the foregoing makes perfectly clear, anyone who procures or solicits engagements for an artist is carrying on the occupation of a talent agency and must be licensed.

It is evident that the functional scope of the TAA admits of no exceptions and encompasses the procurement activities of respondent, even though he is an attorney. In this regard, it is of no moment that some of the skills respondent may have brought to the negotiations on behalf of petitioner are the result of skills for which he has been licensed as an attorney. As Labor Code section 1700.44 makes unequivocally clear, when someone who is not licensed under the TAA wishes to bring such skills to bear on the negotiation of an artist's contract, he must do so "in conjunction with, and at the request of, a licensed talent agency." Here, respondent acted entirely on his own and without a talent agency license; consequently, his conduct constituted a clear violation of the licensure requirements of section 1700.5.

The consequences that flow from a violation of the TAA are well settled. When a person contracts to act as a talent agent without first having obtained a talent agency license as required by the TAA, the contract that has been entered into is illegal, void, and unenforceable. "Since the clear object of the Act is to prevent improper persons from becoming [talent agents] and to regulate such activity for the protection of the public, a contract between an unlicensed [talent agent] and an artist is void." *(Buchwald v. Superior Court* 254 Cal.App. 2d 347, 351(1967).).

As recognized in *Marathon Entertainment, Inc. v. Blasi, supra,* in some cases there may be a basis for severing the illegal portions of a contract violative of the TAA's licensure requirements from the other parts of the contract. However, this will be permissible only where there are both illegal and legal aspects to the contract and where the two aspects can be properly severed in accordance with the legal standards governing application of the severance doctrine.

There is no basis for applying the doctrine of severability in the circumstances of this case. It is established law that if the central purpose of a contract is illegal, the entire contract is void and will not be enforced. In the present case, the central purpose of the engagement contract was to enable respondent to act as petitioners' unlicensed talent agent. This illegal purpose contaminated the entire contract, and rendered it void and unenforceable. In addition, in this case respondent is seeking to preserve his right to recover certain commissions under the engagement contract; the commissions that he seeks to protect are based on the income that respondent generated for petitioner through his illegal procurement activities. Plainly, respondent cannot capitalize on and gain a benefit from illegal conduct under a contract; in these circumstances, the illegality permeates the entire engagement contract and renders it void and unenforceable. In light of these conclusions, it is unnecessary to consider whether, in rendering services under the engagement contract, respondent engaged in other conduct violative of the TAA.

In sum, for the reasons stated above, it is determined that' in entering into the engagement contract with petitioner, and in performing under that contract, respondent engaged in the occupation of a talent agency without having obtained a license from the Labor Commissioner. Because it was pervaded by illegality, the entire contract is found to be void and unenforceable....

The contract between petitioner and respondent is declared to be illegal, void and unenforceable, and respondent is barred from enforcing or seeking to enforce the contract against petitioner in any manner.

Notes and Questions

a. As was the case with attorney Kurnit, lawyers who provide services other than traditional legal services, or who change their relationship with clients during the course of the representation, run the risk of violating rules of professional responsibility as well as the Talent Agencies Act. Nonetheless, these additional services are not uncommon among lawyers. What steps might an attorney take to protect against claims of any breach of ethical or legal duties?

b. Not every claim filed against the lawyer results in liability or the barring of attorneys' fees. For a claim upholding the one-third contingency fee earned for successfully challenging the royalty residuals owed to members of Lynyrd Skynyrd, see *King v. Fox*, No. 97 Civ. 4134, 2004 U.S. Dist. LEXIS 462 (S.D.N.Y. Jan. 16, 2004).

c. The one-year statute of limitations under the Talent Agency Act impacts the ability of artists to recover from payments made in violation of the act brought more than a year after the payment. To what extent does entering into a void talent agent agreement violate other attorney obligations that might extend the statute of limitations?

d. How much can a lawyer do for a client before becoming a conspirator? For a recent unpublished case involving the firm of Lowy and Zucker and the firm's representations to SAG and DGA, see *Parmet v. Lapin*, 2004 Cal. App. Unpub. LEXIS 5217 (Cal. Ct. App. June 1, 2004).

Problem IV-B

Having avoided signing with a representative purporting to be both talent agent and manager, Bryce receives an opportunity to run a motion picture company in a state which has no specific talent agency law. Bryce is told to seek local legal counsel to negotiate the agreement if Bryce plans to relocate to the home of the production company. The attorney Bryce calls offers to negotiate the contract for a five percent commission on Bryce's earnings (from any source) during the term of the employment agreement, including any extensions to that agreement. The retainer letter provides that local law applies to the engagement letter, so California law does not apply.

Explain to Bryce what terms are reasonable for a talent agent agreement and for a management agreement, describing the difference(s) between the two roles.

C. Enforcement of Contracts for Minors

Expansion of Coogan Laws

Federal employment law does not govern the wages or working conditions for minors in the entertainment industry. Under 29 U.S.C. § 213(c)(1)(C)(3) of the Fair Labor Standards Act, federal employment law "relating to child labor shall not apply to any child employed as an actor or performer in motion pictures or theatrical productions, or in radio or television productions." The exclusion regarding child media productions shifts all legislation to the states.

In the area of minors' contracts, the laws have improved since the first Coogan Law was passed in 1939. California updated its law in 2000 and New York adopted a Coogan Law for the first time in 2003. Jackie Coogan, who starred with Charlie Chaplin in *The Kid* at the age of four, never saw any of his childhood fortune because the adults who were supposed to be protecting him spent it.

> In California a law designed to protect the earnings of child actors, known as the Coogan Law was enacted in 1939. The law was named for child actor Jackie Coogan, who filed suit against his parents to recover the $4 million fortune he had made as a popular child actor. However the law was ineffective and the Screen Actors Guild lobbied to have it amended. California's new Coogan Law (SB 1162) became effective on January 1, 2000 and it ensures that every time young performers work under an entertainment contract, 15% of the gross earnings will be set aside for them until they reach legal majority. The bill also makes it clear that the earnings of a minor are the legal property of the minor and not his parents.

Alliance of Canadian Cinema, Television and Radio Artists, Minor's Trust Frequently Asked Questions.[5]

---

5. http://www.actra.ca/main/prs/minors-trust/minors-trust-faq/ (last visited Dec. 16, 2013).

In September 2003, New York joined California with new legislation for the protection of minors. As summarized in a press release from the Actors Equity Association, the law creates the second of the Coogan Laws:

> Similar to the California "Coogan Law," named after child star Jackie Coogan, the New York law requires that 15% of all child performers' earnings be set aside until the age of majority (18 years of age), protecting the earnings of the minor. On the education front, employers must provide a teacher, who is either New York State certified or has credentials recognized by the State, to any child performer who cannot attend school due to his or her employment (when a teacher is provided, the performers will not be marked absent from school while working). Parents will be responsible for getting work permits from the Department of Labor for their children, renewable after six months. Employers will apply to the Labor Department for certificates of eligibility to employ a child, which lasts three years. The law [took effect] on March 28, 2004.

Actors Equity Association News, *Stars, Union Officials and Child Performers Celebrate Passage of NY State's New "Coogan" Law*.[6] Despite these improvements, only two states have such laws. (Florida has a much weaker provision.) In addition, there is not a pattern yet established to ensure that most child workers have their contracts treated appropriately under the new laws.

California Family Code § 6750

(a) This chapter applies to the following contracts entered into between an unemancipated minor and any third party or parties on or after January 1, 2000:

> (1) A contract pursuant to which a minor is employed or agrees to render artistic or creative services, either directly or through a third party, including, but not limited to, a personal services corporation (loan-out company), or through a casting agency. "Artistic or creative services" includes, but is not limited to, services as an actor, actress, dancer, musician, comedian, singer, stunt-person, voice-over artist, or other performer or entertainer, or as a songwriter, musical producer or arranger, writer, director, producer, production executive, choreographer, composer, conductor, or designer.

> (2) A contract pursuant to which a minor agrees to purchase, or otherwise secure, sell, lease, license, or otherwise dispose of literary, musical, or dramatic properties, or use of a person's likeness, voice recording, performance, or story of or incidents in his or her life, either tangible or intangible, or any rights therein for use in motion pictures, television, the production of sound recordings in any format now known or hereafter devised, the legitimate or living stage, or otherwise in the entertainment field.

> (3) A contract pursuant to which a minor is employed or agrees to render services as a participant or player in a sport.

(b) (1) If a minor is employed or agrees to render services directly for any person or entity, that person or entity shall be considered the minor's employer for purposes of this chapter.

> (2) If a minor's services are being rendered through a third-party individual or personal services corporation (loan-out company), the person to whom or entity to which that third party is providing the minor's services shall be considered the minor's employer for purposes of this chapter.

---

6. http://www.actorsequity.org/TheatreNews/coogans_11-20-2003.html (Nov. 20, 2003).

(3) If a minor renders services as an extra, background performer, or in a similar capacity through an agency or service that provides one or more of those performers for a fee (casting agency), the agency or service shall be considered the minor's employer for the purposes of this chapter.

(c) (1) For purposes of this chapter, the minor's "gross earnings" shall mean the total compensation payable to the minor under the contract or, if the minor's services are being rendered through a third-party individual or personal services corporation (loan-out company), the total compensation payable to that third party for the services of the minor.

(2) Notwithstanding paragraph (1), with respect to contracts pursuant to which a minor is employed or agrees to render services as a musician, singer, songwriter, musical producer, or arranger only, for purposes of this chapter, the minor's "gross earnings" shall mean the total amount paid to the minor pursuant to the contract, including the payment of any advances to the minor pursuant to the contract, but excluding deductions to offset those advances or other expenses incurred by the employer pursuant to the contract, or, if the minor's services are being rendered through a third-party individual or personal services corporation (loan-out company), the total amount payable to that third party for the services of the minor.

New York Arts and Cultural Affairs Law § 35.03. Judicial approval of certain contracts for services of infants; effect of approval; guardianship of savings

1. A contract made by an infant or made by a parent or guardian of an infant, or a contract proposed to be so made, under which (a) the infant is to perform or render services as an actor, actress, dancer, musician, vocalist or other performing artist, or as a participant or player in professional sports, or (b) a person is employed to render services to the infant in connection with such services of the infant or in connection with contracts therefor, may be approved by the supreme court or the surrogate's court as provided in this section where the infant is a resident of this state or the services of the infant are to be performed or rendered in this state. If the contract is so approved the infant may not, either during his minority or upon reaching his majority, disaffirm the contract on the ground of infancy or assert that the parent or guardian lacked authority to make the contract. A contract modified, amended or assigned after its approval under this section shall be deemed a new contract....

California Labor Code § 2855. Enforcement of contract to render personal service; time limit

(a) ... [A] contract to render personal service, ... may not be enforced against the employee beyond seven years from the commencement of service under it. Any contract, otherwise valid, to perform or render service of a special, unique, unusual, extraordinary, or intellectual character, which gives it peculiar value and the loss of which can not be reasonably or adequately compensated in damages in an action at law, may nevertheless be enforced against the person contracting to render the service, for a term not to exceed seven years from the commencement of service under it. If the employee voluntarily continues to serve under it beyond that time, the contract may be referred to as affording a presumptive measure of the compensation.

(b) Notwithstanding subdivision (a):

(1) Any employee who is a party to a contract to render personal service in the production of phonorecords in which sounds are first fixed, as defined in Section 101 of Title 17 of the United States Code, may not invoke the provisions of subdivision (a) without first giving written notice to the employer in accordance with Section 1020

of the Code of Civil Procedure, specifying that the employee from and after a future date certain specified in the notice will no longer render service under the contract by reason of subdivision (a).

(2) Any party to such a contract shall have the right to recover damages for a breach of the contract occurring during its term in an action commenced during or after its term, but within the applicable period prescribed by law.

(3) In the event a party to such a contract is, or could contractually be, required to render personal service in the production of a specified quantity of the phonorecords and fails to render all of the required service prior to the date specified in the notice provided in paragraph (1), the party damaged by the failure shall have the right to recover damages for each phonorecord as to which that party has failed to render service in an action which, notwithstanding paragraph (2), shall be commenced within 45 days after the date specified in the notice.

Scott Eden Management v. Kavovit
N.Y.S.2d 1001 (1990)

In this case of first impression, an infant actor has disaffirmed a personal services contract. He thereby seeks to avoid responsibility to his manager for commissions due in the future on income from performance contracts already obtained for him by the manager.

The salient facts are not in dispute. In 1984, when defendant Andrew M. Kavovit was 12 years of age, he and his defendant parents entered into a contract with plaintiffs (Scott Eden) whereby Scott Eden became the exclusive personal manager to supervise and promote Andrew's career in the entertainment industry. This agreement ran from February 8, 1984 to February 8, 1986 with an extension for another three years to February 8, 1989. It provided that Scott Eden was entitled to a 15% commission on Andrew's gross compensation. "With respect to contracts entered into by [Andrew] ... during the term of this agreement ... [Scott Eden] shall be entitled to [its] commission from the residuals or royalties of such contracts, the full term of such contracts, including all extensions or renewals thereof, notwithstanding the earlier termination of this agreement."

In 1986, Andrew signed an agency contract with the Andreadis Agency, a licensed agent selected by Scott Eden pursuant to industry requirements. This involved an additional 10% commission. Thereafter, Andrew signed several contracts for his services. The most important contract, from a financial and career point of view, secured a role for Andrew on "As the World Turns," a long-running television soap opera. Income from this employment contract appears to have commenced on December 28, 1987 and continues through December 28, 1990, with a strong possibility for renewal.

One week before the contract with Scott Eden was to expire, Andrew's attorney notified Scott Eden that his "clients hereby disaffirm the contract on the grounds [sic] of infancy". Up until then, the Andreadis Agency had been forwarding Scott Eden its commissions, but by letter of February 4, 1989, Andrew's father, David Kavovit, advised Andreadis that Andrew's salary would go directly to Andrew and that he would send Andreadis its 10%. Needless to say, no further commissions were sent to Scott Eden.

The complaint seeks money damages for (1) all sums due plaintiffs for commissions relating to Andrew's personal appearances prior to February 8, 1989, the date of disaffirmance, (2) all sums due plaintiff for commissions with respect to contracts entered into by Andrew in the entertainment or promotion fields during the term of his contract with plaintiffs, "i.e., commissions from the residuals or royalties of such contracts—the full term of such contracts—including all extensions or renewals thereof", and (3) $50,000 for tortious interference with the relationship between plaintiff and the Andreadis Agency....

An infant's contract is voidable and the infant has an absolute right to disaffirm. This aspect of the law of contracts was well entrenched in the common law as early as the 15th century. In bringing this action, and defending the motion, plaintiffs fully recognize the principle of law involved here and in no way challenge the infant's right to disaffirm. Rather, plaintiffs rely upon a corollary to the main rule, which also evolved early in the common law

> "After disaffirmance, the infant is not entitled to be put in a position superior to such a one as he would have occupied if he had never entered into his voidable agreement. He is not entitled to retain an advantage from a transaction which he repudiates. 'The privilege of infancy is to be used as a shield and not as a sword.'"

As stated differently by the same court in an earlier case involving an infant's disaffirmance:

> "The theory of a rescission is that the party proceeded against shall be restored to his original position. The plaintiff cannot rescind if he retains in himself or withholds through another any fruit of the contract."

The restoration of consideration requirement found voice in *CPLR 3004* which states that the infant need not tender restoration of benefits received prior to disaffirmance "but the court may make a tender of restoration a condition of its judgment, and may otherwise in its judgment so adjust the equities between the parties that unjust enrichment is avoided." The restoration of consideration principle, as interpreted by the courts, has resulted in the infant being responsible for wear and tear on the goods returned by him. In the event that the minor cannot return the benefits obtained, he is effectively precluded from disaffirming the contract in order to get back the consideration he has given. In *Vichnes v Transcontinental & W. Air* (173 Misc 631) the infant paid the air fare from New York to Los Angeles. On returning to New York she demanded the return of her money. Appellate Term granted summary judgment to defendant because "there is no basis for rescission here in view of the concession that the reasonable value of the transportation was the sum paid by plaintiff."

The parties have not cited, nor has the court found, a case dealing with the exact issue at bar, i.e., whether disaffirmance may void the contractual obligation to pay agents' commissions without any concomitant exchange being made. However, an analogy may be drawn from the case of *Mutual Milk & Cream Co. v Prigge* (112 App Div 652). There, a minor had entered the employ of the plaintiff as a milk wagon driver and had signed a contract which included a restrictive covenant wherein the minor agreed not to solicit plaintiff's customers within three years after leaving plaintiff's employ. Several months after entering into the contract, the minor quit, pursuant to the terms of the contract, but then went to work for plaintiff's rival and solicited business from plaintiff's customers.

The Appellate Division affirmed the issuance of an injunction against the minor, who had pleaded infancy in avoidance of the contractual obligations. The court considered that the issue was not one of liability of an infant for a breach of his contract, but whether an infant should be allowed to repudiate his contract without restoring what he had received and, if restoration could not be made, without being enjoined from making use of the information he had gained from his employment by the plaintiff to the latter's damage. The court held that the infant should be enjoined "from making use of that information in violation of his agreement made at the time when he desired and obtained employment and upon the faith of which he obtained the information and acquaintance." The court further noted that "No man would engage the services of an infant if he could not impose the same condition for his own protection against the use of his formulas, trade secrets, and lists of customers that he could exact of an adult."

The rationale of the *Mutual Milk* case is applicable to this case. The work a personal manager does for and with his client is preparatory to the performance contract. Once a performance contract has been signed, the personal manager is entitled to his percentage fee, subject only to the condition subsequent that the client performs and earns his fee. This is clearly the understanding in the industry, unlike, for example, the standard in the insurance field where the initial commission is disproportionately high and the subsequent, smaller commissions are viewed as consideration for continued efforts in keeping the insurance contract current. When the client signs a performance contract, it is with the understanding that the gross amount to be paid is not solely for him. It is the expectation of all parties—the agent, the performer and, in this case, the soap opera production company, that 15% of that gross amount belongs to the personal manager. To the extent that the performer obtains that 15% for himself, he is unjustly enriched.

Here, the position adopted by defendants is no different than that advanced on behalf of the infant who had taken the airplane ride and wanted her money back or the truck driver who had milked his employer's efforts and tutelage and then refused to honor his reciprocal commitment. In each case, the infant consumed the fruits of the contract and refused to pay for that fruit, to the clear prejudice of the other party. In this case, the infant will continue to reap the benefits of his contract with plaintiff but is using his infancy as an excuse not to honor the promise made in return for that benefit.

If the argument asserted by defendants were adopted by the court, the infant would be put in a position superior to that which he would have occupied had he never entered into the contract with plaintiff. He would be retaining an advantage from the repudiated transaction, i.e., using the privilege of infancy as a sword rather than a shield. Not only is this manifestly unfair, but it would undermine the policy underlying the rule allowing disaffirmance. If the infant may rescind the contract with the manager immediately after a lucrative performance contract is signed, yet still retain the benefits of the performance contract, no reputable manager will expend any efforts on behalf of an infant.

In this case, adjustment of the equities so as to prevent unjust enrichment, as suggested by *CPLR 3004*, leads to the conclusion that defendants must continue to pay to plaintiffs all commissions to which plaintiffs would be entitled under their contract, as they become due. Thus, on the first two causes of action summary judgment is denied to defendants and is granted to plaintiffs to the extent that they shall be restored to their original condition. Moreover, inasmuch as plaintiffs will no longer be involved in the day-to-day personal management of the infant, they will be entitled to periodic statements regarding Andrew's income and the sources thereof and they shall have the right to annual inspections of the books and records kept with regard to Andrew's income.

The third cause of action is dismissed. Plaintiffs have come forward with no proof to buttress their conclusory claim that defendants have tortiously interfered with their business relationship with the Andreadis Agency.

The court notes that this entire situation may have arisen due to a misreading of a statute which is related to the problem at hand but irrelevant to its determination. The affidavit of David J. Kavovit makes reference to *Arts and Cultural Affairs Law § 35.03* as a bar to this action and that "I am advised that the agreement was void at its inception by reason of the fact that its term, including options to extend, exceeded a three year period of time."

Section 35.03 provides for judicial approval of infants' contracts in order to avoid later disaffirmance. However, no such contract may be approved if it extends for a period of more than three years, whether by option or otherwise. However, the purpose of the statute was to limit the infant's right to disaffirm. If there is no judicial approval, for whatever reason, then the statute has no effect upon the infant's contract or upon his right to disaffirm.

Berg v. Traylor
148 Cal.App.4th 809 (2007)

Appellants Meshiel Cooper Traylor (Meshiel) and her minor son Craig Lamar Traylor (Craig) appeal the judgment confirming an arbitration award in favor of Craig's former personal manager, respondent Sharyn Berg (Berg), for unpaid commissions under a contract between Berg, Meshiel and Craig and unrepaid loans from Berg. Because we find that Craig had the statutory right as a minor to disaffirm both the original contract and the arbitration award, we reverse the judgment against Craig. We affirm the judgment against Meshiel.

On January 18, 1999, Berg entered into a two-page "Artist's Manager's Agreement" (agreement) with Meshiel and Craig, who was then 10 years old. Meshiel signed the agreement and wrote Craig's name on the signature page where he was designated "Artist." Craig did not sign the agreement. Pursuant to the agreement, Berg was to act as Craig's exclusive personal manager in exchange for a commission of 15 percent of all gross monies or other consideration paid to him as an artist during the three-year term of the agreement, as well as income from merchandising or promotional efforts or offers of employment made during the term of the agreement, regardless of when Craig received such monies. The agreement expressly provided that any action Craig "may take in the future pertaining to disaffirmance of this agreement, whether successful or not," would not affect Meshiel's liability for any commissions due Berg. The agreement also provided that any disputes concerning payment or interpretation of the agreement would be determined by arbitration in accordance with the rules of Judicial Arbitration and Mediation Services, Inc. (JAMS).

On or about June 13, 2001, Craig obtained a recurring acting role on the Fox Television Network show "Malcolm in the Middle" (show). On September 11, 2001, four months prior to the expiration of the agreement, Meshiel sent a certified letter to Berg stating that while she and Craig appreciated her advice and guidance, they no longer needed her management services and could no longer afford to pay Berg her 15 percent commission because they owed a "huge amount" of taxes. On September 28, 2001, Berg responded, informing appellants that they were in breach of the agreement.

In 2004, Berg filed suit against Meshiel and Craig for breach of the agreement, breach of the implied covenant of good faith and fair dealing, breach of an oral loan agreement, conversion and declaratory relief....

Because appellants had failed to pay their share of the arbitration fees, Berg did not anticipate their appearance and did not retain a court reporter. Though Meshiel and Craig's counsel failed to appear at the hearing, Meshiel personally appeared with Craig's talent agent, Steven Rice. Craig did not appear. According to Meshiel, the arbitrator denied her request for a two-week continuance. The arbitrator permitted Meshiel to use Rice's assistance and advice in presenting her case. Rice asserted that the agreement was invalid because Craig was a minor at the time it was executed and there had been no court approval of the agreement....

The arbitrator awarded Berg commissions and interest of $154,714.15, repayment of personal loans and interest of $5,094, and attorney fees and costs of $13,762. He also awarded Berg $405,000 "for future earnings projected on a minimum of 6 years for national syndication earnings," and stated that this part of the award would "vest and become final, as monies earned after February 7, 2005, become due and payable." On February 20, 2005, the arbitrator served a clarification of the award, stating that "all monies earned by Craig Traylor, pursuant to the contract with Ms. Berg, are paid directly to Ms. Berg.... After deduction of fees and commissions, etc., the balance of the funds shall be forwarded to the client."...

On July 8, 2005, Berg served a petition to confirm the arbitration award, which was filed on July 12, 2005.... Appellants then filed a motion to vacate the judgment pursuant to Code of Civil Procedure section 473. While the motion was pending, appellants filed a notice of appeal from the judgment. In a January 2006 order, the trial court determined that it had no jurisdiction to rule on the matter in light of the appeal and ordered the motion off calendar.

Simply stated, one who provides a minor with goods and services does so at her own risk. The agreement here expressly contemplated this risk, requiring that Meshiel remain obligated for commissions due under the agreement regardless of whether Craig disaffirmed the agreement. Thus, we have no difficulty in reaching the conclusion that Craig is permitted to and did disaffirm the agreement and any obligations stemming therefrom, while Meshiel remains liable under the agreement and resulting judgment. Where our difficulty lies is in understanding how counsel, the arbitrator and the trial court repeatedly and systematically ignored Craig's interests in this matter. From the time Meshiel signed the agreement, her interests were not aligned with Craig's. That no one—counsel, the arbitrator or the trial court—recognized this conflict and sought appointment of a guardian ad litem for Craig is nothing short of stunning. It is the court's responsibility to protect the rights of a minor who is a litigant in court.

Our review of an arbitrator's award is generally limited. In *Aguilar v. Lerner* 32 Cal.4th 974, 981–982 (2004), the Supreme Court stated: "When parties choose to forgo the traditional court system and arbitrate their claims, it is assumed they wish to have a final and conclusive resolution of their dispute. The Legislature has recognized this underlying assumption of finality and has, by statute, limited the grounds for judicial review of an arbitrator's award. (Code Civ. Proc., §1286.2.) Consistent with this legislative intent, we recognized the general rule that 'an arbitrator's decision cannot be reviewed for errors of fact or law.' (*Moncharsh v. Heily & Blase* 3 Cal.4th 1, 11 (1992).) We explained that because the Legislature has provided certain statutory grounds to overturn or modify an arbitrator's decision, courts should not subject such decisions to standard judicial review. In addition, however, to the statutory grounds for vacating an arbitrator's award, we explained in *Moncharsh* 'that there may be some limited and exceptional circumstances justifying judicial review of an arbitrator's decision.... Such cases would include those in which granting finality to an arbitrator's decision would be inconsistent with the protection of a party's *statutory rights*.'"...

The trial court denied appellants' petition to vacate the arbitration award on the ground that it was untimely. Code of Civil Procedure section 1288 provides that a petition to vacate or correct an arbitration award must be served and filed no later than 100 days after the date of service of a signed copy of the award on the petitioner. Code of Civil Procedure section 1290.6 provides that a response to a petition to confirm an award must be served and filed within 10 days after service of the petition. Here, the arbitration award was served on February 14, 2005 and the clarification of the award was served on February 20, 2005. Berg's petition to confirm the award was served on July 8, 2005 and filed on July 12, 2005. It is undisputed that by the time appellants' fourth and current counsel substituted into the action and thereafter filed a petition to vacate the arbitration award and response to the petition to confirm it on August 18, 2005, both of these statutory deadlines had passed.

Appellants contend that despite the lapse of these deadlines, Craig had the statutory right as a minor to disaffirm both the original agreement with Berg containing the arbitration provision and the arbitration award itself. We agree. Craig's minority status entitled him to disaffirm the agreement and his minority status coupled with the absence of the appointment of guardian ad litem entitled him to disaffirm the arbitration award and judgment even after the statutory deadline for moving to vacate the arbitration award had passed.

"As a general proposition, parental consent is required for the provision of services to minors for the simple reason that minors may disaffirm their own contracts to acquire such services." (*Ballard v. Anderson* 4 Cal.3d 873, 878 (1971).) According to Family Code section 6700, "a minor may make a contract in the same manner as an adult, subject to the power of disaffirmance" provided by Family Code section 6710. In turn, Family Code section 6710 states: "Except as otherwise provided by statute, a contract of a minor may be disaffirmed by the minor before majority or within a reasonable time afterwards or, in case of the minor's death within that period, by the minor's heirs or personal representative." Sound policy considerations support this provision: "The law shields minors from their lack of judgment and experience and under certain conditions vests in them the right to disaffirm their contracts. Although in many instances such disaffirmance may be a hardship upon those who deal with an infant, the right to avoid his contracts is conferred by law upon a minor 'for his protection against his own improvidence and the designs of others.' It is the policy of the law to protect a minor against himself and his indiscretions and immaturity as well as against the machinations of other people and to discourage adults from contracting with an infant. Any loss occasioned by the disaffirmance of a minor's contract might have been avoided by declining to enter into the contract." (*Niemann v. Deverich* 98 Cal.App.2d 787, 793 (1950).)

Berg offers two reasons why the plain language of Family Code section 6710 is inapplicable, neither of which we find persuasive. First, she argues that a minor may not disaffirm an agreement signed by a parent. She relies on two cases to support her position, both of which are inapposite because they address discrete public policy concerns not at issue here [*e.g.,* a healthcare contract containing an arbitration provision signed by the minor's father and a liability release signed by a parent relating to a minor's participation in a school program]. Further, because there is a statutory procedure governing contracts in which minors agree to render artistic or creative services, there is no danger that talent managers will decline to contract with minors absent their parents contracting on their behalf. (See Fam.Code, §§ 6750, 6751, subd. (a).)[7]

Second, Berg argues that Craig cannot disaffirm the agreement because it was for his and his family's necessities. Family Code section 6712 provides that a valid contract cannot be disaffirmed by a minor if all of the following requirements are met: the contract is to pay the reasonable value of things necessary for the support of the minor or the minor's family, the things have actually been furnished to the minor or the minor's fam-

---

7. While we recognize that the agreement here does not fall within the parameters of the contracts specified by Family Code section 6750, subdivision (a), which generally involve the employment of a minor to render artistic services, there was evidence below that parties to agreements for the provision of personal management services in the entertainment industry routinely seek court approval for the protection of all involved.

ily, and the contract is entered into by the minor when not under the care of a parent or guardian able to provide for the minor or the minor's family. These requirements are not met here. The agreement was not a contract to pay for the necessities of life for Craig or his family.... Family Code section 6712 does not bar the minor's disaffirmance of the contract....

We find that Craig was entitled to and did disaffirm the agreement which, among other things, required him to arbitrate his disputes with Berg. On this basis alone, therefore, the judgment confirming the arbitration award must be reversed.

Although it is unnecessary to our disposition, we further find that Craig was entitled to and did disaffirm the arbitration award because he was never represented by an appointed guardian ad litem.

Code of Civil Procedure section 372, subdivision (a) requires that a minor who is a party to a lawsuit "shall appear either by a guardian or conservator of the estate or by a guardian ad litem appointed by the court in which the action or proceeding is pending, or by a judge thereof, in each case." As aptly explained in *Keane v. Penha* 76 Cal.App.2d 693, 696 (1946): "It is the general rule that an omission to cause the appointment of a guardian if there be none is fatal to all subsequent steps taken in the action.... Unless a minor is 'duly represented as provided by law' at the time a judgment is entered against him his right to disaffirm such judgment 'continues until barred by laches after the minor has attained the age of majority.' Such a judgment is voidable and may be disaffirmed. The right of disaffirmance by a minor of a judgment rendered voidable by the fact that he was not represented by a guardian in the action is absolute, and such right continues throughout his minority.

Berg contends that no appointment of a guardian ad litem was necessary because Meshiel functioned as Craig's "guardian." She relies on a declaration submitted in support of appellants' petition to vacate the arbitration award in which Meshiel averred that she was "the natural mother and guardian of Craig." Meshiel's self-characterization in no way obviated the need for the appointment of a guardian ad litem to represent Craig's interests. Code of Civil Procedure, section 372, subdivision (a) provides that "[a] guardian ad litem may be appointed in any case when it is deemed by the court in which the action or proceeding is prosecuted, or by a judge thereof, expedient to appoint a guardian ad litem to represent the minor, ... notwithstanding that the person may have a guardian or conservator of the estate and may have appeared by the guardian or conservator of the estate."

Such an appointment was required here due to the inherent conflict of interest between Craig and Meshiel. The agreement expressly provided that if even Craig disaffirmed, Meshiel would remain liable for commissions due Berg. It was therefore not in Meshiel's interest to have Craig disaffirm the agreement because Berg would look to her, personally, for satisfaction of Craig's obligations under the agreement. As such, Meshiel's interests in the lawsuit were in direct conflict with those of her son's. It is clear that Meshiel, as Craig's guardian, could not adequately represent his interests. "'When there is a potential conflict between a perceived parental responsibility and an obligation to assist the court in achieving a just and speedy determination of the action,' a court has the right to select a guardian ad litem who is not a parent if that guardian would best protect the child's interests." (*Williams v. Superior Court, supra.* 147 Cal.App.4th at 49.) As such, it was necessary for Craig to have a guardian ad litem appointed to separately represent his interest with respect to Berg's claims....

Appellants do not generally distinguish their arguments between mother and son, apparently assuming that if Craig disaffirms the agreement and judgment, Meshiel would be permitted to escape liability as well. But a disaffirmance of an agreement by a minor does not operate to terminate the contractual obligations of the parent who signed the agreement. The agreement Meshiel signed provided that Craig's disaffirmance would not serve to void or avoid Meshiel's obligations under the agreement and that Meshiel remained liable for commissions due Berg regardless of Craig's disaffirmance. Accordingly, we find no basis for Meshiel to avoid her independent obligations under the agreement.

Appellants remaining challenges to the arbitration award do not mandate reversal of the judgment as to Meshiel. They argue that the award must be vacated because the arbitrator refused to postpone the hearing despite sufficient cause being shown. (Code Civ. Proc., § 1286.2, subd. (a)(5).) They also raise the defense that the agreement was unenforceable because Berg was allegedly performing the acts of an unlicensed agent in violation of the Talent Agencies Act (Lab.Code, § 1700 et seq.) (the Act), an issue not raised at the arbitration.[8] But Meshiel fails to explain how these issues can be considered after she stipulated to the finality of the arbitration award. More importantly, her failure to file a timely petition to vacate the arbitration award bars her from challenging the judgment confirming the award on appeal.

While we conclude that Craig nevertheless had the right to disaffirm the arbitration award and the subsequent judgment as an unrepresented minor, Meshiel has not provided us with any authority that would permit her now to challenge the award against her. Accordingly, the judgment confirming the arbitration award is affirmed as to Meshiel. The judgment is reversed as to Craig and affirmed as to Meshiel. The parties to bear their own costs on appeal.

Notes and Questions

a. California has a similar statutory provision to that discussed above.

> A minor cannot disaffirm a contract, otherwise valid, entered into during minority, either during the actual minority of the minor entering into such contract or at any time thereafter, with a duly licensed talent agency as defined in Section 1700.4 to secure him engagements to render artistic or creative services in motion pictures, television, the production of phonograph records, the legitimate or living stage, or otherwise in the entertainment field including, but without being limited to, services as an actor, actress, dancer, musician, comedian, singer, or other performer or entertainer, or as a writer, director, producer, production executive, choreographer, composer, conductor or designer, the blank form of which has been approved by the Labor Commissioner pursuant to Section 1700.23, where such contract has been approved by the superior court of the county where such minor resides or is employed.

Cal. Lab. Code § 1700.37 (2003).

b. The language in both California Labor Code § 1700.37 and New York Arts and Cultural Affairs Law § 35.03 provides that a court approved contract involving a minor cannot be disaffirmed. After *Scott Eden Management v. Kavovit*, is there any remaining need

---

8. In its amicus curiae brief, SAG raises for the first time the issue that this defense must be resolved by the California Labor Commissioner, who has exclusive authority to hear disputes arising under the Act. Appellants never raised this issue below and we decline to consider it. "California courts refuse to consider arguments raised by amicus curiae when those arguments are not presented in the trial court, and are not urged by the parties on appeal.["]

to seek court approval for manager contracts or talent agency contracts? So long as the talented minor enters into a role prior to the disaffirmance, the *Scott Eden Management* decision suggests the manager remains entitled to that income stream in perpetuity despite the lack of any judicial approval. Would a California court give this same construction to the meaning of its statute?

Problem IV-C

Bryce stops by your office holding a folded-up contract. Bryce explains that last year, at the age of seventeen, Bryce agreed to a three-year contract to appear in direct-to-video films being shot in California. Bryce appeared in the first of the films, an adult-oriented comedy. Although Bryce was not featured in any of the film's scenes that involved nudity or more mature content, Bryce feels the film was terrible and embarrassing both personally and professionally. Bryce has recently been asked to appear in the second film. Even though Bryce had not appeared nude in the first film, the signed contract included a nudity rider, specifically authorizing the filmmakers to photograph Bryce nude in the film. The contract was signed in California, the same state where Bryce had acted in the first film.

Bryce wants to repudiate the contract, get out of any future filming obligation, and ideally have Bryce's name removed from any future copies of the first film. Bryce is not asking to enjoin the distribution of the first film or to have the film re-edited.

Inform Bryce of the basis for terminating the agreement or disaffirming the obligations under the agreement and whether the California courts would allow the disaffirmance.

D. Bibliography and Links

Donald E. Biederman, *Agents v. Managers Revisited,* 1 Vand. J. Ent. L. & Prac. 5 (1999).

William A. Birdthistle, *A Contested Ascendancy: Problems with Personal Managers Acting as Producers,* 20 Loy. L.A. Ent. L. Rev. 493 (2000).

Christopher C. Cianci, *Entertainment or Exploitation?: Reality Television and the Inadequate Protection of Child Participants Under the Law,* 18 S. Cal. Interdis. L.J. 363 (2009).

Saira Din, *Review of Selected 2003 California Legislation: Family Chapter 667: Instituting Proper Trust Funds and Safeguarding the Earnings of Child Performers from Dissipation by Parents, Guardians and Trustees,* 35 McGeorge L. Rev. 473 (2004).

Shayne J. Heller, *Legislative Updates: The Price Of Celebrity: When a Child's Star-Studded Career Amounts to Nothing,* 10 DePaul-LCA J. Art & Ent. L. 161 (1999).

Erin M. Jacobson, *360 Deals and the California Talent Agencies Act Are Record Labels Procuring Employment?,* 29 Ent. & Sports Law. 9 (2011).

Edwin F. McPherson, *The Talent Agencies Act: Time for a Change,* 19 Hastings Comm. & Ent. L.J. 899 (1997).

Kimberlianne Podlas, *Does Exploiting a Child Amount to Employing a Child? The FLSA's Child Labor Provisions and Children on Reality Television,* 17 UCLA Ent. L. Rev. 39 (2010).

Maria A. Sanders, *Singing Machines: Boy Bands and the Struggle for Artistic Legitimacy,* 20 Cardozo Arts & Ent. L.J. 525 (2002).

Matthew H. Schwartz, *Beaten to "Submissions": Talent Agents Score a Victory over Managers on Submissions of Motion Picture Screenplays,* 22 J. Nat'l Ass'n Admin L. Judges 145 (2002).

Koh Siok Tian Wilson, *Symposium Selected Issues in Labor Relations in the Motion Picture and Television Industries: Talent Agents as Producers: A Historical Perspective of Screen Actors Guild Regulation and the Rising Conflict with Managers,* 21 Loy. L.A. Ent. L.J. 401 (2001).

Symposium: The Uniform Athlete Agents Act, 13 Seton Hall J. Sports L. 345 (2003).

Chapter V

First Amendment Aspects of the Entertainment Industry

A. First Amendment Recognition of the Entertainment Industries

Mutual Film Corp. v. Ohio Indus'l Comm.
236 U.S. 230 (1915)

Mr. Justice McKenna, after stating the case as above, delivered the opinion of the court:

Complainant directs its argument to three propositions: (1) The statute in controversy imposes an unlawful burden on interstate commerce; (2) it violates the freedom of speech and publication guaranteed by § 11, art. 1, of the Constitution of the state of Ohio;[1] and (3) it attempts to delegate legislative power to censors and to other boards to determine whether the statute offends in the particulars designated.

It is necessary to consider only §§ 3, 4, and 5. Section 3 makes it the duty of the board to examine and censor motion picture films to be publicly exhibited and displayed in the state of Ohio. The films are required to be exhibited to the board before they are delivered to the exhibitor for exhibition, for which a fee is charged.

Section 4. "Only such films as are, in the judgment and discretion of the board of censors, of a moral, educational, or amusing and harmless character shall be passed and approved by such board." The films are required to be stamped or designated in a proper manner.

Section 5. The board may work in conjunction with censor boards of other states as a censor congress, and the action of such congress in approving or rejecting films shall be considered as the action of the state board, and all films passed, approved, stamped, and numbered by such congress, when the fees therefore are paid, shall be considered approved by the board.

By § 7 a penalty is imposed for each exhibition of films without the approval of the board, and by § 8 any person dissatisfied with the order of the board is given the same rights and remedies for hearing and reviewing, amendment or vacation of the order "as is provided in the case of persons dissatisfied with the orders of the Industrial Commission."

---

1. Section 11. Every citizen may freely speak, write, and publish his sentiments on all subjects, being responsible for the abuse of the right; and no law shall be passed to restrain or abridge the liberty of speech, or of the press. In all criminal prosecutions for libel the truth may be given in evidence to the jury, and if it shall appear to the jury that the matter charged as libelous is true, and was published with good motives and for justifiable ends, the party shall be acquitted.

The censorship, therefore, is only of films intended for exhibition in Ohio, and we can immediately put to one side the contention that it imposes a burden on interstate commerce. It is true that, according to the allegations of the bill, some of the films of complainant are shipped from Detroit, Michigan, but they are distributed to exhibitors, purchasers, renters, and lessors in Ohio, for exhibition in Ohio, and this determines the application of the statute. In other words, it is only films which are "to be publicly exhibited and displayed in the state of Ohio" which are required to be examined and censored. It would be straining the doctrine of original packages to say that the films retain that form and composition even when unrolling and exhibiting to audiences, or, being ready for renting for the purpose of exhibition within the state, could not be disclosed to the state officers. If this be so, whatever the power of the state to prevent the exhibition of films not approved,—and for the purpose of this contention we must assume the power is otherwise plenary,—films brought from another state, and only because so brought, would be exempt from the power, and films made in the state would be subject to it. There must be some time when the films are subject to the law of the state, and necessarily when they are in the hands of the exchanges, ready to be rented to exhibitors, or have passed to the latter, they are in consumption, and mingled as much as from their nature they can be with other property of the state.

It is true that the statute requires them to be submitted to the board before they are delivered to the exhibitor, but we have seen that the films are shipped to 'exchanges' and by them rented to exhibitors, and the 'exchanges' are described as "nothing more or less than circulating libraries or clearing houses." And one film "serves in many theaters from day to day until it is worn out."

The next contention is that the statute violates the freedom of speech and publication guaranteed by the Ohio Constitution. In its discussion counsel have gone into a very elaborate description of moving picture exhibitions and their many useful purposes as graphic expressions of opinion and sentiments, as exponents of policies, as teachers of science and history, as useful, interesting, amusing, educational, and moral. And a list of the "campaigns," as counsel call them, which may be carried on, is given. We may concede the praise. It is not questioned by the Ohio statute, and under its comprehensive description, "campaigns" of an infinite variety may be conducted. Films of a "moral, educational, or amusing and harmless character shall be passed and approved," are the words of the statute. No exhibition, therefore, or "campaign" of complainant will be prevented if its pictures have those qualities. Therefore, however missionary of opinion films are or may become, however educational or entertaining, there is no impediment to their value or effect in the Ohio statute. But they may be used for evil, and against that possibility the statute was enacted. Their power of amusement, and, it may be, education, the audiences they assemble, not of women alone nor of men alone, but together, not of adults only, but of children, make them the more insidious in corruption by a pretense of worthy purpose or if they should degenerate from worthy purpose. Indeed, we may go beyond that possibility. They take their attraction from the general interest, eager and wholesome it may be, in their subjects, but a prurient interest may be excited and appealed to. Besides, there are some things which should not have pictorial representation in public places and to all audiences. And not only the state of Ohio, but other states, have considered it to be in the interest of the public morals and welfare to supervise moving picture exhibitions. We would have to shut our eyes to the facts of the world to regard the precaution unreasonable or the legislation to effect it a mere wanton interference with personal liberty.

We do not understand that a possibility of an evil employment of films is denied, but a freedom from the censorship of the law and a precedent right of exhibition are asserted, subsequent responsibility only, it is contended, being incurred for abuse. In other words, as we have seen, the Constitution of Ohio is invoked, and an exhibition of films is assimilated to the freedom of speech, writing, and publication assured by that instrument, and for the abuse of which only is there responsibility, and, it is insisted, that as no law may be passed "to restrain the liberty of speech or of the press," no law may be passed to subject moving pictures to censorship before their exhibition.

We need not pause to dilate upon the freedom of opinion and its expression, and whether by speech, writing, or printing. They are too certain to need discussion—of such conceded value as to need no supporting praise. Nor can there be any doubt of their breadth, nor that their underlying safeguard is, to use the words of another, "that opinion is free, and that conduct alone is amenable to the law."

Are moving pictures within the principle, as it is contended they are? They, indeed, may be mediums of thought, but so are many things. So is the theater, the circus, and all other shows and spectacles, and their performances may be thus brought by the like reasoning under the same immunity from repression or supervision as the public press,—made the same agencies of civil liberty.

Counsel have not shrunk from this extension of their contention, and cite a case in this court where the title of drama was accorded to pantomime; and such and other spectacles are said by counsel to be publications of ideas, satisfying the definition of the dictionaries,—that is, and we quote counsel, a means of making or announcing publicly something that otherwise might have remained private or unknown,—and this being peculiarly the purpose and effect of moving pictures, they come directly, it is contended, under the protection of the Ohio constitution.

The first impulse of the mind is to reject the contention. We immediately feel that the argument is wrong or strained which extends the guaranties of free opinion and speech to the multitudinous shows which are advertised on the billboards of our cities and towns, and which regards them as emblems of public safety, to use the words of Lord Camden, quoted by counsel, and which seeks to bring motion pictures and other spectacle into practical and legal similitude to a free press and liberty of opinion.

The judicial sense supporting the common sense of the country is against the contention.... The exercise of the power upon moving picture exhibitions has been sustained.... It cannot be put out of view that the exhibition of moving pictures is a business, pure and simple, originated and conducted for profit, like other spectacles, not to be regarded, nor intended to be regarded by the Ohio Constitution, we think, as part of the press of the country, or as organs of public opinion. They are mere representations of events, of ideas and sentiments published and known; vivid, useful, and entertaining, no doubt, but, as we have said, capable of evil, having power for it, the greater because of their attractiveness and manner of exhibition. It was this capability and power, and it may be in experience of them, that induced the state of Ohio, in addition to prescribing penalties for immoral exhibitions, as it does in its Criminal Code, to require censorship before exhibition, as it does by the act under review. We cannot regard this as beyond the power of government.

It does not militate against the strength of these considerations that motion pictures may be used to amuse and instruct in other places than theaters,—in churches, for instance, and in Sunday schools and public schools. Nor are we called upon to say on this record whether such exceptions would be within the provisions of the statute, nor to anticipate that it will be so declared by the state courts, or so enforced by the state officers....

[The Court also finds the legislation is a proper exercise of state authority.]

Joseph Burstyn, Inc. v. Wilson
343 U.S. 495 (1952)

[The decision overturning The Mutual is presented in Chapter I, *supra*, where the Supreme Court extends First Amendment protections to all forms of speech, including entertainment.]

Interstate Circuit v. Dallas
390 U.S. 676 (1968)

MR. JUSTICE MARSHALL delivered the opinion of the Court.

Appellants are an exhibitor and the distributor of a motion picture named "Viva Maria," which, pursuant to a city ordinance, the Motion Picture Classification Board of the appellee City of Dallas classified as "not suitable for young persons." A county court upheld the Board's determination and enjoined exhibition of the film without acceptance by appellants of the requirements imposed by the restricted classification. The Texas Court of Civil Appeals affirmed, and we noted probable jurisdiction, to consider the First and Fourteenth Amendment issues raised by appellants with respect to appellee's classification ordinance.

That ordinance, adopted in 1965, may be summarized as follows. It establishes a Motion Picture Classification Board, composed of nine appointed members, all of whom serve without pay. The Board classifies films as "suitable for young persons" or as "not suitable for young persons," young persons being defined as children who have not reached their 16th birthday. An exhibitor must be specially licensed to show "not suitable" films.

The ordinance requires the exhibitor, before any initial showing of a film, to file with the Board a proposed classification of the film together with a summary of its plot and similar information. The proposed classification is approved if the Board affirmatively agrees with it, or takes no action upon it within five days of its filing.

If a majority of the Board is dissatisfied with the proposed classification, the exhibitor is required to project the film before at least five members of the Board at the earliest practicable time. At the showing, the exhibitor may also present testimony or other support for his proposed classification. Within two days the Board must issue its classification order. Should the exhibitor disagree, he must file within two days a notice of nonacceptance. The Board is then required to go to court within three days to seek a temporary injunction, and a hearing is required to be set on that application within five days thereafter; if the exhibitor agrees to waive notice and requests a hearing on the merits of a permanent injunction, the Board is required to waive its application for a temporary injunction and join in the exhibitor's request. If an injunction does not issue within 10 days of the exhibitor's notice of nonacceptance, the Board's classification order is suspended. The ordinance does not define the scope of judicial review of the Board's determination, but the Court of Civil Appeals held that *de novo* review in the trial court was required. If an injunction issues and the exhibitor seeks appellate review, or if an injunction is refused and the Board appeals, the Board must waive all statutory notices and times, and join a request of the exhibitor, to advance the case on the appellate court's docket, *i.e.*, do everything it can to assure a speedy determination.

The ordinance is enforced primarily by a misdemeanor penalty: an exhibitor is subject to a fine of up to $200 if he exhibits a film that is classified "not suitable for young persons" without advertisements clearly stating its classification or without the classification being clearly posted, exhibits on the same program a suitable and a not suitable film, knowingly admits a youth under age 16 to view the film without his guardian or spouse accompanying him, makes any false or willfully misleading statement in submitting a film for classification, or exhibits a not suitable film without having a valid license therefor.

The same penalty is applicable to a youth who obtains admission to a not suitable film by falsely giving his age as 16 years or over, and to any person who sells or gives to a youth under 16 a ticket to a not suitable film, or makes any false statements to enable such a youth to gain admission.

Other means of enforcement, as against the exhibitor, are provided. Repeated violations of the ordinance, or persistent failure "to use reasonable diligence to determine whether those seeking admittance to the exhibition of a film classified "not suitable for young persons" are below the age of sixteen," may be the basis for revocation of a license to show not suitable films. Such a persistent failure, or exhibition of a not suitable film by an exhibitor with three convictions under the ordinance, *inter alia*, are defined as "public nuisances," which the Board may seek to restrain by a suit for injunctive relief.

The substantive standards governing classification are as follows:

"Not suitable for young persons" means:

(1) Describing or portraying brutality, criminal violence or depravity in such a manner as to be, in the judgment of the Board, likely to incite or encourage crime or delinquency on the part of young persons; or

(2) Describing or portraying nudity beyond the customary limits of candor in the community, or sexual promiscuity or extra-marital or abnormal sexual relations in such a manner as to be, in the judgment of the Board, likely to incite or encourage delinquency or sexual promiscuity on the part of young persons or to appeal to their prurient interest.

A film shall be considered "likely to incite or encourage" crime delinquency or sexual promiscuity on the part of young persons, if, in the judgment of the Board, there is a substantial probability that it will create the impression on young persons that such conduct is profitable, desirable, acceptable, respectable, praiseworthy or commonly accepted. A film shall be considered as appealing to "prurient interest" of young persons, if in the judgment of the Board, its calculated or dominant effect on young persons is substantially to arouse sexual desire. In determining whether a film is "not suitable for young persons," the Board shall consider the film as a whole, rather than isolated portions, and shall determine whether its harmful effects outweigh artistic or educational values such film may have for young persons."

Appellants attack those standards as unconstitutionally vague. We agree. Motion pictures are, of course, protected by the First Amendment, and thus we start with the premise that "precision of regulation must be the touchstone." And while it is true that this Court refused to strike down, against a broad and generalized attack, a prior restraint requirement that motion pictures be submitted to censors in advance of exhibition, there has been no retreat in this area from rigorous insistence upon procedural safeguards and judicial superintendence of the censor's action.

In *Winters v. New York,* 333 U.S. 507 (1948), this Court struck down as vague and indefinite a statutory standard interpreted by the state court to be "criminal news or stories of deeds of bloodshed or lust, so massed as to become vehicles for inciting violent and depraved crimes...." In *Joseph Burstyn, Inc.* v. *Wilson, supra,* the Court dealt with a film licensing standard of "sacrilegious," which was found to have such an all-inclusive definition as to result in "substantially unbridled censorship." Following *Burstyn,* the Court held the following film licensing standards to be unconstitutionally vague: "of such character as to be prejudicial to the best interests of the people of said City," *Gelling v. Texas,* 343 U.S. 960 (1952); "moral, educational or amusing and harmless," *Superior Films, Inc. v. Department of Education,* 346 U.S. 587 (1954); "immoral," and "tend to corrupt morals," *Commercial Pictures Corp.* v. *Regents,* 346 U.S. 587 (1954); "approve such films ... [as] are moral and proper; ... disapprove such as are cruel, obscene, indecent or immoral, or such as tend to debase or corrupt morals," *Holmby Productions, Inc.* v. *Vaughn,* 350 U.S. 870 (1955).

The vice of vagueness is particularly pronounced where expression is sought to be subjected to licensing. It may be unlikely that what Dallas does in respect to the licensing of motion pictures would have a significant effect upon film makers in Hollywood or Europe. But what Dallas may constitutionally do, so many other cities and States. Indeed, we are told that this ordinance is being used as a model for legislation in other localities. Thus, one who wishes to convey his ideas through that medium, which of course includes one who is interested not so much in expression as in making money, must consider whether what he proposes to film, and how he proposes to film it, is within the terms of classification schemes such as this. If he is unable to determine what the ordinance means, he runs the risk of being foreclosed, in practical effect, from a significant portion of the movie-going public. Rather than run that risk, he might choose nothing but the innocuous, perhaps save for the so-called "adult" picture. Moreover, a local exhibitor who cannot afford to risk losing the youthful audience when a film may be of marginal interest to adults—perhaps a "Viva Maria"—may contract to show only the totally inane. The vast wasteland that some have described in reference to another medium might be a verdant paradise in comparison. The First Amendment interests here are, therefore, broader than merely those of the film maker, distributor, and exhibitor, and certainly broader than those of youths under 16.

Of course, as the Court said in *Joseph Burstyn, Inc.* v. *Wilson,* "it does not follow that the Constitution requires absolute freedom to exhibit every motion picture of every kind at all times and all places." What does follow at the least, as the cases above illustrate, is that the restrictions imposed cannot be so vague as to set "the censor ... adrift upon a boundless sea...." In short, as Justice Frankfurter said, "legislation must not be so vague, the language so loose, as to leave to those who have to apply it too wide a discretion...," one reason being that "where licensing is rested, in the first instance, in an administrative agency, the available judicial review is in effect rendered inoperative [by vagueness]." Thus, to the extent that vague standards do not sufficiently guide the censor, the problem is not cured merely by affording *de novo* judicial review. Vague standards, unless narrowed by interpretation, encourage erratic administration whether the censor be administrative or judicial; "individual impressions become the yardstick of action, and result in regulation in accordance with the beliefs of the individual censor rather than regulation by law."

The dangers inherent in vagueness are strikingly illustrated in these cases. Five members of the Board viewed "Viva Maria." Eight members voted to classify it as "not suitable for young persons," the ninth member not voting. The Board gave no reasons for its determination. Appellee alleged in its petition for an injunction that the classification was warranted because the film portrayed "sexual promiscuity in such a manner as to be in the judgment of the Board likely to incite or encourage delinquency or sexual promiscuity on the part of young persons or to appeal to their prurient interests." Two Board members, a clergyman and a lawyer, testified at the hearing. Each adverted to several scenes in the film which, in their opinion, portrayed male-female relationships in a way contrary to "acceptable and approved behavior." Each acknowledged, in reference to scenes in which clergymen were involved in violence, most of which was farcical, that "sacrilege" might have entered into the Board's determination. And both conceded that the asserted portrayal of "sexual promiscuity" was implicit rather than explicit, *i.e.*, that it was a product of inference by, and imagination of, the viewer.

So far as "judicial superintendence" and *de novo* review are concerned, the trial judge, after viewing the film and hearing argument, stated merely: "Oh, I realize you gentlemen might be right. There are two or three features in this picture that look to me would be unsuitable to young people.... So I enjoin the exhibitor ... from exhibiting it." Nor did the Court of Civil Appeals provide much enlightenment or a narrowing definition of the ordinance.

United Artists argued that the obscenity standards similar to those set forth in *Roth v. United States,* 354 U.S. 476 (1957), and other decisions of this Court ought to be controlling. The majority of the Court of Civil Appeals held, alternatively, (1) that such cases were not applicable because the legislation involved in them resulted in suppression of the offending expression rather than its classification; (2) that if obscenity standards were applicable then "Viva Maria" was obscene as to adults (a patently untenable conclusion) and therefore entitled to no constitutional protection; and (3) that if obscenity standards were modified as to children, the film was obscene as to them, a conclusion which was not in terms given as a narrowing interpretation of any specific provision of the ordinance. In regard to the last alternative holding, we must conclude that the court in effect ruled that the "portrayal ... of sexual promiscuity as acceptable," is in itself obscene as to children. The court also held that the standards of the ordinance were "sufficiently definite."

Thus, we are left merely with the film and directed to the words of the ordinance. The term "sexual promiscuity" is not there defined and was not interpreted in the state courts. It could extend, depending upon one's moral judgment, from the obvious to any sexual contacts outside a marital relationship. The determinative manner of the "describing or portraying" of the subjects covered by the ordinance, including "sexual promiscuity," is defined as "such a manner as to be, in the judgment of the Board, likely to incite or encourage delinquency or sexual promiscuity on the part of young persons." A film is so "'likely to incite or encourage' crime delinquency or sexual promiscuity on the part of young persons, if, in the judgment of the Board, there is a substantial probability that it will create the impression on young persons that such conduct is profitable, desirable, acceptable, respectable, praiseworthy or commonly accepted." It might be excessive literalism to insist, as do appellants, that because those last six adjectives are stated in the disjunctive, they represent separate and alternative subtle determinations the Board is to make, any of which results in a not suitable classification. Nonetheless, "what may be to one viewer the glorification of an idea as being 'desirable, acceptable or proper' may to the notions of another be entirely devoid of such a teaching. The only limits on the censor's discretion is his understanding of what is included within the term 'desirable, acceptable or proper.' This is nothing less than a roving commission...."

Vagueness and the attendant evils we have earlier described are not rendered less objectionable because the regulation of expression is one of classification rather than direct suppression. Nor is it an answer to an argument that a particular regulation of expression is vague to say that it was adopted for the salutary purpose of protecting children. The permissible extent of vagueness is not directly proportional to, or a function of, the extent of the power to regulate or control expression with respect to children. As Chief Judge Fuld has said:

"It is ... essential that legislation aimed at protecting children from allegedly harmful expression—no less than legislation enacted with respect to adults—be clearly drawn and that the standards adopted be reasonably precise so that those who are governed by the law and those that administer it will understand its meaning and application."

The vices—the lack of guidance to those who seek to adjust their conduct and to those who seek to administer the law, as well as the possible practical curtailing of the effectiveness of judicial review—are the same.

It is not our province to draft legislation. Suffice it to say that we have recognized that some believe "motion pictures possess a greater capacity for evil, particularly among the youth of a community, than other modes of expression," and we have indicated more generally that because of its strong and abiding interest in youth, a State may regulate the dissemination to juveniles of, and their access to, material objectionable as to them, but which a State clearly could not regulate as to adults. Here we conclude only that "the absence of narrowly drawn, reasonable and definite standards for the officials to follow," is fatal.

Appellants also assert that the city ordinance violates the teachings of *Freedman v. Maryland* because it does not secure prompt state appellate review. The assurance of a "prompt final judicial decision" is made here, we think, by the guaranty of a speedy determination in the trial court (in this case nine days after the Board's classification). Nor is *Freedman* violated by the requirement that the exhibitor file a notice of nonacceptance of the Board's classification. To be sure, it is emphasized in *Freedman* that "only a procedure requiring a judicial determination suffices to impose a valid final restraint" and here if the exhibitor chooses not to file the notice of nonacceptance, the Board's determination is final without judicial approval. But we are not constrained to view that procedure as invalid in the absence of a showing that it has any significantly greater effect than would the exhibitor's decision not to contest in court the Board's suit for a temporary injunction. The ordinance provides that the Board has the burden of going to court to seek a temporary injunction, once the exhibitor has indicated his nonacceptance, and there it has the burden of sustaining its classification.

The judgment of the Texas Court of Civil Appeals is reversed and the cases are remanded for further proceedings not inconsistent with this opinion.

Southeastern Promotions, Ltd. v. Conrad
420 U.S. 546 (1975)

MR. JUSTICE BLACKMUN delivered the opinion of the Court. The issue in this case is whether First Amendment rights were abridged when respondents denied petitioner the use of a municipal facility in Chattanooga, Tenn., for the showing of the controversial rock musical "Hair." It is established, of course, that the Fourteenth Amendment has made applicable to the States the First Amendment's guarantee of free speech.

Petitioner, Southeastern Promotions, Ltd., is a New York corporation engaged in the business of promoting and presenting theatrical productions for profit. On October 29, 1971, it applied for the use of the Tivoli, a privately owned Chattanooga theater under long-term lease to the city, to present "Hair" there for six days beginning November 23. This was to be a road company showing of the musical that had played for three years on Broadway, and had appeared in over 140 cities in the United States.

Twice previously, petitioner informally had asked permission to use the Tivoli, and had been refused. In other cities, it had encountered similar resistance and had successfully sought injunctions ordering local officials to permit use of municipal facilities. The musical had been presented in two Tennessee cities, Memphis and Nashville.

Respondents are the directors of the Chattanooga Memorial Auditorium, a municipal theater. Shortly after receiving Southeastern's application, the directors met, and, after a brief discussion, voted to reject it. None of them had seen the play or read the script, but they understood from outside reports that the musical, as produced elsewhere, involved nudity and obscenity on stage. Although no conflicting engagement was scheduled for the Tivoli, respondents determined that the production would not be "in the best interest of the community." Southeastern was so notified but no written statement of reasons was provided.

On November 1 petitioner, alleging that respondents' action abridged its First Amendment rights, sought a preliminary injunction from the United States District Court for the Eastern District of Tennessee. Respondents did not then file an answer to the complaint. A hearing was held on November 4. The District Court took evidence as to the play's content, and respondent Conrad gave the following account of the board's decision:

> We use the general terminology in turning down the request for its use that we felt it was not in the best interest of the community and I can't speak beyond that. That was the board's determination.
>
> "Now, I would have to speak for myself, the policy to which I would refer, as I mentioned, basically indicates that we will, as a board, allow those productions which are clean and healthful and culturally uplifting, or words to that effect. They are quoted in the original dedication booklet of the Memorial Auditorium."[2]

The court denied preliminary relief, concluding that petitioner had failed to show that it would be irreparably harmed pending a final judgment since scheduling was "purely a matter of financial loss or gain" and was compensable.

Southeastern some weeks later pressed for a permanent injunction permitting it to use the larger auditorium, rather than the Tivoli, on Sunday, April 9, 1972. The District Court held three days of hearings beginning April 3. On the issue of obscenity vel non, presented to an advisory jury, it took evidence consisting of the full script and libretto, with production notes and stage instructions, a recording of the musical numbers, a souvenir program, and the testimony of seven witnesses who had seen the production elsewhere. The jury returned a verdict that "Hair" was obscene. The District Court agreed. It concluded that conduct in the production—group nudity and simulated sex—would violate city ordinances and state statutes making public nudity and obscene acts criminal offenses. This criminal conduct, the court reasoned, was neither speech nor symbolic speech, and was to be viewed separately from the musical's speech elements. Being pure

---

2. The Memorial Auditorium, completed in 1924, was dedicated to the memory of Chattanooga citizens who had "offered their lives" in World War I. The booklet referred to is entitled Souvenir of Dedication of Soldiers & Sailors Auditorium Chattanooga, Tenn. It contains the following:

"It will be [the board's] endeavor to make [the auditorium] the community center of Chattanooga; where civic, educational, religious, patriotic and charitable organizations and associations may have a common meeting place to discuss and further the upbuilding and general welfare of the city and surrounding territory.

"It will not be operated for profit, and no effort to obtain financial returns above the actual operating expenses will be permitted. Instead its purpose will be devoted for cultural advancement, and for clean, healthful, entertainment which will make for the upbuilding of a better citizenship."

conduct, comparable to rape or murder, it was not entitled to First Amendment protection. Accordingly, the court denied the injunction.

On appeal, the United States Court of Appeals for the Sixth Circuit, by a divided vote, affirmed. The majority relied primarily on the lower court's reasoning. Neither the judges of the Court of Appeals nor the District Court saw the musical performed. Because of the First Amendment overtones, we granted certiorari.

Petitioner urges reversal on the grounds that (1) respondents' action constituted an unlawful prior restraint, (2) the courts below applied an incorrect standard for the determination of the issue of obscenity *vel non*, and (3) the record does not support a finding that "Hair" is obscene. We do not reach the latter two contentions, for we agree with the first. We hold that respondents' rejection of petitioner's application to use this public forum accomplished a prior restraint under a system lacking in constitutionally required minimal procedural safeguards. Accordingly, on this narrow ground, we reverse.

Respondents' action here is indistinguishable in its censoring effect from the official actions consistently identified as prior restraints in a long line of this Court's decisions. In these cases, the plaintiffs asked the courts to provide relief where public officials had forbidden the plaintiffs the use of public places to say what they wanted to say. The restraints took a variety of forms, with officials exercising control over different kinds of public places under the authority of particular statutes. All, however, had this in common: they gave public officials the power to deny use of a forum in advance of actual expression.

Invariably, the Court has felt obliged to condemn systems in which the exercise of such authority was not bounded by precise and clear standards. The reasoning has been, simply, that the danger of censorship and of abridgment of our precious First Amendment freedoms is too great where officials have unbridled discretion over a forum's use. Our distaste for censorship — reflecting the natural distaste of a free people — is deep-written in our law.

In each of the cited cases the prior restraint was embedded in the licensing system itself, operating without acceptable standards. In *Shuttlesworth* [*v. Birmingham,* 394 U.S. 147, 150–151 (1969),] the Court held unconstitutional a Birmingham ordinance which conferred upon the city commission virtually absolute power to prohibit any "parade," "procession," or "demonstration" on streets or public ways. It ruled that "a law subjecting the exercise of First Amendment freedoms to the prior restraint of a license, without narrow, objective, and definite standards to guide the licensing authority, is unconstitutional." In *Hague v. CIO,* 307 U.S. 496 (1939), a Jersey City ordinance that forbade public assembly in the streets or parks without a permit from the local director of safety, who was empowered to refuse the permit upon his opinion that he would thereby prevent " 'riots, disturbances or disorderly assemblage,' " was held void on its face.

In *Cantwell v. Connecticut,* 310 U.S. 296 (1940), a unanimous Court held invalid an act which proscribed the solicitation of money or any valuable thing for "any alleged religious, charitable or philanthropic cause" unless that cause was approved by the secretary of the public welfare council. The elements of the prior restraint were clearly set forth:

> It will be noted, however, that the Act requires an application to the secretary of the public welfare council of the State; that he is empowered to determine whether the cause is a religious one, and that the issue of a certificate depends upon his affirmative action. If he finds that the cause is not that of religion, to solicit for it becomes a crime. He is not to issue a certificate as a mat-

ter of course. His decision to issue or refuse it involves appraisal of facts, the exercise of judgment, and the formation of an opinion.

The elements of prior restraint identified in *Cantwell* and other cases were clearly present in the system by which the Chattanooga board regulated the use of its theaters. One seeking to use a theater was required to apply to the board. The board was empowered to determine whether the applicant should be granted permission—in effect, a license or permit—on the basis of its review of the content of the proposed production. Approval of the application depended upon the board's affirmative action. Approval was not a matter of routine; instead, it involved the "appraisal of facts, the exercise of judgment, and the formation of an opinion" by the board.

The board's judgment effectively kept the musical off stage. Respondents did not permit the show to go on and rely on law enforcement authorities to prosecute for anything illegal that occurred. Rather, they denied the application in anticipation that the production would violate the law.

Respondents' action was no less a prior restraint because the public facilities under their control happened to be municipal theaters. The Memorial Auditorium and the Tivoli were public forums designed for and dedicated to expressive activities. There was no question as to the usefulness of either facility for petitioner's production. There was no contention by the board that these facilities could not accommodate a production of this size. None of the circumstances qualifying as an established exception to the doctrine of prior restraint was present. Petitioner was not seeking to use a facility primarily serving a competing use. Nor was rejection of the application based on any regulation of time, place, or manner related to the nature of the facility or applications from other users.

Whether petitioner might have used some other, privately owned, theater in the city for the production is of no consequence. There is reason to doubt on this record whether any other facility would have served as well as these, since none apparently had the seating capacity, acoustical features, stage equipment, and electrical service that the show required. Even if a privately owned forum had been available, that fact alone would not justify an otherwise impermissible prior restraint. "[One] is not to have the exercise of his liberty of expression in appropriate places abridged on the plea that it may be exercised in some other place."

Thus, it does not matter for purposes of this case that the board's decision might not have had the effect of total suppression of the musical in the community. Denying use of the municipal facility under the circumstances present here constituted the prior restraint. That restraint was final. It was no mere temporary bar while necessary judicial proceedings were under way.

Also important, though unessential to our conclusion, are the classificatory aspects of the board's decision. A licensing system need not effect total suppression in order to create a prior restraint. In *Interstate Circuit v. Dallas*, 390 U.S. 676, 688 (1968), it was observed that the evils attendant on prior restraint "are not rendered less objectionable because the regulation of expression is one of classification rather than direct suppression." In that case, the Court held that a prior restraint was created by a system whereby an administrative board in Texas classified films as "suitable for young persons" or "not suitable for young persons." The "not suitable" films were not suppressed, but exhibitors were required to have special licenses and to advertise their classification in order to show them. Similarly, in *Bantam Books, Inc. v. Sullivan*, 372 U.S. 58 (1963), the Court held that a system of "informal censorship" working by exhortation and advice sufficiently inhibited expression to constitute a prior restraint and warrant injunctive relief. There, the Court held unconstitutional a system in which a commission was charged with reviewing material "manifestly tending to the corruption of the youth"; it did not have direct regulatory or suppressing functions, but operated by persuasion and intimidation, and these informal methods were found effective.

In the present case, the board classified the musical as unfit for showing in municipal facilities. It did not make a point of publicizing its finding that "Hair" was not in the "best interest" of the public, but the classification stood as a warning to all concerned, private theater owners and general public alike. There is little in the record to indicate the extent to which the board's action may have affected petitioner's ability to obtain a theater and attract an audience. The board's classification, whatever the magnitude of its effect, was not unlike that in *Interstate Circuit* and *Bantam Books*.

Only if we were to conclude that live drama is unprotected by the First Amendment— or subject to a totally different standard from that applied to other forms of expression— could we possibly find no prior restraint here. Each medium of expression, of course, must be assessed for First Amendment purposes by standards suited to it, for each may present its own problems. By its nature, theater usually is the acting out— or singing out— of the written word, and frequently mixes speech with live action or conduct. But that is no reason to hold theater subject to a drastically different standard. For, as was said in *Burstyn, supra*, at 503, when the Court was faced with the question of what First Amendment standard applies to films:

> [The] basic principles of freedom of speech and the press, like the First Amendment's command, do not vary. Those principles, as they have frequently been enunciated by this Court, make freedom of expression the rule. There is no justification in this case for making an exception to that rule.

Labeling respondents' action a prior restraint does not end the inquiry. Prior restraints are not unconstitutional *per se*. We have rejected the contention that the First Amendment's protection "includes complete and absolute freedom to exhibit, at least once, any and every kind of motion picture ... even if this film contains the basest type of pornography, or incitement to riot, or forceful overthrow of orderly government...."

Any system of prior restraint, however, "comes to this Court bearing a heavy presumption against its constitutional validity." The presumption against prior restraints is heavier—and the degree of protection broader—than that against limits on expression imposed by criminal penalties. Behind the distinction is a theory deeply etched in our law: a free society prefers to punish the few who abuse rights of speech *after* they break the law than to throttle them and all others beforehand. It is always difficult to know in advance what an individual will say, and the line between legitimate and illegitimate speech is often so finely drawn that the risks of freewheeling censorship are formidable.

In order to be held lawful, respondents' action, first, must fit within one of the narrowly defined exceptions to the prohibition against prior restraints, and, second, must have been accomplished with procedural safeguards that reduce the danger of suppressing constitutionally protected speech. We do not decide whether the performance of "Hair" fits within such an exception or whether, as a substantive matter, the board's standard for resolving that question was correct, for we conclude that the standard, whatever it may have been, was not implemented by the board under a system with appropriate and necessary procedural safeguards.

The settled rule is that a system of prior restraint "avoids constitutional infirmity only if it takes place under procedural safeguards designed to obviate the dangers of a censorship system." *Freedman v. Maryland,* 380 U.S. 51, 58 (1965). In *Freedman* the Court struck down a state scheme for the licensing of motion pictures, holding "that, because only a judicial determination in an adversary proceeding ensures the necessary sensitivity to freedom of expression, only a procedure requiring a judicial determination suffices to impose a valid final restraint." We held in *Freedman*, and we reaffirm here, that a system of prior restraint runs afoul of the First Amendment if it lacks certain safeguards: *First*, the burden of instituting judicial proceedings, and of proving that the material is unprotected, must rest on the censor. Second, any restraint prior to judicial review can be imposed only for a specified brief period and only for the purpose of preserving the status quo. Third, a prompt final judicial determination must be assured....

The theory underlying the requirement of safeguards is applicable here with equal if not greater force. An administrative board assigned to screening stage productions—and keeping off stage anything not deemed culturally uplifting or healthful—may well be less responsive than a court, an independent branch of government, to constitutionally protected interests in free expression. And if judicial review is made unduly onerous, by reason of delay or otherwise, the board's determination in practice may be final.

Insistence on rigorous procedural safeguards under these circumstances is "but a special instance of the larger principle that the freedoms of expression must be ringed about with adequate bulwarks." Because the line between unconditionally guaranteed speech and speech that may be legitimately regulated is a close one, the "separation of legitimate from illegitimate speech calls for ... sensitive tools." The perils of prior restraint are well illustrated by this case, where neither the Board nor the lower courts could have known precisely the extent of nudity or simulated sex in the musical, or even that either would appear, before the play was actually performed.

Procedural safeguards were lacking here in several respects. The board's system did not provide a procedure for prompt judicial review. Although the District Court commendably held a hearing on petitioner's motion for a preliminary injunction within a few days of the board's decision, it did not review the merits of the decision at that time. The question at the hearing was whether petitioner should receive *preliminary* relief, *i. e.,* whether there was likelihood of success on the merits and whether petitioner would suffer irreparable injury pending full review. Effective review on the merits was not obtained until more than five months later. Throughout, it was petitioner, not the board, that bore the burden of obtaining judicial review. It was petitioner that had the burden of persuasion at the preliminary hearing if not at the later stages of the litigation. Respondents did not file a formal answer to the complaint for five months after petitioner sought review. During the time prior to judicial determination, the restraint altered the status quo. Petitioner was forced to forgo the initial dates planned for the engagement and to seek to schedule the performance at a later date. The delay and uncertainty inevitably discouraged use of the forum.

The procedural shortcomings that form the basis for our decision are unrelated to the standard that the board applied. Whatever the reasons may have been for the board's exclusion of the musical, it could not escape the obligation to afford appropriate procedural safeguards. We need not decide whether the standard of obscenity applied by respondents or the courts below was sufficiently precise or substantively correct, or whether the production is in fact obscene. The standard, whatever it may be, must be implemented under a system that assures prompt judicial review with a minimal restriction of First Amendment rights necessary under the circumstances. *Reversed.*

Ward v. Rock Against Racism

491 U.S. 781 (1989)

JUSTICE KENNEDY delivered the opinion of the Court. In the southeast portion of New York City's Central Park, about 10 blocks upward from the park's beginning point at 59th Street, there is an amphitheater and stage structure known as the Naumberg Acoustic Bandshell. The bandshell faces west across the remaining width of the park. In close proximity to the bandshell, and lying within the directional path of its sound, is a grassy open area called the Sheep Meadow. The city has designated the Sheep Meadow as a quiet area for passive recreations like reclining, walking, and reading. Just beyond the park, and also within the potential sound range of the bandshell, are the apartments and residences of Central Park West.

This case arises from the city's attempt to regulate the volume of amplified music at the bandshell so the performances are satisfactory to the audience without intruding upon those who use the Sheep Meadow or live on Central Park West and in its vicinity.

The city's regulation requires bandshell performers to use sound-amplification equipment and a sound technician provided by the city. The challenge to this volume control technique comes from the sponsor of a rock concert. The trial court sustained the noise control measures, but the Court of Appeals for the Second Circuit reversed. We granted certiorari to resolve the important First Amendment issues presented by the case.

Rock Against Racism, respondent in this case, is an unincorporated association which, in its own words, is "dedicated to the espousal and promotion of antiracist views." Each year from 1979 through 1986, RAR has sponsored a program of speeches and rock music at the bandshell. RAR has furnished the sound equipment and sound technician used by the various performing groups at these annual events.

Over the years, the city received numerous complaints about excessive sound amplification at respondent's concerts from park users and residents of areas adjacent to the park. On some occasions RAR was less than cooperative when city officials asked that the volume be reduced; at one concert, police felt compelled to cut off the power to the sound system, an action that caused the audience to become unruly and hostile.

Before the 1984 concert, city officials met with RAR representatives to discuss the problem of excessive noise. It was decided that the city would monitor sound levels at the edge of the concert ground, and would revoke respondent's event permit if specific volume limits were exceeded. Sound levels at the concert did exceed acceptable levels for sustained periods of time, despite repeated warnings and requests that the volume be lowered. Two citations for excessive volume were issued to respondent during the concert. When the power was eventually shut off, the audience became abusive and disruptive.

The following year, when respondent sought permission to hold its upcoming concert at the bandshell, the city declined to grant an event permit, citing its problems with noise and crowd control at RAR's previous concerts. The city suggested some other city-owned facilities as alternative sites for the concert. RAR declined the invitation and filed suit in United States District Court against the city, its mayor, and various police and parks department officials, seeking an injunction directing issuance of an event permit. After respondent agreed to abide by all applicable regulations, the parties reached agreement and a permit was issued.

The city then undertook to develop comprehensive New York City Parks Department Use Guidelines for the Naumberg Bandshell. A principal problem to be addressed by the guidelines was controlling the volume of amplified sound at bandshell events. A major concern was that at some bandshell performances the event sponsors had been unable to "provide the amplification levels required and 'crowds unhappy with the sound became disappointed or unruly.'" The city found that this problem had several causes, including inadequate sound equipment, sound technicians who were either unskilled at mixing sound outdoors or unfamiliar with the acoustics of the bandshell and its surroundings, and the like. Because some performers compensated for poor sound mix by raising volume, these factors tended to exacerbate the problem of excess noise.

The amplified sound heard at a rock concert consists of two components, volume and mix. Sound produced by the various instruments and performers on stage is picked up by microphones and fed into a central mixing board, where it is combined into one signal and then amplified through speakers to the audience. A sound technician is at the mixing board to select the appropriate mix, or balance, of the various sounds produced on stage, and to add other effects as desired by the performers. In addition to controlling the sound mix, the sound technician also controls the overall volume of sound reaching the audience. During the course of a performance, the sound technician is continually manipulating various controls on the mixing board to provide the desired sound mix and volume. The sound technician thus plays an important role in determining the quality of the amplified sound that reaches the audience.

The city considered various solutions to the sound-amplification problem. The idea of a fixed decibel limit for all performers using the bandshell was rejected because the impact on listeners of a single decibel level is not constant, but varies in response to changes in air temperature, foliage, audience size, and like factors. The city also rejected the possibility of employing a sound technician to operate the equipment provided by the various sponsors of bandshell events, because the city's technician might have had difficulty satisfying the needs of sponsors while operating unfamiliar, and perhaps inadequate, sound equipment. Instead, the city concluded that the most effective way to achieve adequate but not excessive sound amplification would be for the city to furnish high quality sound equipment and retain an independent, experienced sound technician for all performances at the bandshell. After an extensive search the city hired a private sound company capable of meeting the needs of all the varied users of the bandshell.

The Use Guidelines were promulgated on March 21, 1986. After learning that it would be expected to comply with the guidelines at its upcoming annual concert in May 1986, respondent returned to the District Court and filed a motion for an injunction against the enforcement of certain aspects of the guidelines. The District Court preliminarily enjoined enforcement of the sound-amplification rule on May 1, 1986. Under the protection of the injunction, and alone among users of the bandshell in the 1986 season, RAR was permitted to use its own sound equipment and technician, just as it had done in prior years. RAR's 1986 concert again generated complaints about excessive noise from park users and nearby residents.

After the concert, respondent amended its complaint to seek damages and a declaratory judgment striking down the guidelines as facially invalid. After hearing five days of testimony about various aspects of the guidelines, the District Court issued its decision upholding the sound-amplification guideline. The court found that the city had been "motivated by a desire to obtain top-flight sound equipment and experienced operators" in selecting an independent contractor to provide the equipment and technician for bandshell events, and that the performers who did use the city's sound system in the 1986 season, in performances "which ran the full cultural gamut from grand opera to salsa to reggae," were uniformly pleased with the quality of the sound provided.

Although the city's sound technician controlled both sound volume and sound mix by virtue of his position at the mixing board, the court found that "[t]he City's practice for events at the Bandshell is to give the sponsor autonomy with respect to the sound mix: balancing treble with bass, highlighting a particular instrument or voice, and the like," and that the city's sound technician "does all he can to accommodate the sponsor's desires in those regards." Even with respect to volume control, the city's practice was to confer with the sponsor before making any decision to turn the volume down. In some instances, as with a New York Grand Opera performance, the sound technician accommodated the performers' unique needs by integrating special microphones with the city's equipment. The court specifically found that "[t]he City's implementation of the Bandshell guidelines provides for a sound amplification system capable of meeting RAR's technical needs and leaves control of the sound 'mix' in the hands of RAR." Applying this Court's three-part test for judging the constitutionality of government regulation of the time, place, or manner of protected speech, the court found the city's regulation valid.

The Court of Appeals reversed. After recognizing that "[c]ontent neutral time, place and manner regulations are permissible so long as they are narrowly tailored to serve a substantial government interest and do not unreasonably limit alternative avenues of expression," the court added the proviso that "the method and extent of such regulation must be reasonable, that is, it must be the least intrusive upon the freedom of expression as is reasonably necessary to achieve a legitimate purpose of the regulation." Applying this test, the court determined that the city's guideline was valid only to the extent necessary to achieve the city's legitimate interest in controlling excessive volume, but found there were various alternative means of controlling volume without also intruding on respondent's ability to control the sound mix. For example, the city could have directed respondent's sound technician to keep the volume below specified levels. Alternatively, a volume-limiting device could have been installed; and as a "last resort," the court suggested, "the plug can be pulled on the sound to enforce the volume limit." In view of the potential availability of these seemingly less restrictive alternatives, the Court of Appeals concluded that the sound-amplification guideline was invalid because the city had failed to prove that its regulation "was the least intrusive means of regulating the volume."

We granted certiorari to clarify the legal standard applicable to governmental regulation of the time, place, or manner of protected speech. Because the Court of Appeals erred in requiring the city to prove that its regulation was the least intrusive means of furthering its legitimate governmental interests, and because the ordinance is valid on its face, we now reverse.

Music is one of the oldest forms of human expression. From Plato's discourse in the Republic to the totalitarian state in our own times, rulers have known its capacity to appeal to the intellect and to the emotions, and have censored musical compositions to serve the needs of the state. The Constitution prohibits any like attempts in our own legal order. Music, as a form of expression and communication, is protected under the First Amendment. In the case before us the performances apparently consisted of remarks by speakers, as well as rock music, but the case has been presented as one in which the constitutional challenge is to the city's regulation of the musical aspects of the concert; and, based on the principle we have stated, the city's guideline must meet the demands of the First Amendment. The parties do not appear to dispute that proposition.

We need not here discuss whether a municipality which owns a bandstand or stage facility may exercise, in some circumstances, a proprietary right to select performances and control their quality. Though it did demonstrate its own interest in the effort to insure high quality performances by providing the equipment in question, the city justifies its guideline as a regulatory measure to limit and control noise. Here the bandshell was open, apparently, to all performers; and we decide the case as one in which the bandshell is a public forum for performances in which the government's right to regulate expression is subject to the protections of the First Amendment. Our cases make clear, however, that even in a public forum the government may impose reasonable restrictions on the time, place, or manner of protected speech, provided the restrictions "are justified without reference to the content of the regulated speech, that they are narrowly tailored to serve a significant governmental interest, and that they leave open ample alternative channels for communication of the information." We consider these requirements in turn.

The principal inquiry in determining content neutrality, in speech cases generally and in time, place, or manner cases in particular, is whether the government has adopted a regulation of speech because of disagreement with the message it conveys. The government's purpose is the controlling consideration. A regulation that serves purposes unrelated to the content of expression is deemed neutral, even if it has an incidental effect on some speakers or messages but not others. Government regulation of expressive activity is content neutral so long as it is *justified* without reference to the content of the regulated speech."

The principal justification for the sound-amplification guideline is the city's desire to control noise levels at bandshell events, in order to retain the character of the Sheep Meadow and its more sedate activities, and to avoid undue intrusion into residential areas and other areas of the park. This justification for the guideline "ha[s] nothing to do with content," and it satisfies the requirement that time, place, or manner regulations be content neutral.

The only other justification offered below was the city's interest in "ensur[ing] the quality of sound at Bandshell events." Respondent urges that this justification is not content neutral because it is based upon the quality, and thus the content, of the speech being regulated. In respondent's view, the city is seeking to assert artistic control over performers at the bandshell by enforcing a bureaucratically determined, value-laden conception of good sound. That all performers who have used the city's sound equipment have been completely satisfied is of no moment, respondent argues, because "[t]he First Amendment does not permit and cannot tolerate state control of artistic expression merely because the State claims that [its] efforts will lead to 'top-quality' results."

While respondent's arguments that the government may not interfere with artistic judgment may have much force in other contexts, they are inapplicable to the facts of this case. The city has disclaimed in express terms any interest in imposing its own view of appropriate sound mix on performers. To the contrary, as the District Court found, the city requires its sound technician to defer to the wishes of event sponsors concerning sound mix. On this record, the city's concern with sound quality extends only to the clearly content-neutral goals of ensuring adequate sound amplification and avoiding the volume problems associated with inadequate sound mix. Any governmental attempt to serve purely esthetic goals by imposing subjective standards of acceptable sound mix on performers would raise serious First Amendment concerns, but this case provides us with no opportunity to address those questions. As related above, the District Court found that the city's equipment and its sound technician could meet all of the standards requested by the performers, including RAR.

Respondent argues further that the guideline, even if not content based in explicit terms, is nonetheless invalid on its face because it places unbridled discretion in the hands of city officials charged with enforcing it. According to respondent, there is nothing in the language of the guideline to prevent city officials from selecting wholly inadequate sound equipment or technicians, or even from varying the volume and quality of sound based on the message being conveyed by the performers.

As a threshold matter, it is far from clear that respondent should be permitted to bring a facial challenge to this aspect of the regulation. Our cases permitting facial challenges to regulations that allegedly grant officials unconstrained authority to regulate speech have generally involved licensing schemes that "ves[t] unbridled discretion in a government official over whether to permit or deny expressive activity." The grant of discretion that respondent seeks to challenge here is of an entirely different, and lesser, order of magnitude, because respondent does not suggest that city officials enjoy unfettered discretion to deny bandshell permits altogether. Rather, respondent contends only that the city, by exercising what is concededly its right to regulate amplified sound, could choose to provide inadequate sound for performers based on the content of their speech. Since respondent does not claim that city officials enjoy unguided discretion to deny the right to speak altogether, it is open to question whether respondent's claim falls within the narrow class of permissible facial challenges to allegedly unconstrained grants of regulatory authority.

We need not decide, however, whether the "extraordinary doctrine" that permits facial challenges to some regulations of expression should be extended to the circumstances of this case, for respondent's facial challenge fails on its merits. The city's guideline states that its goals are to "provide the best sound for all events" and to "insure appropriate sound quality balanced with respect for nearby residential neighbors and the mayorally decreed quiet zone of [the] Sheep Meadow." While these standards are undoubtedly flexible, and the officials implementing them will exercise considerable discretion, perfect clarity and precise guidance have never been required even of regulations that restrict expressive activity. By its own terms the city's sound-amplification guideline must be interpreted to forbid city officials purposely to select inadequate sound systems or to vary the sound quality or volume based on the message being delivered by performers. The guideline is not vulnerable to respondent's facial challenge.

Even if the language of the guideline were not sufficient on its face to withstand challenge, our ultimate conclusion would be the same, for the city has interpreted the guideline in such a manner as to provide additional guidance to the officials charged with its enforcement. The District Court expressly found that the city's policy is to defer to the sponsor's desires concerning sound quality. With respect to sound volume, the city retains ultimate control, but city officials "mak[e] it a practice to confer with the sponsor if any questions of excessive sound arise, before taking any corrective action." The city's goal of ensuring that "the sound amplification [is] sufficient to reach all listeners within the defined concertground," serves to limit further the discretion of the officials on the scene. Administrative interpretation and implementation of a regulation are, of course, highly relevant to our analysis, for "[i]n evaluating a facial challenge to a state law, a federal court must ... consider any limiting construction that a state court or enforcement agency has proffered." Any inadequacy on the face of the guideline would have been more than remedied by the city's narrowing construction.

The city's regulation is also "narrowly tailored to serve a significant governmental interest." Despite respondent's protestations to the contrary, it can no longer be doubted that government "ha[s] a substantial interest in protecting its citizens from unwelcome noise." This interest is perhaps at its greatest when government seeks to protect "'the well-being, tranquility, and privacy of the home,'" but it is by no means limited to that context, for the government may act to protect even such traditional public forums as city streets and parks from excessive noise.

We think it also apparent that the city's interest in ensuring the sufficiency of sound amplification at bandshell events is a substantial one. The record indicates that inadequate sound amplification has had an adverse effect on the ability of some audiences to hear and enjoy performances at the bandshell. The city enjoys a substantial interest in ensuring the ability of its citizens to enjoy whatever benefits the city parks have to offer, from amplified music to silent meditation.... Lest any confusion on the point remain, we reaffirm today that a regulation of the time, place, or manner of protected speech must be narrowly tailored to serve the government's legitimate, content-neutral interests but that it need not be the least restrictive or least intrusive means of doing so.

Rather, the requirement of narrow tailoring is satisfied "so long as the ... regulation promotes a substantial government interest that would be achieved less effectively absent the regulation." To be sure, this standard does not mean that a time, place, or manner regulation may burden substantially more speech than is necessary to further the government's legitimate interests. Government may not regulate expression in such a manner that a substantial portion of the burden on speech does not serve to advance its goals. So long as the means chosen are not substantially broader than necessary to achieve the government's interest, however, the regulation will not be invalid simply because a court concludes that the government's interest could be adequately served by some less-speech-restrictive alternative. "The validity of [time, place, or manner] regulations does not turn on a judge's agreement with the responsible decisionmaker concerning the most appropriate method for promoting significant government interests" or the degree to which those interests should be promoted....

The court squarely rejected respondent's claim that the city's "technician is not able properly to implement a sponsor's instructions as to sound quality or mix," finding that "[n]o evidence to that effect was offered at trial; as noted, the evidence is to the contrary." In view of these findings, which were not disturbed by the Court of Appeals, we must conclude that the city's guideline has no material impact on any performer's ability to exercise complete artistic control over sound quality. Since the guideline allows the city to control volume without interfering with the performer's desired sound mix, it is not "substantially broader than necessary" to achieve the city's legitimate ends, and thus it satisfies the requirement of narrow tailoring.

The final requirement, that the guideline leave open ample alternative channels of communication, is easily met. Indeed, in this respect the guideline is far less restrictive than regulations we have upheld in other cases, for it does not attempt to ban any particular manner or type of expression at a given place or time. Rather, the guideline continues to permit expressive activity in the bandshell, and has no effect on the quantity or content of that expression beyond regulating the extent of amplification. That the city's limitations on volume may reduce to some degree the potential audience for respondent's speech is of no consequence, for there has been no showing that the remaining avenues of communication are inadequate.

The city's sound-amplification guideline is narrowly tailored to serve the substantial and content-neutral governmental interests of avoiding excessive sound volume and providing sufficient amplification within the bandshell concert ground, and the guideline leaves open ample channels of communication. Accordingly, it is valid under the First Amendment as a reasonable regulation of the place and manner of expression. The judgment of the Court of Appeals is *Reversed*.

U.S. v. Stevens

559 U.S. 460 (2010)

Chief Justice ROBERTS delivered the opinion of the Court.

Congress enacted 18 U.S.C. § 48 to criminalize the commercial creation, sale, or possession of certain depictions of animal cruelty. The statute does not address underlying acts harmful to animals, but only portrayals of such conduct. The question presented is whether the prohibition in the statute is consistent with the freedom of speech guaranteed by the First Amendment.

Section 48 establishes a criminal penalty of up to five years in prison for anyone who knowingly "creates, sells, or possesses a depiction of animal cruelty," if done "for commercial gain" in interstate or foreign commerce. § 48(a). A depiction of "animal cruelty" is defined as one "in which a living animal is intentionally maimed, mutilated, tortured, wounded, or killed," if that conduct violates federal or state law where "the creation, sale, or possession takes place." § 48(c)(1). In what is referred to as the "exceptions clause," the law exempts from prohibition any depiction "that has serious religious, political, scientific, educational, journalistic, historical, or artistic value."

The legislative background of § 48 focused primarily on the interstate market for "crush videos." According to the House Committee Report on the bill, such videos feature the intentional torture and killing of helpless animals, including cats, dogs, monkeys, mice, and hamsters. Crush videos often depict women slowly crushing animals to death "with their bare feet or while wearing high heeled shoes," sometimes while "talking to the animals in a kind of dominatrix patter" over "[t]he cries and squeals of the animals, obviously in great pain." Apparently these depictions "appeal to persons with a very specific sexual fetish who find them sexually arousing or otherwise exciting." The acts depicted in crush videos are typically prohibited by the animal cruelty laws enacted by all 50 States and the District of Columbia. But crush videos rarely disclose the participants' identities, inhibiting prosecution of the underlying conduct.

This case, however, involves an application of § 48 to depictions of animal fighting. Dogfighting, for example, is unlawful in all 50 States and the District of Columbia, and has been restricted by federal law since 1976....

The Government's primary submission is that § 48 necessarily complies with the Constitution because the banned depictions of animal cruelty, as a class, are categorically unprotected by the First Amendment. We disagree.

The First Amendment provides that "Congress shall make no law ... abridging the freedom of speech." "[A]s a general matter, the First Amendment means that government has no power to restrict expression because of its message, its ideas, its subject matter, or its content." *Ashcroft v. American Civil Liberties Union*, 535 U.S. 564, 573, (2002) (internal quotation marks omitted). Section 48 explicitly regulates expression based on content: The statute restricts "visual [and] auditory depiction[s]," such as photographs, videos, or sound recordings, depending on whether they depict conduct in which a living animal is intentionally harmed. As such, § 48 is "'presumptively invalid,' and the Government bears the burden to rebut that presumption." *United States v. Playboy Entertainment Group, Inc.*, 529 U.S. 803, 817, (2000).

From 1791 to the present, however, the First Amendment has permitted restrictions upon the content of speech in a few limited areas, and has never included a freedom to disregard these traditional limitations. These historic and traditional categories long familiar to the bar,—including obscenity, defamation, fraud, incitement, and speech integral to criminal conduct,—are well-defined and narrowly limited classes of speech, the prevention and punishment of which have never been thought to raise any Constitutional problem. [Internal quotations and citation omitted.]

The Government argues that "depictions of animal cruelty" should be added to the list. It contends that depictions of "illegal acts of animal cruelty" that are "made, sold, or possessed for commercial gain" necessarily "lack expressive value," and may accordingly "be regulated as *unprotected* speech." The claim is not just that Congress may regulate depictions of animal cruelty subject to the First Amendment, but that these depictions are outside the reach of that Amendment altogether—that they fall into a "'First Amendment Free Zone.'" *Board of Airport Comm'rs of Los Angeles v. Jews for Jesus, Inc.,* 482 U.S. 569, 574 (1987)....

The Government thus proposes that a claim of categorical exclusion should be considered under a simple balancing test: "Whether a given category of speech enjoys First Amendment protection depends upon a categorical balancing of the value of the speech against its societal costs."

As a free-floating test for First Amendment coverage, that sentence is startling and dangerous. The First Amendment's guarantee of free speech does not extend only to categories of speech that survive an ad hoc balancing of relative social costs and benefits. The First Amendment itself reflects a judgment by the American people that the benefits of its restrictions on the Government outweigh the costs. Our Constitution forecloses any attempt to revise that judgment simply on the basis that some speech is not worth it. The Constitution is not a document "prescribing limits, and declaring that those limits may be passed at pleasure." *Marbury v. Madison,* 1 Cranch 137, 178 (1803).

To be fair to the Government, its view did not emerge from a vacuum. As the Government correctly notes, this Court has often *described* historically unprotected categories of speech as being "'of such slight social value as a step to truth that any benefit that may be derived from them is clearly outweighed by the social interest in order and morality.'" *R.A.V., supra,* at 383. In *New York v. Ferber,* 458 U.S. 747 (1982), we noted that within these categories of unprotected speech, "the evil to be restricted so overwhelmingly outweighs the expressive interests, if any, at stake, that no process of case-by-case adjudication is required," because "the balance of competing interests is clearly struck." The Government derives its proposed test from these descriptions in our precedents.

But such descriptions are just that—descriptive. They do not set forth a test that may be applied as a general matter to permit the Government to imprison any speaker so long as his speech is deemed valueless or unnecessary, or so long as an ad hoc calculus of costs and benefits tilts in a statute's favor.

When we have identified categories of speech as fully outside the protection of the First Amendment, it has not been on the basis of a simple cost-benefit analysis. In *Ferber,* for example, we classified child pornography as such a category. We noted that the State of New York had a compelling interest in protecting children from abuse, and that the value of using children in these works (as opposed to simulated conduct or adult actors) was *de minimis.* But our decision did not rest on this "balance of competing interests" alone. We made clear that *Ferber* presented a special case: The market for child pornography was "intrinsically related" to the underlying abuse, and was therefore "an integral part of the production of such materials, an activity illegal throughout the Nation."

Our decisions in *Ferber* and other cases cannot be taken as establishing a freewheeling authority to declare new categories of speech outside the scope of the First Amendment. Maybe there are some categories of speech that have been historically unprotected, but have not yet been specifically identified or discussed as such in our case law. But if so, there is no evidence that "depictions of animal cruelty" is among them. We need not foreclose the future recognition of such additional categories to reject the Government's highly manipulable balancing test as a means of identifying them. . . .

To succeed in a typical facial attack, Stevens would have to establish "that no set of circumstances exists under which [§ 48] would be valid," *United States v. Salerno*, 481 U.S. 739, 745, (1987), or that the statute lacks any "plainly legitimate sweep," *Washington v. Glucksberg*, 521 U.S. 702, 740, n. 7, (1997). Which standard applies in a typical case is a matter of dispute that we need not and do not address, and neither *Salerno* nor *Glucksberg* is a speech case. Here the Government asserts that Stevens cannot prevail because § 48 is plainly legitimate as applied to crush videos and animal fighting depictions. Deciding this case through a traditional facial analysis would require us to resolve whether these applications of § 48 are in fact consistent with the Constitution.

In the First Amendment context, however, this Court recognizes "a second type of facial challenge," whereby a law may be invalidated as overbroad if "a substantial number of its applications are unconstitutional, judged in relation to the statute's plainly legitimate sweep." *Washington State Grange v. Washington State Republican Party*, 552 U.S. 442, 449, n. 6, (2008). Stevens argues that § 48 applies to common depictions of ordinary and lawful activities, and that these depictions constitute the vast majority of materials subject to the statute. The Government makes no effort to defend such a broad ban as constitutional. Instead, the Government's entire defense of § 48 rests on interpreting the statute as narrowly limited to specific types of "extreme" material. As the parties have presented the issue, therefore, the constitutionality of § 48 hinges on how broadly it is construed. It is to that question that we now turn.

As we explained two Terms ago, "[t]he first step in overbreadth analysis is to construe the challenged statute; it is impossible to determine whether a statute reaches too far without first knowing what the statute covers." *United States v. Williams*, 553 U.S. 285, 293 (2008). Because § 48 is a federal statute, there is no need to defer to a state court's authority to interpret its own law.

We read § 48 to create a criminal prohibition of alarming breadth. To begin with, the text of the statute's ban on a "depiction of animal cruelty" nowhere requires that the depicted conduct be cruel. That text applies to "any . . . depiction" in which "a living animal is intentionally maimed, mutilated, tortured, wounded, or killed." § 48(c)(1). "[M]aimed, mutilated, [and] tortured" convey cruelty, but "wounded" or "killed" do not suggest any such limitation. . . .

[T]he phrase "wounded . . . or killed" at issue here contains little ambiguity. The Government's opening brief properly applies the ordinary meaning of these words, stating for example that to "'kill' is 'to deprive of life.'" We agree that "wounded" and "killed" should be read according to their ordinary meaning. Nothing about that meaning requires cruelty.

While not requiring cruelty, § 48 does require that the depicted conduct be "illegal." But this requirement does not limit § 48 along the lines the Government suggests. There are myriad federal and state laws concerning the proper treatment of animals, but many of them are not designed to guard against animal cruelty. Protections of endangered species, for example, restrict even the humane "wound[ing] or kill[ing]" of "living animal[s]."

§ 48(c)(1). Livestock regulations are often designed to protect the health of human beings, and hunting and fishing rules (seasons, licensure, bag limits, weight requirements) can be designed to raise revenue, preserve animal populations, or prevent accidents. The text of § 48(c) draws no distinction based on the reason the intentional killing of an animal is made illegal, and includes, for example, the humane slaughter of a stolen cow.

What is more, the application of § 48 to depictions of illegal conduct extends to conduct that is illegal in only a single jurisdiction. Under subsection (c)(1), the depicted conduct need only be illegal in "the State in which the creation, sale, or possession takes place, regardless of whether the ... wounding ... or killing took place in [that] State." A depiction of entirely lawful conduct runs afoul of the ban if that depiction later finds its way into another State where the same conduct is unlawful. This provision greatly expands the scope of § 48, because although there may be "a broad societal consensus" against cruelty to animals, there is substantial disagreement on what types of conduct are properly regarded as cruel. Both views about cruelty to animals and regulations having no connection to cruelty vary widely from place to place.

In the District of Columbia, for example, all hunting is unlawful. Other jurisdictions permit or encourage hunting, and there is an enormous national market for hunting-related depictions in which a living animal is intentionally killed. Hunting periodicals have circulations in the hundreds of thousands or millions, and hunting television programs, videos, and Web sites are equally popular....

The only thing standing between defendants who sell such depictions and five years in federal prison — other than the mercy of a prosecutor — is the statute's exceptions clause. Subsection (b) exempts from prohibition "any depiction that has serious religious, political, scientific, educational, journalistic, historical, or artistic value." The Government argues that this clause substantially narrows the statute's reach: News reports about animal cruelty have "journalistic" value; pictures of bullfights in Spain have "historical" value; and instructional hunting videos have "educational" value. Thus, the Government argues, § 48 reaches only crush videos, depictions of animal fighting (other than Spanish bullfighting), and perhaps other depictions of "extreme acts of animal cruelty." ...

Quite apart from the requirement of "serious" value in § 48(b), the excepted speech must also fall within one of the enumerated categories. Much speech does not. Most hunting videos, for example, are not obviously instructional in nature, except in the sense that all life is a lesson. According to Safari Club International and the Congressional Sportsmen's Foundation, many popular videos "have primarily entertainment value" and are designed to "entertai[n] the viewer, marke[t] hunting equipment, or increas[e] the hunting community." The National Rifle Association agrees that "much of the content of hunting media ... is merely *recreational* in nature." The Government offers no principled explanation why these depictions of hunting or depictions of Spanish bullfights would be *inherently* valuable while those of Japanese dogfights are not....

The Government explains that the language of § 48(b) was largely drawn from our opinion in *Miller v. California*, 413 U.S. 15 (1973), which excepted from its definition of obscenity any material with "serious literary, artistic, political, or scientific value." According to the Government, this incorporation of the *Miller* standard into § 48 is therefore surely enough to answer any First Amendment objection.

In *Miller* we held that "serious" value shields depictions of sex from regulation as obscenity. Limiting *Miller*'s exception to "serious" value ensured that "'[a] quotation from Voltaire in the flyleaf of a book [would] not constitutionally redeem an otherwise obscene publication.'" We did not, however, determine that serious value could be used as a general precondition to protecting *other* types of speech in the first place. *Most* of what we say to one another lacks "religious, political, scientific, educational, journalistic, historical, or artistic value" (let alone serious value), but it is still sheltered from government regulation.... Thus, the protection of the First Amendment presumptively extends to many forms of speech that do not qualify for the serious-value exception of § 48(b), but nonetheless fall within the broad reach of § 48(c).

Not to worry, the Government says: The Executive Branch construes § 48 to reach only "extreme" cruelty, and it "neither has brought nor will bring a prosecution for anything less," The Government hits this theme hard, invoking its prosecutorial discretion several times. But the First Amendment protects against the Government; it does not leave us at the mercy of *noblesse oblige*. We would not uphold an unconstitutional statute merely because the Government promised to use it responsibly....

Our construction of § 48 decides the constitutional question; the Government makes no effort to defend the constitutionality of § 48 as applied beyond crush videos and depictions of animal fighting. It argues that those particular depictions are intrinsically related to criminal conduct or are analogous to obscenity (if not themselves obscene), and that the ban on such speech is narrowly tailored to reinforce restrictions on the underlying conduct, prevent additional crime arising from the depictions, or safeguard public mores. But the Government nowhere attempts to extend these arguments to depictions of any other activities—depictions that are presumptively protected by the First Amendment but that remain subject to the criminal sanctions of § 48.

Nor does the Government seriously contest that the presumptively impermissible applications of § 48 (properly construed) far outnumber any permissible ones.... We therefore need not and do not decide whether a statute limited to crush videos or other depictions of extreme animal cruelty would be constitutional. We hold only that § 48 is not so limited but is instead substantially overbroad, and therefore invalid under the First Amendment.

Justice ALITO, dissenting.

The Court strikes down in its entirety a valuable statute, 18 U.S.C. § 48, that was enacted not to suppress speech, but to prevent horrific acts of animal cruelty—in particular, the creation and commercial exploitation of "crush videos," a form of depraved entertainment that has no social value. The Court's approach, which has the practical effect of legalizing the sale of such videos and is thus likely to spur a resumption of their production, is unwarranted. Respondent was convicted under § 48 for selling videos depicting dogfights.... Instead of applying the doctrine of overbreadth, I would vacate the decision below and instruct the Court of Appeals on remand to decide whether the videos that respondent sold are constitutionally protected. If the question of overbreadth is to be decided, however, I do not think the present record supports the Court's conclusion that § 48 bans a substantial quantity of protected speech....

In holding that § 48 violates the overbreadth rule, the Court declines to decide whether, as the Government maintains, § 48 is constitutional as applied to two broad categories of depictions that exist in the real world: crush videos and depictions of deadly animal fights....

[I]f the hunting of wild animals were otherwise covered by § 48(a), I would hold that hunting depictions fall within the exception in § 48(b) for depictions that have "serious" (*i.e.*, not "trifling") "scientific," "educational," or "historical" value. While there are certainly those who find hunting objectionable, the predominant view in this country has long been that hunting serves many important values, and it is clear that Congress shares that view.

I do not have the slightest doubt that Congress, in enacting § 48, had no intention of restricting the creation, sale, or possession of depictions of hunting. Proponents of the law made this point clearly....

[W]e have a duty to interpret § 48 so as to avoid serious constitutional concerns, and § 48 may reasonably be construed not to reach almost all, if not all, of the depictions that the Court finds constitutionally protected. Thus, § 48 does not appear to have a large number of unconstitutional applications....

In sum, § 48 may validly be applied to at least two broad real-world categories of expression covered by the statute: crush videos and dogfighting videos.... Accordingly, I would reject respondent's claim that § 48 is facially unconstitutional under the overbreadth doctrine.

Notes and Questions

a. The twin First Amendment rules that arise from *Southeastern Promotions, Ltd. v. Conrad* and *Ward v. Rock Against Racism* result in First Amendment interpretation that bars public or governmental facilities from banning shows from government-owned facilities because of questions of taste. See *Marilyn Manson, Inc. v. New Jersey Sports & Exposition Auth.*, 971 F. Supp. 875 (D.N.J. 1997).

b. The scope of First Amendment protection is not limited to questions of prior restraint. In *Iota Xi Chapter of Sigma Chi Fraternity v. George Mason Univ.*, 993 F.2d 386, 390–91 (4th Cir. 1993), the Fourth Circuit affirmed a district court decision annulling punishment meted out by a public university against a fraternity chapter for an "'ugly woman contest' with racist and sexist overtones." The decision is a good reminder of the difference between the power to encourage taste and community rather than the power to prohibit or punish speech. The Court stated:

> The involved Fraternity members appeared in the contest dressed as caricatures of different types of women, including one member dressed as an offensive caricature of a black woman. He was painted black and wore stringy, black hair decorated with curlers, and his outfit was stuffed with pillows to exaggerate a woman's breasts and buttocks. He spoke in slang to parody African-Americans.... The Fraternity, which later apologized to the University officials for the presentation, conceded during the litigation that the contest was sophomoric and offensive.

> Following the contest, a number of students protested to the University that the skit had been objectionably sexist and racist. Two hundred forty-seven students, many of them members of the foreign or minority student body, executed a petition, which stated: "We are condemning the racist and sexist implications of this event in which male members dressed as women. One man in particular wore a black face, portraying a negative stereotype of black women."

The Court explained that even tasteless programs are protected by the First Amendment. "First Amendment principles governing live entertainment are relatively clear: short of obscenity, it is generally protected.... [T]he low quality of entertainment does not necessarily weigh in the First Amendment inquiry. It would seem, therefore, that the Fraternity's skit, even as low-grade entertainment, was inherently expressive and thus entitled to First Amendment protection."

c. Similar limitations have curbed the license schemes for the sale of artwork. See *Bery v. City of New York*, 97 F.3d 689 (2d Cir. N.Y. 1996). The City of New York could not enforce its licensing for artwork sold on the streets because it failed to meet the standards of *Ward v. Rock Against Racism*. But the scope of the *Bery* injunction prohibiting enforcement of the licensing law against vendors of "paintings, photographs, prints and/or sculpture" has been substantially narrowed "to the narrowest definitions of those terms, as understood by 'plain meaning and normal usage....'" *People v. Ndiaye*, 887 N.Y.S.2d 832, 839–40 (N.Y.Crim.Ct. 2009).

> [Under *Ndiaye*,] there are three categories of merchandise for purposes of determining whether the License Law may be validly applied to its sale. First, newspapers, periodicals, books, pamphlets or other similar written matter are expressly exempt by [statute]. Second, paintings, photographs, prints and sculpture, narrowly defined, are exempt by the terms of the *Bery* injunction. And third, everything else, including jewelry, may constitutionally be made subject to licensure as a reasonable time, place or manner restriction.

d. Most of the court decisions determining the scope of reasonable time, place, and manner restrictions in the entertainment context involve nude dancing, which is afforded some degree of First Amendment protection as a form of expression. That discussion is beyond the scope of this book.

e. For issues of venue access, the First Amendment protections apply only to state action, generally requiring that the property be owned by the government or under the control of the government, and that it be generally available for public use either as an open public forum, or in some more limited forum. To what extent, if any, do these rules affect private property?

f. For additional regulations affecting First Amendment interpretation, see Chapter XV regarding the regulation of television and cable television.

g. The next medium impacted by expansion of First Amendment protection is video gaming. See Chapter XVIII, Section C.

h. Does the First Amendment protect the advertisements for motion pictures, even if the critic's quotes were falsified? For an interesting debate on the topic, see *Rezec v. Sony Pictures Entm't, Inc.*, 116 Cal. App. 4th 135, 10 Cal. Rptr. 3d 333 (2004).

Problem V-A

Bryce is interested in the development of a new project. Bryce has written a script set in a junior high school and is interested in developing it into both a stage play and an independent film screenplay. Working with a company of local, non-union actors, Bryce plans to stage the play at the State Theatre, a city-owned auditorium, and to film the video at Abraham Lincoln Junior High School.

Unfortunately, because of the subject matter of the play, Bryce has received some negative feedback. The play, titled *Juliet Prescott*, is a modern adaptation of *Romeo & Juliet*.[3] Romeo comes from a Catholic Mexican-American family, while Juliet's parents are white and Protestant. Pregnant by Romeo, Juliet's family is encouraging her to have an abortion. Adding fuel to the fire, Bryce has conceived the cleric who secretly marries the couple as an African-American Baptist minister. Bryce assures you that the marriage ceremony is a musical extravaganza that rivals "the church scene in *Blues Brothers*."

---

3. Those unfamiliar with the play should read it and then go see a quality, professional production.

Although neither the State Theatre nor the junior high school had originally requested a copy of the script when first approached, both are now demanding a copy. Bryce believes that a write-up in the local weekly arts magazine overstated the risqué and controversial nature of the play, which depicts no nudity. Concerned local citizens mailed the article to members of the city council and school board to complain about the proposed production. The school is threatening to cancel the location agreement it had signed. The State Theatre has not cancelled yet, but it is demanding a copy of the script, written permission slips from the parents of each minor cast member, and a bond or advance payment. The State Theatre's complaint is based on the highly controversial subject matter, the inclusion of minors in the cast, and the semi-comic tone used through much of the production. (Like *Romeo & Juliet*, however, the script ends tragically.)

Bryce wants the production to go forward and is hoping that the controversy will boost sales. Nonetheless, the costs of the bond and difficulties caused by losing the school for filming could derail the project. Advise Bryce on the legal issues involved in using the theatre and school, as well as how best to proceed.

B. Claims for Injuries Caused by Media Content

James v. Meow Media, Inc.
300 F.3d 683 (6th Cir. 2002)

On December 1, 1997, Michael Carneal walked into the lobby of Heath High School in Paducah, Kentucky, and shot several of his fellow students, killing three and wounding many others. The parents and estate administrators of Carneal's victims—Jessica James, Kayce Steger, and Nicole Hadley—(hereinafter collectively referred to as "James") appeal the judgment of the district court dismissing, for failing to state claims on which relief could be granted, their actions against several video game, movie production, and internet content-provider firms. According to James's complaint, Carneal regularly played video games, watched movies, and viewed internet sites produced by the defendant firms. These activities, James argues, "desensitized" Carneal to violence and "caused" him to kill the students of Heath High School. James claims that the distribution of this material to impressionable youth like Carneal constitutes actionable negligence under Kentucky law, entitling James to recover wrongful death damages from the distributing firms. Moreover, James contends that the defendant firms purveyed defective "products," namely the content of video games, movies, and internet sites, triggering strict product liability under Kentucky law.

The defendant firms argue that they owe no duty to protect third parties from how players, watchers or viewers process the ideas and images presented in their video games, movies, and internet sites. Specifically, the defendants contend that Carneal's actions were not sufficiently foreseeable to trigger the defendants' liability. Even if they were to owe such a duty to protect third parties from the consumers of their ideas and images, the defendants argue that Carneal's independent decision to kill his fellow students constitutes a superseding cause of the claimed damages and defeats the proximate cause element of James's *prima facie* case. The defendants further contend that tort liability for the non-defamatory ideas and images communicated in their respective media would raise significant First Amendment questions that ought to be avoided. Finally, the defendants note that James's theory of product liability is flawed as they have not distributed "products" under Kentucky law.

For the reasons set forth below, we affirm the district court's dismissal of James's actions....

Carneal regularly played "Doom," "Quake," "Castle Wolfenstein," "Redneck Rampage," "Nightmare Creatures," "Mech Warrior," "Resident Evil," and "Final Fantasy," which are interactive computer games that, in various ways, all involve the player shooting virtual opponents. Carneal also possessed a video tape containing the movie, "The Basketball Diaries," in a few minutes of which the high-school-student protagonist dreams of killing his teacher and several of his fellow classmates. Investigators examined Carneal's computer and discovered that he had visited "www.persiankitty.com," which appears to catalogue and link to sites with sexually-suggestive material. It also appeared that through "www.adultkey.com," a site operated by Network Authentication Systems and designed to restrict access to certain websites to viewers over certain ages, Carneal was granted age verification sufficient to visit many other pornographic sites....

First, James alleged that the defendants had been negligent in that they either knew or should have known that the distribution of their material to Carneal and other young people created an unreasonable risk of harm to others. James alleged that exposure to the defendants' material made young people insensitive to violence and more likely to commit violent acts. But for Carneal's steady diet of the defendants' material, James contended, Carneal would not have committed his violent acts.

Second, James asserted that the video game cartridges, movie cassettes, and internet transmissions that the defendants produced and distributed were "products" for purposes of Kentucky product liability law. According to James, the violent features of the movie, games, and internet sites were product defects. The defendants, as producers and distributors of the "products," are strictly liable under Kentucky law for damages caused by such product defects....

The legal questions under review in this case are questions of Kentucky law. When faced with the resolution of these state law issues, our inquiry is in part hypothetical. Specifically, we are charged to decide these questions of Kentucky state law as Kentucky state courts would....

James contends that the defendants in this case acted negligently, perhaps in producing, but at least in distributing to young people, their materials. It was this negligence, according to James, that caused Carneal to undertake his violent actions and that thereby caused the deaths of the plaintiffs' daughters. In order to establish an actionable tort under Kentucky law, the plaintiff must establish that the defendant owed a duty of care to the plaintiff, that the defendant breached that duty of care, and that the *defendant's breach* was the proximate cause of the plaintiff's damages.

A. The Existence of a Duty of Care

The district court held that James's allegations, even if assumed to be true, failed to establish the first element of the *prima facie* case. Specifically, the district court determined that the defendants were under no duty to protect James, Steger, and Hadley from Carneal's actions. James argues that the district court erred as a matter of Kentucky law in this regard....

Kentucky courts have held that the determination of whether a duty of care exists is whether the harm to the plaintiff resulting from the defendant's negligence was "foreseeable." Foreseeability is an often invoked, but not terribly well defined, concept in the common law of tort. Some common law tort regimes use foreseeability as the standard for determining proximate causation. Kentucky's particular use of foreseeability in the duty inquiry finds its roots in perhaps the most famous application of the foreseeability principle. In *Palsgraf v. Long Island Railroad Co.*, 248 N.Y. 339 (N.Y. 1928), then-Judge Cardozo determined that the defendant's duty is to avoid "risks reasonably to be perceived." ... Cardozo determined that the railroad simply did not owe a duty to Palsgraf to protect against *the injury that she suffered*. For Cardozo, the harm that Palsgraf suffered was not sufficiently probable that the railroad employees could have been expected to anticipate it occurring from their actions. Cardozo's reasoning, although implying that Palsgraf was the unforeseeable plaintiff, rested on the improbability of the *harm* that she suffered arising from the defendant's particular actions. For Cardozo too, the existence of a duty of care was a creature of circumstance....

Kentucky courts have struggled with the formless nature of this inquiry. At bottom, Kentucky courts have conceded, deciding the existence of a duty of care is "essentially a policy determination." Rather than the sophisticated weighing of probabilities, the content of that policy determination "is but a conclusion of whether a plaintiff's interests are entitled to legal protection against the defendant's conduct."

Thus, we are called, as best we can, to implement Kentucky's duty of care analysis in this case. Our inquiry is whether the deaths of James, Steger, and Hadley were the reasonably foreseeable result of the defendants' creation and distribution of their games, movie, and internet sites. Whether an event was reasonably foreseeable is not for us to determine with the assistance of hindsight. The mere fact that the risk may have materialized does little to resolve the foreseeability question.

Kentucky courts, in resolving foreseeability questions, have consistently inquired into the relative likelihood of the injuries produced. Of particular interest in this case are cases in which plaintiffs have sought to hold defendants liable for the actions of third parties, allegedly enabled or encouraged by the defendants. A line of cases in this vein concerns dram shops. In *Grayson* [*Fraternal Order of Eagles v. Claywell*, 736 S.W.2d 328 (Ky 1987),] the Kentucky Supreme Court held that an automobile accident injuring third parties was a reasonably foreseeable result of the negligent act of serving alcohol to an intoxicated individual. In contrast, the court later held that an intoxicated patron fighting with and shooting a fellow customer was simply not a foreseeable result of continuing to serve the patron alcohol. According to the court, the violent fighting and shooting was so much less likely a result from the serving of alcohol than the negligent operation of a motor vehicle that it was not reasonably foreseeable. Accordingly, the court held that dram shops, although negligent in serving alcohol to the obviously intoxicated, do not have a duty to protect third parties from the intentional violent acts of their intoxicated patrons.

Intentional violence is less likely to result from intoxication than negligent operation of a motor vehicle. Yet, the Kentucky Supreme Court never makes clear how unlikely is too unlikely for a particular type of harm to be unforeseeable. The cases do not create a principle, portable to the context of this case, for evaluating the probability of harm.

This court has encountered this foreseeability inquiry under Kentucky law before in a situation similar to this case. In *Watters v. TSR, Inc.*, 904 F.2d 378 (6th Cir. 1990), the mother of a suicide victim sued TSR for manufacturing the game "Dungeons and Dragons." The suicide victim regularly played the game. The mother contended that the game's violent content "desensitized" the victim to violence and caused him to undertake the violent act of shooting himself in the head. We held that the boy's suicide was simply not a reasonably foreseeable result of producing the game, notwithstanding its violent content. To have held otherwise would have been "to stretch the concepts of foreseeability and ordinary care to lengths that would deprive them of all normal meaning."

Foreseeability, however, is a slippery concept. Indeed, it could be argued that we ourselves confused it with some concept of negligence. We noted in *Watters*: "The defendant cannot be faulted, obviously, for putting its game on the market without attempting to ascertain the mental condition of each and every prospective player." We almost appeared to say that the costs of acquiring such knowledge would so outweigh the social benefits that it would not be negligent to abstain from such an investigation. We can put the *foreseeability* point a little more precisely, however. It appears simply impossible to predict that these games, movie, and internet sites (alone, or in what combinations) would incite a young person to violence. Carneal's reaction to the games and movies at issue here, assuming that his violent actions were such a reaction, was simply too idiosyncratic to expect the defendants to have anticipated it. We find that it is simply too far a leap from shooting characters on a video screen (an activity undertaken by millions) to shooting people in a classroom (an activity undertaken by a handful, at most) for Carneal's actions to have been reasonably foreseeable to the manufacturers of the media that Carneal played and viewed.

At first glance, our conclusion also appears to be little more than an assertion. Mental health experts could quite plausibly opine about the manner in which violent movies and video games affect viewer behavior. We need not stretch to imagine some mixture of impressionability and emotional instability that might unnaturally react with the violent content of the "Basketball Diaries" or "Doom." Of course, Carneal's reaction was not a normal reaction. Indeed, Carneal is not a normal person, but it is not utter craziness to predict that someone like Carneal is out there.

We return, however, to the Kentucky court's observation that the existence of a duty of care reflects a judicial policy judgment at bottom. From the Kentucky cases on foreseeability, we can discern two relevant policies that counsel against finding that Carneal's violent actions were the reasonably foreseeable result of defendants' distribution of games, movies, and internet material.

1. The Duty to Protect Against Intentional Criminal Actions

First, courts have held that, except under extraordinary circumstances, individuals are generally entitled to assume that third parties will not commit intentional criminal acts. The reasons behind this general rule are simple enough. The first reason is a probabilistic judgment that foreseeability analysis requires. Individuals generally are significantly deterred from undertaking intentional criminal conduct given the sanctions that can follow. The threatened sanctions make the third-party intentional criminal conduct sufficiently less likely that, under normal circumstances, we do not require the putative tort defendant to anticipate it. Indeed, this statistical observation explains the distinction drawn by Kentucky courts in the dram shop liability cases.

The second reason is structural. The system of criminal liability has concentrated responsibility for an intentional criminal act in the primary actor, his accomplices, and his co-conspirators. By imposing liability on those who did not endeavor to accomplish the intentional criminal undertaking, tort liability would diminish the responsibility placed on the criminal defendant. The normative message of tort law in these situations would be that the defendant is not entirely responsible for his intentional criminal act.

Does this case involve the extraordinary circumstances under which we would require the defendants to anticipate a third party's intentional criminal act? Kentucky courts have found such circumstances when the tort defendant had previously developed "a special relationship" with the victim of a third-party intentional criminal act. This duty to protect can be triggered by placing the putative plaintiff in custody or by taking other affirmative steps that disable the plaintiff from protecting himself against third-party intentional criminal acts. Of course, a special relationship can be created by a contract between the plaintiff and the defendant. Finally, some states have imposed a duty to protect others from third-party intentional criminal acts on members of discrete professions who become aware of the third-party's intention to engage in criminal conduct against a specific person. We can find nothing close to a "special relationship" in this case. The defendants did not even know James, Steger, and Hadley prior to Carneal's actions, much less take any affirmative steps that disabled them from protecting themselves.

Courts have held, under extremely limited circumstances, that individuals, notwithstanding their relationship with the victims of third-party violence, can be liable when their affirmative actions "create a high degree of risk of [the third party's] intentional misconduct." Generally, such circumstances are limited to cases in which the defendant has given a young child access to ultra-hazardous materials such as blasting caps or firearms. Even in those cases, courts have relied on the third party's severely diminished capacity to handle the ultra-hazardous materials. With older third parties, courts have found liability only where defendants have vested a particular person, under circumstances that made his nefarious plans clear, with the tools that he then quickly used to commit the criminal act. Arguably, the defendants' games, movie, and internet sites gave Carneal the ideas and emotions, the "psychological tools," to commit three murders. However, this case lacks such crucial features of our jurisprudence in this area. First, the defendants in this case had no idea Carneal even existed, much less the particular idiosyncrasies of Carneal that made their products particularly dangerous in his hands. In every case that this court has discovered in which defendants have been held liable for negligently creating an unreasonably high risk of third-party criminal conduct, the defendants have been specifically aware of the peculiar tendency of a particular person to commit a criminal act with the defendants' materials.

Second, no court has ever held that ideas and images can constitute the tools for a criminal act under this narrow exception. Beyond their intangibility, such ideas and images are at least one step removed from the implements that can be used in the criminal act itself. In the cases supporting this exception, the item that the defendant has given to the third-party criminal actor has been the direct instrument of harm.

2. First Amendment Problems

Moreover, we are loath to hold that ideas and images can constitute the tools for a criminal act under this exception, or even to attach tort liability to the dissemination of ideas. We agree with the district court that attaching tort liability to the effect that such ideas have on a criminal actor would raise significant constitutional problems under the First Amendment that ought to be avoided. Although the plaintiffs' contentions in this case do not concern the absolute proscription of the defendants' conduct, courts have made clear that attaching tort liability to protected speech can violate the First Amendment.

The first inquiry is whether the defendants' activity constitutes protected speech under the First Amendment. One thing is perfectly clear to this court: the plaintiffs' argument does not seek to attach liability to the cassettes and cartridges distributed by the defendants, but the ideas and images communicated to Carneal by those products. Although the defendants' products may be a mixture of expressive and inert content, the plaintiffs' theory of liability isolates the expressive content of the defendants' products.

Expression, to be constitutionally protected, need not constitute the reasoned discussion of the public affairs, but may also be for purposes of entertainment. Clearly, the various media distributed in this case fall along a spectrum of expressive content. It is long settled that movies can constitute protected speech. Of more recent, but no less definitive, resolution is that internet sites are similarly entitled to protection. The constitutional status of video games has been less litigated in federal courts. Yet most federal courts to consider the issue have found video games to be constitutionally protected.

Extending First Amendment protection to video games certainly presents some thorny issues. After all, there are features of video games which are not terribly communicative, such as the manner in which the player controls the game. The plaintiffs in this case, however, complain about none of those non-expressive features. Instead, they argue that the video game, somehow, communicated to Carneal a disregard for human life and an endorsement of violence that persuaded him to commit three murders. Because the plaintiffs seek to attach tort liability to the communicative aspect of the video games produced by the defendants, we have little difficulty in holding that the First Amendment protects video games in the sense uniquely relevant to this lawsuit. Our decision here today should not be interpreted as a broad holding on the protected status of video games, but as a recognition of the particular manner in which James seeks to regulate them through tort liability.

To say that the features of the defendants' products of which the plaintiffs complain are protected by the First Amendment is not necessarily to say that attaching tort liability to those features raises significant constitutional problems. The plaintiffs' argument is more nuanced: they do not seek to hold the defendants responsible merely for distributing their materials to anyone, but to young, impressionable children or, even more specifically, to Carneal. The protections of the First Amendment have always adapted to the audience intended for the speech. Specifically, we have recognized certain speech, while fully protected when directed to adults, may be restricted when directed towards minors. We have also required, however, that such regulations be narrowly tailored to protecting minors from speech that may improperly influence them and not effect an "unnecessarily broad suppression of speech" appropriate for adults.

Of course, the measure here intended to protect minors from the improper influence of otherwise protected speech is quite different from the regulations that we have countenanced in the past. Those regulations were the product of the reasoned deliberation of democratically elected legislative bodies, or at least regulatory agencies exercising authority delegated by such bodies. It was legislative bodies that had demarcated what otherwise protected speech was inappropriate for children and that had outlined in advance the measures that speakers were required to take in order to protect children from the speech.

...

With the movie and video game defendants, James contends that their material is excessively violent and constitutes obscene, non-protected speech. We decline to extend our obscenity jurisprudence to violent, instead of sexually explicit, material. Even if we were to consider such an expansion, James's arguments are not conceptually linked to our obscenity jurisprudence. The concept of obscenity was designed to permit the regulation of "offensive" material, that is, material that people find "disgusting" or "degrading." James's argument, on the other hand, is that the violent content of these video games and the movie shapes behavior and causes its consumers to commit violent acts. This is a different claim than the obscenity doctrine, which is a limit on the extent to which the community's sensibilities can be shocked by speech, not a protection against the behavior that the speech creates.

This is not to say that protecting people from the violence that speech might incite is a completely impermissible purpose for regulating speech. However, we have generally handled that endeavor under a different category of our First Amendment jurisprudence, excluding from constitutional protection those communicated ideas and images that incite others to violence. Speech that falls within this category of incitement is not entitled to First Amendment protection. The Court firmly set out the test for whether speech constitutes unprotected incitement to violence in *Brandenburg v. Ohio,* 395 U.S. 444 (1969). In protecting against the propensity of expression to cause violence, states may only regulate that speech which is "*directed to* inciting or producing *imminent* lawless action and *is likely to incite* or produce such action."

The violent material in the video games and *The Basketball Diaries* falls well short of this threshold. First, while the defendants in this case may not have exercised exquisite care regarding the persuasive power of the violent material that they disseminated, they certainly did not "intend" to produce violent actions by the consumers, as is required by the *Brandenburg* test. Second, the threat of a person like Carneal reacting to the violent content of the defendants' media was not "imminent." Even the theory of causation in this case is that persistent exposure to the defendants' media gradually undermined Carneal's moral discomfort with violence to the point that he solved his social disputes with a gun. This glacial process of personality development is far from the temporal imminence that we have required to satisfy the *Brandenburg* test. Third, it is a long leap from the proposition that Carneal's actions were foreseeable to the *Brandenburg* requirement that the violent content was "likely" to cause Carneal to behave this way....

B. Proximate Causation

Even if this court were to find that the defendants owed a duty to protect James, Steger, and Hadley from Carneal's violent actions, the plaintiffs likely have not alleged sufficient facts to establish the third element of a *prima facie* tort case: proximate causation.... Our determination regarding the idiosyncratic nature of Carneal's reaction to the defendants' media would likely compel us to hold that his action constitutes a superseding cause. We, however, need not reach this question because we have determined that the defendants did not owe a duty to protect the decedents.

James also contends that the district court erred in dismissing his products liability claims.... James has failed to demonstrate a prior requirement, that the video games, movies, and internet sites are "products" for purposes of strict liability. This was the basis on which the district court dismissed James's products liability claims, holding that the video games, movie, and internet transmissions were not "products," at least in the sense that James sought to attach liability to them.

This court has already substantially resolved the question of Kentucky law presented. In *Watters v. TSR,* 904 F.2d 378 (6th Cir. 1990), this court held that "words and pictures" contained in a board game could not constitute "products" for purposes of maintaining a strict liability action. We cannot find any intervening Kentucky authority that persuades us that *Watters* no longer correctly states Kentucky law. James's theory of liability, that the ideas conveyed by the video games, movie cassettes and internet transmissions, caused Carneal to kill his victims, attempts to attach product liability in a nearly identical way.... The video game cartridges, movie cassette, and internet transmissions are not sufficiently "tangible" to constitute products in the sense of their communicative content.

For all the foregoing reasons, we AFFIRM the district court's dismissal of all James's claims.

Waller v. Osbourne

763 F. Supp. 1144 (M.D. Ga. 1991) *aff'd*, 958 F.2d 1084 (11th Cir. 1992)

Plaintiffs Thomas and Myra Waller in the above captioned action allege that the defendants proximately caused the wrongful death of their son Michael Jeffery Waller by inciting him to commit suicide through the music, lyrics, and subliminal messages contained in the song "Suicide Solution" on the album "Blizzard of Oz." Defendants deny all allegations of wrongdoing on their part and now have pending before the court a joint motion for summary judgment.

Plaintiffs filed their original complaint in this case on April 28, 1988, following the death of their son Michael Jeffery Waller on May 3, 1986, as the result of a self-inflicted pistol wound to his head. In that original complaint, plaintiffs alleged that their son's suicide occurred after he had repeatedly listened to an Ozzy Osbourne cassette tape which contained audible and perceptible lyrics that directed Michael Waller to take his own life.[4]

Defendants Ozzy Osbourne, CBS Inc., and CBS RECORDS Inc., responded to the plaintiffs' complaint by moving the court to dismiss the complaint pursuant to Federal Rule of Civil Procedure 12(b)(6) because it failed to state a claim upon which relief could be granted. Before the court acted on the motion to dismiss, however, plaintiffs filed a motion to amend their complaint which the court authorized.

The modified complaint discarded the claim that the lyrics which allegedly incited their son to commit suicide were audible and perceptible and instead charged that those same lyrics represent a subliminal message that is consciously intelligible only when the music is electronically adjusted. The amended complaint further alleges that as a result of the dissemination of the music, lyrics, and subliminal message in the song "Suicide Solution" on the album "Blizzard of Oz," defendants are liable to the plaintiffs for causing the pain and suffering of their deceased son; inciting his wrongful death; encouraging persons to physically harm themselves or commit suicide; and engaging in fraud, invasion of privacy, and nuisance....

In determining whether or not the court should grant the joint summary judgment motion of the defendants in this case, the court must initially resolve the issue of whether, as a matter of law, the song "Suicide Solution" on the album "Blizzard of Oz" contains subliminal messages as alleged by plaintiffs. The court finds this step necessary because it is convinced that the presence of a subliminal message, whose surreptitious nature makes it more akin to false and misleading commercial speech and other forms of speech extremely limited in their social value, would relegate the music containing such to a class worthy of little, if any, first amendment constitutional protection.

Plaintiffs attempt to establish the presence of subliminal messages in the song "Suicide Solution" contained on the "Blizzard of Oz" album primarily through the deposition testimony of two expert witnesses. Plaintiffs' expert, Mr. Hall, however, fails to create an issue of fact concerning the existence of a subliminal message when his specific find-

---

4. The alleged lyrics that were audible and perceptible during a twenty-eight second interlude in the song "Suicide Solution" on the album titled "Blizzard of Oz" went as follows:
   Ah know people
   You really know where it's at
   You got it
   Why try, why try
   Get the gun and try it
   Shoot, shoot, shoot.

ing is that since the lyrics in question in this case are audible, they cannot be a subliminal message as plaintiffs allege.

Plaintiffs' other expert, Ms. Evans, is equally unsuccessful in creating a genuine issue of fact since she contends that the lyrics in question are a subliminal message precisely because they are barely heard but not decipherable. While the court was unable to find a precise legal definition of a subliminal message, it is clear from the definition of subliminal that lyrics which are audible enough to make one consciously aware of their presence, though they may not necessarily be intelligible, do not qualify as a subliminal message.

According to *Webster's Ninth New Collegiate Dictionary*, (1985 Edition), subliminal is actually defined as "inadequate to produce a sensation or perception" and "existing or functioning below the threshold of conscious awareness." *Random House Dictionary* (1987 Edition) defines subliminal as "existing or operating below the threshold of consciousness; being or employing stimuli insufficiently intense to produce a discrete sensation but often being or designed to be intense enough to influence the mental processes or the behavior of the individual." If, as defined, a subliminal message must exist below the threshold of conscious awareness then it must follow that lyrics distinct enough to be heard and reacted to — even though garbled or unclear, are not a subliminal message. The most important character of a subliminal message is that it sneaks into the brain while the listener is completely unaware that he has heard anything at all. If the message is heard to any extent, even if garbled and unintelligible, the listener consciously attempts to discern a meaning from that which he hears. One is then dealing, not with a subliminal message, but rather the interpretation of an abstract medium which is akin to spotting objects in cloud formations.

Possibly a visual subliminal message such as the words "eat popcorn" on a reel of movie film can be proved more easily than an audio one such as the one alleged here. If the film is stopped and one holds each frame up to the light somewhere there must be at least one frame that says "eat popcorn." Here, there is nothing that says what the plaintiffs contend unless one uses his imagination. Therefore, despite her desire to label the lyrics contained in the twenty eight second interlude on the song "Suicide Solution" a subliminal message, the fact that Ms. Evans found that those lyrics are audible means that she has proved just the opposite — that the lyrics are not a subliminal message.

Furthermore, honoring Ms. Evans definition of subliminal message would mean that all rock music, or any music for that matter, which contains unintelligible lyrics could be found to contain a subliminal message, thereby, subjecting an endless number of performers and producers to possible law suits. It would be an understatement to say such a ruling would open the flood gates of litigation....

The court noted in its order denying defendants' motion to dismiss that the plaintiffs would be hard-pressed to avoid summary judgment in this action absent the presence of a subliminal message in the music of the defendants. Such is the case because music in the form of entertainment represents a type of speech that is generally afforded first amendment constitutional protection.

The first amendment protection that shields those who produce, perform, and distribute music is not however absolute. Music legally classified as obscene or defamatory, or that which represents fighting words or incites imminent lawless activity is either entitled to diminished first amendment constitutional protection or none at all. Therefore, even though the court has found that defendants' music does not contain subliminal messages, plaintiffs can strip away the first amendment protection defendants now stand behind if they can demonstrate that defendants music fits into one of the above categories.

Plaintiffs contend that the song "Suicide Solution" on the album "Blizzard of Oz" is properly categorized as speech which incites imminent lawless activity thereby depriving defendants of any legitimate claim to first amendment protection. The removal of first amendment protection from defendants' music on such a basis is contingent on a finding that it was "directed to inciting or producing imminent lawless action and is likely to incite or produce such action." Subsequent Supreme Court decisions have further indicated that in making such a finding the primary focus of the court should be on the imminence of the threat.

In *Hess* [*v. Indiana*, 414 U.S. 105 (1973)], the Court was forced to decide whether an antiwar demonstrator's first amendment rights were violated when the state of Indiana arrested him for shouting, "We'll take the fucking street later [or again]," to a crowd the police were attempting to disperse. In upholding the demonstrator's first amendment right to make that statement the court concluded that:

> Since the uncontroverted evidence showed that Hess' statement was not directed to any person or group of persons, it cannot be said that he was advocating, in the normal sense, any action. And since there was no evidence or rational inference from the import of the language, that his words were intended to produce, and likely to produce, *imminent* disorder, those words could not be punished by the state on the ground that they had 'a tendency to lead to violence.'

A careful examination of the defendants' music in accordance with the test developed in *Brandenburg* and refined in *Hess* leads this court to conclude that the defendants did not engage in culpable incitement. There is no indication whatsoever that defendants' music was directed toward any particular person or group of persons. Moreover, there is no evidence that defendants' music was intended to produce acts of suicide, and likely to cause *imminent* acts of suicide; nor could one rationally infer such a meaning from the lyrics. There, in fact, is no evidence nor even any allegations in this case that Michael Jeffery Waller committed suicide immediately after listening to defendants' music.

Viewing the facts in a light most favorable to the plaintiffs, the song "Suicide Solution" can be perceived as asserting in a philosophical sense that suicide may be a viable option one should consider in certain circumstances. And a strong argument can certainly be made that in light of the almost epidemic proportion of teenage suicides now occurring in this country it is irresponsible and callous for a musician with a large teenage following such as Ozzy Osbourne to portray suicide in any manner other than a tragic occurrence. Nevertheless, an abstract discussion of the moral propriety or even moral necessity for a resort to suicide, is not the same as indicating to someone that he should commit suicide and encouraging him to take such action. That, however, is what the law requires the plaintiffs to demonstrate in order to hold the defendants liable for inciting their son to commit suicide through the dissemination of their music. Plaintiffs have made no such showing and have failed to demonstrate any manner in which defendants' music can be categorized as speech which incites imminent lawless activity. Accordingly, the court finds as a matter of law that defendants are protected by the first amendment from liability for culpable incitement.

Absent the allegation that defendants' music represents speech that incites imminent lawless activities, plaintiffs have no other plausible basis in this case upon which they can overcome the broad first amendment protection generally afforded speech in the form of music. Plaintiffs put forth other theories of liability such as negligence, nuisance, fraud, and invasion of privacy. However, all of those tort based theories, as asserted by plaintiffs, fail to overcome the defendants' imposition of a valid first amendment defense.

Numerous courts have pointed out that any attempt to impose tort liability on persons engaged in the dissemination of protected speech involves too great a risk of seriously chilling all free speech....

Plaintiffs failed to demonstrate the existence of a subliminal message or that defendants' music incites imminent lawless activity, and were thereby left with the difficult task of attempting to impose liability on the defendants based on their dissemination of speech fully protected by the first amendment. It was a task plaintiffs were unable to accomplish.

Having ruled on the matter before the court, this order cannot be signed without an expression of sympathy for the parents of Michael Jeffery Waller who have shown their devotion to his memory by the filing and prosecution of this lawsuit. The court has no doubt as to the sincerity of their motives in following through with what must be an extremely painful course of action. The death of anyone before he has had a full measure of life is tragic and especially so if the person is a much loved teenaged son. If the death is by suicide the pain and grief to those left behind is almost unbearable. Although the court must render all its decisions without regard to sympathy, that does not mean it loses its capacity to experience that emotion.

Winter v. G.P. Putnam's Sons
938 F.2d 1033 (9th Cir. 1991)

Plaintiffs are mushroom enthusiasts who became severely ill from picking and eating mushrooms after relying on information in *The Encyclopedia of Mushrooms*, a book published by the defendant. Plaintiffs sued the publisher and sought damages under various theories. The district court granted summary judgment for the defendant. We affirm.

The Encyclopedia of Mushrooms is a reference guide containing information on the habitat, collection, and cooking of mushrooms. It was written by two British authors and originally published by a British publishing company. Defendant Putnam, an American book publisher, purchased copies of the book from the British publisher and distributed the finished product in the United States. Putnam neither wrote nor edited the book.

Plaintiffs purchased the book to help them collect and eat wild mushrooms. In 1988, plaintiffs went mushroom hunting and relied on the descriptions in the book in determining which mushrooms were safe to eat. After cooking and eating their harvest, plaintiffs became critically ill. Both have required liver transplants.

Plaintiffs allege that the book contained erroneous and misleading information concerning the identification of the most deadly species of mushrooms. In their suit against the book publisher, plaintiffs allege liability based on products liability, breach of warranty, negligence, negligent misrepresentation, and false representations. Defendant moved for summary judgment asserting that plaintiffs' claims failed as a matter of law because 1) the information contained in a book is not a product for the purposes of strict liability under products liability law; and 2) defendant is not liable under any remaining theories because a publisher does not have a duty to investigate the accuracy of the text it publishes. The district court granted summary judgment for the defendant. Plaintiffs appeal. We affirm.

A book containing Shakespeare's sonnets consists of two parts, the material and print therein, and the ideas and expression thereof. The first may be a product, but the second is not. The latter, were Shakespeare alive, would be governed by copyright laws; the laws of libel, to the extent consistent with the First Amendment; and the laws of misrepresentation, negligent misrepresentation, negligence, and mistake. These doctrines applicable to the second part are aimed at the delicate issues that arise with respect to intangibles such as ideas and expression. Products liability law is geared to the tangible world.

A. *Products Liability*

The language of products liability law reflects its focus on tangible items. In describing the scope of products liability law, the Restatement (Second) of Torts lists examples of items that are covered. All of these are tangible items, such as tires, automobiles, and insecticides. The American Law Institute clearly was concerned with including all physical items but gave no indication that the doctrine should be expanded beyond that area.

The purposes served by products liability law also are focused on the tangible world and do not take into consideration the unique characteristics of ideas and expression. Under products liability law, strict liability is imposed on the theory that "the costs of damaging events due to defectively dangerous products can best be borne by the enterprisers who make and sell these products." *Prosser & Keeton on The Law of Torts*, § 98, at 692–93 (W. Keeton ed. 5th ed. 1984). Strict liability principles have been adopted to further the "cause of accident prevention ... [by] the elimination of the necessity of proving negligence." Additionally, because of the difficulty of establishing fault or negligence in products liability cases, strict liability is the appropriate legal theory to hold manufacturers liable for defective products. Thus, the seller is subject to liability "even though he has exercised all possible care in the preparation and sale of the product." It is not a question of fault but simply a determination of how society wishes to assess certain costs that arise from the creation and distribution of products in a complex technological society in which the consumer thereof is unable to protect himself against certain product defects.

Although there is always some appeal to the involuntary spreading of costs of injuries in any area, the costs in any comprehensive cost/benefit analysis would be quite different were strict liability concepts applied to words and ideas. We place a high priority on the unfettered exchange of ideas. We accept the risk that words and ideas have wings we cannot clip and which carry them we know not where. The threat of liability without fault (financial responsibility for our words and ideas in the absence of fault or a special undertaking or responsibility) could seriously inhibit those who wish to share thoughts and theories. As a New York court commented, with the specter of strict liability, "would any author wish to be exposed ... for writing on a topic which might result in physical injury? *e.g.* How to cut trees; How to keep bees?" One might add: "Would anyone undertake to guide by ideas expressed in words either a discrete group, a nation, or humanity in general?"

Strict liability principles even when applied to products are not without their costs. Innovation may be inhibited. We tolerate these losses. They are much less disturbing than the prospect that we might be deprived of the latest ideas and theories.

Plaintiffs suggest, however, that our fears would be groundless were strict liability rules applied only to books that give instruction on how to accomplish a physical activity and that are intended to be used as part of an activity that is inherently dangerous. We find such a limitation illusory. Ideas are often intimately linked with proposed action, and it would be difficult to draw such a bright line. While "How To" books are a special genre, we decline to attempt to draw a line that puts "How To Live A Good Life" books beyond the reach of strict liability while leaving "How To Exercise Properly" books within its reach.

Plaintiffs' argument is stronger when they assert that *The Encyclopedia of Mushrooms* should be analogized to aeronautical charts. Several jurisdictions have held that charts which graphically depict geographic features or instrument approach information for airplanes are "products" for the purpose of products liability law. Plaintiffs suggest that *The Encyclopedia of Mushrooms* can be compared to aeronautical charts because both items contain representations of natural features and both are intended to be used while engaging in a hazardous activity. We are not persuaded.

Aeronautical charts are highly technical tools. They are graphic depictions of technical, mechanical data. The best analogy to an aeronautical chart is a compass. Both may be used to guide an individual who is engaged in an activity requiring certain knowledge of natural features. Computer software that fails to yield the result for which it was designed may be another. In contrast, *The Encyclopedia of Mushrooms* is like a book on how to use a compass or an aeronautical chart. The chart itself is like a physical "product" while the "How to Use" book is pure thought and expression.[5]

Given these considerations, we decline to expand products liability law to embrace the ideas and expression in a book. We know of no court that has chosen the path to which the plaintiffs point.

B. *The Remaining Theories*

As discussed above, plaintiffs must look to the doctrines of copyright, libel, misrepresentation, negligent misrepresentation, negligence, and mistake to form the basis of a claim against the defendant publisher. Unless it is assumed that the publisher is a guarantor of the accuracy of an author's statements of fact, plaintiffs have made no case under any of these theories other than possibly negligence. Guided by the First Amendment and the values embodied therein, we decline to extend liability under this theory to the ideas and expression contained in a book.

In order for negligence to be actionable, there must be a legal duty to exercise due care. The plaintiffs urge this court that the publisher had a duty to investigate the accuracy of *The Encyclopedia of Mushrooms*' contents. We conclude that the defendants have no duty to investigate the accuracy of the contents of the books it publishes. A publisher may of course assume such a burden, but there is nothing inherent in the role of publisher or the surrounding legal doctrines to suggest that such a duty should be imposed on publishers. Indeed the cases uniformly refuse to impose such a duty. Were we tempted to cre-

---

5. In reversing a lower court opinion that aeronautical charts are not products, the *Fluor court* made the following comments:

> [The trial court] explained that it believed strict liability principles are applicable only to items whose physical properties render them innately dangerous, e.g., mechanical devices, explosives, combustible or flammable materials, etc. This belief was erroneous.... Although a sheet of paper might not be dangerous, per se, it would be difficult indeed to conceive of a salable commodity with more inherent lethal potential than an aid to aircraft navigation that, contrary to its own design standards, fails to list the highest land mass immediately surrounding a landing site.

Fluor Corp. v. Jeppesen & Co., 170 Cal. App. 3d 468, 475–76, 216 Cal. Rptr. 68, 71–72 (1985). Plaintiffs argue that this language shows that California courts would not draw a line between physical products and intangible ideas.

The *Fluor* language, however, cannot be stretched that far. The court was simply discussing the fact that under products liability law, the injury does not have to be caused by impact from the physical properties of the item. In other words, the injury does not have to result because a compass explodes in your hand, but can result because the compass malfunctions and leads you over a cliff. This is quite different from saying that liability can be imposed for such things as ideas which have no physical properties at all.

ate this duty, the gentle tug of the First Amendment and the values embodied therein would remind us of the social costs.

Finally, plaintiffs ask us to find that a publisher should be required to give a warning 1) that the information in the book is not complete and that the consumer may not fully rely on it or 2) that this publisher has not investigated the text and cannot guarantee its accuracy. With respect to the first, a publisher would not know what warnings, if any, were required without engaging in a detailed analysis of the factual contents of the book. This would force the publisher to do exactly what we have said he has no duty to do — that is, independently investigate the accuracy of the text. We will not introduce a duty we have just rejected by renaming it a "mere" warning label. With respect to the second, such a warning is unnecessary given that *no* publisher has a duty as a guarantor.

For the reasons outlined above, the decision of the district court is AFFIRMED.

Notes and Questions

a. The court, in *James v. Meow Media, Inc.*, explained that "Learned Hand's famous conception of negligence would hold conduct negligent if the harm that the conduct threatens to create, discounted by the *ex ante* probability of the harm's non-occurrence, outweighs the utility created by the conduct." *James v. Meow Media, Inc.* (citing *United States v. Carroll Towing Co.*, 159 F.2d 169 (2d Cir. 1947)). Assuming the probability-utility formula, does the utility of free speech outweigh the low-risk but extremely high cost of incidents such as the murders at Columbine High School in Colorado and Heath High School in Paducah, Kentucky? Can the answer for general free speech be reframed for violence-based content?

b. Although only briefly discussed by the courts, another question exists as to whether there is a sufficiently direct, causal link between the objectionable content and the violent, criminal activity. While there are numerous studies indicating a correlation, legally sufficient causation is much less likely to be established.

c. On the issue of injury stimulated by violent content, there is a troubling litany of cases. Perhaps the most shocking was the mass-murder and suicide which occurred in Columbine High School in Littleton, Colorado in 1999. Seventeen-year-old high school students Dylan Klebold and Eric Harris "approached the school armed with multiple guns and other 'weapons of destruction' including explosive devices, [shot] at people outside the school, [then] entered the school building and continued their deadly assault inside Columbine. Twelve students and teacher William Sanders were killed. Dozens of others were injured." *Sanders v. Acclaim Entm't, Inc.*, 188 F. Supp. 2d 1264, 1268 (D. Colo. 2002). Others include:

Wilson v. Midway Games, Inc., 198 F. Supp. 2d 167 (D. Conn. 2002) (thirteen-year-old stabbed by a friend allegedly addicted to the video game *Mortal Kombat*);

Pahler v. Slayer, 29 Media L. Rep. 2627 (Cal. Super. Ct. 2001) (denial of liability for musical group Slayer for the rape and murder of a young girl by three teenaged boys);

Watters v. TSR, Inc., 904 F.2d 378 (6th Cir. 1990) (*Dungeons and Dragons* gamer committed suicide and the mother brought an unsuccessful strict products liability claim);

McCollum v. CBS, Inc., 202 Cal. App. 3d 989, 249 Cal. Rptr. 187, (Cal. App. 2d Dist. 1988) (Ozzy Osbourne fan shot himself after listening to *Blizzard of Oz* and *Diary of a Madman*);

Bill v. Superior Court, 137 Cal. App. 3d 1002, 187 Cal. Rptr. 625 (1983) (scene from the motion picture *Boulevard Nights* was copied, resulting in the shooting death of a young girl);

Olivia N. v. National Broadcasting Co., 126 Cal. App. 3d 488, 178 Cal. Rptr. 888 (1981) (imitation of a scene from the motion picture *Born Innocent* depicting the sexual assault of a young girl with a bottle); and

DeFilippo v. National Broadcasting Co., Inc., 446 A.2d 1036 (R.I. 1982) (imitation of a stunt performed on the Tonight Show which resulted in a young boy accidentally hanging himself).

e. In the context of speech that loses First Amendment protection, the courts do not treat all media the same. Although music is constantly blamed for violent behavior, only once has it been deemed obscene. In *Skywalker Records, Inc. v. Navarro,* 739 F.Supp. 578 (S.D. Fla. 1990), the album *Nasty as They Wanna Be* by 2 Live Crew was adjudicated obscene, but this was reversed in *Luke Records, Inc. v. Navarro,* 960 F.2d 134, 135 (11th Cir. 1992).

Problem V-B

Bryce has been diligently working on the set for *Juliet Prescott.* Since Bryce is not an expert at set design, Bryce purchased a detailed manual entitled *Set Construction for Amateur and Professional Theatre* written by a local university professor. Bryce carefully followed the instructions for the design of a moving wall. Unfortunately, the drawing in the book had been transposed and by following the directions in the text, Bryce failed to put the proper bracing on the set. The set piece crashed during rehearsal, injuring one of the actors.

Bryce calls you for advice. Bryce wishes to interplead the book author, bookstore, and book publisher in the event Bryce is sued for the injury. Explain what liability, if any, the various participants in the authoring and sale of the book might have to the injured party.

C. Limits on First Amendment Deference

National Endowment for the Arts v. Finley
524 U.S. 569 (1998)

JUSTICE O'CONNOR delivered the opinion of the Court.

The National Foundation on the Arts and Humanities Act, as amended in 1990, requires the Chairperson of the National Endowment for the Arts (NEA) to ensure that "artistic excellence and artistic merit are the criteria by which [grant] applications are judged, taking into consideration general standards of decency and respect for the diverse beliefs and values of the American public." In this case, we review the Court of Appeals' determination that §954(d)(1), on its face, impermissibly discriminates on the basis of viewpoint and is void for vagueness under the First and Fifth Amendments. We conclude that §954(d)(1) is facially valid, as it neither inherently interferes with First Amendment rights nor violates constitutional vagueness principles.

With the establishment of the NEA in 1965, Congress embarked on a "broadly conceived national policy of support for the ... arts in the United States," pledging federal funds to "help create and sustain not only a climate encouraging freedom of thought, imagination, and inquiry but also the material conditions facilitating the release of ... creative talent." The enabling statute vests the NEA with substantial discretion to award grants; it identifies only the broadest funding priorities, including "artistic and cultural significance, giving emphasis to American creativity and cultural diversity," "professional excellence," and the encouragement of "public knowledge, education, understanding, and appreciation of the arts."

Applications for NEA funding are initially reviewed by advisory panels composed of experts in the relevant field of the arts. Under the 1990 Amendments to the enabling statute, those panels must reflect "diverse artistic and cultural points of view" and include "wide geographic, ethnic, and minority representation," as well as "lay individuals who are knowledgeable about the arts." The panels report to the 26-member National Council on the Arts (Council), which, in turn, advises the NEA Chairperson. The Chairperson has the ultimate authority to award grants but may not approve an application as to which the Council has made a negative recommendation.

Since 1965, the NEA has distributed over three billion dollars in grants to individuals and organizations, funding that has served as a catalyst for increased state, corporate, and foundation support for the arts. Congress has recently restricted the availability of federal funding for individual artists, confining grants primarily to qualifying organizations and state arts agencies, and constraining sub-granting. By far the largest portion of the grants distributed in fiscal year 1998 were awarded directly to state arts agencies. In the remaining categories, the most substantial grants were allocated to symphony orchestras, fine arts museums, dance theater foundations, and opera associations.

Throughout the NEA's history, only a handful of the agency's roughly 100,000 awards have generated formal complaints about misapplied funds or abuse of the public's trust. Two provocative works, however, prompted public controversy in 1989 and led to congressional revaluation of the NEA's funding priorities and efforts to increase oversight of its grant-making procedures. The Institute of Contemporary Art at the University of Pennsylvania had used $30,000 of a visual arts grant it received from the NEA to fund a 1989 retrospective of photographer Robert Mapplethorpe's work. The exhibit, entitled *The Perfect Moment*, included homoerotic photographs that several Members of Congress condemned as pornographic. Members also denounced artist Andres Serrano's work *Piss Christ*, a photograph of a crucifix immersed in urine. Serrano had been awarded a $15,000 grant from the Southeast Center for Contemporary Art, an organization that received NEA support.

When considering the NEA's appropriations for fiscal year 1990, Congress reacted to the controversy surrounding the Mapplethorpe and Serrano photographs by eliminating $45,000 from the agency's budget, the precise amount contributed to the two exhibits by NEA grant recipients. Congress also enacted an amendment providing that no NEA funds "may be used to promote, disseminate, or produce materials which in the judgment of [the NEA] may be considered obscene, including but not limited to, depictions of sadomasochism, homoeroticism, the sexual exploitation of children, or individuals engaged in sex acts and which, when taken as a whole, do not have serious literary, artistic, political, or scientific value." The NEA implemented Congress' mandate by instituting a requirement that all grantees certify in writing that they would not utilize federal funding to engage in projects inconsistent with the criteria in the 1990 appropriations bill. That certification requirement was subsequently invalidated as unconstitutionally vague by a Federal District Court, and the NEA did not appeal the decision....

Ultimately, Congress adopted the Williams/Coleman Amendment, a bipartisan compromise between Members opposing any funding restrictions and those favoring some guidance to the agency. In relevant part, the Amendment became § 954(d)(1), which directs the Chairperson, in establishing procedures to judge the artistic merit of grant applications, to "take into consideration general standards of decency and respect for the diverse beliefs and values of the American public."[6]

The NEA has not promulgated any official interpretation of the provision, but in December 1990, the Council unanimously adopted a resolution to implement § 954(d)(1) merely by ensuring that the members of the advisory panels that conduct the initial review of grant applications represent geographic, ethnic, and aesthetic diversity. John Frohnmayer, then Chairperson of the NEA, also declared that he would "count on [the] procedures" ensuring diverse membership on the peer review panels to fulfill Congress' mandate.

The four individual respondents in this case, Karen Finley, John Fleck, Holly Hughes, and Tim Miller, are performance artists who applied for NEA grants before § 954(d)(1) was enacted. An advisory panel recommended approval of respondents' projects, both initially and after receiving Frohnmayer's request to reconsider three of the applications. A majority of the Council subsequently recommended disapproval, and in June 1990, the NEA informed respondents that they had been denied funding. Respondents filed suit, alleging that the NEA had violated their First Amendment rights by rejecting the applications on political grounds, had failed to follow statutory procedures by basing the denial on criteria other than those set forth in the NEA's enabling statute, and had breached the confidentiality of their grant applications through the release of quotations to the press, in violation of the Privacy Act of 1974. Respondents sought restoration of the recommended grants or reconsideration of their applications, as well as damages for the alleged Privacy Act violations. When Congress enacted § 954(d)(1), respondents, now joined by the National Association of Artists' Organizations (NAAO), amended their complaint to challenge the provision as void for vagueness and impermissibly viewpoint based....

Respondents raise a facial constitutional challenge to § 954(d)(1), and consequently they confront "a heavy burden" in advancing their claim. Facial invalidation "is, manifestly, strong medicine" that "has been employed by the Court sparingly and only as a last resort." To prevail, respondents must demonstrate a substantial risk that application of the provision will lead to the suppression of speech.

Respondents argue that the provision is a paradigmatic example of viewpoint discrimination because it rejects any artistic speech that either fails to respect mainstream values or offends standards of decency. The premise of respondents' claim is that § 954(d)(1) constrains the agency's ability to fund certain categories of artistic expression. The NEA, however, reads the provision as merely hortatory, and contends that it stops well short of an absolute restriction. Section 954(d)(1) adds "considerations" to the grant-making process; it does not preclude awards to projects that might be deemed "indecent" or "dis-

---

6. Title 20 U.S.C. § 954(d) provides in full that:

"No payment shall be made under this section except upon application therefor which is submitted to the National Endowment for the Arts in accordance with regulations issued and procedures established by the Chairperson. In establishing such regulations and procedures, the Chairperson shall ensure that—

"(1) artistic excellence and artistic merit are the criteria by which applications are judged, taking into consideration general standards of decency and respect for the diverse beliefs and values of the American public; and

"(2) applications are consistent with the purposes of this section. Such regulations and procedures shall clearly indicate that obscenity is without artistic merit, is not protected speech, and shall not be funded."

respectful," nor place conditions on grants, or even specify that those factors must be given any particular weight in reviewing an application. Indeed, the agency asserts that it has adequately implemented §954(d)(1) merely by ensuring the representation of various backgrounds and points of view on the advisory panels that analyze grant applications. See Declaration of Randolph McAusland, Deputy Chairman for Programs at the NEA, (stating that the NEA implements the provision "by ensuring that the peer review panels represent a variety of geographical areas, aesthetic views, professions, areas of expertise, races and ethnic groups, and gender, and include a lay person"). We do not decide whether the NEA's view — that the formulation of diverse advisory panels is sufficient to comply with Congress' command — is in fact a reasonable reading of the statute. It is clear, however, that the text of §954(d)(1) imposes no categorical requirement. The advisory language stands in sharp contrast to congressional efforts to prohibit the funding of certain classes of speech. When Congress has in fact intended to affirmatively constrain the NEA's grant-making authority, it has done so in no uncertain terms.

Furthermore, like the plain language of §954(d), the political context surrounding the adoption of the "decency and respect" clause is inconsistent with respondents' assertion that the provision compels the NEA to deny funding on the basis of viewpoint discriminatory criteria. The legislation was a bipartisan proposal introduced as a counterweight to amendments aimed at eliminating the NEA's funding or substantially constraining its grant-making authority. The Independent Commission had cautioned Congress against the adoption of distinct viewpoint-based standards for funding, and the Commission's report suggests that "additional criteria for selection, if any, should be incorporated as part of the selection process (perhaps as part of a definition of 'artistic excellence'), rather than isolated and treated as exogenous considerations." In keeping with that recommendation, the criteria in §954(d)(1) inform the assessment of artistic merit, but Congress declined to disallow any particular viewpoints. As the sponsors of §954(d)(1) noted in urging rejection of the Rohrabacher Amendment, "if we start down that road of prohibiting categories of expression, categories which are indeed constitutionally protected speech, where do we end? Where one Member's aversions end, others with different sensibilities and with different values begin." ([the Court cites a] statement of Rep. Williams) (arguing that the Rohrabacher Amendment would prevent the funding of Jasper Johns' flag series, "The Merchant of Venice," "Chorus Line," "Birth of a Nation," and the "Grapes of Wrath"). In contrast, before the vote on §954(d)(1), one of its sponsors stated: "If we have done one important thing in this amendment, it is this. We have maintained the integrity of freedom of expression in the United States."

That §954(d)(1) admonishes the NEA merely to take "decency and respect" into consideration, and that the legislation was aimed at reforming procedures rather than precluding speech, undercut respondents' argument that the provision inevitably will be utilized as a tool for invidious viewpoint discrimination. In cases where we have struck down legislation as facially unconstitutional, the dangers were both more evident and more substantial. In *R. A. V. v. St. Paul*, 505 U.S. 377, 120 L. Ed. 2d 305, 112 S. Ct. 2538 (1992), for example, we invalidated on its face a municipal ordinance that defined as a criminal offense the placement of a symbol on public or private property "'which one knows or has reasonable grounds to know arouses anger, alarm, or resentment in others on the basis of race, color, creed, religion, or gender.'" That provision set forth a clear penalty, proscribed views on particular "disfavored subjects," and suppressed "distinctive ideas, conveyed by a distinctive message."

In contrast, the "decency and respect" criteria do not silence speakers by expressly "threatening censorship of ideas." Thus, we do not perceive a realistic danger that §954(d)(1) will compromise First Amendment values. As respondents' own arguments demonstrate, the considerations that the provision introduces, by their nature, do not engender the kind of directed viewpoint discrimination that would prompt this Court to invalidate a statute on its face. Respondents assert, for example, that "one would be hard-pressed to find two people in the United States who could agree on what the 'diverse beliefs and values of the American public' are, much less on whether a particular work of art 'respects' them"; and they claim that "'decency' is likely to mean something very different to a septuagenarian in Tuscaloosa and a teenager in Las Vegas." The NEA likewise views the considerations enumerated in §954(d)(1) as susceptible to multiple interpretations. Accordingly, the provision does not introduce considerations that, in practice, would effectively preclude or punish the expression of particular views. Indeed, one could hardly anticipate how "decency" or "respect" would bear on grant applications in categories such as funding for symphony orchestras.

Respondents' claim that the provision is facially unconstitutional may be reduced to the argument that the criteria in §954(d)(1) are sufficiently subjective that the agency could utilize them to engage in viewpoint discrimination. Given the varied interpretations of the criteria and the vague exhortation to "take them into consideration," it seems unlikely that this provision will introduce any greater element of selectivity than the determination of "artistic excellence" itself. And we are reluctant, in any event, to invalidate legislation "on the basis of its hypothetical application to situations not before the Court."

The NEA's enabling statute contemplates a number of indisputably constitutional applications for both the "decency" prong of §954(d)(1) and its reference to "respect for the diverse beliefs and values of the American public." Educational programs are central to the NEA's mission. Permissible applications of the mandate to consider "respect for the diverse beliefs and values of the American public" are also apparent. In setting forth the purposes of the NEA, Congress explained that "it is vital to democracy to honor and preserve its multicultural artistic heritage." The agency expressly takes diversity into account, giving special consideration to "projects and productions ... that reach, or reflect the culture of, a minority, inner city, rural, or tribal community," as well as projects that generally emphasize "cultural diversity." Respondents do not contend that the criteria in §954(d)(1) are impermissibly applied when they may be justified, as the statute contemplates, with respect to a project's intended audience.

We recognize, of course, that reference to these permissible applications would not alone be sufficient to sustain the statute against respondents' First Amendment challenge. But neither are we persuaded that, in other applications, the language of §954(d)(1) itself will give rise to the suppression of protected expression. Any content-based considerations that may be taken into account in the grant-making process are a consequence of the nature of arts funding. The NEA has limited resources and it must deny the majority of the grant applications that it receives, including many that propose "artistically excellent" projects. The agency may decide to fund particular projects for a wide variety of reasons, "such as the technical proficiency of the artist, the creativity of the work, the anticipated public interest in or appreciation of the work, the work's contemporary relevance, its educational value, its suitability for or appeal to special audiences (such as children or the disabled), its service to a rural or isolated community, or even simply that the work could increase public knowledge of an art form."

As the dissent below noted, it would be "impossible to have a highly selective grant program without denying money to a large amount of constitutionally protected expression." The "very assumption" of the NEA is that grants will be awarded according to the "artistic worth of competing applications," and absolute neutrality is simply "inconceivable."

Respondent's reliance on our decision in *Rosenberger v. Rector and Visitors of Univ. of Va.*, 515 U.S. 819, 132 L. Ed. 2d 700, 115 S. Ct. 2510 (1995), is therefore misplaced. In *Rosenberger*, a public university declined to authorize disbursements from its Student Activities Fund to finance the printing of a Christian student newspaper. We held that by subsidizing the Student Activities Fund, the University had created a limited public forum, from which it impermissibly excluded all publications with religious editorial viewpoints. Although the scarcity of NEA funding does not distinguish this case from *Rosenberger*, the competitive process according to which the grants are allocated does. In the context of arts funding, in contrast to many other subsidies, the Government does not indiscriminately "encourage a diversity of views from private speakers." The NEA's mandate is to make aesthetic judgments, and the inherently content-based "excellence" threshold for NEA support sets it apart from the subsidy at issue in *Rosenberger*—which was available to all student organizations that were "'related to the educational purpose of the University,'"— and from comparably objective decisions on allocating public benefits, such as access to a school auditorium or a municipal theater, or the second class mailing privileges available to "'all newspapers and other periodical publications.'"

Respondents do not allege discrimination in any particular funding decision. (In fact, after filing suit to challenge §954(d)(1), two of the individual respondents received NEA grants. Thus, we have no occasion here to address an as-applied challenge in a situation where the denial of a grant may be shown to be the product of invidious viewpoint discrimination. If the NEA were to leverage its power to award subsidies on the basis of subjective criteria into a penalty on disfavored viewpoints, then we would confront a different case. We have stated that, even in the provision of subsidies, the Government may not "aim at the suppression of dangerous ideas," and if a subsidy were "manipulated" to have a "coercive effect," then relief could be appropriate. In addition, as the NEA itself concedes, a more pressing constitutional question would arise if government funding resulted in the imposition of a disproportionate burden calculated to drive "certain ideas or viewpoints from the marketplace." Unless and until §954(d)(1) is applied in a manner that raises concern about the suppression of disfavored viewpoints, however, we uphold the constitutionality of the provision.

Finally, although the First Amendment certainly has application in the subsidy context, we note that the Government may allocate competitive funding according to criteria that would be impermissible were direct regulation of speech or a criminal penalty at stake. So long as legislation does not infringe on other constitutionally protected rights, Congress has wide latitude to set spending priorities....

The lower courts also erred in invalidating §954(d)(1) as unconstitutionally vague. Under the First and Fifth Amendments, speakers are protected from arbitrary and discriminatory enforcement of vague standards. The terms of the provision are undeniably opaque, and if they appeared in a criminal statute or regulatory scheme, they could raise substantial vagueness concerns. It is unlikely, however, that speakers will be compelled to steer too far clear of any "forbidden area" in the context of grants of this nature.... In the context of selective subsidies, it is not always feasible for Congress to legislate with clarity. Indeed, if this statute is unconstitutionally vague, then so too are all government programs awarding scholarships and grants on the basis of subjective criteria such as "cxccllcncc." ... Section 954(d)(1) merely adds some imprecise considerations to an already subjective selection process. It does not, on its face, impermissibly infringe on First or Fifth Amendment rights. Accordingly, the judgment of the Court of Appeals is reversed and the case is remanded for further proceedings consistent with this opinion. *It is so ordered.*

JUSTICE SOUTER, dissenting.

The question here is whether the italicized segment of this statute is unconstitutional on its face: "artistic excellence and artistic merit are the criteria by which applications [for grants from the National Endowment for the Arts] are judged, *taking into consideration general standards of decency and respect for the diverse beliefs and values of the American public*." It is. The decency and respect proviso mandates viewpoint-based decisions in the disbursement of government subsidies, and the Government has wholly failed to explain why the statute should be afforded an exemption from the fundamental rule of the First Amendment that viewpoint discrimination in the exercise of public authority over expressive activity is unconstitutional....

Notes and Questions

a. One recurring issue of state-sponsored discrimination occurs in the context of school facilities that are made available for some, but not all, outside groups. These restrictions may range from prohibitions of religious content to restrictions of plays or film productions based on the content of the activity. See *Lamb's Chapel v. Center Moriches Union Free School Dist.*, 508 U.S. 384, 386 (1993) and *Southeastern Promotions, Ltd. v. Conrad*, 420 U.S. 546, 555 (1975).

b. Another of the state activities declared unconstitutional was the so-called "Son of Sam" legislation, which attempted to bar a convicted felon of the profits earned by selling the book or film rights. See *Simon & Schuster, Inc. v. Members of N. Y. State Crime Victims Bd.*, 502 U.S. 105 (1991). Despite the unconstitutionality of such legislation, states may generally provide legislation for victim restitution and may expand the time-period of such payments to include income earned while in prison from all activities—including the sale of film or book rights. So long as the legislation does not single out the expressive activities, such legislation should be constitutional.

c. Despite the public assumptions regarding the First Amendment, the ability of the government to selectively fund speech, to protect minors, to ban obscenity, and to regulate broadcast media continues to give the government a significant role in the shape of content. Because the broadcast industries, the music industries, and the motion picture industry also rely heavily on the government to promote international trade and copyright policies abroad, these industries are particularly sensitive to the political concerns of elected officials. Voluntary rating systems and other industry self-regulation often stem from the need to appear responsive to the political power that is not shielded by the First Amendment.

The motion picture rating system operated by the Motion Picture Association of America provides guidance for the public—primarily designed to inform parents about the adult nature of motion pictures. With the expansion of the adult or "X" rated film and the attempt by the motion picture industry to market adult films that were adult in tone rather than merely pornographic, the MPAA created the NC-17 rating.

One of the reasons for this change is the policy enforced by most daily newspapers not to advertise films that are either unrated or rated X. Most television stations have a similar policy. As a result, marketing such films successfully is nearly impossible. The advertising ban does not appear to extend to "uncut" versions of previously rated films on DVD. As a result, such uncut DVDs have become a new submarket in recent years.

d. Compare the voluntary rating system employed by the Motion Picture Association and the Association of Broadcasters to the statutes at issue in *Interstate Circuit*. How has the voluntary ratings system changed the availability and content of films available?

e. Because the advertising in mass transportation systems is in a designated public forum, the transportation authority has limited discretion in which advertising to reject. Faced with challenges to a marijuana ad and a religious ad, which ad would be more likely to withstand the refusal to be displayed? See *Ridley v. Mass. Bay Transp. Auth.*, 390 F.3d 65 (1st Cir. 2004).

Problem V-C

Bryce is interested to know whether the play, *Juliet Prescott*, can be the subject of a grant application from the National Endowment for the Arts, the National Endowment for the Humanities, or the two similar state agencies. Bryce is particularly concerned that the play would have to be revised as a condition of accepting such funding. Advise Bryce as to whether the granting agencies could require Bryce to edit the play as a condition of receiving these funds.

D. Bibliography and Links

David A. Anderson, *First Amendment Limitations on Tort Law*, 69 BROOK. L. REV. 755 (2004).

Marc Jonathan Blitz, *A First Amendment for Second Life: What Virtual Worlds Mean for the Law of Video Games*, 11 VAND. J. ENT. & TECH. L. 779 (2009).

Clay Calvert, *The First Amendment, the Media and the Culture Wars: Eight Important Lessons from 2004 About Speech, Censorship, Science and Public Policy*, 41 CAL. W. L. REV. 325 (2005).

Clay Calvert & Robert D. Richards, *Violence and Video Games 2006: Legislation and Litigation*, 8 TEX. REV. ENT. & SPORTS L. 49 (2007).

Peter DiCola, *Copyright Equality: Free Speech, Efficiency, and Regulatory Parity in Distribution*, 93 B.U. L. REV. 1837, 1838 (2013).

Michelle Freeman, *Administrative Law Discussion Forum: First Amendment Protection for the Arts after NEA v. Finley*, 38 BRANDEIS L.J. 405 (2000).

Patrick M. Garry, *The First Amendment and Non-Political Speech: Exploring a Constitutional Model That Focuses on the Existence of Alternative Channels of Communication*, 72 MO. L. REV. 477 (2007).

Gregory K. Laughlin, *Playing Games with the First Amendment: Are Video Games Speech and May Minors' Access to Graphically Violent Video Games Be Restricted?*, 40 U. RICH. L. REV. 481 (2006).

William E. Lee, *Books, Video Games, and Foul-Mouthed Hollywood Glitteratae: The Supreme Court and the Technology-Neutral Interpretation of the First Amendment*, 14 COLUM. SCI. & TECH. L. REV. 295 (2013).

Lisa P. Ramsey, *Increasing First Amendment Scrutiny of Trademark Law*, 61 SMU L. REV. 381 (2008).

Robert D. Richards & Clay Calvert, *Columbine Fallout: The Long-Term Effects on Free Expression Take Hold in Public Schools*, 83 B.U.L. REV. 1089 (2003).

Kevin W. Saunders, *Regulating Youth Access to Violent Video Games: Three Responses to First Amendment Concerns*, 2003 L. REV. M.S.U.-D.C.L. 51 (2003).

Chapter VI

Attention to Non-Literary Rights

A. Defamation

Introduction[1]

A statement is defamatory if "it tends so to harm the reputation of another as to lower him in the estimation of the community or to deter third persons from associating or dealing with him."[2] At common law, a statement is defamatory if it held one out for hatred, ridicule, or contempt. Only a living person may be defamed. A related doctrine known as trade libel applies to businesses. To be defamatory in the U.S., the person alleging the defamation must prove that the statement is false as well as that it is harmful, that it pertains to the person suing, and that it has been published to someone other than the person suing.

Once a person has died, his heirs may not pursue the claim. Any publication to a third person, such as through publication in a script, on a website, or through sending a letter or email, will give rise to liability if the publication is a false defamatory statement of or concerning the defamed person. Republishing a false defamatory statement will give rise to a new claim for defamation. As a result, a filmmaker is responsible for any defamatory material in the work he creates, licenses, or borrows.

Filmmakers face different legal challenges depending on the nature of the party who objects to the characterization or statements. Public officials, such as the President or state officeholders, and public figures such as O.J. Simpson or Ralph Nader, can only win a lawsuit for defamation against the filmmaker if the filmmaker is found to have published defamatory material intentionally—with knowledge it was false—or recklessly—with reckless disregard toward the truth or falsity of the statement.[3] If the publication is about a private individual involving some matter of public interest, then the filmmaker can be liable if he is merely negligent in failing to ascertain the truth[4] or in the manner in which the truth was altered to fit the dramatic needs of the film.[5] The party suing the

---

1. Jon M. Garon, THE INDEPENDENT FILMMAKER'S LAW AND BUSINESS GUIDE: FINANCING, SHOOTING, AND DISTRIBUTING INDEPENDENT AND DIGITAL FILMS (2007) (excerpts).

2. Restatement (Second) Torts §559 (1977). Under California law, "libel is a false and unprivileged publication by writing ... which exposes any person to hatred, contempt, ridicule, or obloquy, or which causes him to be shunned or avoided, or which has a tendency to injure him in his occupation." Cal. Civ. Code §45 (West 1999).

3. New York Times Co. v. Sullivan, 376 U.S. 254, 279–80 (1964).

4. Gertz v. Robert Welch, Inc., 418 U.S. 323, 344 (1974).

5. Davis v. Costa-Gavras, 654 F. Supp. 653, 655 (S.D.N.Y. 1987).

filmmaker for defamation must prove that the statements or depictions are libelous. If the jury believes the film is accurate, the filmmaker will not lose the lawsuit.

One particularly insidious form of libel is to falsely attribute quotes to a person. The Supreme Court has held that otherwise unobjectionable statements could be deemed libelous when they were transformed into quotes.[6] Attributing dialogue to a character in a film can easily achieve this effect. When a film character is based on a living person, the dialogue may include statements that were originally made by critics of that person, but are now portrayed as self-deprecating comments made by the character. This increases the amount of material included in a documentary to which objections may be made.

Fictionalization may also result in the creation of composite characters—fictional characters that embody attributes of a number of live individuals. Because of the requirement that the statement be of or concerning the person claiming defamation, a common practice is to create fictional characters to stand in for unsavory conduct that may have been undertaken by real people. If the fictional character or composite character is identifiable as a real person involved in the situation, then the fictionalization only adds to the potential for liability.[7] This appears to occur most frequently when the fictional character's name bears some resemblance to the living person's name.

Fortunately for filmmakers, courts tend to disfavor defamation awards. This may be a result of the strong respect held by the courts for the First Amendment. It may also reflect respect for the detailed investigative process that major motion picture studios and television networks go through for their docudramas and fact-based works. Needless to say, the institutional respect for filmmakers will not extend to guerilla filmmakers and individuals shooting on-the-fly films on shoestring budgets. For this reason it is vital that when producing a fact-based story, the filmmaker document every step taken to verify the truth of the story before creating the script and shooting the film. As discussed below, having the actual people who are depicted or identified sign agreements will reduce the risk that those people will sue for defamation, but unless every character depicted in a fact-based story has signed a release, the risk of a defamation claim remains.

Expansion of the *N.Y. Times* Standard

Excerpt from Gertz v. Robert Welch, Inc.
418 U.S. 323 (1974)

Three years after *New York Times*, a majority of the Court agreed to extend the constitutional privilege to defamatory criticism of "public figures." This extension was announced in *Curtis Publishing Co. v. Butts* and its companion, *Associated Press v. Walker*, 388 U.S. 130, 162 (1967). The first case involved the Saturday Evening Post's charge that Coach Wally Butts of the University of Georgia had conspired with Coach 'Bear' Bryant of the University of Alabama to fix a football game between their respective schools. Walker involved an erroneous Associated Press account of former Major General Edwin Walker's participation in a University of Mississippi campus riot. Because Butts was paid by a private alumni association and Walker had resigned from the Army, neither could be classified as a 'public official' under *New York Times*. Although Mr. Justice Harlan an-

---

6. Masson v. New Yorker Magazine, 501 U.S. 496, 522 (1991).
7. Springer v. Viking Press, 90 A.D.2d 315, 457 N.Y.S.2d 246 (1st Dept. 1982) aff'd, 60 N.Y.2d 916, 470 N.Y.S.2d 579 (1983).

nounced the result in both cases, a majority of the Court agreed with Mr. Chief Justice Warren's conclusion that the New York Times test should apply to criticism of 'public figures' as well as 'public officials.' The Court extended the constitutional privilege announced in that case to protect defamatory criticism of nonpublic persons who 'are nevertheless intimately involved in the resolution of important public questions or, by reason of their fame, shape events in areas of concern to society at large.'

New York Times and later cases explicated the meaning of the new standard. In *New York Times* the Court held that under the circumstances the newspaper's failure to check the accuracy of the advertisement against news stories in its own files did not establish reckless disregard for the truth. In *St. Amant v. Thompson,* 390 U.S. 727, 731 (1968), the Court equated reckless disregard of the truth with subjective awareness of probable falsity: 'There must be sufficient evidence to permit the conclusion that the defendant in fact entertained serious doubts as to the truth of his publication.'

In *Beckley Newspapers Corp. v. Hanks,* 389 U.S. 81 (1967), the Court emphasized the distinction between the New York Times test of knowledge of falsity or reckless disregard of the truth and 'actual malice' in the traditional sense of ill-will.

Garrison v. Louisiana, 379 U.S. 64 125 (1964), made plain that the new standard applied to criminal libel laws as well as to civil actions and that it governed criticism directed at 'anything which might touch on an official's fitness for office.'

Finally, in *Rosenblatt v. Baer,* 383 U.S. 75, 85 (1966), the Court stated that 'the 'public official' designation applies at the very least to those among the hierarchy of government employees who have, or appear to the public to have, substantial responsibility for or control over the conduct or governmental affairs.'

In *Time, Inc. v. Hill,* 385 U.S. 374 (1967), the Court applied the *New York Times* standard to actions under an unusual state statute. The statute did not create a cause of action for libel. Rather, it provided a remedy for unwanted publicity. Although the law allowed recovery of damages for harm caused by exposure to public attention rather than by factual inaccuracies, it recognized truth as a complete defense. Thus, nondefamatory factual errors could render a publisher liable for something akin to invasion of privacy. The Court ruled that the defendant in such an action could invoke the *New York Times* privilege regardless of the fame or anonymity of the plaintiff. Speaking for the Court, Mr. Justice Brennan declared that this holding was not an extension of *New York Times* but rather a parallel line of reasoning applying that standard to this discrete context:

> This is neither a libel action by a private individual nor a statutory action by a public official. Therefore, although the First Amendment principles pronounced in New York Times guide our conclusion, we reach that conclusion only by applying these principles in this discrete context. It therefore serves no purpose to distinguish the facts here from those in *New York Times*. Were this a libel action, the distinction which has been suggested between the relative opportunities of the public official and the private individual to rebut defamatory charges might be germane. And the additional state interest in the protection of the individual against damage to his reputation would be involved.

Huckabee v. Time Warner Entertainment Co., L.P.

43 Tex. Sup. Ct. J. 674 (Tex. 2000)

We must decide whether a media defendant sued for defamation by a public official is entitled on the facts of this record to summary judgment on the issue of actual malice. Because the defendant produced evidence negating actual malice as a matter of law, and because the plaintiff did not produce controverting evidence raising a fact issue, we affirm the summary judgment granted by the court of appeals.

When this claim arose, Charles Dean Huckabee was presiding judge of the 247th District Court of Harris County, which by statute gives preference to family law matters. Judge Huckabee claims that Respondent, HBO, defamed him by broadcasting the documentary *Women on Trial* on its premium cable channel. This hour-long program chronicled four southeast Texas cases in which family courts granted custody of a child to the father after the mother accused the father of child abuse. Three of these cases arose in Harris County, and Judge Huckabee presided over two of them. Judge Huckabee principally claims that the documentary defamed him in its report on his decision regarding the custody of four-year-old Wayne Hebert ("*Hebert*").

The *Hebert* case began in 1988, when Sandra Hebert discovered that Wayne had sustained an injury to his penis. The day before, Wayne had returned from visiting Michael Hebert, his father and Sandra's ex-husband. Wayne had gone with Michael to visit his grandmother's home in Louisiana. Believing that Michael caused Wayne's injury, Sandra consulted with her friend Sherry Turner, a Houston police officer who specialized in sexual abuse cases. Turner, interviewing Wayne alone, videotaped Wayne's statement that Michael had injured him while taking a bath. In two other videotaped interviews, Wayne also told social worker Cheryl Bennett and Child Protective Services caseworker Wilma Smith that Michael caused the injury. After investigating further, Smith concluded that Wayne had been abused, but that the abuser could not be identified. Because Michael was a Houston police officer, the Houston Police Department's Internal Affairs Department also investigated the incident and likewise determined that the abuser could not be identified.

Alleging that Michael had abused Wayne, Sandra moved to modify the custody order to restrict Michael's visitation rights. After a three-day hearing in March 1988, Judge Huckabee rendered a temporary order that not only made Michael rather than Sandra the managing conservator of Wayne, but went on to deny Sandra all access to her child, even though Michael had not sought either of these changes. Sandra unsuccessfully sought a writ of mandamus from the court of appeals to overturn the temporary order. She did not seek a subsequent modification of the order, and it was still in effect when *Women on Trial* was broadcast in 1992.

In late 1990, Lee Grant, the director of *Women on Trial*, first began work on a documentary about divorce. Hoping to examine how once happily married couples later ended up in bitter divorces, Grant secured her husband's production company, Joseph Feury Productions (JFP), to produce the film. Grant assigned JFP employee Virginia Cotts to find suitable stories for the program. In March 1991, Cotts met in Houston with Joleen Reynolds, the leader of Citizens Organized for Divorce Ethics and Solutions (CODES), a support group for men and women who felt that the Houston family courts had treated them unfairly. Reynolds discussed a number of cases with Cotts, including the *Hebert* case. After meeting with Reynolds, Cotts wrote a three-page summary of Sandra Hebert's situation.

Sandra Hebert's story was included along with several others submitted by Cotts and Grant to HBO in April 1991. In her summary of the Hebert story, Cotts included the following bullet points: (1) "Police ex-husband abused son"; (2) "Corrupt Judge gave custody to father/abuser"; (3) and "Sandy lost all rights to see her child." Sandra Hebert's story particularly impressed the HBO executives. After reading it, HBO vice-president Sheila Nevins wrote on her copy: "Great story. Do at once." Nevins's assistant, Cis Wilson, wrote: "Great, sad story." After considering the proposal, HBO agreed to purchase the film. Throughout the rest of the film's production, Cotts and Grant regularly met with Wilson and Nevins.

Cotts and Grant both came to Houston to film interviews. In addition to Joleen Reynolds, Sandra Hebert, and her current and former attorneys, they also interviewed Ivy Raschke, another woman who had been denied access to her children by Judge Huckabee after accusing the children's father of abuse. Cotts also continued her research into other allegations of impropriety in the Harris County family courts, including those reported by local print and broadcast media.

In September 1991, JFP delivered a "rough cut" of the film to HBO. Cotts's contemporaneous status report revealed tension between Lee Grant and Sheila Nevins over the film's direction. Grant apparently wanted to present a broad picture of divorce that showed both the fathers' and the mothers' perspectives, but Nevins wanted a narrower piece that focused on mothers who believed the family court system had treated them unfairly. Nothing in the status report, however, indicated that Grant, Cotts, or anyone at HBO believed anything in the documentary to be false or entertained serious doubts about the truth of any of the film's allegations.

In November 1991, Grant and Cotts returned to Houston and videotaped Judge Huckabee. While Judge Huckabee stated that he could not talk specifically about the *Hebert* case because it was pending in his court, he did agree to talk about it in "hypothetical" terms. He then explained that all of his decisions in this and other cases were based on the best interests of the children. HBO did not include these statements in the final version. Instead, it aired this response by Judge Huckabee to a question about a "hypothetical" version of the *Hebert* case:

> I have to do what's best for the child. If someone, is, uh, brainwashing the a [sic] child to the same extent that it causes psychological and emotional problems with the child, especially coupled with some physical abuse, in my opinion the child has to be removed from that situation.

The broadcast also aired Judge Huckabee's explanation of his criteria for determining when a mother in that situation could see her children again:

> Well, if its [sic] a person who has mental health problems, they're going to have to seek mental health, uh, care. If its [sic] a person sexually abusing a child, they're probably going to have to seek mental health care.

Finally, the broadcast aired Judge Huckabee's statement that he took the decision to deny access to a parent very seriously, but that he was satisfied that he had made the correct decision in every case in which he had done so.

The filmmakers also interviewed Dr. Kit Harrison, a psychologist appointed by Judge Huckabee in *Hebert* and in many other cases. Four months after Judge Huckabee rendered the temporary order denying Sandra Hebert access to Wayne, Dr. Harrison issued a report concluding that Michael had not caused Wayne's injury. Rather, the report concluded that Wayne's older brother John committed the abuse while Wayne was in Sandra's custody. Based on this belief, Dr. Harrison agreed with Judge Huckabee's decision to transfer Wayne to his father's custody and deny Sandra access to the child. Although the final version mentioned Dr. Harrison's recommendation approving of the judge's order, it did not detail Dr. Harrison's reasons.

Finally, Cotts and Grant interviewed Houston attorney Randy Burton, an outspoken critic of the Houston family courts. Among other things, Burton accused the Harris County family court judges of practicing cronyism and disregarding the best interests of the children before them.

After these interviews, Cotts and Grant recut the film to include some of the new footage. From April to September 1991, HBO and JFP's lawyers reviewed the film, finally allowing the film to air in October 1991. HBO also agreed to indemnify JFP should a judgment arise from the film in excess of JFP's errors-and-omissions insurance coverage.

Women on Trial aired on October 28, 1992. In addition to the Sandra Hebert and Ivy Raschke segments, the film included two other stories. In one, another Harris County family district court judge, Allen Daggett, had transferred custody of Mary Frances Parker's child to her ex-husband, a convicted rapist, even though she claimed that he was abusing the child. In the other, Sherry Nance was convicted of murdering her ex-husband and his father after a Bee County jury awarded custody of her son to the ex-husband. Nance claimed that she killed her ex-husband to save her son from continuing sexual abuse. The documentary did not name the judge in the Bee County case....

To recover for defamation, a public figure or public official, such as Judge Huckabee, must prove that the defendant published a false and defamatory statement with actual malice. As we resolve this case solely on the issue of whether HBO negated actual malice as a matter of law, we assume without deciding that the documentary either expressly or implicitly made false statements about Judge Huckabee. We also do not reach the issue of whether any of these statements, even if false, were not defamatory because the documentary's overall portrayal of Judge Huckabee was substantially true.

Actual malice in a defamation case is a term of art. Unlike common-law malice, it does not include ill-will, spite, or evil motive. Rather, to establish actual malice, a plaintiff must prove that the defendant made the statement "with knowledge that it was false or with reckless disregard of whether it was true or not." Reckless disregard is also a term of art. To establish reckless disregard, a public official or public figure must prove that the publisher "entertained serious doubts as to the truth of his publication." Finally, to prevail at trial, a plaintiff must establish actual malice by clear and convincing evidence.

In Texas, under our traditional summary judgment procedure, defendants can obtain summary judgment only if they conclusively negate one of the elements of the plaintiff's claim. A libel defendant can negate actual malice as a matter of law by presenting evidence that he or she did not publish the statement with knowledge of its falsity or reckless disregard for its truth. Once the defendant has produced evidence negating actual malice as a matter of law, the burden shifts to the plaintiff to present controverting proof raising a genuine issue of material fact....

HBO supported its motion for summary judgment with affidavits from Lee Grant, Sheila Nevins, Cis Wilson, and Virginia Cotts. Grant's affidavit stated that she neither believed the film to have contained a false statement nor entertained any doubts about the truth of any statement regarding Judge Huckabee. Her sources for the Sandra Hebert story included the transcript of the March 1988 hearing, information from Sandra's current and former lawyers, and research by Virginia Cotts.

Sheila Nevins's affidavit stated that as vice-president for documentaries and family programming for HBO, she relied on the favorable reputations for accuracy and truthfulness of both Grant and JFP and her own favorable personal experience with their earlier work. She was aware of Grant and Cotts's efforts to ensure the film's accuracy, and she neither believed any statement in the documentary to be untrue nor harbored any doubts about the film's truthfulness. Cis Wilson's affidavit contained similar statements.

HBO presented two extensive affidavits from Virginia Cotts. In her first affidavit, Cotts explained the steps she took in researching the stories presented in *Women on Trial*. To ensure that the film's account of the *Hebert* case was accurate, she (1) reviewed the transcript from the March 1988 hearing, (2) interviewed Sandra and her attorneys, (3) viewed all three videotapes of Wayne Hebert, (4) reviewed articles in the Houston press describing problems in the family courts, and (5) read Dr. Harrison's deposition in the *Hebert* case. In all, Cotts reviewed over two thousand pages of documents in connection with the Texas cases. From this extensive review, Cotts stated that she believed that the film's depiction of the *Hebert* case was accurate and that she had no doubts regarding this account.

Cotts's second affidavit detailed her reasons for doubting Dr. Harrison's conclusion that Wayne's brother was the abuser, such as (1) her own viewing of the videotapes in which Wayne identified his father as the abuser; (2) the improbability of Harrison's theory that Wayne's older brother John had injured him using a favorite toy; (3) the fact that Wayne's initial description of events was similar to stories that John had told Cotts about abuse from his father; (4) Dr. Harrison's own statement in a scholarly paper that children often recant after disclosing sexual abuse; and (5) the fact that Wayne had sustained a similar injury once before. Cotts buttressed her conclusion by attaching her own notes from the Harrison interview, indicating that she did not believe his explanation even as the interview was in progress.

Because these affidavits are from interested witnesses, they will negate actual malice as a matter of law only if they are "clear, positive, and direct, otherwise credible and free from contradictions and inconsistencies, and [able to be] readily controverted." In actual malice cases, such affidavits must establish the defendant's belief in the challenged statements' truth and provide a plausible basis for this belief. As all four of HBO's affidavits satisfied the Rule 166a(c) requirements, HBO negated actual malice as a matter of law.

Thus, the burden shifted to Judge Huckabee to present evidence to raise a fact issue. He offered six categories of allegedly controverting evidence: (1) HBO and JFP's alleged desire to portray him in an unflattering light; (2) editorial choices by HBO and JFP that left a false impression of events; (3) the filmmakers' disregard for Judge Huckabee's and Dr. Harrison's explanations for Judge Huckabee's order; (4) JFP's and HBO's alleged purposeful avoidance of the truth; (5) HBO's extensive legal review of the film, the film's many rewrites, and the indemnification agreement between HBO and JFP; and (6) HBO's and JFP's decision to air the film despite the knowledge that it contained inaccurate statements. In determining whether the evidence presents a fact issue, we assume that all facts favorable to the nonmovant are true and indulge all reasonable inferences in that party's favor. Even under this lenient standard, we are persuaded that Judge Huckabee has not raised a genuine issue of material fact on any of his categories.

1. HBO's desire to portray Judge Huckabee in an unflattering light.

In claiming that JFP and HBO intended to portray him unfairly, Judge Huckabee first points to Virginia Cotts's three-page summary of the *Hebert* case describing him to HBO executives Sheila Nevins and Cis Wilson as a "corrupt judge." He also points to Cotts's September 1991 status report regarding the disagreement between Grant and Nevins over the film's artistic direction. Neither of these documents, however, indicates actual malice. While Cotts's original memo might suggest personal ill-will toward Judge Huckabee, nothing in either of these documents suggests that Cotts or Grant had any doubts about the truth of the broadcast.

Likewise, Nevins's insistence that the filmmakers focus on divorce from the women's perspective is no evidence of actual malice. Without more, mere evidence of pressure to produce stories from a particular point of view, even when they are hard-hitting or sensationalistic, is no evidence of actual malice. Although evidence that HBO directed Grant to produce a sensational story *without regard for its truth* would raise a fact question, Judge Huckabee has not produced any such evidence.

2. Editorial choices.

Next, Judge Huckabee complains of HBO's choice of material for the documentary. His principal complaint is that *Women on Trial* did not discuss much of the evidence presented at the 1988 *Hebert* hearing, including (1) Wayne's initial treating physician's testimony that Wayne had denied that his father caused the injury; (2) Child Protective Services case worker Wilma Smith's testimony that in his videotaped interview Wayne said that his mother told him to say that his father had abused him (although Wayne still maintained that such abuse occurred); (3) Smith's further testimony that in a subsequent interview with Wayne, he told her that his father had not abused him during the Christmas holidays, but that his father had touched his private area in July 1987; (4) Smith and social worker Cheryl Bennett's testimony that Wayne and his brother John often fought after Wayne returned from Michael; (5) Bennett's testimony that Sandra told her that she preferred that Michael not be allowed visitation rights and had inquired about what was necessary to terminate them; and (6) Wayne's grandmother's testimony that Michael had not bathed Wayne during their visit to her home. By failing to include this evidence, Judge Huckabee claims that HBO intentionally made it look like he was presented with an open-and-shut case against Michael Hebert, when in fact much of the evidence justified his order.

Further, Judge Huckabee complains about the film's failure to clarify two facts: first, that his statements in the interview with Grant came in response to questions about a "hypothetical" case; and second, that Sandra did not move to modify the temporary order in the three years after the court of appeals denied her petition for mandamus. Because of all these omissions, Judge Huckabee claims that the viewers saw him falsely as a judge who flouted his legal duty to render decisions in the best interests of children.

A broadcaster's omission of facts may be actionable if it so distorts the viewers' perception that they receive a substantially false impression of the event. As a public official, however, Judge Huckabee may recover for such an omission only by making the familiar showing that the publisher selected the material with actual malice, *i.e.*, the awareness that the omission could create a substantially false impression. This standard does not, therefore, prevent liability if a media organization selectively omits facts from the record to portray falsely a judge's opinion as arbitrary and unreasonable. Even if a defamation defendant is not persuaded by the evidence which supports a judge's decision, he or she may not deliberately omit all reference to this evidence in order to portray the decision as arbitrary, when in fact it was not. But in the absence of evidence that the defendant selected the material to portray the judge's record falsely, the First Amendment protects the organization's choice of which material to include in its broadcast.

In this case, there is no evidence that HBO chose its material for the broadcast with actual malice. We recognize that an omission may be so glaring and may result in such a gross distortion that by itself it constitutes some evidence of actual malice. For example, when an article reported that an FBI memorandum mentioned plaintiff several times in connection with Jimmy Hoffa's disappearance, the newspaper's decision not to report that the memorandum also cleared plaintiff of wrongdoing was held to be evidence of actual malice. In such a case, the omission so changes the character of the story that one could infer that the defendant knew, or at least suspected, that the omission would convey a false impression. Here, HBO's omissions did not change the character of the story to such an extent. Although the facts omitted might or might not have led a reasonable viewer to suspend judgment or even to reach an opposite conclusion regarding Judge Huckabee's order, their omission did not grossly distort the story. At most, HBO's failure to capture accurately all the story's details suggests an error in judgment, which is no evidence of actual malice. Moreover, the broadcasters did acknowledge Judge Huckabee's explanation for his decision when they aired the portion of the interview responding to questions about the "hypothetical" *Hebert* case. Although the documentary did not convey Judge Huckabee's position as strongly as it could have, the law did not require it to do so....

[3]. Purposeful avoidance.

Next, Judge Huckabee contends that the filmmakers purposefully avoided discovering the truth about the *Hebert* case. Under *Harte-Hanks*, evidence showing that HBO purposefully avoided the truth would be some evidence of actual malice. In *Harte-Hanks*, a newspaper published a story claiming that Daniel Connaughton, a candidate for municipal judge, had promised two sisters, Alice Thompson and Patsy Stephens, jobs and vacations in return for making allegations of corruption against the incumbent judge's court administrator. The newspaper's only source for this story was Thompson. Before the newspaper published the story, Connaughton produced five witnesses who were present when Thompson claimed that Connaughton offered her and Stephens the gifts. All the witnesses denied Thompson's story. Connaughton also produced a tape recording of the conversation in which Thompson accused the administrator of corruption. The newspaper failed to listen to this recording even though it would have confirmed or denied many of Thompson's claims, such as her claims that Connaughton had selectively turned the recorder on and off during various parts of the interview and that her allegations of corruption against the court administrator had come in response to leading questions from him. More importantly, the newspaper failed to interview Stephens, the one person not associated with Connaughton who could have confirmed or denied Thompson's allegations against Connaughton. According to the Court, the newspaper's failure to consult the two sources that could have objectively verified the story was evidence that the newspaper purposefully avoided learning facts that would have shown the story to be false. Upholding a jury verdict against the newspaper, the Court held that this purposeful avoidance of the truth was enough to suggest that the newspaper doubted the story's accuracy, and hence was evidence of actual malice.

Judge Huckabee has not presented a purposeful avoidance case. Unlike *Harte-Hanks*, in which the newspaper based its story on the testimony of a single unreliable source, here the summary judgment evidence reveals that the filmmakers interviewed several people on both sides of the story, including Judge Huckabee and Dr. Harrison. They also read, among other documents, the transcript of the *Hebert* hearing. Such extensive research precludes a finding of purposeful avoidance....

[4]. Legal Review, Rewrites, and Indemnification

Next, we turn to the evidence that Judge Huckabee believes established "institutional doubt" on the part of HBO regarding the truth of *Women on Trial*. According to Judge

Huckabee, HBO's extensive legal review of the film, the editorial rewrites that accompanied this review, and the indemnification agreement between HBO and JFP all suggest that HBO entertained serious doubts about the film's content. We disagree.

That the film underwent a lengthy legal review does not by itself provide evidence of actual malice. HBO could have wished merely to confirm the film's controversial and potentially damaging allegations before its release. This same conclusion also applies to the indemnification agreement. Judge Huckabee can point to no evidence that JFP and HBO entered into the agreement because they entertained serious doubts about the film's truthfulness. Individuals and business organizations enter into indemnification agreements for various reasons; doing so, without more, simply presents no evidence of actual malice....

Davis v. Costa-Gavras
654 F. Supp. 653 (S.D.N.Y. 1987)

This is a libel case brought by a public figure which presently is before the Court on a motion by the defendants for summary judgment in their favor pursuant to Rule 56 of the Federal Rules of Civil Procedure.

Following the submission of affidavits and deposition testimony on the motion, the Court determined that an oral evidentiary hearing was needed under Rule 43(e) of the Federal Rules of Civil Procedure to aid in determining with a fair degree of specificity what plaintiff is able to present at a trial that is provable, clear and convincing affirmative evidence of actual malice on the part of the defendants in publishing the alleged defamation.

Absent such evidence, the action cannot be maintained as a matter of law, and the existence of such evidence is appropriately determined on a motion for summary judgment. The only remaining defamation charged in the complaint is that in their film, "Missing," defendants allegedly portrayed with actual malice that plaintiff, the Commander of the United States Military Group and Chief of the United States Mission to Chile at the time of the 1973 coup in Chile, ordered or approved a Chilean order to kill Charles Horman, an American residing in Chile.

It is now clear that this is a case devoid of any evidence of actual malice. There is no evidence thereof to be considered; no prima facie case at all is supplied on any standard of proof on the requirement of actual malice, be it a preponderance or clear and convincing.

Summary judgment should be granted when the evidence propounded is "of insufficient caliber or quality to allow a rational finder of fact to find actual malice by clear and convincing evidence;" there then is "no genuine issue." A jury could not properly return a verdict herein in plaintiff's favor; the evidence is so one-sided that defendants must prevail as a matter of law.

Actual malice is established in a public figure defamation litigation only where defendant publishes a statement "with knowledge that it was false or with reckless disregard of whether it was false or not." Reckless disregard in such a case means that a defendant published after he "in fact entertained serious doubts as to the truth of his publication."

The paper record on this motion consists of an enormous mass of words. The Rule 43(e) hearing was ordered to permit plaintiff to present or designate any clear and convincing evidence of actual malice detached from the obscure and semantic allusions thereto in the moving papers, and so as to allow the Court to assess the record expeditiously and accurately.

At the Rule 43(e) hearing, the plaintiff conceded that he had no evidence to offer on the requisite standard beyond what was contained in the papers and depositions submitted in opposition to the motion—plaintiff called no witnesses. A prolix and cloudy paper response will not suffice to defeat a motion for summary judgment to dismiss a public figure libel claim. The Rules obligated the nonmoving party to designate "specific facts showing that there is a genuine issue for trial." No such facts have been furnished.

Designated Evidence Offered by Plaintiff

Plaintiff alleges that there are four general categories of purported evidence in the paper defense to the motion from which to find actual malice on behalf of defendants: (1) that defendants' "entire purpose in making 'Missing' was to show plaintiff as responsible for Charles Horman's death"; (2) that defendants' reliance on Thomas Hauser's book *The Execution of Charles Horman* ("*Execution*") was unreasonable; (3) that defendants never consulted with plaintiff on the facts presented in the film; and (4) that "Missing" contains scenes portraying certain episodes which defendants knew were embroidered.

An analysis of the record shows that to accept the plaintiff's opposition to summary judgment would require a distortion of the proofs, deviation from applicable law, and wrenching of the film out of its plain context.

A. *The Thesis of the Film*

Plaintiff has produced no evidence in his papers to substantiate his assertion that the purpose of "Missing" was to make a non-fictional film establishing that Ray Davis, the plaintiff, was responsible for Charles Horman's death. To the contrary, the papers unalterably establish that the film is not a non-fictional documentary or aimed at Ray Davis as an individual, and that it cannot be understood as other than a dramatization of a true story. The film includes fictional characters and a composite portrayal of the American military presence in Chile at the time of the uprising and Allende coup.

The theme of the film is the search for a missing man by his father and his wife. The man who disappeared is finally found to have been executed by the Chilean military. The film is *based upon* a true story. It is only in that setting that the composite conduct of the American governmental representatives in Chile at the time and the degree of their assistance in that search comes under scrutiny and criticism. There is no person named Ray Davis referred to in the film at any time. Ray Tower, with whom the plaintiff associates himself, is a symbolic fictional composite of the entire American political and military entourage in Chile.

The film derives from and is solidly documented and supported by the stories relied on by the filmmakers, taken from the acts and statements of the concerned father and the anguished wife set forth in detail in Thomas Hauser's book, *Execution*. Those sources are shown to have been heavily investigated and confirmed by the filmmakers, who entertained no serious doubts of their truth or knowledge to the contrary of what they portrayed....

B. *Defendants' Reliance on Hauser's Book*

"Missing" is a dramatic portrayal of events and interpretations detailed in Thomas Hauser's book, *Execution*. The substance of the movie's scenes is extracted directly from *Execution*. To meet those facts, plaintiff purports to suggest that defendants' reliance on Hauser's book was unreasonable and that Hauser's credentials would have disclosed him to be "suspect" had a good faith search by defendants been made.

As a matter of law, to prevail on a defamation claim against a public official a plaintiff must do more than propound potential avenues of investigation that a defendant might have pursued. "Mere proof of failure to investigate, without more, cannot establish reckless disregard for the truth." "Rather, a public figure defamation plaintiff must show either that the publisher actually entertained serious doubts about the veracity of the publication, or that there are *obvious* reasons to doubt the veracity of the informant or the accuracy of his reports."

There is nothing in the record tending to show that the filmmakers questioned Hauser's credentials or his book in any respect at the time "Missing" was made. The record is to the contrary. The filmmakers met with Hauser, went over his investigation and sources, supplied him with drafts of the script under preparation and were satisfied that there was no reason to doubt his work. No evidence whatever challenges those facts. Certainly the filmmakers obtained no knowledge contradicting the veracity or accuracy of Hauser's book and the stories of the Hormans as told to them and reflected in the book. There is no suggestion to the contrary from any provable sources. Indeed, nothing in plaintiff's papers demonstrates that either Hauser's credentials or his book, which was nominated for a Pulitzer Prize, are in fact "suspect" in any way.

The filmmakers knew that Hauser was a lawyer who had served as a judicial clerk in the Chambers of a Federal Judge and then worked for a prestigious Wall Street law firm. They knew that Hauser interviewed Captain Ray Davis, as well as other United States officials in Chile and numerous other persons when preparing *Execution*. The filmmakers also knew that no legal action whatsoever was taken against the book in the approximately four years since its publication. In an August 1980 meeting where Costa-Gavras, the film's director, and Stewart, the co-scriptwriter, met with Hauser to verify the accuracy of his book, Hauser described his meticulous research methods and broad inquiries. There is no evidence to the contrary.

The filmmakers then met with Charles Horman's parents, his wife, and one Terry Simon, a close friend who was in Chile with Charles around the time of his disappearance. Each of these individuals made clear to Costa-Gavras and Stewart that Hauser's book accurately and reliably depicted events as they knew and believed them. There is no evidence that any of defendants' further research and review of documents regarding Horman and events in Chile during the coup caused them to doubt the veracity of Hauser's book.

Plaintiff argues that an effective search of Hauser's background would have disclosed "fraudulent letters" sent by Hauser to political figures and The New York Times. This allusion is to Hauser's political satires where he had written on public issues to officials in the voice of a nine-year old boy, "Martin Bear." The New York Times, in fact, solicited from Hauser and published on its "op-ed" page one of these satirical pieces, which can hardly be reason to "suspect" the veracity of his book.

In any event, plaintiff has neither presented nor designated specific facts suggesting or from which it could be reasonably inferred and found that defendants entertained serious doubts as to Hauser's account or that there were obvious reasons to doubt the veracity or accuracy of Hauser's book. Absent such evidence, reliance on *Execution* is not evidence of actual malice.

C. *Failure to Consult Plaintiff Prior to Making Film*

Plaintiff argues that defendant's failure to consult plaintiff personally prior to presentation of the film is evidence of actual malice. However, plaintiff cannot prove actual malice merely by asserting that a publisher failed to contact the subject of his work. The actual malice standard cannot be satisfied by evidence of a failure to check with third parties prior to publication without proof that a publisher knew his publication was false, entertained serious doubts as to its truth, or had obvious reasons to doubt the veracity or accuracy of the source of published information.

While "verification of facts" of a story with its subjects and with others is a desirable and responsible practice and "an important reporting standard, a reporter, without a 'high degree of awareness of their probable falsity,' may rely on statements made by a single source even though they reflect only one side of the story without fear of libel prosecution...." Plaintiff has not designated specific facts suggesting an awareness or even suspicion by defendants of probable falsity of their source material.

D. *Scenes in "Missing" as Evidence of Actual Malice*

Plaintiff enumerates nine scenes in "Missing" which the filmmakers allegedly created, or in which they distorted the context, or made baseless suggestions. None of these scenes provides or contributes to the requisite evidence of actual malice.

It should be made clear that "Missing" is not a documentary, but a dramatization of the Horman disappearance and search. The film does not purport to depict a chronology of the events precisely as they actually occurred; it opens with the prologue: "This film is *based on* a true story. The incidents and facts are documented. Some of the names have been changed to protect the innocent and also to protect the film." No one challenged the accuracy and veracity of Hauser's book to the knowledge of defendants. Defendants concede that although the substance of the film's scenes is extracted almost directly from Thomas Hauser's book, not everything in their film is literally faithful to the actual historical record as if in a documentary. That is not to say that which was not historical was set out in bad faith, portrayed with actual malice, or established or increased the defamatory impact.

The film is not a documentary. A documentary is a non-fictional story or series of historical events portrayed in their actual location; a film of real people and real events as they occur. A documentary maintains strict fidelity to fact.

"Missing," on the other hand, is an art form sometimes described as "Docu-Drama." The line separating a documentary from a docudrama is not always sharply defined, but is nonetheless discernible. Both forms are necessarily selective, given the time constraints of movies and the attention span of the viewing audience. The docudrama is a dramatization of an historical event or lives of real people, using actors or actresses. Docudramas utilize simulated dialogue, composite characters, and a telescoping of events occurring over a period into a composite scene or scenes. This treatment is singularly appropriate and unexceptionable if the context is not distorted when dealing with public and political figures.

Self-evidently a docudrama partakes of author's license — it is a creative interpretation of reality — and if alterations of fact in scenes portrayed are not made with serious doubts of truth of the essence of the telescoped composite, such scenes do not ground a charge of actual malice.

Each scene questioned by the plaintiff is a telescoped composite of events, personalities, and of the American representatives in Chile who are involved therein. Each uses permissible literary license to fit historical detail into a suitable dramatic context. Such dramatic embellishments as are made do not distort the fundamental story being told — the frantic search by his family for a missing man who has suddenly disappeared, their emotions, anxieties, impatience, frustration, and doubts of assistance from American officialdom. The scenes are thus a hybrid of fact and fiction which however do not materially distort the analysis. Always to be remembered is that they fairly represent the source materials for the film believed to be true by the filmmakers. Leeway is properly afforded to an author who thus attempts to recount a true event.

As a matter of law, the dramatic overlay supplied by the film does not serve to increase the impact of what plaintiff charges as defamatory since it fairly and reasonably portrays the unassailable beliefs of the Hormans, the record thereof in the Hauser book, and the corroborative results of the authors' inquiries. In docudrama, minor fictionalization cannot be considered evidence or support for the requirement of actual malice.

The nine scenes selected by plaintiff as support for the requirement of actual malice do no such thing. Each is related solely and unquestionably to the theme of this film. The movie's Ray Tower character is a fictional composite of the American presence operating in Chile at the time. He is a symbolic figure. The artistic input in the scenes questioned is found in permissible syntheses and composite treatment in the film. Although in actuality particular individuals were not physically present when certain dialogue occurred, in the movie scene the composite character portrayed was.

The content of the film reflects what happened according to the book, the persons who complained, and the sources relied on by defendants. While the actual persons involved in the events portrayed do not appear in on-scene interviews to describe their experiences, actions, and motivations, the real names of some individuals are employed. But the name Ray Davis is never mentioned. Real life personalities are accordingly represented by telescoped composites in many instances.

The cases on point demonstrate that the First Amendment protects such dramatizations and does not demand literal truth in every episode depicted; publishing a dramatization is not of itself evidence of actual malice. In *Street v. National Broadcasting Co.,* 645 F.2d 1227 (6th Cir.), *cert. granted,* 454 U.S. 815, *cert. dismissed,* 454 U.S. 1095, (1981), the Court of Appeals affirmed a ruling on a directed verdict that the dramatization embodied in defendant's broadcast program on the Scottsboro rape trial was protected by the *New York Times v. Sullivan* standard, and not chargeable with actual malice. While the dramatization contained certain literal falsehoods, including undocumented statements and conversations, *Street,* the movie was based "in all material respects" on the Judge's findings in the Scottsboro case, and a book by a historian documenting the Scottsboro trial. *See also Reader's Digest Association v. Superior Court,* 37 Cal. 3d 244, 264, 690 P.2d 610, 623, 208 Cal. Rptr. 137, 150 (1984) (summary judgment granted, and no triable issue of actual malice presented where published material "falls within an acceptable range of literary license."); *Leopold v. Levin,* 45 Ill. 2d 434, 259 N.E.2d 250, 256 (1970) (insufficient evidence of actual malice to overcome summary judgment where fictionalized episodes could be "traced in a substantial way" to a recorded source).

Similarly, in *Meeropol v. Nizer,* 381 F. Supp. 29 (S.D.N.Y. 1974), *aff'd,* 560 F.2d 1061 (2d Cir. 1977), *cert. denied,* 434 U.S. 1013 (1978), summary judgment was granted for a defendant sued for defamation of a public figure based on plaintiff's inability to designate specific evidence of actual malice. Defendant had written a book based on letters written by Ethel and Julius Rosenberg, convicted spies. The book contained "minor fictionalizations or approximations of conversations." The court held that these do not supply the requisite specific evidence of actual malice:

> Such techniques do not rise to the constitutional level of clear and convincing showing of reckless disregard.... Deviations from or embellishments upon the information obtained from the primary sources relied upon were miniscule and can be attributed to the leeway afforded an author who attempts to recount and popularize an historic event.

Hotchner v. Castillo-Puche, 551 F.2d 910 (2d Cir.), *cert. denied,* 434 U.S. 834 (1977), was an appeal of a judgment entered after a jury verdict for plaintiff. Defendant published a book which purported to quote derogatory remarks by Ernest Hemingway about plaintiff. Defendant did not print the literal words used by Hemingway, and "was fictionalizing to some extent." The Court of Appeals held that such fictionalization or dramatization does not satisfy the requirement of clear and convincing evidence from which a jury might reasonably find that defendant published the alleged libel with actual malice. Actual malice could not be inferred because "the change did not increase the defamatory impact or alter the substantive content" of Hemingway's original statement which defendants relied upon.

The issue on the motion is not the truth of whether Davis (qua Ray Tower) ordered or approved a Chilean order to kill Charles Horman because he "knew too much" about alleged American involvement in the Chilean coup; the issue is whether the filmmakers intentionally portrayed such a defamatory suggestion, knowing that it was false or with serious doubts of its truth. There is no doubt that Ed Horman, the father of the missing man, asserted such a theory and that assertion is documented in Hauser's book. Plaintiff has not presented evidence that defendants knew the theory of the father was false, or entertained serious doubts as to its truth. There is no evidence that defendants acted with actual malice or disbelieved what the Hormans thought and said or what Hauser wrote.

In sum, returning to the *ratio decidendi*; no provable, clear and convincing, affirmative evidence nor specific facts showing actual malice on the part of the defendants in publishing the alleged defamation have been shown, and the complaint by plaintiff, a public figure, falls as not sustainable under the law....

Pippen v. NBCUniversal Media LLC
734 F.3d 610 (2013)

Scottie Pippen, who won six championship rings with the Chicago Bulls and was named in 1996 to the National Basketball Association's list of the 50 greatest players in its history, has encountered financial reverses since his playing days ended in 2004. He has lost through bad investments a large portion of the fortune he amassed during his playing days. In an effort to recoup some of these losses, he has pursued multiple lawsuits against former financial and legal advisors who he believes led him astray. The media caught wind of Pippen's woes, and several news organizations reported that he had filed for bankruptcy. This is false; he has not.

Pippen contends that the false reports have impaired his ability to earn a living through product endorsements and personal appearances. He filed this suit against multiple defendants under the diversity jurisdiction in the Northern District of Illinois, contending that he was defamed and cast in a false light. The district court dismissed the complaint. It found that the falsehoods did not fit within any of the categories of statements recognized by Illinois law to be so innately harmful that damages may be presumed. The district court also concluded that the complaint did not plausibly allege that the defendants had published the falsehoods with actual malice—a term that looks as if it might mean "ill will" but in fact means knowledge the statement is false or reckless disregard of whether it is false. Demonstrating actual malice is a requirement for a public figure such as Pippen to recover damages for defamation, and to make out a claim of false light under Illinois law.

There are two types of action for defamation. The first, called defamation *per quod*, requires a plaintiff to show that the false statements caused him harm. Some statements, however, expose the subject to such great obloquy that they are actionable without proof of injury. This is defamation *per se*. Let us begin with the latter type.

Illinois recognizes five categories of defamation *per se*, but only two are of interest here: (1) statements that suggest that the subject can't perform his job because of lack of ability or want of integrity, and (2) statements that prejudice the subject in the pursuit of his trade or profession. The difference between the two is subtle. The former seems to imply some sort of on-the-job malfeasance; the latter covers suitability for a trade or profession. Pippen argues that this court has already established in *Giant Screen Sports v. Canadian Imperial Bank of Commerce*, 553 F.3d 527 (7th Cir.2009), that false accusations of bankruptcy fit into one of these categories.

But the statements at issue in *Giant Screen Sports* were not about bankruptcy; instead, they repeated false accusations that a company willfully defaulted on a credit agreement it was not a party to. The statements depicted the company as one that shirked its contractual obligations; a reader might reasonably think twice about doing business with the company. A similar taint does not attach to the reputation of people who go bankrupt. Many innocent reasons lead to financial distress. Readers of the defendants' statements who mistakenly believe that Pippen is insolvent readily could conclude that his advisers bear the blame.

What's more, Pippen was reported to be personally bankrupt. To succeed under Illinois law without the need to prove injury, he must show that he was falsely accused of lacking ability in his trade or of doing something bad while performing his job. Pippen has been employed since he retired from basketball as a goodwill ambassador for the Chicago Bulls, a basketball analyst, and a celebrity product endorser. Bankruptcy does not imply that he lacks the competence or integrity to perform any of these jobs.

Sometimes personal and professional ability or integrity are linked. When the subject of the false statements is employed in an occupation (schoolteacher for example) that requires certain personal traits, such as trustworthiness, accusations of being a scam artist or an inveterate liar could lead to unemployment. Pippen does not contend that his is such a situation. His post-retirement employability derives from his pre-retirement stardom (for his endorsement and appearance work) and basketball knowledge (for his work as an analyst), not his financial prudence or investment savvy. Reports of personal bankruptcy would not so impugn his job performance that they necessarily constitute defamation.

This leaves the second type of defamation (*per quod*).... The district court dismissed these claims after concluding that Pippen had failed to allege special damages in sufficient detail. We think this a mistake.... Pippen's complaint alleges that his endorsement and personal-appearance opportunities dwindled as a result of the defendants' false reports. In a proposed amended complaint, Pippen itemized losses that in his view flowed from defendants' statements; he identified specific business opportunities that had been available to him earlier but that, following the defendants' statements, were available no more. This is more than a general allegation of economic loss; it is an allegation that third parties have ceased to do business with him because of the defendants' actions. This contention may be substantively inadequate. It appears to be an example of the *post hoc ergo propter hoc* fallacy: since Pippen's opportunities diminished after the statements were made, he believes they must have diminished *because* the statements were made. This theory of causation is weak for professional athletes, whose earnings related to past stardom drop as time passes since their playing days. But, as a matter of pleading, Pippen did enough.

The district court had a second reason, however, and it is stronger. The judge observed that Pippen is a public figure, which he concedes. Thus he must show that the defendants published the defamatory statements with actual malice—in other words, that the defendants either knew the statements to be false or were recklessly indifferent to whether they are true or false. States of mind may be pleaded generally, but a plaintiff still must point to details sufficient to render a claim plausible.

Defendants had many ways to learn whether Pippen had filed for bankruptcy. For example, all bankruptcy court dockets can be searched simultaneously through the federal courts' PACER service. And then there's the tried-and-true journalistic practice of asking a story's subject. If rather than relying on the rumor mill the defendants had conducted even a cursory investigation, they would have discovered that Pippen had not declared bankruptcy—and they concede this. But failure to investigate is precisely what the Supreme Court has said is insufficient to establish reckless disregard for the truth.

The Supreme Court also has said that actual malice cannot be inferred from a publisher's failure to retract a statement once it learns it to be false. Thus the fact that Pippen alerted the defendants by email *after* publication that he had not entered bankruptcy does not help him establish actual malice at the time of publication. And Illinois has adopted the Uniform Single Publication Act, 740 ILCS 165/1, which provides that a claim for relief for defamation is complete at the time of first publication; later circulation of the original publication does not trigger fresh claims. The Act protects speakers and writers from repeated litigation arising from a single, but mass-produced, defamatory publication.

Pippen argues that the Act does not apply to statements on the Internet, where all defendants made their reportage available. Online publishers do not face the same logistical hurdles or costs in correcting a false statement as their old-media counterparts. Print publishers would need to hunt down every physical copy of a book, magazine, or newspaper in circulation, while Internet publishers can alter their sites with relative ease. In Pippen's view, then, every day that an unaltered defamatory statement remains online after a publisher learns of its falsity constitutes an actionable republication.

Illinois courts have not yet considered how the single-publication rule applies to Internet publications, so our job is to predict how the state's highest court would answer the question if asked. In the absence of any Illinois authority on the question, decisions from other jurisdictions may prove instructive. We conclude that, if presented with the opportunity, the Supreme Court of Illinois would deem the single-publication rule applicable to the Internet.

Every state court that has considered the question applies the single-publication rule to information online. And those federal courts that have addressed the topic have concluded that the relevant state supreme court would agree. Pippen does not alert us to any authority supporting his view, and we have found none.

The theme of these decisions is that excluding the Internet from the single-publication rule would eviscerate the statute of limitations and expose online publishers to potentially limitless liability. This same concern previously led courts to apply the single-publication rule to books. They did so despite the fact that book publishers have greater post-publication control over the circulation of their content than do newspaper publishers. All copies of a single newspaper edition are made available to the public on one day; in contrast, book publishers hold stock in reserve and release batches to the public over months or years. In Pippen's view, the single-publication rule ought not have been extended to book publishers because they could pulp the books they kept in stock, while newspaper publishers had no leftover stock to destroy. But no court saw it that way, and no court has been persuaded that the even greater control that Internet publishers have over their content—and the much lower cost of editing or deleting that content—is a reason to exclude them from the Act's coverage. Indeed, courts have drawn the opposite conclusion: the Internet's greater reach comes with an "even greater potential for endless retriggering of the statute of limitations, multiplicity of suits and harassment of defendants." *Firth* [*v. State,*] 98 N.Y.2d 365, 370 (2002)]; the more reason that the single-publication rule should apply.

A publisher's degree of control over its content does not matter to Illinois's test for whether redistribution of a defamatory statement amounts to a republication. Instead, courts must ask whether the "act of the defendant [was] a conscious independent one". *Winrod v. Time Inc.*, 334 Ill.App. 59 (1948). Courts have grappled with what degree of affirmative act constitutes a republication. The defendants in those cases changed the URL where the statements were posted but left the statements unaltered. In *Firth*, the defendants added an unrelated story to the web page hosting the allegedly defamatory statement. None of those acts was sufficient to count as a republication. Pippen does not contend that the defendants took any action beyond initially posting the stories to their web sites, and we conclude that Illinois would deem the passive maintenance of a web site not a republication.

Notes and Questions

a. The standards for defamation are quite clear in the abstract, but very difficult to adapt to the world of novelization, motion pictures, and dramatic license. Even the less controversial characters are sometimes put into question. In the film *The Hurricane*, former middleweight champion Joey Giardello sued for the allegedly false portrayal of his title fight against Ruben Hurricane Carter. The case was eventually settled, reportedly with changes to the DVD version of the movie, including a voice-over by director Norman Jewison which alludes to an admission that the fight scene in the movie was inaccurate. See Matthew Stohl, *False Light Invasion of Privacy in Docudramas: The Oxymoron Which Must Be Solved*, 35 AKRON L. REV. 251 (2002). Similar issues occurred with *Boys Don't Cry*, *Erin Brockovich*, *The Perfect Storm*, and many other stories based on true events.

b. In Matthew Stohl's account of the controversy involving Joey Giardello, the descriptions are not likely to meet the actual malice standard. As former middleweight champion, it is likely that Giardello would have been treated as a public figure and therefore unable to prove his case. Unlike Giardello, minor characters who claim defamation are not typically public figures or public officials. As private figures, plaintiffs need only prove negligence to have a claim—something much more likely to occur during the constant change of editing or filmmaking.

c. What role does a film's disclaimer serve to limit tort liability? In *Davis v. Costa-Gavras*, the district court put a good deal of stock in the "based upon" language of the film's description—assuming that the public understood what a dramatization implies about specific incidents. Other books, plays, and motion pictures use much broader disclaimers. One such formulation, from the book *Rush*, provides that the book "is a work of fiction. Any resemblance its characters may have to persons living or dead is purely coincidental."

d. The motion picture *Harry Potter and the Sorcerer's Stone* uses a fittingly more British approach: "The story, all names, characters & incidents portrayed in this production are fictitious. No identification with actual persons, places, buildings & products is intended or should be inferred." The *Harry Potter* disclaimer is interesting in its expansive scope. To what extent do the disclaimers impact the outcome of litigation or attempts to bring litigation? Does the addition of buildings and places suggest new potential claims for invasion of legal interests? Will such a disclaimer serve to avoid trademark issues or concerns about product disparity?

e. Defamation remains in the eye of the beholder. Described by the Ninth Circuit as a "compliment," famed daredevil Evel Knievel did not appreciate ESPN's form of attention. As the Court explained,

> Famed motorcycle stuntman Evel Knievel and his wife Krystal were pho-
> tographed when they attended ESPN's Action Sports and Music Awards in 2001.
> The photograph depicted Evel, who was wearing a motorcycle jacket and rose-
> tinted sunglasses, with his right arm around Krystal and his left arm around an-
> other young woman. ESPN published the photograph on its "extreme sports"
> website with a caption that read "Evel Knievel proves that you're never too old
> to be a pimp."

Knievel v. ESPN, 393 F.3d 1068, 1070 (9th Cir. 2005). The Court reminded Knievel that
an assessment of defamation must take the context of the website into account, and the
remainder of the website used an "overwhelming presence of slang and non-literal language," along with such terms as "hardcore" and "scoping," and slang phrases such as
"throwing down a pose," "put a few back," and "hottie of the year...." *Id.* at 1077.

f. What is based upon a true story? Given the facts and standards of the dispute between little league volunteer Robert Muzikowski and Paramount Pictures, the standard
is evidently very low. In a bitterly contested defamation claim, the plaintiff objected to the
conversion of the "nonfiction novel" *Hardball: A Season in the Projects* into the fictional
movie *Hardball. Muzikowski v. Paramount Pictures Corp.*, 477 F.3d 899 (7th Cir. 2007). Having denied that Muzikowski is represented in any fashion in the fictionalization — to avoid
the claims of defamation — Paramount claims the movie is based on the true story of the
baseball team.

> Muzikowski claimed that Paramount's promotion of the *Hardball* movie as "in-
> spired by a true story" was false because of the extent to which Muzikowski's life
> story was changed in the film. The district court concluded that these theories
> failed too, because Muzikowski had neither demonstrated that Paramount's ad-
> vertisement was false nor that consumers who viewed the advertisements had
> been deceived.
>
> In order to establish a claim of false or deceptive advertising under § 43(a)
> of the Lanham Act, a plaintiff must show that the defendant made a mater-
> ial false statement of fact in a commercial advertisement and that the false
> statement deceived or had the tendency to deceive a substantial segment of
> its audience. The district court held, and we have previously assumed with-
> out deciding, that this analysis also applies to Illinois false advertising claims.
> Because Muzikowski does not argue to the contrary, we assume the same in
> this case.
>
> In granting summary judgment to Paramount on the false advertising claims,
> the district court reasoned that Paramount's statement "inspired by a true story"
> is "literally true," observing that neither party disputes the veracity of the state-
> ment. Paramount insists that its advertisement represents the film as "the story
> of ... the [Little League] team featured in Coyle's book." Muzikowski, on the
> other hand, contends that the advertisements "lead viewers to believe that the
> story is his." Since Muzikowski does not in any event contest the district court's
> conclusion that Paramount's advertising for *Hardball* did not contain a false
> statement of fact, we conclude that he has waived both this argument and his
> false advertising claims generally.

Id. at 907–08.

Eighteen affidavits did little to convince the judge that a substantial portion of the
viewers knew about Muzikowski or cared that it was based upon a true story, making enforcement of the "based on a true story" pronouncement much less likely. See *Id.*

g. To what extent can the use of images to illustrate a story be defamatory of those depicted in the photographs if they are not related to the story itself? See *Stanton v. Metro Corp.*, 438 F.3d 119 (1st Cir. 2006) (depicting teens at a high school party in an unrelated story about teenage promiscuity).

Problem VI-A

Angered and frustrated by the response to Bryce's *Juliet Prescott* (see Problem V-A), Bryce tried to strike back. Bryce added a scene to the script set in the city hall depicting characters whose first names were those of actual local city officials. Other than in the matter of first names, none of Bryce's characterizations bear any direct relation or resemblance to the city council members. Bryce never performed any background research on the city council members. The play's new city council characters are generally depicted as racist and illiterate. At the end of the scene, the city council voted to "deport Romeo — at least to New Mexico." Bryce has shown you the scene (which you acknowledge is a clever satire of the city council) to ask your advice. Advise Bryce regarding the extent to which the scene is actionable as defamatory.

B. Parody and Satire

Hustler Magazine v. Falwell
485 U.S. 46 (1988)

Chief Justice REHNQUIST delivered the opinion of the Court.

Petitioner Hustler Magazine, Inc., is a magazine of nationwide circulation. Respondent Jerry Falwell, a nationally known minister who has been active as a commentator on politics and public affairs, sued petitioner and its publisher, petitioner Larry Flynt, to recover damages for invasion of privacy, libel, and intentional infliction of emotional distress. The District Court directed a verdict against respondent on the privacy claim, and submitted the other two claims to a jury. The jury found for petitioners on the defamation claim, but found for respondent on the claim for intentional infliction of emotional distress and awarded damages. We now consider whether this award is consistent with the First and Fourteenth Amendments of the United States Constitution.

The inside front cover of the November 1983 issue of Hustler Magazine featured a "parody" of an advertisement for Campari Liqueur that contained the name and picture of respondent and was entitled "Jerry Falwell talks about his first time." This parody was modeled after actual Campari ads that included interviews with various celebrities about their "first times." Although it was apparent by the end of each interview that this meant the first time they sampled Campari, the ads clearly played on the sexual double entendre of the general subject of "first times." Copying the form and layout of these Campari ads, Hustler's editors chose respondent as the featured celebrity and drafted an alleged "interview" with him in which he states that his "first time" was during a drunken incestuous rendezvous with his mother in an outhouse. The Hustler parody portrays respondent and his mother as drunk and immoral, and suggests that respondent is a hypocrite who preaches only when he is drunk. In small print at the bottom of the page, the ad contains the disclaimer, "ad parody — not to be taken seriously." The magazine's table of contents also lists the ad as "Fiction; Ad and Personality Parody." ...

This case presents us with a novel question involving First Amendment limitations upon a State's authority to protect its citizens from the intentional infliction of emotional distress. We must decide whether a public figure may recover damages for emotional harm caused by the publication of an ad parody offensive to him, and doubtless gross and repugnant in the eyes of most. Respondent would have us find that a State's interest in protecting public figures from emotional distress is sufficient to deny First Amendment protection to speech that is patently offensive and is intended to inflict emotional injury, even when that speech could not reasonably have been interpreted as stating actual facts about the public figure involved. This we decline to do....

We conclude that public figures and public officials may not recover for the tort of intentional infliction of emotional distress by reason of publications such as the one here at issue without showing in addition that the publication contains a false statement of fact which was made with "actual malice," i.e., with knowledge that the statement was false or with reckless disregard as to whether or not it was true. This is not merely a "blind application" of the *New York Times* standard, see *Time, Inc. v. Hill,* 385 U.S. 374, 390, (1967), it reflects our considered judgment that such a standard is necessary to give adequate "breathing space" to the freedoms protected by the First Amendment.

Here it is clear that respondent Falwell is a "public figure" for purposes of First Amendment law. The jury found against respondent on his libel claim when it decided that the Hustler ad parody could not "reasonably be understood as describing actual facts about [respondent] or actual events in which [he] participated." The Court of Appeals interpreted the jury's finding to be that the ad parody "was not reasonably believable," and in accordance with our custom we accept this finding. Respondent is thus relegated to his claim for damages awarded by the jury for the intentional infliction of emotional distress by "outrageous" conduct. But for reasons heretofore stated this claim cannot, consistently with the First Amendment, form a basis for the award of damages when the conduct in question is the publication of a caricature such as the ad parody involved here. The judgment of the Court of Appeals is accordingly Reversed.

Farah v. Esquire Magazine

736 F.3d 528 (2013)

This case is principally a defamation action based on the publication of an article by journalist Mark Warren on *Esquire Magazine*'s Politics Blog. The article was posted one day after the release of a book entitled "*Where's the Birth Certificate? The Case that Barack Obama is not Eligible to Be President,*" written by Jerome Corsi and published by Joseph Farah's WND Books. Farah's website, WorldNetDaily, announced the book launch with the headline, "**It's out! The book that proves Obama's ineligible:** Today's the day Corsi is unleashed to tell all about that 'birth certificate'" (emphasis in original). Approximately three weeks earlier, President Obama had released his long-form birth certificate showing that he was born in Hawaii. Warren's article was entitled "**BREAKING: Jerome Corsi's Birther Book Pulled from Shelves!**" (emphasis in original). It stated, in part: "In a stunning development one day after the release of [the Corsi book], [Farah] has announced plans to recall and pulp the entire 200,000 first printing run of the book, as well as announcing an offer to refund the purchase price to anyone who has already bought ... the book." Approximately ninety minutes later, *Esquire* published an "update" on its blog "for those who didn't figure it out," that Warren's article was "satire"; the "update" clarified that the article was untrue and referenced other "serious" *Esquire* articles on the birth certificate issue. Farah observed the same day that he thought the blog post was a "poorly executed parody." Also that day, Warren told *The Daily Caller* that he had no regrets about publishing the fictitious article and expressed his negative view of the book's author; his statements were published on *The Daily Caller* website that day and the following day.

Farah and Corsi filed suit for compensatory and punitive damages alleging defamation.... *Esquire* for all defendants moved to dismiss on several grounds, and the district court dismissed the complaint.... Upon *de novo* review, we hold that the complaint was properly dismissed pursuant to Federal Rule of Civil Procedure 12(b)(6) for failure to state a claim because the blog post was fully protected political satire and the "update" and Warren's statements are protected opinion. The complaint also fails to state a claim for violation of the Lanham Act. Accordingly, we affirm the dismissal of the complaint....

Esquire published an online article by Mark Warren entitled "**BREAKING: Jerome Corsi's Birther Book Pulled from Shelves!**" The article contained "false and misleading facts" about Corsi's book. The article, on "The Politics Blog," was accompanied by a copy of the "Drudge Siren" above an image of the book's cover. It read in full:

> **In a stunning development** one day after the release of *Where's the Birth Certificate? The Case that Barack Obama is not Eligible to be President,* by Dr. Jerome Corsi, World Net Daily Editor and Chief Executive Officer Joseph Farah has announced plans to recall and pulp the entire 200,000 first printing run of the book, as well as announcing an offer to refund the purchase price to anyone who has already bought either a hard copy or electronic download of the book.

> In an exclusive interview, a reflective Farah, who wrote the book's foreword and also published Corsi's earlier best-selling work, *Unfit for Command: Swift Boat Veterans Speak out Against John Kerry* and *Capricorn One: NASA, JFK, and the Great "Moon Landing" Cover-Up,* said that after much serious reflection, he could not go forward with the project. "I believe with all my heart that Barack Obama is destroying this country, and I will continue to stand against his administration at every turn, but in light of recent events, this book has become problematic, and contains what I now believe to be factual inaccuracies," he said this morning. "I cannot in good conscience publish it and expect anyone to believe it."

> When asked if he had any plans to publish a corrected version of the book, he said cryptically, "There is no book." Farah declined to comment on his discussions of the matter with Corsi.

> A source at WND, who requested that his name be withheld, said that Farah was "rip-shit" when, on April 27, President Obama took the extraordinary step of personally releasing his "long-form" birth certificate, thus resolving the matter of Obama's legitimacy for "anybody with a brain."

> "He called up Corsi and really tore him a new one," says the source. "I mean, we'll do anything to hurt Obama, and erase his memory, but we don't want to look like fucking idiots, you know? Look, at the end of the day, bullshit is bullshit."

> Corsi, who graduated from Harvard and is a professional journalist, could not be reached for comment.

According to the complaint, "[i]mmediately" after the blog posting, "news organizations, readers of WorldNetDaily, purchasers and distributors of WND Books and others began contacting [ ] Farah for confirmation of the story and comment." Also, "consumers began requesting refunds[,] ... book supporters began attacking Farah and Corsi[,] [and] [b]ook stores ... began pulling the book from their shelves, or not offering it for sale at all." Only after Farah "issued a statement saying he was exploring legal options against *Esquire* and Warren did they purport to issue a disclaimer." This "so-called disclaimer" was "as false[ ][and] misleading ... as the initial story that was published" on the website. *Id.* It read in full:

> DEVELOPING ...
>
> *UPDATE, 12:25 p.m., for those who didn't figure it out yet, and the many on Twitter for whom it took a while:* We committed satire this morning to point out the problems with selling and marketing a book that has had its core premise and reason to exist gutted by the news cycle, several weeks in advance of publication. Are its author and publisher chastened? Well, no. They double down, and accuse the President of the United States of perpetrating a fraud on the world by having released a forged birth certificate. Not because this claim is in any way based on reality, but to hold their terribly gullible audience captive to their lies, and to sell books. This is despicable, and deserves only ridicule. That's why we committed satire in the matter of the Corsi book. Hell, even the president has a sense of humor about it all. Some more serious reporting from us on this whole "birther" phenomenon here, here, and here.
>
> **Tags:** birther book, jerome corsi, where's the birth certificate, drudge without context, birthers, wingnuts, humor

... On June 28, 2011, Farah and Corsi sued Esquire Magazine, Inc., Hearst Communications, Inc., and Warren (together "*Esquire*") for defamation, ... The complaint sought in excess of $100 million for actual and compensatory damages, and punitive damages in excess of $20 million....

To meet the requirements for defamation under District of Columbia law, a plaintiff must prove (1) that he was the subject of a false and defamatory statement; (2) that the statement was published to a third party; (3) that publishing the statement was at least negligent; and (4) that the plaintiff suffered either actual or legal harm. A statement is "defamatory" if it tends to injure the plaintiff in his trade, profession or community standing, or to lower him in the estimation of the community. This court, in reviewing the dismissal of the complaint, "must assume, as the complaint alleges, the falsity of any express or implied factual statements made" in the publications at issue. The court must also assume that *Esquire* made such statements with the requisite state of mind. And, "[i]n determining whether a complaint states a claim, the court may consider the facts alleged in the complaint, documents attached thereto or incorporated therein, and matters of which it may take judicial notice." *Abhe & Svoboda, Inc. v. Chao*, 508 F.3d 1052, 1059 (D.C.Cir.2007) Judicial notice is properly taken of publicly available historical articles such as were attached to *Esquire*'s motions to dismiss....

Esquire maintains that Farah and Corsi have no cognizable defamation claim because the blog post is fully protected satire. "Satire" is a long-established artistic form that uses means such as "ridicule, derision, burlesque, irony, parody, [or] caricature" to censure the "vices, follies, abuses, or shortcomings" of an individual or society. *Satire*, ENCYC. BRITANNICA ONLINE, http://www.britannica.com/EBchecked/topic/524958/satire (last visited Nov. 1, 2013). Although satire has been employed since the time of Ancient Greece, it remains "one of the most imprecise" of all literary designations — a notoriously broad and complex genre whose "forms are as varied as its victims." *Id.* Sometimes satire is funny. *See, e.g., Saturday Night Live* (NBC television broadcast); THE ONION, http://

www.theonion.com (last visited Nov. 1, 2013). Other times it may seem cruel and mocking, attacking the core beliefs of its target. And sometimes it is absurd, as in the classic example of Jonathan Swift's proposal to "solve" the problem of Irish poverty by killing and eating Irish children. *See* JONATHAN SWIFT, A MODEST PROPOSAL (1729). Satire's unifying element is the use of wit "to expose something foolish or vicious to criticism." *Satire*, ENCYC. BRITANNICA ONLINE. A "parody" is to the same effect: the style of an individual or work is closely imitated for comic effect or in ridicule. *See* MERRIAM WEBSTER'S COLLEGIATE DICTIONARY at 846 (10th ed.1993) ("parody"); *see id.* at 1038 ("satire").

Despite its literal falsity, satirical speech enjoys First Amendment protection. Consistent with the "actual facts" requirement, "the 'statement' that the plaintiff must prove false ... is not invariably the literal phrase published but rather what a reasonable reader would have understood the author to have said." *Milkovich* [v. Lorain Journal Co., 497 U.S. 1, 23–24 (1990)]. Thus, a satire or parody must be assessed in the appropriate context; it is not actionable if it "cannot reasonably be interpreted as stating actual facts about an individual." *Milkovich*, 497 U.S. at 20. In light of the special characteristics of satire, of course, "what a reasonable reader would have understood" is more informed by an assessment of her well-considered view than by her immediate yet transitory reaction. Without First Amendment protection, there is a risk that public debate would "suffer for lack of 'imaginative expression'" and "the 'rhetorical hyperbole' which has traditionally added much to the discourse of our Nation." *Id.* (quoting *Hustler Magazine*, 485 U.S. at 53–55).

Farah and Corsi do not suggest that satire, as a genre, lacks constitutional protection. Rather, in their view *Esquire*'s *particular attempt* at satire is not protected because reasonable readers would take the fictitious blog post literally. They point to the inquiries they received following the blog post, as well as to *Esquire*'s own "update" clarifying that the post was satire, as evidence that many actual readers were misled by *Esquire*'s story. But it is the nature of satire that not everyone "gets it" immediately. For example, when Daniel Defoe first published *The Shortest Way with the Dissenters*, an anonymous satirical pamphlet against religious persecution, it was initially welcomed by the church establishment Defoe sought to ridicule. Similarly, Benjamin Franklin's "Speech of Miss Polly Baker," a fictitious news story mocking New England's harsh treatment of unwed mothers, was widely republished in both England and the United States as actual news.

Indeed, satire is effective as social commentary precisely because it is often grounded in truth. In a similar case involving a satirical news article, the Texas Supreme Court observed that satire works by "distort[ing] ... the familiar with the pretense of reality in order to convey an underlying critical message." *New Times v. Isaacks*, 146 S.W.3d 144, 151 (Tex.2004). Here, too, *Esquire*'s story conveyed its message by layering fiction upon fact. The test, however, is not whether some actual readers were misled, but whether the hypothetical reasonable reader could be (after time for reflection). And to the extent Farah and Corsi rely on *Esquire*'s "update" to demonstrate reader confusion, *Esquire* can hardly be penalized for attempting to set the record straight and *avoid* confusion by those readers who did not at first "get" the satirical nature of Warren's article.

Considering the blog post in its context, the reasonable reader could not understand Warren's article to be conveying "real news" about Farah and Corsi. The article's primary intended audience—that is, readers of "The Politics Blog"—would have been familiar with *Esquire*'s history of publishing satirical stories, with recent topics ranging from Osama Bin Laden's television-watching habits to "Sex Tips from Donald Rumsfeld." At the same time, followers of "The Politics Blog" were politically informed readers. The "update" notes that *Esquire*.com had previously featured several "serious" reports on the birth certificate issue. Farah and Corsi acknowledge that they were well-known leaders of the movement questioning President Obama's eligibility, and admit that readers of *Esquire*.com would have been familiar with WorldNetDaily and its positions,. The postings on Farah's own website show that he has been writing on the issue for years, and Corsi's then-forthcoming book had recently received publicity on the Drudge Report. It defies common sense to suppose that readers of "The Politics Blog" were unaware of the birth certificate controversy or the heated debate it had provoked.

With that baseline of knowledge, reasonable readers of "The Politics Blog" would recognize the prominent indicia of satire in the Warren article. Most notably, the very substance of the story would alert the reasonable reader to the possibility that the post was satirical. The essence of the fictitious story was that Farah, a self-described leader (along with Corsi) of the movement to challenge President Obama's eligibility to serve, had suddenly and without any warning decided to recall and "pulp" the Corsi book the very day after it was released. The supposed basis for this decision was President Obama's earlier release of his long-form birth certificate; yet that release occurred three weeks before Corsi's book was published, and, as Farah acknowledges, he and Corsi remained (and still remain) committed to the book even after that event. *After* the release of the birth certificate, Farah appeared on MSNBC and published more than 40 articles on WorldNet-Daily continuing to promote the book. The day of the Corsi book's release—the day before *Esquire* posted its fictitious story—WorldNetDaily announced the publication on its website with an article entitled, "**It's out! The book that proves Obama's ineligible:** Today's the day Corsi is unleashed to tell all about that 'birth certificate.'" It is inconceivable that Farah would reverse course so abruptly, as *Esquire*'s fictitious story claimed. Readers of "The Politics Blog" would have recognized that the article was "reporting" events and statements that were totally inconsistent with Farah's and Corsi's well-publicized views, and could not reasonably have taken the story literally.

A number of humorous or outlandish details in the blog post also betray its satirical nature. The story attributes to Corsi an obviously fictitious book entitled, *Capricorn One: NASA, JFK, and the Great "Moon Landing" Cover-Up.* Of all prominent cover-ups featured in the news in recent years, a moon cover-up—much less "the Great 'Moon Landing' Cover-Up"—was not among them. Further, the story includes incredible counter-factual statements like, "[Farah] said cryptically, 'There is no book.'" Farah had published and released the book and then confirmed the next day to *The Daily Caller* that the book "was selling briskly. I am 100 percent behind it." The story repeatedly attributes to a "source at WND" quotes that are highly unorthodox for a real news story, such as Farah was "rip-shit," "bullshit is bullshit," and "we don't want to look like fucking idiots, you know?" …

Even if none of these elements standing alone—the story's substance, outlandish and humorous details, stylistic elements—would convince the reasonable reader that the blog post was satirical, taken in context and as a whole they could lead to no other conclusion. Farah immediately recognized the blog post as a "parody," although he told *The Daily Caller* that in his view it was "a very poorly executed" one. Admittedly, apart from its headline, the article did not employ the sort of imitation and exaggerated mimicry that are typical of parody. But satire is a far broader concept than parody, incorporating a variety of literary forms and devices. And poorly executed or not, the reasonable reader would have to suspend virtually all that he or she knew to be true of Farah's and Corsi's views on the issue of President Obama's eligibility to serve in order to conclude the story was reporting true facts.

Because the reasonable reader could not, in context, understand *Esquire*'s blog post to be conveying "real news" — that is, actual facts about Farah and Corsi — the blog post was not actionable defamation. To the contrary, almost everything about the story and the nature of the issue itself showed it was political speech aimed at critiquing Farah's and Corsi's public position on the issue of President Obama's eligibility to hold office even after he had released his long-form birth certificate showing he was born in Hawaii. Farah and Corsi were entitled to express their opinion that its delayed release signaled it was a forgery, but they could not then sue for defamation because *Esquire* conveyed its contrary view by using satire, rather than straightforward attack. Because the blog post was entitled to First Amendment protection, the district court properly dismissed the defamation count as to the blog post for failure to state a claim.

Notes and Questions

a. *Hustler v. Falwell* was proceeded by two other decisions which together help frame the parody analysis of defamation law. See *Greenbelt Cooperative Publishing Assn., Inc. v. Bresler*, 398 U.S. 6 (1970) (rhetorical hyperbole should not be construed as factual assertions); *Letter Carriers v. Austin*, 418 U.S. 264 (1974) (false representation of fact required for defamation so opinion or hyperbole not actionable).

b. *Mink v. Knox* summarized the *Greenbelt, Letter Carriers,* and *Falwell* line of cases as follows:

> As to the constitutional limits on the *type* of speech which may be the subject of state defamation actions, the line of cases provides protection for statements, such as parody, fantasy, rhetorical hyperbole, and imaginative expressions, that cannot reasonably [be] interpreted as stating actual facts' about an individual. Because no reasonable person would take these types of speech as true, they simply cannot impair one's good name. This provides assurance that public debate will not suffer for lack of 'imaginative expression' or the 'rhetorical hyperbole' which has traditionally added much to the discourse of our Nation."

Mink v. Knox, 613 F.3d 995, 1005 (10th Cir. 2010) (internal quotations and citations omitted).

c. Does satire and parody apply differently to private individuals rather than public officials or regarding matters that are not of public concern? With social media allowing any person to publish content available to large groups of people, topics that are non-public involving private individuals are commonly published. How should parody be viewed? See *Pring v. Penthouse Intern., Ltd.*, 695 F.2d 438, 443 (10th Cir. 1982).

Problem VI-B

Like many artists, Bryce maintains a significant presence on social media. Bryce publishes information about upcoming events, future projects, and personal musings. Some of these posts talk about the many artists with whom Bryce collaborates. Frustrated late one evening, Bryce wrote a fictional dialogue between Bryce's producer and distributor. The essence of the discussion was how funny the producer and distributor thought it was to watch artists dedicate their lives to content that would be sold for pennies and what little money was paid by the distributor to the producer would be kept far away from the artists. The dialogue was written in Seussian Rhyme. Bryce's producer has threatened to bring a lawsuit for defamation and demanded a significant financial settlement, an apology, and the removal of the post. Please advise Bryce regarding the best strategy to address the problem.

C. Privacy

Time, Inc. v. Hill

385 U.S. 374 (1967)

MR. JUSTICE BRENNAN delivered the opinion of the Court.

The question in this case is whether appellant, publisher of Life Magazine, was denied constitutional protections of speech and press by the application by the New York courts of §§ 50–51 of the New York Civil Rights Law[8] to award appellee damages on allegations that Life falsely reported that a new play portrayed an experience suffered by appellee and his family.

The article appeared in Life in February 1955. It was entitled "True Crime Inspires Tense Play," with the subtitle, "The ordeal of a family trapped by convicts gives Broadway a new thriller, 'The Desperate Hours.'" The text of the article reads as follows:

Three years ago Americans all over the country read about the desperate ordeal of the James Hill family, who were held prisoners in their home outside Philadelphia by three escaped convicts. Later they read about it in Joseph Hayes's novel, *The Desperate Hours*, inspired by the family's experience. Now they can see the story re-enacted in Hayes's Broadway play based on the book, and next year will see it in his movie, which has been filmed but is being held up until the play has a chance to pay off.

---

8. The complete text of the New York Civil Rights Law §§ 50–51 is as follows:

§ 50. Right of privacy

    A person, firm or corporation that uses for advertising purposes, or for the purposes of trade, the name, portrait or picture of any living person without having first obtained the written consent of such person, or if a minor of his or her parent or guardian, is guilty of a misdemeanor.

§ 51. Action for injunction and for damages

    Any person whose name, portrait or picture is used within this state for advertising purposes or for the purposes of trade without the written consent first obtained as above provided may maintain an equitable action in the supreme court of this state against the person, firm or corporation so using his name, portrait or picture, to prevent and restrain the use thereof; and may also sue and recover damages for any injuries sustained by reason of such use and if the defendant shall have knowingly used such person's name, portrait or picture in such manner as is forbidden or declared to be unlawful by the last section, the jury, in its discretion, may award exemplary damages. But nothing contained in this act shall be so construed as to prevent any person, firm or corporation, practicing the profession of photography, from exhibiting in or about his or its establishment specimens of the work of such establishment, unless the same is continued by such person, firm or corporation after written notice objecting thereto has been given by the person portrayed; and nothing contained in this act shall be so construed as to prevent any person, firm or corporation from using the name, portrait or picture of any manufacturer or dealer in connection with the goods, wares and merchandise manufactured, produced or dealt in by him which he has sold or disposed of with such name, portrait or picture used in connection therewith; or from using the name, portrait or picture of any author, composer or artist in connection with his literary, musical or artistic productions which he has sold or disposed of with such name, portrait or picture used in connection therewith.

The play, directed by Robert Montgomery and expertly acted, is a heart-stopping account of how a family rose to heroism in a crisis. LIFE photographed the play during its Philadelphia tryout, transported some of the actors to the actual house where the Hills were besieged. On the next page scenes from the play are re-enacted on the site of the crime.

The pictures on the ensuing two pages included an enactment of the son being "roughed up" by one of the convicts, entitled "brutish convict," a picture of the daughter biting the hand of a convict to make him drop a gun, entitled "daring daughter," and one of the father throwing his gun through the door after a "brave try" to save his family is foiled.

The James Hill referred to in the article is the appellee. He and his wife and five children involuntarily became the subjects of a front-page news story after being held hostage by three escaped convicts in their suburban, Whitemarsh, Pennsylvania, home for 19 hours on September 11–12, 1952. The family was released unharmed. In an interview with newsmen after the convicts departed, appellee stressed that the convicts had treated the family courteously, had not molested them, and had not been at all violent. The convicts were thereafter apprehended in a widely publicized encounter with the police which resulted in the killing of two of the convicts. Shortly thereafter the family moved to Connecticut. The appellee discouraged all efforts to keep them in the public spotlight through magazine articles or appearances on television.

In the spring of 1953, Joseph Hayes' novel, The Desperate Hours, was published. The story depicted the experience of a family of four held hostage by three escaped convicts in the family's suburban home. But, unlike Hill's experience, the family of the story suffer violence at the hands of the convicts; the father and son are beaten and the daughter subjected to a verbal sexual insult.

The book was made into a play, also entitled The Desperate Hours, and it is Life's article about the play which is the subject of appellee's action. The complaint sought damages under §§ 50–51 on allegations that the Life article was intended to, and did, give the impression that the play mirrored the Hill family's experience, which, to the knowledge of defendant " ... was false and untrue." Appellant's defense was that the article was "a subject of legitimate news interest," "a subject of general interest and of value and concern to the public" at the time of publication, and that it was "published in good faith without any malice whatsoever...." A motion to dismiss the complaint for substantially these reasons was made at the close of the case and was denied by the trial judge on the ground that the proofs presented a jury question as to the truth of the article.

The jury awarded appellee $50,000 compensatory and $25,000 punitive damages. On appeal the Appellate Division of the Supreme Court ordered a new trial as to damages but sustained the jury verdict of liability. The court said as to liability:

> Although the play was fictionalized, *Life's* article portrayed it as a re-enactment of the Hills' experience. It is an inescapable conclusion that this was done to advertise and attract further attention to the play, and to increase present and future magazine circulation as well. It is evident that the article cannot be characterized as a mere dissemination of news, nor even an effort to supply legitimate newsworthy information in which the public had, or might have a proper interest.

At the new trial on damages, a jury was waived and the court awarded $30,000 compensatory damages without punitive damages.

The New York Court of Appeals affirmed the Appellate Division "on the majority and concurring opinions at the Appellate Division," two judges dissenting. We noted probable jurisdiction of the appeal to consider the important constitutional questions of freedom of speech and press involved. After argument last Term, the case was restored to the docket for reargument, We reverse and remand the case to the Court of Appeals for further proceedings not inconsistent with this opinion....

Although "Right of Privacy" is the caption of §§ 50–51, the term nowhere appears in the text of the statute itself. The text of the statute appears to proscribe only ... the appropriation and use in advertising or to promote the sale of goods, of another's name, portrait or picture without his consent. An application of that limited scope would present different questions of violation of the constitutional protections for speech and press.

The New York courts have, however, construed the statute to operate much more broadly. In *Spahn* the Court of Appeals stated that "Over the years since the statute's enactment in 1903, its social desirability and remedial nature have led to its being given a liberal construction consonant with its over-all purpose...." Specifically, it has been held in some circumstances to authorize a remedy against the press and other communications media which publish the names, pictures, or portraits of people without their consent. Reflecting the fact, however, that such applications may raise serious questions of conflict with the constitutional protections for speech and press, decisions under the statute have tended to limit the statute's application. "Ever mindful that the written word or picture is involved, courts have engrafted exceptions and restrictions onto the statute to avoid any conflict with the free dissemination of thoughts, ideas, newsworthy events, and matters of public interest."

In the light of questions that counsel were asked to argue on reargument, it is particularly relevant that the Court of Appeals made crystal clear in the *Spahn* opinion that truth is a complete defense in actions under the statute based upon reports of newsworthy people or events. The opinion states: "The factual reporting of newsworthy persons and events is in the public interest and is protected." Constitutional questions which might arise if truth were not a defense are therefore of no concern....

We find applicable here the standard of knowing or reckless falsehood, not through blind application of *New York Times Co.* v. *Sullivan*, relating solely to libel actions by public officials, but only upon consideration of the factors which arise in the particular context of the application of the New York statute in cases involving private individuals. This is neither a libel action by a private individual nor a statutory action by a public official. Therefore, although the First Amendment principles pronounced in *New York Times* guide our conclusion, we reach that conclusion only by applying these principles in this discrete context....

II. Turning to the facts of the present case, the proofs reasonably would support either a jury finding of innocent or merely negligent misstatement by Life, or a finding that Life portrayed the play as a re-enactment of the Hill family's experience reckless of the truth or with actual knowledge that the portrayal was false. The relevant testimony is as follows:

Joseph Hayes, author of the book, also wrote the play. The story theme was inspired by the desire to write about "true crime" and for years before writing the book, he collected newspaper clippings of stories of hostage incidents. His story was not shaped by any single incident, but by several, including incidents which occurred in California, New York, and Detroit. He said that he did not consciously portray any member of the Hill family, or the Hill family's experience, although admitting that "in a very direct way" the Hill experience "triggered" the writing of the book and the play.

The Life article was prepared at the direction and under the supervision of its entertainment editor, Prideaux. He learned of the production of the play from a news story. The play's director, Robert Montgomery, later suggested to him that its interesting stage setting would make the play a worthwhile subject for an article in Life. At about the same time, Prideaux ran into a friend of author Hayes, a free-lance photographer, who told Prideaux in casual conversation that the play had a "substantial connection with a true-life incident of a family being held by escaped convicts near Philadelphia." As the play was trying out in Philadelphia, Prideaux decided to contact the author. Hayes confirmed that an incident somewhat similar to the play had occurred in Philadelphia, and agreed with Prideaux to find out whether the former Hill residence would be available for the shooting of pictures for a Life article. Prideaux then met with Hayes in Philadelphia where he saw the play and drove with Hayes to the former Hill residence to test its suitability for a picture story. Neither then nor thereafter did Prideaux question Hayes about the extent to which the play was based on the Hill incident. "A specific question of that nature was never asked, but a discussion of the play itself, what the play was about, in the light of my own knowledge of what the true incident was about, confirmed in my mind beyond any doubt that there was a relationship, and Mr. Hayes' presence at this whole negotiation was tacit proof of that."

Prideaux sent photographers to the Hill residence for location photographs of scenes of the play enacted in the home, and proceeded to construct the text of the article. In his "story file" were several news clippings about the Hill incident which revealed its nonviolent character, and a New York Times article by Hayes in which he stated that the play "was based on various news stories," mentioning incidents in New York, California, Detroit and Philadelphia.

Prideaux's first draft made no mention of the Hill name except for the caption of one of the photographs. The text related that a true story of a suburban Philadelphia family had "sparked off" Hayes to write the novel, that the play was a "somewhat fictionalized" account of the family's heroism in time of crisis. Prideaux's research assistant, whose task it was to check the draft for accuracy, put a question mark over the words "somewhat fictionalized." Prideaux testified that the question mark "must have been" brought to his attention, although he did not recollect having seen it. The draft was also brought before the copy editor, who, in the presence of Prideaux, made several changes in emphasis and substance. The first sentence was changed to focus on the Hill incident, using the family's name; the novel was said to have been "inspired" by that incident, and the play was referred to as a "re-enactment." The words "somewhat fictionalized" were deleted.

Prideaux labeled as "emphatically untrue" defense counsel's suggestion during redirect examination that from the beginning he knew that the play had no relationship to the Hill incident apart from being a hostage incident. Prideaux admitted that he knew the play was "between a little bit and moderately fictionalized," but stated that he thought beyond doubt that the important quality, the "heart and soul" of the play, was the Hill incident.

The jury might reasonably conclude from this evidence—particularly that the New York Times article was in the story file, that the copy editor deleted "somewhat fictionalized" after the research assistant questioned its accuracy, and that Prideaux admitted that he knew the play was "between a little bit and moderately fictionalized"—that Life knew the falsity of, or was reckless of the truth in, stating in the article that "the story re-enacted" the Hill family's experience. On the other hand, the jury might reasonably predicate a finding of innocent or only negligent misstatement on the testimony that a statement was made to Prideaux by the free-lance photographer that linked the play to an incident in

Philadelphia, that the author Hayes cooperated in arranging for the availability of the former Hill home, and that Prideaux thought beyond doubt that the "heart and soul" of the play was the Hill incident.

We do not think, however, that the instructions confined the jury to a verdict of liability based on a finding that the statements in the article were made with knowledge of their falsity or in reckless disregard of the truth. The jury was instructed that liability could not be found under §§ 50–51 "merely because of some incidental mistake of fact, or some incidental incorrect statement," and that a verdict of liability could rest only on findings that (1) Life published the article, "not to disseminate news, but was using plaintiffs' names, in connection with a fictionalized episode as to plaintiffs' relationship to The Desperate Hours"; the Court variously restated this "fictionalization" requirement in terms such as whether appellant "altered or changed the true facts concerning plaintiffs' relationship to The Desperate Hours, so that the article, as published, constituted substantially fiction or a fictionalized version...," whether the article constituted "fiction," or was "fictionalized"; and that (2) the article was published to advertise the play or "for trade purposes." This latter purpose was variously defined as one "to amuse, thrill, astonish or move the reading public so as to increase the circulation of the magazine or for some other material benefit," "to increase circulation or enhance the standing of the magazine with its readers," and "for the publisher's profits through increased circulation, induced by exploitation of the plaintiffs."

The court also instructed the jury that an award of punitive damages was justified if the jury found that the appellant falsely connected appellee to the play "knowingly or through failure to make a reasonable investigation," adding "You do not need to find that there was any actual ill will or personal malice toward the plaintiffs if you find a reckless or wanton disregard of the plaintiffs' rights."

Appellee argues that the instructions to determine whether Life "altered or changed" the true facts, and whether, apart from incidental errors, the article was a "substantial fiction" or a "fictionalized version" were tantamount to instructions that the jury must find that Life knowingly falsified the facts. We do not think that the instructions bear that interpretation, particularly in light of the marked contrast in the instructions on compensatory and punitive damages. The element of "knowingly" is mentioned only in the instruction that punitive damages must be supported by a finding that Life falsely connected the Hill family with the play "knowingly or through failure to make a reasonable investigation."

Moreover, even as to punitive damages, the instruction that such damages were justified on the basis of "failure to make a reasonable investigation" is an instruction that proof of negligent misstatement is enough, and we have rejected the test of negligent misstatement as inadequate. Next, the trial judge plainly did not regard his instructions as limiting the jury to a verdict of liability based on a finding of knowing or reckless falsity; he denied appellant's motion to dismiss after the close of the evidence because he perceived that it was for the jury to find "whether the Life article was true or whether an inference could be obtained from reading it that it was not true." This implies a view that "fictionalization" was synonymous with "falsity" without regard to knowledge or even negligence, except for the purpose of an award of punitive damages. Finally, nothing in the New York cases decided at the time of trial limited liability to cases of knowing or reckless falsity and *Spahn*, decided since, has left the question in doubt.

The requirement that the jury also find that the article was published "for trade purposes," as defined in the charge, cannot save the charge from constitutional infirmity.

"That books, newspapers, and magazines are published and sold for profit does not prevent them from being a form of expression whose liberty is safeguarded by the First Amendment." ...

The judgment of the Court of Appeals is set aside and the case is remanded for further proceedings not inconsistent with this opinion.

Leopold v. Levin
259 N.E.2d 250 (Ill. 1970)

Nathan F. Leopold, Jr., the plaintiff, brought an action in the circuit court of Cook County, which was in the nature of a suit alleging a violation of the right of privacy. The defendants included: the author, publishers and several local distributors of a novel and a play, entitled "Compulsion," and the producer, distributor and Chicago area exhibitors of a related motion picture of the same name. The trial court granted the plaintiff's motion for a summary judgment on the question of liability and reserved the issue as to the amount of damages. The defendants appealed to this court but on the plaintiff's motion the appeal was dismissed on the ground that the judgment was interlocutory and, hence, unappealable. When remanded, the case was assigned to a different judge of the circuit court for pretrial consideration on the question of damages. The defendants at that point contested the judgment which had been entered by the predecessor judge. After extended proceedings the succeeding judge vacated the summary judgment in favor of the plaintiff and granted the motions of the defendants for summary judgment and judgment on the pleadings. A direct appeal has been taken by the plaintiff to this court, as a constitutional question is involved.

In 1924, Richard Loeb, who is deceased, and Nathan F. Leopold, Jr., the plaintiff, pleaded guilty to the murder and kidnapping for ransom of a 14-year-old boy, Bobby Franks. Following a presentence proceeding, each was given consecutive prison sentences of life and 99 years. The luridness of the crime, the background of the defendants, their representation by the most prominent criminal advocate of the day, the "trial," and its denouement attracted international notoriety. Public interest in the crime and its principals did not wane with the passage of time and the case became an historical *cause celebre*.

The novel "Compulsion" was first published in hardcover in October 1956. The author was the defendant Meyer Levin, who had been a fellow student of Loeb and Leopold and who had served as a reporter for a Chicago newspaper at the time of the crime. All concerned in this appeal agree that the basic framework of the novel, as well as of the subsequently produced movie, was factually provided by the kidnapping and murder of Bobby Franks, the events leading to the apprehension of Leopold and Loeb, and their prosecution. However, as the author himself, in the foreword of the book, wrote: "Though the action is taken from reality, it must be recognized that thoughts and emotions described in the characters come from within the author, as he imagines them to belong to the personages in the case he has chosen." And, "I follow known events. Some scenes are, however, total interpolations, and some of my personages have no correspondence to persons in the case in question. This will be recognized as the method of the historical novel. I suppose *Compulsion* may be called a contemporary historical novel or a documentary novel, as distinguished from a *roman a clef*. [That is, a novel drawing upon actual occurrences or real persons under the guise of fiction.]"

Neither the name of Loeb or Leopold appear in the foreword, and fictitious names are used in the novel itself for all persons who may have been involved in the case. However, the names of Loeb and the plaintiff were used in advertising the novel. Illustrative of this, on the paper jacket to the hardcover edition it was said: "This book is a novel suggested by what is possibly the most famous and certainly one of the most shocking crimes ever committed in America—the Leopold-Loeb murder case." On the page preceding the title page of the paperback edition of "Compulsion," which was first published in 1958, the following appeared: "In his novel based upon the Leopold-Loeb case, Meyer Levin seeks to discover the psychological motivation behind this monstrous deed." The back cover of the paperback noted that "'Compulsion' is a spellbinding fictionalized account of one of the most famous and shocking crimes of our age—the Leopold-Loeb murder case."

The case had been of interest to other authors. For example, in 1957, a novel, "Nothing But The Night," by James Yaffe was published. It bore a fictionalized resemblance to the Leopold-Loeb case, but had a different locale and no reference was apparently made in the advertising of it to the actual case. In the same year a factual account of the life and crimes of Leopold and Loeb by Maureen McKernan, entitled, "The Amazing Crime and Trial of Leopold and Loeb" was published and widely advertised. In 1957, too, an account of the kidnapping, murder and prosecution written by the plaintiff for compensation appeared in serialized form for several weeks in a Chicago newspaper. Story captions included: "Leopold Tells Own Story—How It Felt To Be A Killer"; "Leopold Arrested; Time For Him To Use Alibi"; "Darrow Makes Masterful Plea For Understanding." He was granted parole in 1958 and that year his autobiographical story, "Life Plus 99 Years," which included a description of his detection and prosecution and their personal consequences, was published. It was given extensive publicity.

The motion picture "Compulsion" was released in April, 1959. Several major characters in the film, including the one corresponding to the appellant, were styled to resemble actual persons in the case. Fictitious names were used, though, and no photographs of the appellant or any other person connected with the case appeared in the movie or in any material used to promote the film. The promotional material did refer to the crime. In a brochure prepared for movie exhibitors, entitled "Vital Statistics," 20th Century Fox Film Corporation, a defendant, outlined the likenesses and differences between the movie and the actual events, and declared: "It should be made clear emphatically that 'Compulsion' is not an effort to reproduce the crime of Leopold and Loeb, nor their trial. The screenplay was taken from a recognized work of fiction 'suggested' by the Leopold-Loeb case, but neither the author of the book nor the producer of the film has attempted anything but to tell a dramatic story.... The picture is in no way a documentary and its makers have attempted only to translate the book into terms of good dramaturgy." One motion picture exhibitor, the Woods Theatre in Chicago, owned by a defendant here, in advertising the movie used a photographic enlargement of the back cover of the paperback book edition of "Compulsion" in which the plaintiff's name was used, as has been described. It displayed also a blow-up or enlargement of portions of reviews given the movie in which the plaintiff's name had been mentioned. His name also was introduced during personal, radio and television interviews in various cities by certain of the defendants in the course of their promotion of the motion picture.

The plaintiff acknowledges that a documentary account of the Leopold-Loeb case would be a constitutionally protected expression, since the subject events are matters of public record. Also constitutionally protected, the plaintiff continues, would be a completely fictional work inspired by the case if matters such as the locale would be changed and if there would be no promotional identification with the plaintiff. Leopold's claim is that the constitutional assurances of free speech and press do not permit an invasion of his privacy through the exploitation of his name, likeness and personality for commercial gain in "knowingly fictionalized accounts" of his private life and through the appropriation of his name and likeness in the advertising materials. Denying him redress would deprive him, he argues, of his right to pursue and obtain happiness, guaranteed by section 1 of article II of the constitution of Illinois.

While the question of a right of privacy has not until now been considered by this court, such a right has been recognized in other courts of this State. It was first acknowledged at the appellate level in the case of *Eick v. Perk Dog Food Co.* (1952), 347 Ill. App. 293, and there has been implicit recognition of it by the legislature through its enactment of a statute of limitations for suits complaining of violations of privacy. A right of privacy has been recognized in more than 30 States in addition to the District of Columbia.

The dimensions of the right in Illinois have thus far been conservatively interpreted under the appellate courts' decisions. In *Eick*, where the interest in privacy was first admitted, a blind girl's photograph was used without her consent in promoting the sale of dog food. The court held that the allegation of these facts stated a good cause of action for violation of the right of privacy. The court observed, though, that the right of privacy is a limited one in areas of legitimate public interest, as where there is a legitimate news interest in one's photograph or likeness as a public figure. Later, in *Bradley v. Cowles Magazines Inc.*(1960), 26 Ill. App. 2d 331, a case holding that a mother had no cognizable claim that her right of privacy had been violated by the publisher of *Look* magazine when it publicized the murder of her son, the court stated that *Eick*, itself, was limited to its conclusion — "that a private person would be protected against the use of his portrait for commercial advertising purposes." It was observed in *Bradley* too, that the purpose underlying the right of privacy action was "To find an area within which the citizen must be left alone" and that, viewing the possible development of the right, "It is important ... that in defining the limits of this right, courts proceed with caution." There have been no appellate court cases subsequent to *Bradley*, which have admitted a broader right than was announced in *Eick*.

We agree that there should be recognition of a right of privacy, a right many years ago described in a limited fashion by Judge Cooley with utter simplicity as the right "to be let alone." Privacy is one of the sensitive and necessary human values and undeniably there are circumstances under which it should enjoy the protection of law. However, we must hold here that the plaintiff did not have a legally protected right of privacy. Considerations which in our judgment require this conclusion include: the liberty of expression constitutionally assured in a matter of public interest, as the one here; the enduring public attention to the plaintiff's crime and prosecution, which remain an American *cause celebre*; and the plaintiff's consequent and continuing status as a public figure....

In *Time, Inc.* v. *Hill*, the Supreme Court for the first time had occasion to consider directly the effect of the constitutional guarantees for speech and press upon the rights of privacy. There, as will be seen, the right of privacy when involved with the publication of a matter of public interest was viewed narrowly and cautiously by the court. That decisional attitude toward publication is consistent with other first amendment holdings of the court in recent years, especially in the areas of libel and obscenity, where the announced objective was to insure "uninhibited, robust and wide-open" discussion of legitimate public issues or to protect published materials unless they are "utterly without redeeming social value."

It is of importance here, too, that the plaintiff became and remained a public figure because of his criminal conduct in 1924. No right of privacy attached to matters associated with his participation in that completely publicized crime. The circumstances of the crime and the prosecution etched a deep public impression which the passing of time did not extinguish. A strong curiosity and social and news interest in the crime, the prosecution, and Leopold remained. It is of some relevance, too, in this consideration, that the plaintiff himself certainly did not appear to seek retirement from public attention. The publication of the autobiographical story and other writings and his providing interviews unquestionably contributed to the continuing public interest in him and the crime. Having encouraged public attention "'he cannot at his whim withdraw the events of his life from public scrutiny.'"

A carefully narrowed argument of the plaintiff appears to be that the defendants through "knowingly fictionalized accounts" caused the public to identify the plaintiff with inventions or fictionalized episodes in the book and motion picture which were so offensive and unwarranted as to "outrage the community's notions of decency." However, the core of the novel and film and their dominating subjects were a part of the plaintiff's life which he had caused to be placed in public view. The novel and film were derived from the notorious crime, a matter of public record and interest, in which the plaintiff had been a central figure. Further, as the trial court appeared to do, we consider that the fictionalized aspects of the book and motion picture were reasonably comparable to, or conceivable from facts of record from which they were drawn, or minor in offensiveness when viewed in the light of such facts.

Sidis, upon which the plaintiff bottomed this argument of outraging "the community's notions of decency," involved the publishing of a "profile" of a one-time prodigy. A magazine article disclosed his undistinguished achievement as an adult and described some of his eccentricities. The court held the publication proper but in a dictum observed: "Revelations may be so intimate and so unwarranted in view of the victim's position as to outrage the community's notions of decency." Even if one were to accept the validity of the dictum for the purpose of discussing it, the genesis of the fictionalized episodes in "Compulsion," as we have observed, can be traced in a substantial way to the exposed conduct of Leopold. Argument that the community's notions of decency were outraged here must be regarded as fanciful.

The contention that a right of privacy was violated by an appropriation, without consent, of the plaintiff's name and likeness for the commercial gain of the defendants through their advertisements must also fail. The circumstances here obviously are distinguishable from those in cases such as *Eick* v. *Perk Dog Food Co.*, which the plaintiff cites. There, as has been noted, a likeness, *i.e.*, a photograph of a girl who was clearly not a public figure, was "appropriated" to promote a purely commercial product. Unlike here, no question of freedom of expression was presented. The reference to the plaintiff in the advertising material concerned the notorious crime to which he had pleaded guilty. His participation was a matter of public and, even, of historical record. That conduct was without benefit of privacy.

We consider that *Time, Inc. v. Hill,* 385 U.S. 374, 17 L. Ed. 2d 456, to which reference has been made, does not support the plaintiff's positions. *Hill* and his family had been held in their home as hostages for 19 hours by escaped convicts. Their captors did not mistreat them in any way. After the incident Hill moved to another State and discouraged all attempts to keep his family in public view. A book and later a play partly drawn, it would appear, from the incident were published and *Life* magazine carried an article about the play. In the play the author had some members of the captive family subjected to violence and a daughter to verbal abuse. *Life's* article allegedly gave the false impression that the play did reflect what had happened to the Hill family. The Supreme Court held that the constitutional protections of free speech and press prevented Hill's recovering under the New York privacy statute because of this false report of a matter of public interest, unless upon remand of the case there was a showing that the magazine had published the report with knowledge of its falsity or in reckless disregard of the truth. It is clear that *Time, Inc.* involved a situation essentially dissimilar from the one here. The case involved what was claimed to be a false but purportedly factual account of the Hill incident. Here, the motion picture, play and novel, while "suggested" by the crime of the plaintiff, were evidently fictional and dramatized materials and they were not represented to be otherwise. They were substantially creative works of fiction and would not be subject to the "knowing or reckless falsity" or actual malice standards discussed in *Time, Inc.* v. *Hill*, where the court considered an untrue but supposedly factual magazine account ...

We conclude that the judgment of the circuit court of Cook County which vacated the summary judgment for the plaintiff on the issue of liability and granted summary judgment and judgment on the pleadings in favor of the defendants was proper. Accordingly, the judgment is affirmed.

Judgment affirmed.

Polydoros v. Twentieth Century Fox Film Corp.

67 Cal. App. 4th 318 (Ct. App. 2d 1997)

In 1993, respondents released The Sandlot, a comedic coming-of-age story set in the San Fernando Valley in the 1960s. The film's protagonists are a motley group of boys on a sandlot baseball team who, in the course of one summer, overcome various adversaries, including a disdainful, well-funded opposing team and a gigantic, ferocious dog that has taken possession of the team's baseballs and secreted them in a neighboring yard. One of the boys on the sandlot team is a character named Michael Palledorous, nicknamed "Squints." The Palledorous character is one of the team's leaders, and spearheads the team's valiant efforts to reclaim a baseball autographed by Babe Ruth from the slavering canine next door.

Appellant Michael Polydoros grew up in a setting similar to that described in the film. Appellant was a schoolmate of respondent David Mickey Evans. Evans wrote and directed The Sandlot. A photograph of appellant dating from the 1960s is similar to a photograph of the Palledorous character in the movie, right down to appellant's eyeglasses and the color and design of his shirt. Appellant played baseball with friends on a sandlot when he was a child, swam in a community pool like the one shown in the movie, and was somewhat obstreperous, like the "Squints" character. Other than the similarity in names and attire, the enjoyment of baseball and swimming, and the brash nature of the "Squints" character, appellant cannot point to any other aspects in which the film accurately depicts his life. Appellant concedes that the work is fiction. He also concedes that he has not been financially damaged by the motion picture.

Piqued by the similarities in name and by the physical likeness of the "Squints" character to himself as a child, appellant filed suit in March of 1994. The operative pleading asserts causes of action for commercial appropriation of identity, invasion of privacy, negligence and defamation. Appellant alleges that the nickname "Squints" used in the film "is a blatantly derogatory moniker derived from the thick glasses the character wears throughout the film" and that people began teasing appellant by calling him "Squints." Appellant felt "embarrassed and humiliated" by the nickname. To make matters worse, in appellant's view, respondents used the "Squints" Palledorous character as their principal advertising image for the film....

Invasion of privacy claims have been rejected by the courts when there is merely alleged to be some resemblance between an actual person and a character in a work of fiction. In *Aguilar*, for example, the plaintiff alleged that the movie Zoot Suit (Universal Pictures 1981) invaded her privacy by exposing "unsavory incidents" from her adolescence through the use of a character who shared plaintiff's surname. The court observed that the plaintiff, a grown woman, was not the 13-year-old person shown in the movie, although plaintiff was 13 at the time of the historical incident recreated in the movie. Because there was no consonance between the plaintiff's present age and the movie character's age or physical appearance, and because plaintiff's actual experiences diverged in many respects from those of the character who shared her name, no trier of fact could reasonably draw a connection between the two.

We find particularly compelling the reasoning in the New York case of *People v. Charles Scribner's Sons*, 205 Misc. 818 [130 N.Y.S.2d 514] (1954), which involved the interpretation of a commercial appropriation of likeness statute. The complainant in that case, Joseph A. Maggio, served in the United States Army in Hawaii in the early 1940s in the same Army company as James Jones. Jones thereafter authored a successful book entitled, From Here to Eternity (1951) which was made into a motion picture. The book tells a story about Army personnel stationed in Hawaii in the early 1940s. One of the characters portrayed in the book and film is called "Angelo Maggio" or "Maggio." Despite the obvious similarities in name and his former contact with the author, Maggio did not claim that the story portrayed acts performed by him: "Except for the alleged identity of name, none of the things which the character 'Angelo Maggio' does in the book, nor any of the details of the background and life of 'Angelo Maggio' as set forth in the book, are claimed by the complainant to be a portrayal of him or of his life and do not in any wise point to or identify him as the person intended or referred to." As the court noted, if the author had not chosen the name "Maggio" for his fictional character, "the complainant could not by any stretch of the imagination have implied any identity of the character with himself."

The court rejected the misappropriation of name charge made against the book publisher and the motion picture company. It wrote,

> It is generally understood that novels are written out of the background and experiences of the novelist. The characters portrayed are fictional, but very often they grow out of real persons the author has met or observed. This is so also with respect to the places which are the setting of the novel. The end result may be so fictional as to seem wholly imaginary, but the acorn of fact is usually the progenitor of the oak, which when fully grown no longer has any resemblance to the acorn. In order to disguise the acorn and to preserve the fiction, the novelist disguises the names of the actual persons who inspired the characters in his book. Since a novel is not biography, the details of the character's life and deeds usually have, beyond possible faint outlines, no resemblance to the life and deeds of the actual person known to the author. Thus, the public has come to accept novels as pure fiction and does not attribute their characters to real life.

For the reasons cited in *Aguilar* and *Maggio*, the cases above, appellant cannot state a claim that respondents invaded his privacy by appropriating his name or likeness for commercial purposes. First, there was a marked difference in age and appearance between our appellant, the 40-year-old Michael Polydoros, and the 10-year-old character of Squints Palledorous. No person seeing this film could confuse the two. Second, the rudimentary similarities in locale and boyhood activities do not make The Sandlot a film about appellant's life. This is a universal theme and a concededly fictional film. The faint outlines appellant has seized upon do not transform the fiction into fact.

Film is a "significant medium for the communication of ideas" and, whether exhibited in theaters or on television, is protected by constitutional guarantees of free expression. Popular entertainment is entitled to the same constitutional protection as the exposition of political ideas: "It is clear that works of fiction are constitutionally protected in the same manner as political treatises and topical news stories."

The plaintiff in *Guglielmi* was the nephew of deceased silent picture star Rudolph Valentino and had a proprietary interest in the commercial use of Valentino's name and likeness. He sued the defendants after they exhibited a film purporting to recreate a portion of the life of Valentino using Valentino's name, likeness and personality. Plaintiff alleged that the film did not truthfully portray Valentino's life and that Valentino's name and likeness were used to sell or commercially exploit the film for defendants' profit.

At the heart of *Guglielmi* was the fictional nature of the film exhibited by the defendants. Four justices of the Supreme Court agreed that plaintiff was protected by the common law right of publicity. Nevertheless, the context and nature of the defendants' use of Valentino's name and likeness in a *fictional* work of art, even if created *for financial gain*, was protected by the constitutional right to free expression, the justices concluded. They observed, "The First Amendment is not limited to those who publish without charge. Whether the activity involves newspaper publication or motion picture production, it does not lose its constitutional protection because it is undertaken for profit. The fact that respondents sought to profit from the production and exhibition of a film utilizing Valentino's name and likeness is not constitutionally significant."

Guglielmi unequivocally prevents appellant from proceeding on his claim for commercial appropriation of identity. There is no question that The Sandlot is a fanciful work of fiction and imagination. In the movie, the dog next door to the sandlot assumes the proportions of a grizzly bear (having been magnified by the boys' fear); baseball hero Babe Ruth appears and offers advice (notwithstanding Ruth's death some 20 years before the movie takes place); the dog's owner just happens to be a former teammate of Babe Ruth; the "Squints" character fakes his own drowning death in order to sneak a kiss from the pretty female lifeguard, and so on. Appellant does not attempt to suggest that any of this is true or actually happened to him. Because the film is obvious fantasy, appellant could not reasonably suffer injury to his feelings or his peace of mind. This film is not a portrait of appellant's life and reveals no private facts about appellant: His name and former physical appearance are not private facts.

Appellant is especially vexed because respondents used photographs of "his" character in particular to advertise and promote public viewing of The Sandlot. This issue is addressed in *Guglielmi*. A filmmaker's use of photographs of an actor resembling an actual personage to promote a fictional work is "merely an adjunct to the exhibition of the film." "Having established that any interest in financial gain in producing the film did not affect the constitutional stature of respondents' undertaking, it is of no moment that the advertisements may have increased the profitability of the film. It would be illogical to allow respondents to exhibit the film but effectively preclude any advance discussion or promotion of their lawful enterprise. Since the use of Valentino's name and likeness in the film was not an actionable infringement of Valentino's right of publicity, the use of his identity in advertisements for the film is similarly not actionable."

In sum, appellant is not entitled to recover under a commercial appropriation of name or likeness theory merely because respondents used a name that sounds like appellant's name or employed an actor who resembles appellant at the age of 10. Because respondents were creating a fictionalized artistic work, their endeavor is constitutionally protected. This right was not diminished when respondents advertised then sold their work as mass public entertainment. . . .

The judgment is affirmed.

Notes and Questions

a. One of the preliminary questions that must be asked in a defamation or invasion of privacy case is whether the plaintiff was in fact the party depicted, or put another way, whether a reasonable person viewing the work would understand the character depicted was the plaintiff. In *Aguilar v. Universal City Studios, Inc.*, 174 Cal. App. 3d 384, 388 (1985), the California Court of Appeals explained this preliminary step.

> Plaintiff, Bertha Aguilar, claims she is the character "Bertha" and that she is falsely portrayed in the film ['Zoot Suit'] as "a fornicating woman of loose morals." The motion picture "Zoot Suit" is a work of fiction based on the sensational 1942 Sleepy Lagoon murder case and the ensuing "zoot suit" riots. . . . The screen play was adapted by Luis Valdez from his play of the same name. . . . The gist of Ms. Aguilar's libel complaint is that the character "Bertha" is depicted as unchaste. This allegation is based on a single reference to "Bertha" which implies she had had sexual relations with another character in the back seat of a car. Ms. Aguilar also contends the film invaded her privacy by exposing "unsavory incidents" from her past. . . .

> In order to succeed on any of her causes of action, Ms. Aguilar must first establish she is portrayed in the film "Zoot Suit." The test is whether a reasonable person, viewing the motion picture, would understand the character "Bertha" was, in actual fact, Bertha Aguilar conducting herself as described. . . .

> In support of her argument summary judgment was improper Ms. Aguilar makes three points relating to the issue of identity. The film uses the name "Bertha"; Ms. Aguilar was a participant in the Sleepy Lagoon incident; and other persons have concluded she is the character "Bertha." [T]his evidence is insufficient to raise a triable issue as to whether Ms. Aguilar is portrayed in the film. . . .

> [A]s a matter of law, mere similarity or even identity of names is insufficient to establish a work of fiction is of and concerning a real person. . . .

> There Is No Similarity Between Ms. Aguilar and "Bertha" in Terms of Age or Physical Appearance. . . . Ms. Aguilar was 13 years of age at the time of the Sleepy Lagoon incident. "Bertha" is not a 13 year-old-girl. Even Ms. Aguilar admits she is "much older than 13." She also admits at the time of the Sleepy Lagoon incident she did not look or dress like "Bertha." . . .

> Ms. Aguilar's Involvement in the Sleepy Lagoon Incident Bears No Resemblance to the Involvement of "Bertha." Close parallels between real and fictional events may establish a reasonable belief in identity despite the author's efforts to hide the real person through alteration of name or physical appearance. . . .

Finally, there is the uncontradicted testimony of the author, Luis Valdez, he had never heard of Ms. Aguilar until after the play was written. The similarity in names appears to have been purely coincidental....

b. The four distinct privacy torts give rise to a variety of claims. For a discussion on the limited right to be free from prying videotape cameras, see *Sanders v. American Broadcasting Companies*, 20 Cal. 4th 907, 85 Cal. Rptr. 2d 909, 978 P.2d 67 (1999). A key issue in these cases is the newsworthiness of the event being publicly broadcast or presented. The offshoot of privacy torts that has evolved into the right of publicity is treated separately in Chapter V, *supra*.

c. Notwithstanding the broad First Amendment protection afforded to novelizations and dramatizations, what steps should be taken by authors, producers, and distributors of these works? How would you recommend a client proceed to develop a fictionalized version of a true story?

d. The courts continue to struggle with the application of the *N.Y. Times v. Sullivan* actual malice standard to intentionally fictionalized material. It is axiomatic that intentionally fictionalized material is knowingly false. If that intentional fictionalization is defamatory about a person, it will be actionable. As *Time v. Hill* and other cases demonstrate, however, many intentional falsehoods are not defamatory, but remain objectionable. To what extent does *N.Y. Times v. Sullivan* continue to shield authors, producers, and distributors from "false light invasion of privacy" when the material is knowingly false? Can Michael Polydoros' claims be reconciled with *Time v. Hill*, or is there a broader shield provided by the First Amendment than that articulated in *Time v. Hill* and *N.Y. Times v. Sullivan*?

e. False light invasion of privacy is often subsumed by defamation analysis. In some states, however, the cause of action remains discrete. With local news stations seeking to make stories more newsworthy than the facts provide, the lead-ins to those stories may be grounds for liability even though the story is more factually accurate. See *Grogan v. KOKH, LLC*, 256 P.3d 1021, 1029 (Okla. App. Div. 2 2011), where a misunderstanding between students and a coach escalated to a lead-in on local television tying the story to terrorism. Such a stretch was capable of creating a false light invasion of privacy.

f. Notwithstanding constitutional protection, most publishers and producers go to extensive efforts to eliminate risk of litigation by checking names and locations for any possible connections with real persons and by purchasing the right to portray persons involved in the story. While the case law suggests that these portrayal agreements are not necessary, prudence and risk management suggest that motion picture companies, in particular, are often better served by acquiring the releases of those portrayed rather than to rely solely on the constitutional privilege of portraying the events.

Problem VI-C

Bryce stops by your office. (By now you know the problem is worse if Bryce stops in rather than merely calling.) Bryce acknowledges that the idea for *Juliet Prescott*, the Romeo & Juliet concept project, came to Bryce after learning that a sixteen-year-old classmate, Julie, had become pregnant by a boy of another race. Only a few students knew of Julie's pregnancy; Bryce only found out accidentally while waiting at the doctor's office. Bryce does not want to cancel or rewrite the play but is concerned about being liable to Julie. Please advise Bryce regarding the legal implications of the play for Julie and any legal recourse she may have.

D. Bibliography and Links

Josh Blackman, *Omniveillance, Google, Privacy in Public, and the Right to Your Digital Identity: A Tort for Recording and Disseminating an Individual's Image Over the Internet*, 49 Santa Clara L. Rev. 313 (2009).

David A. Elder, *Truth, Accuracy and Neutral Reportage: Beheading the Media Jabberwock's Attempts to Circumvent New York Times v. Sullivan*, 9 Vand. J. Ent. & Tech. L. 551 (2007).

Lawrence M. Friedman, *The One-Way Mirror: Law, Privacy, and the Media*, 82 Wash. U. L.Q. 319 (2004).

Jon M. Garon, *Tidying up the Internet: Take Down of Unauthorized Content under Copyright, Trademark and Defamation Law*, 41 Capital U. L. Rev. 513 (2013).

Jon M. Garon, *Star Wars: Film Permitting, Prior Restraint and Government's Role in the Entertainment Industry*, 17 Loyola Ent. L. J. 1 (1996).

Sonia K. Katyal, *Privacy vs. Piracy*, 9 Int'l J. Comm. L. & Pol'y 7 (2004/2005).

Joseph H. King, *Defamation Claims Based on Parody and Other Fanciful Communications Not Intended to Be Understood As Fact*, 2008 Utah L. Rev. 875 (2008).

David Kohler, *Forty Years after New York Times v. Sullivan: The Good, the Bad, and the Ugly*, 83 Or. L. Rev. 1203 (2004).

Laura E. Little, *Just A Joke: Defamatory Humor and Incongruity's Promise*, 21 S. Cal. Interdisc. L.J. 95 (2011).

William L. Prosser, *Privacy*, 48 Cal. L. Rev. 383 (1960) (articulating the four distinct branches of privacy).

George P. Smith, *The Extent of Protection of the Individual's Personality against Commercial Use: Toward a New Property Right*, 54 S.C.L. Rev. 1 (Fall 2002).

Samuel D. Warren & Louis D. Brandeis, *The Right to Privacy*, 4 Harv. L. Rev. 193 (1890) (the law review article which originated or discovered the right of privacy).

Websites

Federal Communications Commission, www.fcc.gov

Media Watch, www.mediawatch.com (a website dedicated to fighting censorship in the media, discusses current cases against the media)

Privacy Rights.Org, www.privacyrights.org

Chapter VII

Trademarks & Publicity

A. Trademarks

Introduction

Unlike copyright, which protects expression, and patent law, which generally protects inventions and improvements to existing inventions, trademarks are brand names and graphical designs which are applied to products or used in connection with services. A trademark includes any word, name, symbol, or device, or any combination, used, or intended to be used, in commerce to identify the source of the goods. Trademarks are brand names, logos or marks that allow the consumer to identify the source of goods or services and distinguish between competing brands. A service mark provides the same consumer information as to the source of services.

A person's name is not generally recognized as a federal trademark because more than one person often share the same name, but a name can become a trademark if it is associated with particular products or services.

In addition to the federal trademark system, states have statutory or common law trademarks. Common law rights arise from actual use of a mark. Generally, the first to use a mark in commerce has priority for use of that mark. For federal trademarks, an intent to use application may be filed up to six months prior to the actual use. Assuming the proper forms are filed, federal trademark protection may last indefinitely.

One of the most important aspects of trademark law in the entertainment industry flows from the protection afforded to the use of unregistered marks. Section 43(a) of the Lanham Act, the Federal Trademark Act, allows for federal actions involving unregistered marks. These claims for "false designation of origin" allow plaintiffs to object to the use of names, likenesses, unregistered trademarks, service marks, phrases, and artwork when the use creates a likelihood of confusion "as to the origin, sponsorship, or approval of his or her goods, services, or commercial activities by another person."

Such cases have included actions by Elvis Presley Enterprises for the unauthorized use of Elvis' name in aspects of a live stage show and in the bar, "The Velvet Elvis," *Estate of Elvis Presley v. Russen,* 513 F. Supp. 1339 (D.N.J. 1981) and *Elvis Presley Enters., Inc. v. Capece,* 141 F.3d 188, 193 (5th Cir. 1998); Woody Allen's objection to look-alikes in video store advertising, *Allen v. Nat'l Video, Inc.,* 610 F. Supp. 612, 624–25 (S.D.N.Y. 1985); George Wendt and John Ratzenberger allowed to go to trial on their complaint that animatronic characters in the *Cheers* bars created confusion as to the sponsorship of the bars by the actors, *Wendt v. Host Int'l, Inc.,* 125 F.3d 806, 812 (9th Cir. 1997); and basketball star Kareem Abdul Jabbar objecting to the use of his childhood name, Lew Alcindor, in a car commercial, *Abdul-Jabbar v. Gen. Motors Corp.*, 85 F.3d 407, 410 (9th Cir. 1996).

Other uses of the Lanham Act are not so successful. When a performer's distinctive name or likeness is used as part of the content for another party's project or to comment, criticize, or parody a work, then courts are likely to view the First Amendment interests of the speaker as more significant than the trademark interests of the performer. For example, Ginger Rogers' claim against the movie title *Ginger and Fred* did not create any actionable Lanham Act confusion. See *Rogers v. Grimaldi*, 875 F.2d 994 (2d Cir. N.Y. 1989). Similarly, parody is also sometimes a successful defense when the trademark is used in the context of another work. In *Cardtoons, L.C. v. Major League Baseball Players Ass'n*, 95 F.3d 959, 966 (10th Cir. 1996), parodies of the players overcame objections to the use of their valuable trademark images. In another situation, the Danish rock band, Aqua, produced the song *Barbie Girl* on the album Aquarium. Mattel objected to the use, but in a blistering opinion Judge Kozinski rejected each of Mattel's arguments as well as generally chided the Ninth Circuit for allowing trademark and publicity law to overexpand. See *Mattel, Inc. v. MCA Records*, 296 F.3d 894 (9th Cir. Cal. 2002) ("If this were a sci-fi melodrama, it might be called Speech-Zilla meets Trademark Kong."). See also *Wendt v. Host Int'l, Inc.*, 197 F.3d 1284 (9th Cir. Cal. 1999) (Kozinski, dissenting to denial of rehearing en banc) ("We pass up yet another opportunity to root out this weed. Instead, we feed it Miracle-Gro. I dissent.").

As can be seen below, many of the considerations involving trademark's relationship to copyright and First Amendment interests have only been addressed in the last few years. This will now be one of the most fertile areas of litigation and confusion for years to come.

Dastar Corp. v. Twentieth Century Fox Film Corp.
539 U.S. 23 (2003)

Justice Scalia delivered the opinion of the Court.

In this case, we are asked to decide whether § 43(a) of the Lanham Act, *15 U.S.C. § 1125(a)*, prevents the unaccredited copying of a work, and if so, whether a court may double a profit award under§ *1117(a)*, in order to deter future infringing conduct.

In 1948, three and a half years after the German surrender at Reims, General Dwight D. Eisenhower completed Crusade in Europe, his written account of the allied campaign in Europe during World War II. Doubleday published the book, registered it with the Copyright Office in 1948, and granted exclusive television rights to an affiliate of respondent Twentieth Century Fox Film Corporation (Fox). Fox, in turn, arranged for Time, Inc., to produce a television series, also called Crusade in Europe, based on the book, and Time assigned its copyright in the series to Fox. The television series, consisting of 26 episodes, was first broadcast in 1949. It combined a soundtrack based on a narration of the book with film footage from the United States Army, Navy, and Coast Guard, the British Ministry of Information and War Office, the National Film Board of Canada, and unidentified "Newsreel Pool Cameramen." In 1975, Doubleday renewed the copyright on the book as the "'proprietor of copyright in a work made for hire.'" Fox, however, did not renew the copyright on the Crusade television series, which expired in 1977, leaving the television series in the public domain.

In 1988, Fox reacquired the television rights in General Eisenhower's book, including the exclusive right to distribute the Crusade television series on video and to sub-license others to do so. Respondents SFM Entertainment and New Line Home Video, Inc., in turn, acquired from Fox the exclusive rights to distribute Crusade on video. SFM obtained the negatives of the original television series, restored them, and repackaged the series on videotape; New Line distributed the videotapes.

Enter petitioner Dastar. In 1995, Dastar decided to expand its product line from music compact discs to videos. Anticipating renewed interest in World War II on the 50th anniversary of the war's end, Dastar released a video set entitled World War II Campaigns in Europe. To make Campaigns, Dastar purchased eight beta cam tapes of the *original* version of the Crusade television series, which is in the public domain, copied them, and then edited the series. Dastar's Campaigns series is slightly more than half as long as the original Crusade television series. Dastar substituted a new opening sequence, credit page, and final closing for those of the Crusade television series; inserted new chapter-title sequences and narrated chapter introductions; moved the "recap" in the Crusade television series to the beginning and retitled it as a "preview"; and removed references to and images of the book. Dastar created new packaging for its Campaigns series and (as already noted) a new title.

Dastar manufactured and sold the Campaigns video set as its own product. The advertising states: "Produced and Distributed by: *Entertainment Distributing*" (which is owned by Dastar), and makes no reference to the Crusade television series. Similarly, the screen credits state "DASTAR CORP presents" and "an ENTERTAINMENT DISTRIBUTING Production," and list as executive producer, producer, and associate producer, employees of Dastar. The Campaigns videos themselves also make no reference to the Crusade television series, New Line's Crusade videotapes, or the book. Dastar sells its Campaigns videos to Sam's Club, Costco, Best Buy, and other retailers and mail-order companies for $25 per set, substantially less than New Line's video set.

In 1998, respondents Fox, SFM, and New Line brought this action alleging that Dastar's sale of its Campaigns video set infringes Doubleday's copyright in General Eisenhower's book and, thus, their exclusive television rights in the book. Respondents later amended their complaint to add claims that Dastar's sale of Campaigns "without proper credit" to the Crusade television series constitutes "reverse passing off"[1] in violation of §43(a) of the Lanham Act, and in violation of state unfair-competition law. On cross-motions for summary judgment, the District Court found for respondents on all three counts, treating its resolution of the Lanham Act claim as controlling on the state-law unfair-competition claim because "the ultimate test under both is whether the public is likely to be deceived or confused." The court awarded Dastar's profits to respondents and doubled them pursuant to §35 of the Lanham Act to deter future infringing conduct by petitioner.

The Court of Appeals for the Ninth Circuit affirmed the judgment for respondents on the Lanham Act claim, but reversed as to the copyright claim and remanded. (It said nothing with regard to the state-law claim.) With respect to the Lanham Act claim, the Court of Appeals reasoned that "Dastar copied substantially the entire *Crusade in Europe* series created by Twentieth Century Fox, labeled the resulting product with a different name and marketed it without attribution to Fox [,and] therefore committed a 'bodily appropriation' of Fox's series." It concluded that "Dastar's 'bodily appropriation' of Fox's original [television] series is sufficient to establish the reverse passing off." The court also affirmed the District Court's award under the Lanham Act of twice Dastar's profits. We granted certiorari.

---

1. Passing off (or palming off, as it is sometimes called) occurs when a producer misrepresents his own goods or services as someone else's. "Reverse passing off," as its name implies, is the opposite: The producer misrepresents someone else's goods or services as his own.

The Lanham Act was intended to make "actionable the deceptive and misleading use of marks," and "to protect persons engaged in ... commerce against unfair competition." While much of the Lanham Act addresses the registration, use, and infringement of trademarks and related marks, §43(a), is one of the few provisions that goes beyond trademark protection. As originally enacted, *§43(a)* created a federal remedy against a person who used in commerce either "a false designation of origin, or any false description or representation" in connection with "any goods or services." As the Second Circuit accurately observed with regard to the original enactment, however—and as remains true after the 1988 revision—*§43(a)* "does not have boundless application as a remedy for unfair trade practices." "Because of its inherently limited wording, *§43(a)* can never be a federal 'codification' of the overall law of 'unfair competition,'" but can apply only to certain unfair trade practices prohibited by its text.

Although a case can be made that a proper reading of *§43(a)*, as originally enacted, would treat the word "origin" as referring only "to the geographic location in which the goods originated," the Courts of Appeals considering the issue, beginning with the Sixth Circuit, unanimously concluded that it "does not merely refer to geographical origin, but also to origin of source or manufacture," thereby creating a federal cause of action for traditional trademark infringement of unregistered marks. Moreover, every Circuit to consider the issue found *§43(a)* broad enough to encompass reverse passing off. *The Trademark Law Revision Act of 1988* made clear that *§43(a)* covers origin of production as well as geographic origin.[2] Its language is amply inclusive, moreover, of reverse passing off—if indeed it does not implicitly adopt the unanimous court-of-appeals jurisprudence on that subject.

Thus, as it comes to us, the gravamen of respondents' claim is that, in marketing and selling Campaigns as its own product without acknowledging its nearly wholesale reliance on the Crusade television series, Dastar has made a "false designation of origin, false or misleading description of fact, or false or misleading representation of fact, which ... is likely to cause confusion ... as to the origin ... of his or her goods."

That claim would undoubtedly be sustained if Dastar had bought some of New Line's Crusade videotapes and merely repackaged them as its own. Dastar's alleged wrongdoing, however, is vastly different: it took a creative work in the public domain—the Crusade television series—copied it, made modifications (arguably minor), and produced its very own series of videotapes. If "origin" refers only to the manufacturer or producer of the physical "goods" that are made available to the public (in this case the videotapes), Dastar was the origin. If, however, "origin" includes the creator of the underlying work that Dastar copied, then someone else (perhaps Fox) was the origin of Dastar's product. At bottom, we must decide what *§43(a)(1)(A) of the Lanham Act* means by the "origin" of "goods."

---

2. *Section 43(a) of the Lanham Act* now provides:

"Any person who, on or in connection with any goods or services, or any container for goods, uses in commerce any word, term, name, symbol, or device, or any combination thereof, or any false designation of origin, false or misleading description of fact, or false or misleading representation of fact, which—

"(A) is likely to cause confusion, or to cause mistake, or to deceive as to the affiliation, connection, or association of such person with another person, or as to the origin, sponsorship, or approval of his or her goods, services, or commercial activities by another person, or

"(B) in commercial advertising or promotion, misrepresents the nature, characteristics, qualities, or geographic origin of his or her or another person's goods, services, or commercial activities, shall be liable in a civil action by any person who believes that he or she is or is likely to be damaged by such act." *15 U.S.C. §1125(a)(1)*.

The dictionary definition of "origin" is "the fact or process of coming into being from a source," and "that from which anything primarily proceeds; source." Webster's New International Dictionary 1720–1721 (2d ed. 1949). And the dictionary definition of "goods" (as relevant here) is "[w]ares; merchandise." We think the most natural understanding of the "origin" of "goods"—the source of wares—is the producer of the tangible product sold in the marketplace, in this case the physical Campaigns videotape sold by Dastar. The concept might be stretched (as it was under the original version of § 43(a)) to include not only the actual producer, but also the trademark owner who commissioned or assumed responsibility for ("stood behind") production of the physical product. But as used in the Lanham Act, the phrase "origin of goods" is in our view incapable of connoting the person or entity that originated the ideas or communications that "goods" embody or contain. Such an extension would not only stretch the text, but it would be out of accord with the history and purpose of the Lanham Act and inconsistent with precedent.

Section 43(a) of the Lanham Act prohibits actions like trademark infringement that deceive consumers and impair a producer's goodwill. It forbids, for example, the Coca-Cola Company's passing off its product as Pepsi-Cola or reverse passing off Pepsi-Cola as its product. But the brand-loyal consumer who prefers the drink that the Coca-Cola Company or PepsiCo sells, while he believes that that company produced (or at least stands behind the production of) that product, surely does not necessarily believe that that company was the "origin" of the drink in the sense that it was the very first to devise the formula. The consumer who buys a branded product does not automatically assume that the brand-name company is the same entity that came up with the idea for the product, or designed the product—and typically does not care whether it is. The words of the Lanham Act should not be stretched to cover matters that are typically of no consequence to purchasers.

It could be argued, perhaps, that the reality of purchaser concern is different for what might be called a communicative product—one that is valued not primarily for its physical qualities, such as a hammer, but for the intellectual content that it conveys, such as a book or, as here, a video. The purchaser of a novel is interested not merely, if at all, in the identity of the producer of the physical tome (the publisher), but also, and indeed primarily, in the identity of the creator of the story it conveys (the author). And the author, of course, has at least as much interest in avoiding passing-off (or reverse passing-off) of his creation as does the publisher. For such a communicative product (the argument goes) "origin of goods" in § 43(a) must be deemed to include not merely the producer of the physical item (the publishing house Farrar, Straus and Giroux, or the video producer Dastar) but also the creator of the content that the physical item conveys (the author Tom Wolfe, or—assertedly—respondents).

The problem with this argument according special treatment to communicative products is that it causes the Lanham Act to conflict with the law of copyright, which addresses that subject specifically. The right to copy, and to copy without attribution, once a copyright has expired, like "the right to make [an article whose patent has expired]—including the right to make it in precisely the shape it carried when patented—passes to the public." "In general, unless an intellectual property right such as a patent or copyright protects an item, it will be subject to copying." The rights of a patentee or copyright holder are part of a "carefully crafted bargain," under which, once the patent or copyright monopoly has expired, the public may use the invention or work at will and without attribution. Thus, in construing the Lanham Act, we have been "careful to caution against misuse or over-extension" of trademark and related protections into areas traditionally occupied by patent or copyright. "The Lanham Act," we have said, "does not exist to reward manufacturers for their innovation in creating a particular device; that is the purpose of the patent law and its period of exclusivity."

Federal trademark law "has no necessary relation to invention or discovery," but rather, by preventing competitors from copying "a source-identifying mark," "reduce[s] the customer's costs of shopping and making purchasing decisions," and "helps assure a producer that it (and not an imitating competitor) will reap the financial, reputation-related rewards associated with a desirable product." Assuming for the sake of argument that Dastar's representation of itself as the "Producer" of its videos amounted to a representation that it originated the creative work conveyed by the videos, allowing a cause of action under§ 43(a) for that representation would create a species of mutant copyright law that limits the public's "federal right to 'copy and to use,'" expired copyrights.

When Congress has wished to create such an addition to the law of copyright, it has done so with much more specificity than the Lanham Act's ambiguous use of "origin." The *Visual Artists Rights Act of 1990*, § 603(a), provides that the author of an artistic work "shall have the right ... to claim authorship of that work." That express right of attribution is carefully limited and focused: It attaches only to specified "works of visual art," *§ 101*, is personal to the artist, *§§ 106A(b) and (e)*, and endures only for "the life of the author," at *§ 106A(d)(1)*. Recognizing in *§ 43(a)* a cause of action for misrepresentation of authorship of noncopyrighted works (visual or otherwise) would render these limitations superfluous. A statutory interpretation that renders another statute superfluous is of course to be avoided.

Reading "origin" in *§ 43(a)* to require attribution of uncopyrighted materials would pose serious practical problems. Without a copyrighted work as the basepoint, the word "origin" has no discernable limits. A video of the MGM film Carmen Jones, after its copyright has expired, would presumably require attribution not just to MGM, but to Oscar Hammerstein II (who wrote the musical on which the film was based), to Georges Bizet (who wrote the opera on which the musical was based), and to Prosper Merimee (who wrote the novel on which the opera was based). In many cases, figuring out who is in the line of "origin" would be no simple task. Indeed, in the present case it is far from clear that respondents have that status. Neither SFM nor New Line had anything to do with the production of the Crusade television series—they merely were licensed to distribute the video version.

While Fox might have a claim to being in the line of origin, its involvement with the creation of the television series was limited at best. Time, Inc., was the principal if not the exclusive creator, albeit under arrangement with Fox. And of course it was neither Fox nor Time, Inc. that shot the film used in the Crusade television series. Rather, that footage came from the United States Army, Navy, and Coast Guard, the British Ministry of Information and War Office, the National Film Board of Canada, and unidentified "Newsreel Pool Cameramen." If anyone has a claim to being the *original* creator of the material used in both the Crusade television series and the Campaigns videotapes, it would be those groups, rather than Fox. We do not think the Lanham Act requires this search for the source of the Nile and all its tributaries.

Another practical difficulty of adopting a special definition of "origin" for communicative products is that it places the manufacturers of those products in a difficult position. On the one hand, they would face Lanham Act liability for *failing* to credit the creator of a work on which their lawful copies are based; and on the other hand they could face Lanham Act liability for *crediting* the creator if that should be regarded as implying the creator's "sponsorship or approval" of the copy. In this case, for example, if Dastar had simply "copied [the television series] as Crusade in Europe and sold it as Crusade in Europe," without changing the title or packaging (including the original credits to Fox), it is hard to have confidence in respondents' assurance that they "would not be here on a Lanham Act cause of action."

Finally, reading *§ 43(a) of the Lanham Act* as creating a cause of action for, in effect, plagiarism — the use of otherwise unprotected works and inventions without attribution — would be hard to reconcile with our previous decisions. For example, in *Wal-Mart Stores, Inc. v. Samara Brothers, Inc.,* 529 U.S. 205 (2000), we considered whether product-design trade dress can ever be inherently distinctive. Wal-Mart produced "knockoffs" of children's clothes designed and manufactured by Samara Brothers, containing only "minor modifications" of the original designs. We concluded that the designs could not be protected under *§ 43(a)* without a showing that they had acquired "secondary meaning," so that they "'identify the source of the product rather than the product itself.'" This carefully considered limitation would be entirely pointless if the "original" producer could turn around and pursue a reverse-passing-off claim under exactly the same provision of the Lanham Act. Samara would merely have had to argue that it was the "origin" of the designs that Wal-Mart was selling as its own line. It was not, because "origin of goods" in the Lanham Act referred to the producer of the clothes, and not the producer of the (potentially) copyrightable or patentable designs that the clothes embodied.

Similarly under respondents' theory, the "origin of goods" provision of *§ 43(a)* would have supported the suit that we rejected in *Bonito Boats,* where the defendants had used molds to duplicate the plaintiff's unpatented boat hulls (apparently without crediting the plaintiff). And it would have supported the suit we rejected in *TrafFix:* The plaintiff, whose patents on flexible road signs had expired, and who could not prevail on a trade-dress claim under *§ 43(a)* because the features of the signs were functional, would have had a reverse-passing-off claim for unattributed copying of his design.

In sum, reading the phrase "origin of goods" in the Lanham Act in accordance with the Act's common-law foundations (which were *not* designed to protect originality or creativity), and in light of the copyright and patent laws (which *were*), we conclude that the phrase refers to the producer of the tangible goods that are offered for sale, and not to the author of any idea, concept, or communication embodied in those goods. To hold otherwise would be akin to finding that *§ 43(a)* created a species of perpetual patent and copyright, which Congress may not do.

The creative talent of the sort that lay behind the Campaigns videos is not left without protection. The original film footage used in the Crusade television series could have been copyrighted, as was copyrighted (as a compilation) the Crusade television series, even though it included material from the public domain. Had Fox renewed the copyright in the Crusade television series, it would have had an easy claim of copyright infringement. And respondents' contention that Campaigns infringes Doubleday's copyright in General Eisenhower's book is still a live question on remand. If, moreover, the producer of a video that substantially copied the Crusade series were, in advertising or promotion, to give purchasers the impression that the video was quite different from that series, then one or more of the respondents might have a cause of action — not for reverse passing off under the "confusion … as to the origin" provision of *§ 43(a)(1)(A)*, but for misrepresentation under the "misrepresents the nature, characteristics [or] qualities" provision of *§ 43(a)(1)(B)*. For merely saying it is the producer of the video, however, no Lanham Act liability attaches to Dastar.

Because we conclude that Dastar was the "origin" of the products it sold as its own, respondents cannot prevail on their Lanham Act claim. We thus have no occasion to consider whether the Lanham Act permitted an award of double petitioner's profits. The judgment of the Court of Appeals for the Ninth Circuit is reversed, and the case is remanded for further proceedings consistent with this opinion. It is so ordered.

Notes and Questions

a. The interpretation of *Dastar* may have far-reaching impact on the entertainment industries. As the Court explained, purchasing copies of plaintiff's videotapes and repackaging them would survive the decision, but the language suggests that this is true only if the videotapes were of copyrighted works.

To the extent the Court rejects § 43(a) as a remedy for plagiarism, it suggests that the republishing of public domain works under new names and titles gives the prior authors, publishers, and producers no surviving claim. Future courts may interpret the decision more narrowly, perhaps by requiring that such republications have some annotation of origin so that the public is not deceived that it is purchasing a new work.

b. Already *Dastar* has been interpreted to change the non-contractual rights to credit. See *Williams v. UMG Recordings, Inc.,* 281 F. Supp. 2d 1177 (C.D. Cal. 2003).

c. As courts continue to interpret *Dastar*, the implications are beginning to be explored. For a discussion of palming off, reverse palming off, and copyright preemption, see *Aagard v. Palomar Builders, Inc.*, 344 F. Supp. 2d 1211 (E.D. Cal. 2004), involving the theft of architectural plans. See also *A Slice of Pie Prods. v. Wayans Bros. Entm't*, 392 F. Supp. 2d 297, 323–24 (D. Conn. 2005) (unpublished screenplay); *Gen. Universal Sys., Inc. v. Lee*, 379 F.3d 131, 148–49 (5th Cir. 2004) (computer software).

d. The distinction between copyrighted works and public domain works was not made by the Supreme Court and therefore lower courts have not opted to make the distinction. Does a distinction remain regarding the corporate publisher of a work, rather than the author of the work? See *Hustlers, Inc. v. Thomasson*, 73 U.S.P.Q. 2d 1923 (N.D. Ga. 2004).

e. How far does a trademark extend? Ishmael Butler and Maryann Vieira wrote the jazz/hip-hop song "Rebirth of Slick (Cool like Dat)." They performed in commercials for Target Stores using the song, for which they gave permission, but they claim that the song title and lyrics were used in slogans and signage without permission in violation of the Lanham Act, a claim the court did not dismiss. *Butler v. Target Corp.*, 323 F. Supp. 2d 1052 (C.D. Cal. 2004).

f. In *Herb Reed Enterprises, LLC v. Florida Entertainment Management Inc.*, 736 F.3d 1239 (9th Cir. 2013), the Ninth Circuit extended a limitation on injunctive relief to trademark. In *eBay Inc. v. MercExchange, L.L.C.*, 547 U.S. 388 (2006), the Supreme Court rejected a tradition that allowed intellectual property plaintiffs to rely on a presumption of irreparable injury when seeking preliminary and permanent injunctions. The Supreme Court rejected the presumption for patent litigants and lower courts have extended *eBay* to copyright and trademark as well. The result requires the owner of the trademark for the musical group, The Platters, to establish irreparable harm before enjoining former band members from using the mark. See *Salinger v. Colting*, 607 F.3d 68, 77 (2d Cir. 2010) (applying eBay to copyright actions in both preliminary and permanent injunctions).

Problem VII-A

Bryce has recently become interested in the opportunities that are available through capturing public domain material. Tyrell Jones has approached Bryce about creating a new project for a local school, called the "New Masters" series, which is intended to teach music and literary history. Under Bryce's supervision, selected students from the school will rewrite Gilbert & Sullivan operettas using well-recognized modern stories. The students will create new arrangements, adding jazz, rock, hip-hop, and pop sensibilities to the music. The students plan to write original stories based on such literary characters as Peter Pan, Sherlock Holmes, Frankenstein, Dracula, and the Phantom of the Opera, as well as those narratives traditionally associated with them. Only a few plan to use the original Gilbert & Sullivan plots.

Bryce has researched the material and correctly identified that all the written materials are in the public domain. Each work's copyright has expired in the United States. Nonetheless, Bryce has read that there are estates and companies which claim ownership of some trademarks in some of these works. Bryce seeks your advice on whether there are any limitations on the public domain materials. Since some of these works have also been used in more modern works which continue to be protected by copyright, you should also explain the scope of the public domain and the impact of trademark interests on Bryce's upcoming project.

B. Publicity

Zacchini v. Scripps-Howard Broadcasting Co.
433 U.S. 562, 573 (1977)

[The case of the "Human Cannonball" is presented in Chapter I. One particular passage restates the importance of the right of publicity:] [T]he State's interest in permitting a "right of publicity" is in protecting the proprietary interest of the individual in his act in part to encourage such entertainment. As we later note, the State's interest is closely analogous to the goals of patent and copyright law, focusing on the right of the individual to reap the reward of his endeavors and having little to do with protecting feelings or reputation. Second, the two torts differ in the degree to which they intrude on dissemination of information to the public. In "false light" cases the only way to protect the interests involved is to attempt to minimize publication of the damaging matter, while in "right of publicity" cases the only question is who gets to do the publishing. An entertainer such as petitioner usually has no objection to the widespread publication of his act as long as he gets the commercial benefit of such publication.

[New York] Civil Rights Law
§§ 50, 51 McKinney (2003)

§ 50. A person, firm or corporation that uses for advertising purposes, or for the purposes of trade, the name, portrait or picture of any living person without having first obtained the written consent of such person, or if a minor of his or her parent or guardian, is guilty of a misdemeanor.

§ 51. Any person whose name, portrait, picture or voice is used within this state for advertising purposes or for the purposes of trade without the written consent first obtained as above provided may maintain an equitable action in the supreme court of this state against the person, firm or corporation so using his name, portrait, picture or voice, to prevent and restrain the use thereof; and may also sue and recover damages for any injuries sustained by reason of such use and if the defendant shall have knowingly used such person's name, portrait, picture or voice in such manner as is forbidden or declared to be unlawful by section fifty of this article, the jury, in its discretion, may award exemplary damages. But nothing contained in this article shall be so construed as to prevent any person, firm or corporation from selling or otherwise transferring any material containing such name, portrait, picture or voice in whatever medium to any user of such name, portrait, picture or voice, or to any third party for sale or transfer directly or indirectly to such a user, for use in a manner lawful under this article; nothing contained in this article shall be so construed as to prevent any person, firm or corporation, practicing the profession of photography, from exhibiting in or about his or its establishment specimens of the work of such establishment, unless the same is continued by such person, firm or corporation after written notice objecting thereto has been given by the person portrayed; and nothing contained in this article shall be so construed as to prevent any person, firm or corporation from using the name, portrait, picture or voice of any manufacturer or dealer in connection with the goods, wares and merchandise manufactured, produced or dealt in by him which he has sold or disposed of with such name, portrait, picture or voice used in connection therewith; or from using the name, portrait, picture or voice of any author, composer or artist in connection with his literary, musical or artistic productions which he has sold or disposed of with such name, portrait, picture or voice used in connection therewith. Nothing contained in this section shall be construed to prohibit the copyright owner of a sound recording from disposing of, dealing in, licensing or selling that sound recording to any party, if the right to dispose of, deal in, license or sell such sound recording has been conferred by contract or other written document by such living person or the holder of such right. Nothing contained in the foregoing sentence shall be deemed to abrogate or otherwise limit any rights or remedies otherwise conferred by federal law or state law.

California Civil Code
§ 3344 Deering (2012)

(a) Any person who knowingly uses another's name, voice, signature, photograph, or likeness, in any manner, on or in products, merchandise, or goods, or for purposes of advertising or selling, or soliciting purchases of, products, merchandise, goods or services, without such person's prior consent, or, in the case of a minor, the prior consent of his parent or legal guardian, shall be liable for any damages sustained by the person or persons injured as a result thereof. In addition, in any action brought under this section, the person who violated the section shall be liable to the injured party or parties in an amount equal to the greater of seven hundred fifty dollars ($750) or the actual damages suffered by him or her as a result of the unauthorized use, and any profits from the unauthorized use that are attributable to the use and are not taken into account in computing the actual damages. In establishing such profits, the injured party or parties are required to present proof only of the gross revenue attributable to such use, and the person who violated this section is required to prove his or her deductible expenses. Punitive damages may also be awarded to the injured party or parties. The prevailing party in any action under this section shall also be entitled to attorney's fees and costs.

(b) As used in this section, "photograph" means any photograph or photographic reproduction, still or moving, or any videotape or live television transmission, of any person, such that the person is readily identifiable.

(1) A person shall be deemed to be readily identifiable from a photograph when one who views the photograph with the naked eye can reasonably determine that the person depicted in the photograph is the same person who is complaining of its unauthorized use.

(2) If the photograph includes more than one person so identifiable, then the person or persons complaining of the use shall be represented as individuals rather than solely as members of a definable group represented in the photograph. A definable group includes, but is not limited to, the following examples: a crowd at any sporting event, a crowd in any street or public building, the audience at any theatrical or stage production, a glee club, or a baseball team.

(3) A person or persons shall be considered to be represented as members of a definable group if they are represented in the photograph solely as a result of being present at the time the photograph was taken and have not been singled out as individuals in any manner.

(c) Where a photograph or likeness of an employee of the person using the photograph or likeness appearing in the advertisement or other publication prepared by or in behalf of the user is only incidental, and not essential, to the purpose of the publication in which it appears, there shall arise a rebuttable presumption affecting the burden of producing evidence that the failure to obtain the consent of the employee was not a knowing use of the employee's photograph or likeness.

(d) For purposes of this section, a use of a name, voice, signature, photograph, or likeness in connection with any news, public affairs, or sports broadcast or account, or any political campaign, shall not constitute a use for which consent is required under subdivision (a).

(e) The use of a name, voice, signature, photograph, or likeness in a commercial medium shall not constitute a use for which consent is required under subdivision (a) solely because the material containing such use is commercially sponsored or contains paid advertising. Rather it shall be a question of fact whether or not the use of the person's name, voice, signature, photograph, or likeness was so directly connected with the commercial sponsorship or with the paid advertising as to constitute a use for which consent is required under subdivision (a).

(f) Nothing in this section shall apply to the owners or employees of any medium used for advertising, including, but not limited to, newspapers, magazines, radio and television networks and stations, cable television systems, billboards, and transit ads, by whom any advertisement or solicitation in violation of this section is published or disseminated, unless it is established that such owners or employees had knowledge of the unauthorized use of the person's name, voice, signature, photograph, or likeness as prohibited by this section.

(g) The remedies provided for in this section are cumulative and shall be in addition to any others provided for by law.[3]

---

3. *See also* Cal Civ. Code 3344.1 (Deerings 2012) (extending these rights to decedents' estates).

Downing v. Abercrombie & Fitch
265 F.3d 994 (9th Cir. 2001)

Appellants brought this diversity action against Abercrombie and Fitch ("Abercrombie") for publishing a photograph of them, with identification of their names, for Abercrombie's commercial benefit without the Appellants' authorization. They allege a violation of California's common law and statutory prohibition against misappropriation of a person's name and likeness for commercial purposes, a violation of the Lanham Act for confusion and deception indicating sponsorship of Abercrombie goods, and a claim for negligence and defamation. The district court entered summary judgment for Abercrombie, holding that their California state claims were foreclosed because Abercrombie's use of the photograph was protected by the First Amendment, and those claims were also preempted by the federal Copyright Act; that Hawaii law was the proper choice of law for some of these claims; that the Lanham Act claim was precluded by the First Amendment and it was also precluded by the nominative fair use doctrine; and that there was insufficient evidence to sustain the negligence or defamation claims. The district court had jurisdiction under 28 U.S.C. § 1332, and we have appellate jurisdiction under 28 U.S.C. § 1291. We reverse the grant of summary judgment and remand for trial.

I. Factual Background

Abercrombie is an outfitter catering to young people. The upscale retailer sells casual apparel for men and women, including shirts, khakis, jeans, and outerwear. In addition to sales in approximately 200 stores nationwide, Abercrombie also sells merchandise through its subscription catalog, the "Abercrombie and Fitch Quarterly" ("Quarterly").

The Quarterly is Abercrombie's largest advertising vehicle. It accounts for approximately 80% of Abercrombie's overall advertising budget. The primary purpose of the Quarterly is to build brand awareness and increase sales. Each issue is over 250 pages in length and embraces a theme such as collegiate lifestyle, back to school, or winter wear. The Quarterly contains photographs of models wearing Abercrombie's garments as well as pictures of the clothing displayed for sale. In addition, approximately one-quarter of each issue is devoted to stories, news and other editorial pieces.

In 1998, Michael Jeffries, Abercrombie's CEO, developed a surfing theme for the upcoming Quarterly. Abercrombie held the photo shoot for the upcoming issue at San Onofre Beach, California. While at the photo shoot, Abercrombie employees Sam Shahid and Savas Abadsidis looked through a compilation of surfing photographs by surf photographer LeRoy Grannis. The photo book contained a picture of Appellants which Grannis had taken at the 1965 Makaha International Surf Championship in Hawaii. Sam Shahid purchased the photograph, along with three other photographs from the book, for $100 each. LeRoy Grannis then handwrote the names of Appellants at the bottom of the photograph.

Subsequently, Sam Shahid showed Appellants' photograph to Jeffries who decided to use the photograph in the upcoming Quarterly. Abercrombie did not obtain Appellants' permission. Jeffries also decided to create t-shirts, exactly like those worn by the Appellants in the photograph, for sale in the upcoming issue. Abercrombie labeled the t-shirts" Final Heat Tees." The t-shirts were advertised for sale in the Quarterly.

The Spring 1999 Quarterly, "Spring Fever," contains a section entitled "Surf Nekkid." The "Surf Nekkid" section includes an article recounting the history of surfing. Abercrombie also included a 700-word story, entitled "Your Beach Should Be This Cool," describing the history of Old Man's Beach at San Onofre, California. The following page exhibits the photograph of Appellants. The two pages immediately thereafter feature the "Final Heat Tees."

The "Spring Fever" issue contains other articles about the surfing lifestyle. An article entitled "Beachcombing" documents the efforts of the Surfrider Foundation, an ecological group founded by surfers. Still another article entitled "Where the Wild Things Are," written by the editor of Surfer Magazine, describes various surfer "types." Also contained in the issue is an interview of Nat Young, former world surfing champion and the first professional surfer. The interview is accompanied by photographs of Young and his son wearing Abercrombie clothing. . . .

On appeal, Appellants contend: (1) Abercrombie's use of the photograph is not protected under the First Amendment; (2) the state law publicity claims are not preempted by the Copyright Act; (3) California law is the proper choice of law for the claim under California Civil Code § 3344; (4) triable issues of fact exist with regard to the Lanham Act claims. . . .

The district court's grant of summary judgment is reviewed de novo. We must determine, viewing the evidence in the light most favorable to the nonmoving party, whether there are any genuine issues of material fact and whether the district court correctly applied the relevant substantive law.

ANALYSIS

I. First Amendment and Right of Publicity Claims

The district court concluded that Abercrombie's use of the photograph containing Appellants' names and likenesses was proper because it constituted expression protected under the First Amendment. We disagree.

California has long recognized a common law right of privacy for protection of a person's name and likeness against appropriation by others for their advantage. To sustain a common law cause of action for commercial misappropriation, a plaintiff must prove: "(1) the defendant's use of the plaintiff's identity; (2) the appropriation of plaintiff's name or likeness to defendant's advantage, commercially or otherwise; (3) lack of consent; and (4) resulting injury."

In addition to the common law cause of action, California has provided a statutory remedy for commercial misappropriation under California Civil Code § 3344. The remedies provided for under California Civil Code § 3344 complement the common law cause of action; they do not replace or codify the common law. Section 3344 provides in relevant part, "any person who knowingly uses another's name, voice, signature, photograph, or likeness, in any manner . . . for purposes of advertising . . . without such person's prior consent . . . shall be liable for any damages sustained by the person." Under section 3344, a plaintiff must prove all the elements of the common law cause of action. In addition, the plaintiff must allege a knowing use by the defendant as well as a direct connection between the alleged use and the commercial purpose.

Under both the common law cause of action and the statutory cause of action "no cause of action will lie for the publication of matters in the public interest, which rests on the right of the public to know and the freedom of the press to tell it." This First Amendment defense extends "to almost all reporting of recent events," as well as to publications about "people who, by their accomplishments, mode of living, professional standing or calling, create a legitimate and widespread attention to their activities. However, the defense is not absolute; we must find "a proper accommodation between [the] competing concerns" of freedom of speech and the right of publicity.

In the instant case, Abercrombie defends on the basis of the First Amendment arguing that the photograph illustrates an article about surfing, a matter in the public interest. To support its defense, Abercrombie relies on *Dora v. Frontline Video, Inc.,* 15 Cal. App. 4th 536 (Ct. App. 1993). In Dora, the court held that a surfing documentary was in the public interest because it was "about a certain time and place in California history and, indeed, in American legend." Dora involved a surfing legend, Mickey Dora, who sued the producer of a video documentary on surfing claiming common law and statutory appropriation of his name and likeness. The trial court entered summary judgment for the film's producer and the California Court of Appeal affirmed. In addressing the First Amendment issue, the court found that the documentary was about a matter of public interest, specifically surfing, and, therefore, the producer was protected by the defense. In so concluding the court stated:

> surfing is of more than passing interest to some. It has created a life-style that influences speech, behavior, dress, and entertainment, among other things. A phenomenon of such scope has an economic impact, because it affects purchases, travel, and the housing market. Surfing has also had a significant influence on the popular culture, and in that way touches many people. It would be difficult to conclude that a surfing documentary does not fall within the category of public affairs.

Although the theme of Abercrombie's catalog was surfing and surf culture, a matter of public interest, the use of Appellants' names and pictures is quite different from that involved in the *Dora* case. In *Dora*, Mickey Dora's contribution to the development of the surf life-style and his influence on the sport was "the point of the program." Dora was depicted in the documentary because his identity directly contributed to the story about surfing which came within the protected public interest.

In the current action, there is a tenuous relationship between Appellants' photograph and the theme presented. Abercrombie used Appellants' photograph essentially as window-dressing to advance the catalog's surf-theme. The catalog did not explain that Appellants were legends of the sport and did not in any way connect Appellants with the story preceding it. In fact, the catalog incorrectly identifies where and when the photograph was taken. We conclude that the illustrative use of Appellants' photograph does not contribute significantly to a matter of the public interest and that Abercrombie cannot avail itself of the First Amendment defense.

This case is also distinguishable from *Hoffman v. L.A. Magazine,* 255 F.3d 1180, slip op. at 8591 (9th Cir. 2001), in which the defendant magazine successfully asserted a First Amendment defense to Dustin Hoffman's claim of misappropriation. In that case, L.A. Magazine used a digitally-altered picture of Hoffman, as "Tootsie," in a current designer dress to illustrate its "Grand Illusions" article. We concluded that such use was noncommercial speech entitled to full First Amendment protection. In contrast to the present case, where Abercrombie, itself, used Appellants' images in its catalog to promote its clothing, L.A. Magazine was unconnected to and received no consideration from the designer for the gown depicted in the article. Further, while L.A. Magazine merely referenced a shopping guide buried in the back of the magazine that provided stores and prices for the gown, Abercrombie placed the Appellants' photograph on the page immediately preceding the "Final Heat Tees" for sale. Based on these factors, we conclude that Abercrombie's use was much more commercial in nature and, therefore, not entitled to the full First Amendment protection accorded to L.A. Magazine's use of Hoffman's image.

Accordingly, we reverse the district court's grant of summary judgment in favor of Abercrombie.

II. Federal Copyright Preemption

Abercrombie contends that its right to reproduce and publish the photograph of the Appellants is governed by the federal Copyright Act, and that Appellants' state law claims are preempted by federal copyright law....

The photograph itself, as a pictorial work of authorship, is subject matter protected by the Copyright Act. However, it is not the publication of the photograph itself, as a creative work of authorship, that is the basis for Appellants' claims, but rather, it is the use of the Appellants' likenesses and their names pictured in the published photograph.... [The] point is made in McCarthy's Treatise on Right of Publicity and Privacy:

> The "subject matter" of a Right of Publicity claim is not a particular picture or photograph of plaintiff. Rather, what is protected by the Right of Publicity is the very identity or persona of the plaintiff as a human being ... While copyright in a given photograph may be owned by the person depicted in it, the exact image in that photograph is not the underlying "right" asserted in a Right of Publicity case. To argue that the photograph is identical with the person is to confuse illusion and illustration with reality. Thus, assertion of infringement of the Right of Publicity because of defendant's unpermitted commercial use of a picture of plaintiff is not assertion of infringement of copyrightable "subject matter" in one photograph of plaintiff.

McCarthy, Rights of Publicity and Privacy §11.13[C] at 11-72–73 (1997).

A recent case in the Fifth Circuit [(*Brown v. Ames*, 201 F.3d 654, 661 (5th Cir. 2000))] held that the Texas tort of misappropriation, which provides protection from the unauthorized appropriation of one's name, image, or likeness was not preempted by the Copyright Act. The case involved a record company's misappropriation of the names and likenesses of individual musicians, song writers, and music producers on the company's CD's, tapes, catalogs, and posters. The court stated that "the tort of misappropriation of a name or likeness protects a person's *persona*. A persona does not fall within the subject matter of copyright." Thus, the court held that §301 preemption does not apply.

A similar result was reached in a case decided by a California Court of Appeal, *KNB Enterprises v. Matthews*, 78 Cal. App. 4th 362 (2000). The California Court of Appeals held that the state law right of publicity claims were not pre-empted by the Copyright Act. The copyright owner of erotic photographs, which had been displayed without authorization and for profit on an Internet website, brought suit against the website's operator asserting a misappropriation claim under California Civil Code §3344. The court applied the two-part test for determining preemption and found that neither condition had been met. The court found that "because a human likeness is not copyrightable, even if captured in a copyrighted photograph, the models' section 3344 claims against the unauthorized publisher of their photographs are not the equivalent of a copyright infringement claim and are not preempted by federal copyright law."

We agree with the approach taken by the Fifth Circuit and the reasoning employed in KNB Enterprises. The subject matter of Appellants' statutory and common law right of publicity claims is their names and likenesses. A person's name or likeness is not a work of authorship within the meaning of 17 U.S.C. §102. This is true notwithstanding the fact that Appellants' names and likenesses are embodied in a copyrightable photograph. The same concept is specifically embodied in 17 U.S.C. §103, which provides that the copyright in derivative works extends only to the material contributed by the author as distinguished from preexisting material employed in the work.

Abercrombie relies on the California case of *Fleet v. CBS*, 50 Cal. App. 4th 1911 (Ct. App. 1996). This case was distinguished by both the Fifth Circuit in Brown, and the California Court of Appeals in KNB Enterprises. In *Fleet*, the plaintiffs were actors in a copyrighted film. The claims of the plaintiffs were based on their dramatic performance in a film CBS sought to distribute. The court stated:

> We agree that as a general proposition Civil Code section 3344 is intended to protect rights which cannot be copyrighted and that claims made under its provisions are usually not preempted. But appellants' analysis crumbles in the face of one obvious fact: their individual performances in the film White Dragon were copyrightable. Since their section 3344 claims seeks only to prevent CBS from reproducing and distributing their performances in the film, their claims must be preempted by federal copyright law.

This is clearly distinguishable from this case where the Appellants' claim is based on the use of their names and likenesses, which are not copyrightable....

IV. Lanham Act

Appellants contend that the district court erred in denying their claim under section 43(a) of the Lanham Act.... It is perhaps clearer to restate the eight factors as applicable to the celebrity case, which can be stated as:

1. the level of recognition that the plaintiff has among the segment of the society for whom the defendant's product is intended;

2. the relatedness of the fame or success of the plaintiff to the defendant's product;

3. the similarity of the likeness used by the defendant to the actual plaintiff;

4. evidence of actual confusion;

5. marketing channels used;

6. likely degree of purchaser care;

7. defendant's intent on selecting the plaintiff; and

8. likelihood of expansion of the product lines.

Although these are all factors that are appropriate for consideration in determining the likelihood of confusion, they are not necessarily of equal importance, nor do they necessarily apply to every case.

"The Lanham Act's likelihood of confusion standard is predominantly factual in nature." Thus, summary judgment is inappropriate when a jury could reasonably conclude that there is a likelihood of confusion. Application of the eight factors to the current action leads us to conclude that the district court erred in rejecting Appellants' Lanham Act claim at the summary judgment stage.

In applying the factors to this case we reach the following conclusions. First, in considering the recognition that the Appellants have among those persons toward whom the Abercrombie catalog is directed, Appellants cite to a declaration submitted by surf historian Steve Pezman. In the declaration, Pezman asserts that Appellants "are considered legends in the surf community and are still highly well-known and regarded." This declaration from a surf historian provides some evidence that Appellants' names and images enjoy a high level of recognition among average members of society as a whole. In addition, it is undisputed that Appellants are legendary surfers, and thus there is a reasonable inference that Appellants would be known to the young people to whom the Quarterly is directed and who would be purchasing Abercrombie's surf wear.

The second factor is the relatedness of the Appellants' fame and success to the Defendant's product. Appellants' fame is due to their surfing success. Appellants' surfing success could be seen as closely-related to the Abercrombie's surf-related clothing.

Applying the third factor, the similarity of the likeness, to the Appellants is clear because it is an actual photograph of the Appellants with their names designated.

The fourth factor, evidence of actual confusion, also supports Appellants' position. Appellants provided declarations demonstrating that several individuals actually believed that Appellants were endorsing Abercrombie merchandise.

Under the fifth factor, marketing channels used, the catalog was the only marketing channel. It is therefore the likelihood of confusion in that marketing channel that is at issue.

In applying the sixth factor, the inquiry is whether consumers are likely to be particularly careful in determining who endorses the Abercrombie surf apparel, making confusion as to Appellants' endorsement more likely. A jury could reasonably find that young consumers are not likely to be particularly careful when purchasing surf-related clothing.

As to the seventh factor, the relevant question is whether the Defendants intended to profit by confusing consumers concerning the endorsement of the Abercrombie apparel. A jury could reasonably find that Abercrombie intended to indicate to consumers that these legendary surfers were endorsing Abercrombie's merchandise.

The eighth factor is the likelihood of expansion of the product lines. Neither party discusses this factor, however, no evidence has been produced that Abercrombie intends to utilize these photographs in additional product lines.

Application of these factors, leads us to conclude that the district court erred in rejecting Appellants' Lanham Act claim at the summary judgment stage. Viewing the evidence in the light most favorable to Appellants, we conclude that Appellants have raised a genuine issue of material fact concerning a likelihood of confusion as to their endorsement.

V. Doctrine of Nominative Fair Use

The district court concluded that Appellants' Lanham Act claim was barred by the doctrine of nominative fair use. In support of its position that the district court was correct in concluding that Appellants' Lanham Act claim was barred, Abercrombie relies upon *New Kids on the Block v. News America Publishing, Inc.*, 971 F.2d 302 (9th Cir. 1992). In *New Kids*, two newspapers conducted "900" number telephone polls concerning their readers' reactions to the musical group "New Kids on the Block." The newspapers charged their readers 95 cents per minute to respond to the poll. The band, which had its own competing "900" numbers for its fans, filed Lanham Act claims against the two newspapers. The district court granted summary judgment for the defendant newspapers on First Amendment grounds. On appeal, we affirmed on a non-constitutional ground, as appropriate when the constitutional issue can be avoided. We concluded that the newspapers' use of the band name constituted a nominative fair use.

We found that where the defendant uses a trademark to describe the plaintiff's product rather than its own product, a commercial user is entitled to a nominative fair use defense provided the defendant meets three requirements:

1. the product or service in question must be one not readily identifiable without use of the trademark;

2. only so much of the mark or marks may be used as is reasonably necessary to identify the product or service; and

3.   the user must do nothing that would, in conjunction with the mark, suggest sponsorship or endorsement by the trademark holder.

Applying the three-part test, we concluded that the newspaper was entitled to the nominative fair use defense.

Abercrombie argues that its use of the photograph was nominative fair use in the same manner as the defendants' purported infringement in New Kids. We disagree. In New Kids, we stated that the test applies only "where the defendant uses a trademark to describe the plaintiff's product, rather than its own." Here, Abercrombie used the photograph in its catalog that was intended to sell its goods. As we have noted in this case involving a celebrity endorsement claim, the mark being protected is the Appellants' names and pictures. There is a genuine issue of material fact as to whether the third criterion is met, whether Abercrombie did nothing that would in conjunction with the Appellants' names and pictures suggest sponsorship or endorsement by the Appellants....

Neither the California state law claims or the Lanham Act claim are precluded by the First Amendment; [and] the California state claims are not preempted by the federal Copyright Act.... REVERSE AND REMAND FOR TRIAL.

Notes and Questions

a. The *Abercrombie* decision provides a roadmap for the entire chapter, by putting the claims of California's common law publicity, statutory publicity, and Lanham Act side-by-side, as well as thoughtfully discussing the First Amendment defense and the defense of nominative trademark fair use. Each of these claims will be briefly noted, in turn.

b. Common law publicity. Although the New York Court of Appeals quickly rejected the common law discovery of privacy and publicity rights, many other states began to recognize these common law claims. The first was Georgia, in *Pavesich v. New England Life Ins. Co.,* 50 S.E. 68 (Ga. 1905). The Court adopted the right of publicity as described by Warren and Brandeis, recognizing the formulation provided by their law review article. As a common law rule, the range of potential for identification may be broader than that provided by statute. See *Midler v. Ford Motor Co.,* 849 F.2d 460 (9th Cir. 1988) (unique voice); *Motschenbacher v. R.J. Reynolds Tobacco Co.,* 498 F.2d 821 (9th Cir. 1974) (combination of race car and driver).

c. Statutory publicity issues. New York provides only a statutory right of publicity whereas California recognizes both. One of the difficulties of publicity law is that it continues to be a matter of first impression for many states. As a result, states may have an established rule recognizing publicity rights, but no interpretation as to the descendibility or the interest. New York provides statutory law which appears very clear and narrow in scope, but subsequent court interpretation suggests that it embraces all the privacy and publicity rights enumerated by Warren and Brandeis. See *Spahn v. Julian Messner, Inc.,* 221 N.E.2d 543 (N.Y. 1966).

d. Section 43(a) of the Lanham Act. Decisions following *Dastar* have not focused on the facts of the decision but rather the sweeping rhetoric which suggests trademark rights are unavailable to authors. Decisions following *Dastar* have embraced its broad, sweeping effect. See *Williams v. UMG Recordings, Inc.,* 281 F. Supp. 2d 1177, 1185 (C.D. Cal. 2003) ("[T]he Supreme Court's holding did not depend on whether the works were copyrighted or not.... Rather ... the Court noted that protection for communicative products was available through copyright claims."); *Romero v. Buhimschi,* 396 Fed. Appx.

224, 233 (6th Cir. 2010) (unpublished) ("Assuming that a portion of Romero's pleadings could fall under §43(a)(1)(B)'s advertising prong, the misconduct alleged in the pleadings would have to relate to the "nature, characteristics, qualities, or geographic origin" of the manuscript."); *Sybersound Records, Inc. v. UAV Corp.*, 517 F.3d 1137, 1144 (9th Cir. 2008).

e. Nominative Trademark Fair Use. The use of another party's trademark is not always actionable. One common defense is the correct usage of a competitor's or third party's trademark even when done without its permission. For example, a consumer products magazine can identify the products reviewed in each issue by the products' trademarks. This nominative use — identifying the product by its correct name — is permitted even over the objection of the trademark holder. This defense also allows for comparative advertising. This is particularly important in the context of commercial speech which may have less First Amendment protection than other forms of speech. See *Mattel, Inc. v. Walking Mt. Productions*, 353 F.3d 792, 809 (9th Cir. 2003) ("a defendant's use of a plaintiff's mark is nominative where he or she used the plaintiff's mark to describe the plaintiff's product, even if the defendant's ultimate goal is to describe his own product.") (internal citation and quotation omitted).

f. First Amendment Concerns. The leading cases in this area are developed in detail, below. Procedurally, these cases allow the defendant to raise the First Amendment as a shield, an affirmative defense which essentially informs the court that it may not interpret the law in a manner that would force the trademark law to become a law abridging the freedom of speech or press. The courts strive to interpret the laws in a manner that does not suggest content regulation. As this area of law continues to be developed, courts might begin to treat trademark law as a form of content-neutral, time, place, or manner restriction. Would this provide greater guidance to courts and parties?

g. There are many examples of publicity and trademark infringement litigation. The following list of cases may not be long, but it is illustrious. A brief chronology sampled from among the leading cases provides an interesting timeline:

- *Motschenbacher v. R.J. Reynolds Tobacco Co.*, 498 F.2d 821 (9th Cir. 1974) (recognizing right of publicity for a sports car driver, identified in part based on his car rather than his name or likeness).

- *Groucho Marx Productions, Inc. v. Day & Night Co.*, 523 F. Supp. 485 (S.D.N.Y. 1981), rev'd on other grounds, 689 F.2d 317 (2d Cir. 1982) (addressing right to use real persons in a fictional stage play) (reversed because the Second Circuit determined that New York law should be applied and New York's publicity law is not descendible).

- *Estate of Presley v. Russen*, 513 F. Supp. 1339 (D.N.J. 1981) (contrasting publicity and trademark rights in Elvis Presley and those trademarks used by him, but refusing to prohibit the continued look-alike performances).

- *Carson v. Here's Johnny Portable Toilets, Inc.*, 698 F.2d 831 (6th Cir. 1983) (affirming §43(a) and other claims for use of a pun on Carson's "Here's Johnny" introduction).

- *Stephano v. News Group Publications*, 64 N.Y.2d 174 (N.Y. 1984) (photograph of professional model not used as advertising or in trade where it accompanied a news article on fashion rather than a paid advertisement).

- *Allen v. National Video, Inc.*, 610 F. Supp. 612 (S.D.N.Y. 1985) (addressing use of look-alikes in advertisements).

- *White v. Samsung Electronics America, Inc.,* 971 F.2d 1395 (9th Cir. 1992) (permitting identity claim to be presented to the jury where the likeness was based on the pearls and hand gesture of a vaguely female robot).

- *Wendt v. Host Int'l, Inc.,* 125 F.3d 806, 812 (9th Cir. 1997) (actors from *Cheers* may have publicity interests in robotic dolls).

- *Seale v. Gramercy Pictures,* 949 F. Supp. 331 (E.D. Pa. 1996) (although no publicity rights claim was recognized for a docudrama of the Black Panther Party founded by plaintiff Bobby Seale and Huey P. Newton, court allowed trial to proceed on whether the soundtrack album using Seale's name and likeness was similarly protected).

h. Drawing fine distinctions in publicity rights and the First Amendment continues to baffle courts and commentators. For example, in *Doe v. TCI Cablevision,* 110 S.W.3d 363 (Mo. 2003), professional hockey player "enforcer" Tony Twist argued that his name had been co-opted by the Spawn comic for the character "Anthony 'Tony Twist' Twistelli," a mafia don and enforcer. Although the defamation claim was denied on First Amendment grounds, the right of publicity claim survived. On substantially the same facts, the Missouri Supreme Court rejected the California decision finding First Amendment protection for the comic book. The Missouri Supreme Court explained:

> Right to publicity cases, both before and after *Zacchini*, focus instead on the threshold legal question of whether the use of a person's name and identity is "expressive," in which case it is fully protected, or "commercial," in which case it is generally not protected. For instance, the use of a person's identity in news, entertainment, and creative works for the purpose of communicating information or expressive ideas about that person is protected "expressive" speech. On the other hand, the use of a person's identity for purely commercial purposes, like advertising goods or services or the use of a person's name or likeness on merchandise is rarely protected.

> Several approaches have been offered to distinguish between expressive speech and commercial speech. The RESTATEMENT, for example, employs a "relatedness" test that protects the use of another person's name or identity in a work that is "related to" that person. The catalogue of "related" uses includes "the use of a person's name or likeness in news reporting, whether in newspapers, magazines, or broadcast news ... use in entertainment and other creative works, including both fiction and nonfiction ... use as part of an article published in a fan magazine or in a feature story broadcast on an entertainment program ... dissemination of an unauthorized print or broadcast biography, [and use] of another's identity in a novel, play, or motion picture...." RESTATEMENT (THIRD) OF UNFAIR COMPETITION sec. 47 cmt. c at 549. The proviso to that list, however, is that "if the name or likeness is used solely to attract attention to a work that is *not related* to the identified person, the user may be subject to liability for a use of the other's identity in advertising...." *Id.* (emphasis added).

> California courts use a different approach, called the "transformative test," ... "'what is essentially a balancing test between the First Amendment and the right of publicity based on whether the work in question adds significant creative elements so as to be transformed into something more than a mere celebrity likeness or imitation.'" ...

> The weakness of the RESTATEMENT's "relatedness" test and California's "transformative" test is that they give too little consideration to the fact that many uses of a person's name and identity have both expressive and commercial components. These tests operate to preclude a cause of action whenever the use of

the name and identity is in any way expressive, regardless of its commercial exploitation. Under the relatedness test, use of a person's name and identity is actionable only when the use is solely commercial and is otherwise unrelated to that person. Under the transformative test, the transformation or fictionalized characterization of a person's celebrity status is not actionable even if its sole purpose is the commercial use of that person's name and identity. Though these tests purport to balance the prospective interests involved, there is no balancing at all—once the use is determined to be expressive, it is protected. At least one commentator, however, has advocated the use of a more balanced balancing test—a sort of predominant use test—that better addresses the cases where speech is both expressive and commercial:

> If a product is being sold that predominantly exploits the commercial value of an individual's identity, that product should be held to violate the right of publicity and not be protected by the First Amendment, even if there is some "expressive" content in it that might qualify as "speech" in other circumstances. If, on the other hand, the predominant purpose of the product is to make an expressive comment on or about a celebrity, the expressive values could be given greater weight.

Id. at 373–74 (quoting Mark S. Lee, *Agents of Chaos: Judicial Confusion in Defining the Right of Publicity-Free Speech Interface*, 23 LOY. L.A. Ent. L. Rev. 471, 488–98 (2003)). See also *Winter v. D.C. Comics*, 30 Cal. 4th 881, 69 P.3d 473 (2003). On remand in *Doe v. TCI Cablevision*, a St. Louis jury again found for Twist. In January 2005, the $15,000,000 verdict for Twist's publicity rights against Todd McFarlane Productions Inc. drew the Spawn publisher into bankruptcy protection.

Problem VII-B

In posters and flyers for Bryce's "New Masters" series, the name for the reconceived Gilbert & Sullivan series (see Problem VII-A), some of the students used a mock-up of Universal Pictures *Frankenstein* poster and a photograph of Boris Karloff's image as Frankenstein to promote the new play. Redrawn in pen and ink, the poster shows a recognizable Karloff-like monster sporting a Mohawk and nose ring. It does not use Universal's name or logo. Instead the students copied the poster style of the early 1930s. (Copies of the poster art may be viewed or purchased on eBay.)

Tyrell Jones, the faculty member in charge of the project, has called Bryce. The school has been subject to a number of copyright and trademark infringement complaints in recent years, so the central administration is quite sensitive to activity that may invite more complaints. Tyrell has been hearing of objections regarding the mocked-up artwork. Bryce asks your advice and counsel. Explain to Bryce the grounds for objection to the artwork and the extent to which such grounds are supported by law.

C. Sound Alikes

Midler v. Ford Motor Co.
849 F.2d 460 (9th Cir. 1988)

This case centers on the protectibility of the voice of a celebrated chanteuse from commercial exploitation without her consent. Ford Motor Company and its advertising agency, Young & Rubicam, Inc., in 1985 advertised the Ford Lincoln Mercury with a series of nineteen 30 or 60 second television commercials in what the agency called "The Yuppie Campaign." The aim was to make an emotional connection with Yuppies, bringing back memories of when they were in college. Different popular songs of the seventies were sung on each commercial. The agency tried to get "the original people," that is, the singers who had popularized the songs, to sing them. Failing in that endeavor in ten cases the agency had the songs sung by "sound alikes." Bette Midler, the plaintiff and appellant here, was done by a sound alike.

Midler is a nationally known actress and singer. She won a Grammy as early as 1973 as the Best New Artist of that year. Records made by her since then have gone Platinum and Gold. She was nominated in 1979 for an Academy award for Best Female Actress in The Rose, in which she portrayed a pop singer. Newsweek in its June 30, 1986 issue described her as an "outrageously original singer/comedian." Time hailed her in its March 2, 1987 issue as "a legend" and "the most dynamic and poignant singer-actress of her time."

When Young & Rubicam was preparing the Yuppie Campaign it presented the commercial to its client by playing an edited version of Midler singing "Do You Want To Dance," taken from the 1973 Midler album, "The Divine Miss M." After the client accepted the idea and form of the commercial, the agency contacted Midler's manager, Jerry Edelstein. The conversation went as follows: "Hello, I am Craig Hazen from Young and Rubicam. I am calling you to find out if Bette Midler would be interested in doing ...? Edelstein: "Is it a commercial?" "Yes." "We are not interested."

Undeterred, Young & Rubicam sought out Ula Hedwig whom it knew to have been one of "the Harlettes" a backup singer for Midler for ten years. Hedwig was told by Young & Rubicam that "they wanted someone who could sound like Bette Midler's recording of [Do You Want To Dance]." ... At the direction of Young & Rubicam, Hedwig made a record for the commercial. The Midler record of "Do You Want To Dance" was first played to her. She was told to "sound as much as possible like the Bette Midler record," leaving out only a few "aahs" unsuitable for the commercial. Hedwig imitated Midler to the best of her ability. ...

Neither the name nor the picture of Midler was used in the commercial; Young & Rubicam had a license from the copyright holder to use the song. At issue in this case is only the protection of Midler's voice. The district court described the defendants' conduct as that "of the average thief." They decided, "If we can't buy it, we'll take it." The court nonetheless believed there was no legal principle preventing imitation of Midler's voice and so gave summary judgment for the defendants. Midler appeals.

The First Amendment protects much of what the media do in the reproduction of likenesses or sounds. A primary value is freedom of speech and press. The purpose of the media's use of a person's identity is central. ... Moreover, federal copyright law pre-empts much of the area. "Mere imitation of a recorded performance would not constitute a copyright infringement even where one performer deliberately sets out to simulate another's performance as exactly as possible." It is in the context of these First Amendment and federal copyright distinctions that we address the present appeal.

Nancy Sinatra once sued Goodyear Tire and Rubber Company on the basis of an advertising campaign by Young & Rubicam featuring "These Boots Are Made For Walkin'," a song closely identified with her; the female singers of the commercial were alleged to have imitated her voice and style and to have dressed and looked like her. The basis of Nancy Sinatra's complaint was unfair competition; she claimed that the song and the arrangement had acquired "a secondary meaning" which, under California law, was protectible. This court noted that the defendants "had paid a very substantial sum to the copyright proprietor to obtain the license for the use of the song and all of its arrangements." To give Sinatra damages for their use of the song would clash with federal copyright law. Summary judgment for the defendants was affirmed.

If Midler were claiming a secondary meaning to "Do You Want To Dance" or seeking to prevent the defendants from using that song, she would fail like Sinatra. But that is not this case. Midler does not seek damages for Ford's use of "Do You Want To Dance," and thus her claim is not preempted by federal copyright law. Copyright protects "original works of authorship fixed in any tangible medium of expression." A voice is not copyrightable. The sounds are not "fixed." What is put forward as protectible here is more personal than any work of authorship.

Bert Lahr once sued Adell Chemical Co. for selling Lestoil by means of a commercial in which an imitation of Lahr's voice accompanied a cartoon of a duck. Lahr alleged that his style of vocal delivery was distinctive in pitch, accent, inflection, and sounds. The First Circuit held that Lahr had stated a cause of action for unfair competition, that it could be found "that defendant's conduct saturated plaintiff's audience, curtailing his market." That case is more like this one. But we do not find unfair competition here. One-minute commercials of the sort the defendants put on would not have saturated Midler's audience and curtailed her market. Midler did not do television commercials. The defendants were not in competition with her.

California Civil Code section 3344 is also of no aid to Midler. The statute affords damages to a person injured by another who uses the person's "name, voice, signature, photograph or likeness, in any manner." The defendants did not use Midler's name or anything else whose use is prohibited by the statute. The voice they used was Hedwig's, not hers. The term "likeness" refers to a visual image not a vocal imitation. The statute, however, does not preclude Midler from pursuing any cause of action she may have at common law; the statute itself implies that such common law causes of action do exist because it says its remedies are merely "cumulative." ... Appropriation of such common law rights is a tort in California....

California will recognize an injury from "an appropriation of the attributes of one's identity." ... [D]efendants here used an imitation to convey the impression that Midler was singing for them.

Why did the defendants ask Midler to sing if her voice was not of value to them? Why did they studiously acquire the services of a sound-alike and instruct her to imitate Midler if Midler's voice was not of value to them? What they sought was an attribute of Midler's identity. Its value was what the market would have paid for Midler to have sung the commercial in person.

A voice is more distinctive and more personal than the automobile accouterments protected in *Motschenbacher* [*v. R.J. Reynolds Tobacco Co.*, 498 F.2d 821 (9th Cir. 1974)]. A voice is as distinctive and personal as a face. The human voice is one of the most palpable ways identity is manifested. We are all aware that a friend is at once known by a few words on the phone.... A fortiori, these observations hold true of singing, especially singing by a singer of renown. The singer manifests herself in the song. To impersonate her voice is to pirate her identity.

We need not and do not go so far as to hold that every imitation of a voice to advertise merchandise is actionable. We hold only that when a distinctive voice of a professional singer is widely known and is deliberately imitated in order to sell a product, the sellers have appropriated what is not theirs and have committed a tort in California. Midler has made a showing, sufficient to defeat summary judgment, that the defendants here for their own profit in selling their product did appropriate part of her identity.

Waits v. Frito-Lay, Inc.
978 F.2d 1093 (9th Cir. 1992)

Defendants Frito-Lay, Inc., and Tracy-Locke, Inc., appeal a jury verdict and award of $2.6 million in compensatory damages, punitive damages, and attorney's fees, in favor of singer Tom Waits. Waits sued the snack food manufacturer and its advertising agency for voice misappropriation and false endorsement following the broadcast of a radio commercial for SalsaRio Doritos which featured a vocal performance imitating Waits' raspy singing voice. On appeal, the defendants mount attacks on nearly all aspects of the judgment....

Tom Waits is a professional singer, songwriter, and actor of some renown. Waits has a raspy, gravelly singing voice, described by one fan as "like how you'd sound if you drank a quart of bourbon, smoked a pack of cigarettes and swallowed a pack of razor blades.... Late at night. After not sleeping for three days." Since the early 1970s, when his professional singing career began, Waits has recorded more than seventeen albums and has toured extensively, playing to sold-out audiences throughout the United States, Canada, Europe, Japan, and Australia. Regarded as a "prestige artist" rather than a musical superstar, Waits has achieved both commercial and critical success in his musical career. In 1987, Waits received *Rolling Stone* magazine's Critic's Award for Best Live Performance, chosen over other noted performers such as Bruce Springsteen, U2, David Bowie, and Madonna. *SPIN* magazine listed him in its March 1990 issue as one of the ten most interesting recording artists of the last five years....

Frito-Lay, Inc. is in the business of manufacturing, distributing, and selling prepared and packaged food products, including Doritos brand corn chips. Tracy-Locke, Inc. is an advertising agency which counts Frito-Lay among its clients. In developing an advertising campaign to introduce a new Frito-Lay product, SalsaRio Doritos, Tracy-Locke found inspiration in a 1976 Waits song, "Step Right Up." ...

The story of Tracy-Locke's search for a lead singer for the commercial suggests that no one would do but a singer who could not only capture the feeling of "Step Right Up" but also imitate Tom Waits' voice.... Stephen Carter was among those who auditioned.... When Carter auditioned, members of the Tracy-Locke creative team "did a double take" over Carter's near-perfect imitation of Waits, and remarked to him how much he sounded like Waits....

On the day the commercial was due for release to radio stations across the country, Grossman had a ten-minute long-distance telephone consultation with Tracy-Locke's attorney, asking him whether there would be legal problems with a commercial that sought to capture the same feeling as Waits' music. The attorney noted that there was a "high profile" risk of a lawsuit in view of recent case law recognizing the protectability of a distinctive voice. Based on what Grossman had told him, however, the attorney did not think such a suit would have merit, because a singer's style of music is not protected....

Waits' claim, like Bette Midler's, is for infringement of voice, not for infringement of a copyrightable subject such as sound recording or musical composition. Moreover, the legislative history of section 114 indicates the express intent of Congress that "[t]he evolving common law rights of 'privacy,' 'publicity,' and trade secrets ... remain unaffected [by the preemption provision] as long as the causes of action contain elements, such as an invasion of personal rights ... that are different in kind from copyright infringement." Waits' voice misappropriation claim is one for invasion of a personal property right: his right of publicity to control the use of his identity as embodied in his voice. The trial's focus was on the elements of voice misappropriation, as formulated in Midler: whether the defendants had deliberately imitated Waits' voice rather than simply his style and whether Waits' voice was sufficiently distinctive and widely known to give him a protectable right in its use. These elements are "different in kind" from those in a copyright infringement case challenging the unauthorized use of a song or recording. Waits' voice misappropriation claim, therefore, is not preempted by federal copyright law.

The defendants next contend that the district court committed prejudicial error by rejecting their proposed jury instructions on three elements of the Midler tort: the deliberate misappropriation for commercial purposes of (1) a voice, that is (2) distinctive and (3) widely known. We consider jury instructions as a whole to determine if they are misleading or inadequate. We review challenges to the formulation of jury instructions for abuse of discretion. Whether a jury instruction misstates the elements that must be proved at trial, however, is a question of law which we review *de novo*....

[R]ead as a whole, the instructions were not misleading. In charging the jury, the court repeatedly noted that two claims were presented for determination and gave separate instructions on each claim. The court's voice misappropriation instructions limited the jury's consideration to voice, and in no way implied that it could consider style. Indeed, in addressing the jury in closing argument, Waits' attorney agreed with the defendants that style was not protected. Moreover, the court included an additional instruction that effectively narrowed the jury's focus to Waits' voice and indicated that style imitation alone was insufficient for tort liability. For the defendants to be liable for voice misappropriation, the court stated, the imitation had to be so good that "people who were familiar with plaintiff's voice who heard the commercial *believed plaintiff performed it*. In this connection it is not enough that they were reminded of plaintiff or thought the singer sounded like plaintiff...." (emphasis added). This instruction effectively added an additional element to Midler's formulation of voice misappropriation: actual confusion. The validity of this instruction is not before us in this appeal and we express no opinion on this issue. Even if the jury were initially confused about whether the defendants could be liable simply for imitating Waits' style, this instruction would have disabused them of this notion....

The defendants next argue that reputational damages are available only in defamation actions and that since Waits did not allege or prove defamation, they were unavailable here. Further, they argue, there was no evidence to support the award of such damages because Waits did not show that his career had suffered. Again, we reject these contentions.

We have no doubt, in light of general tort liability principles, that where the misappropriation of identity causes injury to reputation, compensation for such injury is appropriate. Reputational damages, moreover, have been awarded in right of publicity cases. The central issue is not whether these damages were available, but whether the evidence was sufficient to establish injury to Waits' reputation. As we noted above, the jury could have inferred from the evidence that the commercial created a public impression that Waits was a hypocrite for endorsing Doritos. Moreover, it also could have inferred damage to his artistic reputation, for Waits had testified that "part of my character and personality and image that I have cultivated is that I do not endorse products." Finally, from the testimony of Waits' expert witness, the jury could have inferred that if Waits ever wanted to do a commercial in the future, the fee he could command would be lowered by $50,000 to $150,000 because of the Doritos commercial. This evidence was sufficient to support the jury's award of $75,000 for injury to Waits' goodwill and future publicity value.

The jury awarded Waits a total of $2 million in punitive damages for voice misappropriation: $1.5 million against Tracy-Locke and $500,000 against Frito-Lay. The defendants ask that we vacate this award, arguing that punitive damages are unavailable as a matter of law, and alternatively, that the evidence was insufficient to support their award.

In California, exemplary or punitive damages are available "where it is proven by clear and convincing evidence that the defendant has been guilty of oppression, fraud, or malice." The statute defines "malice" in pertinent part as "despicable conduct which is carried on by the defendant with a *willful and conscious disregard of the rights* or safety of others." The defendants contend that because Midler was so recently decided and so imprecise in the scope of its holding, they could not have been aware of the rights they were infringing upon in broadcasting the commercial. Thus, they reason, their conduct was not in "conscious disregard" of Waits' property right in his voice.

Where an issue is one of first impression or where a right has not been clearly established, punitive damages are generally unavailable. The right of a well-known professional singer to control the commercial use of a distinctive voice, however, was not an "issue of first impression" in this case. The right had been established clearly by Midler. The evidence was unequivocal that, although Midler was decided just three months before the conduct at issue, Tracy-Locke personnel responsible for making the Doritos commercial were familiar with the Midler decision. Tracy-Locke was concerned enough that the commercial could result in voice misappropriation liability that it cautioned Frito-Lay of the legal risks in choosing the Carter version. At the same time, however, Tracy-Locke stated its readiness to indemnify Frito-Lay against damages. Frito-Lay, reassured by the indemnification, chose to proceed with the Carter version. In going forward with the commercial, the defendants knowingly took a calculated risk, thereby consciously disregarding the effect of these actions on Waits' legally recognized rights.

The defendants argue, however, that although they may have been aware that legal risks were involved, they had a good faith belief that Waits' rights would not be infringed because they read the legal precedents differently. This argument leaves us unpersuaded. Good faith cannot be manufactured by looking to the law of other jurisdictions to define the rights of California residents. Midler could not be more clear that, in California at least, a well-known singer with a distinctive voice has a property right in that voice. Waits is a California resident, a fact of which Tracy-Locke personnel were aware. The defendants made a conscious decision to broadcast a vocal performance imitating Waits in markets across the country, including San Francisco and Los Angeles. This evidence is sufficient to raise at least a prima facie showing that defendants acted in conscious disregard of rights recognized in California.

Even if punitive damages are available, the defendants argue, the award must be vacated because it is not supported by clear and convincing evidence, as required by California law. Clear and convincing evidence means evidence sufficient to support a finding of "high probability." ...

The evidence the jury heard included testimony that Carter, the Waits' impersonator, told Brenner that Waits had a policy against doing commercials and would not like this one. Brenner knew of Waits' policy because he had tried unsuccessfully to hire him for another commercial. In the face of Brenner's warnings that the commercial sounded too much like Waits and presented serious legal concerns, Grossman called a lawyer. Although the lawyer thought the scenario Grossman painted him did not present a colorable legal problem, Grossman had not told the lawyer that the commercial featured a voice that sounded like Waits—only that the "feeling" of the music was the same. Grossman urged Frito-Lay to choose the Carter version over one that did not sound like Waits. ...

We believe that, viewed most favorably to Waits, this evidence was adequate to support a finding of high probability that Tracy-Locke and Frito-Lay acted with malice. Despicability reflects a moral judgment, "conscious disregard" a state of mind. A rational jury could have found the defendants' conduct despicable because they knowingly impugned Waits' integrity in the public eye. A rational jury also could have found that the defendants, in spite of their awareness of Waits' legal right to control the commercial use of his voice, acted in conscious disregard of that right by broadcasting the commercial. We therefore affirm the award of punitive damages.

II. *Lanham Act Claim*

Section 43(a) of the Lanham Act, prohibits the use of false designations of origin, false descriptions, and false representations in the advertising and sale of goods and services. Waits' claim under section 43(a) is premised on the theory that by using an imitation of his distinctive voice in an admitted parody of a Tom Waits song, the defendants misrepresented his association with and endorsement of SalsaRio Doritos. The jury found in Waits' favor and awarded him $100,000 in damages. The district court also awarded him attorneys' fees under section 35 of the Lanham Act. On appeal, the defendants argue that Waits lacks standing to bring a Lanham Act claim, that Waits' false endorsement claim fails on its merits, that the damage award is duplicative, and that attorneys' fees are improper. Before we address these contentions, however, we turn to the threshold issue of whether false endorsement claims are properly cognizable under section 43(a) of the Lanham Act, a question of first impression in this circuit. ... Section 43(a) now expressly prohibits, *inter alia,* the use of any symbol or device which is likely to deceive consumers as to the association, sponsorship, or approval of goods or services by another person. Moreover, the legislative history of the 1988 amendments also makes clear that in retaining the statute's original terms "symbol or device" in the definition of "trademark," Congress approved the broad judicial interpretation of these terms to include distinctive sounds and physical appearance. In light of persuasive judicial authority and the subsequent congressional approval of that authority, we conclude that false endorsement claims, including those premised on the unauthorized imitation of an entertainer's distinctive voice, are cognizable under section 43(a). ...

A false endorsement claim based on the unauthorized use of a celebrity's identity is a type of false association claim, for it alleges the misuse of a trademark, *i.e.,* a symbol or device such as a visual likeness, vocal imitation, or other uniquely distinguishing characteristic, which is likely to confuse consumers as to the plaintiff's sponsorship or approval of the product. Standing, therefore, does not require "actual competition" in the traditional sense; it extends to a purported endorser who has an economic interest akin to that of a trademark holder in controlling the commercial exploitation of his or her identity. Moreover, the wrongful appropriator is in a sense a competitor of the celebrity, even when the celebrity has chosen to disassociate himself or herself from advertising products as has Waits. They compete with respect to the use of the celebrity's name or identity. They are both utilizing or marketing that personal property for commercial purposes. Accordingly, we hold that a celebrity whose endorsement of a product is implied through the imitation of a distinctive attribute of the celebrity's identity, has standing to sue for false endorsement under section 43(a) of the Lanham Act. Tom Waits, therefore, need not be a competitor in the traditional sense to sue under the Lanham Act for the imitation of his voice on the theory that its use falsely associated him with Doritos as an endorser. Rather, his standing was sufficiently established by the likelihood that the wrongful use of his professional trademark, his unique voice, would injure him commercially....

This evidence was sufficient to support the jury's finding that consumers were likely to be misled by the commercial into believing that Waits endorsed SalsaRio Doritos....

The defendants urge us to vacate the damage award on Waits' Lanham Act claim as duplicative of those damages awarded for voice misappropriation representing the fair market value of Waits' services. Waits does not contest this point. Standing by the representations he made to the jury at trial that he was not seeking a double recovery, he asserts on appeal that he "does not oppose a reduction of the final judgment in the amount of $100,000 based on the overlapping Lanham Act award."

In instructing the jury on Waits' Lanham Act claim, the court stated that it could award damages for the fair market value of Waits' services. The jury awarded Waits $100,000 on this claim. It also awarded Waits $100,000 for the fair market value of his services on his voice misappropriation claim. The damages awarded under the Lanham Act, therefore, are duplicative. Accordingly, we vacate this portion of the judgment....

Waits' voice misappropriation claim and his Lanham Act claim are legally sufficient. The court did not err in instructing the jury on elements of voice misappropriation. The jury's verdict on each claim is supported by substantial evidence, as are its damage awards. Its award of damages on Waits' Lanham Act claim, however, is duplicative of damages awarded for voice misappropriation; accordingly we vacate it. Finally, the court did not abuse its discretion in awarding attorneys' fees under the Lanham Act....

Notes and Questions

a. Frito-Lay continued to struggle with the sound-alike cases. In *Oliveira v. Frito-Lay, Inc.,* 251 F.3d 56 (2d Cir. N.Y. 2001), Astrud Oliveira (or Astrud Gilberto) did not fare as well as Tom Waits. The Second Circuit rejected her distinctive voice claim. Her second attempt at Lanham Act protection was more inventive, but also rejected. She claimed her song, "The Girl from Ipanema," was her trademark song such that the use by Frito-Lay created an implied endorsement by her. The court shied away from the novel claim. As it explained:

> We cannot say it would be unthinkable for the trademark law to accord to a performing artist a trademark or service mark in her signature performance.... But for a court now to "recognize" the previously unknown existence of such a right would be profoundly disruptive to commerce. Numerous artists who could assert claims similar to Gilberto's would bring suit against entities that had paid bona fide license fees to all known holders of rights. Indeed, artists who had licensed users under their copyrights and had received fees for the copyright license could bring suits claiming additional compensation for infringement of trademark rights. Immense unforeseen liabilities might accrue, upsetting reasonable commercial expectations.

Id. at 62–63.

The Second Circuit pointed to both the lack of prior case law and the potential disruption for the marketplace. Nonetheless, the claim may be less extreme than that. The court recognized that commercial jingles ("You Deserve a Break Today") or public domain songs ("William Tell Overture" for the Lone Ranger and "Sweet Georgia Brown" for the Harlem Globetrotters) are recognized as trademarks. The distinction is that the song relates to the product or service rather than back to the singer.

Perhaps one-hit wonders like Nancy Sinatra or Astrud Gilberto can be marketed using their signature songs as trademarks. Would the result be different if the song in question was used in commercials and registered as a trademark for those advertised services?

b. The *Waits* Court expanded the liability for sound-alikes, moving past the position it had previously held in *Cher v. Forum Int'l, Ltd.,* 692 F.2d 634 (9th Cir. 1982) (finding for Cher for state unfair competition law and refusing to decide the Lanham Act claim). In this case, an interview granted by the singer/actress was subsequently sold to a hard-core adult magazine and not published by the magazine she believed to be publishing the interview.

c. If a movie distributor changes the rating for a motion picture, does that change give rise to any Lanham Act claim for false endorsement of the motion picture? See *Halicki v. United Artists Communications, Inc.,* 812 F.2d 1213 (9th Cir. 1987). What if the anticipated PG-13 film was edited in a manner to receive a rating of X or NC-17?

d. On the topic of endorsements, to what extent does the use of a song serve as an endorsement of a motion picture or its home video version? Can a composer object to the unintended endorsement created by her song when the song is used in a project the composer finds objectionable? See *Storball v. Twentieth Century Fox Film Corp.,* 1993 U.S. Dist. LEXIS 20455, 30 U.S.P.Q.2d (BNA) 1394 (C.D. Cal. 1993).

e. Modern courts continue to struggle with preemption of copyright and the extent to which the performer's voice can be licensed by the sound recording company without first acquiring the performer's publicity rights in the performance. Should such claims to one's vocal performance be assigned to the sound recording company as a matter of copyright law? See *Laws v. Sony Music Entm't, Inc.,* 448 F.3d 1134 (9th Cir. 2006); *E.S.S. Entm't 2000, Inc. v. Rock Star Videos, Inc.,* 547 F.3d 1095 (9th Cir. 2008) (reproduced in Chap. 18, Sec. C, *infra*).

Problem VII-C

Bryce has stopped by your office with a serious problem. Three years ago, Bryce modeled a very flashy outfit. Last month, a friend showed Bryce a photograph that looked almost the same as the original photograph, except that Bryce's flashy outfit appears to have been modified so as to appear nearly transparent (though not quite pornographic) and the backdrop digitally altered to resemble what can best be described as a bordello. The photograph appears in an adult-content magazine.

Bryce tells you that at the time of the photo-shoot, Bryce signed an agreement licensing name, likeness, and identity in association with the marketing and sales of the modeled clothing. Bryce is convinced that the outfit has been digitally altered to seem much more revealing than the outfit as originally worn. Worse, if Tyrell Jones, the faculty member in charge of the New Masters project, learns of the pictures, Bryce is sure to be fired. Advise Bryce regarding the legal ability to enjoin the distribution of the magazine and to stop all future uses of the offending photograph.

D. Tension between Publicity and Free Speech

Comedy III Prods., Inc. v. Gary Saderup, Inc.
25 Cal. 4th 387 (2001)

... I. THE STATUTE

In this state the right of publicity is both a statutory and a common law right.... Section 990 declares broadly that "Any person who uses a deceased personality's name, voice, signature, photograph, or likeness, in any manner, on or in products, merchandise, or goods, or for purposes of advertising or selling, or soliciting purchases of, products, merchandise, goods, or services, without prior consent from the person or persons specified in subdivision (c), shall be liable for any damages sustained by the person or persons injured as a result thereof." The amount recoverable includes "any profits from the unauthorized use," as well as punitive damages, attorney fees, and costs....

The statute provides a number of exemptions from the requirement of consent to use. Thus a use "in connection with any news, public affairs, or sports broadcast or account, or any political campaign" does not require consent. Use in a "commercial medium" does not require consent solely because the material is commercially sponsored or contains paid advertising; "Rather it shall be a question of fact whether or not the use ... was so directly connected with" the sponsorship or advertising that it requires consent. Finally, subdivision (n) provides that "[a] play, book, magazine, newspaper, musical composition, film, radio or television program," work of "political or newsworthy value," "[s]ingle and original works of fine art," or "[a]n advertisement or commercial announcement" for the above works are all exempt from the provisions of the statute.

Plaintiff Comedy III Productions, Inc. (hereafter Comedy III), brought this action against defendants Gary Saderup and Gary Saderup, Inc. (hereafter collectively Saderup), seeking damages and injunctive relief for violation of section 990 and related business torts.... Comedy III is the registered owner of all rights to the former comedy act known as The Three Stooges, who are deceased personalities within the meaning of the statute. Saderup is an artist with over 25 years' experience in making charcoal drawings of celebrities. These drawings are used to create lithographic and silkscreen masters, which in turn are used to produce multiple reproductions in the form, respectively, of lithographic prints and silkscreened images on T-shirts. Saderup creates the original drawings and is actively involved in the ensuing lithographic and silkscreening processes.

Without securing Comedy III's consent, Saderup sold lithographs and T-shirts bearing a likeness of The Three Stooges reproduced from a charcoal drawing he had made. These lithographs and T-shirts did not constitute an advertisement, endorsement, or sponsorship of any product. Saderup's profits from the sale of unlicensed lithographs and T-shirts bearing a likeness of The Three Stooges was $75,000 and Comedy III's reasonable attorney fees were $150,000.

On these stipulated facts the court found for Comedy III and entered judgment against Saderup awarding damages of $75,000 and attorney fees of $150,000 plus costs.... Saderup ... contends that enforcement of the judgment against him violates his right of free speech and expression under the First Amendment. He raises a difficult issue, which we address below.

The right of publicity is often invoked in the context of commercial speech when the appropriation of a celebrity likeness creates a false and misleading impression that the celebrity is endorsing a product. Because the First Amendment does not protect false and misleading commercial speech, and because even nonmisleading commercial speech is generally subject to somewhat lesser First Amendment protection, the right of publicity may often trump the right of advertisers to make use of celebrity figures.

But the present case does not concern commercial speech. As the trial court found, Saderup's portraits of The Three Stooges are expressive works and not an advertisement for or endorsement of a product. Although his work was done for financial gain, "[t]he First Amendment is not limited to those who publish without charge.... [An expressive activity] does not lose its constitutional protection because it is undertaken for profit."

The tension between the right of publicity and the First Amendment is highlighted by recalling the two distinct, commonly acknowledged purposes of the latter. First, "'to preserve an uninhibited marketplace of ideas' and to repel efforts to limit the '"uninhibited, robust and wide-open" debate on public issues.'" Second, to foster a "fundamental respect for individual development and self-realization. The right to self-expression is inherent in any political system which respects individual dignity. Each speaker must be free of government restraint regardless of the nature or manner of the views expressed unless there is a compelling reason to the contrary."

The right of publicity has a potential for frustrating the fulfillment of both these purposes. Because celebrities take on public meaning, the appropriation of their likenesses may have important uses in uninhibited debate on public issues, particularly debates about culture and values. And because celebrities take on personal meanings to many individuals in the society, the creative appropriation of celebrity images can be an important avenue of individual expression. As one commentator has stated:

> Entertainment and sports celebrities are the leading players in our Public Drama. We tell tales, both tall and cautionary, about them. We monitor their comings and goings, their missteps and heartbreaks. We copy their mannerisms, their styles, their modes of conversation and of consumption. Whether or not celebrities are 'the chief agents of moral change in the United States,' they certainly are widely used—far more than are institutionally anchored elites—to symbolize individual aspirations, group identities, and cultural values. Their images are thus important expressive and communicative resources: the peculiar, yet familiar idiom in which we conduct a fair portion of our cultural business and everyday conversation.

(Madow, *Private Ownership of Public Image: Popular Culture and Publicity Rights* 81 Cal. L. Rev. 125, 128 (1993) (Madow), italics and fns. omitted.)

As Madow further points out, the very importance of celebrities in society means that the right of publicity has the potential of censoring significant expression by suppressing alternative versions of celebrity images that are iconoclastic, irreverent, or otherwise attempt to redefine the celebrity's meaning. (Madow, *supra, 81 Cal. L.Rev. at pp. 143–145.*) A majority of this court recognized as much in *Guglielmi [v. Spelling-Goldberg Productions, 25 Cal. 3d 860, 869 (1979)]*: "The right of publicity derived from public prominence does not confer a shield to ward off caricature, parody and satire. Rather, prominence invites creative comment."

For similar reasons, speech about public figures is accorded heightened First Amendment protection in defamation law.... Giving broad scope to the right of publicity has the potential of allowing a celebrity to accomplish through the vigorous exercise of that right the censorship of unflattering commentary that cannot be constitutionally accomplished through defamation actions.

Nor do Saderup's creations lose their constitutional protections because they are for purposes of entertaining rather than informing. As Chief Justice Bird stated in *Guglielmi*, invoking the dual purpose of the First Amendment: "Our courts have often observed that entertainment is entitled to the same constitutional protection as the exposition of ideas. That conclusion rests on two propositions. First, '[t]he line between informing and entertaining is too elusive for the protection of the basic right. Everyone is familiar with instances of propaganda through fiction. What is one man's amusement, teaches another doctrine.'" "Second, entertainment, as a mode of self-expression, is entitled to constitutional protection irrespective of its contribution to the marketplace of ideas. 'For expression is an integral part of the development of ideas, of mental exploration and of the affirmation of self. The power to realize his potentiality as a human being begins at this point and must extend at least this far if the whole nature of man is not to be thwarted.'" ...

Nor does the fact that Saderup's art appears in large part on a less conventional avenue of communications, T-shirts, result in reduced First Amendment protection. As Judge Posner stated in the case of a defendant who sold T-shirts advocating the legalization of marijuana, "its T-shirts ... are to [the seller] what the *New York Times* is to the Sulzbergers and the Ochs—the vehicle of her ideas and opinions." First Amendment doctrine does not disfavor nontraditional media of expression.

But having recognized the high degree of First Amendment protection for noncommercial speech about celebrities, we need not conclude that all expression that trenches on the right of publicity receives such protection. The right of publicity, like copyright, protects a form of intellectual property that society deems to have some social utility. "Often considerable money, time and energy are needed to develop one's prominence in a particular field. Years of labor may be required before one's skill, reputation, notoriety or virtues are sufficiently developed to permit an economic return through some medium of commercial promotion. For some, the investment may eventually create considerable commercial value in one's identity."

The present case exemplifies this kind of creative labor. Moe and Jerome (Curly) Howard and Larry Fein fashioned personae collectively known as The Three Stooges, first in vaudeville and later in movie shorts, over a period extending from the 1920s to the 1940s....

Although surprisingly few courts have considered in any depth the means of reconciling the right of publicity and the First Amendment, we follow those that have in concluding that depictions of celebrities amounting to little more than the appropriation of the celebrity's economic value are not protected expression under the First Amendment. We begin with *Zacchini v. Scripps-Howard Broadcasting Co.*, 433 U.S. 562, 576 (1977)....

To be sure, *Zacchini* was not an ordinary right of publicity case: the defendant television station had appropriated the plaintiff's entire act, a species of common law copyright violation. Nonetheless, two principles enunciated in *Zacchini* apply to this case: (1) state law may validly safeguard forms of intellectual property not covered under federal copyright and patent law as a means of protecting the fruits of a performing artist's labor; and (2) the state's interest in preventing the outright misappropriation of such intellectual property by others is not automatically trumped by the interest in free expression or dissemination of information; rather, as in the case of defamation, the state law interest and the interest in free expression must be balanced, according to the relative importance of the interests at stake.

Guglielmi adopted a similar balancing approach. The purported heir of Rudolph Valentino filed suit against the makers of a fictional film based on the latter's life. *Guglielmi* concluded that the First Amendment protection of entertainment superseded any right of publicity. This was in contrast to the companion *Lugosi* case, in which Chief Justice Bird concluded in her dissenting opinion that there may be an enforceable right of publicity that would prevent the merchandising of Count Dracula using the likeness of Bela Lugosi, with whom that role was identified. *Guglielmi* proposed a balancing test to distinguish protected from unprotected appropriation of celebrity likenesses: "an action for infringement of the right of publicity can be maintained only if the proprietary interests at issue clearly outweigh the value of free expression in this context." …

On the other side of the equation, the court recognized that [in *Estate of Presley v. Russen*, 513 F. Supp. 1339 (D.N.J. 1981) (*Russen*),] the Elvis impersonation, as in *Zacchini*, represented "'what may be the strongest case for a "right of publicity"—involving, not the appropriation of an entertainer's reputation to enhance the attractiveness of a commercial product, but the appropriation of the very activity by which the entertainer acquired his reputation in the first place.'" Thus, in balancing the considerable right of publicity interests with the minimal expressive or informational value of the speech in question, the *Russen* court concluded that the Presley estate's request for injunctive relief would likely prevail on the merits.

In *Groucho Marx Productions, Inc. v. Day & Night Co. (S.D.N.Y. 1981)* 523 F. Supp. 485, reversed on other grounds (2d Cir. 1982) *689 F.2d 317,* the court considered a right of publicity challenge to a new play featuring characters resembling the Marx Brothers. The court found in favor of the Marx Brothers' heirs, rejecting a First Amendment defense. In analyzing that defense, the court posed a dichotomy between "works … designed primarily to promote the dissemination of thoughts, ideas or information through news or fictionalization," which would receive First Amendment protection, and "use of the celebrity's name or likeness … largely for commercial purposes, such as the sale of merchandise," in which the right of publicity would prevail. In creating this dichotomy, the court did not appear to give due consideration to forms of creative expression protected by the First Amendment that cannot be categorized as ideas or information. Moreover, the court, borrowing from certain copyright cases, seemed to believe that the validity of the First Amendment defense turned on whether the play was a parody, without explaining why other forms of creative appropriation, such as using established characters in new theatrical works to advance various creative objectives, were not protected by the First Amendment. Nonetheless, the case is in line with *Zacchini, Guglielmi* and *Russen* in recognizing that certain forms of commercial exploitation of celebrities that violate the state law right of publicity do not receive First Amendment protection.

It is admittedly not a simple matter to develop a test that will unerringly distinguish between forms of artistic expression protected by the First Amendment and those that must give way to the right of publicity. Certainly, any such test must incorporate the principle that the right of publicity cannot, consistent with the First Amendment, be a right to control the celebrity's image by censoring disagreeable portrayals. Once the celebrity thrusts himself or herself forward into the limelight, the First Amendment dictates that the right to comment on, parody, lampoon, and make other expressive uses of the celebrity image must be given broad scope. The necessary implication of this observation is that the right of publicity is essentially an economic right. What the right of publicity holder possesses is not a right of censorship, but a right to prevent others from misappropriating the economic value generated by the celebrity's fame through the merchandising of the "name, voice, signature, photograph, or likeness" of the celebrity.

Beyond this precept, how may courts distinguish between protected and unprotected expression? Some commentators have proposed importing the fair use defense from copyright law, which has the advantage of employing an established doctrine developed from a related area of the law. Others disagree, pointing to the murkiness of the fair use doctrine and arguing that the idea/expression dichotomy, rather than fair use, is the principal means of reconciling copyright protection and First Amendment rights.

We conclude that a wholesale importation of the fair use doctrine into right of publicity law would not be advisable. At least two of the factors employed in the fair use test, "the nature of the copyrighted work" and "the amount and substantiality of the portion used" seem particularly designed to be applied to the partial copying of works of authorship "fixed in [a] tangible medium of expression" it is difficult to understand why these factors would be especially useful for determining whether the depiction of a celebrity likeness is protected by the First Amendment.

Nonetheless, the first fair use factor—"the purpose and character of the use"—does seem particularly pertinent to the task of reconciling the rights of free expression and publicity. As the Supreme Court has stated, the central purpose of the inquiry into this fair use factor "is to see, in Justice Story's words, whether the new work merely 'supersede[s] the objects' of the original creation, or instead adds something new, with a further purpose or different character, altering the first with new expression, meaning, or message; it asks, in other words, whether and to what extent the new work is 'transformative.' Although such transformative use is not absolutely necessary for a finding of fair use, the goal of copyright, to promote science and the arts, is generally furthered by the creation of transformative works." (*Campbell v. Acuff-Rose Music, Inc.,* 510 U.S. 569, 579 (1994)).

This inquiry into whether a work is "transformative" appears to us to be necessarily at the heart of any judicial attempt to square the right of publicity with the First Amendment. As the above quotation suggests, both the First Amendment and copyright law have a common goal of encouragement of free expression and creativity, the former by protecting such expression from government interference, the latter by protecting the creative fruits of intellectual and artistic labor. The right of publicity, at least theoretically, shares this goal with copyright law. When artistic expression takes the form of a literal depiction or imitation of a celebrity for commercial gain, directly trespassing on the right of publicity without adding significant expression beyond that trespass, the state law interest in protecting the fruits of artistic labor outweighs the expressive interests of the imitative artist.

On the other hand, when a work contains significant transformative elements, it is not only especially worthy of First Amendment protection, but it is also less likely to interfere with the economic interest protected by the right of publicity. As has been observed, works of parody or other distortions of the celebrity figure are not, from the celebrity fan's viewpoint, good substitutes for conventional depictions of the celebrity and therefore do not generally threaten markets for celebrity memorabilia that the right of publicity is designed to protect. Accordingly, First Amendment protection of such works outweighs whatever interest the state may have in enforcing the right of publicity. The right-of-publicity holder continues to enforce the right to monopolize the production of conventional, more or less fungible, images of the celebrity.

There is a fourth factor in the fair use test not yet mentioned, "the effect of the use upon the potential market for or value of the copyrighted work," that bears directly on this question. We do not believe, however, that consideration of this factor would usefully supplement the test articulated here. If it is determined that a work is worthy of First

Amendment protection because added creative elements significantly transform the celebrity depiction, then independent inquiry into whether or not that work is cutting into the market for the celebrity's images — something that might be particularly difficult to ascertain in the right of publicity context — appears to be irrelevant. Moreover, this "potential market" test has been criticized for circularity: it could be argued that if a defendant has capitalized in any way on a celebrity's image, he or she has found a potential market and therefore could be liable for such work....

Cardtoons, [*L.C. v. Major League Baseball Players Ass'n*, 95 F.3d 959 (10th Cir. 1996) (*Cardtoons*)], cited by Saderup, is consistent with this "transformative" test. There, the court held that the First Amendment protected a company that produced trading cards caricaturing and parodying well-known major league baseball players against a claim brought under the Oklahoma right of publicity statute. The court concluded that "[t]he cards provide social commentary on public figures, major league baseball players, who are involved in a significant commercial enterprise, major league baseball," and that "[t]he cards are no less protected because they provide humorous rather than serious commentary." The *Cardtoons* court weighed these First Amendment rights against what it concluded was the less-than-compelling interests advanced by the right of publicity outside the advertising context — especially in light of the reality that parody would not likely substantially impact the economic interests of celebrities — and found the cards to be a form of protected expression. While *Cardtoons* contained dicta calling into question the social value of the right of publicity, its conclusion that works parodying and caricaturing celebrities are protected by the First Amendment appears unassailable in light of the test articulated above.

We emphasize that the transformative elements or creative contributions that require First Amendment protection are not confined to parody and can take many forms, from factual reporting to fictionalized portrayal, from heavy-handed lampooning to subtle social criticism.

Another way of stating the inquiry is whether the celebrity likeness is one of the "raw materials" from which an original work is synthesized, or whether the depiction or imitation of the celebrity is the very sum and substance of the work in question. We ask, in other words, whether a product containing a celebrity's likeness is so transformed that it has become primarily the defendant's own expression rather than the celebrity's likeness. And when we use the word "expression," we mean expression of something other than the likeness of the celebrity.

We further emphasize that in determining whether the work is transformative, courts are not to be concerned with the quality of the artistic contribution — vulgar forms of expression fully qualify for First Amendment protection. On the other hand, a literal depiction of a celebrity, even if accomplished with great skill, may still be subject to a right of publicity challenge. The inquiry is in a sense more quantitative than qualitative, asking whether the literal and imitative or the creative elements predominate in the work.

Furthermore, in determining whether a work is sufficiently transformative, courts may find useful a subsidiary inquiry, particularly in close cases: does the marketability and economic value of the challenged work derive primarily from the fame of the celebrity depicted? If this question is answered in the negative, then there would generally be no actionable right of publicity. When the value of the work comes principally from some source other than the fame of the celebrity — from the creativity, skill, and reputation of the artist — it may be presumed that sufficient transformative elements are present to warrant First Amendment protection. If the question is answered in the affirmative, how-

ever, it does not necessarily follow that the work is without First Amendment protection—it may still be a transformative work.

In sum, when an artist is faced with a right of publicity challenge to his or her work,
he or she may raise as affirmative defense that the work is protected by the First Amendment inasmuch as it contains significant transformative elements or that the value of the
work does not derive primarily from the celebrity's fame....

[T]he inquiry is into whether Saderup's work is sufficiently transformative. Correctly anticipating this inquiry, he argues that all portraiture involves creative decisions, that therefore no portrait portrays a mere literal likeness, and that accordingly all portraiture, including
reproductions, is protected by the First Amendment. We reject any such categorical position. Without denying that all portraiture involves the making of artistic choices, we find it
equally undeniable, under the test formulated above, that when an artist's skill and talent
is manifestly subordinated to the overall goal of creating a conventional portrait of a celebrity
so as to commercially exploit his or her fame, then the artist's right of free expression is outweighed by the right of publicity. As is the case with fair use in the area of copyright law, an
artist depicting a celebrity must contribute something more than a "merely trivial" variation,
[but must create] something recognizably "his own" in order to qualify for legal protection.

On the other hand, we do not hold that all reproductions of celebrity portraits are unprotected by the First Amendment. The silkscreens of Andy Warhol, for example, have as
their subjects the images of such celebrities as Marilyn Monroe, Elizabeth Taylor, and Elvis
Presley. Through distortion and the careful manipulation of context, Warhol was able to
convey a message that went beyond the commercial exploitation of celebrity images and became a form of ironic social comment on the dehumanization of celebrity itself. Such expression may well be entitled to First Amendment protection. Although the distinction
between protected and unprotected expression will sometimes be subtle, it is no more so
than other distinctions triers of fact are called on to make in First Amendment jurisprudence.

Turning to Saderup's work, we can discern no significant transformative or creative
contribution. His undeniable skill is manifestly subordinated to the overall goal of creating literal, conventional depictions of The Three Stooges so as to exploit their fame.
Indeed, were we to decide that Saderup's depictions were protected by the First Amendment, we cannot perceive how the right of publicity would remain a viable right other than
in cases of falsified celebrity endorsements.

Moreover, the marketability and economic value of Saderup's work derives primarily
from the fame of the celebrities depicted. While that fact alone does not necessarily mean
the work receives no First Amendment protection, we can perceive no transformative elements in Saderup's works that would require such protection.

Saderup argues that it would be incongruous and unjust to protect parodies and other
distortions of celebrity figures but not wholesome, reverential portraits of such celebrities. The test we articulate today, however, does not express a value judgment or preference for one type of depiction over another. Rather, it reflects a recognition that the
Legislature has granted to the heirs and assigns of celebrities the property right to exploit
the celebrities' images, and that certain forms of expressive activity protected by the First
Amendment fall outside the boundaries of that right. Stated another way, we are concerned not with whether conventional celebrity images should be produced but with who
produces them and, more pertinently, who appropriates the value from their production.
Thus, under section 990, if Saderup wishes to continue to depict The Three Stooges as
he has done, he may do so only with the consent of the right of publicity holder.

The judgment of the Court of Appeal is affirmed.

Winter v. DC Comics
30 Cal.4th 881 (2003)

Celebrities have a statutory right of publicity by which they can prohibit others from using their likeness. An obvious tension exists between this right of publicity and the First Amendment to the United States Constitution. In *Comedy III,* we considered when constitutional free speech rights may trump the statutory right of publicity. We formulated "what is essentially a balancing test between the First Amendment and the right of publicity based on whether the work in question adds significant creative elements so as to be transformed into something more than a mere celebrity likeness or imitation." In that case, we concluded that lithographs and T-shirts bearing the likeness of The Three Stooges were not sufficiently transformative to receive First Amendment protection.

In this case, we apply the same balancing test to comic books containing characters that evoke musician brothers Johnny and Edgar Winter. We conclude that, in contrast to a drawing of The Three Stooges, the comic books do contain significant creative elements that transform them into something more than mere celebrity likenesses. Accordingly, the comic books are entitled to First Amendment protection.

In the 1990s, DC Comics published a five-volume comic miniseries featuring "Jonah Hex," a fictional comic book "anti-hero." The series contains an outlandish plot, involving giant worm-like creatures, singing cowboys, and the "Wilde West Ranch and Music and Culture Emporium," named for and patterned after the life of Oscar Wilde. The third volume ends with a reference to two new characters, the "Autumn brothers," and the teaser, "Next: The Autumns of Our Discontent." The cover of volume 4 depicts the Autumn brother characters, with pale faces and long white hair. (See append., *post;* the Autumn brothers are the two lower figures.) One brother wears a stovepipe hat and red sunglasses, and holds a rifle. The second has red eyes and holds a pistol. This volume is entitled, Autumns of Our Discontent, and features brothers Johnny and Edgar Autumn, depicted as villainous half-worm, half-human offspring born from the rape of their mother by a supernatural worm creature that had escaped from a hole in the ground. At the end of volume 5, Jonah Hex and his companions shoot and kill the Autumn brothers in an underground gun battle.

Plaintiffs, Johnny and Edgar Winter, well-known performing and recording musicians originally from Texas, sued DC Comics and others alleging several causes of action including, as relevant here, appropriation of their names and likenesses under Civil Code section 3344. They alleged that the defendants selected the names Johnny and Edgar Autumn to signal readers the Winter brothers were being portrayed; that the Autumn brothers were drawn with long white hair and albino features similar to plaintiffs'; that the Johnny Autumn character was depicted as wearing a tall black top hat similar to the one Johnny Winter often wore; and that the title of volume 4, Autumns of Our Discontent, refers to the famous Shakespearian phrase, "the winter of our discontent." They also alleged that the comics falsely portrayed them as "vile, depraved, stupid, cowardly, subhuman individuals who engage in wanton acts of violence, murder and bestiality for pleasure and who should be killed." ...

We granted the defendants' petition for review to decide whether the comic books are protected under the *Comedy III* transformative test.

Civil Code section 3344 provides as relevant: "(a) Any person who knowingly uses another's name, voice, signature, photograph, or likeness, in any manner, on or in products, merchandise, or goods, or for purposes of advertising or selling, or soliciting purchases of, products, merchandise, goods or services, without such person's prior consent ... shall be liable for any damages sustained by the person or persons injured as a result thereof."

In *Comedy III,* ... [w]e developed a test to determine whether a work merely appropriates a celebrity's economic value, and thus is not entitled to First Amendment protection, or has been transformed into a creative product that the First Amendment protects. The "inquiry is whether the celebrity likeness is one of the 'raw materials' from which an original work is synthesized, or whether the depiction or imitation of the celebrity is the very sum and substance of the work in question. We ask, in other words, whether a product containing a celebrity's likeness is so transformed that it has become primarily the defendant's own expression rather than the celebrity's likeness. And when we use the word 'expression,' we mean expression of something other than the likeness of the celebrity." ...

We made two important cautionary observations. First, "the right of publicity cannot, consistent with the First Amendment, be a right to control the celebrity's image by censoring disagreeable portrayals. Once the celebrity thrusts himself or herself forward into the limelight, the First Amendment dictates that the right to comment on, parody, lampoon, and make other expressive uses of the celebrity image must be given broad scope. The necessary implication of this observation is that the right of publicity is essentially an economic right. What the right of publicity holder possesses is not a right of censorship, but a right to prevent others from misappropriating the economic value generated by the celebrity's fame through the merchandising of the 'name, voice, signature, photograph, or likeness' of the celebrity." Second, "in determining whether the work is transformative, courts are not to be concerned with the quality of the artistic contribution — vulgar forms of expression fully qualify for First Amendment protection. On the other hand, a literal depiction of a celebrity, even if accomplished with great skill, may still be subject to a right of publicity challenge. The inquiry is in a sense more quantitative than qualitative, asking whether the literal and imitative or the creative elements predominate in the work." ...

We then summarized the rule. "In sum, when an artist is faced with a right of publicity challenge to his or her work, he or she may raise as [an] affirmative defense that the work is protected by the First Amendment inasmuch as it contains significant transformative elements or that the value of the work does not derive primarily from the celebrity's fame....

Application of the test to this case is not difficult.... Although the fictional characters Johnny and Edgar Autumn are less-than-subtle evocations of Johnny and Edgar Winter, the books do not depict plaintiffs literally. Instead, plaintiffs are merely part of the raw materials from which the comic books were synthesized. To the extent the drawings of the Autumn brothers resemble plaintiffs at all, they are distorted for purposes of lampoon, parody, or caricature. And the Autumn brothers are but cartoon characters — half-human and half-worm — in a larger story, which is itself quite expressive. The characters and their portrayals do not greatly threaten plaintiffs' right of publicity. Plaintiffs' fans who want to purchase pictures of them would find the drawings of the Autumn brothers unsatisfactory as a substitute for conventional depictions. The comic books are similar to the trading cards caricaturing and parodying prominent baseball players that have received First Amendment protection. Like the trading cards, the comic books "'are no less protected because they provide humorous rather than serious commentary.'" ...

Plaintiffs also argue, and the Court of Appeal found, that the record contains evidence that defendants were trading on plaintiffs' likenesses and reputations to generate interest in the comic book series and increase sales. This, too, is irrelevant to whether the comic books are constitutionally protected. The question is whether the work is transformative, not how it is marketed. If the work is sufficiently transformative to receive legal protection, "it is of no moment that the advertisements may have increased the profitability of the [work]." (*Guglielmi v. Spelling-Goldberg Productions, supra,* 25 Cal.3d at p. 860, 873 (1979) (conc. opn. of Bird, C.J.).) If the challenged work is transformative, the way it is advertised cannot somehow make it nontransformative. Here, as we have explained, the comic books are transformative and entitled to First Amendment protection.

Accordingly, we conclude that the Court of Appeal erred in finding the existence of triable issues of fact.... As in *Comedy III,* courts can often resolve the question as a matter of law simply by viewing the work in question and, if necessary, comparing it to an actual likeness of the person or persons portrayed. Because of these circumstances, an action presenting this issue is often properly resolved on summary judgment or, if the complaint includes the work in question, even demurrer. This is one of those cases.

The artist in *Comedy III* essentially sold, and devoted fans bought, pictures of The Three Stooges, not transformed expressive works by the artist. Here, by contrast, defendants essentially sold, and the buyers purchased, DC Comics depicting fanciful, creative characters, not pictures of the Winter brothers. This makes all the difference. The comic books here are entitled to First Amendment protection.

Parks v. Laface Records
329 F.3d 437 (2003)

This is a dispute over the name of a song. Rosa Parks is a civil rights icon who first gained prominence during the Montgomery, Alabama bus boycott in 1955. She brings suit against LaFace Records, a record producer, and OutKast, a "rap" (or "hip-hop") music duo, as well as several other named affiliates, for using her name as the title of their song, *Rosa Parks.* Parks contends that Defendants' use of her name constitutes false advertising under §43(a) of the Lanham Act, and intrudes on her common law right of publicity under Michigan state law. Defendants argue that they are entitled to summary judgment because Parks has failed to show any violation of the Lanham Act or her right of publicity. Defendants further argue that, even if she has shown such a violation, their *First Amendment* freedom of artistic expression should be a defense as a matter of law to each of these claims. Parks also contends that Defendants' conduct renders them liable under Michigan law for defamation and tortious interference with a business relationship; Defendants have also denied liability with respect to these claims....

Rosa Parks is an historical figure who first gained prominence as a symbol of the civil rights movement in the United States during the 1950s and 1960s. In 1955, while riding in the front of a segregated bus in Montgomery, Alabama, she refused to yield her seat to a white passenger and move to the back of the bus as blacks were required to do by the then-existing laws requiring segregation of the races. A 381-day bus boycott in Montgomery flowed from that one event, which eventually became a catalyst for organized boycotts, sit-ins, and demonstrations all across the South. Her single act of defiance has garnered her numerous public accolades and awards, and she has used that celebrity status to promote various civil and human rights causes as well as television programs and books inspired by her life story. She has also approved a collection of gospel recordings by various artists entitled *Verity Records Presents: A Tribute to Mrs. Rosa Parks* (the "*Tribute*" album), released in 1995.

Defendants are OutKast, comprised of recording artists Andre "Dre" Benjamin and Antwan "Big Boi" Patton; their record producers, LaFace, founded by and named after Antonio "L.A." Reid and Kenny "Babyface" Edmonds; and LaFace's record distributors, Arista Records and BMG Entertainment (collectively "Defendants"). In September 1998, Defendants released the album *Aquemini*. The album's first single release was a song titled *Rosa Parks*, described as a "hit single" by a sticker on the album. The same sticker that contained the name *Rosa Parks* also contained a Parental Advisory warning of "explicit content." ...

[A]. The Lanham Act

Section 43(a) of the Lanham Act creates a civil cause of action against any person who identifies his or her product in such a way as to likely cause confusion among consumers or to cause consumers to make a mistake or to deceive consumers as to association of the producer of the product with another person or regarding the origin of the product or the sponsorship or approval of the product by another person. The language of §43(a) is broad....

[T]he scope of §43(a) extends beyond disputes between producers of commercial products and their competitors. It also permits celebrities to vindicate property rights in their identities against allegedly misleading commercial use by others. Celebrities have standing to sue under §43(a) because they possess an economic interest in their identities akin to that of a traditional trademark holder.

In order to prevail on a false advertising claim under §43(a), a celebrity must show that use of his or her name is likely to cause confusion among consumers as to the "affiliation, connection, or association" between the celebrity and the defendant's goods or services or as to the celebrity's participation in the "origin, sponsorship, or approval" of the defendant's goods or services. Consumer confusion occurs when "consumers ... believe that the products or services offered by the parties are affiliated in some way," or "when consumers make an incorrect mental association between the involved commercial products or their producers." A "likelihood" means a "probability" rather than a "possibility" of confusion.

Parks contends that Defendants have violated the Lanham Act because the *Rosa Parks* title misleads consumers into believing that the song is about her or that she is affiliated with the Defendants, or has sponsored or approved the *Rosa Parks* song and the *Aquemini* album. She argues that the risk of confusion is enhanced by the fact that her authorized *Tribute* album is in the marketplace alongside Defendants' album featuring the *Rosa Parks* single. As additional evidence for her claim, Parks points to Defendants' concession that they have used the *Rosa Parks* title to advertise and promote both the song and the *Aquemini* album. She also supplies twenty-one affidavits from consumers affirming that they either believed Defendants' song was about Parks or was connected to the *Tribute* album authorized by her....

1. *Trademark Right In and Trademark Use of Parks' Name*

... We find Parks' prior commercial activities and international recognition as a symbol of the civil rights movement endow her with a trademark interest in her name the same as if she were a famous actor or musician. Therefore, even though Rosa Parks' name might not be eligible for registration as a trademark, and even though Defendants were not selling Rosa Parks-brand CD's, a viable cause of action also exists under §43(a) if consumers falsely believed that Rosa Parks had sponsored or approved the song, or was somehow affiliated with the song or the album. We turn then to Defendants' second argument, that even if Parks could establish some likelihood of confusion, the *First Amendment* protects Defendants' choice of title.

2. *The First Amendment Defense — Three Approaches*

Defendants allege that even if Parks' evidence demonstrates some likelihood of consumer confusion regarding their song and album, their *First Amendment* right of artistic expression trumps that concern. Defendants make an arguable point. From ancient times, music has been a means by which people express ideas. As such, music is firmly ensconced within the protections of the *First Amendment.* However, the *First Amendment* cannot permit anyone who cries "artist" to have *carte blanche* when it comes to naming and advertising his or her works, art though it may be. As the Second Circuit sagely observed, "the purchaser of a book, like the purchaser of a can of peas, has a right not to be misled as to the source [or endorsement] of the product." Courts have adopted three approaches to balance *First Amendment* interests with the protections of the Lanham Act: (a) the "likelihood of confusion" test; (b) the "alternative avenues" test; and (c) the *Rogers v. Grimaldi* test. We will examine each one in turn.

One approach is to rely solely on the "likelihood of confusion" factors applied in other, more traditional, trademark cases.... Based upon that evidence, we then decide if the plaintiff has raised a genuine issue of material fact as to the likelihood of consumer confusion. Under this approach, we do not pay special solicitude to an asserted *First Amendment* defense.... A second approach is the "alternative avenues" test. This is the test urged upon us by Parks, and endorsed by a panel of the Eighth Circuit. Under the "alternative avenues" test, a title of an expressive work will not be protected from a false advertising claim if there are sufficient alternative means for an artist to convey his or her idea....

We conclude that neither the first nor the second approach accords adequate weight to the *First Amendment* interests in this case. The first approach — unmodified application of the likelihood of confusion factors in trademark cases — gives no weight to *First Amendment* concerns. Instead, it treats the name of an artistic work as if it were no different from the name of an ordinary commercial product. However, this approach ignores the fact that the artistic work is *not* simply a commercial product but is also a means of communication....

The second approach, the "alternative avenues" test ... is premised on the notion that, just as a real property owner may exclude a speaker from a shopping mall so long as other locations exist for the speaker to deliver his message, a celebrity may prohibit use of his or her name so long as alternative ways exist for the artist to communicate his or her idea.... To suggest that other words can be used as well to express an author's or composer's message is not a proper test for weighing *First Amendment* rights. As Mark Twain observed, "The difference between the almost-right word and the right word is really a large matter — it's the difference between the 'lightning-bug' and the 'lightning.'" J. Bartlett, *Familiar Quotations* 527 (16th ed.1992). Finally, adopting the "alternative avenues" test would needlessly entangle courts in the process of titling works of art; courts would be asked to determine not just whether a title is reasonably "artistic" but whether a title is "necessary" to communicate the idea. We therefore reject the alternative avenues test.

Finally, a third approach is the one developed by the Second Circuit in *Rogers v. Grimaldi* and adopted by the district court in this case. Under *Rogers*, a title will be protected unless it has "no artistic relevance" to the underlying work or, if there is artistic relevance, the title "explicitly misleads as to the source or the content of the work." ...

In *Rogers*, the plaintiff was dancer and film star Ginger Rogers. Italian movie maker Federico Fellini made a fictional movie titled *Ginger and Fred* about the reunion of two erstwhile cabaret dancers who became known to their fans as Fred and Ginger because they imitated Fred Astaire and Ginger Rogers in their act. Rogers' complaint alleged, *inter alia*, that the title misled viewers into thinking that the movie was about her famous collaboration with Fred Astaire, in violation of the Lanham Act, and that the use of her name infringed her right of publicity. The *Rogers* court, finding that overextension of Lanham Act restrictions in the area of titles might intrude on *First Amendment* values and that the "alternative avenues" test is insufficient to accommodate the public's interest in free expression, adopted a two-pronged test:

> In the context of allegedly misleading titles using a celebrity's name, that balance [between avoiding consumer confusion and protecting free expression] will normally not support application of the Act unless [1] the title has no artistic relevance to the underlying work whatsoever, or, if it has some artistic relevance, unless [2] the title explicitly misleads as to the source or the content of the work.

Courts in the Second Circuit have routinely applied the *Rogers* test to other Lanham Act cases. The Fifth Circuit has followed suit. In addition, a panel of the Ninth Circuit recently adopted the Rogers test in *Mattel, Inc. v. MCA Records*, Inc. In *Mattel*, the manufacturer of the well-known "Barbie" doll, sued a Danish band, Aqua, for their song Barbie Girl, which, among other things, contained lines that portrayed Barbie in a negative light. Mattel alleged that Aqua's use of the name "Barbie" in the title had confused consumers into believing that Mattel was affiliated with the song. Mattel argued that the song was not about "Barbie" and hence could not be protected by the First Amendment. In the district court, as support, Mattel introduced statements by Aqua band members in interviews that "the song isn't about the doll. We're making fun of the glamorous life." Mattel also supplied evidence that purported to show that individuals were misled into believing Mattel and the song were affiliated in some way. Among the evidence was a survey of 556 persons of various ages in six states, 17% of whom believed that Mattel or "Barbie" was the source of, connected with, or gave permission for the Barbie Girl song.

On appeal from a summary judgment in favor of the defendant, the Ninth Circuit, applying *Rogers*, concluded that the First Amendment outweighed any risk of confusion between Mattel and the song title. Specifically it found:

> Under the first prong of *Rogers*, the use of Barbie in the song title clearly is relevant to the underlying work, namely, the song itself.... The song is about Barbie and the values Aqua claims she represents. The song title does not explicitly mislead as to the source of the work; it does not, explicitly or otherwise, suggest that it was produced by Mattel. The only indication that Mattel might be associated with the song is the use of Barbie in the title; if this were enough to satisfy this prong of the *Rogers* test, it would render *Rogers* a nullity.

The application of *Rogers* in *Mattel*, as well as in cases decided in other circuits, persuades us that *Rogers* is the best test for balancing Defendants' and the public's interest in free expression under the First Amendment against Parks' and the public's interest in enforcement of the Lanham Act. We thus apply the *Rogers* test to the facts before us.

3. *Application of the* Rogers *Test*

The first prong of *Rogers* requires a determination of whether there is any artistic relationship between the title and the underlying work. Parks contends that a cursory review of the Rosa Parks title and the lyrics demonstrates that there is no artistic connection between them. Parks also submits two articles in which members of OutKast are purported to have admitted that the song was not about her. As further evidence, she offers a "translation" of the lyrics of the song Rosa Parks, derived from various electronic "dictionaries" of the "rap" vernacular to demonstrate that the song truly has nothing to do with Parks herself. The "translation" of the chorus reads as follows:

> Be quiet and stop the commotion. OutKast is coming back out [with new music] so all other MCs [mic checkers, rappers, Master of Ceremonies] step aside. Do you want to ride and hang out with us? OutKast is the type of group to make the clubs get hyped-up/excited.

Defendants respond that their use of Parks' name is "metaphorical" or "symbolic." They argue that the historical association between Rosa Parks and the phrase "move to the back of the bus" is beyond dispute and that Parks' argument that the song is not "about" her in a biographical sense is simply irrelevant....

Contrary to the opinion of the district court, we believe that the artistic relationship between the title and the content of the song is certainly not obvious and, indeed, is "open to reasonable debate" for the following reasons.

It is true that the phrase "move to the back of the bus" is repeatedly used in the "hook" or chorus of the song. When the phrase is considered *in the context of the lyrics*, however, the phrase has absolutely nothing to do with Rosa Parks. There could be no stronger, no more compelling, evidence of this fact than the admission of "Dre" (Andre "Dre" Benjamin) that, "We (OutKast) never intended for the song to be about Rosa Parks or the civil rights movement. It was just symbolic, meaning that we comin' back out, so all you other MCs move to the back of the bus." The composers did *not* intend it to be about Rosa Parks, and the lyrics are *not* about Rosa Parks. The lyrics' sole message is that OutKast's competitors are of lesser quality and, therefore, must "move to the back of the bus," or in other words, "take a back seat."

We believe that reasonable persons could conclude that there is no relationship of any kind between Rosa Parks' name and the content of the song—a song that is nothing more and nothing less than a paean announcing the triumph of superior people in the entertainment business over inferior people in that business. *Back of the Bus*, for example, would be a title that is obviously relevant to the content of the song, but it also would not have the marketing power of an icon of the civil rights movement. Choosing Rosa Parks' name as the title to the song unquestionably enhanced the song's potential sale to the consuming public.

The *Rogers* court made an important point which clearly applies in this case. The court said, "poetic license is not without limits. The purchaser of a book, like the purchaser of a can of peas, has a right not to be misled as to the source of the product." The same is also true regarding the content of a song. The purchaser of a song titled *Rosa Parks* has a right not to be misled regarding the content of that song....

We do not mean to imply that Rosa Parks must always be displayed in a flattering manner, or that she should have the ability to prevent any other characterization of her. She is a celebrity and, as such, she cannot prevent being portrayed in a manner that may not be pleasing to her.... The present case, however, does not involve any claim of caricature, parody or satire. It involves, instead, the use of a celebrity's name as the title to a song when it reasonably could be found that the celebrity's name has no artistic relevance to the content of the song. It involves, in short, a reasonable dispute whether the use of Rosa Parks' name was a misrepresentation and false advertising or whether it was a legitimate use of a celebrity's name in some recognized form of artistic expression protected by the *First Amendment*....

There is a genuine issue of material fact whether the use of Rosa Parks' name as a title to the song and on the cover of the album is artistically related to the content of the song or whether the use of the name Rosa Parks is nothing more than a misleading advertisement for the sale of the song....

[B]. Right of Publicity

The right of publicity protects the identity of a celebrity from exploitive commercial use. "The theory of the right is that a celebrity's identity can be valuable in the promotion of products, and the celebrity has an interest that may be protected from the unauthorized commercial exploitation of that identity." As such, the common law right of publicity forms a species of property right. The right of publicity is governed by state law. Michigan has indicated that it would recognize a right of publicity, and the parties have not questioned that Plaintiff has a right of publicity. The dispute is over its application to the facts of this case.

Parks' right of publicity argument tracks that of her Lanham Act claim. She alleges that Defendants have profited from her fame by using her name solely for a commercial purpose. She supplies much the same evidence in support of her right of publicity claim as she did for her Lanham Act claim: the lyrics of *Rosa Parks*, the "translation," and the press clippings quoting OutKast members. Defendants do not deny that they have used the title *Rosa Parks* commercially, but argue that Parks has produced no evidence that their use was *solely* commercial. Instead, they argue that the choice was also artistic, and that they therefore have a complete defense in the *First Amendment.*

The district court agreed with Defendants. The district court applied *Rogers*, which, in addition to the false advertising claim under § 43(a), also dealt with a right of publicity action arising under Oregon state law. Under *Rogers,* with respect to a right of publicity claim, a title that uses a celebrity's name will be protected by the *First Amendment* unless the title is "wholly unrelated" to the content of the work or was "simply a disguised commercial advertisement for the sale of goods or services." The district court found that, as a matter of law, there was an artistic relationship between the title and the content of the song, and therefore it could not be considered "simply a disguised commercial advertisement." Defendants' use of the title to promote the album did not change this result.

A right of publicity claim is similar to a false advertising claim in that it grants a celebrity the right to protect an economic interest in his or her name. However, a right of publicity claim does differ from a false advertising claim in one crucial respect; a right of publicity claim does not require any evidence that a consumer is likely to be confused. All that a plaintiff must prove in a right of publicity action is that she has a pecuniary interest in her identity, and that her identity has been commercially exploited by a defendant.

The parties have stipulated that Parks is famous and that she has used her name to promote other goods and services. She has therefore established an economic interest in her name. Furthermore, Defendants admit that they have used Parks' name as the name of their song, and have used that name to sell the song and their album. They argue, however, that, as with the Lanham Act claim, their *First Amendment* right of artistic expression should prevail over Parks' claim.

Because a plaintiff bears a reduced burden of persuasion to succeed in a right of publicity action, courts and commentators have recognized that publicity rights carry a greater danger of impinging on *First Amendment* rights than do rights associated with false advertising claims. We have recognized the importance of a *First Amendment* defense to right of publicity actions in a recent case. In *Ruffin-Steinback v. dePasse,* [82 F. Supp. 2d 723, 726–27 (E.D. Mich. 2000), aff'd, 267 F.3d 457 (6th Cir. 2001)] friends and family members of the Motown group, the "Temptations," sued the makers of a televised miniseries for the manner in which they and the former group members were portrayed in the film. The plaintiffs alleged that their likenesses were appropriated to endorse a product, the film, without their permission. The court found in that case that the plaintiffs could not overcome the defendant's *First Amendment* defense, even where the portrayal of the plaintiffs was partly fictionalized, and even where the likenesses of the plaintiffs were used to promote a videocassette version of the mini-series. As with the Lanham Act, then, we must conduct another balancing of interests—Parks' property right in her own name versus the freedom of artistic expression.

In *Rogers*, the Second Circuit held that movie titles are protected from right of publicity actions unless the title is "wholly unrelated" to the content of the work or was "simply a disguised commercial advertisement for the sale of goods or services." This test is supported in the context of other expressive works by *comment c of § 47 of the Restatement (Third) of Unfair Competition*. It states that "use of another's identity in a novel, play, or motion picture is ... not ordinarily an infringement [of the right of publicity, unless] the name or likeness is used solely to attract attention to a work that is not related to the identified person." ...

For the same reasons we have stated earlier and need not repeat, we believe that Parks' right of publicity claim presents a genuine issue of material fact regarding the question of whether the title to the song is or is not "wholly unrelated" to the content of the song. A reasonable finder of fact, in our opinion, upon consideration of all the evidence, could find the title to be a "disguised commercial advertisement" or adopted "solely to attract attention" to the work....

For the reasons stated, as to Rosa Parks' Lanham Act claim and her common law right of publicity claim, the judgment of the District Court is reversed and this case is remanded for future proceedings not inconsistent with this Opinion....

Tyne v. Time Warner Entm't Co. L.P.
901 So. 2d 802 (Fla. 2005)

We have for review a question of Florida law certified by the United States Eleventh Circuit Court of Appeals that is determinative of a cause pending in that court and for which there appears to be no controlling precedent. We have jurisdiction. See art. V, §3(b)(6), Fla. Const.

The pertinent facts of this case, as set forth by the Eleventh Circuit, are as follows:

> In October, 1991, a rare confluence of meteorological events led to a "massively powerful" weather system off the New England coast. The fishing vessel known as the Andrea Gail was caught in this storm and lost at sea. All six of the crewmembers on board the *Andrea Gail*, including Billy Tyne and Dale Murphy, Sr., were presumed to have been killed. Newspaper and television reports extensively chronicled the storm and its impact. Based on these reports, and personal interviews with meteorologists, local fisherman, and family members, Sebastian Junger penned a book, entitled *The Perfect Storm: A True Story of Men Against the Sea*, recounting the storm and the last voyage of the *Andrea Gail* and its crew. The book was published in 1997.

> That same year, Warner Bros. purchased from Junger and his publisher the rights to produce a motion picture based on the book. Warner Bros. released the film, entitled *The Perfect Storm*, for public consumption in 2000. The Picture depicted the lives and deaths of Billy Tyne and Dale Murphy, Sr., who were the main characters in the film. It also included brief portrayals of each individual that is a

party to this appeal. Nonetheless, Warner Bros. neither sought permission from the individuals depicted in the picture nor compensated them in any manner.

Unlike the book, the Picture presented a concededly dramatized account of both the storm and the crew of the *Andrea Gail*. For example, the main protagonist in the Picture, Billy Tyne, was portrayed as a down-and-out swordboat captain who was obsessed with the next big catch. In one scene, the Picture relates an admittedly fabricated depiction of Tyne berating his crew for wanting to return to port in Gloucester, Massachusetts. Warner Bros. took additional liberties with the land-based interpersonal relationships between the crewmembers and their families.

While the Picture did not hold itself out as factually accurate, it did indicate at the beginning of the film that "THIS FILM IS BASED ON A TRUE STORY." A disclaimer inserted during the closing credits elaborated on this point with the following statement: "This film is based on actual historical events contained in 'The Perfect Storm' by Sebastian Junger. Dialogue and certain events and characters in the film were created for the purpose of fictionalization."

On August 24, 2000, the Tyne and Murphy children, along with Tigue and Kosko, filed suit against Warner Bros. [in the United States District Court for the Middle District of Florida] seeking recompense under Florida's commercial misappropriation law [section 540.08, Florida Statutes (2000)] and for common law false light invasion of privacy.

Tyne v. Time Warner Entertainment Co., L.P., 336 F.3d 1286, 1288–89 (11th Cir. 2003).

[W]e rephrase the certified question to the specific issue that we conclude is presented by this case.

> DOES THE PHRASE "FOR PURPOSES OF TRADE OR FOR ANY COMMERCIAL OR ADVERTISING PURPOSE" IN SECTION 540.08(1), FLORIDA STATUTES, INCLUDE PUBLICATIONS WHICH DO NOT DIRECTLY PROMOTE A PRODUCT OR SERVICE?

The question before this Court is a narrow one. As noted by the federal courts, the Fourth District Court of Appeal considered the applicability of section 540.08, Florida Statutes,[4] to a publication which did not directly promote a product or service, but this Court has not directly addressed this question.

---

4. [*540.08*. Unauthorized publication of name or likeness.

    (1) No person shall publish, print, display or otherwise publicly use for purposes of trade or for any commercial or advertising purpose the name, portrait, photograph, or other likeness of any natural person without the express written or oral consent to such use given by:

    (a) Such person; or

    (b) Any other person, firm or corporation authorized in writing by such person to license the commercial use of her or his name or likeness; or

    (c) If such person is deceased, any person, firm or corporation authorized in writing to license the commercial use of her or his name or likeness, or if no person, firm or corporation is so authorized, then by any one from among a class composed of her or his surviving spouse and surviving children.

    (2) In the event the consent required in subsection (1) is not obtained, the person whose name, portrait, photograph, or other likeness is so used, or any person, firm, or corporation authorized by such person in writing to license the commercial use of her or his name or likeness, or, if the person whose likeness is used is deceased, any person, firm, or corporation having the right to give such consent, as provided hereinabove, may bring an action to enjoin such unauthorized publication, printing, display or other public use, and to recover damages for any loss or injury sustained by reason thereof, including an amount which would

In *Loft* [*v. Fuller*, 408 So. 2d 619 (Fla. Dist. Ct. 1981)], Dorothy Loft and her two children brought an action for, among other things, violation of section 540.08 for the alleged unauthorized publication of the name and likeness of the Lofts' deceased husband and father, Robert Loft. Robert Loft had been the captain of an Eastern Airlines flight that crashed while en route from New York to Miami in 1972. The crash was followed by reports of the appearance of apparitions of the flight's crew members, including Robert Loft, on subsequent flights. Subsequent to the press stories, *The Ghost of Flight 401* was published in 1976. The book was a nonfictionalized account by the author of his investigation of the reports. A movie was also made based on this book. *Loft*, 408 So. 2d at 620.

The Fourth District held as follows:

> In our view, section 540.08, by prohibiting the use of one's name or likeness for trade, commercial or advertising purposes, is designed to prevent the unauthorized use of a name to directly promote the product or service of the publisher. Thus, the publication is harmful not simply because it is included in a publication that is sold for a profit, but rather because of the way it associates the individual's name or his personality with something else. Such is not the case here.

> While we agree that at least one of the purposes of the author and publisher in releasing the publication in question was to make money through sales of copies of the book and that such a publication is commercial in that sense, this in no way distinguishes this book from almost all other books, magazines or newspapers and simply does not amount to the kind of commercial exploitation prohibited by the statute. We simply do not believe that the term "commercial," as employed by Section 540.08, was meant to be construed to bar the use of people's names in such a sweeping fashion. We also believe that acceptance of appellants' view of the statute would result in substantial confrontation between this statute and the *first amendment to the United States Constitution* guaranteeing freedom of the press and of speech. Having concluded that the

---

have been a reasonable royalty, and punitive or exemplary damages.

(3) The provisions of this section shall not apply to:

(a) The publication, printing, display, or use of the name or likeness of any person in any newspaper, magazine, book, news broadcast or telecast, or other news medium or publication as part of any bona fide news report or presentation having a current and legitimate public interest and where such name or likeness is not used for advertising purposes;

(b) The use of such name, portrait, photograph, or other likeness in connection with the resale or other distribution of literary, musical, or artistic productions or other articles of merchandise or property where such person has consented to the use of her or his name, portrait, photograph, or likeness on or in connection with the initial sale or distribution thereof; or

(c) Any photograph of a person solely as a member of the public and where such person is not named or otherwise identified in or in connection with the use of such photograph.

(4) No action shall be brought under this section by reason of any publication, printing, display, or other public use of the name or likeness of a person occurring after the expiration of 40 years from and after the death of such person.

(5) As used in this section, a person's "surviving spouse" is the person's surviving spouse under the law of her or his domicile at the time of her or his death, whether or not the spouse has later remarried; and a person's "children" are her or his immediate offspring and any children legally adopted by the person. Any consent provided for in subsection (1) shall be given on behalf of a minor by the guardian of her or his person or by either parent.

(6) The remedies provided for in this section shall be in addition to and not in limitation of the remedies and rights of any person under the common law against the invasion of her or his privacy.]....

publication as alleged is not barred by Section 540.08, we need not decide if, under the allegations of the complaint, the book was of current and legitimate public interest, thus removing it entirely from the scope of the statute.

Loft, 408 So. 2d at 622–23 (emphasis added) (citations omitted).

We approve the Fourth District's logical construction of section 540.08 in *Loft*. This construction has been applied to cases construing the statute for more than thirty years, and the statute has remained unchanged by the Legislature for this period. For example, in *Valentine v. C.B.S., Inc.*, 698 F.2d 430 (11th Cir. 1983), at issue was a song written by Bob Dylan and Jacques Levy depicting the murder trial of prizefighter Rubin "Hurricane" Carter. The plaintiff, a witness in the murder trial, brought an action alleging a violation of section 540.08 because the song falsely implied that she participated in a conspiracy to unjustly convict Carter. The Eleventh Circuit held that the plaintiff's claim was not actionable under section 540.08....

We disagree with appellants' argument that to uphold the construction given to the statute in Loft renders the exceptions contained in section 540.08(3)(a) and (b) superfluous. Applying the statute to only those situations that "directly promote a product or service" does not necessarily mean that the use is in an advertisement. For example, in *Ewing v. A-1 Management, Inc.*, 481 So. 2d 99 (Fla. 1986), the defendants published the names and addresses of the plaintiffs as parents of a fugitive from justice on a wanted poster distributed by the defendant surety company after the plaintiff's son fled while on bail. The Third District Court of Appeal concluded that while this use of the plaintiffs' names fell within the scope of section 540.08(1), the use was exempted under the newsworthiness exemption of section 540.08(3)(a). Thus, as appellees argue, the newsworthiness exemption served an entirely practical, nonredundant function....

Moreover, it should be emphasized that the Legislature enacted section 540.08 in 1967. Since that time, the only amendment to the statute was to rephrase it in gender neutral terms. The Legislature has not amended the statute in response to the decisions that have required that the statute apply to a use that directly promotes a product or service. This inaction may be viewed as legislative acceptance or approval of the judicial construction of the statute. *Goldenberg v. Sawczak*, 791 So. 2d 1078, 1083 (Fla. 2001).

Finally, as recognized by United States District Court Judge Conway in the decision of the United States District Court, we find that defining the term "commercial purpose" in section 540.08 to apply to motion pictures or similar works raises a fundamental constitutional concern.... It is ... clear that the Picture is entitled to First Amendment protection, and would therefore, be excepted from liability under § 540.08. This provides another basis for this Court's conclusion that Defendants are entitled to summary judgment on these claims....

Notes and Questions

a. Many of the most recent cases involving the tension between First Amendment and publicity rights doctrines occur in the context of video games. Those cases are addressed in Chapter XVIII.

b. One of the more significant recent cases to address the shifting attitude in the relation between publicity rights and First Amendment interests has been *Cardtoons, L.C. v. Major League Baseball Players Ass'n,* 95 F.3d 959, 976 (10th Cir. 1996). The Tenth Circuit upheld the right to sell parody trading cards, recognizing a First Amendment interest notwithstanding the commercial and nontraditional format of the parody. As the court explained:

The cards use similar names, recognizable caricatures, distinctive team colors, and commentary about individual players. For example, the card parodying San Francisco Giants' outfielder Barry Bonds calls him "Treasury Bonds," and features a recognizable caricature of Bonds, complete with earring, tipping a bat boy for a 24 carat gold "Fort Knoxville Slugger." The back of the card has a team logo (the "Gents"), and the following text:

Redemption qualities and why Treasury Bonds is the league's most valuable player:

1. Having Bonds on your team is like having money in the bank.

2. He plays so hard he gives 110 percent, compounded daily.

3. He turned down the chance to play other sports because he has a high interest rate in baseball.

4. He deposits the ball in the bleachers.

5. He is into male bonding.

6. He is a money player.

7. He has a 24-karat Gold Glove.

8. He always cashes in on the payoff pitch.

In an opinion fairly contemptuous of both publicity rights and major league baseball, the Tenth Circuit found that the First Amendment interests transcended any publicity rights which may have existed under Oklahoma's law, which closely paralleled California statutes.

c. Courts and legislatures struggle to distinguish commercial activity from expressive activity with regard to publicity rights. *Spahn v. Julian Messner, Inc.*, 221 N.E.2d 543 (N.Y. 1966), may reflect the low point for the New York Court of Appeals' attempts to understand the scope of publicity rights. There, the publication of a fictionalized biography of a real person—a famous baseball player—was construed as essentially a commercial appropriation of that person's identity. The implication is that where the mention of a person's name is incidental to the larger work of fiction, no appropriation will be found; but where the name is used to define and call attention to the work, a court may find appropriation. Given that the item in question was a book rather than a commercial product, the lack of appropriate First Amendment consideration was shocking.

d. In contrast to *Spahn*, the Ninth Circuit dealt with an even more outrageous falsification in *Hoffman v. L.A. Magazine*, 255 F.3d 1180 (9th Cir. 2001). There, L.A. Magazine used Dustin Hoffman's cross-dressing image from "Tootsie" in a digitally added new gown, as the photo illustration for an article entitled "Grand Illusions." As noncommercial speech, the Ninth Circuit found there could not be a claim for invasion of publicity rights from the expressive use of Mr. Hoffman's likeness.

e. Another significant decision was *Montana v. San Jose Mercury News, Inc.*, 34 Cal. App. 4th 790, 792 (Cal. App. 1995). The newspaper printed commemorative posters celebrating Joe Montana's four Super Bowl victories. Originally appearing as a pull-out, these were later sold as $5.00 posters. Seventy percent were given away to charity while the remainder was sold. The decision turned on the nature of the posters:

Although we have been unable to locate any cases directly on point, several cases discuss First Amendment implications of the sale of posters, videotapes or movies of recognizable individuals without their consent. *Paulsen v. Per-*

sonality Posters, Inc. 59 Misc.2d 444 [299 N.Y.S.2d 501] (1968) is illustrative. There, comedian Pat Paulsen sought a preliminary injunction to bar a poster marketer from selling posters of him with the words "For President" written at the bottom. Paulsen had conducted a mock campaign for the presidency in 1968. In discussing whether Paulsen's statutorily defined "right of privacy" had been abridged, the court observed "that the statute was not intended to limit activities involving the dissemination of news or information concerning matters of public interest.... [S]uch activities are privileged and do not fall within 'the purposes of trade' contemplated by Section 51 [New York's equivalent of California Civil Code section 3344], notwithstanding that they are also carried on for a profit.... Applying those principles to the poster of Paulsen, the court stated: "When a well-known entertainer enters the presidential ring, tongue in cheek or otherwise, it is clearly newsworthy and of public interest. A poster which portrays plaintiff in that role, and reflects the spirit in which he approaches said role, is a form of public interest presentation to which protection must be extended."

The same could be said here. When Joe Montana led his team to four Super Bowl championships in a single decade, it was clearly a newsworthy event. Posters portraying the 49'ers' victories are, like the poster in Paulsen, a "form of public interest presentation to which protection must be extended."

A similar conclusion was reached in *Jackson v. MPI Home Video,* 694 F.Supp. 483 (N.D.Ill. 1988). In that case, the Reverend Jesse Jackson sought an injunction against the unauthorized distribution of videocassettes of a copyrighted speech he gave at the 1988 Democratic National Convention. The court granted the injunction based on Jackson's copyright claims. At the same time, it noted that Jackson's "chances of success on [his] right to publicity claim appear less than negligible" as the "defendants[ ] claim[ed] that they were engaged in news reporting...." The court explained that the right of publicity "is based upon the plaintiff's right to use his own name and likeness for his own benefit, and this right is violated when one, without leave, uses it for his benefit and not the plaintiff's. Public figures possess this right with respect to commercial use of their names and likeness. But public figures do not retain the right of publicity against the use of name and likeness in the news media." ...

At the hearing on the summary judgment motion in this case, SJMN submitted undisputed evidence that it sold the posters to advertise the quality and content of its newspaper. The posters were effective in this regard: they were exact reproductions of pages from the paper. They contained no additional information not included on the newspaper pages themselves, and they did not state or imply that Montana endorsed the newspaper. SJMN also submitted evidence showing it set the price of the posters with the intent simply to recover its costs. Where, as here, a newspaper page covering newsworthy events is reproduced for the purpose of showing the quality and content of the newspaper, the subsequent reproduction is exempt from the statutory and common law prohibitions.

f. Another example of the fine line between commercial speech and content was decided in *Astaire v. Best Film & Video Corp.,* 116 F.3d 1297 (9th Cir. 1997). The widow of Fred Astaire sued to enjoin the sale of dance instructional videotapes featuring Astaire's performances. The district court found that the use was not a violation of the California right of publicity, and the Ninth Circuit found there was neither a publicity claim nor any other claim. The testamentary right of publicity in California has since been amended in a manner which may reverse this decision. See Cal. Civ. Code § 3344.1 (2004).

g. To what extent is the original work of art, as marketed through lithographs, serigraphs, and similar works, still free to be marketed when these works involve the images of well-known sports figures? See *ETW Corp. v. Jireh Publ'g, Inc.*, 332 F.3d 915 (6th Cir. 2003).

Problem VII-D

Bryce calls you with a quick question. One of the students involved with the New Masters series elected to use modern celebrities rather than literary characters. The project included a scene between Al Pacino and Quentin Tarantino where the Tarantino character sings a highly disparaging song, calling Pacino "old, angry, and ugly." The two characters continue to trade insults until the Pacino character picks up a stage prop and beats Tarantino to death — singing all the while. Bryce wants to know if the school, students, or anyone else can be in legal trouble for the scene. Bryce is also interested to know whether the answer will change if a proposed DVD version of the production is actually sold. Advise Bryce of the potential liability for both a live stage version of the scene, as well as a commercial version of the production sold on DVD.

E. Bibliography

Mark Bartholomew, *A Right Is Born: Celebrity, Property, and Postmodern Lawmaking*, 44 Conn. L. Rev. 301 (2011).

Joseph J. Beard, *Clones, Bones and Twilight Zones: Protecting the Digital Persona of the Quick, the Dead and the Imaginary*, 16 Berkeley Tech. L.J. 1165 (2001).

F. Jay Dougherty, *All the World's Not a Stooge: The "Transformativeness" Test for Analyzing a First Amendment Defense to a Right of Publicity Claim against Distribution of a Work of Art*, 27 Colum. J.L. & Arts 1 (2003).

Sheldon W. Halpern, *Trafficking in Trademarks: Setting Boundaries for the Uneasy Relationship Between "Property Rights" and Trademark and Publicity Rights*, 58 DePaul L. Rev. 1013 (2009).

Rita Heimes, *Trademarks, Identity, and Justice*, 11 J. Marshall Rev. Intell. Prop. L. 133, 134 (2011).

Laura A. Heymann, *Naming, Identity, and Trademark Law*, 86 Ind. L.J. 381 (2011).

Sarah Konsky, *Publicity Dilution: A Proposal for Protecting Publicity Rights*, 21 Santa Clara Computer & High Tech. L.J. 347 (2005).

Roberta Rosenthal Kwall, *Symposium: Intellectual Property Challenges in the Next Century: Article Preserving Personality and Reputational Interests of Constructed Personas Through Moral Rights: A Blueprint for the Twenty-First Century*, 2001 U. Ill. L. Rev. 151 (2001).

Bela G. Lugosi, *Competing Perspectives and Divergent Analyses California Expands the Statutory Right of Publicity for Deceased Celebrities while its Courts are examining the First Amendment Limitations of that Statute*, 10 DePaul-LCA J. Art & Ent. L. 259 (2000).

Viva R. Moffat, *Mutant Copyrights and Backdoor Patents: The Problem of Overlapping Intellectual Property Protection*, 19 Berkeley Tech. L.J. 1473 (2004).

Richard A. Posner, *Misappropriation: A Dirge*, 40 Hous. L. Rev. 621 (2003).

Michael Suppappola, *Is Tiger Wood's Swing Really a Work of Art? Defining the Line Between the Right of Publicity and the First Amendment*, 28 W. New Eng. L. Rev. 57 (2005).

Eugene Volokh, *Freedom of Speech and the Right of Publicity*, 40 Hous. L. Rev. 903 (2003).

W. Mack Webner & Leigh Ann Lindquist, *Transformation: The Bright Line Between Commercial Publicity Rights and the First Amendment*, 37 Akron L. Rev. 171 (2004).

Chapter VIII

Contracts: Credit & Control

This chapter reflects the casebook's transition from the purely legal doctrinal focus of the first seven chapters to the industry-specific focus of the remaining chapters. The underlying legal framework remains contract law. While the primary focus is on employment law, certain aspects of these agreements may be focused on partnership agreements, reflecting yet another legal discipline in the practice.

A. The Negotiated Areas for Talent Contracts — Credit, Compensation, & Control

Regardless of the media in question, most talent contracts turn on three fundamental issues—credit, compensation, and control. Given that so many industries are highly unionized, issues such as working conditions, job descriptions, and other more typical negotiable items tend to be handled at the collective bargaining level rather than through private negotiation.

The corollary of the collective nature of this bargaining is that a contract dispute often involves not only the two parties to the transaction, but the rules set out in various collective bargaining and regulatory settings.

This area of law may be undergoing a rapid transformation. In the wake of *Dastar Corp. v. Twentieth Century Fox Film Corp.* (see Chapter V), courts are dramatically shifting the analysis of claims for credit. Nonetheless, because this shift is so recent and the response to it thus far may not fully reflect any long-term trends, the materials contained in the remainder of this casebook explain the analysis of claims for credit prior to and in wake of the *Dastar* decision.

The influence on credit in *Dastar* also fails to address the interpretation of contracts providing the right to credit and the implications for the public regarding the overstating of credit.

1. Credit

The right to have one's name listed prominently in association with a work is a prized economic and professional benefit. Parties negotiate over the scope and placement of credit both on the work and on advertisements for the work. In film, the results of negotiated billing appear in the opening credits; in theatre, the negotiated credit can be seen on the marquee and in the playbill; in publishing, the negotiations involve the dust jacket; and in sound recordings, the billing disputes focus on the CD cover. Whatever media is in question, the concepts regarding size and placement of billing are fairly universal.

The most heavily negotiated credit is for "above the title" billing, a term that refers to the positioning of a star's name before the name of the work on a film or above the name of the work on a marquee or in print. If there are two top stars involved in a work, the upper left position is considered the first position in terms of billing. The size of type used for the billing is often a source of discussion as well, with the type size often being negotiated as a percentage of the size of the title credits.

As indicated from the cases below, credits are often used as the basis for future contract negotiations. As a result, the content and position of credits can have a significant financial impact on an artist's future revenue opportunities.

2. Compensation

Compensation is obviously the source of most entertainment negotiation. The negotiations for compensation for sound recordings are so unique that they are treated separately in Chapter XII. For the other industries, compensation is generally paid in three increments: A non-refundable advance upon execution of the initial production agreement; a salary for the completion of the production; and royalties or profit participation for sharing in the success of the project.

All highly successful artists have a wealth of opportunities. As a result, the decision to participate in any one project necessarily precludes the participation in other projects. Because of this, most artists demand an advance of some form to compensate for the opportunity cost, meaning the lost opportunity caused by agreeing to participate in a future project. This may range from a very modest fee to a significant pay-or-play provision that essentially commits the producer to pay the artist the entire fee whether the production goes forward or not.

The salary is the most traditional employment income, typically paid weekly during the course of a film's production or a play's rehearsal and performance run. Publishers do not typically pay salary to authors. Although the rehearsal period is often more work than production, salary is typically lower during the rehearsal period than during film production or a theatrical run.

Royalties and profit participation are based on the income of the project. Publishing royalties typically range from 10% to 20% of the suggested retail price of a book. Theatrical royalties often run 2% to 6% of all box office receipts for the playwright, director, and star cast members. Motion picture profit participation can be based on some formula of the distributor's adjusted gross income or net income. In the motion picture industry, the deductions before profit participation have become the focus of much controversy because so many expenses are deducted. Whether calculated as a royalty or as a form of profit participation, the purpose of these fees is to reward the artists for the success of the project. These have the second benefit of reducing the cost of production by deferring some of the artist overhead until the income is generated.

3. Control

Control is one of the more controversial aspects of negotiations. Some negotiations for control are overt, such as negotiations over approval of other participants in the project. Other areas for control are over scheduling and locations.

The more difficult area for control focuses on artistic control of the overall project. For example, playwrights have virtually absolute control over the text of their plays, based on a non-negotiable, standardized agreement. Film directors vie for final cut, the ability to control the final editing of the motion picture.

Control is negotiated both directly and indirectly. Often times, powerful stars will only agree to participate in a project once certain preconditions have been met. Although the contract never specifies these conditions, the producer's willingness to engage in negotiations over these preconditions is itself evidence of the star's exercise of significant control over the project.

In every industry, the producers or financiers of projects are the source of power and therefore control all projects at the outset. The ability to fund or withhold funding of a project is the ultimate source of power. This power is immediately limited to the extent it has been negotiated away through collective bargaining agreements or standardized contracts. Further, to launch a project, some of the producer's control must be shared with the creative talent that will develop the project.

An attorney negotiating in the entertainment industry must learn both the express control provisions of contracts and the unexpressed realities through which some participants have *de facto* authority throughout the course of a project's development. Marquee stars, who may have no contractual authority over any aspect of the production, still may have the power to have a director or co-star fired because the value of that actor's goodwill is more tangible than any contractual right. Only by understanding both the express and implicit areas of negotiation can an attorney fully appreciate the nuances of each negotiation.

The other aspect of control may come from the terms of the employment's scope. In *Ahn v. Midway Mfg. Co.,* 965 F. Supp. 1134 (N.D. Ill. 1997), the actors involved in the creation of a video game gave their publicity rights for coin-operated machines. The district court determined the scope of the contract included publicity rights to home computer and video games as well. In contrast, former wrestler and governor Jesse Ventura was able to encourage the opposite result. In *Ventura v. Titan Sports,* 65 F.3d 725 (8th Cir. 1995), the Eighth Circuit found that the performance and television contracts did not extend to home video tape for the performances staged for wrestling.

Perhaps the most interesting of all the talent cases litigated involved Raquel Welch's termination by David Begelman, from *Cannery Row.* In a decision decertified and inconsistent with established California precedent, the court found a conspiracy to improperly terminate the aging star and found the defendants acted with sufficient bad faith to award punitive damages. Enjoy *Welch v. Metro-Goldwyn-Mayer Film Co.,* 207 Cal. App. 3d 164 (Cal. App. 2d Dist. 1988), *decertified,* 769 P.2d 932 (Cal. 1989), *and transferred,* 782 P.2d 594 (Cal. 1989).

Sample Associate Producer Agreement[1]

[This simple agreement assumes that a small production company owned by the writer/ director of a project is hiring the person to produce the project. Various aspects of the compensation, credit, and control are represented by the excerpt from the contract.]

This Agreement is made and entered into as of the date first ascribed below, by and between [XYZ Film Company, LLC, 1234 Main Street, Hollywood, California 90210] ("Com-

---

1. JON M. GARON, INDEPENDENT FILMMAKER'S LAW AND BUSINESS GUIDE 380 (2d. ED. CHICAGO REVIEW PRESS 2009).

pany") and [John Doe, an individual, 5678 W. 46th St., New York, NY 10021] ("Producer"), with reference to the following facts:

Company is a wholly owned limited liability company owned by Jane Roe ("Writer/Director").

Company has or will acquire rights to a screenplay to be written and directed by Writer/Director and desires to make such screenplay into a motion picture (the "Picture"); and

Producer has extensive professional experiences as a line producer and producer of feature motion pictures.

Now Therefore, In consideration of the mutual covenants, conditions, and undertakings hereinafter set forth, the parties hereto agree as follows:

1. Services Provided. Company hereby employs the services of Producer, and Producer hereby accepts such employment, for the purpose of serving as associate producer and line producer of the Picture, for the period of [three (3)] weeks of preproduction, [five (5)] weeks of principal photography on an exclusive basis, and such postproduction as is reasonably necessary for completion of the Picture on a nonexclusive but first-priority basis. Each week shall include six working days. The Producer will provide such services as are generally per-formed by producers, including his service coordinating the creative, financial, technological, and administrative process throughout the term of this agreement, subject to the direction and control of Company and such other contracts as Company shall enter with other parties.

2. Term. The term of this Agreement shall commence on the date hereof and shall continue thereafter until Producer has fully completed all services required hereunder, unless sooner terminated in accordance with the provisions of this Agreement.

3. Credit. Provided Producer completes all services required hereunder and the Picture is completed by Company, then Producer shall receive credit on the screen, in motion picture trailers, and in paid print advertising issued by Company and under Company's control which is at least 10 inches or larger. The credit shall be "John Doe, Associate Producer." On the screen such credit shall be displayed above or before the title of the Picture in a size of type not less than fifty percent (50%) of the size of type used to display the title of the Picture. At its sole discretion, Company may assign "Produced by" and "Associate Producer" credit to one or more additional persons in addition to Producer in the event Company determines such other person or persons provided substantial producer services in addition to Producer. No casual or inadvertent failure to comply with the provisions of this clause shall be deemed to be a breach of this Agreement by Company. Producer shall notify Company of any breach of this paragraph, after which Company shall take reasonable steps to correct all new prints, copies, and advertising on a prospective basis, but Company shall not be required to recall or alter any prints, copies, or advertisements in production or distribution. No monetary damages are available for breach of Company's duties under this paragraph.

4. Consideration. In consideration for Producer's services hereunder and provided Producer is not in default hereunder, Company shall pay Producer as follows:

   (a) Fixed Consideration. Producer shall receive a stipend of [$100.00] per day actually worked during preproduction and principal photography, not to exceed [Forty-Eight Hundred ($4,800.00)] Dollars. The payment shall be paid on a weekly basis.

(b) Net Profits. If Producer fulfills all Producer's obligations pursuant to this agreement and if Company produces the Picture, Producer shall receive an amount equal to [ten percent (10%)] of one hundred percent (100%) of Net Profits in the Gross Receipts of the Company in the Picture or [One Hundred Thousand ($100,000)] Dollars, whichever is lower.

   (i)   Gross Receipts means all income, if any, actually received by Company from the sale, exhibition, or distribution of the Picture in theaters, video/DVD or similar format, broadcast television, satellite, cable exhibition, or any other method of exhibition, display, or performance now known or hereafter created. Gross Receipts does not include income from any other source related to the Picture, including, without limitation, income derived from sale of sequel, prequel, or remake rights, publishing interests such as novelizations, comic books, etc., sales of the screenplay, "making of" or other related projects, or any other spin-offs or related Company projects or activities.

   (ii) The term Net Profits shall mean the Gross Receipts, less the deductions of all Company expenses of every kind related to the Picture. Without limiting the foregoing, the deductions shall include all costs, charges, and expenses paid or incurred in connection with the preparation, production, completion, and delivery of the Picture, deferred compensation, charges for any services, union or trade obligations, interest expenses, obligations to any completion guarantor, legal and accounting charges, the cost of all material, services, facilities, labor, insurance, taxes (other than income, franchise, and like taxes), copyright royalties attributable to the Picture for music, artwork, script, or other, judgments, marketing and promotional expenses, distribution fees, recoveries, settlements, losses, costs, and expenses, including reasonable attorneys' fees, sustained or incurred by Company in connection with the Picture or anything used therein and in connection with the production thereof. Company shall pay Producer twice annually all amounts due hereunder for all monies accrued during the preceding six-month period, not later than forty-five (45) days following the end of each such period.

(c) Reimbursements. Producer shall be reimbursed for all reasonable advances or expenses incurred in the production of the Picture, such as for location scouting, equipment rental, and the like, provided such expenses have been approved by Company in advance and Producer provides adequate documentation and receipts of the expense.

5. Authority. Company shall coordinate with Producer throughout the production to the greatest extent practicable throughout production; provided, however, Company reserves final approval of all essential production elements including, without limitation, script, budget, casting, locations, and film editing. Subject to direction of Company, Producer shall comply with all contractual and union and guild obligations and Company requirements.

6. Termination.

(a) This Agreement may be terminated by Company at any time, with or without cause. If Company elects to terminate this Agreement and Producer is not in default hereunder, Company shall pay Producer his accrued fixed compensation and a pro rata proportion of the contingent compensation.

(By way of example, if Producer is terminated after 12 days, he will receive 12/48 of his contingent compensation, equal to 25% of 10%, meaning 2.5% of the Net Profits.) The costs of additional producer(s) shall be added to the cost of production. In the event Company determines Producer has materially breached his obligations hereunder, no contingent compensation shall be paid.

(b) This Agreement may be terminated by Producer upon seven days' advanced written notice. Unless otherwise agreed in writing by the parties, in the event Producer terminates this Agreement, he shall receive only his accrued fixed compensation, but shall not be eligible for any contingent compensation.

7. Work Made for Hire. Company shall own the copyright in the Picture without any claim by Producer. Producer is employed as on a work made for hire as a specially commissioned audiovisual or motion picture work and acknowledges that the copyright in the Picture shall vest exclusively in Company as author.

(a) The Picture shall be registered for copyright in Company's name both in the United States and elsewhere.

(b) To the extent Producer has created any copyrighted elements incorporated into the Picture and such work made for hire provision is not recognized by the jurisdiction, Producer hereby assigns all rights or the maximum rights allowed under that jurisdiction's laws to Company, including, without limitation, Rental Lending Rights if recognized, rights to enforce any claim of attribution and integrity, or rights to exploit any interest in the Picture in any media now known or hereafter developed.

8. Unique Services. It is hereby agreed and understood that Producer's services to be furnished hereunder are special, extraordinary, unique, and not replaceable, and that there is no adequate remedy at law for breach of this contract by Producer.

(a) Company shall be entitled to both legal and equitable remedies as may be available, including both injunctive relief and damages. Company may elect not to submit to arbitration for the purpose of seeking emergency, preliminary, or temporary injunctive relief.

(b) Producer's services shall be in such time, place, and manner as Company may reasonably direct in accordance with customary motion picture industry practice. Such services shall be rendered in an artistic, conscientious, efficient, and punctual manner to the best of Producer's ability to adhere to the budget and shooting schedule.

(c) Producer grants to Company the perpetual nonexclusive right to use and license others to use Producer's name, biography, and reproductions of Producer's physical likeness and voice in connection with the production, exhibition, advertising, promotion, or other exploitation of the Picture and all subsidiary and ancillary rights therein and thereto; provided, however, Company shall not use or authorize the use of Producer's name or likeness as a direct endorsement of any product or service without Producer's prior consent.

9. Resolution of Disputes. ANY AND ALL DISPUTES HEREUNDER SHALL BE RESOLVED BY ARBITRATION OR REFERENCE. ANY PARTY HERETO ELECTING TO COMMENCE AN ACTION SHALL GIVE WRITTEN NOTICE TO THE OTHER PARTY HERETO. THEREUPON, IF ARBITRATION IS SE-

LECTED BY THE PARTY COMMENCING THE ACTION, THE CLAIM ("ARBITRATION MATTER") SHALL BE SETTLED BY ARBITRATION IN ACCORDANCE WITH THE THEN RULES OF THE AMERICAN ARBITRATION ASSOCIATION ("AAA"). The arbitrator or the referee shall diligently pursue determination of any Arbitration under consideration and shall render a decision within one hundred twenty (120) days after the arbitrator or referee is selected. The determination of the arbitrator on all matters referred to it hereunder shall be final and binding on the parties hereto. The award of such arbitrator may be confirmed or enforced in any court of competent jurisdiction. The referee, arbitrator, or its designee shall have full access to such records and physical facilities of the parties hereto as may be required. The costs and expenses of the referee or arbitrator, and the attorneys' fees and costs of each of the parties incurred in such, may be apportioned between the parties by such arbitrator, as the case may be, based upon such arbitrator's determination of the merits of their respective positions.

10. Confidentiality; Publicity. Company shall have the exclusive right to issue and to license others to issue advertising and publicity with respect to the Picture, and Producer shall not circulate, publish, or otherwise disseminate any such advertising or publicity without Company's prior written consent.

11. Assignment. Producer agrees that Company shall have the right to assign, license, delegate, lend, or otherwise transfer all or any part of its rights or duties under this Agreement at any time to any person. Producer acknowledges that the personal services to be rendered by Producer hereunder are of the essence of this Agreement and agrees that he shall not assign this Agreement, in whole or in part, to any person, and that any purported assignment or delegation of duties by Producer shall be null and void and of no force and effect whatsoever. This Agreement shall inure to the benefit of Company's successors, assigns, licensees, grantees, and associated, affiliated, and subsidiary companies.

12. No Obligation. Company agrees to uses all reasonable efforts to cause the Picture to be produced, however, the parties recognize that the production of an independent motion picture is an inherently difficult undertaking. Company is under no obligation to produce the Picture hereunder. In the event Company abandons production of the Picture hereunder, Producer is entitled to such fixed compensation as had previously accrued and is not entitled to any additional compensation, damage, or loss as a result of such failure to undertake or complete the Picture.

13. Assurances. Each party shall execute all documents and certificates and perform all acts deemed appropriate by the Company or required by this Agreement in connection with this Agreement and the production of the Picture.

Lee v. Marvel Enterprises, Inc.

386 F. Supp. 2d 235 (S.D.N.Y. 2005)
aff'd, 471 Fed. Appx. 14, 15 (2d Cir. 2012) (unpublished)

The defendant Marvel Enterprises, Inc. ("Marvel") has moved for partial summary judgment in accordance with Rule 56(a), Fed. R. Civ. P., dismissing the claims in the complaint seeking a profit participation from licensing of its characters for merchandising. The plaintiff Stan Lee ("Lee") has cross-moved for partial summary judgment declaring that he is entitled to 10% participation in profits derived by Marvel from television or movie productions, not limited by so-called "Hollywood Accounting," including film/television merchandising when the profits do not result from a fee for licensing. For the reasons set forth below, Marvel's motion is denied, and Lee's cross-motion is granted in part and denied in part.

As of the time these motions were filed, Lee continued to serve as Marvel's chairman emeritus. As discussed below, Lee has contributed significantly to Marvel's growth since his initial employment in 1940. Initially, Marvel's predominant business was publishing comic books, many of which featured characters created by Lee—*e.g.* Spider-Man, the Incredible Hulk, the X-Men, and the Fantastic Four. Marvel has subsequently expanded the use of its characters into movies, television, and merchandising. Lee had a contract with Marvel that permitted him to share in certain of these endeavors. Marvel then suffered the vicissitudes of a control contest and bankruptcy. When it emerged from bankruptcy with new leadership, it entered into a new contract with Lee (the "Agreement"). It is paragraph 4(f) of the Agreement, executed on November 17, 1998, that is the central focus of the present action. Paragraph 4(f) states:

> [Lee] shall be paid a participation equal to 10% of the profits derived during [his] life by Marvel (including subsidiaries and affiliates) from the profits of any live action or animation television or movie (including ancillary rights) productions utilizing Marvel Characters. This participation is not to be derived from the fee charged by Marvel for the licensing of the product or of the characters for merchandise or otherwise …

This deceptively simple language, drafted by a company and an executive both skilled and experienced in the industry, has given rise to a multimillion dollar controversy because of changes in the way Marvel has conducted business since the execution of the Agreement in November, 1998.

According to Marvel, paragraph 4(f) entitles Lee to 10% participation in only those television and motion picture production deals where Marvel has been afforded rights of net profit participation. (Such net profit participation arrangements are commonly referred to as "Hollywood Accounting" deals.[2]) Lee argues that paragraph 4(f) entitles him to 10% of all profits—including gross profits or gross proceeds—derived from contingent payments to Marvel in connection with the use of Marvel characters in film or television productions.

According to Marvel, pursuant to the second sentence of paragraph 4(f), Lee is barred from any profits from merchandising. According to Lee, he is entitled to participate in all revenue from film/television merchandising with the exception of profits resulting from fees from licensing for merchandise.

---

2. One commentator has provided the following description of the typical provisions of a "Hollywood accounting" deal:

> The basic net profits formula subtracts from the studio's (distributor's) adjusted gross receipts the production costs, distribution expenses, and distribution fees.… Production costs are all costs directly attributed to the particular film (plus overhead). Production costs include the payments to all other participants in a film including the contingent compensation of gross participants. So, for example, [if a given actor] had fifteen gross points for [a given movie] (that is, he received 15[%] of the gross receipts), every dollar of revenue that the film generated pushed the net profits breakeven point back fifteen cents. Thus, if a film has significant gross participants, the breakeven point quickly recedes. Almost all the box office smashes that failed to produce net profits had significant gross participants.

Victor P. Goldberg, *The Net Profits Puzzle*, 97 Colum. L. Rev. 524, 528–529 (1997).

Skilled counsel for both sides praise the clarity of the language of paragraph 4(f) to reach directly contrary results. What follows is an effort to clarify and determine the terms of the contractual language under the applicable principles of procedure and construction. This determination has the potential to affect substantially the financial fortunes of the parties....

Prior to the 1994 bankruptcy, the parties entered into an agreement granting Lee a share of Marvel's profits. In 1995, pursuant to this agreement, Marvel paid Lee a 10% participation, which was based on revenue received by Marvel under an arrangement with Danchuk Productions. Under this arrangement, Lee received a percentage of gross receipts. The payments to Marvel were characterized as "profit participation." Marvel remitted 10% ($4,994) to Lee without any deduction for costs. Marvel stated to Lee that this sum "represented your 10% of the profits." The executory portion of this prior agreement was rejected by Marvel during the bankruptcy.

After Marvel emerged from bankruptcy, the parties on November 17, 1998 executed the Agreement. In addition to paragraph 4(f), the Agreement contains other relevant provisions. Under paragraph 2, Lee is required to devote ten to fifteen hours per week to Marvel's affairs. As consideration for his services, Lee is entitled to receive an annual base salary of $810,000 for the years beginning November 1, 1998 and 1999, $850,000 for the year beginning November 1, 2000, $900,000 for the year beginning November 1, 2001, and $1,000,000 for the year beginning November 1, 2002 and each year thereafter until his death. Upon Lee's death, the Agreement provides for Lee's wife to receive survivor payments in an amount equal to 50% of Lee's base salary as of the time of his death through the time of her death, and for Lee's daughter thereafter to receive survivor payments of $100,000 per year for five years. Under paragraph 4(c) of the Agreement, Lee received 150,000 valuable stock options which Lee has already exercised for a net gain of approximately $1.4 million.

Between November 17, 1998 and today, Marvel has entered into over a thousand merchandising agreements pursuant to which it has licensed to third parties the right to use its characters in connection with various toys, games, collectibles, apparel, interactive games, arcade games and electronics, stationery and school products, health and beauty products, snack foods and beverages, sporting goods, party supplies, and amusement destinations. Merchandising has generated hundreds of millions of dollars in revenue to Marvel during this period.

In August 1998, the film *Blade*, which was based on a Marvel character, was released. Despite the fact that *Blade* apparently generated considerable profits, Marvel was not entitled to participate in these profits based on the terms of the profit-participation provision of the production agreement. This profit-participation provision, which Marvel has characterized as a "Hollywood accounting" provision, entitled Marvel to a share of *Blade's* "net profits," as that term was defined by the language of the production agreement. Marvel's Rule 30(b)(6) witness stated that "Hollywood accounting" can be interpreted "to mean that you will never see anything—you will never see—the company would not see any revenues from the studio...." Marvel's chief creative officer, Avi Arad, testified that "Hollywood accounting is—is the term used to—studio's deduct everything possible out of film revenues, from cost of the movie to getting a star flowers to—you name it and its in there. And it's expensive and it's hard to monitor, and therefore I'm allergic to it."

Coincident with *Blade's* box-office success, a determination was made by Marvel to avoid "Hollywood accounting" treatment for the use of the Marvel characters. In its 2001 annual report, Marvel advised that its new movie venture agreements were either "gross profit participation 'dollar one,'" "real profit participation," or "equity (ownership) interests in the films themselves." As stated by Marvel, these new agreements "represent an exciting new source of high margin revenue and are a major departure from the past when [Marvel] made little or no money for such projects."

Marvel's contract with Sony for use of the character Spider-Man (generally regarded as Marvel's most valuable asset) contained a gross-profit participation provision. *Spider-Man: The Movie*, which was released in May, 2002, proved to be a huge box-office hit, earning $114.8 million in its opening weekend (at the time, the largest domestic opening of all time) and more than $800 million in worldwide box-office gross. Based on these receipts, the profit participation provision that Marvel negotiated with Sony has yielded more than $50,000,000 to Marvel.

In its October 30, 2002 press release announcing Marvel's quarterly financial results, Marvel's then president and CEO, Peter Cuneo ("Cuneo"), stated that "Marvel's resurgence throughout 2002 has been supported by the overwhelming popularity and success of *Spider-Man: The Movie*, which has spurred licensing and toy revenues; the expanding scope of our publishing efforts; and our strong and growing line-up of entertainment projects scheduled for release in 2003 and beyond." As set forth in its 2002 annual report, Marvel's toy division alone reported over $100 million in sales of *Spider-Man: The Movie* toys. Marvel's 2003 results were similarly strong, driven by the popularity of the films *X-Men 2*, *Daredevil*, and *Hulk*, all of which featured Marvel characters....

[A.] Profit Participation Pursuant To The First Sentence Of Paragraph 4(f) Is Not Limited to Net Profit Participation.

According to Lipson, Marvel's *30(b)(6)* witness, Marvel's construction of the first sentence of paragraph 4(f) is based on the plain meaning of the text. According to Lipson, Lee is entitled to participation pursuant to paragraph 4(f) only when a payment by a studio (or producer) to Marvel is the result of a calculation of profit based on "Hollywood Accounting." Marvel argues that Lee is not entitled to share in profits arising from the contingent compensation provision in the Spider-Man agreement (and others like it) because such provisions entail participation in gross receipts and not profits.

However, the first sentence of paragraph 4(f) does not state that Lee's participation is limited to net profits earned by the producer or studio. Nor is the word "profits" defined in the Agreement. Moreover, the first, and therefore preferred, dictionary definition for "profit" is "an advantageous gain or return; benefit" (The American Heritage College Dictionary (3d ed. 2000)); or "a valuable return: gain." (Merriam-Webster Online Dictionary). As demonstrated by the evidence proffered by Lee, these dictionary definitions are consistent with Marvel's own consistent practice in treating all forms of contingent compensation as profit participation.In short, the first sentence of paragraph 4(f) is not ambiguous. It provides that Lee is entitled to share in the results of Marvel's arrangements for movie and television productions involving Marvel characters, however those arrangements may have been characterized as between Marvel and the third party, as long as there is a valuable gain or return, a benefit to Marvel.

It is also apparent that a determination of the profits to which Lee is entitled cannot be made on the basis of the present record.

[B.] "Ancillary Rights" Include Merchandising

The parties differ as to whether the term "ancillary rights," as used in the first sentence of paragraph 4(f), includes merchandising rights. According to Marvel, pursuant to the first sentence of paragraph 4(f), "ancillary rights" are properly defined as whatever rights are granted by Marvel to a licensee under a given film/television production agreement. Marvel argues that "ancillary rights" neither necessarily include nor exclude merchandising; rather, the terms of each individual film or television production agreement determines the substance of these rights. In contrast, Lee argues that the phrase "ancillary rights" describes all rights beyond a film/television production's initial intended distribution, and that such rights are understood in the entertainment industry to necessarily include merchandising....

[T]he phrase "ancillary rights" includes rights ancillary to the basic film or television production itself. According to Lee's expert, it is understood in the motion picture and television industries that such "ancillary rights" include soundtrack, music, and merchandising revenues. Although Marvel's expert asserts that "there is no fixed and accepted definition" of the term "ancillary rights" he admits that the term is understood in the entertainment industry to include "all rights beyond the right to produce and distribute the motion picture for theatrical release." Furthermore, Marvel's expert states that "there are instances where merchandising rights are expressly excluded from the grant of ancillary rights[,]" thereby strongly suggesting that, in general, ancillary rights are understood to include merchandising.

Based on this expert testimony proffered by Lee and Marvel concerning common usage in the relevant industries, it is determined that the phrase "ancillary rights," as used in the first sentence of paragraph 4(f), necessarily includes merchandising rights....

B. Performer's Rights to Credit

Williams v. UMG Recordings, Inc.
281 F. Supp. 2d 1177 (C.D. Cal. 2003)

This action is brought by Plaintiff Kelvin Williams d/b/a Uprise Productions ("Plaintiff") against Defendants UMG Recordings, Inc., Universal Music & Video Distribution, Inc., Cash Money Records, Inc., Jeffrey Panzer, Ronald Williams, Bryan Williams, Gary Huckaby and Elston Howard....

Plaintiff styles himself as "a talented young film director/writer/editor." Defendant Cash Money is a record label whose principals are Defendants Ronald and Bryan Williams. Cash Money has a contract with non-party Universal Records, Inc. ("Universal"), pursuant to which Cash Money pays Defendant UMG Recordings, Inc. ("UMG") (of which Universal is a division) to manufacture and distribute its products. Defendant Panzer is a Senior Vice President of Music Video Production for Universal who also does free-lance work for the Cash Money Defendants. Defendant Universal Music & Video Distribution, Corp. ("UMVD"), an affiliate of UMG, actually distributed the film that is the subject of this suit.

In February of 2000, Plaintiff, Panzer and the Cash Money Defendants collaborated on the production of a documentary. A dispute over Plaintiff's compensation subsequently developed, apparently resulting in bad blood between Plaintiff and Panzer. In the meantime, around March 2000, Plaintiff got involved in another project with Panzer and the Cash Money Defendants involving post-production work on a film entitled "Baller Blockin.'"

The parties disagree as to the nature and extent of Plaintiff's involvement in the Baller Blockin' project. Plaintiff claims that Defendants contracted with him to restructure the entire film. Plaintiff contends that he re-edited and re-scored the entire film and that it incorporates his copyrighted narration script ("Narration Script"). After Baller Blockin' was released [only on DVD and home video (not in theaters)], Plaintiff discovered his name was not listed in the film's credits and initiated this lawsuit....

Defendants seek reconsideration in part of the July Order dismissing in part Plaintiff's Second Claim for Relief for violation of the Lanham Act.... Specifically, after the issuance of July Order, the United States Supreme Court issued its opinion in *Dastar v. Twentieth Century Fox,* 539 U.S. 23 (2003), and Defendants claim that *Dastar* bars Plaintiff's Lanham Act claim as a matter of law.

Under the Lanham Act, Plaintiff alleges that Defendants engaged in unfair trade practices and unfair competition for appropriating his "copyrighted Narration Script, re-sequencing of scenes and re-scoring of musical content[.]" Specifically, Plaintiff alleges "reverse passing off" based on Defendants' misattribution of film credits for authorship and direction of Baller Blockin' solely to Robert and Bryan Williams.

In the July Order, the Court explained that Section 43(a) of the Lanham Act reaches "'reverse passing off,' which occurs when a person removes or obliterates the original trademark, without authorization, before reselling goods produced by someone else." It further explained that "'mere omission'" of credit, "which obscures the contribution of another to the final product," is actionable under this theory. The Court, acknowledging that the Lanham Act does not create a right of express attribution, held that to recover on his Lanham Act claim, Plaintiff must demonstrate that his alleged contributions in writing the Narration Script and re-editing and re-scoring the film were partially or wholly attributed to others. In other words, Plaintiff cannot seek a remedy under the Lanham Act for credit for contributions not attributed to others. The Court concluded as follows: "The only potentially relevant credit given in the film and on its packaging is that given for 'story/screenplay' and 'editing.'... A triable issue of fact exists as to whether Plaintiff's alleged contributions fall within the categories of 'story/screenplay' and 'editing' such that failure to include Plaintiff's name in the credits constitutes misattribution under the Lanham Act."...

In *Dastar,* plaintiff Twentieth Century Fox ("Fox") produced a 26-episode television series called "Crusade in Europe," which initially aired in 1949, featuring military film footage. The copyright on the series expired in 1977, leaving the series in the public domain. Fox later granted to co-plaintiffs SFM Entertainment ("SFM") and New Line Home Video ("New Line") the exclusive right to sell the "Crusade" series on video.

Defendant Dastar sought to compete directly with the SFM and New Line videos by purchasing tapes of the original "Crusade" series and copying and editing them—retaining much of the original series by adding new opening and closing sequences, credits, chapter-title sequences, and narrated introductions, and making a few other cosmetic changes. Dastar also created new packaging and a new title, selling its version as "World War II Campaigns in Europe."...

The Supreme Court ... acknowledged that the plaintiffs' claim would undoubtedly be sustained if Dastar had bought some of New Line's Crusade videotapes and merely repackaged them as its own. This is because "origin" would refer to the manufacturer or producer of the physical goods that are made available to the public—the videotapes. However, it stated that Dastar's alleged wrongdoing is "vastly different" in that it took a creative work in the public domain—the Crusade television series—copied it, made minor modifications and produced its very own series of videotapes. Under this scenario, if "origin" includes the creator of the underlying work that Dastar copied, then someone else was the origin of Dastar's product. The Supreme Court then determined that the most natural understanding of the "origin" of "goods" is the producer of the tangible product sold in the marketplace (i.e., the videotapes sold by Dastar). It stated that the phrase "origin of goods" in the Lanham Act is "incapable of connoting the person or entity that originated the ideas or communications that 'goods' embody or contain."

The Court then examined the argument that communicative products—products that are valued not primarily for its physical qualities but for the intellectual content that it conveys such as a book or video—should be accorded special treatment. In other words, for a communicative product, "origin of goods" must be deemed to include not merely the producer of the physical item (the video producer Dastar) but also the creator of the content that the physical item conveys (assertedly, the plaintiffs). The Supreme Court rejected this and found that the "problem with this argument ... is that it causes the Lanham Act to conflict with the law of copyright, which addresses that subject specifically." ...

The Court noted the serious practical problems of defining "origin" to require attribution of uncopyrighted materials. It "did not think the Lanham Act requires this search for the source of the Nile and all its tributaries."

The Supreme Court then concluded as follows:

> In sum, reading the phrase 'origin of goods' in the Lanham Act in accordance with the Act's common-law foundations (which were *not* designed to protect originality or creativity), and in light of the copyright and patent laws (which *were*), we conclude that the phrase refers to the producer of the tangible goods that are offered for sale, and not to the author of any idea, concept, or communication embodied in those goods.... To hold otherwise would be akin to finding that *§ 43(a)* created a species of perpetual patent and copyright, which Congress may not do.

Defendants argue that *Dastar* invalidates Plaintiff's Lanham Act claim. This Court agrees with Defendants.... Plaintiff's Lanham Act claim is based on the misattribution of credits for "story/screenplay" and "editing" on the Baller Blockin' film. Plaintiff alleges that he should be given credit for "the authoring of the 'Narration Script' ..., editing film sequences and re-scoring the music." Under *Dastar*, however, the Supreme Court specifically held that the phrase "origin of goods" "refers to the producer of tangible goods that are offered for sale, and not to the author of any idea, concept, or communication embodied in those goods." As such, Plaintiff would have a claim if Defendants purchased copies of Plaintiff's goods (i.e. the film) and repackaged them as their own. By contrast, Plaintiff does not have a claim for his authorship and direction embodied in that film. His claim, therefore, is barred as a matter of law.

In his Opposition, Plaintiff argues that *Dastar* is not a broad sweeping dismissal of reverse passing off claims but rather is limited to defining "origin of goods," not the origin of services. He claims that the Supreme Court's sole focus was on the term "origin of goods," and that it did not address the origin of services, which is at issue here. This Court disagrees with Plaintiff. As Defendants assert, the Supreme Court in *Dastar* was concerned with a claim materially identical to Plaintiff's claim here. The claim was that Dastar had made false or misleading representations on its own goods (Dastar's Campaigns videotapes)—just as Plaintiff here claims that Defendants made false or misleading representations on Defendants' own goods (the Baller Blockin' video and DVD). The "goods" are the defendants', not the plaintiff's. *Dastar* makes clear that a claim that a defendant's failure to credit the plaintiff on the defendant's goods is actionable only where the defendant literally repackages the plaintiff's goods and sells them as the defendant's own—not where, as here, Defendants are accused only of failing to identify someone who contributed not goods, but ideas or communications (or, for that matter, "services") to Defendants' product.

Contrary to Plaintiff's argument, based on the *Dastar* Court's holding, the Ninth Circuit cases cited by Plaintiff would be overruled to the extent they find a reverse passing off claim based on the failure to credit the author of any idea, concept or communication embodied in the tangible goods.

Plaintiff contends that his claim survives *Dastar* because he provided "services" as opposed to "goods." However, to the contrary, his claim fails for this reason. All he allegedly provided was "services," rather than goods which Defendants repackaged and resold as their own. Indeed, in *Dastar*, the defendant did exactly what Plaintiff accuses Defendants of doing here—attributing to itself and its employees various "services" that the plaintiffs claimed they, in fact, provided on the defendant's videotapes. The Supreme Court held that the plaintiffs' claim that these credits were misleading because the plaintiffs really provided those services was non-actionable. As Defendants state, Plaintiff's attempt to differentiate the "services" of an "executive producer" or "producer" at issue in Dastar from his alleged "services" as an "editor" and "writer" is a distinction without a difference.

Plaintiff then asserts that "if defendants [sic] argument were accepted, a talented director who directs a Summer blockbuster for example can be deprived of the immense value of such a credit in the entertainment industry, simply because the producer decides to name himself as the director.... A reading that the Lanham Act does not protect those people who provide services on films permits a form of anarchy in the entertainment industry, where anybody could be credited for anyone else's work and have their credit obliterated." However, the Supreme Court directly addressed Plaintiff's assertion. "The problem with this argument according special treatment to communicative products is that it causes the Lanham Act to conflict with the law of copyright, which addresses that subject specifically." In Plaintiff's hypothetical, the director has options to protect his interest—obtaining a contractual right to a credit, relying on the regulation of credits in union collective bargaining agreements (e.g., the Directors Guild) or maintaining the copyright in the film. In light of *Dastar*, this hypothetical director cannot bring a claim under the Lanham Act.

Finally, Plaintiff attempts to distinguish *Dastar* by claiming that "the Court focused its analysis of the case on the concept that the involved works were uncopyrighted and the difficulties associated with the origin of the product." To the contrary, the Supreme Court's holding did not depend on whether the works were copyrighted or not. While the film footage at issue in *Dastar* was not copyrighted at the time of distribution by *Dastar*, the Court's holding is in no way limited to uncopyrighted material. Rather, in being careful not to extend trademark protections, the Court noted that protection for communicative products was available through copyright claims. In fact, this protection would only be available if a valid copyright existed. Indeed, the Court stated:

> The creative talent of the sort that lay behind the Campaigns videos is not left without protection. The original film footage used in the Crusade television series could have been copyrighted,..., as was copyrighted (as a compilation) the Crusade television series, even though it included material from the public domain,.... Had Fox renewed the copyright in the Crusade television series, it would have had an easy claim of copyright infringement.

Here, Plaintiff does have a copyright claim. As was set forth in the July Order, "a triable issue of fact exists as to whether Defendants are liable for copyright infringement since the filing of this law suit [sic] in April 2001." As *Dastar* makes clear, Plaintiff's claim is more appropriately addressed under copyright law rather than under the Lanham Act. Therefore, this Court concludes that Defendants are the "origin" of the Baller Blockin' film insofar as that term is used to define the manufacturer or producer of the physical goods that were made available to the public, and no Lanham Act liability attaches to them. Plaintiff's claim under the Lanham Act fails as a matter of law, and Defendants are entitled to summary judgment with respect to the claim.

Plaintiff argues that in pleading a cause of action for Lanham Act violation, he properly relied on existing law. He states that rather than plead duplicative claims for relief, he opted for the federal Lanham Act claim rather than the statutory unfair business practice and deceptive advertising claims.... Plaintiff's desired statutory unfair business practice claim would be futile. The Ninth Circuit has consistently held that state law unfair competition claims are "congruent" with Lanham Act claims; Plaintiff's putative unfair competition claim would fail for the same reasons his Lanham Act claim fails....

Accordingly, this Court grants Defendants ... Motion for Reconsideration and dismisses Plaintiff's Second Claim for Relief for violation of the Lanham Act.

Notes and Questions

a. Marybeth Peters, when Register of Copyright, commented on the difficulty created by *Dastar*. "[T]he longstanding understanding prior to *Dastar* [was] that section 43(a) is an important means for protecting the moral rights of attribution and integrity."[3] The importance of the §43(a) claim is the pressure it puts on the producers of a project to provide contractual credit.

b. While the *Dastar* Court is correct that contract law and copyright law provide protection, such protection is not always sufficient. (See *Fleet v. CBS*, below, for more on this topic.)

c. Although *Williams* rejects the idea that *Dastar* involved the re-use of public domain material, should trademark law imply that copyrighted works originate from the copyright holders for trademark purposes or should copyright holders be limited to contractual rights, if any? See *Gilliam v. ABC*, 538 F.2d 14 (2d Cir. 1976).

d. In *Teter v. Glass Onion, Inc.*, 723 F. Supp. 2d 1138 (W.D. Mo. 2010), the district court applied traditional trademark law for a living artist who objected to a gallery's creation of online thumbnails of the artist's works for promotion. The court recognized that LEE TETER was a trademark which had acquired secondary meaning. Reluctantly, the plaintiff was allowed to survive the motion for summary judgment as to whether the use of the trademark created confusion as to an affiliation between the artist and the gallery which sold the artist's work without authorization.

e. The *Dastar* and *Williams* decisions specifically eliminate claims for reverse passing off. A similar, but slightly distinct claim can be made for false advertising. To what extent does this claim survive? See *Lamothe v. Atlantic Recording Corp.*, 847 F.2d 1403 (9th Cir. 1988), vacated, 760 F. Supp. 45 (1991).

f. The right of attribution extends far beyond copyright. Indeed, it may very well be that performers have a much greater stake in the right to credit than do the authors of pro-

---

3. Statement of Marybeth Peters, Register of Copyrights before the Subcommittee on Courts, The Internet and Intellectual Property of the House Committee on the Judiciary, June 17, 2004, *available at* http://www.copyright.gov/docs/regstat061704.html.

jects. The law provides little other protection to performers, so stripping them of attribution rights when the question was not before the court seems unkind as well as unnecessary. Unfortunately, the facts in the case provided a poor basis for making these determinations. The footage in *Dastar* was predominantly government war footage or anonymous stock footage. Presumably, copyright in the footage had never existed because the film was public domain governmental works, because the newsreels were never copyrighted (at a time when such formalities had to be followed), or because there had been no renewals of copyright in the stock footage incorporated into the film.

g. Do states have the ability to enforce or amend their unfair competition laws to reach the "false designation of author" or to make the intentional falsification of a credit a civil tort? What would such a statute include?

Problem VIII-B

Bryce is concerned about some rumors floating around the local dance club scene. One of Bryce's friends, Alan, has been provided a recording contract at a major studio. Bryce had served as producer for Alan's demo. At the time, Bryce had offered to do the producer work without compensation to assist the friend. Bryce had not asked Alan for any payment, nor had anything been said about the copyright in the sound recording. Bryce had correctly assumed that the record company would professionally rerecord the demo, so that Bryce's work would not be widely marketed.

A problem has arisen, however. Alan has represented that he produced the album himself. Worse, Alan said that Bryce assisted on an earlier demo CD that Bryce considers to be of very inferior quality. Bryce does not want credit on the earlier album and is angered that Alan has taken credit on the second album. Because of the potential that significant money will eventually be involved, Bryce wants to know all of the available options with regard to Alan and the record company. Advise Bryce.

C. Loss of Credit Despite Express Contract

Fleet v. CBS, Inc.

50 Cal. App. 4th 1911 (Cal. App. 1996)

In this case we are asked to decide a very narrow issue: whether an actor may bring an action for misappropriation of his or her name, image, likeness, or identity under *section 3344 of the Civil Code* when the only alleged exploitation occurred through the distribution of the actor's performance in a motion picture. The trial court concluded that to the extent California law would permit such claim, it was preempted by federal copyright law. We agree with the trial court and affirm.

The crucial facts are not disputed. In 1985, Legend Productions (Legend), a partnership comprised of Robert Fleet and his wife, Alina Szpak-Fleet (Szpak), entered into a co-production agreement with certain Polish film entities to co-produce two motion pictures, one of which is the subject of this lawsuit.... CBS paid $1,250,000 for these rights. The film commenced shooting on location in Poland in September 1985. Appellant Stephan Fleet is the son of Robert Fleet and Szpak. He and appellant Archie Lee Simpson appeared as actors in the film.

White Dragon Productions entered into separate agreements with one Tadeusz Bugaj to provide financing and with a company known as Performance Guarantees, Inc., to ensure that the film would be completed on time and on budget. In March of 1986, Performance Guarantees stepped in to complete the film and refused to pay the salaries owed to appellants.... CBS went ahead and released the film on videotape under the title "Legend of the White Horse" and, according to the complaint, included a picture of Stephan Fleet on the box.

Appellants brought a complaint against CBS, two of its divisions, and CBS/Fox Video, Inc. (collectively referred to hereafter as CBS) in November of 1993. Insofar as appellants' claims are concerned, the complaint alleges that CBS was notified in March of 1990 that it was not authorized to use the performances of actors Stephan Fleet or Archie Simpson; that Performance Guarantees had breached the terms of the completion bond; that CBS had breached the terms of the distribution agreement; and that "CBS was not authorized to exploit or utilize the Motion Picture in any fashion until the problems and breaches were corrected." The complaint specifically stated that the reason CBS was not authorized to utilize the name, voice, photograph, likeness or performance of appellants in the motion picture was because they were not fully paid. Stephan Fleet further alleged that CBS failed to accord him the credit to which he was contractually entitled on videotape releases of the motion picture; that CBS made unauthorized use of his photograph and likeness on the packaging and advertising materials for the motion picture; and that CBS acquiesced in the redubbing of all his speaking parts without his permission.

Based on these allegations, the complaint contended that CBS violated *section 3344 of the Civil Code*. Section 3344 makes it unlawful to "knowingly use[ ] another's name, voice, signature, photograph, or likeness, in any manner, on or in products, merchandise, or goods, or for purposes of advertising or selling, or soliciting purchases of, products, merchandise, goods or services, without such person's prior consent, or, in the case of a minor, the prior consent of his parent or legal guardian...." The complaint also contained a claim for unfair business practices based on the asserted violation of *Civil Code section 3344*. Appellants, along with the other plaintiffs, sought an accounting and a constructive trust.

CBS filed a cross-complaint against Robert Fleet, Szpak, Legend, White Dragon Productions, Krakowski, Eisenhower, Performance Guarantees, and Lawrence Vanger alleging that to the extent CBS did not have the right to distribute the film, it was owed indemnification under its distribution agreement or was entitled to rescind the distribution agreement and obtain refund of the moneys paid thereunder, including interest.

CBS moved for summary judgment. In its separate statement of undisputed facts, CBS set forth the following fact which went undisputed by appellants: "CBS owns the copyright in the Motion Picture pursuant to federal copyright law." The court granted the motion for summary adjudication as to the causes of action for violation of *Civil Code section 3344* on the ground that appellants' performances were within the scope of copyright protection in that they were "fixed in a tangible medium of expression" and further found that the rights asserted were equivalent to the exclusive rights of copyright. Thus, the court believed, appellants' claims met the two-pronged test for preemption by the federal copyright law. Because the grant of summary adjudication resolved all of the claims between appellants and CBS, they brought an appeal from the order entered.

Before we begin our analysis, we must emphasize that we are resolving at appellants' insistence only the very narrow issue outlined above. Appellants have repeatedly stressed that "[t]his is not a copyright infringement case" and that their claims are solely a matter of violation of *Civil Code section 3344*, California's "right to publicity" statute. They assert no interest in the copyright for the motion picture or in any copyright which may cover the individual performances therein....

Under California law, an individual's right to publicity is invaded if another appropriates for his advantage the individual's name, image, identity or likeness. This is an actionable tort under both common law and *Civil Code section 3344.*

"A common law cause of action for appropriation of name or likeness may be pleaded by alleging (1) the defendant's use of the plaintiff's identity; (2) the appropriation of plaintiff's name or likeness to defendant's advantage, commercially or otherwise; (3) lack of consent; and (4) resulting injury. In addition, to plead the statutory remedy provided in *Civil Code section 3344,* there must also be an allegation of a knowing use of the plaintiff's name, photograph or likeness for purposes of advertising or solicitation or purchases. Furthermore, recent judicial construction of section 3344 has imposed an additional requirement. A 'direct' connection must be alleged between the use and the commercial purpose."

California law concerning right to publicity, as any state statute or law, is subject to preemption under the supremacy clause of the United States Constitution if it "actually conflicts with a valid federal statute" or "'"stands as an obstacle to the accomplishment and execution of the full purposes and objectives of Congress."'" In addition, "when acting within constitutional limits, Congress is empowered to pre-empt state law by so stating in express terms." *17 United States Code section 301,* part of the 1976 Copyright Act (hereafter referred to as the Act) expressly prohibits states from legislating in the area of copyright law. It provides: "On and after January 1, 1978, all legal or equitable rights that are equivalent to any of the exclusive rights within the general scope of copyright as specified by section 106 in works of authorship that are fixed in a tangible medium of expression and come within the subject matter of copyright as specified by sections 102 and 103, whether created before or after that date and whether published or unpublished, are governed exclusively by this title. Thereafter, no person is entitled to any such right or equivalent right in any such work under the common law or statutes of any State."

Thus, for preemption to occur under the Act, two conditions must be met: first, the subject of the claim must be a work fixed in a tangible medium of expression and come within the subject matter or scope of copyright protection as described in sections 102 and 103 of 17 United States Code, and second, the right asserted under state law must be equivalent to the exclusive rights contained in section 106.

Appellants insist that neither of these conditions is met and that their claims pose no threat to the federal scheme because a person's name, voice, likeness, and overall persona are not copyrightable and assertion of these rights cannot be equivalent to those that fall under the Act's protection. We agree that as a general proposition *Civil Code section 3344* is intended to protect rights which cannot be copyrighted and that claims made under its provisions are usually not preempted. But appellants' analysis crumbles in the face of one obvious fact: their individual performances in the film White Dragon were copyrightable. Since their section 3344 claims seeks only to prevent CBS from reproducing and distributing their performances in the film, their claims must be preempted by federal copyright law.

Section 102 of the Act, by its express terms, protects "original works of authorship fixed in any tangible medium of expression ... from which they can be perceived, reproduced, or otherwise communicated, either directly or with the aid of a machine or device." A "work of authorship" is specifically defined to include "dramatic works[.]" A work is fixed in tangible medium of expression "when its embodiment in a copy or phonorecord, by or under the authority of the author, is sufficiently permanent or stable to permit it to be perceived, reproduced, or otherwise communicated for a period of more than transitory duration."

There can be no question that, once appellants' performances were put on film, they became "dramatic work[s]" "fixed in [a] tangible medium of expression" that could be "perceived, reproduced, or otherwise communicated" through "the aid of a machine or device." At that point, the performances came within the scope or subject matter of copyright law protection.

The case of *Zacchini v. Scripps-Howard Broadcasting Co.* 433 U.S. 562 (1977), relied on by appellants, does not point to a different conclusion. There, a performer sued a television station for violating his right of publicity by taping and broadcasting the entirety of his human cannonball act, and the Supreme Court upheld his right to do so. The important distinction between Zacchini's situation and appellants' is that Zacchini had not consented to the taping. A work is fixed in a tangible of expression for purposes of the Act, only if recorded "by or under the authority of the author." Here, appellants' performances in the film were recorded with their active participation and consent.

Appellants deny that the rights which they are asserting under *Civil Code section 3344* are equivalent to the rights available under copyright law, but their denial rings hollow. Appellants seek to protect the physical images of their performances captured on film in the subject motion picture and no others. CBS seeks to display or reproduce those images and no others. The owner of a copyright — either the "author" (actor) or his employer (the producer) — is vested with the exclusive rights to, among other things, "reproduce the copyrighted work" and "display the copyrighted work publicly." Appellants may choose to call their claims misappropriation of right to publicity, but if all they are seeking is to prevent a party from exhibiting a copyrighted work they are making a claim "equivalent to an exclusive right within the general scope of copyright."

To support their contention that their right to sue for appropriation of their name, voice, likeness, or persona survives the fixing of their performance in a tangible medium, appellants quote Professor Nimmer's treatise in which it is said that a "name and likeness does not become a work of authorship simply because it is embodied in a copyrightable work such as a photograph." (1 Nimmer on Copyright (1996) § 1.01[B][1][c], pp. 1-22 to 1-23, fn. omitted.) Again, we have no quarrel with this general proposition, but see no basis for its application here. The celebrity who has merely had his picture taken has not engaged in a "dramatic work" or other "work of authorship," and, as Professor Nimmer said, would be afforded no protection under federal copyright law. Thus, if not for state law, he would have no remedy against those who would misappropriate his image for their own gain. Here, in contrast, it was not merely appellants' likenesses which were captured on film — it was their dramatic performances which are, as we have seen, copyrightable. An actor who wishes to protect the use of the image contained in a single, fixed dramatic performance need simply retain the copyright.

The authorities cited by appellants support our understanding. In *Eastwood v. Superior Court,* 149 Cal. App. 3d 409 [(Cal. Ct. App.)], defendant used a photograph of the well-known actor Clint Eastwood, along with his name and likeness, to sell their newspaper. Since neither his name nor his likeness and image as portrayed in the photograph were copyrightable, no issue of preemption arose. The same was true in *Abdul-Jabbar v. General Motors Corp.* 85 F.3d 407 (9th Cir. 1996), wherein defendants used the name "Lew Alcindor" in a television commercial without consent; *Cher v. Forum International, Ltd.* 692 F.2d 634 (9th Cir. 1982), wherein the actress/singer's photograph was used to solicit subscribers to a magazine in such a way as to convey the misimpression that she endorsed the magazine; and *Clark v. Celeb Publishing, Inc.,* 530 F. Supp. 979 (S.D.N.Y. 1981), wherein the photograph of a model was used without her permission to solicit subscribers to a hard core pornographic magazine. Numerous other cases hold that where the defendant uses a lookalike or soundalike, the person whose voice or image is being imitated may state a claim for misappropriation of publicity rights. The state law claims in these cases were not preempted because it was plaintiffs' image or likeness — and not his or her copyrightable dramatic or musical performance — which had been appropriated.

Appellants cite these cases for the proposition that where "the plaintiff neither owns, nor claims to own, the copyright, there is no preemption and the plaintiff is entitled to pursue his or her claim for wrongful appropriation of the rights of privacy and/or publicity even though the medium in which the offending misappropriation has occurred is itself, copyrightable or even copyrighted." Appellants misapprehend the lesson to be drawn from the cases. In each of the cited cases, the right sought to be protected was not copyrightable — Clint Eastwood's likeness captured in a photograph; Kareem Abdul-Jabbar's former name; Bette Midler's distinctive vocal style; Vanna White's distinctive visual image, etc. The plaintiffs in those cases asserted no copyright claims *because they had none to assert.* Here, by contrast, appellants seek to prevent CBS from using performances captured on film. These performances were copyrightable and appellants could have claimed a copyright in them as have the numerous performers whom we discuss in the following section.

We turn to a discussion of the Seventh Circuit's landmark decision in *Baltimore Orioles v. Major League Baseball Players,* 805 F.2d 663 (7th Cir. 1986).... The court in *Baltimore Orioles* concluded that since the games were copyrightable and since the clubs owned the copyrights under the works made for hire doctrine, the players could not prevent the clubs from exploiting the works by asserting a state law claim for violation of the right to publicity. Contrary to what appellants would have us believe, there is nothing controversial about that aspect of the opinion. It follows inescapably from the Act and the conclusions that the players' performances in the baseball games were works of authorship fixed in a tangible medium of expression and that the clubs held the copyright. "By virtue of being videotaped ... the players' performances are fixed in tangible form, and any rights of publicity in their performances that are equivalent to the rights contained in the copyright of the telecast are preempted."

Nor is the Seventh Circuit the only court to have come to the obvious conclusion that a party who does not hold the copyright in a performance captured on film cannot prevent the one who does from exploiting it by resort to state law. In *Brown v. Twentieth Century Fox Film Corp.,* 799 F. Supp. 166 (D.D.C. 1992), James Brown (the Godfather of Soul) brought suit when a clip of his performance of the song *Please, Please, Please,* originally performed in a '60s television show appeared, without his consent, in the 1991 movie The Commitments about a fictional rock and roll band. The court first analyzed his copyright claims and concluded the producer of the television show held the rights to the performance pursuant to the parties' 1964 agreement. Brown alternatively argued that use of his name, likeness, and persona violated his "right of publicity" under a New York law similar to California's. The court concluded that "[b]ecause defendants lawfully acquired the right to use the [television] Show performance ... the alleged violation of the right of publicity cannot be based on their use of that performance."

In *Rooney v. Columbia Pictures Industries, Inc.,* 538 F. Supp. 211 (S.D.N.Y. 1982) actor Mickey Rooney accused several studios of wrongly refusing to deal with him regarding his "publicity rights" in pre-1960 films, and contended they had wrongfully shown the films on commercial and cable television and distributed them on videocassette. The court concluded that the contracts signed by Rooney were broad enough to include transfer of rights covering television and videocassette display of his performances. Turning to the cause of action alleging misappropriation of Rooney's common law "right of publicity," THE COURT HELD: "[A]ny such rights were assigned or waived by the contracts granting defendants all rights in the pre-1960 films." ...

Although they did not all say so expressly, we believe that all these courts would agree with the Seventh Circuit that "[b]ecause a performance is fixed in tangible form when it is recorded, a right of publicity in [such] performance ... is subject to preemption." We concur with these authorities, and also with Professor Nimmer (1 Nimmer on Copyright, *supra*, § 1.01[B][1], p. 1-14), in holding that a right is equivalent to rights within the exclusive province of copyright when it is infringed by the mere act of reproducing, performing, distributing, or displaying the work at issue. A claim asserted to prevent nothing more than the reproduction, performance, distribution, or display of a dramatic performance captured on film is subsumed by copyright law and preempted. For all the foregoing reasons, the judgment of the trial court is affirmed.

Tamarind Lithography Workshop, Inc. v. Sanders
143 Cal. App. 3d 571 (Cal. App. 2d Dist. 1983)

The essence of this appeal concerns the question of whether an award of damages is an adequate remedy at law in lieu of specific performance for the breach of an agreement to give screen credits. Our saga traces its origin to March of 1969, at which time appellant, and cross-complainant below, Terry Sanders (hereinafter Sanders or appellant), agreed in writing to write, direct and produce a motion picture on the subject of lithography for respondent, Tamarind Lithography Workshop, Inc. (hereinafter referred to as Tamarind or respondent).

Pursuant to the terms of the agreement, the film was shot during the summer of 1969, wherein Sanders directed the film according to an outline/treatment of his authorship, and acted as production manager by personally hiring and supervising personnel comprising the film crew. Additionally, Sanders exercised both artistic control over the mixing of the sound track and overall editing of the picture.

After completion, the film, now titled "Four Stones for Kanemitsu," was screened by Tamarind at its 10th anniversary celebration on April 28, 1970. Thereafter, a dispute arose between the parties concerning their respective rights and obligations under the original 1969 agreement. Litigation ensued and in January 1973 the matter went to trial. Prior to the entry of judgment, the parties entered into a written settlement agreement, which became the premises for the instant action. Specifically, this April 30, 1973, agreement provided that Sanders would be entitled to a screen credit entitled "A Film by Terry Sanders."

Tamarind did not comply with its expressed obligation pursuant to that agreement, in that it failed to include Sanders' screen credits in the prints it distributed. As a result a situation developed wherein Tamarind and codefendant Wayne filed suit for declaratory relief, damages due to breach of contract, emotional distress, defamation and fraud. Sanders cross-complained, seeking damages for Tamarind's breach of contract, declaratory relief, specific performance of the contract to give Sanders screen credits, and defamation. Both causes were consolidated and brought to trial on May 31, 1977. A jury was impaneled for purposes of determining damage issues and decided that Tamarind had breached the agreement and awarded Sanders $25,000 in damages.

The remaining claims for declaratory and injunctive relief were tried by the court. The court made findings that Tamarind had sole ownership rights in the film, that "both June Wayne and Terry Sanders were each creative producers of the film, that Sanders shall have the right to modify the prints in his personal possession to include his credits." All other prayers for relief were denied. It is the denial of appellant's request for specific performance upon which appellant predicates this appeal....

[T]he issue is whether the jury's damage award adequately compensates Sanders, not only for injuries sustained as a result of the prior exhibitions of the film without Sanders' credits, but also for future injuries which may be incurred as a result of any future exhibitions of the film without his credit. Commensurate with our discussion below, we find that the damages awarded raise an issue that justifies a judgment for specific performance. Accordingly, we reverse the judgment of the lower court and direct it to award appellant the injunctive relief he now seeks.

Our first inquiry deals with the scope of the jury's $25,000 damage award. More specifically, we are concerned with whether or not this award compensates Sanders not only for past or preexisting injuries, but also for future injury (or injuries) as well.

Indeed, it is possible to categorize respondent's breach of promise to provide screen credits as a single failure to act from which all of Sanders' injuries were caused. However, it is also plausible that damages awarded Sanders were for harms already sustained at the date of trial, and did not contemplate injury as a result of future exhibitions of the film by respondent, without appropriate credit to Sanders.

Although this was a jury trial, there are findings of facts and conclusions of law necessitated by certain legal issues that were decided by the court. Finding of fact No. 12 states: "By its verdict the jury concluded that Terry Sanders and the Terry Sanders Company are entitled to the sum of $25,000.00 in damages for all damages suffered by them arising from Tamarind's breach of the April 30th agreement."

The exact wording of this finding was also used in conclusion of law No. 1. Sanders argues that use of the word "suffered" in the past tense is positive evidence that the jury assessed damages only for breach of the contract up to time of trial and did not award possible future damages that might be suffered if the film was subsequently exhibited without the appropriate credit.

Tamarind, on the other hand, contends that the jury was instructed that if a breach occurred the award would be for *all* damages past and future arising from the breach. The jury was instructed: "For the breach of a contract, the measure of damages is the amount which will compensate the party aggrieved, for the economic loss, directly and proximately caused by the breach, or which, in the ordinary course of things, would be likely to result therefrom" and " ... economic benefits including enhancement of one's professional reputation resulting in increased earnings as a result of screen credit, if their loss is a direct and natural consequence of the breach, may be recovered for breach of an agreement that provides for screen credit. Economic benefits lost through breach of contract may be estimated, and where the plaintiff [Tamarind], by its breach of the contract, has given rise to the difficulty of proving the amount of loss of such economic benefit, it is proper to require of the defendant [Sanders] only that he show the amount of damages with reasonable certainty and to resolve uncertainty as to the amount of economic benefit against the plaintiff [Tamarind]."

The trial court agreed with Tamarind's position and refused to grant the injunction because it was satisfied that the jury had awarded Sanders all the damages he was entitled to including past and possible future damages. The record does not satisfactorily resolve the issue. However, this fact is not fatal to this appeal because, as we shall explain, specific performance as requested by Sanders will solve the problem.

The availability of the remedy of specific performance is premised upon well established requisites. These requisites include: A showing by plaintiff of (1) the inadequacy of his legal remedy; (2) an underlying contract that is both reasonable and supported by adequate consideration; (3) the existence of a mutuality of remedies; (4) contractual terms which are sufficiently definite to enable the court to know what it is to enforce; and (5) a substantial similarity of the requested performance to that promised in the contract.

It is manifest that the legal remedies available to Sanders for harm resulting from the future exhibition of the film are inadequate as a matter of law. The primary reasons are twofold: (1) that an accurate assessment of damages would be far too difficult and require much speculation, and (2) that any future exhibitions might be deemed to be a continuous breach of contract and thereby create the danger of an untold number of lawsuits.

There is no doubt that the exhibition of a film, which is favorably received by its critics and the public at large, can result in valuable advertising or publicity for the artists responsible for that film's making. Likewise, it is unquestionable that the nonappearance of an artist's name or likeness in the form of screen credit on a successful film can result in a loss of that valuable publicity. However, whether that loss of publicity is measurable dollar wise is quite another matter.

By its very nature, public acclaim is unique and very difficult, if not sometimes impossible, to quantify in monetary terms. Indeed, courts confronted with the dilemma of estimating damages in this area have been less than uniform in their disposition of same. Nevertheless, it is clear that any award of damages for the loss of publicity is contingent upon those damages being reasonably certain, specific, and unspeculative.

The varied disposition of claims for breach of promise to provide screen credits encompasses two schools of thought. On the one hand, there is the view that damages can be ascertained (to within a reasonable degree of certainty) if the trier of fact is given sufficient factual data. On the other hand, there is the equally strong stance that although damages resulting from a loss of screen credits might be identifiable, they are far too imponderable and ethereal to define in terms of a monetary award. If these two views can be reconciled, it would only be by an independent examination of each case on its particular set of facts.

In *Paramount Productions, Inc. v. Smith, supra,* 91 F.2d 863, 866–867, the court was provided with evidence from which the " ... jury might easily compute the advertising value of the screen credit." The particular evidence presented included the earnings the plaintiff/writer received for his work on a previous film in which he did not contract for screen credits. This evidence was in turn easily compared with earnings that the writer had received for work in which screen credits were provided as contracted. Moreover, evidence of that artist's salary, prior to his receipt of credit for a play when compared with earnings received subsequent to his actually receiving credit, was " ... if believed, likewise sufficient as a gauge for the measure of damages."

In another case dealing with a request for damages for failure to provide contracted-for screen credits, the court in *Zorich v. Petroff,* 152 Cal. App. 2d 806 [313 P.2d 118] (1957) demonstrated an equal awareness of the principle. The court emphasized "... that there was no evidence from which the [trial] court could have placed a value upon the screen credit to be given plaintiff as an associate producer. Incident to this fact, the court went on to surmise that because the motion picture which was at the root of the litigation was an admitted financial failure, screen credit, if given, ... could reasonably have been regarded as a detriment to him."

At the other extreme, it has been held that failure to give an artist screen credit *would* constitute irreparable injury. In *Poe v. Michael Todd Co.*, 151 F. Supp. 801 [(S.D.N.Y. 1957)], the New York district court was similarly faced with an author's claim that his contractual right to screen credit was violated. The court held: "Not only would money damages be difficult to establish, but at best they would hardly compensate for the real injury done. A writer's reputation, which would be greatly enhanced by public credit for authorship of an outstanding picture, is his stock in trade, it is clear that irreparable injury would follow the failure to give screen credit if in fact he is entitled to it."

Notwithstanding the seemingly inflexible observation of that court as to the compensability of a breach of promise to provide screen credits, all three cases equally demonstrate that the awarding of damages must be premised upon calculations, inferences or observations that are logical. Just how logical or reasonable those inferences are regarded serves as the determining factor. Accordingly, where the jury in the matter *sub judice* was fully apprised of the favorable recognition Sanders' film received from the Academy of Motion Picture Arts and Sciences, the Los Angeles International Film Festival, and public television, and further, where they were made privy to an assessment of the value of said exposure by three experts, it is reasonable for the jury to award monetary damages for that ascertainable loss of publicity. However, pecuniary compensation for Sanders' future harm is not a fully adequate remedy.

We return to the remaining requisites for Sanders' entitlement to specific performance. The need for our finding the contract to be reasonable and supported by adequate consideration is obviated by the jury's determination of respondent's breach of that contract. The requisite of mutuality of remedy has been satisfied in that Sanders had fully performed his obligations pursuant to the agreement (i.e., release of all claims of copyright to the film and dismissal of his then pending action against respondents. Similarly, we find the terms of the agreement sufficiently definite to permit enforcement of the respondent's performance as promised.

In the present case it should be obvious that specific performance through injunctive relief can remedy the dilemma posed by the somewhat ambiguous jury verdict. The injunction disposes of the problem of future damages, in that full compliance by Tamarind moots the issue. Of course, violation of the injunction by Tamarind would raise new problems, but the court has numerous options for dealing with the situation and should choose the one best suited to the particular violation.

In conclusion, the record shows that the appellant is entitled to relief consisting of the damages recovered, and an injunction against future injury.... The judgment denying appellants' prayer for injunctive relief is hereby reversed....

Notes and Questions

a. Since most of the disputes arising in the context of this section come from the failure to provide appropriate credit, the primary tools for solving these problems come from well-drafted written agreements. Typically, contracts providing credit also provide that "no inadvertent omission of the credit awarded pursuant to this agreement shall be deemed a breach of this agreement." Inadvertent omission is useful compromise language, because any intentional omission remains actionable while the paragraph should eliminate most litigation over simple mistakes.

b. In cases involving writers' credit for motion pictures, the Writers Guild provides very stringent rules for arbitration of credit claims. In most of these disputes, the producer or distributor of the motion picture has very little interest in which party receives the credit. Instead, the dispute is typically between the various writers who contributed during the life of the project. By resorting to the arbitration process, the producer and distributor can essentially remain out of the dispute and avoid taking sides with any particular writer. In the context of songs and other media, no such third-party procedure is mandated by a collectively bargained agreement.

c. Contract law and copyright law also collide on occasion. To what extent may the author of a work sue the co-author for failure to attribute the work, for copyright infringement, or for breach of contract? Co-authors cannot infringe the copyright of one another. Assuming any such action survives *Dastar*, does omission of one party constitute a form of reverse passing off? See *Cleary v. News Corp.*, 30 F.3d 1255 (9th Cir. 1994) (involving a dispute over the attribution and updated versions of Robert's Rules of Order).

d. The outcome of *Fleet v. CBS* may be fully consistent with both prior case law and industry custom; however, the language of the case suggests some potentially odd results. Would actors from *Legend of White Horse* have a cause of action if their images taken from *Legend of White Horse* were transferred onto tee-shirts, mugs, or clocks? Perhaps these uses do not capture the dramatic performance. If so, what would be the result if clips were sold as part of a computer screen-saver program? See *Brown v. Twentieth Century Fox Film Corp.*, 799 F. Supp. 166 (D.D.C. 1992), *aff'd without opinion*, 15 F.3d 1159 (D.C. Cir. 1994).

Problem VIII-C

Bryce has been asked to compile and edit a series of music videos for a local band named Soundfyre. Bryce has decided to use clips from old black-and-white movies as the visual backdrops for most of the videos, inter-cutting these clips with the footage Bryce filmed of Soundfyre in performance. Bryce is coloring (or colorizing) some of the clips, running some in their original black-and-white configuration, and digitally altering others.

Bryce has confirmed that each of the films selected is in the public domain, but remains concerned that the original filmmakers or actors might object to the use of the clips in the music videos. In addition, Soundfyre has licensed one of the music videos to a local auto dealership to use as the background for its upcoming television commercial.

Advise Bryce on the extent to which additional licenses may be needed to use the public domain film clips as requested.

D. Limiting Credit Exploitation

King v. Innovation Books
976 F.2d 824 (2d Cir. 1992)

Defendants-appellants, Allied Vision, Ltd. and New Line Cinema Corporation, appeal from an order of the United States District Court for the Southern District of New York (Motley, J.) granting a preliminary injunction in favor of plaintiff-appellee Stephen King in connection with King's claims under the Lanham Act and New York law. King, who is the author of such best-selling horror thrillers as "The Shining," "Carrie," and "Salem's Lot," contended that Allied and New Line falsely designated him as the originator of the motion picture "The Lawnmower Man," which was produced by Allied and distributed in North America by New Line. The injunction, which prohibits any use of King's name "on or in connection with" the movie, encompasses two forms of credit to which King objected: (i) a possessory credit, describing the movie as "Stephen King's The Lawnmower Man," and (ii) a "based upon" credit, representing that the movie is "based upon" a short story by King. For the reasons that follow, we affirm the district court's order to the extent that it prohibits use of the possessory credit, but reverse the order to the extent that it prohibits use of the "based upon" credit.

In 1970, King wrote a short story entitled "The Lawnmower Man" (the "Short Story")…. In 1978, King assigned to Great Fantastic Picture Corporation the motion picture and television rights for the Short Story. The assignment agreement, which provided that it was to be governed by the laws of England, allowed the assignee the "exclusive right to deal with the [Short Story] as [it] may think fit," including the rights

　　(i) to write film treatments [and] scripts and other dialogue versions of all descriptions of the [Short Story] and at all times to add to[,] take from[,] use[,] alter[,] adapt … and change the [Short Story] and the title[,] characters[,] plot[,] theme[,] dialogue[,] sequences and situations thereof.…

　　(ii) to make or produce films of all kinds … incorporating or based upon the [Short Story] or any part or parts thereof or any adaptation thereof.

In return, King received an interest in the profits of "each" film "based upon" the Short Story.

In February 1990, Great Fantastic transferred its rights under the assignment agreement to Allied, a movie production company organized under the laws of the United Kingdom and having offices in London. In May 1990, Allied commissioned a screenplay for a feature-length film entitled "The Lawnmower Man." The screenplay was completed by August 1990, and pre-production work on the movie began in January 1991. By February 1991, Allied began to market the forthcoming movie by placing advertisements in trade magazines and journals. The picture generally was described as "Stephen King's The Lawnmower Man," and as "based upon" a short story by King. Actual filming of the movie began in May 1991.…

King initiated the instant suit on May 28, 1992, seeking damages as well as injunctive relief. He claimed that the possessory and "based upon" credits violated section 43(a) of the Lanham Act, *see* 15 U.S.C. *§ 1125*(a), as well as the New York common law of unfair competition and contracts, the New York General Business Law, and the New York Civil Rights Law.… The district court agreed with King on all of his claims and granted the injunction on July 2.…

We review a district court's issuance of a preliminary injunction for abuse of discretion. Such an abuse of discretion ordinarily consists of either applying an incorrect legal standard or relying on a clearly erroneous finding of fact. As the district court observed, a party such as King seeking an injunction "must demonstrate (1) irreparable harm should the injunction not be granted, and (2) either (a) a likelihood of success on the merits, or (b) sufficiently serious questions going to the merits and a balance of hardships tipping decidedly toward [that] party.…"

The district court correctly noted that a false reference to the origin of a work, or a reference which, while not literally false, is misleading or likely to confuse, may form the basis of a claim under section 43(a) of the Lanham Act.

We perceive no error in the district court's conclusion that King is likely to succeed on the merits of his objection to the possessory credit. The district court was entirely entitled to conclude, from the testimony at the preliminary injunction hearing, that a possessory credit ordinarily is given to the producer, director or writer of the film; and that the credit at a minimum refers to an individual who had some involvement in, and/or gave approval to, the screenplay or movie itself. In contrast to other films for which he has been given a possessory credit, King had no involvement in, and gave no approval of, "The Lawnmower Man" screenplay or movie.

Under the circumstances, therefore, the arguments advanced by Allied and New Line as to why the possessory credit is not false — that the other movie credits make clear that King was not the producer, director or writer of the film, and that King has in the past received a possessory credit where he merely approved in advance of the screenplay or movie — do not alter the conclusion that King is likely to succeed on his challenge to the possessory credit. Appellants also contend that King offered no evidence of public confusion in relation to the possessory credit. As will be detailed in our discussion of irreparable harm, however, there was some such evidence offered. In any event, as the district court recognized, no evidence of public confusion is required where, as is the case with the possessory credit, the attribution is false on its face.

As the district court recognized, a "based upon" credit by definition affords more "leeway" than a possessory credit. The district court nevertheless concluded that the "based upon" credit at issue here is misleading and likely to cause confusion to the public, reasoning in essence that the "climactic scene from the Short Story is inserted into the film in a manner wholly unrelated to the Plot of the film," and that the credit "grossly exaggerates" the relationship between the Short Story and the film. While particular findings of fact are subject to the clearly erroneous standard of review, we have said that the weighing of factors in "the ultimate determination of the likelihood of confusion is a legal issue subject to *de novo* appellate review." We believe that in so heavily weighing the proportion of the film attributable to the Short Story in the course of finding the "based upon" credit to be misleading and confusing, the district court applied a standard without sufficient support in the testimony and applicable law.

John Breglio, an attorney of the law firm of Paul, Weiss, Rifkind, Wharton & Garrison specializing in entertainment law, testified as an expert witness for King. Breglio opined that the term "based upon," in the context of royalty obligations under King's assignment agreement, was not identical to the term "based upon" in a movie credit. After speaking of a test of "substantial similarity" between the literary work and movie, and opining that there was not substantial similarity between the Short Story and the film, Breglio went on to state that the industry standard for determining the meaning of a "based upon" movie credit is very similar to that used by copyright lawyers in examining issues of copyright infringement. Breglio further explained that this standard involved looking "at the work as a whole and how much protected material *from the underlying work* appears in the derivative work."

Indeed, in cases of alleged copyright infringement it has long been appropriate to examine the quantitative and qualitative degree to which the allegedly infringed work has been borrowed from, and not simply the proportion of the allegedly infringing work that is made up of the copyrighted material. Accordingly, the propriety of the "based upon" credit should have been evaluated with less emphasis on the proportion of the film attributable to the Short Story, and with more emphasis on the proportion, in quantitative and qualitative terms, of the Short Story appearing in the film. Where a movie draws in material respects from a literary work, both quantitatively and qualitatively, a "based upon" credit should not be viewed as misleading absent persuasive countervailing facts and circumstances. Our concern is the possibility that under the district court's apparent approach, substantially all of a literary work could be taken for use in a film and, if unrelated ideas, themes and scenes are tacked on or around the extracted work, a "based upon" credit would be deemed misleading.

In the case before us, the apparent "core" of the ten page Short Story—a scene in which a character called "the lawnmower man" uses psychokinetic powers to chase another character through his house with a running lawnmower and thereby kill him—is used in the movie. In both the movie and the Short Story, the remains of the murdered man (who is named Harold Parkette in both works) are found in the birdbath by the police; the two police officers in both works have the same names and engage in substantially similar dialogue. As King himself described it, "the core of my story, such as it is, is in the movie." The red lawnmower seen in the movie also appears to be as described in the Short Story. A brief reference to the Pan mythology of the Short Story appears in the movie as well; dialogue between Jobe and another character includes a reference to "Pan pipes of the little people in the grass."

We recognize that several important and entertaining aspects of the Short Story were not used in the film, and that conversely the film contains a number of elements not to be found in the Short Story. However, when the resemblances between the Short Story and the motion picture at issue here are considered together, they establish to our satisfaction that the movie draws in sufficiently material respects on the Short Story in both qualitative and quantitative aspects.

Nor are there any persuasive countervailing facts or circumstances in the record to lead us away from the conclusion that the "based upon" credit is proper in this case. King himself apparently was not bothered much (if at all) by the "based upon" credit, in marked contrast to his sustained and strong objections to the possessory credit, until shortly before he initiated this suit. He has not pointed us to evidence in the record of industry or public perception of, or confusion over, the "based upon" credit beyond the thoughts offered by Breglio....

It is undoubtedly the case that King's assignment agreement does not permit Allied to use King's name fraudulently, and we express no view as to the degree of overlap between the term "based upon" in the King assignment agreement and the term "based upon" in a theatrical credit. However, we do note that the agreement contemplates substantial alterations to the Short Story, and even obligates Allied to give King credit in the case of a film "based wholly or substantially upon" the Short Story. We think that King would have cause to complain if he were *not* afforded the "based upon" credit.

As the district court observed, a presumption of irreparable harm arises in Lanham Act cases once the plaintiff establishes likelihood of success on a claim of literal falseness, as King has established with respect to the possessory credit. Nothing in the record persuades us that the district court erred in concluding that this presumption was not rebutted....

The order of the district court granting a preliminary injunction is affirmed to the extent it prohibits use of the possessory credit, but reversed to the extent it prohibits use of a "based upon" credit.

Miramax Films Corp. v. Columbia Pictures Entertainment
996 F. Supp. 294 (S.D.N.Y. 1998)

Miramax Films Corp. sues Columbia Pictures Entertainment, Inc., and Mandalay Entertainment, Inc., for unfair competition under Section 43(a) of the Lanham Act, for common law unfair competition, and for trademark infringement.

Plaintiff moves preliminarily to enjoin defendants from conducting an allegedly false and misleading advertising campaign for the motion picture "I Know What You Did Last

Summer" (hereafter "Summer"), which defendants produced and are distributing throughout the world. Plaintiff complains that defendants' advertising campaign falsely designates "Summer" as originating from the same "creator" as the motion picture "Scream," a motion picture that plaintiff developed and distributed. Plaintiff's grievance is that defendants are seeking to profit from the popularity of "Scream" by inducing potential viewers of horror movies to patronize "Summer" in the false belief that it originated from the same source as "Scream" and is associated with "Scream." Defendants oppose plaintiff's motion on the ground that plaintiff has failed to establish that the advertisements are misleading and has failed to show irreparable harm. For the reasons discussed below, plaintiff's motion for a preliminary injunction is granted.

A preliminary injunction may issue only when the movant demonstrates (a) irreparable harm and (b) either (i) a likelihood of success on the merits of the claim, or (ii) sufficiently serious questions going to the merits of the claim to make it fair ground for litigation, and the balance of the hardships tips decidedly in favor of the movant. A higher standard applies when an injunction will alter, rather than maintain, the *status quo*. Such an injunction should issue only upon a clear showing that the moving party is entitled to the relief requested....

False advertising is actionable under the Lanham Act both for an advertisement that is literally false and for a literally true advertisement which is likely to mislead or confuse customers. The deceptive representation must materially affect consumers' purchasing decisions. A misleading reference to the origin of a work may also form the basis of a claim under the Lanham Act....

Plaintiff is an international developer and distributor of motion pictures. In December 1996, plaintiff released for distribution in the United States the motion picture "Scream," a film of the "horror movie" genre. "Scream" was directed by Wes Craven, an internationally renowned director of horror movies, including the film "Nightmare on Elm Street."

In an attempt to exploit Wes Craven's fame, plaintiff aggressively marketed "Scream" as a Wes Craven product, both in the United States and abroad. For example, promotional materials referred to the film as "The Highly Acclaimed New Thriller From Wes Craven" and "Wes Craven's Scream." As explained by plaintiff's chairman of worldwide film distribution Richard Sands, plaintiff views Wes Craven as "a director that I protect and I use as a commodity." Numerous film critics in the United States and the United Kingdom have identified Wes Craven as the creative force behind "Scream."

By any measure, "Scream" was an extraordinary success. In addition to being praised by film critics, "Scream" grossed over $100 million at the box office domestically, and, as of December 18, 1997, had grossed approximately $65 million overseas. In the United Kingdom, as of December 18, 1997, "Scream" had grossed $13.5 million at the box office, making it the highest grossing horror movie ever shown in the United Kingdom. Because of the extraordinary success of the film, plaintiff is planning a merchandising campaign associated with the film, and expects to produce clothing, accessories, and games under the "Scream" label. As of December 18, 1997, "Scream" was still in box office release in the United Kingdom, and it continues to proceed through the various stages of "ancillary" distribution, home video rental, home video sale, pay-per-view, pay cable, and free television in the United States and the United Kingdom.

On October 17, 1997, defendants, producers and distributors of motion pictures, released "Summer" in the United States. Shortly before October 17, 1997, plaintiff discovered that defendants were marketing "Summer" as "From the Creator of Scream." The marketing campaign preceding the release of "Summer" described the film, in television, radio, and newspaper advertisements, as being "From the Creator of 'Scream,'" and with such lines as "Last Time He Made you Scream, This Time You Won't Have the Chance" and "From the Creator of 'Scream' Comes a New Chapter in Terror." These advertisements (hereafter "'Scream' catchphrases") dominate the written portions of both the television and print advertisements. In the print advertisements, "From the Creator of Scream" is the headline in large print. At one juncture in the television advertisement shown both in the United States and the United Kingdom, the screen fills with the phrase "From the creator of Scream," with a voice-over stating the same information, but without naming the creator.

The only link between "Scream" and "Summer" is the screenwriter Kevin Williamson. Williamson wrote an original screenplay for "Scream," and adapted a novel by Lois Duncan for the screenplay of "Summer." In the television and print advertisements, Williamson's name appears in the small-print "credit block" as the screenwriter of "Summer," but he is never named or otherwise identified as the "creator" to whom the advertisements refer.

In two affidavits in support of plaintiff's position, Williamson himself describes as "quite different" his roles with respect to each of the films. He does not consider himself to be the "creator" of "Summer." Williamson affirms that Wes Craven is the person most reasonably perceived to be the "creator" of "Scream." ...

[P]laintiff presented a consumer survey designed by Dr. Jerry Wind, a professor at the Wharton School of the University of Pennsylvania, and conducted by Data Development Corporation. To the extent indicated below, I accept certain findings of the consumer survey as accurate and reliable.

The survey involved two studies. The first (hereafter "first study") is a study of consumers who saw "Summer" during its opening weekend of October 17, 1997. This survey was conducted between October 26, 1997 and November 4, 1997. The second (hereafter "second study") is a study of consumers standing in line waiting to view "Summer" between October 31, 1997 and November 6, 1997. Both surveys were directed to fifteen to forty year olds in the top 180 motion picture markets of the United States.

According to the first study, 17% of those answering open-ended questions thought that the advertising for "Summer" communicated that "Summer" was the sequel to "Scream," that the creator of "Summer" produced "Scream," that the creator of "Summer" directed "Scream," or that the creator of "Summer" was Wes Craven. Only 2% of those responding to open-ended questions thought that the advertising for "Summer" communicated that "Summer" was by the writer of "Scream" or by Kevin Williamson.

According to the second study, 20% of those answering open-ended questions thought that the advertising for "Summer" communicated that "Summer" was the sequel to "Scream," that the creator of "Summer" produced "Scream," that the creator of "Summer" directed "Scream," or that the creator of "Summer" was Wes Craven. Only 1% of those responding to open-ended questions thought that the advertising for "Summer" communicated that "Summer" was by the writer of "Scream" or by Kevin Williamson....

This case is not easy to pigeon-hole. It is clearly a false advertising case because the misleading words appear in advertisements and promotional materials. Additionally, because the advertisements identify the origin of "Summer" with the origin of "Scream," cases involving false designation of origin and false endorsement provide valuable analogies. Finally, regardless of whether plaintiff is correct that it owns a trademark in "Scream," the fact that defendants' advertisements identify source makes trademark law analogous as well.

Plaintiff is likely to succeed on its claim that the "Scream" catchphrases are misleading and are likely to mislead potential viewers of horror films to believe that "Summer" comes from the same source as "Scream."

First, plaintiff has shown that an appreciable number of consumers hold false beliefs as to the connection between the two films. Virtually no consumers discerned from the advertisements the only accurate link between the films, namely that Williamson wrote both screenplays. By contrast, 17% of those in the first study and 20% of those in the second study perceived a specific creative link which was false.

Second, plaintiff has established that the advertising campaign is the source of the consumer confusion. Defendants' advertisements are likely to confuse because they fail to name Kevin Williamson, or the writer of the movie script, as the only link between "Scream" and "Summer." Defendants could easily have advised the public that the screenwriter of "Summer" and "Scream" was the same person. Instead, defendants' advertisements imply that the films are more closely related.

This is a case in which irreparable harm may be presumed.... As noted, plaintiff's claim is analogous to three types of Lanham Act claims in which irreparable harm has been presumed if the plaintiff establishes likelihood of success on the merits, namely false advertising, false designation of origin, and false endorsement. For the purpose of evaluating irreparable harm, the case most analogous to this case is King. In King, the defendant entitled its motion picture, and advertised it as, "Stephen King's The Lawnmower Man," a designation of origin which was literally false because King had had no involvement in, and had not approved, the screenplay or the movie.

Those facts warranted a presumption of irreparable harm. The harm which presumptively faced King and [Woody] Allen in [*Allen v. Nat'l Video, Inc.,* 610 F. Supp. 612, 624–25 (S.D.N.Y. 1985)] is present here, namely the wrongful attribution of responsibility for a movie over which plaintiff has no control and the potential for loss of reputation with the public.

The fact that the designation of origin in King was literally false, whereas the designation here is misleading, does not diminish the likelihood that plaintiff has been harmed; nor does the fact that in both King and Allen the designation was to a named person, whereas here it is to the more ambiguous "creator" of "Scream." The fact that the false designation in King was literally false and referred by name to Stephen King is relevant to the determination of whether the designation was "likely to cause confusion" within the meaning of *15 U.S.C. § 1125*(a)(1)(A). Although plaintiff cannot rely on the presumption of confusion which would be available in a case of literal falseness such as King, plaintiff has affirmatively demonstrated that defendants' advertisements have confused consumers in the relevant market about the source of "Summer." The type of harm which flows from this confusion does not depend on whether the confusion results from a literally false designation of origin as opposed to a "misleading" designation of origin. While a literally false designation might, depending on the circumstances of any given case, be presumed to cause a greater *degree* of harm, it is the type of harm — not its degree — that permits the reviewing court to presume irreparable injury....

In sum, the harm to be avoided in this case is of the same type as the harm to be avoided in King and Allen. The false advertising and trademark cases discussed above provide guidance as well. Plaintiff has an interest in protecting itself from deceptive association with a product it does not control. Additionally, plaintiff has an interest in protecting "Scream" from source confusion. Under all the circumstances of this case, irreparable harm may be presumed....

NOW, upon all prior submissions in this action, it is ordered, that Columbia Pictures Entertainment, Inc. and Mandalay Entertainment, Inc. immediately direct, in writing, all agents, representatives, successors, assignees, licensees, distributees, and persons or entities to whom any of the above has supplied advertising materials or promotional materials for the film "I Know What You Did Last Summer" in territories appearing on the release lists to remove the "Scream" catchphrases from all advertising materials and promotional materials for the film; and ... immediately cease to distribute any advertising materials or promotional materials containing the "Scream" catchphrases.

Notes and Questions

a. Does the decision in *Dastar Corp. v. Twentieth Century Fox Film Corp.* have any impact on the decisions provided above? Should it?

b. In most cases, the individual negotiating the credit strongly desires the maximum recognition possible. For Stephen King, and arguably for Kevin Williamson, the inflated credit became an embarrassment rather than a source of pride. To what extent does the participant in a project have the ability to correct inflation of the credit? See *Follett v. New American Library, Inc.*, 497 F. Supp. 304 (S.D.N.Y. 1980).

c. In the case of Stephen King, and in other situations which arise on occasion, the problem of unwelcome attribution stems from subsequent fame. The arrangement negotiated at the time of the contract was beneficial, but in later years the talent's market worth has increased considerably and the earlier contract rights now take on new meaning. While the contract could limit all changes to the agreed-upon credit so that credit could not be improved, it might prove difficult to negotiate such a contract. Nonetheless, there is probably some compromise language that can be developed considering that the courts interpret credit provisions as assuming that the rights granted are not misleading.

d. In contrast to the normal situation for performers, it is sometimes the vendors that complain. To what extent does an endorsement agreement to promote high fashion or jewelry extend into the performer's personal life? See *Raymond Weil, S.A. v. Theron*, 585 F. Supp. 2d 473 (S.D.N.Y. 2008).

Problem VIII-D

As Bryce's business has grown, Bryce has come across an opportunity to purchase a very small, local record company (sometimes called a record label). In reviewing the assets of the record label, your office has spent some time reviewing the contracts for each of the records produced or distributed by the company. The due diligence identified one hidden surprise. A back-up singer on one of the lesser known recordings has gone on to become a Grammy-winning recording artist.

Bryce would like to re-release this album with the name of the star prominently featured. The signed recording agreement included a release by the artist to use her name, likeness, voice, and signature in conjunction with the marketing of the album, so Bryce would like to create new artwork for the cover featuring a photograph of this artist.

Advise Bryce on the extent to which the photograph of this Grammy-winning recording artist can be used, as well as what legal limitations might arise.

E. Post-Partnership Ownership: Band Names

Brother Records, Inc. v. Jardine
318 F.3d 900 (9th Cir. 2003)

Alan Jardine appeals the district court's grant of summary judgment in favor of Brother Records, Inc. ("BRI"), on BRI's Lanham Act, trademark infringement action alleging that Jardine infringed BRI's "The Beach Boys" trademark. Jardine also appeals the district court's grant of summary judgment in favor of BRI on Jardine's counterclaims that BRI breached a lifetime employment agreement and license agreement. Finally, Jardine appeals the district court's denial of his motion to amend his counterclaim to add third-party claims and an additional counterclaim. We have jurisdiction under *28 U.S.C. § 1291*, and we affirm.

In 1961, Al Jardine, Mike Love, Brian Wilson, Carl Wilson, and Dennis Wilson formed The Beach Boys. The band shortly thereafter achieved huge commercial success, producing numerous hit songs and touring to huge audiences throughout the country. In 1967, the members of the Beach Boys incorporated BRI to hold and administer the intellectual property rights for The Beach Boys. Currently, BRI is equally owned by four shareholders, who are also its directors: Al Jardine, Mike Love, Brian Wilson, and the estate of Carl Wilson. BRI is the registered owner of "The Beach Boys" trademark.

Over the years, personal difficulties arose between some of the members, and some members of the band decided to not tour full time, or at all. In 1991, the members of the Beach Boys incorporated Brother Tours, Inc., which handled their touring and distributed their touring income. In 1993, the directors of BRI agreed to devote a certain percentage of the touring income to the corporation for use of the trademark and designated a larger percentage of the income to those members who actually toured. By 1998, Carl Wilson had died, Love and Jardine no longer wanted to tour together, and Brian Wilson did not want to tour at all. Love began negotiating with BRI the terms of a license to use "The Beach Boys" trademark in connection with his own band.

BRI's directors met on July 14, 1998, to discuss how the trademark should be used. The representative of Carl Wilson's estate suggested that BRI issue non-exclusive licenses to each shareholder on the same terms and conditions as the license that was being negotiated with Love, thus giving each member an equal right to tour. Three of the four board members, including Jardine, voted to grant each Beach Boy a non-exclusive license. On October 1, 1998, BRI executed a non-exclusive license agreement with Love (the "Love license"). The Love license contained clauses designed to protect the value of the trademark, requiring the licensee to preserve The Beach Boys style and to choose from a list of approved booking agencies and managers.

The parties dispute whether BRI and Jardine entered into a non-exclusive license agreement. After the July 1998 BRI board meeting, Jardine began touring with his own band, using a booking agent and manager that were not included in the list approved by the Love license. On October 25, 1998, Jardine's attorney sent BRI a letter saying that Jardine would be performing as "Beach Boys Family and Friends," and that therefore, "a license from BRI [was] unnecessary." On October 28, 1998, BRI told Jardine that his unlicensed use of the trademark would be an infringement....

Jardine and his band continued to perform using names that included "The Beach Boys" trademark. The performances were promoted under names such as: Al Jardine of the Beach Boys and Family & Friends; The Beach Boys "Family and Friends"; Beach Boys Family & Friends; The Beach Boys, Family & Friends; Beach Boys and Family; as well as, simply, The Beach Boys. Jardine and his band performed in locations and on dates close to Love's "The Beach Boys" shows. With two bands touring as The Beach Boys or as a similar-sounding combination, show organizers sometimes were confused about what exactly they were getting when they booked Jardine's band. A number of show organizers booked Jardine's band thinking they would get The Beach Boys along with special added guests, but subsequently canceled the booking when they discovered that Jardine's band was not what they thought it was. Numerous people who attended one of Jardine's shows said that they had been confused about who was performing. During this time period, BRI sent Jardine cease and desist letters objecting to Jardine's use of the trademark.

On April 9, 1999, BRI filed its complaint in the district court alleging that Jardine was infringing its trademark.... The district court granted summary judgment in favor of BRI and issued a permanent injunction against Jardine's use of the trademark. This timely appeal followed....

Jardine contends that his use of BRI's trademark is protected by either the classic fair use doctrine or the nominative fair use doctrine. In *New Kids on the Block v. News Am. Publ'g Inc.*, 971 F.2d 302 (9th Cir. 1992), we noted that the classic fair use defense could not be applied in that case because "this is not the classic fair use case where the defendant has used the plaintiff's mark to describe the defendant's own product." We then held that, "where the defendant uses a trademark to describe the plaintiff's product, rather than its own ... a commercial user is entitled to a nominative fair use defense." ...

To illustrate this distinction, we cited a number of cases that applied the nominative fair use analysis. For example, in *New Kids*, the defendant newspapers used the New Kids trademark to refer to the music band New Kids itself in order to describe the defendants' own telephone polls about the band. In *Volkswagenwerk AG v. Church*, 411 F.2d 350 (9th Cir. 1969), the defendant car repair shop used the plaintiff's trademarked name "Volkswagen" in a sign that said "Modern Volkswagen Porsche Service." In *Smith v. Chanel, Inc.*, 402 F.2d 562 (9th Cir. 1968), a seller of imitation perfumes advertised its "2d Chance" perfume as indistinguishable from the trademarked "Chanel No. 5" perfume. In *WCVB-TV v. Boston Athletic Ass'n*, 926 F.2d 42 (1st Cir. 1991), a television station referred to and made broadcasts of the trademarked "Boston Marathon." In all these cases, the defendant used the plaintiff's trademark to refer to the plaintiff's product, and therefore the nominative fair use analysis applied.

Following *New Kids*, we have applied the nominative fair use defense in a number of cases. In most of these cases, the nominative fair use defense, as opposed to the classic fair use defense, clearly applied because the defendant used the plaintiff's mark undeniably to refer to the plaintiff's product, even though the defendant's ultimate goal was to describe his own product. In *Abdul-Jabbar v. Gen. Motors Corp.*, 85 F.3d 407 (9th Cir. 1996), the defendant automobile manufacturer referred to plaintiff, a basketball star who had won an award three years in a row, in a commercial for a car that also had won an award three years in a row. In *Downing v. Abercrombie & Fitch*, 265 F.3d 994 (9th Cir. 2001), the defendant clothing company used the trademarked names and photograph of plaintiffs, surfing champions, to market shirts copied from those worn by plaintiffs in the photograph. These were not cases in which the defendant used the plaintiff's mark only to describe the defendant's own product, and not at all to describe the plaintiff's product. Rather, these were cases in which the defendant used the plaintiff's mark to describe the plaintiff's product—Kareem Abdul-Jabbar himself and the surfing champions themselves—even though the ultimate goal was to describe the defendant's own product....

Here, Jardine argues that either the classic fair use *or* the nominative fair use defense applies. As in *Playboy*, whether the defendant's use of the mark refers to the plaintiff's product at all — and thus whether classic fair use analysis or nominative fair use analysis applies — is not clear. Jardine illustrates this point with his conflicting arguments (1) that his use of "The Beach Boys" mark describes the Beach Boys' product, thus requiring application of the nominative fair use analysis, and (2) that, in the alternative, his use of "The Beach Boys" mark describes only himself — a founding member of the Beach Boys — and not at all to describe the Beach Boys' product, thus requiring application of the classic fair use analysis. Where the defendant uses his or her own title, which happens also to be plaintiff's trademark, defendant can argue convincingly both that the use refers to defendant and that the use refers not at all to defendant. In these situations, the reference-to-trademark-holder distinction often proves more frustrating than helpful.

Rather than contorting ourselves into finding either that Jardine used "The Beach Boys" mark to describe the Beach Boys or that Jardine used "The Beach Boys" mark only to describe himself and not at all to describe the Beach Boys, we analyze each defense separately. We note first that the classic fair use defense, codified in the Lanham Act, *15 U.S.C. § 1115*(b)(4), applies only to marks that possess both a primary meaning and a secondary meaning — and only when the mark is used in its primary descriptive sense rather than its secondary trademark sense. Section 1115(b)(4) allows the defense to trademark infringement that

> the use of the name, term or device charged to be an infringement is a use, otherwise than as a mark ... of a term or device which is descriptive of and used fairly and in good faith only to describe the goods or services of such party, or their geographic origin.

We have explained that "the primary cost of recognizing property rights in trademarks is the removal of words ... from our language." We therefore recognized that the classic fair use defense "in essence, forbids a trademark registrant to appropriate a descriptive term for his exclusive use and so prevent others from accurately describing a characteristic of their goods." "If the trademark holder were allowed exclusive rights in such use, the language would be depleted in much the same way as if generic words were protectable." ...

Here, as in Playboy and New Kids, Jardine does not use the trademark in any primary, descriptive sense. That is, Jardine does not use "The Beach Boys" trademark to denote its primary, descriptive meaning of "boys who frequent a stretch of sand beside the sea." Instead, Jardine uses "The Beach Boys" trademark in its secondary, trademark sense, which denotes the music band — and its members — that popularized California surfing culture. This is true regardless of whether Jardine's use of the mark refers to Jardine himself or to the band. Because Jardine does not use the mark in its primary, descriptive sense, the classic fair use defense does not apply.

Where the defendant uses the trademark not in its primary, descriptive sense, but rather in its secondary, trademark sense, the nominative fair use analysis applies.... In *New Kids*, we articulated the three requirements of the nominative fair use defense:

> First, the product or service in question must be one not readily identifiable without use of the trademark; second, only so much of the mark or marks may be used as is reasonably necessary to identify the product or service; and third, the user must do nothing that would, in conjunction with the mark, suggest sponsorship or endorsement by the trademark holder.

Just as it is virtually impossible to refer to the New Kids on the Block, the Chicago Bulls, Volkswagens, or the Boston Marathon without using the trademarked names, so too is it virtually impossible to refer to the Beach Boys without using the trademark, and Jardine therefore meets the first requirement. Also, BRI does not allege that Jardine uses any distinctive logo "or anything else that isn't needed" to identify the Beach Boys, and Jardine therefore satisfies the second requirement.

Jardine fails, however, to meet the third requirement. Jardine's promotional materials display "The Beach Boys" more prominently and boldly than "Family and Friends," suggesting sponsorship by the Beach Boys. Also, there is evidence that Jardine uses "The Beach Boys" trademark to suggest that his band is in fact sponsored by the Beach Boys, as Jardine's management testified that they recommended including the trademark "The Beach Boys" in the name of Jardine's band in order to create or enhance marquee value. Finally, Jardine's use of the trademark caused actual consumer confusion, as both event organizers that booked Jardine's band and people who attended Jardine's shows submitted declarations expressing confusion about who was performing.

Because Jardine's use of the trademark suggested sponsorship or endorsement by the trademark holder, Jardine's nominative fair use argument fails. "The plain language of Rule 56(c) mandates the entry of summary judgment ... against a party who fails to make a showing sufficient to establish the existence of an element essential to that party's case, and on which that party will bear the burden of proof at trial." The district court did not err in concluding that Jardine's use of the Beach Boys' trademark was an infringement. No genuine issue of material fact exists regarding Jardine's suggestion of sponsorship or endorsement by BRI. We therefore affirm the district court's grant of summary judgment in favor of BRI on BRI's trademark infringement claim....

Because no genuine issue of material fact exists regarding the likelihood of confusion, we affirm the district court's grant of summary judgment in favor of BRI on the trademark infringement claim....

Jardine v. Love

2003 Cal. App. Unpub. LEXIS 10223 (2003)

This appeal arises out of a dispute between appellant Jardine and respondents Mike Love ("Love"), Brian Wilson, Melinda Wilson, Bernard Gudvi, The Carl Wilson Trust, and Brother Records, Inc. ("BRI") (collectively, "respondents," unless otherwise individually designated). Jardine was one of the founding members of the world-renowned singing group known as "The Beach Boys," and performed with various incarnations of the group until approximately early 1998, when Love declared he no longer wanted to appear onstage with Jardine. BRI, which was formed by the founding members of the group in or about 1974, and which owned the rights to the trademarked name "The Beach Boys," then voted to give Jardine, Love, and Brian Wilson, the surviving founding members of the group, each a non-exclusive license until December 31, 1999, to tour separately as "The Beach Boys."

BRI sent Jardine a contract outlining the terms of the license agreement, which he eventually signed and returned to BRI for signature. However, BRI demanded further assurances from Jardine that he would meet the conditional terms of the contract, and refused to sign until such assurances were received. Jardine apparently failed to provide such assurances, but began touring under the name "Beach Boy Family and Friends." BRI then sued Jardine in federal court, seeking to prevent Jardine from using the name "The Beach Boys," or any form thereof.

Jardine asserted counterclaims against BRI for breach of employment contract, breach of license agreement, and declaratory relief. Later Jardine sought to amend his answer and counterclaims to include a counterclaim against BRI and third-party claims against BRI's directors for breach of fiduciary duty. However, Jardine's motion for leave to amend was denied by the court on the ground that granting the motion would have caused an undue delay in the proceedings. Jardine's original counterclaims were either dismissed by the federal court in its final judgment or declared moot (with respect to the breach of license claim).

Jardine then filed a complaint in state court against respondents for breach of fiduciary duty. He alleged respondents, acting as majority shareholders and directors of BRI, breached the fiduciary duties they owed to Jardine as a minority shareholder when they turned over control of the business to Love, began to exclude Jardine from live appearances and concerts, and refused to pay Jardine his share of receipts from performances of The Beach Boys in which he was not allowed to take part.

Respondents filed a demurrer to Jardine's complaint, arguing Jardine was raising issues decided in the federal action, and under the transactional analysis theory, his claims were barred by the doctrines of res judicata and collateral estoppel since they arose from the same acts. Jardine responded that the primary rights theory, and not the transactional analysis theory, applied in California state court. He argued that under the primary rights theory his claims were not barred, since his primary right in the federal court lawsuit was the right to perform under his employment contract with BRI, while his primary right in the state court lawsuit was the right to have respondents perform rather than breach the fiduciary duties they owed to Jardine as a minority shareholder in BRI....

With respect to Jardine's claim against the individual respondents, they assert he cannot state a claim as a matter of law because Jardine is an "equal" shareholder in BRI in view of the fact he and the individual respondents each own 25 percent of the stock in the company. Contrary to respondent's claim, determining whether someone is a majority, minority or equal shareholder for a breach of fiduciary duty claim does not turn *solely* on the amount of stock owned. A "minority shareholder" is one who "owns less than half the total shares outstanding and thus cannot control the corporation's management or single handedly elect directors." A court must look at the corporate shareholders as a whole and determine which persons are directing corporate activities. The majority shareholder can either be a single shareholder or a group of shareholders "*acting in concert to accomplish a joint purpose*." Here, Jardine has alleged the individual respondent shareholders, Love, B. Wilson, M. Wilson, and Gudvi are acting together to control the management of BRI and as such they may be considered "majority" shareholders of BRI and therefore, Jardine is the "minority" shareholder of BRI for the purposes of this claim.

Moreover, there is no question that a minority shareholder may assert a cause of action against the controlling majority shareholders for breach of fiduciary duty. The fiduciary duties of majority shareholders in California was clearly enumerated in *Jones v. HF Ahmanson*[, 1 Cal.3d 93, 108, 81 Cal. Rptr. 592, 460 P.2d 464 (1969):]

> majority shareholders, either singly or acting in concert to accomplish a joint-purpose, have a fiduciary responsibility to the minority and to the corporation to use their ability to control the corporation in a fair, just, and equitable manner. Majority shareholders may not use their power to control corporate activities to benefit themselves or in a manner detrimental to the minority. Any use to which they put the corporation or their power to control the corporation must benefit all shareholders proportionately and must not conflict with the proper conduct of the corporation's business.

[The majorities'] dealings with the minority shareholders are subject to rigorous scrutiny. Where any of their contracts or engagements with the minority is challenged, the burden is on the director or stockholder not only to prove the good faith of the transaction, but also to show its inherent fairness from the viewpoint of the corporation and those interested therein.

'"The essence of the test is whether or not under all the circumstances the transaction carries the earmarks of an arm's length bargain. If it does not, equity will set it aside."'

Thus, the majority shareholders do in fact owe a fiduciary duty to the minority shareholder. Consequently, Jardine may bring a claim against the individual respondents for breach of that duty.

This notwithstanding, as currently pled, Jardine has not stated a breach of fiduciary duty claim against BRI. We cannot say as a matter of law, however, there is no theory upon which Jardine may be able to assert a claim.... The judgment is reversed and this matter is remanded to the trial court for further proceedings....

In re Applications of Atlantic Recording Corp.
747 N.Y.S.2d 889 (N.Y. Sup. Ct. 2002)

In March of 2000, five teenagers who wished to embark upon a music career, with the support of their parents, sought and secured judicial approval of several agreements regarding the group and a recording contract under the procedures applicable to contracts for child performers. Despite the apparent great success of the group, discord arose between the parents of three of the five youths and the group's producer-manager.

Although both sides consent to end the future professional relationship between these three young men and the producer-manager, as stated on the record, each side asks to be permitted to retain rights to the group name and the right to perform together under that name, which are significant rights in the music and recording industry.

The essential facts are undisputed. The young men performed under the music group name of Dream Street and Dream Street became a hit. Their album "Dream Street" was listed on Billboard as the Top Independent Album on July 28, 2001; their video was a Most Requested Video on Nickelodeon's internet site Nick.com. Appearances were sponsored or sponsorship offered by such prestigious corporations as McDonalds, Nabisco, Kraft and K Mart. New recording opportunities were presented by Disney and Sony.

This success was not merely fortuitous. Dream Street is a "concept group" created by a manager-promoter who hires performers to play the roles in the group and directs its performance, much like Menudo, the Monkees and the Spice Girls. In this case, Dream Street Entertainment, Inc., was the organizer, promoter and manager, and was responsible for the group's style and characteristics. As acknowledged in the contracts signed by these parents and the promoter which were approved by the court, Dream Street Entertainment, Inc. (Producer), "conceived of" and "created" a group known as "Dream Street" and selected the five teenagers originally making up Dream Street; the agreement between the parents of these three teenagers and the Producer acknowledged that, even if any youth or youths were to depart from the group, the Producer "shall continue to own all right, title and interest in the name Dream Street, at all times, solely and exclusively, including all associated trademark and trade name interests." It stands unrefuted that the Producer expended over two million dollars to create, produce and promote the group, from the Producer's first open call for prospective members of the group in November of

1998, through the selection and training of group members, and to date. The rights of the Producer extend somewhat beyond the term of the recording contract.

This proceeding primarily concerns three group members, i.e., Frank John Galasso, Matthew Ballinger and Gregory Raposo. Christopher Pask, known as Christopher Trousdale, remains as the lead singer and does not desire to leave Dream Street. Jesse McCartney resigned from the group to pursue other highly attractive opportunities and is found to lack standing to join in this application.

Given that there is no dispute that these three musicians are free to leave Dream Street, the first critical issue is that they and their parents, apparently with the support of their personal managers, request that they be able to continue to use the name Dream Street. The use of a group name by departing members cannot be authorized here. The clear concepts applicable to ownership of a common-law mark in a group name are detailed in *Marshak v. Treadwell,* 240 F.3d 184 (3rd Cir. 2001), which concerned "The Drifters," a singing group particularly well known for their 1950s and early 1960s hit songs "Under the Boardwalk," "On Broadway," and "Save the Last Dance for Me." Although not a concept group, The Drifters' composition changed over the course of time, giving rise to a dispute as to who had rights to the group name. The court held that, to demonstrate ownership of a common-law mark in a group name, a claimant must show "(1) that [the] mark was valid and legally protectable; (2) that they owned the mark; and (3) that [another's] use of the mark to identify his group was likely to create confusion concerning their origin." Once created, the right to the mark continues until the mark is clearly abandoned. This statement of the law is consistent with governing copyright, trademark and Lanham Act concepts.

Under this standard, the Producer has a clear common-law right to the Dream Street name, and the use of that name by another would constitute infringement. Indeed, the performers and their parents originally acknowledged that Dream Street is a trademarked name and they have no rights to such name even under a partnership or joint venture theory. Explicit recognition of ownership of a group name by the promoters of a concept group is legally appropriate where, as here, it is undisputed that, (1) the public associates with the group characteristics or a style which (2) is or are controlled by the promoter group New Edition was not a concept group, band members controlled distinctive personality and performing style of the individual members and owned group name.

The second issue is the professed desire of the departing members to continue to perform together, which was advanced without the presentation of details of the planned operation of a new group. The failure to address the name to be used by such a group is reason to forestall judicial action, for many possible group names could trample on the Producer's rights addressed above. Even former group members must be prohibited from using a variation of a group's original name.

Further, without placing concrete details before the court, the request merely seeks an advisory opinion. The court has insufficient basis to frame and issue a binding determination which would block the Producer from the future assertion of a claim of improper conduct or wrongful interference.... The lack of a proposal also leaves the Producer at a disadvantage, for it wishes to retain any contractual exclusivity rights it may have and is willing to make concessions, but cannot frame any particularized response because of the unstructured nature of the applicant's request.

Finally, given that the artists are still minors, the court cannot approve an informal and unstructured concept without presentation and close review of an actual contract regarding a child performer in compliance with the Arts and Cultural Affairs Law. The very purpose of this type of proceeding is to secure judicial approval of a contract "to provide a degree of certainty for parties contracting with infants in the entertainment industry so that the validity of such contracts would not be rendered doubtful or subject to subsequent litigation concerning reasonableness" and "to completely eliminate the power to disaffirm under certain circumstances." A further goal of this type of "elaborate court proceedings" is a determination of what part of the contract remuneration should be set aside for an infant performing artist. Accordingly, this branch of the application is denied as insufficient.

Given the current posture of the parties, the court declares that the three petitioning young men are no longer members of the group for they have withdrawn from participation. This determination "shall not affect any right of action existing at the date of" this ruling upon the application for revocation of approval and does not constitute a revocation of approval.

Moreover, given that these young men have refused to participate in the group and have neglected to make any constructive effort to achieve a resolution of the behavior they reportedly find objectionable, the court finds suspect their assertion that their "well-being ... is being impaired" by the contract. The charges made against the Producer show all the signs of a creative attempt to avoid contractual obligations, in the same vein as the recently popular attempt to use bankruptcy proceedings to try to avoid a no longer desired executory personal services contract. It adds no degree of comfort that, despite being challenged to do so, no explanation has been tendered justifying the presentation of the motion papers on the applicants' behalf to the media, which resulted in the exposure to non-parties of references to and copies of papers which had been ordered sealed by the court order of September 8, 2000.... This conduct is a further sign that the applicants were attempting to create public pressure to achieve what they have been unable to gain by well-reasoned and legal argument, supported by carefully crafted proposals and documents ready for court approval.

Based upon the foregoing, it is declared that the three applicants are released prospectively from their obligations under the previously approved contracts. The balance of the requests for relief in the motion and cross motion are denied. To the extent that the court has not addressed any specific request for relief, such request is either rendered moot by the result reached or inadequately supported.

Although this decision is not sealed, all motion papers and exhibits shall be sealed and access restricted to the parties and their counsel absent specific order of the court.

Kassbaum v. Steppenwolf Productions, Inc.

236 F.3d 487 (9th Cir. 2000)

This case raises the issue of whether a contract between the parties or section 32(1)(a) of the Lanham Trade-Mark Act, ("Lanham Act"), bars Nicholas Kassbaum ("Kassbaum"), a former member of the rock band "Steppenwolf," from referring to himself in promotional materials for a new band as "formerly of Steppenwolf," an "original member of Steppenwolf," or an "original founding member of Steppenwolf." ... We hold that Kassbaum is not barred by contract or by the Lanham Act from truthfully referring to himself, in promotional materials or otherwise, as a former member of Steppenwolf.

In 1967, John Kay, Jerry Edmonton, Michael Monarch and Goldie McJohn formed a musical band called "Steppenwolf." In 1968, Nicholas Kassbaum, who is professionally known as "Nick St. Nicholas," joined Steppenwolf as a bass player. That year, the band members entered into a partnership agreement whereby the members became co-equal partners and owners in Steppenwolf, and agreed to share equally the band's expenses and income. Also in 1968, the band members signed a recording agreement with Dunhill Records both as partners and as Steppenwolf band members.

From late 1968 until late April 1970, Steppenwolf, with Kassbaum as its bass player, toured the world in concerts and recorded Steppenwolf's well-received music. Kassbaum appeared prominently on Steppenwolf record album covers and authored Steppenwolf compositions. In 1971, John Kay, who had asserted control over Steppenwolf, excluded Kassbaum from the band.

In 1975, after Kassbaum and Michael Monarch had been excluded, and John Kay had stopped performing as Steppenwolf, Kassbaum and Goldie McJohn began to perform as "The New Steppenwolf." This began a series of legal disputes over the different band members' use of the name Steppenwolf.

In 1976, Kassbaum filed a complaint against SI and SPI to obtain an order prohibiting SPI from interfering with Kassbaum's performances as The New Steppenwolf. In 1977, Kassbaum paid $17,500.00 to John Kay and SPI in exchange for their agreement to grant Goldie McJohn and Kassbaum the exclusive right to the use of the name Steppenwolf for the purposes of live performances and recordings.

In 1979, Kassbaum entered into a second agreement whereby SI and SPI granted The New Steppenwolf, Inc. the exclusive right to use the name Steppenwolf until 1981 in connection with recording, production, manufacture, sale and distribution of records and tapes containing performances of a musical group. Kassbaum performed as Steppenwolf from 1977 through 1980.

On May 27, 1980, Kassbaum, The New Steppenwolf, Inc., SI and SPI entered into a third contract ("the 1980 contract") which states, in relevant part:

ACKNOWLEDGEMENT [sic] AND WAIVER.

[KASSBAUM], THE NEW STEPPENWOLF, INC. and GEOFFREY EMORY hereby acknowledge and agree that [SI] and [SPI] own all right, title and interest in the name "STEPPENWOLF". [KASSBAUM], THE NEW STEPPENWOLF, INC., and GEOFFREY EMORY hereby acknowledge and agree that [SI] and [SPI] have the sole and exclusive right to use the name "STEPPENWOLF" in connection with the production, manufacture and distribution of phonograph records, in live, in-concert performances of a musical group, and all other uses of the name "STEPPENWOLF" in the entertainment industry. [KASSBAUM], THE NEW STEPPENWOLF, INC. and GEOFFREY EMORY now and forever, waive, relinquish and release any and all of their individual or collective rights in the name "STEPPENWOLF" or any other word or phrase incorporating the name "STEPPENWOLF" for any purpose whatsoever. [KASSBAUM], THE NEW STEPPENWOLF, INC. and GEOFFREY EMORY hereby agree to waive, relinquish and release any trademark, trade name, service mark, or service name rights any or all of them may have in the name "STEPPENWOLF." [KASSBAUM], THE NEW STEPPENWOLF, INC. and GEOFFREY EMORY further agree to transfer or assign all such trademark, trade name, service mark or service name rights they may have in the name "STEPPENWOLF" to [SI] and [SPI]. Notwithstanding anything to the contrary in the foregoing, nothing contained herein shall be deemed an acknowledgment on the part of [SI] and [SPI] that [KASSBAUM], THE NEW STEPPENWOLF, INC., and/or GEOFFREY EMORY, ever acquired or held any such trademark, trade name, service mark or service name right in the name "STEPPENWOLF."

The contract also provided that, in exchange for this acknowledgment and waiver, "[SI] and [SPI] agree to pay [KASSBAUM], THE NEW STEPPENWOLF, INC. and GEOFFREY EMORY the sum of THREE THOUSAND DOLLARS ($3,000.00)."

From 1980, when the contract was executed, until 1996, Kassbaum performed as "Lone Wolf." During that time, without objection from the parties to the 1980 contract, Kassbaum referred to his historical association with Steppenwolf, describing himself as a "former member of" or "previous member of" Steppenwolf.

From 1996 until the present, Kassbaum has performed in a group called World Classic Rockers. The group is comprised of former members of various musical groups well known to rock music fans including: Randy Meiser, a former member of "Wings;" Spencer Davis, a former member of the "Spencer Davis Group;" Bruce Gary, a former member of "Knack;" and Michael Monarch and Kassbaum, former members of Steppenwolf. While performing as the World Classic Rockers, Kassbaum and the other band members often identified themselves by referring to their former musical associations. For example, one advertisement identifies Kassbaum as "NICK ST. NICHOLAS former member of Steppenwolf." Kassbaum also promoted himself as being a "Former Original Member of Steppenwolf," "Original Founding Member of Steppenwolf," and "Formerly of Steppenwolf."

In response to these promotional claims, SPI and SI sent Kassbaum cease and desist letters asserting that Kassbaum's historical references to Steppenwolf violated federal trademark law and the 1980 contract. Kassbaum then filed a complaint in federal district court seeking a declaration that he is entitled to refer to himself as "Formerly of Steppenwolf," an "Original Member of Steppenwolf," and an "Original Founding Member of Steppenwolf." SPI answered and filed a counterclaim alleging trademark infringement, unfair competition and breach of contract. Thereafter, SPI and SI moved for summary judgment on Kassbaum's complaint for declaratory relief and SPI's counterclaim for breach of contract. SPI and SI also sought permanently to enjoin Kassbaum and his agents from using the name Steppenwolf. . . .

We must decide whether either the 1980 contract or the Lanham Act bars Kassbaum from referring to himself as a former member of Steppenwolf.

As described above, the parties entered into the 1980 contract on May 28, 1980. We must decide whether, by the terms of the contract, Kassbaum agreed that he would not identify himself, for promotional purposes or otherwise, with a true statement that he is a former member of the band Steppenwolf.

We review decisions to grant or deny declaratory relief de novo. Contract interpretation is a question of law we review de novo. We also review grants of summary judgment de novo. "Summary judgment is appropriate when the contract terms are clear and unambiguous, even if the parties disagree as to their meaning." Under California law, we interpret the 1980 contract by examining the contract's language, the parties' clear intentions as expressed in the contract and the circumstances under which the parties contracted.

As Kassbaum concedes, there is no doubt that the 1980 contract "absolutely precludes" Kassbaum from "performing, sponsoring, or endorsing a band entitled Steppenwolf." The question is whether the contracting parties intended that broad language such as "waive, relinquish and release any and all ... rights in the name 'STEPPENWOLF' or any other word or phrase incorporating the name 'STEPPENWOLF' for any purpose whatsoever" would bar Kassbaum from such things as truthfully answering a question about his past (for example) on a talk show, distributing a resume, or truthfully describing his past musical affiliations in promotional materials connected with the World Classic Rockers.

Taken out of context, the language "name 'STEPPENWOLF'" and "for any purposes whatsoever," might be read so broadly as to preclude Kassbaum from writing "Steppenwolf" on the sidewalk in chalk. While SPI and SI do not advocate a restriction that broad, they do appear to contend that the contract language prohibits virtually any reference by Kassbaum to the name Steppenwolf in the context of the "entertainment industry." Thus, SPI and SI contend that Kassbaum contracted away his ability to refer to his past association with Steppenwolf in a resume sent to a recording company, or in a music industry interview touching upon his background, or, at the center of this case, in his promotional references relating to his performance with World Classic Rockers.

We must read the words of the 1980 contract in context. We may not read the contract in a manner that leads to an absurd result. Rather, when we encounter broad language such as "for any purposes whatsoever," we must extend the meaning of such language to cover only those things which it appears the parties intended to contract. When broad language is at issue, we must look to the circumstances under which the parties contracted to determine their intentions at the time of contracting.

Here, those circumstances are a continuing dispute between the parties about ownership and control over the trade name Steppenwolf. Over the years, such ownership and control was transferred from party to party through a series of contracts. First, all of the original band members owned the trade name Steppenwolf. Then, in 1977, after Kassbaum was asked to leave Steppenwolf and began to perform as The New Steppenwolf, the parties resolved a dispute over the right to the trade name Steppenwolf by having Kassbaum pay $17,500.00 to SPI in exchange for the exclusive right to perform as Steppenwolf for the purpose of live performances and recordings. The parties entered into a second agreement in 1979, whereby SI and SPI granted Kassbaum and The New Steppenwolf, Inc. the exclusive right to use the name Steppenwolf in connection with recording, production, manufacture, sale and distribution of records and tapes embodying performance of a musical group until 1981. At the time the parties entered into the 1980 contract, Kassbaum owned the trade name Steppenwolf to the extent specified by the 1979 contract, and had been performing as The New Steppenwolf. The 1980 contract effected the transfer of the trade name Steppenwolf from Kassbaum and The New Steppenwolf to SPI and SI. Thereafter, Kassbaum discontinued his performances as The New Steppenwolf, and began to perform as Lone Wolf and later as a part of the World Classic Rockers.

Under these circumstances, it is clear that the contract's broad language "for any purposes whatsoever," and "all other uses of the name 'STEPPENWOLF' in the entertainment industry" refers to use of the *trade name* Steppenwolf, and not to the simple use of the name to provide accurate historical information that would not lead reasonable people to think Kassbaum's new band was Steppenwolf. The terms of the contract do not bar Kassbaum from referring to his former membership in Steppenwolf in the entertainment industry or otherwise. We therefore hold that the district court erred by granting summary judgment to SPI and SI on the contract counterclaim and by dismissing Kassbaum's complaint for declaratory relief on contract grounds.

Kassbaum's complaint requests, inter alia, a declaratory judgment that section 32(1)(a) of the Lanham Act, does not bar him from stating, particularly in promotional materials, that he was "Formerly of Steppenwolf," an "Original Member of Steppenwolf," or an

"Original Founding Member of Steppenwolf." The district court dismissed Kassbaum's complaint and granted SPI and SI's motion for summary judgment. We reverse.

The Lanham Act provides, in pertinent part:

(1) Any person who shall, without the consent of the registrant—

(a) use in commerce any reproduction, counterfeit, copy, or colorable imitation of a registered mark in connection with the sale, offering for sale, distribution, or advertising of any goods or services on or in connection with which such use is likely to cause confusion, or to cause mistake, or to deceive ... shall be liable in a civil action by the registrant....

The purpose of a trademark is to allow customers to identify the manufacturer or sponsor of a good or the provider of a service. Actual consumer confusion is not required for profit recovery; it is sufficient to show a likelihood of confusion combined with willful infringement. For the reasons that follow, we believe that Kassbaum's references to himself in promotional materials as "Formerly of Steppenwolf," an "Original Member of Steppenwolf," and an "Original Founding Member of Steppenwolf," do not cause a likelihood of confusion.[4]

First, we believe the phrases "Formerly of," "Original Member of," and "Original Founding Member of," immediately preceding the name "Steppenwolf" in the promotional materials for World Classic Rockers greatly reduce the likelihood of confusion about the source of the band's music.

Additionally, the context of the historical references to Kassbaum's affiliation with Steppenwolf in World Classic Rockers' promotional materials further reduces any likelihood of confusion between these two bands. In all promotional materials presented to the district court, references to World Classic Rockers are more prominent than are references to Steppenwolf. The materials display the title "World Classic Rockers" on the top or at the center of the page, while references to the band members' former groups, including Steppenwolf, are displayed on the bottom or around the edges of the page. Also, the title "World Classic Rockers" appears in large and bold lettering, while smaller and plainer lettering is used for the titles of the former groups, including Steppenwolf. Finally, while the materials mention multiple former groups, the materials promote only World Classic Rockers, not Steppenwolf, or any other former band.

Our holding is supported by cases in similar contexts. For example, in *Kingsmen v. K-Tel International Ltd.*, 557 F. Supp. 178 (S.D.N.Y. 1983), the district court distinguished the likelihood of confusion that exists when a former member of a band re-records a song under the name of the original band from the likelihood of confusion that exists when the former member re-records a song under his own name with the designation "formerly of" the original band displayed on the recording. The first situation, the court stated, created a likelihood of confusion under the Lanham Act, while the latter, although not then before the court, would not.

In *Playboy Enterprises, Inc. v. Welles*, 7 F. Supp. 2d 1098 (S.D. Cal. 1998), the district court addressed concerns regarding the differences between commercial trademark use and descriptions of individuals that use trade names. In that case, the publisher of Playboy sued

---

4. We consider the following factors to test for likelihood of confusion under the Lanham Act: (1) strength of the mark; (2) proximity of the goods; (3) similarity of the marks; (4) evidence of actual confusion; (5) marketing channels used; (6) type of goods and the degree of care likely to be exercised by the purchaser; (7) defendant's intent in selecting the mark; and (8) likelihood of expansion of the product lines.

a former "Playmate of the Year" for so designating herself on her personal web site, asserting various claims related to trademark. In denying the publisher's motion for preliminary injunction, the court held that defendant was entitled to the "fair use" defense. In holding that the "fair use" defense applied, the court noted that "[i]n the case at bar, Ms. Welles has used the trademark term Playmate of the Year to identify and describe herself.... Ms. Welles earned the title of 'Playboy Playmate of the Year' in 1981 and has used that title ever since, without objection." Because the court applied the "fair use" defense, it found it unnecessary to determine the likelihood of confusion under the Lanham Act. The court, however, went on to state that it did not see any likelihood of confusion under this circuit's eight-factor test.

Finally, we wholeheartedly agree with Justice Holmes's statement about the limits of trademark protection in *Prestonettes, Inc. v. Coty,* 264 U.S. 359, 368, 44 S. Ct. 350, 68 L.Ed. 731 (1924): "When the mark is used in a way that does not deceive the public we see no such sanctity in the word as to prevent its being used to tell the truth. It is not taboo." We reverse the district court's order granting summary judgment to SPI and SI and dismissing Kassbaum's complaint for declaratory judgment as to the Lanham Act issue.

The district court granted SPI and SI's request for a permanent injunction precluding Kassbaum and his agents from using the designations "Formerly of Steppenwolf," "Original Member of Steppenwolf," and "Original Founding Member of Steppenwolf" in promotional materials. Because we hold that Kassbaum is not barred by contract or by the Lanham Act from using these designations, we reverse....

Notes and Questions

a. The battles over band names remain hard-fought, as the two principal cases above demonstrate. The interjection of claims involving fiduciary obligations by Jardine raises a new framework for litigation which has not been tried previously.

b. The variations on the names may clue the audience in as to the relationship between the performer and the band, but these appellations often seem confusing. See *Marshak v. Reed,* 2001 U.S. Dist. LEXIS 880 (E.D.N.Y. 2001), *reinstated,* 229 F. Supp. 2d 179, (E.D.N.Y. 2002), *aff'd,* 87 Fed. Appx. 208 (2d Cir. N.Y. 2004), for a long discussion of the ongoing battles involving the embattled musicians and their heirs to interests in the band, the Platters.

c. In some situations the owner of the trademark is no longer related to the musicians themselves. See *Stetson v. Howard D. Wolf & Assocs.,* 955 F.2d 847 (2d Cir. 1992) (the Diamonds) and *In re Polar Music Int'l AB,* 714 F.2d 1567 (Fed. Cir. 1983) (ABBA).

d. In the unpublished opinion of *Cash v. Brooks,* 1996 WL 684447 (E.D.Tenn. 1996), the court adjudicated a fight over competing former band members involved with The Temptations and noted the similar claims of other bands. A similar history has occurred with The Platters. See *Herb Reed Enterprises, Inc. v. Monroe Powell's Platters, LLC,* 842 F.Supp.2d 1282 (2012); *Robi v. Five Platters, Inc.,* 918 F.2d 1439 (9th Cir. 1990) (The Platters); *Robi v. Five Platters, Inc.,* 838 F.2d 318 (9th Cir. 1988) (The Platters); *The Five Platters v. Purdie,* 419 F. Supp. 372 (D.Md 1976) (The Platters).

The Beach Boys, The Temptations, and The Platters are not alone. Many groups end up fighting over these assets long after the music has grown old. Among the cases involving litigation similar to that here are *Marshak v. Treadwell,* 1995 WL 428639 (E.D.N.Y. 1995) (The Drifters); *Baker v. Parris,* 777 F. Supp. 299 (S.D.N.Y. 1991) (The Five Satins); *Marshak v. Admiral Cruises,* 1991 WL 191233 (S.D.N.Y. 1991) (The Drifters); *Grondin v.*

Rossington, 690 F. Supp. 200 (S.D.N.Y. 1988) (Lynyrd Skynyrd); *Marshak v. Sheppard,* 666 F. Supp. 590 (S.D.N.Y. 1987) (The Drifters); *Marshak v. Sheppard,* 659 F. Supp. 907 (S.D.N.Y. 1987) (the Drifters); *Coasters v. Claridge Hotel,* 1986 WL 9783 (D.N.J. 1986) (The Coasters); *Rick v. Buchansky,* 609 F. Supp. 1522 (S.D.N.Y. 1985) (Vito and The Salutations); *Kingsmen v. K-Tel Intern. Ltd.,* 557 F. Supp. 178 (S.D.N.Y. 1983) (the Kingsmen); *Marshak v. Green,* 505 F. Supp. 1054 (S.D.N.Y. 1981) (The Drifters); *Rare Earth v. Hoorelbeke,* 401 F. Supp. 26 (S.D.N.Y. 1975) (Rare Earth); and *Noone v. Banner,* 398 F. Supp. 260 (S.D.N.Y. 1975) (Herman's Hermits).

e. What structures can be put into band membership agreements to limit the litigation that may affect leaving band members? Assuming that the band is sufficiently sophisticated to negotiate a formal agreement, how does the changing membership over time shape the way in which the agreement should be drafted?

f. The court involved in the minor agreements for Dream Street had little problem dismissing the notion that the performers had wrested the ownership and control of the trademark away from the producer of the concept band. To what extent, if at all, does the public's perception of a band such as the Monkees attach to the performers rather than the contractual trademark holder? Does such public perception alter a judicial enforcement of a signed trademark agreement?

Problem VIII-E

Among the contracts purchased as part of Bryce's record company purchase is a recording agreement for the 1950s band, the "DreamWeavers." Bryce is convinced that the DreamWeavers had a sound and sensibility that was never fully appreciated. Bryce has at least fifteen previously unreleased recordings of the DreamWeavers that Bryce can release contractually. The record label also owns many songs that were released, but could also be re-released. The DreamWeavers last performed together in 1967.

Bryce has noticed, however, that songs recorded during the fifties were generally produced using a rhythm that feels too slow for today's audience. Bryce often comments on the rhythmic differences between the Los Lobos versions of Richie Valens songs and the original recordings as an example of the phenomenon. Rather than merely digitally remastering the songs, Bryce wants to add some new performers and reinvent the DreamWeavers. The contract allows Bryce to control the recording and content of all songs, so the addition or re-recording of the songs is contractually permissible.

Bryce seeks your advice. Bryce would like to re-record the songs and launch a new DreamWeavers touring band. Because the company controls the entire DreamWeavers catalog, the success of the new album could generate potential catalog sales of the other albums as well. DreamWeavers recorded five albums. Only two of the original five DreamWeavers are living, so Bryce will also have to determine how to get permission if necessary. Advise Bryce whether permission is needed from any original members of DreamWeavers, either to record and release the album or to start a touring band using the DreamWeavers name. Also explain the terms such a request for permission might entail if you determine permission is necessary or appropriate.

F. Bibliography and Links

Donald C. Farber, Entertainment Industry Contracts (Looseleaf).

Yafit Lev-Aretz, *Second Level Agreements*, 45 Akron L. Rev. 137 (2012).

Adam Seth Bialow, *Illusory Profits: Net Profit Agreements in Light of Buchwald v. Paramount*, 10 U. Miami Ent. & Sports L. Rev. 51 (1993).

Stacey L. Dogan & Mark A. Lemley, *The Merchandising Right: Fragile Theory or Fait Accompli?*, 54 Emory L.J. 461 (2005).

Ellen P. Goodman, *Commercial Speech in an Age of Emerging Technology and Corporate Scandal: Intellectual Property & Cyberlaw*, 58 S.C. L. Rev. 683 (2007).

Alex Kozinski, *Essay: Trademarks Unplugged*, 68 N.Y.U.L. Rev. 960 (1993).

Henry H. Perritt, Jr., *Cut in Tiny Pieces: Ensuring That Fragmented Ownership Does Not Chill Creativity*, 14 Vand. J. Ent. & Tech. L. 1 (2011).

Lisa P. Ramsey, *Descriptive Trademarks and the First Amendment*, 70 Tenn. L. Rev. 1095 (2003).

Kelli Shope, *The Final Cut: How SAG's Failed Negotiations with Talent Agents Left the Contractual Rights of Rank-And-File Actors on the Cutting Room Floor*, 26 J. NAALJ 123 (2006).

Natalie J. Spears & S. Roberts Carter III, *This Brand is my Brand: Litigating Product Image*, 31 Litig. 31 (2005).

L. Lee Wilson, *Music: Naming Names: How Trademarks Go Platinum*, 1 Vand. J. Ent. L. & Prac. 33 (1999).

Websites

Steppenwolf, http://www.steppenwolf.com

Beach Boys, http://thebeachboys.com

Richie Valens at the Rockabilly Hall of Fame, http://www.rockabillyhall.com/Ritchie Valens.html

Part II
Industry Practice in Entertainment

Chapter IX

Professional Live Theatre

A. Overview

Theatrical performances are the oldest form of organized entertainment, reaching back through the history of western society to the dawn of literate civilization. Originally tied to the religious ceremonies of Greece, theatrical productions lost their former prestige and were eventually reduced to a state of disrepute and penury by, and throughout most of, the Middle Ages. Although heavily regulated, the quality and importance of theatrical productions gradually gained respect beginning in the sixteenth century, and then more so throughout the nineteenth and twentieth.

The rise of the motion picture and television industries dramatically reversed the importance of professional theatre. Nonetheless, stage plays still remain as the primary venue where most aspiring actors first apply their craft, and theatre still serves as a leading cultural and artistic medium. Because of theatre's significant historical role, many of the business conventions incorporated into the music industry, motion picture industry, and television originated with practices started in professional theatre.

1. Broadway Theatre

Today, professional theatre is divided into two large and distinct communities—for-profit and nonprofit. Professional theatre continues to be dominated by the New York Broadway theatrical district. Broadway is defined by both its geographic area, covering an area from 42nd Street to 53rd Street and between 6th and 8th Avenues, and by its theater size, requiring a minimum seating capacity of 500 or more seats. In this small section of Manhattan, which is also referred to as the Great White Way, the Shubert Organization dominates the professional theatrical market. The Shubert Organization owns seventeen of the 40 Broadway theatres and also owns additional theatres outside New York.

With 10 theatres, the Nederlander Organization controls the second largest block of Broadway theatres, while the Jujamcyn Theatres company owns five venues. Roundabout Theatre Co. now owns three of the theatres, including the former dance club Studio 54, which has been converted into a Broadway house. Disney Theatrical Group owns only the New Amsterdam Theatre but often presents additional productions in neighboring houses. This cadre of theatrical real estate owners produce or house almost all Broadway theatre. Independent producers often co-produce with one of these companies.

In addition to the Broadway theatres, a second class of professional theatres exists throughout New York. Called "Off-Broadway," these are professional theatres which are smaller in size, generally seating between 200–499 patrons. Besides the size of the venues, the other difference between Broadway and Off-Broadway are the terms of the primary collective bargaining agreements. Generally speaking, the salaries paid for Off-Broadway are considerably lower than for Broadway productions. This allows more modest productions to be produced at a profit in the Off-Broadway venues which could not happen on Broadway.

2. Touring Companies

A third tier of professional theatre exists outside of New York. Generally referred to as touring companies, most of the for-profit professional productions which appear throughout the United States are organized as touring companies. Each company visits a venue for anywhere between a day and a month, setting up shop in a commercial theatre, trucking in the sets, costumes, lights, and actors. When the production is over, the entire show is struck, loaded into trucks, and moved to the next stop on the tour.

Touring companies represent the largest shift and point of greatest controversy in professional for-profit theatre today. Although touring companies historically accounted for only 10% of the industry revenue, it may now account for as much as 40% of theatrical revenue and as much as two-thirds of the professional theatre audience.

In recent years, the tradition of serving all major cities with union-organized professional casts has eroded as new tour producers have entered the market. On January 20, 2004, Actors Equity Association ordered a boycott by its members against Big League Theatricals, NETworks, and Troika, the three primary non-union touring producers. Unlike the historical two-tiered structure in which union companies would first tour the major cities before non-union companies were given access to these scripts for smaller markets, these three producers are generally regarded for high-quality productions that use less experienced, non-union casts.

In addition to the boycott, Actors Equity Association has brought a charge of unfair labor practices before the National Labor Relations Board against Clear Channel Entertainment, Dodger Stage Holdings Theatricals, Inc., and the Nederlander Organization. In each case, Actors Equity asserts that the Broadway producer illegally or unfairly diverted the production to a non-union producer in violation of its signed union agreement.

Whatever the outcome of these complaints, the changing economics of touring and the increasing revenue from this source are likely to significantly change future labor negotiations and could reshape the Broadway profession.

3. Nonprofit Professional Theatre

Although for-profit theatre is the part of theatre that is most visible and famous, the most vibrant aspect of American theatre today flows from the nonprofit sector. Nonprofit theatre includes volunteer, community theatres; educational programs, such as college stages; and professional theatres loosely organized through the League of Resident Theatres.

The League of Resident Theatres ("LORT") is nonprofit but highly professional. The actors are members of Equity, and other professionals are typical member of other trade unions. These include the Guthrie Theatre in Minneapolis, the Goodman Theatre in Chicago, the La Jolla Playhouse in San Diego, and Lincoln Center in New York. While not every LORT theatre has a resident company of actors, many do; these represent some of the most innovative and lucrative productions developed in the United States in recent years. The modern production cycle often finds new plays originating at one of the LORT theatres and then transferring to Broadway if the show is believed to have a chance to be a smash hit.

Nonprofit theatres generally rely on season ticket holders and charitable donations to protect themselves from the vagaries of season and taste. A healthy, nonprofit theatre should receive at least half its annual budget from donations. If season ticket sales account for 75% or more of the ticket sales, the theatre can afford to take significant risks in developing new works. Few investors today can match the resources of the LORT theatres.

Interestingly, the notion that each theatre employ a resident company of actors is not an organizational component of the resident theatre's membership requirements, notwithstanding this important traditional distinction and between the itinerant New York houses and the stable theatrical companies that operated on the season-production basis. Instead, to be a LORT theatre, the theatre must be a nonprofit, tax exempt organization operating under the LORT — Actor's Equity Association contract. In addition, each season must run at least twelve weeks and each individual production must have at least a three-week rehearsal period. While most LORT theatres greatly exceed these minimums, they provide some consistency for the financial scope and production quality that can be expected from a LORT theatre.

4. The Participants

The character most central to theatre is the playwright. The collective bargaining history of theatre has left the playwright as the undisputed king of the medium. Although the Dramatists Guild is not a union, the Dramatists Guild Approved Production Contract governs all playwright agreements with Broadway producers. Under this contract, no additions, omissions, or alterations may be made to a script without the playwright's consent. The playwright retains ownership of the play or musical, retains control of subsequent productions, and shares approval of the cast, director, and designers with the producer. As a result, the playwright is far more influential for theatre than the screenwriter is for film or the composer is for music.

In a musical, there may be three individuals who collectively become the playwright. The author of the 'book' or dialogue; the composer of the musical score; and the lyricist who writes the words put to music. Some musicals continue to have all three participants while others are written by teams of two or by single individuals.

In collaboration with the playwright, the theatrical director integrates the creative elements of set and production design, casting, and character development to create the completed theatrical performance. The stage director supervises all of the creative elements of the project, but unlike the film director, the process under the stage director's supervision is subject to much greater influence by the playwright. The primary voice for the production cannot contractually shift from the writer to the director as it does in film.

For-profit, professional theatre is highly unionized. The League of American Theatres and Producers, Inc., represents the producers and also serves as the parent organization for the annual Tony awards. Actors' Equity Association ("AEA" or "Equity") represents the actors, and the Dramatists Guild of America, though technically not a union, provides standardization for playwright agreements. The Society of Stage Directors and Choreographers represents directors and choreographers. Additional trade unions represent every other aspect of the theatre experience.

Some of the confusion surrounding the legal agreements in for-profit theatrical production stems from the interlocking collective bargaining agreements used in New York, for-profit theatre. The relatively small number of producers, in tandem with close control of the unions and guilds result in contractual language that is often baffling to the outsider. For example, the Dramatists Guild Approved Production Contract for Plays, which is used by every Broadway production, relies heavily on terms only defined in the collective bargaining agreement between the producers and Equity. For a student interested in the inner workings of Broadway, a careful understanding of each collective bargaining agreement is essential.

Problem IX-A

The success of Bryce's *Juliet Prescott* (see Problem V-A) has served as something of both a blessing and curse for Bryce. The play has caught the attention of New York producers who would like to see it developed for a New York run. Bryce believes that the show is good, but could not survive a New York Times theatrical review in its present condition. Given the pressures of New York, Bryce would like to try to develop the play in a workshop or move it to a small regional or LORT theatre.

Bryce also acknowledges that all the funding for any project would have to come from the theatres or from investors; Bryce has no personal funds to invest. Bryce has asked that you explain the various producing options and how to give the play its best chance of being successful in New York. Also explain how these different choices affect how the play would be financed and how Bryce would be compensated.

B. Employment in the Theatre

This Is Me v. Taylor
157 F.3d 139 (2d Cir. 1998)

Actress Cicely Tyson, through her personal services corporation, plaintiff-appellant This Is Me, Inc., agreed to undertake the lead role in a Broadway production of "The Corn is Green" and in a contemplated taping of the production for television, and sues to recover unpaid fees for her services. Several contracts are arguably in issue; some are standard Actors' Equity (sometimes "Equity") form contracts, others are not; all are signed by and on behalf of various persons and entities as producers. At issue is the unpaid portion of a so-called "pay or play" guarantee of $750,000 payable if (as happened) the show closed before Tyson earned $750,000 in salary. Among the sufficiency of evidence issues are (i) whether the various contracts are sufficiently interrelated that they may be read together; (ii) whether the contractual phrase "a contract made in relation to the Play" includes a contract governing the videotaping; and (iii) who is bound in respect of the $750,000 pay or play guarantee.

Elizabeth Taylor, the actress, and Zev Bufman, the Broadway producer, formed a theater group to produce live performances of plays on the legitimate stage and video and television versions of the same plays. They chose "The Corn is Green" as their second production, and cast Cicely Tyson in the lead role. The play soon closed, and the video was never made.

This Is Me, the corporation through which Ms. Tyson provides her services, sued Taylor and Bufman (and Zev Bufman Entertainment, Inc.) under the pay or play guarantee. Plaintiff's arguments convinced the jury, which found Taylor and Bufman personally liable. The district court, however, issued judgment as a matter of law in favor of defendants on the grounds that the individual defendants were not signatories to the only contract that contained the guarantee, and that Tyson's arguments linking Taylor and Bufman to that undertaking are barred by the parol evidence rule.

We conclude that there was sufficient evidence from which the jury could find liability, and we therefore reverse. That evidence consists of the underlying and well-disclosed purpose of the enterprise to produce the play on stage as well as on videotape, the drafting history of the contracts, the contemporaneity of the undertakings, the cross-referencing between and among the contracts, and the background undertakings of the Actors' Equity rules, accepted by all the parties, that bind the individual signatories (as producers), as well as any partnership or venture controlled by them, to employment contracts.

Following a prior collaboration as producer and actor, Zev Bufman and Elizabeth Taylor decided to "put a theater group together" to produce plays on Broadway. They agreed generally that Bufman "would take care of the business end of it" and Taylor "would take care of the artistic end of it," specifically by "trying to get people to participate and become involved in the group."

Taylor and Bufman entered into a letter of intent providing that: (i) "all profits and losses will be shared equally between us;" (ii) the primary purpose of the Group was "the production of legitimate stage plays and television/film versions of such plays;" (iii) the Group would "produce three (3) plays each year;" (iv) it would be "of the essence at this time that we do not consider any play unless we are able to acquire or have an option to acquire the rights to televise such productions;" and (v) Taylor and Bufman would "be co-producers of every project" and would "each consult with the other with respect to all major decisions." Taylor testified that upon receiving the letter of intent, she scratched out the word "losses" on her copy before signing; she maintains that therefore she is not responsible for any losses. The letter of intent contemplated a more formal contract and the formation of a "new corporation" to carry out the venture, but neither eventuality came to pass.

For the Group's second project—a live production and videotape of Emlyn Williams's play, "The Corn is Green"—Bufman and Taylor decided to seek Cicely Tyson's services to star in the play. Taylor took the lead in recruiting Tyson, with whom she had worked before. In several phone calls and a lunch meeting, Taylor played a key role in reconciling creative differences between Tyson and the author of the play regarding whether use of the original screenplay would be appropriate. Throughout these discussions, Taylor referred to Bufman as her partner and noted that they were in this "50-50."

Tyson agreed to appear in the live theater production and the videotape production of "The Corn is Green," and exacted the $750,000 "pay or play" guarantee. The guarantee reflected that Tyson, who was at the height of her career, would have to turn down other opportunities in film, television, and stage, and commit nearly a year to "The Corn is Green."

An initial contract—later superseded—addressed all the undertakings concerning the stage and videotape performances of the play. This contract (hereinafter the "superseded contract") was dated December 9, 1982, and was executed by Cicely Tyson on behalf of This Is Me and by Zev Bufman on behalf of Zev Bufman Entertainment, Inc. Ms. Tyson also signed an inducement letter to bind herself personally, which is addressed to "Zev Bufman Entertainment, Inc. d/b/a The Elizabeth Theatre Group." The obligations of the superseded contract were afterward bifurcated and expressed in two new contracts executed contemporaneously in August 1983, which provided that they were to be read together to constitute the entire agreement covering This Is Me's services in "The Corn is Green."

The first of these contracts was a standard Actors' Equity document, a run of the play contract that guaranteed Tyson's weekly salary for the Broadway run, without guaranteeing the length of the run. The producer listed on this contract was an entity called "The Corn Company" and the individual signatory was Zev Bufman.

The second of these contracts related to the video production, and contained the pay or play guarantee in the amount of the difference between $750,000 and salary paid under the run of the play contract (the "video contract"). This contract was between Zev Bufman Entertainment, Inc. and This Is Me.

Two further undertakings are potentially implicated as well, both of which arise from the efforts of Actors' Equity to protect its members from defaulting producers:

> It is conceded that the relationship between the actors and the producers in this production was governed by the Actors' Equity Association Agreement and Rules Governing Employment Under the Production Contract (the "Equity Agreement and Rules"). Bufman testified that "in order to put on a play in an Equity playhouse," he "had to abide by the collective bargaining agreement."

The "Security Agreement" (also an industry standard agreement), signed by Zev Bufman, requires the producer to "promptly pay to the Actors any and all sums due," including sums due under employment agreements "made in relation to the Play," and defines "producer" broadly to "include[ ] the individual, firm, partnership or corporation or any combination thereof producing or controlling the production of said Play."

After out-of-town tryouts, "The Corn is Green" had a short run on Broadway, and its closing was unlamented by the critics. The video was never made, and Ms. Tyson received only the weekly salary payments made under the run of the play agreement.

Later, Tyson commenced an arbitration against Bufman, Taylor and Zev Bufman Entertainment, Inc. She won an award of $607,078.86 against Zev Bufman Entertainment, Inc., and at the behest of the individual defendants, agreed to permanently stay the arbitration as against Bufman and Taylor (preserving, however, the right of This Is Me to pursue claims against Bufman and Taylor in court).

The present action followed. The jury found that both Taylor and Bufman were liable to Tyson for "the unpaid balance of the $750,000 she was to receive for performing in the Corn is Green," but the district court granted judgment as a matter of law dismissing the complaint on the grounds that (1) only the video agreement contained the pay or play guarantee; (2) that agreement unambiguously bound only Zev Bufman Entertainment, Inc.; and (3) the Security Agreement could not be "reasonably read to require anything more than the payments due under the Run-of-the Play (sic) Contract that it was designed to secure." This Is Me appealed; for the reasons that follow, we reverse.

Federal Rule of Civil Procedure 50 provides that if a jury returns a verdict for which there is not a legally sufficient evidentiary basis, the district court may either order a new trial or direct the entry of judgment as a matter of law. "The same standard that applies to a pretrial motion for summary judgment pursuant to Fed. R. Civ. P. 56 also applies to motions for judgment as a matter of law during or after trial pursuant to Rule 50." A district court may not grant a motion for a judgment as a matter of law unless "the evidence is such that, without weighing the credibility of the witnesses or otherwise considering the weight of the evidence, there can be but one conclusion as to the verdict that reasonable [persons] could have reached." Weakness of the evidence does not justify judgment as a matter of law; as in the case of a grant of summary judgment, the evidence must be such that "a reasonable juror would have been compelled to accept the view of the moving party." We review a grant of judgment as a matter of law de novo....

Under New York law, all writings forming part of a single transaction are to be read together. The district court properly instructed the jury on this principle:

> New York law requires that all writings which form part of a single transaction and are designed to effectuate the same purpose be read together, even though they were executed on different dates and were not all between the same parties. It is for you to determine whether the Actors' Equity run of the play contract, the Actors' Equity security agreement and the contractual obligation to pay This Is Me $750,000 were each intended to be binding on all the same parties, and were intended to impose the same obligations on each of the parties, even though they were set forth in different documents.

We conclude that there was sufficient evidence—the drafting history and chronology, the cross-referencing of the agreements, the integral nature of the undertakings for the stage and video performance, the relationships among the producing parties and entities, and the background assumptions furnished by the Equity rules—for the jury, as properly instructed, to find that Taylor and Bufman were personally liable on the pay or play guarantee. That conclusion requires a further look at the terms of the various contracts, and their cross-referencing of each other.

A. The Superseded Contract

The original contract for Tyson's services in the production, a letter agreement dated December 9, 1982 between This Is Me and Zev Bufman Entertainment, Inc., provided that Tyson would perform in the stage production and that a performance of that stage production would be videotaped. Zev Bufman Entertainment, Inc. undertook to pay salary for the run of the play, but not less than $750,000, installments of which would be paid at specified intervals "whether or not the Artist is actually performing":

> We guaranty to "pay or play" to [This Is Me] for the services of [Tyson], the total sum of Seven Hundred Fifty Thousand ($750,000) Dollars plus Actors Equity Minimum Rehearsal Salary during the period of rehearsals....

This document also provided that the parties would enter into a standard Actors' Equity Association run of the play contract, but that the pay or play obligation would supersede the run of the play agreement "notwithstanding any provisions therein to the contrary."

This original agreement was split into two superseding agreements, one concerned with the stage performances and undertaking to pay weekly salary for the run of the play, the other concerned with the video performance and undertaking the pay or play guarantee. Conflicting evidence was offered to explain this drafting history, but the jury was free to credit testimony that the producers wanted to keep the pay or play guarantee out of the run of the play contract that would be filed with Actors' Equity in order to reduce the bond required under the Equity rules.

B. The Run of the Play Contract

The run of the play contract was signed by Tyson on behalf of This Is Me and by Bufman on behalf of The Corn Company as "producer," a word left undefined by the contract, except that in Paragraph 9 the binding effect is said to reach the individual signatory as well as persons for whom the signatory acts:

> Individual signature required. The Producer agrees that execution of this Contract binds not only the producing company, but the individual signator to this Contract as well as any person under whose authority this Contract is executed. The jury could find that Zev Bufman was personally bound because he affixed his signature, and that Taylor was bound because Bufman acted on her authority.

The run of the play contract incorporates by reference the Actors' Equity agreement and rules, and recites that they are the essence of the contractual relationship between the parties, that they set forth the minimum conditions under which the actor may work for the producer, and that they may not be waived or modified without Equity's written consent. It is therefore significant that Paragraph 7 of the Equity rules extends the binding effect of contracts beyond their signatories:

> All contracts of employment signed pursuant to these Rules are binding not only upon the signers on the face thereof, but upon any and all corporations, co-partnerships, enterprises and/or groups which said signers or each of them directs, controls, or is interested in, and are hereby agreed to be adopted as their contract by each of them.

By virtue of that clause, the run of the play contract is unquestionably binding upon Taylor and Bufman as producers, but that fact is of limited import, because the pay or play guarantee that this suit seeks to enforce does not appear in the run of the play contract. For reasons stated later in this opinion, however, there was sufficient evidence from which the jury could find that the video agreement, which contains the pay or play guarantee, cross-references the run of the play contract, which in turn incorporates the Equity rules. The interlocking nature of the agreements and the Equity rules is further confirmed by the fact that the Equity agreement and rules prohibit the videotaping of any production in which members of Equity are employed without the express permission of Equity and without adhering to the terms and conditions established by Equity.

C. The Video Contract

The video contract, signed on behalf of Zev Bufman Entertainment, Inc., guarantees payment to This Is Me of the difference between $750,000 and the salary paid pursuant to the run of the play contract. The contract recites that it constitutes the parties' "full and binding agreement with respect to … our proposed film and/or video recording of 'The Corn is Green,'" and that it is "intended to be executed concurrently with a 'Run of the Play' Actors Equity Association contract with respect to the Artist's services in a live stage production of the play." …

When the contracts are read together in light of the other evidence, there are two entirely sufficient analyses that can support the jury verdict against Taylor and Bufman.

First, the video contract (which contains the $750,000 guarantee) cross-references the run of the play contract, which in turn expressly incorporates the Actors' Equity rules. And the run of the play contract, which does not say that it constitutes the parties' full and binding agreement, can be read to incorporate the video contract without contradicting its own express terms. Paragraph 9 of the run of the play contract provides that an individual who signs it in a representative capacity is also bound, and Paragraph 7 of the Equity rules extends the binding power of any employment agreement still further to any partnership or enterprise directed by the signatory. Thus the jury could have concluded that Zev Bufman's signature on the video contract on behalf of Zev Bufman Entertainment, Inc. also bound: (i) himself and (ii) the Elizabeth Theatre Group, an enterprise in which he was a partner. The jury could then further have assessed individual liability against Taylor as derivative of the Elizabeth Theatre Group's liability, because there was evidence (including Taylor's own statements to Tyson) from which the jury could conclude that Ms. Taylor was a partner in the Elizabeth Theatre Group.

Alternatively, the jury could have relied on the Security Agreement (read in conjunction with the run of the play contract and video contract). The Security Agreement provides that it applies to all "individual employment contracts," and defines such contracts as "any agreement of employment heretofore or hereafter entered into between an Actor and the Guarantor or Producer in relation to the Play." The pertinent inquiry under this theory is whether evidence was presented from which the jury reasonably could conclude: (i) that the video contract, in addition to the run of the play contract, was an agreement "in relation to the Play;" and (ii) that Taylor and Bufman fit the definition of producers....

For these reasons, the jury was free to find that Bufman and Taylor were producers, and that the video contract was an employment agreement made in relation to the play. The district court's view—that only the run of the play contract is a contract "in relation to the Play"—may be fairer, and better supported by evidence; but that is not for us to say. As long as there is some evidence based upon which the jury could have held Zev Bufman and Elizabeth Taylor individually liable, we must reinstate the verdict....

The judgment of the district court is reversed, and the jury's verdict reinstated.

H. A. Artists & Associates, Inc. v. Actors' Equity Ass'n
451 U.S. 704 (1981)

JUSTICE STEWART delivered the opinion of the Court.

The respondent Actors' Equity Association (Equity) is a union representing the vast majority of stage actors and actresses in the United States. It enters into collective-bargaining agreements with theatrical producers that specify minimum wages and other terms and conditions of employment for those whom it represents. The petitioners are independent theatrical agents who place actors and actresses in jobs with producers. The Court of Appeals for the Second Circuit held that the respondents' system of regulation of theatrical agents is immune from antitrust liability by reason of the statutory labor exemption from the antitrust laws. We granted certiorari to consider the availability of that exemption in the circumstances presented by this case.

Equity is a national union that has represented stage actors and actresses since early in this century. Currently representing approximately 23,000 actors and actresses, it has collective-bargaining agreements with virtually all major theatrical producers in New York City, on and off Broadway, and with most other theatrical producers throughout the United States. The terms negotiated with producers are the minimum conditions of employment (called "scale"); an actor or actress is free to negotiate wages or terms more favorable than the collectively bargained minima.

Theatrical agents are independent contractors who negotiate contracts and solicit employment for their clients. The agents do not participate in the negotiation of collective-bargaining agreements between Equity and the theatrical producers. If an agent succeeds in obtaining employment for a client, he receives a commission based on a percentage of the client's earnings. Agents who operate in New York City must be licensed as employment agencies and are regulated by the New York City Department of Consumer Affairs pursuant to New York law, which provides that the maximum commission a theatrical agent may charge his client is 10% of the client's compensation.

In 1928, concerned with the high unemployment rates in the legitimate theater and the vulnerability of actors and actresses to abuses by theatrical agents, including the extraction of high commissions that tended to undermine collectively bargained rates of compensation, Equity unilaterally established a licensing system for the regulation of agents. The regulations permitted Equity members to deal only with those agents who obtained Equity licenses and thereby agreed to meet the conditions of representation prescribed by Equity. Those members who dealt with nonlicensed agents were subject to union discipline.

The system established by the Equity regulations was immediately challenged. In *Edelstein v. Gillmore*, 35 F.2d 723 [(2d. Cir. 1929)], the Court of Appeals for the Second Circuit concluded that the regulations were a lawful effort to improve the employment conditions of Equity members. In an opinion written by Judge Swan and joined by Judge Augustus N. Hand, the court said:

> "The evils of unregulated employment agencies (using this term broadly to include also the personal representative) are set forth in the defendants' affidavits and are corroborated by common knowledge.... Hence the requirement that, as a condition to writing new business with Equity's members, old contracts with its members must be made to conform to the new standards, does not seem to us to justify an inference that the primary purpose of the requirement is infliction of injury upon plaintiff, and other personal representatives in a similar situation, rather than the protection of the supposed interests of Equity's members. *The terms they insist upon are calculated to secure from personal representatives better and more impartial service, at uniform and cheaper rates, and to improve conditions of employment of actors by theater managers.* Undoubtedly the defendants intend to compel the plaintiff to give up rights under existing contracts which do not conform to the new standards set up by Equity, but, as already indicated, *their motive in so doing is to benefit themselves and their fellow actors in the economic struggle.* The financial loss to plaintiff is incidental to this purpose."

The essential elements of Equity's regulation of theatrical agents have remained unchanged since 1928. A member of Equity is prohibited, on pain of union discipline, from using an agent who has not, through the mechanism of obtaining an Equity license (called a "franchise"), agreed to comply with the regulations. The most important of the regulations requires that a licensed agent must renounce any right to take a commission on an employment contract under which an actor or actress receives scale wages.[1] To the extent a

---

1. The minimum, or "scale," wage varies. In August 1977, for example, the minimum weekly salary was $335 for Broadway performances, and $175 for performances off Broadway. Scale wages are set by a collective-bargaining agreement between Equity and the producers, to which the agents are not parties. When an agent represents an actor or actress whose professional reputation is not sufficient to demand a salary higher than scale, the agent hopes to develop a relationship that will become continually more remunerative as the performer's professional reputation grows, and with it the power to demand an ever higher salary. No agent is required to represent an actor or actress whom he does not wish to represent.

contract includes provisions under which an actor or actress will sometimes receive scale pay—for rehearsals or "chorus" employment, for example—and sometimes more, the regulations deny the agent any commission on the scale portions of the contract. Licensed agents are also precluded from taking commissions on out-of-town expense money paid to their clients. Moreover, commissions are limited on wages within 10% of scale pay, and an agent must allow his client to terminate a representation contract if the agent is not successful in procuring employment within a specified period. Finally, agents are required to pay franchise fees to Equity. The fee is $200 for the initial franchise, $60 a year thereafter for each agent, and $40 for any subagent working in the office of another. These fees are deposited by Equity in its general treasury and are not segregated from other union funds.

In 1977, after a dispute between Equity and Theatrical Artists Representatives Associates (TARA)—a trade association representing theatrical agents—a group of agents, including the petitioners, resigned from TARA because of TARA's decision to abide by Equity's regulations. These agents also informed Equity that they would not accept Equity's regulations, or apply for franchises. The petitioners instituted this lawsuit in May 1978, contending that Equity's regulations of theatrical agents violated §§ 1 and 2 of the Sherman Act, 26 Stat. 209, as amended, *15 U. S. C. §§ 1 and 2....*

Labor unions are lawful combinations that serve the collective interests of workers, but they also possess the power to control the character of competition in an industry. Accordingly, there is an inherent tension between national antitrust policy, which seeks to maximize competition, and national labor policy, which encourages cooperation among workers to improve the conditions of employment. In the years immediately following passage of the Sherman Act, courts enjoined strikes as unlawful restraints of trade when a union's conduct or objectives were deemed "socially or economically harmful." In response to these practices, Congress acted, first in the Clayton Act, and later in the Norris-LaGuardia Act, to immunize labor unions and labor disputes from challenge under the Sherman Act.

Section 6 of the Clayton Act, *15 U. S. C. § 17,* declares that human labor "is not a commodity or article of commerce," and immunizes from antitrust liability labor organizations and their members "lawfully carrying out" their "legitimate [objectives]." Section 20 of the Act prohibits injunctions against specified employee activities, such as strikes and boycotts, that are undertaken in the employees' self-interest and that occur in the course of disputes "concerning terms or conditions of employment," and states that none of the specified acts can be "held to be [a] [violation] of any law of the United States." This protection is re-emphasized and expanded in the Norris-LaGuardia Act, which prohibits federal-court injunctions against single or organized employees engaged in enumerated activities, and specifically forbids such injunctions notwithstanding the claim of an unlawful combination or conspiracy. While the Norris-LaGuardia Act's bar of federal-court labor injunctions is not explicitly phrased as an exemption from the antitrust laws, it has been interpreted broadly as a statement of congressional policy that the courts must not use the antitrust laws as a vehicle to interfere in labor disputes.

In *United States v. Hutcheson,* 312 U.S. 219, the Court held that labor unions acting in their self-interest and not in combination with nonlabor groups enjoy a statutory exemption from Sherman Act liability.... The Court explained that this exemption derives not only from the Clayton Act, but also from the Norris-LaGuardia Act, particularly its definition of a "labor dispute," in which Congress "reasserted the original purpose of the Clayton Act by infusing into it the immunized trade union activities as redefined by the later Act." Thus under *Hutcheson,* no federal injunction may issue over a "labor dispute," and "§ 20 [of the Clayton Act] removes all such allowable conduct from the taint of being a 'violation of any law of the United States,' including the Sherman [Act]."

The statutory exemption does not apply when a union combines with a "non-labor group." Accordingly, antitrust immunity is forfeited when a union combines with one or more employers in an effort to restrain trade. In *Allen Bradley Co.* v. *Electrical Workers*, 325 U.S. 797, for example, the Court held that a union had violated the Sherman Act when it combined with manufacturers and contractors to erect a sheltered local business market in order "to bar all other business men from [the market], and to charge the public prices above a competitive level." The Court indicated that the union efforts would, standing alone, be exempt from antitrust liability, but because the union had not acted unilaterally, the exemption was denied. Congress "intended to outlaw business monopolies. A business monopoly is no less such because a union participates, and such participation is a violation of the Act."

Court of Appeals properly recognized that the threshold issue was to determine whether or not Equity's franchising of agents involved any combination between Equity and any "non-labor groups," or persons who are not "parties to a labor dispute." And the court's conclusion that the trial court had not been clearly erroneous in its finding that there was no combination between Equity and the theatrical producers to create or maintain the franchise system is amply supported by the record.

The more difficult problem is whether the combination between Equity and the agents who agreed to become franchised was a combination with a "nonlabor group." The answer to this question is best understood in light of *Musicians v. Carroll,* 391 U.S. 99. There, four orchestra leaders, members of the American Federation of Musicians, brought an action based on the Sherman Act challenging the union's unilateral system of regulating "club dates," or one-time musical engagements. These regulations, *inter alia*, enforced a closed shop; required orchestra leaders to engage a minimum number of "sidemen," or instrumentalists; prescribed minimum prices for local engagements;[2] prescribed higher minimum prices for traveling orchestras; and permitted leaders to deal only with booking agents licensed by the union.

Without disturbing the finding of the Court of Appeals that the orchestra leaders were employers and independent contractors, the Court concluded that they were nonetheless a "labor group" and parties to a "labor dispute" within the meaning of the Norris-LaGuardia Act, and thus that their involvement in the union regulatory scheme was not an unlawful combination between "labor" and "nonlabor" groups. The Court agreed with the trial court that the applicable test was whether there was "job or wage competition or some other economic interrelationship affecting legitimate union interests between the union members and the independent contractors."

The Court also upheld the restrictions on booking agents, who were *not* involved in job or wage competition with union members. Accordingly, these restrictions had to meet the "other economic interrelationship" branch of the disjunctive test quoted above. And the test was met because those restrictions were "'at least as intimately bound up with the subject of wages'... as the price floors." The Court noted that the booking agent re-

---

2. These consisted of a minimum scale for sidemen, a "leader's fee," which was twice the sidemen's scale in orchestras of at least four, and an additional 8% for social security, unemployment insurance, and other expenses. In addition, if a leader did not appear but designated a subleader, and four or more musicians performed, the leader was required to pay from his leader's fee 1.5 times the sidemen's scale to the subleader.

strictions had been adopted, in part, because agents had "charged exorbitant fees, and booked engagements for musicians at wages ... below union scale."

The restrictions challenged by the petitioners in this case are very similar to the agent restrictions upheld in the *Carroll* case. The essential features of the regulatory scheme are identical: members are permitted to deal only with agents who have agreed (1) to honor their fiduciary obligations by avoiding conflicts of interest, (2) not to charge excessive commissions, and (3) not to book members for jobs paying less than the union minimum. And as in *Carroll*, Equity's regulation of agents developed in response to abuses by employment agents who occupy a critical role in the relevant labor market. The agent stands directly between union members and jobs, and is in a powerful position to evade the union's negotiated wage structure.

The peculiar structure of the legitimate theater industry, where work is intermittent, where it is customary if not essential for union members to secure employment through agents, and where agents' fees are calculated as a percentage of a member's wage, makes it impossible for the union to defend even the integrity of the minimum wages it has negotiated without regulation of agency fees.

The Court of Appeals found that "the union *cannot* eliminate wage competition among its members without regulation of the fees of the agents." Wage competition is prevented not only by the rule precluding commissions on scale jobs. Actors and actresses could also compete over the percentage of their wages they were willing to cede to an agent, subject only to the restrictions imposed by state law.

The regulations are "brought within the labor exemption [because they are] necessary to assure that scale wages will be paid...." They "embody ... a direct frontal attack upon a problem thought to threaten the maintenance of the basic wage structure." Agents must, therefore, be considered a "labor group," and their controversy with Equity is plainly a "labor dispute" as defined in the Norris-LaGuardia Act: "representation of persons in negotiating, fixing, maintaining, changing, or seeking to arrange terms or conditions of employment, regardless of whether or not the disputants stand in the proximate relation of employer and employee."

Agents perform a function—the representation of union members in the sale of their labor—that in most nonentertainment industries is performed exclusively by unions. In effect, Equity's franchise system operates as a substitute for maintaining a hiring hall as the representative of its members seeking employment.

Finally, Equity's regulations are clearly designed to promote the union's legitimate self-interest. In a case such as this, where there is no direct wage or job competition between the union and the group it regulates, the *Carroll* formulation to determine the presence of a nonlabor group—whether there is "'some ... economic interrelationship affecting legitimate union interests ...'"

The question remains whether the fees that Equity levies upon the agents who apply for franchises are a permissible component of the exempt regulatory system. We have concluded that Equity's justification for these fees is inadequate. Conceding that *Carroll* did not sanction union extraction of franchise fees from agents, Equity suggests, only in the most general terms, that the fees are somehow related to the basic purposes of its regulations: elimination of wage competition, upholding of the union wage scale, and promotion of fair access to jobs. But even assuming that the fees no more than cover the costs of administering the regulatory system, this is simply another way of saying that without the fees, the union's regulatory efforts would not be subsidized—and that the dues of Equity's members would perhaps have to be increased to offset the loss of a general revenue source. If Equity did not impose these franchise fees upon the agents, there is no reason to believe that any of its legitimate interests would be affected....

For the reasons stated, the judgment of the Court of Appeals is affirmed in part and reversed in part, and the case is remanded for proceedings consistent with this opinion.

It is so ordered.

Makarova v. United States

201 F.3d 110 (2d Cir. 2000)

In 1982, Natalia Makarova was injured when a piece of scenery fell on her shoulder at the Kennedy Center for the Performing Arts in Washington, D.C. At the time of the injury, Makarova was performing in a production of the musical "On Your Toes," and a witness for Makarova asserts that she was widely regarded as the world's best prima ballerina.

The Kennedy Center was the producer of "On Your Toes." As producer, it: (1) contracted with the estates of the musical's authors for the right to "produce and present" the show; (2) contracted directly with the director and stage manager; (3) arranged a letter of credit for bond coverage for the show; (4) paid performers throughout the Washington, D.C. run of the show; and (5) maintained workers' compensation coverage for the show's performers and workers.

The contract for Makarova's services was between the Kennedy Center, as producer, and "NMK Productions, Inc. f/s/o Natalia Makarova." NMK Productions, Inc. was Makarova's "personal services corporation," and the term "f/s/o" means "for the services of."

Makarova personally signed a rider to the contract, certifying "that she [had] read and approved all the terms and conditions of said contract, and agreed to perform her services, as performing actress in 'On Your Toes', in accordance with said contract and the Rules of the Actors' Equity Association ... *as though the undersigned had entered into this contract*" (emphasis added). The rider further provided that Makarova would "perform services hereunder in accordance with the terms and conditions of Actors' Equity Association's Standard Run-of-the-Play Contract," which incorporated by reference a standardized set of protocols called the "Agreement and Rules Governing Employment" ("Agreement and Rules").

The incorporated Agreement and Rules provided that the "producer agrees to obtain and maintain Workmen's Compensation Insurance Coverage for all Actors ... in his employ." The Agreement and Rules also included a choice of law provision for employment contracts stating that "all contracts of employment shall be subject to, be construed by, and all the rights of the parties thereto shall be determined by the laws of the State of New York."

Her contract required Makarova to: (1) play a specific part in the musical; (2) maintain a contractually specified rehearsal and performance schedule; (3) have her hair styled in accord with the time period of the show; (4) wear shoes and make-up provided by the Kennedy Center; and (5) provide her exclusive services to the Kennedy Center during the term of the contract.

The Kennedy Center ("United States") is part of the Smithsonian Institution, which is owned and operated by the federal government. In 1984, Makarova filed a federal administrative claim against the Kennedy Center for her injuries. In 1997, thirteen years later, Makarova filed a civil suit against the United States pursuant to the Federal Tort Claims Act, *28 U.S.C. § 1346* (1994) ("FTCA"), in the United States District Court for the

Southern District of New York (Preska, J.). Makarova claimed that the United States government was responsible for the injuries that she sustained during her fateful performance....

It is undisputed that the Kennedy Center is an entity of the United States government. However, "the United States, as sovereign, is immune from suit save as it consents to be sued ..., and the terms of its consent to be sued in any court define that court's jurisdiction to entertain the suit." The doctrine of sovereign immunity is jurisdictional in nature, and therefore to prevail, the plaintiff bears the burden of establishing that her claims fall within an applicable waiver. The FTCA waives the government's sovereign immunity only for:

> claims against the United States, for money damages ... for injury or loss of property, or personal injury or death caused by the negligent or wrongful act or omission of any employee of the Government while acting within the scope of his office or employment, under circumstances where the United States, if a private person, would be liable to the claimant in accordance with the law of the place where the act or omission occurred.

Both parties concede that the FTCA governs Makarova's complaint, and that, accordingly, subject matter jurisdiction exists only if a private defendant could have been sued by Makarova in Washington, D.C.—"the place where the act or omission occurred."

Under the FTCA, courts are bound to apply the law of the state (or here, the district) where the accident occurred. Under District of Columbia law, the exclusive remedy for an "employee" seeking damages from her employer for a work-related injury is the District Workers' Compensation Act. If Makarova was an "employee" of the Kennedy Center, then her remedy lay with the District of Columbia Workers' Compensation Act and not the FTCA.

Pointing to the choice of law provision in the contract, the United States argues, and the district court found, that the question of whether Makarova was an "employee" is governed by New York law.

For her part, Makarova contends that the contract's choice of law provision should not be triggered until we first determine under District of Columbia law whether she was a party to an "employment contract." She also maintains, that in any event, she was not an "employee" of the Kennedy Center under either New York or District of Columbia law....

Under New York law, "there is no absolute rule for determining whether one is an independent contractor or an employee." However, the typical test of whether one is an independent contractor lies in the control exercised by the employer, and in who has the right to direct what will be done and when and how it will be done.

Applying these principles, Makarova was an "employee" rather than an independent contractor. She was: (1) required to play a specific part in a specific musical; (2) required to meet a contractually specified rehearsal and performance schedule; (3) contractually obligated to have her hair styled in accord with the time period of the show; (4) required to wear shoes and make-up provided by the Kennedy Center; and (5) obligated to provide her exclusive services to the Kennedy Center during the term of her contract. Although Makarova had a significant say over her own dancing and acting, the director and the Kennedy Center maintained artistic control over the show, including Makarova's performance.

Indeed, New York courts have repeatedly found performance artists to be "employees." A performer who has entered into a written contract with a producer for a stipulated sum and a time certain, with the time and place of work to be determined by the producer, has been held to be the producer's "employee." As long as the employer exercises control over such aspects of the workers' employment as the dates and times of performances and the work to be performed, New York law would appear to treat him or her as an employee. The Kennedy Center exercised sufficient control over Makarova to render her an employee as a matter of New York law.

Under District of Columbia law, an "employee" is "every person ... in the service of another under any contract of hire or apprenticeship, written or implied, in the District of Columbia."

Makarova satisfied this definition. She is a person, who was "in the service of another," performing for the Kennedy Center in the District of Columbia. Makarova was also "under a contract of hire," having agreed to play a specific role in "On Your Toes" for a specific amount of time.

The Kennedy Center also qualified as Makarova's "employer" under the District of Columbia Workers' Compensation Act, because it was an "individual, firm, association, or corporation ... using the service of another for pay." The Kennedy Center was the producer of "On Your Toes," and paid Makarova to perform in it....

Moreover, there are equitable considerations compelling the conclusion that Makarova was an "employee" of the Kennedy Center—she had earlier accepted the benefits of being one. On that occasion, Makarova hurt her chin during a rehearsal. Part of the medical treatment that she received for that injury was paid for by the Kennedy Center's workers' compensation insurer, which covered the Kennedy Center's "Players, Entertainers or Musicians" and "all other employees." Having accepted the workers' compensation benefits of being a Kennedy Center employee, Makarova cannot now argue that she should be free of the strictures of that same workers' compensation regime.

Makarova maintains that she was paid by the Kennedy Center as an independent contractor. The evidence of this, however, is equivocal. It is unclear whether Makarova was paid as an independent contractor, an employee, or both, because the Kennedy Center's payroll records prior to 1983 are not in the record. In 1983, after she had rejoined the cast of "On Your Toes" while it was touring, Makarova was listed haphazardly as both an "independent contractor" and a "regular employee" by the Kennedy Center. Makarova did receive an IRS form 1099 in 1982, listing $1275.00 in "nonemployee compensation." However, that amount represented less than her salary from the Kennedy Center for a single two-week pay period. Such a modest sum of "nonemployee compensation" does not establish whether Makarova was classified by the Kennedy Center as an employee or an independent contractor for its payroll purposes. In any event, the occasional characterization of Makarova as an independent contractor in the Kennedy Center's records would be insufficient to classify her under either New York or District of Columbia law as an independent contractor rather than an employee.

Makarova tenders other considerations which she believes make her an independent contractor, including the argument that she was a "star," which somehow apparently makes her something less of an employee. None of these arguments are persuasive. We conclude that Makarova was an employee of the Kennedy Center and, as such, was covered by its workers' compensation insurance. She could not have brought suit against a private employer in Washington, D.C., and therefore, under the FTCA, she could not have done so against the government.

For the foregoing reasons, the district court did not err when it granted the government's motion to dismiss Makarova's complaint.... Accordingly, we AFFIRM the grant of appellee's motion for dismissal for lack of subject matter jurisdiction.

Gennaro v. Rosenfield
600 F. Supp. 485 (S.D.N.Y 1984)

In the eyes of many, Hollywood's heyday was the era of the musical, often based on the Broadway show. One of the preeminent films of that era, "Singin' In The Rain," starred Gene Kelly, Debbie Reynolds, and Donald O'Connor. This litigation concerns an apparently new phenomenon—the proposed stage adaptation of that now legendary film.

The plaintiffs, Peter Gennaro, and his company, Geannie Productions, Inc., allege that Mr. Gennaro has contracted to choreograph the proposed Broadway production of "Singin' In The Rain" for the defendant, Maurice Rosenfield. The plaintiffs claim that the defendant has breached this contract and, therefore, seek damages for breach of contract and defamation. Presently before the Court is the plaintiffs' motion for a preliminary injunction which, in essence, would prevent the defendant from engaging any other choreographer pending the outcome of the litigation. The Court must deny this motion for the reasons stated below.

The individual plaintiff, Peter Gennaro, is a choreographer and dancer. He has choreographed a number of well-known Broadway musicals, including "Fiorello," "The Unsinkable Molly Brown," and "Annie" (for which he won a Tony Award). Mr. Gennaro is also the president of the corporate plaintiff, Geannie Productions, Inc. The defendants, Maurice and Lois Rosenfield, are husband and wife. Mr. Rosenfield is a Broadway producer. Among his credits are the 1980 Broadway musical "Barnum" and the 1983 revival of Tennessee Williams's "The Glass Menagerie." In 1980, Mr. Rosenfield acquired the right to adapt "Singin' In The Rain" for stage presentation from Metro-Goldwyn-Mayer and Robbins Music Company. Rosenfield subsequently granted a license to Harold Fielding for the London production of "Singin' In The Rain."

The events giving rise to the instant controversy commenced in November 1980, when Ian Bevan, a British theatrical agent and manager, contacted Mr. Gennaro's agent and attorney, Robert M. Cavallo. According to Mr. Cavallo, Mr. Bevan said that Mr. Fielding wanted Peter Gennaro to choreograph the London production. Mr. Cavallo relayed this offer to Mr. Gennaro, who allegedly said that he would agree to choreograph the London production only on the condition that he also receive the option to choreograph any first-class stage production of "Singin' In The Rain" in the United States, including any Broadway production. Mr. Gennaro alleges that Mr. Bevan proceeded to negotiate with Mr. Cavallo for Mr. Gennaro's services and with Mr. Rosenfield to obtain the desired option. The plaintiff further alleges that an agreement was reached on both counts and that the option agreement was embodied in a January 20, 1983, letter signed by both Bevan and Rosenfield.

On February 2, 1983, Mr. Fielding forwarded a copy of the January 20 letter to Mr. Gennaro along with his own letter confirming an agreement between himself and Mr. Gennaro. According to this letter, Mr. Bevan had "negotiated conditions for [Mr. Gennaro to choreograph] the American and other first-class productions of "Singin' In The Rain" which [would] be separately confirmed to [Mr. Gennaro] by the American producer, Mr. Maurice Rosenfield." On April 5, 1983, Ronald Taft, Mr. Rosenfield's attorney, forwarded a draft contract to Mr. Cavallo and requested Mr. Cavallo's comments. According to Mr. Rosenfield, this contract concerned both the London and American productions. Mr. Gennaro maintains that the April 5 draft only concerned the London production. For unknown reasons, Mr. Cavallo informed Mr. Taft that he would not comment on the draft. At the same time, Mr. Cavallo was negotiating with Mr. Fielding. On April 14, 1984, Harold Fielding, Ltd. and Geannie Productions, Inc. entered into a written agreement with regard to Mr. Gennaro's role in the London production. Mr. Gennaro alleges that this agreement formalized the January 20 letter with respect to the American production.

In early June, Mr. Rosenfield visited Mr. Cavallo in his New York office. Precisely what transpired at that meeting is unclear. Soon thereafter, Mr. Cavallo sent Mr. Taft a letter commenting on the April 5 draft. There were no further discussions about that document.

The London production opened on June 30, 1983, and is still running. Mr. Gennaro has met twice with Mr. and Mrs. Rosenfield since the opening, once in June 1983, and again in December 1983. Precisely what was said at those meetings is also in dispute.

During the summer of 1984, Mr. Cavallo heard that the American production of "Singin' In The Rain" was being planned and that the plans did not involve Peter Gennaro. On September 17, 1984, Mr. Cavallo sent a mailgram to Mr. Rosenfield advising him that Mr. Gennaro had elected to exercise the option to choreograph the American production. On September 20, 1984, Mr. Taft responded for Mr. Rosenfield in a letter that stated, "Mr. Rosenfield has not asked Mr. Gennaro whether he would like to choreograph the production of "Singin' In The Rain" which Mr. Rosenfield plans to produce in New York." The plaintiffs then brought the instant action by order to show cause seeking, *inter alia*, a preliminary negative injunction enjoining the defendants and their agents from

> (a) producing any American first-class stage production of the musical "Singin' In The Rain" (the "American production") with choreography by any choreographer other than Peter Gennaro;

> (b) entering into any contract for choreography of the American production with any choreographer other than Peter Gennaro;

> (c) advertising, promoting or otherwise publicizing the American production, in print or any other media, whereby the actual or prospective choreography is represented as by any choreographer other than Peter Gennaro....

A court will grant preliminary injunctive relief if a plaintiff can show (a) irreparable harm and (b) either (1) likelihood of success on the merits or (2) sufficiently serious questions going to the merits to make them a fair ground for litigation and a balance of hardships tipping decidedly toward the party requesting the preliminary relief. Even if the plaintiffs have established irreparable harm, they have shown neither a likelihood of success on the merits, nor a balance of hardships tipping decidedly in their favor.

A. Irreparable Harm

An inadequate remedy at law is a necessary prerequisite to a showing of irreparable harm. Mr. Gennaro argues that he will continue to suffer two wrongs for which money damages will not compensate: harm to his reputation and erosion of his professional skills. While it may be that the harm to the plaintiff's reputation constitutes irreparable harm, we do not believe that erosion of his skills constitutes such harm.

Although courts recognize that atrophy of professional skills could constitute irreparable harm, we are aware of only one case finding that, under the facts established, such atrophy constitutes irreparable harm. In that case, *Neeld v. American Hockey League,* 439 F. Supp. 459 (W.D.N.Y. 1977), the court found that a young hockey player would suffer irreparable harm were he denied the right to play professional hockey during the pendency of his lawsuit challenging certain league restrictions that would have prevented him from playing.... Mr. Gennaro argues that the alleged breach of contract will limit his opportunities for work, thereby denying him the chance to develop and refine his skills. The plaintiff's situation, however, differs markedly from the young hockey player's in *Neeld*. The plaintiff, an established choreographer with a first class reputation, will not be denied the opportunity to embark on a promising artistic career. Nor are his skills likely to diminish or atrophy. Since he has already choreographed the London production, the Broadway production represents less than a unique opportunity to develop his skills. In addition, as a top flight choreographer, he is likely to gain other work during the time he would be choreographing "Singin' In The Rain." Thus, we decline to follow *Neeld*. The plaintiff has not established that his skills will diminish so as to cause him irreparable harm.

Mr. Gennaro also asserts that his reputation has been irreparably harmed. In his words,

> The world of theatre is small, and its every event is illuminated by the bright spotlight of public curiosity. Reputations which have been built up over many years can be torn apart overnight when it appears that other artists are more desirable. Colleagues have been asking me why I was "replaced" as choreographer for the American production. The situation is painfully embarrassing to me and is severely damaging the first-class reputation and professional credibility I have worked so hard to establish over so many years. I have no traditional monetary remedy, since no amount of money can fully compensate me for this injury; indeed, its subtle effects can never be fully known.

Several cases from this circuit establish that damage to reputation often constitutes irreparable injury and justifies injunctive relief.... Peter Gennaro has worked for many years to establish a reputation as a first class choreographer. His reputation is of great commercial value to him. The apparent replacement of the plaintiff could damage his reputation in the theatre community. Those who had thought Mr. Gennaro would choreograph the production may now hold him in lower esteem. As the plaintiffs correctly point out, such damage to reputation is difficult if not impossible to measure in money terms.

On the other hand, show business arrangements often take into account considerations other than artistic merit. One bad review cannot tarnish the image of an established artist such as Peter Gennaro. Theatre people may well find fault with Mr. Rosenfield in this situation—particularly in light of the success of the London production. This situation resembles that where a baseball manager replaces the starting pitcher in the late innings despite the fact that he is pitching a shut out and has a comfortable lead. If the relief pitcher fails, the manager looks terrible.

B. The Likelihood of Success on the Merits

Setting aside the question of irreparable harm, we next consider whether the plaintiffs have demonstrated a likelihood of success on the merits. We conclude that they have not.

The nub of this case is a dispute over whether Mr. Rosenfield ever contracted with Mr. Gennaro. In determining whether a contract exists, the objective intent of the parties as manifested by their expressed words and deeds at the time of the alleged contract controls. If the parties' expressions and conduct would lead a reasonable person to determine that they intended to reach a binding agreement, their agreement will be enforced.

Mr. Gennaro asserts that the January 20 letter from Ian Bevan to Maurice Rosenfield countersigned by Mr. Rosenfield, standing alone, constitutes a binding contract. That letter states, in part:

> I write to record the heads of agreement I have reached on your behalf in negotiations with Mr. Robert M. Cavallo ... for the services of Mr. Peter Gennaro as choreographer for the above production [("Singin' In The Rain")].

His services have been engaged by Harold Fielding Ltd. for the London production.... Subject to that production running not less than 100 consecutive performances, you undertake to offer Mr. Gennaro a contract to choreograph the first American and/or Broadway production....

This letter is to record in "heads of agreement" style the basic terms agreed between you and Mr. Gennaro, which terms will now be converted into a formal document or documents in such form as shall be to the approval of your respective legal advisers. By our respective signatures to this letter we confirm to each other and to Mr. Gennaro that the basic terms to be incorporated into the formal documentation are those outlined in this letter.

The letter further specified Gennaro's fee and his share of the royalties. No other terms were detailed.

Acknowledging that this letter contemplated more formal documentation, the plaintiffs nevertheless contend that it constitutes a binding agreement. They rely on authority to the effect that a letter containing the essential terms of a contract may create a binding obligation although the parties may have contemplated executing a more formal agreement at a later date. The plaintiffs argue that the evidence conclusively establishes that the parties intended the January 20 letter to be a contract. The plaintiffs point out that the letter contained the material financial terms of the deal and that Mr. Gennaro's agent made it known to Mr. Fielding that Mr. Gennaro would not choreograph the London production unless he had an option to choreograph the Broadway production. To buttress this position, Mr. Cavallo and Mr. Gennaro also offer their recollection of several conversations with Mr. Rosenfield allegedly confirming the agreement. The plaintiffs also submit a letter from Mr. Bevan that purports to support their position. Standing alone, their evidence might establish the likelihood of success on the merits.

However, the defendants make a number of points in rebuttal. They thus make clear that whether the January 20 letter is a contract is, at most, a serious question going to the merits and a fair ground for litigation.

The defendants first argue that the behavior of the parties subsequent to January 20, 1983, indicated their intention *not* to be bound by the January 20 letter. They also take issue with the plaintiffs' characterization of the January 20 letter. According to the defendants, "the January 20 letter is not a contract because it expressly provides that it is to be followed by a detailed agreement to be crafted and approved by counsel and to contain additional terms." "[Such] an agreement ... does not bind the parties until such documentation and approval are accomplished." ... Whether the parties intended to contract is a serious question for the factfinder.

The defendants also claim that the January 20 letter is not sufficiently definite to constitute a binding agreement. Under the general principles of contract law, there can be no contract if the parties fail to agree on all the essential terms. The January 20, 1983, letter specifies only the fee and royalty terms. Mr. Cavallo asserts that this accords with industry practice, an assertion that the defendants vigorously dispute. We are not sure who has the better of this dispute, but we are certain that the plaintiffs have not demonstrated that they are likely to prevail.

The plaintiffs also argue that, even if the January 20 letter is too indefinite to constitute a contract, the April 14 long form agreement between Geannie Productions, Inc. and Harold Fielding Ltd. is sufficiently definite. This detailed agreement contains the essential terms necessary for a binding contract. However, the defendants argue that Fielding lacked actual or apparent authority to bind Rosenfield. In rebuttal, the plaintiffs argue that, even if Fielding lacked actual authority, he had apparent authority. The *Restatement (Second) of the Law of Agency § 8* defines apparent authority as "the power to affect the legal relations of another person by transactions with third persons, professedly as agent for the other, arising from and in accordance with the other's manifestations to such third persons." According to Mr. Gennaro, Mr. Rosenfield manifested Mr. Fielding's authority in his January 20 letter. The defendants, of course, reject this contention. They claim that the plaintiffs have alleged no act by Mr. Rosenfield whereby he conferred authority upon Mr. Fielding to act as his agent or whereby he communicated that authority to Mr. Gennaro or Mr. Cavallo. Again, the facts are so vague that to draw any conclusion with regard to the likelihood of either side prevailing on the authority issue is impossible....

The foregoing discussion leaves no doubt that the plaintiffs have not established the likelihood of success on the merits. There exist too many unresolved factual questions to justify any such conclusion.

C. The Balance of Hardships

Given our conclusion regarding the likelihood of success on the merits, we may grant the requested relief only if the plaintiff can "show that the harm which he would suffer from the denial of his motion is 'decidedly' greater than the harm which [the defendants] would suffer if the motion was granted." In this case, the balance of hardships does not tip decidedly in favor of the plaintiffs. We therefore decline to grant the requested relief.

If the motion is denied, the plaintiffs may suffer some additional irreparable harm. However, even if we accept Mr. Gennaro's assertion of irreparable harm, most of the damage to his reputation has already been done. No doubt, if we grant the requested relief, a group of individuals who would otherwise learn of Mr. Gennaro's alleged dismissal will remain uninformed (assuming the defendants choose to go ahead with the production). A denial of injunctive relief will harm the plaintiff's reputation among this group. However, the plaintiff's primary concern is his reputation among those in the theatre industry. That group is well informed, and has by now learned of this controversy. Thus, the denial of injunctive relief will do little to mitigate the total harm the plaintiff will suffer as a result of his alleged replacement.

On the other hand, should we grant the requested relief, the defendants will have two choices. They may hire Mr. Gennaro, or abandon the production. Abandonment, while not unrealistic—given the assertions to this effect in Mr. Rosenfield's papers—would constitute self-inflicted harm. We do not believe such harm is cognizable or relevant to our determination. Assuming Mr. Rosenfield opts to have Mr. Gennaro choreograph his production, Mr. Rosenfield would find himself in the uncomfortable position of working closely with someone whom he allegedly had replaced, had litigated against, and had no desire to work with. In addition, Mr. Rosenfield would be forced to abandon any discussions or contract into which he might have already entered with another choreographer. He would then suffer the obvious consequences of such an action. In our view, the defendants will suffer at least as much if not more harm from a grant of injunctive relief than the plaintiffs will suffer from a denial.

Although our judgment about the relative harms each party would suffer is subjective, we think it clear that the plaintiff has failed to show that the balance of hardships tips decidedly in his favor. Therefore, we decline to grant the requested prohibitive injunctive relief.

The plaintiffs' motion for preliminary injunctive relief is denied. We will endeavor to schedule a trial of the factual issues as soon as the parties indicate that they have completed discovery and are ready. SO ORDERED.

Notes and Questions

a. The life of the stage actor remains a difficult one, with extremely high unemployment, long hours during rehearsal, and a high risk that a play may be closed within days of opening. The Equity agreements interpreted in *This is Me v. Taylor*, remain standard for the industry. Central to these are the provisions that minimum weekly pay cannot be waived and that there is personal rather than merely corporate liability.

b. Productions such as *Phantom of the Opera* and *Cirque Du Soleil* are modern examples of the classic stage extravaganza. Flying actors and death-defying stunts are part of the allure. Nonetheless, the activities of actors are that of any other workers and therefore covered by worker's compensation insurance and limits on liability. See *Eckis v. Sea World Corp.*, 64 Cal. App. 3d 1 (Cal. App. 4th Dist. 1976) (injury "sustained while riding Shamu the Whale" limited to worker's compensation system, despite evidence that Sea World knew the whale would attack divers who did not wear wet suits and still asked Ms. Eckis to ride the whale wearing a bikini for publicity pictures).

c. Consider *Bailey v. Disney Worldwide Shared Services*, 950 N.Y.S.2d 607 (N.Y. Sup. Ct. 2012). The Court summarizes the accident and resulting litigation as follows:

> On May 20, 2008, plaintiff, Adrian Bailey, an actor performing in The Little Mermaid, a Broadway musical, walked out onto a bridge suspended 35-feet over the stage in order to get ready for his role in a matinee performance of the play. Trap doors on the bridge, known as the "Eric trap," after a character in the play who descends through the trap doors, had been left open after a pre-show test. Plaintiff fell through the open trap doors and suffered serious injuries. A backstage automation operator controlled the trap doors. The automation operator failed to look at the display monitors showing that the trap doors had not been closed after the pre-show check, as he was playing a video game on his personal computer instead of checking the monitors.

> Showman, pursuant to a purchasing agreement with Disney, built the bridge along with its trap doors. Niscon, which did not have a direct contractual relationship with Disney, provided the automation system, known as Raynok, that allowed the trap doors on the bridge to be remotely operated. Disney then sold the bridge to Buena Vista Theatrical Group, LTD (Buena Vista), another Disney entity which produced the Little Mermaid; Buena Vista was the employer of both plaintiff and the automation operator who failed to check his monitor. The Nederlander entities leased the theater used in The Little Mermaid and provided some union labor to the production, including a stage hand who was supposed to check the bridge before allowing actors on to it.

> Plaintiff's allegations in the amended complaint and bill of particulars are made generally against all defendants. Plaintiff alleges that defendants are liable in negligence (first cause of action), as well as for breach of the warranties of fitness for a particular use (the second cause of action) and merchantability (the third cause of action); finally, plaintiff alleges that defendants are liable under a theory of strict products liability (fourth cause of action).

Which parties will be liable for the injuries, if any, sustained by the performer Adrian Bailey?

d. Because of the strength of the theatrical unions, this industry is generally better than most others in having its agreements in writing. A second aspect of this structure is that only a few of the many possible terms involving theatrical production are actually negotiable. Despite the express language of such contracts that they must be signed to be binding, does an oral promise to enter into an approved collective bargaining agreement serve to bind the parties? See *Elvin Associates v. Franklin*, 735 F. Supp. 1177 (S.D.N.Y. 1990) (Aretha Franklin agreed to appear in *Sing Mahalia Sing*, based on the life of Mahalia Jackson. The producer relied on oral promises and arranged the production. Franklin ultimately dropped out of the production as a result of her fear of flying and inability to travel.).

e. The hiring process for theatre is complicated by the very particular needs for each part, more general employment law, and the competing interests of directors, playwrights, and producers. Producers may be seeking marquee value, playwrights see the images of the actors who were in their imagination while writing, and directors need a cast which blends together and meets the director's vision. Noted director Harold Clurman wrote that "the writer, who contractually has the last word in the matter, must sometimes be persuaded that the actor the director wants is the right choice for a particular role." Harold Clurman, On Directing 66 (Fireside ed., 1997).

f. Federal employment antidiscrimination law under Title VII of the Civil Rights Act of 1964, generally prohibits all forms of discrimination in hiring. An exception exists, however, so that "[i]t shall not be an unlawful employment practice for an employer to hire and employ employees ... on the basis of his religion, sex, or national origin in those certain instances where religion, sex, or national origin is a bona fide occupational qualification reasonably necessary to the normal operation of that particular business or enterprise...." 42 U.S.C. § 2000e-2(e) (1994). Race is not included in the exception. To what extent would the courts be compelled to read race into the statute under First Amendment principles, or on a similar basis? Would the decision change based on whether the part was for a principal part rather than merely a chorus member?

g. Sometimes performers themselves become controversial. See *Redgrave v. Boston Symphony Orchestra, Inc.*, 855 F.2d 888, 904 (1988) (en banc). The Boston Symphony Orchestra found grudging legal support after it cancelled Vanessa Redgrave's performance in response to her support of the Palestine Liberation Organization.

h. Like every art form, some performances are only about the reward. Does an actor in a one-person show have any legitimate grounds to demand his right to be considered for a Tony award? See *Mason v. American Theatre Wing*, 165 Misc. 2d 432, 627 N.Y.S.2d 539 (N.Y. Sup. Ct. 1995).

Problem IX-B

Based on the suggestions you provided to Bryce, *Juliet Prescott* has been added to the upcoming theatrical season of the Kernochan Theatre, a premiere LORT theatre in upper Manhattan. Bryce is serving as director for the production. Bryce has been paid $2,500 for three weeks of rehearsal, as well as the LORT minimums in the dual capacity of director and playwright.

Bryce was having a great time working with accomplished professional talent during the rehearsal. The creativity of the cast has resulted in Bryce's changing a good deal of the stage direction and even some of the script to capture the thoughts and suggestions of the cast.

Unfortunately, at the end of the second week of rehearsal, Bryce fell off a platform that had been constructed but not yet secured on the set. The theatre engineer has acknowledged that the platform should not have been available for use until it had been secured and has sent an apology to Bryce and Bryce's family.

From the hospital, you have received a telephone call. Bryce's mother wants Bryce to sue the theatre for the accident. Bryce is primarily concerned about keeping control of the production as director and playwright. Bryce wants the production to be postponed. While Bryce is hopeful the hospital stay will only last a few days, Bryce wants to know what will happen if the injury is much worse. Advise Bryce regarding (i) the potential to sue the theatre for negligence and (ii) the theatre's ability to continue to stage the play without Bryce, including the theatre's ability to modify the script. (You may find it helpful to preview the discussion involving the Approved Production Contract, below, on the question of modification of the script.)

C. Playwrights

1. The Approved Production Contract

In explaining the central tenets of the Approved Production Contract to potential member playwrights, the Dramatists Guild explains the agreements as follows:

The Guild maintains standard or model contracts for all levels of productions: First-Class/Broadway, regional, and smaller houses nationwide; plus other important model contracts such as commission agreements and collaboration agreements — the most comprehensive contracts in the world. Under these contracts:

- No additions, omissions, or alterations to your script may be made without your consent.

- You and the producer have the approval of the cast, director, and designers, and will confer on many elements of the production.

- The rights granted to the producer cease if you are not paid your royalties.

- You own the copyright and all other rights to the play.

- You reserve the right to control the play for all other performances and uses.

The influence provided to playwrights pursuant to these agreements cannot be understated. No other media allows the creative writer such authority and autonomy.

Perhaps the most striking aspect of the Approved Production Contract is that the provisions granting approval have no requirements of reasonability, while ensuring that no changes can be made without the author's approval.

Sections 8.01(b) and 8.01(c) provide that a dissatisfied producer can object to the playwright's position to the Dramatists Guild. While the Dramatists Guild can confer with the playwright, it "shall have no power to compel Author to agree to such change." Powerful contract language, indeed.

Childress v. Taylor
945 F.2d 500 (2d Cir. 1991)

This appeal requires consideration of the standards for determining when a contributor to a copyrighted work is entitled to be regarded as a joint author. The work in question is a play about the legendary Black comedienne Jackie "Moms" Mabley. The plaintiff-appellee Alice Childress claims to be the sole author of the play. Her claim is disputed by defendant-appellant Clarice Taylor, who asserts that she is a joint author of the play. Taylor, Paul B. Berkowsky, Ben Caldwell, and the "Moms" Company appeal from the February 21, 1991, judgment of the District Court for the Southern District of New York (Charles S. Haight, Jr., Judge) determining, on motion for summary judgment, that Childress is the sole author. We affirm.

Defendant Clarice Taylor has been an actress for over forty years, performing on stage, radio, television, and in film. After portraying "Moms" Mabley in a skit in an off-off-Broadway production ten years ago, Taylor became interested in developing a play based on Mabley's life. Taylor began to assemble material about "Moms" Mabley, interviewing her friends and family, collecting her jokes, and reviewing library resources.

In 1985, Taylor contacted the plaintiff, playwright Alice Childress, about writing a play based on "Moms" Mabley. Childress had written many plays, for one of which she won an "Obie" award. Taylor had known Childress since the 1940s when they were both associated with the American Negro Theatre in Harlem and had previously acted in a number of Childress's plays....

Taylor turned over all of her research material to Childress, and later did further research at Childress's request. It is undisputed that Childress wrote the play, entitled "Moms: A Praise Play for a Black Comedienne." However, Taylor, in addition to providing the research material, which according to her involved a process of sifting through facts and selecting pivotal and key elements to include in a play on "Moms" Mabley's life, also discussed with Childress the inclusion of certain general scenes and characters in the play. Additionally, Childress and Taylor spoke on a regular basis about the progress of the play....

Childress filed for and received a copyright for the play in her name. Taylor produced the play at the Green Plays Theatre in Lexington, New York, during the 1986 summer season and played the title role. After the play's run at the Green Plays Theatre, Taylor planned a second production of the play at the Hudson Guild Theatre in New York City.

At the time Childress agreed to the project, she did not have any firm arrangements with Taylor, although Taylor had paid her $2,500 before the play was produced. On May 9, 1986, Taylor's agent, Scott Yoselow, wrote to Childress's agent, Flora Roberts, stating:

> Per our telephone conversation, this letter will bring us up-to-date on the current status of our negotiation for the above mentioned project:
>
>   1. CLARICE TAYLOR will pay ALICE CHILDRESS for her playwriting services on the MOMS MABLEY PROJECT the sum of $5,000.00, which will also serve as an advance against any future royalties.
>
>   2. The finished play shall be equally owned and be the property of both CLARICE TAYLOR and ALICE CHILDRESS.
>
> It is my understanding that Alice has commenced writing the project. I am awaiting a response from you regarding any additional points we have yet to discuss.

Flora Roberts responded to Yoselow in a letter dated June 16, 1986:

> As per our recent telephone conversation, I have told Alice Childress that we are using your letter to me of May 9, 1986 as a partial memo preparatory to our future good faith negotiations for a contract. There are two points which I include herewith to complete your two points in the May 9th letter, i.e.:
>
>   1) The $5,000 advance against any future royalties being paid by Clarice Taylor to Alice Childress shall be paid as follows. Since $1,000 has already been

paid, $1,500 upon your receipt of this letter and the final $2,500 to be paid upon submission of the First Draft, but in no event later than July 7, 1986.

2) It is to be understood that pending the proper warranty clauses to be included in the contract, Miss Childress is claiming originality for her words only in said script....

In March 1987, Childress rejected the draft agreement proposed by Taylor, and the parties' relationship deteriorated. Taylor decided to mount another production of the play without Childress. Taylor hired Ben Caldwell to write another play featuring "Moms" Mabley; Taylor gave Caldwell a copy of the Childress script and advised him of elements that should be changed....

Taylor contended that she was a joint author with Childress, and therefore shared the rights to the play....

Co-authorship was well known to the common law. An early formulation, thought by Learned Hand to be the first definition of "joint authorship," [as] "a joint laboring in furtherance of a common design." Judge Hand endorsed that formulation in the District Court, concluding that the book for the comic opera "Sweethearts" was a work of joint authorship.... The [1976] Copyright Act defines a "joint work" as

a work prepared by two or more authors with the intention that their contributions be merged into inseparable or interdependent parts of a unitary whole....

In common with many issues arising in the domain of copyrights, the determination of whether to recognize joint authorship in a particular case requires a sensitive accommodation of competing demands advanced by at least two persons, both of whom have normally contributed in some way to the creation of a work of value. Care must be taken to ensure that true collaborators in the creative process are accorded the perquisites of co-authorship and to guard against the risk that a sole author is denied exclusive authorship status simply because another person rendered some form of assistance. Copyright law best serves the interests of creativity when it carefully draws the bounds of "joint authorship" so as to protect the legitimate claims of both sole authors and coauthors.

Some aspects of the statutory definition of joint authorship are fairly straightforward. Parts of a unitary whole are "inseparable" when they have little or no independent meaning standing alone. That would often be true of a work of written text, such as the play that is the subject of the pending litigation. By contrast, parts of a unitary whole are "interdependent" when they have some meaning standing alone but achieve their primary significance because of their combined effect, as in the case of the words and music of a song....

The legislative history also clarifies other aspects of the statutory definition, but leaves some matters in doubt. Endeavoring to flesh out the definition, the committee reports state:

[A] work is "joint" if the authors collaborated with each other, or if *each* of the authors prepared his or her contribution with the knowledge and *intention* that it would be merged with the contributions of other authors as "inseparable or interdependent parts of a unitary whole." The touchstone here is the *intention, at the time the writing is done,* that the parts be absorbed or combined into an integrated unit....

This passage appears to state two alternative criteria—one focusing on the act of collaboration and the other on the parties' intent. However, it is hard to imagine activity that would constitute meaningful "collaboration" unaccompanied by the requisite intent on the part of both participants that their contributions be merged into a unitary whole, and the case law has read the statutory language literally so that the intent requirement applies to all works of joint authorship.

A more substantial issue arising under the statutory definition of "joint work" is whether the contribution of each joint author must be copyrightable or only the combined result of their joint efforts must be copyrightable. . . .

The insistence on copyrightable contributions by all putative joint authors might serve to prevent some spurious claims by those who might otherwise try to share the fruits of the efforts of a sole author of a copyrightable work, even though a claim of having contributed copyrightable material could be asserted by those so inclined. More important, the prevailing view strikes an appropriate balance in the domains of both copyright and contract law. In the absence of contract, the copyright remains with the one or more persons who created copyrightable material. Contract law enables a person to hire another to create a copyrightable work, and the copyright law will recognize the employer as "author." Similarly, the person with non-copyrightable material who proposes to join forces with a skilled writer to produce a copyrightable work is free to make a contract to disclose his or her material in return for assignment of part ownership of the resulting copyright. And, as with all contract matters, the parties may minimize subsequent disputes by formalizing their agreement in a written contract.

It seems more consistent with the spirit of copyright law to oblige all joint authors to make copyrightable contributions, leaving those with non-copyrightable contributions to protect their rights through contract.

There remains for consideration the crucial aspect of joint authorship—the nature of the intent that must be entertained by each putative joint author at the time the contribution of each was created. The wording of the statutory definition appears to make relevant only the state of mind regarding the unitary nature of the finished work—an intention "that their contributions be merged into inseparable or interdependent parts of a unitary whole." However, an inquiry so limited would extend joint author status to many persons who are not likely to have been within the contemplation of Congress. For example, a writer frequently works with an editor who makes numerous useful revisions to the first draft, some of which will consist of additions of copyrightable expression. Both intend their contributions to be merged into inseparable parts of a unitary whole, yet very few editors and even fewer writers would expect the editor to be accorded the status of joint author, enjoying an undivided half interest in the copyright in the published work.

Similarly, research assistants may on occasion contribute to an author some protectable expression or merely a sufficiently original selection of factual material as would be entitled to a copyright, yet not be entitled to be regarded as a joint author of the work in which the contributed material appears. What distinguishes the writer-editor relationship and the writer-researcher relationship from the true joint author relationship is the lack of intent of both participants in the venture to regard themselves as joint authors.

Focusing on whether the putative joint authors regarded themselves as joint authors is especially important in circumstances, such as the instant case, where one person (Childress) is indisputably the dominant author of the work and the only issue is whether that person is the sole author or she and another (Taylor) are joint authors. This concern requires less exacting consideration in the context of traditional forms of collaboration, such as between the creators of the words and music of a song. . . .

Though joint authorship does not require an understanding by the co-authors of the legal consequences of their relationship, obviously some distinguishing characteristic of the relationship must be understood in order for it to be the subject of their intent. In many instances, a useful test will be whether, in the absence of contractual agreements concerning listed authorship, each participant intended that all would be identified as co-authors. Though "billing" or "credit" is not decisive in all cases and joint authorship can exist without any explicit discussion of this topic by the parties, consideration of the topic helpfully serves to focus the fact-finder's attention on how the parties implicitly regarded their undertaking. . . .

Examination of whether the putative co-authors ever shared an intent to be co-authors serves the valuable purpose of appropriately confining the bounds of joint authorship arising by operation of copyright law, while leaving those not in a true joint authorship relationship with an author free to bargain for an arrangement that will be recognized as a matter of both copyright and contract law. Joint authorship entitles the co-authors to equal undivided interests in the work. That equal sharing of rights should be reserved for relationships in which all participants fully intend to be joint authors. The sharing of benefits in other relationships involving assistance in the creation of a copyrightable work can be more precisely calibrated by the participants in their contract negotiations regarding division of royalties or assignment of shares of ownership of the copyright. . . .

Childress was asked to write a play about "Moms" Mabley and did so. To facilitate her writing task, she accepted the assistance that Taylor provided, which consisted largely of furnishing the results of research concerning the life of "Moms" Mabley. As the actress expected to portray the leading role, Taylor also made some incidental suggestions, contributing ideas about the presentation of the play's subject and possibly some minor bits of expression. But there is no evidence that these aspects of Taylor's role ever evolved into more than the helpful advice that might come from the cast, the directors, or the producers of any play. A playwright does not so easily acquire a co-author.

Judge Haight was fully entitled to bolster his decision by reliance on the contract negotiations that followed completion of the script. Though his primary basis for summary judgment was the absence of any evidence supporting an inference that Childress shared "Taylor's notion that they were co-authors," he properly pointed to the emphatic rejection by Childress of the attempts by Taylor's agent to negotiate a co-ownership agreement and Taylor's acquiescence in that rejection. Intent "at the time the writing is done" remains the "touchstone," but subsequent conduct is normally probative of a prior state of mind.

Taylor's claim of co-authorship was properly rejected, and with the rejection of that claim, summary judgment for Childress was properly entered on her copyright and unfair competition claims, and on defendants' counterclaim. The judgment of the District Court is affirmed.

Thomson v. Larson
147 F.3d 195 (2d Cir. 1998)

Rent, the Pulitzer Prize and Tony Award-winning Broadway modern musical based on Puccini's opera *La Boheme*, began in 1989 as the joint project of Billy Aronson and composer Jonathan Larson. Aronson and Larson collaborated on the work until their amicable separation in 1991. At that time, Larson obtained Aronson's permission to develop the play on his own. By written agreement, Larson promised that the title would always be

"RENT a rock opera by Jonathan Larson. Original concept and additional lyrics by Billy Aronson." In return, Aronson agreed that he would "not … be considered [an] active collaborator or co-author of RENT."

In the summer of 1992, Larson's *Rent* script was favorably received by James Nicola, Artistic Director of the New York Theatre Workshop ("NYTW"), a nonprofit theater company in the East Village. Larson continued to develop and revise the "workshop version" of his *Rent* script. In the spring of 1993, Nicola urged Larson to allow the NYTW to hire a playwright or a bookwriter to help revamp the storyline and narrative structure of the play. But Larson "absolutely, vehemently and totally rejected [Nicola's] suggestion of hiring a bookwriter" and "was insistent on making RENT entirely his own project." Larson received a grant in the spring of 1994 to pay for a workshop production of *Rent*, which was presented to the public in the fall of 1994 in a series of ten staged performances produced by the NYTW and directed by Michael Greif. "The professional consensus concerning the show, after the studio production, was that it was, at a minimum, very promising and that it needed a great deal of work." Artistic Director Nicola once again suggested to Larson that he consider working with a bookwriter, which Larson "adamantly and steadfastly refused, consistently emphasizing his intention to be the only author of RENT."

In May 1995, in preparation for *Rent*'s off-Broadway opening scheduled for early 1996, Larson agreed to the NYTW's hiring of Lynn Thomson, a professor of advanced playwrighting at New York University, as a dramaturg[3] to assist him in clarifying the storyline of the musical. Thomson signed a contract with the NYTW, in which she agreed to provide her services with the workshop production from May 1, 1995, through the press opening, scheduled for early February of 1996. The agreement stated that Thomson's "responsibilities shall include, but not be limited to: Providing dramaturgical assistance and research to the playwright and director." In exchange, the NYTW agreed to pay "a fee" of $2000, "in full consideration of the services to be rendered" and to provide for billing credit for Thomson as "Dramaturg." The Thomson/NYTW agreement was silent as to any copyright interests or any issue of ownership with respect to the final work.

In the summer and fall of 1995, Thomson and Larson worked extremely intensively together on the show. For the most part, the two worked on the script alone in Larson's apartment. Thomson testified that revisions to the text of *Rent* didn't begin until early August 1995. Larson himself entered all changes directly onto his computer, where he kept the script, and Thomson made no contemporaneous notes of her specific contributions of language or other structural or thematic suggestions. Thomson alludes to the "October Version" of *Rent* as the culmination of her collaborative efforts with Larson. That new version was characterized by experts as "a radical transformation of the show."

A "sing-through" of the "October Version" of *Rent* took place in early November 1995. And on November 3, 1995, Larson signed a contract with the NYTW for ongoing revisions to *Rent*. This agreement identified Larson as the "Author" of *Rent* and made no reference to Thomson. The contract incorporated by reference an earlier draft author's agreement that set forth the terms that would apply if the NYTW opted to produce *Rent*. The earlier draft author's agreement gave Larson approval rights over all changes in text, provided that any changes in text would become his property, and assured him billing as "sole author."

---

3. Dramaturgs provide a range of services to playwrights and directors in connection with the production and development of theater pieces. According to Thomson's testimony, the role of the dramaturg "can include any number of the elements that go into the crafting of a play," such as "actual plot elements, dramatic structure, character details, themes, and even specific language."

The final dress rehearsal was held on January 24, 1996. Just hours after it ended, Larson died suddenly of an aortic aneurysm. Over the next few weeks, Nicola, Greif, Thomson, and musical director Tim Weil worked together to fine-tune the script.[4] The play opened off-Broadway on February 13, 1996, to rave reviews. On February 23, *Rent*'s move to Broadway was announced. Since its opening on Broadway on April 29, 1996, the show has been "an astounding critical, artistic, and commercial success."

Before the Broadway opening, Thomson, in view of her contributions to *Rent*, sought compensation and title page dramaturgical credit from the Broadway producers. And on April 2, 1996, she signed a contract in which the producers agreed to pay her $10,000 plus a nominal $50/week for her dramaturgical services. Around the same time, upon the producers' advice, Thomson approached Allan S. Larson, Nanette Larson, and Julie Larson McCollum ("Larson Heirs"), the surviving members of Jonathan Larson's family, to request a percentage of the royalties derived from the play. In a letter to the Larson family, dated April 8, 1996, Thomson stated that she believed Larson, had he lived, would have offered her a "small percentage of his royalties to acknowledge the contribution I made." In reply, the Larson Heirs offered Thomson a gift of 1% of the author's royalties. Negotiations between Thomson and the Larson Heirs, however, broke down.

After the parties failed to reach a settlement, Thomson brought suit against the Larson Heirs, claiming that she was a co-author of *Rent* and that she had never assigned, licensed, or otherwise transferred her rights. Thomson sought declaratory relief and a retroactive and on-going accounting under the Copyright Act. Specifically, she asked that the court declare her a "co-author" of *Rent* and grant her 16% of the author's share of the royalties....

The district court properly defined the principal question in this case as: "not whether Lynn Thomson made a great contribution to the show. It is not whether she has been or ought to be compensated differently than she has been compensated. It is about whether what happened between Lynn Thomson and Jon Larson met the statutory definition as it has been construed by the higher courts of a joint work." In analyzing this issue, the district court made numerous findings of fact and then applied the *Childress* test to these facts.

... [The Court first reviews the standard provided in *Childress v. Taylor*.]

The potential danger of allowing anyone who makes even a minimal contribution to the writing of a work to be deemed a statutory co-author — as long as the two parties intended the contributions to merge — motivated the court to set forth a two-pronged test. A co-authorship claimant bears the burden of establishing that each of the putative co-authors (1) made independently copyrightable contributions to the work; and (2) fully intended to be co-authors. The court attempted to strike a balance between "ensuring that true collaborators in the creative process are accorded the perquisites of co-authorship," while at the same time, "guarding against the risk that a sole author is denied exclusive authorship status simply because another person renders some form of assistance."

1. Independently Copyrightable Contributions

Childress held that collaboration alone is not sufficient to establish joint authorship. Rather, the contribution of each joint author must be independently copyrightable. Without

---

4. All four agreed that they would not claim authorship in any of the material created during this time. Accordingly, before *Rent* opened off-Broadway, Nancy Dickmann, Managing Director of the NYTW, asked each of them to sign waivers disclaiming any copyright interest in the material they contributed. Thomson alone refused.

making specific findings as to any of Thomson's claims regarding lyrics or other contributions, the district court concluded that Thomson "made at least some non-*de minimis* copyrightable contribution," and that Thomson's contributions to the *Rent* libretto were "certainly not zero." Once having said that, the court decided the case on the second *Childress* prong — mutual intent of co-authorship. It hence did not reach the issue of the individual copyrightability of Thomson's varied alleged contributions (plot developments, thematic elements, character details, and structural components).

2. Intent of the Partiesa. Mutual Intent Requirement

Childress mandates that the parties "entertain in their minds the concept of joint authorship." This requirement of mutual intent recognizes that, since co-authors are afforded equal rights in the co-authored work, the "equal sharing of rights should be reserved for relationships in which all participants fully intend to be joint authors." ...

The [*Childress*] court stated that "in many instances, a useful test will be whether, in the absence of contractual arrangements concerning listed authorship, each participant intended that all would be identified as co-authors." But it is also clear that the intention standard is not strictly subjective. In other words, co-authorship intent does not turn solely on the parties' own words or professed state of mind. Rather, the *Childress* court suggested a more nuanced inquiry into factual indicia of ownership and authorship, such as how a collaborator regarded herself in relation to the work in terms of billing and credit, decision making, and the right to enter into contracts....

b. Evidence of Larson's Intent

i. Decision making Authority

An important indicator of authorship is a contributor's decision making authority over what changes are made and what is included in a work. The district court determined that Larson "retained and intended to retain at all times sole decision-making authority as to what went into [*Rent*]." In support of its conclusion, the court relied upon Thomson's statement that she was "flattered that [Larson] was asking [her] to contribute actual language to the text" and found that this statement demonstrated that even Thomson understood "that the question whether any contribution she might make would go into the script was within Mr. Larson's sole and complete discretion."[5] Moreover, as the court recognized, the November agreement between Larson and the NYTW expressly stated that Larson had final approval over all changes to *Rent* and that all such changes would become Larson's property.

In this respect, the district court also credited a telephone interview Larson gave in October 1995 to a high school student, in which Larson "said, in substance, that he wrote everything in *Rent* and distinguished writers in the theater from writers in the other media by saying that in the theater the writer is the king." ("In theater, as opposed to film and television, dramatists retain copyright to their work, [and] are independent contractors....") The district court found this statement significant because it "evidences Mr. Larson's view that *Rent* in all respects was his, he was the king."

---

5. There was also documentary evidence before the district court that confirmed the advisory nature of Thomson's role. Thus, a set of notes Thomson wrote to Larson began, "Please know that everything is intended as a question but might sound differently in the shorthand of the writing." And other notes, addressed to Nicola and Grief, read: "Usual disclaimer; the following is meant to generate discussion. Even when I offer 'solutions' what I mean is only to communicate a response by example...."

ii. Billing

… The district court found … that the billing was unequivocal: "Every script brought to [the court's] attention says "*Rent*, by Jonathan Larson." In addition, Larson "described himself in the biography he submitted for the playbill in January 1996, nine days before he died, as the author/composer, and listed Ms. Thomson on the same document as dramaturg." And while, as Ms. Thomson argues, it may indeed have been highly unusual for an author/composer to credit his dramaturg with a byline, we fail to see how Larson's decision to style her as "dramaturg" on the final page in *Rent* scripts reflects a co-authorship intent on the part of Larson. The district court properly concluded that "the manner in which [Larson] listed credits on the scripts strongly supports the view that he regarded himself as the sole author."

iii. Written Agreements with Third Parties

Just as the parties' written agreements with each other can constitute evidence of whether the parties considered themselves to be co-authors, so the parties' agreements with outsiders also can provide insight into co-authorship intent, albeit to a somewhat more attenuated degree.

The district court found that Larson "listed himself or treated himself as the author in the November 1995 revisions contract that he entered into with the NYTW, which in turn incorporated the earlier draft author's agreement that had not been signed." That agreement identifies Larson as Rent's "Author" and does not mention Thomson.…

c. Conclusion

Based on all of the evidence, the district court concluded that "Mr. Larson never regarded himself as a joint author with Ms. Thomson." We believe that the district court correctly applied the *Childress* standards to the evidence before it and hold that its finding that Larson never intended co-authorship was not clearly erroneous.…

[Thomson also asserted rights to her portions of Rent used in the production. The court dismissed these claims because they had not been brought out at trial, but suggesting that Thomson may have exclusive rights to some portions of Rent that can be asserted.]

Notes and Questions

a. Perhaps one of the greatest changes from the Minimum Basic Production Contract to the Approved Production Contract was the formulation for a producer's rights to subsidiary income. As the financial risk for producing Broadway plays has increased dramatically in the past few decades, producers need the potential windfall that a play might have if adapted as a movie or television series. Nonetheless, questions remain as to the scope of these provisions. See *Houlihan v. McCourt,* 2002 U.S. Dist. LEXIS 13850 (N.D. Ill. July 23, 2002) (involving the rights to receive book and motion picture income where the book and film were based on the life story of the author but not his autobiographical play).

b. Although issues of joint authorship occur from time to time in every industry, it has been theatrical productions that have generated the most significant legal issues. This is likely caused by the fact that film, television, and recording industries are large business enterprises which contractually assign copyright to the corporate entity, aggregating the copyright interests acquired from the various participants. If every potential joint author has signed an assignment of copyright for the benefit of the corporate producer, it is far less relevant what the technical copyright status had been for each of the assignees.

Nonetheless, there have been a few instances of litigation involving joint authorship in media other than theatre. See *Corwin v. Quinonez*, 858 F. Supp. 2d 903 (N.D. Ohio 2012) (after band's demise, plaintiff band member sought declaratory judgment that he was joint author of compositions recorded by band); *Gaiman v. McFarlane*, 360 F.3d 644 (7th Cir. 2004) (author Neil Gaiman sought declaratory judgment that he was joint author of certain comic book characters used by Todd McFarlane); *Aalmuhammed v. Lee*, 202 F.3d 1227 (9th Cir. 1999) (participant in production of *Malcolm X* claimed joint authorship with filmmaker Spike Lee).

c. *Aalmuhammed v. Lee* provides some insights into the difference between theatrical and motion picture production.

In 1991, Warner Brothers contracted with Spike Lee and his production companies to make the movie *Malcolm X*, to be based on the book, *The Autobiography of Malcolm X*. Lee co-wrote the screenplay, directed, and co-produced the movie, which starred Denzel Washington as Malcolm X. Washington asked Jefri Aalmuhammed to assist him in his preparation for the starring role because Aalmuhammed knew a great deal about Malcolm X and Islam. Aalmuhammed, a devout Muslim, was particularly knowledgeable about the life of Malcolm X, having previously written, directed, and produced a documentary film about Malcolm X.

Aalmuhammed joined Washington on the movie set. The movie was filmed in the New York metropolitan area and Egypt. Aalmuhammed presented evidence that his involvement in making the movie was very extensive. He reviewed the shooting script for Spike Lee and Denzel Washington and suggested extensive script revisions. Some of his script revisions were included in the released version of the film; others were filmed but not included in the released version. Most of the revisions Aalmuhammed made were to ensure the religious and historical accuracy and authenticity of scenes depicting Malcolm X's religious conversion and pilgrimage to Mecca.

Aalmuhammed submitted evidence that he directed Denzel Washington and other actors while on the set, created at least two entire scenes with new characters, translated Arabic into English for subtitles, supplied his own voice for voice-overs, selected the proper prayers and religious practices for the characters, and edited parts of the movie during post production. Washington testified in his deposition that Aalmuhammed's contribution to the movie was "great" because he "helped to rewrite, to make more authentic." Once production ended, Aalmuhammed met with numerous Islamic organizations to persuade them that the movie was an accurate depiction of Malcolm X's life.

Aalmuhammed never had a written contract with Warner Brothers, Lee, or Lee's production companies, but he expected Lee to compensate him for his work. He did not intend to work and bear his expenses in New York and Egypt gratuitously. Aalmuhammed ultimately received a check for $25,000 from Lee, which he cashed, and a check for $100,000 from Washington, which he did not cash....

Aalmuhammed claimed that the movie *Malcolm X* was a "joint work" of which he was an author, thus making him a co-owner of the copyright. He sought a declaratory judgment to that effect, and an accounting for profits. He is not claiming copyright merely in what he wrote or contributed, but rather in the whole work, as a co-author of a "joint work." The district court granted defendants summary judgment against Mr. Aalmuhammed's copyright claims....

A "joint work" in this circuit "requires each author to make an independently copyrightable contribution" to the disputed work. *Malcolm X* is a copyrightable work, and it is undisputed that the movie was intended by everyone involved with it to be a unitary whole. It is also undisputed that Aalmuhammed made substantial and valuable contributions to the movie, including technical help, such as speaking Arabic to the persons in charge of the mosque in Egypt, scholarly and creative help, such as teaching the actors how to pray properly as Muslims, and script changes to add verisimilitude to the religious aspects of the movie.... The best objective manifestation of a shared intent, of course, is a contract saying that the parties intend to be or not to be co-authors. In the absence of a contract, the inquiry must of necessity focus on the facts.... Aalmuhammed was not the person who has actually formed the picture by putting the persons in position, and arranging the place.... Spike Lee was, so far as we can tell from the record. Aalmuhammed, like Larson's dramaturg, could make extremely helpful recommendations, but Spike Lee was not bound to accept any of them, and the work would not benefit in the slightest unless Spike Lee chose to accept them. Aalmuhammed lacked control over the work, and absence of control is strong evidence of the absence of co-authorship....

Warner Brothers required Spike Lee to sign a "work for hire" agreement, so that even Lee would not be a co-author and co-owner with Warner Brothers. It would be illogical to conclude that Warner Brothers, while not wanting to permit Lee to own the copyright, intended to share ownership with individuals like Aalmuhammed who worked under Lee's control, especially ones who at the time had made known no claim to the role of co-author. No one, including Aalmuhammed, made any indication to anyone prior to litigation that Aalmuhammed was intended to be a co-author and co-owner....

The broader construction that Aalmuhammed proposes would extend joint authorship to many "overreaching contributors," like the dramaturg in *Thomson*, and deny sole authors "exclusive authorship status simply because another person rendered some form of assistance." Claim jumping by research assistants, editors, and former spouses, lovers and friends would endanger authors who talked with people about what they were doing, if creative copyrightable contribution were all that authorship required.

Id. at 1229–36.

d. In both *Childress* and *Thomson*, the actual cases turned much more on intent than on questions of independent copyrightability. Perhaps the position advanced by Professor Nimmer then is more appropriate: that the combined work need be copyrightable, but that each contribution need not be. In the event one party provides a highly abstract outline of characters, plots, and settings to the second author, who creates the copyrighted expression based on that work, what is the legal status of each author?

Assuming that the intent of the parties to create a joint work was manifest, should the court enforce that understanding or strip the first partner of her efforts? Assuming there is a written agreement between the parties to be treated as joint authors, does the Second Circuit approach require that the court deny the terms of the agreement if it cannot find independent creation of authorship from each party?

e. Because the Dramatists Guild is not a union, it does not operate under an exemption from the anti-trust laws. To address this decades-old problem, legislation entitled "The Playwrights' Licensing Relief Act of 2002" was drafted to allow collective bargaining by the Dramatists Guild notwithstanding its non-union status. The legislation has yet to be enacted, and the Dramatists Guild remains in its precarious position.

f. In contrast to *Aalmuhammed*, the role of a band or musical performer as joint author may raise additional interests in the filming of that performance. Does an actor have a copyright interest in her filmed performance? What if the actor is also a performing musician? See *Morrill v. Smashing Pumpkins*, 157 F. Supp. 2d 1120, 2001 U.S. Dist. LEXIS 16720 (C.D. Cal. 2001).

g. Like *Childress v. Taylor*, the problem of joint authorship seems exacerbated in the highly collaborative environment of smaller, non-union theatres. Does the hiring of a playwright to create a script specifically for the theatre add to the suggestion of joint authorship or provide a justification of a work for hire relationship? See *Cabrera v. Teatro del Sesenta, Inc.*, 914 F. Supp. 743 (D.P.R. 1995).

Problem IX-C

Fortunately for Bryce, the injury sustained from the fall during rehearsal was less problematic than initially feared. Bryce recovered quickly enough for *Juliet Prescott* to be delayed only one week. Good reviews and an enthusiastic producer have kept the show running for an additional three weeks.

While the New York producers were impressed with the current, LORT version of *Juliet Prescott*, they would like it to be expanded into a full-blown Broadway musical. They introduced Bryce to a few possible composers to assist Bryce in punching up the musical numbers, perhaps add an additional opening number to the second act, and "improve the sophistication of a few refrains."

Bryce is unsure of what this would mean in terms of control of the production. Bryce is also unsure what financial and control interest this new composer would have in the musical if they did decide to work together. Bryce would like you to explain the status of the ownership of the show, both under the Approved Production Contract and under any contractual proposal you would suggest. All the suggested composers are themselves members of the Dramatists Guild, so the agreement would need to be consistent with the terms of the Approved Production Contract for both Bryce and the composer. Finally, Bryce is open to any advice you might wish to give on whether working with one of these composers would make sense for the project.

D. Bibliography and Links

Donald C. Farber, Producing Theatre: A Comprehensive Legal and Business Guide (1997).

Donald C. Farber, From Option to Opening: A Guide to Producing Plays Off-Broadway (1989).

Charles Grippo, The Stage Producer's Business & Legal Guide (2002).

Michael W. Carroll, *Copyright's Creative Hierarchy in the Performing Arts*, 14 Vand. J. Ent. & Tech. L. 797 (2012).

Carolyn Casselman, *Staffing the 21st Century Theater: Technological Evolution and Collective Bargaining*, 25 Colum. J.L. & Arts 401 (2003).

Shun-Ling Chen, *Collaborative Authorship: From Folklore to the Wikiborg*, 2011 U. Ill. J.L. Tech. & Policy 131 (2011).

Mary LaFrance, *Authorship, Dominance, and the Captive Collaborator: Preserving the Rights of Joint Authors*, 50 Emory L.J. 193 (2001).

Susan P. Liemer, *Understanding Artists' Moral Rights: A Primer*, 7 B.U. Pub. Int. L.J. 41 (1998).

Carter Anne McGowan, Twittergate: *Rethinking the Casting Director Contract*, 21 Fordham Intell. Prop. Media & Ent. L.J. 365 (2011).

Talia Yellin, *New Directions for Copyright: The Property Rights of Stage Directors*, 24 Colum.-VLA J.L. & Arts 317 (2001).

Websites

The Dramatists Guild, www.dramatistsguild.org ("the only professional association for playwrights, composers, and lyricists. Membership is open to all dramatic writers, regardless of their production history.")

Live Broadway Online, www.livebroadway.com (sponsored by the League of American Theatres and Producers, Inc.)

Off Broadway Online, www.offbroadwayonline.com/home.php ("the official website of Off Broadway, presented by the Alliance of Resident Theatres/New York")

League of Resident Theatres, www.Lort.org

BackStage, www.backstage.com

Playbill, www.Playbill.com

Business Committee for the Arts, Inc., http://www.bcainc.org

Chapter X

Film Production Rights, Financing & Distribution

A. Overview

1. The Industry at a Glance[1]

The billions of dollars funneled into local economies by the entertainment industry are spent in modest increments through on-location productions and the rare, but spectacular, creation of production studios. Such studios consist of permanent production offices, production shops for creating sets and costumes, and sound stages where filming can take place in a controlled environment.

a. The Studio Production

Studios may also have outdoor back lots where semi-permanent sets are left standing for use in various productions on a regular basis. The term "studio" represents both the dominant corporations in the motion picture industry as well as the physical structures those companies utilize in creating their film product. Studios may mean "the larger, fully integrated production, distribution and marketing companies," as well as the soundstages, back lots, offices, and editing rooms such companies control....

The positive economic impact of a studio can be attributed to direct employment by the studio ... as well as the indirect impact of employment from service providers to the studio's activities. Such service providers include film laboratories, construction houses, prop rentals, and other related industries, as well as those support services that are the same for any large employer, including construction, housing, restaurants, catering, and retail....

Unfortunately, the high cost of constructing a new studio is only the first obstacle to creating a significant local production facility. The industrial infrastructure is necessary to make the studio operate productively. This infrastructure includes trained production staff with expertise in the skill crafts, carpenters, artists, electricians, and access to communities where professional acting talent lives or will purchase second homes. Industrial support services must also be located within a convenient distance, including film laboratories, equipment rental houses for lighting and other equipment, and other ancillary companies....

---

1. Jon M. Garon, *Star Wars: Film Permitting, Prior Restraint & Government's Role in the Entertainment Industry*, 17 Loy. L.A. Ent. L.J. 1 (1996) (most footnotes omitted, others renumbered) (reprinted with author's permission).

b. The Location Production

To film "on location" simply means that the filming takes place somewhere other than a soundstage. Unlike a soundstage, the production company does not own the location; thus, the property owner must approve any necessary modifications to the property. [Locations often need to be painted, redecorated, or distressed to match the desired look for the film. High voltage electric cables need to be used during the filming and larger productions often require additional bathroom facilities to accommodate the needs of a large cast and crew.] For cities, counties, and states vying to get a toehold in location productions, the primary selling tool is the scenic nature of the landscape. The success of Astoria, Oregon illustrates the point.

When New Line Cinema chose Astoria, Ore. over Wilmington, N.C. for principal location shooting for … "Teenage Mutant Ninja Turtles III," it was because the studio needed something different. Wilmington, the site of the first two [Turtles] movies, could not offer proximity to both ocean and mountains. Oregon's rugged Coastal Range and powerful coastline gave the location scouts exactly what they were looking for.

Similarly, the Maine Film Office highlights the features of its region. "Natural assets including mountains, coastline, forests, farms, rivers, lakes, villages, cities and people provide a stunning backdrop for work or play." Nevada's brochure and production guide carries a similar theme, as reflected in the "message from the Governor" printed in the Nevada Production Directory: "We take pride in offering a variety of unique locations, dazzling neon, isolated ghost towns, majestic mountain ranges and desolate dry lake beds. You'll find it all!" For locations in areas that have studios and significant resident production, convenience becomes more critical than scenery. Virtually anything filmed can be shot on-location rather than in the studio; thus, many of the mundane areas become film locations for those production companies already in the area. Every project has specific needs, most of which are not particularly exotic.

c. The Various Media

Like locations, the types of projects also differ greatly from medium to medium. The location requirements and the economic impact of filming will vary greatly depending on the type of production and the purpose of the filming. The various media that comprise the entertainment industry can be categorized into a number of distinct production types. While they all share many of the same characteristics, each has a distinct economic impact.

i. Feature Motion Pictures

Feature motion pictures are movies most commonly thought of as the product of Hollywood. Budgets for feature films range from a few hundred thousand dollars when made by small, independent film companies to more than $100 million for the largest spectaculars. [This number has risen above $200 million in recent years.] … Feature films typically use dozens, if not hundreds, of different locations.

Nevada's Motion Picture and Television Division claims a feature motion picture has six release windows. These include: "domestic and international theatrical release" through first-run motion picture theaters; "pay-per-view," which allows for films to be seen in the home via cable television; "video store rental," which provides copies of the film for sale or rental through retail outlets; "cable television premieres" on premium movie stations such as HBO or Showtime; "network television release" broadcast over the air on television paid for through commercial sponsorship rather than by the viewers; and "syndi-cated television release" broadcast on local television stations unaffiliated with networks or at times in the television schedule not controlled by the networks. Increasingly, inde-pendent films are being created specifically for the video market. Such films will cycle through some or all the stages listed above, with the exception of the first-run domestic theaters.

ii. Industrial Films

A significant segment of production in areas like New York City, Chicago, and the pe-riphery of Hollywood (such as Orange County) is industrial films (or industrials) that traditionally include projects produced as training programs, educational films, and sim-ilar non-broadcast markets. The area has expanded tremendously with the advent of home videotape.

Today, "industrials" include corporate image pieces shown to a broad general public, traditional training films, motivational and sales projects, point-of-purchase videos, prod-uct demos, employee benefits programs, interactive videos, tape cut-ins for live telecon-ferences (sometimes global via satellite uplink), and laser disc, CDI and CD/ROM recordings—in short, anything and everything that can go on tape, film, or disc but isn't made for TV or for theatrical release.

While budgets for industrials are significantly lower than for most feature films, the tech-nical requirements and "below the line budget" (which excludes star, director, and pro-ducer salaries) are often very similar to that of feature films. As a result, the amount of local spending on a per day basis remains competitive with that of feature films.

iii. Television Production

Television production includes a wide variety of different projects, including specials, one-hour series, half-hour comedies, talk shows, and music videos. Television produc-tions have significantly lower budgets than motion pictures and work on a much tighter time schedule. Unlike feature films and industrials, however, many television produc-tions require weekly or even daily projects. As a result, a regular location for a long-running television show will generate significant local revenue. For example, the recent version of the television series "The Untouchables" generated an estimated $25 million an-nually for Chicago during its two-year run in 1985–86, while providing significant long-term employment for local production workers. Similar success was generated by "Miami Vice" for Dade County in Southern Florida....

iv. Commercials

As a distinct type of television production, television commercials are actually the most expensive medium as judged on a cost-per-minute basis, generating $2 billion in an-nual production revenue. The top commercials may have as many locations as a televi-sion episode or industrial film with crew sizes and expenditures comparable to that of a feature film. Commercials are the most frequently shot motion picture form. Television commercials for local retailers are created in virtually every television market in the coun-try. National advertising campaigns tend to be created in the major markets such as Los Angeles, New York City, Miami, and Chicago because of the access to talent and pro-duction companies. A commercial usually entails only one day of location shooting with a total budget averaging $90,000 per thirty to sixty-second spot. Commercials involving complex special effects may take anywhere from days to months in post-production at considerable extra expense.

v. Print Photography

Still photography for print advertising, magazines, marketing materials, and book jackets involves a significant component of the film production around the country.... Photography has the added advantage of requiring few props, relatively small lighting equipment, and great mobility. Some jurisdictions view commercial photography as an "invisible industry" because it generates revenue while requiring virtually no services or resources.

vi. Multimedia Software

As one of the most explosive new forms of entertainment, multimedia software applications for CD-ROM, online services, and the Internet have been touted as the future of entertainment and commerce. Multimedia uses digitized pictures shot on or in a manner similar to videotape. The technology and sophistication of image production for multimedia currently ranges from home video production to that of feature films. As this industry continues to grow, however, the expertise and production value will also increase. This industry is particularly important to areas such as Seattle, San Francisco, and Orange County, California where the industrial base already has a strong foundation in software, electronic hardware, and intellectual property.

Each of these segments of the motion picture industry can be found at work in communities throughout the United States and Canada. Every day, productions are filming in one city or another. Most of the productions involve few city or county resources and operate in an efficient, unobtrusive manner. Whatever the type of production, local revenue is generated, jobs are created, and the greater economy is improved. Because of the high stakes involved in this $21 billion industry, a battle rages to attract and retain production companies in each jurisdiction.

2. The Film Industry: Key Participants[2]

[1. Producers.] The producer provides the key leadership, management, and supervision for the entire film project. This includes the "creative, financial, technological and administrative [process] ... throughout all phases of production from inception to completion, including coordination, supervision and control of all other talents and crafts, subject to the provisions of their collective bargaining agreements and personal service contracts."[3] Like the CEO or president of a corporation, the producer is responsible for all final executive decisions and personally participates in many of the choices made in every aspect of the project.

A good producer must have a solid grasp of the financial, artistic, and technical aspects of filmmaking. Often the task requires that the producer bring strong-willed profession-

---

2. JON GARON, THE INDEPENDENT FILMMAKER'S LAW & BUSINESS GUIDE TO FINANCING, SHOOTING, & DISTRIBUTING INDEPENDENT & DIGITAL FILMS ___ (2d Ed. CHICAGO REVIEW PRESS 2009) (reprinted with author's permission).

3. Producers Guild of America, "Frequently Asked Questions," www.producersguild.org/pg/about_a/faq.asp (accessed September 12, 2008).

als together to make hard decisions that balance the filmmaker's vision against the financial resources and technical limitations of the project. Experience, problem-solving skills, and strong management techniques are the essential qualities of a good producer.

Executive producers, on the other hand, are generally involved in the project only indirectly, helping raise funds or coordinating multiple films at the conceptual level. Few independent films have executive producers, except as a way of securing additional capital by providing the credit to inactive but essential financial participants. Occasionally, executive producer credit is provided to important cast members who use their influence to sign the remaining members of the cast and crew. By taking an extra hand in the production, these actors empower the film to go forward.

Associate producer is a title that is often liberally distributed to production participants who undertake many of the producer's duties, whether in coordination with the producer or by their own initiative. Although this credit is sometimes used in bargaining, independent filmmakers may wish to grant associate producer status to the individual who stands out throughout the production process, the unsung hero who went well beyond the job description or who paid to ensure that the project was completed.

The Producers Guild of America distinguishes between entrepreneurial producers and employee producers. In the independent filmmaking context, the entrepreneurial producer is the filmmaker—the person who takes it upon herself to initiate the project. An employee producer is a person hired by the financier of the project to manage the film's production.

If the filmmaker is not an entrepreneurial producer, then she must entrust the producing responsibilities to an employee producer, and take pains to ensure that he is under her direction and employ, rather than under the authority of the distributor or other financier of the project. The producer's control of the budget gives him primary authority over the film, so the filmmaker can retain control only to the extent that the producer answers to her and no one else.

This is not to suggest that the filmmaker should not employ a producer at all. If she (like most artists) lacks the experience, problem-solving skills, or management strength to do the job herself, an independent professional will add perspective to the project, enabling the filmmaker to make prudent, responsible choices. Even if the producer can be overruled, his advice and alternative viewpoints will prove invaluable....

The motion picture writer may be the loneliest person in Hollywood. Although the job may include the development of the story, the preparation of the treatment, or the writing of the shooting script, each of these tasks is done in relative isolation. To protect its members from loss of credit and status, the Writers Guild insists that the writer's work be highly restricted and noncollaborative. While this does not stop collaboration from occurring, it does illustrate the solitary nature of the writer's role in the process. The job for the writer will depend significantly on the relationship of the story to the screenplay. The writer of an original screen-play will typically play a much more central role than a person adapting a novel or dramatizing a true story....

[2. Writers.] If a writer is a member of the Writers Guild, then union rules prohibit her from working with a nonunion company. Whether the individual writer chooses to follow this rule, however, is her choice rather than the concern of the production company. The only danger in working with a union writer on a nonunion production is that she could change her mind and refuse to deliver a script unless the film company signs the WGA Theatrical and Television Basic Agreement (commonly called the Writers Guild Minimum Basic Agreement, or WGA-MBA). A film company may become a signatory to the

WGA-MBA simply by contacting the Writers Guild. The WGA-MBA provides an excellent structure for negotiations whether or not the writer is actually a member of the union....

[3. Directors.] According to the Directors Guild of America, the job of the director is "to contribute to all of the creative elements of a film and to participate in molding and integrating them into one cohesive dramatic and aesthetic whole."[4] This somewhat vague description nonetheless captures the essence of the director's role. The director (typically the filmmaker but not always, as described previously), supervises all the creative elements of the production, imprinting his vision of the story, sound, design, and essence of the film onto the project. Technically, the director need only be responsible for the actions of the cast and the camera; in reality, the director remains integral to the entire production.

Unlike with screenwriters, the use of multiple directors occurs rarely and results in significant confusion in those unfortunate situations where it is required. The director is usually attached to the project early and thereafter participates in all the other employment arrangements for the production. The director should know about, or help decide, virtually all issues involved with the production, including the casting, employment of other creative personnel, and creative decisions involving script, locations, set design, scheduling, and postproduction editing. The producer generally has authority over the director, but throughout most of preproduction and principal photography, the director has practical control over much of the project....

Since its inception in 1939, the role of the Directors Guild has traditionally been to provide representation on issues of credit, control, and finances. The DGA represents directors, assistant directors, and unit production managers. Because the motion picture has evolved into a director's medium more than the medium of any other artist, the union focuses primarily on its relationship with the studios. Within the independent filmmaking arena, the filmmakers are typically the directors, so the union has little to do in that respect. Nonetheless, the DGA Minimum Basic Agreement can serve as a useful guide even in the context of low-budget nonunion filmmaking, and is mandatory for any union production. The DGA-MBA provides for compensation minimums, mandatory credit, and rules on the relationship between the director and the production company.

The DGA also offers a side letter that serves as a rider to the DGA-MBA, providing reduced director minimums. The side letter has changed in recent years to improve the opportunities for union directors to participate in low-budget productions. The side letter ... provides various minimum fees depending on the budget of the production. It also allows for the deferral of some of the director's payments....

[4. Assistants.] The team of unit production manager (UPM) and first assistant director (AD) fill out the senior management of the film production. The UPM implements the decisions of the producer, and the first AD implements those of the director.

The UPM oversees the logistical details of the production, working through the budget, scheduling, finance, travel, and myriad additional issues that affect the film. She will negotiate many of the agreements for the production and arrange (and rearrange) the production schedule. On union productions, despite their budgetary role, UPM positions are governed by the Directors Guild.

---

4. Directors Guild of America, DGA Basic Agreement, § 7-101, available at www.dga.org/contracts/agreements_ctr.php3 in both PDF and online formats (accessed September 12, 2008).

A related position to the UPM is that of line producer. On an independent film, there is likely to be only a line producer or a UPM, but not both. In a larger production, the UPM may be a standing employee of the producer who moves from one film project to the next, serving each project exclusively while the producer provides nonexclusive services to a number of films at various stages of development. In this situation, the film company may also hire a line producer who has on-set operational responsibility for the film's expenses.

The first assistant director runs the set, ensuring that each day's schedule is ready for the director—that the call times for shooting, costuming, and makeup are coordinated so each cast member can be costumed and ready in time for his scheduled appearance. The first AD works with the cast and serves as an intermediary between cast and crew whenever necessary....

[5. Actors.] The actors portray the characters in the film. More formally, acting may be defined as "the performing art in which movement, gesture, and intonation are used to realize a fictional character for the stage, for motion pictures, or for television."[5] The task is as simple as that, but it remains perhaps the most difficult role in the creative arts. Some film roles may be portrayed by experienced professionals with years of training to project their emotions on film. Others are portrayed by untrained individuals who simply appear onscreen in the manner sought by the director of the film. Casting choices are often the most fundamental to the success of the entire project....

3. The Antitrust Experience in Hollywood

For all its glamour, Hollywood has always been a small town, with everyone knowing each other's business. This aphorism was historically too accurate, with the industry being the subject of repeated antitrust actions. The most significant of these was *U.S. v. Paramount Pictures, Inc.*, 334 U.S. 131 (1948). Although the Supreme Court noted in passing that the motion picture was entitled to First Amendment protection, the Court quickly moved past this issue to ban the horizontal and vertical price fixing by the motion picture companies. As the Court explained, "The District Court found that two price-fixing conspiracies existed—a horizontal one between all the [the major motion picture distributors]; a vertical one between each distributor-defendant and its licensees." The Court, therefore, banned the practice of setting the minimum price for theatre tickets charged by the exhibitors. Similarly, it required the distributors divest themselves of their major ownership of the exhibitors to eliminate the vertical price fixing.

Another of the practices banned was block-booking. The Court explained that "[b]lock-booking is the practice of licensing, or offering for license, one feature or group of features on condition that the exhibitor will also license another feature or group of features released by the distributors during a given period. The films are licensed in blocks before they are actually produced." A corollary practice was blind-selling, described as "a practice whereby a distributor licenses a feature before the exhibitor is afforded an opportunity to view it." The practice was also barred:

> Where a high quality film greatly desired is licensed only if an inferior one is taken, the latter borrows quality from the former and strengthens its monopoly by drawing on the other. The practice tends to equalize rather than differentiate the reward for the individual copyrights. Even where all the films included in the package are of equal quality, the requirement that all be taken if one is de-

---

5. *Encyclopedia Britannica Online*, s.v. "acting," www.britannica.com/EBchecked/topic/4329/acting (accessed September 12, 2008).

sired increases the market for some. Each stands not on its own footing but in whole or in part on the appeal which another film may have. As the District Court said, the result is to add to the monopoly of the copyright in violation of the principle of the patent cases involving tying clauses.

Finally, the Court banned all practices that discriminated against the smaller, independent theatre chains, requiring the studios to engage in open, competitive bidding for the films once they were completed and available for viewing. The results of *U.S. v. Paramount* swept through Hollywood, fundamentally altering the financial structure of the old studios and paving the way for the rise of independent producers.

The continuing antitrust activities remained the focus of significant court action. In *United States v. Loew's, Inc.*, 371 U.S. 38 (1962), the Supreme Court barred the practice of block-booking to television stations. The Court summed up the antitrust violation simply: "To use the trial court's apt example, forcing a television station which wants 'Gone With The Wind' to take 'Getting Gertie's Garter' as well is taking undue advantage of the fact that to television as well as motion picture viewers there is but one 'Gone With The Wind.'" The Court allowed motion pictures to be sold in blocks or groups, but only if "there is no requirement, express or implied, for the purchase of more than one film." This caveat allowed the film studios to copy the copyright licensing approach of the performing rights societies such as ASCAP and BMI — licensing each work individually or in groups to maximize efficiency.

Notes and Questions

a. Although many of these cases seem to be part of Hollywood's ancient lore, the battles and antitrust accusations continue. See *Six West Retail Acquisition, Inc. v. Sony Theatre Mgmt. Corp.*, 203 F.R.D. 98, 51 Fed. R. Serv. 3d (Callaghan) (S.D.N.Y. 2001) (Sony, which now owns some of the Loews theaters, was accused of block-booking and refusing to deal with a small, exhibitor chain).

b. Many states also regulated the practices of exclusive theatrical runs, blind-bidding, block-booking, and other anticompetitive activities. These statutes have generally been upheld as constitutional. See *Associated Film Distribution Corp. v. Thornburgh*, 614 F. Supp. 1100 (E.D. Pa. 1985); *Allied Artists Pictures Corp. v. Rhodes*, 496 F. Supp. 408 (S.D. Ohio 1980). Nonetheless, recent changes to copyright jurisprudence have brought some of these decisions into question. See *Orson, Inc. v. Miramax Film Corp.*, 189 F.3d 377 (3d Cir. 1999) (determining that the exhibition regulations were preempted by federal copyright law).

c. Given the requirements that distributors no longer engage in blind-selling, the studios regularly screen movies prior to their sale. Nonetheless, the distributors often try to promote these films to the greatest extent possible. At what point does the promise of the next big blockbuster move from hype to guarantee? See *Presidio Enterprises, Inc. v. Warner Bros. Distributing Corp.*, 784 F.2d 674 (5th Cir. 1986).

B. Production Agreements and Budgets

1. Film Finance and Control

Despite comments that film is primarily a filmmaker's medium, production expenses and marketing expenses can sometimes exceed $250 million, making each major film a huge financial commitment. As a result, the motion picture studios/distributors wield tremendous influence on every aspect of the film.

A small percentage of films are created directly by the motion picture studio itself. The more typical arrangement, however, is the negative pick-up agreement whereby an independent film company is formed for purpose of creating a film. This is the type of agreement litigated in *Filmline (Cross-Country) Productions, Inc. v. United Artists*, below. In this arrangement, the distributor agrees to purchase the final film (at the completed negative stage) in exchange for a set price. This assures the distributor that any overruns are paid by the producer rather than the distributor. At each stage in the process, the distributor must verify and approve of compliance with the budget and the agreed-upon script. Payments are made in increments, which are timed to the production schedule.

Smaller films are often financed independently of the distributors and sold to distributors after they are completed. While a few independent films reap both critical acclaim and financial windfalls for their creators and financial backers, the vast majority of these films are never exhibited to the general public and result in complete financial losses for their investors.

2. Final Cut

Depending on the contractual arrangement, the director's influence over the final project will vary. For a director, the most important aspect of control stems from the concept of final cut. The most successful or most influential of directors negotiate the final approval rights over the content of their films. Even these rights are not absolute. The directors must meet all the contractual preconditions to exercise such control. Typically, this means that the film must be edited to an agreed length (typically somewhere between 93–120 minutes), conform to an agreed MPAA rating (most likely PG-13), come within budget (including all pre-approved overages), and substantially contain the same scenes and dialogue as provided in the final shooting script.

Woody Allen is famous for his absolute control over the content of his films and the ability to deliver a film every year on schedule. Steven Spielberg exercised such a degree of final cut over *Schindler's List* that he retained the right to personally supervise the film's adaptation into every foreign language and every foreign censorship edit. Because disputes over final cut are covered by the Directors Guild collective bargaining agreement, these cases are not typically reported. The few reported cases involve editing for television. Chapter XIV details the leading cases involving final cut and the editing for television that regularly occur.

The most significant benefit to directing an independently financed film is the autonomy it affords. Because there is no distributor financing, there rarely is the type of editorial pressure on the filmmaker that occurs with studio pictures. Nonetheless, distributors will sometimes insist on changes to films as a condition of purchasing them for distribution. In this vein, the director is never completely free from outside influences.

3. Motion Picture Budgets

The motion picture budget can range from a few thousand dollars for digital equipment rental and pizza to hundreds of millions of dollars. Whatever the budget, the primary structure and approach remain the same.

The budgets are divided into halves — above the line and below the line. Above the line expenses are those marquee components of the motion picture, such as the fees for the stars, director, writer, and producer. Everything else is below the line. Typical Hollywood budgeting sets the above the line and below the line costs in an informal equilibrium. As the budget for stars and director grow more lavish, so do the expenses below the line for locations, designs, travel, costumes and other elements of the production.

The rise of the special effects movie, exemplified by trilogies such as *The Matrix* and *Lord of the Rings*, suggests a new model for budgeting, with special effects constituting such a large starring role and percentage of the budget that the above the line expenses must be reduced to afford production. Steven Spielberg's *Jurassic Park* established this new approach by casting dinosaurs as the stars and forgoing the costs of hiring a bankable cast.

At the other end of the spectrum, a 35mm independent film can still be made for $5–$10 million with the production values and professional cast and crew comparable to that of the blockbuster. Films shot using digital technology can be made with less equipment and simpler lighting and power requirements, so these films can be shot at an even lower budget. As a result, the costs that determine the budget of a motion picture may emphasize the cost for the cast members, the cost for the locations, the cost for the special effects, or a combination of all those attributes.

Filmline (Cross-Country) Productions, Inc. v. United Artists Corp.

865 F.2d 513 (2d Cir. 1989)

This is an action for damages resulting from an alleged breach of contract. Defendants appeal from a judgment ... awarding plaintiffs damages in the amount of $2,189,889 plus $869,900 in prejudgment interest after a trial without a jury....

The subject matter of this suit is a letter agreement dated as of February 11, 1982 [for a "negative pick-up agreement] (the "Agreement"), as amended, between defendant United Artists Corp. ("UA") and plaintiffs Filmline (Cross-Country) Productions, Inc. ("Filmline") and Yellowbill Finance Limited ("Yellowbill") for the production of a film entitled "Cross Country" (the "Picture"). The Agreement called for Filmline to produce the Picture, with interim financing to be provided by Yellowbill, and obliged UA to purchase the Picture if Filmline produced it in accordance with the terms of the Agreement. Provision for the interim financing was made in a separate contract between Filmline and Yellowbill.

The Picture was produced, but UA acted to terminate the Agreement as production drew to a conclusion, asserting unacceptable variation from "an approved screenplay." The district court found that UA's stated reason for repudiating the contract was a pretext, the real reason being that UA sought to avoid a financial commitment to the picture. The district court held that while UA had a right to terminate prior to filming, it waived that right by failing to exercise it in a timely fashion and by participating in the actual filming of the picture. Thus, UA's later repudiation of its obligation to purchase and distribute the picture was deemed to constitute a breach of the contract. We affirm.

The basic events underlying this dispute are the formation of the Agreement between Filmline, UA and Yellowbill for the production of the Picture, an ensuing period during which the screenplay was revised, the actual filming of the Picture which began on May 11, 1982, and UA's repudiation of the Agreement on June 24, 1982 when the filming of the Picture was two days from completion. The Agreement provided that Yellowbill would finance the film, that Filmline would produce it, and that UA would purchase the Picture upon completion. Central to the case is UA's right of approval of the screenplay for the Picture under the Agreement.

Section 5 of the Agreement states that "UA shall have the following approvals with respect to the production of the Picture," specifying the director of the Picture, the screenplay writer, lead actors and actresses, the director of photography, the production designer and the film editor, but not the screenplay itself. Section 2 of the Agreement, which deals with development of the screenplay, provides:

> UA shall read and submit to [Filmline] such comments, if any, as it may have with respect to each draft of the screenplay. [Filmline] shall cause each draft of the screenplay to be rewritten in accordance with UA's suggested changes. The foregoing procedure shall be repeated until such time as UA and [Filmline] are satisfied with the final screenplay to be utilized for the production of the picture. UA and [Filmline] agree to accomplish the foregoing as promptly as reasonably possible so as not to frustrate the timely production of the Picture.

Section 15 of the Agreement states Filmline's obligation to produce the picture in conformity with the approved screenplay, and UA's resulting obligation to purchase, in the following terms:

> Provided that the Picture shall be produced in strict conformity with the approved screenplay and story board (except only for such minor changes as may be required by the exigencies of production), and provided further that [Filmline] has performed all of its obligations hereunder and is not in breach of any representation, warranty, covenants or agreements hereunder, UA agrees to pay to [Filmline] upon full delivery of the Picture ... a sum ... in an amount equal to the final certified negative cost of the Picture ... up to the sum of Two Million Five Hundred Thousand Dollars ($2,500,000)....

Similarly, Section 3(b) of the financing agreement between Filmline and Yellowbill provides that "the Film shall be based on the Script, as approved pursuant to the UA Agreement, except for minor deviations of the kind usual in the course of production of a film."

Section 4.01 of UA's "Standard Terms and Conditions" (the "Terms") provides in part:

> In the event [Filmline] shall breach or become in default of performance of any material term, condition or covenant contained in this Agreement, or shall breach any representation or warranty contained in this Agreement, and shall fail to cure, correct or remedy such breach or default *within thirty (30) days after service of written notice specifying same,* ... United may:
>
> (1) terminate this Agreement in its entirety and be relieved of any obligations to advance or cause to be advanced any further monies or to pay the Purchase Price for the Picture or any part thereof....
>
> All rights and remedies to United under this agreement are cumulative and the exercise of one shall not limit or affect its right concurrently or subsequently to exercise any other rights or remedies as it may have at law, in equity, under this Agreement or otherwise (emphasis added).

Section 8.04 of the Terms states that "this Agreement shall be construed and interpreted under the laws of the State of New York governing agreements which are wholly executed and performed therein."

UA entered into the Agreement based upon its evaluation of an initial draft of the screenplay. UA's agent in these activities was Charles Lippincott, vice president of acquisitions, who reviewed the initial screenplay and subsequent alterations. After reviewing the initial draft of the screenplay, Lippincott requested a number of alterations. On April 17, 1982, Lippincott met with Pieter Kroonenberg, one of the principals of Filmline, to discuss a revised draft of the screenplay dated April 13, 1982. Lippincott expressed his dissatisfaction with the April 13th screenplay and repeated requests for certain modifications. On April 19, 1982, UA (for whom Lippincott acted), Filmline and Yellowbill entered into an amendment (the "April Amendment") to the Agreement which provides in part:

> This will confirm the approval by UA of the following elements:
>
> (a) The April 13, 1982 revised screenplay, as further revised in accordance with the changes agreed to by UA and Filmline on April 17, 1982, provided that it is acknowledged that UA reserves the right to request minor changes to said screenplay prior to the confirmed May 11, 1982 start date of principal photography....

The April Amendment also included approvals of the casting as to four characters, the "story board as to Scenes 1B through 35C," the director of photography, the production designer and the film editor (subject to the later enlistment of a supervisory film editor "at UA's request and subject to UA's approval").

Some revisions were made to the April 13 screenplay, resulting in a final screenplay, to be used for filming, dated May 7, 1982. Lippincott reviewed this final screenplay on May 11, 1982, which was also the date for commencement of filming. The district court determined that the May 7th screenplay did not make the orally agreed changes required by the April Amendment. Thus, after Lippincott's May 11th review, UA had the right to terminate the contract, subject to a thirty day right of cure by Filmline. Lippincott chose, however, not to give notice of termination. Instead, Lippincott actively participated in the filming, reviewing further revisions of the screenplay and appearing on the scene of shooting from May 11 to May 16 and June 1 to June 4. On several occasions, Lippincott assured plaintiffs that production was proceeding acceptably. Only on June 20, 1982, did Lippincott complain to plaintiffs that he did not believe that the picture was working out as he had hoped.

On June 24, 1982, independent developments within UA precipitated the termination. UA's senior management had evidently been misinformed as to the existence of a UA commitment to purchase the Picture. Discovery of the commitment by Lippincott's superiors was followed by a telephone conversation with Lippincott in which he apprised senior management of his growing pessimism about the commercial prospects for the film. Immediately thereafter, UA transmitted a termination notice to Filmline which stated in part:

> It has come to our attention that (A) the Picture is not being produced *in strict conformity with the approved screenplay* and storyboard, (B) you have failed to perform certain of your obligations under the Agreement (including, without limitation, your obligation to obtain UA's approval as to certain production and creative elements and to fully and in good faith consult with UA as to certain other creative elements), and (C) you have breached certain of your representations, warranties, covenants and agreements contained in the Agreement (including, without limitation, the covenants relating to (A) and (B) above).

> Based on the foregoing, this is to advise you that UA's obligations under the Agreement are hereby terminated and that US [sic] will not accept delivery of the Picture if and when completed. Nor will UA pay you the Cash Purchase Price (as defined in paragraph 15 of the Agreement) for the Picture in the event you attempt to tender delivery of the completed Picture to UA.

UA's purported notice of termination included no provision for Filmline to cure, correct or remedy its asserted defaults. Filmline's counsel responded promptly in writing, denying any breach on Filmline's part and contending that UA's purported notice of termination was itself an anticipatory breach of the Agreement.

Filmline and Yellowbill subsequently arranged for alternate distribution, but the Picture was a commercial failure. On January 26, 1983, Filmline and Yellowbill commenced the instant litigation. Prior to the trial of the case, the district court denied a motion by UA to dismiss or stay the action in favor of a California state court action initiated by UA, or alternatively for a transfer of the action to the United States District Court for the Central District of California pursuant to *28 U.S.C. § 1404*(a) (1982). After trial, the district court ruled that UA had waived its right to terminate for failure of the screenplay to conform with the provisions of the April Amendment, determined the various damages issues tendered by the parties, and concluded that UA was liable to Filmline and Yellowbill in the amount of $2,189,889, plus pre-judgment interest on that amount from January 26, 1983. This appeal followed.

It is undisputed that this diversity action is governed by New York law. Indeed, as noted earlier, Section 8.04 of the Terms explicitly so provides.

UA's purported notice of termination specified that the Picture was "not being produced in strict conformity with the approved screenplay and storyboard...." Both at trial, and on appeal, however, UA contended that there was never an approved screenplay, because the requirement stated in the April Amendment that the screenplay be "further revised in accordance with the changes agreed to by UA and Filmline on April 17, 1982" had never been fulfilled. UA contends that it allowed Filmline to go forward with screening of the Picture and attempt to bring it into conformity with "the changes agreed to by UA and Filmline on April 17, 1982," and legitimately terminated the Agreement and UA's responsibilities thereunder when Filmline failed in that attempt. The district court rejected that position, concluding that New York law required an election by UA either to terminate on May 11, 1982, prior to the inception of filming, or to waive the breach that had by then become manifest and continue performance under the contract.

We concur in the district court's general view of New York law. UA, however, cites to us New York authorities which mitigate the rigor of this rule. *Lenkay Sani Products Corp. v. Benitez,* 47 A.D.2d 524, 362 N.Y.S.2d 572 (2d Dep't 1975), is typical. In *Lenkay,* machines were delivered which did not function properly, and the buyer offered the manufacturer an opportunity to remedy the defects. When this effort failed, the buyer sued to recover the partial payments it had made for the machinery, and the manufacturer counterclaimed for the balance of the purchase price, claiming acceptance by the buyer and waiver of the defects. The Appellate Division rejected this contention, stating:

> Where a buyer has knowledge that the goods do not conform to the contract specifications, but nevertheless accepts them, he may revoke his acceptance and rescind the contract if the acceptance was on the reasonable assumption that the nonconformity would be seasonably cured, but cure was not effected.

Although this decision was premised upon a specific provision of the Uniform Commercial Code, other New York cases apply the principle more broadly. We applied this rule in *S.D. Hicks & Son Co. v. J.T. Baker Chemical Co.*, 307 F.2d 750 (2d Cir. 1962), a diversity case governed by New York law. In that case, defendant undertook to construct a chemical processing plant and guaranteed its performance. Defendant then sought additional compensation for bringing the finished plant into compliance with the guarantee, contending that the buyer's initial acceptance of the plant constituted a waiver of the guarantee. We rejected that contention, stating:

> [T]here is no warrant for the position that a party to a contract waives his rights under the contract by failing to insist upon performance at the due date and by urging and encouraging the other party to perform thereafter.

We would have some difficulty in applying the rule for which UA contends to the facts of this case, given the equivocal conduct of the parties at the inception of the shooting of the Picture, and the foreknowledge of all parties that Filmline would incur the bulk of its expense in performing the Agreement by shooting the Picture. We deem the inquiry mooted, however, because even on the assumption that Filmline was in breach and UA was entitled to terminate when it purported to do so on June 24, 1982, it is clear that UA's notice of termination did not conform to the Agreement and was therefore ineffective under New York law.

Specifically, UA's purported notice of termination made no effort to comply with the explicit requirement, stated in section 4.01 of the Terms, that Filmline was to be accorded an opportunity "to cure, correct or remedy such breach or default within thirty days of written notice specifying same...." Under New York law, that defect is fatal to UA's position.

In *General Supply and Constr. Co. v. Goelet*, 241 N.Y. 28, 148 N.E. 778 (1925), remittitur amended, 241 N.Y. 507, 150 N.E. 532 (1925), the defendant purported to terminate a contract for the construction of a building. As the court described it, the contract provided "that the owner might terminate the contract at any time upon certificate of the architect that the work was being unreasonably delayed and that such delay was sufficient ground for termination of the contract." 241 N.Y. at 34, 148 N.E. at 779. Rejecting the owner's purported termination of the contract without obtaining the contractually required certificate, the Court of Appeals stated:

> Though [the owner] may have been justified ... in his belief that the contractor would not thereafter mend his ways and finish the work within a reasonable time, yet where such delay did not amount to abandonment [the owner] could not rescind the contract for that reason, *except according to its terms....* Having indicated purpose to keep the contract alive in spite of delays on the part of the contractor, the owner could not suddenly abandon the purpose and treat as essential an element of the contract which he had previously waived, as ground for termination. The termination of the contract in this case without the required previous notice and without a certificate from the architect *in accordance with the terms of the contract* was wrongful....

We conclude that on this record, New York courts would apply the clear New York rule requiring termination of a contract in accordance with its terms[ ].... Accordingly, since UA's purported termination was in violation of the terms of the Agreement, it was inoperative and plaintiffs are entitled to recover for breach of contract.

The district court reached this result by a different route, concluding that by allowing the filming of the Picture to proceed on May 11, 1982, UA waived Filmline's failure to conform the Picture to the requirements of the April Amendment.[6] As indicated earlier, we do not deem it necessary to resolve the waiver issue. That is, we conclude that whether or not UA waived Filmline's failure to conform the screenplay to the requirements of the April Amendment, UA's purported notice of termination dated June 24, 1982 was in any event ineffective under New York law because it did not comply with the Agreement. It is settled that we may affirm on any basis that is supported by the record, regardless of the ground upon which the trial court relied.

UA contends that the district court vastly overstated the damages properly recoverable, assuming a breach of contract. Specifically, UA argues that the district court erroneously rejected UA's contention that "the plaintiffs' damages must be reduced by the amount it would cost plaintiffs to reshoot the entire Picture in strict conformity with the May 7 screenplay." The district court concluded that "had UA not wrongfully terminated the contract, UA would have and in good faith could have only required Filmline to conform to the May 7 screenplay the eleven scenes which [UA] actually preferred in the May 7 version," at a cost of $20,901. These determinations are not clearly erroneous, and are accordingly affirmed.... The judgment of the district court is affirmed.

Buchwald v. Paramount Pictures, Corp.

1990 Cal. App. LEXIS 634; 13 U.S.P.Q.2D (BNA) 1497 (1990)

At the outset the Court desires to indicate what this case is and is not about. It is not about whether Art Buchwald or Eddie Murphy is more creative. It is clear to the Court that each of these men is a creative genius in his own field and each is an uniquely American institution. This case is also not about whether Eddie Murphy made substantial contributions to the film "Coming to America." The Court is convinced he did. Finally, this case is not about whether Eddie Murphy "stole" Art Buchwald's concept "King for a Day." Rather, this case is primarily a breach of contract case between Buchwald and Paramount (not Murphy) which must be decided by reference to the agreement between the parties and the rules of contract construction, as well as the principals of law enunciated in the applicable legal authorities.

As indicated, the starting point for the analysis of this case is the contract between Buchwald and Paramount. Pursuant to this agreement Buchwald transferred to Paramount "the sole and exclusive motion picture and other rights" to the "original story and concept written by Art Buchwald ... tentatively entitled "KING FOR A DAY", also known as "It's a Crude, Crude World" (which material, as defined in said Standard Terms is hereinafter called the 'Work')." In the agreement Buchwald warranted "[t]hat the Work is original with Author; that neither the Work nor any part thereof are taken from or based upon any other material or any motion picture...." As is pertinent to the present case, the agreement provided that:

---

6. The district court also found that UA's purported notice of termination was pretextual, although not relying upon that finding for its conclusion as to liability. This finding was amply supported by the record, especially by testimony from an arbitration to which UA was a party, introduced into evidence at the trial below, which demonstrated that UA's notice of termination was motivated by a desire to extricate UA from its obligations under the Agreement when UA's senior management belatedly learned its provisions on or about June 24, 1982. Again, in view of the failure of UA's purported notice of termination to comply with the requirements of the Agreement, we need not reach the question whether a pretextual motivation might in some circumstances invalidate an otherwise effective termination.

> "'Work' means the aforementioned Material and includes all prior, present and future versions, adaptations and translations thereof (whether written by Author or by others), its theme, story, plot, characters and their names, its title or titles and subtitles, if any,..., and each and every part of all thereof. 'Work' does not include the material referred to in paragraph 2 (f) above, written or prepared by Purchaser or under Purchaser's Authority."

Finally, the agreement entitled Buchwald to certain "contingent consideration" "[f]or the first theatrical motion picture (the 'Picture'): If, but only if, a feature length theatrical motion picture shall be produced based upon Author's Work."

Since the agreement provided Buchwald was entitled to payment only if Paramount produced "a feature length theatrical motion picture" "based upon Author's Work," the threshold inquiry in this case is what is meant by the term "based upon." Because the term is not defined in the contract, it was the Court's hope that the term had a specific meaning in the entertainment industry and that the experts who testified would so indicate. Unfortunately, there was as little agreement among the experts concerning the meaning of this term as there was between plaintiffs and Paramount concerning whether "Coming to America" is based upon Buchwald's treatment. For example, David Kirkpatrick testified that his understanding of "based upon," as used in the entertainment industry, is that "there exists some underlying antecedents that triggered the realization of the story in a screenplay." ...

Since the Court found the testimony of the entertainment experts, both individually and collectively, to be of little value with respect to the "based upon" issue, the Court turned to the appellate decisions of this State for guidance. Fortunately, that guidance existed. Indeed, as will be discussed more fully below, the Court believes these decisions provide a road map through the "based upon" mine field.

In cases involving infringement, which this case is not, it has been held that an inference of copying may arise where there is proof of access to the material with a showing of similarity.... These same rules have been applied in a case involving a cause of action alleging breach of an express contract.

In the present case, there is no real issue concerning Eddie Murphy's access to Buchwald's concept. Indeed, the evidence is that Murphy knew about Buchwald's concept. Specifically, it is undisputed that in the spring of 1983, Paramount creative executives Kirkpatrick and Katzenberg met with Murphy and his manager, Robert Wachs, at the Ma Maison Restaurant and discussed Buchwald's concept with them. In fact, it was reported that Murphy was positively responsive to the "King for a Day" presentation and indicated that he liked playing the African character in the movie "Trading Places." Murphy himself testified (by way of deposition) that he had "a very vague recollection, maybe of Jeff [Katzenberg] going into the "King for a Day" thing. 'You'd be great in it.'" Murphy further testified that Katzenberg "liked the idea of it, I guess, 'cause I remember."

There is other, persuasive evidence on the issue of access. For example, on June 6, 1983, Kirkpatrick sent Wachs a short outline of Buchwald's "King for a Day." Wachs admitted that he read at least part of the Buchwald's treatment. Finally, there is evidence that Kirkpatrick discussed "King for a Day" with Eddie Murphy on at least three occasions subsequent to the meeting at the Ma Maison Restaurant in the spring of 1983.

Since there is no real issue concerning access, the focus must then be on the question of similarity. Similarity is, of course, a question of fact for the trier of fact to determine. The parties have directed a substantial amount of their attention to the issue of similarity. Paramount contends that there must be substantial similarity between Buchwald's treatment and "Coming to America" in order for Buchwald to succeed in this case....

Although the Court believes the cases relied upon by Paramount are inapplicable to the issue of the extent of similarity that is required in this case, the Court has concluded the two controlling cases with respect to this issue are *Fink* [*v. Goodson-Todman Enterprises, Ltd., 9 Cal. App. 3d 996, 1013* (1970)], and *Weitzenkorn* [*v. Lesser, 40 Cal. 2d 778* (1953)].

In *Fink*, as in the present case, the contract between the parties obligated the defendant to compensate the plaintiff if the defendant created a series "based on Plaintiff's Program or any material element contained in [it]." The Court stated that a "'[m]aterial element' could range from a mere basic theme up to an extensively elaborated idea, depending upon what might be proved as the concept of the parties." With respect to the contract cause of action, the Court framed the issue: "[W]hether ... defendants have based their series on a material element of plaintiff's program." The Court noted that its "based on any material element" test was "quite close to the concept of 'inspiration for' which was the key to the upholding of an implied contract count in *Minniear v. Tors, 266 Cal. App. 2d 495, 505* [(1968)]."

Similarly, in *Weitzenkorn, supra,* the contract obligated the defendants to pay for plaintiffs' composition "if they used it or any portion of it, regardless of its originality."

Based on the decisions in *Fink* and *Weitzenkorn*, and the contract involved in this case, the Court concludes that Paramount's obligation to pay Buchwald arose if "Coming to America" is based upon a material element of or was inspired by Buchwald's treatment. As the Court in Fink noted, this determination is to be made by searching for "points of similarity" both quantitatively and qualitatively. It is to this search that the Court now turns.

Before engaging in a comparison of "King for a Day" and "Coming to America," the Court wishes to state the obvious. Specifically, plaintiff has the burden of proving similarity by a preponderance of the evidence. "'Preponderance of the evidence' means evidence that has more convincing force than that opposed to it."

In Buchwald's treatment, a rich, educated, arrogant, extravagant, despotic African potentate comes to America for a state visit. After being taken on a grand tour of the United States, the potentate arrives at the White House. A gaffe in remarks made by the President infuriates the African leader. His sexual desires are rebuffed by a black woman State Department officer assigned to him. She is requested by the President to continue to serve as the potentate's United States escort. While in the United States, the potentate is deposed, deserted by his entourage and left destitute. He ends up in the Washington ghetto, is stripped of his clothes, and befriended by a black lady. The potentate experiences a number of incidents in the ghetto, and obtains employment as a waiter. In order to avoid extradition, he marries the black lady who befriended him, becomes the emperor of the ghetto and lives happily ever after.

In "Coming to America" the pampered prince of a mythical African kingdom (Zamunda) wakes up on his 21st birthday to find that the day for his prearranged marriage has arrived. Discovering his bride to be very subservient and being unhappy about that fact, he convinces his father to permit him to go to America for the ostensible purpose of sowing his "royal oats." In fact, the prince intends to go to America to find an independent woman to marry. The prince and his friend go to Queens, New York, where their property is stolen and they begin living in a slum area. The prince discovers his true love, Lisa, whose father—McDowell—operates a fast-food restaurant for whom the prince and his friend begin to work. The prince and Lisa fall in love, but when the King and Queen come to New York and it is disclosed who the prince is, Lisa rejects the prince's marriage invitation. The film ends with Lisa appearing in Zamunda, marrying the prince and apparently living happily ever after.

There are, to be sure, differences between Buchwald's "King for a Day" and "Coming to America." However, as noted above, where, as here, the evidence of access is overwhelming, less similarity is required. Moreover, "'[E]ven if the similar material is quantitatively small, if it is qualitatively important ... the trier of fact ... may properly find substantial similarity.'"

In his opening statement, counsel for plaintiffs made the following comparison of "King for a Day" and "Coming to America":

> Both are modern day comedies. The protagonist is a young black member of royalty from a mythical African kingdom, pampered and extremely wealthy, well-educated. They both come to a large city on the American East Coast. And they arrive as a fish out of water from this foreign kingdom.
>
> Abruptly, finding themselves without royal trappings of money and power, they end up in the black, urban American ghetto, about as far culturally as they could ever hope to be from their pampered, royal status in their mythical kingdom. Each character abandons his regal attitudes. Both live in the ghetto as poor blacks experiencing the realities of ghetto life.
>
> Each takes a menial job as (sic) a series of harrowing and comedic adventures in the ghetto, is humanized and enriched by his experiences. Love always triumphing over all, each meets and falls in love with a beautiful young American woman whom he will marry and make his Queen and live happily ever after in his mythical African kingdom.

The Court agrees with this comparison. In fact, the Court believes that these similarities alone, given the language of the contract involved in this case and the law that liability in a contract case can arise even if a non-substantial element is copied, might well be sufficient to impose contract liability on Paramount. The fact is, however, that other compelling evidence of similarity exists.

In the original script written by Tab Murphy that was indisputably based upon Buchwald's treatment, the king ends up as an employee of a fast food restaurant where he ultimately foils a robbery attempt by use of a mop. In "Coming to America" the prince is also employed by a fast food restaurant and foils a robbery attempt by use of a mop. These similar "gimmicks" provide compelling evidence that the evolution of plaintiffs' idea provided an inspiration for "Coming to America." ...

There are other factors that are present in this case that strongly support plaintiffs' position that Buchwald's original concept and its subsequent development at Paramount was the inspiration for "Coming to America". For example, the evidence is overwhelming that for two years Paramount considered "King for a Day" to be a project that was being developed for Eddie Murphy. In fact, when "Coming to America" was made, its star was Eddie Murphy. Additionally, during the development of "King for a Day" it was contemplated Murphy would portray multiple characters. In "Coming to America" he did.

Moreover, when "King for a Day" was under development, Paramount sought to interest John Landis in directing the movie. On July 1, 1983, David Kirkpatrick of Paramount sent to Landis a description of "King for a Day." In fact, Landis directed "Coming to America". The fact that Landis was aware of Buchwald's concept for "King for a Day" is important. Since the evidence revealed that Landis had creative input into "Coming to America," it is his access and knowledge, in addition to Eddie Murphy's, that it is relevant to the issue of similarity.

It is also important to observe that one of the promotional ideas utilized in connection with "Coming to America" was a "King for a Day" concept where a prize winner was afforded the opportunity to go on a shopping spree.

As indicated above, there are differences between Buchwald's treatment and "Coming to America." One of the principal differences is that the king in Buchwald's original treatment was despotic, while the prince in "Coming to America" is kind and naive. The fact is, however, that early in the development process Paramount desired to make Buchwald's king more likable. Indeed, by the time Francis Veber submitted his second script, which was clearly based upon Buchwald's original treatment, the king had none of his despotic characteristics. As indicated above the Court believes that "Coming to America" must be compared with the Buchwald treatment as it was developed in the Tab Murphy and Veber scripts.

The other significant difference between Buchwald's treatment and "Coming to America" is the motivation that brought the principal character to America. In Buchwald's treatment the motivation was to obtain military weapons from the United States. In "Coming to America" it was to find an independent wife. This dissimilarity does not, however, require a finding that "Coming to America" is not "based upon" Buchwald's work.

In many ways, the decision in *Weitzenkorn, supra,* is similar to the present case. *Weitzenkorn* was a breach of contract case in which the plaintiff sued to recover damages by reason of the defendant's use of her Tarzan/Fountain of Youth idea. Although both plaintiff's idea and the defendant's movie involved Tarzan, there were striking dissimilarities between the two. In plaintiff's story, Tarzan entered the area where the Fountain of Youth was located because he was captured by the evil persons who dwelled in the area. By contrast, in the defendant's version Tarzan voluntarily entered the area which was occupied by a king who was a friend of Tarzan. In plaintiff's version, Tarzan undertook his journey to rescue Boy. In defendant's version, Tarzan was on a mission of mercy to find a missing aviatrix. In plaintiff's version, the evil queen and her subjects disintegrated when Tarzan destroyed the Fountain of Youth. In defendant's version, the ending was totally different.

In *Weitzenkorn* the Court found no similarity as to form and manner of expression between plaintiff's composition and defendant's movie. Although both works included the same characters in Africa being involved with a mythical Fountain of Youth, the moral of each was entirely different. Specifically, the moral of plaintiff's work was that eternal youth was not a blessing. The moral of defendant's work was that eternal youth was a reward for good.

In spite of the significant differences between plaintiff's and defendant's work, the Court concluded that the trial court had erroneously sustained the demurrers of the defendants without leave to amend. Because the defendants had expressly agreed to compensate the plaintiff if they used plaintiff's composition, or any portion of it, the Court concluded that plaintiff's complaint stated a cause of action "no matter how slight or commonplace the portion which" the defendants used.

Finally, *Blaustein v. Burton,* 9 Cal. App. 3d 961 (1970) is also instructive. In this case plaintiff's idea of using Richard Burton and Elizabeth Taylor as the stars of "Taming of the Shrew," together with several ideas with respect to how and where the movie should be made, was held to give rise to contract liability.

Based upon the authorities discussed above and the provisions of the contract involved in this case, the Court concludes that "Coming to America" is a movie that was "based upon"

Buchwald's treatment "King for a Day." "Bearing in mind the unlimited access ... [proved] in this case and the rule that the stronger the access the less striking and numerous the similarities need be, ... [the Court concludes that Paramount has] appropriated and used a qualitatively important part of plaintiff's material in such a way that features discernible in ... [Paramount's] work are substantially similar thereto."[7]

Finally, the Court wishes again to emphasize that its decision is in no way intended to disparage the creative talent of Eddie Murphy. It was Paramount and not Murphy who prepared the agreement in question. It is Paramount and not Murphy that obligated itself to compensate Buchwald if any material element of Buchwald's treatment was utilized in or inspired a film produced by Paramount. "Coming to America" is no less the product of Eddie Murphy's creativity because of the Court's decision than it was before this decision was rendered....

The Court understands there will now be an accounting phase of this case. The Court desires to make it clear that, depending on the evidence adduced during the accounting phase, the possibility exists that Paramount's accounting practices may make the imposition of tort damages appropriate.

Notes and Questions

a. Both the *based upon* clause and the *pay or play* clause of production agreements create significant controversy. These terms are traditional entertainment clauses which have no corollary in copyright law or in any other professions or industries. As a result, courts struggle to interpret them, often with only the vaguest notions of industry trade and custom.

b. Pay or Play agreements reflect the opportunity costs associated with agreeing to participate in a project without knowing whether it will actually take place. As discussed in Chapter V, producing a movie is a chicken-or-the-egg proposition. Without the right cast, no one will finance or green-light the project; without the financing and green-light, no top talent will agree to commit to the project. There are two methods available to break this impasse. First, the agreement may be conditional. For example, the financing of a film may be conditioned on the commitment of a particular cast or director. The obligation cannot be invoked unless the condition is satisfied.

The second method is through the pay or play clause in an employment agreement. Here, the star performer or director is guaranteed a salary whether or not the project begins. This compensates the individual for the work which might be given up because the scheduled commitment interferes with other possible projects. (This is the opportunity cost associated with each project.) As reflected in *Locke v. Warner Bros.*, the pay or play clause may result in a sizable payment to the artist, but it still does not reflect the true value that the completed project would have provided—particularly if the project had received widespread acclaim. To the extent that some projects flop, the difference between the guaranteed payment and the potential value of the contract is necessarily speculative.

c. As the court identified in *Buchwald*, based upon credit and the compensation which follows is only roughly analogous to the substantial similarity test of copyright. While ac-

---

7. The statement by Judge Learned Hand in *Fred Fisher, Inc. v. Dillingham*, 293 F.145 (1924) is appropriate to quote at this point. Judge Hand stated: "Everything registers somewhere in our memories, and no one can tell what may evoke it." Eddie Murphy, with commendable candor, admitted as much when he testified (by way of deposition) that he did not know "what triggers my subconscious."

cess is a critical element, similarity is not nearly as important as paternity. Projects can transform significantly from the first treatment to the final cut. Writers, actors, directors, and producers are constantly adding new material. Nonetheless, if the conceptual strands of the original, contractual project still exist at the end of the project, then the based upon credit and contractual obligations should survive.

d. Regarding *Coming to America*, others made claims of infringement. Because these claims were based on copyright infringement rather than contract law, the evidence of substantial similarity required a much higher degree of similarity than Buchwald's claim that there was a contractual relationship between the two works. See *Beal v. Paramount Pictures Corp.*, 20 F.3d 454 (11th Cir. 1994).

e. Alternatives to *based upon* clauses might be appropriate in some contracts. Producers are reluctant to owe money and to have too many claimants on a project. Just as the Writers Guild of America has rules limiting writers' credits, producers might elect to place limits on the eligibility for based upon credit. Such limitations might be based on time, content, or paternity. First, the acquisition agreement could provide that based upon credit will only be available if principle photography for the motion picture begins within a short time period, typically one to two years from the inception of the contract. Time may be a reasonable limiting tool on the assumption that the longer a project takes, the less likely the original submission was the creative spark for the project and the more likely other people have become responsible for the project's success.

Second, contracts could define based upon as requiring substantial similarity between the submission and the final project. While much more limited than the based upon clause in *Buchwald*, the test would be more stringent and more likely to be understood.

Third, *based upon* could be awarded on a good faith chain of paternity. Essentially, such a clause would provide that so long as the producers did not purchase a third party's treatment or script, then based upon credit would be available. Under this test, if a third party's material was also purchased, an arbitration would be held and the material most substantially incorporated into the final project would receive the based upon credit. This last test is closest in concept to the method that the Writers Guild of America employs in its arbitrations. The requirement of the arbitration helps avoid the bad faith purchase of other rights simply to break the chain of paternity.

f. Studios often try very hard to lure the most successful talent. These deals sometimes include transactions for third parties, entered into as favors for the valuable star. If those transactions do not go well, might it raise questions of good faith regarding the studio's commitment to that transaction? See *Locke v. Warner Bros., Inc.*, 57 Cal. App. 4th 354 (Cal. App. 2d Dist. 1997).

g. To what extent can a motion picture studio ensure good press? What possible legal or ethical issues are raised by this license agreement provision used by The Walt Disney Company in its licensing of movie trailers to website retailers?

> The Website in which the Trailers are used may not be derogatory to or critical of the entertainment industry or of [Disney] (and its officers, directors, agents, employees, affiliates, divisions and subsidiaries) or of any motion picture produced or distributed by [Disney] ... [or] of the materials from which the Trailers were taken or of any person involved with the production of the Underlying Works. Any breach of this paragraph will render this license null and void and Licensee will be liable to all parties concerned for defamation and copyright infringement, as well as breach of contract....

Video Pipeline, Inc. v. Buena Vista Home Entm't, Inc., 342 F.3d 191, 203 (3d Cir. 2003).

h. The large revenues earned by theatrical revenue for a motion picture must be divided between the producer, distributor, and exhibitor of the film. In an article for IFP, independent film expert Mark Litwak explains some of the transformation occurring in the financial arrangements between distributor and exhibitor:

> [E]xhibitors and distributors have competing interests. The exhibitor and distributor enter into a lengthy and complex agreement, which sets out how they share revenue. The agreement may require the exhibitor to give certain advances or guarantees to the distributor to secure a film. Additionally, the exhibitor may agree to play the film for a minimum number of weeks. In the past, a distributor releasing a major motion picture would split revenues on a sliding scale, with a 90/10 ratio for the first few weeks after the theater owner deducted its overhead costs. The distributor received 90% of the revenue and the exhibitor 10%. In subsequent weeks, the split would become more favorable for the exhibitor, shifting to 70/30, 60/40, or 50/50.

> This sliding scale formula gave exhibitors an incentive to retain the picture for a long run. As the weeks pass, the exhibitor's share increases. Of course, for major studio films, revenues tend to drop sharply after the initial few weeks. Giving the exhibitor a larger share of revenue in later weeks makes sense because the distributor wants to encourage the theatre owner to exhibit the film as long as possible.

> However, major studios have now adopted a new formula for sharing revenue with exhibitors. The revenues are split according to the magnitude of the overall national box office. The distributor receives 48% to 63% of box office receipts, with more receipts earning the distributor a larger percentage. On average, a major studio receives 53% of the box office gross. For art house fare, distributors average around 45%. The exhibitor no longer has the same incentive to hold a picture, and pictures tend to be released wider and pay off faster. For major studio films, 80% of the box office revenue is often received in the first two weeks of a picture's release.

> One aspect of exhibition has not changed. The exhibitor retains 100% of all sales at the concession stand. This is a major profit center for theaters; it can be said that theater owners are really in the fast food business. The candy and popcorn they sell have huge profit margins. However, nobody goes to the theater for the food. So, theater owners have an incentive to fill the house with a lot of moviegoers, even if they only earn a relative minor portion of the ticket price. This is why they prefer major studio films designed for mass consumption rather than art house fare that appeals to a niche audience.[8]

Problem X-B

Based on the reception to *Juliet Prescott* (see Problem V-A), Bryce has been offered the opportunity to modernize, adapt and direct another Shakespearean-based tragedy. This time, Bryce is working on *Leer*, a contemporary retelling of the classic story centered around a somewhat bizarre musical family. Obviously based upon *King Lear*, Bryce has

---

8. Mark Litwak, *Domestic Distribution Part 2*, IFP Resources, Oct. 17, 2012 at http://www.ifp.org/resources/domestic-distribution-part-2/.

written *Leer* as a modern day parable about society's descent and degeneration into an overly sex-focused pop culture. In the story, a film mogul who was once powerful at the height of the studio era had married a jazz singer who died of a drug overdose shortly after the birth of their third daughter. The eldest daughter, a pop diva, marries her record producer, and cuts her father out of her production deals; the middle daughter buys her father's former studio from a bankruptcy auction, only to cut, remake, and colorize his films; the third daughter, however, refuses not only to buy into the industry, but also to assist her aging father in making his long sought-after comeback.

To attract the cast needed to successfully complete this project, Bryce has tried to structure a contract that can attract the quality actor needed to play Leer. Since the budget will be modest, Bryce asks you to outline the deal points necessary to land the leading player.

In addition, Bryce is worried because the screenplay is not yet completed. Bryce is very concerned that the producer may use the *Leer* structure with another writer/director, so Bryce asks you to outline a deal memo that will protect Bryce even if the *Leer* concept is utilized by the producers with someone other than Bryce. Provide Bryce with a deal memo outlining the star's contract and a deal memo outlining the producer's agreement with Bryce as writer and director.

C. Derivative Interests and Bundling of Motion Picture Interests

Russell v. Price
612 F.2d 1123 (9th Cir. 1979)

Defendants distributed copies of the film "Pygmalion," the copyright for which had expired. They were sued by the owners of the renewal copyright in the George Bernard Shaw play upon which the film was based....

In 1913 Shaw registered a copyright on his stage play "Pygmalion." The renewal copyright on the play, obtained in 1941 and originally scheduled to expire in 1969, was extended by Congressional action to the year 1988. Shaw died in 1950 and the plaintiffs, except for Janus Films, are current proprietors of the copyright. Janus Films is a licensee.

In 1938 a derivative version of the play, a motion picture also entitled "Pygmalion," was produced under a license from Shaw; neither the terms nor the licensee's identity appear in the record. The film was produced by Gabriel Pascal, copyrighted by Loew's, and distributed by Metro-Goldwyn-Mayer ("MGM"). For undisclosed reasons, the film's copyright was allowed to expire in 1966. When and if the original film rights agreement expired is also not disclosed....

Defendants' main contention on the primary issue in this litigation is simply stated: Because the film copyright on "Pygmalion" has expired, that film is in the public domain, and, consequently, prints of that film may be used freely by anyone. Thus, they argue that their renting out of the film does not infringe the statutory copyright on Shaw's play.

Defendants admit that any new motion picture or other derivative work produced without the permission of the proprietors of the copyright on Shaw's play would infringe that underlying copyright. Defendants rely almost entirely on the recent opinion of Judge

Friendly in *Rohauer v. Killiam Shows, Inc.,* 551 F.2d 484 (2d Cir.), *cert. denied,* 431 U.S. 949 (1977). However, in so relying, they ignore or fail to appreciate the significant differences between that case and this one.

In *Rohauer* the author of a novel which was statutorily copyrighted in 1925 assigned exclusive movie rights to one Moskowitz, specifically promising in the contract to reassign to him or his successor in interest all film rights for the novel's copyright renewal term. A successful silent film was made under that assignment and separately copyrighted in 1926 by an assignee of Moskowitz. Unfortunately, the novel's author died prior to the end of the novel's first copyright term. The author's daughter, as statutory beneficiary of the right to renew, inherited the renewal term free from the film license granted by her mother. The daughter then granted exclusive movie and television rights for the renewal term to Rohauer. Killiam Shows, Inc., successor in interest to the 1926 film's renewal copyright, allowed the film to be shown on educational television without Rohauer's or the daughter's authorization, whereupon the latter two brought a copyright infringement action against Killiam.

The Second Circuit held on those facts that the derivative film's independent copyright entitled the defendant to continue showing the film without infringing rights under the renewal copyright in the underlying novel. Defendants here understand by this that a derivative copyright covers more than the new matter which the producer of the derivative work added to the underlying work. Thus, they say that when the derivative copyright expires the whole product enters the public domain free of the monopoly protection of any subsisting copyright in the underlying work. The court's opinion in *Rohauer,* however, makes it clear that this is simply not the case.

First, the *Rohauer* court placed heavy emphasis on the nongratuitous intent of the nonsurviving author to convey film rights in the novel's renewal term, a promise which had been bargained for in the initial assignment. The defendants here have never bargained with Shaw or his successors for anything, nor do they enjoy any relationship with anyone who had so bargained.

A second important difference between the favored party in Rohauer and the defendants here is that the defendant Killiam there was the proprietor of the still valid copyright in the film. By virtue of that copyright, Killiam was held to have sufficient rights in the matter derived from the novel to continue showing it as part of the film. A prominent rationale in that case for awarding those limited rights in favor of the owner of the derivative copyright is the protection and encouragement of the "large and independently copyrightable" "literary, musical and economic" contributions of the "person who with the consent of the author has created an opera or a motion picture film" from a copyrighted novel. However, whatever place sympathy for the position of creators of derivative works might properly have under the 1909 Copyright Act, the defendants here can take advantage of none, having contributed nothing to the production of the film "Pygmalion".

Nor is it apparent under *Rohauer* that such sympathy should have any place at all when the independent copyright on the derivative work has been allowed to expire. For then there is no longer a conflict between two copyrights, each apparently granting "their proprietors overlapping "exclusive' rights to use whatever underlying material ... had been incorporated into the derivative film." *Comment, Derivative Copyright and the 1909 Act New Clarity or Confusion?,* 44 Brooklyn L.Rev. 905, 912 (1978) (footnote omitted). Thus, the persons who might have had standing to raise the *Rohauer* claim here could, consistently with that case, be held to have forfeited it by their failure to renew the derivative copyright. Defendants here could never have laid claim to the right recognized in *Ro-*

hauer, and we perceive no reason to award it to them at the expense of the holders of the renewal copyright which still covers the Shaw play.

Thus, we reaffirm, without finding it necessary to repeat the rationale, the well-established doctrine that a derivative copyright protects only the new material contained in the derivative work, not the matter derived from the underlying work. Thus, although the derivative work may enter the public domain, the matter contained therein which derives from a work still covered by statutory copyright is not dedicated to the public. The established doctrine prevents unauthorized copying or other infringing use of the underlying work or any part of that work contained in the derivative product so long as the underlying work itself remains copyrighted. Therefore, since exhibition of the film "Pygmalion" necessarily involves exhibition of parts of Shaw's play, which is still copyrighted, plaintiffs here may prevent defendants from renting the film for exhibition without their authorization.

Defendants seek finally to avoid this result by citing *Classic Film Museum, Inc. v. Warner Bros., Inc.,* 597 F.2d 13 (1st Cir. 1979), *Aff'g* 453 F. Supp. 852 (D. Me. 1978). That decision concerned "the legal effect of an expired statutory copyright on work derived from an underlying work in which there exists a common-law copyright." Although defendants would have us ignore the major difference between an underlying common-law copyright and an underlying statutory copyright (the former extending in perpetuity, the latter restricted in length) that difference is the linchpin of the court's holding in Classic Film that a person could exhibit the motion picture "A Star is Born," on which the film copyright had expired, without infringing the common-law copyright in the unpublished screenplay and musical score from which the film was derived. The court found the Ricordi doctrine inapplicable for the following reason:

> "… Any protection offered by the Ricordi doctrine was limited to the fixed life of the underlying copyright (28 years plus the renewal period). The Ricordi doctrine is not equally applicable where there is an underlying common-law copyright which might extend indefinitely. Such unending protection of the derivative work would allow the Ricordi exception to swallow the rule of limited monopoly found in the constitution and copyright statutes."

The underlying statutory copyright in the instant case will expire in 1988. After that time Budget may freely distribute its copies of the 1938 film. The result we reach here does not conflict with the limited monopoly policy rooted in the Copyrights Clause of the constitution and advanced in the congressional acts.

For the foregoing reasons, we conclude that defendants' activities here infringed the subsisting copyright in Shaw's play and were properly enjoined....

Affirmed.

Stewart v. Abend

495 U.S. 207 (1990)

JUSTICE O'CONNOR delivered the opinion of the Court.

The author of a pre-existing work may assign to another the right to use it in a derivative work. In this case the author of a pre-existing work agreed to assign the rights in his renewal copyright term to the owner of a derivative work, but died before the commencement of the renewal period. The question presented is whether the owner of the derivative work infringed the rights of the successor owner of the pre-existing work by continued distribution and publication of the derivative work during the renewal term of the pre-existing work.

Cornell Woolrich authored the story "It Had to Be Murder," which was first published in February 1942 in Dime Detective Magazine. The magazine's publisher, Popular Publications, Inc., obtained the rights to magazine publication of the story and Woolrich retained all other rights. Popular Publications obtained a blanket copyright for the issue of Dime Detective Magazine in which "It Had to Be Murder" was published.

The Copyright Act of 1909 (1909 Act) provided authors a 28-year initial term of copyright protection plus a 28-year renewal term. In 1945, Woolrich agreed to assign the rights to make motion picture versions of six of his stories, including "It Had to Be Murder," to B. G. De Sylva Productions for $9,250. He also agreed to renew the copyrights in the stories at the appropriate time and to assign the same motion picture rights to De Sylva Productions for the 28-year renewal term. In 1953, actor Jimmy Stewart and director Alfred Hitchcock formed a production company, Patron, Inc., which obtained the motion picture rights in "It Had to Be Murder" from De Sylva's successors in interest for $10,000.

In 1954, Patron, Inc., along with Paramount Pictures, produced and distributed "Rear Window," the motion picture version of Woolrich's story "It Had to Be Murder." Woolrich died in 1968 before he could obtain the rights in the renewal term for petitioners as promised and without a surviving spouse or child. He left his property to a trust administered by his executor, Chase Manhattan Bank, for the benefit of Columbia University. On December 29, 1969, Chase Manhattan Bank renewed the copyright in the "It Had to Be Murder" story pursuant to *17 U.S.C. § 24*. Chase Manhattan assigned the renewal rights to respondent Abend for $650 plus 10% of all proceeds from exploitation of the story.

"Rear Window" was broadcast on the ABC television network in 1971. Respondent then notified petitioners Hitchcock (now represented by co-trustees of his will), Stewart, and MCA Inc., the owners of the "Rear Window" motion picture and renewal rights in the motion picture, that he owned the renewal rights in the copyright and that their distribution of the motion picture without his permission infringed his copyright in the story. Hitchcock, Stewart, and MCA nonetheless entered into a second license with ABC to rebroadcast the motion picture. In 1974, respondent filed suit against these same petitioners, and others, in the United States District Court for the Southern District of New York, alleging copyright infringement. Respondent dismissed his complaint in return for $25,000.

Three years later, the United States Court of Appeals for the Second Circuit decided *Rohauer v. Killiam Shows, Inc.*, 551 F. 2d 484, *cert. denied*, 431 U.S. 949 (1977), in which it held that the owner of the copyright in a derivative work may continue to use the existing derivative work according to the original grant from the author of the pre-existing work even if the grant of rights in the pre-existing work lapsed. Several years later, apparently in reliance on Rohauer, petitioners re-released the motion picture in a variety of media, including new 35 and 16 millimeter prints for theatrical exhibition in the United States, videocassettes, and videodiscs. They also publicly exhibited the motion picture in theaters, over cable television, and through videodisc and videocassette rentals and sales.

Respondent then brought the instant suit in the United States District Court for the Central District of California against Hitchcock, Stewart, MCA, and Universal Film Exchanges, a subsidiary of MCA and the distributor of the motion picture. Respondent's complaint alleges that the release of the motion picture infringes his copyright in the story because petitioners' right to use the story during the renewal term lapsed when Woolrich died before he could register for the renewal term and transfer his renewal rights to them.

Respondent also contends that petitioners have interfered with his rights in the renewal term of the story in other ways. He alleges that he sought to contract with Home

Box Office (HBO) to produce a play and television version of the story, but that petitioners wrote to him and HBO stating that neither he nor HBO could use either the title, "Rear Window" or "It Had to Be Murder." Respondent also alleges that petitioners further interfered with the renewal copyright in the story by attempting to sell the right to make a television sequel and that the re-release of the original motion picture itself interfered with his ability to produce other derivative works.... The issue before the court, therefore, was whether petitioners were entitled to distribute and exhibit the motion picture without respondent's permission despite respondent's valid copyright in the pre-existing story. Relying on the renewal provision of the 1909 Act, *17 U.S.C. § 24*, respondent argued before the Court of Appeals that because he obtained from Chase Manhattan Bank, the statutory successor, the renewal right free and clear of any purported assignments of any interest in the renewal copyright, petitioners' distribution and publication of "Rear Window" without authorization infringed his renewal copyright. Petitioners responded that they had the right to continue to exploit "Rear Window" during the 28-year renewal period because Woolrich had agreed to assign to petitioners' predecessor in interest the motion picture rights in the story for the renewal period....

Petitioners would have us read into the Copyright Act a limitation on the statutorily created rights of the owner of an underlying work. They argue in essence that the rights of the owner of the copyright in the derivative use of the pre-existing work are extinguished once it is incorporated into the derivative work, assuming the author of the pre-existing work has agreed to assign his renewal rights. Because we find no support for such a curtailment of rights in either the 1909 Act or the 1976 Act, or in the legislative history of either, we affirm the judgment of the Court of Appeals....

The right of renewal found in § 24 provides authors a second opportunity to obtain remuneration for their works. Section 24 provides:

> "[T]he author of [a copyrighted] work, if still living, or the widow, widower, or children of the author, if the author be not living, or if such author, widow, widower, or children be not living, then the author's executors, or in the absence of a will, his next of kin shall be entitled to a renewal and extension of the copyright in such work for a further term of twenty-eight years when application for such renewal and extension shall have been made to the copyright office and duly registered therein within one year prior to the expiration of the original term of copyright."

17 U.S.C. § 24 (1976 ed.)

Since the earliest copyright statute in this country, the copyright term of ownership has been split between an original term and a renewal term.... The 1831 renewal provisions created "an entirely new policy, completely dissevering the title, breaking up the continuance ... and vesting an absolutely new title eo nomine in the persons designated." In this way, Congress attempted to give the author a second chance to control and benefit from his work. Congress also intended to secure to the author's family the opportunity to exploit the work if the author died before he could register for the renewal term. "The evident purpose of [the renewal provision] is to provide for the family of the author after his death. Since the author cannot assign his family's renewal rights, [it] takes the form of a compulsory bequest of the copyright to the designated persons."

In its debates leading up to the Copyright Act of 1909, Congress elaborated upon the policy underlying a system comprised of an original term and a completely separate renewal term. See *G. Ricordi & Co. v. Paramount Pictures, Inc.,* 189 F. 2d 469, 471 (CA2) (the renewal right "creates a new estate, and the ... cases which have dealt with the subject assert that the new estate is clear of all rights, interests or licenses granted under the original copyright"), *cert. denied*, 342 U.S. 849 (1951). "It not infrequently happens that the author sells his copyright outright to a publisher for a comparatively small sum." H.R. Rep. No. 2222, 60th Cong., 2d Sess., 14 (1909). The renewal term permits the author, originally in a poor bargaining position, to renegotiate the terms of the grant once the value of the work has been tested. "[U]nlike real property and other forms of personal property, [a copyright] is by its very nature incapable of accurate monetary evaluation prior to its exploitation." 2 M. Nimmer & D. Nimmer, Nimmer on Copyright § 9.02, p. 9-23 (1989) (hereinafter Nimmer). "If the work proves to be a great success and lives beyond the term of twenty-eight years, ... it should be the exclusive right of the author to take the renewal term, and the law should be framed ... so that [the author] could not be deprived of that right." H.R. Rep. No. 2222, *supra*, at 14. With these purposes in mind, Congress enacted the renewal provision of the Copyright Act of 1909. With respect to works in their original or renewal term as of January 1, 1978, Congress retained the two-term system of copyright protection in the 1976 Act.

Applying these principles in *Miller Music Corp. v. Charles N. Daniels, Inc.*, 362 U.S. 373 (1960), this Court held that when an author dies before the renewal period arrives, his executor is entitled to the renewal rights, even though the author previously assigned his renewal rights to another party. "An assignment by an author of his renewal rights made before the original copyright expires is valid against the world, if the author is alive at the commencement of the renewal period. If the author dies before that time, the "next of kin obtain the renewal copyright free of any claim founded upon an assignment made by the author in his lifetime. These results follow not because the author's assignment is invalid but because he had only an expectancy to assign; and his death, prior to the renewal period, terminates his interest in the renewal which by § 24 vests in the named classes." The legislative history of the 1909 Act echoes this view: "The right of renewal is contingent. It does not vest until the end [of the original term]. If [the author] is alive at the time of renewal, then the original contract may pass it, but his widow or children or other persons entitled would not be bound by that contract." Thus, the renewal provisions were intended to give the author a second chance to obtain fair remuneration for his creative efforts and to provide the author's family a "new estate" if the author died before the renewal period arrived.

An author holds a bundle of exclusive rights in the copyrighted work, among them the right to copy and the right to incorporate the work into derivative works. By assigning the renewal copyright in the work without limitation, as in Miller Music, the author assigns all of these rights. After *Miller Music*, if the author dies before the commencement of the renewal period, the assignee holds nothing. If the assignee of all of the renewal rights holds nothing upon the death of the assignor before arrival of the renewal period, then, a fortiori, the assignee of a portion of the renewal rights, e.g., the right to produce a derivative work, must also hold nothing.

Application of this rule to this case should end the inquiry. Woolrich died before the commencement of the renewal period in the story, and, therefore, petitioners hold only an unfulfilled expectancy. Petitioners have been "deprived of nothing. Like all purchasers of contingent interests, [they took] subject to the possibility that the contingency may not occur."

The reason that our inquiry does not end here, and that we granted certiorari, is that the Court of Appeals for the Second Circuit reached a contrary result in *Rohauer v. Killiam Shows, Inc.*, 551 F. 2d 484 (1977). Petitioners' theory is drawn largely from *Rohauer*. The Court of Appeals in *Rohauer* attempted to craft a "proper reconciliation" between the owner of the pre-existing work, who held the right to the work pursuant to *Miller Music*, and the owner of the derivative work, who had a great deal to lose if the work could not be published or distributed. Addressing a case factually similar to this case, the court concluded that even if the death of the author caused the renewal rights in the pre-existing work to revert to the statutory successor, the owner of the derivative work could continue to exploit that work. The court reasoned that the 1976 Act and the relevant precedents did not preclude such a result and that it was necessitated by a balancing of the equities:

> "[T]he equities lie preponderantly in favor of the proprietor of the derivative copyright. In contrast to the situation where an assignee or licensee has done nothing more than print, publicize and distribute a copyrighted story or novel, a person who with the consent of the author has created an opera or a motion picture film will often have made contributions literary, musical and economic, as great as or greater than the original author.... [T]he purchaser of derivative rights has no truly effective way to protect himself against the eventuality of the author's death before the renewal period since there is no way of telling who will be the surviving widow, children or next of kin or the executor until that date arrives."

The Court of Appeals for the Second Circuit thereby shifted the focus from the right to use the pre-existing work in a derivative work to a right inhering in the created derivative work itself. By rendering the renewal right to use the original work irrelevant, the court created an exception to our ruling in *Miller Music* and, as petitioners concede, created an "intrusion" on the statutorily created rights of the owner of the pre-existing work in the renewal term.

Though petitioners do not, indeed could not, argue that its language expressly supports the theory they draw from *Rohauer*, they implicitly rely on §6 of the 1909 Act, *17 U.S.C. §7* (1976 ed.), which states that "dramatizations ... of copyrighted works when produced with the consent of the proprietor of the copyright in such works ... shall be regarded as new works subject to copyright under the provisions of this title." Petitioners maintain that the creation of the "new," i.e., derivative, work extinguishes any right the owner of rights in the pre-existing work might have had to sue for infringement that occurs during the renewal term.

We think, as stated in Nimmer, that "[t]his conclusion is neither warranted by any express provision of the Copyright Act, nor by the rationale as to the scope of protection achieved in a derivative work. It is moreover contrary to the axiomatic copyright principle that a person may exploit only such copyrighted literary material as he either owns or is licensed to use." 1 Nimmer §3.07[A], pp. 3-23 to 3-24 (footnotes omitted). The aspects of a derivative work added by the derivative author are that author's property, but the element drawn from the pre-existing work remains on grant from the owner of the pre-existing work. See *Russell v. Price*, 612 F. 2d 1123, 1128 (CA9 1979) (reaffirming "well-established doctrine that a derivative copyright protects only the new material contained in the derivative work, not the matter derived from the underlying work"), *cert. denied*, 446 U.S. 952 (1980). So long as the pre-existing work remains out of the public domain, its use is infringing if one who employs the work does not have a valid license or assignment for use of the pre-existing work. It is irrelevant whether the pre-existing work is inseparably intertwined with the derivative work. Indeed, the plain language of §7 supports the view that the full force of the copyright in the pre-existing work is preserved despite incorporation into the derivative work....

In fact, if the 1976 Act's termination provisions provide any guidance at all in this case, they tilt against petitioners' theory. The plain language of the termination provision itself indicates that Congress assumed that the owner of the pre-existing work possessed the right to sue for infringement even after incorporation of the pre-existing work in the derivative work.

> "A derivative work *prepared* under authority of the grant before its termination may continue to be utilized under the terms of the grant after its termination, but this privilege does not extend to the preparation after the termination of other derivative works based upon the copyrighted work covered by the terminated grant." § 304(c)(6)(A) (emphasis added).

Congress would not have stated explicitly in § 304(c)(6)(A) that, at the end of the renewal term, the owner of the rights in the pre-existing work may not terminate use rights in existing derivative works unless Congress had assumed that the owner continued to hold the right to sue for infringement even after incorporation of the pre-existing work into the derivative work.

Accordingly, we conclude that neither the 1909 Act nor the 1976 Act provides support for the theory set forth in *Rohauer*. And even if the theory found some support in the statute or the legislative history, the approach set forth in *Rohauer* is problematic. Petitioners characterize the result in *Rohauer* as a bright-line "rule." The Court of Appeals in *Rohauer*, however, expressly implemented policy considerations as a means of reconciling what it viewed as the competing interests in that case. While the result in *Rohauer* might make some sense in some contexts, it makes no sense in others. In the case of a condensed book, for example, the contribution by the derivative author may be little, while the contribution by the original author is great. Yet, under the *Rohauer* "rule," publication of the condensed book would not infringe the pre-existing work even though the derivative author has no license or valid grant of rights in the pre-existing work. Thus, even if the *Rohauer* "rule" made sense in terms of policy in that case, it makes little sense when it is applied across the derivative works spectrum. Indeed, in the view of the commentators, *Rohauer* did not announce a "rule," but rather an "interest-balancing approach."

Finally, petitioners urge us to consider the policies underlying the Copyright Act. They argue that the rule announced by the Court of Appeals will undermine one of the policies of the Act—the dissemination of creative works—by leading to many fewer works reaching the public. Amicus Columbia Pictures asserts that "[s]ome owners of underlying work renewal copyrights may refuse to negotiate, preferring instead to retire their copyrighted works, and all derivative works based thereon, from public use. Others may make demands—like respondent's demand for 50% of petitioners' future gross proceeds in excess of advertising expenses ...—which are so exorbitant that a negotiated economic accommodation will be impossible." These arguments are better addressed by Congress than the courts....

For the foregoing reasons, the judgment of the Court of Appeals is affirmed, and the case is remanded for further proceedings consistent with this opinion.

Notes and Questions

a. The Second Circuit had quickly followed *Russel v. Price* with *Filmvideo Releasing Corp. v. Hastings,* 668 F.2d 91 (2d Cir. 1981) (Hopalong Cassidy motion pictures), which set the stage for the Supreme Court decision to clarify the role played by a pre-existing grant of copyright.

b. As noted in *Stewart v. Abend*, Congress eliminated the renewal provision, replacing it with a right to terminate the grant of a copyright. The termination provisions seek to introduce the same Congressional policy of providing copyright holders a second opportunity to benefit from the copyrighted work created. Because no such rights exist for works-made-for-hire, the characterization of a transfer as an assignment or as a work for hire may have tremendous significance. These issues persist. See *Marvel Characters, Inc. v. Simon,* 310 F.3d 280 (2d Cir. 2002) (remanding to trial the issue of work for hire status of the creation of Captain America).

c. One of the more difficult areas to reconcile *Russel v. Price* and *Stewart v. Abend* has been with the industry practice regarding unpublished screenplays. The Ninth Circuit and Second Circuit have both concluded that the common-law copyrights in these screenplays cannot be recognized. As the Second Circuit explained:

> In *Batjac [Prods. Inc. v. Goodtimes Home Video Corp.,* 160 F.3d 1223, 1225, 1236 (9th Cir. 1998)]*, the Ninth Circuit ruled that the publication of a motion picture publishes so much of the underlying screenplay as was disclosed in the motion picture. The court reasoned that a contrary rule would turn on its head the copyright principle of limited monopoly, in that "the copyright in any film that has entered the public domain under the 1909 Act could be resurrected by an unpublished screenplay." We find this reasoning persuasive and consonant with the principles approved in our prior cases, to wit, that when the author consents to the inclusion of his work in a derivative work, the publication of the derivative work, to the extent that it discloses the original work, also constitutes publication of that underlying work. We conclude in the present case, based on the statute and the principles underlying the scope of copyright protection, that if a previously unpublished screenplay is embodied in a motion picture, so much of the screenplay as is disclosed in the motion picture is published when the motion picture is published. This interpretation is also consistent with the long-standing approach apparently taken by the Copyright Office, that the publication of a derivative work constitutes publication of so much of the underlying work as is disclosed in the derivative work.

Shoptalk, Ltd. v. Concorde-New Horizons Corp., 168 F.3d 586, 592 (2d Cir. 1999). A somewhat different analysis may be required if the rights to the screenplay were not fully transferred to the production company. See *Welles v. Turner Entertainment Co.*, 503 F.3d 728 (2007) (reviewing rights reserved to Orson Welles for the screenplay to Citizen Kane).

d. The issues of pre-existing literary works are not the only problems faced by filmmakers incorporating copyrighted images. For example, a documentary filmmaker captured a 75-second performance of a musician's act which was included in the motion picture without the musician's consent. In a subsequent action for violation of her rights of publicity and trademark, what is the expected result? Compare *Man v. Warner Bros., Inc.,* 317 F. Supp. 50 (S.D.N.Y. 1970) (documentary *Woodstock*), with *Zacchini v. Scripps-Howard Broadcasting Co.,* 433 U.S. 562 (1977) (human cannonball).

e. Like documentary footage, incorporation may sometimes come from prior staged performances. One common problem occurs when a filmmaker desires to use scenes filmed during the shooting of its motion picture as part of an upcoming sequel. None of the actors in the original film have been hired to appear in the sequel, but have signed a contract allowing for the use of their names and likenesses. Does the film company need an additional agreement with each of the actors? See *Donahue v. Artisan Entm't, Inc.,* 2002 U.S. Dist. LEXIS 5930 (S.D.N.Y. Apr. 3, 2002).

f. Still images may create the same concerns. Compare *Brown v. McCormick,* 87 F. Supp. 2d 467 (D. Md. 2000), *aff'd* 243 F.3d 536 (4th Cir. 2001) (finding infringement for use of copyrighted quilt patterns in film but awarding a surprisingly low award of damages for the various infringing activities stemming from the motion picture entitled *How to Make an American Quilt*) with *Sandoval v. New Line Cinema Corp.,* 147 F.3d 215 (2d Cir. 1998) (brief showing of photographs in background of scene *de minimis* given how indistinguishable the images appeared).

Problem X-C

Bryce has been diligently working on *Leer*. Bryce has become very concerned that since Shakespeare's original play is in the public domain, the newly drafted screenplay and film will not be protected by copyright. Advise Bryce on the extent to which copyright will protect both the *Leer* screenplay and the finished motion picture.

D. Character Licensing

New Line Cinema Corp. v. Easter Unlimited, Inc.
17 U.S.P.Q.2D (BNA) 1631 (E.D.N.Y. 1989)

… The Elm Street Venture and the Fourth New-Line-Heron Venture are joint ventures and registered the series of four motion pictures in the United States Copyright Office of the Library of Congress based on assignments of rights in New Line Cinema Corporation. The plaintiffs collectively own all the copyrights to the four films issued.

The theme of the films is the terror expressed through viewing Freddy and the mystery and confusion between reality and dreams. Freddy is the only means of expressing the idea. The appearance of Freddy that expresses the idea gives copyright protection to the character of Freddy, independent of the films' copyright protection.… *Walt Disney Productions v. Air Pirates,* 581 F.2d 751, 755 (9th Cir. 1978), *cert. denied,* 439 U.S. 1132 (1979) (A comic book character which contains "unique elements of expression" is protectible).

Freddy's character is revealed through the expression of his scarred face and glove with protruding razor blades (a copy is appended). Copyright protection is extended to the component part of the character which significantly aids in identifying the character.

Copyright Protection

Copyright infringement may be established by showing access to the protected work and substantial similarity. The wide circulation of the films and the Freddy products distributed in the trade gave Easter access to Freddy and the Freddy glove.

The recorded conversation on May 3, 1989 between Anthony Spiesman, a private investigator employed by New Line, and Mitchell Schiff, an Easter employee, convinced this court that Easter copied the Freddy glove.

In answer to Spiesman's question as to whether Easter designs the items it sells, Schiff replied: "Some of the time. Some items we just see around. You know capturing someone else's ideas and modifying it to what we think is better. The Krueger stuff is gone to the movies.… Yeah and like the Nightmare thing, you know everybody puts this little name on it and you don't have any royalty involved."

Copying may also be established by showing access and substantial similarity. Easter claims the difference in the gloves defeats plaintiff's claim of substantial similarity, i.e., the Freddy glove consists of "brown cloth with armor-like articulations and openings on the inner side of the fingers and the palm.... By contrast the HAND is a glove of tightfitting black nylon with no openings. The visual impression of the black nylon is more elegant, with a vampirish ghoulish effect as opposed to the utilitarian look and feel of Freddy's glove.

"The extensions to the black fabric of the HAND are more like thin flat nails. They could be made to flop about and by way of construction, lay flat on a place perpendicular to the "knives" extending from the Freddy glove. Freddy's knives on the other hand look like rigid steel stilettos."

Easter places undue emphasis on the dissimilarity of the two gloves. "Even if a copied portion be relatively small in proportion to the entire work, if qualitatively important, the finder of fact may find substantial similarity." Since copyright protects the "expression of [an] idea," where the copy is of "the expression of the idea," substantial similarity is established no matter how little is copied.

In *Warner Bros. v. American Broadcasting Companies,* 720 F.2d 231, 241 (2d Cir. 1983) in a claim of infringement, the court, finding a sufficient dissimilarity between the copyrighted character of Superman, and the fictional character of Ralph Hinkley, the principal figure in the television series, "The Greatest American Hero," noted:

> A somewhat paradoxical aspect of infringement disputes, especially pertinent to claims of character infringement, concerns the attention courts give both to similarities and differences in the two works at issue. Professor Nimmer categorically asserts as a proposition, "It is entirely immaterial that in many respects plaintiff's and defendant's works are dissimilar if in other respects similarity as to a substantial element of plaintiff's work can be shown." 3 Nimmer § 13.03(B) at 13-38. In Hand's pithy phrase, "No plagiarist can excuse the wrong by showing how much of his work he did not pirate." *Sheldon v. Metro-Goldwyn Pictures Corp.,* 81 F.2d 49, 56 (2d Cir.), *cert. denied,* 298 U.S. 669, 56 S. Ct. 835, 80 L.Ed. 1391 (1936). Yet Professor Nimmer also recognizes, as a second proposition, that "a defendant may legitimately avoid infringement by intentionally making sufficient changes in a work which would otherwise be regarded as substantially similar to that of the plaintiff's, 3 Nimmer § 13.03(B) at 13-38.1 to -38.2.

We find that Easter attempted to avoid infringement and failed.

Trademark Infringement and Unfair Competition

The Lanham Act claim is based on section 43(a) of the Lanham Act. The section protects unregistered as well as registered marks. Registration gives jurisdictional and procedural advantages to the registrant. The right to trademark protection however arises from use and not from registration.

We find that an appreciable number of ordinarily prudent purchasers of items found in novelty stores during the Halloween season are likely to be mislead or confused as to the source of Easter's glove. This is particularly true when presented with the attachment on which the glove is inserted showing the word NIGHTMARE in a form of print similar to New Line's presentation of Freddy's glove. In examining both gloves presented to the potential market of teenagers and young adults, the likelihood of confusion is apparent.

New Line has a valuable property right in the character Freddy Krueger and the Freddy glove acquired over a period of about five years at great expense. Easter with full knowledge of New Line's right designed a glove with a view to appropriating that right for its own gain and resulting in New Line's loss.

New Line has shown (a) the possibility of irreparable injury and (b) likelihood of success on the merits and is therefore entitled to preliminary injunctive relief. The motion for a preliminary injunction is granted....

Gary Friedrich Enterprises, LLC v. Marvel Characters, Inc.
716 F.3d 302 (2013)

In 1972, the Marvel Comics Group published a comic book featuring the "Ghost Rider"—a motorcycle-riding superhero with supernatural powers and a flaming skull for a head. The issue—which sold for twenty cents—told the story of Johnny Blaze, a motorcycle stunt rider who promised his soul to the devil to save his adoptive father from cancer.... Gary Friedrich contends that he conceived the Ghost Rider, the related characters, and the origin story, and that he owns the renewal term copyrights in those works. While acknowledging that Friedrich contributed his ideas, defendant-counter-claimant-appellee Marvel Characters, Inc. ("Marvel") contends that the Ghost Rider characters and story were created through a collaborative process with Marvel personnel and resources, and that Marvel owns the renewal rights in question....

The facts are heavily disputed. They are presented here in the light most favorable to Friedrich, with all reasonable inferences drawn in his favor. To the extent Friedrich argues that he is entitled to summary judgment on the issue of authorship, we construe the facts in Marvel's favor and set forth that alternative version below....

Friedrich was a part-time freelance comic book writer, scripting issues of existing comic book serials when solicited by Marvel and other publishers. In 1971, Friedrich decided to try to publish a comic book starring his flaming-skulled hero after the Comics Code Authority relaxed its standards to permit comic books to contain more adult-themed and supernatural content. After refining the origin story and the characters' appearances, Friedrich created a written synopsis on his own initiative and at his own expense. The synopsis detailed Ghost Rider's origin story and the main characters' appearances.

Friedrich presented his written synopsis to his friend Roy Thomas, an assistant editor at Magazine Management Co., Inc. ("Magazine Mgmt."), the then-publisher of Marvel comics. Thomas liked the idea, so he gave the synopsis to Marvel chief Stan Lee and arranged for Lee to meet with Friedrich. Lee agreed to publish the Ghost Rider comic book in the series *Marvel Spotlight*, a vehicle used to audition new superheroes. In return, Friedrich agreed to assign his rights in the Ghost Rider characters to Marvel. Friedrich and Lee never discussed renewal rights and did not execute a written agreement....

The first Ghost Rider comic was published in Marvel Spotlight, Vol. 1, No. 5 ("*Spotlight* 5") in April 1972, bearing a copyright notice in favor of "Magazine Management Co., Inc. Marvel Comics Group." The first page of the comic, reproduced above, contained a credit box that included the following:

CONCEIVED & WRITTEN

GARY FRIEDRICH

At the same time *Spotlight* 5 was published, Marvel advertised the new superhero in a contemporaneous issue of *The Amazing Spider-Man*. In a feature called "Marvel Bullpen Bulletins," Marvel encouraged fans to read *Spotlight* 5 and acknowledged that Friedrich had "dreamed the whole thing up." Ghost Rider quickly became one of Marvel's most popular comic book heroes. After *Spotlight* 5, Ghost Rider stories appeared in the next six issues of *Marvel Spotlight*. By May 1973, Marvel launched a separate *Ghost Rider* comic book series.…

Friedrich continued to write Ghost Rider and other superhero stories for Marvel on a freelance basis until approximately 1978. In 1976, Congress repealed the 1909 Copyright Act and replaced it with the current Copyright Act. Under the 1976 Act, which took effect on January 1, 1978, *id.* § 102 (codified at note preceding 17 U.S.C.), a work created outside the scope of employment was considered a "work-for-hire" only if the parties had executed an express written agreement to that effect, *see* 17 U.S.C. § 101 (defining "work made for hire"). Thus, in 1978, Cadence Industries, Inc. ("Cadence"), the then-publisher of Marvel comics, required Friedrich and all of its other freelance artists to sign a form work-for-hire agreement.

The full agreement was a page long and read in pertinent part:

> MARVEL is in the business of publishing comic and other magazines known as the Marvel Comics Group, and SUPPLIER wishes to have MARVEL order or commission either written material or art work as a contribution to the collective work known as the Marvel Comics Group. MARVEL has informed SUPPLIER that MARVEL only orders or commissions such written material or art work on an employee-for-hire basis.

> THEREFORE, the parties agree as follows:

> In consideration of MARVEL's commissioning and ordering from SUPPLIER written material or art work and paying therefor, SUPPLIER acknowledges, agrees and confirms that any and all work, writing, art work material or services (the "Work") which have been or are in the future created, prepared or performed by SUPPLIER for the Marvel Comics Group have been and will be specially ordered or commissioned for use as a contribution to a collective work and that as such Work was and is expressly agreed to be considered a work made for hire.

> SUPPLIER expressly grants to MARVEL forever all rights of any kind and nature in and to the Work, the right to use SUPPLIER's name in connection therewith and agrees that MARVEL is the sole and exclusive copyright proprietor thereof having all rights of ownership therein. SUPPLIER agrees not to contest MARVEL's exclusive, complete and unrestricted ownership in and to the Work.

July 31, 1978 Agreement between Friedrich & Marvel (the "Agreement"). Cadence told Friedrich that the Agreement only covered future work and that he had to sign it without alteration if he wanted to obtain further freelance work from them. Thus, Friedrich filled in his name and address by hand as the "Supplier" and signed the Agreement on July 31, 1978. Friedrich was not paid anything for signing the Agreement. After he signed, neither Cadence nor any subsequent Marvel publisher solicited any more freelance work from him.

The initial copyright term for Ghost Rider expired at the end of 2000, twenty-eight years after *Spotlight* 5's original publication in 1972. *See* 17 U.S.C. § 304(a)(1)(A). Beginning in 2001, the renewal copyright would have vested in Friedrich, as the original author, by operation of law. *See id.* § 304(a)(1)(C)(i), (2)(B)(ii). Nonetheless, Marvel exploited the Ghost Rider character after 2000 by: publishing reprints of *Spotlight* 5 in 2001, 2004, and 2005; publishing six issues of a new *Ghost Rider* comic series that ran from August 2001 to January 2002; offering a single Ghost Rider toy for sale in catalogs in 2003 and 2004; having Ghost Rider make cameo appearances in other characters' video games released in 2000 and 2006; filming the *Ghost Rider* movie in 2005 and releasing it in 2007 (pursuant to a licensing agreement entered into in 2000); and releasing a *Ghost Rider* video game, based on the movie, in 2007. While most of these items did not credit Friedrich, all the *Spotlight* 5 reprints published during the renewal term contained Friedrich's "Conceived & Written" credit.

Friedrich was not aware of Marvel's use of the Ghost Rider character during the renewal period until around 2004, when he learned Marvel was preparing to make the *Ghost Rider* movie. On April 6, 2004, Friedrich's attorney wrote a letter to Sony Pictures, the company producing the movie, asserting Friedrich's rights to the Ghost Rider copyright. In a response dated April 14, 2004, Marvel advised Friedrich that Ghost Rider was a work-for-hire. Despite taking this position, however, Marvel paid Friedrich with checks labeled "roy," meaning "royalties," when it reprinted *Spotlight* 5 in 2005.

Friedrich first learned about the concept of renewal rights in 2005 or 2006. He filed for, and received, a Renewal Copyright Registration in *Spotlight* 5 and Ghost Rider in February 2007. He then assigned the rights to his company, Gary Friedrich Enterprises, LLC....

We review *de novo* both the grant of summary judgment and the district court's interpretation of the Agreement. In reviewing a grant of summary judgment, we must construe the evidence in the light most favorable to the non-moving party and draw all reasonable inferences in its favor.

For artistic works still in their initial term of copyright protection on January 1, 1978, the Copyright Act establishes two terms of protection: an initial term of twenty-eight years from "the date [the copyright] was originally secured" and a renewal term of sixty-seven years. The renewal term of a copyright is "not merely an extension of the original copyright term but a 'new estate ... clear of all rights, interests or licenses granted under the original copyright.'" *P.C. Films Corp.*, 138 F.3d at 456–57. Its purpose is "to 'provide authors a second opportunity to obtain remuneration for their works'" and "'to renegotiate the terms of the grant once the value of the work has been tested.'" *Id.* at 457.

An author may assign his renewal rights during the copyright's initial term, but "there is a strong presumption against the conveyance of renewal rights." *Corcovado Music Corp. v. Hollis Music, Inc.*, 981 F.2d 679, 684 (2d Cir.1993). This presumption may be rebutted by an express assignment of "renewals of copyright" or "extensions of copyright," or by "general words of assignment," such as "forever," "hereafter," or "perpetual," if the parties' clear intent was to convey renewal rights. *P.C. Films Corp.*, 138 F.3d at 457. In *Siegel*, we explained that words like "forever" may be indicative of an intent to convey renewal rights, but this "intent is to be determined by the trier of the facts." In *P.C. Films Corp.*, we affirmed the district court's conclusion, reached after a bench trial, that the term "perpetual" indicated a clear intent to convey renewal rights. There, the parties had agreed to use the term "perpetual" after "months of negotiations conducted by sophisticated and expert parties, each represented by counsel." Furthermore, there was undisputed testimony that the assignee would not have entered the agreement "for less than a perpetual term and that, in his understanding, the term 'perpetual'... was not coterminous with the initial copyright term." ...

The Agreement is ambiguous on its face. First, the critical sentence defining the "Work" covered by the Agreement is ungrammatical and awkwardly phrased:

> In consideration of MARVEL's commissioning and ordering from SUPPLIER written material or art work and paying therefor, SUPPLIER acknowledges, agrees and confirms that any and all work, writing, art work material or services (the "Work") which have been or are in the future created, prepared or performed by

SUPPLIER for the Marvel Comics Group have been and will be specially ordered or commissioned for use as a contribution to a collective work and that as such Work was and is expressly agreed to be considered a work made for hire.

This opaque cluster of clauses is simply not clear and parsing through its dense provisions does little to elucidate its meaning.

Second, the language is ambiguous as to whether it covered a work published six years earlier. The introductory recitals indicate that the "SUPPLIER *wishes to have* MARVEL order or commission" work and that "MARVEL only *orders or commissions* such ... work on an employee-for-hire basis." There is no explicit acknowledgement that the generic "SUPPLIER" ever performed work for Marvel previously, and certainly no specific mention of the Ghost Rider works. Marvel attempts to extract the phrase "all work ... which have [sic] been ... created, prepared or performed by SUPPLIER for the Marvel Comics Group" from the dense sentence quoted above, but the entire agreement suggests that this was a forward-looking contract only intended to cover work submitted after the Agreement was signed. Read in this context, work that "have [sic] been ... created"—to the extent the phrase has a discernible meaning—may refer to work that was in-progress when the Agreement was executed, even though Marvel may have commissioned that work, and the freelance artist may have begun working on it, before the Agreement was formally reduced to writing. *See, e.g.,* Agreement ("MARVEL has informed SUPPLIER that MARVEL only orders ... work on an employee-for-hire basis.... SUPPLIER acknowledges, agrees and confirms that any and all work ... have [sic] been and will be specially ordered or commissioned ... [as] a work made for hire.").

Third, the language is ambiguous as to whether it conveys renewal rights. The contract contains no explicit reference to renewal rights and most of the language merely tracks the 1976 Act's definition of "work made for hire." If the contract only covers "work made for hire," Marvel would be the statutory author, and the "SUPPLIER" would not have any renewal rights that could be assigned to Marvel.

Finally, Marvel relies heavily on the provision "grant[ing] to MARVEL *forever* all rights of any kind and nature in and to the Work." In context, however, for the reasons discussed above, it is not clear whether this broad language applies to work performed by Friedrich some six years earlier. The broadness of the language would be of no help to Marvel if the Agreement were intended to cover only future work. Moreover, that sentence goes on to provide that "Marvel is the sole and exclusive copyright proprietor thereof having all rights of ownership therein," which again suggests Marvel is the statutory author by virtue of the fact that the work was "made for hire." Thus, the Agreement could reasonably be construed as a form work-for-hire contract having nothing to do with renewal rights. Accordingly, the language by itself fails to overcome the "strong presumption against the conveyance of renewal rights."

Because the Agreement is reasonably susceptible of more than one meaning, it is ambiguous and we next look to extrinsic evidence in the record to determine whether there is a genuine dispute regarding the parties' intent at the time of the Agreement.

Here, the record demonstrates that Cadence extended this same one-page, forward-looking form contract to all its freelance artists to ensure that commissioned work would be deemed a "work made for hire" under the new 1976 Copyright Act. It did so shortly after the 1976 Act took effect on January 1, 1978. When Friedrich signed the Agreement, he was doing other freelance work for Marvel and he believed the Agreement would only cover future work because that was what Cadence told him at the time. He was not paid anything separately for signing the Agreement. Moreover, *Spotlight* 5 had been published six years earlier by a different corporate entity (Magazine Mgmt.) and had grown so popular that Marvel had already reprinted it once and had launched a separate *Ghost* Rider comic book series. Given that context, it is doubtful the parties intended to convey rights in the valuable Ghost Rider copyright without explicitly referencing it. It is more likely that the Agreement only covered ongoing or future work. Hence, there is a genuine dispute regarding the parties' intent for this form contract to cover Ghost Rider.

Even if the parties intended the definition of "Work" to extend to Ghost Rider, that alone would not mean that they intended the Agreement to convey Friedrich's remaining renewal rights in that work. First, the Agreement appears to create an "employee for hire" relationship, but the Agreement could not render Ghost Rider a "work made for hire" *ex post facto,* even if the extrinsic evidence shows the parties had the intent to do so. The 1909 Act governs whether works created and published before January 1, 1978 are "works made for hire," and that Act requires us to look to agency law and "the actual relationship between the parties, rather than the language of their agreements," in determining the authorship of the work. Thus, regardless of the parties' intent in 1978, the evidence must prove Ghost Rider was actually a "work made for hire" at the time of its creation. But the circumstances surrounding the creation of the work are genuinely in dispute....

Second, there is little extrinsic evidence to suggest that the parties actually intended to assign anything other than an initial term of copyright and much evidence to suggest that they did not. Friedrich was unrepresented by counsel, was told that the Agreement only covered future work, and did not learn about the concept of renewal rights until 2005. There was no discussion about renewal rights when he signed the Agreement in 1978. A jury could reasonably conclude that the parties never even considered renewal rights when they made this contract. Accordingly, the district court erred in granting summary judgment based on the Agreement....

[Marvel challenged the claim on the basis of the three year copyright statute of limitations. Sporadic royalty payment to Friedrich made it unclear whether Marvel denied his claim as author or joint author of the work.] Hence, a jury could find that a reasonably diligent person would not have known that Marvel was exploiting Ghost Rider, without paying royalties, during the renewal term but before April 4, 2004. Because there are genuine disputes regarding whether Friedrich should have known about Marvel's repudiation of his claim of ownership, his claim is not untimely as a matter of law.

On appeal, Friedrich also asks us to review the district court's decision to deny his cross-motion for summary judgment on the issue of authorship. Friedrich contends that the record establishes as a matter of law that he was the author, or at least a joint author, of the Ghost Rider work....

Although the 1976 Act requires the parties to execute an express agreement that a work is "made for hire," works created prior to 1978 are governed by the 1909 Copyright Act. That Act did not require an express agreement; instead, "[t]he copyright belong[ed] to the person at whose 'instance and expense' the work was created." "A work is made at the hiring party's 'instance and expense' when the employer induces the creation of the work and has the right to direct and supervise the manner in which the work is carried out," even if that right is never exercised.

We agree with the district court that there are genuine disputes of material fact that preclude granting summary judgment on the issue of authorship. While Friedrich points to evidence that would demonstrate that he was the sole author or a joint author of the work, Marvel has presented evidence supporting the following contradictory account of the creation of Ghost Rider:

Marvel had published comic books starring a cowboy named Ghost Rider since 1966. In 1971, Friedrich was working on an issue of *Daredevil* when he approached Thomas with an idea, not a written proposal, for a motorcycle-riding villain named Ghost Rider. Thomas thought the character was better suited as a superhero in his own comic book and arranged a meeting with Lee. Lee authorized the comic book, deciding Ghost Rider's alter ego would be named "Johnny Blaze," even though both Friedrich and Thomas disliked that name. Friedrich began writing Ghost Rider's origin story only after this meeting. Thomas and Ploog scheduled a meeting to design the character, but Friedrich failed to attend that meeting and did not provide any instruction on what Ghost Rider should look like beforehand. Therefore, Ploog modeled the new character after the original cowboy, incorporating Thomas's idea for an Elvis-like leather jump suit and a skull head, and then spontaneously drawing flames to frame the skull. The rest of the book was produced according to the "Marvel method," with Marvel retaining editorial control throughout and paying all costs, including a page rate for Friedrich's contributions as a freelance writer.

When construed in Marvel's favor, the record reveals that Friedrich had nothing more than an uncopyrightable idea for a motorcycle-riding character when he presented it to Marvel because he had not yet fixed the idea into a tangible medium. A jury could find that Marvel then "induce[d] the creation of" the flaming-skulled superhero Ghost Rider and *Spotlight* 5, and had "the right to direct and supervise the manner in which the work [was] carried out." *Martha Graham Sch.,* 380 F.3d at 635. Under this version of the facts, Thomas, a Marvel employee, was the one who decided that Ghost Rider should be a superhero in his own comic book. Lee, the head of Marvel, commissioned the work by authorizing the comic's production. Ghost Rider's appearance and origin story developed through the collaborative efforts of Friedrich, Thomas, Lee, and Ploog, all of whom were paid by Marvel. If accepted as true, a jury could easily conclude from these facts that Ghost Rider was a "work made for hire" and thus that Marvel was the sole statutory author. Accordingly, we affirm the district court's denial of Friedrich's motion for summary judgment.

We conclude that the district court erred in granting summary judgment because the Agreement is ambiguous and there are genuine disputes of material fact regarding the parties' intent to assign renewal rights in that Agreement, the timeliness of Friedrich's ownership claim, and the authorship of the work. Accordingly, the judgment is VACATED and the case is REMANDED for trial.

Notes and Questions

a. Comic book rights have engendered a great deal of litigation. See *Lee v. Marvel Enterprises, Inc.,* 765 F. Supp. 2d 440, 445 (S.D.N.Y. 2011) aff'd, 471 Fed. Appx. 14 (2d Cir. 2012) (unpublished); *Abadin v. Marvel Entertainment, Inc.,* No. 09 Civ. 715, 2010 WL 1257519 (S.D.N.Y. March 31, 2010); *Stan Lee v. Marvel Enterprises, Inc.,* 386 F.Supp.2d 235 (S.D.N.Y.2005) (involving various claims related to Stan Lee's ownership of rights to the Marvel universe); *Marvel Characters, Inc. v. Kirby,* 726 F.3d 119 (2d Cir. 2013) (involving work of Jack Kirby on Fantastic Four and other projects for Marvel); *Siegel v. Warner Bros. Ent. Inc.,* 658 F. Supp. 2d 1036 (C.D. Cal. 2009) (involving origins and ownership of Superman).

b. Different film projects may result in very different merchandise. In *Twentieth Century Fox Film Corp. v. Suarez Corp.,* 46 U.S.P.Q.2d (BNA) 1312 (S.D.N.Y. Mar. 19, 1998), a mail-order jeweler quickly created a design to mimic that worn by the star of *Titanic*. While the court refused to order a preliminary injunction against the jeweler, that was only because the court found the voluntary steps taken to withdraw from the marketplace made the injunction redundant and overreaching. As a result, Fox suddenly found itself in the jewelry business.

c. One of the most difficult aspects of character licensing is understanding the scope of such licenses. Literary characters are created within their literary world, but they often have the ability to transcend these worlds. In the bitter dispute between Marvel Comics and Twentieth Century Fox, this battle waged on for the supremacy of the *X-Men* characters as these superheroes transcended the confines of the *X-Men* comic books, animated television series and feature films by appearing in a live-action television series called *Mutant X*. Whereas the *X-Men* characters are endowed with superpowers, mere mortal lawyers are ultimately left struggling to determine these superheroes' final fates through the interpretation of licensing agreements contested between warring protagonists. See *Twentieth Century Fox Film Corp. v. Marvel Enters.*, 155 F. Supp. 2d 1 (S.D.N.Y. 2001), *aff'd in part, rev'd in part*, 277 F.3d 253 (2d Cir. 2002).

d. A deeper understanding of the licensing of characters can be gleaned from the ownership dispute involving the Jim Henson characters, Wilkins and Wontkins, created for John H. Wilkins Company coffee advertisements:

> In the late 1950s, when a copyright user wanted to obtain perpetual rights in a character (distinct from rights in a work in which the character appeared) it was the practice of the copyright bar to spell this out in no uncertain terms. One compelling reason for this is that in 1954, the Ninth Circuit had issued its opinion in *Warner Bros. Pictures, Inc. v. Columbia Broadcasting Pictures, Inc. v. Columbia Broadcasting System, Inc.*, 216 F.2d 945 (9th Cir. 1954), which held that the clearest possible language was needed to divest Dashiell Hammet of his rights in his detective character Sam Spade, the principal character in The Maltese Falcon, and that his grant of motion picture, radio and television rights in The Maltese Falcon to Warner Bros. did not, as asserted by Warner Bros., give it the exclusive right to use Sam Spade in those media. In the wake of this watershed case, the copyright bar was on notice that there was the strongest presumption that even when an author transferred the copyright in a work in which a character was fully delineated, the author retained the right to use the character in sequels or other works. After that decision any copyright lawyer representing a user wishing to buy exclusive rights in a character would make certain that the assignment documents said so unmistakably and unequivocally.

Jim Henson Prods. v. John T. Brady & Assocs., 16 F. Supp. 2d 259, 277 (S.D.N.Y. 1997).

e. Characters also leave themselves open to significant claims of parody. Recent examples include *World Wrestling Fedn. Entm't, Inc. v. Big Dog Holdings, Inc.*, 280 F. Supp. 2d 413 (W.D. Pa. 2003) (wrestling characters); *Warner Bros. v. American Broadcasting Companies*, 720 F.2d 231 (2d Cir. 1983) (Superman parody); *Mattel Inc. v. Walking Mt. Prods.*, 2003 U.S. App. LEXIS 26294 (9th Cir. 2003) (Barbie doll).

f. Another point regarding character licensing is the difficulty of knowing which characters will prove successful and unsuccessful when promoted for marketing. Despite the vagaries of popularity, the contractual obligations to promote characters may not be readily ignored just because of changing market conditions. See *Marsu, B.V. v. Walt Disney Co.*, 185 F.3d 932 (9th Cir. 1999) (obligation to promote European characters through creation of television show).

The opposite problem also occurs from time to time. In *Tom Doherty Assocs. v. Saban Entertainment*, 60 F.3d 27 (2d Cir. 1995), what had been a reasonable licensing agreement to turn children's television into modestly popular children's books became far less interesting to the licensor when its Mighty Morphin Power Rangers suddenly became the must-have characters among the pre-school set. Nonetheless, Saban's attempt to ignore the preexisting book publishing agreement could not be ignored simply because the characters were suddenly economic superheroes.

Problem X-D

Bryce has called with an interesting issue that has developed during the creation of *Leer*. In writing material for the screenplay (*e.g.*, the scenes for the three sisters and the character sketches), Bryce believes the basis for a spin-off project has arisen. Entitled *Regan's Revenge*, Bryce outlined a novel based on Leer's second daughter, the villainous movie mogul. Bryce has also completed the first three chapters of the novel. The novel uses the relationship between Regan and Leer (derived from the relationship between Regan and Lear in Shakespeare's stage play) as the background for a dark comic look at Hollywood.

Bryce has received an offer to publish the novel, along with a publishing contract that requires a right of first refusal on motion picture rights to the novel. The production agreement for *Leer* assigns the copyright in the screenplay to the producers, including all sequel and prequel rights. The present screenplay for *Leer* has only three scenes with Regan. Bryce believes the character could be reduced even more, if necessary. Advise Bryce on the extent to which copyright law, trademark law, or customary industry contractual provisions would treat Bryce's development of *Regan's Revenge* as separate from *Leer*, and on Bryce's possible courses of action.

E. Ratings

Maljack Prods. v. Motion Picture Ass'n of Am.
52 F.3d 373 (D.C. Cir. 1995)

Maljack, an independent movie and video production company, sued the industry's major trade association, the Motion Picture Association of America, for breach of contract. Maljack asserted that the Association's film-rating arm had discriminated against it because it was not a member of the Association. The district court dismissed the complaint under Fed. R. Civ. P. 12(b)(6) for failure to state a claim, holding that Maljack's assertions of discrimination—that its movie had received an "X" rating for violence, while more violent films produced by companies belonging to the Association had been given "R"s—were not adequate to allege a breach of the ratings contract. We reverse....

Maljack is an Illinois corporation primarily engaged in distributing videocassettes to the home market. Its first major venture into the production of general-release films came in the mid-1980s, when it produced Henry: Portrait of a Serial Killer, a movie depicting, in documentary style, the life of a fictional serial murderer loosely based on a person on death row in Texas. Maljack concedes that Henry contains several explicit scenes of physical violence, including depictions of two rapes and several brutal murders.

The Motion Picture Association of America is a New York-incorporated trade association consisting of many of the largest American producers and distributors of television programs and motion pictures. Maljack is not a member. Among its other activities, the Association operates the Code and Rating Administration ("CARA"), located in California, which reviews movies prior to their release and evaluates their suitability for viewing by children. At the time of the events at issue, CARA rated movies either "G," "PG," "PG-13," "R," or "X" — with the exception of the last, all federally registered certification marks owned by the Association. Submission of a film to CARA is wholly voluntary, and producers are free to distribute movies without obtaining an Association rating.

In March 1988 Maljack submitted Henry to CARA for rating and paid a fee calibrated to the film's production costs. CARA gave Henry an "X" on grounds of its violence. That marked it, according to the Association's published general description of the rating, as having an "accumulation of brutal or sexually connected language, or of explicit sex or excessive and sadistic violence" that rendered it "patently an adult film." A representative of CARA explained that four sequences in the movie were particularly offensive and would have to be cut before CARA would even consider giving Henry an "R," the next most restrictive rating. Maljack refused to make the cuts and instead appealed the "X" rating to the Association's Classification and Rating Appeals Board. The Appeals Board affirmed the "X" rating.

In February 1989 Maljack surrendered the ratings certificate for Henry and chose instead to distribute the movie unrated. Maljack alleges that the picture was not as successful as it would have been if the Association had given Henry an "R": a substantial number of movie theaters will not show films that either are "X"-rated or lack a CARA rating altogether. Maljack maintains that the Association denied Henry an "R" rating because it was a small, independent production company that did not belong to the Association.

Maljack filed a two-count complaint against the Association in May 1990. Count I asked the court to cancel the Association's registered certification mark for the "R" rating on the grounds that the defendant applied its ratings in an illegally discriminatory fashion; the trial court dismissed this count on jurisdictional grounds, and Maljack does not appeal that ruling. Count II alleged that the Association's discrimination breached a covenant of good faith and fair dealing implied by law in CARA's agreement to rate Henry for a set fee. The district court also dismissed this count, holding that the complaint was devoid of non-conclusory factual allegations capable of supporting an inference that the Association had acted unfairly or in bad faith. Maljack moved to amend its complaint, but the district court denied leave to amend on the ground that the proposed amended complaint suffered from the same basic flaw.

Maljack now appeals both the dismissal of its original complaint and the denial of leave to amend. We need reach only the first issue. . . .

We review de novo the district court's dismissal of the complaint for failure to state a claim. At this stage of the litigation the plaintiff's burden is relatively light. . . . At the same time, we are not to accept inferences drawn by Maljack if they are unsupported by the alleged facts, nor will we accept purely legal conclusions masquerading as factual allegations.

The parties and the district court have so far assumed that California law governs the rating agreement, and we will proceed on the same assumption. Under California law, "all contracts contain an implied covenant of good faith and fair dealing [that] '"requires each contracting party to refrain from doing anything to injure the right of the other to receive the benefits of the agreement.'" A complaint alleging breach of this covenant must plead deliberate and conscious bad faith on the part of the defendant:

[A]llegations which assert such a claim must show that the conduct of the defendant, whether or not it also constitutes a breach of a consensual contract term, demonstrates a failure or refusal to discharge contractual responsibilities, prompted not by an honest mistake, bad judgment or negligence but rather by a conscious and deliberate act, which unfairly frustrates the agreed common purposes and disappoints the reasonable expectations of the other party thereby depriving that party of the benefits of the agreement.

If the Association deliberately gave Henry an "X" rating instead of an "R" because Maljack was not a member, it breached this implied covenant. The Association's assertion that Maljack "bargained to receive CARA's subjective judgment and nothing more" is inaccurate: as it stated in its complaint, Maljack reasonably expected that CARA would rate Henry in good faith based upon the content of the film alone and not the identity of its producer and that producer's links (or lack of links) to the Association. This expectation of fair dealing is protected under California law as if it were an explicit obligation of the contract.

The question, then, is whether the original complaint adequately alleged the sort of discrimination that would violate the implied covenant. Maljack pled the following:

- That it did not belong to the Association,

- That although Henry contained some violent scenes, "the scenes were neither overly explicit or gory as compared to other films produced or released by members of the [Association] and given a "R" rating by the [Association],"

- That because of the small ($1,100) rating fee paid by Maljack under CARA's production-cost-based sliding scale, CARA was aware that Henry was not a major-studio "big budget" film,

- That CARA gave Henry an "X" rating without ever explaining "why other films containing equal or greater violence and released by member companies of the [Association] had received an "R" rating," [and]

- That the Association breached the covenant of good faith and fair dealing implied in the rating agreement "by rating [Henry] in a discriminatory manner when compared to other films it had given an 'R' rating to." The Association objects to the conclusory tone of this last paragraph and faults Maljack for never stating explicitly that it was discriminated against because it did not belong to the Association. This is too stingy a reading of the complaint. The context makes clear the plaintiff's claim that the discrimination mentioned in the last paragraph flowed from Maljack's non-member status.

The Association's more serious objection is that the mere fact that Henry received an "X" while more violent films by member companies were rated "R" cannot logically support an inference that CARA acted with improper motive. It is true, as the Association points out, that the complaint would have been stronger if it had alleged that the rating criteria were biased against independent producers, or that CARA had a pattern of giving unwarranted "X" ratings to similar movies, or that the Association's member companies had a financial interest in sabotaging Henry, or that there was some direct communication from the Association indicating bad faith.

But the absence of such confirming data does not nullify what has been alleged. Disparate treatment is the essence of all discrimination claims: at their core is always the assertion that the defendant has treated like cases differently on the basis of some impermissible criterion. And this is exactly what Maljack's complaint has alleged. The fact, which we must take as true, that the Association routinely assigned "R" ratings to member films more violent than Henry certainly suggests that it may have applied a different standard to Henry because of the identity of its producer. Later on, of course, at the summary judgment or trial phase of this litigation, it will not be easy for Maljack to show so skewed a ratings pattern as to support the inference necessary to meet California's quite demanding requirements for demonstrating bad faith, but federal pleading standards do not require the plaintiff to stuff its complaint with all of the details establishing the discrepancy. This is especially true in a case where, as here, the alleged discriminator is applying rather broad and amorphous criteria (e.g., "excessive ... violence"), so that countless details may be needed to support an inference of discrimination.

The Association effectively conceded at oral argument that this method of proof—comparing treatment in an individual case to the pattern of related decisions—is meaningful in this context. When asked to consider a hypothetical case in which a children's film like Snow White was given an "X" rating, Association counsel acknowledged that an observer could legitimately say something was amiss: Snow White's "X" would be so out of line with CARA's other decisions as to raise a compelling inference of something more than a simple judgment error or difference of opinion. Such logic is no different from that contained in Maljack's complaint. Henry the Serial Killer may be no Snow White (nor even her wicked stepmother), but the degree of difference is a question of fact, and we must now take the facts to be as Maljack alleges.

We therefore reverse the district court's order dismissing the original complaint and remand the case for further proceedings.

So ordered.

2. From Hays Onward[9]

Taking their cue from the baseball scandal involving the Chicago White Sox [in which professional baseball hired former federal judge Kenesaw Mountain Landis as the first baseball commissioner to "clean up the game"], the film producers decided that the best antidote for their Jewish, immoral product was a commissioner of film who was beyond reproach. The choice was Will Hays, former postmaster general of the United States. Hays had most recently served as President Harding's campaign manager. As a Republican and a Presbyterian elder, he represented the perfect image for the Jewish film industry. Hays was elected president of the Motion Picture Producers and Distributors of America. The members were the major studios, Columbia (now Sony), Metro-Goldwyn-Mayer, Paramount, RKO (now also owned by Paramount's parent company Viacom), Twentieth Century-Fox, United Artists, Universal, and Warner Bros. With the addition of Disney and the merger of United Artists into Metro-Goldwyn-Mayer, the list has remained essentially unchanged.

The Hays Office, as the organization was generally known, undertook to clean up the image of the film industry. Initially, this was a rather ad hoc process of reviewing movies and clearing them for distribution, with a healthy dose of public relations thrown in at every step. By 1927, however, the Hays Office began to formalize its practices. In 1927, the Hays Office promulgated the Production Code, an official document outlining the principles of film production for approved films in the United States....

9. Jon M. Garon, *Entertainment Law*, 76 Tul. L. Rev. 559, 649 (2002) (reprinted with author's permission).

The Hays Office established a comprehensive process of prior review of source material to ensure that plays and novels were acceptable before they were purchased as the subjects for future films. The Production Code banned scenes, such as a man and woman sharing a bed (even if married); topics such as promiscuity, brutality, or pleasant depictions of immorality; and words ranging from "God" and "sex" to "guts," "nuts," "nerts," and "louse." Hays Office members were fined as much as $25,000 for violating the Code. These exacting rules and fines applied to every major studio and distributor in the United States. With detailed constraints and complete participation, there is no doubt that the films produced were more highly scrutinized than any governmental regulation could have created....

The greatest problem of the Production Code was its success. Although it has been significantly modified in response to the concerns that only Will Hays and a few deputies dictated the tastes and morality for the entire company, the reality is that the current Motion Picture Association of America (MPAA) has not significantly modified the effects of this system to this day.... The success of the Production Code existed before the films were granted protection by free speech. It was designed as a fence around a fence, crafted to ensure that Hollywood films were not censored by the governmental review boards out of fear of the negative press that would ensue and of the difficulties a finding of immorality would have on the already negotiated distribution agreements. As such, it resulted in far greater censorship than would have been required by the government, probably more stringent than would have been tolerated by the public of its elected officials. But as a voluntary activity, it was not in the interest of the filmmakers, distributors, exhibitors, or government officials to complain....

For the public, two important imprints were left by the Hays Office legacy. The first deals with voluntary censorship. The notion that voluntary censorship is a benign, unintrusive model designed to promote positive values without sacrificing free expression or democratic values has been sold to us since 1922. In addition to motion pictures, the media has added voluntary ratings to television, music, and video games, often at the urging of Congress....

Following the massacre of high school students in Littleton, Colorado in 1999, President Clinton pressured the National Association of Theater Owners to enforce the so-called voluntary movie-ratings restrictions by requiring photographic identification. Under the policy now enforced by the vast majority of theater exhibitors ... [p]arents who wish to encourage their teenage children to attend appropriate but mature films must accompany them to the theater. While still technically voluntary, the system urged by the President seems much like the governmental ban on alcohol and tobacco from which it is modeled.

The second legacy of the Hays Office was to weaken the impact of state-sponsored censorship. The fence within the fence of the Hays Office effectively marginalized the state and local film boards. Their threat kept the Hays Office humming, but only so no film board could have an opportunity to complain about the content of a Hollywood film. The effect was to desensitize the public and the courts to the real censorship taking place....

Notes and Questions

a. While the decision to allow adult films to be designated by anyone as "X" made sense, the pervasive nature of the ratings made the NC-17 inevitable. At the same time, the very need for the NC-17 rating reinforces how much more significant the ratings actually are than suggested by the MPAA. Rather than merely serving as a voluntary guide for concerned parents, the ratings may take on unintended roles. To what extent do the MPAA rating guidelines provide an unintended seal of approval for theatrical motion pictures? For another example of the problems caused by the X rating for mainstream films, see *Miramax Films Corp. v. Motion Picture Ass'n*, 148 Misc. 2d 1, 560 N.Y.S.2d 730 (N.Y. Sup. Ct. 1990).

b. Why is it critical that the MPAA has trademarked each of the ratings it uses within the rating system? Do these marks actually meet the legal standards for being registered trademarks as either the source of goods or an endorsement thereof?

c. Enterprising businesses might see other opportunities to make use of the ratings designation. Could a clothing manufacturer design a line of children's clothes rated "PG-13" and a lower-cut line rated "R"? See *Motion Picture Ass'n. v. Rated R Clothing, Inc.*, 646 F. Supp. 22 (S.D.N.Y. 1986).

d. The ratings are used by parents as a guide to let them and their children select appropriate viewing material, as well as by most exhibitors looking to control who is permitted to enter the theatre. Is such a restriction by the theatrical exhibitors free of any First Amendment concerns? Is the failure to enforce the rating restrictions the potential cause for liability? See *Delgado v. American Multi-Cinema, Inc.*, 72 Cal. App. 4th 1403, 85 Cal. Rptr. 2d 838 (Cal. Jud. Council 1999); *Rosen v. Budco, Inc.*, 10 Phila. 112 (Pa. C.P. 1983).

e. Colleges and universities sometimes play the role of *in loco parentis*, serving as surrogate parents for the students on campus. Can a college campus prohibit the showing of X or NC-17 films in school facilities? Does it matter if the school is a private institution or a publicly funded state college? See *Swope v. Lubbers*, 560 F. Supp. 1328 (W.D. Mich. 1983).

f. With the advent of DVDs, a new sub-market has developed for R rated films. Distributors now market DVDs that have both exhibition rated and unrated versions in video stores. To what extent will this trend undermine the impact of the MPAA? Will rules be forthcoming to bar the two-rating distribution of DVDs?

g. In addition to the MPAA, ratings systems now exist for music, broadcast television and cable, and video games. Have these additional ratings regimes improved the usefulness of the ratings? Do these guides have the impact intended by their advocates?

h. In addition to the rating system, the MPAA also operates a title registry service. The MPAA's Title Registration Bureau is voluntary, but all members of the MPAA use it. The system allows any member to object to the use of a registered title or title similar to that of a registered title. Studios tend to use the system aggressively to make naming new films somewhat difficult. In the case of the dispute between The Weinstein Company and Warner Bros., the movie originally entitled *The Butler* received a notice of objection by Warner Bros. because it was the same title as one used in 1916 for a short, silent film. An arbitration hearing determined that The Weinstein Company could use *Lee Daniels' The Butler* because that title had also been registered by The Weinstein Company and Warner Bros. had failed to object to the use of the phrase "the butler" as part of another title. Because The Weinstein Company had marketed the movie under its original title during the pendency of the arbitration, however, it received a $400,000 fine.

Problem X-E

Bryce received a green light to proceed with the screenplay for *Leer* as a filmed musical in the genre of modern rock opera as popularized by *Chicago*, *American Idiot*, or *Book of Mormon*. Bryce now faces a problem. Bryce's rewrites of the script and extensive character development made certain scenes more graphic and sexual than the initial draft. The producers are objecting to the explicit content of the revisions. They believed the original script served to condemn the immoral lifestyle of the characters while Bryce's most recent changes seem to celebrate that immorality. Because of these new explicit scenes, the producers are concerned that Bryce may not be able to deliver an "R" rated film.

The contract specified that Bryce would use best efforts to deliver a "PG-13" rated film, but required the producers to accept delivery of the finished film with an "R" rating if Bryce could not, in good faith, edit the film in a manner that was consistent with the approved screenplay, if such edit resulted in an "R" rating.

Bryce seeks your advice. To what extent can the production agreement require editing of a film to receive a particular MPAA rating, and what can Bryce do to avoid creating an "NC-17" film or having the production cancelled? Provide Bryce with guidance on how to best address the situation.

F. Bibliography and Links

Paul A. Baumgarten, Donald C. Farber & Mark Fleischer, Producing, Financing & Distributing Film — A Comprehensive Legal & Business Guide (2d ed. 1992).

Jon Garon, The Independent Filmmaker's Law & Business Guide to Financing, Shooting, & Distributing Independent & Digital Films (2d Ed. 2009).

Gregory Goodell, Independent Feature Film Production (1982) (this is a wonderfully thoughtful text, and although out of print, well worth utilizing as a solid reference).

Schuyler M. Moore, The Biz: The Basic Business, Legal & Financial Aspects of the Film Industry (2000).

Peter Decherney, *Auteurism on Trial: Moral Rights and Films on Television*, 2011 Wis. L. Rev. 273 (2011).

Catherine L. Fisk, *The Role of Private Intellectual Property Rights in Markets for Labor and Ideas: Screen Credit and the Writers Guild of America, 1938–2000*, 32 Berkeley J. Emp. & Lab. L. 215 (2011).

Howard M. Frumes, *Surviving Titanic: Independent Production in an Increasingly Centralized Film Industry*, 19 Loy. L.A. Ent. L. Rev. 523 (1999).

Michael J. Fucci, *Facing the Future: An Analysis of the Television Ratings System*, 6 UCLA Ent. L. Rev. 1 (1998).

Jon M. Garon, *Star Wars: Film Permitting, Prior Restraint & Government's Role in the Entertainment Industry*, 17 Loy. L.A. Ent. L. Rev. 1 (1996).

Allan R. Grogan & Sam C. Mandel, *Representing the New Media Company, Hollywood Online*, PLI Order No. G4-4031(1998).

Richard M. Mosk, *The Jurisprudence of Ratings Symposium Part I: Motion Picture Ratings in the United States*, 15 Cardozo Arts & Ent. L.J. 135 (1997).

Jenica Yurcic, *Co-Productions: The Future Feature*, 5 Vand. J. Ent. L. & Prac. 76 (2002).

Websites

Motion Picture Association of America, http://www.mpaa.org

The Producers Guild of America, http://www.producersguild.org

Writers Guild of America, west http://www.wga.org/

Directors Guild of America, http://www.dga.org/

Screen Actors Guild, http://www.sag.org

IATSE, http://www.iatse.lm.com

California Film Commission, http://commerce.ca.gov/film/

TV Parental Guidelines: About the TV Ratings and V-Chip, http://www.tvguidelines.org/
   default.asp

The Entertainment Software Rating Board (ESRB) ratings, http://www.esrb.org/esrbratings.asp

Recording Industry Association of America: Parental Advisory, http://www.riaa.com/issues/
   parents/default.asp

Chapter XI

Music Publishing

A. Overview of the Music Industries

1. The Industry at a Glance

Music is generally divided into two discrete industries: the music publishing business and the record business. Music publishing includes printed music, the income generated from the public performance of music, and more generally the business activities of composers and lyricists. The record business or sound recording business includes the manufacture and distribution of CDs, DVDs, and more generally the business activities related to bands and performing artists.

The music industries are the most complex and rapidly changing in the entertainment industries, and arguably in the entire economy. According to Billboard Magazine, the global music market has three primary distributors of recorded music (such as CDs, albums, or digital audio files): Universal Music Group (38.9%); Sony Music Entertainment (29.5%), which acquired EMI in 2012; and Warner Music Group (18.7%). Independent companies comprise 12.3% share of recorded music ownership, but a healthy 35% market share of the distribution. These recorded music distributors also own the three largest music publishing companies. Sony's acquisition of EMI has made it the largest music publisher, followed by Universal Music Group and Warner/Chappell Music.

The music industries have contracted substantially since 1999 when peer-to-peer file sharing was first introduced. 2013 was the first year since 1999 that the international revenue for music saw an increase in income. File sharing, the shift from album to single sales made popular through digital marketplaces, and the growth of streaming services for music and music videos, have combined to restructure the music industry in the past decade. These changes have occurred in the music publishing industry, the record distribution system, and the law governing exemptions from copyright for public performances of music.

2. Ownership of a CD/MP3

A music CD (or its digital counterpart) actually contains a number of different rights. The breakdown of these interests will help students and lawyers understand both the complexity of negotiating transactions and of reformulating the industry's current structure.

A CD begins with written musical compositions. Many songs have two writers, a composer who writes the music and a lyricist who writes the words for the song. These two components of each song are typically written together with the intention that a single copyrighted work is created, so the composer and lyricist are joint authors of the song. Often, one person serves as both composer and lyricist. (This person is referred to as composer or songwriter throughout the text.)

Once a song is written, it must be arranged for performance by multiple musical instruments. In some situations, this is little more than adding chord structure to the melody, but in other situations it entails having an arranger write a complex series of orchestrations and additional parts for various instruments to play. If the arrangement and orchestrations embody original works of authorship, these may also be subject to copyright protection. Because the arrangements are dependent on the original song, commonly the arranger is hired as an employee in a work-made-for-hire capacity so that no additional copyright owner is added.

With the arrangement completed, the song is now ready for recording. A producer is hired (sometimes for the entire CD, but increasingly for each particular song). The producer then helps shape the arrangement, directs the recording artist, selects takes, and serves as the controlling authority over the sound of the final master tape. The producer is typically the copyright holder for the master tape of the finished song. The recording artist has a much more limited copyright in the performance, limited to when the work is performed publicly by means of a digital audio transmission. On occasion, however, the performing artist undertakes the editorial and authorial functions of the producer and may therefore share the producer's copyright. If the song digitally copies portions of the music, rhythm or other component from a different recording, then this digital sample must be licensed from its copyright holder. In some situations, the sample's copyright holder can earn as much as 50% of the recording copyright, although payments ranging from 10% to 33% are more typical.

Background singers and musicians are not likely to have any copyright interest in the work, but will be entitled to royalties for sales and public performances based on collective bargaining agreements negotiated by the American Federation of Musicians, or other unions. They will also have a modest royalty due for the digital public performance rights.

Assuming that a CD has ten songs or cuts collected for a single performing artist, the masters may have ten different producers and ten different composer/lyricist teams. The record label is the company that aggregates these rights, arranges for the manufacturing of the CD, pays for its marketing, provides for its distribution, and collects income for the use of the recording in other media. The record label will also purchase the necessary copyrights or licenses, hire the musicians, and control the selection and order of the songs.

Finally, the record label will hire writers to create liner notes and artists to design the album cover, and will attach its trademarks to indicate the source of the record manufacture and distribution.

As a result of this process, there are two different music industries—the publishing industry and the recording industry. On the publishing side, the composer and lyricist typically retain the copyright in their songs and enter into a publishing agreement. In the most typical arrangement, they assign the copyright in the song to the publisher in exchange for 50% of the royalties. The publisher exploits the written song in at least four markets: (1) print sheet-music sales; (2) blanket licenses through the performing rights societies for television, radio, and public performances; (3) direct licenses for films, DVDs, home video, and theatrical productions (grand rights); and (4) mechanical licenses for the right to include the song on CDs. In this example, the composer and lyricist are entitled to a payment for each copy of the song embodied in a CD, vinyl album, MP3 file, or other format.

The recording industry, however, is governed by the labels rather than the publishers. The label must license the song from the publisher, paying a mechanical royalty for the right to embody the song in each recording.

The performing artist enters into a contract with the label, assigning any copyright interest for an interest in the royalties generated through the sale of the copies of the recording and through direct licensing of the recording in any other medium. The label also acquires the copyright interest of each producer, each musician, the arranger, and all others who contributed to the recording of each rendition of the song.

Finally, in many modern recording agreements, the performing artist is also the composer and lyricist for some or all of the compositions. As a result, the line between publishing rights and recording rights sometimes blurs.

Although most attention has been paid to the recording industry, changes in technology have also affected the music publishing industry as well. Composers and lyricists have not been compensated when songs are distributed as unauthorized MP3 files, resulting in a loss of income as dramatic as that recently experienced in the recording industry. The Internet's competition with television and radio may erode these income sources as well.

3. Exclusive Writing Agreements

From the 1920s to the 1940s, the height of Tin Pan Alley, musicians would sell the copyright in their songs outright for a few dollars, never to see another payment or royalty. The anomalous two-term copyright protection provided by the 1909 Copyright Act helped to limit the negative consequences to a small degree. The transfer of copyright could not bind the composer unless the transfer of the second term was in writing. In addition, the writing bound only the transferor, so if the composer died prior to the beginning of the second copyright term, then the right to renew passed to the composer's spouse or as otherwise provided under the statute. This had only a modest impact on the law, but it provided some minimal relief.

To avoid any possible loss of copyright, the music publishing companies turned to the work for hire doctrine. By employing composers full-time, in their music writing capacity, these writers were employees in every legal sense, and as a result, the copyright vested in the publisher as employer. The employee never was an owner of the copyright and no renewal rights were created in these employees.

While this practice is largely gone, some issues of exclusivity remain. The most important is the scope of the music publishing agreement. The agreement may provide that every song written during the term of the contract is subject to the terms of the agreement. If the music publisher is providing comprehensive service by promoting all of the composer's songs, managing the mechanical royalties, and generally aiding the songwriting career, then this may be a reasonable provision. If the publisher is really working to administrate the songs from a single album or particular albums, then this exclusivity may become a form of overreaching that musicians should seek to avoid.

4. Relations with Recording Companies

The music publishing industry is sufficiently independent of the sound recording industry that most agreements to record a band's albums are not tied to owning the publishing rights as well. Oddly, this may be the only area in which some form of tying is not the presumptive model. Nonetheless, these functions are discrete and a musician is generally better served by licensing publishing rights separately from recording rights.

5. Mechanical Licenses and Making Records

To produce an album, the sound recording company (the "record company" or "label") needs the permission of the composer to reproduce the composition in recorded form on each tape and CD copy manufactured. This is called the mechanical recording right. On behalf of the composer, the publisher typically manages the mechanical rights.

If the composition has never been recorded before, then copyright law provides that the right to license the composition remains exclusively with the composer or the composer's publisher. Once the composition has been recorded and publicly distributed, the law allows anyone who wishes to make his or her own sound recording using the composition to do so merely by following the notice and payment guidelines of § 115 of the Copyright Act. In practice, most parties avoid the need for working through the Copyright Office and instead arrange these licenses through the Harry Fox Agency, a division of the National Music Publishers' Association. The fee charged is typically the fee set through the Copyright Royalty Board.[1] Limelight, a service offered through Rightsflow by Google, also provides simplified mechanical licenses and related services. The mechanical rights fees can theoretically be negotiated upward or downward by the parties, though in practice, the statutory rate operates as an upper limit on the payments made to artists for mechanical rights.

If an album includes ten cuts, the current royalty owed to the composers is $0.91 per album (i.e., 10 x $0.091). On a gold album of 500,000 copies manufactured and sold, that equals a payment of $455,000 from the label to the publisher. The amount would increase to $591,500 if there were thirteen songs on the album. The publisher typically retains fifty percent of the income and the composer retains the other fifty percent.

6. Controlled Composition Clauses

The controlled composition clause is actually a provision of the sound recording agreement rather than the publishing agreement; however, its importance to the revenue structure for a recording artist makes the discussion of this provision and its application clearer in the context of the publishing industry.

The rock and roll era changed the music industry. Bands were generally expected to have written the songs they performed. As a result, the labels no longer wanted to pay

---

1. Until changed by the Copyright Royalty Board, the rate is 9.1 cents per song or 1.75 cents per minute of playing time or fraction thereof, whichever is greater.

for the mechanical rights, since the recording artists were also the composers and were being paid for using the band's own songs.

Out of this tension arose the controlled composition clause. Pursuant to this provision of the agreement, a recording artist is limited in the total payment that the label will pay for mechanical rights on any given album. The label may limit the payment to a percentage of the total amount due, the total number of songs, or both. For example, a contract may provide that the label will pay for 85% of the total mechanical license fee for the first ten songs, and no mechanical fees for additional songs. If the songs are written by the recording artist, then this provision results in a reduction of mechanical royalties. If instead, other composer's songs are used, then this may result in significant recording expenses being shifted from the label to the artist.

Under the worst circumstances, assume thirteen songs are on an album which is subject to both the percentage and song limitation. In that case, the royalties owed for thirteen songs on a gold album are $591,500. From that, the label will pay for only 85% of ten songs and therefore cover only $386,750 of the total amount due. The remaining $204,750 will be deducted from the recording artist's royalties.

This example illustrates how the interplay between the publishing agreements and the recording agreements is essential to fully understanding the implications of most music contracts.

B. Publisher Agreements

Folkways Music Publishers, Inc. v. Weiss
989 F.2d 108 (2d Cir. 1993)

Plaintiff, Folkways Music Publishers, Inc. ("Folkways") appeals from an order of the Southern District of New York, John F. Keenan, *Judge,* confirming an arbitration award and granting summary judgment to defendants, George David Weiss, June Peretti, Luigi Creatore (the "Songwriters"), and Abilene Music Corporation. The district court found that the arbitrators, who had granted renewal rights in the song "The Lion Sleeps Tonight" to the Songwriters, had not exceeded their authority or manifestly disregarded the law. We affirm.

This appeal involves a song entitled "The Lion Sleeps Tonight" (the "Lion version") written by the Songwriters which Folkways claims infringes its copyright in the songs "Mbube" and "Wimoweh." According to Folkways, the underlying music for the latter two songs was composed by Solomon Linda who assigned all rights, title, and interest in his song, called "Mbube," to Gallo Africa, Ltd. ("Gallo") in 1952. On May 7, 1952, Gallo registered a claim to copyright "Mbube" in the United States. After the expiration of the original term on December 31, 1980, the renewal rights in the song vested in Linda's widow. Allegedly, she thereafter assigned Folkways all of her rights in "Mbube."

In 1951, Pete Seeger and the Weavers, under the pseudonym Paul Campbell ("Campbell") wrote a new arrangement of "Mbube" entitled "Wimoweh." Campbell assigned all rights and copyright interests in "Wimoweh" to Folkways which subsequently registered a claim to copyright the song on January 17, 1952. On November 30, 1979, the original term of the copyright was renewed in Campbell's name and thereafter assigned to Folkways.

In 1961, the Songwriters wrote another version of "Wimoweh," the Lion version, which was published by Token Music Publishing Company ("Token"). Token registered a claim to copyright on October 17, 1961, and licensed the use of the Lion version for phonograph records and public performance. On October 31, 1961, Folkways alerted Token of its claim that the Lion version infringed its copyright in "Wimoweh."

In response, Token ceded its rights as publisher of the Lion version to Folkways and the Songwriters entered into the agreement which is the subject of this suit. The Songwriters allegedly executed five documents, including acknowledgments of the infringement and assignments of rights in the Lion version to Folkways. Two of these documents are central to the disposition of this case. On November 6, 1961, Folkways drafted a letter which was signed by the Songwriters, providing for a distribution of public performance royalties payable by Broadcast Music, Inc., Folkways' performing rights society, for uses of the Lion version. In addition, the parties entered into a "Standard Popular Songwriter Contract" ("the Agreement") also dated November 6, 1961. This contract transferred and assigned all rights in the Lion version to Folkways, including "the right to secure copyright therein throughout the entire world and to have and to hold the said copyright and all rights of whatsoever nature thereunder existing, subject to the terms of this agreement." On December 18, 1961, Folkways registered a claim to copyright in the Lion version. This original term expired on December 31, 1989.

Folkways alleges that in October 1989, Weiss on behalf of the Songwriters notified it that he believed Folkways' rights to be limited to the original term of the copyright. He stated that, subsequent to the expiration of the initial copyright term, the Songwriters would exercise their rights in the Lion version absent payment from Folkways for rights in the renewal term. Folkways refused and the Songwriters filed a demand for arbitration on September 13, 1990 pursuant to the 1961 Agreement.

In their demand, the Songwriters sought a declaration that they were "the sole and exclusive owners of all rights in and to the [Lion version], including worldwide copyright, since the composition entered its United States renewal term of copyright." They also sought to compel Folkways to notify its licensees that it no longer had any interest in the copyright in the Lion version. Lastly, the Songwriters requested they be awarded all revenue Folkways had received since the beginning of the renewal term stemming from use of the Lion version. Folkways then filed a copyright infringement action in the district court. Folkways argued that the Songwriters' use of the Lion version since the beginning of the renewal term infringed on its rights not only in the Lion version but also in "Mbube," "Wimoweh," and one other version of the song owned by Folkways ("the underlying works"). Folkways also asked the district court to stay the arbitration or limit its scope to renewal rights in the Lion version. The district court granted the Songwriters' demand for arbitration and denied Folkway's motion.

The arbitration panel ruled that rights to the Lion version had reverted to the Songwriters at the end of the initial copyright term and that the Songwriters "shall have the right to exploit the Composition free of any and all claims from Folkways...." The award, however, did not explicitly discuss whether the Songwriters' use of the Lion version would infringe on Folkways' copyrights in the underlying works. Nonetheless, the arbitrators did say quite plainly that Folkways would have no claims against the Songwriters' use of the Lion version....

Folkways appeals from the affirmance [of the arbitration by the district court] on alternative grounds: first, it argues that the district court misinterpreted the award in finding that it resolved rights to the underlying music; second, it contends that if the district court was correct in its finding that the award determined the rights to the underlying music, then the arbitrators exceeded their powers; third, it claims that if the district court's interpretation was correct then the award is irrational and in manifest disregard of the law

Initially, Folkways contends that the district court misunderstood the import of the arbitration award. The award stated that "all rights in and to the composition 'The Lion Sleeps Tonight' (the 'Composition') shall revert to [the Songwriters].... CLAIMANTS shall have the right to exploit the Composition free of any and all claims from Folkways...." The district court found that this language clearly barred any infringement claims by Folkways against the Songwriters based on rights to the underlying music. In opposition, Folkways argues that the district court misread the words "composition" and "revert," ignoring the "obvious" meaning they have in the award. According to Folkways, "composition" can only refer to the original material added by the songwriters to the Lion version and not to the aspects of the Lion version which stem from the underlying works. Moreover, they argue that material never owned by the Songwriters cannot "revert" to them. As the district court noted, however, the arbitrators determined that the Songwriters had the right to exploit the composition "free of *any* and *all*' claims" from *Folkways.* In finding that the award encompassed rights to the underlying works, the district court properly interpreted the award.

In effect, Folkways argues that this is an improper understanding of the law of copyright, that the arbitrators could not have been mistaken as to the law, and thus that the district court incorrectly interpreted the award. As the district court's reading of the award is proper, this argument is really a challenge to the validity of the arbitrators' award and not to the district court's review. We deal with this challenge below.

Folkways' second argument focuses on the arbitration award itself, attacking the breadth of the arbitrators' determination ...

Folkways, as the party challenging the award, bears a heavy burden of proof. In the order to proceed with arbitration, the district court stated that the arbitrators may pass on the issue of rights to the underlying music. The district court found that the broad language of the Agreement, which required arbitration as to "'any and all differences, disputes or controversies arising out of this contract' ..." permitted such a determination. We agree that this language granted the arbitrators the scope to determine rights in the underlying works. As such, we cannot say that the arbitrators exceeded their authority in reaching this issue.

Lastly, Folkways contends that the arbitrators' decision was in "manifest disregard" of the law. In order to advance the goals of arbitration, courts may vacate awards only for an overt disregard of the law and not merely for an erroneous interpretation. As we noted in *Merrill Lynch, Pierce, Fenner & Smith, Inc. v. Bobker,* 808 F.2d 930 (2d Cir. 1986), "'manifest disregard of the law' by arbitrators is a judicially-created ground for vacating their arbitration award.... [I]t clearly means more than error or misunderstanding with respect to the law. The error must have been obvious and capable of being readily and instantly perceived by the average person qualified to serve as an arbitrator."

In order to vacate for "manifest disregard," a court must find that the arbitrators knew of a governing legal principle yet refused to apply it or ignored it altogether. Moreover, the law ignored by the arbitrators must be "well defined, explicit, and clearly applicable" if the award is to be vacated....

The district court did not misconstrue the arbitration award and that award was not in manifest disregard of the law of copyright. In light of the above discussion, we uphold the district court's confirmation of the arbitration award and grant of summary judgment to the Songwriters.

Notes and Questions

a. The publishing industry has not had nearly the litigation tradition as that of the recording industry. As a result, the few courts that have had to deal with publishing issues have struggled to understand the context of the issue, as these excerpts illustrate. In a footnote, the Second Circuit explained the situation as follows:

> The parties and the District Court called the first category "Performance Royalties" and the second category "Publishing Royalties." The Court's opinion defined "Performance Royalties" as "monies directly generated by record sales and other sound recordings" and "Publishing Royalties" as "monies generated by the exploitation of the musical compositions themselves—that is, the words and the music of the songs." The Court explained that "in the music industry, Publishing Royalties are typically created through the efforts of a musical publishing company or administrator who licenses use of the work to third parties. Such licenses include: (a) mechanical licenses that allow other record companies to use the work ('cover' songs), (b) public performance fees when a song is played on the radio or in a concert, (c) sampling rights that permit other artists to use pieces of the song, and (d) synchronization rights when a musical work is used in a movie, commercial or television show." We do not think clarity is promoted by using the phrase "Performance Royalties" to mean income from record sales and at the same time using the phrase "Publishing Royalties" to include "public performance fees."
>
> We note that although the terms "performance royalties" and "publishing royalties" have been used in a few reported appellate opinions, these terms are not terms of art with precise meanings. Indeed, they have not been given consistent meanings. We have said that "performance royalties" are "paid by the performer to performing rights societies such as [ASCAP], of which the songwriter and publisher are members.... ASCAP's practice is to distribute half of the performance royalties to the songwriter ('writer distributions'), and the remaining half to the publisher ('publisher distributions').... The songwriter and publisher may by contract alter the allocation of performance royalties." *Larry Spier, Inc. v. Bourne Co.,* 953 F.2d 774, 776 (2d Cir. 1992). By "performer" we refer not only to the person who sings the song but also to "radio stations, television stations, restaurants, stores and other entities that 'perform' music publicly." *Woods v. Bourne Co.,* 60 F.3d 978, 984 (2d Cir. 1995). The Ninth Circuit has used "performance royalties" to refer to the income due a song composer for licensing the synchronization right that permits a song to be recorded on the soundtrack of a movie.
>
> Appellate courts have used the phrase "publishing royalties" in the context of music to have various meanings. The Nimmer treatise categorizes the primary sources of revenue for the owner of a copyright in a musical composition as "public performance income, mechanical licenses, synchronization licenses, ... and print publishing revenues." 6 Nimmer on Copyright § 30.02[F], at 30–102 (2002).

Jasper v. Bovina Music, Inc., 314 F.3d 42, 44 (2d Cir. 2002).

b. Compare this description with that in *Larry Spier, Inc. v. Bourne Co.,* 953 F.2d 774, 776 (2d Cir. 1992):

> Plaintiff-appellant Larry Spier, Inc. appeals from a summary judgment entered in the United States District Court for the Southern District of New York (Haight, J.) in favor of defendant-appellee Bourne Company. Both parties are music

publishers, and the district court concluded that Bourne was entitled to judgment as a matter of law because the Copyright Act of 1976, prohibits recognition of the assignment under which Spier claims ownership of certain disputed copyrights....

This case recalls the bygone era of Tin Pan Alley and the popular music of another day. Between 1925 and 1931, successful songwriter Dave Dreyer joined with some famous co-authors in assigning to Irving Berlin, Inc., as publisher, copyrights for five songs still popular enough to generate royalties worth fighting over: "Cecelia," written with Herman Ruby; "Me and My Shadow," "Back in Your Own Back Yard," and "There's a Rainbow 'Round My Shoulder," written with Billy Rose and Al Jolson; and "Wabash Moon," written with Morton Downey and Billy McKenney. Irving Berlin, Inc. is the predecessor in interest of defendant-appellee Bourne Company. The initial term of each copyright was 28 years, and the five copyrights therefore were scheduled to expire between 1953 and 1959. In 1951, prior to the expiration of the initial term of the copyrights, Dreyer assigned to Bourne the right to renew the copyrights. Like the original assignment agreements, the 1951 agreements allocated the various types of royalties to be earned from the songs between Dreyer, as co-author, and Bourne, as publisher. The royalties earned from the manufacture and sale of records of the songs (known as "mechanical royalties") were split evenly between Dreyer and Bourne, as were royalties from licenses for use of the songs in broadcasts and movies. Dreyer was paid a royalty for each copy of the sheet music sold as well.

The Dreyer songs also generated royalties from public performances of the songs (known as "performance royalties"). In the music business, performance royalties are paid by the performer to performing rights societies such as the American Society of Composers, Authors, and Publishers ("ASCAP"), of which the songwriter and publisher are members. Dreyer and Bourne were members of ASCAP. ASCAP's practice is to distribute half of the performance royalties to the songwriter ("writer distributions"), and the remaining half to the publisher ("publisher distributions"). While the songwriter and publisher may by contract alter the allocation of the performance royalties, Dreyer and Bourne did not do so. Under the assignment agreement, Bourne was entitled to retain all of the publisher distributions made by ASCAP. The agreement further provided that its terms were subject to any existing arrangements between Dreyer or Bourne and ASCAP, apparently meaning that Dreyer was entitled to retain all writer distributions made by ASCAP. In any event, Dreyer and Bourne interpreted the agreement over the years in this manner, with writer distributions being paid to Dreyer and publisher distributions to Bourne.

It appears that Bourne duly renewed the copyrights prior to expiration. Under the copyright laws then in effect, the so-called "renewal term" of the copyrights would have continued until 1981–87. The most recent Copyright Act further extends the life of the Dreyer copyrights until 2000–2006.

[The remainder of the dispute involved which party had the right to license the music in the renewal term of the agreement. The Second Circuit interpreted § 304(c) of the Copyright Act to allow the children of the copyright holder to terminate the earlier grants of publishing rights and transfer them to a different publishing company.]

Id.

c. It is common for bands to form companies to hold the rights of their members' copyrights and distribute the income from those companies. What techniques are available to protect a songwriter who is also a member of a band from loss of control when the copyrights are assigned to the band? See *Cusano v. Klein,* 280 F. Supp. 2d 1035 (C.D. Cal. 2003) (dismissing former KISS guitarist and songwriter's claims for improper assignment of song copyrights and failure to properly account for royalties).

d. Is the publisher's fee worth 50% of the royalties? The costs associated with collection and licensing are significant, but so are the benefits of having a publisher actively market a composition for recording by other bands or for use in commercials, films, and in other formats. Nonetheless, for successful composers, an alternative is to form a wholly-owned publishing company.

The composer can then choose to do without a third-party publisher, or the composer can have his or her publishing company enter into a co-publishing agreement with a third-party publisher. In this manner, the composer keeps the 50% of the royalties earned as the composer and splits the remaining 50% earned by the two publishing companies, retaining 75% of the total available royalties. A similar agreement, known as an administration agreement, provides for a limited term (typically 3–5 years) during which the commercial publisher assists the wholly owned publishing house.

e. In addition to the more traditional troubles confronting a performing artist, a few musicians have been sued over the content of their lyrics on copyright and trademark grounds. See *Mattel, Inc. v. MCA Records,* 296 F.3d 894 (9th Cir. 2002) (use of Barbie name in song challenged but allowed); *Parks v. LaFace Records,* 329 F.3d 437 (6th Cir. 2003) (reviewing use of the name of Civil Rights icon Rosa Parks in song lyrics).

f. The Lion Never Sleeps — According to press reports, Disney is the first of what may be many defendants in an action to reclaim the copyright in the songs *Wimoweh* and *Mbue* for the estate of Solomon Linda, the author of the underlying composition popularized as *The Lion Sleeps Tonight*. As shown in *Folkways Music Publishers, Inc. v. Weiss,* 989 F.2d 108 (2d Cir. 1993), this has been a musical legacy fraught with intrigue.

The latest chapter stems from the application of British imperial copyright law to the claims. The Guardian reports copyright expert Dr. Dean as explaining that "all rights to a song revert[ ] to the composer's estate 25 years after his death."[2] The author, Zulu composer Solomon Linda, died in 1962. He had named the song *Mbue* from the Zulu word for lion. Pete Seeger transcribed the song for his folk band, The Weavers, who corrupted the word to *Wimoweh*. Although Disney chose not to reproduce the song on the *Lion King* soundtrack album, it used the song in both the film and the live stage version of the production. The lawsuit was settled in 2006, bringing Linda's estate royalties for the ongoing use of the song.

g. In testimony before Congress, the Register of Copyright noted the congressional effort to mitigate the controlled composition clause:

> Congress also addressed the common industry practice of incorporating controlled composition clauses into a songwriter/performer's recording contract, whereby a recording artist agrees to reduce the mechanical royalty rate payable when the record company makes and distributes phonorecords including songs written by the performer. In general, the DPRA provides that privately negotiated contracts entered into after June 22, 1995, between a recording company and a recording artist who is the author of the musical work cannot include a rate for the making and distribution of the musical work below that established for

---

2. *Lion Takes on Mouse in Copyright Row. Poverty-stricken descendants of enduring hit song's composer could make fortune from Disney,* GUARDIAN (July 2, 2004), http://www.buzzle.com/editorials/7-2-2004-56177.asp.

the compulsory license. There is one notable exception to this general rule. A recording artist-author who effectively is acting as her own music publisher may accept a royalty rate below the statutory rate if the contract is entered into after the sound recording has been fixed in a tangible medium of expression in a form intended for commercial release.

17 U.S.C. § 115(c)(3)(E).[3]

h. Renewal and termination rights continue to vex publishers and authors alike. The rules are complex, confusingly drafted, and intended to force renegotiations more than to allow authors to reclaim their works. Renewal rights under the 1909 Copyright Act were assignable whereas termination rights under the 1976 Copyright Act are not. But the transfer of the renewal right requires the transferring artist to be living. In *Roger Miller Music, Inc. v. Sony/ATV Pub., LLC,* 672 F.3d 434 (6th Cir. 2012), a court addresses what happens when the artist dies after the renewal is filed but before that renewal takes effect:

> This case presents an interstitial issue of copyright law. Miller's assignment of the renewal copyright would indisputably have been made effective if he had still been living at the commencement of the renewal term on January 1, 1993. Equally indisputable is that the assignment would have been rendered ineffective if Miller had died before 1992. This case is before us because Miller was still living at the time in 1992 that his assignee applied to register the copyright, but Miller died before the start of the renewal term. RMMI contends that Miller must have been living at the start of the renewal term to effectuate his assignment to Sony, but Sony counters that Miller needed to survive only until the time at which the application was filed. Sony is correct that the Copyright Act supports the effectiveness of assignments in such circumstances.

Roger Miller Music, Inc. v. Sony/ATV Pub., LLC, 672 F.3d 434, 437 (6th Cir. 2012).

Problem XI-B

Bryce is interested in cutting a demo CD featuring six songs that Bryce wrote: two hip-hop versions of 1890s Gilbert & Sullivan songs and four songs written by various popular folk writers from the 1960s. Bryce expects to sell a few thousand copies of the CD, if lucky, and to give away an additional 500. Advise Bryce how to obtain the necessary rights to license the songs for Bryce's demo CD, explaining how many of the copies would have to be paid for under the license.

---

3. Statement of Marybeth Peters, The Register of Copyrights before the Subcommittee on Intellectual Property, Committee on the Judiciary, United States Senate 109th Congress, 1st Session July 12, 2005, *available at* http://www.copyright.gov/docs/regstat071205.html.

C. Performing Rights Societies & Copyright Enforcement

Introduction

As defined by the Copyright Act, "[a] 'performing rights society' is an association, corporation, or other entity that licenses the public performance of nondramatic musical works on behalf of copyright owners of such works, such as the American Society of Composers, Authors and Publishers (ASCAP), Broadcast Music, Inc. (BMI), and SESAC, Inc." (17 U.S.C. § 101). ASCAP was the first of these societies in the United States, formed through the leadership of Victor Herbert in 1914. By joining the songwriters (both composers and lyricists) together in one collective organization, it enabled this organization to use its negotiating leverage against restaurants, theatres, movie-houses, and other venues in which music was performed either for an admission fee or as part of the value provided in the cost of the food or drink.

Part of ASCAP's troubles stemmed from its own success. To create a competitor to ASCAP, BMI was founded in 1939. By 1941, however, some of ASCAP's practices had gained the attention of the U.S. Justice Department. The 1941 consent decree created ongoing federal jurisdiction over many of the activities of the organization. Through a myriad of court cases and amendments to the consent decree in 1950, 1960, and 2001 the federal government and the industry set out the structural rules under which ASCAP and BMI operate. Continuing jurisdiction is vested in the Southern District of New York, which serves as the rate-setting court for disputes involving the royalties paid for licenses. Increasingly, these rate determination proceedings struggle to keep up with the changing demands of technology as music is now delivered via digital radio, on cable systems, and through online streaming on the Internet in addition to the traditional venues of radio, television, and retail shops such as restaurants and retailers. The summary of the consent decrees can be seen in any of the ASCAP or BMI license agreements (available online at www.ASCAP.com or www.BMI.com). The most important aspects of the antitrust limitations are as follows:

1. No exclusivity;

2. No discriminatory pricing — similar license for similar licensee;

3. Broadcasters must have choice of per program or blanket license;

4. Membership requirements must be open and subject to court control;

5. Performing rights societies are prohibited from licensing to motion pictures or theatrical productions. Dramatic rights (grand rights) are prohibited and instead must be source licensed;

6. A licensee can complain that fees are unreasonable to the District Court, and the performing rights society has the burden to establish fairness of fees; and

7. Royalties must be fairly and objectively distributed.

Broadcast Music, Inc. v. Weigel Broadcasting Co.

488 F.Supp.2d 411 (2007)

Broadcast Music Inc.'s petition seeks an order exercising the Court's rate-setting authority under article XIV of the BMI Consent Decree,[4] setting reasonable music license terms and fees for Weigel Broadcasting Company's two local commercial television stations for the time period of April 1, 1999 to December 31, 2004 and, on an interim basis, from January 1, 2005 on....

BMI is a non-profit music licensing organization that, on behalf of approximately 300,000 composers, songwriters and music publishers, licenses non-exclusive rights to publicly perform approximately 4.5 million musical works to a variety of music users, including local commercial television stations. BMI offers a blanket license and a per program license to local commercial television stations for monthly fees. Stations that choose the blanket license may, for a pre-determined flat fee, perform all of the music in BMI's repertoire as often as they like during the license period. Those that choose a per program license can also perform all of BMI's music as often as they like, but their fees are based on the percentage of their total revenues that derived from programs with performances of BMI music (other than music for which they held a license from another source, such as the composer).

Weigel is a television broadcasting company that operates two full-power television stations, WCIU-TV in Chicago, Illinois and WDJT-TV in Milwaukee, Wisconsin. WCIU is not affiliated with a television network, such as NBC, ABC or CBS. It airs primarily syndicated programming, which it obtains from television producers, studios or other third parties. That programming, like most commercial television programming, contains copyrighted music in BMI's repertoire, for which WCIU obtains a blanket license from BMI.

BMI's ability to license the public performance rights in its music is governed by a consent decree that settled an antitrust suit brought by the United States ("BMI Consent Decree" or "Decree"). Under the Decree, BMI is required to make licenses available for public performances of its music and to provide applicants with proposed license fees upon request. BMI Consent Decree Arts. VIII(B), XIV(A). If BMI and an applicant cannot agree on a license fee, either party may apply to this court for the determination of reasonable or interim license terms and fees. *Id.* at Art. XIV(A).

Because television programming often contains copyrighted music, the television industry formed a non-profit volunteer association to negotiate music license terms and fees with performing rights organizations such as BMI and its chief competitor, the American Society of Composers, Authors and Publishers ("ASCAP"). That association has existed in one form or another since before the BMI Consent Decree was entered, and is now known as the Television Music Licensing Committee ("TMLC"). The majority of the approximately 1,300 full-power local commercial television stations[5] in the United States now authorize the TMLC to negotiate on their behalf, and virtually all others agree to be bound by the outcome of the TMLC's negotiations with BMI or a rate-court proceeding between the TMLC and BMI.

Historically, local television stations represented by the TMLC or its predecessors paid music license fees to BMI and ASCAP equal to a percentage of each station's revenues. In 1993, however, the ASCAP rate court rejected the percentage of revenue fee and set a flat license fee for the entire local commercial television industry. Following that decision, the TMLC told BMI that it would no longer negotiate music license fees on a percentage

---

4. United States v. Broadcast Music, Inc., 1966 Trade Cas. (CCH) ¶ 71,941 (S.D.N.Y.1966), as amended by, 1996-1 Trade Cas. (CCH) ¶ 71,378 (S.D.N.Y.1994).

5. The ABC, NBC and CBS television networks have separate licenses to perform BMI music.

of revenue basis, and instead demanded a single, overall industry-wide fee, which the TMLC would then allocate among the individual stations.

In April 2002, BMI and the TMLC concluded three years of negotiations and reached an agreement for an annual industry-wide blanket-license fee of $85 million, which the industry would yield to BMI for its aggregate annual use of BMI-licensed music if all stations chose the blanket license. Under that agreement, in 2002 through 2004 a portion of that $85 million base fee would be allocated to every station in the industry.

The negotiation and agreement upon the industry-wide fee terminated BMI's contribution to the process: the allocation among the members of their respective contributions toward that amount was devised by, and carried out by, the Television Music License Committee.

The TMLC devised an allocation formula based primarily on television "ratings," which measure the size of a television audience. Taking ratings data compiled by Nielsen, each of the roughly 210 markets in the country as measured by Nielsen was placed in one of nine categories, each of which was arithmetically weighted "to reflect, within a broad parameter, that a household in the 150th market does not represent the same value as a household in the New York market." (The word "value," of course, refers to the desirability to advertisers, and the amount they will pay, for air time.) Within each market a series of computations apportioned the total blanket license fee assigned to that market among the stations in it, according to each station's share of the viewing audience at different times during the average day.

Oversimplifying the process, it resulted in allocating each market's portion of the total $85 million among the stations in that market, according to the portion they enjoyed of that market's television audience.

From 1995 to April 1, 1999, Weigel agreed to be bound by the outcome of the TMLC's negotiations with BMI, and executed a blanket BMI license agreement for WCIU. The terms of the license and allocation formula for the 1995–1999 period were essentially the same as those for the 1999–2004 period, except for increases in BMI's industry-wide blanket base fee.

In May 1998, WCIU's monthly blanket fees under its 1995–1999 BMI license increased from $5,882 to $9,002. Weigel rejected the increase.... Despite subsequent communications and meetings, the parties have been unable to agree on music license fees for the period of April 1, 1999 to the present. On November 19, 2004, BMI filed its petition for an order setting reasonable license fees for Weigel's stations.

The relationship between BMI and Weigel is governed by, and BMI has limited flexibility under, the Decree. The general method of setting a reasonable fee is well-recognized in case law. Essentially, it proceeds from prices paid in other transactions between willing sellers and buyers more or less similarly situated to the particular case. Those transactions (called "benchmarks") are evaluated, their differences from the present case are weighed, and a process of triangulation and adjustment develops the proper figure for the case at hand.

As described in *United States v. Broadcast Music, Inc. (Music Choice)*, 316 F.3d 189, 194 (2d Cir.2003):

> In making a determination of reasonableness (or of a reasonable fee), the court attempts to make a determination of the fair market value — "the price that a willing buyer and a willing seller would agree to in an arm's length transaction." [*ASCAP v. Showtime/The Movie Channel*, 912 F.2d 563, 569 (2d Cir.1990)]. This determination is often facilitated by the use of a benchmark — that is, reasoning by analogy to an agreement reached after arms' length negotiation be-

tween similarly situated parties. Indeed, the benchmark methodology is suggested by the BMI consent decree itself, of which article VIII(A) enjoins disparate treatment of similarly situated licensees.

That is the usual, and approved, method. As the court continued:

> While in some instances there may be reason to approximate fair market value on the basis of something other than the prices paid by consumers, in the absence of factors suggesting a different measure the price willing buyers and sellers agree upon in arm's-length transactions appears to be the best measure.

Music Choice, 316 F.3d at 195 (citing authority).

Since the most appropriate benchmarks may not exactly fit the case at hand, they may need adjustment to produce a proper figure. Examples of such adjustments are given in a later opinion of the Court of Appeals in the same *Music Choice* case, 426 F.3d 91, 97 (2d Cir.2005), elaborating on the rate court's duty:

> In choosing a benchmark and determining how it should be adjusted, a rate court must determine "the degree of comparability of the negotiating parties to the parties contending in the rate proceeding, the comparability of the rights in question, and the similarity of the economic circumstances affecting the earlier negotiators and the current litigants[.]"

Id. at 95, quoting *Buffalo Broadcasting,* 1993 U.S. Dist LEXIS 2566, at *61.

These principles are encapsulated in article VIII(A) of the Decree, which forbids BMI from making or honoring any agreement resulting in different fees between similar licensees. That is not a matter of discretion or business preference, but a prohibition BMI must follow, on pain of contempt:

> Defendant shall not enter into, recognize as valid or perform any performing rights license agreement which shall result in discriminating in rates or terms between licensees similarly situated ...

BMI Consent Decree Art. VIII(A).

But the prohibition does not stop there. It recognizes that within the same principle there is the corollary that different fees must be allowed for licensees whose situations are different. The proviso allows for adjustments based upon business factors which justify them:

> ... provided, however, that differentials based upon applicable business factors which justify different rates or terms shall not be considered discrimination within the meaning of this section[.]

Id.

Accordingly, BMI must give Weigel the same rate it gives all others who are similarly situated; but equally, its rate to Weigel must recognize any business factors affecting Weigel which justify treating Weigel differently.

In this case there is only one available "benchmark." It consists of the uniform process to which each of the 1,300 members of the industry have agreed, and which operates neutrally as to each of them. The dollar figure to be paid by each station is calculated once for the following year and billed monthly.

Thus, the only "benchmark" in the industry lies in the acceptance by all its members (save Weigel) of their respective portions of the overall fee obligation. Of course that does not mean that the process produced a reasonable rate with respect to Weigel. If it did not, a reasonable rate must be set for Weigel, regardless whether that results in the other members of the industry bearing a greater or lesser proportion of the $85 million.

However, the virtual unanimity (even Weigel, up to a point) of the industry's acceptance of the negotiation-and-allocation method and its results, when each member had the ability to opt-out and make a rate court challenge as Weigel ultimately did, has two consequences. It provides hundreds of "benchmark" transactions in support of that method, and it leaves an absence of competing benchmarks.

Thus the question in this case is simple: whether, under article VIII(A) of the Decree there are "differentials based upon applicable business factors which justify different rates or terms" in Weigel's case. If there are, Weigel should pay a different, reasonable rate. If there are not, BMI is prohibited from offering different terms to Weigel.

The differences which Weigel perceives between its business and that of the other stations in the industry are not apparent when viewing the evidence as a whole. Nor are they shown, even when aggregated, to present "differentials based upon applicable business factors which justify different rates or terms" in the words of article VIII(A) of the Decree.

Like many other stations, WCIU has no local news program, which requires a large initial and continuing investment. Similarly, its sports programming contracts are not unique, and they allow WCIU to avoid substantial costs while attracting a large audience. Some of its advertisers choose (or not) to advertise on those of WCIU's programs which primarily target African-Americans, as "other stations around the country do as well." Its programming "has been, and had been, shown on numerous other stations across the country." Many other stations in the country are family-owned and privately held. Its programming generates less than average revenue at certain times of day, but is "exceptionally competitive" at others.

Even though each factor Weigel mentions is unexceptional in the industry, their individual or cumulative effect upon Weigel might justify an adjustment to the benchmark for Weigel. Whether that is the case is best determined by comparing WCIU's license fees, as a percentage of its revenues, to the percentages of their revenues that are paid as fees by the other stations in the industry. All parties agree that the percentages-of-revenues comparisons are the most meaningful, because the firms' revenues capture the net effect of all their business variations.

As a percentage of WCIU's revenues, its BMI license fees are equal to or less than the license fees paid by many other stations in the industry. Of all blanket-license stations in the top 50 markets in the country, 104 paid a higher percentage of their program revenues in BMI fees in at least one year during the years 1999–2004 than the highest percentage of WCIU's revenues billed to it by BMI during any of those years....

Weigel asks the court to set a rate for WCIU based on the total BMI fees paid by the entire local television industry over the 1999–2004 time period as a percentage (approximately 0.33% to 0.41% by different calculations) of the industry's estimated program revenues during that period, instead of what WCIU was billed: 0.59% of its revenues in 1999, 0.54% in 2000, 0.49% in 2001, 0.69% in 2002, 0.63% in 2003, and 0.68% in 2004.

The concept is unrealistic. That percentage represents an amalgam of those stations who paid more and those who paid less than the average, and there is no support for the assumption that a reasonable fee for Weigel would fall at the middle. The more refined and ramified process employed by the TMLC in allocating the portions of the overall fee treated Weigel more rationally than merely arbitrarily selecting an average....

For the foregoing reasons, the petition is granted and weigel is directed to pay BMI at the rates established by the BMI/TMLC license agreement and allocation from April 1, 1999 to date, with interest at the legal rate, but with credit for the payments already made. So ordered.

MOB Music Pub. v. Zanzibar on the Waterfront, LLC
698 F.Supp.2d 197 (2010)

This is an action for copyright infringement arising under the United States Copyright Act, 17 U.S.C. § 101. Plaintiffs allege that defendants infringed their copyrights by giving unauthorized public performances of six musical compositions at defendants' establishment, Zanzibar on the Waterfront Restaurant. Pending before the Court is Plaintiffs' Motion for Summary Judgment. Upon consideration of the motion, the response and reply thereto, the applicable law, and the entire record, the Court hereby **GRANTS** Plaintiff's Motion for Summary Judgment.

Plaintiffs are the purported owners of six musical compositions at issue in this action.... Defendant Zanzibar on the Waterfront, LLC is the owner and operator of Zanzibar on the Waterfront Restaurant—a nightclub and restaurant located in the District of Columbia, where live music is routinely performed. Defendant Michel L. Daley is the managing member of Zanzibar on the Waterfront. In his capacity as managing member, Defendant Daley performs a variety of functions for Zanzibar on the Waterfront Restaurant, including obtaining insurance, making bank deposits, signing checks, hiring and firing employees, marketing and promoting the restaurant, entering into licensing agreements for the restaurant, and handling all legal matters—including lawsuits.

Each plaintiff in this action is a member of the American Society of Composers, Authors and Publishers ("ASCAP"), to which they have granted a nonexclusive right to license non-dramatic public performances of their copyrighted musical compositions. On behalf of plaintiffs and its more than 360,000 members, ASCAP issues licenses to thousands of television networks, radio stations, nightclubs, restaurants, and other establishments whose owners desire to have public performances of copyrighted musical compositions in the ASCAP repertory.

Defendants were licensed to have live performances of any of the hundreds of thousands of works in the ASCAP repertory for periods prior to August 15, 2006. Effective August 15, 2006, however, ASCAP terminated defendants' license for failure to pay license fees. Although ASCAP representatives made repeated offers to reinstate the license of Zanzibar on the Waterfront, defendants have failed to renew their ASCAP license. Accordingly, defendants have been without a license to have live performances of musical compositions in the ASCAP repertory since August 15, 2006.

On the evening of November 16, 2007, an investigator for ASCAP visited Zanzibar on the Waterfront Restaurant for the purpose of "making a contemporaneous list of the titles of all musical compositions performed during [his] visit which [he] was able to recognize." During his visit, the ASCAP investigator heard performances of five songs in the ASCAP repertory.... Plaintiffs filed suit against defendants on September 19, 2008, alleging that these musical compositions were performed in violation of the Copyright Act....

On August 24, 2009, plaintiffs filed a motion for summary judgment. Plaintiffs seek (i) statutory damages in the amount of $10,000 for each cause of action, for a total of $60,000; (ii) an injunction prohibiting further infringing performances of any copyrighted musical compositions in the ASCAP repertory; and (iii) reasonable attorney's fees and costs.... Plaintiffs' motion for summary judgment is now ripe for determination by the Court....

"A plaintiff seeking to establish copyright infringement must prove '(1) ownership of a valid copyright, and (2) copying of constituent elements of the work that are original.'" *Stenograph LLC v. Bossard Assoc., Inc.*, 144 F.3d 96, 99 (D.C.Cir.1998) (quoting *Feist Publ'ns, Inc. v. Rural Tel. Serv. Co.*, 499 U.S. 340, 361, (1991)). In the music performance context, these requirements have been alternatively stated as: (1) originality and authorship of the compositions involved; (2) compliance with the formalities required to secure a copyright; (3) plaintiff's ownership of the copyright; and (4) defendant's public performance of the compositions.

To establish ownership of valid copyrights to the musical compositions at issue in this case, plaintiffs have filed copies of the copyright registration certificates for each musical composition as well as other pertinent documents demonstrating chain of title. Because these copyright registration certificates constitute prima facie evidence of plaintiffs' valid copyrights, defendants have the burden of establishing the invalidity of plaintiffs' titles....

Because plaintiffs are listed as the copyright claimants on the certificates of registration, they have satisfied their initial burden of demonstrating copyright ownership. As the leading treatise on this issue explains:

> If the plaintiff was the author of the work in issue, he has no problem of proof beyond proving such authorship in establishing his ownership of the copyright. Where, however, the plaintiff claims not as author but as a direct or mesne assignee of the author, the question arises as to where the burden of proof lies in establishing the chain of title. Here, a distinction must be observed between a plaintiff who, as assignee of the copyright, (either common law or statutory), first registered a claim of statutory copyright in his name, and a plaintiff who was merely an assignee of a previously registered copyright. As the former has obtained a certificate of registration that constitutes *prima facie* evidence of the validity of his copyright, and of the facts stated therein, the defendant has the burden of controverting the plaintiff's chain of title. However, an assignee of a previously registered statutory copyright has the burden of proving his chain of title because nothing in the registration certificate evidences his right to claim through the original copyright claimant. Once such evidence is offered by the plaintiff, the burden shifts to the defendant to establish the invalidity of plaintiff's title.

3–12 Nimmer on Copyright § 12.11[C]. As defendants have produced no evidence to controvert plaintiffs' chain of title to the songs "Cha Cha Slide," "Around the Way Girl," "In Da Club," and "Big Poppa," the Court concludes that plaintiffs have established their ownership of valid copyrights for these musical compositions. [The Court also rejects defendant's claim that plaintiffs did not have proper chain of title for Bob Marley works "Jamming" and "Is This Love."] Accordingly, the Court finds that plaintiffs have established proof of ownership of all musical compositions at issue in this case.

In order to establish copyright infringement, plaintiffs must also establish that the six copyrighted musical compositions owned by plaintiffs were performed at the Zanzibar on the Waterfront Restaurant without plaintiffs' permission. The affidavits of Kevin McDonough and Mark Eanes—the [ASCAP] investigators—establish proof of the infringing behavior. Although defendants have generally denied that the musical compositions were performed at the restaurant on the dates alleged, they have offered no affirmative proof that the compositions were not performed. Nor have defendants offered any evidence that they received permission from the individual plaintiffs to perform the disputed musical compositions. Defendants, therefore, have failed to raise a genuine issue of fact necessary to defeat plaintiffs' motion for summary judgment.

In sum, the Court concludes that plaintiffs' have established that defendants unlawfully infringed upon their copyrights for "Cha Cha Slide," "Around the Way Girl," "In Da Club," "Big Poppa," "Jamming," and "Is This Love" through the unauthorized performance of these musical compositions at Zanzibar on the Waterfront Restaurant on November 17, 2007 and February 1, 2009. Accordingly, the Court hereby **GRANTS** plaintiffs' motion for summary judgment. . . .

With respect to Defendant Daley, plaintiffs argue that he may be held vicariously liable for the copyright infringements because, *inter alia,* (i) he is the managing member of Zanzibar on the Waterfront, LLC and is held out to the public as such; (ii) he has a supervisory role with respect to the operations of Zanzibar on the Waterfront Restaurant; (iii) he has the right and ability to supervise the decision of which music is performed at Zanzibar on the Waterfront Restaurant; and (iv) he derives a direct financial benefit from the operation of Zanzibar on the Waterfront in the form of a salary and dividends. Defendants do not dispute these facts, nor do they respond to plaintiffs' arguments in their opposition brief. The Court will nevertheless, however, briefly review the law of vicarious liability.

It is well established that an individual may be held vicariously liable for copyright infringement if he (i) has the "right and ability" to supervise the infringing activity and (ii) has a "direct financial interest" in such activities. The imposition of liability on a controlling individual is based upon the belief that the individual is in a position to control the conduct of the entity which is the primary infringer. Lack of knowledge of the infringing activity, however, is not a defense; nor is the fact that independent contractors hired by defendants performed the infringing musical compositions. Indeed, "[e]ven when a restaurant proprietor instructs band members not to perform copyrighted music at his establishment, or inserts a provision to that effect in the band's contract, such proprietor cannot escape vicarious liability when he has a right to supervise and a financial interest in such performance." [*EMI April Music, Inc. v. White,* 618 F.Supp.2d 497, 507 (E.D.Va.2009)] (citing cases). Accordingly, the fact that "[t]he selection of songs played at the Defendants' club is determined by non-employee, independent contractors who are hired to play music at the club," does not absolve Defendant Daley of liability. Therefore, because it is undisputed that Defendant Daley had the right and ability to supervise the infringing activity, and because Defendant Daley had a financial interest in the infringing activity through his operation of the profit-making establishment, the Court concludes that Defendant Daley is jointly and severally liable, along with his co-defendant Zanzibar on the Waterfront, LLC, for the copyright infringements that are the subject of this action.

Having found defendants jointly and severally liable for the infringing behavior, the Court will now address the question of damages and relief.

Plaintiffs seek statutory damages pursuant to 17 U.S.C. § 504(c)(1). Section 504(c)(1) directs the Court to award a copyright owner an amount "not less than $750 or more than $30,000" for each piece of work infringed. 17 U.S.C. § 504(c)(1). In a case where a defendant has willfully violated a copyright, the Court "may increase the award of statutory damages to a sum of not more than $150,000" for each piece of work infringed.

It is important to note that statutory damages "are intended not merely for the restitution of reparation of injury, but to deter wrongful conduct." *EMI April Music,* 618 F.Supp.2d at 508 (internal quotation marks omitted). As the Supreme Court has long recognized:

> [A] rule of liability which merely takes away the profits from an infringement would offer little discouragement to infringers. It would fall short of an effective sanction for enforcement of the copyright policy. The statutory rule, formulated after long experience, not merely compels restitution of profit and reparation for injury but also is designed to discourage wrongful conduct.

F.W. Woolworth Co. v. Contemporary Arts, 344 U.S. 228, 233 (1952). Indeed, in cases such as this, courts have routinely awarded statutory damages in amounts between two and three times the license fees.

Plaintiffs represent that had defendants been properly licensed by ASCAP to date, defendants would owe approximately $26,395.15 in license fees and finance charges. Plaintiffs argue that an award of damages equivalent to the ASCAP license fees, however, is insufficient to deter defendants from continued infringement of copyrighted music, and urge the Court to award damages of $10,000 per infringement—for a total of $60,000.

The Court agrees that damages in the amount of the ASCAP license fee, alone, are insufficient to deter defendants from additional copyright infringements. Indeed, after this lawsuit was filed, plaintiffs had to amend their complaint to add an additional claim of copyright infringement which occurred on February 1, 2009—five months after plaintiffs had instituted this action. Accordingly, the Court concludes that damages in the amount of $6,000 per infringement are warranted for the unlawful performances of "Cha Cha Slide," "Around the Way Girl," "In Da Club," "Jamming," and "Is This Love," which occurred on November 16, 2007, for a total of $30,000 (which is slightly more than the total ASCAP license fee "saved"). The Court concludes that damages in the amount of $10,000 are warranted for the unlawful performance of "Big Poppa," which occurred several months after this lawsuit was filed and therefore after defendants were put on notice of their infringing activity. Defendants are therefore jointly and severally liable in the amount of $40,000 in statutory damages.

Plaintiffs also seek a permanent injunction prohibiting defendants from publicly performing any of the copyrighted musical compositions in the ASCAP repertory. Pursuant to 17 U.S.C. §502(a), the Court may grant "temporary and final injunctions on such terms as it may deem reasonable to prevent or restrain infringement of a copyright." 17 U.S.C. §502(a). Because plaintiffs have established that defendants have repeatedly infringed upon their copyrights by unlawfully performing their musical compositions, and in view of defendants' unwillingness to renew their ASCAP license despite ASCAP's repeated efforts, the Court concludes that a permanent injunction is warranted. Accordingly, the Court hereby **ORDERS** that defendants and all persons acting under the direction, control, permission, or authority of defendants are permanently **ENJOINED AND RESTRAINED** from publicly performing, or causing to be performed, or aiding and abetting the public performance of, any and all music in the ASCAP repertory without proper authorization.

Finally, plaintiffs seek reasonable costs and attorney's fees in the amount of $74,712.22. 17 U.S.C. §505 permits "the court in its discretion" to award "the recovery of full costs by or against any party" as well as "reasonable attorney's fees to the prevailing party." 17 U.S.C. §505. Considering all the facts in this case, including plaintiffs' interest in vindicating the rights provided to them by Congress in the Copyright Act, plaintiffs' need to amend its complaint to add an additional infringement, and the protracted nature of this litigation, the Court concludes that an award of costs and attorney's fees is warranted. Having carefully reviewed the Declaration of Mr. Zelenko, the Court concludes that an award of attorney's fees in the amount of $69,145.00 and costs of $5,567.22 is reasonable. Defendants are therefore jointly and severally liable in the amount of $74,712.22 for attorney's fees and costs.

For the foregoing reasons, plaintiffs' motion for summary judgment is **GRANTED**.

Notes & Questions

a. Under the 1909 Copyright Act, one of the threshold issues for enforcement of a copyrighted work was whether the use of the work was for profit. Section 110 of the current Copyright Act provides similar limitations on the copyright holder by making certain rights unenforceable against nonprofit use. The seminal start of ASCAP's licensing power began when the Supreme Court recognized that an orchestra playing music in nightclubs constituted a for-profit use of the copyrighted works:

> These two cases present the same question: whether the performance of a copyrighted musical composition in a restaurant or hotel without charge for admission to hear it infringes the exclusive right of the owner of the copyright to perform the work publicly for profit.... The plaintiff owns the copyright of a lyric comedy in which is a march called "From Maine to Oregon." It took out a separate copyright for the march and published it separately. The defendant hotel company caused this march to be performed in the dining room of the Vanderbilt Hotel for the entertainment of guests during meal times, in the way now common, by an orchestra employed and paid by the company. It was held by the Circuit Court of Appeals, reversing the decision of the District Court, that this was not a performance for profit within the meaning of the act. The other case is similar so far as the present discussion is concerned. The plaintiffs were the composers and owners of a comic opera entitled "Sweethearts," containing a song of the same title as a leading feature in the performance. There is a copyright for the opera and also one for the song which is published and sold separately. This the Shanley Company caused to be sung by professional singers, upon a stage in its restaurant on Broadway, accompanied by an orchestra....
>
> If the rights under the copyright are infringed only by a performance where money is taken at the door they are very imperfectly protected. Performances not different in kind from those of the defendants could be given that might compete with and even destroy the success of the monopoly that the law intends the plaintiffs to have. It is enough to say that there is no need to construe the statute so narrowly. The defendants' performances are not eleemosynary. They are part of a total for which the public pays, and the fact that the price of the whole is attributed to a particular item which those present are expected to order, is not important. It is true that the music is not the sole object, but neither is the food, which probably could be got cheaper elsewhere. The object is a repast in surroundings that to people having limited powers of conversation or disliking the rival noise give a luxurious pleasure not to be had from eating a silent meal. If music did not pay it would be given up. If it pays it pays out of the public's pocket. Whether it pays or not the purpose of employing it is profit and that is enough. Decrees reversed.

Herbert v. Shanley Co., 242 U.S. 591 (1917).

b. The first battle was waged between the musicians and the restaurateurs, and battles between the two have continued since *Shanley* was decided. In 1998, as part of the statutory package that increased the length of the copyright term by twenty years, Congress changed the statutory balance back in favor of the restaurants and shops. The Fairness in

Music Licensing Act of 1998 created a music licensing exception for restaurants and other establishments meeting either size specifications or equipment limitations. Section 110(5) provides as follows:

(5)(A) except as provided in subparagraph (B), communication of a transmission embodying a performance or display of a work by the public reception of the transmission on a single receiving apparatus of a kind commonly used in private homes, unless—

(i) a direct charge is made to see or hear the transmission; or

(ii) the transmission thus received is further transmitted to the public;

(B) communication by an establishment of a transmission or retransmission embodying a performance or display of a nondramatic musical work intended to be received by the general public, originated by a radio or television broadcast station licensed as such by the Federal Communications Commission, or, if an audiovisual transmission, by a cable system or satellite carrier, if—

(i) in the case of an establishment other than a food service or drinking establishment, either the establishment in which the communication occurs has less than 2,000 gross square feet of space (excluding space used for customer parking and for no other purpose), or the establishment in which the communication occurs has 2,000 or more gross square feet of space (excluding space used for customer parking and for no other purpose) and—

(I) if the performance is by audio means only, the performance is communicated by means of a total of not more than 6 loudspeakers, of which not more than 4 loudspeakers are located in any 1 room or adjoining outdoor space; or

(II) if the performance or display is by audiovisual means, any visual portion of the performance or display is communicated by means of a total of not more than 4 audiovisual devices, of which not more than 1 audiovisual device is located in any 1 room, and no such audiovisual device has a diagonal screen size greater than 55 inches, and any audio portion of the performance or display is communicated by means of a total of not more than 6 loudspeakers, of which not more than 4 loudspeakers are located in any 1 room or adjoining outdoor space;

(ii) in the case of a food service or drinking establishment, either the establishment in which the communication occurs has less than 3,750 gross square feet of space (excluding space used for customer parking and for no other purpose), or the establishment in which the communication occurs has 3,750 gross square feet of space or more (excluding space used for customer parking and for no other purpose) and—

(I) if the performance is by audio means only, the performance is communicated by means of a total of not more than 6 loudspeakers, of which not more than 4 loudspeakers are located in any 1 room or adjoining outdoor space; or

(II) if the performance or display is by audiovisual means, any visual portion of the performance or display is communicated by means of a total of not more than 4 audiovisual devices, of which not more than 1 audiovisual device is located in any 1 room, and no such audiovisual device has a diagonal screen size greater than 55 inches, and any audio portion of the performance or display is communicated by means of a total of not more than 6 loudspeakers, of which not more than 4 loudspeakers are located in any 1 room or adjoining outdoor space;

(iii) no direct charge is made to see or hear the transmission or retransmission;

(iv) the transmission or retransmission is not further transmitted beyond the establishment where it is received; and

(v) the transmission or retransmission is licensed by the copyright owner of the work so publicly performed or displayed;

17 U.S.C. § 110(5). In addition, Congress added § 513 to assist these companies in their rate hearings. It allows the restaurant owner to sue in his home district rather than in New York and guarantees that the restaurant can continue to perform the music:

Pending the completion of such proceeding, the individual proprietor shall have the right to perform publicly the copyrighted musical compositions in the repertoire of the performing rights society by paying an interim license rate or fee into an interest bearing escrow account with the clerk of the court, subject to retroactive adjustment when a final rate or fee has been determined, in an amount equal to the industry rate, or, in the absence of an industry rate, the amount of the most recent license rate or fee agreed to by the parties.

17 U.S.C. § 513(5).

c. What does ASCAP or BMI have to prove to show that the defendant is willfully liable? See *Jobete Music Co. v. Johnson Communs., Inc.,* 285 F. Supp. 2d 1077 (S.D. Oh. 2003).

d. Wait staff at commercial restaurants (or the guests themselves) will frequently sing the copyrighted tune "Happy Birthday." If the restaurant does not have an ASCAP license and the wait staff sings the song, is the restaurant liable? See *Bonneville Intern. Corp. v. Peters,* 347 F.3d 485, 487 (3d Cir. 2003) ("every time you hear the ubiquitous refrain from "Happy Birthday" in a public performance, a subsidiary of AOL/TimeWarner cashes a royalty check."). What if family members sing it at the restaurant; is that actionable against the family members, the restaurant, or both?

e. The history behind the Fairness in Music Licensing Act may provide some insight to the current law. The Supreme Court addressed the scope of the performance license in *Twentieth Century Music Corp. v. Aiken,* 422 U.S. 151 (1975).

George Aiken owns and operates a small fast-service food shop in downtown Pittsburgh, Pa., known as "George Aiken's Chicken." Some customers carry out the food they purchase, while others remain and eat at counters or booths. Usually the "carry-out" customers are in the restaurant for less than five minutes, and those who eat there seldom remain longer than 10 or 15 minutes.

A radio with outlets to four speakers in the ceiling receives broadcasts of music and other normal radio programming at the restaurant. Aiken usually turns on the radio each morning at the start of business. Music, news, entertainment, and commercial advertising broadcast by radio stations are thus heard by Aiken, his employees, and his customers during the hours that the establishment is open for business.

On March 11, 1972, broadcasts of two copyrighted musical compositions were received on the radio from a local station while several customers were in Aiken's establishment. Petitioner Twentieth Century Music Corp. owns the copyright on one of these songs, "The More I See You"; petitioner Mary Bourne the copyright on the other, "Me and My Shadow." Petitioners are members of the American Society of Composers, Authors and Publishers (ASCAP), an association that licenses the performing rights of its members to their copyrighted works. The station that broadcast the petitioners' songs was licensed by ASCAP to broadcast them. Aiken, however, did not hold a license from ASCAP....

The precise statutory issue in the present case is whether Aiken infringed upon the petitioners' exclusive right, under the Copyright Act of 1909, 17 U.S.C. § 1(e), "[t]o perform the copyrighted work publicly for profit." We may assume that the radio reception of the musical compositions in Aiken's restaurant occurred "publicly for profit." When this statutory provision was enacted in 1909, its purpose was to prohibit unauthorized performances of copyrighted musical compositions in such public places as concert halls, theaters, restaurants, and cabarets. An orchestra or individual instrumentalist or singer who performs a copyrighted musical composition in such a public place without a license is thus clearly an infringer under the statute.

The entrepreneur who sponsors such a public performance for profit is also an infringer — direct or contributory.... With the advent of commercial radio, a broadcast musical composition could be heard instantaneously by an enormous audience of distant and separate persons operating their radio receiving sets to reconvert the broadcast to audible form.... [It] was soon established in the federal courts that the broadcast of a copyrighted musical composition by a commercial radio station was a public performance of that composition for profit — and thus an infringement of the copyright if not licensed....

To hold in this case that the respondent Aiken "performed" the petitioners' copyrighted works would ... result in a regime of copyright law that would be both wholly unenforceable and highly inequitable.

The practical unenforceability of a ruling that all of those in Aiken's position are copyright infringers is self-evident. One has only to consider the countless business establishments in this country with radio or television sets on their premises — bars, beauty shops, cafeterias, car washes, dentists' offices, and drive-ins — to realize the total futility of any evenhanded effort on the part of copyright holders to license even a substantial percentage of them.

The Court of Appeals observed that ASCAP now has license agreements with some 5,150 business establishments in the whole country, noting that these include "firms which employ on premises sources for music such as tape recorders and live entertainment." As a matter of so-called "policy" or "practice," we are told, ASCAP has not even tried to exact licensing agreements from commercial establishments whose radios have only a single speaker.

Id.

As a result of the Supreme Court ruling, the practice arose that ASCAP and BMI limited the licensing of radios to those stores and restaurants which had more than four speakers or otherwise exceeded the usage made by Mr. Aiken.

f. The online music industry is creating many tensions and new definitions around the various aspects of music copyright. For a discussion of the separation of public performance rights (which are subject to the licensing mechanisms of the performance rights societies) as distinct from the reproduction rights on a computer, see *Country Rd. Music,*

Inc. v. MP3.com, Inc., 279 F. Supp. 2d 325, 327–28 (S.D.N.Y. 2003) ("[T]he performing rights licenses themselves, as their name implies, explicitly authorize public performance only, do not purport to grant a reproduction right in musical compositions.... Moreover, the performing rights societies themselves do not, and do not purport to have, the authority to grant such a right.").

g. New technologies continue to create challenges to the licensing from the performing rights societies. These include Internet streaming (*United States v. ASCAP in re AOL, RealNetworks and Yahoo! Inc.*, 559 F. Supp. 2d 332, 562 F. Supp. 2d 413 (S.D.N.Y. 2008) (AOL, Yahoo!)) and online videos (*United States v. ASCAP* by United States v. Am. Soc'y of Composers, 2010 U.S. App. LEXIS 19983 (2d Cir., Sept. 28, 2010) (YouTube)). As streaming grows in economic importance, the legal issues in these licenses will take on increased importance as well.

h. A critical question for the performance rights societies has been the characterization of digital downloads. While online streaming of content is undoubtedly a public performance of the content, what about the ephemeral performance of music content as it is made available to a consumer's computer or mobile device?

> In answering the question of whether a download is a public performance, we turn to Section 101 of the Copyright Act, which states that "[t]o 'perform' a work means to recite, render, play, dance, or act it, either directly or by means of any device or process." 17 U.S.C. § 101. A download plainly is neither a "dance" nor an "act." Thus, we must determine whether a download of a musical work falls within the meaning of the terms "recite," "render," or "play." ...
>
> The ordinary sense of the words "recite," "render," and "play" refer to actions that can be perceived contemporaneously. To "recite" is "to repeat from memory or read aloud esp[ecially] before an audience," Webster's Third New International Dictionary 1895 (1981); to "render" is to "say over: recite, repeat," 9 *id.* at 1922; and to "play" is to "perform on a musical instrument," "sound in performance," "reproduce sound of recorded material," or "act on a stage or in some other dramatic medium," *id.* at 1737. All three actions entail contemporaneous perceptibility....
>
> Because the electronic download itself involves no recitation, rendering, or playing of the musical work encoded in the digital transmission, we hold that such a download is not a performance of that work, as defined by § 101.

United States v. Am. Soc'y of Composers, 627 F.3d 64, 71–73 (2d Cir. 2010).

i. New forms of technology are creating new licensing requirements. In *ASCAP v. MobiTV, Inc.*, 2012 U.S. App. LEXIS 10307 (2d Cir. May 22, 2012), the Court addresses the appropriate royalty rates for mobile devices (phone handsets). The decision describes both the financial structure of content delivery for mobile devices and analyzes the methods for valuing content delivered on those platforms. See *United States v. Broad. Music, Inc.*, 316 F.3d 189 (2d Cir. 2003), and *United States v. Broadcast Music, Inc.*, 426 F.3d 91 (2d Cir. 2005), for a similar discussion regarding cable and satellite broadcast technology that applied a different royalty formulation.

Problem XI-C

For the past two months, Bryce has been earning extra money by managing a local bar several nights each week. To keep the customers amused, Bryce occasionally brings in an electric guitar and plays songs. In fact, as Bryce explains to you over the telephone, it worked so well that Bryce invited some local bands to liven the place up. Bryce swears that the only songs played were songs written by Bryce or others in the bands. Bryce was amazed that letters from both ASCAP and BMI arrived at the bar.

The bar owner and manager are both quite upset. While Bryce does not remember singing the songs listed in the cease and desist letters, Bryce does remember talking with the college kids who had notepads and were listening to the songs very intently. The bar has stopped Bryce and all other bands from appearing. The owner wants to know what is likely to happen if he ignores the letters or how he can go about correcting Bryce's mistake. Bryce is fairly confident that the owner will go after Bryce for any costs, so Bryce wants you to provide advice which Bryce can use to negotiate with ASCAP, BMI, and the bar owner.

D. Antitrust Regulation of the Performing Rights Societies

United States v. ASCAP

2001 U.S. Dist. LEXIS 23707, 2001-1 Trade Cas. (CCH) P73474, 2001-2 Trade Cas. (CCH) P73474 (S.D.N.Y. 2001)

Plaintiff having filed its complaint herein on February 26, 1941, the original defendants having appeared and filed their answer to the complaint denying the substantive allegations thereof, all parties having consented, without trial or adjudication of any issue of fact or law therein, to the entry of a Civil Decree and Judgment, filed March 4, 1941, to the entry of an Amended Final Judgment on March 14, 1950, as subsequently amended and modified and to the entry of an Order thereunder issued on January 7, 1960, as subsequently amended and modified;

The parties having moved the Court to amend the Amended Final Judgment,

NOW, THEREFORE, before the taking of any testimony, and without trial or adjudication of any issue of fact or law herein, without admission by the defendant American Society of Composers, Authors and Publishers with respect to any such issue, and upon consent of all remaining parties hereto, it is hereby

ORDERED, ADJUDGED, AND DECREED that the Amended final Judgment be amended as follows:

I. Jurisdiction. This Court has jurisdiction of the subject matter hereof and of all parties hereto. The complaint states a claim upon which relief may be granted against ASCAP under Section 1 of the Sherman Act, *15 U.S.C. § 1.*

II. Definitions. As used in this Second Amended Final Judgment:

(A) "ASCAP" means the American Society of Composers, Authors and Publishers;

(B) "ASCAP music" means any work in the ASCAP repertory;

(C) "ASCAP repertory" means those works the right of public performance of which ASCAP has or hereafter shall have the right to license at the relevant point in time;

(D) "Background/foreground music service" means a person that transmits performances of music to subscribers and that furnishes to those subscribers equipment not otherwise available to the general public that enables subscribers to make the transmitted performances on their premises. A background/foreground music service does not include radio or television stations or networks, cable television networks or systems, persons that transmit renditions of music to private homes, apartments, or hotel or motel guest rooms, or persons that transmit renditions of music to subscribers that charge admission;

(E) "Blanket License" means a non-exclusive license that authorizes a music user to perform ASCAP music, the fee for which does not vary depending on the extent to which the music user in fact performs ASCAP music;

(F) "Broadcaster" means any person who transmits audio or audio-visual content substantially similar to content that is transmitted by over-the-air or cable radio or television stations or networks as they existed on the date of entry of this Second Amended Final Judgment or that transmits the signal of another broadcaster: (1) over the air, (2) via cable television or direct broadcast satellite, or (3) via other existing or yet-to-be-developed transmission technologies, to audiences using radios, television sets, computers, or other receiving or playing devices;

(G) "Music user" means any person that (1) owns or operates an establishment or enterprise where copyrighted musical compositions are performed publicly, or (2) is otherwise directly engaged in giving public performances of copyrighted musical compositions;

(H) "On-line music user" means a person that publicly performs works in the ASCAP repertory via the Internet or similar transmission facility including any succeeding transmission technologies developed after entry of this Second Amended Final Judgment;

(I) "Performing rights organization" means an association or corporation, such as ASCAP, Broadcast Music, Inc., or SESAC, Inc., that collectively licenses rights of public performance on behalf of numerous copyright owners;

(J) "Per-program license" means a non-exclusive license that authorizes a broadcaster to perform ASCAP music in all of the broadcaster's programs, the fee for which varies depending upon which programs contain ASCAP music not otherwise licensed for public performance;

(K) "Per-segment license" means a non-exclusive license that authorizes a music user to perform any or all works in the ASCAP repertory in all segments of the music users's activities in a single industry, the fee for which varies depending upon which segments contain ASCAP music not otherwise licensed for public performance;

(L) "Person" means an individual, partnership, firm, association, corporation or other business or legal entity;

(M) "Program" means either a discrete program exhibited by a broadcaster or on-line music user or, if such broadcaster or on-line music user does exhibit discrete programs, such other portion of the transmissions made by the broadcaster or on-line music user as shall be agreed to by ASCAP and the broadcaster or on-line music user or as shall be determined by the Court in a proceeding conducted under Section IX of this Second Amended Final Judgment;

(N) "Public list" means such records that indicate the title, date of U.S. copyright registration, if any, writer and current publisher or other copyright owner of all works in the ASCAP repertory, including, but not limited to, the public electronic list;

(O) "Public electronic list" means separate databases of: (1) works in the ASCAP repertory that have been registered with ASCAP since January 1, 1991, or identified in ASCAP's surveys of performed works since January 1, 1978, identifying the title, writer, and current publisher or other copyright owner of each work; and (2) current ASCAP members;

(P) "Representative music user" means a music user whose frequency, intensity and type of music usage is typical of a group of similarly situated music users;

(Q) "Right of public performance" means, and "perform" refers to, the right to perform a work publicly in a nondramatic manner, sometimes referred to as the "small performing right," and any equivalent rights under foreign copyright law, including, but not limited to, rights known as the rights of transmission, retransmission, communication, diffusion and rediffusion;

(R) "Similarly situated" means music users or licenses in the same industry that perform ASCAP music and that operate similar businesses and use music in similar ways and with similar frequency; factors relevant to determining whether music users or licensees are similarly situated include, but are not limited to, the nature and frequency of musical performances, ASCAP's cost of administering licenses, whether the music users or licensees complete with one another, and the amount and source of the music users' revenue;

(S) "Through-to-the-Audience License" means a license that authorizes the simultaneous or so-called "delayed" performances of ASCAP music that are contained in content transmitted or delivered by a music user to another music user with whom the licensee has an economic relationship relating to that content;

(T) "Total license fee" means the sum of all fees paid by the music user in connection with the license, including any fee for ambient or incidental uses but excluding the administrative charges authorized by Section VII(B) of this Second Amended Final Judgment;

(U) "Work" means any copyrighted musical composition; and

(V) "Writer" means a person who has written the music or lyrics of a work.

III. Applicability. The provisions of this Second Amended Final Judgment shall apply to ASCAP, its successors and assigns, and to each of its officers, directors, agents, employees, and to all other persons in active concert or participation with any of them who shall have received actual notice of this Second Amended Final Judgment by personal service or otherwise. Except as provided an Sections IV (A) and (B) of this Second Amended Final Judgment, none of the injunctions or requirements herein imposed upon ASCAP shall apply to the acquisition or licensing of the right to perform musical compositions publicly solely outside the United States of America, its territories or possessions.

IV. Prohibited Conduct. ASCAP is hereby enjoined and restrained from:

(A) Holding, acquiring, licensing, enforcing, or negotiating concerning any foreign or domestic rights in copyrighted musical compositions other than rights of public performance on a non-exclusive basis; provided; however, that ASCAP may collect and distribute royalties for home recording devices and media to the extent such royalty collection is required or authorized by statute;

(B) Limiting, restricting, or interfering with the right of any member to issue, directly or through an agent other than a performing rights organization, non-exclusive licenses to music users for rights of public performance;

(C) Entering into, recognizing, enforcing or claiming any rights under any license for rights of public performance which discriminates in license fees or other terms and conditions between licensees similarly situated;

(D) Granting any license to any music user for rights of public performance in excess of five years' duration;

(E) Granting to, enforcing against, collecting any monies from, or negotiating with any motion picture theater exhibitor concerning the right of public performance for music synchronized with motion pictures;

(F) Asserting or exercising any right or power to restrict from public performance by any licensee of ASCAP any work in order to exact additional consideration for the performance thereof, or for the purpose of permitting the fixing or regulating of fees for the recording or transcribing of such work; nothing in this Section IV(F) shall be construed to prevent ASCAP, when so directed by the member in interest in respect of a work, from restricting performances of a work in order reasonably to protect the work against indiscriminate performances, or the value of the public performance rights therein, or the dramatic or "grand" performing rights therein or to prevent ASCAP from restricting performances of a work so far as may be reasonably necessary in connection with any claim or litigation involving the performing rights in any such work;

(G) Instituting, threatening to institute, maintaining, continuing, sponsoring, funding or providing any legal services for any suit or proceeding against any motion picture theater exhibitor for copyright infringement relating to the nondramatic public performance of any work contained in a motion picture, provided, however, that nothing this Section IV(G) shall preclude ASCAP from pursuing its own *bona fide* independent interest in any such suit or proceeding; and

(H) Issuing to any broadcaster any license the fee for which is based upon a percentage of the income received by the licensee from programs that include no ASCAP music unless the broadcaster to whom such license shall be issued shall desire a license on such a basis; provided, however, that this Section IV(H) shall not limit the discretion the Court in a proceeding conducted under Section IX of this Second Amended Final Judgment to determine a license fee on any appropriate basis.

V. Through-to-the-Audience Licenses. ASCAP is hereby ordered and directed to issue upon request, a through-to-the-audience license to a broadcaster, an on-line user, a background/foreground music service, and an operator of any yet-to-be-developed technology that transmits content to other music users with whom it has an economic relationship relating to that content; provided, however, that, in accordance with Section III of this Second Amended Final Judgment, ASCAP shall not be required to issue a through-to-the-audience license to perform ASCAP music outside the United States. The fee for a through-to-the-audience license shall take into account the value of all performances made pursuant to the license.

VI. Licensing. ASCAP is hereby ordered and directed to grant to any music user making a written request therefor a non-exclusive license to perform all of the works in the ASCAP repertory; provided, however, that ASCAP shall not be required to issue a license to any music user that is in material breach or default of any license agreement by failing to pay to ASCAP any license fee that is indisputably owed to ASCAP. ASCAP shall not grant to any music user a license to perform one or more specified works in the ASCAP repertory, unless both the music user and member or members in interest shall have requested ASCAP in writing to do so, or unless ASCAP, at the written request of the prospective music user shall have sent a written notice of the prospective music user's request for a license to each such member at the member's last known address, and such member shall have failed to reply within thirty (30) days thereafter.

VII. Per-Program and Per-Segment Licenses.

(A) ASCAP is ordered and directed to offer, upon written request:

(1) To a broadcaster, a per-program license that shall, in addition, cover ambient and incidental uses and shall not require any record-keeping or monitoring of ambient and incidental uses; and

(2) To a background/foreground music service or to an on-line music user, a per-segment license if (a) the music user's performances of music can be tracked and monitored to determine with reasonable accuracy which segments of the music user's activity are subject to an ASCAP license fee; (b) the music user's performances of music can be attributed to segments commonly recognized within the music user's industry for which a license fee can be assessed; and (c) administration of the license will not impose an unreasonable burden on ASCAP, the per-segment license shall, in addition, cover ambient and incidental uses without any record-keeping or monitoring of those uses if that is reasonably necessary to afford a genuine choice among the types of licenses offered, or of the benefits of any of those types of licenses, if a portion of any on-line music user's transmissions consists of programs substantially similar to those transmitted by over-the-air or cable radio or television stations or networks as they existed on the date of entry of this Second Amended Final Judgment, or is a retransmission of any broadcaster's programs, it shall be presumed that each individual program shall constitute a segment and for those segments the on-line music user need not meet the requirements of subsections (a), (b) and (c) of this section.

(B) ASCAP may charge any music user that selects a per-program license or a per-segment license a fee to recover its reasonable cost of administering the license.

(C) Nothing in this Second Amended Final Judgment shall prevent ASCAP and any music user from agreeing on any other form of license.

(D) The fee for a per-program license and for any per-segment license issued to an on-line user shall be at the option of ASCAP either:

(1) Expressed in terms of dollars, requiring the payment of a specified amount for each program or segment that contains works in the ASCAP repertory not otherwise licensed for public performance; or

(2) Expressed as a percentage of the music user's revenue attributable to each program or segment that contains works in the ASCAP repertory not otherwise licensed for public performance.

VIII. Genuine Choice.

(A) ASCAP shall use its best efforts to avoid any discrimination among the various types of licenses offered to any group of similarly situated music users that would deprive those music users of a genuine choice among the various types of licenses offered, or of the benefits of any of those types of licenses.

(B) For a representative music user, the total license fee for a per-program or per-segment license shall, at the time the license fee is established, approximate the fee for a blanket license; for the purpose of making that approximation, it shall be assumed for the purposes of this Section VIII(B) that all of the music user's programs or segments that contain performances of ASCAP music are subject to an ASCAP fee.

(C) ASCAP shall maintain an up-to-date system for tracking music use by per-program and per-segment licenses; ASCAP shall not be required to incur any unreasonable costs in maintaining such system; ASCAP may require its members and such licensees to provide ASCAP with all information reasonably necessary to administer the per-program or per-segment license including, but not limited to:

(1) cue sheets or music logs;

(2) the date of performance of a work and identification of the program or other segment of the music user's activities that contained the performance;

(3) the title of the work performed; and

(4) the writer, publisher or performing artist;

such requirements shall be designed to avoid unreasonable burdens on ASCAP, ASCAP members and licenses.

(D) The terms and requirements of any license shall be designed to avoid imposing any unreasonable burdens or costs on licensees or ASCAP.

IX. Determination of Reasonable Fees.

(A) ASCAP shall, upon receipt of a written request for a license for the right of public performance of any, some or all of the works in the ASCAP repertory, advise the music user in writing of the fee that it deems reasonable for the license requested or the information that it reasonably requires in order to quote a reasonable fee. In the event ASCAP requires such additional information, it shall so advise the music user in writing, and shall advise the music user in writing of the fee that it deems reasonable within sixty (60) days of receiving such information. If the parties are unable to reach agreement within sixty (60) days from the date when the request for a license is received by ASCAP, or within sixty (60) days of ASCAP's request for information, whichever is later, the music user may apply to the Court for a determination of a reasonable fee retroactive to the date of the written request for a license, and ASCAP shall, upon receipt of notice of the filing of such request, promptly give notice of the filing to the Assistant Attorney General in charge of the Antitrust Division. If the parties are unable to agree upon a reasonable fee within ninety (90) days from the date when ASCAP advises the music user of the fee that it deems reasonable or requests additional information from the music user, and if the music user has not applied to the Court for a determination of a reasonable fee, ASCAP may apply to the Court for the determination of a reasonable fee retroactive to the date of a written request for a license and ASCAP shall upon filing such application promptly give notice of the filing to the Assistant Attorney General in charge of the Antitrust Division.

(B) In any such proceeding, the burden of proof shall be on ASCAP to establish the reasonableness of the fee it seeks except that, where a music user seeks a per-segment license, the music user shall have the burden of demonstrating that is performances of music can be tracked and monitored to determine with reasonable accuracy which segments of the music user's activity are subject to an ASCAP fee and of demonstrating that the music user's performances of music can be attributed to segments commonly recognized within the music user's industry for which a license fee can be assessed.

(C) The fees negotiated by ASCAP and any music user during the first five years that ASCAP licenses music users in that industry shall not be evidence of the reasonableness of any fees (other than an interim fee as provided in Section IX(F) of this Second Amended Final Judgment) for any license in any proceeding under this Section IX.

(D) Should ASCAP not establish that the fee it requested is reasonable, then the Court shall determine a reasonable fee based upon all the evidence.

(E) The parties shall have the matter ready for trial by the Court within one year of the filing of the application unless ASCAP and at least one music user request that the Court delay the trial for an additional period not to exceed one year. No other delay shall be granted unless good cause is shown for extending such schedule. Pending the completion of any such negotiations or proceedings, the music user shall have the right to perform any, some or all of the works in the ASCAP repertory to which its application pertains, without payment of any fee or other compensation, but subject to the provisions of Section IX(F) of this Second Amended Final Judgment, and to the final order or judgment entered by the Court in such proceeding.

(F) When a music user has the right to perform works in the ASCAP repertory pending the completion of any negotiations or pending proceeding provided for in Section IX(A) of this Second Amended Final Judgment, either the music user or ASCAP may apply to the Court to fix an interim fee pending final determination or negotiation of a reasonable fee. The Court shall then fix an interim fee within ninety (90) days of such application for an interim fee retroactive to the date of the written request for a license, allowing only such limited discovery, if any, that the Court deems necessary to the fixing of such interim fee. In fixing such interim fee, there shall be a presumption that the last existing license (if any) between the music user and ASCAP, or between licensees similarly situated to the music user and ASCAP, sets forth the appropriate interim fee. If the Court fixes such interim fee, ASCAP shall then issue and the music user shall accept a license providing for the payment of a fee at such interim rate from the date of the request by such music user for a license pursuant to Section IX(A) of this Second Amended Final Judgment. If the music user fails to accept such a license or fails to pay the interim fee in accordance therewith, such failure shall be ground for the dismissal of its application for a reasonable fee, if any.

(G) When a reasonable fee has been determined by the Court, ASCAP shall be required to offer a license at a comparable fee to all other similarly situated music users who shall thereafter request a license of ASCAP; provided, however, that any license agreement that has been executed between ASCAP and another similarly situated music user prior to such determination by the Court shall not be deemed to be in any way affected or altered by such determination for the term of such license agreement.

(H) Nothing in this Section IX shall prevent any applicant or licensee from attacking in the aforesaid proceedings or in any other controversy the validity of the copyright of any of the compositions in the ASCAP repertory, nor shall this Second Amended Final Judgment be construed as importing any validity or value to any of said copyrights.

(I) Pursuant to its responsibility to monitor and ensure compliance with this Second Amended Final Judgment, the United States may participate fully in any proceeding brought under this Section IX. Any order or agreement governing the confidentiality of documents or other products of discovery in any such proceeding shall contain the following provisions:

(1) The Department of Justice (the "Department") may make a written request for copies of any documents, deposition transcripts or other products of discovery ("products of discovery") produced in the proceeding. If the Department makes such a request to a party other than the party who produced the materials in the proceeding or to a deponent ("the producing party"), the Department and the party to whom it directed the request shall provide a copy of the request to the producing party. The producing party must file any objection to the request with the Court within thirty days of receiving the request; if the producing party does not file such an objection, the person to whom the Department directed its request shall provide the materials to the Department promptly;

(2) Any party to the proceeding may provide the Department with copies of any products of discovery produced in the proceeding. Any party who provides the Department with copies of any product of discovery shall inform the other parties to the proceeding within fifteen days of providing such materials to the Department. The producing party must file any objection to the production within fifteen days of receiving such notice; and

(3) The Department shall not disclose any products of discovery that it obtains under this order that have been designated as "confidential" in good faith or as otherwise protectable under Fed. R. Civ. P. 26(c)(7) to any third party without the consent of the producing party, except as provided in the Antitrust Civil Process Act, *15 U.S.C. §1313*(c), (d), or as otherwise required by law.

X. Public Lists.

(A) Within 90 days of entry of this Second Amended Final Judgment, ASCAP shall, upon written request from any music user or prospective music user:

(1) Inform that person whether any work identified by title and writer is in the ASCAP repertory; or

(2) Make a good faith effort to do so if identifying information other than title and writer is provided.

(B) Within 90 days of entry of this Second Amended Final Judgment, ASCAP shall:

(1) Make the public list available for inspection at ASCAP's offices during regular business hours, maintain it thereafter, and update it annually; and

(2) Make the public electronic list available through on-line computer access (*e.g.*, the Internet), update it weekly, make copies of it available in a machine-readable format (*e.g.*, CD-ROM) for the cost of reproduction, and update the machine-readable copies semi-annually.

(C) Beginning 90 days after entry of this Second Amended Final Judgment, the first written offer of a license that ASCAP makes to a music user or prospective music user shall describe how to gain access to the public list and public electronic list and describe the variety of works in the ASCAP repertory, including, but not limited to, a list of writers, genres of music and works that illustrates that variety.

(D) After the date on which ASCAP makes the public electronic list available pursuant to Section X(B)(2) of this Second Amended Final Judgment, ASCAP shall not institute or threaten to institute, maintain, continue, sponsor, fund (wholly or partially, directly or indirectly) or provide any legal services for, any suit or proceeding against any music user for copyright infringement relating to the right of nondramatic public performance of any work in the ASCAP repertory that is not, at the time of the alleged infringement, identified on the public electronic list; provided, however, that nothing in this Section X shall preclude ASCAP from pursuing its own *bona fide* independent interest in any such suit or proceeding. This Section X(D) shall not apply to any such suit or proceeding pending on the date of entry of this Second Amended Final Judgment.

XI. Membership.

A. ASCAP is hereby ordered and directed to admit to membership, non-participating or otherwise:

(1) Any writer who shall have had at least one work regularly published, whether or not performance of the work has been recorded in an ASCAP survey; or

(2) Any person actively engaged in the music publishing business, whose musical publications have been used or distributed on a commercial scale for at least one year, and who assumes the financial risk involved in the normal publication of musical works.

B. (1) ASCAP shall distribute to its members the monies received by licensing rights of public performance, less its costs, primarily on the basis of performances of its members' works (excluding those works licensed by the member directly) as indicated by objective surveys of performances periodically made by or for ASCAP, provided, however, that ASCAP may make special awards of its distributable revenues to writers and publishers whose works have a unique prestige value, or which make a significant contribution to the ASCAP repertory. Distribution of ASCAP's distributable revenue based on such objective surveys shall reflect the value to ASCAP of performances in the various media, and the method or formula for such distribution shall be fully and clearly disclosed to all members. Upon written request of any member, ASCAP shall disclose information sufficient for that member to determine exactly how that member's payment was calculated by ASCAP.

(2) Where feasible, ASCAP shall conduct, or cause to have conducted, a census or a scientific, randomly selected sample of the performances of the works of its members. Such census or sample shall be designed to reflect accurately the number and identification of performances and the revenue attributable to those performances, made in accordance with a design made and periodically reviewed by an independent and qualified person.

(3) ASCAP shall not restrict the right of any member to withdraw from membership in ASCAP at the end of any calendar year upon giving three months' advance written notice to ASCAP; provided, however, that any writer or publisher member who resigns from ASCAP and whose works continue to be licensed by ASCAP by reason of the continued membership of a co-writer, writer or publisher of any such works, may elect to continue receiving distribution for such works on the same basis and with the same elections as a member would have, so long as the resigning member does not license the works to any other performing rights licensing organization for performance in the United States. ASCAP may require a written acknowledgment from such resigning member that the works have not been so licensed.

(a) A resigning member shall receive distribution from ASCAP for performances occurring through the last day of the member's membership in ASCAP, regardless of the date the revenue are received.

(b) ASCAP shall not, in connection with any member's resignation, change the valuation of that member's works or the basis on which distribution is made to that member, unless such changes are part of similar changes applicable to all members in the resigning member's classification.

(c) Notwithstanding the foregoing, for any member who resigns from ASCAP, ASCAP is enjoined and restrained from requiring that member to agree that the withdrawal of such works be subject to any rights or obligations existing between ASCAP and its licensees, provided, however, that ASCAP may make withdrawal of any works from the ASCAP repertory subject to any license agreement between ASCAP and any licensee that is in effect on the date that this provision becomes effective.

C. Each provision of Section XI(B) of this Second Amended Final Judgment shall only be effective upon entry of an order in *United States v. Broadcast Music, Inc.,* 2001 U.S. Dist. LEXIS 10368, No. 64 Civ. 3787 (S.D.N.Y.), that contains a substantially identical provision. Until the provisions of Section XI(B)(3) of this Second Amended Final Judgment become effective, ASCAP shall not enter into any contract with a writer or publisher requiring such writer or publisher to grant to ASCAP performing rights for a period in excess of five years.

D. Notwithstanding the provisions of Section XI (B)(3) and (C) of this Second Amended Final Judgment, a member who requests and receives an advance from ASCAP shall remain a member of ASCAP and shall be entitled to exercise any right to resign until the advance has been fully recouped or repaid....

XIV. Retention of Jurisdiction. Jurisdiction of this cause is retained for the purpose of enabling any of the parties to this Second Amended Final Judgment to make application to the Court for such further orders and directions as may be necessary or appropriate in relation to the construction of or carrying out of this Second Amended Final Judgment, for the modification thereof, for the enforcement of compliance therewith and for the punishment of violations thereof. It is expressly understood, in addition to the foregoing, that:

(A) The plaintiff may at any time after entry of this Second Amended Final Judgment, upon reasonable notice, apply to the Court for the vacation of said Judgment, or its modification in any respect, including the dissolution of ASCAP; and

(B) If, at any time after the entry of this Second Amended Final Judgment, a stipulated amended final judgment is entered in United States v. Broadcast Music, Inc., 2001 U.S. Dist. LEXIS 10368, No. 64 Civ. 3787 (S.D.N.Y.), ASCAP may move the Court, and the Court shall grant such motion, to substitute the relevant terms of that stipulated amended final judgment for those of this Second Amended Final Judgment.

XV. Effective Date. This Second Amended Final Judgment shall become effective three months from the date of entry hereof whereupon the Amended Final Judgment entered on March 14, 1950, all modifications or amendments thereto, the Order entered thereunder on January 7, 1960, and all modifications and amendments thereto (collectively the "Amended Final Judgment") and the Final Judgment in *United States v. The American Society of Composers, Authors and Publishers,* (formerly Civ. No. 42-245 (S.D.N.Y.)) entered on March 14, 1950 and all modifications and amendments thereto (the "Foreign Decree") shall be vacated. This Second Amended Final Judgment shall not be construed to make proper or lawful or sanction any acts which occurred prior to the date hereof which were enjoined, restrained or prohibited by the Amended Final Judgment or the Foreign Decree.

Notes and Questions

a. The 1941 ASCAP consent decree set forth the basic structure of the performing rights societies which still governs today. At its heart, the original consent decree provided:

> [ASCAP] shall not, with respect to any musical composition, acquire or assert any exclusive performing right as agent, trustee or otherwise on behalf of any copyright owner ... to pay for such right a share of, or an amount measured by, the receipts or revenues of said defendants.... [ASCAP] shall not enter into, recognize as valid or perform any performing license agreement which shall result in discriminating in price or terms between licensees similarly situated; provided, however, that differentials based upon applicable business factors which justify different prices or terms shall not be considered discriminations within the meaning of this subparagraph; and provided further that nothing contained in this sub-paragraph shall prevent price changes from time to time by reason of changing conditions affecting the market for or marketability of performing rights.

United States v. ASCAP, 1941 U.S. Dist. LEXIS 3944, 1941 Trade Cas. (CCH) P56104 (S.D.N.Y. 1941). The 1941 decree introduced the blanket license, per program license, and per segment or per-use licensing structure, although the terms for these practices have varied over the years.

b. BMI has a similar but unique history. Although founded to be a better partner for radio than ASCAP, that distinction did not last long.

> BMI, founded in 1939, is a not-for-profit organization, which functions as the representative of the owners of copyrighted music to license performances of the recordings. BMI issues non-exclusive licenses to music users and distributes its revenues as royalties to its affiliated composers and music publishers, who are the owners of the copyrights. BMI typically issues blanket licenses, that is, licenses to broadcast, for a finite period of time, any and all of the approximately 4.5 million musical works in its portfolio. Because of unique conditions recognized as potentially anti-competitive, BMI's business operations, like those of its chief competitor, the American Society of Composers, Authors and Publishers (ASCAP), are regulated by a court-approved consent decree....

United States v. Broad. Music, Inc., 316 F.3d 189, 190 (2d Cir. 2003).

The 1966 action against BMI illustrates both the similarities and the original differences between the two organizations. The 1966 consent decree focused primarily on radio licensing structures with only passing references to public performances and exclusive licenses. Instead, the additional prohibitions concern BMI's activities as a record producer or music publisher. See *United States v. Broadcast Music, Inc.,* 1966 Trade Cas. (CCH) P 71,941 (S.D.N.Y. 1966):

> IV. Defendant [BMI] is enjoined and restrained from:
>
> (A) Failing to grant permission, on the written request of all writers and publishers of a musical composition including the copyright proprietor thereof, allowing such persons to issue to a music user making direct performances to the public a non-exclusive license permitting the making of specified performances of such musical composition by such music user directly to the public, provided that the defendant shall not be required to make payment with respect to performances so licensed.

(B) Engaging in the commercial publication or recording of music or in the commercial distribution of sheet music or recordings.

V. (A) Defendant shall not refuse to enter into a contract providing for the licensing by defendant of performance rights with any writer who shall have had at least one copyrighted musical composition of his writing commercially published or recorded, or with any publisher of music actively engaged in the music publishing business whose musical publications have been commercially published or recorded and publicly promoted and distributed for at least one year, and who assumes the financial risk involved in the normal publication of musical works; provided, however, that defendant shall have the right to refuse to enter into any such contract with any writer or publisher who does not satisfy reasonable standards of literacy and integrity if the defendant is willing to submit to arbitration in the County, City and State of New York the reasonableness and applicability of such standards, under the rules then prevailing of the American Arbitration Association, with any writer or publisher with who defendant has refused so to contract....

VI. (A) Defendant shall not acquire rights of public performance in any musical compositions from any publisher under a contract which requires the officers, directors, owners or employees of such publisher to refrain from publishing or promoting musical works licensed through another performing rights organization, provided that nothing contained in this paragraph shall prevent defendant from entering into a contract with a publishing entity which requires such entity not to license any performance rights through any other performing rights organization during the terms of the contract, and requiring that any works licensed by such officers, directors, owners or employees through another performing rights organization be licensed by a separate publishing entity which does not have a name identical with or similar to the name of any publishing entity with which defendant has contracted.

(B) Defendant shall not enter into any agreement for the acquisition or the licensing of performing rights which requires the recording or public performance of any stated amount or percentage of music, the performing rights in which are licensed or are to be licensed by defendant.

VII. (A) Defendant shall make available at reasonable intervals, to all writers and publishers who have granted performance rights to it, a complete statement of the performance rates (to writers, those applicable to writers, and to publishers, those applicable to publishers), currently utilized by it for all classifications of performance and musical compositions.

(B) Defendant will not offer or agree to make payments in advance for a stated period for future performing rights which are not either repayable or to be earned by means of future performance to any writer or publisher who, at the time of such offer or agreement, is a member of or under direct contract for the licensing of such performing rights with any other United States performing rights licensing organization, provided that this restriction shall not apply (1) in the case of any such writer or publisher who at any time prior to said offer or agreement had licensed performing rights through defendant or (2) in the case of any such writer or publisher who is a member of or directly affiliated with any other United States performing rights licensing organization which makes offers or makes payments similar to those forbidden in this subparagraph to writers or publishers then under contract to defendant.

(C) Defendant shall include in all contracts which it tenders to writers, publishers and music users relating to the licensing of performance rights a clause requiring the parties to submit to arbitration in the City, County and State of New York under the then prevailing rules of the American Arbitration Association, all disputes of any kind, nature or description in connection with the terms and conditions of such contracts or arising out of the performance thereof or based upon an alleged breach thereof.

VIII. (A) Defendant shall not enter into, recognize as valid or perform any performing rights license agreement which shall result in discriminating in rates or terms between licensees similarly situated; provided, however, that differentials based upon applicable business factors which justify different rates or terms shall not be considered discrimination within the meaning of this section; and provided further that nothing contained in this section shall prevent changes in rates or terms from time to time by reason of changing conditions affecting the market for or marketability of performing rights.

(B) Defendant shall, upon the request of any unlicensed broadcaster, license the rights publicly to perform its repertory by broadcasting on either a per program or per programming period basis, at defendant's option. The fee for this license shall relate only to programs (including announcements), or to programming periods, during which a licensed composition is performed. The fee shall be expressed, at defendant's option, either (1) in dollars, (2) as a percentage of the revenue which the broadcaster received for the use of its broadcasting facilities or (3), in the case of sustaining programs or programming periods, as a percentage of the applicable card rate had the program or programming period been commercially sponsored. In the event defendant offers to license broadcasters on bases in addition to a per program or per programming period basis, defendant shall act in good faith so that there shall be a relationship between such per program or such per programming period basis and such other bases, justifiable by applicable business factors including availability, so that there will be no frustration of the purpose of this section to afford broadcasters alternative bases of license compensation.

IX. (A) Defendant shall not license the public performance of any musical composition or compositions except on a basis whereby, insofar as network broadcasting by a regularly constituted network is concerned, the issuance of a single license, authorizing and fixing a single license fee for such performance by network broadcasting, shall permit the simultaneous broadcasting of such performance by all stations on the network which shall broadcast such performance, without requiring separate licenses for such several stations for such performance.

(B) With respect to any musical composition in defendant's catalogue of musical compositions licensed for broadcasting and which is or shall be lawfully recorded for performance on specified commercially sponsored programs on an electrical transcription or on other specially prepared recordation intended for broadcasting purposes, defendant shall not refuse to offer to license the public performance by designated broadcasting stations of such compositions by a single license to any manufacturer, producer or distributor of such transcription or recordation or to any advertiser or advertising agency on whose behalf such transcription or recordation shall have been made who may request such license, which single license shall authorize the broadcasting of the recorded composition by means of such transcription or recordation by all stations enumerated by the licensee, on terms and conditions fixed by defendant, without requiring separate licenses for such enumerated stations.

(C) Defendant shall not, in connection with any offer to license by it the public performance of musical compositions by music users other than broadcasters, refuse to offer a license at a price or prices to be fixed by defendant with the consent of the copyright proprietor for the performance of such specific (i.e., per piece) musical compositions, the use of which shall be requested by the prospective licensee.

X.(A) Defendant shall not assert or exercise any right or power to restrict from public performance by any licensee of defendant any copyrighted musical composition in order to exact additional consideration for the performance thereof, or for the purpose of permitting the fixing or regulating of fees for the recording or transcribing of such composition; provided, however, that nothing in this paragraph shall prevent defendant from restricting performances of a musical composition in order reasonably to protect the work against indiscriminate performance or the value of the public performance rights therein or to protect the dramatic performing rights therein, or, as may by reasonably necessary in connection with any claim or litigation involving the performance rights in any such composition.

(B) Defendant, during the term of any license agreements with any class of licensees, shall not make any voluntary reductions in the fees payable under any such agreements, provided, however, that nothing herein shall prevent defendant from lowering any fees or rates to any or all classes of licensees in response to changing conditions affecting the value or marketability of its catalogue to such class or classes, or where necessary to meet competition....

c. The Southern District of New York continues to have jurisdiction as the so-called rate court, setting the fees for the use of the various ASCAP and BMI licenses. To what extent does the rapid change in technologies modify the rate setting of the court? Compare *United States v. Broad. Music, Inc.,* 316 F.3d 189, 190 (2d Cir. 2003), with *ASCAP v. Showtime/The Movie Channel, Inc.,* 912 F.2d 563 (2d Cir. 1990).

d. Do the changes caused by the Internet to music distribution change the antitrust posture of ASCAP and BMI, or should they continue to be governed by the consent decrees first enforced in 1941 and 1966? If either organization were formed today, would such formation and operation violate the Sherman Antitrust Act?

Problem XI-D

Having recorded a demo CD, Bryce now wishes to begin making income from the performing rights of the compositions. Even though no one is presently broadcasting or performing Bryce's compositions, Bryce is both hopeful and eager. Advise Bryce on how to join a performing rights society, and which society might be the best fit.

E. Grand Performing Rights v. Small Performing Rights

Introduction

The distinction between grand performing rights and small performing rights becomes significant, because the source from which to license the music may change depending on the nature of the rights. The Copyright Act does not use these terms.

Instead, it uses the undefined term "nondramatic rights" but makes no effort to interpret this term.

The ASCAP consent decree references the copyright concept of nondramatic rights under the industry term "small performing rights" without explaining either term. Nonetheless, the antitrust prohibitions which limit the scope of the performing rights societies' licensing eliminate their ability to provide any licenses to cover grand performing rights. As a result, this distinction sometimes results in significant confusion and occasional litigation.

Frank Music Corp. v. Metro-Goldwyn-Mayer, Inc.
772 F.2d 505 (9th Cir. 1985)

This copyright infringement suit arises out of defendants' use of five songs from plaintiffs' dramatico-musical play *Kismet* in a musical revue staged at defendant MGM Grand Hotel in 1974–76. After a bench trial, the district court found infringement and awarded the plaintiffs $22,000 as a share of defendants' profits. Plaintiffs appeal and defendants cross-appeal. We affirm in part, reverse in part, and remand.

The original version of *Kismet* was a dramatic play, written by Edward Knoblock in 1911. Knoblock copyrighted the play as an unpublished work in that year and again as a published work in 1912. Knoblock's copyright expired in 1967, and the dramatic play *Kismet* entered the public domain.

In 1952, plaintiff Edwin Lester acquired the right to produce a musical stage production of the dramatic play *Kismet*. Lester hired plaintiffs Luther Davis and Charles Lederer to write the libretto and plaintiffs Robert Wright and George Forrest to write the music and lyrics for the musical adaptation. In 1953 and 1954, Lederer and Davis copyrighted their dramatico-musical play *Kismet*, and in 1953, Wright and Forrest assigned to plaintiff Frank Music Corporation the right to copyright all portions of the musical score written for *Kismet*. Frank Music subsequently obtained copyrights for the entire musical score and for each of the songs in the score.

In 1954, Lederer, Wright, and Forrest entered into a license agreement with Loew's, Inc., a predecessor of Metro-Goldwyn-Mayer, Inc., ("MGM, Inc.") granting to it the right to produce a musical motion picture based on plaintiffs' play. MGM released its motion picture version of *Kismet*, starring Howard Keel and Ann Blyth, in 1955.

The story presented in the MGM film and in plaintiffs' dramatico-musical play is essentially the same as that told in Knoblock's dramatic play. It is the tale of a day in the life of a poetic beggar named Hajj and his daughter, Marsinah. The story is set in ancient Baghdad, with major scenes in the streets of Baghdad, the Wazir's palace, an enchanted garden, and the Wazir's harem.

On April 26, 1974, defendant MGM Grand Hotel premiered a musical revue entitled *Hallelujah Hollywood* in the hotel's Ziegfeld Theatre. The show was staged, produced, and directed by defendant Donn Arden. It featured ten acts of singing, dancing, and variety performances. Of the ten acts, four were labeled as "tributes" to MGM motion pictures of the past, and one was a tribute to the "Ziegfeld Follies." The remaining acts were variety numbers, which included performances by a live tiger, a juggler, and the magicians, Siegfried and Roy.

The Ziegfeld Theatre, where *Hallelujah Hollywood* was performed, is a lavish showplace. Its special features, including huge elevators used to raise or lower portions of the stage and ceiling lifts capable of lowering performers down into the audience during the shows, reportedly provide impressive special effects.

Act IV of *Hallelujah Hollywood*, the subject of this lawsuit, was entitled "Kismet," and was billed as a tribute to the MGM movie of that name. Comprised of four scenes, it was approximately eleven and one-half minutes in length. It was set in ancient Baghdad, as was plaintiffs' play, and the characters were called by the same or similar names to those used in plaintiffs' play. Five songs were taken in whole or in part from plaintiffs' play. No dialogue was spoken during the act, and, in all, it contained approximately six minutes of music taken directly from plaintiffs' play.

The total running time of *Hallelujah Hollywood* was approximately 100 minutes, except on Saturday nights when two acts were deleted, shortening the show to 75 minutes. The show was performed three times on Saturday evenings, twice on the other evenings of the week.

On November 1, 1974, plaintiffs informed MGM Grand that they considered *Hallelujah Hollywood* to infringe their rights in *Kismet*. MGM Grand responded that it believed its use of plaintiffs' music was covered by its blanket license agreement with the American Society of Composers, Authors and Publishers ("ASCAP"). In 1965, plaintiffs had granted to ASCAP the right to license certain rights in the musical score of their play *Kismet*.

Plaintiffs filed this action, alleging copyright infringement, unfair competition, and breach of contract. MGM Grand continued to present *Hallelujah Hollywood*, including Act IV "Kismet," until July 16, 1976, when the hotel substituted new music in Act IV. In all, the "Kismet" sequence was used in approximately 1700 performances of the show.

A. *Scope of the ASCAP License*

Paragraph one of the ASCAP license gives MGM Grand the right to perform publicly "non-dramatic renditions of the separate musical compositions" in the ASCAP repertory.

> Society grants and Licensee accepts for a period commencing as of January 1, 1974 and ending December 31, 1978 a license to perform publicly by means of live entertainment or mechanical music (as defined in paragraph 2), and by no other means, at or in any part of section of the hotel or motel known as MGM Grand Hotel, 3645 Las Vegas Blvd. So., Las Vegas, Nv. 29109 non-dramatic renditions of the separate musical compositions copyrighted or composed by members of Society and of which Society shall have the right to license the performing rights.

Paragraph three excludes from the license "dramatico-musical works, or songs [accompanied by] visual representation of the work from which the music is taken...."

> This license shall not extend to or be deemed to include: (a) Oratorios, choral, operatic or dramatico-musical works (including plays with music, revues and ballets) in their entirety, or songs or other excerpts from operas or musical plays accompanied either by words, pantomime, dance, or visual representation of the work from which the music is taken; but fragments of instrumental selections from such works may be instrumentally rendered without words, dialogue, costume, accompanying dramatic action or scenic accessory, and unaccompanied by any stage action or visual representation (by motion picture or otherwise) of the work of which such music forms a part. (b) Any work (or part thereof) whereof the stage presentation and singing rights are reserved.

> ...

Act IV "Kismet" was accompanied by "visual representation" of plaintiffs' play. Accordingly, defendants' use was excluded from the ASCAP license by the express terms of paragraph three. We conclude, however, that there is no reason to consider, as the district court did, whether Act IV was "non-dramatic."

The district court found the following "visual representations": plaintiffs' songs were performed in *Hallelujah Hollywood* by singers identified as characters from plaintiffs' *Kismet*, dressed in costumes designed to recreate *Kismet*, and the performance made use of locale, settings, scenery, props, and dance style music of the type used in plaintiffs' work.

The defendants do not challenge the finding that their production contained these visual representations. They argue, instead, that the district court failed to give sufficient consideration to whether the visual representations in Act IV were "of the work from which the music is taken," i.e., plaintiffs' *Kismet*. Defendants suggest that this distinction is important because plaintiffs' *Kismet* is a derivative work. They argue that many of the visual representations, (e.g., street scenes in ancient Baghdad, swarming bazaars, and an oriental palace), could be said to be derived from Edward Knoblock's 1911 dramatic version of *Kismet* rather than from plaintiffs' *Kismet*. Since Knoblock's play is in the public domain, defendants contend these visual representations are not protectable by plaintiffs' copyright. Defendants further argue that other elements of the "visual representations," such as choreography style and character names, also are not protectable by copyright.

... [D]efendants' argument is unpersuasive because it is simply irrelevant. The question we face is not whether the "visual representations" are copyrightable, but whether the use of a copyrighted work exceeds the scope of an ASCAP license because visual representations accompanied the songs. The license agreement does not refer to "copyrightable" visual representations. The district court was not clearly erroneous in finding that Act IV "Kismet" was accompanied by sufficient[6] visual representations derived from plaintiffs' play to place the songs' use beyond the scope of the ASCAP license.

The district court properly concluded that defendants infringed plaintiffs' copyrights in *Kismet*.

[On remand the district court recalculated the damages only to have that decision again overturned as the Circuit Court increased the portion of the revenue earned by the hotel to the portion of the musical improperly performed. See *Frank Music Corp. v. Metro-Goldwyn-Mayer, Inc.,* 886 F.2d 1545, 1557 (9th Cir. Cal. 1989), *cert. denied Metro-Goldwyn-Mayer, Inc. v. Frank Music Corp.,* 494 U.S. 1017, (1990) ("We vacate the damages award. We conclude that the proper apportionment entitles plaintiffs to 9% of the direct profits from *Hallelujah Hollywood....* Accordingly, plaintiffs are entitled to $551,844.54 as their share of direct profits and $699,963.10 as their share of indirect profits.")]

Robert Stigwood Group, Ltd. v. Sperber
457 F.2d 50 (2d Cir. 1972)

The rock opera *Jesus Christ Superstar* and several of its individual musical compositions have enjoyed large commercial success as well as substantial critical acclaim. More than two million records and tape cartridges of the full opera have been sold, the authorized touring production grossed over one million dollars in its first four weeks, and tickets to

---

6. Whether some visual representations, less significant than those presented here (*e.g.,* performance of the same five songs as those performed here by a single character dressed in ancient Arabian costume), would be enough to take a performance out of the ASCAP license is a more difficult question, which we need not resolve.

the Broadway version have been among the more difficult to acquire. We can understand, therefore, the desire of promoters and producers throughout the country to capitalize on the success of *Jesus Christ Superstar*, and it is not surprising that one consequence of its explosive yet impermanent popularity is litigation. The role of the courts must be to prevent exploitation of the opera in a manner that infringes the rights of the creators of the work and their assignees.

Timothy Rice wrote the libretto for *Jesus Christ Superstar* and Andrew Lloyd Webber composed the score of the opera's overture and 22 songs which depict the last seven days in the life of Christ. Rice and Webber assigned the rights in the work (except "King Herod's Song") to Leeds Music Limited which duly obtained United States copyrights for the opera as a "dramatico-musical composition" pursuant to *17 U.S.C. §5*(d) and for several of the individual songs as "musical compositions" pursuant to *17 U.S.C. §5*(e). Leeds Music Limited assigned the United States copyrights to Leeds Music Corporation. The Robert Stigwood Group Limited ("Stigwood") acquired the rights for stage productions and dramatic presentations of the opera, and its rights are those allegedly infringed. Defendant Betty Sperber is a booking agent doing business as "The Original American Touring Company" ("OATC") and concerts presented by it are represented as being performed by The Original American Touring Company. The business details of the concerts are handled by Betty Sperber Management of which Sperber is President. Each OATC so-called concert consists of 20 of the 23 songs from *Jesus Christ Superstar*, sung sequentially with one exception, and three additional religious works. Sperber avers that other programs not involving *Jesus Christ Superstar* are planned by OATC.

Stigwood brought this suit, *inter alia*, to enjoin: one, OATC's performance of *Jesus Christ Superstar* or portions thereof; two, any references to *Jesus Christ Superstar* in advertisements for OATC performances; and three, use of the name The Original American Touring Company. The district court's preliminary injunction, issued pursuant to *17 U.S.C. §112*, barred only the references to *Jesus Christ Superstar* in OATC advertisements, and both parties appealed.

OATC's claim that its productions do not infringe Stigwood's rights is based upon the usual and customary agreement between the American Society of Composers, Authors and Publishers ("ASCAP") and Leeds Music Corporation, an ASCAP member. Although a complete description of the purpose of ASCAP and its methodology are unnecessary to our decision, some understanding of its function is vital to an examination of the agreements it makes with its members. The Copyright Act of 1909 granted several rights to the holders of copyrights in works including the exclusive right "to perform the copyrighted work publicly for profit if it be a musical composition."

Composers and publishers soon realized it was impractical for each copyright holder to attempt to enforce this right since he could not possibly police all public performances for profit of every musical composition throughout the United States. ASCAP was formed to meet this need. By obtaining licenses from its members, this organization, staffed for the purpose, could enforce the performing rights of its members. It was believed, however, that each copyright owner could appropriately police and license performances of musical comedies or operas because of the relative infrequency of such productions and the lengthy preparation and publicity which must precede these productions. *See*, Nimmer, "Copyright 1955," *43 Cal. L. Rev. 791, 798 (1955).*

In any event, ASCAP is authorized by its members to license only nondramatic performing rights of compositions in its repertory. Consequently, pursuant to the standard ASCAP agreement utilized here, ASCAP was authorized by Leeds to give:

1. (b) The non-exclusive right of public performance of the separate numbers, songs, fragments or arrangements, melodies or selections forming part or parts of musical plays and dramatico-musical compositions, the Owner reserving and excepting from this grant the right of performance of musical plays and dramatico-musical compositions in their entirety, or any part of such plays or dramatico-musical compositions on the legitimate stage.

Thus, while ASCAP licensees can perform the individual songs from *Jesus Christ Superstar*, whether copyrighted individually or merely as part of the opera as a whole, paragraph 3 of the standard license indicates that it does not extend to presentations of:

(a) Oratorios, choral, operatic, or dramatico-musical works ..., in their entirety or songs or other excerpts from operas or musical plays accompanied either by word, pantomime, dance or visual representation of the work from which the music is taken; but fragments or instrumental selections from such works may be instrumentally rendered without words, dialogue, costume, accompanying dramatic action or scenic accessory and unaccompanied by any stage action or visual representation (by motion picture or otherwise) of the work of which such music forms a part.

Both parties and the court agree, therefore, that selections from *Jesus Christ Superstar* can be properly presented by ASCAP licensees if they are presented in "nondramatic" performances. Accordingly, we must decide if OATC's performances fall into the "dramatic" or "nondramatic" category.

The Copyright Act distinguishes between "musical" and "dramatico-musical" works. Dramatico-musical works are considered dramas for the purpose of *17 U.S.C. § 1*(d). ["Musical" works] are infringed only by public performances for profit whereas ["dramatico-musical" works] are infringed by any public performance.

In our effort to find some guidance in distinguishing between musical and dramatico-musical productions, we were soon to learn of the dearth of cases on the subject. We received some aid, however, from Judge Learned Hand's statement that a performance in "words and music alone may constitute a dramatic performance, and it did not matter that the performance was only of a scene or part of a scene." *Herbert v. Shanley,* 222 F. 344, 345 (S.D.N.Y. 1915) (citations omitted), affirmed, *229 F. 340 (2d Cir. 1916),* reversed on other grounds, *242 U.S. 591 (1917).* The Supreme Court's reversal of *Herbert,* however, nipped this line of cases in the bud by construing the "for profit" language so liberally that it obviated the need for further litigation over what was "dramatic" or "nondramatic."

The only case cited to us which discusses the scope of the ASCAP license is *April Productions, Inc. v. Strand Enterprises, Inc.,* 221 F.2d 292 (2d Cir. 1955). In *April* the copyright owner of *The Student Prince* sued the proprietor of a cabaret, "The Harem," for infringement based upon performances there of a medley of songs from *The Student Prince.* The medley was a small part of one of ten scenes of the nightclub's show, and was not connected by a story line or otherwise. The Court stated:

Even if The Harem put on a dramatic performance, [the entire show of ten scenes], the selections ... were not part of it. The worst that could be said would be that they were sung in an intermission between the acts of a dramatic performance. Such a rendition is "nondramatic" within the meaning of the license.

In the opinion, Judge Dimock (District Judge, sitting by designation), laboring without guidance or precedent, of course, was unable to cite us to a single authority.

In any event, Strand's use of several songs from *The Student Prince* pales by comparison with Sperber's use of almost the entire score from *Jesus Christ Superstar*. The twenty musical compositions from *Superstar* were almost the entire OATC performance rather than less than one-tenth as in "The Harem" club's show. Moreover, *April* has been severely criticized as inadequately protective of and virtually extinguishing dramatic performing rights with respect to musical compositions. As Professor Nimmer puts it:

> Under the rule of this case one could by simply obtaining an ASCAP license perform in a new musical play all of the music from "South Pacific" providing the "book" for the new production is not borrowed from "South Pacific." The ASCAP membership could hardly have intended to permit the performance of their musical compositions in Broadway musicals or similar productions in return for mere payment of the ASCAP fee.

M. Nimmer, Copyright § 125.6 (1971).

Where the defendant has not even supplied a *new* "book" in its performances, a determination that dramatic rights have been infringed would seem simple. But, OATC asserts that plaintiff's "book" is not used either and insists that there is no story line whatever to defendant's performances. Recently, in *Rice v. American Program Bureau,* 446 F.2d 685 (2d Cir. 1971) a panel of this court in a 2–1 decision, favored this contention of defendants. *Rice* also dealt with performances of *Jesus Christ Superstar* allegedly executed pursuant to the ASCAP license. Because of the sparse record before it, the majority was unable to conclude that the performance was "dramatic." It did however, make clear that "presentation of all of the songs from the opera *Jesus Christ Superstar* without costumes, words, or scenery, but in sequence could arguably develop the overall plot of the opera, and … might possibly be 'dramatic.'" We have come to the conclusion that the fuller record before us establishes that a dramatic story is developed by defendant's productions, as Judge Smith in his dissenting opinion in *Rice* would have found and District Judge Motley did find even on the skimpier record there.

… [Twenty] of 23 *Superstar* selections are performed in defendant's concert, all but one in identical sequence as in the copyrighted opera. The conclusion is inescapable that the story of the last seven days in the life of Christ is portrayed in the OATC performances substantially as in *Superstar*. One might appropriately ask why, if OATC did not intend that the same story be told, would it insist on preserving the sequence of the songs presented in *Jesus Christ Superstar*, which when performed in that fashion, tell the story even in the absence of intervening dialogue? As *Rice* instructed, the lack of scenery or costumes in the OATC production does not *ipso facto* prevent it from being dramatic. Indeed, radio performances of operas are considered dramatic, because the story is told by the music and lyrics. There can be no question that the OATC concerts, in which singers enter and exit, maintain specific roles and occasionally make gestures, and in which the story line of the original play is preserved by the songs which are sung in almost perfect sequence using 78 of the 87 minutes of the original copyrighted score, is dramatic. And, the admitted desire of defendants to make reference to the opera in its advertisement provides further evidence that the performance is intended to come as close as possible to the original dramatico-musical....

In view of our disposition of the primary issue in this case and the accompanying discussion, our resolution of the remaining issues may be of only academic interest. Nevertheless, we feel obliged to affirm the conclusion reached below and in *Rice* that defendants cannot make reference to *Jesus Christ Superstar* in its advertisements. Sperber argues that there can be no copyright in titles, and, for the first time on appeal, claims that no protection can be afforded on any other theory because of Supreme Court decisions in *Sears, Roebuck & Co. v. Stiffel Co.,* 376 U.S. 225 (1964) and *Compco Corp. v. Day-Brite Lighting, Inc.,* 376 U.S. 234 (1964). We disagree. *Sears* and *Compco* prevent protection outside of the copyright laws, of works which Congress could have protected but chose not to. It may be that titles are not "writings" in the constitutional sense and thus cannot be protected by copyright but can be protected under unfair competition doctrine. In any event, *Sears* and *Compco* carved out a specific exemption for trademarks and labels of products which can be protected to prevent deception of the public. That is precisely the situation we have here. Thus, while Sears could manufacture a pole lamp identical to Stiffel's, it could not call it a Stiffel pole lamp. Similarly, OATC may perform songs under the ASCAP license but may not indicate that they are from the opera. The Senate Judiciary Committee, in its proposed general revision of the Copyright Law, preserves the right to regulate deceptive trade practices outside of the copyright laws. Since the title *Jesus Christ Superstar* may well be associated with the opera as a whole and thus a "secondary meaning" has developed, we agree with the district court that defendants must be enjoined from directly or indirectly advertising or in any way representing any presentation as being from *Jesus Christ Superstar* or any song, instrumental selection or excerpt as taken therefrom in whole or in part. We also agree, however, that subject to the conditions we have set forth in Part I, the individual song titles can be listed.

Finally, although we do not doubt that the defendants chose the name "The Original American Touring Company" with the hope of misleading the public, we agree with the district court that there is insufficient evidence in the record to support an inference of likelihood of confusion strong enough to underpin a preliminary injunction to restrain the use of that name, provided the restrictions we have set forth are observed.... The preliminary injunction is modified as we have indicated. The mandate shall issue forthwith.

Notes and Questions

a. In *Gershwin v. Whole Thing Co.,* 208 U.S.P.Q. 557 (C.D. Cal. 1980), the Whole Thing Company created a forty-song musical tribute to George and Ira Gershwin entitled *Let's Call the Whole Thing Gershwin* (the "Play"), which was produced at the Westwood Playhouse. On behalf of the Gershwin interests, George Gershwin originally objected, but relented sufficiently to allow a limited run at the Westwood Playhouse. When Broadway backers contacted the play's producers, the relationship broke down and the producers sought to rely upon the small performing rights ASCAP license to continue to produce the show. In granting a preliminary injunction, the court rejected this approach:

> To show that serious questions are raised sufficient to require litigation (and to show probable success on the merits), Mr. Gershwin makes three principal arguments. First, Mr. Gershwin argues that performances of the Play after January 31, 1980 infringe his copyrights. Mr. Gershwin argues that Whole Thing is required to have a license from Mr. Gershwin even though Whole Thing has a license from music publishers. The copyright laws permit an owner of a copyright to transfer some or all of the rights comprised in a copyright, and Mr. Gershwin had previously transferred some rights to certain music publishers. In general, the publishers have been granted small performing rights (or non-dramatic rights) to certain Gershwin songs. Mr. Gershwin contends that he gen-

erally retains grand performing rights (also known as grand rights or dramatic rights).

There are two basic tests to determine whether grand rights are required. Grand rights are required if: (1) a song is used to tell a story, M. Nimmer, Nimmer on Copyrights § 10.10(G), at 10–92 (1979); or (2) a song is performed with dialogue, scenery, or costumes, Finkelstein [ASCAP's former general attorney], The Composer and the Public Interest — Regulation or Performing, *19 L. & Contemp. Prob. 275, 283 n.32 (1954)*. In response, Whole Thing argues that the music publishers have granted it grand rights.

Id.

b. Courts are often forced to make subjective decisions. See *April Productions, Inc. v. Strand Enterprises, Inc.,* 221 F.2d 292 (2d Cir. 1955) (night club performance of medley from *The Student Prince* as one scene in a ten scene show not a dramatic use, so ASCAP license sufficient). See also *Rice v. American Program Bur.,* 446 F.2d 685 (2d Cir. 1971) (modifying an injunction against the performance of a concert version of *Jesus Christ Superstar*, but allowing multiple songs to be performed in sequence, without costume or staging).

c. The Riverview Dinner Club, a licensee of both ASCAP and BMI, is trying to increase business by changing the floor shows and musical entertainment. The first proposal is to have so-called theme nights, where a particular artist's music is featured all evening. Beatles nights, Cole Porter nights, and Beach Boys nights are planned under this proposal. Are the ASCAP and BMI licenses sufficient? Would there be any change if the evening features the life story of any of the featured artists?

d. A second proposal recommends that the evenings be themed with "love," "new romance," "old friends," or similar motifs. The performers would create characters that would relate to each other through the lyrics of the selected songs. All the songs would come from the ASCAP and BMI repertories. Are the existing ASCAP and BMI licenses sufficient? Would there be any difference if a cover charge were required?

e. In 1888, in *Kennedy v. McTammany,* 33 F. 584 (Cir. D. Mass. 1888), the Circuit Court for the District of Massachusetts reviewed the copyright protection for piano rolls. "The sole question in issue is whether these perforated sheets of paper are an infringement of copyrighted sheet music. To the ordinary mind it is certainly a difficult thing to consider these strips of paper as sheet music. There is no clef, or bars, or lines, or spaces, or other marks which are found in common printed music, but only plain strips of paper with rows of holes or perforations." As a result, no copyright protection was found.

Twenty years later, in 1908, the Supreme Court endorsed the *Kennedy v. McTammany* result in *White-Smith Music Pub. Co. v. Apollo Co.,* 209 U.S. 1, 9 (1908). According to the White-Smith Court, in "1902 from seventy to seventy-five thousand [player pianos] were in use in the United States, and that from one million to one million and a half of such perforated musical rolls ... were made in this country in that year." Given the widespread use of these piano rolls and the public's reliance on this free source of entertainment, the Court felt incapable of reversing the practice. The decision anticipates much of the *Sony v. Universal* discussion which was to follow seven decades later.

The 1909 Copyright Act reversed *White-Smith Music Publishing.* Section 1(e) of the 1909 Act provided copyright protection to musical works embodied in "any system of notation or any form of record in which the thought of an author may be recorded and from which it may be read or reproduced." This covered both piano rolls and the newly developed wax cylinders that were the first step in the creation of sound recordings, phonograms, and albums.

Congress wished to grant copyright holders the exclusive right to record their work on piano rolls or phonograph records, but feared that the large musical publishers would then be able to dominate the marketplace for popular music. As a compromise, the exclusive right to record the musical composition was initially vested in the copyright holder. Once exercised, however, any other recording company willing to pay the fee set by Congress could also exercise the right to record the composition. This mandatory permission became the first compulsory license under the Copyright Act. This rule is embodied in the current Copyright Act as § 114, providing a statutory royalty rate and structure for making cover recordings.

Immediately, companies began paying the two-cent per copy fee. Some companies chose to physically copy the piano rolls manufactured by others, particularly those owned by the Aeolian Co., the largest owner of piano roll copyrights. In *Aeolian Co. v. Royal Music Roll Co.,* 196 F. 926 (W.D.N.Y. 1912), the court interpreted the Copyright Act compulsory mechanical license to cover only the copyrighted work embodied in the piano roll. The payment did not give permission to physically copy the piano roll itself. To create a physical copy of the piano roll required a license that could only be purchased through direct negotiation with the piano roll manufacturer. The piano roll was protected by this interpretation of the Copyright Act and by state unfair competition law. In 1971, Congress extended copyright protection directly to the phonograph album.

f. Producers of a play based on the life of Sam Cooke wanted Cooke's music as part of the show, but they did not wish to obtain grand performing rights for the production. Was the strategy to perform a musical medley onstage prior to the opening of the play a reasonable solution? See *ABKCO Music, Inc. v. Washington,* 2011 U.S. Dist. LEXIS 120081, 100 U.S.P.Q.2d (BNA) 1669 (E.D. Mich. Oct. 18, 2011).

Problem XI-E

With the success of Bryce's *Juliet Prescott,* Bryce has been approached to write and direct a musical for the Prometheus Theatre. Candi, the executive director, is planning an entire season of George Gershwin, including both piano concerts and musicals. As the kickoff for the season, she wants to create a review, tentatively entitled *From Ira to George,* celebrating the brother composer's early life and George's transformation from a song plugger to Broadway star and classical composer.

Candi has asked Bryce to write the book for the musical, incorporating all or some of the many songs written by the composing duo. The Prometheus Theatre is licensed by both ASCAP and BMI, so Candi told Bryce no additional rights are needed. Bryce seeks your advice. To what extent can Bryce write such a production under the ASCAP or BMI licenses? What else must Bryce do?

F. Bibliography and Links

Al Kohn & Bob Kohn, Kohn on Music Licensing (3d Ed. 2002).

Donald S. Passman, All You Need to Know About the Music Business (5th Ed. 2003).

Mark Halloran, The Musician's Business & Legal Guide (2001).

Todd Brabec & Jeffrey Brabec, *The New and Complex World of Television Music Licensing*, 27 Ent. & Sports Law 1 (2009).

Daniel Cantor, *How Many Guests May Attend a Wedding Reception Before ASCAP Shows Up? Or, What Are the Limits of the Definition of Perform "Publicly" Under 17 U.S.C. § 101?*, 27 Colum. J.L. & Arts 79 (2003).

Neil Conley, *The Future of Licensing Music Online: The Role of Collective Rights Organizations and the Effect of Territoriality*, 25 J. Marshall J. Computer & Info. L. 409 (2008).

Peter Dicola, *Money from Music: Survey Evidence on Musicians' Revenue and Lessons About Copyright Incentives*, 55 Ariz. L. Rev. 301, 304 (2013).

Jon M. Garon, *Normative Copyright: A Conceptual Framework for Copyright Philosophy and Ethics,* 88 Cornell L. Rev. 1278 (2003).

Douglas Lichtman and William Landes, *Indirect Liability for Copyright Infringement: An Economic Perspective,* 16 Harv. J. Law & Tec. 395 (2003).

Jay Mason *All Again, from the Top! The Continuing Pursuit of a General Public Performance Right in Sound Recordings*, 22 Alb. L.J. Sci. & Tech. 1 (2012).

Stuart M. Maxey, *That Carp Is No Keeper: Copyright Arbitration Royalty Panels-Change Is Needed, Here Is Why, and How,* 10 J. Intell. Prop. L. 385 (2003).

Douglas Okorocha, *A Full 360: How the 360 Deal Challenges the Historical Resistance to Establishing a Fiduciary Duty Between Artist and Label*, 18 UCLA Ent. L. Rev. 1 (2010/11).

Dotan Oliar & Nicholas Matich, *Copyright Preregistration: Evidence and Lessons from the First Seven Years*, 2005–2012, 55 Ariz. L. Rev. 1073 (2013).

Cydney A. Tune, *Music Licensing—From the Basics to the Outer Limits, Part 1:* 21 Ent. & Sports L. 1 (2003).

Cydney A. Tune, *Music Licensing—From the Basics to the Outer Limits, Part 2: Key Considerations for Potential Licensees and Licensors of Music*, 21 Ent. & Sports L. 3 (2004).

Cydney A. Tune, *Music Licensing—From the Basics to the Outer Limits, Part 3: The Myriad World of Music Licenses*, 22 Ent. & Sports L. 5 (2004).

Websites

ASCAP, www.ascap.org

BMI, www.bmi.com

Harry Fox Agency, www.nmpa.org/hfa.html

Billboard, http://www.billboard.com/

Musician Magazine, http://www.musicianmag.com/

Rolling Stone Magazine, www.rollingstone.com/

Chapter XII

Sound Recording Industry

As discussed in Chapter XI on Music Publishing, the recording industry and the music publishing industry are closely entwined but distinct in revenue and structure. The recording industry derives its income from the exploitation of music, but makes most of its income on the sale of recordings. Since the biggest story in the recording industry has become the battle to stop illegal copying and sharing of digital music files, this material has been segregated into a separate chapter. See Chapter XIII, infra.

Although illegal downloading and file sharing impact songwriters and publishers, the loss of record sales reflects only a small portion of the music publisher's income. In contrast, the sale of physical records reflects the vast majority of the recording industry income so that piracy poses a much greater threat to this industry.

A. Finances in the Recording Industry

1. Production Agreements: General Structures

a. Producer Agreement

The producer agreement is the contract between the record producer (who may hold the copyright to the master tape or master recording) and either the recording artist or the record company (label). Typically the producer is selected by mutual agreement between the label and the recording artist. This is often a function of influence, such that junior artists are more typically assigned producers based on the label's needs while senior artists have the ability to command particular producers to help create or maintain their sound.

In recent years, it has become increasingly common for the producer to work on a particular song or group of songs, leaving the recording artist and the label more control over the totality of the CD. As packaging has created multiple editions of the CDs (including videos, bonus songs, and other material), the CD no longer has the integrity as a cohesive product that the LP once had.

The goal of the label is to acquire the copyrights to all aspects of the CD, so it will typically require the producer to assign the copyright to the label in exchange for payment. Similarly, the recording artist agreement assigns all copyright interest of the recording artist to the label (see below). Because the performing artist may also share in the joint copyright ownership of the master tape with the producer, this arrangement provides significant efficiency. Assignments of both joint authors' copyrights are necessary to fully exploit the work.

b. Pressing and Distribution Agreement

Smaller labels will sometimes enter into Pressing and Distribution Agreements with the larger distributors. These arrangements serve as upstream sub-licensing agreements, allowing the smaller label to specialize in particular talent, while relying on the larger distributor's infrastructure for distribution and advertising. The small label will assign the right to the mechanical license for advertising and distribution by the distributor.

c. Master Purchase Agreement

This arrangement allows the owner of a particular master tape to assign the copyright, including the mechanical rights and all other uses of the artist's performance in exchange for the royalties along with an advance or fee. Such agreements can be used to assign master tapes from the performing artists to labels (particularly when the master was created as a demo). Similar deals can be used to move master tapes from one label to another.

d. Recording Artist Agreement

The recording artist agreement is the most significant contract in the life of the performing and recording artist. The terms of this agreement are responsible for the financial future of the artist and generally represent the most troubling aspects of the recording industry. Typically, these exclusive agreements provide for the production of a single CD with the option of the label to order additional CDs to be created by the artist. Although the contract covers a band as a group, it is structured to control each of the individual members of the group — even if members leave or join.

The recording artist is typically given a lump-sum budget (not necessarily the cash) as an advance. This large advance payment is used to pay for the production expenses of creating the CD. The actual payment budgeted for the recording artist may be quite modest, particularly if the production costs, studio musicians, studio recording time, producer fees, and incidental expenses start to exceed the original budgets. A $150,000 advance can quickly begin to disappear. At $3,000–$5,000 per song, the producer may earn $30,000–$65,000 of the advance depending on the rate and number of songs on the CD. Studio time, musicians, studio rentals, and engineering fees can easily cost at least $100,000, resulting in little or no payments to the recording artist. Further, since this payment is an advance against future royalties, the entire amount must be recouped before the recording artist will begin to earn royalties from the sale of the CD.

2. Recording Artist Contracts: Budgets and Income to the Recording Artist

The details of the recording artist agreement reflect some of the most Byzantine contracting practices of the entertainment industries. Recording artists suffer from royalty deductions for items such as breakage fees that date back to the lacquer records of the 1920s but continue to be included in poorly negotiated form agreements.

The law review article by Lynn Morrow, *The Recording Artist Agreement: Does it Empower or Enslave?* 3 VAND. J. ENT. L. & PRAC. 40 (2001) ("Morrow"), provides an excellent summary of the costs and practices of the field. As Morrow points out, the label pays all production expenses for a CD only as an advance. The label recoups (or collects) these costs before the recording artist receives any income from the sales of the CD. In contrast, the marketing expenses for the CD are label overhead, not charged back to the recording artist. Music videos, which serve as both marketing and product, are the subject of much negotiation.

There are a number of key provisions over which the entertainment attorney needs to be particularly watchful. Donald Passman, Lynn Morrow, and other analysts focus on these provisions because they are likely to be the areas where negotiations are most likely to reduce the costs expected to be borne by the recording artist and because they seem the least reasonable. At the end of the day, however, real financial success for the artist can be measured by the size of the cash advance actually received and the limitation on the length of the contract.

(i) The Advance. As discussed earlier, the advance is more accurately described as a budget for the production of the CD from which all other expenses must be paid, including studio musicians, song producers, arrangers, engineers, and studio rental expenses. A large advance can quickly disappear if the recording process goes slowly. Teaching a client that time wasted in a studio comes directly out of the client's pocket may change some of the recording artist's behavior. This is where good management is critical.

(ii) Royalties and Deductions. The recording artist typically receives a royalty rate based on either the suggested retail price of the album or the wholesale price of the album to retailers. Against this royalty, a number of deductions are made, so that the actual royalty is often a small fraction of the theoretical percentage of retail sales.

First, since the royalty is typically "all in," other royalty participants are deducted. If the record producer receives a 3% royalty, then the 12% "all in" royalty of the artist has a 9% effective rate. (Morrow at 45.)

Second, the total income against which the royalty is calculated is reduced for free goods (2 of 10 given free for promotion), packaging expenses (10%–15% reduction), and breakage expenses (10%–20% reduction). No royalties are paid on copies of a work sold through record clubs or in discounted mid-price sales (*i.e.*, discount racks). These charges can reduce the potential income from a CD by half.

Third, since the mechanical fees are charged for the number of times each composition is recorded and produced, not the number sold, the reductions for free goods, breakage, and record clubs do not reduce the mechanical royalty rate owed to the publisher.

Finally, the label will reserve significant income against the prospect of returned CDs so that money actually due to be paid to the artist may be delayed as long as two years. The cumulative effect of all these charges and deductions is that it far too common for a recording artist to never receive a royalty check. Only the most popular and best managed of recording artists earn significant income from their recording contracts.

(iii) Cross-collateralization. Instead of receiving actual royalties, the recording artist earns money from other sources, such as from the mechanical license fees for writing the songs, the performance fees from touring, product license fees from tee-shirts and souvenirs, and through advances on future albums. The recording budget generally increases with each successful prior album. Both Morrow and Passman provide useful charts and typical contract language.

Morrow provides an excellent explanation of how these fees are cross-collateralized, so that the expense for each album is charged against royalty income for future albums:

> [A]ny unrecouped sums payable to a record company in connection with one album may be recouped from royalties earned by any of the artist's other albums.

> Record companies use cross-collateralization so that an artist's success helps to cover any previous or future losses.

(Morrow at 44.) The result of cross-collateralization is that even one unsuccessful album will generally absorb the royalty income for the artist.

The lesson for the entertainment attorney is to recognize that some of these reductions against royalties can be eliminated and that the recording artist's production management can greatly affect the financial success or failure of the artist's career.

3. Deal Structures and the Rise of the 360 Deal

In defense of the record company business model, in 2010, IFPI published a booklet, Investing in Music, to explain the business model of the sound recording industry. IFPI tries to make the economic case that recording companies' success involves significant investment and a good deal of risk. IFPI reports that few artists are ultimately successful, with a success ratio among successful acts hovering somewhere between one-in-five to one-in-ten.

Artists are paid royalties based on the sale of their music. In addition, the record company will invest its own funds on marketing and promotion for the sale of the artist. These investments include direct advertising, investing in public relations and media events, financial relationships with broadcasters, and merchandising. The record company will also advance additional funds—loans that will be deducted from the artist's royalties as advance payments to the artist, payment for the recording costs, and payment for the production videos. (Production videos can be negotiated to be treated as marketing costs and therefore not deductible from royalties.)

In recent years, as the revenue from sales of CDs has declined and cassettes tapes disappeared, record companies have sought to gain a portion of the artist's revenue from additional sources, specifically tour income and public performance income. Tour income had historically been reserved exclusively for the artist, while public performance revenue was historically collected through the performing rights societies and managed by the music publishing companies.

These new arrangements go by a number of different labels, including Multiple Rights Agreements, Broad Rights Agreements, or 360 Deals. In essence, the record company promises broader economic support and a one-stop-shop for the artist's services in exchange for a percentage of revenue from all of the artist's revenue streams.

> Broad rights or "360 degree" deals are increasingly widespread. The terms of these agreements commit music companies to greater investment across a range of artists' activities in return for a proportion of the revenue stream from all of them. This diverse investment benefits an artist's longevity and means there is not the same pressure on an artist to go into the recording studio in order to recoup their heavy investment costs.
>
> This form of non-traditional licensing income is becoming an increasingly important revenue channel for music companies.[1]

Potentially any company can enter into a full-service agreement with any musical artist. The broadcasting and touring giant Live Nation demonstrated this with very aggressive

---

1. JOHN KENNEDY & ALISON WENHAM, INVESTING IN MUSIC, IFPI 19 (Mar. 2010).

deals for Madonna and Jay-Z. Most of such deals, however, are coming from the record companies as they seek to maintain control over the changing musical landscape.

For artists without the market clout of a superstar, the value of a 360 Deal must be carefully scrutinized. The risks of cross-collateralization are magnified when all revenue streams are combined. Similarly, the artist bears a much greater risk of failure if the record company underperforms, fails to adequately invest, adopts a strategy that does not fully fit with the artist's vision, or simply misses its target. At the same time, if the artist receives a substantially larger advance and a binding commitment to invest in marketing, promotion, and tour support that is measurably larger than competing offers without the 360 Deal components (and subject to rigorous audit rights to assure compliance), then such an offer may be worth considering.

The 360 Deal and the expansion of record label control of the artist comes at a time when artists have much greater access to equipment, self-promotion, and direct marketing than ever before. Today, the vast majority of musicians record their own music, book their own tours, and use guerilla marketing to promote their professional activities. As such, the recording industry of today is becoming more highly stratified between the artists signed to labels and those who are truly independent. This trend is likely to continue as the ramifications to changes in technology and music consumption continue to transform the industries built on music.

Notes and Questions

a. From the label's perspective, it is better if the producer is an employee of the record company for copyright purposes, so that the copyright in the master is created as a work for hire, because copyright law does not support the practice of merely declaring an independent producer a provider of a specially commissioned work. Section 101 provides two separate definitions of work for hire. The first situation covers "a work prepared by an employee within the scope of his or her employment" which vests copyright authorship in the employer for employees engaged in their professional activities.

The second situation is the one which is more controversial. It provides nine special categories[2] under which the parties can agree in writing in advance. The nine categories do not include sound recording. In 1999, an attempt was made to insert this tenth category as a technical amendment to the Satellite Home Viewer Improvement Act of 1999. The response to this addition was fierce, resulting in The Work Made for Hire and Copyright Corrections Act of 2000, which not only deleted "as a sound recording" from the definition, but explicitly applied the deletion retroactively to negate any introduction of the term.

b. What legal rights might a label have if it entered into a work-for-hire agreement in December 1999 when the "as a sound recording" category existed in the definition of work-

---

2. [A] work specially ordered or commissioned for use as a contribution to a collective work, as a part of a motion picture or other audiovisual work, as a translation, as a supplementary work, as a compilation, as an instructional text, as a test, as answer material for a test, or as an atlas, if the parties expressly agree in a written instrument signed by them that the work shall be considered a work made for hire. For the purpose of the foregoing sentence, a "supplementary work" is a work prepared for publication as a secondary adjunct to a work by another author for the purpose of introducing, concluding, illustrating, explaining, revising, commenting upon, or assisting in the use of the other work, such as forewords, afterwords, pictorial illustrations, maps, charts, tables, editorial notes, musical arrangements, answer material for tests, bibliographies, appendixes, and indexes, and an "instructional text" is a literary, pictorial, or graphic work prepared for publication and with the purpose of use in systematic instructional activities. 17 U.S.C. § 101.

for-hire, but which was subsequently and retroactively deleted? Does the December 1999 agreement constitute an assignment, or does the copyright remain with the producer?

c. IFPI reports that digital delivery of music has become the cause for optimism in the record industry with a number of positive economic trends:

- Digital music revenues to record companies grew by 8 per cent globally in 2011 to an estimated US$5.2 billion. This compares to growth of 5 per cent in 2010 and represents the first time the year-on-year growth rate has increased since IFPI started measuring digital revenues in 2004

- IFPI estimates that 3.6 billion downloads were purchased globally in 2011, an increase of 17 percent (combining singles and albums downloads)

- Some markets now see more than half of their revenues derive from digital channels, notably the US (52%) and South Korea (53%) ...

- Many major markets are seeing healthy growth in single track download sales: the US up 8 per cent in volume; the UK up 10 per cent; France up 23 per cent

- Consumer demand for an artist's body of work remains strong in the digital world. Digital album volume sales grew by an estimated 24 per cent globally in 2011, with the US and UK up by 19 and 27 per cent respectively and France up 71 per cent

- The global number of paying subscribers for music services has grown by 65 per cent, from an estimated 8.2 million in 2010 to over 13.4 million in 2011

- Subscription has caught on exceptionally well in some markets, particularly in Scandinavia. In Sweden, for example, subscription accounted for 84 per cent of digital revenues in the first ten months of 2011, boosted by its national champion Spotify. Other markets saw sharp growth in subscription revenues, such as France with growth of more than 90 per cent in the first 11 months of 2011

IFPI Digital Music Report 2012, Key Facts and Figures, IFPI, available at http://ifpi.org/content/library/DMR2012_key_facts_and_figures.pdf (last visited Dec. 27, 2012).

d. At the 2004 Midwest Art, Entertainment & Sports Law Institute—Signing and Developing Artists in a Download Economy, attorney Peter Strand commented that a $300,000 production budget "shrinks in the dryer," so that a $30,000 production budget for an independent label would be "a good deal."[3] He explained that independent budgets often range from $15,000 to $50,000, though the upper range would be rather rare. The panel made a few additional points:

1. Less than 15% of all sound recordings released by major record companies will even make back their costs.

2. There were 38,857 albums released in 2002, 7000 from the majors and 31,857 from the [independent record labels]. Out of all of these releases, only 233 sold over 250,000 units and only 437 sold over 100,000 units. That means that less than 1% of the time for the total recording industry that an album returns makes significant sales (in terms of recouping costs and turning a clean profit)....

3. A typical album released by a major label often costs in excess of $300,000 to record plus an advance to the artists which often runs in the hundreds of thousands of dollars. In addition, for each CD released, a major label typically spends,

---

3. *Midwest Art, Entertainment & Sports Law Institute—Signing and Developing Artists in a Download Economy*, MSBA Art & Entertainment Law Section, Minnesota State Bar Association, July 9, 2004.

in the aggregate, several hundred thousand dollars on marketing, promotion, and publicity (e.g., print, TV, and radio advertising, videos, independent radio promotion services, etc.), distribution and tour support for the artist. In total, the overall costs incurred in connection with a single album released by a major often runs well over a $1,000,000. Based on the odds set forth in Paragraph 2, above, it is highly unlikely that the label ever breaks even on its investment....[4]

Problem XII-A

A local band has begun covering some of Bryce's songs. Bryce is thrilled. The band, Soundfyre, is a five-member rock and blues band. On occasion Bryce would join the band, playing bass, sax, and keyboards. To Bryce's surprise, Soundfyre has invited Bryce to join the band. Bryce needs advice.

The band has a recording contract and has already produced one CD. The CD sold only about 75,000 units but the label is willing to give Soundfyre a chance with a second album. Bryce really wants Soundfyre to use Bryce's songs but is not sure if joining the band is the best plan. Advise Bryce regarding the financial and business implications of joining the band and what options might be available.

B. Producers and Copyright Ownership

Systems XIX, Inc. v. Parker
30 F. Supp. 2d 1225 (N.D. Ca. 1998)

Plaintiff Maritime Hall Productions (Maritime) owns Maritime Hall, a combined amphitheater and recording studio in San Francisco, California. Defendants are Lawrence Parker (Parker), a performer of rap music who performs under the name "KRS-ONE", and Zomba Recording Corporation (Zomba), the record company responsible for the marketing and distribution of Parker's songs. Zomba is the copyright owner of Parker's musical compositions and recordings.

In mid-January 1997, Albert Cook, a concert promoter, contacted Maritime's president, Boots Hughston, to arrange a concert involving Parker at the Maritime Hall. Over the course of the next four weeks, Cook, Hughston, and Wesley Powell, Parker's road manager, negotiated the terms of the performance contract.

According to Hughston, Cook explained to Hughston during the negotiations that Parker was creating a new album and that if Maritime were to record Parker's performance, those recordings might be used on the new album. Hughston informed Cook that Maritime would require compensation and producer credits if Parker included a Maritime Hall recording on an album. Although the parties' negotiations were reduced to an Artist Engagement Contract, neither party signed the agreement due, in part, to an inability to agree on terms relating to the production and recording of Parker's live performance.

Parker states that he customarily records his performances for purposes of self-evaluation. On March 15, 1997, the day of the concert, Parker claims that since Parker's own sound

---

4. *Id.*

engineer was absent, Powell requested Maritime to record the concert. Maritime proceeded to set up its recording equipment, including stage and audience microphones, audio lines and video cameras. Powell and Hughston then discussed the recording process for the concert. According to Hughston, Powell observed the pre-concert recording set-up, asked some questions about the video cameras, but appeared primarily concerned with receiving "the master" of the performance. A "master" tape refers to a professional sound quality digital audio tape that has been mixed and equalized.

Maritime recorded the concert and provided Powell with a master tape of the concert after the show. In the summer of 1997, Parker released an album "I Got Next" (the album). Two tracks on the album were taken from the sound recording of the concert on March 15, 1997. Although each of the remaining sixteen tracks on the album listed producer credits, the two tracks from the Maritime Hall concert sound recording contained no reference to producer credits or venue. Following the release of the album, Maritime requested compensation and producer credit listing from Zomba for its use of the sound recording on the album. Zomba did not reply to Maritime's request.

Maritime filed this action for declaratory relief and damages against Parker and Zomba on October 30, 1997. Maritime seeks a judicial determination of its rights under the Copyright Act with respect to the sound recording. In the alternative, Maritime seeks recovery in *quantum meruit* for Zomba's allegedly unauthorized use of the sound recording. Defendants filed the instant motion for summary judgment on August 7, 1998....

1. Maritime's rights under the Copyright Act

Maritime claims joint copyright ownership of the sound recordings. Defendants respond that Maritime is not a joint author of the sound recordings because Zomba and Parker lacked the requisite intent to create a joint work and never authorized Maritime to use the underlying musical compositions to make the sound recording.

Section 101 of the Copyright Act of 1976 (Act) defines a 'joint work' as: "a work prepared by two or more authors with the intention that their contributions be merged into inseparable or interdependent parts of a unitary whole." A party claiming joint authorship must establish that the authors 1) intended to merge their contributions into a unitary whole and 2) contributed copyrightable subject matter to the joint work.

A. Intention of the parties

i. The applicable standard

For a joint work to exist, the putative authors must have intended to merge their respective contributions into a unitary whole. Defendants first argue that under *Childress v. Taylor*, 945 F.2d 500 (2nd Cir. 1991), the parties' intent turns on their subjective expectations. Maritime responds that the courts scrutinize the subjective intent of the parties under the heightened *Childress* test only where the copyright claimant does not occupy a traditional authorship role as contemplated by Congress. In the case of sound recordings, Maritime argues that since Congress explicitly recognized the potential joint authorship roles of producer and artist, the *Childress* test is inapplicable to the instant facts. Rather than a subjective standard, Maritime contends that the parties' intent should be measured against an objective, factual standard as contemplated by the Act.

The Court agrees with Maritime that the subjective standard under *Childress* does not apply to the instant facts. *Childress* involved an actress/research assistant who claimed joint authorship of a play. The *Childress* court evaluated the intention of the parties based on a subjective standard to prevent the extension of "joint authorship status to many persons who are not likely to have been within the contemplation of Congress."

In contrast to the playwright/research assistant relationship in *Childress*, the producer/performer relationship here was under the specific contemplation of Congress as joint authors of a sound recording under the Act. Congress discussed in the Act's legislative history that "the copyrightable elements of a sound recording will usually, though not always, involve 'authorship' both on the part of the performers whose performance is captured and on the part of the record producer responsible for setting up the session, capturing and electronically processing the sounds, and compiling and editing them to make a final sound recording." H.R. Rep. No. 94-1476, 94th Cong., 2nd Sess. 56 (1976).

The standard by which the intent of the parties is measured is not strictly subjective as urged by Defendants. Rather, the requisite intent will be found if, based on an objective, factual standard, the parties prepared the sound recording "with the intention that their contributions be merged into inseparable or interdependent *parts of a unitary whole.*"

ii. Did Zomba possess the requisite intent to create a joint work?

Defendants contend that they did not share a mutual intent with Maritime to create a joint work in the sound recordings. Defendants argue that since neither Zomba nor Parker ever had any direct communication with Maritime, much less asked Maritime to professionally record the concert, defendants could not have intended the creation of a joint work with Maritime.

Maritime responds that defendants did share an intention with Maritime to co-author the sound recording, as demonstrated by copyright practice, industry custom, and the factual circumstances in which the sound recording was produced.

Maritime first argues that sound recordings by their nature are usually joint works. For example, according to the United States Copyright Office, "[s]ound recording authorship may be contributed by the performer or the record producer. Usually, authorship is contributed by both performer and producer." Compendium of Copyright Office Practices, United States Copyright Office, § 495.01 at 400-37 (1984).

Maritime next argues that as an experienced artist, Parker understood the inherently collaborative nature of producing a live performance. Parker was aware of both the technical and creative efforts that are customarily required of producers, as well as the acknowledgment of those efforts through the industry practice of 1) crediting producers on an album for their contribution in recording a particular track and 2) requesting third party producers to transfer their rights in the track in exchange for royalty payments.

Finally, Maritime contends that when Parker requested, through his road manager, that Maritime record his performance, Parker intended to create a collaborative joint work with Maritime, in accordance with copyright practice and industry custom. Powell, the road manager, claims that he did not request a professional recording, but merely asked Maritime to activate a tape recorder. Maritime points out, however, that both Parker and Powell knew prior to the concert that Parker was going to be professionally recorded because the recording equipment, including large microphones and video cameras, was plainly visible from the stage.

After the concert, Parker's road manager left with the "master" tape. Parker and Zomba ultimately used the sound recording on the album. Maritime concludes that by requesting a recording of the concert, which was later commercially released, defendants intended that the parties merge their creative efforts in the production of a sound recording.

The Court finds that Maritime has demonstrated the existence of triable issues of fact with respect to the intention of the parties. Contrary to defendants' contentions, whether

Zomba or Parker ever directly asked Maritime to record the concert is not dispositive of the question of the parties' intent.

Maritime has submitted evidence that Parker requested Maritime to record him. Parker knew Maritime was employing professional equipment while he was being recorded. Parker, through his road manager, sought out the tape after the concert, and ultimately used the tape on his album. From these circumstances a jury could reasonably conclude that Parker/Zomba and Maritime shared an implied agreement to jointly create a sound recording of the concert through the interdependent contributions of Parker's performance and Maritime's recordation and production thereof.

B. Copyrightable contribution

Copyright protection applies only to those claimants that have made an original contribution. Maritime argues that it contributed copyrightable subject matter to the sound recordings through the arrangement and administration of recording equipment, the electronic processing of sounds, and the balancing, equalization, and integration of vocal, instrumental and audience components into a blended whole.

Defendants contend, however, that as a matter of law, Maritime is precluded from making copyrightable contributions to the sound recording because Maritime did not have Zomba's consent to make those contributions. Zomba owns the exclusive copyright to the musical compositions that form the basis of the sound recording. Defendants correctly maintain that to assert a claim of joint authorship over the sound recordings, Maritime must have obtained Zomba's permission to use Parker's musical compositions in the sound recordings. Defendants conclude that since Zomba did not authorize Maritime to use the underlying compositions in the sound recording, Maritime had no legal right to make copyrightable contributions in the production of the sound recording.

Permission to employ pre-existing copyrighted material in a sound recording need not be in writing, but can be granted orally or implied from conduct in the form of a non-exclusive license. Maritime argues that it received a non-exclusive license from defendants to use Parker's underlying musical compositions in the sound recording. Maritime contends that its license was implied from the following conduct: 1) Parker's road manager asked Maritime to record the performance; 2) Parker performed in front of two highly conspicuous audience microphones; and 3) Parker and Zomba accepted and released the sound recordings.

Defendants argue that since Zomba owned the copyrights to Parker's musical compositions, only Zomba could grant Maritime a license to use the compositions. Defendants contend that Maritime has presented evidence of an implied license based only on the conduct of Powell and Parker, and not of Zomba.

The Court finds that whether Maritime had an implied license to use Parker's musical compositions based on the conduct of Zomba or its agents is a question of fact that cannot be resolved on summary judgment. It is true that Zomba owns the copyright to Parker's musical compositions. Zomba, however, also vested Parker with the authority to perform those compositions at Maritime's venue. At the venue, Parker requested that Maritime record his musical compositions. Since Parker states that he "customarily" records his own performances, it should have come as no surprise to Zomba that Parker asked Maritime to record the concert.

From these facts, a jury could reasonably conclude that Parker, vested with Zomba's authority to perform the copyrighted compositions, acted as Zomba's agent when he requested Maritime to record the concert. In light of Zomba's later acceptance and commercial exploitation of the sound recordings, it is a question of fact whether Parker's request to record the performance constituted an implied license for Maritime to use the underlying compositions to produce the sound recording.

2. Maritime's unjust enrichment claim

Defendants contend that Maritime's equitable claim for unjust enrichment is preempted by the Copyright Act under *17 U.S.C. § 301*. Maritime responds that preemption does not apply because the subject matter of its state law claim falls outside the scope of the Act....

The Court finds that the rights which Maritime seeks to enforce in its claim for unjust enrichment is equivalent to the rights of a copyright owner under §§ 106(1) and 106(3) of the Act. Section 106(1) ensures a copyright owner the right "to reproduce the copyrighted work in copies or phonorecords." Section 106(3) protects the right of copyright owners to distribute those copies to the public for sale.

In its state law claim, Maritime seeks recovery from defendants for their wrongful profits from Maritime's interest in the sound recording. Under the Act, Maritime, as putative joint author, possesses the right under §§ 106(1) and 106(3) to share in the profits of Zomba's reproduction and distribution of the sound recordings. Under federal copyright law or in *quantum meruit*, Maritime is seeking the same thing: compensation for the reproduction and distribution of the sound recordings. Under the third prong, therefore, the rights Maritime asserts under its state law claim are equivalent to rights within the general scope of copyright as specified in § 106.

The sound recording is a work of authorship fixed in a tangible medium of expression and the work comes within the subject matter of copyright under § 102(a)(7). Further, the rights sought to be vindicated in Maritime's unjust enrichment claim are rights involving reproduction and distribution that are clearly equivalent to the rights prescribed by §§ 106(1) and 106(3). Consequently, § 301(a) preempts Maritime's unjust enrichment claim....

Forward v. Thorogood
985 F.2d 604 (1st Cir. 1993)

This is an appeal from a final judgment determining the copyright ownership of certain unpublished tape recordings of the musical group George Thorogood and the Destroyers (the "Band"). The district court ruled that the Band held the copyright to the tapes and enjoined appellant John Forward from making commercial use of the recordings. We affirm.

The basic facts can be briefly stated. Forward is a music aficionado and record collector with a special interest in blues and country music. In 1975, Forward was working as a bus driver when he first met Thorogood at a Boston nightclub where the Band was performing. Forward was immediately taken with the Band's act and struck up a friendship with Thorogood. Thorogood and his fellow band members, a drummer and a guitar player, had been playing together at East Coast colleges and clubs since 1973.

Upon learning that the Band had yet to release its first album, Forward began a campaign to persuade his friends at Rounder Records to sign the Band to a recording contract. Rounder Records is a small, Boston-based record company specializing in blues and folk music. As part of this effort, Forward arranged and paid for two recording sessions for the Band in 1976. The purpose of the sessions was to create a "demo" tape that would capture Rounder Records' interest. At Forward's invitation, one of the principals of Rounder Records attended the Band's second recording session. Other than requesting specific songs to be recorded, Forward's contribution to the sessions was limited to arranging and paying for them.

Rounder Records was impressed by what it heard; the day after the second session, it arranged to sign the Band to a contract. The Band agreed that Forward could keep the tapes for his own enjoyment, and they have remained in his possession ever since. In 1977, the Band's first album was released under the Rounder Records label. Forward was singled out for "special thanks" in the album's acknowledgements. Since then, Thorogood and the Destroyers have released a number of records and gone on to achieve success as a blues/rock band.

The dispute between the parties arose in early 1988, when Forward told the Band that he intended to sell the 1976 tapes to a record company for commercial release. The Band objected, fearing that release of the tapes would harm its reputation; they were, the district court found, of "relatively primitive quality" compared to the Band's published work. On July 5, 1988, Forward filed suit in the district court, seeking a declaratory judgment that he held the common law copyright to the tapes. Determination of copyright ownership is governed by the common law of copyright because the tapes are unpublished and were recorded in 1976, prior to the January 1, 1978, effective date of the Copyright Act of 1976. The Band responded with a counterclaim for declaratory and injunctive relief....

On this appeal, Forward's first theory in support of his claim of copyright ownership is based on his ownership and possession of the tapes. According to Forward, ownership of a copyrightable work carries with it ownership of the copyright. Alternatively, he argues that the evidence mandated a finding that the copyright was implicitly transferred to him along with the demo tapes. We find no merit in either claim.

The creator of a work is, at least presumptively, its author and the owner of the copyright. The performer of a musical work is the author, as it were, of the performance. The courts, in applying the common law of copyright, did in a number of cases infer from an unconditional sale of a manuscript or painting an intent to transfer the copyright. This doctrine, often criticized and subject to various judicial and statutory exclusions is the source of Forward's principal claim. The difficulty for Forward is that even under the doctrine this physical transfer merely created a presumption and the ultimate question was one of intent.

In this case, the district court found that "[n]either the band nor any of its members ever conveyed, or agreed to convey, their copyright interest in the tapes to Forward." Rather the Band allowed Forward to keep the tapes solely for his personal enjoyment. Forward's disregard of this central finding is premised on a highly artificial attempt to claim "constructive possession" of the tapes from the outset and then to argue that any reservation by the Band at the end of the sessions was an invalid attempt to reconvey or qualify his copyright. The reality is that the Band never surrendered the copyright in the first place and the transfer of the tapes' ownership to Forward was not a sharply defined event distinct from the reservation of the Band's rights....

Forward's second theory of copyright ownership involves the "works for hire" doctrine. Under this doctrine, a judicially developed notion later codified in the Copyright Act of 1909, an employer is deemed the "author" and copyright holder of a work created by an employee acting within the scope of employment. Although initially confined to the traditional employer-employee relationship, the doctrine has been expanded to include commissioned works created by independent contractors, with courts treating the contractor as an employee and creating a presumption of copyright ownership in the commissioning party at whose "instance and expense" the work was done.[5] Forward maintains

---

5. The Copyright Act of 1976 altered the works for hire doctrine so that only certain types of commissioned works qualify as works for hire, and then only if the parties have agreed in writing to treat it as such. See *Community for Creative Non-Violence, 490 U.S. at 738.* The Act's provisions on works for hire operate prospectively and do not govern this case.

that the tapes, created at his "instance and expense," are commissioned works to which he holds the copyright.

The district court rejected this claim, finding that the evidence did not support it. The court said that, although Forward booked and paid for the studio time, he neither employed nor commissioned the band members nor did he compensate or agree to compensate them. While the lack of compensation may not be decisive, see, e.g., *Community for Creative Non-Violence*, 490 U.S. at 734 (donated commissioned work), the evidence as a whole amply supports the trial judge's conclusion. Nothing suggests that the tapes were prepared for the use and benefit of Forward. Rather, the purpose was to provide demo tapes to entice a recording company. Forward was a fan and friend who fostered this effort, not the Archbishop of Saltzburg commissioning works by Mozart.

Finally, Forward argues that he is at least a co-owner of the copyright as a "joint author" of the tape recordings.... In appraising this claim, our concern is with Forward's musical or artistic contribution rather than his encouragement to the Band or his logistical support.

The district court found that "Forward made no musical or artistic contribution" to the tapes, explaining that Forward did not serve as the engineer at the sessions or direct the manner in which the songs were played or sung. The trial judge noted that Forward did request that certain songs be played but "the band then played those songs in precisely the same manner that it always played them." The district court's concise and unqualified findings are fully supported by the evidence.

Forward has only one legal prop for his contrary claim and it is a weak one. In the House Report on the Copyright Act of 1976, the committee observed that the copyright in sound recordings "will usually, though not always, involve 'authorship' both ... [by the artist and by] the record producer responsible for setting up the recording session, capturing and electronically processing the sounds, and compiling and editing them to make the final sound recording." H. Rep. No. 94-1476, 94th Cong., 2d Sess. 56 (1976). It is apparent from this passage that the "producer" envisaged by the committee is one who engages in artistically supervising and editing the production. That is exactly what Forward did not do in this case....

In 1995, a legislative compromise amended §§ 106 and 114 to provide a limited copyright. Under § 106, a copyright interest now exists for performers "in the case of sound recordings, to perform the copyrighted work publicly by means of a digital audio transmission." Congress amended the law in 1998 to incorporate the dramatic changes caused by Internet broadcasting to the original regulations. Under § 114 of the Copyright Act, digital performances are regulated in three general categories.

Arista Records, LLC v. Launch Media, Inc.
578 F.3d 148 (2d Cir. 2009)

[Section 114(d)(1)(a) and (b) excepts from any licensing requirement those digital audio signals that are part of a nonsubscription terrestrial broadcast or a retransmission of a broadcast so long as the signal is within a 150-mile radius of the transmitter.

Section 114(d)(2) provides that non-interactive digital transmissions which would not be exempt under (d)(1) are subject to a statutory or compulsory license. The Recording Industry Association of America (RIAA) has undertaken to serve as the collective licensing arm for this right.

The third type of use is for interactive, digital transmissions. These uses must be negotiated directly with the RIAA or the copyright holders and are not subject to the statutory licensing structure.]

We are the first federal appellate court called upon to determine whether a webcasting service that provides users with individualized internet radio stations—the content of which can be affected by users' ratings of songs, artists, and albums—is an interactive service within the meaning of 17 U.S.C. § 114(j)(7). If it is an interactive service, the webcasting service would be required to pay individual licensing fees to those copyright holders of the sound recordings of songs the webcasting service plays for its users. If it is not an interactive service, the webcasting service must only pay a statutory licensing fee set by the Copyright Royalty Board. A jury determined that the defendant does not provide an interactive service and therefore is not liable for paying the copyright holders, a group of recording companies, a licensing fee for each individual song. The recording companies appeal claiming that as a matter of law the webcasting service is an interactive service, and alternatively, that the district court's instruction to the jury, as well as its admission and exclusion of certain evidence and testimony, was harmful error. We affirm; the webcasting service is not an interactive service as a matter of law.

On May 24, 2001 Arista Records, LLC, Bad Boy Records, BMG Music, and Zomba Recording LLC (collectively, "BMG") brought suit against Launch Media, Inc. ("Launch") alleging that Launch violated provisions of the Digital Millennium Copyright Act of 1998, Pub. L. 105-304, 112 Stat. 2860 (1998) (the "DMCA"), codified in relevant part in 17 U.S.C. § 114, by willfully infringing sound recording copyrights of BMG from 1999 to 2001. The United States District Court for the Southern District of New York (Owen, J.) denied the parties' cross-motions for dismissal under Federal Rule of Civil Procedure 12(b)(6) and summary judgment. The case was tried before a jury, and after the district court denied BMG's motion for judgment as a matter of law, the jury returned a verdict for Launch.

Launch operates an internet radio website, or "webcasting" service, called LAUNCHcast, which enables a user to create "stations" that play songs that are within a particular genre or similar to a particular artist or song the user selects. BMG holds the copyrights in the sound recordings of some of the songs LAUNCHcast plays for users.

BMG, as a sound recording copyright holder, has no copyright in the general performance of a sound recording, see 17 U.S.C. §§ 106(4), 114(a), but BMG does have the exclusive right "to perform the copyrighted [sound recording] publicly by means of a digital audio transmission," 17 U.S.C. § 106(6). Launch does not dispute that LAUNCHcast provides a digital audio transmission within the definition of § 106(6). See 17 U.S.C. §§ 101, 114(j)(5). BMG has a right to demand that those who perform—i.e., play or broadcast—its copyrighted sound recording pay an individual licensing fee to BMG if the performance of the sound recording occurs through an "interactive service." See 17 U.S.C. § 114(d)(3)(C).

An interactive service is defined as a service "that enables a member of the public to receive a transmission of a program specially created for the recipient, or on request, a transmission of a particular sound recording..., which is selected by or on behalf of the recipient." Id. § 114(j)(7). If a digital audio transmission is not an interactive service and its "primary purpose ... is to provide to the public such audio or other entertainment programming," id. § 114(j)(6), the transmitter need only pay a compulsory or statutory licensing fee set by the Copyright Royalty Board made up of Copyright Royalty Judges appointed by the Library of Congress.

At trial, BMG claimed that between November 1999 and May 2001 Launch—through LAUNCHcast—provided an interactive service and therefore was required to obtain individual licenses from BMG to play BMG's sound recordings. To demonstrate how LAUNCHcast functioned, BMG submitted an email from Jeff Boulter, Senior Director of Product Development at Launch, in which Boulter described how LAUNCHcast generated a list of songs using the user's preferences. In turn, Launch submitted a report from Margaret L. Johnson, a computer science professor at Stanford University, which also detailed how LAUNCHcast generated songs for a user. There is no material dispute between the parties with regard to how LAUNCHcast works. The jury returned a verdict in favor of Launch....

An "interactive service" according to the statute "is one that enables a member of the public to receive a transmission of a program specially created for the recipient, or on request, a transmission of a particular sound recording, whether or not as part of a program, which is selected by or on behalf of the recipient." 17 U.S.C. § 114(j)(7). The statute provides little guidance as to the meaning of its operative term "specially created." ...

Congress extended the first copyright protection for sound recordings in 1971 by creating a right "[t]o reproduce and distribute" "tangible" copies of sound recordings. Sound Recording Act of 1971 (the "SRA"), Pub. L. 92-140, 85 Stat. 391[.] Notably, unlike the copyright of musical works, the sound recording copyright created by the SRA did not include a right of performance. Therefore, holders of sound recording copyrights—principally recording companies such as BMG—had no right to extract licensing fees from radio stations and other broadcasters of recorded music. The reason for this lack of copyright protection in sound recordings, as the Third Circuit has put it, was that the "recording industry and [radio] broadcasters existed in a sort of symbiotic relationship wherein the recording industry recognized that radio airplay was free advertising that lured consumers to retail stores where they would purchase recordings." *Bonneville Int'l Corp.*, 347 F.3d at 487. As the *Bonneville* court also noted, however, the relationship has been, and continues to be, "more nuanced" and occasionally antagonistic. In response to continued lobbying by the recording industry, Congress and the Copyright Office (the "Office") studied the need for stronger copyright protection for sound recordings for two decades after passage of the SRA. See 141 Cong. Rec. S11,945-04, 11,949 (daily ed. Aug. 8, 1995) (statement of Sen. Hatch).

... Congress enacted the current version of § 114 under the DMCA in 1998. The term "interactive service" was expanded to include "those that are specially created for a particular individual." H.R. Rep. No. 105-796, at 87 (1998) (Conf. Rep.). As enacted, the definition of "interactive service" was now a service "that enables a member of the public to receive a transmission of a program specially created for the recipient, or on request, a transmission of a particular sound recording, whether or not as part of a program, which is selected by or on behalf of the recipient." 17 U.S.C. § 114.

According to the House conference report,

> The conferees intend that the phrase "program specially created for the recipient" be interpreted reasonably in light of the remainder of the definition of "interactive service." For example, a service would be interactive if it allowed a small number of individuals to request that sound recordings be performed in a program specially created for that group and not available to any individuals outside of that group. In contrast, a service would not be interactive if it merely transmitted to a large number of recipients of the service's transmissions a program consisting of sound recordings requested by a small number of those listeners.

H.R. Rep. No. 105-796, at 87–88 (Conf. Rep.).

The House report continued that a transmission is considered interactive "if a transmission recipient is permitted to select particular sound recordings in a prerecorded or predetermined program." *Id.* at 88. "For example, if a transmission recipient has the ability to move forward and backward between songs in a program, the transmission is interactive. It is not necessary that the transmission recipient be able to select the actual songs that comprise the program." *Id....*

[T]he Copyright Office [opined] that in enacting the § 114(j)(7), "Congress sought to identify a service as interactive according to the amount of influence a member of the public would have on the selection and performance of a particular sound recording." However, the Office stated that "the fact that some degree of consumer influence on a service's programming is permissible does not mean that a regulation to clarify that fact is necessary or even desirable." The Copyright Office also noted that "because the law and the accompanying legislative history make it clear that consumers can have some influence on the offerings made by a service without making the service interactive, there is no need to amend the regulations to make this point." ...

In sum, from the SRA to the DMCA, Congress enacted copyright legislation directed at preventing the diminution in record sales through outright piracy of music or new digital media that offered listeners the ability to select music in such a way that they would forego purchasing records....

After creating a username and password, and entering basic information and preferences unrelated to the music LAUNCHcast provides, a LAUNCHcast user is able to create and modify personalized radio stations. First, the user is prompted to select artists whose music the user prefers. The user is then asked which music genres the user enjoys and asked to rate the genres on a scale. The user is also asked the percentage of new music—songs the user has not previously rated—the user would like to incorporate into the user's station (the "unrated quota") and whether the user permits playing songs with profane lyrics. The minimum unrated quota is 20%, meaning no less than 20% of the songs played can be unrated.

Once LAUNCHcast begins playing music based on the user's preferred artists and genres, the user rates the songs, artists, or albums LAUNCHcast plays between zero and 100, with 100 being the best rating. Below the rating field are hyperlinks termed "history," "share," and "buy." The history hyperlink allows the user to see a list of the songs previously played, and the buy hyperlink facilitates the user's purchase of the songs. The share hyperlink allows the user to share the station with other users. This feature facilitates the "subscription" of one user to another user's station. When user A subscribes to the station of user B, user B becomes a "DJ" for user A. The DJ feature of LAUNCHcast does not allow a user to play particular songs for other users, but instead gives users access to each other's stations, which they can modify by rating songs, artists, or albums....

Whenever the user logs into LAUNCHcast and selects a station, LAUNCHcast generates a playlist of fifty songs based on several variables. LAUNCHcast does not provide a list of the pool of songs or of the songs in the generated playlist, and therefore, the user does not know what songs might be played.... LAUNCHcast then generates a list of all songs played for the user within the last thirty days, a list of all DJs, genres, and radio stations to which the user subscribes, and a list of all the ratings of all the songs, artists, and albums rated by either the user or any DJ to which the user subscribes.... All of these songs are initially added to the hashtable. LAUNCHcast then excludes: (1) all songs that the user, or a DJ to which the user subscribes, requests be skipped permanently (rated as zero) and (2) songs played within the last three hours for the user on any LAUNCHcast station. This yields approximately 4,000 songs.

LAUNCHcast then adds to the hashtable the 1,000 most popular songs—songs most highly rated by all LAUNCHcast users—in the bandwidth specified by the user, provided those songs are not already on the hashtable. LAUNCHcast then adds another 5,000 songs. To generate this group of songs, LAUNCHcast first counts the total number of songs contained in each of all the genres the user has selected and divides that number by the total number of songs in LAUNCHcast's database. If the resulting quotient is less than 5% of the number of songs in LAUNCHcast's database then LAUNCHcast picks only songs listed as within the genres the user has selected. This calculation is performed in order to ensure that of the 5,000 "random" songs added to the hashtable, a sufficiently large number are of genres eligible to be selected for inclusion on the final playlist....

The language and development of the DPSR and DMCA make clear that Congress enacted both statutes to create a narrow copyright in the performance of digital audio transmissions to protect sound recording copyright holders—principally recording companies—from the diminution in record sales....

Contrary to BMG's contentions, Congress was clear that the statute sought to prevent further decreases in revenues for sound recording copyright holders due to significant reductions in record sales, perceived in turn to be a result of the proliferation of interactive listening services. If the user has sufficient control over the interactive service such that she can predict the songs she will hear, much as she would if she owned the music herself and could play each song at will, she would have no need to purchase the music she wishes to hear. Therefore, part and parcel of the concern about a diminution in record sales is the concern that an interactive service provides a degree of predictability—based on choices made by the user—that approximates the predictability the music listener seeks when purchasing music....

Launch does not deny that each playlist generated when a LAUNCHcast user selects a radio station is unique to that user at that particular time. However, this does not necessarily make the LAUNCHcast playlist specially created for the user. Based on a review of how LAUNCHcast functions, it is clear that LAUNCHcast does not provide a specially created program within the meaning of § 114(j)(7) because the webcasting service does not provide sufficient control to users such that playlists are so predictable that users will choose to listen to the webcast in lieu of purchasing music, thereby—in the aggregate—diminishing record sales.

First, the rules governing what songs are pooled in the hashtable ensure that the user has almost no ability to choose, let alone predict, which specific songs will be pooled in anticipation for selection to the playlist. At least 60% of the songs in the hashtable are generated by factors almost entirely beyond the user's control. The playlist—a total of fifty songs—is created from a pool of approximately 10,000 songs, at least 6,000 of which (1,000 of the most highly rated LAUNCHcast songs among all users and 5,000 randomly selected songs) are selected without any consideration for the user's song, artist, or album preferences. The user has control over the genre of songs to be played for 5,000 songs, but this degree of control is no different from a traditional radio listener expressing a preference for a country music station over a classic rock station. LAUNCHcast generates this list with safeguards to prevent the user from limiting the number of songs in the list eligible for play by selecting a narrow genre. Also, no more than 20% of the songs the user rates—marked by LAUNCHcast as explicitly rated—can be pooled in the hashtable, and no more than three times the number of explicitly rated songs divided by the total number of rated songs can be in the hashtable. This ensures that a limited number of explicitly rated songs will eventually be selected for the playlist. Ironically, this effectively means that the more songs the user explicitly rates, the less the user can predict which explicitly rated songs will be pooled in the hashtable and played on the playlist.

Second, the selection of songs from the hashtable to be included in the playlist is governed by rules preventing the user's explicitly rated songs from being anywhere near a majority of the songs on the playlist. At minimum, 20% of the songs played on the station are unrated—meaning the user has never expressed a preference for those songs. If the user attempts to increase her chances of hearing a particular song by rating only a small number of songs—making the user's list of explicitly and implicitly rated songs smaller than 100—90% of the songs LAUNCHcast selects for the playlist will be unrated, flooding the playlist with songs for which the user has never expressed a preference.

Even the ways in which songs are rated include variables beyond the user's control. For instance, the ratings by all of the user's subscribed-to DJs are included in the playlist selection process. When the user rates a particular song, LAUNCHcast then implicitly rates all other songs by that artist, subjecting the user to many songs the user may have never heard or does not even like. There are restrictions placed on the number of times songs by a particular artist or from a particular album can be played, and there are restrictions on consecutive play of the same artist or album. Finally, because each playlist is unique to each user each time the user logs in, a user cannot listen to the playlist of another user and anticipate the songs to be played from that playlist, even if the user has selected the same preferences and rated all songs, artists, and albums identically as the other user.... Finally, after navigating these criteria to pool a hashtable and generate a playlist, LAUNCHcast randomly orders the playlist. This randomization is limited by restrictions on the consecutive play of artists or albums, which further restricts the user's ability to choose the artists or albums they wish to hear. LAUNCHcast also does not enable the user to view the unplayed songs in the playlist, ensuring that a user cannot sift through a playlist to choose the songs the user wishes to hear.

It appears the only thing a user can predict with certainty—the only thing the user can control—is that by rating a song at zero the user will not hear that song on that station again. But the ability not to listen to a particular song is certainly not a violation of a copyright holder's right to be compensated when the sound recording is played.

In short, to the degree that LAUNCHcast's playlists are uniquely created for each user, that feature does not ensure predictability. Indeed, the unique nature of the playlist helps Launch ensure that it does not provide a service so specially created for the user that the user ceases to purchase music. LAUNCHcast listeners do not even enjoy the limited predictability that once graced the AM airwaves on weekends in America when "special requests" represented love-struck adolescents' attempts to communicate their feelings to "that special friend." Therefore, we cannot say LAUNCHcast falls within the scope of the DMCA's definition of an interactive service created for individual users.

When Congress created the sound recording copyright, it explicitly characterized it as "narrow." There is no general right of performance in the sound recording copyright. There is only a limited right to performance of digital audio transmission with several exceptions to the copyright, including the one at issue in this case. We find that LAUNCHcast is not an interactive service within the meaning of 17 U.S.C. § 114(j)(7). Because we so conclude, we need not reach the other issues raised by BMG on appeal.

The district court's judgment of May 16, 2007 in favor of Appellee is hereby affirmed with costs.

SoundExchange—The Performing
Rights Society for Sound Recordings

For the licensing fees of public performance in sound recordings involving non-interactive services, the Copyright Royalty Board recognized SoundExchange, a private, nonprofit performing rights society that grew out of the RIAA. SoundExchange provides the following overview:

> SoundExchange is a non-profit performance rights organization that collects statutory royalties from satellite radio (such as SIRIUS XM), Internet radio (like Pandora), cable TV music channels and similar platforms for streaming sound recordings. The Copyright Royalty Board, which is appointed by The U.S. Library of Congress, has entrusted SoundExchange as the sole entity in the United States to collect and distribute these digital performance royalties on behalf of featured and non-featured recording artists, master rights owners (usually record labels), and independent artists who record and own their masters....

> Before 1995, Sound Recording Copyright Owners (SRCOs) in the United States did not have a performance right in any medium. This meant that, unlike their counterparts in most of Europe and other nations around the world, artists and copyright owners did not get paid for the public performance of their works. Service providers used and made money from those works at will, without a dime being paid to the rightful owners of those recordings or the featured artists who performed the recordings that create the backbone of their business.

> The Digital Performance in Sound Recordings Act of 1995 and the Digital Millennium Copyright Act of 1998 granted a performance right in sound recordings in some kinds of digital media. As a result of this forward step, copyright law now requires that certain users of music pay the copyright owner of the sound recording for the public performance of that music via certain digital transmissions. Recognizing the excellent work SoundExchange was doing, the U.S. Copyright Office designated SoundExchange as the sole administrative entity for subscription services' statutory license fees. The Copyright Royalty Board— which governs the fair market rates for recordings—reaffirmed SoundExchange's sole collective status in 2007.

> SoundExchange is the principal administrator of the statutory licenses under Sections 112 and 114 of the Copyright Act. SoundExchange participates in each periodic rate-making proceeding under the Section 112 and 114 licenses to establish rates that appropriately compensate copyright owners and performers for the exploitation of copyrighted sound recordings. Such rate-setting proceedings may be resolved through voluntary multi-party settlements or proceedings involving the Copyright Royalty Board. SoundExchange also participates in Copyright Office rulemakings to establish the terms governing how services operate under the two statutory licenses.

About SoundExchange, SOUNDEXCHANGE, http://www.soundexchange.com (last visited Dec. 27, 2012).

By statute, 50% of the revenue collected through sound recording performance fees are distributed to the copyright holders of the sound recordings (i.e., the record labels), 45% is provided to the featured artists on the recording, and 5% is distributed to the non-featured musicians and background vocalists. SoundExchange explains the featured artist category in its FAQ:

> A "featured artist," "featured recording artist," "contract artist," "royalty artist," or "featured performer" means the performing group or, if not a group or ensemble, the individual performer, identified most prominently in print on, or otherwise in connection with, the sound recording actually being performed. This means that if you are a solo artist and have released songs or albums you would be considered a "featured artist." If instead you are a part of a band then that band would be considered the "featured artist."

> If a sound recording (either musical or spoken word) identifies several featured performers, then the allocation of royalties may be on a pro rata basis among all identified performers. According to the legislative history to the Digital Performance Right in Sound Recordings Act, where "both the vocalist or soloist and the group or ensemble are identified as a single entity and with equal prominence (such as 'Diana Ross and the Supremes'), both the individual and the group qualify as the 'featured recording artist.'" SoundExchange may also distribute royalties according to any splits agreed to among featured recording artists in private agreements, provided that all of the identified featured recording artists agree in writing to SoundExchange's distribution of royalties according to such splits.

FAQ, SoundExchange, http://www.soundexchange.com (last visited Dec. 27, 2012).

Notes and Questions

a. Under traditional copyright law, a musical performing artist holds no copyright in his or her performance. As a result, the performers do not receive any income from radio play or other public performances of their recordings except as negotiated under union recording agreements. Nonetheless, as copyright interests have continued to expand since 1972 when federal law first recognized copyright in sound recordings, an increasing number of possible ownership claims have arisen. State laws often protect sound recording made prior to February 15, 1972.

b. Jenny Smith, a musician, engineer, and record producer, serves as producer for three cuts on a CD. Part of the Producer's Agreement states that the three song masters were created as a work-for-hire as a specially commissioned work. Both Ms. Smith and the label duly sign the agreement. If there is no additional assignment provision in the contract, who is the author of the three song masters? See *Staggers v. Real Authentic Sound*, 77 F. Supp. 2d 57 (D.C. D.C. 1999).

c. Industry custom generally places the copyright ownership of a master tape in the record label to assure all copyright interests are collected into a single entity so the final work may be exploited through reproductions, sales, and licenses. To what extent does this custom govern the interpretation of copyright law?

d. Does the composer of a song have a claim to compensation or control over the sampling of another sound recording embodying some portion of the composer's work? See *Newton v. Diamond*, 349 F.3d 591 (9th Cir. 2003).

e. Does the mechanical license cover any composer's interest in a song sample? Compare the results under 17 U.S.C. § 115 (compulsory license for making and distributing phonorecords) with the type license generally used by the industry as provided by the Harry Fox Agency.

f. The international management of copyrights only compounds the problems for the copyright owners. The copyrights in the underlying compositions must be maintained in each country where the sound recording is sold. These rights are often held by local entities, and the local recording distributor must secure those rights. For an example where Sony was deemed to overreact to the failure to maintain these underlying rights, see *Point Prods. A.G. v. Sony Music Entm't, Inc.*, 93 Civ. 4001 (NRB) (S.D.N.Y. July 20, 2000).

g. In 2009, legislation was introduced to extend a public performance right for radio or "audio transmissions." The effect would be to extend the mandatory statutory licensing to AM and FM radio.

h. Can a person sell a sound recording and still exploit the underlying composition? Not through litigation. The distinction between these two aspects of a song tested the differing standards for sound recordings and the underlying musical compositions. To the extent that these standards can be compared, see *Newton v. Diamond*, 388 F.3d 1189 (9th Cir. 2004).

i. When does a producer's claim of copyright ownership in the master recordings accrue? See *Diamond v. Gillis*, 357 F. Supp. 2d 1003 (E.D. Mich. 2005).

j. In seeking statutory damages for the unauthorized sale of digital albums, what is the work—the individual songs or the compilation as a whole? See *Bryant v. Media Rights Products*, 603 F.3d 135 (2d Cir. 2010).

k. Record companies actively support the marketing of recording artists by distributing many copies of the recordings for free on CD, sending the discs to record stores, broadcasters, and others. To what extent can they restrict the resale of these free copies to avoid flooding the used-CD market? See *UMG Recordings, Inc. v. Augusto*, 628 F.3d 1175 (9th Cir. 2011).

l. For a discussion of the ownership of sound master copyrights and infringement of sound recording prior to the federal copyright protection in 1972, see *Capitol Records, Inc. v. Naxos of Am., Inc. (USCOA)*, Copyright L. Rep. (CCH) ¶ 28,980, 74 U.S.P.Q. 2d (BNA) 1331 (N.Y. 2005).

m. For a discussion of the rights to compulsory license fees for digital performances in sound recordings, see *Beethoven.com LLC v. Librarian of Cong.*, 394 F.3d 939, 942 (D.C.Cir.2005) ("The Digital Millennium Copyright Act of 1998, Pub.L. No. 105-304, 'created a statutory license in performances by webcast,' to serve Internet broadcasters and to provide a means of paying copyright owners."); *Intercollegiate Broad. System, Inc. v. Copy. Royalty Bd.*, 574 F.3d 748, 753 (D.C. Cir. 2009).

Problem XII-B

Bryce is a bit upset. Two of Bryce's songs were rewritten by the drummer in Soundfyre. Bryce acknowledges that late one night after one of the performances, Bryce had said "do whatever you want" regarding the songs, but Bryce did not think it was anything other than bar talk, and Bryce did not consider that the statement was intended to waive fees or rights.

The forthcoming album by Soundfyre includes the two songs in question. The CD lists Bryce and Jeri Thundar as authors of the songs. Bryce is not receiving mechanical royalties. Advise Bryce what options are available to collect on the income from the songs and correct the credits provided on the album.

C. Scope of Prior Licenses

Thomas v. Gusto Records, Inc.

939 F.2d 395 (6th Cir. 1991)

[T]he musicians in this suit have achieved a high degree of success in "popular music." B. J. Thomas is most famous for his recording of the theme song for the movie "Butch Cassidy and the Sundance Kid," "Rain Drops Keep Fallin' on My Head." Burt Bacharach and Hal Davis wrote the song originally for Bob Dylan to record. Thomas also had a number one hit with "Another Somebody Done Somebody Wrong Song." Among his accolades are eleven gold records, two platinum albums, and five Grammy awards....

Thomas and the Shirelles entered into contracts with Scepter Records, Inc. in 1968 and 1961, respectively. The provisions of the two contracts in question are identical, except as to the royalty rate, and provide the following:

> 4. For the rights herein granted and the service to be rendered by you we shall pay you as royalty a sum equal to [4% for the Shirelles] [5% for Thomas] of the net retail list price in the United States of America based on 90% of all double-faced records manufactured and sold by us and paid for, on both faces of which are embodied only the selections recorded hereunder; and one-half of the respective amounts of such royalties of 90% of all records manufactured and sold by us and paid for on only one face of which are embodied only the selections recorded hereunder. In the case of phonograph records and other copies manufactured and sold in foreign countries by any subsidiary, affiliate, licensee or nominees to whom we have supplied a copy or duplicate of a master or matrix or tape of any such recordings, we will pay you one-half of the United States of America royalty rate out of all net license fees paid and received by us for phonograph records and other copies so manufactured and sold....

Gusto and G.M.L. assert that paragraph four is unambiguous with regard to royalties from domestic licensing, arguing that the "obvious implication" of silence on the issue is that the parties agreed there would be no such royalties. We do not find that implication so obvious.

Both parties agree that New York law should be applied to resolve this issue. The resolution of any ambiguity in a written contract is to be determined by the court as a matter of law. Not only are these contracts silent on many issues, e.g. domestic licensing royalties, many of the provisions which the contracts do set forth are perfectly obscure. Paragraph eight of both contracts, for example, if read independently, could be interpreted as a provision in which Thomas and the Shirelles signed away any and all rights. Indeed, the defendants assert this is what the paragraph means with respect to royalties from domestic licensing. Without an integration clause or more evidence in the documents supporting this harsh interpretation, we cannot accept this reading of the contracts. Because of the ambiguities in these contracts, we believe the district court properly looked beyond the written contract to determine the true intentions of the parties.

New York cases have consistently held that custom may be used to clarify ambiguities or to "fill gaps" in an agreement. Gusto asserts these cases are inapposite because custom and practice cannot be used to contradict the express terms of the contracts. The problem with this argument is that the contracts in question are silent with respect to royalties from domestic licensing; there are no express terms in the contracts explaining the parties' intentions on this issue. Paragraph 4 sets forth the royalty rate on the record company's own sales and on *foreign* sales by "any subsidiary, affiliate, licensee or nominee[ ]." ... Because no provision in the contracts of B. J. Thomas or the Shirelles pertains to royalties from domestic licensing income which could be contradicted by incorporating into the contracts the custom in the music industry with respect to that issue, the district court properly accepted the fifty percent royalty rate as the rate intended by the parties....

Greenfield v. Philles Records

98 N.Y.2d 562 (N.Y. 2002)

In this contract dispute between a singing group and their record producer, we must determine whether the artists' transfer of full ownership rights to the master recordings of musical performances carried with it the unconditional right of the producer to redistribute those performances in any technological format. In the absence of an explicit contractual reservation of rights by the artists, we conclude that it did.

In the early 1960s, Veronica Bennett (now known as Ronnie Greenfield), her sister Estelle Bennett and their cousin Nedra Talley, formed a singing group known as "The Ronettes." They met defendant Phil Spector, a music producer and composer, in 1963 and signed a five-year "personal services" music recording contract (the Ronettes agreement) with Spector's production company, defendant Philles Records, Inc. The plaintiffs agreed to perform exclusively for Philles Records and in exchange, Philles Records acquired an ownership right to the recordings of the Ronettes' musical performances. The agreement also set forth a royalty schedule to compensate plaintiffs for their services. After signing with Philles Records, plaintiffs received a single collective cash advance of approximately $15,000.

The Ronettes recorded several dozen songs for Philles Records, including "Be My Baby," which sold over a million copies and topped the music charts. Despite their popularity, the group disbanded in 1967 and Philles Records eventually went out of business. Other than their initial advance, plaintiffs received no royalty payments from Philles Records.

Beyond their professional relationship, however, was the story of the personal relationship between Spector and plaintiff Ronnie Greenfield. They married in 1968 but separated after a few years. Greenfield initiated a divorce proceeding against Spector in California and a settlement was reached in 1974. As part of that agreement, Spector and Greenfield executed mutual general releases that purported to resolve all past and future claims and obligations that existed between them, as well as between Greenfield and Spector's companies.

Defendants subsequently began to capitalize on a resurgence of public interest in 1960s music by making use of new recording technologies and licensing master recordings of the Ronettes' vocal performances for use in movie and television productions, a process known in entertainment industry parlance as "synchronization." The most notable example was defendants' licensing of "Be My Baby" in 1987 for use in the motion picture "Dirty Dancing." Defendants also licensed master recordings to third parties for production and distribution in the United States (referred to as domestic redistribution), and sold compilation albums containing performances by the Ronettes. While defendants earned considerable compensation from such licensing and sales, no royalties were paid to any of the plaintiffs.

As a result, plaintiffs commenced this breach of contract action in 1987, alleging that the 1963 agreement did not provide Philles Records with the right to license the master recordings for synchronization and domestic redistribution, and demanded royalties from the sales of compilation albums. Although defendants initially denied the existence of a contract, in 1992 they stipulated that an unexecuted copy of the contract would determine the parties' rights. Defendants thereafter argued that the agreement granted them absolute ownership rights to the master recordings and permitted the use of the recordings in any format, subject only to royalty rights. Following extensive pretrial proceedings, Supreme Court ruled in plaintiffs' favor and awarded approximately $3 million in damages and interest.

The Appellate Division affirmed, concluding that defendants' actions were not authorized by the agreement with plaintiffs because the contract did not specifically transfer the right to issue synchronization and third-party domestic distribution licenses. Permitting plaintiffs to assert a claim for unjust enrichment, the Court found that plaintiffs were entitled to the music recording industry's standard 50% royalty rate for income derived from synchronization and third-party licensing. We granted leave to appeal.

We are asked on this appeal to determine whether defendants, as the owners of the master recordings of plaintiffs' vocal performances, acquired the contractual right to issue licenses to third parties to use the recordings in connection with television, movies and domestic audio distribution. The agreement between the parties consists of a two-page document, which apparently was widely used in the 1960s by music producers signing new artists. Plaintiffs executed the contract without the benefit of counsel. The parties' immediate objective was to record and market the Ronettes' vocal performances and "[m]ake therefrom phonograph records and/or tape recordings and other similar devices (excluding transcriptions)."[6] The ownership rights provision of the contract provides:

> "All recordings made hereunder and all records and reproductions made therefrom together with the performances embodied therein, shall be entirely [Philles'] property, free of any claims whatsoever by you or any person deriving any rights of interest from you. Without limitation of the foregoing, [Philles] shall have the right to make phonograph records, tape recordings or other reproductions of the performances embodied in such recordings by any method now or hereafter known, and to sell and deal in the same under any trade mark or trade names or labels designated by us, or we may at our election refrain therefrom."

Plaintiffs concede that the contract unambiguously gives defendants unconditional ownership rights to the master recordings, but contend that the agreement does not bestow the right to exploit those recordings in new markets or mediums since the document is silent on those topics. Defendants counter that the absence of specific references to synchronization and domestic licensing is irrelevant. They argue that where a contract grants full ownership rights to a musical performance or composition, the only restrictions upon the owner's right to use that property are those explicitly enumerated by the grantor/artist.

Despite the technological innovations that continue to revolutionize the recording industry, long-settled common-law contract rules still govern the interpretation of agreements between artists and their record producers. The fundamental, neutral precept of contract interpretation is that agreements are construed in accord with the parties' intent....

The pivotal issue in this case is whether defendants are prohibited from using the master recordings for synchronization, and whatever future formats evolve from new tech-

---

6. "Transcriptions" were large discs used for reproducing musical performances for radio broadcasts.

nologies, in the absence of explicit contract language authorizing such uses. Stated another way, does the contract's silence on synchronization and domestic licensing create an ambiguity which opens the door to the admissibility of extrinsic evidence to determine the intent of the parties? We conclude that it does not and, because there is no ambiguity in the terms of the Ronettes agreement, defendants are entitled to exercise complete ownership rights, subject to payment of applicable royalties due plaintiffs.

New York has well-established precedent on the issue of whether a grantor retains any rights to artistic property once it is unconditionally transferred.... A broad grant of ownership rights, coupled with the absence of a reservation clause, was similarly dispositive in *Burnett v Warner Bros. Pictures* (67 N.Y.2d 912, 501 N.Y.S.2d 815, 492 N.E.2d 1231 [1986], affg 113 AD2d 710, 493 N.Y.S.2d 326). In that case, the plaintiffs had assigned all of their rights in a play that was later adapted into a movie, "Casablanca," and subsequently led to the defendant's spinoff television series. We affirmed the Appellate Division's conclusion that if "the plaintiff intended to retain certain rights, specific clauses to that effect should have been included in the agreement" because the parties' contract assigned "all imaginable rights" to *Warner Brothers* (113 A.D.2d at 712–713).

In analogous contexts, other courts have recognized that broad contractual provisions, similar to those in the Ronettes agreement, convey virtually unfettered reproduction rights to license holders in the absence of specific exceptions to the contrary. In *Boosey & Hawkes Music Publs. Ltd. v Walt Disney Co.* (145 F.3d 481 [2d Cir 1998]), the plaintiff granted distribution rights in foreign countries to Igor Stravinsky's musical composition "The Rite of Spring," including the "right, license, privilege and authority to record [the composition] in any manner, medium or form" for use in the motion picture "Fantasia" to the Walt Disney Company. After Disney reproduced the song in videocassette and laser disc versions for foreign distribution, the plaintiff sought breach of contract damages on the basis that the agreement did not explicitly provide for distribution in new technological mediums.

The United States Court of Appeals for the Second Circuit reiterated its precedent that "'licensee[s] may properly pursue any uses which may reasonably be said to fall within the medium as described in the license.'" As applied to the facts of *Boosey*, the Second Circuit concluded that the broad language employed in the contract granted Disney the authority to use the musical composition in the videocassette version of the movie in the absence of any contractual indication otherwise. Thus, the language of the contract was the controlling factor in interpreting the agreement:

> "If the contract is more reasonably read to convey one meaning, the party benefited by that reading should be able to rely on it; the party seeking exception or deviation from the meaning reasonably conveyed by the words of the contract should bear the burden of negotiating for language that would express the limitation or deviation"

We agree with these prevalent rules of contract construction—the unconditional transfer of ownership rights to a work of art includes the right to use the work in any manner unless those rights are specifically limited by the terms of the contract. However, if a contract grants less than full ownership or specifies only certain rights to use the property, then other, unenumerated rights may be retained by the grantor.

In this case, plaintiffs concede that defendants own the master recordings. Notably, the agreement explicitly refers to defendants' "right to make phonograph records, tape recordings or *other reproductions* of the performances embodied in such recordings by *any method now or hereafter known,* and to sell and deal in the same." Plaintiffs contend that the breadth of the ownership provision is limited by the agreement's introductory paragraph, which states that defendants' purpose for purchasing plaintiffs' performances was to make "phonograph records and/or tape recordings and other similar devices." However, when read in conjunction with the ownership provision, a reasonable meaning emerges—the phrase "other similar devices" refers to defendants' right to reproduce the performances by any current or future technological methods. We also reject plaintiffs' assertion that the royalty schedule restricts the scope of defendants' ownership rights. That section of the agreement provides compensation rights to plaintiffs; it does not inhibit defendants' ability to use the master recordings. We therefore hold that the Ronettes agreement, "read as a whole to determine its purpose and intent" is susceptible to only one reasonable interpretation—defendants are authorized to license the performances for use in visual media, such as movies and television commercials or broadcasts, and for domestic release by third parties in audio formats.

Plaintiffs' reliance upon *B.J. Thomas v Gusto Records* (939 F.2d 395 [6th Cir], cert. denied 502 U.S. 984 [1991]) is misplaced. In *Thomas,* the United States Court of Appeals for the Sixth Circuit purportedly applied New York law and held that the parties' agreements were ambiguous regarding the artists' right to royalties from domestic licensing because the contracts were silent on the issue. The dispute in *Thomas*—whether the contract's compensation clause entitled the plaintiffs to royalties from the issuance of domestic licenses—is not the same as the question posed in this case, which concerns the scope of owners' rights to use their property. Furthermore, *Thomas'* suggestion that the failure of a contract to address certain categories of royalties allows a court to look beyond the four corners of the document to discern the parties' true intent conflicts with our established precedent that silence does not equate to contractual ambiguity....

Defendants acknowledge that the royalty schedule for domestic sales encompasses the sale of records, compact discs and other audio reproductions by entities holding domestic third-party distribution licenses from Philles Records. In light of that concession, we remit this case to Supreme Court to recalculate plaintiffs' damages for royalties due on all such sales. Damages should be determined pursuant to the applicable schedule incorporated in the agreement rather than based on industry standards....

FurryRecords, Inc. v. RealNetworks, Inc.

64 U.S.P.Q.2D (BNA) 1382 (S.D.N.Y 2002)

Plaintiffs, a music artist named Hannah Bentley (who previously did business under the name Sam LaHanna) and her personal company, FurryRecords, Inc., allege that the sole remaining defendant in this case, a music promotion company named The Orchard, LLC ("Orchard"), committed various violations of the Copyright Act, 17 U.S.C. § 101 et seq., the Lanham Act, 15 U.S.C. § 1125, and the common law, chiefly by making allegedly unauthorized MP3 copies of plaintiffs' recordings. Ultimately, the viability of all of plaintiffs' claims against Orchard depends on the scope and validity, *vel non*, of a license agreement between Sam LaHanna and Orchard, dated September 3, 1999. Against this background, both sides move for summary judgment. The pertinent portions of the license agreement read:

> You [Sam LaHanna] grant to us [Orchard] throughout the Territory during the Sales Period the NON-EXCLUSIVE rights to sell, distribute and otherwise exploit any and all of your Recordings by any and all means and media (whether now known or existing in the future), including, without limitation, the non-exclusive rights to sell, distribute and otherwise exploit any and all of your Record-

ings throughout E-stores including, but not limited to, those via the Internet, as well as digital storage, download and transmission rights, whether now known or existing in the future....

The following words when used have the following meanings: "You" means the person(s) signing as individual(s) and/ or as member(s) of any group(s). "We" or "Us" means THE ORCHARD, LLC. "Territory" means the Universe. "Signing Date" means the date You sign. "Term" means a period starting on the Signing Date and ending one (1) year from the Signing Date. "Recordings" means each and every compact disc and/ or any other audio and/ or audiovisual recording in any format, in whole or in part (whether now known or existing in the future) which You deliver during the Term. "Sales Period" means the time period beginning on the Signing Date and continuing in perpetuity for each of your Recordings in each country of the Territory ...

Plaintiffs' primary argument is that, because the contract does not expressly provide for "copying" per se, defendant's encoding of plaintiffs' works into MP3 format constitutes copyright infringement (and other, related violations). However, defendant's open-ended right under the contract to "otherwise exploit" plaintiffs' recordings permits such copying. Moreover, any doubt on this score is resolved, so far as MP3 copying is concerned, by the contract's specific grant to defendant to exercise plaintiffs' "storage, download and transmission rights, whether now known or existing in the future."

Plaintiffs' fall-back argument is that the license agreement—a form contract used by Orchard—is unconscionable, and therefore void, chiefly because, while it obligates defendant to promote plaintiffs' recordings for only a one-year period, it permits defendants to sell, distribute, and otherwise exploit plaintiffs' recordings "in perpetuity." But there is nothing inherently unreasonable in a promoter, in return for promoting (here, on a website) musical works of a relatively unknown artist, obtaining, as here, a non-exclusive right to thereafter exploit those works. Furthermore, notwithstanding the "in perpetuity" language, plaintiffs have a federally-protected statutory right to terminate the contract after 35 years.

More generally, Ms. Bentley (LaHanna), a graduate of the Columbia Law School, could not conceivably have been misled as to the nature of the bargain she was entering into in agreeing to this simple, four-page contract. Nor is there any competent evidence that she was subject to high pressure tactics, given a deadline by which she had to accept or reject the contract, or otherwise subject to having her will overborne. Indeed, virtually none of the indicia of unconscionability under New York state law (which governs this contract) is here present....

The Court has considered plaintiffs' other arguments and finds them without merit. Consequently, defendants' motion for summary judgment is granted and plaintiffs' cross-motion is denied. Accordingly, the Clerk of the Court is directed to enter judgment dismissing the case with prejudice.

F.B.T. Prods., LLC v. Aftermath Records

621 F.3d 958 (9th Cir. 2010)

This dispute concerns the percentage of royalties due to Plaintiffs F.B.T. Productions, LLC, and Em2M, LLC, under their contracts with Defendant Aftermath in connection with the recordings of Marshal B. Mathers, III, professionally known as the rap artist Eminem. Specifically, F.B.T. and Aftermath disagree on whether the contracts' "Records Sold" provision or "Masters Licensed" provision sets the royalty rate for sales of Eminem's records in the form of permanent downloads and mastertones. Before trial, F.B.T. moved for summary judgment that the Masters Licensed provision unambiguously applied to permanent downloads and mastertones. The district court denied the motion. At the close of evidence, F.B.T. did not move for judgment as a matter of law, and the jury returned a verdict in favor of Aftermath. On appeal, F.B.T. reasserts that the Masters Licensed provision unambiguously applies to permanent downloads and mastertones. We agree that the contracts are unambiguous and that the district court should have granted summary judgment to F.B.T. We therefore reverse the judgment and vacate the district court's order awarding Aftermath its attorneys' fees.

F.B.T. signed Eminem in 1995, gaining exclusive rights to his recordings. In 1998, F.B.T. signed an agreement transferring Eminem's exclusive recording services to Aftermath. The "Records Sold" provision of that agreement provides that F.B.T. is to receive between 12% and 20% of the adjusted retail price of all "full price records sold in the United States ... through normal retail channels." The agreement further provides that "[n]otwithstanding the foregoing," F.B.T. is to receive 50% of Aftermath's net receipts "[o]n masters licensed by us ... to others for their manufacture and sale of records or for any other uses." The parties refer to this provision as the "Masters Licensed" provision. The contract defines "master" as a "recording of sound, without or with visual images, which is used or useful in the recording, production or manufacture of records." The agreement does not contain a definition of the terms "licensed" or "normal retail channels."

In 2002, Aftermath's parent company, Defendant UMG Recordings, Inc., concluded an agreement with Apple Computer, Inc., that enabled UMG's sound recordings, including the Eminem masters, to be sold through Apple's iTunes store as permanent downloads. Permanent downloads are digital copies of recordings that, once downloaded over the Internet, remain on an end-user's computer or other device until deleted. The contract between UMG and Apple is but one example of the many agreements that Aftermath has concluded to sell sound recordings in digital formats since approximately 2001. Since 2003, Aftermath has also concluded contracts with major cellular telephone network carriers to sell sound recordings as mastertones, which are short clips of songs that can be purchased by users to signal incoming calls, popularly known as ringtones.

In 2003, F.B.T. and Aftermath entered into a new agreement that terminated the 1998 agreement. The 2003 agreement increased some royalty rates, but incorporated the wording of the Records Sold and Masters Licensed provisions from the 1998 agreement. In 2004, the parties amended the agreement to provide that "Sales of Albums by way of permanent download shall be treated as [U.S. Normal Retail Channel] Net Sales for the purposes of escalations." Escalations are increases in the royalty rate when total album sales surpass certain targets. The amendment further provides, "Except as specifically modified herein, the Agreement shall be unaffected and remain in full force and effect."

F.B.T. brought suit after a 2006 audit showed that Aftermath had been applying the Records Sold provision to calculate the royalties due to F.B.T. for sales of Eminem's recordings in the form of permanent downloads and mastertones. Before trial, F.B.T. moved for summary judgment that the Masters Licensed provision unambiguously applied to those sales. Aftermath cross-moved for summary judgment. It argued, in part, that the 2004 amendment showed that the parties intended the Records Sold provision to apply to permanent downloads.

After provisionally reviewing the undisputed extrinsic evidence, the district court concluded that the agreements were reasonably susceptible to either party's interpretation and denied both motions for summary judgment. At trial, only Aftermath moved for judgment as a matter of law at the close of the evidence. The court denied the motion. The jury returned a verdict in favor of Aftermath, and the district court awarded Aftermath its attorneys' fees of over $ 2.4 million. F.B.T. timely appealed the district court's final judgment and award of attorneys' fees. We have jurisdiction pursuant to 28 U.S.C. § 1291 and we reverse....

Turning to the agreements in question, the Records Sold provision contains the royalty rate for "full price records sold in the United States ... through normal retail channels." On summary judgment, Aftermath argued that the Records Sold provision applied because permanent downloads and mastertones are records, and because iTunes and other digital music providers are normal retail channels in the United States.

However, the agreements also provide that "notwithstanding" the Records Sold provision, F.B.T. is to receive a 50% royalty on "masters licensed by [Aftermath] ... to others for their manufacture and sale of records or for any other uses." The parties' use of the word "notwithstanding" plainly indicates that even if a transaction arguably falls within the scope of the Records Sold provision, F.B.T. is to receive a 50% royalty if Aftermath licenses an Eminem master to a third party for "any" use. A contractual term is not ambiguous just because it is broad. Here, the Masters Licensed provision explicitly applies to (1) masters (2) that are licensed to third parties for the manufacture of records "or for any other uses," (3) "notwithstanding" the Record Sold provision. This provision is admittedly broad, but it is not unclear or ambiguous.

Accordingly, to determine whether the Masters Licensed provision applies, we must decide whether Aftermath licensed the Eminem masters to third parties. Aftermath argues that there was no evidence that it or F.B.T. used the term "licensed" in a technical sense. In the ordinary sense of the word, a license is simply "permission to act." WEBSTER'S THIRD NEW INTERNATIONAL DICTIONARY OF THE ENGLISH LANGUAGE 1304 (2002). Aftermath did not dispute that it entered into agreements that permitted iTunes, cellular phone carriers, and other third parties to use its sound recordings to produce and sell permanent downloads and mastertones. Those agreements therefore qualify as licenses under Aftermath's own proposed construction of the term.

The conclusion that Aftermath licensed the Eminem masters to third parties also comports well with and finds additional support in federal copyright law. When one looks to the Copyright Act, the terms "license" and "sale" have well differentiated meanings, and the differences between the two play an important role in the overall structures and policies that govern artistic rights. For example, under the language of the Act and the Supreme Court's interpretations, a "sale" of a work may either be a transfer in title of an individual copy of a work, or a sale of all exclusive intellectual property rights in a work.

There is no dispute that Aftermath was at all relevant times the owner of the copyrights to the Eminem recordings at issue in this case, having obtained those rights through the recording contracts in exchange for specified royalty payments. Pursuant to its agreements with Apple and other third parties, however, Aftermath did not "sell" anything to the download distributors. The download distributors did not obtain title to the digital files. The ownership of those files remained with Aftermath, Aftermath reserved the right to regain possession of the files at any time, and Aftermath obtained recurring benefits in the form of payments based on the volume of downloads.

Much as Section 109 describes a "sale" under the "first sale" doctrine, various other sections of the Copyright Act illuminate the meaning of the term "license." For example, section 114(f), titled "Licenses for Certain Nonexempt Transmissions," describes the statutory authorization for a third party to exercise public performance rights that otherwise remain the exclusive rights of a copyright holder and defines this authorization as a "license." Section 115, titled "Scope of Exclusive Rights in Nondramatic Musical Works: Compulsory License for Making and Distributing Phonorecords," refers directly to the statutory authorization for artists to exercise the copyright owner's right to make and distribute phonorecord "covers" as a license, but again makes it clear that title remains with the copyright owner.

Under our case law interpreting and applying the Copyright Act, too, it is well settled that where a copyright owner transfers a copy of copyrighted material, retains title, limits the uses to which the material may be put, and is compensated periodically based on the transferee's exploitation of the material, the transaction is a license.

It is easily gleaned from these sources of federal copyright law that a license is an authorization by the copyright owner to enable another party to engage in behavior that would otherwise be the exclusive right of the copyright owner, but without transferring title in those rights. This permission can be granted for the copyright itself, for the physical media containing the copyrighted work, or for both the copyright and the physical media.

When the facts of this case are viewed through the lens of federal copyright law, it is all the more clear that Aftermath's agreements with the third-party download vendors are "licenses" to use the Eminem master recordings for specific purposes authorized thereby— i.e., to create and distribute permanent downloads and mastertones—in exchange for periodic payments based on the volume of downloads, without any transfer in title of Aftermath's copyrights to the recordings. Thus, federal copyright law supports and reinforces our conclusion that Aftermath's agreements permitting third parties to use its sound recordings to produce and sell permanent downloads and mastertones are licenses.

Furthermore, the sound recordings that Aftermath provided to third parties qualify as masters. The contracts define a "master" as a "recording of sound ... which is used or useful in the recording, production or manufacture of records." Aftermath admitted that permanent downloads and mastertones are records. The sound recordings that Aftermath supplied to third parties were "used or useful" in the production of permanent downloads and mastertones, so those sound recordings were masters. Because Aftermath permitted third parties to use the Eminem masters to produce and sell records, in the form of permanent downloads and mastertones, F.B.T. is entitled to a 50% royalty under the plain terms of the agreements.

Aftermath argues that the 2004 amendment to the agreements clarified that the Records Sold provision sets the royalty for permanent downloads. However, the 2004 amendment states only that albums sold as permanent downloads are to be counted "for purposes of escalations" under the Records Sold provision, and that "[e]xcept as specifically modified herein, the Agreement shall be unaffected and remain in full force and effect." Read in context, the plain language of the amendment provides that sales of permanent downloads by third parties count towards escalations on the royalty owed when Aftermath itself sells records through normal retail channels. It does not state, and in no way implies, that the royalty rate for the sale of the permanent downloads by third parties is set by the Records Sold provision.

Nor did any of the evidence regarding industry custom or the parties' course of performance support Aftermath's interpretation that the Records Sold provision applies. Aftermath's expert explained that the Masters Licensed provision had in the past been applied "only to compilation records and incorporation into movies, TV shows, and commercials." It was, however, undisputed that permanent downloads and mastertones only came into existence from 2001 to 2003. Consequently, the fact that the Masters Licensed provision had never previously been applied to those forms of licensing is immaterial. There is no indication that the parties intended to confine the contract to the state of the industry in 1998. To the contrary, the contract contemplated advances in technology. It provided that Aftermath had the right to exploit the "masters in any and all forms of media now known and hereinafter developed." Aftermath's evidence of how the Masters Licensed provision had been applied in the past therefore did not cast doubt on its application to permanent downloads and mastertones.

Furthermore, Aftermath renewed its agreement with F.B.T. in 2003, by which time permanent downloads and mastertones were coming into existence. Aftermath argued that subsequent to renewal, F.B.T. had "never objected to Defendants' payment of royalties under the Records Sold provision until the auditor raised the issue in 2006." However, Aftermath provided no evidence that F.B.T. knowingly acquiesced to payment under the Records Sold provision between 2003 and 2006. It showed that F.B.T. had received statements that included royalties for permanent downloads and mastertones, but it was uncontroverted that F.B.T. did not audit those royalty statements until 2006. F.B.T. had no obligation to audit the statements any earlier than it did, and it immediately raised the issue with Aftermath after the audit. Accordingly, Aftermath cannot use F.B.T.'s lack of objection to payments made before 2006 to prove how it interpreted the agreements. The undisputed extrinsic evidence provisionally reviewed by the district court therefore did not support Aftermath's interpretation that the Records Sold provision applies.

In sum, the agreements unambiguously provide that "notwithstanding" the Records Sold provision, Aftermath owed F.B.T. a 50% royalty under the Masters Licensed provision for licensing the Eminem masters to third parties for any use. It was undisputed that Aftermath permitted third parties to use the Eminem masters to produce and sell permanent downloads and mastertones. Neither the 2004 amendment nor any of the parole evidence provisionally reviewed by the district court supported Aftermath's interpretation that the Records Sold provision applied. Because the agreements were unambiguous and were not reasonably susceptible to Aftermath's interpretation, the district court erred in denying F.B.T. summary judgment.

The judgment in favor of Aftermath is REVERSED, the district court's order granting Aftermath its attorneys' fees is VACATED, and the case is REMANDED for further proceedings consistent with this opinion.

[The parties continued to litigate the interpretation of the agreements and the implications for damage calculations. The District Court's opinion on the interpretation of net receipts is illuminating.]

F.B.T. Prods., LLC v. Aftermath Records
2011 U.S. Dist. LEXIS 126159 (C.D. Cal. 2011)

. . .

Net Receipts

The Masters Licensed provision states that FBT and Eminem's "royalty shall be an amount equal to [50%] of our net receipts." The parties dispute what comprises "our net receipts." Defendants argue that net receipts means the revenue Aftermath receives from licensing downloads and mastertones less Aftermath's direct costs from that licensing. These direct costs include mechanical royalties and distribution fees. Plaintiffs argue that neither mechanical royalties nor distribution fees should be deducted from the gross revenue that Aftermath receives from licensing.

First, it is clear that the term "our" refers to Aftermath. Aftermath is the only entity responsible for licensing that signed the agreements. It is also clear that "net receipts" contemplates some type of deduction. The definition of "net" is "free from, or not subject to, any deduction; remaining after all necessary deductions have been made." Oxford English Dictionary at 340 (2d ed. 1989). Moreover, the term "net" was used elsewhere by the parties to denote a subtraction. In the provision dealing with the licensing of videos, the parties defined "net receipts" as "gross receipts solely attributable to Videos hereunder less (1) any and all direct costs and/or third party payments in connection with the creation, manufacture, exploitation or use of said Videos; and (2) an additional fee in lieu of any overhead or distribution fee of twelve percent (12%) of the gross receipts in connection therewith." Similarly, section 16(a) defines "Net Sales" as "gross sales, less returns, credits and reserves against anticipated returns and credits." And section 12(b) defines "net" as "the amount otherwise payable to Artist after deducting all third party reductions." In accord with these definitions, net receipts is reasonably read to mean Aftermath's gross revenue from licensing less Aftermath's direct costs associated with licensing.

Plaintiffs urge a different interpretation of "our net receipts" based on extrinsic evidence. Plaintiffs argue that testimony and exhibits introduced at trial show that Aftermath does not deduct mechanical royalties or distribution fees from the licensing income received from conditional downloads and streams. Thus, Plaintiffs conclude, mechanical royalties and distribution fees should not be deducted when it comes to permanent downloads and mastertones. Plaintiffs' conclusion does not follow from the evidence. The reason Aftermath does not deduct mechanical royalties or distribution fees from income received from licensing conditional downloads and streams is because Aftermath does not pay those costs for licensing conditional downloads and streams. In contrast, it is undisputed Aftermath does have to pay mechanical royalties and distribution fees for permanent downloads and mastertones. Aftermath's practice with regard to costs that do not exist for conditional downloads and streams cannot be relevant to whether Aftermath may deduct costs that indisputably do exist for permanent downloads and mastertones. Accordingly, Aftermath's "net receipts" are its gross revenues from the licensing of masters, less the direct costs of mechanical royalties and distribution fees. . . .

New Medium and Container Charge Deductions

Defendants also argue that other provisions in the agreements should be read to apply to the Masters Licensed royalty rate. Section 5(f) of the 2003 Agreement states "[t]he royalty payable to you for New Mediums will be seventy five percent (75%) of the otherwise applicable royalty rate." New Mediums are "records ... in any software medium (including, without limitation, 'digital audio tape,' 'digital compact disc,' 'and mini-disc' and transmission directly into the home) in which recorded music is not in general commercial distribution in the United States as of January 1, 1997."

Defendants further argue they are entitled to take a deduction known as a "Container Charge." The agreements provide that "[f]or purposes of computing royalties, there will be deducted from the [applicable price] ... twenty-five percent (25%) thereof for records in the form of digital records (including, without limitation, Compact Discs), and for all records in any other form now known or hereafter devised."

The meaning of the New Medium and Container Charge deductions in relation to the Masters Licensed provision is unclear from the plain language of the agreements. In the New Medium definition, the phrase "transmission directly into the home" could be reasonably read to apply to permanent downloads. On the other hand, the types of "records" specifically contemplated by the New Medium provision are audio tapes, compact discs, and mini-discs. These physical mediums suggest the parties contemplated the application of the New Medium deduction to the Records Sold provision and not the Masters Licensed provision. Likewise, the Container Charge provision specifically contemplates compact discs. And even the term "Container Charge," which Defendants themselves use to refer to this charge, suggests a product sold in a "container," not the mere licensing of container-less downloads and mastertones.

Due to the ambiguous language of these clauses, the Court will turn to extrinsic evidence to shed light on their meaning. It is undisputed that the licensing of conditional downloads and streams is covered by and paid under the Masters Licensed provision. It is also undisputed that conditional downloads and streams utilize the same technology as permanent downloads. At trial, Defendants agreed that they pay for conditional downloads and streams "according to the terms of the contract." Lastly, Defendants concede they have never taken a New Medium or Container Charge deduction from royalties for licensing of conditional downloads and streams. Defendants have, therefore, admitted they do not read the agreements to allow for a New Medium or Container Charge deduction from Masters Licensed royalties derived from the licensing of conditional downloads and streams. Defendants do not offer any reason, and the terms of the agreements do not admit of any reason, why these deductions would apply to permanent downloads and mastertones under the Masters Licensed provision, but not to products utilizing the same technology under the same Masters Licensed provision. The Court concludes that Defendants' course of performance demonstrates that, before this litigation arose, Defendants did not understand the agreements to allow for these deductions under the Masters Licensed provision. The parties' pre-dispute understanding of the terms of the agreements controls over the post-dispute interpretation offered by Defendants.

Defendants contend that the Ninth Circuit's *F.B.T.* opinion found that the parties' course of performance could not change the language of a contract and therefore Defendants' past practice in regards to the New Medium and Container Charge deductions is irrelevant. The Ninth Circuit held that none of the evidence offered by the parties "regarding industry custom or the parties' course of performance support[ed] Aftermath's interpretation." As this sentence plainly indicates, the Ninth Circuit did not hold that a parties' course of performance cannot be used to inform the meaning of contractual terms. Rather, the Ninth Circuit only held that the course of performance evidence proffered by Defendants on appeal did not support the contract interpretation urged by Defendants. In contrast, here the course of performance evidence directly supports the interpretation, proffered by Plaintiffs, that the New Medium and Container Charge deductions do not apply to the Masters Licensed provision. Consequently, Defendants may not argue that the New Medium and Container Charge deductions apply, when the parties' performance shows these deductions do not apply to the Masters Licensed provision....

[T]he phrase "our net receipts" in the Masters Licensed provision means Aftermath's gross revenue from licensing, less the direct costs of mechanical royalties and distribution fees; and the New Medium and Container Charge deductions do not apply to the Masters Licensed provision.

IT IS SO ORDERED.

Notes and Questions

a. Since *Boosey-Hawkes*, New York courts have been reluctant to upset large grants of rights on the basis that the contracts were silent or that new technologies were not in existence at the time. See *Maljack Prods. v. GoodTimes Home Video Corp., 81 F.3d 881, 885 (9th Cir 1996)* (music rights granted for synchronization of film included right to synchronize music in videocassette format); *Chambers v. Time Warner,* 123 F. Supp. 2d 198, 200–201 (S.D.N.Y. 2000) (vacated on other grounds, and remanded by, 282 F3d 147 (2d Cir 2002)) (transfer of master recording to digital format not precluded). The trend has remained true even when the change has been the subsequent recognition of a legal interest in the sound recording that had not existed at the time of contract.

b. In the case of a performer's interest in a digital transmission, this right is relatively recent in origin and has not been interpreted, so all recording artists presumably have this interest. The ability of some artists to retain this interest has yet to be litigated.

c. If the band dismisses a member during its recording sessions, should it re-record the songs without the former band member? Does the band or the record label have any duty to the former band member, either before or after delivery of the completed master has occurred? See *Poley v. Sony Music Entertainment, Inc.,* 163 Misc.2d 127, 619 N.Y.S.2d 923 (N.Y. Sup. 1994), *affirmed* 222 A.D.2d 308, 636 N.Y.S.2d 10 (App. Div. 1995).

Problem XII-C

Bryce is interested in creating a more successful and more equitable record distribution system. Bryce is convinced that bands such as Soundfyre would do better avoiding the larger distributors in favor of a greater return from independent companies, even though it would mean a significantly lower marketing budget. As a result, Bryce is willing to earn "far less than the big distributors" if the musicians are willing to join in a collective or collaborative venture whereby everyone helps promote the sales of the albums through a common catalog, website, compilations CDs, and tour promotions.

Bryce is trying to create a local label. Bryce has interested some local investors in the idea. Bryce wants to structure the compensation and promotional terms for the bands that might be interested in the project. Prepare an outline of the key features such a contract might contain that would be attractive to both the bands and the potential investors. If you have other ideas that might be of assistance to Bryce in structuring such a promotion and distribution company, provide those suggestions as well.

D. Promotion and Exploitation of the Recording Artist

Contemporary Mission, Inc. v. Famous Music Corp.
557 F.2d 918 (2d Cir. 1977)

This is an appeal by Famous Music Corporation ("Famous") from a verdict rendered against it in favor of Contemporary Mission, Inc. ("Contemporary"), in the United States District Court for the Southern District of New York, after a jury trial before Judge Richard Owen. Contemporary cross-appeals from a ruling which excluded testimony concerning its prospective damages. The dispute between the parties relates to Famous' alleged breach of two contracts.

Contemporary is a nonprofit charitable corporation organized under the laws of the State of Missouri with its principal place of business in Connecticut. It is composed of a small group of Roman Catholic priests who write, produce and publish musical compositions and recordings. In 1972 the group owned all of the rights to a rock opera entitled VIRGIN, which was composed by Father John T. O'Reilly, a vice-president and member of the group. Contemporary first became involved with Famous in 1972 as a result of O'Reilly's efforts to market VIRGIN.

Famous is ... a wholly-owned subsidiary of the Gulf+Western Corporation, and, until July 31, 1974, it was engaged in the business of producing musical recordings for distribution throughout the United States. Famous' president, Tony Martell, is generally regarded in the recording industry as the individual primarily responsible for the successful distribution of the well-known rock operas TOMMY and JESUS CHRIST SUPERSTAR.... On August 16, 1972, [the parties] executed the so-called "VIRGIN Recording Agreement" ("VIRGIN agreement") on behalf of their respective organizations.

The terms of the VIRGIN agreement were relatively simple. Famous agreed to pay a royalty to Contemporary in return for the master tape recording of VIRGIN and the exclusive right to manufacture and sell records made from the master. The agreement also created certain "Additional Obligations of Famous" which included, inter alia: the obligation to select and appoint, within the first year of the agreement, at least one person to personally oversee the nationwide promotion of the sale of records, to maintain contact with Contemporary and to submit weekly reports to Contemporary; the obligation to spend, within the first year of the agreement, no less than $50,000 on the promotion of records; and the obligation to release, within the first two years of the agreement, at least four separate single records from VIRGIN....

On May 8, 1973, the parties entered into a distribution contract which dealt with musical compositions other than VIRGIN. This, the so-called "Crunch agreement," granted to Famous the exclusive right to distribute Contemporary's records in the United States. Famous agreed to institute a new record label named "Crunch," and a number of records were to be released under it annually. Contemporary agreed to deliver ten long-playing records and fifteen single records during the first year of the contract. Famous undertook to use its "reasonable efforts" to promote and distribute the records. Paragraph 15 of the Crunch agreement stated that a breach by either party would not be deemed material unless the non-breaching party first gave written notice to the defaulting party and the defaulting party failed to cure the breach within thirty days. The notice was to specify the nature of the alleged material breach. The contract prohibited assignment by Contemporary, but it contained no provision relating to Famous' right to assign.

Although neither VIRGIN nor its progeny was ever as successful as the parties had originally hoped, the business relationship continued on an amicable basis until July 31, 1974. On that date, Famous' record division was sold to ABC Records, Inc. (ABC). When O'Reilly complained to Martell that Famous was breaking its promises, he was told that he would have to look to ABC for performance. O'Reilly met with one of ABC's lawyers and was told that ABC was not going to have any relationship with Contemporary. On August 21, 1974, Contemporary sent a letter to Famous pursuant to paragraph 15 of the Crunch agreement notifying Famous that it had "materially breached Paragraph 12, among others, of (the Crunch) Agreement in that (it had) attempted to make a contract or other agreement with ABC-Dunhill Record Corporation (ABC Records) creating an obligation or responsibility in behalf of or in the name of the Contemporary Mission." Paragraph 12 of the Crunch agreement provides, in full, as follows:

> This agreement shall not be construed as one of partnership or joint venture, nor shall it constitute either party as the agent or legal representative of the other. Neither party shall have the right, power or authority to make any contract or other agreement, or to assume or create any obligation or responsibility, express or implied, in behalf of or in the name of the other party or to bind the other party in any manner for anything whatsoever.

This lawsuit followed....

Famous vigorously contends ... that the jury's conclusion, that it had failed to adequately promote VIRGIN prior to the sale to ABC, is at war with the undisputed facts and cannot be permitted to stand. In particular they argue that they spent the required $50,000 and appointed the required overseer for the project. The flaw in this argument is that its focus is too narrow. The obligations to which it refers are but two of many created by the VIRGIN agreement.

Under the doctrine of *Wood v. Lucy, Lady Duff-Gordon*, 222 N.Y. 88, 118 N.E. 214 (1917), Famous had an obligation to use its reasonable efforts to promote VIRGIN on a nationwide basis. That obligation could not be satisfied merely by technical compliance with the spending and appointment requirements of paragraph 14 of the agreement. Even assuming that Famous complied fully with those requirements, there was evidence from which the jury could find that Famous failed to adequately promote VIRGIN. The question is a close one, particularly in light of Martell's obvious commitment to the success of VIRGIN and in light of the efforts that were in fact exerted and the lack of any serious dispute between the parties prior to the sale to ABC. However, there was evidence that Famous prematurely terminated the promotion of the first single record, "Got To Know," shortly after its release, and that Famous limited its promotion of the second record, "Kyrie," to a single city, rather than promoting it nationwide. Moreover, there was evidence that, prior to the sale to ABC, Famous underwent a budget reduction and cut back its promotional staff. From this, the jury could infer that the promotional effort was reduced to a level that was less than adequate. On the whole, therefore, we are not persuaded that the jury's verdict should be disturbed.

There is no dispute that the sale of Famous' record division to ABC constituted an assignment of the Crunch agreement to ABC. The assignment of a bilateral contract includes both an assignment of rights and a delegation of duties. The distinctions between the two are important.

> Perhaps more frequently than is the case with other terms of art, lawyers seem prone to use the word "assignment" inartfully, frequently intending to encompass within the term the distinct (concept) of delegation.... An assignment involves the transfer of rights. A delegation involves the appointment of another to perform one's duties.

J. Calamari & J. Perillo, Contracts § 254 (1970) (footnote omitted). Famous' arguments with respect to the Crunch agreement ignore this basic distinction, and the result is a distortion of several fundamental principles of contract law.

It is true, of course, as a general rule, that when rights are assigned, the assignor's interest in the rights assigned comes to an end. When duties are delegated, however, the delegant's obligation does not end.

> One who owes money or is bound to any performance whatever, cannot by any act of his own, or by any act in agreement with any other person, except his creditor, divest himself of the duty and substitute the duty of another. "No one can assign his liabilities under a contract without the consent of the party to whom he is liable."

> This is sufficiently obvious when attention is called to it, for otherwise obligors would find an easy practical way of escaping their obligations....

3 Williston on Contracts § 411 (3d ed. 1960) (footnote omitted). This is not to say that one may not delegate his obligations. In fact, most obligations can be delegated as long as performance by the delegate will not vary materially from performance by the delegant. The act of delegation, however, does not relieve the delegant of the ultimate responsibility to see that the obligation is performed. If the delegate fails to perform, the delegant remains liable.

Judge Owen correctly charged the jury that "after the assignment of the contract by Famous to ABC, Famous remained liable for any obligation that was not fulfilled by ABC." This was a correct statement of the law, and Famous' assault upon it, while valiant, is without merit....

The problem for Famous, of course, was that, having sold its entire record division to ABC, it had stripped itself of its ability to cure the breach....

During the trial, Contemporary sought to introduce a statistical analysis, together with expert testimony, in order to prove how successful the most successful of its single recordings, "Fear No Evil," would have become if the VIRGIN agreement had not been breached as a result of the sale to ABC. Based upon its projection of the success of that recording, Contemporary hoped to prove what revenues that success would have produced. Judge Owen excluded this evidence on the ground that it was speculative.

There can no dispute that Contemporary "is entitled to the reasonable damage flowing from the breach of" the VIRGIN agreement by Famous, and that "the measure of the damage is the amount necessary to put (Contemporary) in (the) exact position as (it) would have been if the contract had not been breached." ... [U]nder the long-standing New York rule, when the existence of damage is certain, and the only uncertainty is as to its amount, the plaintiff will not be denied a recovery of substantial damages. Moreover, the burden of uncertainty as to the amount of damage is upon the wrongdoer, and the test for admissibility of evidence concerning prospective damages is whether the evidence has any tendency to show their probable amount. The plaintiff need only show a "stable foundation for a reasonable estimate of royalties he would have earned had defendant not breached." ...

We are confident that under the principles enunciated above the exclusion of the evidence proffered by Contemporary was error. This is not a case in which the plaintiff sought to prove hypothetical profits from the sale of a hypothetical record at a hypothetical price in a hypothetical market. At the time of the sale to ABC, the record was real, the price was fixed, the market was buying and the record's success, while modest, was increasing. Even after the promotional efforts ended, the record was withdrawn from the marketplace, it was carried, as a result of its own momentum, to an additional 10,000 sales and to a rise from approximately number 80 on the "Hot Soul Singles" chart of Billboard magazine to number 61. It cannot be gainsaid that if someone had continued to promote it, and if it had not been withdrawn from the market, it would have sold more records than it actually did. Thus, it is certain that Contemporary suffered some damage in the form of lost royalties. The same is not true, however, of the existence of damage in the form of lost opportunities for concert tours, theatrical tours or similar benefits....

The judgment of the district court is affirmed in all respects except as to its ruling with regard to lost royalties, and the case is remanded to the district court for further proceedings in accordance with this opinion....

Notes and Questions

a. The label's duty to promote a work is often framed in the most general of terms, while the label's ability to exploit a work is retained against every conceivable eventuality. As the power and influence of a recording artist increases, these contractual provisions are often the point for new negotiation.

b. The contractual relations between the parties is often quite complex, sometimes involving many participants. In some instances, this may lead to individuals or entities that are not parties to a particular transaction having an influence on its signing or enforcement, which raises the potential for the additional tort, tortious interference with contractual relations. See *TVT Records v. Island Def Jam Music Group*, 279 F. Supp. 2d 366 (S.D.N.Y. 2003).

c. To what extent do parties who are not signatories to these contracts have standing? Depending on the nature of the contract and the conflict, there may be intended third party beneficiaries who have standing to enforce claims or to object to breaches of the contracts.

d. The contract provisions at issue above reflect that a significant portion of an album's marketing occurs when it is first released. However, an album creates an income stream that can potentially last for many years. Approximately half the income generated by sound recordings is derived from back catalog sales. The back catalog is a label's backlist of songs previously produced and distributed but not currently being marketed and promoted. Compilation albums, such as The Beatles 1 CD, constitute yet another important economic source of revenue from the catalog. Given these economics, is it helpful or appropriate for a recording artist to put some limitations or time constraints on the publicity rights granted to the record labels?

e. In many cases, the recording artists deliver more songs than the number of cuts that are included on the album or CD. What happens to those previously unreleased songs? Can the record label create new albums out of unreleased songs, or should unpublished sound recordings expire after a reasonable period of time? See *Levert v. Phila. Int'l Records*, No. 04-1489, 2004 U.S. Dist. LEXIS 11825 (E.D. Pa. Apr. 9, 2004) ("Plaintiffs Edward Levert and Walter Williams are singers and performers who form the musical group known as The O'Jays. The O'Jays have been recording music for more than forty years and ... recorded more than fifty records, including nine 'platinum records' and ten 'gold records.'").

f. Despite the impression that contracts in the music business are rarely enforced, there can be tremendous costs for failing to abide by a contract or failing to renegotiate a new arrangement. In *Smith v. Positive Prods.*, 419 F. Supp. 2d 437 (S.D.N.Y. 2005), the district court allowed the enforcement of an arbitration provision against Jonathan "Lil Jon" Smith for twice failing to participate in a concert tour in Japan. Positive Productions, the Japanese concert promotion company, received $379,874 in an arbitration held under the American Arbitration Association rules. Lil Jon ignored the arbitration proceeding, but he was unsuccessful in vacating the judgment.

Problem XII-D

As a result of the dispute between Bryce and Soundfyre, Soundfyre's label has elected not to exercise the option for the band's third album. Although Bryce never joined the band, Bryce is concerned not only because Soundfyre's success was generating Bryce income (thanks to your expert advice settling the dispute) but also because Bryce was hoping to build on the association with the band. Soundfyre is particularly upset because the label has stopped the advertising campaign for the band's second album.

Bryce is learning a lesson. In talking to potential labels, Bryce wants to ensure that any album is fully under Bryce's control and heavily promoted. Explain to Bryce what provisions can be added to a standard contract to provide the protections Bryce needs, as well as the likely response by most labels.

E. Term, Renewals, and Extensions of Recording Contracts

MCA Records, Inc. v. Newton-John
90 Cal. App. 3d 18 (1979)

Defendant Olivia Newton-John, a singer, appeals a preliminary injunction restraining her from recording for anyone other than plaintiff MCA Records while MCA's action is pending "or until April 1, 1982, if that date shall occur during the pendency of this action." ...

On April 1, 1975, the parties entered the following agreement: Defendant Newton-John would record and deliver to plaintiff master recordings for two albums per year for an initial period of two years, and, at plaintiff's option, further similar recordings for three additional periods of one year each. If defendant failed to deliver a recording when due, plaintiff would become entitled to extend the term of the agreement. In return, plaintiff would pay defendant royalties and a nonreturnable advance of $250,000 for each recording received during the initial two years, and an advance of $100,000 for each recording received during the option years. The cost of producing the recordings would be borne by defendant.

The first three recordings were delivered on schedule; the fourth was delivered late. Plaintiff exercised its first option to renew, but never received another recording. Under the terms of the contract plaintiff paid defendant approximately $2,500,000 in royalties and nonreturnable advances.

On May 31, 1978, the parties filed breach-of-contract actions against one another. Both parties sought damages and injunctive relief, and defendant additionally sought declaratory relief. Plaintiff obtained a preliminary injunction, and defendant has appealed.

Defendant asserts the preliminary injunction was improperly granted because: (1) the agreement failed to guarantee payment of minimum compensation of $6,000 a year; (2) she had already been suspended by the plaintiff and could not be further restrained from engaging in her occupation; and (3) there was no showing or finding that irreparable injury would be imminent if the injunction were not granted.

A. A party to a personal service contract may not be enjoined from rendering personal services to others unless, under the terms of the contract, she is guaranteed minimum annual compensation of $6,000. Defendant argues that the agreement at bench fails to meet the statutory minimum because the cost of producing two recordings a year exceeds $194,000, and when this expense is deducted from the guaranteed $200,000 annual advance, her net compensation becomes less than $6,000 annually.

The trial court found: (1) the "minimum compensation" referred to in the statutes does not mean "net profits"; (2) even if it did, suitable recordings could be made at costs that would net the defendant minimum compensation of $6,000 a year. It is decisive here that under the terms of the agreement exclusive control of production costs remained in defendant's hands at all times. Defendant was free to record in as tight-fisted or as open-handed a manner, costwise, as she chose. Defendant's interpretation of the minimum compensation statutes would allow her to nullify her contract at any time merely by increasing her production expenses, which at all times remained under her exclusive control. We do not believe the Legislature intended to sanction such a one-sided bargain, and we agree with the trial court's ruling in both its aspects....

B. Defendant next contends she cannot be suspended by plaintiff and at the same time enjoined from rendering personal services for others. But defendant has not been suspended. She is still free to record for plaintiff, and, in the event she chooses to record, nothing in the agreement relieves plaintiff from its obligation to compensate her.

C. Defendant maintains the grant of the preliminary injunction was improper because plaintiff failed to show, and the trial court failed to explicitly find, that such relief was necessary to prevent irreparable injury. The grant of a preliminary injunction lies within the discretion of the trial court, and an explicit finding of irreparable harm is not required to sustain the trial court's exercise of that discretion. In requesting injunctive relief plaintiff alleged that if defendant were permitted to record for a competitor, it would suffer irreparable injury, both in loss of profits and loss of goodwill. This allegation was supported by substantial evidence that defendant's services are unique. Absent any indication to the contrary, we can presume from the trial court's order granting the preliminary injunction that the court did in fact find that irreparable injury would be imminent unless the injunction were granted.

Defendant contends that even if the court did not err in granting a preliminary injunction, it erred in authorizing the preliminary injunction to extend beyond the five-year term of the agreement. Plaintiff responds, in effect, that so long as defendant fails to perform her obligations under the contract, the term of the agreement, and thus of the preliminary injunction, may be extended until the seven-year statutory maximum has elapsed.

Because a period of five years has not yet passed since defendant began her employment on April 1, 1975, the issue of the availability to plaintiff of injunctive relief after April 1, 1980, is technically premature. Nevertheless, we consider the language in the preliminary injunction extending its possible duration to April 1, 1982, inappropriate for two reasons:

First, if defendant had performed under the contract, plaintiff would not be entitled to prevent her from recording for competitors at the end of the five-year term of the agreement. We have grave doubts that defendant's failure to perform her obligations under the contract can extend the term of the contract beyond its specified five-year maximum.

Second, the injunction appealed here is merely a preliminary injunction, whose sole function is to preserve the status quo pending a final judgment in the action. Plaintiff's general duty to exercise due diligence in the prosecution of its action and to bring it to conclusion within a reasonable time is particularly strong when, as here, the cause involves injunctive and declaratory relief. To the extent the phrase "until April 1, 1982" suggests that plaintiff, without taking further action, may prevent defendant from recording for competitors until 1982, the phrase is misleading.

The order for preliminary injunction is modified by deleting the phrase, "or until April 1, 1982, if that date shall occur during the pendency of this action," and as so modified, the order is affirmed.

CA. Lab. Code § 2855

§ 2855. Enforcement of contract to render personal service; Personal service in production of phonorecords

(a) Except as otherwise provided in subdivision (b), a contract to render personal service, other than a contract of apprenticeship as provided in Chapter 4 (commencing with Section 3070), may not be enforced against the employee beyond seven years from the commencement of service under it. Any contract, otherwise valid, to perform or render service of a special, unique, unusual, extraordinary, or intellectual character, which gives it peculiar value and the loss of which can not be reasonably or adequately compensated in damages in an action at law, may nevertheless be enforced against the person contracting to render the service, for a term not to exceed seven years from the commencement of service under it. If the employee voluntarily continues to serve under it beyond that time, the contract may be referred to as affording a presumptive measure of the compensation.

(b) Notwithstanding subdivision (a):

(1) Any employee who is a party to a contract to render personal service in the production of phonorecords in which sounds are first fixed, as defined in Section 101 of Title 17 of the United States Code, may not invoke the provisions of subdivision (a) without first giving written notice to the employer in accordance with Section 1020 of the Code of Civil Procedure, specifying that the employee from and after a future date certain specified in the notice will no longer render service under the contract by reason of subdivision (a).

(2) Any party to such a contract shall have the right to recover damages for a breach of the contract occurring during its term in an action commenced during or after its term, but within the applicable period prescribed by law.

(3) In the event a party to such a contract is, or could contractually be, required to render personal service in the production of a specified quantity of the phonorecords and fails to render all of the required service prior to the date specified in the notice provided in paragraph (1), the party damaged by the failure shall have the right to recover damages for each phonorecord as to which that party has failed to render service in an action which, notwithstanding paragraph (2), shall be commenced within 45 days after the date specified in the notice.

Notes and Questions

a. Record labels often exert influence on the composition of the bands under contract. The structure of the Recording Agreement and Band Member Agreements typically bind all band members, whether such a band member tries to leave the label voluntarily or is fired by the band. The most obvious concern for recording artists is the limitation this may have on the rights to produce new work after leaving a band. A label can elect to offer a solo recording contract to the leaving band member on terms very favorable to the label because that label already owns the rights to record that performer. While most deals seem to eventually work out, the agreements put the recording artists in a particularly weak bargaining position.

b. In addition to the lack of leverage, the Band Member Agreements also create a substantial financial risk for the departing band member. If the recording of subsequent CDs goes over budget, then those expenses are treated as advances that the label can recoup from royalties. The Band Member Agreement does not typically put any limits on this liability. A band member such as Bautista who records a solo album for the same label (or another label under common ownership) will see the royalties used to offset that recording artist's share of any unrecouped advances on the former band's albums. This is an example of a cross-collateralization that incorporates the practice of charging all unrecouped expenses from one album to all others produced by the recording artist. Cross-collateralization can quickly make a recording artist a debt-slave to a label. This practice can be truly pernicious when the debts derive from solo activities attributed to the rest of the band.

c. The Recording Agreement and Band Member Agreement are drafted to create a single relationship. Despite the technical reading by the Southern District of New York in *EMI Latin v. Bautista*, 2003 WL 470333 (S.D.N.Y. 2003), Band Member Agreements often provide that they incorporate the terms of the Recording Agreement by reference and any modification of the Recording Agreement serves as an amendment to the Band Member Agreement. Alternatively, at the time of drafting any modification of the Recording Agreement, a rider to the Band Member Agreement can be executed.

These amendments often extend the life of these contracts well beyond their initial terms. Some specifically provide that the modifications of the Band Member Agreements are to be made by a majority vote, or that the band has authorized its manager to negotiate and amend the agreement on behalf of the band. In each case, the general delegation means that the band is more likely to come to terms with the label, but also more likely that individual band members may be bound to terms he or she would consider unacceptable.

d. New York and many other states do not have the same employment statutes as California. As a result, the choice of law provisions of recording agreements may play a significant role. Nonetheless, the California courts tend to see these provisions as significant to public welfare, so that a mere recitation of jurisdiction may not carry weight if the performer resides in California during the term of the agreement.

e. The second provision of § 2855 makes the recording artist liable for damages to the label in the event of non-performance. While the idea that a party to a contract is liable for damages as a result of non-performance is generally not controversial, the provision takes on a different context in the recording business. Typically, poor employment performance results in termination rather than expectation damages. California has singled out recording artists for § 2855 in a rather odd, if not constitutionally suspect manner. Further, as many commentators suggest, the issue of damages is particularly controversial.

The risk of receiving expectation damages from the performing artist, rather than merely being reimbursed for any advances or other *quantum meruit* award, has a significant chilling effect which strengthens the negotiation position of the label and undermines the benefits of § 2855(a). See Note, California Labor Code Section 2855 and Recording Artists' Contracts, 116 Harv. L. Rev. 2632, 2643–45 (2003).

f. California historically required a $6,000 minimum annual income to claim specific performance. Despite this relatively low amount (which once had been a bit more significant before inflation), labels often tried to avoid the direct expense.

In *Foxx v. Williams,* 244 Cal. App. 2d 223, 52 Cal. Rptr. 896 (1966), the court addressed the impact of an agreement for royalties only. It found that the right to receive royalties does not meet the statutory requirement for actually receiving specific minimum compensation. In *MCA Records, Inc. v. Newton-John* (above) the court distinguished the situation:

> [C]omedian Redd Foxx agreed to record comedy routines for Williams, a record manufacturer and distributor. In return, Foxx was to receive royalties from the sale of the records. Foxx sued Williams and Williams' recording company for an accounting, and the company cross-complained for damages and injunctive relief. The lower court enjoined Foxx from recording for anyone other than cross-complainant, but the appellate court reversed for the reason that Foxx' royalty contract did not guarantee him annual compensation of $6,000. Unlike the defendant at bench, who is guaranteed minimum annual compensation of $200,000 in the form of nonreturnable advances in addition to any royalties she may receive, Foxx' sole compensation was in the form of royalties contingent upon prospective sales which could amount to nothing.

MCA Records, Inc. v Newton-John, 153 Cal. Rptr. 153, 155 (1979).

In *Motown Record Corp. v. Brockert,* 160 Cal. App. 3d 123, 132–33 (1984) (often known as the Teena Marie case), the record company attempted to meet the payment minimum by providing itself an option to pay the $6,000 statutory minimum. The court found that this was not the same as the guaranteed minimum payment, so specific performance was ruled unavailable.

g. In 1993, California recognized that the $6,000 requirement had lost much of its market value and amended the statutory threshold of Cal Civ. Code § 3423 for specific performance. It briefly increased the amount to $50,000, but then withdrew that amount in favor of the current statute:

> § 3423. When injunction may not be granted. An injunction may not be granted:
>
> ... (e) To prevent the breach of a contract the performance of which would not be specifically enforced, other than a contract in writing for the rendition of personal services from one to another where the promised service is of a special, unique, unusual, extraordinary, or intellectual character, which gives it peculiar value, the loss of which cannot be reasonably or adequately compensated in damages in an action at law, and where the compensation for the personal services is as follows: (1) As to contracts entered into on or before December 31, 1993, the minimum compensation provided in the contract for the personal services shall be at the rate of six thousand dollars ($6,000) per annum. (2) As to contracts entered into on or after January 1, 1994, the criteria of subparagraph (A) or (B), as follows, are satisfied: (A) The compensation is as follows: (i) The min-

imum compensation provided in the contract shall be at the rate of nine thousand dollars ($9,000) per annum for the first year of the contract, twelve thousand dollars ($12,000) per annum for the second year of the contract, and fifteen thousand dollars ($15,000) per annum for the third to seventh years, inclusive, of the contract. (ii) In addition, after the third year of the contract, there shall actually have been paid for the services through and including the contract year during which the injunctive relief is sought, over and above the minimum contractual compensation specified in clause (i), the amount of fifteen thousand dollars ($15,000) per annum during the fourth and fifth years of the contract, and thirty thousand dollars ($30,000) per annum during the sixth and seventh years of the contract. As a condition to petitioning for an injunction, amounts payable under this clause may be paid at any time prior to seeking injunctive relief. (B) The aggregate compensation actually received for the services provided under a contract that does not meet the criteria of subparagraph (A), is at least 10 times the applicable aggregate minimum amount specified in clauses (i) and (ii) of subparagraph (A) through and including the contract year during which the injunctive relief is sought. As a condition to petitioning for an injunction, amounts payable under this subparagraph may be paid at any time prior to seeking injunctive relief. (3) Compensation paid in any contract year in excess of the minimums specified in subparagraphs (A) and (B) of paragraph (2) shall apply to reduce the compensation otherwise required to be paid under those provisions in any subsequent contract years....

h. The seven-year limitation was enacted into California law in 1931, extending the term from two years to seven. (It harkens back to the biblical proscription on bonded slavery; the slave owner was required to free the slave and provide financial support to give the former slave meaningful economic support. Anyone desiring to remain a slave after the seven-year period had to agree to be marked as a permanent slave by having his ear pierced with an awl.) The law was quickly associated with Hollywood because Olivia de Havilland fought to terminate her studio contract with Warner Bros. Her original contract was for one year, with six additional options, but Warner Bros. added time periods when Ms. de Havilland was unavailable or under suspension. The court found that the law was for seven calendar years and terminated the contract.

The time limitation does not mean seven years of actual service regardless of the time over which such service extends, but means seven calendar years from the commencement of service. *De Havilland v Warner Bros. Pictures, Inc.,* 67 Cal. App. 2d 225, 153 P.2d 983 (1944).

i. Because of the harsh results imposed by the recording contracts, courts do not give the record labels leeway in exercising the options to continue an artist. Essentially, the courts tend to treat these renewal periods as if there were a time-of-the-essence approach. The difficulty of this approach is that the exact date for renewal is often conditioned on an event rather than a date. In *Polygram Records, Inc. v. Buddy Buie Productions,* 520 F. Supp. 248 (S.D.N.Y. 1981), the court was required to interpret the series of events that occurred when the master recording and the "reference lacquer"—a copy of the master tape (essentially a pre-production album) was offered to Polygram as delivery. The renewal period for the contract was based on the date of acceptance, and the Southern District found that receipt of the reference lacquer and payment constituted acceptance. The court rejected the contention that the reference lacquer was at first considered subject to additional editing and therefore not accepted. Polygram's week-late renewal of the contract was not timely and all obligations to Polygram terminated.

Problem XII-E

Bryce is again considering joining Soundfyre. Bryce remains very concerned about inheriting the costs each band member must still recoup from the band's previous recordings. Bryce is also concerned that the association will only last a year or two and does not want to be captive to Soundfyre's record label. Bryce asks you to draft proposed language to provide Soundfyre and its record label that would allow Bryce to join the band but not be bound by the typical band membership agreement with regard to debt and future recording obligations.

F. Accountability under Recording Contracts

In many instances, the combination of advances, low royalty rates, and bookkeeping irregularities resulted in the recording artist never receiving any income after the advance. Renewed popularity of these recordings decades after the initial contract has resulted in significant income that was never distributed to the recording artists. For example, in *Greenfield v. Philles Records,* 98 N.Y.2d 562 (N.Y. 2002), the Ronettes never received any royalties from Phil Spector's Philles Records, Inc. despite a surge in popularity during the 1980s and the marriage of Ronettes' Ronnie Greenfield to Spector. Courts apply different approaches to these cases of failure to account or to pay royalties.

Peterson v. Highland Music, Inc.
140 F. 3d 1313 (9th Cir. 1998)

This case involves an attempt by the Kingsmen, a musical group, to secure a rescission of the contract by which they assigned to others the rights to their popular recording of the hit song, "Louie, Louie." We review three actions consolidated on appeal. In the first, the parties litigated the right to rescind. In the second, the defendants sought a declaratory judgment to limit the effect of the judgment of rescission. In the third, the district court imposed contempt sanctions upon the defendants for their refusal to comply with the judgment of rescission. We affirm the district court in all respects.

The facts of this procedurally convoluted case are relatively simple. The members of the Kingsmen seek to secure their rights to the master recordings (the "Masters") of their hit song, "Louie, Louie." The group made the recording over thirty years ago. They then sold the Masters to one Specter Records ... in return for nine per cent of any profits or licensing fees that the recording might generate. The Kingsmen and Specter entered into their contract in 1968. Specter's interest in the Masters was eventually transferred to Gusto Records and GML, who were the named defendants in the rescission action. The parties do not dispute that the Kingsmen have never received a single penny of the considerable royalties that "Louie, Louie" has produced over the past thirty years.

In 1993, the Kingsmen brought suit in federal district court in California for rescission of the contract, basing their claim entirely on actions (or inactions) by the defendants that fell within the four-year statutory limitations period. After a full trial, the district court ruled in plaintiffs' favor and granted the rescission, restoring possession of the Masters to the Kingsmen....

Defendants [ ] contend that the district court erred in holding that the statute of limitations does not bar a remedy of rescission in this case. In California, the statute of limitations for an action seeking rescission of a contract is four years. *See* Cal. Code Civ. Proc. § 337. Specifically, the statute provides that an aggrieved party must commence such an action within four years "from the date upon which the facts that entitled the aggrieved party to rescind occurred." Both parties agree that the period of limitations has long since run with respect to the first occasions on which defendants breached their agreement. Both parties also agree that defendants have breached their agreement repeatedly over the course of the past thirty years, and did so, repeatedly, within four years of the time that plaintiffs commenced this action. Defendants' claim is that, even in the face of multiple and continuing breaches of the agreement, the California statute should be read to bar any action that is not commenced within four years of the *first* occasion on which an aggrieved party could have requested rescission. Defendants cite no authority for this proposition, and we reject it.

In analyzing requests for rescission where there have been multiple breaches under an installment contract, California courts have held that each breach starts the clock afresh for statute of limitations purposes. In *Conway v. Bughouse, Inc.*, 105 Cal. App. 3d 194, 164 Cal. Rptr. 585 (1980), for example, a California appeals court looked to the manner in which money would be paid under a pension contract in determining how a party's failure to make any given payment should affect the tolling of the statute of limitations.

> The total amount of money to be paid to [the pensioner] is not a fixed sum which is to be paid out over a period of time. To the contrary, the total amount owed is unascertainable until the date of [the pensioner's] death because each payment is separate and contingent upon [the survival of the pensioner and his adherence to the terms of the contract]. As each payment is separable from the others and is not a part of a total payment, the agreement should logically be considered an installment contract for purposes of determination of the application of the statute of limitations.

The same holds true in the present case: There is no fixed amount to be paid out over time under the Kingsmen's contract, but rather a continuing obligation to pay a portion of the profits and royalties on "Louie, Louie" as the recording gets used over time.

The district court in this case made it clear that, in determining whether rescission was warranted and appropriate, it was relying upon breaches that had occurred within the limitations period. To find for defendant under these circumstances would be to hold that California law forever bars a party from seeking a remedy of rescission after it has once passed up the opportunity to do so, regardless of the nature of any future breaches of the other party's obligations. We have found no authority that would support such a reading of California law. We therefore affirm the district court's conclusion that the statute of limitations does not bar rescission of the contract in this case....

On the merits, the district court found that the rescission of the Kingsmen's contract was effective as of the date of the filing of the Kingsmen's complaint. We agree. Under California law, "a party to a contract [can] rescind it and ... such rescission [can] be accomplished by the rescinding party by giving notice of the rescission and offering to restore everything of value which [the rescinding party has] received." When a party gives notice of rescission, it has effected the rescission, and any subsequent judicial proceedings are for the purpose of confirming and enforcing that rescission. Thus, when the Kingsmen filed suit in 1993, they rescinded the contract and became owners of the Masters. The lawsuit that followed confirmed that their rescission was a proper one and resulted in an order enforcing that rescission. The district court correctly ruled that, as the owners of the Masters, the Kingsmen are entitled to all income derived from the exploitation of the recordings following September 29, 1993, the date of the notice of rescission.

[The court also upholds findings of contempt related to the failure to abide by the district court decision.] The district court's rulings in these consolidated actions are well-reasoned and supported by ample evidence in the record. We affirm in all respects.

Cabot v. Jamie Record Co.

1999 U.S. Dist. LEXIS 5549, Copy. L. Rep. (CCH) P27897 (E.D. Pa. 1999)
aff'd 248 F.3d 1129 (3d Cir. 2000) (without opinion)

This court has subject matter jurisdiction over this action by reason of diversity of citizenship and amount pursuant to 28 U.S.C. § 1332. Plaintiff, Gilbert A. Cabot, is a resident and citizen of California. Defendants, Jamie Record Co. and Jamie Music Publishing Co. t/a Dandelion Music Co., are corporations organized and existing under Pennsylvania law with their principal places of business in Philadelphia, Pennsylvania. As pled, the amount in controversy exceeds $50,000, the statutory minimum at the time the complaint was filed. The parties agree and this court finds that the substantive law for Pennsylvania controls. In the late 1960s, Cabot produced a number of phonograph records including "Fireball" and "Love Can Make You Happy" (together "the compositions"). The song, "Love Can Make You Happy," was recorded by the group "The Mercy" pursuant to an agreement between Cabot and the group's manager and songwriter, Jack Sigler, Jr.... In 1969, Cabot, relinquished his copyrights and all other rights in the compositions to Dandelion and Jamie Record in exchange for advances and promises of future royalties. On February 26, 1969, Cabot, under the unregistered trade name, Gil Cabot Enterprises, Inc. (hereinafter "Gil Cabot Enterprises"), entered into a "Master Purchase Agreement" by which he sold the master recordings of the compositions and all rights attendant thereto to Jamie Record [and Cabot's company]. Rendezvous/Tobac entered into a "Participation Agreement" by which it sold to Dandelion the copyrights and rights to copyright, print, publish, sell, use, or license the use of the compositions....

As a successor-in-interest to Gil Cabot Enterprises and Rendezvous/Tobac, Cabot now sues for rescission of the Master Purchase and Participation Agreements (together "the agreements").... Cabot's principle contention is that the agreements should be rescinded and he should be allowed to recapture his copyrights and all other rights in the compositions because of failure of consideration by the defendants at the time the agreements were made. Cabot further contends that an extended period of non-payment and failure to account by defendants, equivalent to Pennsylvania's four-year statute of limitations period for breaches of contract, specifically from 1991 to 1995, constituted a material breach going to the essence of the contract. Cabot also asserts that royalties that were paid prior to this time were not the total of the sums due and owing to him under the agreements....

Under the Master Purchase Agreement ownership of the master recordings of the compositions was transferred from Cabot to Jamie Record. The Master Purchase Agreement provided in relevant part:

(1.) This letter sets forth the agreement between you [Gil Cabot Enterprises, Inc.] and ourselves [Jamie Record], your and our heirs and distributees, successors and assigns, for the sale to us of two phonograph masters recorded by Mercy

(2.) You hereby warrant and represent that you are the sole and exclusive owner of the following master recordings of: Love "Can Make You Happy" b/w Fireball [sic]....

Such masters and all records and reproductions made therefrom together with the performances embodied therein, shall be entirely our property, free of any claims whatsoever by you or any person deriving any rights or interests from you. Without limitation of the foregoing, we shall have the right to make records or other reproductions of the performances embodied in such recordings ... and to sell and deal in the same under any trademarks or trade names or labels designated by us, and perform the same publicly and permit public performance by any method now or hereafter known throughout the world.

... The consideration paid to Gil Cabot Enterprises under the Master Purchase Agreement was a one thousand dollar ($1000) cash advance and royalties derived from the sale and/or licensing of the recordings of the compositions. Generally, Cabot was to receive a seventeen percent (17%) royalty, payable upon the wholesale price, exclusive of taxes, on ninety percent (90%) of all records sold. For sales outside of the United States, Cabot was to receive one-half of the seventeen percent (17%) otherwise payable.... Jamie Record was to provide Gil Cabot Enterprises bi-annually with an accounting and payment of net income due: "Accounts shall be made to you within sixty days after the first day of January and July of each year for the preceding six months period and shall be accompanied by payment of accrued royalties less any then unrecouped advances...." However, Jamie Record did not send out financial statements every six months as required. For earnings from 1972 to 1976, there were no statements issued by it until February 22, 1977. Nonetheless, some payments were received, though not regularly, [b]etween the period 1969 and 1986, ... amounting to approximately $52,000....

Pursuant to the Participation Agreement, Dandelion acquired exclusive ownership of the copyrights and the right to copyright, print, publish, sell, use, or license the use of the compositions anywhere in the world. The Participation Agreement stated, in relevant part:

(1.) [Rendezvous/Tobac] agrees and acknowledges that [Dandelion] is the sole and exclusive owner of the copyright Title: (1) "LOVE 'CAN MAKE YOU HAPPY'" (2) "FIREBALL" ... hereinafter called the "Musical Compositions," for the territory of the World subject only to limitations thereon and the rights of the authors and/or composers set forth in an agreement between [Dandelion] and Authors & Composers....

(2.) [Dandelion] shall have the sole and exclusive right to print, publish, sell, use and license the use of the Musical Composition in the aforementioned territory, and to execute in its own name any and all licenses and agreements whatsoever affecting or respecting the Musical Composition, including but not limited to licenses for mechanical reproduction, public performance, synchronization uses and sub-publication. This statement of exclusive rights being in clarification and amplification of its rights as copyright owner and not in limitation thereof.

The consideration paid to Rendezvous/Tobac under the Participation Agreement was a one thousand dollar ($1000) cash advance and royalties derived from the compositions. Generally, Dandelion received a fee of ten percent (10%) of the total revenues. The remaining ninety percent (90%) was to be divided equally between Rendezvous/ Tobac and Dandelion.

Under that agreement, Rendezvous/Tobac was also to receive direct payments from Broadcast Music, Inc. ("BMI") which was licensed to collect royalties for public performances of the compositions. BMI was to pay a fifty percent (50%) share of any performance income to Dandelion and a fifty percent (50%) share to Rendezvous/Tobac. The Participation Agreement stated that Dandelion was to provide Rendezvous/Tobac bi-annually with an accounting and payment of net income: "All sums payable to [Rendezvous/Tobac] pursuant hereto by [Dandelion], shall be accounted for, in writing and paid at the time of accounting, at the same time as [Dandelion] customarily accounts to authors and composers, but in no event less than twice a year."

Dandelion did not send out statements every six months as required by the Participation Agreement. As with the Master Purchase Agreement, there were no statements issued to Rendezvous/Tobac from 1972 to 1976. One cumulative statement was issued in 1997. Between the period 1969 and 1986, Rendezvous/Tobac received payments amounting to approximately $9,200 from Dandelion under the Participation Agreement. From 1970 to the present, Cabot received payments from BMI under the Participation Agreement. From 1991 to 1995, Cabot received more that $10,500 under the Participation Agreement from BMI directly.

In October 1986, Dandelion decided to suspend payments due to Rendezvous/Tobac under the Participation Agreement, after it suspended the payments to Sundi Records under the Master Purchase Agreement. Accountings were also not issued during that time. On July 10, 1998, this court ordered Dandelion to pay to Rendezvous/Tobac all sums withheld since 1986. Dandelion has tendered payment of those amounts but these sums have not been accepted.

Legal Conclusions

Rescission, an equitable rather than a legal remedy, "amounts to the unmaking of a contract, and is not merely a termination of the rights and obligations of the parties towards each other, but is an abrogation of all rights and responsibilities of the parties towards each other from the inception of the contract." *Metropolitan Property and Liability Insurance Co. v. Commonwealth of Pennsylvania,* 97 Pa. Commw. 219, 509 A.2d 1346, 1348 (Pa. Commw. Ct. 1986), *aff'd,* 517 Pa. 218, 535 A.2d 588 (Pa. 1987). Through equitable powers, a court may intervene to grant rescission when there are allegations of failure of consideration, fraud, and mistake. Cabot has based his claim of rescission on all of these grounds.

This court finds that the defendants' failure to make timely and accurate payments and regular accountings does not justify rescission of the Master Purchase and Participation Agreements. Not every breach of a contract justifies rescission. Under Pennsylvania law, rescission "is appropriate only under extraordinary circumstances when the complaining party has suffered a breach of such a fundamental and material nature that it affects the very essence of the contract and serves to defeat the object of the parties." It is well settled that an executed agreement should not be rescinded on the basis of inadequate consideration in the absence of fraud or mistake. Rescission has been allowed in cases in which a publisher has made none of the royalty payments. The rationale behind such a rescission is that "an essential objective of a contract between a composer and publisher is the payment of royalties, and a complete failure to pay means this objective has not been achieved."

Cabot cannot assert that there has been no payment whatsoever under the contract. Rather, he argues that rescission is warranted because defendants paid nothing between 1991 and 1995, the applicable statute of limitations period. Cabot argues that several other circuits have limited themselves to the statute of limitations period in evaluating whether a defendants' failure to pay and to make regular accounts warrants rescission. Cabot has cited no cases in this circuit that stand for such proposition. Nevertheless, this court finds that defendant's breaches of agreement both over the life of the agreements and during the applicable statute of limitations period, are not sufficient to warrant rescission here.

Between 1969 and 1986, Cabot received approximately $52,000 from defendants under the Master Purchase Agreements and $9,200 under the Participation Agreement. Further, BMI has made payments to Cabot since 1970 under the Participation Agreement. Jamie Record also paid additional consideration to Sigler pursuant to the Master Purchase Agreement. Payments to Sigler from Jamie Record under the Master Purchase Agreement and to Cabot from BMI under the Participation Agreement, continued during the statute of limitations period. In fact, from 1991 to 1995 Cabot received $10,574 from BMI directly.

While the defendants have breached the Master Purchase and Participation Agreements by failing to make timely payments and regular accountings to Cabot, and perhaps have not fully compensated Cabot under the agreements, these breaches only amount to inadequate consideration and failure to comply fully with the contractual provisions. It is well settled that a party may not avail itself of the equity powers of the court if there exists or existed an adequate remedy at law. Here, Cabot could have been, or can be, made whole by an award of damages. In fact, the tender of payments withheld by the defendants since 1986, may have fully compensated Cabot....

Further, rescission is inappropriate in this case because the parties cannot be placed in their pre-contractual positions at this time, as that would mean restoring the 1969 status quo in 1997. Rescission is ordinarily granted only where the parties to the contract can be restored to substantially the same position they occupied when the contract was made. The songs were popular primarily in 1969 and 1970. This success was due in some significant part to the efforts of the defendants. Thus, if rescission was granted, Cabot would necessarily benefit from any value that the defendants have added to the compositions, and the defendants would lose the benefit of those efforts.

Cabot asserts that the defendants had an obligation to exploit or actively solicit and promote interest in the compositions and the Sundi label by maximizing on the past popularity of the compositions.... The only terms for distribution of the compositions and the label are stated briefly in the Master Purchase Agreement at paragraph 15:

> It is understood and agreed that the above recording will be released by Jamie Record Co. on the Sundi label, with the logo 'Nationally distributed by Jamie/Guyden D. Corp.,' and you agree that we shall be exclusive distributors of all recordings on the Sundi label so long as this Agreement is in effect.

No duties were imposed in the agreements regarding exploitation, or active promotion, of the compositions and label. Thus, under the plain language of the Master Purchase Agreement, Jamie Record was bound only to release the compositions on the Sundi label with the described logo, and was given the exclusive right to distribute on the Sundi label. Likewise, the Participation Agreement only provided Dandelion with the "exclusive right to print, publish, sell, use and license the use of the compositions and to execute in its own name any and all licenses and agreements affecting or respecting the Musical Compositions...."

Where the language of a contract is clear and unambiguous, the intent is to be discovered only from the express language of the agreement and the plain meaning of the agreement will be enforced. While Cabot may have expected a subsequent, more formal agreement to be reached regarding distribution under the Master Purchase Agreements, such an agreement would not have altered the Master Purchase Agreements' original terms.

Cabot asserts that even absent an explicit contractual duty, the nature of the relationship of the parties and the transfer of all title and control over the copyrights and master recordings to Jamie Record and Dandelion, created an implied duty for them to exploit. Cabot cites second circuit cases, applying New York law, in an attempt to support his assertion that even in the absence of specific contractual language, the defendants had an implied duty to exploit the compositions and actively to promote distribution of the Sundi label.... At best, the second circuit cases hold that a publisher, holding exclusive rights in a work, has an implied duty to exercise good faith and sound business judgment in working a copyright. Those cases do not stand for the proposition that there is an implied duty to exploit a copyright in the manner that Cabot urged, and that a publisher is obligated to promote the work regardless of circumstances, costs, or other conditions that might erode popularity, such as the passage of time and change in consumer taste....

Cabot's claim for rescission of the Master Purchase Agreement and Participation Agreement is denied....

Notes and Questions

a. Ambiguity in the scope of the license transfers remains a common problem. In *Greenfield v. Philles Records*, the New York Court of Appeals reversed the Appellate Division because it found that the comprehensive assignment left no ambiguity regarding the scope of the rights transfer. Although not discussed in the opinion, the silence on synchronization rights could have been particularly instructive since this was not a new technology, but rather the right to use the sound recordings as part of a motion picture. Producer Phil Spector was certainly aware of the possibility, and undoubtedly, Ms. Greenfield and the other Ronettes also knew of the possibility that the sound recording could be sold for use in movies.

b. Another important aspect of *Greenfield* was the drafting of the agreement. The agreement provided for a transfer of all rights, but provided compensation to the recording artist only in selected income streams. The silence of the contract resulted in all income from the synchronization being kept by Philles Records and no royalties being paid. In this age of rapidly changing technologies, it is appropriate to provide an "other revenue" royalty provision that provides a blended royalty rate for all income streams not otherwise identified in the agreement. This will protect today's recording artists from income opportunities that will develop during the many decades covered by the transfer of the exploitation rights.

c. Interestingly, it might be worth noting the sniping between the Sixth Circuit and the New York Court of Appeals. In response to the criticism of its earlier case in *Greenfield*, the Sixth Circuit responded:

> We recognize that a recent opinion by the New York Court of Appeals, *Greenfield v. Philles Records, Inc.,* No. 114, 98 N.Y.2d 562, 780 N.E.2d 166, 2002 N.Y. LEXIS 3146, 750 N.Y.S.2d 565 (N.Y. October 17, 2002), questioned our earlier decision, *Thomas v. Gusto Records,* 939 F.2d 395 (6th Cir. 1991). To the extent *Greenfield* departs from earlier New York jurisprudence, it has no bearing here because *Greenfield* involved the interpretation of a contract silent on an important issue and thus possibly ambiguous for that reason. The agreements disputed in this case are neither silent on issues important to a resolution of the parties' dispute nor ambiguous.

Thomas v. Lytle, 52 Fed. Appx. 671, 672 n1 (6th Cir. 2002).

d. Despite contract language limiting the audit of books to one year, misleading royalty statements may trigger the delayed discovery doctrine and toll the time provided under the contract. See *Weatherly v. Universal Music Publishing Group*, 125 Cal. App. 4th 913, 23 Cal. Rptr. 3d 157 (2004).

e. To what extent is the presumptive relationship between a band and record company exclusive? In *Bucciarelli-Tieger v. Victory Records, Inc.*, 488 F. Supp. 2d 702 (N.D. Ill. 2007), the court refused to go beyond the text of the agreement. "The agreement contains no exclusivity provision, nor does any of its language appear to prevent plaintiffs from recording elsewhere during the life of the agreement." At the same time, the decision included some practical limitations—not written into the agreement. "Our interpretation does not mean plaintiffs can market the same albums to another record company, or even re-record the same tracks, and plaintiff clarified that this was not their argument. It simply means plaintiffs are free to record other albums or tracks for another record company during the life of the agreement with defendants. Defendants even admit in their motion that within the industry standard there are exceptions to the rule of exclusivity."

f. Sometimes the problem with the accountability exists on both sides of the recording agreement. Such is the saga of the Bay City Rollers, who have been litigating a royalty dispute with Arista Records—at least through 2011—that stemmed from non-payments in 1981. See *Faulkner v. Arista Records LLC*, 797 F. Supp. 2d 299 (S.D.N.Y. 2011).

Problem XII-F

Despite the somewhat contentious relationship between Bryce and Soundfyre, Bryce has agreed to appear as a principal musician on the band's next album and participate in limited appearances. Based on your advice and Bryce's personal career aspirations, Bryce does not wish to join the band or become subject to the exclusive recording agreement.

Prepare a deal memo that can serve as an outline for an agreement that Bryce and Soundfyre can offer to the label so that Bryce can participate on the album without joining the band.

G. Bibliography and Links

Al Kohn & Bob Kohn, Kohn on Music Licensing (3d Ed. 2002).

Donald S. Passman, All You Need to Know About the Music Business (5th Ed. 2003).

Mark Halloran, The Musician's Business & Legal Guide (2001).

Brian Day, *The Super Brawl: The History and Future of the Sound Recording Performance Right*, 16 Mich. Telecomm. Tech. L. Rev. 179 (2009).

Brian C. Drobnik *Art & Industry Forum: Truckin' In Style Along the Avenue: How the Grateful Dead Turned Alternative Business and Legal Strategies Into A Great American Success Story*, 2 Vand. J. Ent. L. & Prac. 242, 20663 (2000).

Seth Ericsson, *Copyright and Specific Industries: The Recorded Music Industry and the Emergence of Online Music Distribution: Innovation in the Absence of Copyright (Reform)*, 79 Geo. Wash. L. Rev. 1783 (2011).

Tonya M. Evans, *Sampling, Looping, and Mashing ... Oh My!: How Hip Hop Music Is Scratching More Than the Surface of Copyright Law*, 21 Fordham Intell. Prop. Media & Ent. L.J. 843 (2011).

Patryk Galuszka *Undisclosed Payments to Promote Records on the Radio: An Economic Analysis of Anti-Payola Legislation*, 11 Va. Sports & Ent. L.J. 38 (2011).

William Henslee, *What's Wrong with U.S.?: Why the United States Should Have a Public Performance Right for Sound Recordings*, 13 Vand. J. Ent. & Tech. L. 739 (2011).

Thomas W. Joo, *Remix Without Romance*, 44 Conn. L. Rev. 415 (2011).

Camalla Kimbrough, *LAUNCH Away: Second Circuit Rules that Degree of User Influence Determines Whether a Webcasting Service Must Obtain Individual Licenses for Performing Sound Recordings*, 12 Tul. J. Tech. & Intell. Prop. 293 (2009).

Nora Miles, *FILM & TV: Pop Goes the Commercial: The Evolution of the Relationship Between Popular Music and Television Commercials*, 5 Vand. J. Ent. L. & Prac. 121 (2003).

Lynn Morrow, *The Recording Artist Agreement: Does it Empower or Enslave?*, 3 Vand. J. Ent. L. & Prac. 40 (2001).

Henry H. Perritt, Jr., *New Business Models for Music*, 18 Vill. Sports & Ent. L.J. 63 (2011).

John P. Strohma, *clearing the way: Acquiring Rights and Approvals for Music use in Media Applications*, 18 J. Intell. Prop. L. 561 (2011).

Cydney A. Tune & Christopher R. Lockard, *Navigating the Tangled Web of Webcasting Royalties*, 27 Ent. & Sports Law 20 (2009).

Websites

Recording Industry of America, www.RIAA.com

Association For Independent Music, http://www.afim.org

IFPI, International Federation of the Phonographic Industry, www.ifpi.org

Chapter XIII

Digital Distribution, Piracy, and Technology

Although this chapter had been conceived primarily with music as its main emphasis, digital distribution has moved to the forefront of distribution for film, television, software, and publishing, so the issues impact the entire entertainment industry. Still, the music industry has historically served as the leading edge for software protection, motion picture legislation, and similar public policy changes. For example, the Record Rental Act of 1984 was drafted to protect both the burgeoning CD and the rapidly developing home software markets. Much of the e-Hollywood era will be dictated by the legal, technical, and social changes which allow profitable enterprise to develop.

An elegant summary of the effect of publishing piracy was written by Harlan Ellison, noted futurist and novelist. On February 22, 2001, in response to the ongoing litigation, *Ellison v. Robertson*, Ellison issued the following statement as part of his plea to finance his lawsuit through Kick Internet Piracy "to protect writers' creative properties."[1]

> [With my lawyer, I] filed a lawsuit against the above parties to stop them from posting my works on the Internet without permission. This is copyright infringement. Rampant. Out of control. Pandemic.
>
> AOL, RemarQ/Critical Path and a host of self-serving individuals seem to think that they can allow the dissemination of writers' work on the internet without authorization, and without payment, under the banner of "fair use" or the idiot slogan "information must be free." A writer's work is not information: it is our creative property, our livelihood and our families' annuity. Why should any artist, of any kind, continue creating new work, eking out an existence in pursuit of a career, following the muse, when little internet thieves, rodents without ethic or understanding, steal and steal and steal, conveniencing themselves and "screw the author?" What we're looking at is the death of the professional writer!
>
> This is not only *my* fight, I'm not the only one whose work is being pirated. Hundreds of writers' stories, entire books, and the work of a lifetime, everyone from Isaac Asimov to Roger Zelazny: Their work has been thrown onto the web by these smartass vandals who find it an imposition to have to pay for the goods. (But gawd forbid you try to appropriate something of *theirs* ... listen to 'em squeal!)
>
> The outcome of this case will affect every writer, editor, photographer, artist, musician, poet, sculptor, actor, book designer, publisher and reader. What we're looking at is the anarchy of ignorant thieves ripping off those who labor for an

---

1. Reprinted with permission of the author.

> honest payday, because they conveniently honor the lie that everything should be theirs for the taking....
>
> Do not, for an instant, buy into the cultural mythology that all artists are rich. A few are, but most have a hard row to hoe just subsisting, holding down second jobs. Most creators practice their art because they love it. If it were only for the bucks, they'd fare better as dentists, plumbers, or steam fitters. I'm fighting for myself, of course, but I'm also doing this for Avram Davidson, who died broke; for Roger Zelazny, who had to work like a dog till the day he pitched over; and for Gerald Kersh, whose work was reprinted and pirated in sixty-five countries, while he had to borrow money from friends to fight off the cancer. This is your fight, too, gang ... and now we need your help!

Mr. Ellison's personalization of the impact of piracy does more than economic models to articulate that the corrosive effect of piracy has already begun to erode the creative markets. The cases and materials below illustrate how far this jurisprudence has come—and how far it has to go.

Other authors and artists take a very different approach. For musicians and performers who can make their artistic living through performance income rather than publication rights, there have been many who embrace free internet content and others who rely on the audience's voluntary payments as sufficient. This description on *Digital Hollywood* provides an example:[2]

> Louis C.K. tried an experiment. A U.S. based comedian and television star, he invested in a premium production of his stage show, which he then sold directly to the public for $5.00, free of any digital rights management or other restrictions.[3] The experiment was a success. Despite $170,000 in direct production expenses and significant additional expenses for web design, processing fees and marketing, the project was profitable within two days of launch[4] and has reportedly earned the artist a pre-tax earnings of $750,000.[5]
>
> The experiment is neither new nor entirely exceptional. DramaFever, Epix, Fandor, Film Fresh, Popcorn Flix and others provide opportunities for filmmakers to distribute their content. Many of these have modest distribution fees that would have been comparable to the costs Louis C.K. incurred by building his own infrastructure.[6] Other comedians such as Ron White have started the direct-to-public marketing strategy.[7] Nonetheless, the experiment is important because it reflects the next wave of content disintermediation. Premium cable television systems such as HBO and Showtime had held a monopoly on first-

---

2. Jon M. Garon, *Digital Hollywood 2.0: Reimagining Film, Music, Television, and Publishing Distribution as a Global Artist Collaborative*, 21 Mich. St. Int'l L. Rev. 563 (2013).

3. Louis C.K., *A Statement from Louis C.K.*, LouisCK.net (Dec. 13, 2011), http://buy.louisck.net/news/a-statement-from-louis-c-k.

4. *Id.*

5. David Carr, *A Comic Distributes Himself*, N.Y. Times, Dec. 19, 2011, at B1, *available at* http://www.nytimes.com/2011/12/19/business/media/louis-ck-plays-a-serious-joke-on-tv-the-media-equation.html?pagewanted=all&_r=0.

6. *See, e.g.*, Tim Appelo, *New Film Site Fandor: A Cross Between Sundance and Netflix, Only Smaller*, Hollywood Rep. (Mar. 8, 2011, 10:19 PM), http://www.hollywoodreporter.com/news/new-film-site-fandor-a-165495.

7. Chris Marlowe, *Ron White becomes latest to sell direct-to-fan downloads*, Digital Media Wire (Sept. 14, 2012, 5:04 AM), http://www.dmwmedia.com/news/2012/09/14/ron-white-becomes-latest-to-sell-direct-to-fan-downloads.

run comedy specials, competing only with basic cable channel Comedy Central.[8] The premium cable channels would promote the shows to encourage monthly subscribers.[9] Once the special had aired and the audience been exhausted, the cable system would license the special for general broadcast on basic cable systems.[10] Often these specials would require some editing to meet the slightly more restrictive censorship requirements.

A number of decisions made by Louis C.K. and Ron White are notable. Both are using Internet-based distribution that eschews digital rights management and country-code controls.[11] This allows for the distribution of the content to any Internet enabled computer in the world, unless the computer is located in a region that is subject to governmental filtering. Louis C.K. is making his content available exclusively on his own, personally branded website. White, in contrast, is using both his own website and a more general content distribution platform in which he is a partner.[12] For less established artists, there may be other services available.[13]

The disintermediation of cable parallels the decline in control by record distributors and book publishers. This has been less true of film and television, but just as comedy specials are a form of television, the Louis C.K. experiment may be a harbinger of change in these industries as well. ...

The ... revolution occurred in 1999 with the launch of Napster, the paradigm-shifting peer-to-peer platform that enabled the public to have access to any content that resided on any other participant's computer system.[14] Napster and its progeny operate outside of territorial boundaries and without the ability to charge for content.[15]

Although Napster itself was successfully sued for its contributory copyright infringement,[16] the legacy of peer-to-peer content distribution made it imperative for content companies to open up their content to Internet distribution.[17] Apple was the first mover to take full advantage of this market pressure, launching

---

8. Deborah Vankin & Dawn C. Chmielewski, *The new comedy stages: YouTube, Twitter, online specials*, SAG Actor Online (Dec. 30, 2012), http://www.sagactoronline.com/2012/09/the-new-comedy-stages-youtube-twitter.html.

9. June Thomas, *How Much Gold Is Game of Thrones Worth?* Slate Mag. (Mar. 29, 2012, 2:00 PM), http://www.slate.com/articles/arts/culturebox/2012/03/game_of_thrones_how_hbo_and_showtime_make_money_despite_low_ratings_.html.

10. *Id.*

11. *See* Louis C.K., *supra* note 4; *see also* Marlowe, *supra* note 8.

12. *See* Marlowe, *supra* note 8 (discussing Ron White).

13. *See, e.g.,* DaCast.com (2013) (offering pay-per-view and subscription services on a web-based platform).

14. *See* Peter K. Yu, *P2P and the Future of Private Copying*, 76 U. Colo. L. Rev. 653, 658 (2005); *see also* Robert A. Heverly, *The Information Semicommons*, 18 Berkeley Tech. L.J. 1127, 1136 (2003); *see generally* Grace J. Bergen, *The Napster Case: The Whole World is Listening*, 15 Transnat'l Law 259, 260–69 (2002).

15. Theodore Hong, *Performance, in* Peer-To-Peer: Harnessing the Benefits of a Disruptive Technology 204 (Andy Oram ed., 2001).

16. A&M Records, Inc., v. Napster, Inc., 284 F.3d 1091, 1098–99 (9th Cir. 2002). *See also* MGM Studios Inc., v. Grokster, Ltd., 545 U.S. 913 (2005) (finding peer-to-peer file sharing service could be liable for inducing copyright infringement even in absence of vicarious or contributory liability).

17. *See* Kimberlianne Podlas, *The Moral of the Story ... Musical Artists must Protect Their own Rights in Digital Music*, 10 Wake Forest Intell. Prop. L.J. 265, 287–88 (2010); *see also* Seth Robert Belzley, *Grokster and Efficiency in Music*, 10 Va. J.L. & Tech. 1, 7 (2005) ("This process of cutting the entertainment industry out of the transactional loop threatens the industry's ability to maintain the

iTunes to make its elegant music player a better value than products from rival Sony or Microsoft.[18] For example, had Sony been in a position to exploit its large music catalog and content holdings by licensing its own content on its music players, it is reasonable to expect that it would have retained significant market share in this competitive environment.[19]

Book distributors, Amazon and Barnes & Noble, have been equally aggressive in establishing book and e-book distribution platforms that have largely consolidated the retail end of book publishing, shifting power to these distributors.[20] Not to be outdone, Apple has moved aggressively to manage book distribution on its iTunes platform as well.[21]

In film, the industry remains much more fragmented. Control remains dominated by nearly the same group of distributors as existed at the time of the *U.S. v. Paramount* decision. The historical legacy of price fixing by the exhibitors has left global audiences with little expectation that there will be meaningful price competition for a movie ticket. Instead, within each city the prices of movie tickets do not reflect popularity or the number of weeks a motion picture has played. Ticket prices are held rather constant and the exhibitor varies the number of seats available to see a popular movie by increasing the number of screens on which the movie will play.[22]

But just as television moved the audience from the communal theater to the living room, Napster initiated a move to the computer screen which technology has further pushed to mobile devices. These mobile devices—smartphones, tablets, and netbooks—serve as platforms for each of the content industries, so control for the mobile device will define the next generation of viewership.[23] Moreover, since television advertising is a ripe target for further disintermediation, it is reasonable if not inevitable to expect that the device companies and content providers will seek to reimagine television sets as extensions of the mobile experience.[24]

---

status quo. And when the status quo changes, there is always a strong chance of creative destruction.").

18. *See* Kristin Thomson & Brian Zisk, *iTunes and Digital Downloads: An Analysis*, FUTURE OF MUSIC COALITION (June 15, 2003), http://www.futureofmusic.org/article/article/itunes-and-digital-downloads-analysis.

19. *See generally* Frank Rose, *The Civil War Inside Sony*, WIRED MAG., Feb. 11, 2003, at 101, *available at* http://www.wired.com/wired/archive/11.02/sony.html; *see also* Steve Hamm & William C. Symonds, *Mistakes Made on the Road to Innovation*, BUS.WK. (Nov. 26, 2006), http://www.business-week.com/stories/2006-11-26/mistakes-made-on-the-road-to-innovation.

20. *See* John Biggs, Nook Media Officially Spins Out Of B&N With Microsoft's Help, Plans To Enter Ten New Markets By Next Year, TECHCRUNCH (Oct. 4, 2012), http://techcrunch.com/2012/10/04/nook-media-officially-spins-out-of-bn-with-microsofts-help-plans-to-enter-ten-new-markets-by-next-year/.

21. *See* Declan McCullagh, DOJ announces three e-book settlements, but not with Apple, CNET (Apr. 11, 2012, 9:27 AM), http://news.cnet.com/8301-13578_3-57412452-38/doj-announces-three-e-book-settlements-but-not-with-apple/.

22. *See* Hay, supra note 27, at 447–50.

23. AARON SMITH & JAN LAUREN BOYLES, THE RISE OF THE "CONNECTED VIEWER," PEW INTERNET & AM. LIFE PROJECT 2 (2012), available at http://pewinternet.org/Reports/2012/Connected-viewers.aspx.

24. *See* Chris Morris, Mobile TV searches for breakthrough, VARIETY (Sept. 29, 2012, 4:00 AM), http://www.variety.com/article/VR1118060011/ ("The history of mobile television has been rocky at best. While the allure of streaming live network programming to viewers over their handheld devices is undeniable, delivering that content in ways that don't abrogate rights agreements and can somehow be monetized has proven mercurial.").

In the not too distant future, the mobile device will also be the preview screen for the large living-room device. Whether broadcast television or cable/satellite resides on the device will depend on the battle over market and design.

A. Unauthorized Recording & Distribution

As part of the 1994 Uruguay Round Agreements enacted pursuant to the General Agreement on Tariffs and Trade (GATT) annexed to the WTO Agreement, additional criminal and civil protections were added to create liability for the unauthorized copying of live musical performances:

1. 18 U.S.C.S. § 2319A (2003)

Unauthorized fixation of and trafficking in sound recordings and music videos of live musical performances:

(a) Offense. Whoever, without the consent of the performer or performers involved, knowingly and for purposes of commercial advantage or private financial gain — (1) fixes the sounds or sounds and images of a live musical performance in a copy or phonorecord, or reproduces copies or phonorecords of such a performance from an unauthorized fixation; (2) transmits or otherwise communicates to the public the sounds or sounds and images of a live musical performance; or (3) distributes or offers to distribute, sells or offers to sell, rents or offers to rent, or traffics in any copy or phonorecord fixed as described in paragraph (1), regardless of whether the fixations occurred in the United States; shall be imprisoned for not more than 5 years or fined in the amount set forth in this title, or both, or if the offense is a second or subsequent offense, shall be imprisoned for not more than 10 years or fined in the amount set forth in this title, or both....

2. 17 U.S.C. § 1101. Unauthorized Fixation and Trafficking in Sound Recordings and Music Videos

(a) Unauthorized Acts. — Anyone who, without the consent of the performer or performers involved —

(1) fixes the sounds or sounds and images of a live musical performance in a copy or phonorecord, or reproduces copies or phonorecords of such a performance from an unauthorized fixation,

(2) transmits or otherwise communicates to the public the sounds or sounds and images of a live musical performance, or

(3) distributes or offers to distribute, sells or offers to sell, rents or offers to rent, or traffics in any copy or phonorecord fixed as described in paragraph (1), regardless of whether the fixations occurred in the United States,

shall be subject to the remedies provided in sections 502 through 505, to the same extent as an infringer of copyright.

United States v. Moghadam

175 F.3d 1269 (11th Cir. 1999)

In 1994, Congress passed a statute criminalizing the unauthorized recording, the transmission to the public, and the sale or distribution of or traffic in unauthorized recordings of live musical performances. *See* 18 U.S.C. §2319A. [Similar civil liability was enacted as well and codified in 17 U.S.C. §1101.] Appellant Ali Moghadam was convicted of violating that law (herein sometimes referred to as the "anti-bootlegging statute") after he pleaded guilty to knowingly distributing, selling, and trafficking in bootleg (unauthorized) compact discs featuring live musical performances by recording artists including Tori Amos and the Beastie Boys. The present appeal challenges the constitutional power of Congress to enact this legislation. In the district court, Moghadam moved to dismiss the indictment, arguing that the statute was unconstitutional because it did not fall within any of the federal legislative powers enumerated in Article I, §8 of the Constitution....

[F]or most of the nation's history, sound recordings were not protected. In 1971, Congress extended copyright protection to sound recordings. Sound Recording Act of 1971, 17 U.S.C. §102(a)(7) (including "sound recordings" in the list of copyrightable "works of authorship"). This meant that persons who made unauthorized reproductions of records or tapes, which is known as "piracy," could be prosecuted or face civil liability for copyright infringement. The copyright law, especially as amended by further statutes, went far toward securing the rights of musicians and recording artists to receive fair benefit from their creative efforts....

[I]n contrast to the six exclusive rights of a copyright owner spelled out in 17 U.S.C. §106, it appears that the only exclusive right created by the anti-bootlegging statute is to record and/or re-communicate one's performance.... [T]he protections that the anti-bootlegging statutes confer on musicians are best described as "quasi-copyright" or *sui generis* protections.

[Although the court discusses the reach of the Copyright Clause to the type of legal protection afforded under the statute, it chooses not to decide whether the statute is a constitutional exercise of authority. Instead, it allows the legislation to be deemed constitutional under the Commerce Clause.] ...

Section 2319A clearly prohibits conduct that has a substantial effect on both commerce between the several states and commerce with foreign nations. The link between bootleg compact discs and interstate commerce and commerce with foreign nations is self-evident. For example, one of the elements of the offense is that the activity must have been done "for purposes of commercial advantage or private financial gain." 18 U.S.C. §2319A(a). If bootlegging is done for financial gain, it necessarily is intertwined with commerce. Bootleggers depress the legitimate markets because demand is satisfied through unauthorized channels. Generally speaking, performing artists who attract bootleggers are those who are sufficiently popular that their appeal crosses state or national lines. The very reason Congress prohibited this conduct is because of the deleterious economic effect on the recording industry. The specific context in which §2319A was enacted involved a treaty with foreign nations, called for by the World Trade Organization, whose purpose was to ensure uniform recognition and treatment of intellectual property in international commerce. The context reveals that the focus of Congress was on interstate and international commerce....

Summarizing our narrow holding in this case, we assume *arguendo*, without deciding, that the anti-bootlegging statute cannot satisfy the fixation requirement of the Copyright Clause; we hold that the statute satisfies the "substantial effects" test of the post-*Lopez*

Commerce Clause jurisprudence; we hold that the Commerce Clause can provide the source of Congressional power in this case because the extension of copyright-like protection here is not fundamentally inconsistent with the fixation requirement of the Copyright Clause; and thus under the circumstances of this case, we reject Moghadam's constitutional challenge to his conviction....

Notes and Questions

a. In addition to the bar on unauthorized fixation, other provisions criminalize the counterfeiting of a copyrighted work, 18 U.S.C. § 2318 (2010), and create RICO predicate jurisdiction. See 18 U.S.C. § 1960(b) (2006).

b. As the *Moghadam* Court explains, "The anti-bootlegging statute grew out of the Agreement on Trade Related Aspects of Intellectual Property ('TRIPs').... TRIPs became law by operation of the Uruguay Round Agreements Act ('URAA'), Pub.L. No. 103-465, 108 Stat. 4809 (1994), a comprehensive act dealing with matters of international trade." In essence, then, the extension of copyright or Commerce Clause protection to the act of fixation, fills the final gap in the creative process and keeps the United States consistent with the other content-producing nations.

c. The discomfort shown by the *Moghadam* Court at extending copyright protection raises interesting issues. One view is that since a derivative work cannot be copyrighted without the express permission of the copyright holder, such a derivative work is an infringement of the source work. Given that precedent, no work can be copyrighted without the express permission of the copyright owner, and the unauthorized work is an infringement of the copyright owner's rights. The other view, however, posits that an author does not exist until the work exists. Therefore, there can be no injury since there is no copyright owner with standing.

The Copyright Clause of the United States Constitution provides Congress the power "to promote the Progress of Science and the useful Arts, by securing for limited Times to Authors and Inventors the exclusive Right to their respective Writings and Discoveries." U.S. Const. art. I, § 8, cl. 8. The question of whether an author cannot exist until the writing is fixed tends to take on a rather theosophical patina, which tends to belie the actual creative process for many authors.

d. Other than the need to conform United States law to the TRIPS treaty, what practical consequence does the statute's extension of protection provide to copyright holders and law enforcement?

e. The FBI has unveiled a new labeling system to reinforce its anti-piracy efforts. Like the copyright warning on videotapes and DVDs, the new logo will be featured on music CDs, software, and other intellectual property products. See http://www.fbi.gov/page2/feb04/pirates021904.htm.

f. Courts have struggled to reconcile the Copyright Clause with the Commerce Clause regarding the constitutionality of the anti-trafficking statutes. Courts continue to uphold the legislation. See *United States v. Martignon*, 492 F.3d 140 (2d Cir. 2007) (upholding 18 U.S.C. § 2319A); *Kiss Catalog, Ltd. v. Passport Int'l Prods.*, 405 F. Supp. 2d 1169 (C.D. Cal. 2005) (upholding 17 U.S.C. § 1101).

> [T]he analysis of The Trade-Mark Cases is more to the point. There, the Supreme Court noted that legislation that could not be permitted under the Copyright Clause could nevertheless pass muster under the Commerce Clause —

if the independent requirements of that clause were met. Under the more restrictive view of the Commerce Clause that prevailed at the time, those requirements were not met. As noted above, modern case law has expanded the interpretation of the Commerce Clause and modem cases upholding trademark protection are based on the Commerce Clause. Therefore, once the Court concludes that the Statute does not fall within the purview of the Copyright Clause, it need no longer consider whether it complies with the limitations of the Copyright Clause. To do so imports into the Commerce Clause limits that clause does not have. That the Statute might provide "copyright-like" or "copyright-related" protection to matters clearly not covered by the Copyright Clause is not important. One need only find an alternative source of constitutional authority. This Court finds such authority in the Commerce Clause.

Kiss Catalog, Ltd. v. Passport Int'l Prods., 405 F. Supp. 2d 1169, 1174–75 (C.D. Cal. 2005).

Problem XIII-A

Bryce and some other members of Soundfyre stop by your office. While surfing the Internet, Bryce came across a multimedia file of Soundfyre's live concert from the previous week. The clip featured Bryce performing duets with Freddi, the bass player. Bryce explained that they know the material had been audiotaped and videotaped the previous week at a private club because they recognized the songs being played and the logo displayed on the back of the stage. Bryce is particularly upset because they had been testing out some new songs that were not even completely finished.

Advise Bryce as to which laws may have been broken, what civil remedies might be available, and how best to proceed.

B. Traditional Bootlegging of Branded Merchandise

Plant v. Does

19 F. Supp. 2d 1316 (S.D. Fla. 1998)

THIS CAUSE comes before the Court upon Plaintiffs' Ex Parte Emergency Motion for Order to Show Cause on Motion for Preliminary Injunction with Temporary Restraining Order ("TRO") and Order of Seizure, filed May 21, 1998. Defendants, as they are unknown and have not been served, were unable to file a response. The Court entertained oral argument from Plaintiffs' counsel on May 21, 1998. At the conclusion of the TRO hearing, the Court announced its decision denying Plaintiff's motion and dismissing the case in open court. The day following the Court's announcement of its ruling, Plaintiff sought and obtained a TRO from the U.S. District Court for the Middle District of Florida, prohibiting unnamed parties from selling souvenir merchandise in Florida, South Carolina, and North Carolina.

Plaintiffs are rock musicians and the companies licensed to sell their souvenir merchandise. Plaintiffs Plant and Page, former members of the rock and roll band Led Zeppelin, are currently on a nationwide music tour. As well as owning the intellectual property rights to their own names and likenesses, Plant and Page are co-owners of the Led Zeppelin trademark. Plaintiffs seek a nationwide injunction directed at as yet unknown "bootleggers" who sell t-shirts and souvenir items bearing Plant and Page likenesses or the Led Zeppelin logo. Plaintiffs ask this Court to authorize the U.S. Marshal or other law enforcement authorities to seize and impound any apparently infringing merchandise sold within a twenty-five mile radius of Page/Plant concerts.... [The Court first upbraided the plaintiffs for filing for the TRO on the eve of the concert and for failing to properly identify the rulings that were adverse to the relief sought.]

That being said, the Court will turn to whether the law permits Plaintiffs to obtain ex parte equitable relief to prevent unknown parties from engaging in what might be illegal behavior in the future. Although other courts have granted such relief, this Court is convinced that doing so would neither comport with federal procedural rules nor the dictates of justice. First, Plaintiffs have not made a sufficient showing that the Court has personal jurisdiction over the unknown Defendants. Plaintiffs have not served Defendants with process, and have elected not to do so until Defendants' property has already been seized. The Court initially notes that although plaintiffs are permitted to use fictitious names in their complaints. "Federal courts do not favor the naming of 'John Doe' defendants." In addition, "a district court does not have jurisdiction over unnamed defendants unless they have been served with a summons and a copy of the complaint." Courts generally permit the use of fictitious names when the only way a plaintiff can obtain the name of a defendant who has harmed him is through the discovery process in a case filed against that defendant as an unnamed party. The use of a fictitious name is not generally permitted as a tool by which a private plaintiff may obtain a broad-based order preventing any and all members of society from engaging in future behavior that might or might not later be found to have violated the plaintiff's rights.

Moreover, in order to survive dismissal for lack of jurisdiction, Plaintiffs must "demonstrate[ ] that they have engaged in a reasonably diligent search to identify the unknown defendants [and] ... inform[ ] the Court of any efforts they have taken to provide these individuals with constructive notice." Furthermore, the requirement that "unknown parties have at least constructive notice is no dispensable formality; rather, it is an essential element of due process without which a court has no jurisdiction to bind the absent parties."

Plaintiffs simply assert that the use of a fictitious name is proper because "said parties cannot be identified until they actually appear at said concerts." In the very same paragraph, however, Plaintiffs state that, unless enjoined, these individuals will "travel[ ] on to the next concert" and sell their merchandise. This clearly indicates that the same individuals follow the band from concert to concert, selling their wares. Plaintiffs give no explanation as to why they are unable to obtain the identities of these individuals. Indeed, Plaintiffs do not indicate that they have even ever attempted to ascertain the identity of these individuals. This Court declines to suspend time-honored procedural rules simply because Plaintiffs did not wish to expend a modest amount of their ample resources to do a routine preliminary factual investigation before bringing suit in this federal Court. Given the considerations discussed above, courts have concluded that they lack personal jurisdiction over these unknown bootleggers. In addition, Plaintiffs' case must fail for lack of justiciability. As the Second Circuit observed in *Heldman v. Sobol,* 962 F.2d 148, 153–54 (2d Cir. 1992):

> Federal courts may decide only actual cases and controversies. See U.S. Const. art. III, §2. The parameters of the case or controversy limitation emerge from the cluster of justiciability doctrines—doctrines that incorporate concerns about the proper role of the judiciary in a democratic society and the need to assure an adversarial presentation of the issues.

Serious justiciability problems arise from the facts that Defendants cannot possibly be here to defend their position, Defendants at this time have not committed any injurious act, and Defendants, for all the Court knows, may never have committed any similar injurious acts in the past. As Judge Clemon observed in his well-reasoned opinion in *Rock Tours, [Ltd. v. Does,* 507 F. Supp. 63, 66 (N.D. Ala. 1981):

> At this point, plaintiffs have no adversaries in this Court. This proceeding has been wholly ex parte. Although the lack of actual defendants has apparently not posed an insurmountable barrier to preliminary injunctive relief in at least sixteen similar federal district court cases, this Court is not so sanguine in an ex parte proceeding. While plaintiffs take comfort in the fact that in those cases there is usually no challenge to the ex parte relief granted by the Courts; in this Court's view, the absence of challenges may simply beg the question of whether the proceedings are truly adversary proceedings....

> Under these circumstances, this Court doubts "... the existence of a sufficient adversary interest to stimulate the parties to a full presentation of the facts and arguments, which in our adversary system is available from the parties." At this time, the instant action is not a justiciable one for purposes of ex parte injunctive relief.

In our uniquely American governmental system of checks and balances, courts play a necessarily limited role. They do not create the law, and they do not execute the law. Rather, courts exist solely to resolve disputes between actual parties involved in actual controversies. They may not issue advisory opinions, and they may not address contingencies or hypothetical situations. The doctrine of justiciability grows out of this recognition that the role of courts is limited.... The relief sought by Plaintiffs extends far beyond the powers of this one federal district Court. Plaintiffs ask this Court first to create a law authorizing the U.S. Marshal to seize on sight any merchandise that reasonably appears to the Marshal to infringe on a trademark and second to execute the law by ordering the Marshal to seize the merchandise. For this reason, Judge Clemon concluded:

> Basically, plaintiffs seek through this Court a mechanism under which to seize and impound the allegedly bootleg merchandise to be sold by the unnamed defendants ... It would appear, therefore, that this controversy is one which may be more appropriately addressed to the legislative or executive branches.

Rock Tours, Inc., 507 F. Supp. at 66.

Finally, policy consideration militate against granting injunctive relief. The public interest can hardly be served by this Court ordering armed police personnel to forcibly confiscate the merchandise of unsuspecting vendors at a rock concert where people are probably already in a rowdy mood. In sum, the hornets' nest of procedural problems and policy implications posed by this case simply prevents the Court from granting the extreme and broad based injective relief requested by Plaintiffs. If district courts are not rigorous in their application of Constitutional standards and enforcement of venerable procedural mandates, it is the individual citizen that bears risk of getting stung. This Court agrees with the poignant opinion in *National Football League Props., Inc. v. Coniglio,* 554 F. Supp. 1224, 1225 (D.D.C. 1983):

> Plaintiff seeks a [seizure] order without notice to any defendant, and before it has even effected service of its complaint on all defendants. Indeed, plaintiff has not even identified all of the potentially numerous defendants to whom this sweeping order would apply other than by the designation "Various John Does and Jane Does, and ABC Companies." Even on the surface, the order requested

by plaintiff would appear to invite catastrophe. It promises a nightmare of jurisdictional flaws, deprivations of due process, and windfall litigation that could ensue for years to come. This is not even to mention the physical spectacle of the United States Marshall Service, which is already greatly overburdened in its work, in the company of paid thugs (euphemistically styled "security representatives") roaming the streets of Washington to confiscate the merchandise of small businessmen and other licensed vendors who sell their wares in the open air. In short, the relief plaintiff seeks would open a veritable Pandora's box of problems that this court cannot even begin to imagine now.

The law should reward reason over haste and adherence to fair procedure over sweeping judicial power. The Court recognizes that bootlegging is a social problem; however, federal litigation is not a cure-all, and judicial authority may not be invoked every time a private litigant wishes to obtain a quick fix to what he perceives to be society's ailments. Federal procedural rules, incorporating the principles of jurisdiction and justiciability, are not mere technicalities, and they cannot be abandoned even in the most compelling of cases. They must not be abandoned in this case. Justice will never be served in the long run by submerging the procedural doctrines which protect all litigants in all cases to one individual's wanton quest to achieve success in his particular case....

SKS Merch, LLC v. Barry

233 F. Supp. 2d 841 (E.D. Ky. 2002)

This matter is before the Court on the Plaintiffs' Motions for a nationwide Preliminary Injunction and a Permanent Injunction. Having reviewed the pleadings in this matter, and having considered the arguments of counsel, the Court will grant both Motions for the reasons set forth below.

Plaintiff Toby Keith Covel, d/b/a Toby Keith ("Keith"), is a country music recording artist and performer. Plaintiff SKS is a Tennessee limited liability company. Authorized by Keith, SKS manufactures, markets and sells t-shirts, hats, and other merchandise bearing Keith's name, photograph, logo, likeness, tour information, and/or image, or which is otherwise associated with Keith's music career. SKS sells the merchandise at Keith's concerts throughout the country; SKS's primary focus is the sale of this concert merchandise, which is unique from other authorized Toby Keith merchandise. SKS remits taxes in each venue in which the merchandise is sold. In many venues, a license is required (and properly obtained) in order for SKS to lawfully sell its merchandise.

As explained by the Affidavit and testimony of Billy Ray Eden ("Eden"), an SKS representative, "bootleggers" have sold and continue to sell unauthorized, unlicensed versions of t-shirts, hats, and other merchandise bearing Keith's name, photograph, logo, likeness, tour information, and/or image. This "bootlegged" merchandise is sold without any authorization or license from SKS or Keith. The bootleggers appear at successive concerts, essentially following Keith on his nationwide concert tour and to other performances. Mr. Eden's Affidavit and testimony explains that bootlegging activities have occurred during concerts in seven (7) different states. The Affidavit details multiple instances of bootlegging at eleven (11) separate Keith concerts, while Mr. Eden's testimony also addressed bootlegging activity at a recent Keith performance in Greenville, South Carolina. Mr. Eden also testified that, at Keith's concert in Ypsilanti, Michigan, on October 17, 2002, Robert P. Conderato ("Conderato") was charged with bootlegging activity. Conderato was observed by a law enforcement officer selling t-shirts featuring Keith's logo. Conderato conceded that he did not have a license or any authorization from SKS to sell the t-shirts. Moreover, the bootleg t-shirts have also appeared on eBay, an internet auction site.

Mr. Eden's testimony also established the difficulty confronted by SKS in obtaining the names and addresses of the bootleg vendors who appear at Keith's concerts and performances. Typically, the bootleg vendors disappear before SKS employees can find them, confiscate their goods, or question them regarding their names and addresses. SKS employees have managed to identify at least some of the bootleggers: named Defendants Mike Barry, Lou Black, and Louie Cutone. At a hearing on the pending Motions, the Plaintiffs produced photographs depicting various persons allegedly engaged in selling bootleg merchandise at and around Keith's concerts. The photographs evidence the Plaintiffs' ongoing but ultimately futile efforts to identify and stop the bootleg vendors.

Mr. Eden also testified that he and other members of the SKS staff have been subjected to threats of violence by the bootleg vendors. Local law enforcement officers in the areas in which Keith performs routinely advise SKS that they will make no effort to identify the bootleg vendors, seize the bootleg merchandise, or charge the vendors with any offense or violation unless the Plaintiffs have an injunction issued by a federal court prohibiting the sale of the bootleg merchandise. Having lacked such an injunction, the Plaintiffs have been unable to consistently persuade local law enforcement to aid them in any predictable way in their attempt to prevent the bootlegging activity at and around Keith's concerts.

Because of its inability to thwart the bootleggers without intervention by a federal court, the Plaintiffs filed a Complaint on November 19, 2002, alleging violations of the Lanham Act by the named and unnamed Defendants. The Plaintiffs also sought a Temporary Restraining Order and a Preliminary Injunction. After a hearing on November 19, 2002, the Court granted the Plaintiffs' request for a Temporary Restraining Order. The Order enjoined the named and unnamed Defendants from selling or offering to sell t-shirts, hats, and other merchandise bearing the photograph, likeness, image, and/or logo of Keith without the Plaintiffs' authorization within a 25-mile radius of Keith's November 23, 2002, performance in Lexington, Kentucky. The Order further authorized law enforcement officers to seize any such merchandise. The Order provided that it, as well as related pleadings, would be served upon the Defendants when and if law enforcement or the Plaintiffs observed the sale of bootleg merchandise. The Temporary Restraining Order was secured by a $500 bond by the Plaintiffs and was set to expire within ten (10) days of its issuance. The Temporary Restraining Order also scheduled a hearing on the Plaintiffs' Motion for a Preliminary Injunction for November 27, 2002.

The Plaintiffs then filed a renewed Motion for a nationwide Preliminary Injunction, as well as a Motion for a Permanent Injunction pertaining to the Eastern District of Kentucky.

Although no bootleg vendors were identified during Keith's November 23, 2002, performance in Lexington, Kentucky, the ongoing and pervasive nature of the bootlegging activity at and around Keith's performances was established by Mr. Eden's Affidavit and his testimony at the November 27, 2002, hearing. At that hearing, the Plaintiffs produced numerous examples of authorized and unauthorized Toby Keith merchandise. The unauthorized merchandise, sold by bootleg vendors, apparently includes t-shirts with torn tags, an indication of poor quality. Some bootleg t-shirts bear erroneous concert dates. Although the bootleg versions are of poorer quality and contain minor inaccuracies, the images and logos printed on the unauthorized merchandise are essentially identical, or at least substantially similar, to those printed on the authorized merchandise.

At the hearing, Mr. Eden explained the difficulty in quantifying and recovering the profits lost by SKS due to the bootleg activity. Because the bootleg vendors flee when approached by the Plaintiffs, the exact number and price of the unauthorized, unlicensed t-shirts, hats, and other merchandise cannot be calculated. Even if such a calculation were possible, the bootleg vendors' refusal to identify themselves or provide addresses make any recovery by the Plaintiffs almost impossible.

I. THE PLAINTIFFS ARE ENTITLED TO A NATIONWIDE PRELIMINARY INJUNCTION RESTRAINING THE SALE OF UNAUTHORIZED, UNLICENSED MERCHANDISE BEARING KEITH'S NAME, LIKENESS, PHOTOGRAPH, TOUR INFORMATION, AND/OR IMAGE

A. The Plaintiffs Satisfy Each Prerequisite for the Issuance of a Preliminary Injunction

A motion for a preliminary injunction requires this Court to consider and balance four factors:

> (1) whether the movant has a strong likelihood of success on the merits; (2) whether the movant would suffer irreparable injury without the injunction; (3) whether issuance of the injunction would cause substantial harm to others [and balancing the harm to the moving party if the injunction is denied against the harm to others if the injunction is granted]; and (4) whether the public interest would be served by the issuance of the injunction.

Although the factors are to be balanced against each other, each factor need not be satisfied to issue a preliminary injunction. As explained below, the Court finds that the Plaintiffs have satisfied each factor relevant to the issuance of a preliminary injunction. The Court also notes, however, that irreparable harm is often presumed when a preliminary injunction is requested to enjoin a violation of the Lanham Act. "Simply fulfilling the requirements of the statute or, in other words, fulfilling the first factor for an injunction to issue—showing a strong likelihood of success on the merits—is all that is needed for the Court to issue an injunction."

Thus, in the context of a Lanham Act claim, a showing of likelihood of confusion as to sponsorship, approval, or association will itself establish the requisite likelihood of success on the merits and a risk of irreparable harm. The Court finds that the Plaintiffs satisfy each prerequisite for the issuance of a nationwide Preliminary Injunction enjoining the unauthorized sale of merchandise bearing Keith's name, photograph, logo, likeness, tour information, and/or image.

1. The Plaintiffs are likely to succeed on the merits of their Lanham Act claim

The Plaintiffs have demonstrated a strong likelihood that they will succeed on the merits of their Lanham Act claim against the named and unnamed Defendants. The Lanham Act generally prohibits the unauthorized sale of merchandise bearing Keith's photograph, image, name, likeness, and/or logo....

The testimony and evidence offered by the Plaintiffs establishes that the sale of bootleg merchandise associated with Keith is a consistent and pervasive problem throughout the nation. A strong likelihood exists that the Defendants have sold and will continue to sell merchandise bearing Keith's name, photograph, image, likeness, tour information, and/or logo which has not been authorized or licensed by the Plaintiffs. For example, Mr. Eden testified that SKS obtained forty-eight (48) t-shirts from bootleg vendors at Keith's November 22, 2002, performance in Greenville, South Carolina. The bootleggers who routinely appear at and around Keith's performances often sell their unauthorized merchandise from parking lots and exit ramps. The Defendants, both named and unnamed, scatter when questioned by SKS employees. Such conduct is hardly consistent with vendors of authorized, licensed merchandise. The Defendants' pattern of conduct establishes a strong likelihood that the bootleg activities will continue throughout Keith's 2003 performance tour.

The Defendants have misappropriated Keith's name, photograph, likeness, and image without authorization or license from the Plaintiffs. Because it appears to be nearly identical to the licensed, authorized merchandise, the bootleg merchandise clearly causes a likelihood of confusion as to Keith's association with and sponsorship and approval of that merchandise. Although the Defendants' outright misappropriation of the Plaintiffs' merchandise designs may make such an analysis unnecessary, the Plaintiffs have satisfied the test set forth in *Frisch's Restaurants, Inc. v. Elby's Big Boy of Steubenville, Inc.,* 670 F.2d 642 (6th Cir. 1982), for determining whether a defendant's goods cause a likelihood of confusion under the Lanham Act.... The Plaintiffs' mark is obviously strong: the t-shirts and other merchandise legitimately sold by the Plaintiffs feature distinctive photographs and images of Keith and his logos and tour information. The goods sold by both parties are clearly related: both the Plaintiffs and the Defendants sell t-shirts, hats and other merchandise bearing Keith's name, photograph, likeness, tour information, and/or image, as evidenced by the t-shirts produced at the hearing. The Defendants' bootleg merchandise is unmistakably similar to the Plaintiffs legitimate merchandise. Mr. Eden's testimony established that actual confusion has resulted from the sale of the bootleg merchandise. Many of Keith's fans reported to SKS that they believed the bootleg merchandise to be "official" Keith merchandise. Both parties almost exclusively use the marketing channels made available at and around Keith's performances. Finally, the merchandise sold by both parties will expand at a concurrent rate, as Keith's career and performances continue.

The most critical *Frisch's* factor is the defendant's intent. If the defendant's mark "was adopted with the intent of deriving benefit from the reputation of [the plaintiff], that fact alone may be sufficient to justify the inference that there is confusing similarity." In other words,

> [A] defendant who purposely chooses a particular mark because it is similar to that of a senior user [the plaintiff] is saying, in effect, that he thinks that there is at least a possibility that he can divert some business from the senior user — and the defendant ought to know at least as much about the likelihood of confusion as the trier of fact.

Little Caesar Enterprises, Inc. v. Pizza Caesar, Inc., 834 F.2d 568, 572 (6th Cir. 1987). Direct testimony is not necessary to establish wrongful intent; instead, the defendant's intent may be inferred from the defendant's acts.

Here, the Defendants' intent is obvious: the Defendants intend to derive a benefit from Keith's reputation and performances. Otherwise, the Defendants would not sell t-shirts and other merchandise which so closely resemble the merchandise sold by the Plaintiffs or which makes use of Keith's likeness, image, photograph, logos, and/or tour information. This fact alone establishes a likelihood of confusion and, correspondingly, the Plaintiffs' likelihood of success on the merits of their Lanham Act claim.

2. *The Plaintiffs will suffer irreparable harm absent the issuance of a nationwide preliminary injunction*

As explained above, irreparable harm may be presumed from a finding of a likelihood of confusion as to the Plaintiffs' sponsorship and approval of and association with the merchandise sold by the Defendants. However, the Plaintiffs have independently established that they will be irreparably harmed absent a Preliminary Injunction enjoining the sale of bootleg merchandise related to Keith throughout the nation. Absent such relief, the

Defendants' bootleg activity will be permitted to continue unabated, in blatant violation of the Lanham Act. Mr. Eden's testimony established that, in several jurisdictions, law enforcement officers expressly stated that no action would be taken against the bootleg vendors absent an injunctive order from a federal court. Even if SKS could identify all of the bootleg vendors, the Plaintiffs could not recover the damages caused by the bootleg activity. Because the Plaintiffs have no way to ascertain the number of t-shirts or hats sold by the bootleg vendors, they cannot calculate the number of legitimate sales to performance attendees which they lost due to the bootleg vendors' activities. Even if such a calculation could be made, the Defendants' nomadic nature and refusal to identify themselves would make any collection of damages by the Plaintiffs exceedingly improbable. The Plaintiffs have also been subjected to threats of violence from the unnamed Defendants, hampering their ability to learn the identity and addresses of the bootleg vendors.

No adequate remedy at law exists. The Plaintiffs' rights under the Lanham Act may be protected only by the issuance of a preliminary injunction against the sale of unauthorized merchandise bearing Keith's name, likeness, photograph, logo, tour information, and/or image throughout the country.

3. *The issuance of a nationwide Preliminary Injunction will not cause substantial harm to others*

The named and unnamed Defendants who appear at Keith's performances with bootleg merchandise for sale can hardly argue that they will be harmed by an order preventing them from violating the Lanham Act. The bootleg vendors have no conceivable right to continue violating the law. In the event that the Defendants are somehow harmed by the presence of the Preliminary Injunction, the Plaintiffs' bond will compensate them. As further set forth below, this Court is authorized to condition its injunction as equitably appropriate. For example, a preliminary injunction is not binding upon any defendant until and unless it is served with this Court's Order granting the injunction. Additionally, the defendants may be supplied with the Plaintiff's pleadings to date and/or notify the Defendants how to contest any seizure of goods or the existence of the Preliminary Injunction.

4. *The issuance of a Preliminary Injunction will serve the public interest*

The issuance of a nationwide Preliminary Injunction will serve the public interest. The public is obviously not served by ongoing violations of the Lanham Act. Further, as established by Mr. Eden's testimony and the t-shirts produced at the November 27, 2002, hearing, the bootleg vendors typically sell inferior and misleading merchandise to often unsuspecting concert attendees who believe they are buying "official" Toby Keith merchandise.

The public interest will also be served by an injunction which ensures the proper licensing and taxation of legitimate vendors of Keith merchandise. Legal vendors of concert merchandise are properly licensed and remit taxes on their sales, while the bootleg vendors are unlicensed and, presumably, remit no taxes.

B. The Preliminary Injunction Issued to the Plaintiffs Must be Nationwide

This Court is authorized to grant a nationwide preliminary injunction against violations of the Lanham Act. Nationwide injunctions have been issued in connection with performance tours in at least three (3) unreported, unpublished district court cases. Some district courts have held that nationwide preliminary injunctions are inappropriate in cases involving nationally touring performers. See *Plant v. Does,* 19 F. Supp.2d 1316 (S.D. Fla. 1998); *Brockum Co. v. Various John Does,* 685 F. Supp. 476 (E.D. Penn. 1988). However, this Court considers *Plant* to be distinguishable from this case. As for *Brockum,* this Court rejects the analysis upon which that opinion was based....

Certainly, Rule 65(d) requires actual notice, by service or otherwise, for an unnamed person acting in concert or participation with a named defendant to be bound by an injunction. Actual notice can and will be given when the nationwide injunction is served upon bootleg vendors throughout the country.

II. THE PLAINTIFFS ARE ENTITLED TO A PERMANENT INJUNCTION AGAINST THE SALE OF UNAUTHORIZED TOBY KEITH MERCHANDISE WITHIN THIS JURISDICTION

In addition to a nationwide Preliminary Injunction against the sale of unauthorized merchandise throughout the United States, the Plaintiffs are also entitled to a Permanent Injunction against such sales within the Eastern District of Kentucky.

To obtain a permanent injunction, an applicant must establish the following: (1) that it has prevailed on the merits; (2) that it will suffer continuing irreparable harm; (3) that it has no adequate remedy at law....

Notes and Questions

a. For many bands, the products sold as part of their concerts and tours are the most important revenue available to them. Unlike the record sales where the band receives a fraction of the total retail and is charged for most of the production costs, the licensee fees for tee-shirts, cups, posters, and other memorabilia is essentially cost-free net revenue to the bands. The licensors assume the risks associated with the sales and returns of the goods. As such, this income may make the difference between a successful and failed career.

b. The debate between the district courts reflects a growing dissatisfaction with the tools available to stop intellectual property theft. To some, these tools are too limited, while to others, the tools are unreasonably broad. See also *Recording Indus. Ass'n of Am. v. Verizon Internet Servs.,* 351 F.3d 1229 (D.C. Cir. 2003) (vacating and quashing subpoenas against Verizon pursuant to 17 U.S.C.S. §512(h), that were used to identify ISP customers who were allegedly involved in illegal downloading).

c. What steps might a band or a venue take to reduce the bootlegging of non-licensed products?

d. Even with a default judgment, there remain significant difficulties in proving actual damages, calculating statutory damages, tracing assets, and identifying the various works being infringed. See *Bravado Int'l Group Merch. Servs. v. Ninna, Inc.,* 655 F. Supp. 2d 177 (E.D.N.Y. 2009) (entering a default judgment against some but not all of the individual defendants and web companies Cmegamall.com, Rocktshirtspunk.com, and Mosh-pitt.com for $300,000 in statutory damages for use of a counterfeit mark on an Iron Maiden tee-shirt and ordering a permanent injunction prohibiting the defendants from "selling, manufacturing, and/or distributing any items bearing the names, trademarks, logos, or likenesses of Morrissey, Metallica, Slayer, Korn, Guns N' Roses, Led Zeppelin, The Clash, Iron Maiden, Motorhead, or Depeche Mode.").

Problem XIII-B

Bryce was approached by a friend with an offer to make some extra money at an upcoming concert of a national mega-tour. Tickets to the show sold out almost immediately, so the chance to attend the concert was nearly as enticing as the chance to make some money working at it.

Bryce was employed by a seller of music paraphernalia. The seller gave Bryce $300.00 to go shopping for souvenirs, in what Bryce originally thought was an attempt by the seller to determine "what were the hottest items going." Having completed the shopping, Bryce now suspects that the goods to be sold at the upcoming concert may be knock-offs of the items Bryce purchased. It is not uncommon today to find knock-offs or pirated goods that include authentic-looking copyright notices, trademark notices, and in some cases, fictitious labels.

After making a few inquiries with the so-called "friend," Bryce felt the earlier suspicions to be confirmed that none of the goods to be sold at the concert have been approved by the bands in the mega-tour, meaning that all the goods are unlicensed bootleg products.

Bryce seeks your advice on how to handle the situation and how to report the suspicious activity. Bryce is unsure whether this constitutes state or federal crimes, or both. Assist Bryce in reporting the criminal activity. In addition, identify the legal or corporate authorities to whom reports of the suspicious conduct should be submitted.

C. Unauthorized Distribution Using Peer-to-Peer File Sharing

Introduction

The rapid rise of digital technology has stripped both courts and Congress of the ability to keep up with the changes. The seminal modern case, *A&M Records v. Napster, Inc.*, no longer reflects the state of the art for peer-to-peer file sharing, but it best captures the doctrinal, technological, and social trends critical to understanding the revolution taking place in music distribution.

Sony Corp. of America v. Universal City Studios, Inc., 464 U.S. 417 (1984), framed the modern debate. There, the Court addressed the introduction of the video tape recorder. In what was drafted to be a very narrow ruling, the Court excused Sony of secondary liability because its machine had substantial noninfringing uses—a concept adapted without authority or precedent from patent law. The Ninth Circuit's discussion of the scope of injunction, below, harkens back to this concept in *Sony* and guides both the design of the Grokster software and the Court's determination of liability. In essence, the *Napster* decision created a structural template for software designers to meet. If the program can eliminate central control and direct benefit to the distributor, then the substantial noninfringing use will preclude liability. The line of *Sony-Napster-Aimster-Grokster* represents a developmental chain in peer-to-peer software jurisprudence.

Napster also represents an important decision in terms of the impact of the software on the music industry. The Ninth Circuit's recognition of market harm and changes to music distribution came well before the impact was truly being felt. Unlike the *Sony* Court, which vastly underestimated the changes to be brought by the video cassette, the Ninth Circuit was much quicker to anticipate the transformative impact of the technology.

In this way, the *Napster* litigation anticipated the changes to the legal doctrines of fair use, the technological innovations which would result from these legal standards, and the social impact or normative effect that the availability of peer-to-peer technology would bring. Although the decision is already dated in terms of subsequent case law, it remains the central, transformative decision in this body of jurisprudence.

A&M Records v. Napster, Inc.
239 F.3d 1004 (9th Cir. Cal. 2001)

Plaintiffs are engaged in the commercial recording, distribution and sale of copyrighted musical compositions and sound recordings. The complaint alleges that Napster, Inc. ("Napster") is a contributory and vicarious copyright infringer. On July 26, 2000, the district court granted plaintiffs' motion for a preliminary injunction. The injunction was slightly modified by written opinion on August 10, 2000. The district court preliminarily enjoined Napster "from engaging in, or facilitating others in copying, downloading, uploading, transmitting, or distributing plaintiffs' copyrighted musical compositions and sound recordings, protected by either federal or state law, without express permission of the rights owner." ... We affirm in part, reverse in part and remand....

In 1987, the Moving Picture Experts Group set a standard file format for the storage of audio recordings in a digital format called MPEG-3, abbreviated as "MP3." Digital MP3 files are created through a process colloquially called "ripping." Ripping software allows a computer owner to copy an audio compact disk ("audio CD") directly onto a computer's hard drive by compressing the audio information on the CD into the MP3 format. The MP3's compressed format allows for rapid transmission of digital audio files from one computer to another by electronic mail or any other file transfer protocol.

Napster facilitates the transmission of MP3 files between and among its users. Through a process commonly called "peer-to-peer" file sharing, Napster allows its users to: (1) make MP3 music files stored on individual computer hard drives available for copying by other Napster users; (2) search for MP3 music files stored on other users' computers; and (3) transfer exact copies of the contents of other users' MP3 files from one computer to another via the Internet. These functions are made possible by Napster's MusicShare software, available free of charge from Napster's Internet site, and Napster's network servers and server-side software. Napster provides technical support for the indexing and searching of MP3 files, as well as for its other functions, including a "chat room," where users can meet to discuss music, and a directory where participating artists can provide information about their music.

In order to copy MP3 files through the Napster system, a user must first access Napster's Internet site and download the MusicShare software to his individual computer. Once the software is installed, the user can access the Napster system. A first-time user is required to register with the Napster system by creating a "user name" and password.

If a registered user wants to list available files stored in his computer's hard drive on Napster for others to access, he must first create a "user library" directory on his computer's hard drive. The user then saves his MP3 files in the library directory, using self-designated file names. He next must log into the Napster system using his user name and password. His MusicShare software then searches his user library and verifies that the available files are properly formatted. If in the correct MP3 format, the names of the MP3 files will be uploaded from the user's computer to the Napster servers. The content of the MP3 files remains stored in the user's computer.

Once uploaded to the Napster servers, the user's MP3 file names are stored in a server-side "library" under the user's name and become part of a "collective directory" of files available for transfer during the time the user is logged onto the Napster system. The collective directory is fluid; it tracks users who are connected in real time, displaying only file names that are immediately accessible....

Plaintiffs claim Napster users are engaged in the wholesale reproduction and distribution of copyrighted works, all constituting direct infringement. Secondary liability for copyright infringement does not exist in the absence of direct infringement by a third party. It follows that Napster does not facilitate infringement of the copyright laws in the absence of direct infringement by its users. The district court agreed. We note that the district court's conclusion that plaintiffs have presented a prima facie case of direct infringement by Napster users is not presently appealed by Napster. We only need briefly address the threshold requirements.

A. Infringement

Plaintiffs must satisfy two requirements to present a prima facie case of direct infringement: (1) they must show ownership of the allegedly infringed material and (2) they must demonstrate that the alleged infringers violate at least one exclusive right granted to copyright holders under *17 U.S.C. § 106*. Plaintiffs have sufficiently demonstrated ownership. The record supports the district court's determination that "as much as eighty-seven percent of the files available on Napster may be copyrighted and more than seventy percent may be owned or administered by plaintiffs."

The district court further determined that plaintiffs' exclusive rights under § 106 were violated: "here the evidence establishes that a majority of Napster users use the service to download and upload copyrighted music.... And by doing that, it constitutes—the uses constitute direct infringement of plaintiffs' musical compositions, recordings." ... Napster users who upload file names to the search index for others to copy violate plaintiffs' distribution rights. Napster users who download files containing copyrighted music violate plaintiffs' reproduction rights. Napster asserts an affirmative defense to the charge that its users directly infringe plaintiffs' copyrighted musical compositions and sound recordings.

B. Fair Use

Napster contends that its users do not directly infringe plaintiffs' copyrights because the users are engaged in fair use of the material. Napster identifies three specific alleged fair uses: sampling, where users make temporary copies of a work before purchasing; space-shifting, where users access a sound recording through the Napster system that they already own in audio CD format; and permissive distribution of recordings by both new and established artists.

The district court considered factors listed in *17 U.S.C. § 107*, which guide a court's fair use determination. These factors are: (1) the purpose and character of the use; (2) the nature of the copyrighted work; (3) the "amount and substantiality of the portion used" in relation to the work as a whole; and (4) the effect of the use upon the potential market for the work or the value of the work. The district court first conducted a general analysis of Napster system uses under § 107, and then applied its reasoning to the alleged fair uses identified by Napster. The district court concluded that Napster users are not fair users. We agree. We first address the court's overall fair use analysis.

1. Purpose and Character of the Use. This factor focuses on whether the new work merely replaces the object of the original creation or instead adds a further purpose or different character. In other words, this factor asks "whether and to what extent the new work is 'transformative.' The district court first concluded that downloading MP3 files

does not transform the copyrighted work. This conclusion is supportable. Courts have been reluctant to find fair use when an original work is merely retransmitted in a different medium. This "purpose and character" element also requires the district court to determine whether the allegedly infringing use is commercial or noncommercial. A commercial use weighs against a finding of fair use but is not conclusive on the issue....

We also note that the definition of a financially motivated transaction for the purposes of criminal copyright actions includes trading infringing copies of a work for other items, "including the receipt of other copyrighted works." See No Electronic Theft Act ("NET Act") (defining "Financial Gain").

2. The Nature of the Use. Works that are creative in nature are "closer to the core of intended copyright protection" than are more fact-based works. The district court determined that plaintiffs' "copyrighted musical compositions and sound recordings are creative in nature ... which cuts against a finding of fair use under the second factor." We find no error in the district court's conclusion.

3. The Portion Used. "While 'wholesale copying does not preclude fair use per se,' copying an entire work 'militates against a finding of fair use.'" The district court determined that Napster users engage in "wholesale copying" of copyrighted work because file transfer necessarily "involves copying the entirety of the copyrighted work." We agree. We note, however, that under certain circumstances, a court will conclude that a use is fair even when the protected work is copied in its entirety.

4. Effect of Use on Market. "Fair use, when properly applied, is limited to copying by others which does not materially impair the marketability of the work which is copied." "[T]he importance of this [fourth] factor will vary, not only with the amount of harm, but also with the relative strength of the showing on the other factors." The proof required to demonstrate present or future market harm varies with the purpose and character of the use:

> A challenge to a noncommercial use of a copy-righted work requires proof either that the particular use is harmful, or that if it should become wide-spread, it would adversely affect the potential market for the copyrighted work.... *If the intended use is for commercial gain, that likelihood [of market harm] may be presumed. But if it is for a noncommercial purpose, the likelihood must be demonstrated.*

Sony, 464 U.S. at 451 (emphases added).

Addressing this factor, the district court concluded that Napster harms the market in "at least" two ways: it reduces audio CD sales among college students and it "raises barriers to plaintiffs' entry into the market for the digital downloading of music." The district court relied on evidence plaintiffs submitted to show that Napster use harms the market for their copyrighted musical compositions and sound recordings....

[T]he district court made sound findings related to Napster's deleterious effect on the present and future digital download market. Moreover, lack of harm to an established market cannot deprive the copyright holder of the right to develop alternative markets for the works. Here, ... the record supports the district court's finding that the "record company plaintiffs have already expended considerable funds and effort to commence Internet sales and licensing for digital downloads." Having digital downloads available for free on the Napster system necessarily harms the copyright holders' attempts to charge for the same downloads....

Accordingly, we next address whether Napster is secondarily liable for the direct infringement under two doctrines of copyright law: contributory copyright infringement and vicarious copyright infringement.

IV. We first address plaintiffs' claim that Napster is liable for contributory copyright infringement. Traditionally, "one who, with knowledge of the infringing activity, induces, causes or materially contributes to the infringing conduct of another, may be held liable as a 'contributory' infringer." Put differently, liability exists if the defendant engages in "personal conduct that encourages or assists the infringement."

The district court determined that plaintiffs in all likelihood would establish Napster's liability as a contributory infringer. The district court did not err; Napster, by its conduct, knowingly encourages and assists the infringement of plaintiffs' copyrights.

A. Knowledge. Contributory liability requires that the secondary infringer "know or have reason to know" of direct infringement. The district court found that Napster had both actual and constructive knowledge that its users exchanged copyrighted music. The district court also concluded that the law does not require knowledge of "specific acts of infringement" and rejected Napster's contention that because the company cannot distinguish infringing from noninfringing files, it does not "know" of the direct infringement.

It is apparent from the record that Napster has knowledge, both actual and constructive, of direct infringement.

The district court found actual knowledge because: (1) a document authored by Napster co-founder Sean Parker mentioned "the need to remain ignorant of users' real names and IP addresses 'since they are exchanging pirated music'"; and (2) the Recording Industry Association of America ("RIAA") informed Napster of more than 12,000 infringing files, some of which are still available. The district court found constructive knowledge because: (a) Napster executives have recording industry experience; (b) they have enforced intellectual property rights in other instances; (c) Napster executives have downloaded copy-righted songs from the system; and (d) they have promoted the site with "screen shots listing infringing files."

Napster claims that it is nevertheless protected from contributory liability by the teaching of *Sony Corp. v. Universal City Studios, Inc.*, 464 U.S. 417, 78 L. Ed. 2d 574, 104 S. Ct. 774 (1984). We disagree. We observe that Napster's actual, specific knowledge of direct infringement renders Sony's holding of limited assistance to Napster. We are compelled to make a clear distinction between the architecture of the Napster system and Napster's conduct in relation to the operational capacity of the system.

The Sony Court refused to hold the manufacturer and retailers of video tape recorders liable for contributory infringement despite evidence that such machines could be and were used to infringe plaintiffs' copyrighted television shows. Sony stated that if liability "is to be imposed on petitioners in this case, it must rest on the fact that they have sold equipment with constructive knowledge of the fact that their customers may use that equipment to make unauthorized copies of copy-righted material." The Sony Court declined to impute the requisite level of knowledge where the defendants made and sold equipment capable of both infringing and "substantial noninfringing uses" (adopting a modified "staple article of commerce" doctrine from patent law).

We are bound to follow Sony, and will not impute the requisite level of knowledge to Napster merely because peer-to-peer file sharing technology may be used to infringe plaintiffs' copyrights. We depart from the reasoning of the district court that Napster failed to demonstrate that its system is capable of commercially significant noninfringing uses. The district court improperly confined the use analysis to current uses, ignoring the system's capabilities. Consequently, the district court placed undue weight on the proportion of current infringing use as compared to current and future noninfringing use.... Regardless of the number of Napster's infringing versus noninfringing uses, the evidentiary record here supported the district court's finding that plaintiffs would likely prevail in establishing that Napster knew or had reason to know of its users' infringement of plaintiffs' copyrights.

... [I]f a computer system operator learns of specific infringing material available on his system and fails to purge such material from the system, the operator knows of and contributes to direct infringement. Conversely, absent any specific information which identifies infringing activity, a computer system operator cannot be liable for contributory infringement merely because the structure of the system allows for the exchange of copyrighted material. To enjoin simply because a computer network allows for infringing use would, in our opinion, violate Sony and potentially restrict activity unrelated to infringing use.

We nevertheless conclude that sufficient knowledge exists to impose contributory liability when linked to demonstrated infringing use of the Napster system. The record supports the district court's finding that Napster has actual knowledge that specific infringing material is available using its system, that it could block access to the system by suppliers of the infringing material, and that it failed to remove the material.

B. Material Contribution. Under the facts as found by the district court, Napster materially contributes to the infringing activity. Relying on *Fonovisa*, the district court concluded that "without the support services defendant provides, Napster users could not find and download the music they want with the ease of which defendant boasts." We agree that Napster provides "the site and facilities" for direct infringement. The district court correctly applied the reasoning in *Fonovisa*, and properly found that Napster materially contributes to direct infringement.

We affirm the district court's conclusion that plaintiffs have demonstrated a likelihood of success on the merits of the contributory copyright infringement claim. We will address the scope of the injunction in part VIII of this opinion.

We turn to the question whether Napster engages in vicarious copyright infringement. Vicarious copyright liability is an "outgrowth" of respondeat superior. In the context of copyright law, vicarious liability extends beyond an employer/employee relationship to cases in which a defendant "has the right and ability to supervise the infringing activity and also has a direct financial interest in such activities." ...

A. Financial Benefit. The district court determined that plaintiffs had demonstrated they would likely succeed in establishing that Napster has a direct financial interest in the infringing activity. We agree. Financial benefit exists where the availability of infringing material "acts as a 'draw' for customers." Ample evidence supports the district court's finding that Napster's future revenue is directly dependent upon "increases in user-base." More users register with the Napster system as the "quality and quantity of available music increases." We conclude that the district court did not err in determining that Napster financially benefits from the availability of protected works on its system.

B. Supervision. The district court determined that Napster has the right and ability to supervise its users' conduct. We agree in part. The ability to block infringers' access to a particular environment for any reason whatsoever is evidence of the right and ability to supervise. Here, plaintiffs have demonstrated that Napster retains the right to control access to its system. Napster has an express reservation of rights policy, stating on its website that it expressly reserves the "right to refuse service and terminate accounts in [its] discretion, including, but not limited to, if Napster believes that user conduct violates applicable law ... or for any reason in Napster's sole discretion, with or without cause."

To escape imposition of vicarious liability, the reserved right to police must be exercised to its fullest extent. Turning a blind eye to detectable acts of infringement for the sake of profit gives rise to liability. The district court correctly determined that Napster had the right and ability to police its system and failed to exercise that right to prevent the exchange of copyrighted material. The district court, however, failed to recognize that the boundaries of the premises that Napster "controls and patrols" are limited. Put differently, Napster's reserved "right and ability" to police is cabined by the system's current architecture. As shown by the record, the Napster system does not "read" the content of indexed files, other than to check that they are in the proper MP3 format.

Napster, however, has the ability to locate infringing material listed on its search indices, and the right to terminate users' access to the system. The file name indices, therefore, are within the "premises" that Napster has the ability to police. We recognize that the files are user named and may not match copyrighted material exactly (for example, the artist or song could be spelled wrong). For Napster to function effectively, however, file names must reasonably or roughly correspond to the material contained in the files, otherwise no user could ever locate any desired music. As a practical matter, Napster, its users and the record company plaintiffs have equal access to infringing material by employing Napster's "search function."

Our review of the record requires us to accept the district court's conclusion that plaintiffs have demonstrated a likelihood of success on the merits of the vicarious copyright infringement claim. Napster's failure to police the system's "premises," combined with a showing that Napster financially benefits from the continuing availability of infringing files on its system, leads to the imposition of vicarious liability. We address the scope of the injunction in part VIII of this opinion. [The Court next addressed and rejected protection for Napster under § 1008 of the Audio Home Recording Act of 1992 and § 512 of the Digital Millennium Copyright Act as well as affirmative defenses of waiver, implied license and copyright misuse.]

The district court correctly recognized that a preliminary injunction against Napster's participation in copyright infringement is not only warranted but required. We believe, however, that the scope of the injunction needs modification in light of our opinion. Specifically, we reiterate that contributory liability may potentially be imposed only to the extent that Napster: (1) receives reasonable knowledge of specific infringing files with copyrighted musical compositions and sound recordings; (2) knows or should know that such files are available on the Napster system; and (3) fails to act to prevent viral distribution of the works. The mere existence of the Napster system, absent actual notice and Napster's demonstrated failure to remove the offending material, is insufficient to impose contributory liability.

Conversely, Napster may be vicariously liable when it fails to affirmatively use its ability to patrol its system and preclude access to potentially infringing files listed in its search index. Napster has both the ability to use its search function to identify infringing musical recordings and the right to bar participation of users who engage in the transmission of infringing files.

The preliminary injunction which we stayed is overbroad because it places on Napster the entire burden of ensuring that no "copying, downloading, uploading, transmitting, or distributing" of plaintiffs' works occur on the system. As stated, we place the burden on plaintiffs to provide notice to Napster of copyrighted works and files containing such works available on the Napster system before Napster has the duty to disable access to the offending content. Napster, however, also bears the burden of policing the system within the limits of the system. Here, we recognize that this is not an exact science in that the files are user named. In crafting the injunction on remand, the district court should recognize that Napster's system does not currently appear to allow Napster access to users' MP3 files.

Based on our decision to remand, Napster's additional arguments on appeal going to the scope of the injunction need not be addressed. We, however, briefly address Napster's First Amendment argument so that it is not reasserted on remand. Napster contends that the present injunction violates the First Amendment because it is broader than necessary. The company asserts two distinct free speech rights: (1) its right to publish a "directory" (here, the search index) and (2) its users' right to exchange information. We note that First Amendment concerns in copyright are allayed by the presence of the fair use doctrine. There was a preliminary determination here that Napster users are not fair users. Uses of copyrighted material that are not fair uses are rightfully enjoined....

Napster contends that the district court should have imposed a monetary penalty by way of a compulsory royalty in place of an injunction.... Imposing a compulsory royalty payment schedule would give Napster an "easy out" of this case. If such royalties were imposed, Napster would avoid penalties for any future violation of an injunction, statutory copyright damages and any possible criminal penalties for continuing infringement. The royalty structure would also grant Napster the luxury of either choosing to continue and pay royalties or shut down. On the other hand, the wronged parties would be forced to do business with a company that profits from the wrongful use of intellectual properties. Plaintiffs would lose the power to control their intellectual property: they could not make a business decision *not* to license their property to Napster, and, in the event they planned to do business with Napster, compulsory royalties would take away the copyright holders' ability to negotiate the terms of any contractual arrangement....

We affirm in part, reverse in part and remand.

MGM Studios, Inc. v. Grokster Ltd.

545 U.S. 913 (2005)

JUSTICE SOUTER delivered the opinion of the Court.

The question is under what circumstances the distributor of a product capable of both lawful and unlawful use is liable for acts of copyright infringement by third parties using the product. We hold that one who distributes a device with the object of promoting its use to infringe copyright, as shown by clear expression or other affirmative steps taken to foster infringement, is liable for the resulting acts of infringement by third parties.

Respondents, Grokster, Ltd., and StreamCast Networks, Inc., defendants in the trial court, distribute free software products that allow computer users to share electronic files through peer-to-peer networks, so called because users' computers communicate directly with each other, not through central servers. The advantage of peer-to-peer networks over information networks of other types shows up in their substantial and growing popularity. Because they need no central computer server to mediate the exchange of information or files among users, the high-bandwidth communications capacity for a server may be dispensed with, and the need for costly server storage space is eliminated. Since copies of a file (particularly a popular one) are available on many users' computers, file requests and retrievals may be faster than on other types of networks, and since file exchanges do not travel through a server, communications can take place between any computers that remain connected to the network without risk that a glitch in the server will disable the network in its entirety. Given these benefits in security, cost, and efficiency, peer-to-peer networks are employed to store and distribute electronic files by universities, government agencies, corporations, and libraries, among others.[25]

Other users of peer-to-peer networks include individual recipients of Grokster's and StreamCast's software, and although the networks that they enjoy through using the software can be used to share any type of digital file, they have prominently employed those networks in sharing copyrighted music and video files without authorization. A group of copyright holders (MGM for short, but including motion picture studios, recording companies, songwriters, and music publishers) sued Grokster and StreamCast for their users' copyright infringements, alleging that they knowingly and intentionally distributed their software to enable users to reproduce and distribute the copyrighted works in violation of the Copyright Act, 17 U.S.C. § 101 et seq. (2000 ed. and Supp. II). MGM sought damages and an injunction.

Discovery during the litigation revealed the way the software worked, the business aims of each defendant company, and the predilections of the users. Grokster's eponymous software employs what is known as FastTrack technology, a protocol developed by others and licensed to Grokster. StreamCast distributes a very similar product except that its software, called Morpheus, relies on what is known as Gnutella technology. A user who downloads and installs either software possesses the protocol to send requests for files directly to the computers of others using software compatible with FastTrack or Gnutella. On the FastTrack network opened by the Grokster software, the user's request goes to a computer given an indexing capacity by the software and designated a supernode, or to some other computer with comparable power and capacity to collect temporary indexes of the files available on the computers of users connected to it. The supernode (or indexing computer) searches its own index and may communicate the search request to other supernodes. If the file is found, the supernode discloses its location to the computer requesting it, and the requesting user can download the file directly from the computer located. The copied file is placed in a designated sharing folder on the requesting user's computer, where it is available for other users to download in turn, along with any other file in that folder.

In the Gnutella network made available by Morpheus, the process is mostly the same, except that in some versions of the Gnutella protocol there are no supernodes....

Although Grokster and StreamCast do not therefore know when particular files are copied, a few searches using their software would show what is available on the networks the software reaches. MGM commissioned a statistician to conduct a systematic search, and his study showed that nearly 90% of the files available for download on the FastTrack system were copyrighted works.[26] Grokster and StreamCast dispute this figure, raising methodological problems and arguing that free copying even of copyrighted works may be authorized by the rightholders. They also argue that potential noninfringing uses of their software are significant in kind, even if infrequent in practice. Some musical per-

---

25. Peer-to-peer networks have disadvantages as well. Searches on peer-to-peer networks may not reach and uncover all available files because search requests may not be transmitted to every computer on the network. There may be redundant copies of popular files. The creator of the software has no incentive to minimize storage or bandwidth consumption, the costs of which are borne by every user of the network. Most relevant here, it is more difficult to control the content of files available for retrieval and the behavior of users.

26. By comparison, evidence introduced by the plaintiffs in A & M Records, Inc. v. Napster, Inc., 239 F.3d 1004 (9th Cir. 2001), showed that 87% of files available on the Napster filesharing network were copyrighted. *Id.* at 1013.

formers, for example, have gained new audiences by distributing their copyrighted works for free across peer-to-peer networks, and some distributors of unprotected content have used peer-to-peer networks to disseminate files, Shakespeare being an example. Indeed, StreamCast has given Morpheus users the opportunity to download the briefs in this very case, though their popularity has not been quantified.

As for quantification, the parties' anecdotal and statistical evidence entered thus far to show the content available on the FastTrack and Gnutella networks does not say much about which files are actually downloaded by users, and no one can say how often the software is used to obtain copies of unprotected material. But MGM's evidence gives reason to think that the vast majority of users' downloads are acts of infringement, and because well over 100 million copies of the software in question are known to have been downloaded, and billions of files are shared across the FastTrack and Gnutella networks each month, the probable scope of copyright infringement is staggering.

Grokster and StreamCast concede the infringement in most downloads, and it is uncontested that they are aware that users employ their software primarily to download copyrighted files, even if the decentralized FastTrack and Gnutella networks fail to reveal which files are being copied, and when. From time to time, moreover, the companies have learned about their users' infringement directly, as from users who have sent e-mail to each company with questions about playing copyrighted movies they had downloaded, to whom the companies have responded with guidance. And MGM notified the companies of 8 million copyrighted files that could be obtained using their software.

Grokster and StreamCast are not, however, merely passive recipients of information about infringing use. The record is replete with evidence that from the moment Grokster and StreamCast began to distribute their free software, each one clearly voiced the objective that recipients use it to download copyrighted works, and each took active steps to encourage infringement.

After the notorious file-sharing service, Napster, was sued by copyright holders for facilitation of copyright infringement, StreamCast gave away a software program of a kind known as OpenNap, designed as compatible with the Napster program and open to Napster users for downloading files from other Napster and OpenNap users' computers. Evidence indicates that "it was always [StreamCast's] intent to use [its OpenNap network] to be able to capture email addresses of [its] initial target market so that [it] could promote [its] StreamCast Morpheus interface to them," indeed, the OpenNap program was engineered "'to leverage Napster's 50 million user base.'"

StreamCast monitored both the number of users downloading its OpenNap program and the number of music files they downloaded. It also used the resulting OpenNap network to distribute copies of the Morpheus software and to encourage users to adopt it. Internal company documents indicate that StreamCast hoped to attract large numbers of former Napster users if that company was shut down by court order or otherwise, and that StreamCast planned to be the next Napster. A kit developed by StreamCast to be delivered to advertisers, for example, contained press articles about StreamCast's potential to capture former Napster users, and it introduced itself to some potential advertisers as a company "which is similar to what Napster was." It broadcast banner advertisements to users of other Napster-compatible software, urging them to adopt its OpenNap. An internal e-mail from a company executive stated: "'We have put this network in place so that when Napster pulls the plug on their free service ... or if the Court orders them shut down prior to that ... we will be positioned to capture the flood of their 32 million users that will be actively looking for an alternative.'"

Thus, StreamCast developed promotional materials to market its service as the best Napster alternative. One proposed advertisement read: "Napster Inc. has announced that it will soon begin charging you a fee. That's if the courts don't order it shut down first. What will you do to get around it?" Another proposed ad touted StreamCast's software as the "# 1 alternative to Napster" and asked "when the lights went off at Napster … where did the users go?" StreamCast even planned to flaunt the illegal uses of its software; when it launched the OpenNap network, the chief technology officer of the company averred that "the goal is to get in trouble with the law and get sued. It's the best way to get in the news."

The evidence that Grokster sought to capture the market of former Napster users is sparser but revealing, for Grokster launched its own OpenNap system called Swaptor and inserted digital codes into its Web site so that computer users using Web search engines to look for "Napster" or "free filesharing" would be directed to the Grokster Web site, where they could download the Grokster software. And Grokster's name is an apparent derivative of Napster.

StreamCast's executives monitored the number of songs by certain commercial artists available on their networks, and an internal communication indicates they aimed to have a larger number of copyrighted songs available on their networks than other file-sharing networks. The point, of course, would be to attract users of a mind to infringe, just as it would be with their promotional materials developed showing copyrighted songs as examples of the kinds of files available through Morpheus. Morpheus in fact allowed users to search specifically for "Top 40" songs, which were inevitably copyrighted. Similarly, Grokster sent users a newsletter promoting its ability to provide particular, popular copyrighted materials.

In addition to this evidence of express promotion, marketing, and intent to promote further, the business models employed by Grokster and StreamCast confirm that their principal object was use of their software to download copyrighted works. Grokster and StreamCast receive no revenue from users, who obtain the software itself for nothing. Instead, both companies generate income by selling advertising space, and they stream the advertising to Grokster and Morpheus users while they are employing the programs. As the number of users of each program increases, advertising opportunities become worth more. While there is doubtless some demand for free Shakespeare, the evidence shows that substantive volume is a function of free access to copyrighted work. Users seeking Top 40 songs, for example, or the latest release by Modest Mouse, are certain to be far more numerous than those seeking a free Decameron, and Grokster and StreamCast translated that demand into dollars.

Finally, there is no evidence that either company made an effort to filter copyrighted material from users' downloads or otherwise impede the sharing of copyrighted files. Although Grokster appears to have sent e-mails warning users about infringing content when it received threatening notice from the copyright holders, it never blocked anyone from continuing to use its software to share copyrighted files. StreamCast not only rejected another company's offer of help to monitor infringement, but blocked the Internet Protocol addresses of entities it believed were trying to engage in such monitoring on its networks. . . .

The District Court held that those who used the Grokster and Morpheus software to download copyrighted media files directly infringed MGM's copyrights, a conclusion not contested on appeal, but the court nonetheless granted summary judgment in favor of Grokster and StreamCast as to any liability arising from distribution of the then current versions of their software. Distributing that software gave rise to no liability in the court's view, because its use did not provide the distributors with actual knowledge of specific acts of infringement.

The Court of Appeals affirmed. In the court's analysis, a defendant was liable as a contributory infringer when it had knowledge of direct infringement and materially contributed to the infringement. But the court read *Sony Corp. of America v. Universal City Studios, Inc.*, 464 U.S. 417 (1984), as holding that distribution of a commercial product capable of substantial noninfringing uses could not give rise to contributory liability for infringement unless the distributor had actual knowledge of specific instances of infringement and failed to act on that knowledge. The fact that the software was capable of substantial noninfringing uses in the Ninth Circuit's view meant that Grokster and Stream-Cast were not liable, because they had no such actual knowledge, owing to the decentralized architecture of their software. The court also held that Grokster and StreamCast did not materially contribute to their users' infringement because it was the users themselves who searched for, retrieved, and stored the infringing files, with no involvement by the defendants beyond providing the software in the first place.

The Ninth Circuit also considered whether Grokster and StreamCast could be liable under a theory of vicarious infringement. The court held against liability because the defendants did not monitor or control the use of the software, had no agreed-upon right or current ability to supervise its use, and had no independent duty to police infringement....

MGM and many of the *amici* fault the Court of Appeals' holding for upsetting a sound balance between the respective values of supporting creative pursuits through copyright protection and promoting innovation in new communication technologies by limiting the incidence of liability for copyright infringement. The more artistic protection is favored, the more technological innovation may be discouraged; the administration of copyright law is an exercise in managing the trade-off.

The tension between the two values is the subject of this case, with its claim that digital distribution of copyrighted material threatens copyright holders as never before, because every copy is identical to the original, copying is easy, and many people (especially the young) use file-sharing software to download copyrighted works. This very breadth of the software's use may well draw the public directly into the debate over copyright policy ... As the case has been presented to us, these fears are said to be offset by the different concern that imposing liability, not only on infringers but on distributors of software based on its potential for unlawful use, could limit further development of beneficial technologies.

The argument for imposing indirect liability in this case is, however, a powerful one, given the number of infringing downloads that occur every day using StreamCast's and Grokster's software. When a widely shared service or product is used to commit infringement, it may be impossible to enforce rights in the protected work effectively against all direct infringers, the only practical alternative being to go against the distributor of the copying device for secondary liability on a theory of contributory or vicarious infringement.

One infringes contributorily by intentionally inducing or encouraging direct infringement, and infringes vicariously by profiting from direct infringement while declining to exercise a right to stop or limit it.[27] Although "the Copyright Act does not

---

27. We stated in *Sony Corp. of America v. Universal City Studios, Inc.*, 464 U.S. 417 (1984), that "'the lines between direct infringement, contributory infringement and vicarious liability are not clearly drawn'.... Reasoned analysis of [the Sony plaintiffs' contributory infringement claim] necessarily entails consideration of arguments and case law which may also be forwarded under the other labels, and indeed the parties ... rely upon such arguments and authority in support of their respec-

expressly render anyone liable for infringement committed by another," *Sony Corp. v. Universal City Studios*, 464 U.S. at 434....

[W]here an article is "good for nothing else" but infringement, there is no legitimate public interest in its unlicensed availability, and there is no injustice in presuming or imputing an intent to infringe. Conversely, the doctrine absolves the equivocal conduct of selling an item with substantial lawful as well as unlawful uses, and limits liability to instances of more acute fault than the mere understanding that some of one's products will be misused. It leaves breathing room for innovation and a vigorous commerce.

The parties and many of the *amici* in this case think the key to resolving it is the *Sony* rule and, in particular, what it means for a product to be "capable of commercially significant noninfringing uses." MGM advances the argument that granting summary judgment to Grokster and StreamCast as to their current activities gave too much weight to the value of innovative technology, and too little to the copyrights infringed by users of their software, given that 90% of works available on one of the networks was shown to be copyrighted. Assuming the remaining 10% to be its noninfringing use, MGM says this should not qualify as "substantial," and the Court should quantify Sony to the extent of holding that a product used "principally" for infringement does not qualify. As mentioned before, Grokster and StreamCast reply by citing evidence that their software can be used to reproduce public domain works, and they point to copyright holders who actually encourage copying. Even if infringement is the principal practice with their software today, they argue, the noninfringing uses are significant and will grow.

We agree with MGM that the Court of Appeals misapplied *Sony*, which it read as limiting secondary liability quite beyond the circumstances to which the case applied. *Sony* barred secondary liability based on presuming or imputing intent to cause infringement solely from the design or distribution of a product capable of substantial lawful use, which the distributor knows is in fact used for infringement. The Ninth Circuit has read *Sony*'s limitation to mean that whenever a product is capable of substantial lawful use, the producer can never be held contributorily liable for third parties' infringing use of it; it read the rule as being this broad, even when an actual purpose to cause infringing use is shown by evidence independent of design and distribution of the product, unless the distributors had "specific knowledge of infringement at a time at which they contributed to the infringement, and failed to act upon that information." Because the Circuit found the StreamCast and Grokster software capable of substantial lawful use, it concluded on the basis of its reading of *Sony* that neither company could be held liable, since there was no showing that their software, being without any central server, afforded them knowledge of specific unlawful uses.

This view of *Sony*, however, was error, converting the case from one about liability resting on imputed intent to one about liability on any theory. Because *Sony* did not displace other theories of secondary liability, and because we find below that it was error to grant summary judgment to the companies on MGM's inducement claim, we do not revisit *Sony* further, as MGM requests, to add a more quantified description of the point of balance between protection and commerce when liability rests solely on distribution

---

tive positions on the issue of contributory infringement," *id.* at 435, n.17 (quoting *Universal City Studios, Inc. v. Sony Corp.*, 480 F. Supp. 429, 457–458 (C.D. Cal. 1979)). In the present case MGM has argued a vicarious liability theory, which allows imposition of liability when the defendant profits directly from the infringement and has a right and ability to supervise the direct infringer, even if the defendant initially lacks knowledge of the infringement. Because we resolve the case based on an inducement theory, there is no need to analyze separately MGM's vicarious liability theory.

with knowledge that unlawful use will occur. It is enough to note that the Ninth Circuit's judgment rested on an erroneous understanding of *Sony* and to leave further consideration of the *Sony* rule for a day when that may be required.

Sony's rule limits imputing culpable intent as a matter of law from the characteristics or uses of a distributed product. But nothing in *Sony* requires courts to ignore evidence of intent if there is such evidence, and the case was never meant to foreclose rules of fault-based liability derived from the common law. Thus, where evidence goes beyond a product's characteristics or the knowledge that it may be put to infringing uses, and shows statements or actions directed to promoting infringement, *Sony's* staple-article rule will not preclude liability.

The classic case of direct evidence of unlawful purpose occurs when one induces commission of infringement by another, or "entices or persuades another" to infringe, Black's Law Dictionary 790 (8th ed. 2004), as by advertising. Thus at common law a copyright or patent defendant who "not only expected but invoked [infringing use] by advertisement" was liable for infringement "on principles recognized in every part of the law."

The rule on inducement of infringement as developed in the early cases is no different today.[28] Evidence of "active steps ... taken to encourage direct infringement," such as advertising an infringing use or instructing how to engage in an infringing use, show an affirmative intent that the product be used to infringe, and a showing that infringement was encouraged overcomes the law's reluctance to find liability when a defendant merely sells a commercial product suitable for some lawful use.

For the same reasons that *Sony* took the staple-article doctrine of patent law as a model for its copyright safe-harbor rule, the inducement rule, too, is a sensible one for copyright. We adopt it here, holding that one who distributes a device with the object of promoting its use to infringe copyright, as shown by clear expression or other affirmative steps taken to foster infringement, is liable for the resulting acts of infringement by third parties. We are, of course, mindful of the need to keep from trenching on regular commerce or discouraging the development of technologies with lawful and unlawful potential. Accordingly, just as *Sony* did not find intentional inducement despite the knowledge of the VCR manufacturer that its device could be used to infringe, mere knowledge of infringing potential or of actual infringing uses would not be enough here to subject a distributor to liability. Nor would ordinary acts incident to product distribution, such as offering customers technical support or product updates, support liability in themselves. The inducement rule, instead, premises liability on purposeful, culpable expression and conduct, and thus does nothing to compromise legitimate commerce or discourage innovation having a lawful promise.

The only apparent question about treating MGM's evidence as sufficient to withstand summary judgment under the theory of inducement goes to the need on MGM's part to adduce evidence that StreamCast and Grokster communicated an inducing message to their software users. The classic instance of inducement is by advertisement or solicitation that broadcasts a message designed to stimulate others to commit violations....

In StreamCast's case, of course, the evidence just described was supplemented by other unequivocal indications of unlawful purpose in the internal communications and advertising designs aimed at Napster users ("When the lights went off at Napster ... where did the users go?") Whether the messages were communicated is not to the point on this record. The function of the message in the theory of inducement is to prove by a defen-

---

28. Inducement has been codified in patent law. *Ibid.*

dant's own statements that his unlawful purpose disqualifies him from claiming protection (and incidentally to point to actual violators likely to be found among those who hear or read the message). Proving that a message was sent out, then, is the preeminent but not exclusive way of showing that active steps were taken with the purpose of bringing about infringing acts, and of showing that infringing acts took place by using the device distributed. Here, the summary judgment record is replete with other evidence that Grokster and StreamCast, unlike the manufacturer and distributor in *Sony*, acted with a purpose to cause copyright violations by use of software suitable for illegal use.

Three features of this evidence of intent are particularly notable. First, each company showed itself to be aiming to satisfy a known source of demand for copyright infringement, the market comprising former Napster users. StreamCast's internal documents made constant reference to Napster, it initially distributed its Morpheus software through an OpenNap program compatible with Napster, it advertised its OpenNap program to Napster users, and its Morpheus software functions as Napster did except that it could be used to distribute more kinds of files, including copyrighted movies and software programs. Grokster's name is apparently derived from Napster, it too initially offered an OpenNap program, its software's function is likewise comparable to Napster's, and it attempted to divert queries for Napster onto its own Web site. Grokster and StreamCast's efforts to supply services to former Napster users, deprived of a mechanism to copy and distribute what were overwhelmingly infringing files, indicate a principal, if not exclusive, intent on the part of each to bring about infringement.

Second, this evidence of unlawful objective is given added significance by MGM's showing that neither company attempted to develop filtering tools or other mechanisms to diminish the infringing activity using their software. While the Ninth Circuit treated the defendants' failure to develop such tools as irrelevant because they lacked an independent duty to monitor their users' activity, we think this evidence underscores Grokster's and StreamCast's intentional facilitation of their users' infringement.[29]

Third, there is a further complement to the direct evidence of unlawful objective. It is useful to recall that StreamCast and Grokster make money by selling advertising space, by directing ads to the screens of computers employing their software. As the record shows, the more the software is used, the more ads are sent out and the greater the advertising revenue becomes. Since the extent of the software's use determines the gain to the distributors, the commercial sense of their enterprise turns on high-volume use, which the record shows is infringing. This evidence alone would not justify an inference of unlawful intent, but viewed in the context of the entire record its import is clear.

The unlawful objective is unmistakable....

In sum, this case is significantly different from *Sony* and reliance on that case to rule in favor of StreamCast and Grokster was error. *Sony* dealt with a claim of liability based solely on distributing a product with alternative lawful and unlawful uses, with knowledge that some users would follow the unlawful course. The case struck a balance between the interests of protection and innovation by holding that the product's capability of substantial lawful employment should bar the imputation of fault and consequent secondary liability for the unlawful acts of others....

---

29. Of course, in the absence of other evidence of intent, a court would be unable to find contributory infringement liability merely based on a failure to take affirmative steps to prevent infringement, if the device otherwise was capable of substantial noninfringing uses. Such a holding would tread too close to the *Sony* safe harbor.

There is substantial evidence in MGM's favor on all elements of inducement, and summary judgment in favor of Grokster and StreamCast was error. On remand, reconsideration of MGM's motion for summary judgment will be in order. The judgment of the Court of Appeals is vacated, and the case is remanded for further proceedings consistent with this opinion.

[The precise role of *Sony* continues to be debated. The Court split between concurrences by Justices Ginsburg and Breyer on whether Grokster's product is "capable of 'substantial' or 'commercially significant' noninfringing uses." Each concurrence had three votes.]

Capitol Records, Inc. v. Thomas-Rasset
692 F.3d 899 (2012)

This appeal arises from a dispute between several recording companies and Jammie Thomas-Rasset. There is a complicated procedural history involving three jury trials, but for purposes of appeal, it is undisputed that Thomas-Rasset willfully infringed copyrights of twenty-four sound recordings by engaging in file-sharing on the Internet. After a first jury found Thomas-Rasset liable and awarded damages of $222,000, the district court granted a new trial on the ground that the jury instructions incorrectly provided that the Copyright Act forbids making sound recordings available for distribution on a peer-to-peer network, regardless of whether there is proof of "actual distribution." A second jury found Thomas-Rasset liable for willful copyright infringement under a different instruction, and awarded statutory damages of $1,920,000. The district court remitted the award to $54,000, and the companies opted for a new trial on damages. A third jury awarded statutory damages of $1,500,000, but the district court ultimately ruled that the maximum amount permitted by the Due Process Clause of the Fifth Amendment was $54,000 and reduced the verdict accordingly. The court also enjoined Thomas-Rasset from taking certain actions with respect to copyrighted recordings owned by the recording companies.

The companies appeal two aspects of the remedy ordered by the district court. They object to the district court's ruling on damages, and they seek an award of $222,000, which was the amount awarded by the jury in the first trial. They also seek a broader injunction that bars Thomas-Rasset from making any of their sound recordings available to the public. For tactical reasons, the companies do not seek reinstatement of the third jury's award of $1,500,000. They urge instead that this court should reverse the district court's order granting a new trial, rule that the Copyright Act does protect a right to "making available" sound recordings, reinstate the first jury's award of $222,000, and direct entry of a broader injunction. In a cross-appeal, Thomas-Rasset argues that *any* award of statutory damages is unconstitutional, and urges us to vacate the award of damages altogether.

For reasons set forth below, we conclude that the recording companies are entitled to the remedies they seek: damages of $222,000 and a broadened injunction that forbids Thomas-Rasset to make available sound recordings for distribution. But because the verdicts returned by the second and third juries are sufficient to justify these remedies, it is unnecessary for this court to consider the merits of the district court's order granting a new trial after the first verdict. Important though the "making available" legal issue may be to the recording companies, they are not entitled to an opinion on an issue of law that is unnecessary for the remedies sought or to a freestanding decision on whether Thomas-Rasset violated the law by making recordings available.

Capitol Records, Inc., Sony BMG Music Entertainment, Arista Records LLC, Inter-scope Records, Warner Bros. Records, and UMG Recordings, Inc., are recording companies that own the copyrights to large catalogs of music recordings. In 2005, they undertook to investigate suspected infringement of these copyrights. MediaSentry, an online investigative firm hired by the recording companies, discovered that an individual with the username "tereastarr" was participating in unauthorized file sharing on the peer-to-peer network KaZaA.

During the relevant time period, KaZaA was a file-sharing computer program that allowed its users to search for and download specific files from other users. KaZaA users shared files using a share folder. A share folder is a location on the user's computer in which the user places files—such as audio or video recordings—that she wants to make available for other users to download. KaZaA allowed its users to access other users' share folders, view the files in the folder, and download copies of files from the folder.

MediaSentry accessed tereastarr's share folder. The investigative firm determined that the user had downloaded copyrighted songs and was making those songs available for download by other KaZaA users. MediaSentry took screen shots of tereastarr's share folder, which included over 1,700 music files, and downloaded samples of the files. But MediaSentry was unable to collect direct evidence that other users had downloaded the files from tereastarr. MediaSentry then used KaZaA to send two instant messages to tereastarr, notifying the user of potential copyright infringement. Tereastarr did not respond to the messages. MediaSentry also determined tereastarr's IP address, and traced the address to an Internet service account in Duluth, Minnesota, provided by Charter Communications. MediaSentry compiled this data in a report that it prepared for the recording companies.

Using the information provided by MediaSentry, the recording companies, through the Recording Industry Association of America (RIAA), issued a subpoena to Charter Communications requesting the name of the person associated with tereastarr's IP address. Charter informed the RIAA that the IP address belonged to Jammie Thomas-Rasset. The RIAA then sent a letter to Thomas-Rasset informing her that she had been identified as engaging in unauthorized trading of music and inviting her to contact them to discuss the situation and settle the matter. Thomas-Rasset contacted the RIAA as directed in the letter and engaged in settlement conversations with the organization. The parties were unable to resolve the matter.

In 2006, the recording companies sued Thomas-Rasset, seeking statutory damages and injunctive relief for willful copyright infringement under the Copyright Act, 17 U.S.C. § 101 *et seq.* They alleged that Thomas-Rasset violated their exclusive right to reproduction and distribution under 17 U.S.C. § 106 by impermissibly downloading, distributing, and making available for distribution twenty-four copyrighted sound recordings.

A jury trial was held in October 2007. At trial, Thomas-Rasset conceded that "tereastarr" is a username that she uses regularly for Internet and computer accounts. She admitted familiarity with and interest in some of the artists of works found in the tereastarr KaZaA account. She also acknowledged that she wrote a case study during college on the legality of Napster—another peer-to-peer file sharing program—and knew that Napster was shut down because it was illegal. Nonetheless, Thomas-Rasset testified that she had never heard of KaZaA before this case, did not have KaZaA on her computer, and did not use KaZaA to download files. The jury also heard evidence from a forensic investigator that Thomas-Rasset removed and replaced the hard drive on her computer with a new hard drive after investigators notified her of her potential infringement. The new hard drive did not contain the files at issue.

At the close of evidence, the district court instructed the jury that one who reproduces or distributes a copyrighted work without license infringes the copyright. The court's instructions defined "reproduction" to include "[t]he act of downloading copyrighted sound recordings on a peer-to-peer network." The court also instructed that the act of "making copyrighted sound recordings available for electronic distribution on a peer-to-peer network, without license from the copyright owners, violates the copyright owners' exclusive right of distribution, regardless of whether actual distribution has been shown." The jury found Thomas-Rasset liable for willful infringement and awarded the recording companies statutory damages of $9,250 per work, for a total of $222,000.

Thomas-Rasset moved for a new trial or, in the alternative, for a remittitur, arguing that the size of the jury's statutory damages award violated her rights under the Due Process Clause. The United States intervened to defend the constitutionality of the statute on statutory damages, 17 U.S.C. § 504(c). The recording companies also filed a post-trial motion, seeking to amend the judgment to include an injunction enjoining Thomas-Rasset from infringing the recording companies' copyrights by "using the Internet or any online media distribution system to reproduce (*i.e.*, download) any of Plaintiffs' Recordings, to distribute (*i.e.*, upload) any of Plaintiffs' Recordings, or to make any of Plaintiffs' Recordings available for distribution to the public."

Several months later, the district court *sua sponte* raised the issue whether it erred by instructing the jury that making sound recordings available for distribution on a peer-to-peer network violates a copyright owners' exclusive right to distribution, "regardless of whether actual distribution has been shown." The parties filed supplemental briefs in which the recording companies defended the court's instruction and Thomas-Rasset argued that the court erred when it instructed the jury on the "making available" issue. After a hearing, the district court granted Thomas-Rasset's motion for a new trial on this alternative ground, holding that making a work available to the public is not "distribution" under 17 U.S.C. § 106(3). The issue whether making copyrighted works available to the public is a right protected by § 106(3) has divided the district courts. *Compare, e.g., Atl. Recording Corp. v. Howell*, 554 F.Supp.2d 976, 981–84 (D.Ariz.2008), *and London-Sire Records v. Doe 1*, 542 F.Supp.2d 153, 176 (D.Mass.2008), *with Motown Record Co. v. DePietro*, No. 04-CV-2246, 2007 WL 576284, at *3 (E.D.Pa. Feb. 16, 2007), *and Warner Bros. Records, Inc., v. Payne*, No. W-06-CA-051, 2006 WL 2844415, at *3 (W.D.Tex. July 17, 2006).

The district court convened a second trial in June 2009, at which the recording companies produced substantially the same evidence of Thomas-Rasset's liability. At this trial, however, Thomas-Rasset attempted to deflect responsibility by suggesting for the first time that her children and former boyfriend might have done the downloading and file-sharing attributed to the "tereastarr" username. The court again instructed the jury that reproduction or distribution constituted copyright infringement. But this time, the court omitted reference to making works available and instructed the jury that "[t]he act of distributing copyrighted sound recordings to other users on a peer-to-peer network, without license from the copyright owners, violates the copyright owners' exclusive distribution right." The jury again found Thomas-Rasset liable for willful infringement, and awarded the recording companies statutory damages of $80,000 per work, for a total of $1,920,000.

Following the second trial, Thomas-Rasset filed a post-trial motion in which she argued that any statutory damages award would be unconstitutional in her case, but in the alternative that the court should reduce the jury's award either through remittitur or based on the Due Process Clause. The district court declined to rule on the constitutional issue and instead remitted damages to $2,250 per work, for a total of $54,000, on the ground that the jury's award was "shocking." The recording companies declined the re-mitted award and exercised their right to a new trial on damages.

A third trial was held in November 2010, and the only question for the jury was the amount of statutory damages. The jury awarded the recording companies statutory dam-ages of $62,500 per work, for a total of $1,500,000.

Thomas-Rasset then moved to alter or amend the judgment, again arguing that any statu-tory damages award would be unconstitutional, but alternatively that the district court should reduce the award under the Due Process Clause. The district court, relying in part on the now-vacated decision in *Sony BMG Music Entm't v. Tenenbaum*, 721 F.Supp.2d 85 (D.Mass.2010), *vacated in relevant part by*, 660 F.3d 487 (1st Cir.2011), granted Thomas-Rasset's motion and reduced the award to $2,250 per work, for a total of $54,000. The court ruled that this amount was the maximum award permitted by the Due Process Clause. The district court also entered a permanent injunction against Thomas-Rasset, but refused to include language enjoining her from "making available" copyrighted works for distri-bution to the public.

The recording companies appeal the judgment of the district court, arguing that the district court erred in (1) granting a new trial based on the "making available" instruc-tion in the first trial, and (2) holding that the Due Process Clause limits statutory dam-ages to $2,250 per infringed work. They request that we reinstate and affirm the first jury's $222,000 award, and remand with instructions to grant an injunction prohibiting Thomas-Rasset from making the copyrighted works available to the public. Thomas-Rasset cross-appeals, arguing that even an award of the minimum statutory damages authorized by the Copyright Act would be unconstitutional....

For the reasons set forth below, we conclude that when the district court entered judg-ment after the verdict in the third trial, the court should have enjoined Thomas-Rasset from making copyrighted works available to the public, whether or not that conduct by itself violates rights under the Copyright Act. We also conclude that statutory damages of at least $222,000 were constitutional, and that the district court erred in holding that the Due Process Clause allowed statutory damages of only $54,000. We therefore will vacate the district court's judgment and remand with directions to enter a judgment that in-cludes those remedies....

After the third trial, the district court entered an injunction that prohibits Thomas-Ras-set from "using the Internet or any online media distribution system to reproduce (*i.e.,* download) any of Plaintiffs' Recordings, or to distribute (*i.e.,* upload) any of Plaintiff's Recordings." The recording companies urged the district court to amend the judgment to enjoin Thomas-Rasset from making any of their sound recordings available for distrib-ution to the public through an online media distribution system. The district court de-clined to do so on the ground that the Copyright Act does not provide an exclusive right to making recordings available. The court further reasoned that the injunction as granted was adequate to address the concerns of the companies....

We conclude that the district court's ruling was based on an error of law. Even as-suming for the sake of analysis that the district court's ruling on the scope of the Copy-right Act was correct, a district court has authority to issue a broad injunction in cases where "a proclivity for unlawful conduct has been shown." The district court is even per-mitted to "enjoin certain otherwise lawful conduct" where "the defendant's conduct has demonstrated that prohibiting only unlawful conduct would not effectively protect the plain-tiff's rights against future encroachment." *Russian Media Grp., LLC v. Cable America, Inc.,* 598 F.3d 302, 307 (7th Cir.2010) (citing authorities). If a party has violated the governing statute, then a court may in appropriate circumstances enjoin conduct that allowed the prohibited actions to occur, even if that conduct "standing alone, would have been unassailable." *EEOC v. Wilson Metal Casket Co.*, 24 F.3d 836, 842 (6th Cir.1994) (internal quotation omitted).

Thomas-Rasset's willful infringement and subsequent efforts to conceal her actions certainly show "a proclivity for unlawful conduct." The recording companies rightly point out that once Thomas-Rasset makes copyrighted works available on an online media distribution system, she has completed all of the steps necessary for her to engage in the same distribution that the court did enjoin. The record also demonstrates the practical difficulties of detecting actual transfer of recordings to third parties even when a party has made large numbers of recordings available for distribution online. The narrower injunction granted by the district court thus could be difficult to enforce.

For these reasons, we conclude that the district court erred after the third trial by concluding that the broader injunction requested by the companies was impermissible as a matter of law. An injunction against making recordings available was lawful and appropriate under the circumstances, even accepting the district court's interpretation of the Copyright Act. Thomas-Rasset does not resist expanding the injunction to include this relief. We therefore will direct the district court to modify the judgment to include the requested injunction.

On the question of damages, we conclude that a statutory damages award of $9,250 for each of the twenty-four infringed songs, for a total of $222,000, does not contravene the Due Process Clause. The district court erred in reducing the third jury's verdict to $2,250 per work, for a total of $54,000, on the ground that this amount was the maximum permitted by the Constitution.

The Supreme Court long ago declared that damages awarded pursuant to a statute violate due process only if they are "so severe and oppressive as to be wholly disproportioned to the offense and obviously unreasonable." *St. Louis, I. M. & S. Ry. Co. v. Williams*, 251 U.S. 63, 67 (1919). Under this standard, Congress possesses a "wide latitude of discretion" in setting statutory damages. *Williams* is still good law, and the district court was correct to apply it.

Thomas-Rasset urges us to consider instead the "guideposts" announced by the Supreme Court for the review of punitive damages awards under the Due Process Clause. When a party challenges an award of punitive damages, a reviewing court is directed to consider three factors in determining whether the award is excessive and unconstitutional: "(1) the degree of reprehensibility of the defendant's misconduct; (2) the disparity between the actual or potential harm suffered by the plaintiff and the punitive damages award; and (3) the difference between the punitive damages awarded by the jury and the civil penalties authorized or imposed in comparable cases." *State Farm Mut. Auto. Ins. Co. v. Campbell*, 538 U.S. 408, 418 (2003).

The Supreme Court never has held that the punitive damages guideposts are applicable in the context of statutory damages. Due process prohibits excessive punitive damages because "'[e]lementary notions of fairness enshrined in our constitutional jurisprudence dictate that a person receive fair notice not only of the conduct that will subject him to punishment, but also of the severity of the penalty that a State may impose.'" *Campbell*, 538 U.S. at 417 [(quotation omitted)]. This concern about fair notice does not apply to statutory damages, because those damages are identified and constrained by the authorizing statute. The guideposts themselves, moreover, would be nonsensical if applied to statutory damages. It makes no sense to consider the disparity between "actual harm" and an award of statutory damages when statutory damages are designed precisely for instances where actual harm is difficult or impossible to calculate. Nor could a reviewing court consider the difference between an award of statutory damages and the "civil penalties authorized," because statutory damages *are* the civil penalties authorized.

Applying the *Williams* standard, we conclude that an award of $9,250 per each of twenty-four works is not "so severe and oppressive as to be wholly disproportioned to the offense and obviously unreasonable." 251 U.S. at 67. Congress, exercising its "wide latitude of discretion," *id.* at 66, set a statutory damages range for willful copyright infringement of $750 to $150,000 per infringed work. 17 U.S.C. § 504(c). The award here is toward the lower end of this broad range. As in *Williams,* "the interests of the public, the numberless opportunities for committing the offense, and the need for securing uniform adherence to [federal law]" support the constitutionality of the award. *Id.* at 67.

Congress's protection of copyrights is not a "special private benefit," but is meant to achieve an important public interest: "to motivate the creative activity of authors and inventors by the provision of a special reward, and to allow the public access to the products of their genius after the limited period of exclusive control has expired." *Sony Corp. of Am. v. Universal City Studios, Inc.,* 464 U.S. 417, 429 (1984). With the rapid advancement of technology, copyright infringement through online file-sharing has become a serious problem in the recording industry. Evidence at trial showed that revenues across the industry decreased by fifty percent between 1999 and 2006, a decline that the record companies attributed to piracy. This decline in revenue caused a corresponding drop in industry jobs and a reduction in the number of artists represented and albums released.

Congress no doubt was aware of the serious problem posed by online copyright infringement, and the "numberless opportunities for committing the offense," when it last revisited the Copyright Act in 1999. To provide a deterrent against such infringement, Congress amended § 504(c) to increase the minimum per-work award from $500 to $750, the maximum per-work award from $20,000 to $30,000, and the maximum per-work award for willful infringement from $100,000 to $150,000. *Id.*

Thomas-Rasset contends that the range of statutory damages established by § 504(c) reflects only a congressional judgment "at a very general level," but that courts have authority to declare it "severe and oppressive" and "wholly disproportioned" in particular cases. The district court similarly emphasized that Thomas-Rasset was "not a business acting for profit, but rather an individual consumer illegally seeking free access to music for her own use." By its terms, however, the statute plainly encompasses infringers who act without a profit motive, and the statute already provides for a broad range of damages that allows courts and juries to calibrate the award based on the nature of the violation. For those who favor resort to legislative history, the record also suggests that Congress was well aware of the threat of noncommercial copyright infringement when it established the lower end of the range. Congressional amendments to the criminal provisions of the Copyright Act in 1997 also reflect an awareness that the statute would apply to noncommercial infringement. *See* No Electronic Theft (NET) Act, Pub.L. No. 105-147, § 2(a), 111 Stat. 2678 (1997).

In holding that any award over $2,250 per work would violate the Constitution, the district court effectively imposed a treble damages limit on the $750 minimum statutory damages award. The district court based this holding on a "broad legal practice of establishing a treble award as the upper limit permitted to address willful or particularly damaging behavior." Any "broad legal practice" of treble damages for statutory violations, however, does not control whether an award of statutory damages is within the limits prescribed by the Constitution. The limits of treble damages to which the district court referred, such as in the antitrust laws or other intellectual property laws, represent congressional judgments about the appropriate maximum in a given context. They do not establish a *constitutional* rule that can be substituted for a different congressional judgment in the area of copyright infringement....

Thomas-Rasset highlights that if the recording companies had sued her based on infringement of 1,000 copyrighted recordings instead of the twenty-four recordings that they selected, then an award of $9,250 per song would have resulted in a total award of $9,250,000. Because that hypothetical award would be obviously excessive and unreasonable, she reasons, an award of $222,000 based on the same amount per song must likewise be invalid. Whatever the constitutionality of the hypothetical award, we disagree that the validity of the lesser amount sought here depends on whether the Due Process Clause would permit the extrapolated award that she posits. The absolute amount of the award, not just the amount per violation, is relevant to whether the award is "so severe and oppressive as to be wholly disproportioned to the offense and obviously unreasonable." *Williams,* 251 U.S. at 67, 40 S.Ct. 71. The recording companies here opted to sue over twenty-four recordings. If they had sued over 1,000 recordings, then a finder of fact may well have considered the number of recordings and the proportionality of the total award as factors in determining where within the range to assess the statutory damages. If and when a jury returns a multi-million dollar award for noncommercial online copyright infringement, then there will be time enough to consider it.

For the foregoing reasons, we conclude that the recording companies are entitled to the remedies that they seek on appeal. The judgment of the district court is vacated, and the case is remanded with directions to enter a judgment for damages in the amount of $222,000, and to include an injunction that precludes Thomas-Rasset from making any of the plaintiffs' recordings available for distribution to the public through an online media distribution system.

Sony BMG Music Entm't v. Tenenbaum
660 F.3d 487 (1st Cir. Mass. 2011)

Plaintiffs, the recording companies Sony BMG Music Entertainment, Warner Brothers Records Inc., Arista Records LLC, Atlantic Recording Corporation, and UMG Recordings, Inc. (together, "Sony"), brought this action for statutory damages and injunctive relief under the Copyright Act, 17 U.S.C. § 101 et seq. Sony argued that the defendant, Joel Tenenbaum, willfully infringed the copyrights of thirty music recordings by using filesharing software to download and distribute those recordings without authorization from the copyright owners.

The district court entered judgment against Tenenbaum as to liability. The jury found that Tenenbaum's infringement of the copyrights at issue was willful and awarded Sony statutory damages of $22,500 for each infringed recording, an award within the statutory range of $750 to $150,000 per infringement that Congress established for willful conduct. See 17 U.S.C. § 504(c).

Upon Tenenbaum's motion for a new trial or remittitur, the district court skipped over the question of remittitur and reached a constitutional issue. It reduced the damage award by a factor of ten, reasoning that the award was excessive in violation of Tenenbaum's due process rights.

The parties have cross-appealed. Sony argues the district court erred, for a number of reasons, in reducing the jury's award of damages and seeks reinstatement of the full award. It defends the liability and willfulness determinations.

Tenenbaum challenges both liability and damages. He challenges the Copyright Act's constitutionality and the applicability of the Copyright Act and its statutory damages provision to his conduct. Tenenbaum also argues that the district court committed various errors that require a new trial, and that a further reduction of the damage award is required by the due process clause.

The United States, intervening to defend the constitutionality of the Copyright Act, argues that the district court erred in bypassing the question of common law remittitur to reach a constitutional issue.

We reject all of Tenenbaum's arguments and affirm the denial of Tenenbaum's motion for a new trial or remittitur based on claims of error as to the application of the Copyright Act and error as to the jury instructions. However, the court erred when it bypassed Tenenbaum's remittitur arguments based on excessiveness of the statutory damages award and reached the constitutional due process issue. We agree with the United States that the doctrine of constitutional avoidance requires consideration of common law remittitur before consideration of Tenenbaum's due process challenge to the jury's award. We reverse the reduction in damages, reinstate the original award, and remand for consideration of the common law remittitur question. We comment that this case raises concerns about application of the Copyright Act which Congress may wish to examine.

[The Court provides an extensive review of the conduct by Tenenbaum as a connoisseur of peer-to-peer file sharing, repeated warnings that such conduct was illegal, and Tenenbaum's myriad claims of Copyright Law unconstitutionality and error. The Court rejected all such claims.]

. . .

After handling the trial with great skill, the district court committed reversible error when, after the jury awarded statutory damages, it bypassed the issue of common law remittitur, and instead resolved a disputed question of whether the jury's award of $22,500 per infringement violated due process, and decided itself to reduce the award. The court declined to adhere to the doctrine of constitutional avoidance on the ground that it felt resolution of a constitutional due process question was inevitable in the case before it. A decision on a constitutional due process question was not necessary, was not inevitable, had considerable impermissible consequences, and contravened the rule of constitutional avoidance. That rule had more than its usual import in this case because there were a number of difficult constitutional issues which should have been avoided but were engaged.

Facing the constitutional question of whether the award violated due process was not inevitable. The district court should first have considered the non-constitutional issue of remittitur, which may have obviated any constitutional due process issue and attendant issues. Had the court ordered remittitur of a particular amount, Sony would have then had a choice. It could have accepted the reduced award. Or, it could have rejected the remittitur, in which case a new trial would have ensued.

In reaching and deciding that due process constitutional question, the district court also unnecessarily decided several related constitutional issues. The court determined that the statutory damage award was effectively a punitive damage award for due process purposes and applied the factors set forth in *BMW v. Gore*, 517 U.S. 559 (1996), to assess its constitutionality. The court declined to apply the *Williams* standard the Supreme Court had previously applied to statutory damage awards. The district court's tack also led to unnecessary resolution of Seventh Amendment issues. The decision to reduce the jury's award without offering Sony a new trial implicitly presupposed that, in reducing a statutory damage award issued by a jury, a court need not offer plaintiffs the option of a new jury trial in order to comport with the Seventh Amendment.

The United States, concerned with defending the constitutionality of the Copyright Act and its statutory damage provision, argues that the district court erred by unnecessarily reaching Tenenbaum's constitutional challenge to the award and bypassing the question of common law remittitur. The United States alternatively argues that, if the due process issue were reached, the district court was required to apply the *Williams* due process standard. The United States points out an inferior federal court may not displace the Supreme Court's on point holding. The United States also raises Seventh Amendment concerns.

We agree with the position of the United States that the district court erred when it prematurely reached a constitutional question of whether the jury's award was excessive so as to violate due process. We reverse the reduction of the award, reinstate the original jury verdict and award, and remand for consideration of the common law remittitur question....

Notes and Questions

a. The court decisions quote *Sony* extensively as the framework for the various interpretations of fair use in the context of a new technology which is being used extensively for copyright piracy, but which also has great potential for substantial noninfringing uses.

b. Two excellent but very different works provide the history and context of the *Sony* decision. Compare PAUL GOLDSTEIN, COPYRIGHT'S HIGHWAY: FROM GUTENBURG TO THE CELESTIAL JUKEBOX 41–44 (1994), with JAMES LARDNER, FAST FORWARD, A MACHINE AND THE COMMOTION IT CAUSED (Revised ed. Pierce Law 2002).

c. These three cases, *Napster*, *Aimster*, and *Grokster*, suggest very different attitudes towards both the plaintiffs and defendants. Was the *Grokster* Court correct in ignoring the choices made by the software designers to create software intentionally to thwart the secondary liability standards of contributory infringement and vicarious liability? In the alternative, did the *Napster* Court overstate the secondary liability standards to stop the direct infringement being conducted?

d. The *Napster* Court discussed the impact that peer-to-peer file sharing may have had on the sale of CDs, but what about the creation of new opportunities, such as live concerts broadcast over the Internet? Did the sudden rise in popularity of these services affect either the value or enforceability of these agreements? See *Profile Publ'g & Mgmt. Corp. APS v. Musicmaker.com, Inc.*, 2003 U.S. Dist. LEXIS 991 (S.D.N.Y. 2003).

e. Significant focus has been on section 1201 of the Digital Millennium Copyright Act which bans the anti-circumvention of copyright protection systems. "Congress enacted three new anti-circumvention prohibitions.... The first two provisions target circumvention of technological measures that effectively control access to a copyrighted work; the third ... [prohibits] the trafficking in and marketing of devices primarily designed to circumvent the use restriction protective technologies." *United States v. Elcom Ltd.*, 203 F. Supp. 2d 1111, 1120 (N.D. Cal. 2002). See also *DVD Copy Control Assn., Inc. v. Bunner*, 31 Cal. 4th 864, 4 Cal. Rptr. 3d 69, 75 P.3d 1 (2003); and *Universal City Studios, Inc. v. Corley*, 273 F.3d 429 (2d Cir. N.Y. 2001). Chapter II, *supra*, provides an overview of these provisions in the international context. As explained in Chapter II, these provisions have been generally upheld by the courts and widely criticized by commentators.

f. In *Ellison v. Robertson*, 357 F.3d 1072 (9th Cir. 2004), RemarQ Communities, Inc. and Critical Path, Inc., settled the case with the following joint statement:

> The copyright infringement action filed by noted author and literary activist Harlan Ellison against Critical Path, Inc. and its subsidiary RemarQ Communities, Inc. has been settled. The action stemmed from the unauthorized posting of some of Ellison's most well-known copyrighted stories on the RemarQ service. Ellison's copyright infringement action is continuing against the remaining defendant, America Online, Inc.

> Among the terms of the settlement, Critical Path will develop software that allows Ellison immediately to delete unauthorized postings of his works of which he becomes aware. Critical Path will also appoint an employee to be available to Ellison as a back up measure.

> Ellison, who has authored 75 books in his distinguished career, noted: "I am pleased to have settled this case with Critical Path and RemarQ and believe we have taken a step forward for writers everywhere in their efforts to protect copyrighted works."

> The settlement did not include any admission of liability. Commenting on the settlement, a Critical Path spokesperson said: "We are pleased to reach a settlement in this case that will aid authors in protecting their intellectual property."

g. The reframing of *Grokster* to use the "inducement of infringement" doctrine has the potential to separate out interesting new technologies and well-intended companies from those sham enterprises that provide noninfringing activities as a smokescreen for the business of profiting from other parties' copyright infringement.

h. On remand, the district court applied the "inducement doctrine" to the claim. "Plaintiffs need prove only that StreamCast distributed the product with the intent to encourage infringement. Since there is no dispute that StreamCast did distribute an infringement-enabling technology, the inquiry focuses on the defendant's intent, which can be shown by evidence of the defendant's expression or conduct." The district court found sufficient intent and issued the injunction. *MGM Studios, Inc. v. Grokster Ltd.*, 454 F. Supp. 2d 966, 985 (C.D. Cal. 2006).

i. An example of this attempt to distinguish between infringement and technical copyright noncompliance was demonstrated in *Chamberlain Group, Inc. v. Skylink Techs., Inc.*, 292 F. Supp. 2d 1040 (N.D. Ill. 2003). Here, a garage door manufacturer used encrypted coding to tie its remote door opener to the door mechanism. The court rejected the tying:

> Under Chamberlain's theory, any customer who loses his or her Chamberlain transmitter, but manages to operate the opener either with a non-Chamberlain transmitter or by some other means of circumventing the rolling code, has violated the DMCA. In this court's view, the statute does not require such a conclusion. GDO transmitters are similar to television remote controls in that consumers of both products may need to replace them at some point due to damage or loss, and may program them to work with other devices manufactured by different companies. In both cases, consumers have a reasonable expectation that they can replace the original product with a competing, universal product without violating federal law.

Id. at 1046. The distinction is not grounded in copyright or fair use, but in the reasonable expectations of consumers. While this is a proper outcome, to what extent can consumer expectation provide a guide for common law development of copyright policy?

Problem XIII-C

In addition to the issues Bryce raised in Problem XIII-A, Bryce also found that two-thirds of Bryce's recorded songs were available free on the Internet. Bryce had originally placed three of those songs on Napster to promote the CD four years earlier, but now wishes to remove them. The other songs were never placed in peer-to-peer networks with permission. To what extent does this information add to the advice you provided pursuant to Problem XIII-A?

D. Consumer Services & Electronics

Introduction

Despite headlines which suggest that the primary threat to the entertainment industry is piracy, the true battle for the future of the United States entertainment industry is being waged against the consumer electronic industry and computer industry. Although the income from the consumer electronic industry and computer industry dwarfs that of all the entertainment companies combined, most consumer electronics equipment would be unneeded and unused without the content of the entertainment industries. In industry parlance, music and video is the "killer app" for consumer electronics and many computer upgrades.

This tension between the content industries and the electronic industries is at the heart of the debate for the future of the industries. Sony is the only company to successfully operate within all industries, but private reports suggest that Sony does not operate so much as an integrated company as it does as a balkanized confederation of competing industries—the battle over control is being fought within the corporate, multinational structure. Similarly, the potential of the AOL-Time/Warner merger went largely unrecognized because the merged entity could not take advantage of the integration.

Perhaps ironically, it was *Sony Corp. of America v. Universal City Studios, Inc.*, which began the series of cases that fostered the consumer electronic industry by permitting the consumer electronics industry to rely on fair use rather than licensed content to promote the growth of the VCR.

Given these cases and the track record of both Sony and AOL/Warner, there is perhaps some reason that other large consumer electronics companies have not directly purchased the media companies. Steve Jobs (1955–2011), co-founder and longtime CEO of Apple Computer and co-founder of Pixar, may have best exemplified the potential leadership needed to meld the two industries. It is inevitable that these mergers will eventually take place, if for no other reason than so that key players in the consumer electronics industry can gain control over archival content. The nature of these eventual mergers will dramatically impact each entertainment industry as it is subsumed. Nonetheless, fair use decisions reduce the incentive to buy the media producers.

Indeed, it may be that losing these lawsuits is the most important thing the entertainment industry can do to remain free from merger mania.

Recording Indus. Ass'n of Am. v. Diamond Multimedia Sys.
180 F.3d 1072 (9th Cir. 1999)

[The Ninth Circuit found that the early digital music players did not violate copyright laws and did not require payments to the copyright holders under the Audio Home Recording Act of 1992.]

Rio's operation is entirely consistent with the Act's main purpose—the facilitation of personal use. As the Senate Report explains, "[t]he purpose of [the Act] is to ensure the right of consumers to make analog or digital audio recordings of copyrighted music for their *private, noncommercial use*." The Act does so through its home taping exemption, which "protects all noncommercial copying by consumers of digital and analog musical recordings." The Rio merely makes copies in order to render portable, or "space-shift," those files that already reside on a user's hard drive. Such copying is paradigmatic noncommercial personal use entirely consistent with the purposes of the Act.

Even though it cannot directly reproduce a digital music recording, the Rio would nevertheless be a digital audio recording device if it could reproduce a digital music recording "from a transmission." ... The parties do not really dispute the definition of transmission, but rather, whether *indirect* reproduction of a transmission of a digital music recording is covered by the Act....

[T]he Rio is not a digital audio recording device subject to the restrictions of the Audio Home Recording Act of 1992. The district court properly denied the motion for a preliminary injunction against the Rio's manufacture and distribution. Having so determined, we need not consider whether the balance of hardships or the possibility of irreparable harm supports injunctive relief.

UMG Recordings, Inc. v. MP3.com, Inc.
92 F. Supp. 2d 349 (S.D.N.Y. 2000)

The complex marvels of cyberspatial communication may create difficult legal issues; but not in this case. Defendant's infringement of plaintiff's copyrights is clear.... [D]efendant MP3.com, on or around January 12, 2000, launched its "My.MP3.com" service, which it advertised as permitting subscribers to store, customize, and listen to the recordings contained on their CDs from any place where they have an Internet connection.... [A]lthough defendant seeks to portray its service as the "functional equivalent" of storing its subscribers' CDs, in actuality defendant is re-playing for the subscribers converted versions of the recordings it copied, without authorization, from plaintiffs' copyrighted CDs. On its face, this makes out a presumptive case of infringement under the Copyright Act of 1976 ...

Viacom Int'l, Inc. v. YouTube, Inc.
676 F.3d 19 (2d Cir. 2012)

This appeal requires us to clarify the contours of the "safe harbor" provision of the Digital Millennium Copyright Act (DMCA) that limits the liability of online service providers for copyright infringement that occurs "by reason of the storage at the direction of a user of material that resides on a system or network controlled or operated by or for the service provider." 17 U.S.C. § 512(c).

… The plaintiffs alleged direct and secondary copyright infringement based on the public performance, display, and reproduction of approximately 79,000 audiovisual "clips" that appeared on the YouTube website between 2005 and 2008. They demanded, *inter alia*, statutory damages pursuant to 17 U.S.C. § 504(c) or, in the alternative, actual damages from the alleged infringement, as well as declaratory and injunctive relief.

… [W]e affirm the District Court's holding that three of the challenged YouTube software functions fall within the safe harbor for infringement that occurs "by reason of" user storage; we remand for further fact-finding with respect to a fourth software function.

BACKGROUND

A. The DMCA Safe Harbors

"The DMCA was enacted in 1998 to implement the World Intellectual Property Organization Copyright Treaty," *Universal City Studios, Inc. v. Corley*, 273 F.3d 429, 440 (2d Cir. 2001), and to update domestic copyright law for the digital age. Title II of the DMCA, separately titled the "Online Copyright Infringement Liability Limitation Act" (OCILLA), was designed to "clarif[y] the liability faced by service providers who transmit potentially infringing material over their networks." S. Rep. No. 105-190 at 2 (1998).… OCILLA established a series of four "safe harbors" that allow qualifying service providers to limit their liability for claims of copyright infringement based on (a) "transitory digital network communications," (b) "system caching," (c) "information residing on systems or networks at [the] direction of users," and (d) "information location tools." 17 U.S.C. §§ 512(a)–(d).

To qualify for protection under any of the safe harbors, a party must meet a set of threshold criteria. First, the party must in fact be a "service provider," defined, in pertinent part, as "a provider of online services or network access, or the operator of facilities therefor." 17 U.S.C. § 512(k)(1)(B). A party that qualifies as a service provider must also satisfy certain "conditions of eligibility," including the adoption and reasonable implementation of a "repeat infringer" policy that "provides for the termination in appropriate circumstances of subscribers and account holders of the service provider's system or network." *Id.* § 512(i)(1)(A). In addition, a qualifying service provider must accommodate "standard technical measures" that are "used by copyright owners to identify or protect copyrighted works." *Id.* §§ 512(i)(1)(B), (i)(2).

Beyond the threshold criteria, a service provider must satisfy the requirements of a particular safe harbor. In this case, the safe harbor at issue is § 512(c), which covers infringement claims that arise "by reason of the storage at the direction of a user of material that resides on a system or network controlled or operated by or for the service provider." *Id.* § 512(c)(1). The § 512(c) safe harbor will apply only if the service provider:

> (A) (i) does not have actual knowledge that the material or an activity using the material on the system or network is infringing;

> (ii) in the absence of such actual knowledge, is not aware of facts or circumstances from which infringing activity is apparent; or

> (iii) upon obtaining such knowledge or awareness, acts expeditiously to remove, or disable access to, the material;

> (B) does not receive a financial benefit directly attributable to the infringing activity, in a case in which the service provider has the right and ability to control such activity; and

> (C) upon notification of claimed infringement as described in paragraph (3), responds expeditiously to remove, or disable access to, the material that is claimed to be infringing or to be the subject of infringing activity.

Id. §§ 512(c)(1)(A)–(C). Section 512(c) also sets forth a detailed notification scheme that requires service providers to "designate[ ] an agent to receive notifications of claimed infringement," *id.* § 512(c)(2), and specifies the components of a proper notification, commonly known as a "takedown notice," to that agent. Thus, actual knowledge of infringing material, awareness of facts or circumstances that make infringing activity apparent, or receipt of a takedown notice will each trigger an obligation to expeditiously remove the infringing material....

B. Factual Background

YouTube was founded in February 2005 by Chad Hurley ("Hurley"), Steve Chen ("Chen"), and Jawed Karim ("Karim"), three former employees of the internet company PayPal. When YouTube announced the "official launch" of the website in December 2005, a press release described YouTube as a "consumer media company" that "allows people to watch, upload, and share personal video clips at www.YouTube.com." Under the slogan "Broadcast yourself," YouTube achieved rapid prominence and profitability, eclipsing competitors such as Google Video and Yahoo Video by wide margins. In November 2006, Google acquired YouTube in a stock-for-stock transaction valued at $1.65 billion. By March 2010, at the time of summary judgment briefing in this litigation, site traffic on YouTube had soared to more than 1 billion daily video views, with more than 24 hours of new video uploaded to the site every minute.

The basic function of the YouTube website permits users to "upload" and view video clips free of charge. Before uploading a video to YouTube, a user must register and create an account with the website. The registration process requires the user to accept YouTube's Terms of Use agreement, which provides, *inter alia*, that the user "will not submit material that is copyrighted ... unless [he is] the owner of such rights or ha[s] permission from their rightful owner to post the material and to grant YouTube all of the license rights granted herein." When the registration process is complete, the user can sign in to his account, select a video to upload from the user's personal computer, mobile phone, or other device, and instruct the YouTube system to upload the video by clicking on a virtual upload "button."

Uploading a video to the YouTube website triggers a series of automated software functions. During the upload process, YouTube makes one or more exact copies of the video in its original file format. YouTube also makes one or more additional copies of the video in "Flash" format, a process known as "transcoding." The transcoding process ensures that YouTube videos are available for viewing by most users at their request. The YouTube system allows users to gain access to video content by "streaming" the video to the user's computer in response to a playback request. YouTube uses a computer algorithm to identify clips that are "related" to a video the user watches and display links to the "related" clips....

We review an order granting summary judgment *de novo*, drawing all factual inferences in favor of the non-moving party.

A. Actual and "Red Flag" Knowledge: § 512(c)(1)(A)

The first and most important question on appeal is whether the DMCA safe harbor at issue requires "actual knowledge" or "aware[ness]" of facts or circumstances indicating "specific and identifiable infringements," *Viacom*, 718 F. Supp. 2d at 523. We consider first the scope of the statutory provision and then its application to the record in this case.

1. The Specificity Requirement

"As in all statutory construction cases, we begin with the language of the statute," *Barn-hart v. Sigmon Coal Co.*, 534 U.S. 438, 450 (2002). Under §512(c)(1)(A), safe harbor protection is available only if the service provider:

> (i) does not have actual knowledge that the material or an activity using the material on the system or network is infringing;

> (ii) in the absence of such actual knowledge, is not aware of facts or circumstances from which infringing activity is apparent; or

> (iii) upon obtaining such knowledge or awareness, acts expeditiously to remove, or disable access to, the material....

17 U.S.C. §512(c)(1)(A). As previously noted, the District Court held that the statutory phrases "actual knowledge that the material ... is infringing" and "facts or circumstances from which infringing activity is apparent" refer to "knowledge of specific and identifiable infringements." *Viacom*, 718 F. Supp. 2d at 523. For the reasons that follow, we substantially affirm that holding.

Although the parties marshal a battery of other arguments on appeal, it is the text of the statute that compels our conclusion. In particular, we are persuaded that the basic operation of §512(c) requires knowledge or awareness of specific infringing activity. Under §512(c)(1)(A), knowledge or awareness alone does not disqualify the service provider; rather, the provider that gains knowledge or awareness of infringing activity retains safe-harbor protection if it "acts expeditiously to remove, or disable access to, the material." 17 U.S.C. §512(c)(1)(A)(iii). Thus, the nature of the removal obligation itself contemplates knowledge or awareness of specific infringing material, because expeditious removal is possible only if the service provider knows with particularity which items to remove. Indeed, to require expeditious removal in the absence of specific knowledge or awareness would be to mandate an amorphous obligation to "take commercially reasonable steps" in response to a generalized awareness of infringement. Such a view cannot be reconciled with the language of the statute, which requires "expeditious[ ]" action to remove or disable *"the material"* at issue. 17 U.S.C. §512(c)(1)(A)(iii) (emphasis added).

On appeal, the plaintiffs dispute this conclusion by drawing our attention to §512(c)(1)(A)(ii), the so-called "red flag" knowledge provision. See *id.* §512(c)(1)(A)(ii) (limiting liability where, "in the absence of such actual knowledge, [the service provider] is not aware of facts or circumstances from which infringing activity is apparent"). In their view, the use of the phrase "facts or circumstances" demonstrates that Congress did not intend to limit the red flag provision to a particular type of knowledge. The plaintiffs contend that requiring awareness of specific infringements in order to establish "aware[ness] of facts or circumstances from which infringing activity is apparent," 17 U.S.C. §512(c)(1)(A)(ii), renders the red flag provision superfluous, because that provision would be satisfied only when the "actual knowledge" provision is also satisfied. For that reason, the plaintiffs urge the Court to hold that the red flag provision "requires less specificity" than the actual knowledge provision.

This argument misconstrues the relationship between "actual" knowledge and "red flag" knowledge.... The phrase "actual knowledge," which appears in §512(c)(1)(A)(i), is frequently used to denote subjective belief. By contrast, courts often invoke the language of "facts or circumstances," which appears in §512(c)(1)(A)(ii), in discussing an objective reasonableness standard.

The difference between actual and red flag knowledge is thus not between specific and generalized knowledge, but instead between a subjective and an objective standard. In other words, the actual knowledge provision turns on whether the provider actually or "subjectively" knew of specific infringement, while the red flag provision turns on whether the provider was subjectively aware of facts that would have made the specific infringement "objectively" obvious to a reasonable person. The red flag provision, because it incorporates an objective standard, is not swallowed up by the actual knowledge provision under our construction of the §512(c) safe harbor. Both provisions do independent work, and both apply only to specific instances of infringement.

The limited body of case law interpreting the knowledge provisions of the §512(c) safe harbor comports with our view of the specificity requirement. Most recently, a panel of the Ninth Circuit addressed the scope of §512(c) in *UMG Recordings, Inc. v. Shelter Capital Partners LLC*, 667 F.3d 1022 (9th Cir. 2011), a copyright infringement case against Veoh Networks, a video-hosting service similar to YouTube. As in this case, various music publishers brought suit against the service provider, claiming direct and secondary copyright infringement based on the presence of unauthorized content on the website, and the website operator sought refuge in the §512(c) safe harbor. The Court of Appeals affirmed the district court's determination on summary judgment that the website operator was entitled to safe harbor protection. With respect to the actual knowledge provision, the panel declined to "adopt[ ] a broad conception of the knowledge requirement," holding instead that the safe harbor "[r]equir[es] specific knowledge of particular infringing activity." The Court of Appeals "reach[ed] the same conclusion" with respect to the red flag provision, noting that "[w]e do not place the burden of determining whether [materials] are actually illegal on a service provider."

Although *Shelter Capital* contains the most explicit discussion of the §512(c) knowledge provisions, other cases are generally in accord. While we decline to adopt the reasoning of those decisions *in toto*, we note that no court has embraced the contrary proposition — urged by the plaintiffs — that the red flag provision "requires less specificity" than the actual knowledge provision.

Based on the text of §512(c)(1)(A), as well as the limited case law on point, we affirm the District Court's holding that actual knowledge or awareness of facts or circumstances that indicate specific and identifiable instances of infringement will disqualify a service provider from the safe harbor.

2. The Grant of Summary Judgment

The corollary question on appeal is whether, under the foregoing construction of §512(c)(1)(A), the District Court erred in granting summary judgment to YouTube on the record presented. For the reasons that follow, we hold that although the District Court correctly interpreted §512(c)(1)(A), summary judgment for the defendants was premature.

i. Specific Knowledge or Awareness

The plaintiffs argue that, even under the District Court's construction of the safe harbor, the record raises material issues of fact regarding YouTube's actual knowledge or "red flag" awareness of specific instances of infringement. To that end, the plaintiffs draw our attention to various estimates regarding the percentage of infringing content on the YouTube website. For example, Viacom cites evidence that YouTube employees conducted website surveys and estimated that 75–80% of all YouTube streams contained copyrighted material. The class plaintiffs similarly claim that Credit Suisse, acting as financial advisor to Google, estimated that more than 60% of YouTube's content was "premium" copyrighted content and that only 10% of the premium content was authorized. These approximations suggest that the defendants were conscious that significant quantities of material on the YouTube website were infringing. But such estimates are insufficient, standing alone, to create a triable issue of fact as to whether YouTube actually knew, or was aware of facts or circumstances that would indicate, the existence of particular instances of infringement.

Beyond the survey results, the plaintiffs rely upon internal YouTube communications that do refer to particular clips or groups of clips. The class plaintiffs argue that YouTube was aware of specific infringing material because, *inter alia*, YouTube attempted to search for specific Premier League videos on the site in order to gauge their "value based on video usage." In particular, the class plaintiffs cite a February 7, 2007 e-mail from Patrick Walker, director of video partnerships for Google and YouTube, requesting that his colleagues calculate the number of daily searches for the terms "soccer," "football," and "Premier League" in preparation for a bid on the global rights to Premier League content. On another occasion, Walker requested that any "clearly infringing, official broadcast footage" from a list of top Premier League clubs—including Liverpool Football Club, Chelsea Football Club, Manchester United Football Club, and Arsenal Football Club—be taken down in advance of a meeting with the heads of "several major sports teams and leagues." YouTube ultimately decided not to make a bid for the Premier League rights—but the infringing content allegedly remained on the website.

The record in the *Viacom* action includes additional examples. For instance, YouTube founder Jawed Karim prepared a report in March 2006 which stated that, "[a]s of today[,] episodes and clips of the following well-known shows can still be found [on YouTube]: Family Guy, South Park, MTV Cribs, Daily Show, Reno 911, [and] Dave Chapelle [sic]." Karim further opined that, "although YouTube is not legally required to monitor content ... and complies with DMCA takedown requests, we would benefit from *preemptively* removing content that is blatantly illegal and likely to attract criticism." He also noted that "a more thorough analysis" of the issue would be required.... A reasonable juror could also conclude that Karim believed the clips he located to be infringing (since he refers to them as "blatantly illegal"), and that YouTube did not remove the content from the website until conducting "a more thorough analysis," thus exposing the company to liability in the interim....

ii. "Willful Blindness"

The plaintiffs further argue that the District Court erred in granting summary judgment to the defendants despite evidence that YouTube was "willfully blind" to specific infringing activity. On this issue of first impression, we consider the application of the common law willful blindness doctrine in the DMCA context.

"The principle that willful blindness is tantamount to knowledge is hardly novel." *Tiffany (NJ) Inc. v. eBay, Inc.*, 600 F.3d 93, 110 n.16 (2d Cir. 2010) (collecting cases). A person is "willfully blind" or engages in "conscious avoidance" amounting to knowledge where the person " 'was aware of a high probability of the fact in dispute and consciously avoided confirming that fact.' " *United States v. Aina-Marshall*, 336 F.3d 167, 170 (2d Cir. 2003) Writing in the trademark infringement context, we have held that "[a] service provider is not ... permitted willful blindness. When it has reason to suspect that users of its service are infringing a protected mark, it may not shield itself from learning of the particular infringing transactions by looking the other way." *Tiffany*, 600 F.3d at 109.

The DMCA does not mention willful blindness. As a general matter, we interpret a statute to abrogate a common law principle only if the statute "speak[s] directly to the question addressed by the common law." *Matar v. Dichter*, 563 F.3d 9, 14 (2d Cir. 2009) (internal quotation marks omitted). The relevant question, therefore, is whether the DMCA "speak[s] directly" to the principle of willful blindness. The DMCA provision most relevant to the abrogation inquiry is § 512(m), which provides that safe harbor protection shall not be conditioned on "a service provider monitoring its service or affirmatively seeking facts indicating infringing activity, except to the extent consistent with a standard technical measure complying with the provisions of subsection (i)." 17 U.S.C. § 512(m)(1). Section 512(m) is explicit: DMCA safe harbor protection cannot be conditioned on affirmative monitoring by a service provider. For that reason, § 512(m) is incompatible with a broad common law duty to monitor or otherwise seek out infringing activity based on general awareness that infringement may be occurring. That fact does not, however, dispose of the abrogation inquiry; as previously noted, willful blindness cannot be defined as an affirmative duty to monitor. Because the statute does not "speak[ ] directly" to the willful blindness doctrine, § 512(m) limits—but does not abrogate— the doctrine. Accordingly, we hold that the willful blindness doctrine may be applied, in appropriate circumstances, to demonstrate knowledge or awareness of specific instances of infringement under the DMCA....

B. Control and Benefit: § 512(c)(1)(B)

...

On appeal, the parties advocate two competing constructions of the "right and ability to control" infringing activity. 17 U.S.C. § 512(c)(1)(B). Because each is fatally flawed, we reject both proposed constructions in favor of a fact-based inquiry to be conducted in the first instance by the District Court.

The first construction, pressed by the defendants, is the one adopted by the District Court, which held that "the provider must know of the particular case before he can control it." The Ninth Circuit recently agreed, holding that "until [the service provider] becomes aware of specific unauthorized material, it cannot exercise its 'power or authority' over the specific infringing item. In practical terms, it does not have the kind of ability to control infringing activity the statute contemplates." *UMG Recordings, Inc. v. Shelter Capital Partners LLC*, 667 F.3d 1022, 1041 (9th Cir. 2011). The trouble with this construction is that importing a specific knowledge requirement into § 512(c)(1)(B) renders the control provision duplicative of § 512(c)(1)(A). Any service provider that has item-specific knowledge of infringing activity and thereby obtains financial benefit would already be excluded from the safe harbor under § 512(c)(1)(A) for having specific knowledge of infringing material and failing to effect expeditious removal. No additional service provider would be excluded by § 512(c)(1)(B) that was not already excluded by § 512(c)(1)(A). Because statutory interpretations that render language superfluous are disfavored, we reject the District Court's interpretation of the control provision.

The second construction, urged by the plaintiffs, is that the control provision codifies the common law doctrine of vicarious copyright liability. The common law imposes liability for vicarious copyright infringement "[w]hen the right and ability to supervise coalesce with an obvious and direct financial interest in the exploitation of copyrighted materials—even in the absence of actual knowledge that the copyright mono[poly] is being impaired." *Shapiro, Bernstein & Co. v. H. L. Green Co.*, 316 F.2d 304, 307 (2d Cir. 1963); *cf. Metro-Goldwyn-Mayer Studios Inc. v. Grokster, Ltd.*, 545 U.S. 913, 930 n.9 (2005).... [A] service provider who has knowledge or awareness of infringing material or who receives a takedown notice from a copyright holder is *required* to "remove, or disable access to, the material" in order to claim the benefit of the safe harbor. But in taking such action, the service provider would—in the plaintiffs' analysis—be admitting the "right and ability to control" the infringing material. Thus, the prerequisite to safe harbor protection under §§ 512(c)(1)(A)(iii) & (C) would at the same time be a disqualifier under § 512(c)(1)(B).

Moreover, if Congress had intended § 512(c)(1)(B) to be coextensive with vicarious liability, "the statute could have accomplished that result in a more direct manner." *Shelter Capital*, 667 F.3d at 1045.

> It is conceivable that Congress ... intended that [service providers] which receive a financial benefit directly attributable to the infringing activity would not, under any circumstances, be able to qualify for the subsection (c) safe harbor. But if that was indeed their intention, it would have been far simpler and much more straightforward to simply say as much.

Id. (alteration in original).

... Accordingly, we conclude that the "right and ability to control" infringing activity under § 512(c)(1)(B) "requires something more than the ability to remove or block access to materials posted on a service provider's website." *MP3tunes, LLC*, 821 F. Supp. 2d 627, 2011 WL 5104616, at *14. The remaining—and more difficult—question is how to define the "something more" that is required.

To date, only one court has found that a service provider had the right and ability to control infringing activity under § 512(c)(1)(B).[30] In *Perfect 10, Inc. v. Cybernet Ventures, Inc.*, 213 F. Supp. 2d 1146 (C.D. Cal. 2002), the court found control where the service provider instituted a monitoring program by which user websites received "detailed instructions regard[ing] issues of layout, appearance, and content." *Id.* at 1173. The service provider also forbade certain types of content and refused access to users who failed to comply with its instructions. Similarly, inducement of copyright infringement under *Metro-Goldwyn-Mayer Studios Inc. v. Grokster, Ltd.*, 545 U.S. 913 (2005), which "premises liability on purposeful, culpable expression and conduct," *id.* at 937, might also rise to the level of control under § 512(c)(1)(B). Both of these examples involve a service provider exerting substantial influence on the activities of users, without necessarily—or even frequently—acquiring knowledge of specific infringing activity.

In light of our holding that § 512(c)(1)(B) does not include a specific knowledge requirement, we think it prudent to remand to the District Court to consider in the first instance whether the plaintiffs have adduced sufficient evidence to allow a reasonable jury to conclude that YouTube had the right and ability to control the infringing activity and received a financial benefit directly attributable to that activity.

C. "By Reason of" Storage: § 512(c)(1)

The § 512(c) safe harbor is only available when the infringement occurs "by reason of the storage at the direction of a user of material that resides on a system or network controlled or operated by or for the service provider." 17 U.S.C. § 512(c)(1). In this case, the District Court held that YouTube's software functions fell within the safe harbor for infringements that occur "by reason of" user storage. For the reasons that follow, we affirm that holding with respect to three of the challenged software functions—the conversion

---

30. Other courts have suggested that control may exist where the service provider is "actively involved in the listing, bidding, sale and delivery" of items offered for sale, Hendrickson v. eBay, Inc., 165 F. Supp. 2d 1082, 1094 (C.D. Cal. 2001), or otherwise controls vendor sales by previewing products prior to their listing, editing product descriptions, or suggesting prices, Corbis Corp., 351 F. Supp. 2d at 1110. Because these cases held that control did not exist, however, it is not clear that the practices cited therein are individually sufficient to support a finding of control.

(or "transcoding") of videos into a standard display format, the playback of videos on "watch" pages, and the "related videos" function. We remand for further fact-finding with respect to a fourth software function, involving the third-party syndication of videos uploaded to YouTube....

The relevant case law makes clear that the §512(c) safe harbor extends to software functions performed "for the purpose of facilitating access to user-stored material." *Id.* Two of the software functions challenged here—transcoding and playback—were expressly considered by our sister Circuit in *Shelter Capital*, which held that liability arising from these functions occurred "by reason of the storage at the direction of a user." 17 U.S.C. §512(c). Transcoding involves "[m]aking copies of a video in a different encoding scheme" in order to render the video "viewable over the Internet to most users." The playback process involves "deliver[ing] copies of YouTube videos to a user's browser cache" in response to a user request. The District Court correctly found that to exclude these automated functions from the safe harbor would eviscerate the protection afforded to service providers by §512(c).

A similar analysis applies to the "related videos" function, by which a YouTube computer algorithm identifies and displays "thumbnails" of clips that are "related" to the video selected by the user. The plaintiffs claim that this practice constitutes content promotion, not "access" to stored content, and therefore falls beyond the scope of the safe harbor.... The record makes clear that the related videos algorithm "is fully automated and operates solely in response to user input without the active involvement of YouTube employees." Furthermore, the related videos function serves to help YouTube users locate and gain access to material stored at the direction of other users. Because the algorithm "is closely related to, and follows from, the storage itself," and is "narrowly directed toward providing access to material stored at the direction of users," we conclude that the related videos function is also protected by the §512(c) safe harbor.

. . .

The District Court correctly determined that a finding of safe harbor application necessarily protects a defendant from all affirmative claims for monetary relief. For the reasons previously stated, further fact-finding is required to determine whether YouTube is ultimately entitled to safe harbor protection in this case. Accordingly, we vacate the order denying summary judgment to the plaintiffs and remand the cause without expressing a view on the merits of the plaintiffs' affirmative claims.

Rulemaking on Exemptions from Prohibition on Circumvention of Technological Measures That Control Access to Copyrighted Works[31]

The Librarian of Congress has announced the classes of works subject to the exemption from the prohibition against circumvention of technological measures that control access to copyrighted works. Persons making noninfringing uses of the following six classes of works will not be subject to the prohibition against circumventing access controls (17 U.S.C. §1201(a)(1)) until the conclusion of the next rulemaking.

---

31. The full ruling is available at http://www.copyright.gov/fedreg/2010/75fr43825.pdf. *See* Exemption to Prohibition on Circumvention of Copyright Protection Systems for Access Control Technologies 37 C.F.R. 201 (2009).

(1) Motion pictures on DVDs that are lawfully made and acquired and that are protected by the Content Scrambling System when circumvention is accomplished solely in order to accomplish the incorporation of short portions of motion pictures into new works for the purpose of criticism or comment, and where the person engaging in circumvention believes and has reasonable grounds for believing that circumvention is necessary to fulfill the purpose of the use in the following instances:

(i) Educational uses by college and university professors and by college and university film and media studies students;

(ii) Documentary filmmaking;

(iii) Noncommercial videos.

(2) Computer programs that enable wireless telephone handsets to execute software applications, where circumvention is accomplished for the sole purpose of enabling interoperability of such applications, when they have been lawfully obtained, with computer programs on the telephone handset.

(3) Computer programs, in the form of firmware or software, that enable used wireless telephone handsets to connect to a wireless telecommunications network, when circumvention is initiated by the owner of the copy of the computer program solely in order to connect to a wireless telecommunications network and access to the network is authorized by the operator of the network.

(4) Video games accessible on personal computers and protected by technological protection measures that control access to lawfully obtained works, when circumvention is accomplished solely for the purpose of good faith testing for, investigating, or correcting security flaws or vulnerabilities, if:

(i) The information derived from the security testing is used primarily to promote the security of the owner or operator of a computer, computer system, or computer network; and

(ii) The information derived from the security testing is used or maintained in a manner that does not facilitate copyright infringement or a violation of applicable law.

(5) Computer programs protected by dongles that prevent access due to malfunction or damage and which are obsolete. A dongle shall be considered obsolete if it is no longer manufactured or if a replacement or repair is no longer reasonably available in the commercial marketplace; and

(6) Literary works distributed in ebook format when all existing ebook editions of the work (including digital text editions made available by authorized entities) contain access controls that prevent the enabling either of the book's read-aloud function or of screen readers that render the text into a specialized format.

Background

The Copyright Office is conducting this rulemaking proceeding mandated by the Digital Millennium Copyright Act, which provides that the Librarian of Congress may exempt certain classes of works from the prohibition against circumvention of technological measures that control access to copyrighted works.

The purpose of this proceeding is to determine whether there are particular classes of works as to which users are, or are likely to be, adversely affected in their ability to make noninfringing uses due to the prohibition on circumvention of access controls. ...

The Notice of Inquiry in this fourth anticircumvention rulemaking requests written comments from all interested parties, including representatives of copyright owners, educational institutions, libraries and archives, scholars, researchers and members of the public, in order to elicit evidence on whether noninfringing uses of certain classes of works are, or are likely to be, adversely affected by this prohibition on the circumvention of measures that control access to copyrighted works.

The entire records of the previous anticircumvention rulemakings are available. The first rulemaking took place in 2000. The second was in 2003. The third was in 2006.

Notes and Questions

a. On remand, the district court granted summary judgment to YouTube. See *Viacom Intern. Inc. v. YouTube, Inc.*, 940 F. Supp. 2d 110, 123 (S.D.N.Y. 2013).

b. Part of the ongoing battle between copyright owners and pirates has been the creation and banning of software designed to circumvent encryption on various products and services. See, *e.g.*, *Universal City Studios, Inc. v. Corley*, 273 F.3d 429 (2d Cir. 2001) (enjoining posting of DVD anti-encryption software); *United States v. Elcom Ltd.*, 203 F. Supp. 2d 1111 (N.D. Cal. 2002) ("Congress banned trafficking in devices that are primarily designed for the purpose of circumventing any technological measure that 'effectively protects a right of a copyright owner,' or that have limited commercially significant purposes other than circumventing use restrictions, or that are marketed for use in circumventing the use restrictions.").

c. In *Universal City Studios, Inc. v. Corley*, 273 F.3d 429 (2d Cir. 2001), the Second Circuit upheld a permanent injunction against Eric Corley, barring him from posting DeCSS, the simple computer program that disabled the encryption software on commercial DVDs. The injunction barred Corley from posting DeCSS on his website or from knowingly linking via a hyperlink to any other website containing DeCSS. Corley was the publisher of "2600: The Hacker Quarterly," and he ran a companion website to the publication. The injunction was largely symbolic since the computer program was widely available on the Internet. Nonetheless, the impact of encryption and decryption software remains one of the most important issues bedeviling the entertainment and software industries.

> The movie studios were reluctant to release movies in digital form until they were confident they had in place adequate safeguards against piracy of their copyrighted movies. The studios took several steps to minimize the piracy threat. First, they settled on the DVD as the standard digital medium for home distribution of movies. The studios then sought an encryption scheme to protect movies on DVDs. They enlisted the help of members of the consumer electronics and computer industries, who in mid-1996 developed the Content Scramble System ("CSS"). CSS is an encryption scheme that employs an algorithm configured by a set of "keys" to encrypt a DVD's contents. The algorithm is a type of mathematical formula for transforming the contents of the movie file into gibberish; the "keys" are in actuality strings of 0's and 1's that serve as values for the mathematical formula. Decryption in the case of CSS requires a set of "player keys" contained in compliant DVD players, as well as an under-

standing of the CSS encryption algorithm. Without the player keys and the algorithm, a DVD player cannot access the contents of a DVD. With the player keys and the algorithm, a DVD player can display the movie on a television or a computer screen, but does not give a viewer the ability to use the copy function of the computer to copy the movie or to manipulate the digital content of the DVD.

The studios developed a licensing scheme for distributing the technology to manufacturers of DVD players. Player keys and other information necessary to the CSS scheme were given to manufacturers of DVD players for an administrative fee. In exchange for the licenses, manufacturers were obliged to keep the player keys confidential. Manufacturers were also required in the licensing agreement to prevent the transmission of "CSS data" (a term undefined in the licensing agreement) from a DVD drive to any "internal recording device," including, presumably, a computer hard drive.

With encryption technology and licensing agreements in hand, the studios began releasing movies on DVDs in 1997, and DVDs quickly gained in popularity, becoming a significant source of studio revenue. By the end of 1997, most if not all DVDs that were released were encrypted with CSS. Moreover, DVD players were projected to be in ten percent of United States homes by the end of 2000. In fact, as of 2000, about thirty-five percent of one studio's worldwide revenues from movie distribution was attributable to DVD sales and rentals.

In 1998, the studios secured added protection against DVD piracy when Congress passed the DMCA, which prohibits the development or use of technology designed to circumvent a technological protection measure, such as CSS....

In September 1999, Jon Johansen, a Norwegian teenager, collaborating with two unidentified individuals he met on the Internet, reverse-engineered a licensed DVD player designed to operate on the Microsoft operating system, and culled from it the player keys and other information necessary to decrypt CSS. The record suggests that Johansen was trying to develop a DVD player operable on Linux, an alternative operating system that did not support any licensed DVD players at that time. In order to accomplish this task, Johansen wrote a decryption program executable on Microsoft's operating system. That program was called, appropriately enough, "DeCSS."

If a user runs the DeCSS program (for example, by clicking on the DeCSS icon on a Microsoft operating system platform) with a DVD in the computer's disk drive, DeCSS will decrypt the DVD's CSS protection, allowing the user to copy the DVD's files and place the copy on the user's hard drive. The result is a very large computer file that can be played on a non-CSS-compliant player and copied, manipulated, and transferred just like any other computer file. DeCSS comes complete with a fairly user-friendly interface that helps the user select from among the DVD's files and assign the decrypted file a location on the user's hard drive. The quality of the resulting decrypted movie is "virtually identical" to that of the encrypted movie on the DVD. And the file produced by DeCSS, while large, can be compressed to a manageable size by a compression software called "DivX," available at no cost on the Internet. This compressed file can be copied onto a DVD, or transferred over the Internet (with some patience).

The history of DeCSS encapsulates the history of digital piracy. Distributors are extremely fearful of releasing products without some promise of anti-theft protection, but those same promises invariably understate the problem or overstate the solution.

d. The *Corley* defense rested, in part, on the fair use purposes to which an unencrypted work could be put. A new form of consumer fair use is developing based upon the purchaser's interest in creating back-up copies of works and the purchaser's interest in using a work (listening to a CD or watching a DVD) on multiple devices. This interest held by the consumer is quite different in form than the fair use of comment and criticism embodied in the preamble to § 107. This new form of fair use is an offshoot of the convenience articulated in *Sony* and *Diamond*. The growth of convenience as the basis for fair use is a significant change in the copyright landscape.

From a commercial standpoint, it was Apple Computer which first identified consumer convenience as a significant marketing issue. When iTunes was introduced, the feature most discussed was the relaxation of proprietary controls by the record studios and increased convenience in moving the music files between computers and other devices. The expansion of convenience was a predominant factor in iTunes' success.

e. Can the increasing court recognition of the CMCA safe harbors for video-sharing ISPs such as YouTube and Veoh be reconciled with the substantial jury verdicts against individuals who use peer-to-peer software as demonstrated in *Tenenbaum* and *Thomas-Rasset*? Or, taken together, is copyright moving towards a model of consumer notice-before-liability (since both cases involving the individual defendants included statements of repeated warnings to desist and findings of willfulness in each case)?

f. The 1995 amendments to §§ 106 and 114 were originally written to take advantage in the dramatic changes made in digital radio technology. Three years earlier, in 1992, the FCC had approved the implementation of Digital Audio Radio Services. The 1995 amendments were designed to allow the recording artists to participate in expected technological innovation. It was not until 1997 that the FCC actually approved the licenses for what are now Sirius Satellite Radio and XM Satellite Radio. Although these two services have begun to gain some market share, the bulk of the activity in digital broadcast moved to the Internet. The ability to stream audio files, download files for permanent storage on the listener's machine, and to create interactive uses forced Congress to amend the law in 1998. Continuing controversy over the pricing structure led to a December 2002 compromise and additional statutory changes.

g. Among the more controversial aspects of the Internet streaming media debate was whether the temporary files created on a user's computer were copies for purposes of the copyright law. Had the temporary file been deemed a copy, then a license would be needed for both the composition and the sound recording of the transmission file. This would essentially double the mechanical licensing fees owed to the composer/lyricist and create an additional licensee fee for the sound recording copyright holders. Were these temporary files considered ephemeral copies, then they would not exist under the law and would not trigger any of these additional rights. In 1998, the Digital Millennium Copyright Act amended § 112 to limit some of this risk for multiple licensing requirements. In the Small Webcaster Settlement Act of 2002, the ephemeral recordings were declared copies that were not entitled to additional statutory licensing fees, at least temporarily ending the controversy.

h. The triennial rule-making process has begun once again. The initial proposals for the 2012 hearing are available at http://www.copyright.gov/1201/2011/initial/.

Problem XIII-D

Bryce is trying to promote the musicians who are popular locally by creating a website. Bryce wants the project to be entirely legal and fully licensed. The goal is to acquire the right to post local musicians' songs to a website, sell them for $0.75 per song, and split the income between the artist and Bryce. Bryce will use the income to promote the site. Bands will also be able to announce concerts, sell memorabilia, and operate chat-rooms.

Advise Bryce as to the types of licenses and agreements which will be needed to allow local bands to participate in the project, including both bands with recording contracts and those which do not yet have recording contracts.

E. Bibliography and Links

Yochai Benkler, *The Public Domain: Through the Looking Glass: Alice and the Constitutional Foundations of the Public Domain*, 66 LAW & CONTEMP. PROB. 173 (2003).

Annemarie Bridy, *Why Pirates (Still) Won't Behave: Regulating P2P in the Decade After Napster*, 40 RUTGERS L.J. 565 (2009).

Edward L. Carter & Scott Lunt, *Podcasting and Copyright: The Impact of Regulation on New Communication Technologies*, 22 SANTA CLARA COMPUTER & HIGH TECH. L.J. 187 (2006).

Jacqueline C. Charlesworth, *The Moral of the Story: What Grokster Has to Teach About the DMCA*, 2011 STAN. TECH. L. REV. 6 (2011).

Craig W. Dallon, *The Anti-Bootlegging Provisions: Congressional Power and Constitutional Limitations*, 13 VAND. J. ENT. & TECH. L. 255 (2011).

James DeBriyn, *Shedding Light on Copyright Trolls: An Analysis of Mass Copyright Litigation in the Age of Statutory Damages*, 19 UCLA ENT. L. REV. 79 (2012).

Craig A. Grossman, *From Sony to Grokster, the Failure of the Copyright Doctrines of Contributory Infringement and Vicarious Liability to Resolve the War Between Content and Destructive Technologies*, 53 BUFF. L. REV. 141 (2005).

Shae Yatta Harvey, *National, Multi-District Preliminary Tour Injunctions: Why the Hesitation?*, 40 IDEA 195 (2000).

John T. Holland, *Making Money Instead of Excuses: A Market-based Alternative to the Digital Millennium Copyright Act that Protects Copyrights without Diminishing Expression*, 7 GEO. J.L. & PUB. POL'Y 279 (2009).

Yafit Lev-Aretz, *Second Level Agreements*, 45 AKRON L. REV. 137 (2012).

Jessica Litman & Pamela Samuelson, *Intellectual Property Law: Toward a "New Deal" for Copyright in the Information Age*, 100 MICH. L. REV. 1488 (2002).

Joseph P. Liu, *The DMCA and the Regulation of Scientific Research*, 18 BERKELEY TECH. L.J. 501 (2003).

Mark S. Nadel, *How Current Copyright Law Discourages Creative Output: The Overlooked Impact of Marketing*, 19 BERKELEY TECH. L.J. 785 (2004).

Jed Rubenfeld, *The Freedom of Imagination: Copyright's Constitutionality*, 112 YALE L.J. 1 (2002).

Shelly Rosenfeld, *Taking the Wind out of the Movie Pirates' Sails: The Constitutionality of Senate Bill 3804*, 36 SETON HALL LEGIS. J. 57 (2012).

Lionel S. Sobel, *DRM As An Enabler Of Business Models: ISPs as Digital Retailers*, 18 BERKELEY TECH. L.J. 667 (2003).

Peter K. Yu, *The Copyright Divide*, 25 CARDOZO L. REV. 331 (2003).

Peter K. Yu, *Digital Copyright and Confuzzling Rhetoric*, 13 VAND. J. ENT. & TECH. L. 881 (2011).

Websites

Electronic Frontier Foundation, http://www.eff.org/

RIAA, www.riaa.com

MPAA, www.mpaa.com

Federal Bureau of Investigation, www.fbi.gov

FBI Investigative Programs Cyber Investigations, http://www.fbi.gov/cyberinvest/cyberhome. htm

Chapter XIV

Television & Cable Production Agreements

A. Structure of the Television and Cable Market

FCC, Annual Assessment of the Status of Competition in the Market for the Delivery of Video Programming
Adopted: July 19, 2013[1]

This is the fifteenth report ("15th Report" or "Report") of the Federal Communications Commission to the United States Congress on the status of competition in the market for the delivery of video programming as required by Section 628(g) of the Communications Act of 1934, as amended (the "Act") [47 U.S.C. § 548(g)]. In this Report, we focus on developments in the video marketplace in 2011 and 2012. As described below, the most significant trends since the last report include the continuing development, and consumer usage, of time and location shifted viewing of video programming, the expansion of digital and high definition programming, and the progress of the online video industry.

Herein, we categorize entities into one of three strategic groups—multichannel video programming distributors ("MVPDs"),[2] broadcast television stations,[3] and online video distributors ("OVDs").[4] ...

MVPDs. Between year-end 2010 and June 2012, the number of subscribers to MVPD service grew from 100.8 million to 101.0 million households. Over that period, however, cable MVPDs lost market share, falling from 59.3 percent of all MVPD video subscribers at the end of 2010 to 57.4 percent at the end of 2011, and 55.7 percent at the end of June

---

1. Paragraph numbering, section headings, and most footnotes omitted.
2. For purposes of this Report, MVPDs are companies that offer multiple channels of video programming to consumers for a subscription fee....
3. The Commission has previously held that broadcast television alone is not sufficiently substitutable with the services provided by MVPDs to constrain attempted MVPD price increases, and hence declined to broaden the MVPD product market. Accordingly, we treat broadcasters as part of a separate group.
4. An "OVD" is any entity that offers video content by means of the Internet or other Internet Protocol (IP)-based transmission path provided by a person or entity other than the OVD. An OVD does not include an MVPD inside its MVPD footprint or an MVPD to the extent it is offering online video content as a component of an MVPD subscription to customers whose homes are inside its MVPD footprint. Consumers need a broadband connection to receive video content from OVDs....

2012. During this period, [direct broadcast satellite service ("DBS")] MVPDs and telephone MVPDs gained both video subscribers and market share. DBS MVPDs had 33.4 million video subscribers, accounting for 33.1 percent of all MVPD subscribers in 2010, increasing to 33.9 million, representing 33.6 percent in 2011, and 34 million, representing an estimated 33.6 percent at the end of June 2012. Telephone MVPDs had approximately 6.9 million video subscribers, representing 6.9 percent of all MVPD subscribers in 2010, increasing to 8.5 million, representing for 8.4 percent in 2011. At the end of June 2012, AT&T's U-verse and Verizon's FiOS services combined had 8.6 million video subscribers.

MVPDs continue to expand their "TV Everywhere" offerings, which allow subscribers of certain MVPD services to access video programming on stationary and mobile Internet-connected devices including televisions, computers, tablets and smartphones.[5] Consumer usage of TV Everywhere continues to increase. SNL Kagan estimates that 5.1 percent of MVPD subscribers qualifying for TV Everywhere access viewed programming through this service in September 2012.

In addition, to free up bandwidth for additional services (*e.g.*, more digital channels, more HD channels, more video-on-demand ("VOD") programming, and faster Internet speeds), some cable MVPDs are transitioning analog channels to all digital. At the end of 2012, the all-digital transition had reached slightly more than half of the collective footprints of the top eight cable MVPDs. Cable operators are also deploying switched digital video ("SDV"), freeing up bandwidth by transmitting only the digital channels that are actually being watched within a given group of homes at any given time, rather than all digital channels to all subscribers all the time. At the end of 2012, SDV served approximately 43 percent of digital cable subscribers of the top eight cable MVPDs.

Broadcast Television Stations. Since the last report, full-power television stations have continued to take advantage of digital broadcasting technology to offer improved service to the public. In addition to high definition ("HD") content, broadcasters are using multicasting to bring more programming to consumers by expanding the availability of established networks and adding new startup digital networks (including networks targeting minorities and programming targeting niche audiences) and Spanish language offerings. As of the end of 2011, 1,501 (82.2 percent) of full-power stations were broadcasting in HD, up from 1,036 stations in 2010.

Patterns of consumer behavior noted in the last report, including increases in the number of households with HD television sets, penetration of digital video recorders (DVRs), and increased availability of broadband and mobile devices, have continued. As of 2012, 85.3 million U.S. television households, or 74.4 percent of such households, have sets capable of displaying and/or receiving digital signals, including HD television signals, up from 75.5 million, or 65.1 percent of television households, in 2011. In 2012, 50.3 million television households had DVRs, representing 43.8 percent of all such households, an increase from the 46.3 million households, or 40.4 percent of all television households, reported in 2011. In addition, broadcasters are using a variety of mechanisms to respond to consumers' desire to watch video on a time-shifted basis either on television sets or on other screens, including mobile DTV, VOD, and online video distribution.

Since the last report, the number of households relying exclusively on over-the-air broadcast service has remained steady at approximately 11.1 million households, although

---

5. "TV Everywhere" refers to an MVPD initiative, which allows subscribers of certain services to access video programming on a variety of fixed and mobile Internet-connected devices. MVPDs market their TV Everywhere initiatives under various brand names (*e.g.*, Verizon's FlexView).

the percentage of all households they represent increased slightly from 9.6 percent in 2011 to 9.7 percent in 2012. Broadcast station revenues appear to have rebounded somewhat in 2012, in part due to increased political advertising, following a decline in 2011, with broadcasters relying chiefly on advertising sales, and, increasingly, retransmission consent fees from MVPDs. Industry revenues fell to $21.31 billion in 2011 from the $22.22 billion in 2010, but were projected to rise to $24.70 billion in 2012.

OVDs. While the OVD industry is still evolving, a few trends emerged during the period covered by this Report. OVDs continue to expand the amount of video content available to consumers through original programming and new licensing agreements with traditional content creators. A few MVPDs now offer OVD services to non-subscribers. Some OVDs have invested in their own servers, content delivery networks, and other infrastructure to facilitate the delivery of video programming. Several technology companies, notably Amazon, Apple, Google, and Microsoft, are delivering end-to-end solutions of Internet infrastructure, software, devices, and video programming.

Viewing of OVDs' video programming on television sets is becoming increasingly prevalent. SNL Kagan estimated that there were 26.6 million Internet-connected television households (*i.e.*, accessed via an Internet-enabled game console, OVD set-top box, television set, or Blu-ray player), representing 22.8 percent of all television households, at the end of 2011, and estimated that by the end of 2012, the number would grow to 41.6 million, or 35.4 percent of television households.

OVDs account for an increasing portion of Internet traffic during peak hours. During the first half of 2012, most major cable multiple system operators ("MSOs") formalized bandwidth caps or usage-based/metered pricing. Several telephone company MVPDs also are implementing bandwidth caps and usage fees....

Our examination of vertical integration in the MVPD industry focuses on common ownership of entities that deliver video programming and entities that supply video programming. Vertical relationships may have beneficial effects, or they may deter competitive entry in the video marketplace or limit the diversity of video programming. In 1992, Congress enacted various provisions related to vertical integration between cable operators and programming networks (*e.g.*, program access, channel occupancy limit). In 1992, a large number of the most popular cable programming networks were owned by cable operators. Congress was concerned that cable operators had the ability and incentive to thwart the competitive development of additional programming networks by refusing to carry unaffiliated networks, by insisting on an ownership stake in return for carriage, or by withholding their most popular programming networks from competing MVPDs.

... We now find that there are 99 national networks (47 of these HD networks) affiliated with the top five cable MVPDs. As of early 2013. we report that Comcast has ownership interests in 50 national networks (23 are HD), Time Warner Cable has ownership interests in four national networks (two are HD), Cox has ownership interests in six national networks (three are HD), Cablevision has ownership interests in ten national networks (five are HD), and Bright House has ownership interests in 29 national networks (14 are HD). In addition, we identified 62 national networks that were affiliated with a DBS MVPD (25 were HD).

Program Carriage. MVPDs must obtain carriage agreements with video programming vendors in order to provide a competitive video service. Section 616 of the Act directs the Commission to regulate the program carriage agreements and related practices between cable operators or other MVPDs and video programming vendors. The Commission's rules prohibit cable operators or other MVPDs from requiring a financial interest in a video programming vendor or obtaining exclusive rights to programming as conditions for carriage. MVPDs also are prevented from discriminating against video programming vendors on the basis of affiliation in the selection, terms, or conditions of carriage if the effect of such conduct is to unreasonably restrain the ability of an unaffiliated video programming vendor to compete fairly. An aggrieved MVPD or video programming vendor may file a complaint for alleged violations....

Retransmission Consent and Must Carry. The ability of MVPDs to access local broadcast programming impacts their entry into the video services marketplace. In 1992, Congress enacted Sections 325, 614, and 615 of the Act to facilitate cable operators' carriage of local broadcast television stations and subsequently adopted a similar carriage regime for DBS providers in 1999. Pursuant to Section 325 of the Act, MVPDs may not retransmit a local broadcaster's signal without the station's express permission. Cable operators are required to carry local television stations in every market they serve unless a station elects retransmission consent. DBS operators need not carry any local television signals. But where a DBS operator chooses to carry any such station, it must carry all stations in that market ("carry one, carry all") except for those stations electing retransmission consent. Under this regime, broadcasters maintain control over their signals. And commercial broadcasters electing retransmission consent may request compensation from MVPDs for the carriage of their signals.

In local television markets, as defined by The Nielsen Company's ("Nielsen's") designated market areas ("DMAs"), every three years commercial television stations must select between the right to grant retransmission consent or the right to mandatory carriage. If a station selects retransmission consent, the broadcaster and MVPD negotiate a carriage agreement; the carriage agreement may include monetary or other types of compensation in return for the right to carry the broadcast signal. Where a station selects must carry, it is generally entitled to carriage but it is prohibited from receiving compensation. Qualified local noncommercial educational ("NCE") stations have a right to mandatory carriage within the same market, but do not have retransmission consent rights. Cable operators also are permitted to negotiate for retransmission consent with any other broadcast station they seek to carry irrespective of the station's television market....

Exclusivity Rules. MVPDs must abide by the Commission's rules protecting the exclusive distribution rights of local broadcast stations. For cable operators, the Commission's network non-duplication rules permit a local broadcast station to request the blackout of duplicated programming in the local station's zone of protection when carried on another station imported by the operator. Similarly, the Commission's syndicated exclusivity rules give a local broadcaster the right to black out its exclusive syndicated programming when that programming is carried on another station imported by a cable operator within its zone of protection. The Commission's sports blackout rule protects a sports team's or sports league's distribution rights to a live sporting event occurring in a local market. The rule prevents a cable operator from providing the live sporting event on a distant signal in a market where the game is blacked out on the local broadcast station. As mandated by Congress, the Commission's network non-duplication, syndicated exclusivity, and sports blackout rules apply to satellite carriers....

The transition from analog to digital service described in the *14th Report* has allowed broadcast television stations to offer more programming, including both HD signals and standard-definition ("SD") multicast signals. Between the end of 2010 and the end of 2011, the number of multicast channels grew from 4,552 to 4,597. Much of this growth has been fueled by the launch of new digital networks and the affiliate expansions of such digital networks, including networks targeting minorities and Spanish language offerings, as well as multicasting by low power stations.

Programming is a critical input for broadcast television stations to compete effectively in the industry. Stations combine local programming, either produced in-house or acquired from independent sources, syndicated programming, and/or network programming. The mix of programming varies by station, and depends on whether the station is affiliated with a network or operates as an independent station. Whether or not a station is affiliated with one of the four major networks (ABC, CBS, FOX, or NBC) has a significant impact on the composition of the station's revenues, expenses, and operations.

Most full-power commercial stations (approximately 92 percent) get at least some of their programming from broadcast networks on their primary signals. Commercial broadcast networks generally fall into five main categories: English-language (*e.g.,* ABC, CBS, FOX, NBC, The CW, and MyNetworkTV); Spanish-language (*e.g.,* Univision, Telemundo, and TeleFutura); shopping (*e.g.,* HSN), religious (*e.g.,* TBN and CTN), and regional specialty networks (*e.g.,* Memorable Entertainment Television). Three of the major networks (ABC, CBS, and NBC) generally provide their affiliates with about 22 hours per week of prime time programming. FOX, MyNetworkTV, and The CW supply affiliates with up to 15 hours per week of prime time programming. In addition, these networks may supply affiliates with daytime programming (*e.g.,* morning news programs, game shows, talk shows (including Sunday public affairs), and late night programs). Spanish language and religious networks provide nearly round-the-clock programming for affiliates.

Broadcast stations also acquire programming from television syndicators that distribute original ("first-run syndication") programming, such as *Jeopardy! and Judge Judy,* or reruns of network television series ("off-net" syndication), such as reruns of *Seinfeld* and *The Simpsons,* to television stations. In addition, local broadcast stations produce programming in-house, such as local newscasts, public affairs shows, and coverage of regional and local sporting events.

National Group Ownership. The Act imposes a cap that limits the percentage of television households that one television station group owner can serve to 39 percent of U.S. television households. According to SNL Kagan, as of 2012, the largest group owners by coverage total of U.S. television households, include ION Media Networks (owned by Avenue Capital, Black Diamond Capital, and Trilogy Capital), Univision Communications (Broadcast Media Partners Inc.), CBS Television Stations (CBS Corp.), FOX Television Stations (News Corp.), NBC Universal Stations (Comcast Corp. and General Electric), Tribune Broadcasting (owned by an Employee Stock Ownership Plan), ABC Owned Television Stations (The Walt Disney Company), Gannett Broadcasting (Gannett Company), Sinclair Broadcast Group, Inc., and Hearst Corp. During the 2011–2012 season, Sinclair increased its coverage of TV households from 19 percent to 25 percent of U.S. television households.

Analyzing the largest group owners in terms of revenue results in a similar list. According to *TVNewsCheck,* the top station groups in 2011 in terms of revenue include Fox, CBS, NBCUniversal, ABC, Tribune, Sinclair, Gannett, Hearst, Belo Corp., and Univision....

Some stations are vertically integrated upstream, with suppliers of programming, as well as downstream, with distributors of programming. For instance, the stations' parent company may have ownership interests in television production studios, movie studios, sports teams, broadcast television networks, cable networks, or syndicators. Similarly, Comcast's acquisition of NBC/Universal resulted in downstream vertical integration of NBC's O&O stations with a cable MVPD.

[The] parent companies of six of the top seven station groups—ION Media Networks, Univision Communications, Inc., CBS Television Stations, FOX Television Stations, NBC Universal Stations, and ABC Owned Television Stations, representing 188 O&Os, own all or part of at least one broadcast television network. Broadcast networks typically own and operate their own stations in the largest television markets. Spanish-language broadcast networks, *e.g.,* Univision and Telemundo, own and operate television stations in the largest Spanish-speaking markets.

In addition to ownership of broadcast networks, a number of owners of local broadcast stations have affiliations with cable networks. Through its ownership of NBC Universal, Comcast has ownership interests in 50 national cable networks. Other broadcast station owners with affiliated cable networks are: The Walt Disney Company with interests in 39 cable networks; Univision with interests in nine affiliated cable networks; and CBS Corporation with interests in 28 cable networks. News Corp. has ownership interests in 29 national cable networks. In addition, since the last report, News Corp. took an interest in the Yankee Entertainment & Sports Network ("Yes Network"), increasing its count of affiliated regional cable networks to 46. Several broadcast television groups owners that are not vertically integrated with broadcast networks also have ownership interests in cable networks. These owners include Hearst Television Inc. (32 cable networks), InterMedia Partners (five cable networks), Tribune Company (six cable networks), Cox Communications Inc. (six cable networks), and Hubbard Broadcasting Corp. (four cable networks). Combined, Hearst, InterMedia, Tribune, Cox, and Hubbard, own 83 stations. Other broadcast station groups operate local and regional cable news channels. Belo Corp., for example, owns 20 television stations and six regional cable news channels.

Both Viacom and E.W. Scripps hold their broadcast television station groups and cable network holdings in separate corporate entities. Because their station groups and cable networks have common corporate directors, however, we consider them to be affiliated. Counting Viacom's 34 cable networks and CBS's 28 cable networks, these affiliated companies have interests in 62 cable networks. Including Scripps Networks Interactive, E.W. Scripps has interests in 11 cable networks.

Comcast is the only distributor of video programming with ownership interests in each mode of video distribution covered by this Report; it is an MVPD that owns and operates 26 full-power television stations (10 NBC O&Os and 16 Telemundo O&Os) and maintains an ownership interest in Hulu, an OVD. News Corp. (which holds 27 broadcast television stations) and Disney/ABC (which holds 8 broadcast television station) also have ownership interests in Hulu. Other than Comcast, Cox Media Holdings is the only MVPD that owns broadcast stations serving a DMA where it also owns a cable system. . . .

Licensing of Broadcast Spectrum. A broadcast station may not operate in the United States without first receiving Commission authorization.[6] The Commission therefore is responsible for licensing broadcast spectrum to respective applicants and ensuring that the spectrum is used to serve the public interest. . . . The Act also prohibits broadcast stations from assigning or transferring control of their licenses without obtaining Commission approval. In addition, certain obligations are imposed on licensees during each license term, which is generally eight years. Under the Act, in order to grant an application for renewal of a broadcast license, the Commission must find that, during the previous license term, the station has served the public interest, convenience, and necessity; there have been no serious violations of the licensee of the Act or the Commission's rules and regu-

---

6. 47 U.S.C. § 301.

lations; and there have been no other violations by the licensee of the Act or the Commission's rules and regulations which, taken together, would constitute a pattern of abuse.

Ownership Limits. The Commission has adopted several rules limiting the ownership interests of broadcasters to further the Act's goals of competition, localism, and diversity. Congress mandates that the Commission review its media ownership rules every four years to determine whether they "are necessary in the public interest as a result of competition." Currently, the Commission's media ownership rules limit local television ownership, local radio ownership, newspaper/broadcast cross-ownership, radio/television cross-ownership, and dual network ownership. The local television ownership rule permits a single entity to own two television stations in the same market only if certain conditions are met. The newspaper/broadcast cross-ownership rule prevents the common ownership of a radio or television broadcast station and a daily newspaper where the station's broadcast signal encompasses the entire community where the newspaper is published. The radio/television cross-ownership rule restricts the common ownership of radio and television broadcast stations in a single market after factoring in the size of the relevant market.

Notes and Questions

a. The full FCC Annual Assessment of the Status of Competition in the Market for the Delivery of Video Programming, contains some other very helpful information to understand the rapidly changing television marketplace:

> The broadcast television station group consists of commercial and noncommercial, full-power, Class A, and low-power stations.... At the end of 2012, there were 1,028 commercial UHF stations, 358 commercial VHF stations, 288 noncommercial UHF stations, 107 noncommercial VHF stations, and 6,609 television translators, Class A stations, and low power television stations. See FCC, *Licensed Broadcast Station Totals*, http://transition.fcc.gov/mb/audio/Broadcast-StationTotals.html....

> Television translator stations typically serve communities that cannot receive the signals of free over-the-air television stations because they are too far away from a full-power television station or because of geographic limitations. [C]ertain qualifying low-power television (LPTV) stations are accorded Class A status, which indicates that these stations have "primary" status as television broadcasters and have a measure of interference protection from full service television stations.

b. Retransmission consent and must-carry provisions are more fully described in other FCC documents. See *In-State Broadcast Programming: Report to Congress Pursuant to Section 304 of the Satellite Television Extension and Localism Act of 2010*, MB Docket No. 10-238, Report, 26 FCC Rcd 11919 (MB 2011) ("*STELA Report*"); *Retransmission Consent and Exclusivity Rules: Report to Congress Pursuant to Section 208 of the Satellite Home Viewer Extension and Reauthorization Act of 2004*, MB Docket No. 05-28 (Sept. 8, 2005), http://hraunfoss.fcc.gov/edocs_public/attachmatch/DOC-260936A1.doc.

c. The FCC has attempted numerous efforts at maintaining vertical and horizontal market concentration rules, but given the difficulty in proving anti-competitive harm and the First Amendment implications of such ownership restrictions, the Commission has had little success in court. See *Comcast Corp. v. FCC*, 579 F.3d 1, 10 (D.C. Cir. 2009); *Time Warner Entm't Co. v. FCC*, 240 F.3d 1126, 1136, 1139 (D.C. Cir. 2001).

Problem XIV-A

Bryce has learned that a local cable channel has been broadcasting an unauthorized video of a live performance recorded of Bryce's band. The channel is either public access or paid access, Bryce is unsure. The program episode that includes Bryce's music also shows audience shots in which questionable and unsavory activity may be taking place. Bryce is unsure what was happening among the patrons but is embarrassed by the use of the band's performance to highlight the lewd, embarrassing conduct.

Bryce has contacted the program's producers but they are uninterested in removing the content. Bryce does not wish to bring a copyright lawsuit or other legal action, but is hoping the cable company might be of assistance. Advise Bryce regarding the options that might be available.

B. Television Writer Agreements

The Writers Guild Standard Writing Services Contract

... The WGAW has created a standard writing services contract, now available via download (below)—which can be tailored to reflect the negotiated terms of any writing services contract you negotiate. We encourage you to use it in place of deal memos or those quickly jotted notes you write to confirm the terms just negotiated. The standard writing services contract is available in two versions—one for directly employed writers and the other for writers employed through loan-outs....

WRITER'S THEATRICAL SHORT-FORM CONTRACT

...

6. COMPENSATION:

A. Guaranteed Compensation (see 11, below): $_____

B. Contingent Compensation (see 11, below): $_____

C. Profit Participation: If sole writing credit, _____% of (Net/Gross) Proceeds; Reducible for shared credit to _____% (see 27, below)

7. Specific material upon which services are to be based, if any _____ (a copy will be sent to Writer under separate cover): _____ ...

13. BONUS:

A. For sole writing credit: $_____

B. For shared writing credit: $_____. Shared credit bonus will be paid on commencement of principal photography if no other writer has been engaged; balance to be paid on determination of writing credit.

C. For "green light" or engagement of an "element": $_____. If Writer is writer of record or is most recent writer on the Project at the time the Project is given a "green light" by a studio or an element is attached on a pay-or-play basis, Writer shall be given a bonus of _____ _____ Dollars ($_____) which may may not be applied against the bonus in A. or B., above....

24. RESULTS AND PROCEEDS: Work-Made-For-Hire: Writer acknowledges that all results, product and proceeds of Writer's services (including all original ideas in connection therewith) are being specially ordered by Producer for use as part of a Motion Pic-

ture and shall be considered a "work made for hire" for Producer as specially commissioned for use as a part of a motion picture in accordance with Sections 101 and 201 of Title 17 of the U.S. Copyright Act. Therefore, Producer shall be the author and copyright owner thereof for all purposes throughout the universe without limitation of any kind or nature. In consideration of the monies paid to Lender hereunder, Producer shall solely and exclusively own throughout the universe in perpetuity all rights of every kind and nature whether now or hereafter known or created in and in connection with such results, product and proceeds, in whatever stage of completion as may exist from time to time, including: (i) the copyright and all rights of copyright; (ii) all neighboring rights, trademarks and any and all other ownership and exploitation rights now or hereafter recognized in any Territory, including all rental, lending, fixation, reproduction, broadcasting (including satellite transmission), distribution and all other rights of communication by any and all means, media, devices, processes and technology; (iii) the rights to adapt, rearrange, and make changes in, deletions from and additions to such results, product and proceeds, and to use all or any part thereof in new versions, adaptations, and other Motion Pictures including Remakes and Sequels; (iv) the right to use the title of the Work in connection therewith or otherwise and to change such title; and (v) all rights generally known as the "moral rights of authors." ...

26. NO INJUNCTIVE RELIEF:

The sole right of Writer as to any breach or alleged breach hereunder by Company shall be the recovery of money damages, if any, and the rights herein granted by Writer shall not terminate by reason of such breach. In no event may Writer terminate this Agreement or obtain injunctive relief or other equitable relief with respect to any breach of Company's obligations hereunder.

27. PROFIT PARTICIPATION: Terms to be negotiated in good faith. If the parties fail to reach agreement ____ months after execution hereof, either party, upon 30 days notice to the other, may submit the matter to what is known as a "baseball arbitration," in which each party presents one profit proposal and the arbitrator is required to adopt one of the two proposals. The arbitrator shall be selected and the arbitration conducted pursuant to the Voluntary Labor Arbitration Rules of the AAA.

Sandy Veith & Vuelta Int'l, Inc. v. MCA Inc.
1997 Cal. App. Unpub. LEXIS 1 (1997)

[Most of the litigation involving television development has to do with ownership of ideas as they evolve into scripts. It is axiomatic that ideas are not protected by copyright whereas written expression has copyright protection. In the collaborative world of television, a great deal of activity and investment occurs around projects that are still in the idea stage of development. Unless the concept's creator is a member of the Writer's Guild of America and protected by a pre-existing contract, the general result is for the idea submission to be unprotected. Copyright cannot protect the ideas, and in most cases there is no sufficient written agreement to protect the creators of television concepts even when the ideas served as the basis for subsequent television series.

The somewhat convoluted factual history of "Northern Exposure" illustrates a contractual dispute involving the development of a hit television series and the difficulties of ascribing origination. The following is an unpublished opinion.]

The defendants, MCA, Inc. and Universal City Studios, Inc. (collectively, "Universal") appeal a judgment in favor of the plaintiffs, Sandy Veith and Vuelta International Inc., entered following a jury verdict in the total sum of $7.29 million. Veith, a television writer and producer, asserted a claim against Universal based upon a breach of contract which involved Universal's failure to pay certain bonus compensation due under Veith's exclusive term contract.

The Writers Guild of America, West, Inc. (herein, "Writer's Guild") has appeared in this matter as amicus curiae. Veith is a member of the Writer's Guild and as such is a third-party beneficiary of a collective bargaining agreement (CBA) between the Writer's Guild and the Alliance of Motion Picture & Television Producers, Inc. Universal is a signatory to the CBA.

The CBA, which was effective August 8, 1988 through May 1, 1992, determines, among other things, (1) minimum rates of payment, (2) rules relating to credit, and (3) rights to "residual" participation, if any, in future exploitation and the profits therefrom. While the CBA sets minimum standards for pay, "in many cases individuals with notable skills and achievements ('track records'), with special relation to particular projects, with multiple creative roles, with combined creative and entrepeneurial roles, or with other sources of bargaining power, can obtain compensation well above the collectively-bargained minimum contractual rates, as well as varying measures of artistic control."

FACTUAL AND PROCEDURAL BACKGROUND

Sometime in late 1980 or early 1981, Veith was approached by William Sackheim, an experienced producer and writer, who asked Veith to collaborate on "Coletta," Bill's idea for a television series.[7] Bill's idea involved a doctor compelled to serve in a rural area for four or five years in order to pay off the scholarship which enabled him to attend medical school. Bill had prepared a written document which he denominated a "presentation" or "back story" on the "Coletta" project, which is less detailed than a "format" or some other type of creative product. A writer who prepares a "presentation" rather than a "format" is not entitled to the so-called "created by" credit. Bill and Veith agreed that Veith would write the project, and began fleshing out the idea and developing a storyline.

In March 1981, Veith, with Bill's assistance, entered into a written exclusive term contract with Universal (the "Agreement"), effective June 1, 1981, to use his creative talents exclusively for Universal to develop original ideas for television programming. The Agreement provided for a one year term, with two successive annual options, the first for an additional year, and the second for an additional two year term. During the term of the Agreement, Universal could use Veith in all media as a writer and as a producer.

Veith was guaranteed a specified annual salary, which was a nonreturnable advance against certain "per assignment" fees set forth in Exhibit A to the Agreement ("Exhibit A").

In other words, if Veith completed sufficient assignments, Universal would pay Veith additional sums based on the completion of such assignments. Exhibit A showed the fees per assignment for work as a writer and as a producer, and differentiated between such creative products as "story & teleplay," "story only," "teleplay only," "treatment," and "format only." Exhibit A also provided that "If Veith should render any services hereunder in collaboration (or as a team) with another artist or artists, fees, percentages, (pursuant to this EXHIBIT 'A' or in the Agreement to which this EXHIBIT 'A' is attached) etc., will be proportionately reduced."

---

7. As a matter of convenience and to avoid confusion we will hereafter refer to William Sackheim simply as "Bill" in order to differentiate him from Ray Sackheim, who is Bill's brother and was, at relevant times, Veith's agent.

Of particular relevance to this appeal, in addition to the guaranteed compensation and additional sums based on the completion of such assignments, Veith was entitled to additional payments under the Agreement if certain conditions were met. Specifically, the Agreement provided that if a prime time television series were to be licensed for exhibition as a direct result of a pilot photoplay for which Veith received sole or partial teleplay credit and sole or partial separation of rights[8] Veith would be entitled to various additional sums (the bonus), as, when and to the extent required by the CBA.

With respect to the bonus, the Agreement provided:

"4. [Veith] shall be entitled to the following additional payments which do not apply against salary listed in Paragraph 2 above.

"a) If a prime time episodic television series is licensed for exhibition as a direct result of a pilot photoplay for which [Veith] receives sole Teleplay credit and additionally receives sole 'separation of rights' on the series, we shall pay [Veith] whichever of the following sequel royalties is applicable: $2,000 for sequels 30 minutes in length, $2,250 for sequels over 30 but not more than 60 minutes in length; $2,500 for sequels over 60 but not more than 90 minutes in length, $2,750 for sequels over 90 minutes in length. One-half of the aforementioned sequel royalty shall be deemed earned for receiving sole 'separation of rights' on the series and one-half shall be deemed earned for receiving sole Teleplay credit on said pilot photoplay. To the extent Veith receives less than sole 'separation of rights' and/or less than sole Teleplay credit on said pilot, the sequel royalty will be proportionately reduced (e.g., if Veith receives sole 'separation of rights' with respect to a series hereunder and one-half Teleplay credit on the pilot photoplay that directly results in a series sale, the 30 minute length sequel royalty would be $1,000 for sole 'separation of rights' and $500 for one-half Teleplay credit, or a total of $1,500). Sequel royalties shall be payable as and when required by the WGA. Any WGA-required sequel royalty or character payment shall be deemed an advance against any contractual sequel royalty hereunder and the converse shall be equally true.

"b) [Veith] shall be entitled to receive residuals on sequel royalties payable as, when and to the extent required by the [CBA].

"c) [Veith] shall be entitled to receive a 'hyphenate bonus' as required by the [CBA] payable as, when and to the extent required by the [CBA].

"d) With respect to all writing assignments hereunder, [Veith] shall receive scale residuals payable as, when and to the extent required by the [CBA]." ...

"6. During the term of this agreement, Veith shall have no right to acquire or dispose of (for his own account or otherwise) whether personally or through a

---

8. "For WGA [Writers Guild Association] screen writers, so-called 'separation of rights' (Article 16(A) of the WGA agreement) is a critical concept. A writer's entitlement to 'separation of rights' depends on the originality and substantiality of the writer's contribution to the film and flow from having written the story. For example, minor rewrites do not qualify. A writer who has 'separation of rights' receives the major package of WGA-negotiated benefits, including novelization, remake, sequel (and perhaps turnaround), etc. The requirements to attain 'separation of rights' are spelled out in detail in the WGA agreement. There are somewhat different but also detailed specifications for 'separation of rights' for television writers." ("Ownership and Control of Intellectual Property Rights in Motion Pictures and Audiovisual Works: Contractual and Practical Aspects—Response of the United States to the ALAI Questionnaire, ALAI Congress, Paris, Sept. 20, 1995," 20 COLUM.-VLA J.L. & ARTS, *supra*, at p. 459, fn. 51).

firm or corporation he controls, rights in and to any literary, motion picture, television and/or related material. All writing and other materials on which he is engaged during the term of this agreement (to the extent not based on source material furnished by us) shall be deemed created by him during the term hereof. Veith agrees to give us forthwith a list of properties owned or controlled by him. With respect to such properties, if during the term he desires to sell or license such properties, he must first offer such properties to us and we shall have a 21-day negotiation with respect to the sale or license of such properties; if thereafter, Veith desires to sell or license said properties to others on terms less favorable to himself than last offered to us, Veith shall advise us in writing of the terms and conditions of such proposed licensing or sale and we shall have a 7-day first refusal with respect to such deal. As to properties not contained in the list, they shall be deemed created during the term....

It is understood that Sandy Veith is an employee of Vuelta International, Inc., and that all material to be written hereunder shall be a work for hire for us and we shall be the owner thereof, ..."

It is Universal's failure to pay such bonus which is at the heart of this case.

At some point before Veith actually began working for Universal, he and Bill met with Warren Littlefield and Jeff Sagansky of the NBC network and pitched the "Coletta" project to them. Littlefield liked it, and asked what Veith and Bill wanted. They wanted NBC to pay for six scripts; he offered to pay for four, and asked where they thought they would be taking "Coletta," that is, what studio would be producing it. Bill told him that Veith was going to Universal, and they therefore would take it to Universal because Bill wanted Universal to produce it.

NBC ultimately purchased an option from Universal to produce "Coletta." Veith, who was by then working for Universal, wrote the story and screenplay for "Coletta," and Bill, who was with another studio, was to supervise the project. This deal was evidenced by a written agreement between NBC and Universal for a half-hour pilot script to be written by Veith and supervised by Bill, and by a second written agreement between NBC and Universal for three backup scripts. Universal also amended Bill's consulting contract to give him additional compensation if "Coletta" was produced as a series.

Veith wrote a "Coletta" story for NBC, which approved it, apparently the preliminary step to beginning work on a teleplay. In January or February of 1982, Veith delivered a pilot teleplay of "Coletta" to NBC. After a note session with people from NBC and Universal, Universal agreed to pay for three back-up scripts, and hired two other writers to work on them, one of whom was a writer named Bill Dial, whose resulting familiarity with "Coletta" became relevant about 8 years later, in 1990. Veith participated in the writing and rewriting of the back-up scripts.

Sometime in 1982, Universal "extended and suspended" its Agreement with Veith so that he could take a year off to produce "Love, Sidney" with Tony Randall in New York. In consideration for being given leave to produce "Love, Sidney," Veith agreed with Universal that he would continue to render required consultative services in connection with "our project 'Coletta'" during the period of his leave, for no additional compensation, and, in fact, he and Bill continued to work on "Coletta" during the year Veith was in New York. However, sometime in 1982, Jeff Sagansky of NBC decided not to go with "Coletta" as a series. In 1983, Universal exercised an option to extend the Agreement and, on June 6, 1983, signed an amendment to the Agreement which increased the remuneration due to Veith under the Agreement (the "Amendment").

After NBC turned down "Coletta," Veith was working for Warner Bros., and was too busy to make changes to "Coletta." However, Veith knew another writer at Universal, Joel Blasberg, whom he thought might be able to revise "Coletta" using a new locale where Veith had grown up. Blasberg wrote a new "Coletta" story, using the same central characters as before, but set the location of the story in the Florida Keys, and it was presented to ABC as a possible half-hour comedy; however, ABC would not commit to the project. Veith and Bill subsequently decided "Coletta" should be made into an hour-long program, to take advantage of the revised, exotic setting. Veith had to rewrite the characters, and Universal introduced him to a "one hour writer," Steve Brown. Veith, Brown, Bill and Charmiane Balian, Universal's vice-president of drama development, then pitched "Coletta" to Greg Mayday at CBS. Bill also met with Michelle Brustin of NBC's drama department about the possibility of making "Coletta" an hour-long program (dramas are usually an hour in length, while comedies are usually half-hour in length). Bill continued to try to sell "Coletta" to a network. In 1985, he met with an executive of ABC and told her about "Coletta." She suggested that he approach Stu Bloomberg, who was in charge of comedy at ABC, so Bill, Blasberg and Bloomberg all met and talked about "Coletta" as set in the Florida Keys. As a result, Bill told Universal's executives that they had a shot at selling "Coletta" to ABC.

In 1986, ABC entered into an option agreement with Universal for another script of "Coletta" set in the Florida Keys. Veith, whose contract with Universal had by this time expired, was then working at Warner Bros. Blasberg, who was working as a writer under contract to Universal, was selected to write the script. Universal asked Veith to sign a letter agreement, dated June 27, 1986, which would give Universal an extension of time within which to commence exploitation of the television sequel rights to "Coletta" related to the rewrite by Blasberg (the Extension Agreement). Veith did not immediately agree to sign the June 27, 1986 agreement. In late June and early July of 1986, although Veith was working at Warner Bros., and although he had not signed the Extension Agreement, he accompanied Blasberg to the Florida Keys for several days, to work on ideas for the rewrite and to show Blasberg how to mine Veith's boyhood home for characters for the series.

Universal continued to pressure Veith to sign some form of an extension agreement, and ultimately Veith did so, granting to Universal two additional extensions of time within which to continue the pilot and series development of "Coletta" for television production. Universal also tried to get Veith to agree to a less remunerative bonus provision, but Veith insisted that he would not give up his existing deal, and Universal finally acceded on this point. Blasberg prepared "Coletta" scripts which were presented to ABC as a possible half-hour comedy series, but in 1987 ABC passed on "Coletta." Thus, by 1987, both NBC and ABC had taken a look at "Coletta" and had passed; the other network, CBS, had also looked at it but had refused to make a commitment.

Apparently all was quiet on the "Coletta" front until the evening of July 12, 1990, when Veith received a telephone call from Bill Dial, one of the writers hired by Universal to work on the "Coletta" back-up scripts in 1982. Dial had just seen the first episode of "Northern Exposure," and called to tell Veith it sounded "an awful lot" like "Coletta." Veith had not seen the show himself, but soon received more calls from other people about the remarkable similarity between "Northern Exposure" and "Coletta." Veith obtained a copy of a "Northern Exposure" script and determined for himself that it was very similar.

On July 13, 1990, one day after the initial broadcast of "Northern Exposure," Veith called the Writer's Guild and then on July 16, he wrote to Stacy Murphy at the Guild, sent him two scripts to compare, and asked what he should do. He had discovered that not only were the scripts similar, but also the same players, other than the writers, had been involved in both projects (i.e. Kerry McCluggage, Richard Lindheim, Charmiane Balian and Brad Johnson of Universal and Jeff Sagansky, who, while at NBC, had bought an option on "Coletta" and who had then, while President of CBS Television, bought "Northern Exposure" in 1989). He also learned that Lee Gabler, his agent at Creative Artists Agency, Inc., represented Joshua Brand and John Falsey, the creators, writers and producers of "Northern Exposure." However, when he first contacted Gabler about the similarity between "Coletta" and "Northern Exposure," Gabler acted as though he had no idea who the writers and producers of "Northern Exposure" might be, and would have to find out.

In January of 1993, Veith filed suit against Universal and Creative Artists Agency, Inc. for breach of written contract, breach of implied contract, breach of fiduciary duty, and for an accounting.[9] His complaint alleged, in relevant part, that pursuant to paragraph 4 (a)–(e) of the Agreement, he was to receive, in addition to a fixed salary, specific dollar amounts *if a prime time episodic television series was licensed as a result of his creative efforts.* Such compensation included sequel royalties, residuals on sequel royalties, series and teleplay bonuses, a hyphenate bonus, scale residuals on writing assignments, a share of Universal's net profits, writing and producing fees and syndication fees.

At trial, substantial evidence was produced from which the jury reasonably could infer that Universal's executives intentionally supplied material amounts of the "Coletta" story and teleplay to Brand and Falsey without telling them that the material came from "Coletta." There was also evidence that Universal was motivated to do so, because it had a significant financial incentive in the form of a blind commitment from ABC in 1987 and from NBC in 1989 to have Brand and Falsey, rather than some other writer or writers, come up with an acceptable idea for a television series. Finally, there was also evidence that the similarities between "Coletta" and "Northern Exposure" were so significant on many different elements of plot, characterization and detail that they could not be the result of a coincidence, and which indicated that the "Northern Exposure" story and teleplay came about as a direct result of Veith's "Coletta" story and teleplay.

Veith put on evidence of damages he suffered not only as a result of his loss of the bonus, but also as a result of the loss of future earning capacity occasioned by not receiving the creative credit for the very successful prime time television series, "Northern Exposure." On direct examination, one of plaintiff's expert witnesses, Veith's agent, Ray Sackheim testified that in his opinion, the future monetary value of being credited as the creator of a show like "Northern Exposure" was $10 to $25 million. He also opined that "Coletta" would have been a better series than "Northern Exposure." Defense counsel did not cross-examine Sackheim on his opinion as to the amount of damages, nor move to strike such opinion, nor is there any indication in the record that Universal made a motion in limine to exclude such evidence.

Robert Schiller, another witness for Veith, who had 45 years of experience in writing and producing many well-known television programs, testified that in his opinion, the future value over a writer's career of receiving credit as the creator of a successful series, i.e., one which ran three or four seasons, was a minimum of $5 million, based on the usefulness of such credit in getting offers of other employment and deals.

---

9. By the time of trial, Veith had dismissed Creative Artists Agency, Inc., as a defendant and had dropped all causes of action against Universal except for breach of contract. This, of course, has no effect on his ability to argue that Universal breached the implied covenant of good faith and fair dealing in the Agreement; there is no reason to assert a separate cause of action for breach of the implied covenant of good faith and fair dealing unless the plaintiff wishes to seek a tort recovery.

In addition to this direct testimony on the damages Veith had suffered as a result of the loss of future earning capacity because of his failure to receive created by credit on "Northern Exposure," there was also circumstantial evidence related to this issue, in the form of testimony related to Veith's and Brand and Falsey's respective careers, i.e., to the different programs on which they had worked as writers and producers and on which they had or had not received various creative credits, and the sums they had earned for their work as their careers progressed.

In 1994, after a five-week trial, the jury returned a special verdict against Universal and awarded Veith $7.29 million in damages, and judgment was entered thereon on October 14, 1994. On November 1, 1994, Universal made a timely motion for judgment notwithstanding the verdict, and at the same time filed its notice of intention to move for new trial. Both motions were denied by the trial court on December 8, 1994.

ISSUES PRESENTED

… First, is there substantial evidence that Universal breached the Agreement with Veith, and prevented Veith from fulfilling the condition precedent to Universal's duty to pay Veith the bonus? Second, can Universal avoid the consequences of its breach of the Agreement by relying on the arbitration provisions of the CBA?…

1. *Substantial Evidence Supports the Jury's Determination that Universal Breached The Agreement and Prevented Veith from Fulfilling the Condition Precedent to Receiving the Bonus Under Paragraph 4 of the Agreement*

"'Every contract imposes upon each party a duty of good faith and fair dealing in its performance and its enforcement.'… The covenant of good faith finds particular application in situations where one party is invested with a discretionary power affecting the rights of another. Such power must be exercised in good faith." In general, the covenant imposes a duty upon all parties to a contract not to deprive the other parties of the contract's benefits. The covenant "'… not only imposes upon each contracting party the duty to refrain from doing anything which would render performance of the contract impossible by any act of his own, but also the duty to do everything that the contract presupposes that he will do to accomplish its purpose.'" In other words, good faith performance of a contract "emphasizes faithfulness to an agreed common purpose and consistency with the justified expectations of the other party." Thus, "a breach of the implied covenant can result from conduct permitted by the express (or implied-in-fact) terms of the contract."

This rule was developed "in the contract arena and is aimed at making effective the agreement's promises." … In short, the covenant is an implied-in-law term of the contract. Therefore, its breach will always result in a breach of the contract, although a breach of a consensual (i.e., an express or implied-in-fact) contract term will not necessarily constitute a breach of the covenant. To establish a breach of the covenant, the obligee must demonstrate "conscious and deliberate" conduct on the part of the obligor which was designed to frustrate the obligee's contract rights, i.e., conduct which constitutes "'unfair dealing rather than mistaken judgment.'" Just what conduct will meet this criteria must be determined on a case by case basis and will depend on the contractual purposes and reasonably justified expectations of the parties.

Here, Universal's promise to pay Veith the bonus was conditioned on (1) the licensing of a prime time television series as a direct result of a pilot photoplay in which Veith was sufficiently involved so as to be entitled to sole or partial teleplay credit and separation of rights, and (2) Veith's actual receipt of sole or partial teleplay and separation of rights credits on such series. Thus, under the implied covenant of good faith and fair dealing, Universal had a duty not only to refrain from doing anything which would render Veith's performance of these conditions impossible, but also the duty to do everything that the contract presupposed would be necessary so that Veith could perform such conditions.

The evidence shows that Universal breached these duties. Specifically, there was substantial evidence that executives from Universal, and possibly Jeff Sagansky from CBS, intentionally "fed" significant aspects of the "Coletta" story and teleplay to Brand and Falsey during the development of the "Northern Exposure" project. There was also substantial evidence that Universal knew that (1) Veith, as the writer of both the "Coletta" story and teleplay, was entitled, at the very least, to be listed in the "Notice of Tentative Writing Credits" (NTWC) and to compete for writing credits and separation of rights on "Northern Exposure" pursuant to the CBA; (2) Brand and Falsey were unaware that they had been given "Coletta" material during the development of the "Northern Exposure" project; (3) Brand and Falsey, as the producers of "Northern Exposure," would fill out the NTWC which would be sent to the Writer's Guild as part of the process of determining final credits; (4) Brand and Falsey, being unaware of the "Coletta/Northern Exposure" connection, had no reason to think that Veith should be listed as a participating writer on the NTWC for "Northern Exposure"; (5) anyone not listed by Brand and Falsey as a participating writer on the NTWC would not be sent a copy of the notice; (6) anyone not sent a copy of the NTWC would not be able to deliver to the Writer's Guild a written protest of the tentative credits and request for arbitration of credits within the extremely short amount of time before the producers' tentative allocation of credits became final; and (7) once the allocation of credits became final, there was no method under the CBA by which the issue of the actual allocation of credits could be reopened.[10]

Thus, there is substantial evidence that Universal engaged in "conscious and deliberate" conduct which frustrated Veith's justifiable expectations under the Agreement by preventing him from fulfilling the condition precedent to Universal's duty to pay him the bonus, i.e., that he receive teleplay credit and separation of rights for his story and teleplay on which "Northern Exposure" was based. Because Universal prevented or made impossible the performance or happening of the condition precedent, the condition was excused. Because the condition precedent was excused, and because the jury found that but for Universal's prevention, Veith would have obtained teleplay credit and separation of rights, Universal was obligated to pay Veith the bonus, and its failure to do so constituted a breach of the Agreement.

2. *Arbitration Under the CBA Was Not Available to Veith Either as the Exclusive Remedy for His Claim Nor as a Method by Which to Mitigate His Damages.*

Universal contends that the judgment must be reversed and a judgment in its favor entered as a matter of law because Veith's right to writing credits is governed exclusively by the CBA, and lawfully cannot be the subject of an individual contract such as the Agreement, nor can Veith seek a judicial remedy for the breach of such right. We agree that in the case of a *dispute* over entitlement to writing credits, only the Writer's Guild can determine who is entitled to such credits. However, if writers who participated in the authorship of a story and/or teleplay unanimously agree on the allocation of writing credits, the Writer's Guild is *not* involved in making an award of credits. (CBA, Television

---

10. The CBA does provide that the allocation of credits can be reopened under circumstances not applicable here, i.e., if material changes have been made in a script after the credits have been determined under the NTWC procedure, then either the company or the participating writer and the Writer's Guild jointly may reopen the credit allocation by making a claim to the Writer's Guild or the company within 48 hours after completion of the writing claimed to justify revision of the credits. (See CBA, Television Schedule A, Television Credits, subparagraph 19.)

Schedule A, Television Credits, subparagraph 6.) In any event, only writers, either through unanimous agreement, or through the Writer's Guild's arbitration of credits process, can award writing credits.

This, however, does not mean that the jury here, *for purposes of calculating Veith's contractual damages,* could not conclude that, but for Universal's conduct, Veith *would* have had a right to particular kinds of creative credits, i.e., "created by," and "written by" as to story and/or teleplay, and to the separation of rights which then flowed from his right to the other kinds of credit. *This is entirely different than awarding Veith the actual credits.* As pointed out by Veith's attorney at oral argument, Veith will *never* receive credit as the sole or partial creator or writer of "Northern Exposure." His name will never appear on the screen each time the program is shown in reruns. All he will receive is *damages.*

Universal also contends that, as a matter of law, the CBA *required* Veith to submit this claim to arbitration. Whether Veith was required to arbitrate this claim under the CBA is a question of law. For the following reasons, we conclude that the CBA does *not* provide for, nor require, arbitration of this particular dispute.

a. *Universal Waived Its Right to Demand Arbitration*

If Universal believed that Veith was required to arbitrate this claim rather than bringing an action at law, its remedy was to file a petition to compel arbitration (which, coincidentally, is exactly what it did in *Universal City Studios, Inc.* v. *Writers Guild of America, Inc.,* U.S.D.C. Case No. CV 96-3732-DT (Ex) (C.D. Cal. July 11, 1996) (the *Blasberg* action), a case of which Universal has asked this court to take judicial notice, and which we discuss, *infra*). For whatever reason, Universal did not do so. The contractual right to demand arbitration may be waived by the failure to demand arbitration within a reasonable time. What constitutes a reasonable time is normally a question of fact requiring an examination of all of the circumstances, including any prejudice the opposing party suffered as a result of the delay. In this case, Universal never demanded arbitration and therefore, we hold, as a matter of law, that Universal waived its right to demand arbitration.

b. The CBA Does Not Provide for nor Require Arbitration of This Particular Dispute.

Article 8 of the CBA is entitled "Credits for Screen Authorship (General)." It provides, in relevant part: "The Company agrees that credits for screen authorship shall be given only pursuant to the terms of and in the manner prescribed in the applicable Schedule A attached hereto and by this reference incorporated herein, with respect to credits for screen authorship finally determined during the term hereof, and with respect to credits for screen authorship finally determined after the expiration of the term hereof involving material written during the term hereof or during the term of a prior collective bargaining agreement between the Company and the Guild; …"

Article 12 of the CBA is entitled "Court Proceedings." Subsection A of Article 12 is entitled "Disputes Concerning Credits." Article 12.A provides, in relevant part: "Nothing in this [CBA] shall limit the rights of the Guild or any writer to assert any and all appropriate legal and equitable rights and remedies to which the Guild or such writer is entitled in courts of competent jurisdiction with regard to an alleged breach of Article 8 and Schedule A of this [CBA] with respect to writing credit; subject, however, to the following conditions and limitations:

> "…

> "2. If the Guild or the writer commences any proceedings in court with respect to any such alleged breach prior to the submission of the dispute to arbitration hereunder, then neither the Guild nor the writer may submit such dispute

to arbitration *and no arbitrator shall have jurisdiction to consider the alleged breach of such credit provision."* (Italics added.) In other words, Veith had the option to litigate any dispute related to screen credits rather than submitting it to arbitration, and if he filed suit before Universal submitted the matter to arbitration, which it had the right to do under Article 12.A.3., then the arbitrator had no jurisdiction over the matter.

In its amicus curiae brief, the Writer's Guild contends that under Article 12.A., a writer may only pursue his or her legal and equitable remedies for breach of credit privileges and benefits *after* credits have been determined, and that neither the Writer's Guild nor the writer "may pursue in court that determination of *entitlement to credit*" (emphasis added). Nothing we hold here is to the contrary. However, the Writer's Guild is the sole arbitor of screen credits so long as the writer is either listed on the NTWC or receives notice that he or she has not been listed and the NTWC has not become final. Under the facts of this case where Veith was neither listed on the NTWC nor given notice he was not so listed *and* where the NTWC has become final, there is nothing in the CBA that prevents Veith from pursuing the only other legal remedy available to him, i.e., filing suit. Furthermore, Veith's claim against Universal was for damages for breach of contract, not for a determination awarding him created by or written by credit on "Northern Exposure," and, in fact, Veith pursued his action for breach of contract against Universal only *after* the credit determination for the credits on "Northern Exposure" had become final, and he had no other remedy.

That Veith had no remedy under the CBA once the credit determination became final is clear. Television Schedule A of the CBA, paragraph 13, provides, in relevant part: "If within the time specified [in the NTWC], a written protest of the tentative credits has not been delivered to the Guild, the tentative writing credits shall become final." The only provision for vacating or otherwise attacking a credit determination that has become final which is made in Television Schedule A, or anywhere else in the CBA for that matter, is found at paragraph 19 of Television Schedule A, which provides:

"In the event that after the screen credits are determined as hereinabove provided, material changes are made in the script, either the Company or a participant and the Guild jointly may reopen the credit determination by making a claim to the Guild or Company as the case may be, within forty-eight (48) hours after completion of the writing claimed to justify the revision of credits, in which case the procedure for determining such revised credits will be the same as that provided for the original determination of credits." Thus, the CBA does not provide for arbitration over entitlement to credit *once the credit determination became final*, except in one circumstance clearly not applicable here.

Our conclusion that, as a matter of law, arbitration under the CBA was simply not available as a method for resolving this particular dispute, puts an end to Universal's argument that Veith could and should have mitigated his damages by pursuing arbitration to try to have the allocation of creative credits changed after such credits became final, and resolves Universal's contentions on appeal that the trial court committed various errors in connection with the mitigation issue.

... [The court addresses and upholds the jury award of damages.]

Jacobs v. CBS Broad., Inc.

291 F.3d 1173 (9th Cir. 2002)

Plaintiffs Mike Jacobs, Jr., William Webb, and Westwind Releasing Corporation filed this action against Defendant CBS Broadcasting, Inc., alleging that CBS had breached a contract to give Plaintiffs production credit when it produced a television series called *Early Edition*. The district court granted summary judgment to CBS on the ground that an earlier nonjudicial proceeding precluded Plaintiffs from bringing their claim to court. We reverse because that nonjudicial proceeding was too informal to have preclusive effect.

Michael Givens is a script writer and a member of the Writers' Guild of America (WGA). Givens wrote a script titled *The Fourth Estate a/k/a/Final Edition* (*Final Edition*). Westwind optioned *Final Edition* for the purpose of securing a television broadcast commitment from a network. Under the agreement between Givens and Westwind, any writing credit to be accorded Givens was to be determined pursuant to the WGA's Minimum Basic Agreement (MBA) credit-determination procedures. Givens was entitled to additional compensation under the contract only if the WGA awarded him a "written by" or "screenplay by" credit.

CBS later agreed with Westwind to acquire the broadcast rights to *Final Edition* (First Agreement). In a second contract, CBS bought all rights to *Final Edition* from Westwind *and* Givens (Second Agreement). The Second Agreement provided that, "*if a project is produced based upon the literary property*, CBS agrees ... to provide credit to William Webb and Mike Jacobs, Jr. as Co-Executive Producers (or Executive Producers at CBS' election) on a shared card" (emphasis added). The Second Agreement also incorporated the provision in the original contract between Givens and Westwind stating that any writing credit for Givens would be governed by the WGA's credit-determination procedures.

CBS eventually participated in the production of a series called *Early Edition*, which shared a common premise with Givens' *Final Edition* script. In *Early Edition* and *Final Edition*, a man is able to predict the future when he comes into possession of the next day's newspaper, and he attempts to alter events that are yet to occur. However, when the Notice of Tentative Writing Credits for *Early Edition* was issued, Givens was not listed as a "participating writer" who was entitled to receive credit. Givens complained to the WGA, citing those provisions of the MBA setting forth the circumstances under which WGA members such as Givens are entitled to writing credit. The WGA responded by suspending the credits process and informing Columbia Tristar, one of the producers of *Early Edition*, that if *Early Edition* aired with credits different from those that the WGA ultimately found to be proper, the WGA would pursue damages on behalf of the WGA-credited writers.

The WGA undertook an investigation and concluded that Givens was not a "participating writer" of *Early Edition*. Givens sought review of the participating-writer decision but, after engaging in additional investigation, the WGA reaffirmed its conclusion that Givens was not entitled to writing credit. After this second determination, Givens asked the WGA to reconsider its decision. The WGA again decided that Givens was not entitled to credit. In a letter to Givens, the WGA noted that its determination that Givens was not a participating writer precluded it from representing him in any subsequent writing-credit arbitration against CBS.

While Givens was pursuing his WGA appeals, Givens, Jacobs, Webb, and Westwind filed this action in Los Angeles County Superior Court. They argued that the *Early Edition* project was "based upon" the literary property *Final Edition* and that, accordingly, CBS had breached its contract by not providing them with writing and production credit. CBS removed the action to federal court. Next, CBS filed a Notice of Initiation of Arbitration, which sought a decision pursuant to the WGA's arbitration procedure on two questions: (1) whether Givens had a right to enforce the contractual provisions of the Second Agreement with respect to *Early Edition* independently of the processes and standards for determining writing credit set forth in the MBA, and (2) whether Givens had a right to pursue a writing-credit claim in a judicial forum. The district court stayed proceedings in federal court pending the outcome of the arbitration.

The WGA arbitrator ruled in favor of CBS. The arbitrator held that allowing Givens to litigate his claims would undermine the finality of the MBA's "fast, fair, and effective system for determining credit." Givens stipulated to an order confirming the arbitration award. Accordingly, Givens is not a party to this appeal.

CBS then filed a motion for summary judgment against the remaining Plaintiffs, who seek production credit regardless of who actually wrote the *Early Edition* scripts. Arguing that Plaintiffs' claims for production credit were entirely derivative of Givens' claim for writing credit, CBS asserted that the formal WGA arbitration had a preclusive effect on Plaintiffs' federal action. The district court rejected that argument, but nonetheless granted summary judgment on the alternate ground that the earlier WGA participating-writer determination involving Givens had a nonmutual collateral estoppel effect on Plaintiffs' action.

Under the doctrine of nonmutual collateral estoppel, it is not necessary that the earlier and later proceedings involve the same parties or their privies. To the contrary, a nonparty to the earlier proceeding may invoke the doctrine *against* a party who *is* bound by the proceeding. The district court in this case applied the doctrine of nonmutual collateral estoppel, holding that, because Plaintiffs were in privity with Givens, CBS could invoke the WGA participating-writer determination against them even though CBS had not been a party to that proceeding. Plaintiffs filed a timely notice of appeal.

We review de novo the district court's grant of summary judgment. We also review de novo the district court's determination that a prior decision has preclusive effect.

A. *California Law on Collateral Estoppel (Issue Preclusion) Applies.*

CBS argues that the WGA's determination that Givens was not a participating writer precludes Plaintiffs from litigating whether *Early Edition* is "based upon" *Final Edition*. To prevail, CBS must establish that the WGA participating-writer proceeding satisfies the requirements for application of collateral estoppel. Because this is a diversity action, state law controls whether the WGA participating-writer determination has a preclusive effect on Plaintiffs' claims for production credit.... Accordingly, we look to California law for the governing principles.

B. *The WGA Participating-Writer Proceeding Is Not Entitled to Preclusive Effect.*

Under California law, CBS must demonstrate that the WGA participating-writer determination was adjudicatory in nature before that determination can have collateral estoppel effect. Additionally, CBS must show that: (1) the issue decided in the WGA proceeding is identical to that presented in Plaintiffs' action; (2) the issue was actually litigated in the WGA proceeding; (3) the issue was necessarily decided in the WGA proceeding; (4) there was a final judgment on the merits in the WGA proceeding; and (5) Plaintiffs were a party or in privity with a party to the WGA proceeding. Plaintiffs argue that the first of these factors is dispositive and that the district court erred in giving the WGA participating-writer determination preclusive effect because that determination lacked the procedural safeguards that California courts require. We agree.

In order to have an issue-preclusive effect in a later judicial action in California, an arbitration must have been conducted with certain procedural safeguards. As the California Supreme Court recently explained:

> Whether collateral estoppel is fair and consistent with public policy in a particular case depends in part upon the character of the forum that first decided the issue later sought to be foreclosed. In this regard, courts consider the judicial nature of the prior forum, i.e., its legal formality, the scope of its jurisdiction, and its procedural safeguards, particularly including the opportunity for judicial review of adverse rulings.

Vandenberg, 982 P.2d at 237. The California Courts of Appeal have similarly noted that it is "appropriate to give collateral estoppel effect to findings made during an arbitration, *so long as the arbitration had the elements of an adjudicatory procedure." Kelly v. Vons Cos.,* 67 Cal. App. 4th 1329, 79 Cal. Rptr. 2d 763, 767 (Ct. App. 1998). The need for procedural safeguards and legal formality is especially acute in the circumstances of this case because "collateral estoppel is invoked by a nonparty to the prior litigation. Such cases require close examination to determine whether nonmutual use of the doctrine is fair and appropriate."

When deciding whether an arbitration was sufficiently adjudicatory in nature, courts apply the same standards used to determine whether an administrative proceeding should have collateral estoppel effect. Accordingly, courts must examine such factors as whether

> (1) the [arbitration] was conducted in a judicial-like adversary proceeding; (2) the proceedings required witnesses to testify under oath; (3) the [arbitral] determination involved the adjudicatory application of rules to a single set of facts; (4) the proceedings were conducted before an impartial hearing officer; (5) the parties had the right to subpoena witnesses and present documentary evidence; and (6) the [arbitrator] maintained a verbatim record of the proceedings. Additional factors include whether the hearing officer's decision was adjudicatory and in writing with a statement of reasons. Finally, [whether] that reasoned decision [was] adopted by the director of the agency with the potential for later judicial review.

Imen v. Glassford, 201 Cal. App. 3d 898, 247 Cal. Rptr. 514, 518 (Ct. App. 1988).

The WGA participating-writer determination did not provide the requisite procedural safeguards to give it issue-preclusive effect in California. The determination was made after an informal "investigation" into Givens' claims. The WGA did not take formal testimony from interested parties but, instead, engaged in "discussions" with Givens, his agent, CBS, and Columbia Tristar. Givens had no opportunity to cross-examine witnesses. Neither did Jacobs or Webb. Further, none of them had a right to examine the evidence presented by CBS and others. Givens and CBS simply provided the WGA with relevant information about the development of each project, and the WGA arrived at its conclusions through an examination of those materials. Finally, the WGA's participating-writer determination was subject to only very limited judicial review.

Thus, although undoubtedly conducted with care and in good faith, the WGA participating-writer proceeding was insufficiently formal and provided too few procedural safeguards to constitute an adjudicatory proceeding. Because the remaining Plaintiffs did not agree to litigate their entitlement to production credit in an informal arbitral forum, under California law the WGA's decision on writing credit does not preclude the litigation of Plaintiffs' claims in a judicial proceeding.

Although Givens *did* agree to arbitrate his entitlement to writing credit, he is no longer a plaintiff in this action. REVERSED and REMANDED for further proceedings consistent with this opinion.

Notes and Questions

a. The principal cases demonstrate the structures used for development of television projects. Significant income and value is ascribed to the final writers on the television pilots. Among professional writers who are members of the Writers Guild of America (WGA), this system works relatively well. Each writer is bound by the collective bargaining agreement to arbitrate the dispute, and the WGA focuses on the extent to which each writer's material exists in the final script as filmed. This question ignores the ownership of the original idea, the chain of development, and the obligations to the writers outside of the actual writing credit. For non-writers or writers who are not members of the union, this process may leave them out of the loop.

b. Another benefit the television networks receive from the writer's credit provisions of the agreement stems from the WGA's role in credit determinations. Whatever the network promises as a contingent reward, it will condition the proffered bonuses, benefits, and interests on the writer receiving exclusive writing credit. In this way, the network can essentially offer everyone involved in a project the same agreement, knowing that the WGA arbitration process will eliminate the risk that more than one person will earn the reward.

In drafting agreements, writers should be careful to separate out "based upon" or other forms of credit as distinct from the writer's credit subject to the WGA arbitration process.

c. In addition to the contractual problems between networks and competing development teams, networks can run afoul of the scope of the rights received when they purchase pre-existing literary rights. See *Twentieth Century Fox Film Corp. v. Marvel Enters.*, 155 F. Supp. 2d 1 (S.D.N.Y. 2001).

d. A television series has been advertised with the same name and concept as one your client pitched to a television network five years earlier. Many of the elements are similar and various executives have moved from the network at which your client had pitched the story to the network which ultimately produced the television series in question. What is the legal challenge you must bring and what is the likely result? See *Shaw v. Lindheim*, 809 F. Supp. 1393 (C.D. Cal. 1992).

Problem XIV-B

Bryce arrives at your office with a box and explains once having tried to write for television. From the box, Bryce shows you a written pilot episode for a television series, a story bible for that series, and a treatment of the series concepts. The story bible is a compendium of characters, settings, and other details that need to take place in each episode to maintain consistency and build story arcs from episode to episode. The treatment contains a three-page summary of the pilot episode's plot and brief introductions to the story's characters.

Unfortunately, Bryce's writing efforts were rejected by Yin/Yang Television. Bryce never had a development contract for this television series. Instead, the entire project had been written "on spec" with the hope that the television show would be picked up.

Bryce is now convinced that a television show about to air this fall is heavily based on—if not outright copied from—the work Bryce submitted to Yin/Yang Television. Bryce does not expect the pilot to be an exact match since so much changes during the development of any show. Nonetheless, Bryce is convinced that between the story bible and treatment, all of the important elements of Bryce's project appear in the new show. Since the producer and show runner have worked with Bryce on projects in the past and both were employed at Yin/Yang, Bryce is convinced that there has been access to the materials and conversations about the project, even though Bryce never formally pitched it to either individual in their official capacity. Explain to Bryce the ability to use the story bible and treatment to prove infringement, as well as what procedural steps are necessary bring any action.

C. TV Substantial Similarity

Willis v. HBO

57 Fed. Appx. 902 (2d. Cir. 2003) (unpublished opinion)

Plaintiff-Appellant Patricia Willis appeals from a judgment of the United States District Court for the Southern District of New York (John S. Martin, Jr., *Judge*) granting summary judgment in favor of Defendant-Appellee Home Box Office ("HBO"). We affirm for substantially the reasons stated by the District Court in its opinion and order of November 5, 2001.

In her complaint, Willis alleges that the HBO television series *Arli$$* infringes on her copyrighted outline for a proposed television series entitled *Schmoozers*. It is true that both works are situation comedies that feature a money-driven talent agent as their primary character, and that satirize the American entertainment industry as being wholly populated by self-absorbed, morally-depraved individuals. It is also true that both works surround the primary character with a supporting cast comprised of a hapless, male sidekick and an intelligent, female assistant. We agree with the District Court, however, that such similarities are based on stereotypical characters and stock themes, and thus any copying by the defendant related to noncopyrightable aspects of Willis' work.

Willis argues that, apart from individual aspects of *Schmoozers*, the "total concept and feel" of the two works are substantially similar. We reject that assertion because we do not think that any reasonable trier of fact could so conclude. As already pointed out, the generalized similarities between *Arli$$* and *Schmoozers* relate to unoriginal elements of Willis' work. More importantly, the distinctive "total concept and feel" of *Arli$$* is shaped primarily by its use of a dramatic device in which each episode of the series is presented as a narrated reading of a chapter from the main character's autobiography. This enables *Arli$$* to take comedic advantage of the sharp contrast between the main character's overblown and self-reverential view of an event in his life—which the audience learns throughout the episode by means of somber voiceover from that character—and the chaotic, immoral manner in which the event actually transpired. In *Schmoozers*, by contrast, the comedic foil to the main character is not the main character himself but a supporting character who occasionally relates direct criticism of her boss's actions to the audience.

Willis also contends that the District Court erred in dismissing her claims under New York law because "[a] state claim based upon an implied-in-fact obligation to compensate a plaintiff for use of an idea is not preempted...." While there is some support for the general principle that an implied-in-fact contract claim is not preempted by federal copyright law, Willis' complaint does not actually plead an implied-in-fact contract claim, nor does it even set forth facts that would arguably support such a claim. As we observed in *Nadel v. Play-By-Play Toys & Novelties, Inc.,* 208 F.3d 368 (2d Cir. 2000), a recent case involving implied-in-fact contracts under New York law:

> Of course, the mere disclosure of an ... idea to a defendant ... will not automatically entitle a plaintiff to compensation upon the defendant's subsequent use of the idea. An implied-in-fact contract requires such elements as consideration, mutual assent, legal capacity and legal subject matter.... The element of mutual assent ... must be inferred from the facts and circumstances of each case, including such factors as the specific conduct of the parties, industry custom, and course of dealing.

Willis' complaint contains nothing from which "a court may justifiably infer that the promise [to pay Willis for subsequent use of her ideas] would have been explicitly made [by HBO], had attention been drawn to it." ...

The judgment of the District Court is hereby affirmed.

Warner Bros., Inc. v. Am. Broad. Cos.
720 F.2d 231 (2d Cir. 1983)

The primary issue raised by this appeal is whether as a matter of law the fictional character Ralph Hinkley, the principal figure in a television series, "The Greatest American Hero," is not sufficiently similar to the fictional character Superman, the hero of comic books, television, and more recently films, so that claims of copyright infringement and unfair competition may be dismissed without consideration by a jury.... Plaintiffs own the copyrights in various works embodying the character Superman and have thereby acquired copyright protection for the character itself. Since the creation of Superman in 1938, plaintiffs have exploited their rights with great success, portraying Superman in several media and licensing the character for a variety of merchandising purposes. Through plaintiffs' efforts, Superman has attained an extremely high degree of exposure and recognition.

In 1978, building on previous Superman works, plaintiff Warner Bros., Inc. released a motion picture entitled "Superman, The Movie" (*Superman I*) and more recently two sequels....

In *Superman I* and in previous Superman works, Superman is portrayed as a brave, fearless hero, endowed with superhuman powers. His strength, speed, vision, and hearing far exceed the physical capabilities of mere mortals. He is impervious to bullets. In early works, Superman displayed extraordinary leaping ability, in later works this skill had become the power of flight, as Superman is regularly seen soaring through the sky, arms stretched ahead, then landing agilely on his feet ready for action. Superman engages in a series of exploits against assorted criminals and villains who pose threats not only to public safety but also to national security and even world peace. Regardless of his adversary, Superman always prevails....

The substantial commercial success of *Superman I* and the attendant publicity prompted many requests for licenses permitting use of the Superman character in connection with the merchandising of toys, greeting cards, apparel, and other products. It also led ABC to seek a license for production of a television series about "Superboy" based on the early adventures of Superman. Plaintiffs, who were planning to make their own sequels and derivative works, refused ABC permission to proceed with its proposed project.

Unable to obtain this license, ABC assigned to Cannell, the principal of the third-party defendant production company, the task of creating a "pilot" program for a TV series involving a superhero. Cannell produced a program, and subsequently a weekly series, entitled "The Greatest American Hero" (*Hero*), which he described as being about "what happens when you [the average person] become Superman." *Hero's* protagonist, Ralph Hinkley, was given attributes intended to identify him as an "ordinary guy." Hinkley is portrayed as a young high school teacher attempting to cope with a recent divorce, a dispute over the custody of his son, and the strain that his domestic problems place upon his work and his relationship with his girlfriend. Although Hinkley is attractive, his physical appearance is not imposing: he is of medium height with a slight build and curly, somewhat unkempt, blond hair.

In the pilot show, as described on the prior appeal:

> Hinkley's van breaks down en route to a high school field trip in the desert. While walking along a road in search of help, Hinkley is nearly run over by an out-of-control automobile driven by Bill Maxwell, an American undercover agent. Maxwell has been searching the desert for his missing FBI partner who, unbeknownst to Maxwell, has been murdered by a band of extremists. Maxwell and Hinkley are suddenly approached by a brightly glowing spaceship from which descends the image of Maxwell's deceased partner. Hinkley is handed a magical caped costume—a red leotard with a tunic top, no boots, and a black cape—which, when worn, endows him with fantastic powers. Unfortunately, however, Hinkley loses the instruction book that accompanied the intergalactic gift and is left only with the verbal instruction that he should use his powers to save the world from self-destruction. Hinkley grudgingly accepts the mission after being importuned to do so by Maxwell.

Hinkley's magical costume endows him with superhuman speed and strength, the ability to fly, imperviousness to bullets, and what Cannell calls "holographic vision, "the power to perceive sights and sounds occurring out of his line of vision. Partly for lack of the instruction book that accompanied the costume and partly because some of his character traits remain dominant when he is wearing the suit, Hinkley as a superhero is not an unqualified success. He uses his superpowers awkwardly and fearfully. When flying, Hinkley shouts with fright and makes crash-landings, sometimes crumpling in a heap or skidding nearly out of control to a stop. Though protected from bullets by his costume, Hinkley cringes and cowers when shot at by villains.

In the pilot episode of *Hero*, the reaction of the first man who sees Hinkley in his costume, which he has put on in a gas station washroom, is fear that Hinkley is some sort of pervert who may harm the man or his seven-year-old son, Jerry. While the man calls for the police, Jerry notices that Hinkley is trying to fly but does not know how. The youngster patiently explains that Hinkley must take three steps and jump vigorously into the air. Hinkley manages to get airborne, has difficulty steering, barely avoids colliding with a fire escape, and finally crashes into a brick wall, knocking himself out. Police officers arrest him and take him to a hospital, where he protests in vain to a nurse that he is not crazy. . . .

The *Hero* series contains several visual effects and lines that inevitably call Superman to mind, sometimes by way of brief imitation, sometimes by mention of Superman or another character from the Superman works, and sometimes by humorous parodying or ironic twisting of well-known Superman phrases. Hinkley's suit invests him with most of Superman's powers, and the suit, like Superman's, is a tight-fitting leotard with a chest insignia and a cape. Their outfits differ in that Superman wears a blue leotard with red briefs, boots, and cape, while Hinkley's costume is a red leotard with a tunic top, no boots, and a black cape. In one scene, as Hinkley is running at super speed, smoke emerges from his footsteps, and the sound of a locomotive is heard. A similar scene occurs in *Superman I*, though even without seeing the movie it would be difficult not to be reminded by the *Hero* scene of Superman, who is regularly described as "more powerful than a locomotive." When Hinkley first views himself in a mirror holding his costume in front of him, he says, "It's a bird ... it's a plane ... it's Ralph Hinkley." The youngster, Jerry, watching Hinkley's unsuccessful first effort to fly, tells him, "Superman wouldn't do it that way." In a scene with his girlfriend, who is aware of the powers that come with the magic costume, Hinkley says, "Look at it this way ... you're already one step up on Lois Lane. She never found out who Clark Kent really was." ...

The basic issues concerning the copyright infringement claim are whether the *Hero* and *Superman* works are substantially similar so as to support an inference of copying and whether the lack of substantial similarity is so clear as to fall outside the range of reasonably disputed fact questions requiring resolution by a jury. The similarity to be assessed must concern the expression of ideas, not the ideas themselves, a distinction easier to assert than to apply. Though the issue of substantial similarity is frequently a fact issue for jury resolution, we have recognized that a court may determine non-infringement as a matter of law on a motion for summary judgment, either because the similarity between two works concerns only "*non*-copyrightable elements of the plaintiff's work," or because no reasonable jury, properly instructed, could find that the two works are substantially similar. Before assessing the District Court's determination that summary judgment was appropriate in this case, we consider the principles that guide decisions in this area.

It is a fundamental objective of the copyright law to foster creativity. However, that law has the capacity both to augment and diminish the prospects for creativity. By assuring the author of an original work the exclusive benefits of whatever commercial success his or her work enjoys, the law obviously promotes creativity. At the same time, it can deter the creation of new works if authors are fearful that their creations will too readily be found to be substantially similar to preexisting works. The idea-expression dichotomy originated in the case law and is now codified in the statute, in an effort to enable courts to adjust the tension between these competing effects of copyright protection. Though imprecise, it remains a useful analytic tool for separating infringing from non-infringing works, especially when the essence of the work sought to be protected is a story and the allegedly infringing work is accused of what Professor Nimmer calls "comprehensive nonliteral similarity," 3 *Nimmer* § 13.03[A] [1], duplicating the "fundamental essence or structure" of a work. Confronting a claim of that sort, courts have often invoked Learned Hand's "abstractions" test, or Professor Chaffee's "pattern" test.[11]

[Judge Hand's abstractions test, *Nichols v. Universal Pictures Corp., supra*, 45 F.2d at 121, provides that] "[u]pon any work, and especially upon a play, a great number of patterns of increasing generality will fit equally well, as more and more of the incident is left out. The last may perhaps be no more than the most general statement of what the play is about, and at times consist only of its title; but there is a point in this series of ab-

---

11. "No doubt, the line does lie somewhere between the author's idea and the precise form in which he wrote it down. I like to say that the protection covers the 'pattern' of the work ... the sequence of events, and the development of the interplay of characters." Chaffee, *Reflections on the Law of Copyright*, 45 Colum. L. Rev. 503, 513–14 (1945).

stractions where they are no longer protected, since otherwise the playwright could prevent the use of his 'ideas,' to which, apart from their expression, his property is never extended."

When, as in this case, the claim concerns infringement of a character, rather than a story, the idea-expression distinction has proved to be especially elusive. In *Nichols*, Hand applied his "abstractions" test in determining that neither the plot nor the characters of "Abie's Irish Rose" were infringed by a similar play called "The Cohens and the Kellys." He noted that no case then decided had found infringement of a character described only by written word, although he recognized the possibility that a literary character could be sufficiently delineated to support a claim of infringement by a second comer, copyrightability of a literary character has on occasion been recognized....

In determining whether a character in a second work infringes a cartoon character, courts have generally considered not only the visual resemblance but also the totality of the characters' attributes and traits. A pertinent consideration, formulated in a case concerning greeting cards in which characters were one element of the art work, is the extent to which the allegedly infringing character captures the "total concept and feel" of the copyrighted character.

A somewhat paradoxical aspect of infringement disputes, especially pertinent to claims of character infringement, concerns the attention courts give both to similarities and differences in the two works at issue. Professor Nimmer categorically asserts as a proposition, "It is entirely immaterial that in many respects plaintiff's and defendant's works are dissimilar if in other respects similarity as to a substantial element of plaintiff's work can be shown." In Hand's pithy phrase, "No plagiarist can excuse the wrong by showing how much of his work he did not pirate." Yet Professor Nimmer also recognizes, as a second proposition, that "a defendant may legitimately avoid infringement by intentionally making sufficient changes in a work which would otherwise be regarded as substantially similar to that of the plaintiff's." The two propositions are not facially inconsistent; the second proposition contemplates a work that *would be* substantially similar if its author had not made changes from the plaintiff's work. Yet in practice the distinction between the two propositions has become somewhat blurred. We have observed that "numerous differences tend to undercut substantial similarity." This observation appears to go beyond Professor Nimmer's second proposition by emphasizing the significance of differences that do not necessarily change features of the plaintiff's work, but may be entirely additional. To that extent, the observation modifies the first proposition.

The tension between these two propositions perhaps results from their formulation in the context of literary works and their subsequent application to graphic and three-dimensional works. A story has a linear dimension: it begins, continues, and ends. If a defendant copies substantial portions of a plaintiff's sequence of events, he does not escape infringement by adding original episodes somewhere along the line. A graphic or three-dimensional work is created to be perceived as an entirety. Significant dissimilarities between two works of this sort inevitably lessen the similarity that would otherwise exist between the total perceptions of the two works. The graphic rendering of a character has aspects of both the linear, literary mode and the multi-dimensional total perception. What the character thinks, feels, says, and does and the descriptions conveyed by the author through the comments of other characters in the work episodically fill out a viewer's understanding of the character. At the same time, the visual perception of the character tends to create a dominant impression against which the similarity of a defendant's character may be readily compared, and significant differences readily noted.

Ultimately, care must be taken to draw the elusive distinction between a substantially similar character that infringes a copyrighted character despite slight differences in appearance, behavior, or traits, and a somewhat similar though non-infringing character whose appearance, behavior, or traits, and especially their combination, significantly differ from those of a copyrighted character, even though the second character is reminiscent of the first one. Stirring one's memory of a copyrighted character is not the same as appearing to be substantially similar to that character, and only the latter is infringement. An entirely separate issue of infringement, also posed by this case, concerns what Professor Nimmer calls "fragmented literal similarity," duplicating the exact or nearly exact wording of a fragment of the protected work. With respect to such claims, courts have invoked two distinct doctrines. First, a *de minimis* rule has been applied, allowing the literal copying of a small and usually insignificant portion of the plaintiff's work. Second, under the "fair use" doctrine, codified in *17 U.S.C. § 107*, courts have allowed the taking of words or phrases when adapted for use as commentary or parody.

The "parody" branch of the "fair use" doctrine is itself a means of fostering the creativity protected by the copyright law. It also balances the public interest in the free flow of ideas with the copyright holder's interest in the exclusive use of his work. Especially in an era of mass communications, it is to be expected that phrases and other fragments of expression in a highly successful copyrighted work will become part of the language. That does not mean they lose all protection in the manner of a trade name that has become generic. No matter how well known a copyrighted phrase becomes, its author is entitled to guard against its appropriation to promote the sale of commercial products. That doctrine enabled the proprietors of the Superman copyright to prevent a discount chain from using a television commercial that parodied well-known lines associated with Superman. *D.C. Comics, Inc. v. Crazy Eddie, Inc.,* 205 U.S.P.Q. (BNA) 1177 (S.D.N.Y. 1979) ("Look! … Up in the sky! … It's a bird! … It's a plane … It's … Crazy Eddie!"). But an original work of authorship with elements of parody, though undoubtedly created in the hope of commercial success, stands on a different footing from the products of a discount chain. Whatever aesthetic appeal such a work may have results from the creativity that the copyright law is designed to promote. It is decidedly in the interests of creativity, not piracy, to permit authors to take well-known phrases and fragments from copyrighted works and add their own contributions of commentary or humor. After all, any work of sufficient notoriety to be the object of parody has already secured for its proprietor considerable financial benefit. According that proprietor further protection against parody does little to promote creativity, but it places a substantial inhibition upon the creativity of authors adept at using parody to entertain, inform, or stir public consciousness.

Applying these principles to this case, we conclude that Chief Judge Motley correctly entered summary judgment for the defendants on the claim of copyright infringement. Plaintiffs make no claim that the *Hero* pilot, subsequent episodes, or "promos" infringed the story of any Superman works. Their contention is that the *Hero* character, Ralph Hinkley, is substantially similar to Superman and that the *Hero* works impermissibly copied what plaintiffs call the "indicia" of Superman, a concept broad enough to include Superman's costume, his abilities, the well-known lines associated with him — in short, anything occurring in the *Hero* works that might remind a viewer of Superman.

The total perception of the Hinkley character is not substantially similar to that of Superman. On the contrary, it is profoundly different. Superman looks and acts like a brave, proud hero, who has dedicated his life to combating the forces of evil. Hinkley looks and acts like a timid, reluctant hero, who accepts his missions grudgingly and prefers to get on with his normal life. Superman performs his superhuman feats with skill, verve, and dash, clearly the master of his own destiny. Hinkley is perplexed by the superhuman powers his costume confers and uses them in a bumbling, comical fashion. In the genre of superheroes, Hinkley follows Superman as, in the genre of detectives, Inspector Clouseau follows Sherlock Holmes....

The unfair competition and trademark dilution claims present slightly different issues, but, as will appear, we agree with Chief Judge Motley that defendants were entitled to summary judgment on these claims as well as on the infringement claims.... [W]e have noted that "the absence of substantial similarity leaves little basis for asserting a likelihood of confusion or palming off" for purposes of a claim under section 43(a) of the Lanham Act. We do not doubt that the image of a cartoon character and some indicia of that character can function as a trademark to identify the source of a work of entertainment. But, as with claims of copyright infringement, courts retain an important authority to monitor the outer limits of substantial similarity within which a jury is permitted to make the factual determination whether there is a likelihood of confusion as to source....

We agree with Chief Judge Motley that a visual comparison of the Superman works with the *Hero* series and "promos" establishes as a matter of law a lack of substantial similarity that would create a likelihood of confusion as to source. Our discussion of the differences in "total concept and feel" of the central characters of Superman and Hinkley applies to the issue of likelihood of confusion as well as to copyright infringement. We do not doubt that there may be some viewers among the television audience who think that the *Hero* series was produced or authorized by those responsible for the Superman movies, television series, or comics. Some may come to that conclusion with respect to every film or television program portraying a character with superhuman abilities. Perhaps some viewers think that every program with a dramatic courtroom lawyer was made by the producers of the Perry Mason series, or that every show featuring a doctor is a spin-off of the Marcus Welby series. The "average lay observer" test, however, must be applied by fact-finders within an outer limit of reasonable fact-finding marked by the courts. Otherwise the scope of protection a competitor is entitled to enjoy would be expanded far beyond what Congress prescribed in the Lanham Act. Thus, as we concluded with respect to the copyright claim, the availability of survey evidence indicating that some viewers associated the *Hero* series with Superman does not create a *reasonably* disputed factual issue of likelihood of confusion as to source when the works are as different as those in this case....

We also recognize that lack of substantial similarity is not a complete answer to a Lanham Act claim, since a second comer can violate section 43(a) by falsely representing his goods as those of the trademark owner. A claim of "passing off" or "palming off" may be established even if the goods are not confusingly similar; the wrong is in the misrepresentation of a common source. However, in this case this aspect of the section 43(a) claim is also defeated as a matter of law by visual comparison of the works in question. Whether a television viewer could be misled into thinking that the *Hero* series was produced or authorized by those responsible for the Superman films depends on the extent to which the *Hero* programs and "promos" convey such a misrepresentation, even if it was not intended. Plainly there is no overt claim in this regard, and we agree with Chief Judge Motley that perceiving the materials through the eyes and ears of the average lay observer does not create a fair jury issue as to whether a misrepresentation of common source or sponsorship has been implied. The works are too fundamentally different, and the references in the *Hero* programs and "promos" to names and fragments of lines associated with Superman are pointedly made for purposes of contrast.

Plaintiffs fare no better to the extent that their claims are based on New York's common law of unfair competition or the state anti-dilution statute. We have recognized the breadth of New York's common law tort of unfair competition and have not hesitated to apply it to pirated audio-visual works, so long as the cause of action was not preempted by the Copyright Act of 1976.... However, to the extent that plaintiffs are relying on state unfair competition law to allege a tort of "passing off," they are not asserting rights equivalent to those protected by copyright and therefore do not encounter preemption. Their claim fails nevertheless on the merits. The lack of a fairly triable issue of fact as to "passing off" defeats this aspect of the state law claim, just as it did the similar theory advanced under the Lanham Act.

Robinson v. Viacom Int'l

1995 U.S. Dist. LEXIS 9781, Copy. L. Rep. (CCH) P27480 (S.D.N.Y. 1995)

... Plaintiffs Tom Robinson ("Robinson") and Phil Herter ("Herter") charge Defendants Viacom International, Inc. ("Viacom"), MTV Networks ("MTV"), Ripe Productions, Inc. ("Ripe"), American Broadcasting Companies, Inc. ("ABC"), Penny Stallings, and Rick Mitz with copyright infringement and other unauthorized use of a "Treatment" and a Script created by the two Plaintiffs for a proposed television series to be titled variously as "Deja Vu" or "Four Characters in Search of a Sitcom" (collectively, "Four Characters") based on the production and telecast of a series titled "Hi Honey! I'm Home" ("Hi Honey") by ABC and Nickelodeon/Nick at Nite ("Nickelodeon").

[Prior dealings between the parties create access to the treatment and script which is not otherwise discussed by the court.]

A. Four Characters

"Four Characters" presents two sharply contrasting families: the Walldenski family, a contemporary American suburban family, and whose house is haunted by the Johnson family, an idealized television family derived from the sitcom archetype dating back to the 1950s. Plaintiffs' work consists of a four-page Treatment of the "Four Characters" series, and a 25-page Script for a pilot episode....

B. Hi Honey.... Episode One of "Hi Honey" introduces the Duffs as a single-parent contemporary American family living in suburban New Jersey. Elaine Duff is a single mother working for the phone company and raising two sons after her husband Ted "ran away." The Duff's house appears quite messy, and several locks are mounted on the front door. Mike, the older son, is a high school sophomore who apparently spends most of his free time watching television, and he is upset to learn that reruns of his favorite old black and white show, called "Hi Honey! I'm Home," have just been cancelled. Mike's 10-year old brother Sidney, who is usually called Skunk, dresses as a rebel and sports a "punk-style" haircut. A homeless man named Malcolm appears at the Duff's door, and provokes a hostile reaction from Elaine.

After returning home from work one day, Elaine drags her two boys to meet their new next-door neighbors, the Nielsons, and to ask them to sign her petition for a woman's right to choose. Honey Nielson greets the Duffs, and invites them into her immaculate house (Elaine rolls her eyes when Honey apologizes for its condition). The decor in the Nielsons' house is dated, and the Nielsons' clothes also reflect fashions from the 1950s. Honey is exuberant and unsophisticated, and constantly offers her guests various baked goods. Mike's suspicions are immediately raised by the Nielsons' resemblance to the "Hi Honey! I'm Home" family, and each detail he observes confirms his feeling that the Nielsons are somehow connected to the show he watches each afternoon. The Nielson children, Chuckie and Babbs, are also naive and wholesome, and Mike immediately shows a love interest in Babbs, his high school classmate....

Stock Themes. Related to the requirement of originality under copyright law is the exclusion of protection for "stock themes." Copyright protection does not extend to "'stock' themes commonly linked to a particular genre." Such customary themes, or "scenes a faire," are not copyrightable as a matter of law. Examples of scenes a faire include disgruntled police officers, superheroes lifting cars to show strength and the setting of a POW camp in Hitler's Germany. "Stock themes" or "scenes a faire" in Plaintiffs' work are not eligible for copyright protection.

Idea v. Expression. Copyright law protects only a "particular expression of ideas, not [ ] the ideas themselves, a distinction easier to state than to apply." To determine whether two works are "so substantially similar as to reveal an infringement of one by the other, courts must decide whether the similarities shared by the works are something more than mere generalized ideas or themes."

Comparison of two works for substantial similarity is "a task generally performed after detailed examination of the works themselves...." To make this determination, a court may break down the works into the following components: plot, characters, total concept and feel (mood), setting, format and pace. A comparison of these components in the Plaintiffs' Treatment and Script with the four episodes of "Hi Honey" reveals the following similarities and differences between the two works.

a. Plot. At the outset, it should be noted that the underlying plot devices used in both parties' works exhibit certain similarities. Both works revolve around the interplay between a contemporary family and a 1950s era television family. Plaintiffs argue that no prior television show was identified by Defendants "which features a television family (qua electronic television images) that comes to exist in the real world.... [or] that has as one of its central characters a television family that is a composite of idealized television sitcom families of the past." However, juxtaposition of the two families constitutes an idea, not an expression, and Plaintiffs may not be granted a monopoly in this idea, even if the Plaintiffs' formulation is novel. Plaintiffs argue that the plots of the two works are the same since they both involve "a modern family in a suburban neighborhood [which] discovers that they are living in proximity to the incarnations of a television sitcom family." Plaintiffs' capsule description abstracts their own plot which involves ghosts haunting the house of a modern family, and which is quite different from Defendants' work where the Nielson family appears to be almost normal to outsiders.

Plaintiffs also attempt to provide specific examples of plot similarities between the two works. Plaintiffs point out that both works begin with one family moving into a new neighborhood, Rips but in "Hi Honey" the newcomers are the television family, while "Four Characters" involves a contemporary family moving into a new home. Plaintiffs contend that in both works the elder contemporary child discovers the identity of the television family, but Plaintiffs do not mention that in "Hi Honey" the older Duff son is the only person who recognizes the Nielsons. Plaintiffs also argue that the plot suggestion in their Treatment for an episode based on shoplifting is similar to Episode Eight of "Hi Honey" in which three boys steal money from a neighbor's house to buy shoes, however this effort to protect a minimally developed plot suggestion would encompass virtually any sitcom plot involving a theft by a young person—an unoriginal storyline common to numerous family-based sitcoms. Other such comparisons by the Plaintiffs are similarly faulty (i.e. the use of brownies as a motif in both works, humorous cooking escapades). Furthermore, this highlighting of similarities chosen from a number of episodes "would seem as a general matter to allow a plaintiff to cast too wide a net." Plot ideas out-lined in Plaintiffs' Treatment are not developed sufficiently to merit protection, especially in light of their derivative nature (most actually constitute cliches gleaned from a long line of family-based sitcoms). Plaintiffs' attempts to note specific similarities between the plots of the two works fail as either too general or because they concern unoriginal com-ponents which are not protectible under copyright law.

Plaintiffs only produced one script, and its plot is significantly different from that used to introduce the characters in Episode One of "Hi Honey." Plaintiffs' plot concerns the Wallden-ski's perception of the Johnsons and their unique view of 1950s values brought into their home by what Herter described as "ghost[s]." Defendants' series involves a 1950s family interacting with all of modern society, and visible to everyone. This is a significant dif-ference in plot between the two works, and prevents a finding of substantial similarity.

b. Characters. Plaintiffs claim that substantial similarity exists between the characters in the two works. In comparing the characters of two works, a court must consider the "totality of their attributes and traits." "No character infringement claim can succeed un-less plaintiff's original conception sufficiently developed the character, and defendants have copied this development and not merely the broader outlines."

Robinson testified that the Johnson family was developed "based [ ] on our joint mem-ory of things that we had seen as reruns." The "Four Characters" Script presents essentially no character development beyond introducing characters clearly derived from a long line of family-based sitcoms. The Treatment similarly compiles attributes which are not orig-inal and relies only on the device of the Johnsons haunting the Walldenskis' house for originality. Plaintiffs may not claim copyright protection for the characters in their work because they lack originality.

Similarities between characters in the two works relate only to non-protectible stock themes. "Copyright law will not protect characters where 'it is virtually impossible to write about a particular fictional theme without employing certain stock or standard literary devices.'" Furthermore, the similarities identified by Plaintiffs between characters in the two works exist only at the abstract level of unprotectible ideas. For example, although Plaintiffs as-sert that the contemporary fathers in the two works are identical, the contemporary fa-ther in "Hi Honey" has run away and never appears on-screen. Plaintiffs argue that the two characters are nevertheless "identical" since they are both undergoing mid-life crises, but at this level of identity all middle-aged father characters are potentially similar. Plain-tiffs also contend that the contemporary younger son, Skunk, in "Hi Honey" "matches precisely" Defendants' description of the contemporary daughter in "Four Characters," Shelia, since Skunk was involved in a theft as was Shelia. The identity perceived here by Plaintiff exists at a level too general to support substantial similarity: the "Four Charac-ters" incident revolved around a shoplifting by the daughter to obtain clothes, whereas the theft in "Hi Honey" was of money in a neighbor's house so that Skunk and his friends could buy sneakers. Plaintiffs argue that the 1950s son in "Hi Honey," Chuckie Nielson, is similar to the athletic 1950s son in "Four Characters" since Chuckie, although over-weight and generally portrayed as an outcast, is seen returning home from a baseball game in uniform. This similarity is also at too abstract a level to merit copyright protection.

c. Total Concept and Feel. Plaintiffs claim that Defendants' work is substantially sim-ilar in its "total concept and feel." As Judge Haight recently noted, "Courts must pay par-ticular attention to summary judgment motions in cases where a plaintiff claims that defendant's work copies the "total concept and feel" of plaintiff's work. Accepting an overly broad scope for protectable "total concept and feel" threatens the basic principal of copyright law: that concepts and ideas may not be copyrighted, and that only a particular expression of an idea may be copyrighted."

The broad theme of a 1950s era sitcom family interacting with a contemporary family is an unprotectible idea. Furthermore, the device of characters appearing in color or black and white to emphasize a temporal contrast has been used in numerous television and motion picture settings.

d. Setting. Plaintiffs claim that the settings in both works are identical: "a middle-class suburb." However, this is not a protectible element since settings such as an opening "with a frontal shot of ... a solid two story house with a well-maintained lawn shaded by stately trees[,]" have been commonly found in sitcoms for over 30 years. Similarly, the type and arrangement of furniture in the living rooms of the two families and the appliances in the kitchen are not ideas original with plaintiffs, and are unprotectible under copyright law.

e. Format. Plaintiffs argue that "the choice of a comedy ... [to] treat the social issues at the heart of the shows in a light manner" renders the two works identical, as does the use of a five-minute prologue to introduce the central conflict for the episode. This format is common to many sitcoms, and is not a protectible element of Plaintiff's work.

f. Pace. The "up-tempo" pace of the two works is common to virtually all sitcoms, and is not a protectible element of Plaintiffs' work.

Conclusion. Defendants have shown that any similarities between "Hi Honey" and "Four Characters" relate only to unprotectible elements, and that no reasonable jury, properly instructed, could find that the works are substantially similar.... [All remaining state court and Lanham Act claims dismissed.]

Notes and Questions

a. A few additional comments from the district court in *Willis v. HBO*, 2001 U.S. Dist. LEXIS 17887 (S.D.N.Y. 2001) may also be of interest:

> Many people would consider the phrase "sleazy talent agent" to be redundant. While this is no doubt as unfair a stereotype as is the "sleazy lawyer," no one could reasonably claim a copyright in the concept of a sleazy talent agent. The question presented here is what degree of detail must an author add to such a well-recognized stock character in order to obtain copyright protection.

> Defendant now moves for summary judgment contending that the only similarity between Arli$$ and Schmoozers is that both employ well-known concepts which no one may copyright. Plaintiff contends, however, that there are such significant similarities in the details of her Treatment for Schmoozers and the series Arli$$ that a trier of fact could conclude that Arli$$ violates her Schmoozers copyright. To support her claim she relies upon the report of an "expert" in television studies who details what he considers to be the significant similarities between Schmoozers and Arli$$ and concludes that the two series are "uniquely alike." ... The problem with Plaintiff's claim and her "expert's" report is that, to the extent that there are similarities, they are found either in stock characters, or themes that are common to the talent agency business, or to situation comedies in general or in trivial detail that are not essential to either series. Plaintiff's arguments also ignore the significant differences between the two series and strain to find similarities where none exist.

Id.

b. Some ideas seem more similar than others. Steve Fischer, creator of the characters Steve and Bluey, and the comic strip "There's a Dog Under my Bed," lost in a claim dispute regarding "Blue's Clues" despite documentation that Fischer had been in correspondence with Nickelodeon U.K. for the production of a children's animated television series. Nickelodeon U.S. is the producer of "Blue's Clues," a children's animated television series originally featuring the human Steve and his dog, Blue. See *Fischer v. Viacom Int'l Inc.,* 115 F. Supp. 2d 535 (D. Md. 2000).

c. When does a character become a sufficiently protected element that the use of a similar character will infringe the copyright? Compare *Rice v. Fox Broad. Co.,* 330 F.3d 1170 (9th Cir. 2003) (competing video and television products for The Mystery Magician), with *Metro-Goldwyn-Mayer, Inc. v. Am. Honda Motor Corp.,* 900 F. Supp. 1287 (C.D. Cal. 1995) (use of secret agent like James Bond), and *Anderson v. Stallone,* 1989 U.S. Dist. LEXIS 11109 (C.D. Cal. 1989) (use of Rocky character in an unauthorized sequel 'spec' script).

d. To what extent is the Fox reality show, *Trading Spouses,* a copy of the British-made and ABC-acquired *Wife Swap*? The world may never know. Trademark, trade dress, and bad etiquette claims were dismissed, though the copyright claim was allowed. See *RDF Media Ltd. v. Fox Broad. Co.,* 372 F. Supp. 2d 556 (C.D. Cal. 2005).

e. Who wants to share in being a millionaire? On the issue of fair dealing when negotiating syndication and related rights for sale to the same conglomerate, see *Celador International Ltd. v. The Walt Disney Co.,* 347 F. Supp. 2d 846 (C.D. Cal. 2004). Owners of *Who Wants to Be a Millionaire* can bring claims for an alleged breach of the covenant of good faith and fair dealing when selling rights to other entities or divisions commonly owned by a party to the agreement.

f. Occasionally the similarity between two broadcast television shows will be so overwhelming that the producer does have a copyright action:

> Infringement can occur where—without copying a single line—the later author borrows wholesale the entire backdrop, characters, inter-relationships, genre, and plot design of an earlier work. Imagine, for example, that the first Sherlock Holmes stories had been penned and copyrighted last year by Sir Arthur Conan Doyle, and Logroño had then written his own sequels carrying everything forward into a new plot. Here, ... "El Condominio" is ... "an unauthorized derivative work. In effect ... both programs are the same with only a difference in name and transmitted via a different channel. Specifically, the setting, character names, costumes, character interactions, comedy line, mood, [and] camera angles are almost identical in both sitcoms."

TMTV, Corp. v. Mass Prods., 645 F.3d 464, 470–471 (1st Cir. 2011) (quoting the District Court).

g. Television programming elicits a great deal of copyright litigation by parties claiming that their unsolicited material has been copied. The courts, therefore, often make a preliminary determination of substantial similarity on motions to dismiss and summary judgment.

> The analysis of [Plaintiff's] copyright infringement claim is straightforward. Whether the "ordinary observer" or "more discerning observer" test is employed, the appropriate inquiry is whether the copying of protectable elements "is quantitatively and qualitatively sufficient to support a finding of infringement." *Nihon Keizai Shimbun, Inc. v. Comline Bus. Data, Inc.,* 166 F.3d 65, 70 (2d Cir.1999) (in-

ternal quotation marks omitted). In applying this test, "we examine the similarities in such aspects as the total concept and feel, theme, characters, plot, sequence, pace and setting." *Williams v. Crichton*, 84 F.3d 581, 588 (2d Cir.1996).

Alexander v. Murdoch, 502 Fed. Appx. 107, 109 (2d Cir. 2012) (unpublished).

Problem XIV-C

Inspired by a cable television marathon, Bryce comes to you for advice. Bryce wants to rewrite the James Bond character to reinvigorate the franchise. Bryce recognizes that the copyright is owned by United Artists, but believes that a fresh and innovative approach to the character will reenergize it in a way that it has lost since the end of the Cold War and the fall of the Berlin Wall.

Bryce says the idea is not another hackneyed return to the Middle East, but instead marries the adventure and gadgetry of Bond's best films with the intrigue and complexity of John LeCarre's Smiley character. Advise Bryce on how best to proceed.

D. Editing for Television

Preminger v. Columbia Pictures Corp.
267 N.Y.S.2d 594 (Sup. Ct. 1966), *aff'd* 25 A.D.2d 830,
269 N.Y.S.2d 913 (App. Div.), *aff'd* 18 N.Y.2d 659 (1966)

The interesting question presented for decision is the right of a producer, in the absence of specific contractual provision, to prevent, by injunction, minor cuts in his motion picture, when shown on television, and the usual breaks for commercials. The litigation involves the production of the motion picture "Anatomy of a Murder."

The complaint alleges that plaintiff Preminger is a producer and director of motion pictures, including the motion picture involved; and plaintiff Carlyle Productions, Inc., a California corporation, was the owner of all rights to the picture, and Carlyle Productions, a limited New York partnership, its assignee; that Carlyle Productions, Inc., entered into a series of agreements with Columbia Pictures Corporation between 1956 and 1959, which are collectively referred to as the contract, copies of which are annexed to the complaint.

Defendant Columbia and defendant Screen Gems, Inc., its subsidiary, the complaint continues, have licensed over 100 television stations to exhibit the motion picture on television, and those license agreements purport to give the licensees the right to cut, to eliminate portions of the picture, and to interrupt the remainder of the picture for commercials and other extraneous matter.

Unless enjoined, the complaint asserts, defendants will (a) detract from the artistic merit of "Anatomy of a Murder"; (b) damage Preminger's reputation; (c) cheapen and tend to destroy Anatomy's commercial value; (d) injure plaintiffs in the conduct of their business; and (e) falsely represent to the public that the film shown is Preminger's film.

It is then alleged, and not denied, that "Anatomy" is one of a very few motion pictures with a rating of AA-1; that it has been licensed in blocks of 60 to 300 pictures; and that the others are artistically and commercially inferior to "Anatomy".

Finally it is alleged that defendants have allocated an unfairly and unreasonably low share of license fees to "Anatomy". This allegation is denied.

All these acts are described as willful and wanton breaches of the contract with Carlyle as owner and Preminger as producer.

Injunctive relief and accounting, for plaintiffs' damages, are prayed for.

Specifically, it is demanded that judgment be granted: (a) enjoining defendants from performing their obligations under the licensing agreements; (b) enjoining defendants from entering into further agreements violative of plaintiffs' rights; (c) enjoining defendants to withdraw all prints previously distributed; (d) directing defendants to account to plaintiffs, for what are presumably plaintiffs' damages; profits are not requested; and (e) other and further relief....

Thus, the only question before the court in this proceeding is the plaintiffs' right to a permanent injunction.

The plaintiffs plant themselves upon article VIII of the contract, which provides: "You [Carlyle] shall have the right to make the final cutting and editing of the Picture, but you shall in good faith consider recommendations and suggestions with respect thereto made by us [Columbia]; nevertheless, you shall have final approval thereof, provided however that notwithstanding the foregoing, in the event that cutting or re-editing is required in order to meet censorship requirements and you shall fail or refuse to comply therewith, then we shall have the right to cut and edit the Picture in order to meet censorship requirements without obligation on our part to challenge the validity of any rule, order, regulation or requirement of any national, state or local censorship authority." The import of the paragraph is that plaintiffs have the right to make the final "cutting and editing" of the picture; giving the defendants the right to make suggestions, only.

This article must be read, however, in juxtaposition with article X of the contract, which provides as follows: "The rights herein granted, without limiting the generality of the foregoing, shall include and embrace all so-called 'theatrical' as well as 'non-theatrical' rights in the Picture (as those terms are commonly understood in the motion picture industry); and shall include the right to use film of any and all gauges. You hereby give and grant to us throughout the entire world the exclusive and irrevocable right during the term herein specified to project, exhibit, reproduce, transmit and perform, and authorize and license others to project, exhibit, reproduce, transmit and perform, the picture and prints thereof by television, and in any other manner, and by any other means, method or device whatsoever, whether mechanical, electrical or otherwise, and whether now known or hereafter conceived or created."

This article, it will be noted, which contains the specific grant of television rights, makes no reference to "cutting and editing".

In these circumstances the court is inclined to the view that the right to the "final" cutting and editing, reserved to the plaintiffs, is limited to the original or theatrical production of the picture, and not to showings on television; and that as to such showings, in the absence of specific contractual provision, the parties will be deemed to have adopted the custom prevailing in the trade or industry.

This view is confirmed by the authorities and fortified by the evidence.

We begin with the proposition that the law is not so rigid, even in the absence of contract, as to leave a party without protection against publication of a garbled version of his work. This, as pointed out by Frank, J., concurring in *Granz v. Harris*, 198 F. 2d 585, 589 [(2d Cir. 1952)] is not novel doctrine.

The court "appreciates that the failure of the community … to protect its gifted men of letters led to tragedies which comprise scars in the history of civilization." And in Granz the United States Court of Appeals for the Second Circuit held that publication of a truncated version of plaintiffs' phonograph recording should be enjoined. In the case at bar, however, the contract must serve as a guide to the intention of the parties.

Thus, where the parties have particularized the terms of a contract, an apparently inconsistent general statement to a different effect must yield. Therefore, the clause in this contract, general in its terms, giving plaintiffs the right to "finally" cut and edit as to the original production of the motion picture, must yield to the specific clause with respect to television showing, which contained no such right. So it is, too, that in the construction of a contract, weight will be given to the custom prevailing in the trade to which it refers. This brings us to a review of the evidence, on which, of course, the burden of proof rests on the plaintiffs.

At the trial, extensive testimony was presented by both sides with respect to the normal customs prevailing in the television and motion picture industries as to the significance of the right to "final cut."

A review of the testimony demonstrates that, at least for the past 15 years, the right to interrupt the exhibition of a motion picture on television for commercial announcements and to make minor deletions to accommodate time segment requirements or to excise those portions which might be deemed, for various reasons, objectionable, has consistently been considered a normal and essential part of the exhibition of motion pictures on television. Implicit in the grant of television rights is the privilege to cut and edit.

No proof has been adduced that this cutting and editing would be done in such a manner as to interfere with the picture's story line.

The licensing agreements provide:

> Licensee shall telecast each print, as delivered by Distributor, in its entirety. However, Licensee may make such minor cuts or elimination as are necessary to conform to time segment requirements or to the orders of any duly authorized public censorship authority and may add commercial material at the places and of the lengths indicated by Distributor, but under no circumstances shall Licensee delete the copyright notice or the credits incorporated in the pictures as delivered by the Distributor, provided, however, in no event may the insertion of any commercial material adversely affect the artistic or pictorial quality of the picture or materially interfere with its continuity.

Defendants' witnesses, Lacey of WCBS, Howard of WNBC and Gilbert of WABC, testified with respect to the practices customarily prevailing throughout the television industry. Plaintiffs' witnesses did not controvert the testimony concerning the customary practices in the trade with regard to interruptions for commercials, and minor cuts. As a matter of fact, Sherwin, one of plaintiffs' witnesses, the program director of KHJ, Los Angeles, testified, as had defendants' witnesses, that his station had never purchased any motion picture without the right to make interruptions as well as minor cuts. Whether or not, in an isolated instance, a picture was exhibited with less than the customary number of commercials is not determinative of the issue. We are concerned not with what might have happened in some rare instance but instead with what was the common practice and custom at the time the parties herein signed their contract....

With respect to the expression "final cut", sufficient testimony was adduced to indicate that this phrase, as used in article VIII of the contract, relates only to a phase in the production of the picture for theatrical showing and has no relation to the interruptions and minor cuts here under discussion. Even plaintiffs' own witnesses identified the "final cutting and editing" of a picture as the last stage in its production for theatrical exhibition.

Although plaintiffs consistently refer to the practice of interrupting and making minor cuts as "mutilation", their own witnesses have conceded that the minor cuts customarily made in a television exhibition of a picture have such a minimal impact upon its overall effect that these are rarely even noticed.

Undisputed is the fact that not a single television station has ever failed to insist upon the right to interrupt for commercials. Similarly unrefuted is defendants' proof to the effect that no station ever purchased a motion picture without reserving to itself the right to interrupt for commercials and to make minor cuts.

Plaintiff Preminger admitted that when he signed the agreement for "Anatomy of a Murder", he was aware that the practice of the television industry was to interrupt motion pictures for commercials and to make minor cuts. Aware of this practice, plaintiffs at the time the instant contract was signed nevertheless did not specifically provide for conditions other than those known to them to be prevalent in the industry.

Two contracts between Preminger and United Artists Corporation were received in evidence. These were contracts pertaining to "Man With The Golden Arm" and "The Moon Is Blue", the last two pictures produced by Preminger prior to "Anatomy of a Murder", which he made for Columbia. In both the contract for "The Moon Is Blue" and the contract for "Man With The Golden Arm", clauses appeared which demonstrate that Preminger was aware of the prevailing practice in the television industry with respect to interrupting motion pictures for commercials and making minor cuts therein for normal television purposes. These contracts further show that when Preminger desired to prevent television distribution in the normal manner, he so provided.

In the contract between the Carlyle corporation and United Artists Corporation, dated December 20, 1954, for "Man With The Golden Arm," it was expressly provided that United Artists' right "to make such changes, additions, alterations, cuts, interpolations and eliminations as may be required for the distribution of the picture in television" should be subject to the approval of producer.... Both Preminger and United Artists were aware that granting the producer this right of approval was tantamount to giving him a veto power over ultimate television distribution of the film, for in other provisions of both of the above contracts it was expressly recognized that television distribution was not to take place without the producer's prior approval. Plaintiffs' entry into the instant contract which failed to contain such a clause may be considered by the court as evidence of the parties' intention....

So standardized has the practice of interrupting films for commercials become, that guidelines have been established in the television industry as to the maximum number of commercials regarded as acceptable in a given time period.

The television industry serves a great public need and its services have ofttimes, and perhaps at some financial sacrifice, been offered in the public interest. Despite such apparent unselfish public service, it should not be overlooked that the industry, like every other business, has as its primary objective the accumulation of profits. Sponsorship of programs, by advertisers, provides a station with its only source of revenue and though it ofttimes interrupts its programs with what some viewers feel to be an inordinate amount of advertising, since its primary purpose is to advertise the products of its sponsors, such interruptions in the absence of governmental or industry regulation can only be controlled by contractual arrangement.

It is of no import that some viewers may not approve of the advertising practices prevalent in the industry—that is, the number and types of commercials. However, the parties to this distribution agreement signed it knowing of the existence of such practices. The plaintiffs, as well as any independent producer or director, could have obviated this problem by specifically prohibiting such cuts or interruptions by contract. This, of course, might have had an adverse effect on the extent of television distribution—an eventuality which most producers would not welcome. Accordingly, in the absence of any contractual provision to the contrary, they must be deemed to have contemplated that what was permissible, under the existing practice, would continue in effect.

The criterion for the determination of what the defendants were likely to do with respect to interrupting and cutting the subject film, in the absence of a specific contractual arrangement, was not what plaintiffs might disapprove of or dislike but, rather, what was the normal custom and practice in the industry.

The issues in the case, in the court's view, are therefore issues of law: i.e., (1) whether plaintiffs may thwart the making of minor cuts or interpolations in the absence of specific contractual provision; the court finds the answer to this question to be in the negative; and (2) whether, under this contract, in the light of the custom in the trade, plaintiffs left to the station masters the right to use their judgment and exercise their discretion, instead of plaintiffs', as to which minor cuts, eliminations, and interpolations are appropriate. In view of the variety of stations, localities, audiences, and commercials, the court answers this question in the affirmative.

The running time of the full motion picture is 161 minutes. The brochure for WABC-TV advertised the picture to potential sponsors as a 100-minute feature. The station master, however, testified, and the court credits his testimony, that this was a mistake; that it was never intended to permit any such extensive cutting. This applies as well to the asserted cutting of the picture to 53 minutes. Obviously such cuts would not be minor and indeed could well be described as mutilation. Should such "mutilation" occur in the future, plaintiffs may make application to this court for injunctive or other relief against such violation as they may be advised....

Gilliam v. ABC
538 F.2d 14 (2d Cir. 1976)

Plaintiffs, a group of British writers and performers known as "Monty Python," appeal from a denial by Judge Lasker in the Southern District of a preliminary injunction to restrain the American Broadcasting Company (ABC) from broadcasting edited versions of three separate programs originally written and performed by Monty Python for broadcast by the British Broadcasting Corporation (BBC). We agree with Judge Lasker that the appellants have demonstrated that the excising done for ABC impairs the integrity of the original work. We further find that the countervailing injuries that Judge Lasker found might have accrued to ABC as a result of an injunction at a prior date no longer exist. We therefore direct the issuance of a preliminary injunction by the district court.

Since its formation in 1969, the Monty Python group has gained popularity primarily through its thirty-minute television programs created for BBC as part of a comedy series entitled "Monty Python's Flying Circus." In accordance with an agreement between Monty Python and BBC, the group writes and delivers to BBC scripts for use in the television series. This scriptwriters' agreement recites in great detail the procedure to be followed when any alterations are to be made in the script prior to recording of the program.[12] The essence of this section of the agreement is that, while BBC retains final authority to make changes, appellants or their representatives exercise optimum control over the scripts consistent with BBC's authority and only minor changes may be made without prior consultation with the writers. Nothing in the scriptwriters' agreement entitles BBC to alter a program once it has been recorded. The agreement further provides that, subject to the terms therein, the group retains all rights in the script.

Under the agreement, BBC may license the transmission of recordings of the television programs in any overseas territory. The series has been broadcast in this country primarily on non-commercial public broadcasting television stations, although several of the programs have been broadcast on commercial stations in Texas and Nevada. In each instance, the thirty-minute programs have been broadcast as originally recorded and broadcast in England in their entirety and without commercial interruption.

In October 1973, Time-Life Films acquired the right to distribute in the United States certain BBC television programs, including the Monty Python series. Time-Life was permitted to edit the programs only "for insertion of commercials, applicable censorship or governmental ... rules and regulations, and National Association of Broadcasters and time segment requirements." No similar clause was included in the scriptwriters' agreement between appellants and BBC. Prior to this time, ABC had sought to acquire the right to broadcast excerpts from various Monty Python programs in the spring of 1975, but the group rejected the proposal for such a disjoined format. Thereafter, in July 1975, ABC agreed with Time-Life to broadcast two ninety-minute specials each comprising three thirty-minute Monty Python programs that had not previously been shown in this country.

Correspondence between representatives of BBC and Monty Python reveals that these parties assumed that ABC would broadcast each of the Monty Python programs "in its entirety." On September 5, 1975, however, the group's British representative inquired of BBC how ABC planned to show the programs in their entirety if approximately 24 min-

---

12. The Agreement provides:

V. When script alterations are necessary it is the intention of the BBC to make every effort to inform and to reach agreement with the Writer. Whenever practicable any necessary alterations (other than minor alterations) shall be made by the Writer. Nevertheless the BBC shall at all times have the right to make (a) minor alterations and (b) such other alterations as in its opinion are necessary in order to avoid involving the BBC in legal action or bringing the BBC into disrepute. Any decision under (b) shall be made at a level not below that of Head of Department. It is however agreed that after a script has been accepted by the BBC alterations will not be made by the BBC under (b) above unless (i) the Writer, if available when the BBC requires the alterations to be made, has been asked to agree to them but is not willing to do so and (ii) the Writer has had, if he so requests and if the BBC agrees that time permits if rehearsals and recording are to proceed as planned, an opportunity to be represented by the Writers' Guild of Great Britain (or if he is not a member of the Guild by his agent) at a meeting with the BBC to be held within at most 48 hours of the request (excluding weekends). If in such circumstances there is no agreement about the alterations then the final decision shall rest with the BBC. Apart from the right to make alterations under (a) and (b) above the BBC shall not without the consent of the Writer or his agent (which consent shall not be unreasonably withheld) make any structural alterations as opposed to minor alterations to the script, provided that such consent shall not be necessary in any case where the Writer is for any reason not immediately available for consultation at the time which in the BBC's opinion is the deadline from the production point of view for such alterations to be made if rehearsals and recording are to proceed as planned.

utes of each 90 minute program were to be devoted to commercials. BBC replied on September 12, "we can only reassure you that ABC have decided to run the programmes 'back to back,' and that there is a firm undertaking not to segment them."

ABC broadcast the first of the specials on October 3, 1975. Appellants did not see a tape of the program until late November and were allegedly "appalled" at the discontinuity and "mutilation" that had resulted from the editing done by Time-Life for ABC. Twenty-four minutes of the original 90 minutes of recording had been omitted. Some of the editing had been done in order to make time for commercials; other material had been edited, according to ABC, because the original programs contained offensive or obscene matter....

We ... reach the question whether there is a likelihood that appellants will succeed on the merits. In concluding that there is a likelihood of infringement here, we rely especially on the fact that the editing was substantial, i.e., approximately 27 per cent of the original program was omitted, and the editing contravened contractual provisions that limited the right to edit Monty Python material. It should be emphasized that our discussion of these matters refers only to such facts as have been developed upon the hearing for a preliminary injunction. Modified or contrary findings may become appropriate after a plenary trial....

Appellants first contend that the question of ownership is irrelevant because the recorded program was merely a derivative work taken from the script in which they hold the uncontested copyright. Thus, even if BBC owned the copyright in the recorded program, its use of that work would be limited by the license granted to BBC by Monty Python for use of the underlying script. We agree.

Section 7 of the [1909] Copyright Law, provides in part that "adaptations, arrangements, dramatizations ... or other versions of ... copyrighted works when produced with the consent of the proprietor of the copyright in such works ... shall be regarded as new works subject to copyright...." Manifestly, the recorded program falls into this category as a dramatization of the script, and thus the program was itself entitled to copyright protection. However, section 7 limits the copyright protection of the derivative work, as works adapted from previously existing scripts have become known, to the novel additions made to the underlying work. Thus, any ownership by BBC of the copyright in the recorded program would not affect the scope or ownership of the copyright in the underlying script.

Since the copyright in the underlying script survives intact despite the incorporation of that work into a derivative work, one who uses the script, even with the permission of the proprietor of the derivative work, may infringe the underlying copyright. If the proprietor of the derivative work is licensed by the proprietor of the copyright in the underlying work to vend or distribute the derivative work to third parties, those parties will, of course, suffer no liability for their use of the underlying work consistent with the license to the proprietor of the derivative work. Obviously, it was just this type of arrangement that was contemplated in this instance. The scriptwriters' agreement between Monty Python and BBC specifically permitted the latter to license the transmission of the recordings made by BBC to distributors such as Time-Life for broadcast in overseas territories.

One who obtains permission to use a copyrighted script in the production of a derivative work, however, may not exceed the specific purpose for which permission was granted.... Appellants herein ... claim that revisions in the script, and ultimately in the program, could be made only after consultation with Monty Python, and that ABC's broadcast of a program edited after recording and without consultation with Monty Python exceeded the scope of any license that BBC was entitled to grant.

The rationale for finding infringement when a licensee exceeds time or media restrictions on his license — the need to allow the proprietor of the underlying copyright to control the method in which his work is presented to the public — applies equally to the situation in which a licensee makes an unauthorized use of the underlying work by publishing it in a truncated version. Whether intended to allow greater economic exploitation of the work, as in the media and time cases, or to ensure that the copyright proprietor retains a veto power over revisions desired for the derivative work, the ability of the copyright holder to control his work remains paramount in our copyright law. We find, therefore, that unauthorized editing of the underlying work, if proven, would constitute an infringement of the copyright in that work similar to any other use of a work that exceeded the license granted by the proprietor of the copyright.

If the broadcast of an edited version of the Monty Python program infringed the group's copyright in the script, ABC may obtain no solace from the fact that editing was permitted in the agreements between BBC and Time-Life or Time-Life and ABC. BBC was not entitled to make unilateral changes in the script and was not specifically empowered to alter the recordings once made; Monty Python, moreover, had reserved to itself any rights not granted to BBC. Since a grantor may not convey greater rights than it owns, BBC's permission to allow Time-Life, and hence ABC, to edit appears to have been a nullity....

ABC next argues that under the "joint work" theory adopted in *Shapiro, Bernstein & Co. v. Jerry Vogel Music, Inc.*, 221 F.2d 569 (2d Cir. 1955), the script produced by Monty Python and the program recorded by BBC are symbiotic elements of a single production. Therefore, according to ABC, each contributor possesses an undivided ownership of all copyrightable elements in the final work and BBC could thus have licensed use of the script, including editing, written by appellants.

The joint work theory as extended in *Shapiro* has been criticized as inequitable unless "at the time of creation by the first author, the second author's contribution [is envisaged] as an integrated part of a single work," and the first author intends that the final product be a joint work. Furthermore, this court appears to have receded from a broad application of the joint work doctrine where the contract which leads to collaboration between authors indicates that one will retain a superior interest. In the present case, the screenwriters' agreement between Monty Python and BBC provides that the group is to retain all rights in the script not granted in the agreement and that at some future point the group may license the scripts for use on television to parties other than BBC. These provisions suggest that the parties did not consider themselves joint authors of a single work. This matter is subject to further exploration at the trial, but in the present state of the record, it presents no bar to issuance of a preliminary injunction.

Aside from the question of who owns the relevant copyrights, ABC asserts that the contracts between appellants and BBC permit editing of the programs for commercial television in the United States. ABC argues that the scriptwriters' agreement allows appellants the right to participate in revisions of the script only *prior* to the recording of the programs, and thus infers that BBC had unrestricted authority to revise after that point. This argument, however, proves too much. A reading of the contract seems to indicate that Monty Python obtained control over editing the script only to ensure control over the program recorded from that script. Since the scriptwriters' agreement explicitly retains for the group all rights not granted by the contract, omission of any terms concerning alterations in the program after recording must be read as reserving to appellants exclusive authority for such revisions.

Finally, ABC contends that appellants must have expected that deletions would be made in the recordings to conform them for use on commercial television in the United States. ABC argues that licensing in the United States implicitly grants a license to insert commercials in a program and to remove offensive or obscene material prior to broadcast. According to the network, appellants should have anticipated that most of the excised material contained scatological references inappropriate for American television and that these scenes would be replaced with commercials, which presumably are more palatable to the American public....

Several of the deletions made for ABC, such as elimination of the words "hell" and "damn," seem inexplicable given today's standard television fare. If, however, ABC honestly determined that the programs were obscene in substantial part, it could have decided not to broadcast the specials at all, or it could have attempted to reconcile its differences with appellants. The network could not, however, free from a claim of infringement, broadcast in a substantially altered form a program incorporating the script over which the group had retained control.

Our resolution of these technical arguments serves to reinforce our initial inclination that the copyright law should be used to recognize the important role of the artist in our society and the need to encourage production and dissemination of artistic works by providing adequate legal protection for one who submits his work to the public. We therefore conclude that there is a substantial likelihood that, after a full trial, appellants will succeed in proving infringement of their copyright by ABC's broadcast of edited versions of Monty Python programs. In reaching this conclusion, however, we need not accept appellants' assertion that any editing whatsoever would constitute infringement. Courts have recognized that licensees are entitled to some small degree of latitude in arranging the licensed work for presentation to the public in a manner consistent with the licensee's style or standards. That privilege, however, does not extend to the degree of editing that occurred here especially in light of contractual provisions that limited the right to edit Monty Python material.

It also seems likely that appellants will succeed on the theory that, regardless of the right ABC had to broadcast an edited program, the cuts made constituted an actionable mutilation of Monty Python's work. This cause of action, which seeks redress for deformation of an artist's work, finds its roots in the continental concept of droit moral, or moral right, which may generally be summarized as including the right of the artist to have his work attributed to him in the form in which he created it.

American copyright law, as presently written, does not recognize moral rights or provide a cause of action for their violation, since the law seeks to vindicate the economic, rather than the personal, rights of authors. Nevertheless, the economic incentive for artistic and intellectual creation that serves as the foundation for American copyright law, cannot be reconciled with the inability of artists to obtain relief for mutilation or misrepresentation of their work to the public on which the artists are financially dependent. Thus courts have long granted relief for misrepresentation of an artist's work by relying on theories outside the statutory law of copyright, such as contract law, or the tort of unfair competition. Although such decisions are clothed in terms of proprietary right in one's creation, they also properly vindicate the author's personal right to prevent the presentation of his work to the public in a distorted form.

Here, the appellants claim that the editing done for ABC mutilated the original work and that consequently the broadcast of those programs as the creation of Monty Python violated the Lanham Act § 43(a), *15 U.S.C. § 1125*(a). This statute, the federal counterpart to state unfair competition laws, has been invoked to prevent misrepresentations that may injure plaintiff's business or personal reputation, even where no registered trademark is concerned. It is sufficient to violate the Act that a representation of a product, although technically true, creates a false impression of the product's origin.

These cases cannot be distinguished from the situation in which a television network broadcasts a program properly designated as having been written and performed by a group, but which has been edited, without the writer's consent, into a form that departs substantially from the original work.... In such a case, it is the writer or performer, rather than the network, who suffers the consequences of the mutilation, for the public will have only the final product by which to evaluate the work. Thus, an allegation that a defendant has presented to the public a "garbled," distorted version of plaintiff's work seeks to redress the very rights sought to be protected by the Lanham Act, *15 U.S.C. § 1125*(a), and should be recognized as stating a cause of action under that statute....

After hearing argument of this appeal, this panel also viewed and compared the two versions. We find that the truncated version at times omitted the climax of the skits to which appellants' rare brand of humor was leading and at other times deleted essential elements in the schematic development of a story line. We therefore agree with Judge Lasker's conclusion that the edited version broadcast by ABC impaired the integrity of appellants' work and represented to the public as the product of appellants what was actually a mere caricature of their talents.

We believe that a valid cause of action for such distortion exists and that therefore a preliminary injunction may issue to prevent repetition of the broadcast prior to final determination of the issues....

Tristar Pictures v. Director's Guild of Am.
160 F.3d 537 (9th Cir. 1998)

Director Michael Apted was unhappy with the way Tristar Pictures edited his film, *Thunderheart,* for television. With the help of the Directors Guild of America (DGA), Apted sought a pseudonym for the director's credit, for as his name is so is he.

Cinephiles believe the director is the true author of a film: It's Coppola's *Godfather,* Spielberg's *Schindler's List* and Verhoeven's *Robocop.* So too when things go badly: It's Coppola's *One from the Heart,* Spielberg's *Lost World* and Verhoeven's *Showgirls.* With his reputation on the line, Apted was concerned when he learned that Tristar would shorten *Thunderheart* by nearly half an hour in order to show it on commercial television.[13] Tristar asked Apted to help trim the movie from 118 minutes, its running time in theatres, down to 90 minutes (a two-hour slot minus commercials). Apted refused and insisted that *Thunderheart* be shown in its entirety. Tristar decided to proceed over Apted's objection and hired an editor who made 270 separate cuts totaling 22 minutes, sped up the credits to steal two more minutes, and compressed the rest of the film elec-

---

13. *Thunderheart* tells the story of a young FBI agent (Val Kilmer) sent to the Pine Ridge Sioux reservation in the 1970s to investigate the violence between traditionalist and progressive factions. The film was shot on location in South Dakota with an indigenous supporting cast. Apted explains that he made a moral commitment to the Sioux about the type of film *Thunderheart* would be, and the cut version wasn't it. For example, Tristar cut a multi-minute pow-wow scene, which Apted says infringed on his creative role as director and violated his moral obligation to present a well-rounded picture of the Sioux tradition.

tronically to gain another four. Apted then asked that his name be taken off the edited picture, but Tristar refused. After an arbitrator ruled in favor of Apted, Tristar brought a petition in state court claiming that the arbitrator had overstepped his authority. The DGA then removed the case to federal court, and the district court upheld the award. Tristar appeals.

Apted's relationship with Tristar is governed by a collective bargaining agreement (the Basic Agreement) negotiated between the studios and the DGA. Two clauses of the agreement are relevant to this appeal. One of them, section 8-211, governs claims by a director that he is entitled to a pseudonym. In order to avail himself of this remedy, a director must first persuade the Director's Council of the DGA that he is entitled to a pseudonym. If the Council assents, the pseudonym question is presented to a joint panel composed of two representatives from the studio and two from the DGA. If a majority of the joint panel sides with the director, the film's directing credit goes to a fictitious director, typically "Alan Smithee." If not, the studio may continue to use the director's name.

The second relevant provision is the Basic Agreement's arbitration clause. Section 2-101 sets forth the arbitrator's jurisdiction, which embraces the capacious range of "all grievances, disputes or controversies over the interpretation or application" of the Basic Agreement. The arbitrator's authority can be invoked under a normal arbitration procedure, set forth in section 2-300 of the Basic Agreement, or under an expedited arbitration procedure, found in section 2-400.

In this case, the Director's Council agreed with Apted and on July 7th called for the convocation of a joint panel to consider whether Apted was entitled to a pseudonym. As of July 12, 1995, however, just six days before *Thunderheart* was scheduled to air, the joint panel had not yet met. The DGA therefore called for expedited arbitration of the dispute under section 2-400. The arbitration took place two days later.

The arbitrator did not rule on Apted's pseudonym claim, explaining that this was a dispute "most appropriately" resolved by the joint panel. But he agreed that Tristar's cuts were so severe as to breach Tristar's duty of good faith and fair dealing set forth in section 7-1502 of the Basic Agreement. As a result, the arbitrator made a conditional award: If the joint panel did not grant Apted a pseudonym, Tristar would have to show a disclaimer that reflected Apted's view of the edited version.[14] The awarded disclaimer read:

> This film is not the version originally released. 22 minutes have been cut out. The director, Michael Apted, believes this alteration changes the narrative and characterization and is not associated with it. The film has also been electronically speeded up. The director believes that this alteration changes the pace of the performance and is not associated with it.

This put Tristar in a box. If it used Apted's name, it would be forced to air the disclaimer, which would make it look as if the film had been butchered. If it used a pseudonym, it would lose the attraction of a respected director. Tristar chose what it saw as the lesser of the two evils, and when *Thunderheart* aired on Fox, sans disclaimer, it carried the label "An Adam Smithy Film."

---

14. Tristar had already indicated that it planned to run a standard disclaimer, reading: "This film has been modified from its original version. It has been formatted to fit this screen and edited to run in the time allotted and for content."

Tristar argues that the arbitrator lacked jurisdiction over the dispute. Under Tristar's reading of the Basic Agreement, all disputes concerning the editing of a film are governed by the pseudonym clause, and the only remedy available to a director unhappy with the studio's editing decision is to seek a pseudonym. While the language of the arbitration clause is very broad, Tristar argues, it should not be read so as to render superfluous the more specific procedure in the pseudonym clause, which is calibrated to resolve disputes about whether edits made to a movie so change its character as to render it no longer the director's work.

Tristar's argument is not without force. The pseudonym procedure does contain a carefully negotiated mechanism for dealing with precisely the type of dispute that arose between Apted and Tristar. Notably, the procedure gives the studio considerable leverage in resisting a claim by the director. Because the joint panel is made up of an equal number of members nominated by the studio and the DGA, a director can only obtain a pseudonym by persuading at least one member nominated by the studio; a tie vote denies the director the pseudonym. By contrast, the studio has no particular leverage for resisting a ruling by the arbitrator — other than the inertial force of being the non-moving party. The pseudonym clause also gives the director only one possible remedy — a pseudonym — while (as we see in this case) the arbitrator can grant other types of relief. Finally, the contract provides no standard for obtaining relief from the joint council, while the arbitrator is limited to any ground available under the terms of the contract and applicable principles of contract law, such as breach of the covenant of good faith and fair dealing. Given these differences, it would seem almost foolish for a director to avail himself of the pseudonym procedure rather than seeking relief under the arbitration clause. Indeed, a director might proceed under the pseudonym procedure and, if unhappy with the result, then seek a separate remedy under the arbitration clause over the same issue.

Tristar also notes that the arbitrator himself saw a tension between the broad sweep of the arbitration clause and the pseudonym procedure. He therefore found that arbitration was not the "most appropriate way" to resolve a dispute over a pseudonym, noting that the parties had established the pseudonym clause as the method for resolving disputes of that sort. Seizing upon this concession by the arbitrator as to the scope of his authority, Tristar argues that the pseudonym provision carves out an area where even the expansive arbitration clause does not reach. By making the arbitration award provisional upon whether a pseudonym is granted, Tristar claims, the arbitrator impermissibly tread upon ground he admitted he had no right to occupy.

Were we interpreting the Basic Agreement in the first instance, this would be a difficult case, but we are not. We are reviewing the award of an arbitrator who ruled on this issue and held that Tristar had violated the implied promise of good faith and fair dealing contained in Article 7 of the Basic Agreement. Tristar's challenge to the arbitrator's jurisdiction fails, not only because of the broad language of the arbitration clause, but also because of Tristar's prior actions. Although Tristar did suggest at the arbitration hearing that the arbitrator had no authority to decide certain issues, it chose to argue that the arbitrator lacked authority rather than simply refusing to come to the table. In this manner, Tristar "by [its] conduct evinced clearly its intent to allow the arbitrator to decide not only the merits of the dispute but also the question of arbitrability." Instead of resting on its present contention that the arbitrator could not grant Apted the relief he sought, Tristar put on evidence of its good faith in editing the film, tacitly admitting that it was plausible for the arbitrator to assume jurisdiction over the dispute.

Tristar's complaint that the arbitrator effectively forced it to grant Apted a pseudonym, thereby circumventing section 8-211 of the Basic Agreement and impermissibly extending the limits of his jurisdiction, also fails. Our review of the scope of an arbitrator's award is extremely narrow: We may ask only "whether the arbitrator's solution can be rationally derived from some plausible theory of the general framework or intent of the agreement." The Basic Agreement gives the arbitrator ample leeway in fashioning remedies: Section 2-501 empowers the arbitrator "to require [the studio] to change or re-do any film titles ... or to order any other reasonable relief the Arbitrator deems appropriate in the circumstances, whether relating to credit on the screen or in advertising or any other arbitrable matter...." This clause invokes the rule that "where it is contemplated that the arbitrator will determine remedies for contract violations that he finds, courts have no authority to disagree with his honest judgment in that respect." The arbitrator's ruling that the covenant of good faith and fair dealing gives an aggrieved director more remedies than just seeking a Smithee is not completely implausible....

Tristar finally argues that affirming this award will create a per se rule prohibiting studios from editing movies for television. We are unconvinced that a single award will have any such effect. Although section 2-309 says that awards interpreting a term of the Basic Agreement are binding on the DGA and the studio, it also instructs that "in any subsequent arbitration ... involving an interpretation of the same term or terms of the [Basic Agreement], the Arbitrator may determine whether or not, as a result of the different combination of facts, the prior arbitration award is relevant or determinative of the issue in such subsequent arbitration." Furthermore, if the arbitrator's decision was indeed so far removed from the spirit of the agreement, the parties are free to renegotiate the governing rules to preclude such awards in the future.

We are bound by the very deferential standard of review that we must give arbitral decisions. "Courts ... do not sit to hear claims of factual or legal error by an arbitrator as an appellate court does in reviewing decisions of lower courts.... That a court is convinced [an arbitrator] committed serious error does not suffice to overturn his decision." Regardless of whether this is the solution that we would come up with through our own independent interpretation of the Basic Agreement, we must abide by the arbitrator's plausible interpretation of the agreement. *AFFIRMED.*

Notes and Questions

a. The transition from a theatrically dominated entertainment experience to one dominated by television was not an easy one. Originally, the motion picture studios attempted to boycott television, refusing to provide the new medium with even their older movies. This allowed the radio industry and talent agencies to take primary control of the new medium. Whether a similar transition has begun again with regard to cable—or perhaps even the Internet—remains to be seen.

b. An early example of the problems inherent in editing for television occurred in *Autry v. Republic Productions, Inc.*, 213 F.2d 667 (9th Cir. 1954). Gene Autry sued to stop having seven of his feature length movies edited down to 53 minutes in length. Seven minutes were dedicated to commercials in each hour of television programming. The court recognized that the studios had the right to edit the films (including the right to edit them down to 53 minutes), but it also recognized that "some such cutting and editing could result in emasculating the motion pictures so that they would no longer contain substantially the same motion and dynamic and dramatic qualities which it was the purpose of the artist's employment to produce." See also *Jaeger v. American Intn'l Pictures, Inc.*, 330 F. Supp. 274 (S.D.N.Y. 1971).

c. The Second Circuit also addressed the contractual control once held by television writers. See *McGuire v. United Artists Television Productions, Inc.,* 254 F. Supp. 270 (S.D. Cal. 1966), for another example of the courts struggling to frame the reservation of rights clause, this time in television contracts.

d. In addition to the implications *Dastar Corp. v. Twentieth Century Fox Film Corp.,* 539 U.S. 23 (2003), has towards copyright and trademark, it also opens the door to potentially renewed interest in mining old films or television episodes for public domain materials.

e. The triggering of the copyright term for television and motion pictures is a bit difficult to track. Prior to the 1976 Copyright Act, works could retain a perpetual, common law copyright. Publication divested this interest. At the point of publication, a work had to be properly registered. Failure to meet the statutory formalities of registration, notice, and deposit would result in the work falling into the public domain. Despite this, a public performance did not constitute publication, so neither a live performance of a play nor a public exhibition of a motion picture constituted a publication.

On the other hand, to reach statutory copyright, the courts and Congress determined that the production and distribution of copies of a work to television broadcasters was a sufficient publication to constitute an act of publication. See *ABC, Inc. v. PrimeTime 24, Joint Venture,* 67 F. Supp. 2d 558, 561 (M.D.N.C. 1999) ("Just as it is clear that mere broadcast does not constitute publication, it is also clear that 'the distribution of copies of a motion picture to television stations for broadcast purposes constitutes an act of publication.'" *Id.* (quoting Nimmer on Copyright § 4.11[B] at 4–57)). If the work is presented to a single broadcaster, however, that did not automatically constitute a publication under the 1909 Copyright Act or the current statute. See *Burke v. National Broadcasting Co.,* 598 F.2d 688 (1st Cir. 1979); 17 U.S.C. § 101 (publication requires an offer "to distribute copies [of the work] to a group of persons for purposes of ... public performance....").

Problem XIV-D

Bryce is hoping someday to be in a position to retain final cut. Given Bryce's current professional status, it generally is not an issue. However, Bryce is both confident and hopeful. To this end, Bryce has asked that you review the film production agreement for Bryce's *Juliet Prescott* (see Problem V-A). Bryce would like to assign all the copyright distribution rights of this film and all of Bryce's other works into a newly formed publishing and distribution company.

Bryce has asked that you provide contracts to that new company. At the moment, Bryce is the sole member and manager of this new Limited Liability Company. Bryce expects to bring on other investors eventually and to use the company to distribute the works. Bryce does not wish to transfer the rights to edit the works, hoping this will create a form of final cut control in the works.

Explain to Bryce the efficacy of this strategy and provide a deal memorandum outlining the terms of the transaction between Bryce and the company. You may wish to consult with your corporate or business associates as well to discuss what fiduciary or other obligations Bryce may have towards the company and future members. Finally, you may wish to review whether any professional conflict of interest exists when representing a client and the client's wholly-owned business when you know that additional owners are going to be invited to join the entity.

E. Bibliography and Links

HOWARD J. BLUMENTHAL AND OLIVER R. GOODENOUGH, THIS BUSINESS OF TELEVISION (2d ed. 1998).

Mark Litwak, Contracts for the Film & Television Industry (2d ed. 1999).

James L. Baughman, *Minow's Viewers: Understanding the Response to the "Vast Wasteland" Address,* 55 FED. COMM. L.J. 449 (2003).

Anna R. Buono & Alonzo Wickers IV, *Montz v. Pilgrim Films & Television, Inc.: Copyright Preemption and Idea Submission Cases,* 28 COMM. LAWYER 4 (2011).

Konrad Gatien, *Internet Killed the Video Star: How In-House Internet Distribution of Home Video Will Affect Profit Participants,* 13 FORDHAM INTELL. PROP. MEDIA & ENT. L.J. 909 (2003).

Jesse Haskins, *Commercial Skipping Technology and the New Market Dynamic: The Relevance of Antitrust Law to an Emerging Technology,* 2009 DUKE L. & TECH. REV. 6 (2009).

Peter M. Hoffman & Lindsee Gendron, *Judicial Review of Arbitration Awards after Cable Connection: Towards a Due Process Model,* 17 UCLA ENT. L. REV. 1 (2010).

Nicholas Johnson, *Forty Years of Wandering in the Wasteland,* 55 FED. COMM. L.J. 521 (2003).

Daniel A. Lyons, *Technology Convergence and Federalism: Who Should Decide the Future of Telecommunications Regulation?,* 43 U. MICH. J.L. REFORM 383 (2010).

Newton N. Minow, *Television and the Public Interest,* 55 FED. COMM. L.J. 395 (2003).

Zahr Said, *Embedded Advertising and the Venture Consumer,* 89 N.C.L. REV. 99 (2010).

Websites

Alliance of Motion Picture and Television Producers, www.amptp.org

Canadian Film and Television Production Association, www.cftpa.ca

Chapter XV

Television & Cable Regulation

A. Overview

The Public and Broadcasting[1]

Introduction

This Manual is published by the Federal Communications Commission (the "FCC" or the "Commission"), the federal agency directed by Congress to regulate broadcasting. It provides a brief overview of the FCC's regulation of broadcast radio and television licensees, describing how the FCC authorizes broadcast stations, the various rules relating to broadcast programming and operations with which stations must comply, and the essential obligation of licensees that their stations serve their local communities....

In exchange for obtaining a valuable license to operate a broadcast station using the public airwaves, each radio and television licensee is required by law to operate its station in the "public interest, convenience and necessity." This means that it must air programming that is responsive to the needs and problems of its local community of license.

To do so, each station licensee must affirmatively identify those needs and problems and then specifically treat those local matters that it deems to be significant in the news, public affairs, political and other programming that it airs. As discussed at page 29 of this Manual,[2] each station must provide the public with information about how it has met this obligation by means of quarterly reports, which contain a listing of the programming that it has aired that the licensee believes provided significant treatment of issues facing the community.... [E]ach station also must maintain and make available to any member of the public for inspection, generally at its studio, a local public inspection file which contains these reports, as well as other materials that pertain to the station's operations and dealings with the FCC and with the community that it is licensed to serve. The public file is an excellent resource to gauge a station's performance of its obligations as a Commission licensee. In the future, television stations with websites will be required to post most of the content of their public files on their websites, or on the website of their state local broadcasters association, if permitted.

---

1. The Media Bureau, Federal Communications Commission, Washington, July 2008. D.C. http://www.fcc.gov/guides/public-and-broadcasting-july-2008.
2. Page numbers in the text below refer to pages in the original PDF version.

The FCC and Its Regulatory Authority

The Communications Act. The FCC was created by Congress in the Communications Act for the purpose of "regulating interstate and foreign commerce in communication by wire and radio so as to make available, so far as possible, to all the people of the United States, without discrimination on the basis of race, color, religion, national origin, or sex, a rapid, efficient, Nation-wide, and world-wide wire and radio communications service...." (In this context, the word "radio" covers both broadcast radio and television.) The Communications Act authorizes the FCC to "make such regulations not inconsistent with law as it may deem necessary to prevent interference between stations and to carry out the provisions of [the] Act." It directs us to base our broadcast licensing decisions on the determination of whether those actions will serve the public interest, convenience, and necessity....

The FCC and the Media Bureau. The FCC has five Commissioners, each of whom is appointed by the President and confirmed by the Senate. Serving under the Commissioners are a number of Offices and operating Bureaus. One of those is the Media Bureau, which has day-to-day responsibility for developing, recommending, and administering the rules governing the media, including radio and television stations. The FCC's broadcast rules are contained in Title 47 of the Code of Federal Regulations ("CFR"), Parts 73 (broadcast) and 74 (auxiliary broadcast, including low power TV, and translator stations). Our rules of practice and procedure can be found in Title 47 CFR, Part 1....

FCC Regulation of Broadcast Radio and Television. The FCC allocates (that is, designates a portion of the broadcast spectrum to) new broadcast stations based upon both the relative needs of various communities for additional broadcast outlets and specified engineering standards designed to prevent interference among stations and to other communications users. As noted above, whenever we review an application—whether to build a new station, modify or renew a license or sell a station—we must determine if its grant would serve the public interest. As discussed earlier, we expect station licensees to be aware of the important problems and issues facing their local communities and to foster public understanding by presenting programming that relates to those local issues. As discussed in this Manual, however, broadcasters—not the FCC or any other government agency—are responsible for selecting the material that they air. By operation of the First Amendment to the U.S. Constitution, and because the Communications Act expressly prohibits the Commission from censoring broadcast matter, our role in overseeing program content is very limited.

FCC Regulation of Broadcast Radio and Television

The FCC allocates (that is, designates a portion of the broadcast spectrum to) new broadcast stations based upon both the relative needs of various communities for additional broadcast outlets and specified engineering standards designed to prevent interference among stations and to other communications users. As noted above, whenever we review an application—whether to build a new station, modify or renew a license or sell a station—we must determine if its grant would serve the public interest. As discussed earlier, we expect station licensees to be aware of the important problems and issues facing their local communities and to foster public understanding by presenting programming that relates to those local issues. As discussed in this Manual, however, broadcasters—not the FCC or any other government agency—are responsible for selecting the material that they air. By operation of the First Amendment to the U.S. Constitution, and because the Communications Act expressly prohibits the Commission from censoring broadcast matter, our role in overseeing program content is very limited.

We license only individual broadcast stations. We do not license TV or radio networks (such as CBS, NBC, ABC or Fox) or other organizations with which stations have relationships (such as PBS or NPR), except to the extent that those entities may also be station licensees. We also do not regulate information provided over the Internet, nor do we intervene in private disputes involving broadcast stations or their licensees. Instead, we usually defer to the parties, courts, or other agencies to resolve such disputes.

The Licensing of TV and Radio Stations

Commercial and Noncommercial Educational Stations. The FCC licenses FM radio and TV stations as either commercial or noncommercial educational ("NCE"). (All AM radio stations are licensed as commercial facilities.) Commercial stations generally support themselves through the sale of advertising. In contrast, NCE stations generally meet their operating expenses with contributions received from listeners and viewers, and also may receive government funding. In addition, NCE stations may receive contributions from for-profit entities, and are permitted to acknowledge such contributions or underwriting donations with announcements naming and generally describing the contributing party or donor. However, NCE stations may not broadcast commercials or other promotional announcements on behalf of for-profit entities ...

Broadcast Programming: Basic Law and Policy

The FCC and Freedom of Speech. The First Amendment, as well as Section 326 of the Communications Act, prohibits the Commission from censoring broadcast material and from interfering with freedom of expression in broadcasting. The Constitution's protection of free speech includes that of programming that may be objectionable to many viewer or listeners. Thus, the FCC cannot prevent the broadcast of any particular point of view. In this regard, the Commission has observed that "the public interest is best served by permitting free expression of views." However, the right to broadcast material is not absolute. There are some restrictions on the material that a licensee can broadcast. We discuss these restrictions below.

Licensee Discretion. Because the Commission cannot dictate to licensees what programming they may air, each individual radio and TV station licensee generally has discretion to select what its station broadcasts and to otherwise determine how it can best serve its community of license. Licensees are responsible for selecting their entertainment programming, as well as programs concerning local issues, news, public affairs, religion, sports events, and other subjects....

Criticism, Ridicule, and Humor Concerning Individuals, Groups, and Institutions. The First Amendment's guarantee of freedom of speech similarly protects programming that stereotypes or may otherwise offend people with regard to their religion, race, national background, gender, or other characteristics. It also protects broadcasts that criticize or ridicule established customs and institutions, including the government and its officials. The Commission recognizes that, under our Constitution, people must be free to say things that the majority may abhor, not only what most people may find tolerable or congenial. However, if you are offended by a station's programming, we urge you to make your concerns known to the station licensee, in writing.

Programming Access. In light of their discretion to formulate their programming, station licensees are not required to broadcast everything that is offered or otherwise suggested to them. Except as required by the Communications Act, including the use of stations by candidates for public office (discussed at pages 13–14 of this Manual), licensees have no obligation to allow any particular person or group to participate in a broadcast or to present that person or group's remarks.

Broadcast Programming: Law and Policy on Specific Kinds of Programming

Broadcast Journalism

Introduction. As noted above, in light of the fundamental importance of the free flow of information to our democracy, the First Amendment and the Communications Act bar the FCC from telling station licensees how to select material for news programs, or prohibiting the broadcast of an opinion on any subject. We also do not review anyone's qualifications to gather, edit, announce, or comment on the news; these decisions are the station licensee's responsibility. Nevertheless, there are two issues related to broadcast journalism that are subject to Commission regulation: hoaxes and news distortion.

Hoaxes. The broadcast by a station of false information concerning a crime or catastrophe violates the FCC's rules if:

- the station licensee knew that the information was false,

- broadcasting the false information directly causes substantial public harm, and

- it was foreseeable that broadcasting the false information would cause such harm.

In this context, a "crime" is an act or omission that makes the offender subject to criminal punishment by law, and a "catastrophe" is a disaster or an imminent disaster involving violent or sudden events affecting the public. The broadcast must cause direct and actual damage to property or to the health or safety of the general public, or diversion of law enforcement or other public health and safety authorities from their duties, and the public harm must begin immediately. If a station airs a disclaimer before the broadcast that clearly characterizes the program as fiction and the disclaimer is presented in a reasonable manner under the circumstances, the program is presumed not to pose foreseeable public harm....

News Distortion. The Commission often receives complaints concerning broadcast journalism, such as allegations that stations have aired inaccurate or one-sided news reports or comments, covered stories inadequately, or overly dramatized the events that they cover. For the reasons noted above, the Commission generally will not intervene in such cases because it would be inconsistent with the First Amendment to replace the journalistic judgment of licensees with our own. However, as public trustees, broadcast licensees may not intentionally distort the news: the FCC has stated that "rigging or slanting the news is a most heinous act against the public interest." The Commission will investigate a station for news distortion if it receives documented evidence of such rigging or slanting, such as testimony or other documentation, from individuals with direct personal knowledge that a licensee or its management engaged in the intentional falsification of the news. Of particular concern would be evidence of the direction to employees from station management to falsify the news. However, absent such a compelling showing, the Commission will not intervene....

Political Broadcasting: Candidates for Public Office. In recognition of the particular importance of the free flow of information to the public during the electoral process, the Communications Act and the Commission's rules impose specific obligations on broadcasters regarding political speech.

Reasonable Access. The Communications Act requires that broadcast stations provide "reasonable access" to candidates for federal elective office. Such access must be made available during all of a station's normal broadcast schedule, including television prime time and radio drive time. In addition, federal candidates are entitled to purchase all classes of time offered by stations to commercial advertisers, such as preemptible and non-preemptible time. The only exception to the access requirement is for bona fide news programming (as defined below), during which broadcasters may choose not to sell airtime to federal candidates. Broadcast stations have discretion as to whether to sell time to candidates in state and local elections.

Equal Opportunities. The Communications Act requires that, when a station provides airtime to a legally qualified candidate for any public office (federal, state, or local), the station must "afford equal opportunities to all other such candidates for that office." The equal opportunities provision of the Communications Act also provides that the station "shall have no power of censorship over the material broadcast" by the candidate. The law exempts from the equal opportunities requirement appearances by candidates during bona fide news programming, defined as an appearance by a legally qualified candidate on a bona fide newscast, interview, or documentary (if the appearance of the candidate is incidental to the presentation of the subject covered by the documentary) or on-the-spot coverage of a bona fide news event (including debates, political conventions and related incidental activities).

In addition, a station must sell political advertising time to certain candidates during specified periods before a primary or general election at the lowest rate charged for the station's most favored commercial advertiser....

Objectionable Programming

Programming Inciting "Imminent Lawless Action." The Supreme Court has held that the government may curtail speech if it is both: (1) intended to incite or produce "imminent lawless action;" and (2) likely to "incite or produce such action." Even when this legal test is met, any review that might lead to a curtailment of speech is generally performed by the appropriate criminal law enforcement authorities, not by the FCC.

Obscene, Indecent, or Profane Programming. Although, for the reasons discussed earlier, the Commission is generally prohibited from regulating broadcast content, the courts have held that the FCC's regulation of obscene and indecent programming is constitutional, because of the compelling societal interests in protecting children from potentially harmful programming and supporting parents' ability to determine the programming to which their children will be exposed at home.

Obscene material is not protected by the First Amendment and cannot be broadcast at any time. To be obscene, the material must have all of the following three characteristics:

- an average person, applying contemporary community standards, must find that the material, as a whole, appeals to the prurient interest;
- the material must depict or describe, in a patently offensive way, sexual conduct specifically defined by applicable law; and
- the material, taken as a whole, must lack serious literary, artistic, political, or scientific value.

Indecent material is protected by the First Amendment, so its broadcast cannot constitutionally be prohibited at all times. However, the courts have upheld Congress' prohibition of the broadcast of indecent material during times of the day in which there is a reasonable risk that children may be in the audience, which the Commission has determined to be between the hours of 6 a.m. and 10 p.m. Indecent programming is defined as "language or material that, in context, depicts or describes, in terms patently offensive as measured by contemporary community standards for the broadcast medium, sexual or excretory organs or activities." Broadcasts that fall within this definition and are aired between 6 a.m. and 10 p.m. may be subject to enforcement action by the FCC.

Profane material also is protected by the First Amendment, so its broadcast cannot be outlawed entirely. The Commission has defined such program matter to include language that is both "so grossly offensive to members of the public who actually hear it as to amount to a nuisance" and is sexual or excretory in nature or derived from such terms. Such material may be the subject of possible Commission enforcement action if it is broadcast within the same time period applicable to indecent programming: between 6 a.m. and 10 p.m....

Violent Programming. Many members of the public have expressed concern about violent television programming and the negative impact such broadcast material may have upon children. In response to these concerns, and at the request of 39 members of the U.S. House of Representatives, the FCC conducted a proceeding seeking public comment on violent programming. In April 2007, the Commission delivered to Congress a Report recommending that the industry voluntarily commit to reducing the amount of such programming viewed by children. The Commission also suggested that Congress consider enacting legislation that would better support parents' efforts to safeguard their children from such objectionable programming....

The V-Chip and TV Program Ratings. In light of the widespread concern about obscene, indecent, profane, violent, or otherwise objectionable programming, in 1996, Congress passed a law to require TV sets with screens 13 inches or larger to be equipped with a "V-Chip"—a device that allows parents to program their sets to block TV programming that carries a certain rating. Since 2000, all such sets manufactured with screens 13 inches or larger must contain the V-Chip technology. This technology, which must be activated by parents, works in conjunction with a voluntary television rating system created and administered by the television industry and others, which enables parents to identify programming containing sexual, violent, or other content that they believe may be harmful to their children. All of the major broadcast networks and most of the major cable networks are encoding their programming with this ratings information to work with the V-Chip. However, some programming, such as news and sporting events, and unedited movies aired on premium cable channels, are not rated. In 2004, the FCC expanded the V-Chip requirement to apply also to devices that do not have a display screen but are used with a TV set, such as a VCR or a digital-to-analog converter box....

Children's Television Programming. Throughout its license term, every TV station must serve the educational and informational needs of children both by means of its overall programming and through programming that is specifically designed to serve those needs. Licensees are eligible for routine staff-level approval of the Children's Television Act portion of their renewal applications if they air at least three hours of "core" children's television programming, per week, or proportionally more if they provide additional free digital programming streams. Core programming is defined as follows:

Educational and Informational. The programming must further the educational and informational needs of children 16 years old and under (this includes their intellectual/cognitive or social/emotional needs).

Specifically Designed to Serve Their Needs. A program is considered "specifically designed to serve the educational and information needs of children" if: (1) that is its significant purpose; (2) it is aired between the hours of 7 a.m. and 10 p.m.; (3) it is a regularly scheduled weekly program; and (4) it is at least 30 minutes in duration.

To ensure that parents and other interested parties are informed of the educational and informational children's programming that their area stations offer, television licensees must identify each program specifically designed to "educate and inform" children by displaying the icon "E/I" throughout the program. In addition, commercial stations must provide information identifying such programs to the publishers of program guides.

During the broadcast of TV programs aimed at children 12 and under, advertising may not exceed 10.5 minutes an hour on weekends and 12 minutes an hour on weekdays.

These rules apply to analog and digital broadcasting. As discussed at page 9 of this Manual, television stations have traditionally operated with analog technology. Television stations, however, are in the process of switching to digital broadcasting, which greatly enhances their capability to serve their communities. Among other things, digital technology permits stations to engage in multicasting, that is, to air more than one stream of programming at the same time. Digital stations that choose to air more than one stream of free, over-the-air video programming must air proportionately more children's educational programming than stations that air only one stream of free, over-the-air video programming....

Tobacco and Alcohol Advertising. Federal law prohibits the airing of advertising for cigarettes, little cigars, smokeless tobacco, and chewing tobacco on radio, TV, or any other medium of electronic communication under the FCC's jurisdiction. However, the advertising of smoking accessories, cigars, pipes, pipe tobacco, or cigarette-making machines is not prohibited. Congress has not enacted any law prohibiting broadcast advertising of any kind of alcoholic beverage, and the FCC does not have a rule or policy regulating such advertisements.

Subliminal Programming. The Commission sometimes receives complaints regarding the alleged use of subliminal perception techniques in broadcast programming. Subliminal programming is designed to be perceived on a subconscious level only. Regardless of whether it is effective, the broadcast of subliminal material is inconsistent with a station's obligation to serve the public interest because it is designed to be deceptive.

Must-Carry or Retransmission Consent Election. The public file for all commercial television stations must also contain documentation of the station's election for carriage over cable and satellite systems. In this regard, there are two ways that a broadcast TV station can choose to be carried over a cable or satellite system: "must-carry" or "retransmission consent." Each is discussed below.

Must carry. TV stations are generally entitled to be carried on cable television systems in their local markets. A station that chooses to exercise this right receives no compensation from the cable system. Satellite carriers may decide to offer local stations in a designated market area. If they choose to offer one station, then they must carry all the stations in that market that request carriage.

Retransmission Consent. Instead of exercising their "must-carry" rights, commercial TV stations may choose to receive compensation from a cable system or satellite carrier in return for granting permission to the cable system or satellite carrier to carry the station. This option is available only to commercial TV stations. Because it is possible that a station that elects this option may not reach an agreement with the cable system, it may ultimately not be carried by the system.

Every three years, commercial TV stations must decide whether their relationship with each local cable system and satellite carrier that offers local service will be governed by must-carry or by retransmission consent agreements. Each commercial station must keep a copy of its decision in the public file for the three-year period to which it pertains.

Noncommercial stations are not entitled to compensation in return for carriage on a cable or satellite system, but they may request mandatory carriage on the system. A noncommercial station making such a request must keep a copy of the request in the public file for the duration of the period to which it applies....

Cable Television Information Bulletin[3]

Federal Communications Commission Fact Sheet, June 2000

EVOLUTION OF CABLE TELEVISION

Cable television (also called CATV or community antenna television) was developed in the late 1940s for communities unable to receive TV signals because of terrain or distance from TV stations. Cable television system operators located antennas in areas with good reception, picked up broadcast station signals and then distributed them by coaxial cable to subscribers for a fee.

In 1950, cable systems operated in only 70 communities in the United States. These systems served 14,000 homes. By October 1998 there were more than 10,700 systems serving more than 65 million subscribers in more than 32,000 communities. Cable systems are operating in every state of the United States and in many other countries, including Austria, Canada, Belgium, Germany, Great Britain, Italy, Japan, Mexico, Spain, Sweden and Switzerland.

Most cable systems are technically capable of offering between 36 and 60 channels. Channel capacity in the industry has increased dramatically in recent years; some systems now offer in excess of 100 channels. Most cable subscribers receive service from a system offering more than 54 channels.

The channel capacity of a cable system makes it possible for a cable television system operator to provide many services. In addition to over-the-air television broadcast signals, most systems also offer diverse program services, including, for example, news, weather, business information, movies, sports, special entertainment features, and programming designed for specific audiences such as children, women, and ethnic and racial groups. Within the past few years, some cable systems have begun offering a full-range of telecommunications services, including high-speed Internet access and local telephone service. High-speed Internet access allows subscribers to connect to the Internet more than 100 times faster than the fastest standard analog modem.

Some cable operators also create their own local programming and provide access channels for public and institutional uses. They also provide leased access channels for "rent" to those wishing to show specific programs. Electronic banking, shopping, utility meter reading, and home security are some of the home services that are possible using the two-way transmission capabilities of cable television systems.

INITIAL JURISDICTION AND RULES

The Federal Communications Commission first established rules in 1965 for cable systems which received signals by microwave antennas. In March 1966, the Commission established rules for all cable systems (whether or not served by microwave). The Supreme Court affirmed the Commission's jurisdiction over cable in *United States v. Southwestern Cable Co.*, 392 U.S. 157 (1968). The Court ruled that "the Commission has reasonably concluded that regulatory authority over CATV is imperative if it is to perform with appropriate effectiveness certain of its responsibilities." The Court found the Commission needed authority over cable systems to assure the preservation of local broadcast service

---

3. Available at http://www.fcc.gov/mb/facts/csgen.html.

and to effect an equitable distribution of broadcast services among the various regions of the country.

In March 1972, new rules regarding cable television became effective. These rules required cable television operators to obtain a certificate of compliance from the Commission prior to operating a cable television system or adding a television broadcast signal. The rules applicable to cable operators fell into several broad subject areas—franchise standards, signal carriage, network program nonduplication and syndicated program exclusivity, nonbroadcast or cablecasting services, cross-ownership, equal employment opportunity, and technical standards. Cable television operators who originated programming were subject to equal time, Fairness Doctrine, sponsorship identification and other provisions similar to rules applicable to broadcasters. Cable operators were also required to maintain certain records and to file annual reports with the Commission concerning general statistics, employment and finances.

In succeeding years, the Commission modified or eliminated many of the rules. Among the more significant actions, the Commission deleted most of the franchise standards in 1977, substituted a registration process for the certificate of compliance application process in 1978, and eliminated the distant signal carriage restrictions and syndicated program exclusivity rules in 1980. In 1983, the Commission deleted its requirement that cable operators file financial information. In addition, court actions led to the deletion of the pay cable programming rules in 1977.

1984 CONGRESSIONAL POLICY AND RULES

In October 1984, the U.S. Congress amended the Communications Act of 1934 by adopting the Cable Communications Policy Act of 1984. The 1984 Cable Act established policies in the areas of ownership, channel usage, franchise provisions and renewals, subscriber rates and privacy, obscenity and lockboxes, unauthorized reception of services, equal employment opportunity, and pole attachments. The new law also defined jurisdictional boundaries among federal, state and local authorities for regulating cable television systems.

1992 CONGRESSIONAL POLICY AND RULES

Following the 1984 Cable Act, the number of households subscribing to cable television systems increased, as did the channel capacity of many cable systems. However, competition among distributors of cable services did not increase, and, in many communities, the rates for cable services far outpaced inflation. Responding to these problems, Congress enacted the Cable Television Consumer Protection and Competition Act of 1992. The 1992 Cable Act mandated a number of changes in the manner in which cable television is regulated.

In adopting the 1992 Cable Act, Congress stated that it wanted to promote the availability of diverse views and information, to rely on the marketplace to the maximum extent possible to achieve that availability, to ensure cable operators continue to expand their capacity and program offerings, to ensure cable operators do not have undue market power, and to ensure consumer interests are protected in the receipt of cable service. The Commission has adopted regulations to implement these goals.

1996 CONGRESSIONAL POLICY AND RULES

In adopting the Telecommunications Act of 1996, Congress noted that it wanted to provide a pro-competitive, de-regulatory national policy framework designed to accelerate rapidly private sector deployment of advanced telecommunications and information technologies and services to all Americans by opening all telecommunications markets to competition. The Commission has adopted regulations to implement the requirements of the 1996 Act and the intent of Congress.

WHAT IS CABLE TELEVISION?

Cable television is a video delivery service provided by a cable operator to subscribers via a coaxial cable or fiber optics. Programming delivered without a wire via satellite or other facilities is not "cable television" under the Commission's definitions.

A **cable television system operator** is any person or group of persons who provides cable service over a cable system and directly or through one or more affiliates owns a significant interest in such cable system, or who otherwise controls or is responsible for, through any arrangement, the management and operation of such a cable system.

Cable service is the transmission to subscribers of video programming, or other programming service. This definition includes any subscriber selection required in choosing video programming or other programming service.

A **cable system** is a facility, consisting of a set of closed transmission paths and associated signal generation, reception, and control equipment that is designed to provide cable service which includes video programming and which is provided to multiple subscribers within a community. This term does not include a facility that serves only to retransmit the television signals of one or more television broadcast stations; a facility that serves subscribers without using any public right-of-way; a facility of a common carrier which is subject in whole or in part, to the provisions of Title II of the Communications Act, except that such facility shall be considered a cable system to the extent such facility is used in the transmission of video programming directly to subscribers; unless the extent of such use is solely to provide interactive on demand services; an open video system; or any facilities of any electric utility used solely for operating its electric utility system.

Cable services are often provided in **tiers**. A tier is a category of cable service or services provided by a cable operator for which a separate rate is charged by the cable operator. There are three types of cable service: basic service, cable programming service, and per-channel or per-program (sometimes called pay-per-view) service. **Basic service** is the lowest level of cable service a subscriber can buy. It includes, at a minimum, all over-the-air television broadcast signals carried pursuant to the must-carry requirements of the Communications Act, and any public, educational, or government access channels required by the system's franchise agreement. It may include additional signals chosen by the operator. Basic service is generally regulated by the local franchising authority (the local or state entity empowered by Federal, State, or local law to grant a franchise to a cable company to operate in a given area). **Cable programming service** includes all program channels on the cable system that are not included in basic service, but are not separately offered as per-channel or per-program services. Pursuant to a 1996 federal law, the rates charged for cable programming services tiers provided after March 31, 1999 are not regulated. There may be one or more tiers of cable programming service.

Per-channel or per-program service includes those cable services that are provided as single-channel tiers by the cable operator, and individual programs for which the cable operator charges a separate rate. Neither of these services is regulated by the local franchising authorities or the Commission.

A **local exchange carrier** (LEC) is a telephone company which provides local telephone service.

A **multichannel video programming distributor** is any person such as, but not limited to, a cable operator, a multichannel multipoint distribution service, a direct broadcast satellite service, or a television receive-only satellite program distributor, who makes available for purchase, by subscribers or customers, multiple channels of video programming....

STATE AND LOCAL REGULATION OF CABLE SYSTEMS

A variety of laws and regulations for cable television exist at the state and local level. Some states, such as Massachusetts, regulate cable television on a comprehensive basis through a state commission or advisory board established for the sole purpose of cable television regulation. In Alaska, Connecticut, Delaware, Nevada, New Jersey, Rhode Island, and Vermont, the agencies are state public utility commissions. In Hawaii, regulation of cable television is the responsibility of the Department of Regulatory Agencies. In other areas of the country, cable is regulated by local governments such as a city cable commission, city council, town council, or a board of supervisors. These regulatory entities are called "local franchising authorities." In addition, at least 30 other states have one or more laws specifically applicable to cable television, dealing most commonly with such subjects as franchising, theft of service, pole attachments, rate regulation and taxation.

The 1992 Cable Act codified, and the Commission has adopted, a regulatory plan allowing local and/or state authorities to select a cable franchisee and to regulate in any areas that the Commission did not preempt. Local franchising authorities have adopted laws and/or regulations in areas such as subscriber service requirements, public access requirements and franchise renewal standards. Under the 1992 Cable Act, local franchising authorities have specific responsibility for regulating the rates for basic cable service and equipment.

The Communications Act requires that no new cable operator may provide service without a franchise and establishes several policies relating to franchising requirements and franchise fees. The Communications Act authorizes local franchising authorities to grant one or more franchises within their jurisdiction. However, a local franchising authority may not grant an exclusive franchise, and may not unreasonably withhold its consent for new service. Included in the grant of a franchise to a cable system are rights relating to the construction of the system, including the local franchising authority's authorization to use public rights-of-way, easements, and to establish the areas to be served. In addition, the law requires just compensation to property owners who have suffered damages as a result of a cable operator's construction, operation, installation, or removal of its cable television facilities. Moreover, franchising authorities are required to ensure that access to cable service is not denied to any group of potential residential cable subscribers on the basis of income class. Although the Communications Act also generally precludes the regulation of cable systems as common carriers, it authorizes the Commission, to require, if it chooses, the filing of informational tariffs for intrastate communications services, other than cable service, which is provided by a cable system.

Franchising authorities may charge the cable operator a fee for the right to operate a cable system in that franchise area; however, the franchise fee paid by the cable system can be no more than five percent of its annual gross revenue. A franchising authority may use the money collected from this fee for any purpose. A cable operator must list any applicable franchise fee as a separate item on the subscriber's bill....

UNAUTHORIZED RECEPTION OF CABLE SERVICES

The 1984 Cable Act provides damages and penalties of up to two years in prison and/or $50,000 in fines to be assessed against anyone determined to be guilty either of the unauthorized interception or reception of cable television services or of the manufacture or distribution of equipment intended to be utilized for such a purpose. The Commission does not prosecute unauthorized reception of cable services. Rather, cable operators aggrieved by a violation may bring an action in a United States district court or in any other court of competent jurisdiction. Knowledge of violations should be reported directly to the cable system.

SIGNAL CARRIAGE REQUIREMENTS

The 1992 Cable Act established new standards for television broadcast station signal carriage on cable systems. Under these rules, each local commercial television broadcast station was given the option of selecting mandatory carriage ("must-carry") or retransmission consent ("may carry") for each cable system serving the same market as the commercial television station. The market of a television station is established by its Area of Dominant Influence ("ADI"), as defined by Arbitron and/or modified by the Commission. Every county in the country is assigned to an ADI, and those cable systems and television stations in the same ADI are considered to be in the same market. Upon the request of a television station or a cable system, the Commission has the authority to change the ADI to which a station is assigned. As a result of Arbitron abandoning the television research business, the Commission has determined that, effective January 1, 2000, the market of a television station shall be its Designated Market Area ("DMA") as determined by Nielsen Media Research.

Must-Carry/Retransmission Consent Election

Every three years, every local commercial television station has the right to elect either must-carry or retransmission consent. The initial election was made on June 17, 1993, and was effective on October 6, 1993. The next election occurred on October 1, 1996, and was effective January 1, 1997. All subsequent elections will occur every three years (October 1 1999, to be effective January 1, 2000; October 1, 2002, to be effective January 1, 2003; etc.).

Election of Must-Carry Status

Generally, if a local commercial television station elects must-carry status, it is entitled to insist on cable carriage in its local market. Each cable system with more than 12 channels must set aside up to one-third of its channel capacity for must-carry stations. For example, if a cable system has 60 channels, it must set aside 20 of those channels for must-carry stations. If there are 25 stations in the market which elected must-carry, the cable operator may choose 20 to carry. On the other hand, if only 15 stations elected must-carry in the market, the cable system would have to carry all 15 of these stations. A must-carry station has a statutory right to a channel position, usually its over-the-air channel number, or another channel number on which it has historically been carried.

Retransmission Consent Election

A cable system is not permitted to carry a commercial station without the station's consent. Therefore, if the local commercial television station elects retransmission consent, the cable system must obtain that station's consent prior to carrying or transmitting its signal. Except for "superstations," a cable system may not carry the signal of any television broadcast station that is not located in the same market as the cable system without that broadcaster's consent. Superstations are transmitted via satellite, usually nationwide, and the cable system may carry such stations outside their local market without their consent. The negotiations between a television station and a cable system are private agreements which may, but need not, include some form of compensation to the television station such as money, advertising time or additional channel access.

Noncommercial Educational Television Stations

Every cable system across the country must carry at least one local noncommercial educational ("NCE") station. A noncommercial station which places a Grade B signal over a cable system's principal headend, or whose city of license is within fifty miles of the cable system's principal headend, is considered "local" for this purpose. Cable systems with more than 36 channels may be required to carry all local noncommercial educational television stations which request carriage. Any cable system operating in a market where no local NCE station is available is required to import one NCE station....

Syndicated Program Exclusivity Protection

With respect to non-network programming, cable systems that serve at least 1,000 subscribers may be required, upon proper notification, to provide syndicated protection to broadcasters who have contracted with program suppliers for exclusive exhibition rights to certain programs within specific geographic areas, whether or not the cable system affected is carrying the station requesting this protection. However, no cable system is required to delete a program broadcast by a station which is either significantly viewed or which places a Grade B or better contour over the community of the cable system.

Network Program Nonduplication

Commercial television station licensees are entitled to protect the network programming they have contracted for by exercising nonduplication rights against more distant television broadcast stations carried on a local cable television system that serves more than 1,000 subscribers. Commercial broadcast stations may assert these nonduplication rights regardless of whether or not their signals are being transmitted by the local cable system and regardless of when, or if, the network programming is scheduled to be broadcast. Generally, the zone of protection for such programming cannot exceed thirty-five miles for stations licensed to a community in the Commission's list of top 100 television markets or fifty-five miles for stations licensed to communities in smaller television markets. In addition, a cable operator does not have to delete the network programming of any station which the Commission has previously recognized as significantly viewed in the cable community.

Sports Programming Blackouts

A cable system located within 35 miles of the city of license of a broadcast station where a sporting event is taking place may not carry the live television broadcast of the sporting event on its system if the event is not available live on a local television broadcast station, if the holder of the broadcast rights to the event, or its agent, requests such a blackout. The holder of the rights is responsible for notifying the cable operator of its request for program deletion at least the Monday preceding the calendar week during which the deletion is desired. If no television broadcast station is licensed to the community in which the sports event is taking place, the 35-mile blackout zone extends from the broadcast station's licensed community with which the sports event or team is identified. If the event or local team is not identified with any particular community (for instance, the New England Patriots), the 35-mile blackout zone extends from the community nearest the sports event which has a licensed broadcast station. The sports blackout rule does not apply to cable television systems serving less than 1,000 subscribers, nor does it require deletion of a sports event on a broadcast station's signal that was carried by a cable system prior to March 31, 1972. The rule does not apply to sports programming carried on nonbroadcast program distribution services such as ESPN. These services, however, may be subject to private contractual blackout restrictions.

For example, if the Boston Celtics are playing the Atlanta Hawks at Boston Gardens in a National Basketball Association ("NBA") game, and the game is not broadcast live on a Boston television station, and the NBA sends a blackout notice to cable systems within 35 miles of Boston, those systems will have to delete the game which is carried on their systems by "superstation" WTBS from Atlanta. If a sports event were carried, for example, on ESPN or a regional subscription sports network, any blackout would be the result of a private contractual agreement between the holder of the rights to the event and the sports network.

Copyright

The Copyright Act requires cable operators to obtain a compulsory license for the carriage of programming. The cable operator pays the fee to the copyright office, for distribution to the copyright holders of the program material. The fee for each cable system is based on the system's "gross receipts" from the carriage of broadcast signals and the number of "distant signal equivalents" a term identifying non-network programming from distant television stations carried by the system.

Under the Commission's must-carry rules, a cable operator is not required to carry a signal of a television broadcast station if that station would be considered a distant signal under the Copyright Act, unless the station agrees to indemnify the cable operator for any increased copyright liability resulting from carriage of the signal....

Program Content Regulations

Cable television system operators generally make their own selection of channels and programs to be distributed to subscribers in response to consumer demands. The Commission does, however, have rules in some areas that are applicable to programming — called "origination cablecasting" that is subject to the editorial control of the system operator. The rules generally do not apply to the contents of broadcast signals or access channels over which the system operator has no editorial control.

Cable subscribers may request a "lockbox" from cable operators to prevent viewing of any channel on which objectional programming may appear. Cable operators are required to make lockboxes available for sale or lease to customers who request them. Lockboxes can also be purchased from other commercial distributors.

The 1996 Act included several provisions that were designed to increase the subscriber's ability to control the programming coming into the home. Section 551 of the 1996 Act required representatives of the broadcast and cable television industries to develop, within one year after enactment of the 1996 Act, voluntary rules to rate programming that contains violence and sexual or other indecent material. The industry proposed the *TV Parental Guidelines* and the proposal was approved by the Commission on March 12, 1998. The *TV Parental Guidelines* (labels and content indicators and respective meanings) are:

TV-Y — This program is designed to be appropriate for all children.

TV-Y7 — This program is designed for children age 7 and above. Note: For those programs where fantasy violence may be more intense or more combative than other programs in this category, such programs will be designated **TV-Y7-FV**.

TV-G — Most parents would find this program suitable for all ages.

TV-PG — This program contains some material that parents may find unsuitable for younger children. The program contains one or more of the following: moderate violence (**V**), some sexual situations (**S**), infrequent coarse language (**L**), or some suggestive dialogue (**D**).

TV-14 — This program contains some material that many parents would find unsuitable for children under 14 years of age. This program contains one or more of the following: intense violence (**V**), intense sexual situations (**S**), strong coarse language (**L**), or intensely suggestive dialogue (**D**).

TV-MA — This program is specifically designed to be viewed by adults and therefore may be unsuitable for children under 17. This program contains one or more of the following: graphic violence (**V**), explicit sexual activity (**S**), or crude indecent language (**L**).

The ratings icons and associated symbols appear for 15 seconds at the beginning of all rated programming. Sports, news, commercials, promotions and unedited movies with a Motion Picture Association of America rating that are aired on premium cable channels are exempt from these ratings.

The 1996 Act also required that television receivers manufactured or imported for use in the United States be equipped with circuitry that is capable of identifying all programs with a common rating and blocking individual channels during selected time periods. This is the circuitry commonly referred to as the "V-chip." This requirement applies to all television sets with a least a 13 inch screen. Manufacturers of such equipment were required to include a v-chip on at least 50% of their products by July 1, 1999 and on the remaining 50% by January 1, 2000. The Commission also required that personal computers that include a television tuner and a 13 inch or larger monitor must also include the v-chip. However, the requirement to rate programming applies only to video transmissions that are delivered to the computer by using the television tuner. Video transmissions delivered over the Internet or via computer networks are not required to be rated.

Section 504 of the 1996 Act required a cable operator to fully scramble or block the audio and video portions of programming services not specifically subscribed to by a household. The cable operator must fully scramble or block the programming in question upon the request of the subscriber and at no charge to the subscriber. In addition, Section 505 states that cable operators or other multichannel video programming distributors who offer sexually explicit programming or other programming that is indecent on any channel(s) primarily dedicated to sexually-oriented programming must fully scramble or block both the audio and video portions of the channels so that someone who does not subscribe to the channel does not receive it. Until a multichannel video distributor complies with this provision, the distributor cannot provide the programming during hours when a significant number of children are likely to view it.

On March 4, 1996, the Commission adopted an *Order and Notice of Proposed Rulemaking* (FCC 96-84) establishing interim rules to implement Section 505 of the 1996 Act. The interim rules established the hours of 6:00 a.m. to 10:00 p.m. as those hours when a significant number of children are likely to have access to and view the programming. However, before the rules could take effect, Section 505 was challenged in the courts and the Commission was subsequently prevented from enforcing the rules because of a temporary restraining order and a number of stays granted by the United States District Court for the District of Delaware. On March 24, 1997, the United States Supreme Court affirmed the District Court's decision to deny the request for a preliminary injunction of section 505. Thus, on April 17, 1997, the Commission adopted an Order establishing May 18, 1997 as the effective date of our rules implementing section 505. However, on December 28, 1998, a federal court in Delaware issued a decision (*Playboy Entertainment Group v. U.S.*) which determined that Section 505 is unconstitutional. Therefore, the Commission's rules based on Section 505 could not be enforced. An appeal of this decision was filed with the U.S. Supreme Court. On May 22, 2000, the U.S. Supreme Court also determined that Section 505 is unconstitutional. Thus, the Commission's rules implementing Section 505 cannot be enforced. However, persons who wish to prevent the viewing of such programming may do so by obtaining a "lockbox" or by exercising the options provided in Section 504 of the 1996 Act.

Finally, Section 506 of the 1996 Cable Act allows cable operators to refuse to transmit any public access or leased access program which contains obscenity, indecency, or nudity. On June 28, 1996, the U.S. Supreme Court issued a decision (*Denver Area Educational Telecommunications Consortium, Inc. v. FCC*) which held that cable operators may decline to carry indecent programming on leased access channels, but cannot exercise the same control over programming on public access channels....

ACCESS AND ORIGINATION CHANNELS

Access channels typically provide community-oriented programming, such as local news, public announcements and government meetings. They are usually programmed by individuals or groups, on either public, educational or governmental access channels or on commercial leased access channels.

Origination channels are usually programmed by the cable system and may include many types of specialized program packages such as movies, sports, national news and public affairs, feature entertainment, children's programming or programming for specific ethnic or other minority groups.

The Commission's rules do not require cable operators to originate programming. Operators who originate programming, however, are required to comply with the Commission's program content rules.

Channels For Public, Educational, Or Governmental Use

Under the 1984 Cable Act, local franchising authorities may require that cable operators set aside channels for public, educational, or governmental ("PEG") use. In addition, franchising authorities may require cable operators to provide services, facilities, and equipment for the use of these channels. Many cable systems include several PEG channels.

In general, cable operators are not permitted to control the content of programming on PEG channels. Cable operators may impose non-content-based requirements, such as minimum production standards, and may mandate equipment user training.

PEG channel capacity which is not in use for its designated purpose may, with the franchising authority's permission, be used by the cable operator to provide other services. Under certain conditions, a franchising authority may authorize the use of unused PEG channels to carry low power commercial television stations and local noncommercial educational television stations that are required by law.

Information relating to PEG channels may be obtained directly from the cable system or the local franchising authority.

Leased Commercial Access

The statutory framework for commercial leased access was established by the 1984 Act and amended by the 1992 Cable Act. The 1984 Cable Act established leased access to assure access to the channel capacity of cable systems by parties unaffiliated with the cable operator who want to distribute video programming free of the editorial control of the cable operator. Channel set-aside requirements were established in proportion to a system's total activated channel capacity, in order to "assure that the widest possible diversity of information sources are made available to the public from cable systems in a manner consistent with the growth and development of cable systems." A cable system operator was permitted to use any unused leased access channel capacity for its own purposes, until such time as a written agreement for a leased channel use was obtained. Each system operator subject to this requirement was to establish the "price, terms, and conditions of such use which are at least sufficient to assure that such use will not adversely affect the operation, financial condition, or market development of the cable system."

The only exception to the leased commercial access channel set-aside provides that up to 33 percent of a system's designated leased commercial access channel capacity may be used for qualified minority or educational programming from sources that may or may not be affiliated with the cable operator. The qualified minority or educational source may be affiliated with the operator.

The 1992 Cable Act amendments broadened the statutory purpose to include "the promotion of competition in the delivery of diverse sources of video programming," and the Commission was provided with expanded authority: (1) to determine the maximum reasonable rates that a cable operator may establish for leased access use, including the rate charged for the billing of subscribers and for the collection of revenue from subscribers by the cable operator for such use; (2) to establish reasonable terms and conditions for leased access, including those for billing and collection; and (3) to establish procedures for the expedited resolution of leased access disputes. The legislative history of the 1992 amendments expresses concern that some cable operators may have established unreasonable terms or may have had financial incentives to refuse to lease channel capacity to potential leased access users based on anticompetitive motives, especially if the operator had a financial interest in the programming services it carried.

Any person aggrieved by the failure or the refusal of a cable operator to make commercial channel capacity available or to charge rates as required by Commission rules may file a petition for relief with the Commission within 60 days of the alleged violation. In order to merit relief, the petition must show by clear and convincing evidence that the operator violated the leased access statutory or regulatory provisions or otherwise acted unreasonably or in bad faith. Relief may be in the form of refunds, injunctive relief or forfeitures. The Commission encourages parties to use alternative dispute resolution procedures such as settlement negotiation, conciliation, facilitation, mediation, fact finding, mini-trials and arbitration. The 1992 Cable Act provides for both judicial and Commission review of leased commercial access disputes....

CABLE SYSTEM OWNERSHIP

The Commission rules restrict the ability of television broadcast stations, national television networks, MMDS, and SMATV systems to own or control interests in cable systems. These rules also restrict the ownership interest of cable operators and their ability to own or control video programming services. While there are no prohibitions on foreign ownership of cable television systems, foreign governments or their representatives may not own CARS stations.

Cable/Telephone Cross-Ownership Restrictions

Pursuant to the 1984 Act, the Commission's rules placed restrictions on telephone companies providing cable television service. In general, telephone companies were prohibited from providing video programming directly to subscribers within their telephone service areas. However, telephone companies were allowed to provide cable television service in rural areas (defined as places of fewer than 2500 persons), or where the telephone company was able to show that cable service could not exist unless provided by the telephone company. Waivers could also be granted for good cause.

The 1996 Act established various options for local exchange carriers to provide video programming to subscribers. They are: common carrier transport, wireless ("MMDS"), cable, and open video systems. The Commission has structured a streamlined regulatory format for open video systems that allows open video system operators to offer their own programming and affords independent programmers the ability to reach subscribers directly. By encouraging entry into the video programming distribution market, the open video system framework will provide competitors to cable operators, direct broadcast satellite systems and wireless cable providers. Open video systems will advance competition in two areas of the video market, distribution and carriage. In the latter, open video systems will afford broad capability for video programming providers to reach subscribers directly, independent of the open video system operator.

Cable/MMDS Cross-Ownership

Commission rules and the Communications Act provisions generally preclude common ownership of a cable television system and a Multichannel Multipoint Distribution Service ("MMDS") system that serves the same area. However, following passage of the 1996 Act, this restriction does not apply to cable systems subject to effective competition in the relevant franchise area.

With MMDS, often referred to as "wireless cable," an omnidirectional microwave signal is sent from a central transmission tower to receiving microwave antennas. The signals involve "line of sight" transmission and, as a result, the signals are subject to degradation when obstructed. On the other hand, absent obstacles, the signals can travel up to 70 miles, providing television pictures comparable to those received through cable television. The microwave signal is a high frequency signal which is converted for television use by a converter located on the subscriber's receiving antenna.

Vertical Ownership Restrictions

To prevent vertically integrated cable systems from unduly favoring their affiliated programmers over non-affiliated program providers, the Commission imposes a 40% limit on the number of channels that can be occupied by video programmers affiliated with the particular cable system. In this context, vertical integration refers to common ownership of both cable systems and program networks, channels, services or production companies. For purposes of determining common ownership, all interests of 5% or greater are recognized unless there is no possibility of such interests exerting control or influence over the cable system....

PROTECTION OF SUBSCRIBER PRIVACY

Cable operators generally are prohibited from using their cable systems to collect personally identifiable information concerning any subscriber without the prior written or electronic consent of the subscriber. However, cable operators may collect this information if necessary to render cable television or other service to the subscriber or to detect unauthorized reception of cable communications.

Cable operators generally are also prohibited from disclosing personally identifiable information without the prior written or electronic consent of the subscriber. However, there are certain circumstances where the cable operator may do so. A cable operator may disclose this information if such disclosure is necessary to render, or conduct a legitimate business activity related to, cable television or other service provided to the subscriber. The operator may also disclose such information pursuant to a court order authorizing the disclosure, however, the subscriber must be notified of such an order by the person to whom the order is directed (such as a government agency or the cable operator). Finally, the cable operator may disclose the names and addresses of subscribers, but the cable operator must provide the subscriber the opportunity to prohibit or limit such disclosure. Moreover, the cable operator must ensure the disclosure does not reveal, directly or indirectly, the extent of any viewing or other use by the subscriber or the nature of any transaction made by the subscriber over the cable system.

At the time of entering into an agreement to provide cable service or any other service to a subscriber, cable operators must notify the subscriber of the following: the nature of any personally identifiable information collected, or that will be collected, regarding the subscriber; the nature of the use of such information; the nature, frequency, and purpose of any possible disclosure of such information; including an identification of the types of persons to whom the disclosure may be made, the period during which such information will be maintained by the cable operator, the times and place at which the subscriber may gain access to such information, and the limitations with respect to collection and disclosure of information by a cable operator and the right of subscribers to enforce these limitations. Notice to the subscriber must be in the form of a separate, written statement and must be clear and conspicuous. Notice must also be given at least once every year that the agreed upon service is provided. "Personally identifiable information" does not include any record of aggregate data which does not identify particular persons....

American Broadcasting Companies, Inc. v. Aereo, Inc.
___ U.S. ___, 134 S. Ct. 896 (2014)

The question presented is:

Whether a company "publicly performs" a copyrighted television program when it retransmits a broadcast of that program to thousands of paid subscribers over the Internet.

The decision below:

WNET, Thirteen v. Aereo, Inc.
712 F.3d 676 (2013)

Aereo, Inc. ("Aereo") enables its subscribers to watch broadcast television programs over the internet for a monthly fee. Two groups of plaintiffs, holders of copyrights in programs broadcast on network television, filed copyright infringement actions against Aereo in the United States District Court for the Southern District of New York. They moved for a preliminary injunction barring Aereo from transmitting programs to its subscribers while the programs are still airing, claiming that those transmissions infringe their exclusive right to publicly perform their works. The district court (Nathan, *J.*) denied the motion, concluding that the plaintiffs were unlikely to prevail on the merits in light of our prior decision in *Cartoon Network LP, LLLP v. CSC Holdings, Inc.*, 536 F.3d 121 (2d Cir.2008) ("*Cablevision* "). We agree and affirm the order of the district court denying the motion for a preliminary injunction.

BACKGROUND

The parties below agreed on all but one of the relevant facts of Aereo's system, namely whether Aereo's antennas operate independently or as a unit. The district court resolved that issue, finding that Aereo's antennas operate independently. The Plaintiffs do not appeal that factual finding. Thus the following facts are undisputed....

Aereo subscribers begin by logging on to their account on Aereo's website using a computer or other internet-connected device. They are then presented with a programming guide listing broadcast television programs now airing or that will air in the future. If a user selects a program that is currently airing, he is presented with two options: "Watch" and "Record." If the user selects "Watch," the program he selected begins playing, but the transmission is briefly delayed relative to the live television broadcast. Thus the user can watch the program nearly live, that is, almost contemporaneously with the over-the-air broadcast. While the user is watching the program with the "Watch" function, he can pause or rewind it as far back as the point when the user first began watching the program. This may result in the user watching the program with the "Watch" feature after the over-the-air broadcast has ended. At any point while watching the program with the "Watch" feature, the user can select the "Record" button, which will cause Aereo's system to save a copy of the program for later viewing. The recorded copy of the program will begin from the point when the user first began watching the program, not from the time when the user first pressed the "Record" button. If a user in "Watch" mode does not press "Record" before the conclusion of the program, the user is not able to watch that program again later....

Aereo's system thus provides the functionality of three devices: a standard TV antenna, a DVR, and a Slingbox-like device. These devices allow one to watch live television with the antenna; pause and record live television and watch recorded programing using the DVR; and use the Slingbox to watch both live and recorded programs on internet-connected mobile devices.

Aereo has large antenna boards at its facility in Brooklyn, New York. Each of these boards contains approximately eighty antennas, which consist of two metal loops roughly the size of a dime. These boards are installed parallel to each other in a large metal housing such that the antennas extend out of the housing and can receive broadcast TV signals. Aereo's facility thus uses thousands of individual antennas to receive broadcast television channels.

When an Aereo user selects a program to watch or record, a signal is sent to Aereo's antenna server. The antenna server assigns one of the individual antennas and a transcoder to the user. The antenna server tunes that antenna to the broadcast frequency of the channel showing the program the user wishes to watch or record. The server transcodes the data received by this antenna, buffers it, and sends it to another Aereo server, where a copy of the program is saved to a large hard drive in a directory reserved for that Aereo user. If the user has chosen to "Record" the program, the Aereo system will create a complete copy of the program for that user to watch later. When the user chooses to view that program, Aereo's servers will stream the program to the user from the copy of the program saved in the user's directory on the Aereo server. If the user instead has chosen to "Watch" the program, the same operations occur, except that once six or seven seconds of programming have been saved in the hard drive copy of the program in the user's directory on the Aereo server, the Aereo system begins streaming the program to the user from this copy. Thus even when an Aereo user is watching a program using the "Watch" feature, he is not watching the feed directly or immediately from the antenna assigned to him. Rather the feed from that antenna is used to create a copy of the program on the Aereo server, and that copy is then transmitted to the user. If at any point before the program ends, the user in "Watch" mode selects "Record," the copy of the program is retained for later viewing. If the user does not press "Record" before the program ends, the copy of the program created for and used to transmit the program to the user is automatically deleted when it has finished playing.

Three technical details of Aereo's system merit further elaboration. First, Aereo assigns an individual antenna to each user. No two users share the same antenna at the same time, even if they are watching or recording the same program.[4] Second, the signal received by each antenna is used to create an individual copy of the program in the user's personal directory. Even when two users are watching or recording the same program, a separate copy of the program is created for each. Finally, when a user watches a program, whether nearly live or previously recorded, he sees his individual copy on his TV, computer, or mobile-device screen. Each copy of a program is only accessible to the user who requested that the copy be made, whether that copy is used to watch the program nearly live or hours after it has finished airing; no other Aereo user can ever view that particular copy....

The outcome of this appeal turns on whether Aereo's service infringes the Plaintiffs' public performance right under the Copyright Act....

I. The Public Performance Right

The 1976 Copyright Act (the "Act") gives copyright owners several exclusive rights and then carves out a number of exceptions. The fourth of these rights, at issue in this appeal, is the copyright owner's exclusive right "in the case of literary, musical, dramatic, and choreographic works, pantomimes, and motion pictures and other audiovisual works, to perform the copyrighted work publicly." 17 U.S.C. § 106(4). The Act defines "perform" as "to recite, render, play, dance, or act [a work], either directly or by means of any device or process or, in the case of a motion picture or other audiovisual work, to show its images in any sequence or to make the sounds accompanying it audible." 17 U.S.C. § 101. The Act also states:

> To perform or display a work "publicly" means—
>
> (1) to perform or display it at a place open to the public or at any place where a substantial number of persons outside of a normal circle of a family and its social acquaintances is gathered; or
>
> (2) to transmit or otherwise communicate a performance or display of the work to a place specified by clause (1) or to the public, by means of any device or process, whether the members of the public capable of receiving the performance or display receive it in the same place or in separate places and at the same time or at different times.

17 U.S.C. § 101. This appeal turns on the second clause of this definition (the "Transmit Clause" or "Clause").

The relevant history of the Transmit Clause begins with two decisions of the Supreme Court, *Fortnightly Corp. v. United Artists Television, Inc.,* 392 U.S. 390 (1968), and *Teleprompter Corp. v. Columbia Broadcasting System, Inc.,* 415 U.S. 394 (1974). These decisions held that under the then-current 1909 Copyright Act, which lacked any analog to the Transmit Clause, a cable television system that received broadcast television signals via antenna and retransmitted these signals to its subscribers via coaxial cable did not "perform" the copyrighted works and therefore did not infringe copyright holders' public performance right. Even before these cases were decided, Congress had begun drafting a new copyright act to respond to changes in technology, most notably, cable television.

---

4. Aereo's system usually assigns these antennas dynamically. Aereo users "share" antennas in the sense that one user is using a particular antenna now, and another may use the same antenna when the first is no longer using it. But at any given time, the feed from each antenna is used to create only one user's copy of the program being watched or recorded. Thus if 10,000 Aereo users are watching or recording the Super Bowl, Aereo has 10,000 antennas tuned to the channel broadcasting it.

These efforts resulted in the 1976 Copyright Act. The Act responded to the emergence of cable television systems in two ways. First, it added the Transmit Clause. The legislative history shows that the Transmit Clause was intended in part to abrogate *Fortnightly* and *Teleprompter* and bring a cable television system's retransmission of broadcast television programming within the scope of the public performance right. H.R. Rep. 94-1476, 1976 U.S.C.C.A.N. 5659, at 63 (1976) ("House Report") ("[A] sing[er] is performing when he or she sings a song; a broadcasting network is performing when it transmits his or her performance (whether simultaneously or from records); a local broadcaster is performing when it transmits the network broadcast; a cable television system is performing when it retransmits the broadcast to its subscribers; and any individual is performing when he or she plays a phonorecord embodying the performance or communicates it by turning on a receiving set."). Second, Congress recognized that requiring cable television systems to obtain a negotiated license from individual copyright holders may deter further investment in cable systems, so it created a compulsory license for retransmissions by cable systems.

Plaintiffs claim that Aereo's transmissions of broadcast television programs while the programs are airing on broadcast television fall within the plain language of the Transmit Clause and are analogous to the retransmissions of network programing made by cable systems, which the drafters of the 1976 Copyright Act viewed as public performances. They therefore believe that Aereo is publicly performing their copyrighted works without a license. In evaluating their claims, we do not work from a blank slate. Rather, this Court in *Cablevision*, 536 F.3d 121, closely analyzed and construed the Transmit Clause in a similar factual context. Thus the question of whether Aereo's transmissions are public performances under the Transmit Clause must begin with a discussion of *Cablevision*.

II. *Cablevision's* Interpretation of the Transmit Clause

In *Cablevision*, 536 F.3d 121, we considered whether Cablevision's Remote Storage Digital Video Recorder ("RS-DVR") infringed copyright holders' reproduction and public performance rights. Cablevision, a cable television system, wished to offer its customers its newly designed RS-DVR system, which would give them the functionality of a stand-alone DVR via their cable set-top box. Before the development of the RS-DVR system, Cablevision would receive programming from various content providers, such as ESPN or a local affiliate of a national broadcast network, process it, and transmit it to its subscribers through coaxial cable in real time. With the RS-DVR system, Cablevision split this stream into two. One stream went out to customers live as before. The second stream was routed to a server, which determined whether any Cablevision customers had requested to record a program in the live stream with their RS-DVR. If so, the data for that program was buffered, and a copy of that program was created for that Cablevision customer on a portion of a Cablevision remote hard drive assigned solely to that customer. Thus if 10,000 Cablevision customers wished to record the Super Bowl, Cablevision would create 10,000 copies of the broadcast, one for each customer. A customer who requested that the program be recorded could later play back the program using his cable remote, and Cablevision would transmit the customer's saved copy of that program to the customer. Only the customer who requested that the RS-DVR record the program could access the copy created for him; no other Cablevision customer could view this particular copy....

The *Cablevision* court began by discussing the language and legislative history of the Transmit Clause. Based on language in the Clause specifying that a transmission may be "to the public ... whether the members of the public capable of receiving the performance ... receive it in the same place or in separate places and at the same time or at different times," 17 U.S.C. § 101, this Court concluded that "it is of no moment that the potential recipients of the transmission are in different places, or that they may receive the transmission at different times." 536 F.3d at 134. As the language makes plain, in determining whether a transmission is to the public it is important "to discern who is 'capable of receiving' the performance being transmitted." *Id.* (quoting 17 U.S.C. § 101). *Cablevision* then decided that "capable of receiving the performance" refers not to the performance of the underlying work being transmitted but rather to the transmission itself, since the "transmission of a performance is itself a performance." *Id.* The Court therefore concluded that "the transmit clause directs us to examine who precisely is 'capable of receiving' *a particular transmission of a performance.*" 536 F.3d at 135 (emphasis added).

In adopting this interpretation of the Transmit Clause, *Cablevision* rejected two alternative readings. First, it considered the interpretation accepted by the district court in that case. According to that view, a transmission is "to the public," not based on the "potential audience of a particular transmission" but rather based on the "potential audience of the underlying work (i.e., 'the program') whose content is being transmitted." *Id.* at 135. The *Cablevision* court rejected this interpretation of the Transmit Clause. Given that "the *potential* audience for every copyrighted audiovisual work is the general public," this interpretation would render the "to the public" language of the Clause superfluous and contradict the Clause's obvious contemplation of non-public transmissions. *Id.* at 135–36....

First and most important, the Transmit Clause directs courts to consider the potential audience of the individual transmission. If that transmission is "capable of being received by the public" the transmission is a public performance; if the potential audience of the transmission is only one subscriber, the transmission is not a public performance, except as discussed below. Second and following from the first, private transmissions—that is those not capable of being received by the public—should not be aggregated. It is therefore irrelevant to the Transmit Clause analysis whether the public is capable of receiving the same underlying work or original performance of the work by means of many transmissions. Third, there is an exception to this no-aggregation rule when private transmissions are generated from the same copy of the work. In such cases, these private transmissions *should* be aggregated, and if these aggregated transmissions from a single copy enable the public to view that copy, the transmissions are public performances. Fourth and finally, "any factor that limits the *potential* audience of a transmission is relevant" to the Transmit Clause analysis.

III. *Cablevision's* Application to Aereo's System

As discussed above, *Cablevision's* holding that Cablevision's transmissions of programs recorded with its RS-DVR system were not public performances rested on two essential facts. First, the RS-DVR system created unique copies of every program a Cablevision customer wished to record. Second, the RS-DVR's transmission of the recorded program to a particular customer was generated from that unique copy; no other customer could view a transmission created by that copy. Given these two features, the potential audience of every RS-DVR transmission was only a single Cablevision subscriber, namely the subscriber who created the copy. And because the potential audience of the transmission was only one Cablevision subscriber, the transmission was not made "to the public."

The same two features are present in Aereo's system. When an Aereo customer elects to watch or record a program using either the "Watch" or "Record" features, Aereo's system creates a unique copy of that program on a portion of a hard drive assigned only to that Aereo user. And when an Aereo user chooses to watch the recorded program, whether (nearly) live or days after the program has aired, the transmission sent by Aereo and received by that user is generated from that unique copy. No other Aereo user can ever receive a transmission from that copy. Thus, just as in *Cablevision,* the potential audience of each Aereo transmission is the single user who requested that a program be recorded.

Plaintiffs offer various arguments attempting to distinguish *Cablevision* from the Aereo system. First, they argue that *Cablevision* is distinguishable because Cablevision had a license to transmit programming in the first instance, namely when it first aired the programs; thus the question was whether Cablevision needed an additional license to retransmit the programs recorded by its RS-DVR system. Aereo, by contrast, has no license. This argument fails, as the question is whether Aereo's transmissions are public performances of the Plaintiffs' copyrighted works. If so, Aereo needs a license to make such public performances; if they are not public performances, it needs no such license. Thus whether Aereo has a license is not relevant to whether its transmissions are public and therefore must be licensed. This argument by the Plaintiffs also finds no support in the *Cablevision* opinion. *Cablevision* did not hold that Cablevision's RS-DVR transmissions were *licensed* public performances; rather it held they were not public performances. It does not appear that the *Cablevision* court based its decision that Cablevision's RS-DVR transmissions were non-public transmissions on Cablevision's license to broadcast the programs live. Indeed, such a conclusion would have been erroneous, because having a license to publicly perform a work in a particular instance, such as to broadcast a television program live, does not give the licensee the right to perform the work again. That Cablevision had a license to transmit copyrighted works when they first aired thus should have no bearing on whether it needed a license to retransmit these programs as part of its RS-DVR system. Indeed, if this interpretation of *Cablevision* were correct, Cablevision would not need a license to retransmit programs using video-on-demand and there would have been no reason for Cablevision to construct an RS-DVR system employing individual copies.

Second, Plaintiffs argue that discrete transmissions should be aggregated to determine whether they are public performances. This argument has two aspects. Plaintiffs first argue that because Aereo's discrete transmissions enable members of the public to receive "the same performance (i.e., Aereo's retransmission of a program)" they are transmissions made "to the public." But this is nothing more than the *Cablevision* plaintiffs' interpretation of the Transmit Clause, as it equates Aereo's transmissions with the original broadcast made by the over-the-air network rather than treating Aereo's transmissions as independent performances. This approach was explicitly rejected by the *Cablevision* court....

IV. The Legislative Intent Behind the 1976 Copyright Act

Plaintiffs also contend that the legislative history of the 1976 Copyright Act shows that Aereo's transmissions should be deemed public performances of the Plaintiffs' copyrighted works. They argue that cable retransmissions are public performances under the Transmit Clause and Aereo is functionally equivalent to a cable system. However, this reading of the legislative history is simply incompatible with the conclusions of the *Cablevision* court.

This view of the legislative history also ignores a contrary strand of the history behind the 1976 Copyright Act. Congress recognized when it drafted the 1976 Act that its broad definition of "performance" could create unintended results. The House Report states that under this definition, "any individual is performing whenever he or she plays a phonorecord embodying the performance or communicates the performance by turning on a receiving set." House Report at 63. But because Congress did not wish to require everyone to obtain a license from copyright holders before they could "perform" the copyrighted works played by their television, Congress was careful to note that a performance "would not be actionable as an infringement unless it were done 'publicly,' as defined in section 101." *id.* "Private" performances are exempted from copyright liability. *Id.* This limitation also applies to performances created by a "transmission," since, as the *Cablevision* court noted, if Congress intended all transmissions to be public performances, the Transmit Clause would not have contained the phrase "to the public." *Cablevision,* 536 F.3d at 135–36.

In the technological environment of 1976, distinguishing between public and private transmissions was simpler than today. New devices such as RS-DVRs and Slingboxes complicate our analysis, as the transmissions generated by these devices can be analogized to the paradigmatic example of a "private" transmission: that from a personal roof-top antenna to a television set in a living room. As much as Aereo's service may resemble a cable system, it also generates transmissions that closely resemble the private transmissions from these devices. Thus unanticipated technological developments have created tension between Congress's view that retransmissions of network programs by cable television systems should be deemed public performances and its intent that some transmissions be classified as private. Although Aereo may in some respects resemble a cable television system, we cannot disregard the contrary concerns expressed by Congress in drafting the 1976 Copyright Act. And we certainly cannot disregard the express language Congress selected in doing so. That language and its legislative history, as interpreted by this Court in *Cablevision,* compels the conclusion that Aereo's transmissions are not public performances....

We conclude that Aereo's transmissions of unique copies of broadcast television programs created at its users' requests and transmitted while the programs are still airing on broadcast television are not "public performances" of the Plaintiffs' copyrighted works under *Cablevision.* As such, Plaintiffs have not demonstrated that they are likely to prevail on the merits on this claim in their copyright infringement action. Nor have they demonstrated serious questions as to the merits and a balance of hardships that tips decidedly in their favor. We therefore affirm the order of the district court denying the Plaintiffs' motion.

CHIN, Circuit Judge:

I respectfully dissent.

Defendant-appellee Aereo, Inc. ("Aereo") captures over-the-air broadcasts of television programs and retransmits them to subscribers by streaming them over the Internet. For a monthly fee, Aereo's customers may "Watch" the programming "live" (that is, with a seven-second delay) on their computers and other electronic devices, or they may "Record" the programs for later viewing. Aereo retransmits the programming without the authorization of the copyright holders and without paying a fee.

The Copyright Act confers upon owners of copyrights in audiovisual works the exclusive right "to perform the copyrighted work publicly." 17 U.S.C. § 106(4). This exclusive right includes the right "to transmit or otherwise communicate a performance ... to the public, by means of any device or process." *Id.* § 101. In my view, by transmitting (or retransmitting) copyrighted programming to the public without authorization, Aereo is engaging in copyright infringement in clear violation of the Copyright Act.

Aereo argues that it is not violating the law because its transmissions are not "public" performances; instead, the argument goes, its transmissions are "private" performances, and a "private performance is not copyright infringement." It contends that it is merely providing a "technology platform that enables consumers to use remotely-located equipment ... to create, access and view their own unique recorded copies of free over-the-air broadcast television programming."

Aereo's "technology platform" is, however, a sham. The system employs thousands of individual dime-sized antennas, but there is no technologically sound reason to use a multitude of tiny individual antennas rather than one central antenna; indeed, the system is a Rube Goldberg-like contrivance, over-engineered in an attempt to avoid the reach of the Copyright Act and to take advantage of a perceived loophole in the law. After capturing the broadcast signal, Aereo makes a copy of the selected program for each viewer, whether the user chooses to "Watch" now or "Record" for later. Under Aereo's theory, by using these individual antennas and copies, it may retransmit, for example, the Super Bowl "live" to 50,000 subscribers and yet, because each subscriber has an individual antenna and a "unique recorded cop[y]" of the broadcast, these are "private" performances. Of course, the argument makes no sense. These are very much *public* performances.

Aereo purports to draw its infringement-avoidance scheme from this Court's decision in *Cablevision*. But, as discussed below, there are critical differences between *Cablevision* and this case. Most significantly, *Cablevision* involved a cable company that paid statutory licensing and retransmission consent fees for the content it retransmitted, while Aereo pays no such fees. Moreover, the subscribers in *Cablevision* already had the ability to view television programs in real-time through their *authorized* cable subscriptions, and the remote digital video recording service at issue there was a supplemental service that allowed subscribers to store that authorized content for later viewing. In contrast, no part of Aereo's system is authorized. Instead, its storage and time-shifting functions are an integral part of an unlicensed retransmission service that captures broadcast television programs and streams them over the Internet.

Aereo is doing precisely what cable companies, satellite television companies, and authorized Internet streaming companies do — they capture over-the-air broadcasts and retransmit them to customers — except that those entities are doing it legally, pursuant to statutory or negotiated licenses, for a fee. By accepting Aereo's argument that it may do so without authorization and without paying a fee, the majority elevates form over substance. Its decision, in my view, conflicts with the text of the Copyright Act, its legislative history, and our case law.

For these and other reasons discussed more fully below, I would reverse the district court's order denying plaintiffs-appellants' motion for a preliminary injunction.

When interpreting a statute, we must begin with the plain language, giving any undefined terms their ordinary meaning. We must "attempt to ascertain how a reasonable reader would understand the statutory text, considered as a whole." *Pettus v. Morgenthau*, 554 F.3d 293, 297 (2d Cir.2009). Where Congress has expressed its intent in "reasonably plain terms, that language must ordinarily be regarded as conclusive." *Negonsott v. Samuels*, 507 U.S. 99, 104 (1993) (internal quotation marks and citation omitted). If we conclude that the text is ambiguous, however, we will look to legislative history and other tools of statutory interpretation to "dispel this ambiguity." *In re Air Cargo Shipping Servs. Antitrust Litig.*, 697 F.3d 154, 159 (2d Cir.2012).

I begin, then, by considering the text of the relevant sections of the Copyright Act. To the extent there is any arguable ambiguity in the statutory language, I next turn to its legislative history. Finally, I conclude with a discussion of *Cablevision* as well as other relevant precedents.

A. *The Statutory Text*

Section 106 of the Copyright Act sets out six exclusive rights held by a copyright owner; these include the right "to perform the copyrighted work publicly." 17 U.S.C. § 106(4).

As defined in section 101, "[t]o perform … a work 'publicly' means," among other things:

> to transmit or otherwise communicate a performance or display of the work … to the public, by means of any device or process, whether the members of the public capable of receiving the performance or display receive it in the same place or in separate places and at the same time or at different times.

Id. § 101. "To 'transmit' a performance" is "to communicate it by any device or process whereby images or sounds are received beyond the place from which they are sent." *Id.* Hence, the use of a device or process to transmit or communicate copyrighted images or sounds to the public constitutes a public performance, whether members of the public receive the performance in the same place or in different places, whether at the same time or at different times.

It is apparent that Aereo's system fits squarely within the plain meaning of the statute. *See, e.g., Fox Television Stations, Inc. v. BarryDriller Content Sys., PLC*, No. CV 12-6921, ___ F.Supp.2d ___, ___, 2012 WL 6784498, at *1–6 (C.D.Cal. Dec. 27, 2012) (holding that a service "technologically analogous" to Aereo's was engaged in public performances). The statute is broadly worded, as it refers to "*any* device or process." 17 U.S.C. § 101 (emphasis added); *see also id.* (defining "device" and "process" as "one now known or later developed"). Aereo's system of thousands of antennas and other equipment clearly is a "device or process." Using that "device or process," Aereo receives copyrighted images and sounds and "transmit [s] or otherwise communicate[s]" them to its subscribers "beyond the place from which they are sent," *id.*, that is, "'beyond the place' of origination," *Columbia Pictures Indus., Inc. v. Prof'l Real Estate Investors, Inc.*, 866 F.2d 278, 282 (9th Cir.1989). The "performance or display of the work" is then received by paying subscribers "in separate places" and "at different times." 17 U.S.C. § 101.

Even assuming Aereo's system limits the potential audience for each transmission, and even assuming each of its subscribers receives a unique recorded copy, Aereo still is transmitting the programming "to the public." *Id.* Giving the undefined term "the public" its ordinary meaning, a transmission to anyone other than oneself or an intimate relation is a communication to a "member[ ] of the public," because it is not in any sense "private."

What Aereo is doing is not in any sense "private," as the Super Bowl example discussed above illustrates. This understanding accords with the statute's instruction that a transmission can be "to the public" even if the "members of the public capable of receiving the performance. receive it in the same place or in separate places and at the same time or at different times." 17 U.S.C. § 101. Because Aereo is transmitting television signals to paying strangers, all of its transmissions are "to the public," even if intervening "device[s] or process[es]" limit the potential audience of each separate transmission to a single "member[ ] of the public." *Id.*

By any reasonable construction of the statute, Aereo is engaging in public performances and, therefore, it is engaging in copyright infringement. *See id.* §§ 106(4), 501(a).

B. *The Legislative History*

Even if the language of the transmit clause were ambiguous as applied to Aereo's system, *see Cablevision,* 536 F.3d at 136 ("[T]he transmit clause is not a model of clarity…."), the legislative history reinforces the conclusion that Aereo is engaging in public performances. The legislative history makes clear that Congress intended to reach new technologies, like this one, that are designed solely to exploit someone else's copyrighted work.

Just before the passage of the 1976 Copyright Act, the Supreme Court held in *Fortnightly* and *Teleprompter* that community antenna television ("CATV") systems—which captured live television broadcasts with antennas set on hills and retransmitted the signals to viewers unable to receive the original signals—did not infringe the public performance right because they were not "performing" the copyrighted work. In reaching this conclusion, the Court reasoned that:

> If an individual erected an antenna on a hill, strung a cable to his house, and installed the necessary amplifying equipment, he would not be 'performing' the programs he received on his television set.... The only difference in the case of CATV is that the antenna system is erected and owned not by its users but by an entrepreneur.

Fortnightly, 392 U.S. at 400. This rationale is nearly identical to the justification advanced by Aereo: each subscriber could legally use his own antenna, digital video recorder ("DVR"), and Slingbox to stream live television to his computer or other device, and so it makes no legal difference that the system is actually "erected and owned not by its users but by an entrepreneur." *Id.*

But Congress expressly rejected the outcome reached by the Supreme Court in *Fortnightly* and *Teleprompter. See Capital Cities Cable, Inc. v. Crisp,* 467 U.S. 691, 709 (1984) ("Congress concluded that cable operators should be required to pay royalties to the owners of copyrighted programs retransmitted by their systems on pain of liability for copyright infringement."). In the 1976 Copyright Act, Congress altered the definitions of "perform" and "publicly" specifically to render the CATV systems' unlicensed retransmissions illegal.

Congress was not only concerned, however, with the then newly-emerging CATV systems. Recognizing that the *Fortnightly* and *Teleprompter* decisions arose in part because of the "drastic technological change" after the 1909 Act, *Fortnightly,* 392 U.S. at 396, Congress broadly defined the term "transmit" to ensure that the 1976 Act anticipated future technological developments:

> The definition of 'transmit'... is broad enough to include all conceivable forms and combinations of wires and wireless communications media, including but by no means limited to radio and television broadcasting as we know them. Each and every method by which the images or sounds comprising a performance or display are picked up and conveyed is a 'transmission,' and if the transmission reaches the public in [any] form, the case comes within the scope of clauses (4) or (5) of section 106.

H.R.Rep. No. 94-1476, at 64, *reprinted in* 1976 U.S.C.C.A.N. at 5678. Further anticipating that there would be changes in technology that it could not then foresee, Congress added that a public performance could be received in different places and at different times. This change was meant to clarify that:

> a performance made available by transmission to the public at large is 'public' even though the recipients are not gathered in a single place, and even if there is no proof that any of the potential recipients was operating his receiving apparatus at the time of the transmission. The same principles apply whenever *the potential recipients of the transmission represent a limited segment of the public,* such as the occupants of hotel rooms or the *subscribers of a cable television service.*

Id. at 64–65, *reprinted at* 1976 U.S.C.C.A.N. at 5678 (emphasis added).

While Congress in 1976 might not have envisioned the precise technological innovations employed by Aereo today, this legislative history surely suggests that Congress could not have intended for such a system to fall outside the definition of a public performance.

To the contrary, Congress made clear its intent to include within the transmit clause "all conceivable forms and combinations of wires and wireless communications media," and if, as here, "the transmission reaches the public in [any] form, the case comes within the scope of clauses (4) or (5) of section 106." H.R.Rep. No. 94-1476, at 64, *reprinted in* 1976 U.S.C.C.A.N. at 5678. Aereo's streaming of television programming over the Internet is a public performance as Congress intended that concept to be defined.

C. *Cablevision*

... *Cablevision* held that the RS-DVR did not infringe either the reproduction or the public performance rights. Unlike the majority here, I do not think we can view *Cablevision*'s analyses of each right in isolation. As *Cablevision* explained, "the right of reproduction can reinforce and protect the right of public performance." *Cablevision*, 536 F.3d at 138. "Given this interplay between the various rights in this context," *id.*, *Cablevision*'s holding that "copies produced by the RS-DVR system are 'made' by the RS-DVR customer," was critical to its holding that "each RS-DVR playback transmission ... made to a single subscriber using a single unique copy *produced by that subscriber* ... [is] not [a] performance[ ] 'to the public,'" *id.* at 139 (emphasis added).

With this concept in mind, it is clear that Aereo's system is factually distinct from Cablevision's RS-DVR system. First, Cablevision's RS-DVR system "exist[ed] only to produce a copy" of material that it already had a license to retransmit to its subscribers, but the Aereo system produces copies to *enable* it to transmit material to its subscribers. Whereas Cablevision promoted its RS-DVR as a mechanism for recording and playing back programs, Aereo promotes its service as a means for watching "live" broadcast television on the Internet and through mobile devices. Unlike Cablevision, however, Aereo has no licenses to retransmit broadcast television. If a Cablevision subscriber wanted to use her own DVR to record programming provided by Cablevision, she could do so through Cablevision's licensed transmission. But an Aereo subscriber could not use her own DVR to lawfully record content received from Aereo because Aereo has no license to retransmit programming; at best, Aereo could only illegally retransmit public broadcasts from its remote antennas to the user. Aereo's use of copies is essential to its ability to retransmit broadcast television signals, while Cablevision's copies were merely an optional alternative to a set-top DVR. The core of Aereo's business is streaming broadcasts over the Internet in real-time; the addition of the record function, however, cannot legitimize the unauthorized retransmission of copyrighted content.

Second, subscribers interact with Aereo's system differently from the way Cablevision's subscribers interacted with the RS-DVR. Cablevision subscribers were already paying for the right to watch television programs, and the RS-DVR gave them the additional option to "record" the programs. In contrast, Aereo subscribers can choose *either* "Watch" or "Record." Both options initiate the same process: a miniature antenna allocated to that user tunes to the channel; the television signal is transmitted to a hard drive; and a full-length, permanent copy is saved for that customer. If the subscriber has opted to "Watch" the program live, the system immediately begins playing back the user's copy at the same time it is being recorded. Aereo will then automatically delete the saved copy once the user is done watching the program, unless the subscriber chooses to save it.

These differences undermine the applicability of Cablevision to Aereo's system. *Cablevision* found that the RS-DVR was indistinguishable from a VCR or set-top DVR because Cablevision's system "exist[ed] only to produce a copy" and its subscribers provided the "volitional conduct" necessary to make a copy by "ordering that system to produce a copy of a specific program." *Cablevision*, 536 F.3d at 131. The RS-DVR was not designed to be a substitute for viewing live television broadcasts. Aereo's system, however, was designed to be precisely that. It does not exist only, or even primarily, to make copies; it exists to stream live television through the Internet. Its users can choose to "Watch" live television instead of "Record" a program, but the system begins to produce a full-length copy anyway because, even under its own theory, Aereo cannot legally retransmit a television signal to them without such a copy. Aereo's system is much different than a VCR or DVR—indeed, as Aereo explains, it is an antenna, a DVR, and a Slingbox rolled into one—and for that reason *Cablevision* does not control our decision here....

Based on the plain meaning of the statute, its legislative history, and our precedent, I conclude that Aereo's transmission of live public broadcasts over the Internet to paying subscribers are unlicensed transmissions "to the public." Hence, these unlicensed transmissions should be enjoined. *Cablevision* does not require a different result. Accordingly, I dissent.

Notes and Questions

a. The overview provided above serves as a roadmap of regular FCC concerns. The FCC is actively involved in promoting localism and diversity of viewpoint, but the net effect may be of questionable value. The FCC has prohibited the networks from programming in the hour prior to prime time. While some of the local stations created original news or other programming, this FCC rule created the opportunity to market game shows and "Entertainment Tonight."

b. The public good premise behind the regulation of the airwaves exists, at least in part, because the extremely valuable broadcast spectrum is provided free of charge to the licensed stations. In exchange, the broadcasts must be in the public interest. Because of First Amendment concerns, however, this has not historically been treated as a public privilege that could be conditioned on the limitations of the broadcaster's free speech interests. Does the recent Supreme Court First Amendment jurisprudence create a new regulatory paradigm for television? Does the advent of cable, satellite, Internet, and mobile television allow regulators to treat broadcast television as only a portion of the television marketplace, or does broadcaster free speech still have a protected place for the courts?

c. As technology has empowered viewers to skip advertising, new methods have arisen to embed advertising in broadcast content. The FCC provides some useful overviews of the various regulations on advertising and related issues:

Sponsorship Identification

The sponsorship identification rule requires the identification of the sponsor of any origination cablecasting which is presented in exchange for money, service or "other valuable consideration." All political spots must contain a visual sponsorship identification in letters equal to at least four percent of the screen height and which are on the air for at least four seconds. Where the cablecast advertises commercial products or services, a mention of the corporate or trade name is usually considered sufficient. Sponsorship identification announcements must also be made before and after certain cablecast material if inducements are given to the cable system in exchange for cablecasting the material.

Commercial Limits in Children's Programs

Regulations implemented pursuant to the Children's Television Act of 1990 restrict the amount of commercial matter that cable operators may cablecast on programs originally produced and broadcast primarily for children 12 years old and younger. Cable operators may transmit no more than 10.5 minutes of commercial matter per hour during children's programming on weekends and no more than 12 minutes of commercial matter per hour on weekdays. Cable systems must maintain records available for public inspection which document compliance with the rule.

Access and Origination Channels

Access channels typically provide community-oriented programming, such as local news, public announcements and government meetings. They are usually programmed by individuals or groups, on either public, educational or governmental access channels or on commercial leased access channels.

Origination channels are usually programmed by the cable system and may include many types of specialized program packages such as movies, sports, national news and public affairs, feature entertainment, children's programming or programming for specific ethnic or other minority groups.

The Commission's rules do not require cable operators to originate programming. Operators who originate programming, however, are required to comply with the Commission's program content rules.

FCC Encyclopedia, Evolution of Cable Television, http://www.fcc.gov/encyclopedia/evolution-cable-television#sec24.

d. Much of the regulation for television and cable stems from an understanding of the demographic market area (DMA). "A DMA is a specific media research area that is used by Nielsen Media Research to identify television stations whose broadcast signals reach a specific area and attract the most viewers. DMA boundaries are widely accepted and used by all types of companies to target and keep track of advertising." *Steak N Shake Co. v. Burger King Corp.*, 323 F. Supp. 2d 983, 986 n.2 (E.D. Mo. 2004).

e. What is the appropriate antitrust marketplace for television and cable: should over-the-air, cable, and satellite be considered a single market or should each be a discrete market for antitrust analysis? If it is one market, then what about the potential competition from Internet content providers and from the telephone companies (known as incumbent local exchange carriers, "LECs" or "ILECs")?

f. Challenges to broadcast television come from cable, telephone, Internet providers and satellite companies. In *Dish Network Corp. v. FCC*, 653 F.3d 771 (9th Cir. 2011), a court summarized the regulation of satellite television:

There are only two major Direct Broadcast Satellite providers in the United States: [DirecTV], which has about 18.5 million subscribers, and DISH, which has about 14.1 million subscribers. They rely on assigned radio frequency bands to transmit signals to consumers from satellites located at designated orbital locations in space. The transmissions are governed by the Federal Communications Commission (FCC) and international regulations.

The United States has been assigned eight orbital locations for providing satellite service. Each location is divided into 32 satellite channels. Transmissions from satellites in the same orbital location may cause signal interference, so Congress has authorized the FCC to grant licenses to satellite service providers assigning them the use of specified channels at particular orbital locations. The licenses are limited in duration and the FCC may grant or renew them only if doing so will serve the public interest, convenience, or necessity.

In 1999, Congress created an exception to copyright law to better enable competition between satellite TV and cable TV. The Satellite Home Viewer Improvement Act of 1999 (SHVIA) amended the Copyright Act to create statutory copyright licenses for satellite carriers that allow them to retransmit a local broadcast station's signal without first getting permission from the individual copyright holders. The copyright license is also subject to statutory and regulatory conditions.

As a condition of their licenses, carriers have certain public obligations. For example, they must also carry, on request, the signals of all other television broadcast stations in the same local market. 47 U.S.C. § 338(a)(1). Additionally, all satellite providers must set aside four to seven percent of their channel capacity for "noncommercial programming of an educational or informational nature." 47 U.S.C. § 335(b). Finally, and particularly relevant to the case at hand, satellite service providers are required to treat all local television stations the same regarding picture quality.

B. Content Regulation

Red Lion Broadcasting Co. v. FCC
395 U.S. 367 (1969)

The Federal Communications Commission has for many years imposed on radio and television broadcasters the requirement that discussion of public issues be presented on broadcast stations, and that each side of those issues must be given fair coverage. This is known as the fairness doctrine, which originated very early in the history of broadcasting and has maintained its present outlines for some time. It is an obligation whose content has been defined in a long series of FCC rulings in particular cases, and which is distinct from the statutory requirement of § 315 of the Communications Act[5] that equal

---

5. Communications Act of 1934, Tit. III, 48 Stat. 1081, as amended, 47 U.S.C. § 301 *et seq*. Section 315 now reads:

"315. Candidates for public office; facilities; rules.

"(a) If any licensee shall permit any person who is a legally qualified candidate for any public office to use a broadcasting station, he shall afford equal opportunities to all other such candidates for that office in the use of such broadcasting station: *Provided*, That such licensee shall have no power of censorship over the material broadcast under the provisions of this section. No obligation is imposed upon any licensee to allow the use of its station by any such candidate. Appearance by a legally qualified candidate on any—

"(1) bona fide newscast,

"(2) bona fide news interview,

"(3) bona fide news documentary (if the appearance of the candidate is incidental to the presentation of the subject or subjects covered by the news documentary), or

"(4) on-the-spot coverage of bona fide news events (including but not limited to political conventions and activities incidental thereto), shall not be deemed to be use of a broadcasting station within the meaning of this subsection. Nothing in the foregoing sentence shall be construed as relieving broadcasters, in connection with the presentation of newscasts, news interviews, news documentaries, and on-the-spot coverage of news events, from the obligation imposed upon them under this chapter to operate in the public interest and to afford reasonable opportunity for the discussion of conflicting views on issues of public importance.

"(b) The charges made for the use of any broadcasting station for any of the purposes set forth in this section shall not exceed the charges made for comparable use of such sta-

time be allotted all qualified candidates for public office. Two aspects of the fairness doctrine, relating to personal attacks in the context of controversial public issues and to political editorializing, were codified more precisely in the form of FCC regulations in 1967. The two cases before us now, which were decided separately below, challenge the constitutional and statutory bases of the doctrine and component rules. Red Lion involves the application of the fairness doctrine to a particular broadcast, and RTNDA arises as an action to review the FCC's 1967 promulgation of the personal attack and political editorializing regulations, which were laid down after the Red Lion litigation had begun.

The Red Lion Broadcasting Company is licensed to operate a Pennsylvania radio station, WGCB. On November 27, 1964, WGCB carried a 15-minute broadcast by the Reverend Billy James Hargis as part of a "Christian Crusade" series. A book by Fred J. Cook entitled "Goldwater—Extremist on the Right" was discussed by Hargis, who said that Cook had been fired by a newspaper for making false charges against city officials; that Cook had then worked for a Communist-affiliated publication; that he had defended Alger Hiss and attacked J. Edgar Hoover and the Central Intelligence Agency; and that he had now written a "book to smear and destroy Barry Goldwater." When Cook heard of the broadcast he concluded that he had been personally attacked and demanded free reply time, which the station refused. After an exchange of letters among Cook, Red Lion, and the FCC, the FCC declared that the Hargis broadcast constituted a personal attack on Cook; that Red Lion had failed to meet its obligation under the fairness doctrine, to send a tape, transcript, or summary of the broadcast to Cook and offer him reply time; and that the station must provide reply time whether or not Cook would pay for it. On review in the Court of Appeals for the District of Columbia Circuit, the FCC's position was upheld as constitutional and otherwise proper.

Not long after the Red Lion litigation was begun, the FCC issued a Notice of Proposed Rule Making, 31 Fed. Reg. 5710, with an eye to making the personal attack aspect of the fairness doctrine more precise and more readily enforceable, and to specifying its rules relating to political editorials. After considering written comments supporting and opposing the rules, the FCC adopted them substantially as proposed. Twice amended, the rules were held unconstitutional in the RTNDA litigation by the Court of Appeals for the Seventh Circuit, on review of the rule-making proceeding, as abridging the freedoms of speech and press.

As they now stand amended, the regulations read as follows:

"Personal attacks; political editorials.

"(a) When, during the presentation of views on a controversial issue of public importance, an attack is made upon the honesty, character, integrity or like personal qualities of an identified person or group, the licensee shall, within a reasonable time and in no event later than 1 week after the attack, transmit to the person or group attacked (1) notification of the date, time and identification of the broadcast; (2) a script or tape (or an accurate summary if a script or tape is not available) of the attack; and (3) an offer of a reasonable opportunity to respond over the licensee's facilities.

"(b) The provisions of paragraph (a) of this section shall not be applicable (1) to attacks on foreign groups or foreign public figures; (2) to personal attacks

---

tion for other purposes.
"(c) The Commission shall prescribe appropriate rules and regulations to carry out the provisions of this section."

which are made by legally qualified candidates, their authorized spokesmen, or those associated with them in the campaign, on other such candidates, their authorized spokesmen, or persons associated with the candidates in the campaign; and (3) to bona fide newscasts, bona fide news interviews, and on-the-spot coverage of a bona fide news event (including commentary or analysis contained in the foregoing programs, but the provisions of paragraph (a) of this section shall be applicable to editorials of the licensee).

"NOTE: The fairness doctrine is applicable to situations coming within [(3)], above, and, in a specific factual situation, may be applicable in the general area of political broadcasts [(2)], above. See, section 315 (a) of the Act, 47 U. S. C. 315 (a); Public Notice: Applicability of the Fairness Doctrine in the Handling of Controversial Issues of Public Importance. 29 F. R. 10415. The categories listed in [(3)] are the same as those specified in section 315 (a) of the Act.

"(c) Where a licensee, in an editorial, (i) endorses or (ii) opposes a legally qualified candidate or candidates, the licensee shall, within 24 hours after the editorial, transmit to respectively (i) the other qualified candidate or candidates for the same office or (ii) the candidate opposed in the editorial (1) notification of the date and the time of the editorial; (2) a script or tape of the editorial; and (3) an offer of a reasonable opportunity for a candidate or a spokesman of the candidate to respond over the licensee's facilities: Provided, however, that where such editorials are broadcast within 72 hours prior to the day of the election, the licensee shall comply with the provisions of this paragraph sufficiently far in advance of the broadcast to enable the candidate or candidates to have a reasonable opportunity to prepare a response and to present it in a timely fashion."

47 CFR §§ 73.123, 73.300, 73.598, 73.679 (all identical).

Believing that the specific application of the fairness doctrine in Red Lion, and the promulgation of the regulations in RTNDA, are both authorized by Congress and enhance rather than abridge the freedoms of speech and press protected by the First Amendment, we hold them valid and constitutional, reversing the judgment below in RTNDA and affirming the judgment below in Red Lion.

The history of the emergence of the fairness doctrine and of the related legislation shows that the Commission's action in the Red Lion case did not exceed its authority, and that in adopting the new regulations the Commission was implementing congressional policy rather than embarking on a frolic of its own.

Before 1927, the allocation of frequencies was left entirely to the private sector, and the result was chaos. It quickly became apparent that broadcast frequencies constituted a scarce resource whose use could be regulated and rationalized only by the Government. Without government control, the medium would be of little use because of the cacophony of competing voices, none of which could be clearly and predictably heard. Consequently, the Federal Radio Commission was established to allocate frequencies among competing applicants in a manner responsive to the public "convenience, interest, or necessity."

... There is a twofold duty laid down by the FCC's decisions and described by the 1949 Report on Editorializing by Broadcast Licensees. The broadcaster must give adequate coverage to public issues, and coverage must be fair in that it accurately reflects the opposing views. This must be done at the broadcaster's own expense if sponsorship is unavailable. Moreover, the duty must be met by programming obtained at the licensee's own initiative if available from no other source. The Federal Radio Commission had imposed these two basic duties on broadcasters since the outset, and in particular respects the personal attack rules and regulations at issue here have spelled them out in greater detail.

When a personal attack has been made on a figure involved in a public issue, both the doctrine of cases such as Red Lion, and also the 1967 regulations at issue in RTNDA require that the individual attacked himself be offered an opportunity to respond. Likewise, where one candidate is endorsed in a political editorial, the other candidates must themselves be offered reply time to use personally or through a spokesman.

These obligations differ from the general fairness requirement that issues be presented, and presented with coverage of competing views, in that the broadcaster does not have the option of presenting the attacked party's side himself or choosing a third party to represent that side. But insofar as there is an obligation of the broadcaster to see that both sides are presented, and insofar as that is an affirmative obligation, the personal attack doctrine and regulations do not differ from the preceding fairness doctrine....

In light of the fact that the "public interest" in broadcasting clearly encompasses the presentation of vigorous debate of controversial issues of importance and concern to the public; the fact that the FCC has rested upon that language from its very inception a doctrine that these issues must be discussed, and fairly; and the fact that Congress has acknowledged that the analogous provisions of §315 are not preclusive in this area, and knowingly preserved the FCC's complementary efforts, we think the fairness doctrine and its component personal attack and political editorializing regulations are a legitimate exercise of congressionally delegated authority. The Communications Act is not notable for the precision of its substantive standards and in this respect the explicit provisions of §315, and the doctrine and rules at issue here which are closely modeled upon that section, are far more explicit than the generalized "public interest" standard in which the Commission ordinarily finds its sole guidance, and which we have held a broad but adequate standard before. We cannot say that the FCC's declaratory ruling in Red Lion, or the regulations at issue in RTNDA, are beyond the scope of the congressionally conferred power to assure that stations are operated by those whose possession of a license serves "the public interest."

The broadcasters challenge the fairness doctrine and its specific manifestations in the personal attack and political editorial rules on conventional First Amendment grounds, alleging that the rules abridge their freedom of speech and press. Their contention is that the First Amendment protects their desire to use their allotted frequencies continuously to broadcast whatever they choose, and to exclude whomever they choose from ever using that frequency. No man may be prevented from saying or publishing what he thinks, or from refusing in his speech or other utterances to give equal weight to the views of his opponents. This right, they say, applies equally to broadcasters.

Although broadcasting is clearly a medium affected by a First Amendment interest, differences in the characteristics of new media justify differences in the First Amendment standards applied to them. For example, the ability of new technology to produce sounds more raucous than those of the human voice justifies restrictions on the sound level, and on the hours and places of use, of sound trucks so long as the restrictions are reasonable and applied without discrimination....

Just as the Government may limit the use of sound-amplifying equipment potentially so noisy that it drowns out civilized private speech, so may the Government limit the use of broadcast equipment. The right of free speech of a broadcaster, the user of a sound truck, or any other individual does not embrace a right to snuff out the free speech of others....

This is not to say that the First Amendment is irrelevant to public broadcasting. On the contrary, it has a major role to play as the Congress itself recognized in § 326, which forbids FCC interference with "the right of free speech by means of radio communication." Because of the scarcity of radio frequencies, the Government is permitted to put restraints on licensees in favor of others whose views should be expressed on this unique medium. But the people as a whole retain their interest in free speech by radio and their collective right to have the medium function consistently with the ends and purposes of the First Amendment. It is the right of the viewers and listeners, not the right of the broadcasters, which is paramount. It is the purpose of the First Amendment to preserve an uninhibited marketplace of ideas in which truth will ultimately prevail, rather than to countenance monopolization of that market, whether it be by the Government itself or a private licensee.... It is the right of the public to receive suitable access to social, political, esthetic, moral, and other ideas and experiences which is crucial here. That right may not constitutionally be abridged either by Congress or by the FCC.

Rather than confer frequency monopolies on a relatively small number of licensees, in a Nation of 200,000,000, the Government could surely have decreed that each frequency should be shared among all or some of those who wish to use it, each being assigned a portion of the broadcast day or the broadcast week. The ruling and regulations at issue here do not go quite so far. They assert that under specified circumstances, a licensee must offer to make available a reasonable amount of broadcast time to those who have a view different from that which has already been expressed on his station. The expression of a political endorsement, or of a personal attack while dealing with a controversial public issue, simply triggers this time sharing. As we have said, the First Amendment confers no right on licensees to prevent others from broadcasting on "their" frequencies and no right to an unconditional monopoly of a scarce resource which the Government has denied others the right to use....

It is strenuously argued, however, that if political editorials or personal attacks will trigger an obligation in broadcasters to afford the opportunity for expression to speakers who need not pay for time and whose views are unpalatable to the licensees, then broadcasters will be irresistibly forced to self-censorship and their coverage of controversial public issues will be eliminated or at least rendered wholly ineffective. Such a result would indeed be a serious matter, for should licensees actually eliminate their coverage of controversial issues, the purposes of the doctrine would be stifled.

At this point, however, as the Federal Communications Commission has indicated, that possibility is at best speculative. The communications industry, and in particular the networks, have taken pains to present controversial issues in the past, and even now they do not assert that they intend to abandon their efforts in this regard.[6] It would be better if the FCC's encouragement were never necessary to induce the broadcasters to meet their responsibility. And if experience with the administration of these doctrines indicates that they have the net effect of reducing rather than enhancing the volume and quality of cov-

---

6. The President of the Columbia Broadcasting System has recently declared that despite the Government, "we are determined to continue covering controversial issues as a public service, and exercising our own independent news judgment and enterprise. I, for one, refuse to allow that judgment and enterprise to be affected by official intimidation." F. Stanton, Keynote Address, Sigma Delta Chi National Convention, Atlanta, Georgia, November 21, 1968. Problems of news coverage from the broadcaster's viewpoint are surveyed in W. Wood, Electronic Journalism (1967).

erage, there will be time enough to reconsider the constitutional implications. The fairness doctrine in the past has had no such overall effect....

Licenses to broadcast do not confer ownership of designated frequencies, but only the temporary privilege of using them. Unless renewed, they expire within three years. The statute mandates the issuance of licenses if the "public convenience, interest, or necessity will be served thereby." In applying this standard the Commission for 40 years has been choosing licensees based in part on their program proposals....

In view of the scarcity of broadcast frequencies, the Government's role in allocating those frequencies, and the legitimate claims of those unable without governmental assistance to gain access to those frequencies for expression of their views, we hold the regulations and ruling at issue here are both authorized by statute and constitutional.[7] The judgment of the Court of Appeals in Red Lion is affirmed and that in RTNDA reversed and the causes remanded for proceedings consistent with this opinion.

Notes and Questions

a. In *Denver Area Educational Telecommunications Consortium, Inc. v. FCC,* 518 U.S. 727 (1996), a plurality of the Supreme Court gave cable operators some control over the mandatory leased access channels.

b. In *Loce v. Time Warner Entm't Advance/Newhouse P'ship*, 191 F.3d 256 (2d Cir.1999), Time Warner addressed allegedly indecent public programming on its Rochester, New York affiliate with a policy prohibiting indecent programming on leased access stations. Plaintiffs sued for violation of their First Amendment Rights. To what extent does the state and federal regulation result in leased access or community access stations becoming state actors for the purpose of First Amendment protections? For a similar question related to the right of a municipality to charge a fee for the access to the station, see *Wilcher v. City of Akron*, 498 F.3d 516, 520–21 (6th Cir. 2007).

c. Cable is only one of many speech areas purportedly regulated by Congress or otherwise subject to First Amendment limitations. The list includes: radio, *National Broadcasting Co. v. United States,* 319 U.S. 190 (1943) (successfully regulated); newspapers, *Miami Herald Publishing Co. v. Tornillo,* 418 U.S. 241 (1974) (not subject to regulation); personal solicitation, *Riley v. National Federation of Blind of N.C., Inc.,* 487 U.S. 781 (1988) (not subject to much regulation); cable, *Turner Broad. Sys. v. FCC,* 520 U.S. 180 (1997) (successfully regulated); Internet, *Reno v. ACLU,* 521 U.S. 844 (1997) (not subject to regulation); and satellite, *Satellite Broad. & Communs. Ass'n v. FCC,* 275 F.3d 337 (4th Cir. Va. 2001) (subject to regulation).

---

7. We need not deal with the argument that even if there is no longer a technological scarcity of frequencies limiting the number of broadcasters, there nevertheless is an economic scarcity in the sense that the Commission could or does limit entry to the broadcasting market on economic grounds and license no more stations than the market will support. Hence, it is said, the fairness doctrine or its equivalent is essential to satisfy the claims of those excluded and of the public generally. A related argument, which we also put aside, is that quite apart from scarcity of frequencies, technological or economic, Congress does not abridge freedom of speech or press by legislation directly or indirectly multiplying the voices and views presented to the public through time sharing, fairness doctrines, or other devices which limit or dissipate the power of those who sit astride the channels of communication with the general public. Cf. *Citizen Publishing Co. v. United States*, 394 U.S. 131 (1969).

d. Given the changes in technology, what is the continuing validity of the scarcity doctrine raised by the *Red Lion* Court? Should the Court look only to television or should media, such as the Internet, be balanced against the risks of scarcity?

e. Clear Channel Communications has become the largest owner of radio stations and networks in the United States. It provides this description on LinkedIn:

> With 243 million monthly listeners in the U.S., Clear Channel Media and Entertainment has the largest reach of any radio or television outlet in America. The company owns and operates 850 broadcast radio stations, serving more than 150 markets throughout the U.S., and more than 140 radio stations in Australia and New Zealand. Plus, iHeartRadio — a free, industry-leading, digital music service — gives users instant access to more than 1,500 live radio stations and allows them to create custom stations inspired by favorite artists or songs, anywhere they are.

On June 4, 2004, it entered into a consent decree with the FCC regarding a large number of ongoing complaints against its personalities and DJs. The consent decree provides in part:

> 1. The Commission has been investigating whether Clear Channel Communications, Inc. and its direct and indirect subsidiaries that hold FCC authorizations ("Clear Channel") may have violated restrictions on the broadcast of obscene, indecent or profane material.[8] ...

> 4. Based on the record before us, in particular Clear Channel's admission that some of the material it broadcast was indecent in violation of 47 C.F.R. § 73.3999, the significant remedial efforts that Clear Channel has already taken and the additional remedial efforts to which Clear Channel has agreed, we conclude that there are no substantial and material questions of fact in regard to these matters as to whether Clear Channel possesses the basic qualifications, including its character qualifications, to hold or obtain any FCC licenses or authorizations....

Consent Decree

> 1. The Federal Communications Commission and Clear Channel Communications, Inc., for itself and on behalf of its direct and indirect subsidiaries that hold FCC authorizations, hereby enter into this Consent Decree for the purpose of resolving and terminating certain forfeiture proceedings, investigations and complaints currently being conducted by, or pending before, the Commission relating to possible violations of the Indecency Laws by Clear Channel Stations....

> 9. Clear Channel represents that it has adopted, and is currently in the process of implementing, a company-wide compliance plan for the purpose of preventing the broadcast of material violative of the Indecency Laws. A summary of that plan is set forth in the Attachment. Clear Channel agrees, to the extent it has not already done so, to implement this compliance plan within thirty (30) days of the Effective Date and to keep such compliance plan in effect for three (3) years after the Effective Date. Clear Channel reserves the right to revise the plan from time to time, provided that the Commission shall be given not less than thirty (30) days advance written notice of any revisions to the plan....

---

8. 18 U.S.C. § 1464; 47 C.F.R. § 73.3999 (2004).

11. Clear Channel waives any and all rights it may have to seek administrative or judicial reconsideration, review, appeal or stay, or to otherwise challenge or contest the validity of this Consent Decree and the Adopting Order, provided no modifications are made to the Consent Decree adverse to Clear Channel or any Clear Channel Station. If the Commission, or the United States acting on its behalf, brings a judicial action to enforce the terms of the Adopting Order or this Consent Decree, or both, Clear Channel will not contest the validity of this Consent Decree or of the Adopting Order and will waive any statutory right to a trial *de novo*. If Clear Channel brings a judicial action to enforce the terms of the Adopting Order or this Consent Decree, or both, the Commission will not contest the validity of this Consent Decree or of the Adopting Order....

Federal Communications Commission, *In the Matter of Clear Channel Communications, Inc.*, FCC 04-128, adopted June 4, 2004.[9]

The concern raised by the Clear Channel consent decree flows from the risks associated with the strategic attempt to chill this marketplace. Company-wide compliance encouraged against the threat of substantial punishment for past and future practices creates the ideal governmental control over the broadcaster. As the largest company in the field, its compliance with the FCC will certainly impact all programming. The consent decree also removes a major source of financial support for other stations which are unwilling to enter into agreements with the government.

f. The Supreme Court struck down the FCC regulations related to fleeting expletives as a violation of the Due Process Clause of the Fifth Amendment. See *FCC v. Fox TV Stations, Inc.*, 132 U.S. 2307 (2012) (finding inadequate notice was provided to broadcasters for regulations relating to the federal law prohibiting the broadcasting of "any ... indecent ... language," 18 U.S.C. § 1464, which includes expletives referring to sexual or excretory activity or organs).

C. Must Carry and Ownership Legislation

Turner Broad. Sys. v. FCC
512 U.S. 622 (1994) (Turner I)

Sections 4 and 5 of the Cable Television Consumer Protection and Competition Act of 1992 require cable television systems to devote a portion of their channels to the transmission of local broadcast television stations. This case presents the question whether these provisions abridge the freedom of speech or of the press, in violation of the First Amendment.

The United States District Court for the District of Columbia granted summary judgment for the United States, holding that the challenged provisions are consistent with the First Amendment. Because issues of material fact remain unresolved in the record as developed thus far, we vacate the District Court's judgment and remand the case for further proceedings.

The role of cable television in the Nation's communications system has undergone dramatic change over the past 45 years. Given the pace of technological advancement

---

9. Available at http://hraunfoss.fcc.gov/edocs_public/attachmatch/FCC-04-128A1.pdf.

and the increasing convergence between cable and other electronic media, the cable industry today stands at the center of an ongoing telecommunications revolution with still undefined potential to affect the way we communicate and develop our intellectual resources....

Broadcast and cable television are distinguished by the different technologies through which they reach viewers. Broadcast stations radiate electromagnetic signals from a central transmitting antenna. These signals can be captured, in turn, by any television set within the antenna's range. Cable systems, by contrast, rely upon a physical, point-to-point connection between a transmission facility and the television sets of individual subscribers. Cable systems make this connection much like telephone companies, using cable or optical fibers strung aboveground or buried in ducts to reach the homes or businesses of subscribers. The construction of this physical infrastructure entails the use of public rights-of-way and easements and often results in the disruption of traffic on streets and other public property. As a result, the cable medium may depend for its very existence upon express permission from local governing authorities....

In contrast to commercial broadcast stations, which transmit signals at no charge to viewers and generate revenues by selling time to advertisers, cable systems charge subscribers a monthly fee for the right to receive cable programming and rely to a lesser extent on advertising. In most instances, cable subscribers choose the stations they will receive by selecting among various plans, or "tiers," of cable service. In a typical offering, the basic tier consists of local broadcast stations plus a number of cable programming networks selected by the cable operator. For an additional cost, subscribers can obtain channels devoted to particular subjects or interests, such as recent-release feature movies, sports, children's programming, sexually explicit programming, and the like. Many cable systems also offer pay-per-view service, which allows an individual subscriber to order and pay a one-time fee to see a single movie or program at a set time of the day.

On October 5, 1992, Congress overrode a Presidential veto to enact the Cable Television Consumer Protection and Competition Act of 1992, (1992 Cable Act or Act). Among other things, the Act subjects the cable industry to rate regulation by the Federal Communications Commission (FCC) and by municipal franchising authorities; prohibits municipalities from awarding exclusive franchises to cable operators; imposes various restrictions on cable programmers that are affiliated with cable operators; and directs the FCC to develop and promulgate regulations imposing minimum technical standards for cable operators. At issue in this case is the constitutionality of the so-called must-carry provisions, contained in §§ 4 and 5 of the Act, which require cable operators to carry the signals of a specified number of local broadcast television stations.

Section 4 requires carriage of "local commercial television stations," defined to include all full power television broadcasters, other than those qualifying as "noncommercial educational" stations under § 5, that operate within the same television market as the cable system. § 4, 47 U.S.C. §§ 534(b)(1)(B), (h)(1)(A) (1988 ed., Supp. IV). Cable systems with more than 12 active channels, and more than 300 subscribers, are required to set aside up to one-third of their channels for commercial broadcast stations that request carriage. § 534(b)(1)(B). Cable systems with more than 300 subscribers, but only 12 or fewer active channels, must carry the signals of three commercial broadcast stations. § 534(b)(1)(A).

If there are fewer broadcasters requesting carriage than slots made available under the Act, the cable operator is obligated to carry only those broadcasters who make the request. If, however, there are more requesting broadcast stations than slots available, the cable operator is permitted to choose which of these stations it will carry. § 534(b)(2). The broadcast signals carried under this provision must be transmitted on a continuous, uninterrupted basis, § 534(b)(3), and must be placed in the same numerical channel position as when broadcast over the air. § 534(b)(6). Further, subject to a few exceptions, a cable operator may not charge a fee for carrying broadcast signals in fulfillment of its must-carry obligations. § 534(b)(10).

Section 5 of the Act imposes similar requirements regarding the carriage of local public broadcast television stations, referred to in the Act as local "noncommercial educational television stations." 47 U.S.C. § 535(a) (1988 ed., Supp. IV).[10] A cable system with 12 or fewer channels must carry one of these stations; a system of between 13 and 36 channels must carry between one and three; and a system with more than 36 channels must carry each local public broadcast station requesting carriage. §§ 535(b)(2)(A), (b)(3)(A), (b)(3)(D). The Act requires a cable operator to import distant signals in certain circumstances but provides protection against substantial duplication of local noncommercial educational stations. As with commercial broadcast stations, § 5 requires cable system operators to carry the program schedule of the public broadcast station in its entirety and at its same over-the-air channel position.

Taken together, therefore, §§ 4 and 5 subject all but the smallest cable systems nationwide to must-carry obligations, and confer must-carry privileges on all full power broadcasters operating within the same television market as a qualified cable system.

Congress enacted the 1992 Cable Act after conducting three years of hearings on the structure and operation of the cable television industry. The conclusions Congress drew from its factfinding process are recited in the text of the Act itself. In brief, Congress found that the physical characteristics of cable transmission, compounded by the increasing concentration of economic power in the cable industry, are endangering the ability of over-the-air broadcast television stations to compete for a viewing audience and thus for necessary operating revenues. Congress determined that regulation of the market for video programming was necessary to correct this competitive imbalance.

In particular, Congress found that over 60 percent of the households with television sets subscribe to cable, and for these households cable has replaced over-the-air broadcast television as the primary provider of video programming. § 2(a)(17). This is so, Congress found, because "most subscribers to cable television systems do not or cannot maintain antennas to receive broadcast television services, do not have input selector switches to convert from a cable to antenna reception system, or cannot otherwise receive broadcast television services." In addition, Congress concluded that due to "local franchising requirements and the extraordinary expense of constructing more than one cable television system to serve a particular geographic area," the overwhelming majority of cable operators exercise a monopoly over cable service. § 2(a)(2). "The result," Congress determined, "is undue market power for the cable operator as compared to that of consumers and video programmers."

According to Congress, this market position gives cable operators the power and the incentive to harm broadcast competitors. The power derives from the cable operator's ability, as owner of the transmission facility, to "terminate the retransmission of the broad-

---

10. "Noncommercial educational television stations" are defined to include broadcast stations that are either (1) licensed by the FCC as a "noncommercial educational television broadcast station" and have, as licensees, entities which are eligible to receive grants from the Corporation for Public Broadcasting; or (2) owned and operated by a municipality and transmit "predominantly noncommercial programs for educational purposes." §§ 535(*l*)(1)(A)–(B).

cast signal, refuse to carry new signals, or reposition a broadcast signal to a disadvantageous channel position." § 2(a)(15). The incentive derives from the economic reality that "cable television systems and broadcast television stations increasingly compete for television advertising revenues." § 2(a)(14). By refusing carriage of broadcasters' signals, cable operators, as a practical matter, can reduce the number of households that have access to the broadcasters' programming, and thereby capture advertising dollars that would otherwise go to broadcast stations. § 2(a)(15).

Congress found, in addition, that increased vertical integration in the cable industry is making it even harder for broadcasters to secure carriage on cable systems, because cable operators have a financial incentive to favor their affiliated programmers. § 2(a)(5). Congress also determined that the cable industry is characterized by horizontal concentration, with many cable operators sharing common ownership. This has resulted in greater "barriers to entry for new programmers and a reduction in the number of media voices available to consumers." § 2(a)(4).

In light of these technological and economic conditions, Congress concluded that unless cable operators are required to carry local broadcast stations, "there is a substantial likelihood that ... additional local broadcast signals will be deleted, repositioned, or not carried," § 2(a)(15); the "marked shift in market share" from broadcast to cable will continue to erode the advertising revenue base which sustains free local broadcast television, §§ 2(a)(13)–(14); and that, as a consequence, "the economic viability of free local broadcast television and its ability to originate quality local programming will be seriously jeopardized." § 2(a)(16).

Soon after the Act became law, appellants filed these five consolidated actions in the United States District Court for the District of Columbia against the United States and the Federal Communications Commission (hereinafter referred to collectively as the Government), challenging the constitutionality of the must-carry provisions. Appellants, plaintiffs below, are numerous cable programmers and cable operators. After additional parties intervened, a three-judge District Court convened under 28 U.S.C. § 2284 to hear the actions....

There can be no disagreement on an initial premise: Cable programmers and cable operators engage in and transmit speech, and they are entitled to the protection of the speech and press provisions of the First Amendment.

Through "original programming or by exercising editorial discretion over which stations or programs to include in its repertoire," cable programmers and operators "seek to communicate messages on a wide variety of topics and in a wide variety of formats." By requiring cable systems to set aside a portion of their channels for local broadcasters, the must-carry rules regulate cable speech in two respects: The rules reduce the number of channels over which cable operators exercise unfettered control, and they render it more difficult for cable programmers to compete for carriage on the limited channels remaining. Nevertheless, because not every interference with speech triggers the same degree of scrutiny under the First Amendment, we must decide at the outset the level of scrutiny applicable to the must-carry provisions....

But the rationale for applying a less rigorous standard of First Amendment scrutiny to broadcast regulation, whatever its validity in the cases elaborating it, does not apply in the context of cable regulation. The justification for our distinct approach to broadcast regulation rests upon the unique physical limitations of the broadcast medium.

As a general matter, there are more would-be broadcasters than frequencies available in the electromagnetic spectrum. And if two broadcasters were to attempt to transmit over the same frequency in the same locale, they would interfere with one another's signals, so that neither could be heard at all....

Although courts and commentators have criticized the scarcity rationale since its inception, we have declined to question its continuing validity as support for our broadcast jurisprudence, and see no reason to do so here. The broadcast cases are inapposite in the present context because cable television does not suffer from the inherent limitations that characterize the broadcast medium. Indeed, given the rapid advances in fiber optics and digital compression technology, soon there may be no practical limitation on the number of speakers who may use the cable medium. Nor is there any danger of physical interference between two cable speakers attempting to share the same channel. In light of these fundamental technological differences between broadcast and cable transmission, application of the more relaxed standard of scrutiny adopted in *Red Lion* and the other broadcast cases is inapt when determining the First Amendment validity of cable regulation.

This is not to say that the unique physical characteristics of cable transmission should be ignored when determining the constitutionality of regulations affecting cable speech. They should not. But whatever relevance these physical characteristics may have in the evaluation of particular cable regulations, they do not require the alteration of settled principles of our First Amendment jurisprudence.

Although the Government acknowledges the substantial technological differences between broadcast and cable, it advances a second argument for application of the *Red Lion* framework to cable regulation. It asserts that the foundation of our broadcast jurisprudence is not the physical limitations of the electromagnetic spectrum, but rather the "market dysfunction" that characterizes the broadcast market. Because the cable market is beset by a similar dysfunction, the Government maintains, the *Red Lion* standard of review should also apply to cable. While we agree that the cable market suffers certain structural impediments, the Government's argument is flawed in two respects. First, as discussed above, the special physical characteristics of broadcast transmission, not the economic characteristics of the broadcast market, are what underlies our broadcast jurisprudence. Second, the mere assertion of dysfunction or failure in a speech market, without more, is not sufficient to shield a speech regulation from the First Amendment standards applicable to nonbroadcast media.

By a related course of reasoning, the Government and some appellees maintain that the must-carry provisions are nothing more than industry-specific antitrust legislation, and thus warrant rational basis scrutiny under this Court's "precedents governing legislative efforts to correct market failure in a market whose commodity is speech," such as *Associated Press v. United States,* 326 U.S. 1 (1945), and *Lorain Journal Co. v. United States,* 342 U.S. 143 (1951). This contention is unavailing. *Associated Press* and *Lorain Journal* both involved actions against members of the press brought under the Sherman Antitrust Act, a law of general application. But while the enforcement of a generally applicable law may or may not be subject to heightened scrutiny under the First Amendment, that single out the press, or certain elements thereof, for special treatment "pose a particular danger of abuse by the State," *Arkansas Writers' Project, Inc. v. Ragland,* 481 U.S. 221, 228 (1987), and so are always subject to at least some degree of heightened First Amendment scrutiny. Because the must-carry provisions impose special obligations upon cable operators and special burdens upon cable programmers, some measure of heightened First Amendment scrutiny is demanded.

The First Amendment, subject only to narrow and well-understood exceptions, does not countenance governmental control over the content of messages expressed by private individuals. Our precedents thus apply the most exacting scrutiny to regulations that suppress, disadvantage, or impose differential burdens upon speech because of its content. Laws that compel speakers to utter or distribute speech bearing a particular message are subject to the same rigorous scrutiny. In contrast, regulations that are unrelated to the content of speech are subject to an intermediate level of scrutiny, because in most cases they pose a less substantial risk of excising certain ideas or viewpoints from the public dialogue.

Deciding whether a particular regulation is content-based or content-neutral is not always a simple task. We have said that the "principal inquiry in determining content-neutrality … is whether the government has adopted a regulation of speech because of [agreement or] disagreement with the message it conveys." See *R. A. V.,* 505 U.S. at 386 ("The government may not regulate [speech] based on hostility—or favoritism—towards the underlying message expressed"). The purpose, or justification, of a regulation will often be evident on its face. But while a content-based purpose may be sufficient in certain circumstances to show that a regulation is content-based, it is not necessary to such a showing in all cases. Nor will the mere assertion of a content-neutral purpose be enough to save a law which, on its face, discriminates based on content.

As a general rule, laws that by their terms distinguish favored speech from disfavored speech on the basis of the ideas or views expressed are content-based. By contrast, laws that confer benefits or impose burdens on speech without reference to the ideas or views expressed are in most instances content-neutral.

Insofar as they pertain to the carriage of full power broadcasters, the must-carry rules, on their face, impose burdens and confer benefits without reference to the content of speech. Although the provisions interfere with cable operators' editorial discretion by compelling them to offer carriage to a certain minimum number of broadcast stations, the extent of the interference does not depend upon the content of the cable operators' programming. The rules impose obligations upon all operators, save those with fewer than 300 subscribers, regardless of the programs or stations they now offer or have offered in the past. Nothing in the Act imposes a restriction, penalty, or burden by reason of the views, programs, or stations the cable operator has selected or will select. The number of channels a cable operator must set aside depends only on the operator's channel capacity, hence, an operator cannot avoid or mitigate its obligations under the Act by altering the programming it offers to subscribers. *Cf. Miami Herald Publishing Co. v. Tornillo,* 418 U.S. at 256–257 (newspaper may avoid access obligations by refraining from speech critical of political candidates).

The must-carry provisions also burden cable programmers by reducing the number of channels for which they can compete. But, again, this burden is unrelated to content, for it extends to all cable programmers irrespective of the programming they choose to offer viewers. And finally, the privileges conferred by the must-carry provisions are also unrelated to content. The rules benefit all full power broadcasters who request carriage—be they commercial or noncommercial, independent or network-affiliated, English or Spanish language, religious or secular.

The aggregate effect of the rules is thus to make every full power commercial and noncommercial broadcaster eligible for must-carry, provided only that the broadcaster operates within the same television market as a cable system.

It is true that the must-carry provisions distinguish between speakers in the television programming market. But they do so based only upon the manner in which speakers transmit their messages to viewers, and not upon the messages they carry: Broadcasters, which transmit over the airwaves, are favored, while cable programmers, which do not, are disfavored. Cable operators, too, are burdened by the carriage obligations, but only because they control access to the cable conduit. So long as they are not a subtle means of exercising a content preference, speaker distinctions of this nature are not presumed invalid under the First Amendment.

The must-carry provisions, on their face, do not burden or benefit speech of a particular content does not end the inquiry. Our cases have recognized that even a regulation neutral on its face may be content-based if its manifest purpose is to regulate speech because of the message it conveys....

Appellants maintain that the must-carry provisions trigger strict scrutiny because they compel cable operators to transmit speech not of their choosing. Relying principally on *Miami Herald Publishing Co. v. Tornillo*, 418 U.S. 241 (1974), appellants say this intrusion on the editorial control of cable operators amounts to forced speech which, if not per se invalid, can be justified only if narrowly tailored to a compelling government interest.

Tornillo affirmed an essential proposition: The First Amendment protects the editorial independence of the press. The right-of-reply statute at issue in *Tornillo* required any newspaper that assailed a political candidate's character to print, upon request by the candidate and without cost, the candidate's reply in equal space and prominence. Although the statute did not censor speech in the traditional sense—it only required newspapers to grant access to the messages of others—we found that it imposed an impermissible content-based burden on newspaper speech. Because the right of access at issue in *Tornillo* was triggered only when a newspaper elected to print matter critical of political candidates, it "exacted a penalty on the basis of ... content." We found, and continue to recognize, that right-of-reply statutes of this sort are an impermissible intrusion on newspapers' "editorial control and judgment."

Tornillo and *Pacific Gas & Electric* do not control this case for the following reasons. First, unlike the access rules struck down in those cases, the must-carry rules are content-neutral in application. They are not activated by any particular message spoken by cable operators and thus exact no content-based penalty. Likewise, they do not grant access to broadcasters on the ground that the content of broadcast programming will counterbalance the messages of cable operators. Instead, they confer benefits upon all full power, local broadcasters, whatever the content of their programming. *Cf. Pacific Gas & Electric, supra, at 14* (access "awarded only to those who disagree with appellant's views and who are hostile to appellant's interests").

Second, appellants do not suggest, nor do we think it the case, that must-carry will force cable operators to alter their own messages to respond to the broadcast programming they are required to carry. Given cable's long history of serving as a conduit for broadcast signals, there appears little risk that cable viewers would assume that the broadcast stations carried on a cable system convey ideas or messages endorsed by the cable operator. Indeed, broadcasters are required by federal regulation to identify themselves at least once every hour, and it is a common practice for broadcasters to disclaim any identity of viewpoint between the management and the speakers who use the broadcast facility. Moreover, in contrast to the statute at issue in *Tornillo*, no aspect of the must-carry provisions would cause a cable operator or cable programmer to conclude that "the safe course is to avoid controversy," and by so doing diminish the free flow of information and ideas.

Finally, the asserted analogy to *Tornillo* ignores an important technological difference between newspapers and cable television. Although a daily newspaper and a cable operator both may enjoy monopoly status in a given locale, the cable operator exercises far greater control over access to the relevant medium. A daily newspaper, no matter how secure its local monopoly, does not possess the power to obstruct readers' access to other competing publications—whether they be weekly local newspapers, or daily newspapers published in other cities. Thus, when a newspaper asserts exclusive control over its own news copy, it does not thereby prevent other newspapers from being distributed to willing recipients in the same locale.

The same is not true of cable. When an individual subscribes to cable, the physical connection between the television set and the cable network gives the cable operator bottleneck, or gatekeeper, control over most (if not all) of the television programming that is channeled into the subscriber's home. Hence, simply by virtue of its ownership of the essential pathway for cable speech, a cable operator can prevent its subscribers from obtaining access to programming it chooses to exclude. A cable operator, unlike speakers in other media, can thus silence the voice of competing speakers with a mere flick of the switch.

Turner Broad. Sys. v. FCC

520 U.S. 180 (1997) (Turner II)

On appeal, we agreed with the District Court that must-carry does not "distinguish favored speech from disfavored speech on the basis of the ideas or views expressed," but is a content-neutral regulation designed "to prevent cable operators from exploiting their economic power to the detriment of broadcasters," and "to ensure that all Americans, especially those unable to subscribe to cable, have access to free television programming—whatever its content." We held that, under the intermediate level of scrutiny applicable to content-neutral regulations, must-carry would be sustained if it were shown to further an important or substantial governmental interest unrelated to the suppression of free speech, provided the incidental restrictions did not "burden substantially more speech than is necessary to further" those interests. Although we "had no difficulty concluding" the interests must-carry was designed to serve were important in the abstract, a four-Justice plurality concluded genuine issues of material fact remained regarding whether "the economic health of local broadcasting is in genuine jeopardy and need of the protections afforded by must-carry," and whether must-carry "'burdens substantially more speech than is necessary to further the government's legitimate interests.'" ...

The District Court oversaw another 18 months of factual development on remand "yielding a record of tens of thousands of pages" of evidence, comprised of materials acquired during Congress' three years of pre-enactment hearings, as well as additional expert submissions, sworn declarations and testimony, and industry documents obtained on remand. Upon consideration of the expanded record, a divided panel of the District Court again granted summary judgment to appellees.

The majority determined "Congress drew reasonable inferences" from substantial evidence before it to conclude that "in the absence of must-carry rules, 'significant' numbers of broadcast stations would be refused carriage." The court found Congress drew on studies and anecdotal evidence indicating "cable operators had already dropped, refused to carry, or adversely repositioned significant numbers of local broadcasters," and suggesting that in the vast majority of cases the broadcasters were not restored to carriage in their prior position. Noting evidence in the record before Congress and the testimony of experts on remand, the court decided the noncarriage problem would grow worse without must-carry because cable operators had refrained from dropping broadcast stations during Congress' investigation and the pendency of this litigation, and possessed increasing incentives to use their growing economic power to capture broadcasters' advertising revenues and promote affiliated cable programmers. The court concluded "substantial evidence before Congress" supported the predictive judgment that a local broadcaster denied carriage "would suffer financial harm and possible ruin." It cited evidence that adverse carriage actions decrease broadcasters' revenues by reducing audience levels, and evidence that the invalidation of the FCC's prior must-carry regulations had contributed to declining growth in the broadcast industry.

The court held must-carry to be narrowly tailored to promote the Government's legitimate interests. It found the effects of must-carry on cable operators to be minimal, noting evidence that: most cable systems had not been required to add any broadcast stations since the rules were adopted; only 1.2 percent of all cable channels had been devoted to broadcast stations added because of must-carry; and the burden was likely to diminish as channel capacity expanded in the future. The court proceeded to consider a number of alternatives to must-carry that appellants had proposed, including: a leased-access regime, under which cable operators would be required to set aside channels for both broadcasters and cable programmers to use at a regulated price; use of so-called A/B switches, giving consumers a choice of both cable and broadcast signals; a more limited set of must-carry obligations modeled on those earlier used by the FCC; and subsidies for broadcasters. The court rejected each in turn, concluding that "even assuming that [the alternatives] would be less burdensome" on cable operators' First Amendment interests, they "are not in any respect as effective in achieving the government's [interests]." Judge Jackson would have preferred a trial to summary judgment, but concurred in the judgment of the court.

This direct appeal followed. We noted probable jurisdiction, and we now affirm.

We begin where the plurality ended in *Turner*, applying the standards for intermediate scrutiny enunciated in *O'Brien*. A content-neutral regulation will be sustained under the First Amendment if it advances important governmental interests unrelated to the suppression of free speech and does not burden substantially more speech than necessary to further those interests. As noted in Turner, must-carry was designed to serve "three interrelated interests: (1) preserving the benefits of free, over-the-air local broadcast television, (2) promoting the widespread dissemination of information from a multiplicity of sources, and (3) promoting fair competition in the market for television programming." We decided then, and now reaffirm, that each of those is an important governmental interest. We have been most explicit in holding that "'protecting noncable households from loss of regular television broadcasting service due to competition from cable systems' is an important federal interest." Forty percent of American households continue to rely on over-the-air signals for television programming. Despite the growing importance of cable television and alternative technologies, "'broadcasting is demonstrably a principal source of information and entertainment for a great part of the Nation's population.'" We have identified a corresponding "governmental purpose of the highest order" in ensuring public access to "a multiplicity of information sources." And it is undisputed the Government has an interest in "eliminating restraints on fair competition..., even when the individuals or entities subject to particular regulations are engaged in expressive activity protected by the First Amendment."

On remand, and again before this Court, both sides have advanced new interpretations of these interests in an attempt to recast them in forms "more readily proven." The Government downplays the importance of showing a risk to the broadcast industry as a whole and suggests the loss of even a few broadcast stations "is a matter of critical importance."

Taking the opposite approach, appellants argue Congress' interest in preserving broadcasting is not implicated unless it is shown the industry as a whole would fail without must-carry, and suggest Congress' legitimate interest in "assuring that the public has access to a multiplicity of information sources," extends only as far as preserving "a minimum amount of television broadcast service."

These alternative formulations are inconsistent with Congress' stated interests in enacting must-carry. The congressional findings do not reflect concern that, absent must-carry, "a few voices," would be lost from the television marketplace. In explicit factual findings, Congress expressed clear concern that the "marked shift in market share from broadcast television to cable television services," resulting from increasing market penetration by cable services, as well as the expanding horizontal concentration and vertical integration of cable operators, combined to give cable systems the incentive and ability to delete, reposition, or decline carriage to local broadcasters in an attempt to favor affiliated cable programmers. Congress predicted that "absent the reimposition of [must-carry], additional local broadcast signals will be deleted, repositioned, or not carried" with the end result that "the economic viability of free local broadcast television and its ability to originate quality local programming will be seriously jeopardized."

At the same time, Congress was under no illusion that there would be a complete disappearance of broadcast television nationwide in the absence of must-carry. Congress recognized broadcast programming (and network programming in particular) "remains the most popular programming on cable systems." Indeed, reflecting the popularity and strength of some broadcasters, Congress included in the Cable Act a provision permitting broadcasters to charge cable systems for carriage of the broadcasters' signals.

Congress was concerned not that broadcast television would disappear in its entirety without must-carry, but that without it, "significant numbers of broadcast stations will be refused carriage on cable systems," and those "broadcast stations denied carriage will either deteriorate to a substantial degree or fail altogether."

Nor do the congressional findings support appellants' suggestion that legitimate legislative goals would be satisfied by the preservation of a rump broadcasting industry providing a minimum of broadcast service to Americans without cable. We have noted that "'it has long been a basic tenet of national communications policy that "the widest possible dissemination of information from diverse and antagonistic sources is essential to the welfare of the public."'" "'Increasing the number of outlets for community self-expression'" represents a "'long-established regulatory goal in the field of television broadcasting.'" Consistent with this objective, the Cable Act's findings reflect a concern that congressional action was necessary to prevent "a reduction in the number of media voices available to consumers." Congress identified a specific interest in "ensuring [the] continuation" of "the local origination of [broadcast] programming," an interest consistent with its larger purpose of promoting multiple types of media, and found must-carry necessary "to serve the goals" of the original Communications Act of 1934 of "providing a fair, efficient, and equitable distribution of broadcast services." In short, Congress enacted must-carry to "preserve the existing structure of the Nation's broadcast television medium while permitting the concomitant expansion and development of cable television."

Although Congress set no definite number of broadcast stations sufficient for these purposes, the Cable Act's requirement that all cable operators with more than 12 channels set aside one-third of their channel capacity for local broadcasters, refutes the notion that Congress contemplated preserving only a bare minimum of stations. Congress' evident interest in "preserving the existing structure," of the broadcast industry discloses a purpose to prevent any significant reduction in the multiplicity of broadcast programming sources available to noncable households....

The dissent proceeds on the assumption that must-carry is designed solely to be (and can only be justified as) a measure to protect broadcasters from cable operators' anti-competitive behavior. Federal policy, however, has long favored preserving a multiplicity of broadcast outlets regardless of whether the conduct that threatens it is motivated by anticompetitive animus or rises to the level of an antitrust violation....

We have no difficulty in finding a substantial basis to support Congress' conclusion that a real threat justified enactment of the must-carry provisions. We examine first the evidence before Congress and then the further evidence presented to the District Court on remand to supplement the congressional determination.

As to the evidence before Congress, there was specific support for its conclusion that cable operators had considerable and growing market power over local video programming markets. Cable served at least 60 percent of American households in 1992, and evidence indicated cable market penetration was projected to grow beyond 70 percent. As Congress noted, cable operators possess a local monopoly over cable households. Only one percent of communities are served by more than one cable system. Even in communities with two or more cable systems, in the typical case each system has a local monopoly over its subscribers. Cable operators thus exercise "control over most (if not all) of the television programming that is channeled into the subscriber's home.... [and] can thus silence the voice of competing speakers with a mere flick of the switch."

Evidence indicated the structure of the cable industry would give cable operators increasing ability and incentive to drop local broadcast stations from their systems, or reposition them to a less-viewed channel. Horizontal concentration was increasing as a small number of multiple system operators (MSO's) acquired large numbers of cable systems nationwide. The trend was accelerating, giving the MSO's increasing market power. In 1985, the 10 largest MSO's controlled cable systems serving slightly less than 42 percent of all cable subscribers; by 1989, the figure was nearly 54 percent.

Vertical integration in the industry also was increasing. As Congress was aware, many MSO's owned or had affiliation agreements with cable programmers. Congress concluded that "vertical integration gives cable operators the incentive and ability to favor their affiliated programming services" a conclusion that even Judge Williams' dissent conceded to be reasonable. Extensive testimony indicated that cable operators would have an incentive to drop local broadcasters and to favor affiliated programmers.

In addition, evidence before Congress, supplemented on remand, indicated that cable systems would have incentives to drop local broadcasters in favor of other programmers less likely to compete with them for audience and advertisers. Independent local broadcasters tend to be the closest substitutes for cable programs, because their programming tends to be similar, and because both primarily target the same type of advertiser: those interested in cheaper (and more frequent) ad spots than are typically available on network affiliates.

Cable systems also have more systemic reasons for seeking to disadvantage broadcast stations: Simply stated, cable has little interest in assisting, through carriage, a competing medium of communication. As one cable-industry executive put it, "'our job is to promote cable television, not broadcast television.'" The incentive to subscribe to cable is lower in markets with many over-the-air viewing options. Evidence adduced on remand indicated cable systems have little incentive to carry, and a significant incentive to drop, broadcast stations that will only be strengthened by access to the 60% of the television market that cable typically controls.

Congress could therefore reasonably conclude that cable systems would drop broadcasters in favor of programmers—even unaffiliated ones—less likely to compete with them for audience and advertisers....

It was more than a theoretical possibility in 1992 that cable operators would take actions adverse to local broadcasters; indeed, significant numbers of broadcasters had already been dropped. The record before Congress contained extensive anecdotal evidence about scores of adverse carriage decisions against broadcast stations. Congress considered an FCC-sponsored study detailing cable system carriage practices in the wake of decisions by the United States Court of Appeals for the District of Columbia Circuit striking down prior must-carry regulations. Substantial evidence demonstrated that absent must-carry the already "serious," problem of noncarriage would grow worse because "additional local broadcast signals will be deleted, repositioned, or not carried." The record included anecdotal evidence showing the cable industry was acting with restraint in dropping broadcast stations in an effort to discourage reregulation....

We think it apparent must-carry serves the Government's interests "in a direct and effective way." Must-carry ensures that a number of local broadcasters retain cable carriage, with the concomitant audience access and advertising revenues needed to support a multiplicity of stations. Appellants contend that even were this so, must-carry is broader than necessary to accomplish its goals. We turn to this question.

The second portion of the *O'Brien* inquiry concerns the fit between the asserted interests and the means chosen to advance them. Content-neutral regulations do not pose the same "inherent dangers to free expression," that content-based regulations do, and thus are subject to a less rigorous analysis, which affords the Government latitude in designing a regulatory solution. Under intermediate scrutiny, the Government may employ the means of its choosing "'so long as the ... regulation promotes a substantial governmental interest that would be achieved less effectively absent the regulation,'" and does not "'burden substantially more speech than is necessary to further'" that interest.

The must-carry provisions have the potential to interfere with protected speech in two ways. First, the provisions restrain cable operators' editorial discretion in creating programming packages by "reducing the number of channels over which [they] exercise unfettered control." Second, the rules "render it more difficult for cable programmers to compete for carriage on the limited channels remaining."

Appellants say the burden of must-carry is great, but the evidence adduced on remand indicates the actual effects are modest. Significant evidence indicates the vast majority of cable operators have not been affected in a significant manner by must-carry. Cable operators have been able to satisfy their must-carry obligations 87 percent of the time using previously unused channel capacity; 94.5 percent of the 11,628 cable systems nationwide have not had to drop any programming in order to fulfill their must-carry obligations; the remaining 5.5 percent have had to drop an average of only 1.22 services from their programming; and cable operators nationwide carry 99.8 percent of the programming they carried before enactment of must-carry. Appellees note that only 1.18 percent of the approximately 500,000 cable channels nationwide is devoted to channels added because of must-carry; weighted for subscribership, the figure is 2.4 percent. Appellees contend the burdens of must-carry will soon diminish as cable channel capacity increases, as is occurring nationwide....

We cannot displace Congress' judgment respecting content-neutral regulations with our own, so long as its policy is grounded on reasonable factual findings supported by evidence that is substantial for a legislative determination. Those requirements were met in this case, and in these circumstances the First Amendment requires nothing more. The judgment of the District Court is affirmed.

JUSTICE O'CONNOR, with whom JUSTICE SCALIA, JUSTICE THOMAS, and JUSTICE GINSBURG join, dissenting.

In sustaining the must-carry provisions of the Cable Television Protection and Competition Act of 1992, Pub. L. 102-385, §§ 4–5, 106 Stat. 1460 (Cable Act), against a First Amendment challenge by cable system operators and cable programmers, the Court errs in two crucial respects. First, the Court disregards one of the principal defenses of the statute urged by appellees on remand: that it serves a substantial interest in preserving "diverse," "quality" programming that is "responsive" to the needs of the local community. The course of this litigation on remand and the proffered defense strongly reinforce my view that the Court adopted the wrong analytic framework in the prior phase of this case.

Second, the Court misapplies the "intermediate scrutiny" framework it adopts. Although we owe deference to Congress' predictive judgments and its evaluation of complex economic questions, we have an independent duty to identify with care the Government interests supporting the scheme, to inquire into the reasonableness of congressional findings regarding its necessity, and to examine the fit between its goals and its consequences. The Court fails to discharge its duty here.

I did not join those portions of the principal opinion in *Turner* holding that the must-carry provisions of the Cable Act are content neutral and therefore subject to intermediate First Amendment scrutiny. The Court there referred to the "unusually detailed statutory findings" accompanying the Act, in which Congress recognized the importance of preserving sources of local news, public affairs, and educational programming. Nevertheless, the Court minimized the significance of these findings, suggesting that they merely reflected Congress' view of the "intrinsic value" of broadcast programming generally, rather than a congressional preference for programming with local, educational, or informational content....

I fully agree that promoting fair competition is a legitimate and substantial Government goal. But the Court nowhere examines whether the breadth of the must-carry provisions comports with a goal of preventing anticompetitive harms. Instead, in the course of its inquiry into whether the must-carry provisions are "narrowly tailored," the principal opinion simply assumes that most adverse carriage decisions are anticompetitively motivated, and that must-carry is therefore a measured response to a problem of anticompetitive behavior. We ordinarily do not substitute unstated and untested assumptions for our independent evaluation of the facts bearing upon an issue of constitutional law....

The *Turner [I]* plurality found that genuine issues of material fact remained as to both parts of the *O'Brien* analysis. On whether must-carry furthers a substantial governmental interest, the *Turner* Court remanded the case to test two essential and unproven propositions: "(1) that unless cable operators are compelled to carry broadcast stations, significant numbers of broadcast stations will be refused carriage on cable systems; and (2) that the broadcast stations denied carriage will either deteriorate to a substantial degree or fail altogether." As for whether must-carry restricts no more speech than essential to further Congress' asserted purpose, the *Turner* plurality found evidence lacking on the extent of the burden that the must-carry provisions would place on cable operators and cable programmers....

Under the standard articulated by the *Turner* plurality, the conclusion that must-carry serves a substantial governmental interest depends upon the "essential proposition" that, without must-carry, "significant numbers of broadcast stations will be refused carriage on cable systems." In analyzing whether this undefined standard is satisfied, the Court focuses almost exclusively on raw numbers of stations denied carriage or "repositioned"—that is, shifted out of their traditional channel positions.

The larger problem with the Court's approach is that neither the FCC study nor the additional evidence on remand canvassed by the Court says anything about the broadcast markets in which adverse carriage decisions take place. The Court accepts Congress' stated concern about preserving the availability of a "multiplicity" of broadcast stations, but apparently thinks it sufficient to evaluate that concern in the abstract, without considering how much local service is already available in a given broadcast market. . . .

I turn now to the second portion of the *O'Brien* inquiry, which concerns the fit between the Government's asserted interests and the means chosen to advance them. The Court observes that "broadcast stations gained carriage on 5,880 channels as a result of must-carry," and recognizes that this forced carriage imposes a burden on cable system operators and cable programmers. But the Court also concludes that the other 30,006 cable channels occupied by broadcast stations are irrelevant to measuring the burden of the must-carry scheme. The must-carry rules prevent operators from dropping these broadcast stations should other more desirable cable programming become available, even though operators have carried these stations voluntarily in the past. The must-carry requirements thus burden an operator's First Amendment freedom to exercise unfettered control over a number of channels in its system, whether or not the operator's present choice is aligned with that of the Government.

Even assuming that the Court is correct that the 5,880 channels occupied by added broadcasters "represent the actual burden of the regulatory scheme," the Court's leap to the conclusion that must-carry "is narrowly tailored to preserve a multiplicity of broadcast stations," is nothing short of astounding. The Court's logic is circular. Surmising that most of the 5,880 channels added by the regulatory scheme would be dropped in its absence, the Court concludes that the figure also approximates the "benefit" of must-carry. Finding the scheme's burden "congruent" to the benefit it affords, the Court declares the statute narrowly tailored. The Court achieves this result, however, only by equating the effect of the statute—requiring cable operators to add 5,880 stations—with the governmental interest sought to be served. The Court's citation of *Ward v. Rock Against Racism*, 491 U.S. 781 (1989), reveals the true nature of the interest at stake. The "evil the Government seeks to eliminate," is not the failure of cable operators to carry these 5,880 stations. Rather, to read the first half of the principal opinion, the "evil" is anticompetitive behavior by cable operators.

As a factual matter, we do not know whether these stations were not carried because of anticompetitive impulses. Positing the effect of a statute as the governmental interest "can sidestep judicial review of almost any statute, because it makes all statutes look narrowly tailored." Without a sense whether most adverse carriage decisions are anticompetitively motivated, it is improper to conclude that the statute is narrowly tailored simply because it prevents some adverse carriage decisions. In my view, the statute is not narrowly tailored to serve a substantial interest in preventing anticompetitive conduct. . . .

Finally, I note my disagreement with the Court's suggestion that the availability of less-speech-restrictive alternatives is never relevant to *O'Brien*'s narrow tailoring inquiry. The *Turner* Court remanded this case in part because a plurality concluded that "judicial findings concerning the availability and efficacy of constitutionally acceptable less restrictive means of achieving the Government's asserted interests" were lacking in the original record. The Court's present position on this issue is puzzling.

As shown above, in this case it is plain without reference to any alternatives that the must-carry scheme is "substantially broader than necessary," to serve the only governmental interest that the principal opinion fully explains—preventing unfair competition. If Congress truly sought to address anticompetitive behavior by cable system operators, it passed the wrong law. Nevertheless, the availability of less restrictive alternatives—a leased-access regime and subsidies—reinforces my conclusion that the must-carry provisions are overbroad. I therefore respectfully dissent, and would reverse the judgment below.

Comcast Corp. v. FCC

579 F.3d 1 (2009)

Comcast Corporation and several intervenors involved in the cable television industry petition for review of a rule in which the Federal Communications Commission capped at 30% of all subscribers the market share any single cable television operator may serve. We agree with Comcast that the 30% subscriber limit is arbitrary and capricious. We therefore grant the petition and vacate the Rule.

I. Background

The Cable Television Consumer Protection and Competition Act of 1992 directed the FCC, "[i]n order to enhance effective competition," 47 U.S.C. § 533(f)(1), to

> prescrib[e] rules and regulations ... [to] ensure that no cable operator or group of cable operators can unfairly impede, either because of the size of any individual operator or because of joint actions by a group of operators of sufficient size, the flow of video programming from the video programmer to the consumer.

Id. § 533(f)(2)(A). The Commission is to "make such rules and regulations reflect the dynamic nature of the communications marketplace." Id. § 533(f)(2)(E).

Several cable operators immediately challenged certain provisions of the Act, in particular arguing the subscriber limit provision was facially unconstitutional as a content-based restriction of speech. We "conclude[d] that the subscriber limits provision is not content-based." Applying "intermediate, rather than strict scrutiny," we upheld the relevant provision of the Act because the plaintiff "ha[d] not demonstrated that the subscriber limits provision is on its face either unnecessary or unnecessarily overburdensome" to speech protected by the First Amendment to the Constitution of the United States.

In 1993 the Commission first exercised its rulemaking authority and set the subscriber limit at 30%. Much has changed in the subscription television industry since 1993: The number of networks has increased five-fold and satellite television companies, which were bit players in the early 90s, now serve one-third of all subscribers. Meanwhile, the FCC has twice changed the formula it uses to determine the maximum number of subscribers a cable operator may serve, but the subscriber limit has always remained at 30%.

In 2001 we considered a petition for review of a then newly revised version of the 30% subscriber limit. *Time Warner Entm't Co. v. FCC (Time Warner II)*, 240 F.3d 1126 (2001). Then, as now, the Commission established the subscriber limit through an "open field" analysis, in which the agency "determines whether a programming network would have access to alternative [video programming distributors] of sufficient size to allow it to successfully enter the market, if it were denied carriage by one or more of the largest cable operators." *Fourth Report and Order and Further Notice of Proposed Rulemaking*, 23 F.C.C.R. 2134, 2143, 73 Fed.Reg. 11,048 (2008) (*Fourth Report*). In *Time Warner II* we described the formula then used by the FCC:

[T]he FCC determines that the average cable network needs to reach 15 million subscribers to be economically viable. This is 18.56% of the roughly 80 million ... subscribers, and the FCC rounds it up to 20% of such subscribers. The FCC then divines that the average cable programmer will succeed in reaching only about 50% of the subscribers linked to cable companies that *agree* to carry its programming, because of channel capacity, programming tastes of particular cable operators, or other factors. The average programmer therefore requires an open field of 40% of the market to be viable (.20/.50 = .40).

Finally, to support the 30% limit that it says is necessary to assure this minimum, the Commission reasons as follows: With a 30% limit, a programmer has an open field of 40% of the market even if the two largest cable companies deny carriage, acting individually or collusively.

240 F.3d at 1131 (internal citations and quotation marks omitted). As is apparent from this description, in order to use the open field approach, the Commission must assign values to three variables: (1) The "minimum viable scale," which is the number of viewers a network must reach to be economically viable; (2) the relevant market, which is the total number of subscribers; and (3) the "penetration rate," which is the percentage of viewers the average cable network reaches once a cable operator decides to carry it.

In establishing the subscriber limit we reviewed in *Time Warner II*, the Commission had sought to ensure a minimum open field of 40% and reasoned that a 30% cap, rather than the seemingly obvious 60% cap, was necessary because the Commission was concerned about the viability of a video programming network if the two largest cable operators denied it carriage. We granted the petition because the record contained no evidence of cable operators' colluding to deny a video programmer carriage and "the legitimate, independent editorial choices" of two or more cable operators, could not be said to "unfairly impede, either because of the size of any individual operator or because of joint actions by a group of operators of sufficient size, the flow of video programming from the video programmer to the consumer," 47 U.S.C. § 533(f)(2)(A). We directed the agency on remand to consider how the increasing market share of direct broadcast satellite (DBS) companies, such as DirecTV and Dish Network, diminished cable operators' ability to determine the economic fate of programming networks.

On remand, the Commission adopted the current version of the 30% subscriber limit. The Rule here under review was designed to ensure that no single cable operator "can, by simply refusing to carry a programming network, cause it to fail." *Fourth Report*, 23 F.C.C.R. at 2154. Based upon the record before the court in *Time Warner II*, the subscriber limit under this standard could not have been lower than 60%. Based upon the present record, however, the Commission concluded no cable operator could safely be allowed to serve—*mirabile dictu*—more than 30% of all subscribers. *Plus ça change, plus c'est la même chose?* ...

Although the Commission recognized "that competition in the downstream market [especially from DBS companies] may affect the ability of a large cable operator to prevent successful entry by a programming network, and that [the] open field analysis does not directly measure this," it decided not to adjust the subscriber limit to account for such competition because doing so would be "quite difficult." *Id.* at 2167–68. The FCC then gave four reasons it did not regard competition from DBS companies as significant: Customers are reluctant to switch from cable service to DBS because (1) switching is costly; and (2) cable operators offer non-video services, such as telephone and internet access, that are not available with DBS; and (3) "video programming is a product, the quality of which cannot be known with certainty until it is consumed." Additionally, (4) "[c]ompetitive pressures from DBS will not provide any assistance to networks that," not having a contract with the largest cable operator, are unable to "launch due to a lack of financing." *Id.* at 2168–69.

Comcast now petitions for review of the Commission's latest version of the 30% subscriber limit. The National Cable & Telecommunications Association, Bright House Networks, the Cable Television & Communications Association of Illinois, Cablevision Systems Corporation, the Indiana, Michigan, Minnesota, and Missouri Cable Telecommunications Associations, and Time Warner have intervened in support of Comcast's petition. The CCTV Center for Media & Democracy, United Church of Christ, and the Center for Creative Community (collectively CCTV Intervenors) have intervened in support of the FCC.

II. Analysis

Comcast suggests the CCTV Intervenors lack standing and argues the 30% subscriber limit is unconstitutional, outside the scope of the FCC's statutory authority, and arbitrary, capricious, and unsupported by substantial evidence. The Commission suggests Comcast lacks standing and, of course, defends the 30% limit on all fronts....

B. The 30% Subscriber Limit

We may set aside the Commission's decision "only if [it] was 'arbitrary, capricious, an abuse of discretion, or otherwise not in accordance with law.'" *Mission Broad. Corp. v. FCC,* 113 F.3d 254, 259–60 (D.C.Cir.1997) (quoting 5 U.S.C. §706(2)(A)). We will not do so if the agency "examined the relevant data and articulated a satisfactory explanation for its action." *Fresno Mobile Radio, Inc. v. FCC,* 165 F.3d 965, 968 (D.C.Cir.1999) (internal quotation marks omitted).

Whether a cable operator serving more than 30% of subscribers can exercise "bottleneck monopoly power," *Turner Broad. Sys. v. FCC (Turner I),* 512 U.S. 622, 661 (1994), depends, as we observed in *Time Warner II,* "not only on its share of the market, but also on the elasticities of supply and demand, which in turn are determined by the *availability* of competition." 240 F.3d at 1134. A cable operator faces competition primarily from non-cable companies, such as those providing DBS service and, increasingly, telephone companies providing fiber optic service. As Comcast points out, DBS companies alone now serve approximately 33% of all subscribers. Recognizing the growing importance particularly of DBS, in *Time Warner II* we said in no uncertain terms that "in revisiting the horizontal rules the Commission will have to take account of the impact of DBS on [cable operators'] market power."

Of the three aspects of the Commission's open field model—minimum viable scale, total number of subscribers, and penetration rate—only the total subscribers measure fully takes account of the competition from DBS companies and companies offering fiber optic services. As Comcast points out, the measure of minimum viable scale relies upon data from 1984–2001 and, as a result, fails to consider the impact of DBS companies' growing market share (from 18% to 33%) over the six years immediately preceding issuance of the Rule, as well as the growth of fiber optic companies. The penetration rate calculation, by the Commission's own admission, leaves out data regarding DBS penetration—an omission the FCC attempts to justify with the question-begging assertion that such data would not have materially changed the penetration rate.

Comcast argues the Commission has offered no plausible reason for its failure to heed our explicit direction in *Time Warner II* to consider the competitive impact of DBS companies. Instead the Commission made the four non-empirical observations we enumerated above. As for the first, transaction costs undoubtedly do deter some cable customers from switching to satellite services, but Comcast points to record evidence that almost 50% of all DBS customers formerly subscribed to cable; in the face of that evidence, the Commission's observation that cost may deter some customers from switching to DBS is feeble indeed. With regard to the second — that some cable consumers may be reluctant to switch to a satellite television service because, unlike cable companies, DBS companies do not offer internet and telephone services — the Commission does not point to any evidence tending to show these inframarginal customers are numerous enough to confer upon cable operators their supposed bottleneck power over programming. Moreover, as Comcast points out, both DirecTV and Dish Network have partnered with telephone companies to offer bundled DBS and telephone services.

The Commission's third justification — that consumers will not switch providers to access new programming because they cannot know the quality of the programming before consuming it — warrants little discussion. As Comcast points out, there is no record support for this conjecture. In any event, it is common knowledge that new video programming is advertised on other television stations and in other media, and can be previewed over the internet, thus providing consumers with information about the quality of competing services. The FCC's fourth reason — that without its subscriber cap an upstart network will have trouble securing financing unless it has a contract with a cable company serving more than 30% of the market — is no more convincing than the other three when one recalls DBS companies already serve more than 30% of the market.

Finally, we note the Commission's observation that assessing competition from DBS companies is difficult — possibly true even if unexplained — does not justify the agency's failure to consider competition from DBS companies in important aspects of its model. That a problem is difficult may indicate a need to make some simplifying assumptions, but it does not justify ignoring altogether a variable so clearly relevant and likely to affect the calculation of a subscriber limit — not to mention one the court had directed the agency to consider.

Comcast, on the other hand, points beyond DBS companies' growing market share to their exclusive arrangements with certain highly sought after programmers as evidence that competition has led and will likely continue to lead subscribers to switch services. Indeed, Commissioner McDowell pointed out in dissent that, as of the date of the Fourth Report, DirecTV and Dish Network each served more customers than any cable company save Comcast itself. Comcast also points to evidence that the number of cable networks has increased by almost 500% since 1992 and has grown at an ever faster rate since 2000, and that a much lower percentage of cable networks are vertically integrated with cable operators than was the case when the Congress passed the 1992 Act. There can be no doubt that consumers are now able to receive far more channels than they could in 1999, let alone 1992.

In sum, the Commission has failed to demonstrate that allowing a cable operator to serve more than 30% of all cable subscribers would threaten to reduce either competition or diversity in programming. First, the record is replete with evidence of ever increasing competition among video providers: Satellite and fiber optic video providers have entered the market and grown in market share since the Congress passed the 1992 Act, and particularly in recent years. Cable operators, therefore, no longer have the bottleneck power over programming that concerned the Congress in 1992. Second, over the same period there has been a dramatic increase both in the number of cable networks and in the programming available to subscribers.

In view of the overwhelming evidence concerning "the dynamic nature of the communications marketplace," 47 U.S.C § 533(f)(2)(E), and the entry of new competitors at both the programming and the distribution levels, it was arbitrary and capricious for the Commission to conclude that a cable operator serving more than 30% of the market poses a threat either to competition or to diversity in programming. Considering the marketplace as it is today and the many significant changes that have occurred since 1992, the FCC has not identified a sufficient basis for imposing upon cable operators the "special obligations," *Turner I,* 512 U.S. at 641, represented by the 30% subscriber limit....

We hold the 30% subscriber limit is arbitrary and capricious because the Commission failed adequately to take account of the substantial competition cable operators face from non-cable video programming distributors. The petition for review is therefore granted and the subscriber limit is, accordingly, *Vacated.*

Notes and Questions

a. What is the purpose of the must carry rules? Why has the issue been so heavily litigated by the cable industry?

b. Was *Turner's* claim of First Amendment compelled speech a credible argument, or was this simply a legal box into which the cable operator wished to frame a tug-of-war over valuable cable licenses?

c. In 1999, Congress extended some of the rules of the cable industry to the burgeoning satellite industry. The Satellite Home Viewer Improvement Act of 1999 (SHVIA) was immediately challenged by industry on grounds similar to that of *Turner.* In *Satellite Broad. & Communs. Ass'n v. FCC,* 275 F.3d 337 (4th Cir. 2001), the court explained that

> By enacting SHVIA, Congress sought to promote competition between the satellite and cable industries by creating a statutory copyright license that allows satellite carriers to carry the signals of local broadcast television stations without obtaining authorization from the holders of copyrights in the individual programs aired by those stations. The Act also imposes a 'carry one, carry all' rule, which was designed to 'preserve free television for those not served by satellite or cable and to promote widespread dissemination of information from a multiplicity of sources.'

The 'carry one, carry all' rule is arguably less intrusive than the must carry provisions for cable regulation because satellite companies have a choice. If they elect to utilize the statutory copyright for any local broadcast, the satellite provider must carry all local stations which request carriage in the local market. The Fourth Circuit found this a content neutral regulation that was narrowly tailored to the continuing mission of maintaining free over-the-air television.

d. With the growing popularity of satellite television and the incipient move to Internet-based delivery of television or television-like programming, will these decisions survive the next wave in technological evolution, or will over-the-air broadcasting always have a unique regulatory scheme?

e. The definitions of local markets impact the must carry regulations and the 'carry one, carry all' rule. In addition, these definitions impact the calculations for advertising revenue and sales coverage for syndicated television programming. A television station on the fringe of a market may benefit from lower costs to obtain programming, but it then risks being omitted from the increasingly critical must carry rules.

f. Given the continuing problems facing digital piracy, the FCC has attempted to intercede with antipiracy technology that prohibits the redistribution of a broadcast signal.

The FCC tried to "assure that DTV broadcast content will not be indiscriminately redistributed over the Internet, while protecting consumers' ability to view and record video content in a manner to which they have become accustomed."[11] The broadcast flag allowed a digital signal to be copied once, but would block a second copying of that program. The regulation, however, has been judged to greatly exceed the FCC's regulatory authority.

> It is axiomatic that administrative agencies may issue regulations only pursuant to authority delegated to them by Congress. The principal question presented by this case is whether Congress delegated authority to the Federal Communications Commission ("Commission" or "FCC") in the Communications Act of 1934, ("Communications Act" or "Act"), to regulate apparatus that can receive television broadcasts when those apparatus are not engaged in the process of receiving a broadcast transmission. In the seven decades of its existence, the FCC has never before asserted such sweeping authority. Indeed, in the past, the FCC has informed Congress that it lacked any such authority. In our view, nothing has changed to give the FCC the authority that it now claims....

> In November 2003, the Commission adopted "broadcast flag" regulations, requiring that digital television receivers and other devices capable of receiving digital television broadcast signals, manufactured on or after July 1, 2005, include technology allowing them to recognize the broadcast flag. The broadcast flag is a digital code embedded in a DTV broadcasting stream, which prevents digital television reception equipment from redistributing broadcast content. The broadcast flag affects receiver devices only *after* a broadcast transmission is complete....

> In this case, all relevant materials concerning the FCC's jurisdiction — including the words of the Communications Act of 1934, its legislative history, subsequent legislation, relevant case law, and Commission practice — confirm that the FCC has no authority to regulate consumer electronic devices that can be used for receipt of wire or radio communication when those devices are not engaged in the process of radio or wire transmission.

Am. Library Ass'n v. FCC, 406 F.3d 689, 691, 708 (D.C. Cir. 2005) (citations omitted).

g. The FCC has been more successful at extending the prohibition against cable systems enforcing exclusive agreements with affiliated cable programming networks or channels. Because cable systems often have local monopolies or near monopolies, the FCC and Congress were concerned about the availability of content from cable programming networks owned by the cable systems. Congress enacted the Cable Television Consumer Protection and Competition Act of 1992, which prohibited many exclusive contracts between cable systems and affiliated programming networks. Despite challenges on a variety of grounds, the extension of the anti-exclusivity prohibitions were upheld, extending the ban for an additional five year period. See *Cablevision Sys. Corp. v. FCC*, 597 F.3d 1306 (D.C. Cir. 2010).

Market changes have made this prohibition less relevant. The FCC has allowed the rule to sunset, opting for "a case-by-case process will remain in place after the prohibi-

---

11. *In the Matter of: Digital Broadcast Content Protection,* 18 FCC Rcd 23550 (2003) (Broadcast Flag Order).

tion expires to assess the impact of individual exclusive contracts." *In the Matter of Rev. of the Commn.'s Program Access R.*, 27 F.C.C. Rcd. 12605, 12608 (F.C.C. 2012).

h. The FCC has been less successful at regulating the cable systems acting as Internet Service Providers (ISPs). In 2007, Comcast reduced or blocked bandwidth to some customers who were deemed by Comcast to make excessive use of the network, generally those using peer-to-peer networks. The FCC brought an action against Comcast because its actions violated the FCC's Internet Policy Statement that "consumers are entitled to access the lawful Internet content of their choice ... [and] to run applications and use services of their choice." The FCC claimed jurisdiction to regulate Comcast's network management practices and resolve the dispute through adjudication rather than through rulemaking. The FCC then found Comcast's bandwidth management violated federal policy. The D.C. Circuit found the FCC did not have the jurisdiction it asserted, dismissing the action against Comcast. See *Comcast Corp. v. FCC*, 600 F.3d 642 (D.C. Cir. 2010).

In response, the FCC Chairman issued a statement[12] outlining a plan for business model regulation of ISPs. Labeled "the third way" by Chairman Genachowski, the proposal calls for regulation focusing on competition and access but refrains from regulating content:

> Consumers do need basic protection against anticompetitive or otherwise unreasonable conduct by companies providing the broadband access service (e.g., DSL, cable modem, or fiber) to which consumers subscribe for *access* to the Internet. It is widely accepted that the FCC needs backstop authority to prevent these companies from restricting lawful innovation or speech, or engaging in unfair practices, as well as the ability to develop policies aimed at connecting all Americans to broadband, including in rural areas....
>
> • Advancing the critical goals of protecting Americans against cyber-attacks, extending 911 coverage to broadband communications, and otherwise protecting the public's safety; and
>
> • Working to preserve the freedom and openness of the Internet through high-level rules of the road to safeguard consumers' right to connect with whomever they want; speak freely online; access the lawful products and services of their choice; and safeguard the Internet's boundless promise as a platform for innovation and communication to improve our education and health care, and help deliver a clean energy future.
>
> At the same time, I have been clear about what the FCC should *not* do in the area of broadband communications: For example, FCC policies should not include regulating Internet content, constraining reasonable network management practices of broadband providers, or stifling new business models or managed services that are pro-consumer and foster innovation and competition. FCC policies should also recognize and accommodate differences between management of wired networks and wireless networks, including the unique congestion issues posed by spectrum-based communications....

Id.

---

12. Julius Genachowski, The Third Way: A Narrowly Tailored Broadband Framework, Statement of FCC Chairman, May 6, 2010, http://hraunfoss.fcc.gov/edocs_public/attachmatch/DOC-297944 A1.pdf.

D. Bibliography and Links

John Blevins, *The New Scarcity: A First Amendment Framework for Regulating Access to Digital Media Platforms*, 79 Tenn. L. Rev. 353 (2012).

Mark Cenite, *Federalizing or Eliminating Online Obscenity Law as an Alternative to Contemporary Community Standards*, 9 Comm. L. & Pol'y 25 (2004).

Rob Frieden, *Adjusting the Horizontal and Vertical in Telecommunications Regulation: A Comparison of the Traditional and a New Layered Approach*, 55 Fed. Comm. L.J. 207 (2003).

Daniel Brenner, *"Gently Down the Stream": When Is an Online Performance Public Under Copyright?*, 28 Berkeley Tech. L.J. 1167, 1168 (2013).

Nick Gamse, *The Indecency of Indecency: How Technology Affects the Constitutionality of Content-Based Broadcast Regulation*, 22 Fordham Intell. Prop. Media & Ent. L.J. 287 (2012).

Patrick M. Garry, *The Flip Side of the First Amendment: A Right to Filter*, 2004 Mich. St. L. Rev. 57 (2004).

Eldar Haber, *Copyrights in the Stream: The Battle on Webcasting*, 28 Santa Clara Computer & High Tech. L.J. 769 (2012).

Michael Kaneb, *Neither Realistic nor Constitutionally Sound: The Problem of the FCC's Community Standard for Broadcast Indecency Determinations*, 49 B.C. L. Rev. 1081 (2008).

Leslie Kendrick, *Content Discrimination Revisited*, 98 Va. L. Rev. 231 (2012).

Matthew S. Schwartz, *A Decent Proposal: The Constitutionality of Indecency Regulation on Cable and Direct Broadcast Satellite Services*, 13 Rich. J.L. & Tech. 17 (2007).

Joel Timmer, *The Seven Dirty Words you can say on Cable and DBS: Extending Broadcast Indecency Regulation and the First Amendment*, 10 Comm. L. & Pol'y 179 (2005).

Hannibal Travis, *The FCC's New Theory of the First Amendment*, 51 Santa Clara L. Rev. 417 (2011).

R. George Wright, *Broadcast Regulation and the Irrelevant Logic of Strict Scrutiny*, 2012, 37 J. Legis. 179 (2012).

Christopher S. Yoo, *Rethinking the Commitment to Free, Local Television*, 52 Emory L.J. 1579 (2003).

Websites

Federal Communications Commission, www.FCC.gov

The European Institute for the Media (EIM), http://www.eim.org/ ("a think tank for research and strategy concerning developments in European media and communications, based in Düsseldorf and Paris")

Columbia Institute for Tele-Information, New York (www.citi.columbia.edu)

Chapter XVI

Publishing

A. Overview

As in every other entertainment industry, the pairing of computers with the Internet has begun to impact publishing, an industry which dates back to the invention of the Gutenberg press. At the retail level, the dominance of Amazon.com and barnesandnoble.com have impacted the retail market, but perhaps less than the importance of Costco, Sam's Club, and Walmart as retail outlets for books and other published materials. The quaint, local bookshop has become a coffee house, and books are sold (along with DVDs, CDs, and other merchandise) at ever-larger discount retail outlets or through the two principal Internet retailers. An even greater upheaval is underway as more readers are turning to tablets, making Amazon and Apple the leaders in electronic book distribution on the Kindle and iPad formats. Barnes & Noble has struggled with the Nook to remain a relevant competitor in ebooks.

Computers have made the production of publications a much less complicated and time-consuming enterprise. The increased pace of production, however, does not necessarily improve the quality of the output. The number of books published has continued to rise steadily in the past few decades, which has added pressure on the publishers to finance and promote an ever-decreasing percentage of the published titles. Just as in other crowded and highly competitive segments of the entertainment industries, publishers have found it is the ability to market and promote that drives success.

Books tend to be perennials. Academic assignments, bibles, Shakespeare, and similar works provide economic balance for publishers and booksellers, which otherwise rely on the hot new books touted on the best-sellers list. As a result, a publisher's "backlist" or catalog of books that are in print from prior years serves as a considerable part the of publisher's revenue. (This is also true in the music recording industry.) New technologies may change this historical balance in two ways. Electronic versions of public domain materials may decrease the value of backlist printings, while efficiencies in print technologies will decrease the manufacturing and distribution costs of copyrighted works. In addition, copyright piracy is eroding the markets for reprints, anthologies, and other secondary sources of author revenues.

1. Bookstores and eBooks

Throughout the last century, legal issues in publishing tended to focus on chain booksellers such as Barnes & Noble and Waldenbooks. *Publishers Weekly* noted that there were 1,100 fewer bookstores in 2011 than in 1991.[1] While Barnes & Noble and Waldenbooks remain the first and second largest chain stores focused on publishing, many of the regional chain stores are no longer in business. Crown Books, Kroch's & Brentano's, Borders Books, and Lauriat's Books are all out of business.

What has emerged is a rapidly growing trend for ebooks read on tablets and mobile devices. Although Amazon.com did not create the first ebook reader, Amazon's integration of the Kindle reader with its online bookstore dominated the marketplace. By 2009, Amazon had 90% of the ebook market share. Apple entered the market with the iPad and a strong movement into book sales in the iTunes marketplace. Barnes & Noble offers a competing service through its Nook devices, but has not become a serious competitor to Amazon or Apple.

The sale of ebooks and the aggressive pricing strategy used by Amazon has resulted in changes to standard publishing agreements by the publishers and to antitrust violations between many of the publishers and Apple.

2. Print-on-Demand

A segment of the publishing industry once known as the vanity press served a specialized niche market that enabled individuals to self-publish books. Printing technology has transformed the ability to produce very small quantities of books economically. This technology has transformed the vanity press industry. Combined with ebooks, these services have eliminated virtually all barriers to publishing.

A number of online publishers provide high quality, low volume self-publishing enterprises which are perfect for small projects or those who wish to direct-market their wares. These companies feature the ability to print-on-demand, allowing the books to be created, packaged and shipped individually as orders arrive. These services typically tie closely with ebook publishing so that the author can offer both online and physical distribution without prohibitively high production and warehouse costs.

Ebooks and print-on-demand technology are forcing publishers and authors to redefine the concept of the term "out of print." Books need not ever be unavailable or go out of print. Future agreements may have to redefine reversionary interests based on a book's sales, the promotional activities of the publisher, or other measures relevant to the particular transaction.

3. Inter-Media Integration

Increasingly, published works tend to be impacted by film, television and other popular media. The book *Seabiscuit* was propelled to many best-sellers lists because of the suc-

---

1. Jim Milliot, Tracking 20 Years of Bookstore Chains, Publishers Weekly, Aug 26, 2011 at http://www.publishersweekly.com/pw/by-topic/industry-news/bookselling/article/48473-tracking-20-years-of-bookstore-chains.html.

cess of the motion picture adaptation. Similarly, the success of each film in the *Lord of the Rings* trilogy further propelled the backlist works of Tolkien. The trend towards inter-media integration is perhaps the strongest trend that will be seen over the next decade. Despite poor internal integration in most media conglomerates, the promotional opportunities are maximized when books, comics, and video/computer games are tied directly to television and motion picture production. These combinations will increasingly drive the need to hit "homeruns" to finance entertainment companies.

4. Changes in Studies on Readership

A series of reports by the National Endowment for the Arts raised dramatic concerns regarding the literary competency of the adult American population. The 2004 report stated that fewer than half of American adults were reading literature, with a 28 percent decline occurring among the youngest age groups.[2] Then the publishing phenomenon of J.K. Rowling's *Harry Potter* series swept through the literary world. Selling at least 400 million books worldwide in 67 languages and over 200 territories, the book spawned movies, games, an explosion of juvenile literature, and reading. While it may ascribe too much to one author, the reversal in the decline of literary reading correlates directly with the popularity of the series. The 2009 report showed that "for the first time in over a quarter-century, our survey shows that literary reading has risen among adult Americans. After decades of declining trends, there has been a decisive and unambiguous increase among virtually every group measured in this comprehensive national survey."

B. Author Agreements and Delivery Requirements

Chodos v. W. Publ. Co.
292 F.3d 992 (9th Cir. 2002)

This case presents the question whether a publisher retains the right to reject an author's manuscript written pursuant to a standard industry agreement, even though the manuscript is of the quality contemplated by both parties. In this case, attorney Rafael Chodos entered into a standard Author Agreement with the Bancroft-Whitney Publishing Company under which he agreed to write a treatise on the intriguing subject of the law of fiduciary duty. The agreement is widely used in the publishing industry for traditional literary works as well as for specialized volumes. Bancroft-Whitney thought that the treatise would be successful commercially and that it would result in substantial profits for both the author and the publisher. After Chodos had spent a number of years fulfilling his part of the bargain and had submitted a completed manuscript, Bancroft-Whitney's successor, the West Publishing Company, came to a contrary conclusion. It declined to publish the treatise, citing solely sales and marketing reasons. Like a good lawyer, Chodos responded by suing for damages, first for breach of contract, and then, after amend-

---

2. NATIONAL ENDOWMENT FOR THE ARTS NEWS ROOM, LITERARY READING IN DRAMATIC DECLINE, ACCORDING TO NATIONAL ENDOWMENT, FOR THE ARTS SURVEY (July 8, 2004), http://www.nea.gov/news/news04/ReadingAtRisk.html.

ing his complaint to drop that claim, in quantum meruit. The district court held that under the terms of the contract West's decision not to publish was within its discretion, and granted summary judgment in West's favor. Chodos appeals, and we reverse.

Rafael Chodos is a California attorney whose specialty is the law of fiduciary duty. His practice consists primarily of matters involving fiduciary issues such as partnership disputes, corporate dissolutions, and joint ventures.... In July, 1995, Bancroft and Chodos entered into an Author Agreement, which both parties agree is a standard form contract used to govern the composition of a literary work for hire.

The Author Agreement provided for no payments to Chodos prior to publication, and a 15% share of the gross revenues from sales of the work. Farber informed Chodos that a typical successful title published by Bancroft grossed $1 million over a five-year period, although Chodos's work, of course, might be more or less successful than the average. Chodos sought publication of the work not only for the direct financial rewards, but also for the enhanced professional reputation he might receive from the publication of a treatise, which in turn might result in additional referrals to his practice and increased fees for him.

From July, 1995 through June, 1998, Chodos's principal professional activity was the writing of the treatise. He significantly limited the time spent on his law practice, and devoted several hours each morning as well as most weekends to the book project. Chodos estimates that he spent at least 3600 hours over the course of three years on writing the treatise and developing the accompanying electronic materials. He did so with the guidance of Bancroft staff. For example, in late 1995 or early 1996, Farber instructed Chodos that because Bancroft viewed the book as a practice aid and not as an academic work, he should delete an introductory chapter that was primarily historical and disperse the historical material throughout the text, in footnote form. As Chodos completed each of the chapters, he submitted them to Bancroft on a CD-ROM; the seventh and final chapter was sent to the publisher in February, 1998. When finished, the book consisted of 1247 pages.

In mid-1996, Bancroft-Whitney was purchased by the West Publishing Group, and the two entities merged at the end of the year. The Bancroft editors, now employed by West, continued to work with Chodos in preparing the work for publication, although West did establish a management position that ultimately had a direct bearing on Chodos's career as a treatise-writer, that of Director of Product Development and Management for the Western Market Center. Between February and June, 1998, after the entire treatise had been submitted, Chodos reviewed the manuscript to ensure that the formatting was consistent and that no substantive gaps existed. In the summer of 1998 the West editors provided him with detailed notes and suggestions, to which he diligently responded. In November, 1998, West again sent Chodos a lengthy letter including substantive editorial suggestions related to the organization of the book. In early December, 1998, West sent Chodos yet another letter, this time apologizing for delays in publication, and assuring him that publication would take place in the first quarter of 1999. Burt Levy, who replaced Farber as Chodos's editor, informed Chodos that copy editors were preparing the manuscript for release in the early part of that year.

After receiving no communication from Levy in January, 1999, Chodos contacted West to check on the status of his treatise. On February 4, 1999, Chodos received a response from Nell Petri, a member of the marketing department. Petri informed Chodos that West had decided not to publish the book because it did not "fit within [West's] current product mix" and because of concerns about its "market potential." West admits, however, that the manuscript was of "high quality" and that its decision was not due to any literary shortcomings in Chodos's work.

The decision not to publish the treatise on fiduciary duty was made by Carole Gamble, who joined West as Director of Product Development and Management for the Western Market Center at about the same time that Chodos completed the manuscript. In late 1998, West developed new internal criteria to guide publication decisions. Applying these criteria, Gamble decided not to go forward with the publication of the treatise. She did not in fact read what Chodos had written, but instead reviewed a detailed outline of the treatise and the original proposal for it. Gamble did not prepare a business analysis prior to making her decision. After Chodos informed West that in his view the publisher had breached its contract, West did prepare an economic projection that concluded that the publication of Chodos's work would be an unprofitable venture. Thus, this legal action was born....

Chodos makes two alternative arguments: first, that the standard Author Agreement is an illusory contract, and second, that if a valid contract does exist, West breached it. Under either theory of liability, Chodos contends that he is entitled to recover in quantum meruit.

A. The Author Agreement Is Not Illusory.

In support of his first argument, Chodos correctly notes that in order for a contract to be enforceable under California law, it must impose binding obligations on each party. The California Supreme Court has held that "if one of the promises leaves a party free to perform or to withdraw from the agreement at his own unrestricted pleasure, the promise is deemed illusory and it provides no consideration." Chodos contends that because the contract required him to produce a work of publishable quality, but allowed West, in its discretion, to decide unilaterally whether or not to publish his work, the contract violates the doctrine of mutuality of obligation and is therefore illusory.

California law, like the law in most states, provides that a covenant of good faith and fair dealing is an implied term in every contract. Thus, a court will not find a contract to be illusory if the implied covenant of good faith and fair dealing can be read to impose an obligation on each party. The covenant of good faith "finds particular application in situations where one party is invested with a discretionary power affecting the rights of another." It is correct that the agreement at issue imposes numerous obligations on the author but gives the publisher "the right in its discretion to terminate" the publishing relationship after receiving the manuscript and determining that it is unacceptable. However, we conclude that the contract is not illusory because West's duty to exercise its discretion is limited by its duty of good faith and fair dealing. More specifically, because the standard Author Agreement obligates the publisher to make a judgment as to the quality or literary merit of the author's work—to determine whether the work is "acceptable" or "unacceptable"—it must make that judgment in good faith, and cannot reject a manuscript for other, unrelated reasons. Thus, Chodos's first argument fails.

B. West Breached the Agreement.

Chodos's alternative argument—that a contract exists and it was breached—is more persuasive. West contends that the Author Agreement allowed it to decline to publish the manuscript after Chodos completed writing it for *any* good-faith reason, regardless of whether the reason was related to the quality or literary merit of Chodos's manuscript. However, West's right to terminate the agreement is a limited one defined in two related provisions of the agreement. The first, the "acceptance clause," establishes that West may decline to publish Chodos's manuscript if it finds the work to be "unacceptable" in form and content. The acceptance clause, paragraph eight of the agreement, provides that:

> After timely receipt of the Work or any portion of the Work prepared by Author, Publisher shall review it as to both form and content, and notify Author whether it is acceptable or unacceptable in form and content under the terms of this Agreement. In the event that Publisher determines that the Work or any portion of the Work is unacceptable, Publisher shall notify Author of Publisher's determination and Publisher may exercise its rights under paragraph 4.

The second relevant provision (referred to in the acceptance clause as West's "rights under paragraph 4") allows West to terminate the publishing agreement if the author does not cure a failure in performance after being given an opportunity to do so. This provision, numbered paragraph four of the contract and entitled "Author's Failure to Perform," states:

> If Publisher determines that the Work or any portion of it is not acceptable to publisher as provided in paragraph 8 [the acceptance clause] ... after thirty (30) days following written notice to author if Author has not cured such failure in performance Publisher has the right in its discretion to terminate this Agreement.

The district court agreed with West that in determining whether a manuscript is satisfactory in form and content under the acceptance clause of the standard Author Agreement, the publisher may in good faith consider solely the likelihood of a book's commercial success and other similar economic factors. We unequivocally reject the view that the relevant provisions of the Author Agreement may be so construed in the absence of additional language or conditions.

The expansive reading of the acceptance clause suggested by West is inconsistent with the language of the two contract clauses. Under the agreement, the publisher may deem a manuscript unacceptable only if it is deficient in "form and content." Thus, had Chodos submitted a badly written, poorly researched, disorganized or substantially incomplete work to West, the publisher would have been well within its rights to find that submission unacceptable under the acceptance clause—as it would were it to reject any work that it believed in good faith lacked literary merit. A publisher bargains for a product of a certain quality and is entitled to reject a work that in its good faith judgment falls short of the bargained-for standard. Nothing in the contract, however, suggests that the ordinary meaning of the words "form and content" was not intended, and nowhere in the contract does it state that the publisher may terminate the agreement if it changes its management structure or its marketing strategy, or if it revises its business or economic forecasts, all matters unrelated to "form and content".

To the contrary, the fact that the contract required West to afford Chodos an opportunity to cure any deficient performance supports our straightforward reading of the acceptance clause as a provision that relates solely to the quality or literary merit of a submitted work. As noted above, if West determined that Chodos's submission was unacceptable, he was to be given a period of time to cure his failure in performance. The inclusion of this provision indicates that a deficiency in "form and content" is one that the author has some power to cure. Chodos has no power to "cure" West's view that the marketplace for books on fiduciary duty had changed; nor could he "cure" a change in West's overall marketing strategy and product mix; nor, indeed, could he be expected to do much about a general downturn in economic conditions. The text and structure of the contract thus demonstrate that West's stated reasons for terminating the agreement were not among those contemplated by the parties.

The uncontroverted evidence in this case is that Chodos worked diligently in cooperation with West—indeed, with West's encouragement—to produce a work that met the highest professional standard, and that he was successful in that venture. His performance was induced by an agreement that permitted rejection of the completed manuscript only for deficiencies in "form and content." Chodos thus labored to complete a work of high quality with the expectation that, if he did so, it would be published. He devoted thousands of hours of labor to the venture, and passed up substantial professional opportunities, only for West to decide that due to the vagaries of its internal reorganizations and changes in its business strategies or in the national economy or the market for legal treatises, his work, albeit admittedly of high quality, was for naught. It would be inequitable, if not unconscionable, for an author to be forced to bear this considerable burden solely because of his publisher's change in management, its poor planning, or its inadequate financial analyses at the time it entered into the contract, or even because of an unexpected change in the market place. Moreover, to allow a publisher to escape its contractual obligations for these reasons would be directly contrary to both the language and the spirit of the standard Author Agreement.

West urges us to affirm the district court's ruling because, in its view, it is well-accepted that, regardless of the contract's failure to mention economic circumstances or market demands, publishers have broad discretion under the acceptance clause of the standard Author Agreement to reject manuscripts for any good faith commercial reason. For this proposition, the district court cited two cases from the Second Circuit involving that same clause. Although at least one of the cases contains dicta that would support the district court's decision, both are distinguishable factually and legally. Moreover, to the extent that either case suggests that a publisher bound by the standard Author Agreement may terminate the contract for *any* reason so long as it acts in good faith, we respectfully reject that view.

In *Doubleday & Co. v. Curtis,* 763 F.2d 495, 496 (2d Cir. 1985), a publisher rejected a manuscript by the well-known actor but neophyte author, Tony Curtis, on the basis of its poor literary quality. There, as here, the publishing agreement allowed the publisher to reject a submission if it was not satisfactory as to "form and content." However, in *Doubleday,* in direct contrast to the circumstances here, it was agreed that the manuscript was *unsatisfactory* in form and content. In *Doubleday,* Curtis's claim was that the publisher had a good-faith obligation under the contract to re-write his admittedly unsatisfactory manuscript and to transform it into one of publishable quality. The Second Circuit held that a publisher's good faith obligation does not stretch that far; thus, the Second Circuit's essential holding in *Doubleday* has no bearing on the present case.

It is true that the Second Circuit appears to have stated its holding in *Doubleday* more broadly than the case before the court warranted. The court said:

> We hold that a publisher may, in its discretion, terminate a standard publishing contract, provided that the termination is made in good faith, and that the failure of an author to submit a satisfactory manuscript was not caused by the publisher's bad faith.

> Still, read in context, the holding does not make it clear whether the court meant that a publisher may reject a manuscript for reasons wholly unrelated to its literary worth or that it may do so only if it determines in good faith that the submitted work is unsatisfactory on its literary merits. If the former is the Second Circuit's view of the law, we respectfully disagree.

The district court also relied on *Random House, Inc. v. Gold,* 464 F. Supp. 1306 (S.D.N.Y. 1979). That case is more apposite than *Doubleday* in that the district court there held that a publisher may consider economic circumstances when evaluating a manuscript's "form and content" under the standard publishing agreement. Although we disagree with that holding for the reasons set forth above, and are certainly not bound by it, we note that even in *Random House* the court did not go so far as to state that economic considerations may be the *sole* reason for a publisher to decline to publish a manuscript that is in every other respect acceptable. In *Random House*, as in *Doubleday*, the submitted manuscript was not of publishable quality. In contrast to Chodos's work, the editor at Random House considered the manuscript at issue to be "shallow and badly designed."

In sum, we reject the district court's determination that West acted within the discretion afforded it by the Author Agreement when it decided not to publish Chodos's manuscript. Because West concedes that the manuscript was of high quality and that it declined to publish it solely for commercial reasons rather than because of any defect in its form and content, we hold as a matter of law that West breached its agreement with Chodos.

C. Chodos May Pursue A Quantum Meruit Claim.

The district court ruled that if West breached the contract, Chodos could proceed in quantum meruit, but only if the damages were not determinable under the contract.... Here, it is impossible to determine even now what those revenues would have been had West not frustrated the completion of the contract. Had West honored its contractual obligations and published the treatise, the revenues would have depended on any number of circumstances, including how West chose to market the book, and how it was received by readers and critics....

It might also be reasonably argued that West's publishing of Chodos's treatise was an additional element of consideration to which Chodos was entitled.... Because West breached its contract with Chodos by rejecting his manuscript for a reason not permitted by the contract between the parties and because Chodos is entitled to recover for the breach in quantum meruit, we REVERSE the district court's grant of summary judgment in West's favor, and REMAND the case to the district court with instructions to enter summary judgment as to liability in Chodos's favor, and for further proceedings consistent with this opinion ...

Helprin v. Harcourt, Inc.
277 F. Supp. 2d 327 (S.D.N.Y. 2003)

Plaintiff Mark Helprin ("Helprin") filed a complaint (the "Complaint") against Defendants Harcourt Brace Jovanovich, Inc. ("HBJ") and Harcourt, Inc. (together with HBJ, "Harcourt") alleging that Harcourt ... breached [a publishing agreement between Helprin and Harcourt the ("Agreement")] by (i) failing to publish Helprin's second work produced pursuant to the Agreement, (ii) improperly accounting for interest that accrued on the unrecouped portion of the advance paid to Helprin under the Agreement (the "Excluded Claim"), and (iii) failing to expend the required amounts for promotion of Helprin's first work produced pursuant to the Agreement....

Both parties acknowledge that Helprin is a world-famous, talented author whose previous works have earned both commercial and critical acclaim. In addition, both parties agree that in 1989, Helprin and Harcourt entered into the Agreement, which obligated Helprin to produce five works (the "Works") over an indefinite time period in exchange for, among other things, a $2,000,000 advance (the "Advance") and royalties from sales of the Works. In conjunction with the signing of the Agreement, Harcourt purchased a $2,000,000 insurance policy (the "Policy") on Helprin's life to protect Harcourt in the event that Helprin died before he was able to fulfill his obligations under the Agreement. Finally, both parties concur that in 1995, Harcourt published the first Work by Helprin under the Agreement, entitled Memoir from Antproof Case (the "First Work"), and Helprin did not submit a draft of his next Work (the "Contested Work") until October 24, 2002. Past those points of agreement lie the contested issues of the instant litigation.

In the Complaint, Helprin alleges he received no response to his submission of the Contested Work until December 17, 2002, when Dan Farley, president of Harcourt, informed Helprin via letter that Harcourt was rejecting the Contested Work for publication because it was "unacceptable as defined in paragraph 16 of the Agreement." In the Agreement, the standard for determining what constitutes an "acceptable" Work is described as follows:

> "A Work shall be "acceptable" under this Agreement if such Work meets a standard comparable to the literary merit of [Helprin's] previous works."

The Agreement further stated that in the event Harcourt did reject a Work because it was not acceptable, Heplrin would regain all rights with respect to such Work upon notice of the rejection. Helprin then would be obligated to use his best efforts to sell the Work to another publisher, and some of the payments he received from such a deal would first go to Harcourt to reimburse it for certain portions of the Advance that went unrecouped because of the rejection.

Helprin alleges that Harcourt's rejection of the Contested Work was a breach of contract motivated by Harcourt's belief that the Contested Work would not be commercially successful and by Harcourt's desire to avoid spending money on advertising and promoting the Contested Work. Helprin also alleges that Harcourt breached the Agreement by failing to make promotional expenditures for the First Work as required under the Agreement, which states:

> [Harcourt] agrees to allocate a budget of not less than one hundred thousand dollars ($100,000.00) per Work to be used at [Harcourt's] discretion for out-of-house advertising and promotion with respect to first hardcover publication of each Work in the United States, including the costs of [Harcourt's] reimbursement of cooperative advertising expenditures of its wholesalers or dealers.

Moreover, Helprin alleges that Harcourt made intentional misstatements in an effort to conceal this failure to expend the required promotional amounts, thus committing fraud....

Helprin's first claim for relief alleges that Harcourt breached the Agreement when it rejected the Contested Work. Harcourt responds that paragraph 8 of the Agreement prevents Helprin from instigating a lawsuit because it provides that

> if a Work is not published within the time provided in Paragraph 6 ... [Helprin] may thereafter request [Harcourt] by written notice ... to publish such Work within six months after [Harcourt's] receipt of [Helprin's] request. If, after receipt of such notice, [Harcourt] fails to publish such Work within such period, this Agreement will terminate with respect to such Work immediately and automatically at the end of such period, all rights to such Work will revert to [Helprin] on the effective date of termination without further obligation or liability on the part of [Harcourt], and [Helprin] will have the right to retain any advances previously paid, but will be entitled to no other compensation, remedy, or damages, and [Helprin] will retain the right to sell such Work to another publisher and retain the proceeds. [Harcourt's] failure to publish a Work that it has accepted according to the provisions of paragraphs 16 and 17 hereof will not alter the conditions under which [Helprin] is deemed to have satisfied his obligation in regard to such Work.

Paragraph 6 requires that "within eighteen months after delivery and acceptance of the final revised manuscript of a Work hereunder, [Harcourt] will publish such Work at its own expense," and Harcourt contends that the Contested Work is an acceptable Work for purposes of paragraphs 6 and 8—despite Harcout's rejection of it—because "Helprin has pleaded [in the Complaint] that [the Contested Work] met the standards of paragraph 16(a) and therefore under that paragraph's express terms it is deemed to be accepted by Harcourt."

1. What Constitutes an "Acceptable" Work?

Harcourt's argument raises the crucial question at the heart of Helprin's claim: what constitutes an "acceptable" work under the Agreement? To answer that question, the Court first looks at paragraph 16(a) of the Agreement, which states as follows:

> [Harcourt] recognizes its obligation to give editorial assistance to [Helprin] in order to assist [him] in making the manuscript of each Work hereunder acceptable for publication by [Harcourt]. However, [Harcourt] reserves the right to determine the amount and usefulness of its editorial assistance and whether or not its editorial intervention will result in an acceptable manuscript that merits publication by [Harcourt]. A Work shall be "acceptable" under this Agreement if such Work meets a standard comparable to the literary merit of [Helprin's] previous works. When the manuscript of a Work meets the foregoing standard, [Harcourt] shall notify [Helprin] of its acceptance thereof in accordance with paragraph 17 hereof. [Helprin] recognizes [his] obligation to deliver manuscripts that are complete and acceptable in accordance herewith and to participate in the editorial process for that purpose.

Helprin contends that this paragraph was drafted in a way that "substantially alter[ed] Harcourt's] discretion in accepting or rejecting a manuscript." However, in reviewing other cases before this Court involving similar contractual obligations, the Court reaches a different conclusion.

… [T]he ultimate acceptance of a "finally" edited work is to be given "by [Harcourt]." In order for Harcourt to accept a submitted Work, it has to execute a written notice signed by an officer of the company explicitly stating Harcourt's acceptance of the Work. The second sentence's clarification that certain preliminary editorial comments and other communications to Helprin that do not explicitly express Harcourt's acceptance "do not constitute acceptance" demonstrates the intent of the parties to make clear that, as a condition precedent, Harcourt had to determine to unequivocally accept the Work in order for the acceptance to qualify under the Agreement's definition.

Another manifestation of this intent is contained in paragraph 16(c), discussed below, governing the procedure to be followed in the event Harcourt does determine that a manuscript of the Work "is not acceptable to [Harcourt]." As a result, for Harcourt now to contend in its response to Helprin's allegations that paragraph 8 is relevant because Helprin has pleaded that the Contested Work is acceptable invokes a form of circular reasoning that the Court rejects. A contract provision cannot be read to have been fulfilled simply because, in a pleading and without more, one party says so. The claim at issue does not involve Helprin's view of the quality of the Contested Work—which would most likely be favorably biased—but rather Harcourt's assertion in its letter dated December 17, 2002 that the Contested Work was not acceptable. Consequently, paragraphs 6 and 8 are inapplicable to the factual situation as Helprin has pleaded it.

2. Harcourt's Good Faith

Having rejected both Helprin's contention that the acceptability clause is distinct from other such clauses in the publishing industry and Harcourt's assertion that paragraphs 6 and 8 should govern the situation presented here, the Court turns to paragraph 16(c), which contemplates a prospect identical to the factual situation at hand:

> In the event that [Harcourt] determines in accordance with this Agreement that the manuscript of a Work is not acceptable to it, it shall so notify [Helprin] and upon such notice all rights with respect to such Work granted or transferred to [Harcourt] under this Agreement will automatically revert to [Helprin].

The paragraph continues by stating that upon such rejection, Helprin is obligated to use his best efforts to sell the Work to another publisher and, if successful, return some of the profits from that sale to Harcourt so Harcourt could recoup the portion of the Advance that applied to the Contested Work. In light of paragraph 16(c), Harcourt might be inclined to argue that it is under no obligation to publish a submission that it finds unacceptable. Harcourt does not make such an argument, perhaps in part because of the existence of a significant body of precedent in this Court that directly addresses when a publisher is permitted to reject a submitted work from an author who is under contract with that publisher.

In at least six cases in recent years with similar fact patterns to the instant case, the Court has interpreted comparable "acceptability" clauses as granting publishers wide discretion to terminate publishing contracts if the submitted draft is not acceptable, "provided that the termination is made in good faith, and that the failure of the author to submit a satisfactory manuscript was not caused by the publisher's bad faith." The Court reached these holdings based in part on analogous breach of contract cases considered by New York courts where the satisfactory performance of one party was to be judged by another party. In such cases, the New York courts required the party terminating the contract to act in good faith.

In Curtis, for example, the Court observed that:

> this principle—that a contract containing a "satisfaction clause" may be terminated only as a result of honest dissatisfaction—would seem especially appropriate in construing publishing agreements. To shield from scrutiny the already chimerical process of evaluating literary value would render the "satisfaction" clause an illusory promise, and place authors at the unbridled mercy of their editors.

Furthermore, testimony at some of the Court's cases established that publishing industry practice has always involved "significant editorial changes, and that it is 'inconceivable'... that a publisher would reject a completed manuscript written under contract, without first offering or providing some editorial assistance to revise it." [S]ee also *Goldwater,* 532 F. Supp. at 624 (observing that both parties' witnesses testified that the "custom of the trade" establishes an implied good faith obligation on the part of a publisher to engage in appropriate editorial work with the author).

Thus, in determining whether the publisher in each of the foregoing cases acted in good faith, the Court focused primarily on the amount of editorial assistance the publisher provided. A publisher that provided a "detailed and lengthy editorial analysis of the shortcomings in the plot, characters and pacing of the submitted draft" demonstrated its good faith in offering sufficient editorial assistance. A publisher that did "nothing approaching any [kind of] sensible editorial activity" and failed to provide any "comments of a detailed nature designed to give the author[ ] an opportunity to remedy defects" failed the test and could be considered in possible breach of its agreement.

Based on the Complaint, the Court finds that Helprin has pled sufficient facts to state a sufficient claim at this point in the litigation that Harcourt did not act in good faith when judging the Contested Work unacceptable. Helprin alleges that he sent the Contested Work to Harcourt, and less than two months later received a letter back saying only that the Contested Work was being rejected because it was unacceptable as defined in paragraph 16 of the Agreement. There is no indication at this stage from either party that Harcourt offered any further editorial comments or assistance, nor has it been alleged by either party that Harcourt allowed Helprin an opportunity to cure whatever defects Harcourt found in the Contested Work. As a result, the Court finds that Helprin has met his burden to state a claim with regard to breach of contract based on rejection of the Contested Work....

Helprin [further] alleges that Harcourt breached the Agreement by not expending the required amounts for the promotion of the first hardcover edition of the First Work.... Harcourt's defense raises several issues, some of which are not addressed by either party. First, does the language of the Agreement's promotion paragraph actually create a definitive contractual obligation for Harcourt to spend the entire promotional budget for the First Work (the "Budget")? Paragraph 30 states that, with regard to out-of-house advertising and promotion for the American hardcover edition of each Work, Harcourt "agrees to allocate a budget of not less than one hundred thousand dollars ($100,000.00) per Work to be used at [Harcourt's] discretion...." The Agreement's use of the verb "allocate"—which Miriam-Webster's Dictionary defines as "apportioning for a specific purpose or to particular persons or things,"—implies that, while Harcourt is obligated to reserve or earmark a minimum amount for promotion, it is not necessarily required to fully spend the money. Indeed, use of the Budget is left completely to Harcourt's discretion and the provision specifies no time frame in which Harcourt is required to spend the entire Budget.

Moreover, Harcourt is not obligated to account for the Budget, as it is required to do with respect to Helprin's royalties, nor is Helprin given any right to request an audit of the Budget, as he is allowed to with regard to his royalties. Such circumstances lend support to the interpretation that the Agreement intended to provide Harcourt free reign in utilizing what Helprin himself alleged "was substantially in excess of the average [promotional budget] in the publishing industry in June 1995, and ... more than the average for Harcourt at that time as well." However, while Helprin's claim that Harcourt breached the Agreement by not spending the full amount may not be sufficient to state a claim, neither party raises the issue of the interpretation of the promotional paragraph in their briefs on the Motion. Consequently, the Court is not inclined to dismiss the claim out of hand without the benefit of the parties' briefing of the matter....

[3. Helprin's request for Recission.]

Helprin seeks rescission of the Agreement on the ground that a material breach has occurred. "Under New York law, 'rescission is an extraordinary remedy, appropriate only where the breach is found to be material and willful, or, if not willful, so substantial and fundamental as to strongly tend to defeat the object of the parties in making the contract.'" "Courts generally permit rescission of a contract only when it appears reasonably feasible to return the parties to their respective positions prior to the contract." Harcourt contests Helprin's request, asserting that the alleged breach is not material, willful, substantial or fundamental, that Helprin has not offered to restore the status quo, and that he has an adequate remedy at law. The Court is not persuaded that the alleged breach is not significant enough to qualify for rescission. The test for determining the materiality of a breach for purposes of rescission is whether the alleged breach is "of such nature and such importance that the contract would not have been made without it." Assuming that Helprin's allegation that Harcourt rejected the Contested Work in bad faith is correct, it is fair to conclude that such a rejection could serve to undermine the entire purpose of the Agreement, which was to produce the Works for Harcourt to publish....

Finally, Harcourt asserts that Helprin's claim for breach of contract based on the rejection of the Contested Work can be adequately remedied by money damages reflecting lost royalties. This argument ignores Helprin's concerns regarding his ability to publish future Works under the Agreement and the possible lost trust between him and Harcourt that could make it difficult for a working relationship to continue in the future. If the trier of fact eventually finds these concerns have merit, money damages may not be sufficient as a remedy. Thus, at this stage of the proceeding, the Court is satisfied that Helprin's allegations on these issues demonstrate that a request for rescission should be maintained as a possible remedy should the instant case be resolved in favor of Helprin....

Dunn v. CCH Inc.

2011 U.S. Dist. LEXIS 137311, 16–30 (E.D. Mich. Nov. 30, 2011)

This is a contract case. Plaintiff Stephen J. Dunn ("Dunn") is suing defendant CCH Incorporated ("CCH") claiming that CCH breached a Publishing Agreement regarding Dunn's authorship of a treatise on IRS Tax Practice and Procedure to be published by CCH. Dunn says CCH improperly terminated the contract. Dunn claims (1) breach of contract and (2) breach of implied covenant of good faith and fair dealing....

The good faith requirement in publishing contracts comes from the implied covenant of good faith and fair dealing. The covenant of good faith and fair dealing requires a party vested with broad discretion to act reasonably and not arbitrarily or in a manner inconsistent with the reasonable expectations of the parties. It cannot, however, create new terms which do not exist in the contract. *Id.* Rather, the covenant is used as an interpretative tool by Illinois courts. Under Illinois law, a party cannot be held liable for a breach of the covenant of good faith where it acts pursuant to the terms of the contract. Therefore, the question of CCH's breach of the Publishing Agreement and its obligations under the implied covenant of good faith and fair dealing are one and the same....

2. Interpretation of Paragraph 1

The parties disagree on the interpretation of paragraph 1 of the Publishing Agreement. As set forth above, paragraph 1 provides in relevant part:

> If the Author has not delivered in form and content acceptable to the Publisher a complete manuscript and all permissions by the delivery date herein agreed to, including any delivery date pursuant to paragraph 8 with respects to any new edition of the Work, the Publisher may, if it so chooses, return all of the unpublished materials that have been submitted to the Publisher by the author and, at its sole option, terminate this Agreement by prior written notice to the Author without any liability whatsoever on the Publisher's part. Alternatively, the Publisher may, at its sole option, extend the manuscript delivery date or give the Author a reasonable amount of additional time to make changes or revisions acceptable to the Publisher (although the Publisher shall not be required to do so). Should the Author be unwilling or unable to meet the new delivery date or make changes or revisions acceptable to the Publisher in that time, the Publisher may return all unpublished materials as provided above and, at its sole option,

terminate this agreement by prior written notice to the Author, without any liability whatsoever on the Publisher's part.

Dunn says that this paragraph gives CCH the right to terminate the Publishing Agreement only if Dunn fails to deliver a completed manuscript by a deadline that is unsatisfactory to CCH. Dunn says that because it is undisputed that there was no deadline and because it is undisputed that Dunn did not fail to timely submit a "complete manuscript," he is entitled to summary judgment on his breach of contract claim because CCH undisputedly breached the Publishing Agreement.

CCH disagrees with Dunn's interpretation. CCH says there is no temporal requirement and that the question of whether CCH breached the Publishing Agreement depends upon whether CCH acted in bad faith. In other words, CCH focuses on the language that CCH could "at its sole option, terminate this Agreement" if Dunn did not "deliver[ ] in form and content acceptable to [CCH] …" and that "[s]hould the Author be unwilling or unable to meet the new delivery date or make changes or revisions acceptable to [CCH] in that time," CCH "may … at its sole option, terminate this agreement by prior written notice to the Author, without any liability whatsoever on the Publisher's part." CCH argues that Dunn's interpretation—which essentially is that CCH could not have terminated the Publishing Agreement until Dunn failed to deliver a complete treatise that was unacceptable by the deadline for the completed treatise—contradicts the express terms in the Publishing Agreement.

The Publishing Agreement could be interpreted to link the temporal element—delivery of a competed work by a deadline—with CCH's right to terminate only if the work is not acceptable when delivered by the deadline. Because it is clear that there was no deadline for the completed treatise, and Dunn had only submitted two chapters, it is not unreasonable to argue that CCH breached the Publishing Agreement by terminating Dunn's contract when it did. However, this interpretation gives [too] much leeway to the author than what reasonably could be contemplated. As CCH suggests in its papers, such an interpretation results in the untenable result that CCH could not terminate a contract, no matter how poor of quality an author's work is submitted, until the very end of the completed project. CCH's interpretation makes sense because the Publishing Agreement says that "[s]hould the Author be unwilling or unable to meet the new delivery date or make changes or revisions acceptable to CCH in that time." Under Dunn's interpretation, CCH could not terminate the Publishing Agreement until Dunn finished the entire treatise and turned in unacceptable work, wasting months of time and work. It is more reasonable that the Publishing Agreement allows CCH to terminate it if it receives unacceptable work that it does not believe can be revised to be made acceptable. Overall, Dunn is not entitled to summary judgment based on his interpretation of the Publishing Agreement.[3]

3. CCH's Good Faith

Dunn goes on, however, to argue that summary judgment is still appropriate because there is no genuine issue of material fact that CCH acted in bad faith. CCH says just the opposite—that it is entitled to summary judgment because there is no genuine issue of

---

3. Part of the problem with the Publishing Agreement as applied to this case is that it appears to be drafted to apply to a single submission, i.e. a single completed manuscript. The nature of the treatise project, as evidenced by the sequence of events, is that there are multiple submissions, i.e. chapter by chapter. Although CCH has not so argued, a reasonable interpretation would be each submitted chapter constitutes a "manuscript" within the meaning of the Publishing Agreement.

material fact that it did not act in bad faith. Both parties cite publishing cases from the Second Circuit, applying New York law. According to CCH, the lead case in this area is *Doubleday & Co. v. Curtis*, 763 F.2d 495 (2d Cir. 1985). In *Doubleday*, the contract provided that Curtis would deliver manuscripts "satisfactory to the Publisher in content and form," a contract described by the Second Circuit as a "standard industry form." The Second Circuit noted that such contracts, which allow the publisher to terminate if the work is not acceptable as to form or content, have an implied good-faith requirement, which stems from the requirement that a party vested with discretion must exercise that discretion in good faith. The Second Circuit held that "a publisher may, in its discretion, terminate a standard publishing contract, provided that the termination is made in good faith, and that the failure of an author to submit a satisfactory manuscript was not caused by the publisher's bad faith." In other words, the Second Circuit said that so long as the publisher terminates the contract due to its "honest dissatisfaction" with the work, there is no breach.

Assuming that this is the standard of good faith to be applied in publishing cases, the record shows that neither party is entitled to summary judgment. Both parties suggest that the issue boils down to one question—was CCH honestly dissatisfied with Dunn's work on the Tax Returns Chapter? There is a clear dispute of material fact as to whether Dunn was unwilling or unable to revise the chapter he submitted to make it acceptable to CCH. In other words, CCH's honest dissatisfaction is disputed. Dunn revised his first chapter to CCH's satisfaction albeit after having to make substantive revisions. However, Bornstein, apparently did not believe that Dunn was willing and/or capable of making the changes necessary to have the Tax Returns Chapter acceptable to CCH. CCH did not offer Dunn an opportunity to make revisions, as it had done with the Testimonial Privileges Chapter. While Dunn did not ask for an opportunity to revise the chapter, CCH simply told Dunn to stop working on the treatise and later terminated the Publishing Agreement. Under these circumstances, reasonable minds could differ on whether CCH breached the Publishing Agreement when it concluded that Dunn was unwilling or unable to make revisions that would be acceptable to CCH. In other words, there is sufficient doubt as to whether CCH was honestly dissatisfied with Dunn's work such that it had the right to terminate the Publishing Agreement.

B. Dunn's Damages

CCH also argues that summary judgment is appropriate because Dunn cannot establish damages. Damages are an essential element of a breach of contract claim under Illinois law. Dunn is seeking damages for lost royalties and for lost business referrals. Given that liability and damages could be bifurcated at trial, the Court declines to make a ruling on Dunn's damages at this time. However, it offers the following as it may assist the parties in charting the future course of this case, including bringing it to a resolution.

As to lost business referrals, under Illinois law, lost profits may be recovered only when there are "criteria by which they can be estimated with reasonable certainty." *Reliable Fire Equip. Co. v. Arredondo*, 405 Ill. App. 3d 708, 719 (2d Dist. 2010) (finding that plaintiff could not recover lost profits because it failed to prove that lost profits were calculable with reasonable certainty). Indeed, Illinois courts "will reverse damage awards that are based on speculation or conjecture," such as where damages are based on "false assumptions or data." *SK Hand Tool Corp. v. Dresser Indus., Inc.*, 284 Ill. App. 3d 417, 426–27 (1st Dist. 1996)....

[I]t would appear that any possible referrals that he might have received as a result of being a co-author of the P&P Treatise are too speculative to be recoverable as a matter of law. Here, discovery has closed and Dunn has not pointed to any evidence of the quantity or monetary value of his alleged lost business referrals. The only evidence is, in Dunn's words, "speculation." Thus, it seems unlikely Dunn can recover for lost business referrals.

As to his claim for future royalties, CCH says that the P&P Treatise and the Expert Treatise Library is a "new business venture" for the company and that under Illinois law, evidence of projected profits of new business ventures attempted by an established business cannot support a damages award based on lost future profits. CCH explains that the P&P Treatise was an entirely new product for CCH, being built from the ground up and, to this date—much less on August 11, 2010, the date Dunn claims CCH breached the Publishing Agreement—has no record of sales or profits because it has not been released. CCH also says that it is undisputed that the Expert Treatises Library itself was an entirely new business venture for CCH. CCH had never before published treatises and had no track record for the sales or profits associated with treatises of any kind. CCH also says that it is undisputed that Dunn's royalties would have been based exclusively on net sales of the P&P Treatise. The Publishing Agreement provided that the entire author team for the P&P Treatise would have collectively been entitled to royalties of 20% of net sales in the first year of publication and 15% of net sales thereafter. Because there are no established record of sales, CCH argues that royalties dependent upon those sales are too speculative under Illinois' new business rule.

Dunn, however, says that his royalty damages are not speculative. He first relies on historical sales of the Saltzman Treatise as a basis for future sales of the P&P Treatise, [citing cases] which hold that a similarly situated business can be used as a proxy for future profits....

Dunn's argument is not particularly persuasive. As CCH points out, while it may established in the publishing field, the venture into the treatise market was new. Illinois law seems to suggest that the new business rule applies in such a circumstance. Moreover, discovery has closed and Dunn has not designated an expert. Overall, using the Saltzman Treatise as a model for Dunn's damages is problematic....

Moreover, the actual sales of the treatises that have been released are a small fraction of the sales anticipated by the 2009 Projections. Where the 2009 Projections hoped for $494,662 in sales for 2010, the projected first year of publication, actual sales for five months of 2011, the actual first year of production were $5,997.

In the end, even if Dunn is able to establish liability, the amount of damages he would be able to recover is very likely to be far lower than the over $600,000 he is seeking.

V. Conclusion

As explained above, reasonable minds could differ on whether CCH terminated the Publishing Agreement because it was honestly dissatisfied with Dunn's work. Because Dunn was not given an opportunity to revise the second chapter and CCH simply told him to stop working altogether, following up later with a termination letter, reasonable minds could question whether CCH's actions were premature. While a full exposition of the facts at trial may show CCH acted appropriately, there is sufficient doubt in the record so as to prevent summary judgment in CCH's favor.

Notes and Questions

a. One of the more well-known disputes over delivery occurred with film star Tony Curtis, who tried his hand as a novelist. See *Doubleday & Co., Inc. v. Curtis,* 599 F. Supp. 779 (S.D.N.Y. 1984). This dispute originally set the New York standards for good faith and the right to refuse a manuscript.

b. As alluded to in the complaint brought by Helprin, the obligation of the publisher may come in the form of promotional obligations rather than merely an advance. For many authors, publishing income is not the goal but rather a step towards an increase in professional stature or public exposure, both of which afford more lucrative financial opportunities. For nonfiction authors, the opportunities may flow from being perceived as an expert in a field. For fiction writers, the larger income opportunities invariably come from either the motion picture industry or through increased paperback sales.

Rather than merely provide a budget account, authors looking for a meaningful promotional guarantee should seek to be sure that the promotional funds are allocated during a fixed period, actually expended during that period, and accounted for in audits on behalf of the author.

c. In *Zilg v. Prentice-Hall, Inc.,* 717 F.2d 671 (2d Cir. 1983), the Second Circuit rejected a claim for breach of contract when a polemic written about the history and influence of the DuPont family saw its advertising and promotional budget greatly reduced in size and the production run decreased. The Second Circuit found no best-efforts obligation to promote, only an obligation of good faith and fair dealing, so it reversed a finding of breach of contract. While the Court alluded to political influence brought by the DuPont family, it relied more heavily on the publisher's aversion to the book rather than any bad-faith actions.

d. How much work must a publisher do? Is there a minimal level of work that must go into a contractual obligation to promote and distribute a line of books, absent claims of bad faith? See *Proteus Books, Ltd. v. Cherry Lane Music Co.,* 873 F.2d 502 (2d Cir. 1989).

Problem XVI-B

Bryce is working on a new project. Through your work together, Bryce now comes to your office regularly as new deals and opportunities develop. Your association together has taught Bryce to seek advice in the earliest stages of each venture, so that problems are addressed early on in the process.

Bryce's current project is a coffee table book, a photojournalistic exposé. Bryce is supplying much of the editorial content. Jesse Yang is the photographer and photo editor. The project is to photograph the famous and near famous of the city and then write a brief introduction and caption for each picture. Some of the subjects will be asked to pose while those who are more camera shy will be photographed paparazzi-style.

The publisher loves the idea and has approved the concept. Bryce and Jesse submitted a list of probable subjects, but they both clearly explained to the publisher that the final selection of subjects would be based on availability of photographic opportunities and content. Bryce and Jesse will jointly own the copyright in the finished work, sharing royalties evenly and making editorial decisions by mutual consent.

Bryce is concerned that the publisher will not treat the book with the investment it needs. Coffee table books are expensive to produce, and Bryce wants assurances as to the quality of the final product, some guarantee that a reasonable number of books will be published, funds will be spent to promote the book, and that the publisher will not try to shorten the project or later back out of the publishing commitment.

Outline a deal memorandum that Bryce can use as a checklist to finalize negotiations with the publisher regarding the project.

C. Termination Issues

Random House, Inc. v. Rosetta Books LLC
150 F. Supp. 2d 613 (S.D.N.Y. 2001), *aff'd* 283 F.3d 490 (2d Cir. 2002)

In this copyright infringement action, Random House, Inc. seeks to enjoin Rosetta Books LLC and its Chief Executive Officer from selling in digital format eight specific works on the grounds that the authors of the works had previously granted Random House—not Rosetta Books—the right to "print, publish and sell the work[s] in book form." Rosetta Books, on the other hand, claims it is not infringing upon the rights those authors gave Random House because the licensing agreements between the publisher and the author do not include a grant of digital or electronic rights. Relying on the language of the contracts and basic principles of contract interpretation, this Court finds that the right to "print, publish and sell the work[s] in book form" in the contracts at issue does not include the right to publish the works in the format that has come to be known as the "ebook." Accordingly, Random House's motion for a preliminary injunction is denied.

In the year 2000 and the beginning of 2001, Rosetta Books contracted with several authors to publish certain of their works—including The Confessions of Nat Turner and Sophie's Choice by William Styron; Slaughterhouse-Five, Breakfast of Champions, The Sirens of Titan, Cat's Cradle, and Player Piano by Kurt Vonnegut; and Promised Land by Robert B. Parker—in digital format over the internet. On February 26, 2001 Rosetta Books launched its ebook business, offering those titles and others for sale in digital format. The next day, Random House filed this complaint accusing Rosetta Books of committing copyright infringement and tortiously interfering with the contracts Random House had with Messrs. Parker, Styron and Vonnegut by selling its ebooks. It simultaneously moved for a preliminary injunction prohibiting Rosetta from infringing plaintiff's copyrights.

Ebooks are "digital book[s] that you can read on a computer screen or an electronic device." Ebooks are created by converting digitized text into a format readable by computer software. The text can be viewed on a desktop or laptop computer, personal digital assistant or handheld dedicated ebook reading device. Rosetta's ebooks can only be read after they are downloaded into a computer that contains either Microsoft Reader, Adobe Acrobat Reader, or Adobe Acrobat eBook Reader software....

While each agreement between the author and Random House differs in some respects, each uses the phrase "print, publish and sell the work in book form" to convey rights from the author to the publisher.

1. Styron Agreements

Forty years ago, in 1961, William Styron granted Random House the right to publish The Confessions of Nat Turner. Besides granting Random House an exclusive license to "print, publish and sell the work in book form," Styron also gave it the right to "license publication of the work by book clubs," "license publication of a reprint edition," "license after book publication the publication of the work, in whole or in part, in anthologies, school books," and other shortened forms, "license without charge publication of the work in Braille, or photographing, recording, and microfilming the work for the physically handicapped," and "publish or permit others to publish or broadcast by radio or television ... selections from the work, for publicity purposes...." ...

The publisher agreed in the contract to "publish the work at its own expense and in such style and manner and at such a price as it deems suitable." The contract also contains a non-compete clause that provides, in relevant part, that "the Author agrees that during the term of this agreement he will not, without the written permission of the Publisher, publish or permit to be published any material in book or pamphlet form, based on the material in the work, or which is reasonably likely to injure its sale." Styron's contract with Random House for the right to publish Sophie's Choice, executed in 1977, is virtually identical to his 1961 contract to publish The Confessions of Nat Turner.

2. Vonnegut Agreements

Kurt Vonnegut's 1967 contract granting Random House's predecessor-in-interest Dell Publishing Co., Inc. the license to publish Slaughterhouse-Five and Breakfast of Champions follows a similar structure to the Styron agreements. Paragraph # 1 is captioned "grant of rights" and contains those rights the author is granting to the book publisher. Certain rights on the publisher's form contract are crossed out, indicating that the author reserved them for himself. One of the rights granted by the author includes the "exclusive right to publish and to license the Work for publication, after book publication ... in anthologies, selections, digests, abridgements, magazine condensations, serialization, newspaper syndication, picture book versions, microfilming, Xerox and other forms of copying, either now in use or hereafter developed."

Vonnegut specifically reserved for himself the "dramatic ... motion picture (silent and sound) ... radio broadcasting (including mechanical renditions and /or recordings of the text) ... [and] television" rights. Unlike the Styron agreements, this contract does not contain a non-compete clause.

Vonnegut's 1970 contract granting Dell the license to publish The Sirens of Titan, Cat's Cradle, and Player Piano contains virtually identical grants and reservations of rights as his 1967 contract. However, it does contain a non-compete clause, which provides that "the Author ... will not publish or permit to be published any edition, adaptation or abridgment of the Work by any party other than Dell without Dell's prior written consent."

3. Parker Agreement

Robert B. Parker's 1982 contract granting Dell the license to publish Promised Land is similar to the 1970 Vonnegut contract. Paragraph # 1 contains the "grant of rights," certain of which have been crossed out by the author. The contract does grant Random House the right to "Xerox and other forms of copying of the printed page, either now in use or hereafter developed." Parker also reserved the rights to the "dramatic ... motion picture (silent and sound) ... radio broadcasting ... television ... mechanical or electronic recordings of the text...." There is also a non-compete clause that provides, in relevant part, that "the Author ... will not, without the written permission of Dell, publish or permit to be published any material based on the material in the Work, or which is reasonably likely to injure its sale." ...

Two elements must be proven in order to establish a prima facie case of infringement: "(1) ownership of a valid copyright, and (2) copying of constituent elements of the work that are original." In this case, only the first element—ownership of a valid copyright—is at issue, since all parties concede that the text of the ebook is identical to the text of the book published by Random House.

It is well settled that although the authors own the copyrights to their works, "the legal or beneficial owner of an exclusive right under a copyright is entitled ... to institute an action for any infringement of that particular right committed while he or she is the owner of it." 17 U.S.C. § 501. The question for resolution, therefore, is whether Random House is the beneficial owner of the right to publish these works as ebooks....

[T]his Court finds that the most reasonable interpretation of the grant in the contracts at issue to "print, publish and sell the work in book form" does not include the right to publish the work as an ebook. At the outset, the phrase itself distinguishes between the pure content—i.e. "the work"—and the format of display—"in book form." The Random House Webster's Unabridged Dictionary defines a "book" as "a written or printed work of fiction or nonfiction, usually on sheets of paper fastened or bound together within covers" and defines "form" as "external appearance of a clearly defined area, as distinguished from color or material; the shape of a thing or person."

Manifestly, paragraph # 1 of each contract—entitled either "grant of rights" or "exclusive publication right"—conveys certain rights from the author to the publisher. In that paragraph, separate grant language is used to convey the rights to publish book club editions, reprint editions, abridged forms, and editions in Braille. This language would not be necessary if the phrase "in book form" encompassed all types of books. That paragraph specifies exactly which rights were being granted by the author to the publisher. Indeed, many of the rights set forth in the publisher's form contracts were in fact not granted to the publisher, but rather were reserved by the authors to themselves. For example, each of the authors specifically reserved certain rights for themselves by striking out phrases, sentences, and paragraphs of the publisher's form contract. This evidences an intent by these authors not to grant the publisher the broadest rights in their works.

Random House contends that the phrase "in book form" means to faithfully reproduce the author's text in its complete form as a reading experience and that, since ebooks concededly contain the complete text of the work, Rosetta cannot also possess those rights. While Random House's definition distinguishes "book form" from other formats that require separate contractual language—such as audio books and serialization rights—it does not distinguish other formats specifically mentioned in paragraph # 1 of the contracts, such as book club editions and reprint editions. Because the Court must, if possible, give effect to all contractual language in order to "safeguard against adopting an interpretation that would render any individual provision superfluous," Random House's definition cannot be adopted.

Random House points specifically to the clause requiring it to "publish the work at its own expense and in such a style and manner and at such a price as [Random House] deems suitable" as support for its position. However, plaintiff takes this clause out of context. It appears in paragraph # 2, captioned "Style, Price and Date of Publication," not paragraph # 1, which includes all the grants of rights. In context, the phrase simply means that Random House has control over the appearance of the formats granted to Random House in the first paragraph; i.e., control over the style of the book.

Random House also cites the non-compete clauses as evidence that the authors granted it broad, exclusive rights in their work. Random House reasons that because the authors could not permit any material that would injure the sale of the work to be published without Random House's consent, the authors must have granted the right to publish ebooks to Random House. This reasoning turns the analysis on its head. First, the grant of rights follows from the grant language alone. Second, non-compete clauses must be limited in scope in order to be enforceable in New York. Third, even if the authors did violate this provision of their Random House agreements by contracting with Rosetta Books — a point on which this Court does not opine — the remedy is a breach of contract action against the authors, not a copyright infringement action against Rosetta Books.

The photocopy clause — giving Random House the right to "Xerox and other forms of copying, either now in use or hereafter developed" — similarly does not bolster Random House's position. Although the clause does appear in the grant language paragraph, taken in context, it clearly refers only to new developments in xerography and other forms of photocopying. Stretching it to include new forms of publishing, such as ebooks, would make the rest of the contract superfluous because there would be no reason for authors to reserve rights to forms of publishing "now in use." This interpretation also comports with the publishing industry's trade usage of the phrase.

Not only does the language of the contract itself lead almost ineluctably to the conclusion that Random House does not own the right to publish the works as ebooks, but also a reasonable person "cognizant of the customs, practices, usages and terminology as generally understood in the particular trade or business," would conclude that the grant language does not include ebooks. "To print, publish and sell the work in book form" is understood in the publishing industry to be a "limited" grant.... In fact, the publishing industry generally interprets the phrase "in book form" as granting the publisher "the exclusive right to publish a hardcover trade book in English for distribution in North America." 1 LINDEY ON ENTERTAINMENT, PUBLISHING AND THE ARTS FORM 1.01-1 (2d ed. 2000) (using the Random House form contract to explain the meaning of each clause).

3. Comparison to Prior "New Use" Caselaw

The finding that the five licensing agreements at issue do not convey the right to publish the works as ebooks accords with Second Circuit and New York case law. Indeed, the two leading cases limned above that found that a particular new use was included within the grant language — *Boosey*, 145 F.3d 481 (2d Cir. 1998), and *Bartsch*, 391 F.2d 150 (2d Cir. 1968) — can be distinguished from this case on four grounds.

First, the language conveying the rights in *Boosey* and *Bartsch* was far broader than here. See *Boosey*, 145 F.3d at 486; *Bartsch*, 391 F.2d at 153. Second, the "new use" in those cases — i.e. display of a motion picture on television or videocassette — fell squarely within the same medium as the original grant. See *Boosey*, 145 F.3d at 486 (describing videocassettes and laser discs as "subsequently developed methods of distribution of a motion picture"); *Bourne*, 68 F.3d at 630 ("The term 'motion picture' reasonably can be understood to refer to 'a broad genus whose fundamental characteristic is a series of related images that impart an impression of motion when shown in succession ... Under this concept the physical form in which the motion picture is fixed — film, tape, discs, and so forth — is irrelevant.'").

In this case, the "new use" — electronic digital signals sent over the internet — is a separate medium from the original use — printed words on paper. Random House's own expert concludes that the media are distinct because information stored digitally can be manipulated in ways that analog information cannot. Ebooks take advantage of the digital medium's ability to manipulate data by allowing ebook users to electronically search the text for specific words and phrases, change the font size and style, type notes into the text and electronically organize them, highlight and bookmark, hyperlink to specific parts of the text, and, in the future, to other sites on related topics as well, and access a dictionary that pronounces words in the ebook aloud. The need for a software program to interact with the data in order to make it usable, as well as the need for a piece of hardware to enable the reader to view the text, also distinguishes analog formats from digital formats. See *Greenberg v. National Geographic Soc'y*, 244 F.3d 1267, 1273 n.12 (11th Cir. 2001) (Digital format is not analogous to reproducing the magazine in microfilm or microfiche because it "requires the interaction of a computer program in order to accomplish the useful reproduction involved with the new medium.")

Therefore, *Boosey* and *Bartsch*, which apply to new uses within the same medium, do not control this case. See, *e.g., Raine*, 25 F. Supp. 2d 434, 445 (S.D.N.Y. 1998) (finding that the right to "television broadcasts" did not include broadcasts on cable television or videocassettes); *General Mills, Inc. v. Filmtel Int'l Corp.*, 195 A.D.2d 251, 252, 599 N.Y.S.2d 820, 821–22 (1st Dep't 1993); *Tele-Pac, Inc. v. Grainger*, 168 A.D.2d 11, 570 N.Y.S.2d 521 (1st Dep't 1991) (distinguishing Second Circuit "new use" doctrine by holding that right to "broadcast[ ] by television or any other similar device now known or hereafter to be made known" was so dissimilar from display on videocassette and videodisc "as to preclude consideration of video rights as even falling within the 'ambiguous penumbra' of the terms used in the agreement").

The third significant difference between the licensee in the motion picture cases cited above and the book publisher in this action is that the licensees in the motion picture cases have actually created a new work based on the material from the licensor. Therefore, the right to display that new work—whether on television or video—is derivative of the right to create that work. In the book publishing context, the publishers, although they participate in the editorial process, display the words written by the author, not themselves.

Fourth, the courts in *Boosey* and *Bartsch* were concerned that any approach to new use problems that "tilts against licensees [here, Random House] gives rise to antiprogressive incentives" insofar as licensees "would be reluctant to explore and utilize innovative technologies." However, in this action, the policy rationale of encouraging development in new technology is at least as well served by finding that the licensors—i.e., the authors—retain these rights to their works. In the 21st century, it cannot be said that licensees such as book publishers and movie producers are ipso facto more likely to make advances in digital technology than start-up companies....

In *Dresser v. William Morrow & Co.*, 278 A.D. 931, 105 N.Y.S.2d 706 (1st Dep't 1951), aff'd 304 N.Y. 603, 107 N.E.2d 89 (N.Y. 1952), the issue was whether an author could receive additional payments for reprint editions of his book when his publishing contract only provided for an "outright fixed payment." The *Dresser* court found that, under the terms of the contract, he could not. The court relied on the fact that the contract was "at variance with the usual pattern of contracts between author and publisher." Here, although each contract is slightly different, none varies greatly from the usual pattern of contracts between author and publisher; therefore, there is no reason to depart from the usual meaning of such contracts....

Notes and Questions

a. The common practice in publishing is to allow the publishing rights to revert to the author after the book has gone out of print. In addition to the technical issues involving the concept that a book may no longer ever be out of print due to ebooks and on-demand printing facilities, standard contracts may fail to address the disposition of income received after the date of the reversion based on license agreements entered into prior to the date of reversion. The rights to those proceeds can be extensive if the license is for adaptation into new media.

b. Remedies for breach of contract may have some interesting termination issues. See *Frankel v. Stein & Day Inc.*, 1980 U.S. Dist. LEXIS 11510 (S.D.N.Y. Apr. 24, 1980) (allowing the publisher to retain a one-third interest in license income despite a revision caused by the publisher's breach of contract).

c. How could a publisher today guard against the publisher's fate in *Random House, Inc. v. Rosetta Books LLC*? Is there any contract language that could prevent technological advances from terminating the publisher's copyright? What is the proper balance between the author, publisher, and society?

d. To better understand the economics of the publishing industry, the Court in *Health Communs., Inc. v. Chicken Soup for the Soul Publ'g, LLC*, 2009 Conn. Super. LEXIS 337 (Conn. Super. Ct. Feb. 6, 2009) provided a helpful summary of publishing economics:

> [I]t helps to become familiar with what constitutes a "front list" book, and what is a "backlist" book.[4] These concepts are known and used in both the publishing industry in general, and also by these parties in particular. The front list and the backlist must be viewed and analyzed two ways: both in the realities of the Chicken Soup series in the book publishing marketplace, and in the often ambiguous or imprecisely drafted definitions and terms of the various contracts between the parties the court is called upon to construe here.
>
> Front list and backlist are the shorthand terms used in the industry to distinguish the lists of book titles offered for sale each year by any given publisher. A series of newly published books offered for sale to the public each year is known as a publisher's "front list." By contrast, a publisher's "backlist" refers to older books from past seasons still in print; that is, they are books that are yet available for purchase through the publisher, if not always currently stocked in bookstores. Both newly published books (the front list) and older books still in print (the backlist) that are sold by a publisher are known and referenced in the book trade in this fashion. As time goes by, the books on a publisher's front list eventually turn into (and add to the inventory of) a publisher's backlist. Like any other property rights that are alienable pursuant to contract, the court notes that it is not unheard of in the publishing industry for the rights to the backlist and the rights to the front list of a particular book series to be owned by two different companies, as is now the situation in this case.
>
> These sales and marketing terms — front list and backlist — are widely used in the book publishing world, and were the subject of testimony by most, if not all, witnesses for both parties at the hearing on this matter. It was covered by extensive (if not exhaustive) questioning by all counsel, both on direct and in cross examination. As to the backlist, the court finds that it is a property interest with somewhat less market value in terms of current sales than the front list

---

4. Unlike "backlist," accepted English usage requires that "front list" be spelled as two words.

catalog. This would seem to be true even with a normal or more typical book cycle, one considered in the absence of litigation such as now clouds the Chicken Soup brand. Backlist titles, by their nature of being on the backlist and with an older date of original publication, are less subject to the current marketing and promotional efforts of a party.

e. The controversy surrounding the *Chicken Soup* book series was likely triggered by too much success rather than too little. Often parties focus too much on the terms for cementing the relationship and too little on the consequences of the post-termination relationships. If a publishing agreement includes a termination provision based on a term of years rather than merely based on the book going out of print, how should the parties treat the rights following publication? See *Health Communs., Inc. v. Chicken Soup for the Soul Publ'g, LLC,* 2009 Conn. Super. LEXIS 337 (Conn. Super. Ct. Feb. 6, 2009).

Problem XVI-C

Bryce and Jesse are continuing to work on the coffee table photo-exposé. (See Problem XVI-B.) Bryce and Jesse understand that this book will not be sold in stores for more than one or two years. If the book somehow becomes popular, there is the opportunity for sequels and updates, but neither Bryce nor Jesse expects this to happen.

Bryce, however, believes that once the book has run its initial course, the material could lend itself very well to a website-based literary project. At the very least, Bryce wants to post the contents of the book on the Internet. Bryce hopes the posting will grow into a viral editing project[5] that will greatly increase exposure for the writers. Bryce also believes posting the book's content online might create a new market for sales of the printed book.

Bryce and Jesse want the opportunity to recapture the rights to the book so that they can create the website marketing. Advise Bryce and Jesse as to what contractual provisions should be in the final agreement to best reflect their interests in a manner that will be acceptable to their publisher.

D. Ownership of Editorial Content

N.Y. Times Co. v. Tasini

533 U.S. 483 (2001)

JUSTICE GINSBURG delivered the opinion of the Court.

This copyright case concerns the rights of freelance authors and a presumptive privilege of their publishers. The litigation was initiated by six freelance authors and relates to articles they contributed to three print periodicals (two newspapers and one magazine). Under agreements with the periodicals' publishers, but without the freelancers' consent, two computer database companies placed copies of the freelancers' articles—along with all other articles from the periodicals in which the freelancers' work appeared—into three databases.

---

5. By viral, Bryce means a self-propagating editorial project in which the viewers of the work are able to add content and promote the work. See Wikipedia.org for an example of the largest viral encyclopedia. ("Wikipedia is a multilingual project to create an accurate and comprehensive free-content encyclopedia.")

Whether written by a freelancer or staff member, each article is presented to, and retrievable by, the user in isolation, clear of the context the original print publication presented.

The freelance authors' complaint alleged that their copyrights had been infringed by the inclusion of their articles in the databases. The publishers, in response, relied on the privilege of reproduction and distribution accorded them by §201(c) of the Copyright Act, which provides:

> "Copyright in each separate contribution to a collective work is distinct from copyright in the collective work as a whole, and vests initially in the author of the contribution. In the absence of an express transfer of the copyright or of any rights under it, the owner of copyright in the collective work is presumed to have acquired only the privilege of reproducing and distributing the contribution as part of that particular collective work, any revision of that collective work, and any later collective work in the same series."

Specifically, the publishers maintained that, as copyright owners of collective works, *i.e.*, the original print publications, they had merely exercised "the privilege" §201(c) accords them to "reproduce and distribute" the author's discretely copyrighted contribution.

In agreement with the Second Circuit, we hold that §201(c) does not authorize the copying at issue here. The publishers are not sheltered by §201(c), we conclude, because the databases reproduce and distribute articles standing alone and not in context, not "as part of that particular collective work" to which the author contributed, "as part of ... any revision" thereof, or "as part of ... any later collective work in the same series." Both the print publishers and the electronic publishers, we rule, have infringed the copyrights of the freelance authors.

Respondents Jonathan Tasini, Mary Kay Blakely, Barbara Garson, Margot Mifflin, Sonia Jaffe Robbins, and David S. Whitford are authors (Authors). Between 1990 and 1993, they wrote the 21 articles (Articles) on which this dispute centers.... The Authors registered copyrights in each of the Articles. The Times, Newsday, and Time (Print Publishers) registered collective work copyrights in each periodical edition in which an Article originally appeared. The Print Publishers engaged the Authors as independent contractors (freelancers) under contracts that in no instance secured consent from an Author to placement of an Article in an electronic database.

At the time the Articles were published, all three Print Publishers had agreements with petitioner LEXIS/NEXIS (formerly Mead Data Central Corp.), owner and operator of NEXIS, a computerized database that stores information in a text-only format. NEXIS contains articles from hundreds of journals (newspapers and periodicals) spanning many years. The Print Publishers have licensed to LEXIS/NEXIS the text of articles appearing in the three periodicals. The licenses authorize LEXIS/NEXIS to copy and sell any portion of those texts.

Pursuant to the licensing agreements, the Print Publishers regularly provide LEXIS/NEXIS with a batch of all the articles published in each periodical edition. The Print Publisher codes each article to facilitate computerized retrieval, then transmits it in a separate file. After further coding, LEXIS/NEXIS places the article in the central discs of its database.

Subscribers to NEXIS, accessing the system through a computer, may search for articles by author, subject, date, publication, headline, key term, words in text, or other criteria....

On December 16, 1993, the Authors filed this civil action in the United States District Court for the Southern District of New York. The Authors alleged that their copyrights were infringed when, as permitted and facilitated by the Print Publishers, LEXIS/NEXIS and UMI (Electronic Publishers) placed the Articles in the NEXIS, NYTO, and GPO databases (Databases). The Authors sought declaratory and injunctive relief, and damages. In response to the Authors' complaint, the Print and Electronic Publishers raised the reproduction and distribution privilege accorded collective work copyright owners by *17 U.S.C. §201*(c). After discovery, both sides moved for summary judgment.

...

Under the Copyright Act, as amended in 1976, "copyright protection subsists ... in original works of authorship fixed in any tangible medium of expression ... from which they can be perceived, reproduced, or otherwise communicated." *17 U.S.C. §102*(a). When, as in this case, a freelance author has contributed an article to a "collective work" such as a newspaper or magazine, the statute recognizes two distinct copyrighted works: "Copyright in *each separate contribution to a collective work* is distinct from copyright in *the collective work as a whole....*" §201(c) (emphasis added). Copyright in the separate contribution "vests initially in the author of the contribution" (here, the freelancer). Copyright in the collective work vests in the collective author (here, the newspaper or magazine publisher) and extends only to the creative material contributed by that author, not to "the preexisting material employed in the work," §103(b).

Prior to the 1976 revision ... authors risked losing their rights when they placed an article in a collective work. Pre-1976 copyright law recognized a freelance author's copyright in a published article only when the article was printed with a copyright notice in the author's name. When publishers, exercising their superior bargaining power over authors, declined to print notices in each contributor's name, the author's copyright was put in jeopardy. The author did not have the option to assign only the right of publication in the periodical; such a partial assignment was blocked by the doctrine of copyright "indivisibility." Thus, when a copyright notice appeared only in the publisher's name, the author's work would fall into the public domain, unless the author's copyright, in its entirety, had passed to the publisher. Such complete transfer might be accomplished by a contract, perhaps one with a provision, not easily enforced, for later retransfer of rights back to the author. Or, absent a specific contract, a court might find that an author had tacitly transferred the entire copyright to a publisher, in turn deemed to hold the copyright in "trust" for the author's benefit.

In the 1976 revision, Congress acted to "clarify and improve [this] confused and frequently unfair legal situation with respect to rights in contributions." The 1976 Act rejected the doctrine of indivisibility, recasting the copyright as a bundle of discrete "exclusive rights," each of which "may be transferred ... and owned separately." Congress also provided, in §404(a), that "a single notice applicable to the collective work as a whole is sufficient" to protect the rights of freelance contributors. And in §201(c), Congress codified the discrete domains of "copyright in each separate contribution to a collective work" and "copyright in the collective work as a whole." Together, §404(a) and §201(c) "preserve the author's copyright in a contribution even if the contribution does not bear a separate notice in the author's name, and without requiring any unqualified transfer of rights to the owner of the collective work."

Section 201(c) both describes and circumscribes the "privilege" a publisher acquires regarding an author's contribution to a collective work:

> "In the absence of an express transfer of the copyright or of any rights under it, the owner of copyright in the collective work is presumed to have acquired *only*

the privilege of reproducing and distributing the contribution as part of that particular collective work, any revision of that collective work, and any later collective work in the same series" (emphasis added).

A newspaper or magazine publisher is thus privileged to reproduce or distribute an article contributed by a freelance author, absent a contract otherwise providing, only "as part of" any (or all) of three categories of collective works: (a) "that collective work" to which the author contributed her work, (b) "any revision of that collective work," or (c) "any later collective work in the same series." In accord with Congress' prescription, a "publishing company could reprint a contribution from one issue in a later issue of its magazine, and could reprint an article from a 1980 edition of an encyclopedia in a 1990 revision of it; the publisher could not revise the contribution itself or include it in a new anthology or an entirely different magazine or other collective work."

Essentially, § 201(c) adjusts a publisher's copyright in its collective work to accommodate a freelancer's copyright in her contribution. If there is demand for a freelance article standing alone or in a new collection, the Copyright Act allows the freelancer to benefit from that demand; after authorizing initial publication, the freelancer may also sell the article to others. It would scarcely "preserve the author's copyright in a contribution" as contemplated by Congress, if a newspaper or magazine publisher were permitted to reproduce or distribute copies of the author's contribution in isolation or within new collective works.

In the instant case, the Authors wrote several Articles and gave the Print Publishers permission to publish the Articles in certain newspapers and magazines. It is undisputed that the Authors hold copyrights and, therefore, exclusive rights in the Articles.[6] It is clear, moreover, that the Print and Electronic Publishers have exercised at least some rights that § 106 initially assigns exclusively to the Authors: LEXIS/NEXIS' central discs and UMI's CD-ROMs "reproduce ... copies" of the Articles, § 106(1); UMI, by selling those CD-ROMs, and LEXIS/NEXIS, by selling copies of the Articles through the NEXIS Database, "distribute copies" of the Articles "to the public by sale," § 106(3); and the Print Publishers, through contracts licensing the production of copies in the Databases, "authorize" reproduction and distribution of the Articles, § 106.

Against the Authors' charge of infringement, the Publishers do not here contend the Authors entered into an agreement authorizing reproduction of the Articles in the Databases. Nor do they assert that the copies in the Databases represent "fair use" of the Authors' Articles. Instead, the Publishers rest entirely on the privilege described in § 201(c). Each discrete edition of the periodicals in which the Articles appeared is a "collective work," the Publishers agree. They contend, however, that reproduction and distribution of each Article by the Databases lie within the "privilege of reproducing and distributing the [Articles] as part of ... [a] revision of that collective work," § 201(c). The Publishers' encompassing construction of the § 201(c) privilege is unacceptable, we conclude, for it would diminish the Authors' exclusive rights in the Articles.

In determining whether the Articles have been reproduced and distributed "as part of" a "revision" of the collective works in issue, we focus on the Articles as presented to,

---

6. The Publishers do not claim that the Articles are "works made for hire." *17 U.S.C. §201*(b). As to such works, the employer or person for whom a work was prepared is treated as the author. The Print Publishers, however, neither engaged the Authors to write the Articles as "employees" nor "commissioned" the Articles through "a written instrument signed by [both parties]" indicating that the Articles shall be considered "work[s] made for hire."

and perceptible by, the user of the Databases. In this case, the three Databases present articles to users clear of the context provided either by the original periodical editions or by any revision of those editions.... One might view the articles as parts of a new compendium—namely, the entirety of works in the Database. In that compendium, each edition of each periodical represents only a miniscule fraction of the ever-expanding Database. The Database no more constitutes a "revision" of each constituent edition than a 400-page novel quoting a sonnet in passing would represent a "revision" of that poem. "Revision" denotes a new "version," and a version is, in this setting, a "distinct form of something regarded by its creators or others as one work." The massive whole of the Database is not recognizable as a new version of its every small part.

Alternatively, one could view the Articles in the Databases "as part of" no larger work at all, but simply as individual articles presented individually. That each article bears marks of its origin in a particular periodical (less vivid marks in NEXIS and NYTO, more vivid marks in GPO) suggests the article was previously part of that periodical. But the markings do not mean the article is currently reproduced or distributed as part of the periodical. The Databases' reproduction and distribution of individual Articles—simply as individual Articles—would invade the core of the Authors' exclusive rights under § 106.

The Publishers press an analogy between the Databases, on the one hand, and microfilm and microfiche, on the other. We find the analogy wanting. Microforms typically contain continuous photographic reproductions of a periodical in the medium of miniaturized film. Accordingly, articles appear on the microforms, writ very small, in precisely the position in which the articles appeared in the newspaper. The Times, for example, printed the beginning of Blakely's "Remembering Jane" Article on page 26 of the Magazine in the September 23, 1990, edition; the microfilm version of the Times reproduces that same Article on film in the very same position, within a film reproduction of the entire Magazine, in turn within a reproduction of the entire September 23, 1990, edition. True, the microfilm roll contains multiple editions, and the microfilm user can adjust the machine lens to focus only on the Article, to the exclusion of surrounding material. Nonetheless, the user first encounters the Article in context. In the Databases, by contrast, the Articles appear disconnected from their original context. In NEXIS and NYTO, the user sees the "Jane" Article apart even from the remainder of page 26. In GPO, the user sees the Article within the context of page 26, but clear of the context of page 25 or page 27, the rest of the Magazine, or the remainder of the day's newspaper. In short, unlike microforms, the Databases do not perceptibly reproduce articles as part of the collective work to which the author contributed or as part of any "revision" thereof.

Invoking the concept of "media neutrality," the Publishers urge that the "transfer of a work between media" does not "alter the character of" that work for copyright purposes. That is indeed true. But unlike the conversion of newsprint to microfilm, the transfer of articles to the Databases does not represent a mere conversion of intact periodicals (or revisions of periodicals) from one medium to another. The Databases offer users individual articles, not intact periodicals. In this case, media neutrality should protect the Authors' rights in the individual Articles to the extent those Articles are now presented individually, outside the collective work context, within the Databases' new media.

The dissenting opinion apparently concludes that, under the banner of "media-neutrality," a copy of a collective work, even when considerably changed, must constitute a "revision" of that collective work so long as the changes were "necessitated by ... the medium." We lack the dissent's confidence that the current form of the Databases is entirely attributable to the nature of the electronic media, rather than the nature of the economic market served by the Databases. In any case, we see no grounding in § 201(c) for a "medium-driven" necessity defense to the Authors' infringement claims. Furthermore, it bears reminder here and throughout that these Publishers and all others can protect their interests by private contractual arrangement....

The Publishers warn that a ruling for the Authors will have "devastating" consequences. The Databases, the Publishers note, provide easy access to complete newspaper texts going back decades. A ruling for the Authors, the Publishers suggest, will punch gaping holes in the electronic record of history.... Notwithstanding the dire predictions from some quarters, it hardly follows from today's decision that an injunction against the inclusion of these Articles in the Databases (much less all freelance articles in any databases) must issue. The parties (Authors and Publishers) may enter into an agreement allowing continued electronic reproduction of the Authors' works; they, and if necessary the courts and Congress, may draw on numerous models for distributing copyrighted works and remunerating authors for their distribution. In any event, speculation about future harms is no basis for this Court to shrink authorial rights Congress established in § 201(c). Agreeing with the Court of Appeals that the Publishers are liable for infringement, we leave remedial issues open for initial airing and decision in the District Court.

We conclude that the Electronic Publishers infringed the Authors' copyrights by reproducing and distributing the Articles in a manner not authorized by the Authors and not privileged by § 201(c). We further conclude that the Print Publishers infringed the Authors' copyrights by authorizing the Electronic Publishers to place the Articles in the Databases and by aiding the Electronic Publishers in that endeavor. We therefore affirm the judgment of the Court of Appeals.

Faulkner v. Nat'l Geographic Soc'y
294 F.Supp.2d 523 (S.D.N.Y. 2003)

The digital revolution has caused substantial growing pains in the law of copyright as the law has sought to adapt to the demands of a new age. This case is yet another example.

Plaintiffs here are freelance photographers or writers who created images or text that originally appeared in the print version of the *National Geographic Magazine* (the "*Magazine*"). While the ownership of the copyrights in their creations in many cases is disputed, all agree that defendant National Geographic Society ("NGS") had the right to publish their works in the *Magazine* regardless of who owns the copyrights.

In the late 1990s, defendants produced and began to market various editions of "The Complete National Geographic" (the "CNG"), a digital archive of all past issues of the *Magazine* on CD-ROM and DVD. Plaintiffs here claim that the production and sale of the CNG infringed their copyrights in and otherwise violated their rights with respect to their contributions to the *Magazine*. The fundamental questions, common to all of the cases, are whether the NGS, as owner of the copyrights in the individual issues of the *Magazine*, is privileged by *Section 201(c) of the Copyright Act of 1976* (the "1976 Act") to market the CNG on the theory that it is a reproduction or revision of the *Magazine* and whether NGS is foreclosed from reliance on *Section 201(c)* by a previous adverse decision in the Eleventh Circuit.

The matter now is before the Court on defendants' motions for partial summary judgment dismissing the copyright infringement and certain other claims and motions by many of the plaintiffs for partial summary judgment determining that defendants are liable for copyright infringement under the 1976 Act.... The principal defendants are NGS and two of its subsidiaries....

The Complete National Geographic

In 1996, NGS developed a proposal to reproduce all issues of the *Magazine* published between 1888 and 1996 in CD-ROM format. The product, now known as the CNG, was produced in significant part through a process of digital scanning. Each issue of the *Magazine* published between 1888 and 1996 was scanned, page by page, into a computer system. The pages were scanned two at a time, so that a user of CNG is presented with the exact same visual experience as if reading from the print version of the *Magazine*. Defendants assert that the scanning process created an "exact image-based reproduction" of each page as it appeared in the *Magazine*....

"The Complete National Geographic: 108 Years of National Geographic Magazine on CD-ROM" ("CD-ROM 108"), which was introduced to the marketplace in 1997, has three components. The first is a multimedia sequence that displays NGS's logo followed by a promotional message for Kodak and a sequence depicting the covers of ten issues of the *Magazine* that transition from one into another (the "Moving Cover Sequence"). The multimedia sequence plays on the first time a user boots up CD-ROM 108 and at the beginning of each subsequent session. In subsequent sessions, however, the user can skip the sequence by clicking on the logo once. The second component, referred to in this opinion as the Replica, consists of the digital reproduction of the pages and issues of the *Magazine*. The third is the computer software that serves as the storage repository and retrieval system for the *Magazine* images.

Since 1997, the NGS has published additional CNG products, principally CD-ROMs and DVDs for the first 109, 110, 111 and 112 years of the *Magazine*. These products have varied slightly from the first with respect to the introductory sequences, which display the NGS's logo, and the Kodak promotional message. Only the 108 and 109 year CD-ROMs contained the Moving Cover Sequence. Beginning with the 110 year product, each version has contained a very short summary of each article that appears on the list of "hits" generated by the search engine in response to user queries. Capabilities have been added to the software. All, however, contain a Replica section....

II. Copyright Infringement

Section 201(c) of the 1976 Act provides:

> Copyright in each separate contribution to a collective work is distinct from copyright in the collective work as a whole, and vests initially in the author of the contribution. In the absence of an express transfer of the copyright or of any rights under it, the owner of copyright in the collective work is presumed to have acquired only the privilege of reproducing and distributing the contribution as part of that particular collective work, any revision of that collective work, and any later collective work in the same series.

It thus distinguishes between the "copyright in each separate contribution to a collective work" and the "copyright in the collective work as a whole." The former "vests initially in the author of the contribution." The owner of the copyright in the collective work, barring an express transfer, is presumed to have acquired from the owner of the copyright in each separate contribution only the privilege of "reproducing and distributing the contribution as part of [1] that particular collective work, [2] any revision of that collective work, and [3] any later collective work in the same series."

The parties agree that NGS acquired from the plaintiffs at least the right to publish their contributions in the *Magazine*. Defendants contend that the CNG is a "reproduction" or "revision" of the *Magazine* and, in consequence, that the infringement claims must be dismissed. Plaintiffs, for their part, maintain that NGS litigated and lost precisely this argument in *Greenberg v. National Geographic Society* and that defendants therefore are collaterally estopped from relying on *Section 201(c)*....

Section 201(c) creates a privilege in the publisher of a collective work for "reproduction" of "that particular collective work, any revision of that collective work, and any later collective work in the same series" but does not define any of those terms. The phrase "that particular collective work" obviously includes "a specific edition or issue of a periodical." The meaning of the remaining terms, however, is far from self evident. Where, as here, the language of the statute is unclear, resort to legislative history is appropriate. The most pertinent indication is in the House Judiciary Committee Report, which states in relevant part:

> Under the language of this clause a publishing company could reprint a contribution from one issue in a later issue of its magazine, and could reprint an article from a 1980 edition of an encyclopedia in a 1990 revision of it; the publisher could not revise the contribution itself or include it in a new anthology or an entirely different magazine or other collective work.

A staff report expressed much the same idea, stating that the privilege did not permit "inclusion of [an author's] contribution in anthologies or other entirely different works."

These comments are instructive. The use of the term "entirely different" to describe a new work not privileged by *Section 201(c)* suggests that the privilege extends to a collective work that is merely somewhat different from the original in which the contribution appeared. This view is supported strongly by the Judiciary Committee's encyclopedia revision example. An encyclopedia typically is a collective work consisting of individual articles dealing with the various subjects treated. As time goes by, some articles become outdated and new subjects come into being. A revised edition of an encyclopedia thus would contain some articles that have been revised to take account of new learning and some entirely new articles, as well as some articles in precisely their original forms. Each revised and new article would be copyrightable independently. Hence, *Greenberg*'s holding—that the presence of independently copyrightable material is inconsistent with a conclusion that the CNG is a "revision" of the print versions of the *Magazine*—cannot be reconciled with the legislative history. Indeed, it "defies the very legislative history" upon which the Eleventh Circuit relied.

What then distinguishes a "revision" from an "entirely different" work? As the Supreme Court noted in *Tasini, Section 201(c)* was a compromise intended "to adjust the balance between" freelancers and publishers so that "if there is demand for a freelance [work] standing alone or in a new collection, the Copyright Act allows the freelancer to benefit from that demand." In determining whether the freelancer's work is part of a new collection as distinguished from a revision, the focus is on the manner in which it is "presented to, and perceptible by, the user." A critical consideration is whether the original contribution is presented in the same context in which it appeared in the initial collective work, at least to such an extent that the new product "perceptibly presents the author's contribution as part of a revision of the collective work." As the Register of Copyright wrote in a letter discussing *Tasini*:

> The legislative history of *§ 201(c)* supports this conclusion [i.e., that the NEXIS database at issue in *Tasini* was not a revision]. It offers, as examples of a revision of a collective work, an evening edition of a newspaper or a later edition of an encyclopedia. *These examples retain elements that are consistent and recognizable*

from the original collective work so that a relationship between the original and the revision is apparent. Unlike NEXIS, they are recognizable as revisions of the originals. But as the Second Circuit noted, all that is left of the original collective works in the databases involved in *Tasini* are the authors' contributions.

It is clear that the databases involved in *Tasini* constitute, in the words of the legislative history, 'new,' 'entirely different' or 'other' works. *No elements of arrangement or coordination of the pre-existing materials contained in the databases provide evidence of any similarity or relationship to the original collective works to indicate they are revisions.*

147 CONG. REC., E182-02, E183 (daily ed. Feb. 14, 2001) (emphasis added).

In this case, with a few immaterial exceptions, each issue of a regional edition of the *Magazine* was scanned, page by page, into a computer system, creating an exact image of each and every page as it appeared in that edition of the *Magazine.* There are no changes to the content, format or appearance of the issues of the *Magazine* reproduced in the CNG. Each page of each issue appears to the user exactly as it was in the scanned print version of the *Magazine,* including all text, images, advertising and attributions....

The fact that this product appears in a new medium makes no difference, in and of itself, as media neutrality is a fundamental principle of the Copyright Act. So what remains is the contention that the user experience with the CNG—its easy searchability and other attractive software-dependent features—is so different from that with the *Magazine* itself that the CNG should be regarded as an "entirely different" work.

It is difficult to see why this should take the CNG out of *Section 201(c).* The predominant differences between the *Magazine* and the CNG are the CNG's convenient physical "package" and the software that provides easy searchability, i.e., the animated opening sequence and other such material and the search engine, respectively.... The fact that more purchasers may be interested because the package is more attractive than a library full of more than 112 years of monthly copies of the *Magazine* is immaterial.

As the Supreme Court said in *Tasini,* the accommodation struck by *Section 201(c)* was to allow a freelancer to benefit where "there is demand for a freelance article standing alone or in a new collection." But the CNG is not a new collection. Nor is it, in words the House Judiciary Committee used to articulate the limits of the *Section 201(c)* privilege, "a new anthology or an entirely different magazine or other collective work." Rather, it is a package that contains substantially everything that made the *Magazine* copyrightable as a collective work—the same original collection of individual contributions, arranged in the same way, with each presented in the same context. It is readily recognizable as a variation of the original. Accordingly, the Court holds that the CNG is a revision of the individual print issues of the *Magazine*; it respectfully disagrees with so much of *Greenburg* as held otherwise.

B. Effect of Section 201(c) on Pre-1978 Works

The Court's previous opinions determined that the NGS owned copyright in some of the Pre-1978 Works while issues of fact exist concerning ownership of others. NGS argues, however, that these issues are immaterial because *Section 201(c)* protects the use of the Pre-1978 Works in the CNG....

The NGS at all relevant times owned the copyrights in issues of the *Magazine* published before and after January 1, 1978. In consequence, the privileges conferred upon it by *Section 201(c)* as the holder of those copyrights govern regardless of when they were published. Accordingly, to whatever extent that *Section 201(c)* protects publication of the

CNG, it does so regardless of whether the NGS or plaintiffs own the copyrights in plaintiffs' individual contributions....

Notes and Questions

a. One of the greatest concerns raised by the dissent in *Tasini* was the fear that large segments of material would become unavailable on the Internet, as well as on Lexis, Westlaw, and similar databases. The Court suggested that there were alternatives to the publisher's losing access to this material. What might some of those options be?

b. The decisions seem to turn on the nature of the display. If the work is reproduced whole, then it is not an infringement. But if the work is disaggregated into individual articles, then the statute does not treat the work as a reprint. Some imaging software does both. The physical pages of a work are photographically reproduced for display. A copy of the text is dumped into the database so that text-based searches can allow the viewer to call up a page through a keyword search. Does this form of visual representation working in tandem with a searchable database fall outside the statutory definition articulated in *Tasini*? If this is also actionable, then note that Google and other online search engines offer functionality of a similar manner in regards to PDF files posted to the Internet.

c. The case of *Faulkner v. Nat'l Geographic Soc'y.*, 294 F. Supp. 2d 523 (S.D.N.Y. 2003), was affirmed, *Faulkner v. Nat'l Geographic Enters.*, 409 F.3d 26 (2d Cir. 2005), though the ongoing litigation continued through numerous additional opinions. In affirming the district court decision, the Second Circuit explained:

> [W]e hold that, because the original context of the Magazines is omnipresent in the CNG and because it is a new version of the Magazine, the CNG is a privileged revision.
>
> "'Revision' denotes a new 'version,' and a version is, in this setting, a "'distinct form of something regarded by its creator or others as one work.'" [*N.Y. Times Co. v. Tasini*, 533 U.S. 483, 500 (2001)] (quoting Webster's Third New International Dictionary 1944, 2545 (1976)). "In determining whether the [underlying works] have been reproduced and distributed 'as part of' a 'revision' of the collective works in issue, we focus on the [underlying works] as presented to, and perceptible by, the user of the [CNG]." *Id.* at 499 (citations omitted)....
>
> Moreover, because the Section 201(c) privilege of reproduction and distribution extends to that collective work and any revision of that collective work, a permissible revision may contain elements not found in the original—for example, a collection of bound volumes of past issues with a copyrightable index to the entire collection.... In the case of the CNG, some images found in the original version of the Magazines are blacked out, and it contains additional elements.... However, these changes do not substantially alter the original context which, unlike that of the works at issue in *Tasini*, is immediately recognizable. The presentation does not, therefore, affect the CNG's status as a revision.

Faulkner v. Nat'l Geographic Enters., 409 F.3d 26, 38 (2d Cir. 2005).

The last round of litigation addressed whether there was a breach of contact for failing to compensate the "further uses" of the photographs. In *Faulkner v. Natl. Geographic Soc.*, 452 F. Supp. 2d 369, 379–81 (S.D.N.Y. 2006), *aff'd sub nom. Ward v. Natl. Geographic Socy.*, 284 Fed. Appx. 822 (2d Cir. 2008) (unpublished), the court found little ambiguity in the contracts and a clear course of dealing that demonstrated which further uses entitled plaintiffs to additional payments.

[B]oth NGS and the plaintiffs rely on extrinsic evidence of the course of dealing between them. Both cite evidence that NGS consistently paid plaintiffs when their contributions to the Magazine were reused in filmstrips, books, slide presentations, and promotional brochures.... [P]laintiffs do not dispute that they were not paid for use of their work in microform, microfiche, or bound compilations of the magazine. No do they provide any evidence to suggest that they requested payment for such uses from NGS. Unlike the subjective intent or post hoc conclusions of contracting parties, the parties' course of dealing throughout the life of a contract is highly relevant to determining the meaning of the terms of the agreement....

This undisputed evidence of the course of dealing between the parties under the contracts at issue compels the conclusion that the "further use" provisions require additional payments only if a new use presents the contributors' works in a context different than the Magazine article in which they originally appeared.

d. The Supreme Court also returned to the case of *New York Times Co. v. Tasini.*

Because of the growing size and complexity of the lawsuit, the [*Tasini*] District Court referred the parties to mediation. For more than three years, the freelance authors, the publishers (and their insurers), and the electronic databases (and their insurers) negotiated. Finally, in March 2005, they reached a settlement agreement that the parties intended "to achieve a global peace in the publishing industry." *In re Literary Works in Electronic Databases Copyright Litigation,* 509 F.3d 116, 119 (2d Cir. 2007).

The parties moved the District Court to certify a class for settlement and to approve the settlement agreement. Ten freelance authors, including Irvin Muchnick (hereinafter Muchnick respondents), objected. The District Court overruled the objections; certified a settlement class of freelance authors under Federal Rules of Civil Procedure 23(a) and (b)(3); approved the settlement as fair, reasonable, and adequate under Rule 23(e); and entered final judgment.... The Muchnick respondents appealed.... Shortly before oral argument, the Court of Appeals *sua sponte* ordered briefing on the question whether § 411(a) deprives federal courts of subject-matter jurisdiction over infringement claims involving unregistered copyrights. All parties filed briefs asserting that the District Court had subject-matter jurisdiction to approve the settlement agreement even though it included unregistered works.... [T]he Court of Appeals concluded that the District Court lacked jurisdiction to certify a class of claims arising from the infringement of unregistered works, and also lacked jurisdiction to approve a settlement with respect to those claims ...

Reed Elsevier, Inc. v. Muchnick, 559 U.S. 154, 130 S. Ct. 1237, 1242–43 (2010). The Supreme Court reversed, finding that § 411(a) of the Copyright Act did not require every work in dispute between parties to be a registered work. "Section 411(a) imposes a precondition to filing a claim that is not clearly labeled jurisdictional, is not located in a jurisdiction-granting provision, and admits of congressionally authorized exceptions. Section 411(a) thus imposes a type of precondition to suit that supports nonjurisdictional treatment under our precedents." In so deciding, the Court allowed the hard fought class action settlement to go into effect.

e. The saga continued in *Literary Works in Elec. Databases Copyright Litig. v. Thomson Corp.*, 654 F.3d 242, 254–255 (2d Cir. 2011). The Second Circuit reversed the class action settlement because it found that the various categories of claimants were not adequately represented.

> The Settlement divides the works at issue ("Subject Works") into three categories: A, B, and C. Category A covers works that authors registered with the U.S. Copyright Office in time to be eligible for statutory damages and attorney's fees under the Copyright Act. At the time of the Settlement, registration cost $30 per work or $30 per group registration covering multiple periodical contributions by one individual over a 12-month period. Category B includes works that authors registered before December 31, 2002, but too late to be eligible for statutory damages. These claims are eligible to recover only actual damages suffered by the author and any profits of the infringer that are not duplicative of the actual damages. All other claims fall into Category C and cannot be litigated for damages purposes unless they are registered with the Copyright Office. If registered, however, these claims—like those in Category B—would be eligible for awards based on authors' actual damages and infringers' profits. Category C claims comprise more than 99% of authors' total claims. Many authors hold claims in more than one category, each claim based on a separate freelance article they sold for publication....
>
> We agree with objectors that the interests of class members who hold only Category C claims fundamentally conflict with those of class members who hold Category A and B claims. Although all class members share an interest in maximizing the collective recovery, their interests diverge as to the distribution of that recovery because each category of claim is of different strength and therefore commands a different settlement value. Named plaintiffs who hold other combinations of claims had no incentive to maximize the recovery for Category C-only plaintiffs, whose claims were lowest in settlement value but eclipsed all others in quantity. The interests of Category C-only plaintiffs could be protected only by the formation of a subclass and the advocacy of independent counsel. We therefore hold that the district court abused its discretion in certifying the class based on its finding that class representation was adequate.

f. To what extent can the sleuthing needed to find previously unpublished works become a part of a compiler's copyright? When Stuart Silverstein published a book of Dorothy Parker's uncollected poems, he did not expect Penguin Books to first reject his manuscript and then publish the same poems in its own anthology. But sleuthing and compiling may not be the same. See *Silverstein v. Penguin Putnam, Inc.*, 368 F.3d 77 (2d Cir. 2004).

g. With the rise of new technology and self-publishing technology, anyone can serve as a publishing house. At what point do the promises of a successful print and promotional campaign become contractual guarantees? For insight into this issue and the risks of interference with an author's rights, see *Lee v. Mt. Ivy Press, L.P.*, 63 Mass.App.Ct. 538 (2005).

Problem XVI-D

Bryce and Jesse are continuing to work on the coffee table photo-exposé. (See Problem XVI-B.) With the book now tentatively entitled *Exposure*, Jesse has photographed 50 subjects. Bryce has written the introduction for the book, photo captions, and a biography for each subject. Because most of the book's subjects know each other, the book has developed a narrative that neither Bryce nor Jesse expected. The book is actually telling the story of an elite subculture in the city.

Bryce and Jesse expected to use only 35 subjects. The publisher is willing to increase the number slightly, but has asked that all 50 of the completed exposés be delivered. It plans to "assist" in the selection process, "subject to the authors' final approval." Based on their working relationship with the publisher thus far, Bryce and Jesse are not concerned about soliciting the advice of the publisher on the selection process. Bryce is concerned, however, that individual exposés are not sold as filler for magazines or used outside of the completed book—at least not without Bryce's and Jesse's approval. Bryce wants to know whether copyright law would allow the publisher to publish the rejected exposés elsewhere and what contractual language should be added to the agreement to stop this from happening.

E. Fair Use in Publishing

Rosemont Enterprises, Inc. v. Random House, Inc.
366 F.2d 303 (2d Cir. 1966)

On May 26, 1966, plaintiff-appellee, Rosemont Enterprises, Inc. (Rosemont) commenced this action in the district court alleging that copyrights which it owned on a series of articles entitled "The Howard Hughes Story" which appeared in Look Magazine in early 1954 were infringed by a book entitled "Howard Hughes—a Biography by John Keats" published on May 23, 1966 by defendant-appellant, Random House, Inc. In June, Rosemont made a motion for a preliminary injunction restraining the sale, publication, distribution and advertisement of the biography pending final determination of the action on the ground that it had made out a prima facie case of infringement. The defendants, Random House, Inc. and John Keats, opposed the motion on the grounds, *inter alia*, that the copying which was done was insubstantial and that, in any event, whatever use was made of the Look articles constituted a fair use and, thus, was privileged. The district court granted the motion for a preliminary injunction and, in rejecting defendants' claim of fair use, narrowly confined the privilege to materials "used for purposes of criticism or comment or in scholarly works of scientific or educational value." In the district court's view, if a work is published "for commercial purposes" and is designed for the popular market, those responsible for its appearance are precluded from invoking the fair use privilege, regardless of the nature of the work involved. Since the court found that the Hughes biography "can scarcely be said to be a scholarly, scientific or educational work," and was designed for the popular market, it concluded that the fair use privilege was inappropriate here. For the reasons set forth below, we reverse.

The only issue presently before this court is: Was the preliminary injunction erroneously issued as a matter of law?

The articles entitled "The Howard Hughes Story" published in three issues of Look Magazine dated February 9, 23 and March 9, 1954, and copyrighted by its publisher, Cowles Communications, Inc., in January and February 1954 and the allegedly offending book, published in 1966, "Howard Hughes—a Biography by John Keats," are before the court. The nature and extent of the infringement, if any, can be gauged by a comparison of the two writings. For the purposes of this appeal, an attempt will be made to restrict the factual statement to those undisputed items which bear upon a preliminary injunction.

The Circumstances Under Which Plaintiff Acquired the Look Copyrights

At the outset, defendants assert that plaintiff's conduct in acquiring the copyrights indicates that they were purchased solely for the purpose of bringing this lawsuit and, hence, plaintiff is deprived "of the right to relief as a matter of law and as a matter of equitable discretion."

From the facts as outlined in the district court's opinion, it appears that for some time prior to 1962 Random House had been considering a biography of Howard Hughes who by reason of his remarkable exploits and achievements, primarily in the aviation and motion picture fields, had become quite a public figure despite a publicized passion for personal anonymity. To prepare such a biography, Random House in September of 1962 engaged the services of Thomas Thompson, a member of the staff of Life Magazine. After submitting his draft manuscript, Thompson for business reasons could not continue with the additional work necessary for its completion. In the latter part of 1964, Random House obtained the services of an author, the defendant, John Keats, who took the Thompson manuscript, news and copyrighted magazine articles, including the 1954 Look articles, and various public documents, and produced the biography now before the court.

Apparently Hughes and/or his attorneys learned of the forthcoming Random House publication, and his attorney warned Random House that Hughes was opposed to the biography "and would make trouble if the book was published." The legal effect of the "trouble" should not be pre-judged at this time, except as certain aspects bear upon the granting of the preliminary injunction. Whether there be any reality to the claim that the plaintiff Rosemont, organized in September 1965 by Hughes' attorney and two officers of his wholly-owned Hughes Tool Company, is engaged in writing a Hughes biography, must await the trial. For the present, it is sufficient to note that in February 1966 plaintiff, having by some means obtained a galley proof of the forthcoming biography, brought an action against defendants in the Supreme Court of New York alleging in substance a plan to exploit commercially the name and personality of Hughes and an invasion of his right of privacy.

On May 20, 1966, plaintiff obtained from Cowles Communications, Inc. (Look), the copyrights to the 1954 Look articles, so advised Random House the next day and brought this suit five days later. Apparently Look had done nothing with the articles since 1954; they had not been compiled into book form or reprinted or offered to the public in any manner except as articles in three February and March 1954 editions of Look. Nor is there any indication that Look, although advised of the proposed Random House biography, intended to bring an infringement action or to seek an injunction. However, whether the "trouble" threatened will have legal consequences sufficient to constitute a defense cannot be determined upon the facts as adduced at this stage. Nevertheless, we have referred with approval to the rule that "'[t]he interference of the court by injunction being founded on pure equitable principles, a man who comes to the court must be able to show that his own conduct in the transaction has been consistent with equity.'"

A Comparison of the 1954 Look Articles and the 1966 Biography

The three 1954 Look articles contain some 13,500 words and would have, if published in book form (which they were not), filled some 36 to 39 book-size pages. The 1966 biography consists of some 116,000 words and 304 pages. The Look articles do not purport to be a biography in the accepted meaning of the word but narrate certain phases or highlights of Hughes' quite eventful career. Naturally, any writing purporting to deal with the life of a public figure is bound to touch upon the same events as have given rise to the publicity. In addition, various incidents of interest to the reading public can usually be developed from friends, neighbors, teachers, business associates, employees, newspaper and magazine articles and public and private records. And so here the biography gives evidence of such source material. Moreover, there can be little doubt that portions of the Look articles were copied. Two direct quotations and one eight-line paraphrase are attributed to Stephen White, the author of the articles. A mere reading of the Look articles, however, indicates that there is considerable doubt as to whether the copied and paraphrased matter constitutes a material and substantial portion of those articles. On the other hand, the material at most forms an insubstantial part of the 304 page biography. Furthermore, while the mode of expression employed by White is entitled to copyright protection, he could not acquire by copyright a monopoly in the narration of historical events. Finally, in an affidavit submitted to the district court, Thompson asserted that he engaged in extensive research while preparing his manuscript, which included personal interviews with many people familiar with Hughes' activities (fifteen of whom he listed by name) and the employment of a Houston newspaper man to conduct additional interviews for him. There is no dispute that defendant Keats, named as author of the biography, was retained solely to revise Thompson's manuscript which, as described in his contract with Random House, was to include rewriting and reorganization; rechecking facts against the sources used; and such additional research as was necessary to "update the work and fill in facts and events." In any event, the extent of Keats' independent research is of little relevance since Thompson's work, embodied in the manuscript, formed the core of the published biography.

While it is undoubtedly true, as the district court observed, that "the book does rely heavily on previously published newspaper and magazine articles and similar material," that fact does not create a presumption of infringement. At this time, we are not prepared to hold that as a matter of law there has been a clear showing of probable success at a trial with respect to the extent and quality of infringement of the Look articles which warrants the grant of a preliminary injunction.

Fair Use

There is no question that material appearing in the Look articles is contained in the Hughes biography. Appellants contend, however, that the district court erred as a matter of law in refusing to honor their claim of fair use on the ground that the court unjustifiably restricted the privilege to scholarly works written and prepared for scholarly audiences. We agree.

"Fair use" is a "privilege in others than the owner of a copyright to use the copyrighted material in a reasonable manner without his consent, notwithstanding the monopoly granted to the owner...." The fundamental justification for the privilege lies in the constitutional purpose in granting copyright protection in the first instance, to wit, "To Promote the Progress of Science and the Useful Arts." To serve that purpose, "courts in passing upon particular claims of infringement must occasionally subordinate the copyright holder's interest in a maximum financial return to the greater public interest in the development of art, science and industry." Whether the privilege may justifiably be applied to particular materials turns initially on the nature of the materials, e.g., whether their distribution would serve the public interest in the free dissemination of information and whether their preparation requires some use of prior materials dealing with the same subject matter. Consequently, the privilege has been applied to works in the fields of science, law, medicine, history and biography.

Biographies, of course, are fundamentally personal histories and it is both reasonable and customary for biographers to refer to and utilize earlier works dealing with the subject of the work and occasionally to quote directly from such works. This practice is permitted because of the public benefit in encouraging the development of historical and biographical works and their public distribution, e.g., so "that the world may not be deprived of improvements, or the progress of the arts be retarded." Indeed, while the Hughes biography may not be a profound work, it may well provide valuable source material for future biographers (if any) of Hughes or for historians or social scientists....

By this preliminary injunction, the public is being deprived of an opportunity to become acquainted with the life of a person endowed with extraordinary talents who, by exercising these talents, made substantial contributions in the fields to which he chose to devote his unique abilities. Inheriting a small fortune in early youth, Hughes can hardly qualify as a Horatio Alger hero in a "From Rags to Riches" story but a narration of his initiative, ingenuity, determination and tireless work to achieve his conception of perfection in whatever he did ought to be available to a reading public which, even in an affluent society, might well be reminded that affluence usually comes from the work of such entrepreneurs in business and industry.

The Keats biography is laudatory and where critical is critical in an understanding fashion. No claim has been made that the biography contains misrepresentations of fact. Judging by the accounts in the Look articles and the biography, Hughes has almost an obsession as to his privacy and his right thereto. However, when one enters the public arena to the extent that he has, the right of privacy must be tempered by a countervailing privilege that the public have some information concerning important public figures. The district court itself recognized that "Howard Hughes is a rather enigmatic contemporary personality of considerable public interest." ...

Random House, Inc. v. Salinger
811 F.2d 90 (2d Cir. 1987)

This appeal presents the issue whether the biographer of a renowned author has made "fair use" of his subject's unpublished letters. The issue arises on an expedited appeal from an order of the District Court for the Southern District of New York (Pierre N. Leval, *Judge*) denying a preliminary injunction sought by the well-known writer, J. D. Salinger, against Ian Hamilton and Random House, Inc., the author and publisher, respectively, of a book about Salinger and his writings. For reasons that follow, we conclude that a preliminary injunction should be issued.

The plaintiff J. D. Salinger is a highly regarded American novelist and short-story writer, best known for his novel, *The Catcher in the Rye*. He has not published since 1965 and has chosen to shun all publicity and inquiry concerning his private life. The defendant Ian Hamilton is a well-respected writer on literary topics. He serves as literary critic of *The London Sunday Times* and has authored a biography of the poet Robert Lowell. In July 1983 Hamilton informed Salinger that he was undertaking a biography of Salinger to be published by Random House and sought the author's cooperation. Salinger refused, informing Hamilton that he preferred not to have his biography written during his lifetime. Hamilton nevertheless proceeded and spent the next three years preparing a biography titled *J. D. Salinger: A Writing Life....*

Ian Hamilton located most, if not all, of the letters in the libraries of Harvard, Princeton, and the University of Texas, to which they had been donated by the recipients or their representatives. Prior to examining the letters at the university libraries, Hamilton signed form agreements furnished by the libraries, restricting the use he could make of the letters without permission of the library and the owner of the literary property rights. The Harvard form required permission "to publish the contents of the manuscript or any excerpt therefrom." The Princeton form obliged the signer "not to copy, reproduce, circulate or publish" inspected manuscripts without permission.

By May 1986 Hamilton had completed a version of his biography. Salinger received a set of the galley proofs of this version (the "May galleys") and learned from the galleys and the footnote citations to his letters that the letters had been donated to university libraries. In response, he took two actions. First, he registered 79 of his unpublished letters for copyright protection. Second, he instructed his counsel to object to publication of the biography until all of Salinger's unpublished materials were deleted.

In response to Salinger's objection, Hamilton and Random House revised the May galleys. In the current version of the biography (the "October galleys"), much of the material previously quoted from the Salinger letters has been replaced by close paraphrasing. Somewhat more than 200 words remain quoted. Salinger has identified 59 instances where the October galleys contain passages that either quote from or closely paraphrase portions of his unpublished letters....

On October 3, 1986, Salinger sued Ian Hamilton and Random House, seeking an injunction against publication of Hamilton's biography and damages.... To a large extent the appropriate legal principles are not in dispute on this appeal, though their application is seriously contested. The author of letters is entitled to a copyright in the letters, as with any other work of literary authorship. Prior to 1978, unpublished letters, like other unpublished works, were protected by common law copyright, but the 1976 Copyright Act preempted the common law of copyright, and brought unpublished works under the protection of federal copyright law, which includes the right of first publication among the rights accorded to the copyright owner. The copyright owner owns the literary property rights, including the right to complain of infringing copying, while the recipient of the letter retains ownership of "the tangible physical property of the letter itself." Having ownership of the physical document, the recipient (or his representative) is entitled to deposit it with a library and contract for the terms of access to it. As with all works of authorship, the copyright owner secures protection only for the expressive content of the work, not the ideas or facts contained therein, a distinction fundamental to copyright law and of special significance in determining whether infringement has occurred in a work of biography or other account of historical or contemporary events.

Central to this appeal is the application of the defense of "fair use" to unpublished works. Though common law, especially as developed in England, appears to have denied the defense of fair use to unpublished works, the 1976 Act explicitly makes all of the rights protected by copyright, including the right of first publication, subject to the defense of fair use. That fair use applies to unpublished works does not determine, however, the scope of the defense as applied to such works. Whatever glimmerings on that subject have appeared in cases decided before May 20, 1985, our guidance must now be taken from the decision of the Supreme Court on that date in *Harper & Row, Publishers, Inc. v. Nation Enterprises,* 471 U.S. 539, 85 L. Ed. 2d 588, 105 S. Ct. 2218 (1985), the Court's first delineation of the scope of fair use as applied to unpublished works.

The Court begins its discussion of fair use by considering the application of the doctrine to unpublished works. The Court observes that "fair use traditionally was not recognized as a defense to charges of copying from an author's as yet unpublished works," but that this "absolute rule" was "tempered in practice by the equitable nature of the fair use doctrine." The Court notes that, under the Copyright Revision Act of 1976, all of the rights protected by copyright, including the right of first publication, are subject to fair use, but explicitly rejects the contention, advanced by *The Nation* that Congress "intended that fair use would apply *in pari materia* to published and unpublished works." "Under ordinary circumstances," the Court states, "the author's right to control the first public appearance of his undisseminated expression will outweigh a claim of fair use." This proposition was emphasized with respect to unpublished letters. Reckoning with *The Nation's* argument that fair use could permissibly be made of President Ford's unpublished memoirs because the imminent publication demonstrated that the author has no interest in nonpublication, the Court said, "This argument assumes that the unpublished nature of copyrighted material is only relevant to letters or other confidential writings not intended for dissemination," an assumption the Court went on to reject. Pertinent to our case is the fact that the Court underscored the idea that unpublished letters normally enjoy insulation from fair use copying.

After emphasizing the insulation of unpublished works from fair use under "ordinary circumstances," the Court considers in turn each of the four factors identified by Congress as "especially relevant," in determining whether a use is fair. Reflecting its earlier discussion, the Court gives special weight to the fact that the copied work is unpublished when considering the second factor, the nature of the copyrighted work.

Following the Supreme Court's approach in *Harper & Row*, we place special emphasis on the unpublished nature of Salinger's letters and proceed to consider each of the four statutory fair use factors. Application of these four factors points in Salinger's favor.

1. *Purpose of the use.* Hamilton's book fits comfortably within several of the statutory categories of uses illustrative of uses that can be fair. The book may be considered "criticism," "scholarship," and "research." The proposed use is not an attempt to rush to the market just ahead of the copyright holder's imminent publication, as occurred in *Harper & Row*. Whether Random House plans to "exploit the headline value of its infringement," as *The Nation* did, is not clear on the record thus far developed. Though no evidence has yet been presented on the advertising materials Random House plans to use, it is hard to believe that some emphasis will not be placed upon the fact that the book draws generously upon Salinger's unpublished letters.

We agree with Judge Leval that Hamilton's purpose in using the Salinger letters to enrich his scholarly biography weighs the first fair use factor in Hamilton's favor, notwithstanding that he and his publisher anticipate profits. However, we do not agree that a biographer faces a dilemma that entitles him to a generous application of the fair use doctrine.… This dilemma is not faced by the biographer who elects to copy only the factual content of letters.

The biographer who copies only facts incurs no risk of an injunction; he has not taken copyrighted material. And it is unlikely that the biographer will distort those facts by rendering them in words of his own choosing. On the other hand, the biographer who copies the letter writer's expression of facts properly faces an unpleasant choice. If he copies more than minimal amounts of (unpublished) expressive content, he deserves to be enjoined; if he "distorts" the expressive content, he deserves to be criticized for "sacrificing accuracy and vividness." But the biographer has no inherent right to copy the "accuracy" or the "vividness" of the letter writer's expression. Indeed, "vividness of description" is precisely an attribute of the author's expression that he is entitled to protect.

The point is sharply, though unwittingly, made by defendant Hamilton in the course of his deposition in this case. On cross-examination, he is pressed as to why he copied a stylistic device that Salinger had employed in one of the letters. He responds: "I wanted to convey the fact that [Salinger] was adopting an ironic term...." When the cross-examiner asks, "Couldn't you have stated that he had an ironic tone," Hamilton replies, "That would make a pedestrian sentence I didn't wish to put my name to." But when dealing with copyrighted expression, a biographer (or any other copier) may frequently have to content himself with reporting only the fact of what his subject did, even if he thereby pens a "pedestrian" sentence. The copier is not at liberty to avoid "pedestrian" reportage by appropriating his subject's literary devices.

In sum, we agree with the District Court that the first fair use factor weighs in Hamilton's favor, but not that the purpose of his use entitles him to any special consideration.

2. *Nature of the Copyrighted Work.* "The fact that a work is unpublished is a critical element of its 'nature.'" Salinger's letters are unpublished, and they have not lost that attribute by their placement in libraries where access has been explicitly made subject to observance of at least the protections of copyright law. In considering this second factor, we encounter some ambiguity arising from the Supreme Court's observation that "the *scope* of fair use is narrower with respect to unpublished works." This could mean either that the circumstances in which copying will be found to be fair use are fewer in number for unpublished works than for published works or that the amount of copyrighted material that may be copied as fair use is a lesser quantity for unpublished works than for published works. Some support for the latter view can be derived from the statement in *Harper & Row* that, though "substantial" quotations might be used in a review of a published work, the author's right to control first publication weighs against "such use" prior to publication. However, we think that the tenor of the Court's entire discussion of unpublished works conveys the idea that such works normally enjoy complete protection against copying any protected expression. Narrower "scope" seems to refer to the diminished *likelihood* that copying will be fair use when the copyrighted material is unpublished.

The District Judge considered the nature of the copyrighted work, especially its unpublished nature, primarily in rejecting the plaintiff's argument that fair use was inapplicable to unpublished works. However, in analyzing and weighing the fair use factors, Judge Leval gave no explicit consideration to this second factor. Since the copyrighted letters are unpublished, the second factor weighs heavily in favor of Salinger.

3. *Amount and Substantiality of the Portion Used.* It is with regard to this third factor that we have the most serious disagreement with the District Judge's legal analysis, both as to the pertinent standard and its application. As to the standard, we start, as did Judge Leval, by recognizing that what is relevant is the amount and substantiality of the copyrighted *expression* that has been used, not the *factual content* of the material in the copyrighted works. However, that protected expression has been "used" whether it has been quoted verbatim or only paraphrased....

We have carefully analyzed all 59 of the passages from Hamilton's book cited by Salinger as instances of infringing copying from 44 of his letters. Of these 44 letters, the Hamilton biography copies (with some use of quotation or close paraphrase) protected sequences constituting at least one-third of 17 letters and at least 10 percent of 42 letters. These sequences are protected, notwithstanding that they include some reporting of facts and an occasional use of a commonplace word or expression. Hamilton's use of these sequences "exceeds that necessary to disseminate the facts." Judge Leval found that "in the rarest case a complete sentence was taken." That is true only with respect to material directly quoted. The material closely paraphrased frequently exceeds ten lines from a single letter. Even if in one or two instances the portions of the letters copied could be said to lack sufficient creativity to warrant copyright protection, there remains sufficient copying of protected material to constitute a very substantial appropriation.

The taking is significant not only from a quantitative standpoint but from a qualitative one as well. The copied passages, if not the "'heart of the book,'" are at least an important ingredient of the book as it now stands. To a large extent, they make the book worth reading. The letters are quoted or paraphrased on at least 40 percent of the book's 192 pages.

In sum, the third fair use factor weighs heavily in Salinger's favor.

4. *Effect on the Market*. The Supreme Court has called the fourth factor—effect on the market for the copyrighted work—"the single most important element of fair use." As Judge Leval recognized, the need to assess the effect on the market for Salinger's letters is not lessened by the fact that their author has disavowed any intention to publish them during his lifetime. First, the proper inquiry concerns the "potential market" for the copyrighted work. Second, Salinger has the right to change his mind. He is entitled to protect his *opportunity* to sell his letters, an opportunity estimated by his literary agent to have a current value in excess of $500,000.

Proceeding from his conclusion that only a few fragments of the letters have been used in Hamilton's book, Judge Leval expressed the view that such use would have "no effect" on the marketability of the letters. Concluding as we do that substantial portions of the letters have been copied, we do not share the District Judge's view that marketability of the letters will be totally unimpaired. To be sure, the book would not displace the market for the letters. Indeed, we think it likely that most of the potential purchasers of a collection of the letters would not be dissuaded by publication of the biography. Yet some impairment of the market seems likely. The biography copies virtually all of the most interesting passages of the letters, including several highly expressive insights about writing and literary criticism. Perhaps few readers of the biography would refrain from purchasing a published collection of the letters if they appreciated how inadequately Hamilton's paraphrasing has rendered Salinger's chosen form of expression. The difficulty, however, is that some readers of the book will gain the impression that they are learning from Hamilton what Salinger has written. Hamilton frequently laces his paraphrasing with phrases such as "he wrote," "said Salinger," "he speaks of," "Salinger declares," "he says," and "he said." For at least some appreciable number of persons, these phrases will convey the impression that they have read Salinger's words, perhaps not quoted verbatim, but paraphrased so closely as to diminish interest in purchasing the originals. The fourth fair use factor weighs slightly in Salinger's favor.

On balance, the claim of fair use as to Salinger's unpublished letters fails. The second and third factors weigh heavily in Salinger's favor, and the fourth factor slightly so. Only the first factor favors Hamilton. We seriously doubt whether a critic reviewing a published collection of the letters could justify as fair use the extensive amount of expressive material Hamilton has copied. However that may be, if fair use is to have a more "limited scope" with respect to unpublished works, it is not available with respect to the current version of Hamilton's proposed biography.

To deny a biographer like Hamilton the opportunity to copy the expressive content of unpublished letters is not, as appellees contend, to interfere in any significant way with the process of enhancing public knowledge of history or contemporary events. The facts may be reported. Salinger's letters contain a number of facts that students of his life and writings will no doubt find of interest, and Hamilton is entirely free to fashion a biography that reports these facts. But Salinger has a right to protect the expressive content of his unpublished writings for the term of his copyright, and that right prevails over a claim of fair use under "ordinary circumstances." Public awareness of the expressive content of the letters will have to await either Salinger's decision to publish or the expiration of his copyright, save for such special circumstances as might fall within the "narrower" scope of fair use available for unpublished works. Evidently, public interest in the expressive content of the letters of a well-known writer remains substantial even fifty years after his death.

Since we conclude that the record establishes Salinger's entitlement to a preliminary injunction on his copyright claim, we need not consider at this stage of the litigation whether he is also entitled to relief by virtue of the library agreements.

Reversed and remanded with directions to issue a preliminary injunction barring publication of the biography in its present form.

Salinger v. Colting

607 F.3d 68 (2010)

Defendants-Appellants Fredrik Colting, Windupbird Publishing Ltd., Nicotext A.B., and ABP, Inc. appeal from an order of the United States District Court for the Southern District of New York (Deborah A. Batts, Judge) granting Plaintiff-Appellee J.D. Salinger's[7] motion for a preliminary injunction. The District Court's judgment is VACATED and REMANDED.

Salinger published The Catcher in the Rye (hereinafter "Catcher") in 1951.... Catcher was an instant success. It was on the New York Times best-seller list for over seven months and sold more than one million copies in its first ten years. To date it has sold over 35 million copies, influenced dozens of literary works, and been the subject of "literally reams of criticism and comment."...

Inseparable from the Catcher mystique is the lifestyle of its author, Salinger. Shortly after publishing Catcher, Salinger did what Holden did not do: he removed himself from society. Salinger has not published since 1965 and has never authorized any new narrative involving Holden or any work derivative of Catcher. Other than a 1949 film adaptation of one of his early short stories, Salinger has never permitted, and has explicitly instructed his lawyers not to allow, adaptations of his works. He has, however, remained in the public spotlight through a series of legal actions to protect his intellectual property. Salinger has registered and duly renewed his copyright in Catcher with the U.S. Copyright Office.

Defendant-Appellant Fredrik Colting wrote 60 Years Later: Coming Through the Rye (hereinafter "60 Years Later") under the pen name "John David California." Colting pub-

---

7. We note that Plaintiff-Appellee J.D. Salinger died during the pendency of this appeal. In a February 18, 2010 order, we granted the motion of Colleen M. Salinger and Matthew R. Salinger, trustees of the J.D. Salinger Literary Trust, to be substituted for Salinger as Appellees. For reasons of convenience, however, we will continue to refer to Salinger as "Plaintiff" or "Appellee" in this opinion.

lished 60 Years Later with his own publishing company, Defendant-Appellant Windup-bird Publishing, Ltd., in England on May 9, 2009. Copies were originally scheduled to be available in the United States on September 15, 2009. Colting did not seek Salinger's permission to publish 60 Years Later.

60 Years Later tells the story of a 76-year-old Holden Caulfield, referred to as "Mr. C," in a world that includes Mr. C's 90-year-old author, a "fictionalized Salinger." The novel's premise is that Salinger has been haunted by his creation and now wishes to bring him back to life in order to kill him. Unsurprisingly, this task is easier said than done. As the story progresses, Mr. C becomes increasingly self-aware and able to act in ways contrary to the will of Salinger. After a series of misadventures, Mr. C travels to Cornish, New Hampshire, where he meets Salinger in his home. Salinger finds he is unable to kill Mr. C and instead decides to set him free. The novel concludes with Mr. C reuniting with his younger sister, Phoebe, and an estranged son, Daniel....

On July 1, 2009, the District Court granted Salinger's motion for a preliminary injunction, barring Defendants from "manufacturing, publishing, distributing, shipping, advertising, promoting, selling, or otherwise disseminating any copy of [60 Years Later], or any portion thereof, in or to the United States." In doing so, it found that (1) Salinger has a valid copyright in Catcher and the Holden Caulfield character, (2) absent a successful fair use defense, Defendants have infringed Salinger's copyright in both Catcher and the Holden Caulfield character, (3) Defendants' fair use defense is likely to fail, and (4) a preliminary injunction should issue....

Having made this determination, the District Court turned to whether a preliminary injunction should issue. According to the Court:

> Under Rule 65, to obtain a preliminary injunction a party must demonstrate: (1) that it will be irreparably harmed if an injunction is not granted, and (2) either (a) a likelihood of success on the merits or (b) sufficiently serious questions going to the merits to make them a fair ground for litigation, and a balance of hardships tipping decidedly in its favor.

Given its findings, the Court deemed the only remaining question to be whether Salinger had shown that he would be irreparably harmed if an injunction was not granted. Because Salinger had established a *prima facie* case of copyright infringement, and in light of how the District Court, understandably, viewed this Court's precedents, the District Court presumed irreparable harm without discussion....

We hold that, although the District Court applied our Circuit's longstanding standard for preliminary injunctions in copyright cases, our Circuit's standard is inconsistent with the "test historically employed by courts of equity" and has, therefore, been abrogated by *eBay, Inc. v. MercExchange, L.L.C.*, 547 U.S. 388, 390 (2006).

The Copyright Act of 1976 authorizes courts to "grant temporary and final injunctions on such terms as [they] may deem reasonable to prevent or restrain infringement of a copyright." 17 U.S.C. §502(a). And, as the District Court stated, this Court has long issued preliminary injunctions in copyright cases upon a finding of (a) irreparable harm and (b) either (1) likelihood of success on the merits or (2) sufficiently serious questions going to the merits to make them a fair ground for litigation and a balance of hardships tipping decidedly toward the party requesting the preliminary relief.

Thus, once a plaintiff establishes a likelihood of success on the merits, the only additional requirement is a showing that the plaintiff will be irreparably harmed if the preliminary injunction does not issue. And traditionally, this Court has presumed that a plaintiff likely to prevail on the merits of a copyright claim is also likely to suffer irreparable harm if an injunction does not issue....

Defendants do not claim that the District Court failed to apply this Circuit's longstanding preliminary injunction standard. Rather, they argue both that this standard is an unconstitutional prior restraint on speech and that it is in conflict with the Supreme Court's decision in *eBay, Inc. v. MercExchange, L.L.C.*, 547 U.S. 388 (2006). We agree that *eBay* abrogated parts of this Court's preliminary injunction standard in copyright cases, and accordingly, this case must be remanded to the District Court to reevaluate Salinger's preliminary injunction motion. In light of that holding, we need not decide whether the preliminary injunction issued by the District Court constituted an unconstitutional prior restraint on speech.

eBay involved the propriety of a permanent injunction after a finding of patent infringement. The United States District Court for the Eastern District of Virginia had ostensibly applied the traditional four-factor test for determining whether a permanent injunction should issue....

Writing for a unanimous Court, Justice Thomas held that neither the district court nor the Federal Circuit correctly applied the equitable factors:

> According to well-established principles of equity, a plaintiff seeking a permanent injunction must satisfy a four-factor test before a court may grant such relief. A plaintiff must demonstrate: (1) that it has suffered an irreparable injury; (2) that remedies available at law, such as monetary damages, are inadequate to compensate for that injury; (3) that, considering the balance of hardships between the plaintiff and defendant, a remedy in equity is warranted; and (4) that the public interest would not be disserved by a permanent injunction.

eBay, 547 U.S. at 391. Although the courts below had articulated the correct standard, they had both, albeit in different ways, applied "broad classifications" that were inconsistent with traditional equitable principles....

We hold today that *eBay* applies with equal force (a) to preliminary injunctions (b) that are issued for alleged copyright infringement.... Moreover, the Court expressly relied upon copyright cases in reaching its conclusion. In response to the Federal Circuit's reasoning that the Patent Act's right to exclude justifies the preference for injunctive relief, the Court stated that "the creation of a right is distinct from the provision of remedies for violations of that right." In support of this distinction, it noted that "[l]ike a patent owner, a copyright holder possesses the right to exclude others from using his property." It further noted that "[l]ike the Patent Act, the Copyright Act provides that courts 'may' grant injunctive relief 'on such terms as it may deem reasonable to prevent or restrain infringement of copyright.'" *Id.* (quoting 17 U.S.C. § 502(a)). Because of these similarities, the Court emphasized that it "has consistently rejected invitations to replace traditional equitable considerations with a rule that an injunction automatically follows a determination that a copyright has been infringed." Whatever the underlying issues and particular circumstances of the cases cited by the Court in *eBay*, it seems clear that the Supreme Court did not view patent and copyright injunctions as different in kind, or as requiring different standards....

The first consideration in the preliminary injunction analysis is the probability of success on the merits. In gauging this, we emphasize that courts should be particularly cognizant of the difficulty of predicting the merits of a copyright claim at a preliminary injunction hearing. *See* [Mark A. Lemley & Eugene Volokh, *Freedom of Speech and Injunctions in Intellectual Property Cases*, 48 Duke L.J. 147, 201–02 (1998)] ("[When deciding whether to grant a TRO or a preliminary injunction,] the judge has limited time for contemplation. The parties have limited time for briefing. Preparation for a typical copyright trial, even a bench trial, generally takes many months; the arguments about why one work isn't substantially similar in its expression to another, or about why it's a fair use of another, are often sophisticated and fact-intensive, and must be crafted with a good deal of thought and effort."). This difficulty is compounded significantly when a defendant raises a colorable fair use defense. "Whether [a] taking[ ] will pass the fair use test is difficult to predict. It depends on widely varying perceptions held by different judges." Pierre N. Leval, *Toward a Fair Use Standard,* 103 Harv. L.Rev. 1105, 1132 (1990).

Next, the court must consider whether the plaintiff will suffer irreparable harm in the absence of a preliminary injunction, and the court must assess the balance of hardships between the plaintiff and defendant. Those two items, both of which consider the harm to the parties, are related. The relevant harm is the harm that (a) occurs to the parties' legal interests and (b) cannot be remedied after a final adjudication, whether by damages or a permanent injunction. The plaintiff's interest is, principally, a property interest in the copyrighted material. But as the Supreme Court has suggested, a copyright holder might also have a First Amendment interest in *not* speaking. *See Harper & Row Publishers, Inc. v. Nation Enters.,* 471 U.S. 539, 559 (1985). The defendant to a copyright suit likewise has a property interest in his or her work to the extent that work does not infringe the plaintiff's copyright. And a defendant also has a core First Amendment interest in the freedom to express him or herself, so long as that expression does not infringe the plaintiff's copyright.

But the above-identified interests are relevant only to the extent that they are not remediable after a final adjudication. Harm might be irremediable, or irreparable, for many reasons, including that a loss is difficult to replace or difficult to measure, or that it is a loss that one should not be expected to suffer. In the context of copyright infringement cases, the harm to the plaintiff's property interest has often been characterized as irreparable in light of possible market confusion....

After *eBay,* however, courts must not simply presume irreparable harm. Rather, plaintiffs must show that, on the facts of their case, the failure to issue an injunction would actually cause irreparable harm. This is not to say that most copyright plaintiffs who have shown a likelihood of success on the merits would not be irreparably harmed absent preliminary injunctive relief. As an empirical matter, that may well be the case, and the historical tendency to issue preliminary injunctions readily in copyright cases may reflect just that....

But by anchoring the injunction standard to equitable principles, albeit with one eye on historical tendencies, courts are able to keep pace with innovation in this rapidly changing technological area. Justice Kennedy, responding to Justice Roberts, made this very point as to patent injunctions in his *eBay* concurrence. Although the "lesson of the historical practice ... is most helpful and instructive when the circumstances of a case bear substantial parallels to litigation the courts have confronted before[,] ... in many instances the nature of the patent being enforced and the economic function of the patent holder present considerations quite unlike earlier cases." Justice Kennedy concluded that changes in the way parties use patents may now mean that "legal damages [are] sufficient to compensate for the infringement."

Finally, courts must consider the public's interest. The object of copyright law is to promote the store of knowledge available to the public. But to the extent it accomplishes this end by providing individuals a financial incentive to contribute to the store of knowledge, the public's interest may well be already accounted for by the plaintiff's interest.

The public's interest in free expression, however, is significant and is distinct from the parties' speech interests. "By protecting those who wish to enter the marketplace of ideas from government attack, the First Amendment protects the public's interest in receiving information." *Pac. Gas & Elec. Co. v. Pub. Utils. Comm'n of Cal.,* 475 U.S. 1, 8 (1986). Every injunction issued before a final adjudication on the merits risks enjoining speech protected by the First Amendment. Some uses, however, will so patently infringe another's copyright, without giving rise to an even colorable fair use defense, that the likely First Amendment value in the use is virtually nonexistent.

Because the District Court considered only the first of the four factors that, under *eBay* and our holding today, must be considered before issuing a preliminary injunction, we vacate and remand the case. But in the interest of judicial economy, we note that there is no reason to disturb the District Court's conclusion as to the factor it did consider—namely, that Salinger is likely to succeed on the merits of his copyright infringement claim.

Most of the matters relevant to Salinger's likelihood of success on the merits are either undisputed or readily established in his favor. Thus, Defendants do not contest either that Salinger owns a valid copyright in *Catcher* or that they had actual access to *Catcher.* And while they argue only that *60 Years Later* and *Catcher* are not substantially similar, that contention is manifestly meritless. "In considering substantial similarity between two items, we review the district court's findings *de novo*—not on the clearly erroneous standard—because what is required is only a visual comparison of the works, rather than credibility, which we are in as good a position to decide as was the district court." *Folio Impressions, Inc. v. Byer Cal.,* 937 F.2d 759, 766 (2d Cir.1991). And for largely the same reasons as the District Court, we affirm the District Court's finding that *Catcher* and *60 Years Later* are substantially similar.

More serious is Defendants' assertion of a fair use defense. And at this preliminary stage, we agree with the District Court that Defendants will not likely be able to make out such a defense. The District Court in its discussion of fair use focused on the first statutory factor: the "purpose and character of the use." 17 U.S.C. § 107(1). In doing this, the Court found that "[i]t is simply not credible for Defendant Colting to assert now that his primary purpose was to critique Salinger and his persona, while he and his agents' previous statements regarding the book discuss no such critique, and in fact reference various other purposes behind the book." Such a finding is not clear error. It may be that a court can find that the fair use factor favors a defendant even when the defendant and his work lack a transformative *purpose.* We need not decide that issue here, however, for when we consider the District Court's credibility finding together with all the other facts in this case, we conclude, with the District Court, that Defendants are not likely to prevail in their fair use defense.

In this preliminary injunction case, the District Court erred by not applying the equitable standard outlined by the Supreme Court in *eBay, Inc. v. MercExchange, L.L. C.* and *Winter v. Natural Resources Defense Council.* Accordingly, we vacate and remand for further proceedings consistent with this opinion. The preliminary injunction will stay in place for ten days following the issuance of the mandate so that Appellees will have an opportunity to apply for a temporary restraining order pending the rehearing of the motion for a preliminary injunction.

Authors Guild, Inc. v. Google Inc.
954 F.Supp.2d 282 (2013)

Since 2004, when it announced agreements with several major research libraries to digitally copy books in their collections, defendant Google Inc. ("Google") has scanned more than twenty million books. It has delivered digital copies to participating libraries, created an electronic database of books, and made text available for online searching through the use of "snippets." Many of the books scanned by Google, however, were under copyright, and Google did not obtain permission from the copyright holders for these usages of their copyrighted works. As a consequence, in 2005, plaintiffs brought this class action charging Google with copyright infringement.

Before the Court are the parties' cross-motions for summary judgment with respect to Google's defense of fair use under § 107 of the Copyright Act, 17 U.S.C. § 107. For the reasons set forth below, Google's motion for summary judgment is granted and plaintiffs' motion for partial summary judgment is denied. Accordingly, judgment will be entered in favor of Google dismissing the case.

1. *The Parties*

[Plaintiffs include three individual authors and The Authors Guild, Inc. The Authors Guild] is the nation's largest organization of published authors and it advocates for and supports the copyright and contractual interests of published writers.

Google owns and operates the largest Internet search engine in the world. Each day, millions of people use Google's search engine free of charge; commercial and other entities pay to display ads on Google's websites and on other websites that contain Google ads. Google is a for-profit entity, and for the year ended December 31, 2011, it reported over $36.5 billion in advertising revenues.

2. *The Google Books Project*

In 2004, Google announced two digital books programs. The first, initially called "Google Print" and later renamed the "Partner Program," involved the "hosting" and display of material provided by book publishers or other rights holders. The second became known as the "Library Project," and over time it involved the digital scanning of books in the collections of the New York Public Library, the Library of Congress, and a number of university libraries.

The Partner Program and the Library Project together comprise the Google Books program ("Google Books"). All types of books are encompassed, including novels, biographies, children's books, reference works, textbooks, instruction manuals, treatises, dictionaries, cookbooks, poetry books, and memoirs. Some 93% of the books are non-fiction while approximately 7% are fiction. Both in-print and out-of-print books are included, although the great majority are out-of-print.

In the Partner Program, works are displayed with permission of the rights holders. The Partner Program is aimed at helping publishers sell books and helping books become discovered. Initially, Google shared revenues from ads with publishers or other rights holders in certain circumstances. In 2011, however, Google stopped displaying ads in connection with all books. Partners provide Google with a printed copy of their books for scanning, or a digital copy if one already exists. Partners decide how much of their books—from a few sample pages to the entire book—are browsable. As of early 2012, the Partner Program included approximately 2.5 million books, with the consent of some 45,000 rights holders.

As for the Library Project, Google has scanned more than twenty million books, in their entirety, using newly-developed scanning technology. Pursuant to their agreement with

Google, participating libraries can download a digital copy of each book scanned from their collections. Google has provided digital copies of millions of these books to the libraries, in accordance with these agreements. Some libraries agreed to allow Google to scan only public domain works, while others allowed Google to scan in-copyright works as well.

Google creates more than one copy of each book it scans from the library collections, and it maintains digital copies of each book on its servers and back-up tapes. Participating libraries have downloaded digital copies of in-copyright books scanned from their collections. They may not obtain a digital copy created from another library's book. The libraries agree to abide by the copyright laws with respect to the copies they make.

Google did not seek or obtain permission from the copyright holders to digitally copy or display verbatim expressions from in-copyright books. Google has not compensated copyright holders for its copying of or displaying of verbatim expression from in-copyright books or its making available to libraries for downloading of digital copies of in-copyright books scanned from their collections.

3. *Google Books*

In scanning books for its Library Project, including in-copyright books, Google uses optical character recognition technology to generate machine-readable text, compiling a digital copy of each book. Google analyzes each scan and creates an overall index of all scanned books. The index links each word or phrase appearing in each book with all of the locations in all of the books in which that word or phrase is found. The index allows a search for a particular word or phrase to return a result that includes the most relevant books in which the word or phrase is found. Because the full texts of books are digitized, a user can search the full text of all the books in the Google Books corpus.

Users of Google's search engine may conduct searches, using queries of their own design. In response to inquiries, Google returns a list of books in which the search term appears. A user can click on a particular result to be directed to an "About the Book" page, which will provide the user with information about the book in question. The page includes links to sellers of the books and/or libraries that list the book as part of their collections. No advertisements have ever appeared on any About the Book page that is part of the Library Project.

For books in "snippet view" (in contrast to "full view" books), Google divides each page into eighths—each of which is a "snippet," a verbatim excerpt. Each search generates three snippets, but by performing multiple searches using different search terms, a single user may view far more than three snippets, as different searches can return different snippets. For example, by making a series of consecutive, slightly different searches of the book *Ball Four,* a single user can view many different snippets from the book.

Google takes security measures to prevent users from viewing a complete copy of a snippet-view book.... In addition, works with text organized in short "chunks," such as dictionaries, cookbooks, and books of haiku, are excluded from snippet view.

4. *The Benefits of the Library Project and Google Books*

The benefits of the Library Project are many. First, Google Books provides a new and efficient way for readers and researchers to find books. It makes tens of millions of books searchable by words and phrases. It provides a searchable index linking each word in any book to all books in which that word appears. Google Books has become an essential research tool, as it helps librarians identify and find research sources, it makes the process of interlibrary lending more efficient, and it facilitates finding and checking citations. Indeed, Google Books has become such an important tool for researchers and librarians that it has been integrated into the educational system—it is taught as part of the information literacy curriculum to students at all levels.

Second, in addition to being an important reference tool, Google Books greatly promotes a type of research referred to as "data mining" or "text mining." Google Books permits humanities scholars to analyze massive amounts of data—the literary record created by a collection of tens of millions of books. Researchers can examine word frequencies, syntactic patterns, and thematic markers to consider how literary style has changed over time. Using Google Books, for example, researchers can track the frequency of references to the United States as a single entity ("the United States is") versus references to the United States in the plural ("the United States are") and how that usage has changed over time. The ability to determine how often different words or phrases appear in books at different times "can provide insights about fields as diverse as lexicography, the evolution of grammar, collective memory, the adoption of technology, the pursuit of fame, censorship, and historical epidemiology." Jean-Baptiste Michel *et al., Quantitative Analysis of Culture Using Millions of Digitized Books,* 331 SCIENCE 176, 176 (2011).

Third, Google Books expands access to books. In particular, traditionally underserved populations will benefit as they gain knowledge of and access to far more books. Google Books provides print-disabled individuals with the potential to search for books and read them in a format that is compatible with text enlargement software, text-to-speech screen access software, and Braille devices. Digitization facilitates the conversion of books to audio and tactile formats, increasing access for individuals with disabilities. Google Books facilitates the identification and access of materials for remote and underfunded libraries that need to make efficient decisions as to which resources to procure for their own collections or through interlibrary loans.

Fourth, Google Books helps to preserve books and give them new life. Older books, many of which are out-of-print books that are falling apart buried in library stacks, are being scanned and saved. These books will now be available, at least for search, and potential readers will be alerted to their existence.

Finally, by helping readers and researchers identify books, Google Books benefits authors and publishers. When a user clicks on a search result and is directed to an "About the Book" page, the page will offer links to sellers of the book and/or libraries listing the book as part of their collections. The About the Book page for *Ball Four,* for example, provides links to Amazon.com, Barnes & Noble.com, Books-A-Million, and IndieBound. A user could simply click on any of these links to be directed to a website where she could purchase the book. Hence, Google Books will generate new audiences and create new sources of income....

B. *Procedural History*

Plaintiffs commenced this action on September 20, 2005, alleging, *inter alia,* that Google committed copyright infringement by scanning copyrighted books and making them available for search without permission of the copyright holders. From the outset, Google's principal defense was fair use under § 107 of the Copyright Act, 17 U.S.C. § 107.

After extensive negotiations, the parties entered into a proposed settlement resolving plaintiffs' claims on a class-wide basis. On March 22, 2011, I issued an opinion rejecting the proposed settlement on the grounds that it was not fair, adequate, and reasonable. *Authors Guild v. Google Inc.,* 770 F.Supp.2d 666 (S.D.N.Y.2011).

Thereafter, the parties engaged in further settlement discussions, but they were unable to reach agreement. [Google settled with most major book publishers and those companies are no longer party to the suit.] ... On July 1, 2013, without deciding the merits of the appeal, the Second Circuit vacated my class certification decision, concluding that "resolution of Google's fair use defense in the first instance will necessarily inform and perhaps moot our analysis of many class certification issues." *Authors Guild, Inc. v. Google Inc.,* 721 F.3d 132, 134 (2d Cir.2013). The Second Circuit remanded the case "for consideration of the fair use issues." ...

DISCUSSION

For purposes of these motions, I assume that plaintiffs have established a *prima facie* case of copyright infringement against Google under 17 U.S.C. § 106. Google has digitally reproduced millions of copyrighted books, including the individual plaintiffs' books, maintaining copies for itself on its servers and backup tapes. *See* 17 U.S.C. § 106(1) (prohibiting unauthorized reproduction). Google has made digital copies available for its Library Project partners to download. *See* 17 U.S.C. § 106(3) (prohibiting unauthorized distribution). Google has displayed snippets from the books to the public. *See* 17 U.S.C. § 106(5) (prohibiting unauthorized display). Google has done all of this, with respect to in-copyright books in the Library Project, without license or permission from the copyright owners. The sole issue now before the Court is whether Google's use of the copyrighted works is "fair use" under the copyright laws. For the reasons set forth below, I conclude that it is.... I discuss each of the four factors separately, and I then weigh them together.

1. *Purpose and Character of Use*

The first factor is "the purpose and character of the use, including whether such use is of a commercial nature or is for nonprofit educational purposes." 17 U.S.C. § 107(1).

Google's use of the copyrighted works is highly transformative. Google Books digitizes books and transforms expressive text into a comprehensive word index that helps readers, scholars, researchers, and others find books. Google Books has become an important tool for libraries and librarians and cite-checkers as it helps to identify and find books. The use of book text to facilitate search through the display of snippets is transformative. The display of snippets of text for search is similar to the display of thumbnail images of photographs for search or small images of concert posters for reference to past events, as the snippets help users locate books and determine whether they may be of interest. Google Books thus uses words for a different purpose — it uses snippets of text to act as pointers directing users to a broad selection of books.

Similarly, Google Books is also transformative in the sense that it has transformed book text into data for purposes of substantive research, including data mining and text mining in new areas, thereby opening up new fields of research. Words in books are being used in a way they have not been used before. Google Books has created something new in the use of book text — the frequency of words and trends in their usage provide substantive information.

Google Books does not supersede or supplant books because it is not a tool to be used to read books. Instead, it "adds value to the original" and allows for "the creation of new information, new aesthetics, new insights and understandings." Leval, *Toward a Fair Use Standard,* 103 Harv. L.Rev. at 1111. Hence, the use is transformative.... [E]ven assuming Google's principal motivation is profit, the fact is that Google Books serves several important educational purposes. Accordingly, I conclude that the first factor strongly favors a finding of fair use.

2. *Nature of Copyrighted Works*

The second factor is "the nature of the copyrighted work." 17 U.S.C. § 107(2). Here, the works are books—all types of published books, fiction and non-fiction, in-print and out-of-print. While works of fiction are entitled to greater copyright protection, here the vast majority of the books in Google Books are non-fiction. Further, the books at issue are published and available to the public. These considerations favor a finding of fair use.

3. *Amount and Substantiality of Portion Used*

The third factor is "the amount and substantiality of the portion used in relation to the copyrighted work as a whole." 17 U.S.C. § 107(3). Google scans the full text of books—the entire books—and it copies verbatim expression. On the other hand, courts have held that copying the entirety of a work may still be fair use. Here, as one of the keys to Google Books is its offering of full-text search of books, full-work reproduction is critical to the functioning of Google Books. Significantly, Google limits the amount of text it displays in response to a search. On balance, I conclude that the third factor weighs slightly against a finding of fair use.

4. *Effect of Use Upon Potential Market or Value*

The fourth factor is "the effect of the use upon the potential market for or value of the copyrighted work." 17 U.S.C. § 107(4). Here, plaintiffs argue that Google Books will negatively impact the market for books and that Google's scans will serve as a "market replacement" for books. It also argues that users could put in multiple searches, varying slightly the search terms, to access an entire book.

Neither suggestion makes sense. Google does not sell its scans, and the scans do not replace the books. While partner libraries have the ability to download a scan of a book from their collections, they owned the books already—they provided the original book to Google to scan. Nor is it likely that someone would take the time and energy to input countless searches to try and get enough snippets to comprise an entire book. Not only is that not possible as certain pages and snippets are blacklisted, the individual would have to have a copy of the book in his possession already to be able to piece the different snippets together in coherent fashion.

To the contrary, a reasonable factfinder could only find that Google Books enhances the sales of books to the benefit of copyright holders. An important factor in the success of an individual title is whether it is discovered—whether potential readers learn of its existence. Google Books provides a way for authors' works to become noticed, much like traditional in-store book displays. Indeed, both librarians and their patrons use Google Books to identify books to purchase. Many authors have noted that online browsing in general and Google Books in particular helps readers find their work, thus increasing their audiences. Further, Google provides convenient links to booksellers to make it easy for a reader to order a book. In this day and age of on-line shopping, there can be no doubt but that Google Books improves books sales. Hence, I conclude that the fourth factor weighs strongly in favor of a finding of fair use.

5. *Overall Assessment*

Finally, the various non-exclusive statutory factors are to be weighed together, along with any other relevant considerations, in light of the purposes of the copyright laws.

In my view, Google Books provides significant public benefits. It advances the progress of the arts and sciences, while maintaining respectful consideration for the rights of authors and other creative individuals, and without adversely impacting the rights of copyright holders. It has become an invaluable research tool that permits students, teachers, librarians, and others to more efficiently identify and locate books. It has given scholars the ability, for the first time, to conduct full-text searches of tens of millions of books. It preserves books, in particular out-of-print and old books that have been forgotten in the bowels of libraries, and it gives them new life. It facilitates access to books for print-disabled and remote or underserved populations. It generates new audiences and creates new sources of income for authors and publishers. Indeed, all society benefits.

Similarly, Google is entitled to summary judgment with respect to plaintiffs' claims based on the copies of scanned books made available to libraries. Even assuming plaintiffs have demonstrated a *prima facie* case of copyright infringement, Google's actions constitute fair use here as well. Google provides the libraries with the technological means to make digital copies of books that they already own. The purpose of the library copies is to advance the libraries' lawful uses of the digitized books consistent with the copyright law. The libraries then use these digital copies in transformative ways. They create their own full-text searchable indices of books, maintain copies for purposes of preservation, and make copies available to print-disabled individuals, expanding access for them in unprecedented ways. Google's actions in providing the libraries with the ability to engage in activities that advance the arts and sciences constitute fair use.

To the extent plaintiffs are asserting a theory of secondary liability against Google, the theory fails because the libraries' actions are protected by the fair use doctrine. Indeed, in the *HathiTrust* case, Judge Baer held that the libraries' conduct was fair use. *See Authors Guild, Inc. v. HathiTrust,* 902 F.Supp.2d 445, 460–61, 464 (S.D.N.Y.2012) ("I cannot imagine a definition of fair use that would not encompass the transformative uses made by Defendants' [Mass Digitization Project] and would require that I terminate this invaluable contribution to the progress of science and cultivation of the arts that at the same time effectuates the ideals espoused by the [Americans with Disabilities Act]."). The fair use analysis set forth above with respect to Google Books applies here as well to the libraries' use of their scans, and if there is no liability for copyright infringement on the libraries' part, there can be no liability on Google's part.

CONCLUSION

For the reasons set forth above, plaintiffs' motion for partial summary judgment is denied and Google's motion for summary judgment is granted....

Notes and Questions

a. The decision in *Random House, Inc. v. Salinger* set off a controversy over the scope of fair use for unpublished works. L. Ron Hubbard was the subject of much litigation in this regard. See *New Era Publications International, ApS v. Henry Holt & Co.,* 695 F. Supp. 1493 (S.D.N.Y. 1988). The District Court did not appear to think much of the Second Circuit's new jurisprudence:

> As to the book overall, were it not for the ruling of the Court of Appeals in *Salinger,* I would conclude that fair use has been adequately demonstrated.... Many of the takings of Salinger's expression were for the purpose of enlivening that text with Salinger's expressive genius.... Hubbard's expression is taken primarily to show character flaws in a manner that cannot be accomplished without use of his words.

Id. at 1524. The Second Circuit did not appreciate the criticism, but affirmed the decision. *New Era Publs. Int'l v. Henry Holt & Co.,* 873 F.2d 576 (2d Cir. N.Y. 1989). See also *Norse v. Henry Holt & Co.,* 847 F. Supp. 142, 147 (N.D. Cal. 1994); *Wright v. Warner Books, Inc.,* 953 F.2d 731 (2d Cir. 1991) (a slightly more balanced decision making a finding of fair use involving the biography of Richard Wright, author of *Native Son* and *Black Boy*).

Congress finally weighed in on the issue, adding language to § 107 which provides "[t]he fact that a work is unpublished shall not itself bar a finding of fair use if such finding is made upon consideration of all the above factors." As unhelpful as this sentence appears, Congress was correct to add this text to clarify its intent to extend the reach of Fair Use to unpublished works. The legislative history criticized *Salinger* and the Second Circuit, yet it also approved of *Wright*, which was not a particularly broad use of unpublished material. The tone of the legislative hearings may have done more than the text of the statutory amendment to liberalize the courts on the availability of fair use for unpublished material.

b. The Second Circuit continued to struggle with its decision in *Random House, Inc. v. Salinger.* In *Wright v. Warner Books, Inc.,* 953 F.2d 731 (2d Cir. 1991), the Second Circuit appeared to liberalize its analysis somewhat. As the Court explained:

> In the words of the district court: This case presents the next chapter in the continuing narrative of this Circuit's treatment of the fair use defense to a charge of copyright infringement." The principal question presented is whether defendants' sparing use of creative expression from the unpublished letters and journals of the late author Richard Wright constitutes fair use as a matter of law.

By framing the question as "sparing use of creative expression," the Court moved the decision factually from *Salinger*. The Court continued to apply the full, four-factored fair use analysis, but found that the sparing paraphrasing by Dr. Margaret Walker, an acquaintance and biographer of Richard Wright, was fair use.

It might also be noted that Dr. Walker first tried to gain the estate's permission and, when refused, edited out large portions of the unpublished materials. Despite this, the first two publishers later withdrew the offer of publication, fearing the inevitable litigation.

c. The public importance of material sometimes has significant impact on a court's willingness to find fair use. For example, see *Time, Inc. v. Bernard Geis Associates,* 293 F. Supp. 130 (S.D.N.Y. 1968) (upholding fair use for illegal access and copying of 22 frames of the Zapruder film).

One of the few cases to anticipate *eBay, Inc. v. MercExchange,* 547 U.S. 388 (2006) in the area of copyright was *Suntrust Bank v. Houghton Mifflin Co.,* 268 F.3d 1257, 1265 (11th Cir. 2001).

> The basic framework for our analysis remains, however, the standard test governing the issuance of preliminary injunctions. Suntrust is not entitled to relief in the form of a preliminary injunction unless it has proved each of the following four elements: "(1) a substantial likelihood of success on the merits, (2) a substantial threat of irreparable injury if the injunction were not granted, (3) that the threatened injury to the plaintiff outweighs the harm an injunction may cause the defendant, and (4) that granting the injunction would not disserve the public interest."

Suntrust Bank v. Houghton Mifflin Co., 268 F.3d 1257, 1265 (11th Cir. 2001), quoting *Am. Red Cross v. Palm Beach Blood Bank, Inc.*, 143 F.3d 1407, 1410 (11th Cir.1998). Here the court found the unauthorized retelling by Alice Randall of Margaret Mitchell's *Gone with the Wind* was fair use. Randall's *The Wind Done Gone* "persuasively claim[ed] that her novel is a critique of [Gone with the Wind's] depiction of slavery and the Civil-War era American South" and as such Randall's novel was not a market substitute for a sequel to *Gone with the Wind*.

d. Which of the two competing demands should hold greater sway: The free speech interests of the biographer or the privacy rights of the original author? See Samuel D. Warren and Louis D. Brandeis, *The Right to Privacy*, 4 Harv. L. Rev. 193 (1890). This groundbreaking law review article discovered the law of privacy, but careful examination shows the authors relied very heavily on the tort of common law copyright infringement. It was the unauthorized publication of private letters and papers that they relabeled "privacy."

e. Secrecy in publishing is generally inconsistent with copyright registration. In the area of copyrighted test books, the two areas conflict a great deal. To what extent can a newspaper "report" the content of such a copyrighted but nonpublic test book? See *Chi. Bd. of Educ. v. Substance, Inc.*, 354 F.3d 624 (7th Cir. 2004). For a discussion regarding competing test preparation companies, see *Mulcahy v. Cheetah Learning LLC*, 386 F.3d 849 (8th Cir. 2004).

f. Fair use in academic publishing has become much more complex as a result of digital archives and electronic reproductions of course packs. For a thorough review of the topic see *Cambridge U. Press v. Becker*, 863 F. Supp. 2d 1190, 1236 (N.D. Ga. 2012), which is presently under appeal ("if a professor used an excerpt representing 10% of the copyrighted work, and this was repeated by others many times, would it cause substantial damage to the potential market for the copyrighted work? The answer is no, because the 10% excerpt would not substitute for the original, no matter how many copies were made.") Compare this with non-digital decisions *Basic Books, Inc. v. Kinko's Graphics Corp.*, 758 F. Supp. 1522 (S.D.N.Y. 1991); *Princeton University Press v. Michigan Document Services, Inc.*, 99 F.3d 1381 (6th Cir. 1996); and *American Geophysical Union v. Texaco Inc.*, 60 F.3d 913 (2d Cir. 1994).

Problem XVI-E

Bryce and Jesse have just received a telephone call from the publisher of *Exposure*. In reviewing the manuscript, the publisher explained it found "a significant number of exposés which pose an editorial problem from a privacy and copyright standpoint." (You shake your head, knowing full well this moment was inevitable, based on the book's premise and structure.) Specifically, the publisher is concerned because (i) twelve of the subjects were photographed without their consent; (ii) three of the photographs depict artists creating their own works, thus publishing the artist's work as background in Jesse's photograph; (iii) four of the narratives written by Bryce include direct quotes from private letters to and from the subject of the exposé; and (iv) one exposé uses the first line and entire rhythm of a poem written by the subject of that exposé.

Bryce wants you to call the publisher's lawyer and explain why this is all fair use and free speech. After a brief discussion with you, Bryce asks that you write an opinion letter explaining that the items objected to above are fair use and therefore not actionable. Explain whether or not you could provide such a letter and the reason for that decision.

Assuming you do not provide an opinion letter to the publisher, draft a letter to Bryce explaining the legal status of the exposés and the options available to both the authors and the publisher.

F. Antitrust Considerations

U.S. v. Apple Inc.
952 F.Supp.2d 638 (2013)

This Opinion explains how and why the prices for many electronic books, or "e-books," rose significantly in the United States in April 2010. Plaintiffs the United States of America ("DOJ") and thirty-three states and U.S. territories (the "States") (collectively, "Plaintiffs"), filed these antitrust suits on April 11, 2012, alleging that defendant Apple Inc. ("Apple") and five book publishing companies conspired to raise, fix, and stabilize the retail price for newly released and bestselling trade e-books in violation of Section 1 of the Sherman Antitrust Act, 15 U.S.C. § 1 ("Sherman Act"), and various state laws. These cases represent two of four related actions brought before this Court alleging the same e-books price-fixing conspiracy between Apple and the publishers. The publishers are Hachette Book Group, Inc. ("Hachette"), HarperCollins Publishers LLC ("HarperCollins"), Holtzbrinck Publishers LLC d/b/a Macmillan ("Macmillan"), Penguin Group (USA), Inc. ("Penguin"), and Simon & Schuster, Inc. ("Simon & Schuster" or "S & S") (collectively, "Publisher Defendants").

Only Apple proceeded to trial; the Publisher Defendants have settled their claims with both the DOJ and the States. This Opinion presents the Court's findings of fact and conclusions of law following the bench trial that was held from June 3 to 20, 2013 to resolve the issue of Apple's liability and the scope of any injunctive relief. As described below, the Plaintiffs have shown that Apple conspired to raise the retail price of e-books and that they are entitled to injunctive relief....

The Plaintiffs have shown that the Publisher Defendants conspired with each other to eliminate retail price competition in order to raise e-book prices, and that Apple played a central role in facilitating and executing that conspiracy. Without Apple's orchestration of this conspiracy, it would not have succeeded as it did in the Spring of 2010.

There is, at the end of the day, very little dispute about many of the most material facts in this case. Before Apple even met with the first Publisher Defendant in mid-December 2009, it knew that the "Big Six" of United States publishing—the Publisher Defendants and Random House (collectively, the "Publishers"[8])—wanted to raise e-book prices, in particular above the $9.99 prevailing price charged by Amazon for many ebook versions of *New York Times* bestselling books ("NYT Bestsellers") and other newly released hardcover books ("New Releases"). Apple also knew that Publisher Defendants were already acting collectively to place pressure on Amazon to abandon its pricing strategy.

---

8. Titles from the Bix Six publishers accounted for over 90% of all U.S. NYT Bestseller book sales in 2010. Random House is the largest of the Big Six, followed, in descending order of size, by Penguin, Simon & Schuster, HarperCollins, Hachette, and Macmillan. When it comes to e-books, the largest of the Big Six in early 2010 was Penguin, followed in descending order by Random House, HarperCollins, Hachette, S & S, and Macmillan.

At their very first meetings in mid-December 2009, the Publishers conveyed to Apple their abhorrence of Amazon's pricing, and Apple assured the Publishers it was willing to work with them to raise those prices, suggesting prices such as $12.99 and $14.99. Over the course of their negotiations in December 2009 and January 2010, Apple and the Publisher Defendants educated one another about their other priorities. Apple strongly hoped to announce its new iBookstore when it launched the iPad on January 27, 2010, but would only do so if it had agreements in place with a core group of Publishers by that date, could assure itself it would make a profit in the iBookstore, and could offer e-book titles simultaneously with their hardcover releases. For their part, if the Publisher Defendants were going to take control of e-book pricing and move the price point above $9.99, they needed to act collectively; any other course would leave an individual Publisher vulnerable to retaliation from Amazon.

Apple and the Publisher Defendants shared one overarching interest—that there be no price competition at the retail level. Apple did not want to compete with Amazon (or any other e-book retailer) on price; and the Publisher Defendants wanted to end Amazon's $9.99 pricing and increase significantly the prevailing price point for e-books. With a full appreciation of each other's interests, Apple and the Publisher Defendants agreed to work together to eliminate retail price competition in the e-book market and raise the price of e-books above $9.99.

Apple seized the moment and brilliantly played its hand. Taking advantage of the Publisher Defendants' fear of and frustration over Amazon's pricing, as well as the tight window of opportunity created by the impending launch of the iPad on January 27 (the "Launch"), Apple garnered the signatures it needed to introduce the iBookstore at the Launch. It provided the Publisher Defendants with the vision, the format, the timetable, and the coordination that they needed to raise e-book prices. Apple decided to offer the Publisher Defendants the opportunity to move from a wholesale model—where a publisher receives its designated wholesale price for each e-book and the retailer sets the retail price—to an agency model, where a publisher sets the retail price and the retailer sells the e-book as its agent.

The agency agreements that Apple and the Publisher Defendants executed on the eve of the Launch divided New Release e-books among price tiers. The top of each tier, or cap, was essentially the new price for New Release e-books. The caps included $12.99 and $14.99 for many books then being sold at $9.99 by Amazon.

The agreements also included a price parity provision, or Most-Favored-Nation clause ("MFN"), which not only protected Apple by guaranteeing it could match the lowest retail price listed on any competitor's e-bookstore, but also imposed a severe financial penalty upon the Publisher Defendants if they did not force Amazon and other retailers similarly to change their business models and cede control over e-book pricing to the Publishers. As Apple made clear to the Publishers, "There is no one outside of us that can do this for you. If we miss this opportunity, it will likely never come again."

Through the vehicle of the Apple agency agreements, the prices in the nascent e-book industry shifted upward, in some cases 50% or more for an individual title. Virtually overnight, Apple got an attractive, additional feature for its iPad and a guaranteed new revenue stream, and the Publisher Defendants removed Amazon's ability to price their e-books at $9.99....

Beginning in at least early 2009, the Publisher Defendants began testing different ways to address what Macmillan termed "book devaluation to $9.99," and to confront what S & S's Reidy described as the "basic problem: how to get Amazon to change its pricing" and move off its $9.99 price point. They frequently coordinated their efforts to increase the pressure on Amazon and decrease the likelihood that Amazon would retaliate — an outcome each Publisher Defendant feared if it acted alone.

One of the strategies that they employed was the elimination of the existing discount on wholesale prices of e-books. This meant that the wholesale price for e-books would equal the wholesale price for physical books, and as a result, the wholesale price that Amazon paid for an e-book would be set at several dollars above Amazon's $9.99 price point. This tactic, however, failed to convince Amazon to change its pricing policies and it continued to sell many NYT Bestsellers as loss leaders at $9.99.... [The discussion of the publisher's efforts to combine in order to change Amazon's pricing structure and Steven Job's coordination of the publishers to change the pricing model is omitted.]

On Monday, January 11, [2010,] Apple sent its proposed eBook Agency Distribution Agreement ("Draft Agreement") to each of the Publishers. With the iPad launch just sixteen days away, Cue told Jobs that his "goal" was to "get at least 2 of them to sign this week."

The Draft Agreement contained all of the essential elements of the contracts that the Publisher Defendants would accept two weeks later, including a "day and date" commitment to prohibit windowing on the Apple iBookstore, price tiers, the 30% commission, and the MFN. Although the Publisher Defendants were able to negotiate around the edges, none of the material terms of the contract changed. Apple insisted that its agency contract be uniform. It assured the Publisher Defendants that they would all be getting the same terms, as would every other publisher who decided to sell e-books through the iBookstore.

In the end, each of the Publisher Defendants simply had to decide whether they wanted to take this opportunity to raise the price of e-books or not. The risks of acting and of failing to act were similarly large. As explained below, if a Publisher accepted Apple's terms it was bound to lose some of the revenue it would otherwise make from selling e-books, and could be assured that it would incur the wrath of Amazon. If the Publisher declined to join Apple it would lose this particular opportunity, backed by Apple, to confront Amazon as one of an organized group of Publishers united in an effort to eradicate the $9.99 price point....

On January 27, Jobs launched the iPad. As part of a beautifully orchestrated presentation, he also introduced the iPad's e-reader capability and the iBookstore. He proudly displayed the names and logos of each Publisher Defendant whose books would populate the iBookstore. To show the ease with which an iTunes customer could buy a book, standing in front of a giant screen displaying his own iPad's screen, Jobs browsed through his iBooks "bookshelf," clicked on the "store" button in the upper corner of his e-book shelf display, watched the shelf seamlessly flip to the iBookstore, and purchased one of Hachette's NYT Bestsellers, Edward M. Kennedy's memoir, *True Compass,* for $14.99. With one tap, the e-book was downloaded, and its cover appeared on Jobs's bookshelf, ready to be opened and read.

When asked by a reporter later that day why people would pay $14.99 in the iBookstore to purchase an e-book that was selling at Amazon for $9.99, Jobs told a reporter, "Well, that won't be the case." When the reporter sought to clarify, "You mean you won't be 14.99 or they won't be 9.99?" Jobs paused, and with a knowing nod responded, "The price will be the same," and explained that "Publishers are actually withholding their books from Amazon because they are not happy." With that statement, Jobs acknowledged his understanding that the Publisher Defendants would now wrest control of pricing from Amazon and raise e-book prices, and that Apple would not have to face any competition from Amazon on price.

The import of Jobs's statement was obvious. On January 29, the General Counsel of S & S wrote to Reidy that she "cannot believe that Jobs made the statement" and considered it "[i]ncredibly stupid." ...

Just as Apple expected, after the iBookstore opened in April 2010, the price caps in the Agreements became the new retail prices for the Publisher Defendants' e-books.... The Publisher Defendants raised more than the prices of just New Release e-books. The prices of some of their New Release *hardcover* books were also raised in order to move the e-book version into a correspondingly higher price tier. And, all of the Publisher Defendants raised the prices of their backlist e-books, which were not governed by the Agreements' price tier regimen....

Jobs himself was frank in explaining how this scheme worked when he spoke to biographer Walter Isaacson the day after the Launch. Jobs described it as an "a[i]kido move" to move all retailers to agency and eliminate price competition with Amazon. In Jobs's own words:

Amazon screwed it up. It paid the wholesale price for some books, but started selling them below cost at $9.99. The publishers hated that—they thought it would trash their ability to sell hardcover books at $28. So before Apple even got on the scene, some booksellers were starting to withhold books from Amazon. So we told the publishers, "We'll go to the agency model, where you set the price, and we get our 30%, and yes, the customer pays a little more, but that's what you want anyway." But we also asked for a guarantee that if anybody else is selling the books cheaper than we are, then we can sell them at the lower price too. So they went to Amazon and said, "You're going to sign an agency contract or we're not going to give you the books."

DISCUSSION

The United States of America has brought a single claim against Apple for violation of Section 1 of the Sherman Act. The States have brought claims against Apple based on violations of the state statutes "to the extent those laws are congruent with Section 1 of the Sherman Act." Following a description of the legal standard for a Section 1 claim, this Opinion will apply that law to the facts presented at trial. After finding that the Plaintiffs' have carried their burden of showing that Apple violated Section 1, the Opinion will address the six principal arguments that Apple has presented in its defense.

Section 1 of the Sherman Act ("Section 1") outlaws "[e]very contract, combination..., or conspiracy, in restraint of trade or commerce among the several States." 15 U.S.C. § 1. To establish a conspiracy in violation of Section 1, then, proof of joint or concerted action is required. In particular, plaintiffs must show (1) "a combination or some form of concerted action between at least two legally distinct economic entities" that, (2) "constituted an unreasonable restraint of trade either per se or under the rule of reason." *Primetime 24 Joint Venture v. Nat'l Broad. Co.*, 219 F.3d 92, 103 (2d Cir.2000).

Notwithstanding its broad language, Section 1 does not disallow any and all agreements; it "outlaws only unreasonable restraints." *Leegin Creative Leather Prods., Inc. v. PSKS, Inc.*, 551 U.S. 877, 885 (2007) (citation omitted). Thus, in many cases, "antitrust plaintiffs must demonstrate that a particular contract or combination is in fact unreasonable and anticompetitive before it will be found unlawful." *Texaco Inc. v. Dagher*, 547 U.S. 1, 5 (2006). Some agreements, however, "are so plainly anticompetitive that no elaborate study of the industry is needed to establish their illegality." *Id.*

(citation omitted). Such agreements are illegal *per se,* and are not subject to the rule of reason. The *per se* rule thus "eliminates the need to study the reasonableness of an individual restraint in light of the real market forces at work." *Leegin,* 551 U.S. at 886, 127 S.Ct. 2705.

By contrast, under the rule of reason, "the plaintiffs bear an initial burden to demonstrate the defendants' challenged behavior had an *actual* adverse effect on competition as a whole in the relevant market." *Geneva Pharms. Tech. Corp. v. Barr Labs. Inc.,* 386 F.3d 485, 506–07 (2d Cir.2004) (citation omitted).

> If the plaintiffs satisfy their initial burden, the burden shifts to the defendants to offer evidence of the procompetitive effects of their agreement. Assuming defendants can provide such proof, the burden shifts back to the plaintiffs to prove that any legitimate competitive benefits offered by defendants could have been achieved through less restrictive means. Ultimately, the fact finder must engage in a careful weighing of the competitive effects of the agreement—both pro and con—to determine if the effects of the challenged restraint tend to promote or destroy competition.

Id. at 507.

Use of the *per se* rule is limited to restraints "that would always or almost always tend to restrict competition and decrease output," and is appropriate "only after courts have had considerable experience with the type of restraint at issue." *Leegin,* 551 U.S. at 886. "Under the Sherman Act a combination formed for the purpose and with the effect of raising, depressing, fixing, pegging, or stabilizing the price of a commodity in interstate or foreign commerce is illegal *per se.*" *United States v. Socony-Vacuum Oil Co.,* 310 U.S. 150, 223, 60 S.Ct. 811, 84 L.Ed. 1129 (1940). Generally speaking, price-fixing agreements or agreements to divide markets that are horizontal in nature—meaning that the parties to the agreement are "competitors at the same level of the market structure," *Anderson News, L.L.C. v. American Media, Inc.,* 680 F.3d 162, 182 (2d Cir.2012) (citation omitted)—are *per se* unlawful. In other words, "they are prohibited despite the reasonableness of the particular prices agreed upon." *Starr,* 592 F.3d at 326 n. 4. Non-price restrictions that are otherwise lawful are also "per se unlawful if undertaken as part of an illegal scheme to fix prices." *Monsanto,* 465 U.S. at 760 n. 6. By contrast, vertical price restraints, such as resale price maintenance agreements, that do not involve price-fixing are subject to the rule of reason. *See Leegin,* 551 U.S. at 882, 127 S.Ct. 2705. A manufacturer has a right to refuse to deal "with whomever it likes, as long as it does so independently." *Monsanto,* 465 U.S. at 761....

The Plaintiffs have shown through compelling evidence that Apple violated Section 1 of the Sherman Act by conspiring with the Publisher Defendants to eliminate retail price competition and to raise e-book prices. There is overwhelming evidence that the Publisher Defendants joined with each other in a horizontal price-fixing conspiracy. Through that conspiracy, the Publisher Defendants raised the prices of many of their New Releases and NYT Bestsellers above the $9.99 price at which they had previously been sold through Amazon. They also raised the prices of many of their backlist e-books. The Plaintiffs have also shown that Apple was a knowing and active member of that conspiracy. Apple not only willingly joined the conspiracy, but also forcefully facilitated it.

There is little dispute that the Publisher Defendants conspired together to raise the prices of their e-books. They shared a common motivation: the elimination of the "wretched" $9.99 retail price that Amazon, the chief distributor of their e-books, chose for many of their New Releases, including NYT Bestsellers. They believed that this price point in the nascent but swiftly growing e-book market would, if left unchallenged, unalterably affect the consumer perception of the value of a book and severely undermine their more profitable physical book business. To protect their then-existing business model, the Publisher Defendants agreed to raise the prices of e-books by taking control of retail pricing....

This price-fixing conspiracy would not have succeeded without the active facilitation and encouragement of Apple. Before Apple even met with the Publisher Defendants in mid-December 2009, it was fully aware that the Publishers were adamantly opposed to Amazon's $9.99 price point and were actively searching for an effective means, including through collective action, to pressure Amazon to raise its prices. Inspired by the impending Launch of the revolutionary iPad, scheduled for January 27, Apple seized the moment....

Without the collective action that Apple nurtured, it is unlikely any individual Publisher would have succeeded in unilaterally imposing an agency relationship on Amazon. Working together, and equipped with Apple's agency Agreements, Apple and the Publisher Defendants moved the largest publishers of trade e-books and their distributors from a wholesale to agency model, eliminated retail price competition, and raised e-book prices.

The evidence of this conspiracy can be found in Jobs's admissions to a reporter, to James Murdoch, and to his biographer; in contemporaneous e-mails pulled from the files of Apple, the Publishers, Amazon, and others; in the web of telephone calls among Publisher Defendants' CEOs surrounding each turning point in the presentation and execution of the Agreements; and as compellingly, in the circumstantial evidence. This circumstantial evidence includes the following: each of the Publisher Defendants shared the identical goal to raise the $9.99 price point to protect its physical book business; the agency Agreements represented an "abrupt shift" from the past model for the distribution of e-books; the Publisher Defendants each demanded that Amazon adopt this new model within days of each other; the agency model protected Apple from price competition; the rise in trade e-book prices to or close to the price caps established in the Agreements was large and essentially simultaneous; in adopting a model that deprived each of them of a stream of expected revenue from the sale of e-books on the wholesale model, the Publisher Defendants all acted against their near-term financial interests; and each of the Publisher Defendants acted in identical ways even though each was also afraid of retaliation by Amazon.

In sum, the Plaintiffs have shown not just by a preponderance of the evidence, but through compelling direct and circumstantial evidence that Apple participated in and facilitated a horizontal price-fixing conspiracy. As a result, they have proven a *per se* violation of the Sherman Act. If it were necessary to analyze this evidence under the rule of reason, however, the Plaintiffs would also prevail....

Notes and Questions

a. Google's book project began with Google's drive to organize all information. The process resulted in an abortive competitive effort from Microsoft, and lawsuits by the Authors Guild and a group of commercial publishers. After three years of negotiations, the litigation resulted in a proposed settlement between the Authors Guild, the Association of American Publishers, and Google. The proposed Amended Settlement Agreement

---

9. Miguel Helft, *Judge Rejects Google's Deal to Digitize Books*, N.Y. TIMES, Mar. 23, 2011 at B1.

received preliminary approval in 2009. However, in 2011 final settlement approval was denied.

> [C]iting copyright, antitrust and other concerns, Judge Denny Chin said that the settlement went too far. He said it would have granted Google a "de facto monopoly" and the right to profit from books without the permission of copyright owners.
>
> Judge Chin acknowledged that "the creation of a universal digital library would benefit many," but said that the proposed agreement was "not fair, adequate and reasonable." He left open the possibility that a substantially revised agreement could pass legal muster. Judge Chin was recently elevated to the United States Court of Appeals for the Second Circuit, but handled the case as a district court judge.
>
> The decision is also a setback for the Authors Guild and the Association of American Publishers, which sued Google in 2005 over its book-scanning project. After two years of painstaking negotiations, the authors, publishers and Google signed a sweeping settlement that would have brought millions of printed works into the digital age.
>
> The deal turned Google, the authors and the publishers into allies instead of opponents. Together, they mounted a defense of the agreement against an increasingly vocal chorus of opponents that included Google rivals like Amazon and Microsoft, as well as academics, some authors, copyright experts, the Justice Department and foreign governments.[9]

b. The focus of the concern for the settlement was not on copyright considerations. Google's action of copying materials which are not in the public domain violates the exclusive rights of authors and publishers, but such violations may be permitted under the law if it constitutes fair use. When the decision finally went to trial, the copying of the books for Google's database and the snippet views of the books did constitute fair use.

> After seven years of litigation, Google and book publishers said on Thursday that they had reached a settlement to allow publishers to choose whether Google digitizes their books and journals.
>
> It was a small step forward for Google's plan to digitize every book and make them readable and searchable online, known as the Google Library Project, but it did not resolve the much bigger issue standing in Google's way—litigation between Google and authors....
>
> The deal allows publishers to choose whether to allow Google to digitize their out-of-print books that are still under copyright protection. If Google does so, it will also provide them with a digital copy for their own use, perhaps to sell on their Web sites.
>
> For books that it has digitized, Google allows people to read 20 percent of them online and purchase the entire books from the Google Play store, and it shares revenue with the publishers. The two parties did not disclose additional financial terms of the agreement, but the publishers had not asked for monetary damages.... [U]nder the settlement, publishers get the benefit of Google digitizing

---

10. Claire Cain Miller, *Google Deal Gives Publishers a Choice: Digitize or Not*, N.Y. Times, Oct. 5, 2012, at B7.

out-of-print books that they might not otherwise have turned into e-books. Meanwhile, Google can expand the library of e-books it sells to consumers.[10]

Had the settlement with the publishers been part of the class action, it would have removed the pricing model and other potentially anti-competitive behavior outside of antitrust scrutiny. The settlement with publishers returns control over publishing distribution largely to the publishers.

c. Amazon.com had entered into an agreement with Borders Books to operate Borders.com, and eventually Waldens.com, because Borders was unsuccessful at running its online book business. Borders hoped to reduce its losses through the Amazon arrangement while maintaining an Internet presence. The district court rejected claims of a *per se* antitrust challenge to the relationship, since the sales prices of the two companies were not fixed by agreement and the pricing was ancillary to the overall legitimate purposes of the agreement. See *Gerlinger v. Amazon.com, Inc.*, 311 F. Supp. 2d 838 (N.D. Cal. 2004). Following the bankruptcy of Borders, the website was purchased by Barnes & Noble.

G. Bibliography and Links

Anne Coale, *Fair Use: Considerations in the Emerging World of EBooks*, 16 St. John's J. Legal Comment. 727 (2002).

Daniel J. Coplan, *When is "Best Efforts" Really "Best Efforts": An Analysis of the Obligation to Exploit in Entertainment Licensing Agreements and an Overview of How the Term "Best Efforts" Has Been Construed in Litigation*, 31 SW. U. L. Rev. 725 (2002).

William M. Cross, *Restoring the Public Library Ethos: Copyright, E-Licensing, and the Future of Librarianship*, 104 Law Libr. J. 195 (2012).

Jane C. Ginsburg, *The Author's Place in the Future of Copyright*, 45 Willamette L. Rev. 381 (2009).

Jane C. Ginsburg, *The Right to Claim Authorship in U.S. Copyright and Trademarks Law*, 41 Hous. L. Rev. 263 (2004).

F. Gregory Lastowka, *Free Access and the Future of* Copyright, 27 Rutgers Computer & Tech. L.J. 293 (2001).

Martin P. Levin, *The Contemporary Guide to Negotiating the Author-Publisher Contract*, 54 N.Y.L. Sch. L. Rev. 447 (2009–10).

Jake Linford, *A Second Look at the Right of First Publication*, 58 J. Copyright Socy. U.S.A. 585, 586 (2011).

Christina Mulligan, *A Numerus Clausus Principle for Intellectual Property*, 80 Tenn. L. Rev. 235 (2013).

Bob Pimm, *Riding the Bullet to the EBook Revolution*, 18 Entertainment and Sports Lawyer 1 (2003).

Pamela Samuelson, *Collective Management of Copyright: Solution or Sacrifice?: Legislative Alternatives to the Google Book Settlement*, 34 Colum. J.L. & Arts 697 (2011).

Pamela Samuelson, *The Dead Souls of the Google Book Search Settlement*, 52 Comm. ACM (July 2009).

Chapter XVII

Visual Arts and Cultural Artifacts

Although somewhat different than the more commercial areas of entertainment law, fine art, visual arts, sculpture, and cultural artifacts play a similar role in society of entertaining and educating the public. Similarly, the laws of copyright, trademark, publicity rights, First Amendment law, contract law, and labor law shape the world of art and the operations of museums in much the same way as the other entertainment industries.

> Between 2008 and 2012, national rates of attendance at visual and performing arts activities dropped slightly, remaining below 2002 levels. In 2012, one in three U.S. adults (33 percent, or about 78 million) visited an art museum or gallery or attended at least one of various types of performing arts events....
>
> As in prior years, more Americans went to visual arts events and activities than attended most types of arts performance. Between 2008 and 2012, however, rates declined for the following activities:
>
> - Visiting an art museum or gallery (21 percent of adults nationwide, or 49.3 million, did this activity at least once in the 2012 survey year)
>
> - Attending a crafts fair or visual arts festival (22.4 percent, or 52.6 million adults) ...
>
> The share of adults who toured a park, monument, building, or neighborhood for historic or design value remained on par with the 2008 level. In 2012, 23.9 percent of all adults (56.2 million) made these kind of trips.[1]

This chapter provides an introduction to a group of issues unique to the fields of visual arts and cultural artifacts. The topic is the subject of entire courses, so these materials are designed to illustrate its intersection with entertainment law and to highlight the stark differences which derive from the unique management obligations of museums and the international issues related to art theft, forgery, and trafficking in stolen or illegally obtained artifacts.

---

1. HOW A NATION ENGAGES WITH ART — HIGHLIGHTS FROM THE 2012 SURVEY OF PUBLIC PARTICIPATION IN THE ARTS, NATIONAL ENDOWMENT FOR THE ARTS RESEARCH REPORT #57, Sep. 2013 (available http://arts.gov/sites/default/files/highlights-from-2012-SPPA.pdf.)

A. Overview of Copyright for Pictoral, Graphic, or Sculptural Arts

Bleistein v. Donaldson Lithographing Co.

188 U.S. 239 (1903)

MR. JUSTICE HOLMES delivered the opinion of the court.

The alleged infringements consisted in the copying in reduced form of three chromolithographs prepared by employees of the plaintiffs for advertisements of a circus owned by one Wallace. Each of the three contained a portrait of Wallace in the corner and lettering bearing some slight relation to the scheme of decoration, indicating the subject of the design and the fact that the reality was to be seen at the circus. One of the designs was of an ordinary ballet, one of a number of men and women, described as the Stirk family, performing on bicycles, and one of groups of men and women whitened to represent statutes. The Circuit Court directed a verdict for the defendant on the ground that the chromolithographs were not within the protection of the copyright law, and this ruling was sustained by the Circuit Court of Appeals....

We shall do no more than mention the suggestion that painting and engraving unless for a mechanical end are not among the useful arts, the progress of which Congress is empowered by the Constitution to promote. The Constitution does not limit the useful to that which satisfies immediate bodily needs. It is obvious also that the plaintiffs' case is not affected by the fact, if it be one, that the pictures represent actual groups—visible things. They seem from the testimony to have been composed from hints or description, not from sight of a performance. But even if they had been drawn from the life, that fact would not deprive them of protection. The opposite proposition would mean that a portrait by Velasquez or Whistler was common property because others might try their hand on the same face. Others are free to copy the original. They are not free to copy the copy. The copy is the personal reaction of an individual upon nature. Personality always contains something unique. It expresses its singularity even in handwriting, and a very modest grade of art has in it something irreducible, which is one man's alone. That something he may copyright unless there is a restriction in the words of the act.

If there is a restriction it is not to be found in the limited pretensions of these particular works.... We assume that the construction of Rev. Stat. § 4952 ... provides that "in the construction of this act the words 'engraving,' 'cut' and 'print' shall be applied only to pictorial illustrations or works connected with the fine arts." We see no reason for taking the words "connected with the fine arts" as qualifying anything except the word "works," but it would not change our decision if we should assume further that they also qualified "pictorial illustrations," as the defendant contends.

These chromolithographs are "pictorial illustrations." The word "illustrations" does not mean that they must illustrate the text of a book, and that the etchings of Rembrandt or Steinla's engraving of the Madonna di San Sisto could not be protected to-day if any man were able to produce them. Again, the act however construed, does not mean that ordinary posters are not good enough to be considered within its scope. The antithesis to "illustrations or works connected with the fine arts" is not works of little merit or of humble degree, or illustrations addressed to the less educated classes; it is "prints or labels designed to be used for any other articles of manufacture." Certainly works are not the less connected with the fine arts because their pictorial quality attracts the crowd and therefore gives them a real use—if use means to increase trade and to help to make money. A picture is none the less a picture and none the less a subject of copyright that it is used for an advertisement. And if pictures may be used to advertise soap, or the theatre, or monthly magazines, as they are, they may be used to advertise a circus. Of course, the ballet is as legitimate a subject for illustration as any other. A rule cannot be laid down that would excommunicate the paintings of Degas....

It would be a dangerous undertaking for persons trained only to the law to constitute themselves final judges of the worth of pictorial illustrations, outside of the narrowest and most obvious limits. At the one extreme some works of genius would be sure to miss appreciation. Their very novelty would make them repulsive until the public had learned the new language in which their author spoke. It may be more than doubted, for instance, whether the etchings of Goya or the paintings of Manet would have been sure of protection when seen for the first time. At the other end, copyright would be denied to pictures which appealed to a public less educated than the judge. Yet if they command the interest of any public, they have a commercial value—it would be bold to say that they have not an aesthetic and educational value—and the taste of any public is not to be treated with contempt. It is an ultimate fact for the moment, whatever may be out hopes for a change. That these pictures had their worth and their success is sufficiently shown by the desire to reproduce them without regard to the plaintiffs' rights. We are of opinion that there was evidence that the plaintiffs have rights entitled to the protection of the law.

The judgment of the Circuit Court of Appeals is reversed; the judgment of the Circuit Court is also reversed and the cause remanded to that court with directions to set aside the verdict and grant a new trial.

DISSENT: MR. JUSTICE HARLAN, with whom concurred MR. JUSTICE McKENNA, dissenting.

[Quoting the Court of Appeals] "What we hold is this: That if a chromo, lithograph, or other print, engraving, or picture has no other use than that of a mere advertisement, and no value aside from this function, it would not be promotive of the useful arts, within the meaning of the constitutional provision, to protect the 'author' in the exclusive use thereof, and the copyright statute should not be construed as including such a publication, if any other construction is admissible.... It must have some connection with the fine arts to give it intrinsic value, and that it shall have is the meaning which we attach to the act of June 18, 1874, amending the provisions of the copyright law. We are unable to discover anything useful or meritorious in the design copyrighted by the plaintiffs in error other than as an advertisement of acts to be done or exhibited to the public in Wallace's show. No evidence, aside from the deductions which are to be drawn from the prints themselves, was offered to show that these designs had any original artistic qualities."... The clause of the Constitution giving Congress power to promote the progress of science and useful arts, by securing for limited terms to authors and inventors the exclusive right to their respective works and discoveries, does not, as I think, embrace a mere advertisement of a circus.

Notes and Questions

a. Initially, the courts must grapple with the definition of art in a number of contexts. As Justice Learned Hand explained, "It is true that 'works of art' is a loose phrase whose perimeter is hard to define; nevertheless ... the mere fact that the meaning of the phrase, 'works of art,' admits of debate does not make it different from many statutes whose interpretation is every day regarded as reviewable by the courts." *Vacheron & Constantin-Le Coultre Watches, Inc. v. Benrus Watch Co.,* 260 F.2d 637, 640 (2d Cir. 1958).

b. Congress and the courts did not hesitate to recognize fine art as within the ambit of copyright protection. The courts extended this protection to artistic photographs as writings within the meaning of the Constitution. *Burrow-Giles Lithographic Co. v. Sarony,* 111 U.S. 53 (1884). Despite this expansion, however, questions remain regarding the scope of this protection and the meaning of "author" for purposes of copyright.

c. To what extent does the reproduction of a public domain work of art entitle the new artist to claim copyright in the completed work? Compare *L. Batlin & Son, Inc. v. Snyder,* 536 F.2d 486 (2d Cir. 1976), with *Durham Indus., Inc. v. Tomy Corp.,* 630 F.2d 905 (2d Cir. 1980), and *Entm't, Inc. v. Genesis Creative Group, Inc.,* 122 F.3d 1211, 1219 (9th Cir. 1997).

B. Artists' Rights to Attribution and Integrity

Introduction

The law protecting visual artists builds on the legal protections afforded to all copyright owners — those protected by § 43(a) of the Lanham Act, as well as the state law protections for publicity rights. In addition to these protections, select works of visual art are protected by the Visual Artists Rights Act, providing protection for an artist's rights of attribution and integrity.

Article 6*bis* of the Berne Convention states the international standard for the protection of moral rights.

> Independently of the author's economic rights, and even after the transfer of the said rights, the author shall have the right to claim authorship of the work and to object to any distortion, mutilation or other modification of, or other derogatory action in relation to, the said work, which would be prejudicial to his honor or reputation.

Berne Convention for the Protection of Literary and Artistic Works, September 9, 1886, art. 6*bis*, S. Treaty Doc. No. 27, 99th Cong., 2d Sess. 41 (1986).

> In the United States, the moral rights of attribution regarding the identity of the author or artist of a work and the moral right of integrity protecting the work from destruction or mutilation are not explicitly recognized under copyright law, except as provided in the Visual Artists Rights Act of 1990, 17 U.S.C. § 106(a) (2000) (VARA).

> Despite this, courts prior to 1990 and courts adjudicating copyright claims outside the coverage of VARA have sometimes recognized aspects of the moral rights of attribution and integrity through an interpretation of contractual provisions, Lanham Act § 43(a) unfair competition claims, or various state law claims. In a report on VARA, the Register of Copyrights provides a useful history of this litigation:

> Although moral rights were not recognized in U.S. copyright law prior to enactment of VARA, some state legislatures had enacted moral rights laws, and a number of judicial decisions accorded some moral rights protection under the-

ories of copyright, unfair competition, defamation, invasion of privacy, and breach of contract. Such cases have continued relevance, not only for historical interest, but also for precedential value because state and common law moral rights protection was not entirely preempted by VARA. Arguably, state laws of defamation, invasion of privacy, contracts, and unfair competition by "passing off" are not preempted. Further, VARA rights endure only for the artist's life, after which preemption ceases.

In *Vargas v. Esquire* [164 F.2d 522, 526 (7th Cir. 1947)], artist Antonio Vargas created a series of calendar girl illustrations for *Esquire* magazine, some of which were published without his signature or credit-line. The U.S. Court of Appeals for the Seventh Circuit ruled the rights of the parties were determined by the contract in which Vargas agreed as independent contractor to furnish pictures and granted all rights in the artwork to *Esquire*. The court rejected theories of implied contract, moral rights, and unfair competition.

In *Granz v. Harris* [198 F.2d 585 (2d Cir. 1952)], a jazz concert was re-recorded with a reduced playing time and content, such that a full eight minutes was omitted. The contract required the defendant to use a credit-line attributing the plaintiff-producer, who sued. The Second Circuit decided that selling abbreviated recordings with the original credit line constituted unfair competition and breach of contract. Whether by contract or by tort, the plaintiff could prevent publication "as his, of a garbled version of his uncopyrighted product."

In *Gilliam v. American Broadcasting Cos.* [538 F.2d 14 (2d Cir. 1976)], ABC broadcast the first of two 90-minute specials, consisting of three 30-minute Monty Python shows each, but cut 24 of the original 90 minutes. Monty Python sued for an injunction and damages. The Second Circuit ruled that ABC's actions contravened contractual provisions limiting the right to edit the program and that a licensee's unauthorized use of an underlying work by publication in a truncated version was a copyright infringement. In a theory akin to moral rights, the court said that a distorted version of a writer's or performer's work may violate rights protected by the Lanham Act and may present a cause of action under that statute. The concurrence cautioned against employing the Lanham Act as a substitute for moral rights, and believed the court should restrict its opinion to contract and copyright issues.

Another case, *Wojnarowicz v. American Family Association* [772 F. Supp. 201 (S.D.N.Y. 1991)], involved a group that protested an artist's work by reproducing 14 fragments in a pamphlet. The U.S. District Court for the Southern District of New York found for the artist under the New York Artists' Authorship Rights Act, but dismissed claims under the Copyright and Lanham Acts.[2]

Carter v. Helmsley-Spear, Inc.
71 F.3d 77 (2d Cir. 1995)

Defendants 474431 Associates and Helmsley-Spear, Inc. (defendants or appellants), as the owner and managing agent respectively, of a commercial building in Queens, New York, appeal from an order of the United States District Court for the Southern District

---

2. Waiver of Moral Rights in Visual Artworks, Executive Summary, Report of the Copyright Office (October 1996), *available at* http://www.copyright.gov/reports/exsum.html.

of New York (Edelstein, J.), entered on September 6, 1994 following a bench trial. The order granted plaintiffs, who are three artists, a permanent injunction that enjoined defendants from removing, modifying or destroying a work of visual art that had been installed in defendants' building by plaintiffs-artists commissioned by a former tenant to install the work. See *Carter v. Helmsley-Spear, Inc.*, 861 F. Supp. 303 (S.D.N.Y. 1994). Defendants also appeal from the dismissal by the trial court of their counterclaim for waste. Plaintiffs cross-appeal from the dismissal of their cause of action for tortious interference with contractual relations and from the denial of their requests to complete the work and for an award of attorney's fees and costs.

On this appeal we deal with an Act of Congress that protects the rights of artists to preserve their works. One of America's most insightful thinkers observed that a country is not truly civilized "where the arts, such as they have, are all imported, having no indigenous life." 7 WORKS OF RALPH WALDO EMERSON, SOCIETY AND SOLITUDE, CHAPT. II CIVILIZATION 34 (AMS. ed. 1968). From such reflection it follows that American artists are to be encouraged by laws that protect their works. Although Congress in the statute before us did just that, it did not mandate the preservation of art at all costs and without due regard for the rights of others.

For the reasons that follow, we reverse and vacate the grant of injunctive relief to plaintiffs and affirm the dismissal by the district court of plaintiffs' other claims and its dismissal of defendants' counterclaim for waste.

BACKGROUND

Defendant 474431 Associates (Associates) is the owner of a mixed use commercial building located at 47-44 31st Street, Queens, New York, which it has owned since 1978. Associates is a New York general partnership. The general partners are Alvin Schwartz and Supervisory Management Corp., a wholly-owned subsidiary of Helmsley Enterprises, Inc. Defendant Helmsley-Spear, Inc. is the current managing agent of the property for Associates.

On February 1, 1990 Associates entered into a 48-year net lease, leasing the building to 47-44 31st Street Associates, L.P. (Limited Partnership), a Delaware limited partnership. From February 1, 1990 until June 1993, Irwin Cohen or an entity under his control was the general partner of the Limited Partnership, and managed the property through Cohen's SIG Management Company (SIG). Corporate Life Insurance Company (Corporate Life) was a limited partner in the Limited Partnership. In June 1993 SIG ceased its involvement with the property and Corporate Life, through an entity controlled by it, became the general partner of the Limited Partnership. The property was then managed by the Limited Partnership, through Theodore Nering, a Corporate Life representative. There is no relationship, other than the lease, between Associates, the lessor, and the Limited Partnership, the lessee.

Plaintiffs John Carter, John Swing and John Veronis (artists or plaintiffs) are professional sculptors who work together and are known collectively as the "Three-J's" or "Jx3." On December 16, 1991 SIG entered into a one-year agreement with the plaintiffs "engaging and hiring the Artists ... to design, create and install sculpture and other permanent installations" in the building, primarily the lobby. Under the agreement plaintiffs had "full authority in design, color and style," and SIG retained authority to direct the location and installation of the artwork within the building. The artists were to retain copyrights to their work and SIG was to receive 50 percent of any proceeds from its exploitation. On January 20, 1993 SIG and the artists signed an agreement extending the duration of their commission for an additional year. When Corporate Life became a general partner of the Limited Partnership, the Limited Partnership assumed the agreement with plaintiffs and in December 1993 again extended the agreement.

The artwork that is the subject of this litigation is a very large "walk-through sculpture" occupying most, but not all, of the building's lobby. The artwork consists of a variety of sculptural elements constructed from recycled materials, much of it metal, affixed to the walls and ceiling, and a vast mosaic made from pieces of recycled glass embedded in the floor and walls. Elements of the work include a giant hand fashioned from an old school bus, a face made of automobile parts, and a number of interactive components. These assorted elements make up a theme relating to environmental concerns and the significance of recycling.

The Limited Partnership's lease on the building was terminated on March 31, 1994. It filed for bankruptcy one week later. The property was surrendered to defendant Associates on April 6, 1994 and defendant Helmsley-Spear, Inc. took over management of the property. Representatives of defendants informed the artists that they could no longer continue to install artwork at the property, and instead had to vacate the building. These representatives also made statements indicating that defendants intended to remove the artwork already in place in the building's lobby.

As a result of defendants' actions, artists commenced this litigation. On April 26, 1994 the district court issued a temporary restraining order enjoining defendants from taking any action to alter, deface, modify or mutilate the artwork installed in the building. In May 1994 a hearing was held on whether a preliminary injunction should issue. The district court subsequently granted a preliminary injunction enjoining defendants from removing the artwork pending the resolution of the instant litigation.

A bench trial was subsequently held in June and July 1994, at the conclusion of which the trial court granted the artists the permanent injunction prohibiting defendants from distorting, mutilating, modifying, destroying and removing plaintiffs' artwork. The injunction is to remain in effect for the lifetimes of the three plaintiffs. Plaintiffs' other claims, including their cause of action for tortious interference and a request for an award of costs and attorney's fees and that they be allowed to continue to add to the artwork in the lobby, as well as defendants' counterclaim for waste, were all dismissed with prejudice. This appeal and cross-appeal followed.

DISCUSSION

I. Artists' Moral Rights

A. History of Artists' Moral Rights

Because it was under the rubric of the Visual Artists Rights Act of 1990 that plaintiffs obtained injunctive relief in the district court, we must explore, at least in part, the contours of that Act. In doing so it is necessary to review briefly the concept of artists' moral rights and the history and development of those rights in American jurisprudence, which led up to passage of the statute we must now examine.

The term "moral rights" has its origins in the civil law and is a translation of the French *le droit moral*, which is meant to capture those rights of a spiritual, non-economic and personal nature. The rights spring from a belief that an artist in the process of creation injects his spirit into the work and that the artist's personality, as well as the integrity of the work, should therefore be protected and preserved. Because they are personal to the artist, moral rights exist independently of an artist's copyright in his or her work.

While the rubric of moral rights encompasses many varieties of rights, two are protected in nearly every jurisdiction recognizing their existence: attribution and integrity.

See Art Law at 420. The right of attribution generally consists of the right of an artist to be recognized by name as the author of his work or to publish anonymously or pseudonymously, the right to prevent the author's work from being attributed to someone else, and to prevent the use of the author's name on works created by others, including distorted editions of the author's original work. The right of integrity allows the author to prevent any deforming or mutilating changes to his work, even after title in the work has been transferred.

In some jurisdictions the integrity right also protects artwork from destruction. Whether or not a work of art is protected from destruction represents a fundamentally different perception of the purpose of moral rights. If integrity is meant to stress the public interest in preserving a nation's culture, destruction is prohibited; if the right is meant to emphasize the author's personality, destruction is seen as less harmful than the continued display of deformed or mutilated work that misrepresents the artist and destruction may proceed.

Although moral rights are well established in the civil law, they are of recent vintage in American jurisprudence. Federal and state courts typically recognized the existence of such rights in other nations, but rejected artists' attempts to inject them into U.S. law. Nonetheless, American courts have in varying degrees acknowledged the idea of moral rights, cloaking the concept in the guise of other legal theories, such as copyright, unfair competition, invasion of privacy, defamation, and breach of contract.

In the landmark case of *Gilliam v. American Broadcasting Companies, Inc.*, 538 F.2d 14 (2d Cir. 1976), we relied on copyright law and unfair competition principles to safeguard the integrity rights of the "Monty Python" group, noting that although the law "seeks to vindicate the economic, rather than the personal rights of authors ... the economic incentive for artistic ... creation ... cannot be reconciled with the inability of artists to obtain relief for mutilation or misrepresentation of their work to the public on which the artists are financially dependent." Because decisions protecting artists rights are often "clothed in terms of proprietary right in one's creation," we continued, "they also properly vindicate the author's personal right to prevent the presentation of his work to the public in a distorted form."

Artists fared better in state legislatures than they generally had in courts. California was the first to take up the task of protecting artists with the passage in 1979 of the California Art Preservation Act, Cal. Civ. Code § 987 et seq. (West 1982 & Supp. 1995), followed in 1983 by New York's enactment of the Artist's Authorship Rights Act, N.Y. Arts & Cult. Aff. Law § 14.03 (McKinney Supp. 1995). Nine other states have also passed moral rights statutes, generally following either the California or New York models.

B. Visual Artists Rights Act of 1990

Although bills protecting artists' moral rights had first been introduced in Congress in 1979, they had drawn little support. The issue of federal protection of moral rights was a prominent hurdle in the debate over whether the United States should join the Berne Convention, the international agreement protecting literary and artistic works. Article 6*bis* of the Berne Convention protects attribution and integrity, stating in relevant part:

> Independently of the author's economic rights, and even after the transfer of the said rights, the author shall have the right to claim authorship of the work and to object to any distortion, mutilation or other modification of, or other derogatory action in relation to, the said work, which would be prejudicial to his honor or reputation.

Berne Convention for the Protection of Literary and Artistic Works, September 9, 1886, art. 6*bis*, S. Treaty Doc. No. 27, 99th Cong., 2d Sess. 41 (1986).

The Berne Convention's protection of moral rights posed a significant difficulty for U.S. adherence. See Copyright Law at 1022 ("The obligation of the United States to provide *droit moral* ... was the single most contentious issue surrounding Berne adherence."); Nimmer at 8D-15 ("During the debate over [the Berne Convention Implementation Act], Congress faced an avalanche of opposition to moral rights, including denunciations of moral rights by some of the bill's most vociferous advocates."); H.R. Rep. No. 514, 101st Cong., 2d Sess. 7 (1990), reprinted in 1990 U.S.C.C.A.N. 6915, 6917 ("After almost 100 years of debate, the United States joined the Berne Convention.... Consensus over United States adherence was slow to develop in large part because of debate over the requirements of Article 6*bis*.").

Congress passed the Berne Convention Implementation Act of 1988, Pub. L. No. 100-568, 102 Stat. 2853 (1988), and side-stepped the difficult question of protecting moral rights. It declared that the Berne Convention is not self-executing, existing law satisfied the United States' obligations in adhering to the Convention, its provisions are not enforceable through any action brought pursuant to the Convention itself, and neither adherence to the Convention nor the implementing legislation expands or reduces any rights under federal, state, or common law to claim authorship of a work or to object to any distortion, mutilation, or other modification of a work.

Two years later Congress enacted the Visual Artists Rights Act of 1990 (VARA or Act), Pub. L. No. 101-650 (tit. VI), 104 Stat. 5089, 5128–33 (1990). Construing this Act constitutes the subject of the present appeal. The Act

> protects both the reputations of certain visual artists and the works of art they create. It provides these artists with the rights of "attribution" and "integrity."...
>
> These rights are analogous to those protected by Article 6*bis* of the Berne Convention, which are commonly known as "moral rights." The theory of moral rights is that they result in a climate of artistic worth and honor that encourages the author in the arduous act of creation.

H.R. Rep. No. 514 at 5 (internal quote omitted). The Act brings to fruition Emerson's insightful observation.

Its principal provisions afford protection only to authors of works of visual art — a narrow class of art defined to include paintings, drawings, prints, sculptures, or photographs produced for exhibition purposes, existing in a single copy or limited edition of 200 copies or fewer. 17 U.S.C. § 101 (Supp. III 1991). With numerous exceptions, VARA grants three rights: the right of attribution, the right of integrity and, in the case of works of visual art of "recognized stature," the right to prevent destruction. 17 U.S.C. § 106A (Supp. III 1991). For works created on or after June 1, 1991 — the effective date of the Act — the rights provided for endure for the life of the author or, in the case of a joint work, the life of the last surviving author. The rights cannot be transferred, but may be waived by a writing signed by the author. Copyright registration is not required to bring an action for infringement of the rights granted under VARA, or to secure statutory damages and attorney's fees. 17 U.S.C. §§ 411, 412 (1988 & Supp. III 1991). All remedies available under copyright law, other than criminal remedies, are available in an action for infringement of moral rights. 17 U.S.C. § 506 (1988 & Supp. III 1991). With this historical background in hand, we pass to the merits of the present litigation.

II. Work of Visual Art

Because VARA is relatively new, a fuller explication of it is helpful. In analyzing the Act, therefore, we will follow in order the definition set forth in § 101, as did the district court when presiding over this litigation. The district court determined that the work of art installed in the lobby of Associates' building was a work of visual art as defined by VARA; that distortion, mutilation, or modification of the work would prejudice plaintiffs' honor and reputations; that the work was of recognized stature, thus protecting it from destruction (including removal that would result in destruction); and that Associates consented to or ratified the installation of the work in its building. The result was that defendants were enjoined from removing or otherwise altering the work during the lifetimes of the three artists.

[ ] The Statutory Definition

A "work of visual art" is defined by the Act in terms both positive (what it is) and negative (what it is not). In relevant part VARA defines a work of visual art as "a painting, drawing, print, or sculpture, existing in a single copy" or in a limited edition of 200 copies or fewer. 17 U.S.C. § 101. Although defendants aver that elements of the work are not visual art, their contention is foreclosed by the factual finding that the work is a single, indivisible whole. Concededly, considered as a whole, the work is a sculpture and exists only in a single copy. Therefore, the work satisfies the Act's positive definition of a work of visual art. We next turn to the second part of the statutory definition—what is not a work of visual art.

The definition of visual art excludes "any poster, map, globe, chart, technical drawing, diagram, model, applied art, motion picture or other audio-visual work." 17 U.S.C. § 101. Congress meant to distinguish works of visual art from other media, such as audio-visual works and motion pictures, due to the different circumstances surrounding how works of each genre are created and disseminated. See H.R. Rep. No. 514 at 9. Although this concern led to a narrow definition of works of visual art,

> the courts should use common sense and generally accepted standards of the artistic community in determining whether a particular work falls within the scope of the definition. Artists may work in a variety of media, and use any number of materials in creating their works. Therefore, whether a particular work falls within the definition should not depend on the medium or materials used.

Id. at 11.

"Applied art" describes "two- and three-dimensional ornamentation or decoration that is affixed to otherwise utilitarian objects." Defendants' assertion that at least parts of the work are applied art appears to rest on the fact that some of the sculptural elements are affixed to the lobby's floor, walls, and ceiling—all utilitarian objects. Interpreting applied art to include such works would render meaningless VARA's protection for works of visual art installed in buildings. A court should not read one part of a statute so as to deprive another part of meaning.

Appellants do not suggest the entire work is applied art. The district court correctly stated that even if components of the work standing alone were applied art, "nothing in VARA proscribes protection of works of visual art that incorporate elements of, rather than constitute, applied art." VARA's legislative history leaves no doubt that "a new and independent work created from snippets of [excluded] materials, such as a collage, is of course not excluded" from the definition of a work of visual art. H.R. Rep. No. 514 at 14. The trial judge correctly ruled the work is not applied art precluded from protection under the Act.

III. Work Made for Hire

Also excluded from the definition of a work of visual art is any work made for hire. A "work made for hire" is defined in the Copyright Act, in relevant part, as "a work prepared by an employee within the scope of his or her employment." Appellants maintain the work was made for hire and therefore is not a work of visual art under VARA. The district court held otherwise, finding that the plaintiffs were hired as independent contractors.

A. Reid Tests

The Copyright Act does not define the terms "employee" or "scope of employment." In *Community for Creative Non-Violence v. Reid*, 490 U.S. 730 (1989), the Supreme Court looked to the general common law of agency for guidance. It held that a multi-factor balancing test was required to determine if a work was produced for hire (by an employee) or was produced by an independent contractor. The Court elaborated 13 specific factors:

> the hiring party's right to control the manner and means by which the product is accomplished.... the skill required; the source of the instrumentalities and tools; the location of the work; the duration of the relationship between the parties; whether the hiring party has the right to assign additional projects to the hired party; the extent of the hired party's discretion over when and how long to work; the method of payment; the hired party's role in hiring and paying assistants; whether the work is part of the regular business of the hiring party; whether the hiring party is in business; the provision of employee benefits; and the tax treatment of the hired party.

Reid, 490 U.S. at 751–52. While all of these factors are relevant, no single factor is determinative. Instead, the factors are weighed by referring to the facts of a given case.

The district court determined that the sculpture was not "work for hire" and therefore not excluded from the definition of visual art. The Reid test is a list of factors not all of which may come into play in a given case. The Reid test is therefore easily misapplied. We are usually reluctant to reverse a district court's factual findings as to the presence or absence of any of the Reid factors and do so only when the district court's findings are clearly erroneous. By contrast, the ultimate legal conclusion as to whether or not the sculpture is "work for hire" is reviewed *de novo*. The district court correctly stated the legal test. But some of its factual findings, we think, were clearly erroneous.

B. Factors Applied

The district court properly noted that *Aymes* established five factors which would be relevant in nearly all cases: the right to control the manner and means of production; requisite skill; provision of employee benefits; tax treatment of the hired party; whether the hired party may be assigned additional projects. Analysis begins with a discussion of these factors. [*Aymes v. Bonelli*, 980 F.2d 857, 861 (2d Cir. 1992).]

First, plaintiffs had complete artistic freedom with respect to every aspect of the sculpture's creation. Although the artists heeded advice or accepted suggestions from building engineers, architects, and others, such actions were not a relinquishment of their artistic freedom. The evidence strongly supports the finding that plaintiffs controlled the work's "manner and means." This fact, in turn, lent credence to their contention that they were independent contractors. While artistic freedom remains a central factor in our inquiry, the Supreme Court has cautioned that "the extent of control the hiring party exercises over the details of the product is not dispositive." *Reid*, 490 U.S. at 752. Hence, resolving the question of whether plaintiffs had artistic freedom does not end the analysis.

The district court also correctly found the artists' conception and execution of the work required great skill in execution. Appellants' contention that the plaintiffs' reliance on assistants in some way mitigates the skill required for this work is meritless, particularly because each of the plaintiffs is a professional sculptor and the parties stipulated that professional sculpting is a highly skilled occupation. The right to control the manner and means and the requisite skill needed for execution of this project were both properly found by the district court to weigh against "work for hire" status.

The trial court erred, however, when it ruled that the defendants could not assign the artists additional projects. First, the employment agreement between SIG Management Company and the artists clearly states that the artists agreed not only to install the sculpture but also to "render such other related services and duties as may be assigned to [them] from time to time by the Company." By the very terms of the contract the defendants and their predecessors in interest had the right to assign other related projects to the artists. The district court incorrectly decided that this language supported the artists' claim to be independent contractors. While the artists' obligations were limited to related services and duties, the defendants nonetheless did have the right to assign to plaintiffs work other than the principal sculpture.

Further, the defendants did, in fact, assign such other projects. The district court concedes as much, explaining that "plaintiffs did create art work on the property other than that in the Lobby." The record shows the artists performed projects on the sixth floor of the building, on the eighth floor, and in the boiler room. Thus, on at least three different occasions the plaintiffs were assigned additional projects, which they completed without further compensation....

We must also consider factors the district court correctly found to favor finding the sculpture to be work for hire. Specifically, the provision of employee benefits and the tax treatment of the plaintiffs weigh strongly in favor of employee status. The defendants paid payroll and social security taxes, provided employee benefits such as life, health, and liability insurance and paid vacations, and contributed to unemployment insurance and workers' compensation funds on plaintiffs' behalf. Moreover, two of the three artists filed for unemployment benefits after their positions were terminated, listing the building's management company as their former employer. Other formal indicia of an employment relationship existed. For instance, each plaintiff was paid a weekly salary. The artists also agreed in their written contract that they would work principally for the defendants for the duration of their agreement on a 40-hour per week basis and they would only do other work to the extent that it would not "interfere with services to be provided" to the defendants. All of these facts strongly suggest the artists were employees....

C. Employee Status

Our review of the legal conclusion drawn from balancing the various Reid factors persuades us that the factors that weigh in favor of finding the artists were employees outweigh those factors supporting the artists' claim that they were independent contractors.... These factors, properly considered and weighed with the employee benefits granted plaintiffs and the tax treatment accorded them, are more than sufficient to demonstrate that the artists were employees, and the sculpture is therefore a work made for hire as a matter of law.

IV. Defendants' Counterclaim and Plaintiffs' Cross-appeal

Finally, since we have determined that the work is one made for hire and therefore outside the scope of VARA's protection, we need not discuss that Act's broad protection of visual art and the protection it affords works of art incorporated into a building. Also, as plaintiffs' sculpture was not protected from removal because the artists were employees and not independent contractors, we need not reach the defendants' Fifth Amendment takings argument.

Moreover, because the sculpture is not protected by VARA from removal resulting in its destruction or alteration, we do not address plaintiffs' contentions that VARA entitles them to complete the "unfinished" portion of the work, that they are entitled to reasonable costs and attorney's fees, and that appellants tortiously interfered with the artists' contract with SIG and the Limited Partnership. Finally, the district court dismissed defendants' counterclaim against the artists for waste, finding, *inter alia*, that such a cause of action under New York law may only be brought by a landlord against a tenant. Appellants have failed to persuade us that it was error to dismiss this counterclaim.

CONCLUSION

Accordingly, the district court's order insofar as it held the work was one not made for hire is reversed and the injunction vacated. In all other respects, the order of the district court is affirmed. Each party to bear its own costs.

Martin v. City of Indianapolis
192 F.3d 608 (7th Cir. 1999)

We are not art critics, do not pretend to be and do not need to be to decide this case. A large outdoor stainless steel sculpture by plaintiff Jan Martin, an artist, was demolished by the defendant as part of an urban renewal project. Plaintiff brought a one-count suit against the City of Indianapolis (the "City") under the Visual Artists Rights Act of 1990 ("VARA"), 17 U.S.C. § 101 *et seq.* The parties filed cross-motions for summary judgment. The district court granted plaintiff's motion and awarded plaintiff statutory damages in the maximum amount allowed for a non-willful statutory violation....

Plaintiff is an artist, but in this instance more with a welding torch than with a brush. He offered evidence to show, not all of it admitted, that his works have been displayed in museums, and other works created for private commissions, including a time capsule for the Indianapolis Museum of Art Centennial. He has also done sculptured jewelry for the Indiana Arts Commission. In 1979, at the Annual Hoosier Salem Art Show, plaintiff was awarded the prize for best of show in any medium. He holds various arts degrees from Purdue University, the Art Institute of Chicago and Bowling Green State University in Ohio. Plaintiff had been employed as production coordinator for Tarpenning-LaFollette Co. (the "Company"), a metal contracting firm in Indianapolis. It was in this position that he turned his artistic talents to metal sculpture fabrication.

In 1984, plaintiff received permission from the Indianapolis Metropolitan Development Commission to erect a twenty-by-forty-foot metal sculpture on land owned by John LaFollette, chairman of the Company. The Company also agreed to furnish the materials. The resulting Project Agreement between the City and the Company granted a zoning variance to permit the erection of plaintiff's proposed sculpture. An attachment to that agreement and the center of this controversy provided as follows:

> Should a determination be made by the Department of Metropolitan Development that the subject sculpture is no longer compatible with the existing land use or that the acquisition of the property is necessary, the owner of the land and the owner of the sculpture will receive written notice signed by the Director of the Department of Metropolitan Development giving the owners of the land and

sculpture ninety (90) days to remove said sculpture. Subject to weather and ground conditions.

Plaintiff went to work on the project and in a little over two years it was completed. He named it "Symphony # 1," but as it turns out in view of this controversy, a more suitable musical name might have been "1812 Overture." Because of the possibility that the sculpture might someday have to be removed, as provided for in the Project Agreement, Symphony # 1 was engineered and built by plaintiff so that it could be disassembled for removal and later reassembled. The sculpture did not go unnoticed by the press, public or art community. Favorable comments admitted into evidence and objected to by the City are now an issue on appeal and their admissibility will be considered hereinafter.

The trouble began in April 1992 when the City notified LaFollette that there would be public hearings on the City's proposed acquisition of various properties as part of an urban renewal plan. One of the properties to be acquired was home to Symphony # 1. Kim Martin, president of the Company and plaintiff's brother, responded to the City. He reminded the City that the Company had paid for Symphony # 1, and had signed the agreement with the Metropolitan Development Corporation pertaining to the eventuality of removal. Martin stated that if the sculpture was to be removed, the Company would be willing to donate it to the City provided the City would bear the costs of removal to a new site, but that plaintiff would like some input as to where his sculpture might be placed. Plaintiff also personally appeared before the Metropolitan Development Commission and made the same proposal. This was followed by a letter from plaintiff to the Mayor reiterating the removal proposal. The Mayor responded that he was referring plaintiff's proposal to his staff to see what could be done.

The City thereafter purchased the land. At the closing, plaintiff again repeated his proposal and agreed to assist so Symphony # 1 could be saved and, if necessary, moved without damage. The City's response was that plaintiff would be contacted in the event the sculpture was to be removed. Shortly thereafter, the City awarded a contract to demolish the sculpture, and demolition followed, all without prior notice to plaintiff or the Company. This lawsuit resulted in which summary judgment was allowed for plaintiff. However, his victory was not entirely satisfactory to him, nor was the City satisfied. The City appealed, and plaintiff cross-appealed.

VARA seems to be a stepchild of our copyright laws, but does not require copyright registration. Some remedies under the Copyright Act, however, including attorney's fees, are recoverable. 17 U.S.C. §§ 504–05. VARA provides: "The author of a work of visual art … shall have the right … to prevent any destruction of a work of recognized stature, and any intentional or grossly negligent destruction of that work is a violation of that right." The district court considered Symphony # 1 to be of *recognized stature* under the evidence presented and thus concluded that the City had violated plaintiff's rights under VARA. That finding is contested by the City.

"Recognized stature" is a necessary finding under VARA in order to protect a work of visual art from destruction. In spite of its significance, that phrase is not defined in VARA, leaving its intended meaning and application open to argument and judicial resolution. The only case found undertaking to define and apply "recognized stature" is *Carter v. Helmsley-Spear, Inc.*, 861 F. Supp. 303 (S.D.N.Y. 1994), *aff'd in part, vacated in part, rev'd in part*, 71 F.3d 77 (2nd Cir. 1995). Involved was an unusual work of art consisting of interrelated sculptural elements constructed from recycled materials, mostly metal, to decorate the lobby of a commercial building in a borough of New York City. Part of the work was "a giant hand fashioned from an old school bus, [and] a face made of automobile parts...." Although the Second Circuit reversed the district court and held that the work was not a work of visual art protected by VARA, the district court presented an informative discussion in determining whether a work of visual art may qualify as one of "recognized stature." That determination is based greatly on the testimony of experts on both sides of the issue, as would ordinarily be expected.

The stature test formulated by the New York district court required:

> (1) that the visual art in question has "stature," i.e. is viewed as meritorious, and (2) that this stature is "recognized" by art experts, other members of the artistic community, or by some cross-section of society. In making this showing, plaintiffs generally, but not inevitably, will need to call expert witnesses to testify before the trier of fact.

Carter I, 861 F. Supp. at 325.

Even though the district court in this present case found that test was satisfied by the plaintiff's evidence, plaintiff argues that the *Carter v. Helmsley-Spear* test may be more rigorous than Congress intended. That may be, but we see no need for the purposes of this case to endeavor to refine that rule. Plaintiff's evidence, however, is not as complete as in *Carter v. Helmsley-Spear*, possibly because Symphony # 1 was destroyed by the City without the opportunity for experts to appraise the sculpture in place.

The City objects to the "stature" testimony that was offered by plaintiff as inadmissible hearsay. If not admitted, it would result in plaintiff's failure to sustain his burden of proof. It is true that plaintiff offered no evidence of experts or others by deposition, affidavit or interrogatories. Plaintiff's evidence of "stature" consisted of certain newspaper and magazine articles, and various letters, including a letter from an art gallery director and a letter to the editor of *The Indianapolis News*, all in support of the sculpture, as well as a program from the show at which a model of the sculpture won "Best of Show." After reviewing the City's objection, the district court excluded plaintiff's "programs and awards" evidence as lacking adequate foundation, but nevertheless found Martin had met his "stature" burden of proof with his other evidence.

Included in the admitted evidence, for example, was a letter dated October 25, 1982 from the Director of the Herron School of Art, Indiana University, Indianapolis. It was written to the Company and says in part, "The proposed sculpture is, in my opinion, an interesting and aesthetically stimulating configuration of forms and structures." *The Indianapolis Star*, in a four-column article by its visual arts editor, discussed public sculpture in Indianapolis. This article included a photograph of Symphony # 1. The article lamented that the City had "been graced by only five pieces of note," but that two more had been added that particular year, one being plaintiff's sculpture. It noted, among other things, that Symphony # 1 had been erected without the aid of "federal grants" and without the help of any committee of concerned citizens. Other public sculptures came in for some criticism in the article. However, in discussing Symphony # 1, the author wrote: "Gleaming clean and abstract, yet domestic in scale and reference, irregularly but securely cabled together, the sculpture shows the site what it might be. It unites the area, providing a nexus, a marker, a designation, an identity and, presumably, a point of pride." ...

Next the City claims that the Project Agreement entered into pre-VARA by plaintiff and the City encompassed many of plaintiff's rights under VARA. Therefore, the City argues, that whereas plaintiff failed to remove his work within the time allowed in the contract, plaintiff waived any cause of action he might have had under VARA. That failure was the City's, not plaintiff's, as under the Agreement the City was obligated to give the owners of the land and the sculpture ninety days to remove the sculpture. The City, after discussing with the Company and plaintiff possible other uses for the tract and the removal proposal, failed to give the required notice and went ahead and demolished the sculpture. Nothing had happened between the parties prior to that which could constitute a waiver of any rights by the Company or plaintiff. Plaintiff had no notice of the City letting a contract for Symphony # 1's demolition and no notice when that demolition would actually occur. After the preliminary and ongoing discussions plaintiff and the Company had with the City, when there was no immediate threat of imminent demolition, plaintiff had the right to continue to rely on the specific notice provided in the Agreement, unless it had been waived, which it was not.

Plaintiff and the Company had proposed a solution if the sculpture was to be moved. That proposal was still pending when the surprise destruction of Symphony # 1 occurred. Prior to the demolition, nothing more had been heard from anyone, including the Mayor. Bureaucratic ineptitude may be the only explanation. Under 17 U.S.C. § 106A(e)(1), an artist may waive VARA rights "in a written instrument signed by the author," specifying to what the waiver applies. There is no written waiver instrument in this case which falls within the VARA requirements. We regard this argument to be without merit.

In spite of the City's conduct resulting in the intentional destruction of the sculpture, we do not believe under all the circumstances, particularly given the fact that the issue of VARA rights had not been raised until this suit, that the City's conduct was "willful," as used in VARA, 17 U.S.C. § 504(c)(2), so as to entitle the plaintiff to enhanced damages. This appears to be a case of bureaucratic failure within the City government, not a willful violation of plaintiff's VARA rights. As far as we can tell from the record, those VARA rights were unknown to the City. The parties proceeded under their pre-VARA agreement which the City breached. However, plaintiff retained his VARA rights. As unfortunate as the City's unannounced demolition of Symphony # 1 was, it does not qualify plaintiff for damages under VARA....

Being fully satisfied with the district court's careful resolution of these unique issues and the resulting judgment, the district court's finding is affirmed in all respects.

DISSENT: MANION, *Circuit Judge*, concurring in part and dissenting in part. Like my colleagues, I am not an art critic. So I begin with the well-worn adage that one man's junk is another man's treasure. No doubt Jan Martin treasured what the city's bulldozers treated as junk. At this point in the litigation this court is not in a position to attach either label (or perhaps one falling somewhere in between) to Symphony # 1. For the Martin sculpture to receive protection under the Visual Arts Rights Act (VARA), it has to rise to the statutory level of "recognized stature." Because at this summary judgment stage, at least, it has clearly not merited the protection that goes with that description, I respectfully dissent.

Another well-worn adage advises that you should never look a gift horse in the mouth. Of course anyone who has ever accepted a gift horse that turns out to be lame or otherwise infirm quickly understands the error of that advice when the feed and veterinary bills arrive. When the City acquired several tracts of land for urban renewal, Martin's Symphony # 1 remained in place on one of the tracts. Martin offered to donate the sculpture to the City if it would remove and relocate it to another site. The City examined this "gift" and determined it would have cost it $8,000 to relocate, so it declined the offer. But it did agree to notify Martin in advance of any renewal project so he could remove Symphony # 1 if he so chose. Although it appears that Martin was fully aware that the sculpture's days were numbered, the City did not send him an official notice before the bulldozer moved in. If this were a simple breach of contract claim (albeit not a federal case), damages could well be in order. Instead, this is a federal claim under VARA, and different standards apply.

I dissent, however, because summary judgment is not appropriate here. A plaintiff cannot satisfy his burden of demonstrating recognized stature through old newspaper articles and unverified letters, some of which do not even address the artwork in question. Rather, as the district court stated in *Carter*, in "making this showing [of recognized stature] plaintiffs generally, but not inevitably, will need to call expert witnesses to testify before the trier of fact." Instances where expert testimony on this point is not necessary will be rare, and this is not one of those exceptional cases where something of unquestioned recognition and stature was destroyed. Furthermore, where newspaper articles are admitted into evidence only to acknowledge recognition but not for the truth of the matter asserted (that the art in question was good or bad), a plaintiff needs more to overcome *a defendant's* motion for summary judgment on a VARA claim, much less prevail on his own summary judgment motion. While the very publication of newspaper articles on a work of art may have bearing on the "recognized" element, there has to be some evidence that the art had stature (i.e., that it met a certain high level of quality)....

For now, however, those who are purchasers or donees of art had best beware. To avoid being the perpetual curator of a piece of visual art that has lost (or perhaps never had) its luster, the recipient must obtain at the outset a waiver of the artist's rights under VARA. Before awarding building permits for erection of sculptures, municipalities might be well advised to obtain a written waiver of the artist's rights too. If not, once destroyed, art of questionable value may acquire a minimum worth of $20,000.00 under VARA.

Cohen v. G & M Realty L.P.
___ F.Supp.2d ___ (2013), 2013 Copr.L.Dec. P 30, 523
(paragraphs substantially reordered)

[This] case has received wide media coverage because the buildings, located in Long Island City, had become the repository of the largest collection of exterior aerosol art (often also referred to as "graffiti art") in the United States, and had consequently become a significant tourist attraction—commonly known as 5 Pointz.... Starting in the early or mid-1990s, the exterior walls had become a place for distasteful graffiti by many self-proclaimed aerosol artists; it was then known as the Phun Phactory. To control this festering problem, [Plaintiff] Cohen approached [Defendant and building owner] Wolkoff in 2002 to become the curator of the works that would be permitted to be painted on the walls. Wolkoff agreed; Cohen, known in the art world as "Meres One," was one of the principal contributors to the aerosol wall paintings and Wolkoff liked his work. Wolkoff "was supportive of creative efforts but wanted somebody responsible to manage it." But nothing was put in writing; it was just the "general understanding that [Cohen] would be allowed to select who would be permitted to paint on the walls." Wolkoff, therefore, gave his oral blessings to permit qualified aerosol artists, under Cohen's control, to display their works on his buildings....

This marks the first occasion that a court has had to determine whether the work of an exterior aerosol artist—given its general ephemeral nature—is worthy of any protection under the law.

Plaintiffs invoke that part of VARA which gives the "author of a work of visual art" the right to sue to prevent the destruction of his or her work if it is one of "recognized stature." VARA recognizes that a work of visual art "may be incorporated in or made part of a building," and includes within its protective reach any such work that was created after its enactment on June 1, 1991, unless a written waiver was obtained from the artist.

Whether a protected work is of "recognized stature," is "best viewed as a gate-keeping mechanism." *Carter v. Helmsley-Spear, Inc.*, 861 F.Supp. 303, 315 (S.D.N.Y.1994), *rev'd and vacated in part and aff'd in part, by* 71 F.3d 77 (2d Cir. 1995). Accordingly, since plaintiffs' works post-dated VARA and no written waivers were obtained, the Court held a preliminary injunction hearing on November 6–8, and ordered the parties "to be prepared to address, *inter alia,* whether each plaintiff's work was of "recognized stature." ...

What the Second Circuit did not do in *Carter* was to address what constitutes a work of "recognized stature," since, unlike the district court, it found that the particular work— a very large "walk-through sculpture," installed in the lobby of a commercial building— was "a work made for hire," meaning "a work prepared by an employee within the scope of his or her employment." *Id.* at 85....

The lower court in *Carter* perceived "recognized stature" to implicitly require the plaintiff to make a two-tiered showing: "(1) that the visual art in question has 'stature,' i.e. is viewed as meritorious, and (2) that this stature is 'recognized' by art experts, other members of the artistic community, or by some cross-section of society." 861 F.Supp. at 325. In this latter regard, the court noted that an earlier version of VARA provided that a "court or other trier of facts may take into account the opinion of artists, art dealers, collectors of fine art, and other persons involved with the creation, appreciation, history, or marketing of works of recognized sources." *Id.* at 325 n. 10 (citations omitted). Although it believed that this provision was eliminated from VARA prior to enactment to provide courts "greater discretion with regard to what sources may be considered in determining whether a given work of visual art is a work of recognized stature," it nonetheless thought that a court "can, and should, consider these sources." *Id.*

The district court concluded that the plaintiffs' experts had established that the sculpture in the lobby was a work of "recognized stature" principally because (1) one of the experts, an art critic and professor of art history, testified that "this was [a] coherent ongoing program," he wanted "everyone to go and see it," the sculpture was "a work of art like almost nothing I've ever seen before," and that it "is an incredible phenomenon and I want to see it again and learn more about it;" (2) another expert, the president of the Municipal Art Society of New York, testified that the Society had organized a tour of the work and was anxious to make the work a permanent part of its tour schedule; (3) a third witness, a professor who taught two- and three-dimensional design, testified that he was "very exhilarated" by the work, "[t]he imagination of the work is tremendous," and it is "overall a very exciting piece." He enumerated the standards, which unfortunately are not identified in the court's decision, that he used to judge whether a given work is a work of recognized stature.

Although the two-tier *Carter* test has been referenced in a handful of subsequent cases, the Court's research has located only one circuit court and two other district courts that have substantively evaluated whether a visual art work was one of "recognized stature." In *Martin v. City of Indianapolis*, 192 F.3d 608 (7th Cir.1999), the Seventh Circuit affirmed the district court's grant of summary judgment and its award of damages for a sculpture that had been destroyed. It noted, however, that as plaintiff contended, "the *Carter v. Helmsley-Spear* test may be more rigorous than Congress intended." *Id.* at 612. But the court did not have to address the issue since it accepted as probative evidence of "stature," under the more vigorous *Carter* test utilized by the district court—in the face of defendant's hearsay objections—"certain newspaper and magazine articles, including a letter from an art gallery director and a letter to the editor of *The Indianapolis News,* all in support of the sculpture." *Id.* The circuit court also referenced a letter from the Director of Indiana University's Herron School of Art, who opined that the sculpture was "an interesting and aesthetic stimulating configuration of forms and structures," and an article by the visual arts editor of the *The Indianapolis News* describing the sculpture as "[g]leaming, clean and abstract, yet domestic in scale and reference," which "unites the area, providing a nexus, a marker, a designation, an identity and, presumably, a point of pride." *Id.* at 613.

In *Pollara v. Seymour,* 206 F.Supp.2d 333 (N.D.N.Y. 2002), Judge Hurd held, as a matter of law, after a bench trial, that even under the *Carter* formulation, the particular mural in that case was not of recognized stature because "while plaintiff's work was unquestionably meritorious," it was "intended solely as a display piece for a one-time event." *Id.* at 336. The court reasoned, therefore, that "[i]t defies the underlying purpose of VARA to assume that the statute was intended to protect works of artistic merit *without regard* to whether such works were ever intended as 'art' or whether they were intended to be displayed as art or were otherwise intended to be preserved for posterity as works of artistic merit." *Id.* And in *Scott v. Dixon,* 309 F.Supp.2d 395 (E.D.N.Y. 2004), the court dismissed plaintiff's VARA suit on the merits after a bench trial because the artist's sculpture had been commissioned for placement in the defendants' private backyard, which was obscured by hedges from public view. The court reasoned, therefore, that under VARA "it is not enough that works of art authored by the plaintiff, other than the work sought to be protected, have achieved [recognized] stature. Instead, it is the artwork that is the subject of the litigation that must have acquired this stature." *Id.* at 406. Thus, "while the Sculpture may have had artistic merit, it was not a work of recognized stature within the meaning of VARA" since it had never been exposed to the public....

When it came to whether any of the 24 works were of "recognized stature," much of the testimony did not differentiate between these discrete words, and by and large assumed that if the work had artistic merit it was *ipso facto* of recognized stature....

The focus of whether any of plaintiffs' 24 paintings were not only works of stature, but had also achieved the requisite recognition to bring them within the embrace of VARA, centered on the testimony of each party's proffered art expert....

The evidence adduced at the preliminary injunction hearing leads the Court to conclude that at least some of the 24 works, which plaintiffs contend were of recognized stature, such as Lady Pink's "Green Mother Earth," present "sufficiently serious questions going to the merits to make them a fair ground for litigation." *Salinger,* 607 F.3d at 79. The final resolution of whether any do indeed qualify as such works of art is best left for a fuller exploration of the merits after the case has been properly prepared for trial, rather than at the preliminary injunction stage. Since VARA does not define "recognized stature," the court ultimately will have to decide whether to embrace the strictures of the academic views espoused by the defendants or the more expansive ones suggested by the plaintiffs....

C. The Works' Duration

Wolkoff was emphatic that he told Cohen when he agreed in 2002 to let him control the work, that he was "going to be knocking down the building," and "it was always temporary."... Cohen testified that when Wolkoff put him in charge "there was no discussion of any life span, and at the time [Cohen] really didn't have any long-lived expectations." However, "[e]very year [he] heard the building was coming down."

Cohen explained at length about how he decided who would be allowed to paint on the walls and where their works would be located. Some of the walls were "quickly rotating walls, which could last a day to a week;" they were purely "temporary," and meant to be turned over. Others he deemed to be "permanent," meaning that they would last "[a]s long as [he was] there and the operation's there." For those, he chose special places — mostly high up. It was all his decision. And for a "permanent" work, only the artist could thereafter decide whether it could be painted over.

The 24 works here at issue are the ones that were designated by Cohen to be preserved. Upon questioning, Cohen clarified that they were "scattered around the building," and he therefore acknowledged that in order to preserve them the "[m]ajority" of the whole building would have to be kept in place "just to accommodate" them....

The Court could not have issued a preliminary injunction unless the plaintiffs demonstrated "either (a) likelihood of success on the merits or (b) sufficiently serious questions going to the merits to make them a fair ground for litigation and a balance of hardships tipping decidedly in the [p]laintiff's favor." *Salinger v. Colting*, 607 F.3d 68, 79 (2d Cir.2010) (internal citation omitted). If so, "the court may issue the injunction only if the plaintiff has demonstrated that he is likely to suffer irreparable harm in the absence of the injunction." In that regard, the Court "must actually consider the injury the plaintiff will suffer if he or she loses in the preliminary injunction but ultimately prevails on the merits, paying particular attention to whether the remedies available at law, such as monetary damages, are inadequate to compensate for that injury." Next, a Court "must consider the balance of hardships between the plaintiff and defendant and issue the injunction only if the balance of hardships tips in the plaintiff's favor." Finally, the Court "must ensure that the public interest would not be disserved."

Picasso believed that "[t]he purpose of art is washing the dust of daily life off our souls." He surely would have supported applying VARA to protect the works of the modern aerosol artist. As Congress recognized, whether a particular work falls within the definition of *visual art*, "should not depend on the medium or materials used," since "[a]rtists may work in a variety of media, and use any number of materials in creating their work." This fits the aerosol artist to a "T," and our souls owe a debt of gratitude to the plaintiffs for having brought the dusty walls of defendants' buildings to life.

But VARA only protects a *work* of visual art. 17 U.S.C. § 106A; *see also* 17 U.S.C. § 202 ("ownership of a copyright, or any of the exclusive rights under a copyright, is distinct from ownership of any material object in which the work is embodied."). The Court regrettably had no authority under VARA to preserve 5Pointz as a tourist site. That authority is vested in state or local authorities, and since 5Pointz had become such a scenic attraction, the City probably could have exercised its power of eminent domain to acquire the site outright. It chose not to. Although the Court was taken by the breadth and visual impact of 5Pointz, its authority under VARA is consequently limited to determining whether a particular *work* of visual art that was destroyed was one of "recognized stature," and if so, what monetary damages the creator of each work is entitled to.

The Court had to determine, therefore, whether the plaintiffs demonstrated that they were likely to suffer irreparable harm.... Although the works have now been destroyed — and the Court wished it had the power to preserve them — plaintiffs would be hard-pressed to contend that no amount of money would compensate them for their paintings; and VARA — which makes no distinction between temporary and permanent works of visual art — provides that significant monetary damages may be awarded for their wrongful destruction. In any event, paintings generally are meant to be sold. Their value is invariably reflected in the money they command in the marketplace. Here, the works were painted for free, but surely the plaintiffs would gladly have accepted money from the defendants to acquire their works, albeit on a wall rather than on a canvas.

Moreover, plaintiffs' works can live on in other media. The 24 works have been photographed, and the court, during the hearing, exhorted the plaintiffs to photograph all those which they might wish to preserve. All would be protected under traditional copyright law and could be marketed to the general public—even to those who had never been to 5Pointz.

Finally, whether viewed as bearing upon the issue of irreparable harm or the balancing of the hardships, the ineluctable factor which precludes either preliminary or permanent injunctive relief was the transient nature of the plaintiffs' works. Regardless of Cohen's belief that the 24 works were to be permanently displayed on the buildings, he always knew that the buildings were coming down—and that his paintings, as well as the others which he allowed to be placed on the walls, would be destroyed. Particularly disturbing is that many of the paintings were created as recently as this past September, just weeks after the City Planning Commission gave final approval to the defendants' building plans. In a very real sense, plaintiffs' have created their own hardships.

But this does not mean that defendants do not share some responsibility. After all, Wolkoff gave his blessings to Cohen and the aerosol artists to decorate the buildings, and he did not choose to protect himself from liability by requiring VARA waivers. Moreover, while he was supportive of the artists and appreciated their work, he also stood to benefit economically from all the attention that had been drawn to the site as he planned to market the new buildings' residences. Since, as defendants' expert correctly acknowledged, VARA protects even temporary works from destruction, defendants are exposed to potentially significant monetary damages if it is ultimately determined after trial that the plaintiffs' works were of "recognized stature."

As for the public, its general interests will be served by the new apartments, including the 75 affordable housing units, and while the present walls will no longer exist, the public's aesthetic interests were addressed by the City Planning Commission by requiring 3,300 square feet of the exterior of the new buildings to be made available for art. Defendants can do even more. They can make much more space available, and give written permission to Cohen to continue to be the curator so that he may establish a large, permanent home for quality work by him and his acclaimed aerosol artists. For sure, the Court would look kindly on such largesse when it might be required to consider the issue of monetary damages; and 5Pointz, as reincarnated, would live.

Report Waiver of Moral Rights in Visual Artworks

Executive Summary, Report of the Copyright Office (October 1996)[3]

On June 10, 1992, eighteen months after VARA's enactment, the [Copyright Office (Office)] published a Request for Information in the Federal Register seeking comments on artists' bargaining power relative to that of commercial users of artworks, on parties' awareness of the VARA rights and their inclusion of waiver provisions in contracts, on the contractual compliance with the law's requirements that works and uses subject to waivers be specifically identified, on the actual exercise of waivers, and on the relative numbers

---

3. *Id.*

of waivers granted for rights of attribution and integrity for moveable works of visual art and for art works incorporated into buildings. We asked for empirical evidence on the kinds of contracts that include waivers and on the economic impact of those waivers; and we requested parties' assessment of whether the artist's renown affected his or her waiver of rights, and on what factors influence artists' decisions to waive rights. Finally, we asked for comments on possible constitutional problems that might arise if waivers were prohibited. . . .

More than 1,000 persons filed written responses to the survey. Responses were received from 47 states and the District of Columbia, and 955 respondents were self-described visual artists. Most artists grossed less than $10,000 annually from their artwork and most had multiple sources of income.

About three-fourths of the respondents claimed awareness of moral rights, although many who elaborated in written comments stressed the need for more education of artists. Fewer than half knew that moral rights could be waived. Seven percent of those who answered the question said waiver clauses were routinely included in artists' contracts, but nearly 40 percent said waiver clauses were part of contracts for commissioned works.

Nearly one quarter of artists covered by VARA knew of artists who had been asked to waive their moral rights. Thirteen percent of artists covered by VARA said they had refused contracts because they included waivers and a similar number had insisted that a waiver clause be struck from a contract. These artists were generally those who earned more than $25,000 annually from their art or who were represented by an agent. More than half of those who had rejected a request for waiver said such rejection voided the deal. In general, those participants who filed written commentary believe that VARA does little to enhance the artist's inferior bargaining position relative to the buyer.

More than half of the respondents who had experienced waivers said they complied with the specificity requirements of VARA, and about one-third said contracts contained a separate price for the waiver of moral rights. However, most art contracts continue to be oral and therefore cannot contain valid waiver clauses under the terms of VARA. Many artists decried the complexity of art contracts and stated that legal requirements were too burdensome and legal advice too costly. . . .

On June 21, 1995, the Copyright Office held a public hearing to solicit comments on the effect of the waiver of moral rights provision of VARA. . . . Most saw the need for the sec. 113 waiver provisions for works incorporated into buildings. For one attorney, however, the fact that most contracts for major commissions will now routinely require waivers means that the sec. 113 waiver provision should be tightened, if not repealed. . . .

Many panelists believed that repeal of sec. 113 waiver would result in a chilling effect on creation of art, since property owners may be unwilling to commit to a permanent structure. On the other hand, there may be a chilling effect even if building owners have secured a waiver: several artists reported that, had they been operating under a waiver, they would have undertaken the project, but with a different scale and design. Some predicted a standard term in landlord-tenant contracts requiring tenants to get waivers or refrain from installing art.

Other recommendations were made for VARA. For example, several parties agreed that one joint author should not have the ability to waive for all co-authors. Others believed VARA should apply to print or broadcast reproductions of works, thus covering distortions in books, magazines and electronic media. . . .

Notes and Questions

a. To what extent do the cases identified by the Register of Copyright regarding U.S. moral rights law compare to the treaty obligation to adhere to Article *6bis* of the Berne Convention?

b. The Supreme Court has significantly revised the role the Lanham Act § 43(a) can play with regard to protection for the attribution of a motion picture video cassette, providing that the source of goods is the distributor of those cassettes. Does the same source of goods analysis apply to the creation of a work of art? Does it matter whether the work is incorporated into a utilitarian object (such as the base of a lamp or a piece of jewelry) or if the work is a more traditional oil painting or photograph? See *Dastar Corp. v. Twentieth Century Fox Film Corp.*, 539 U.S. 23 (2003).

c. When an artist's clay model for a sculpture is left outdoors, does this constitute a violation of VARA? In this case the model was a 35-foot clay model for a statue's head made for the "purpose of memorializing the life of Catherine of Braganza, Princess of Portugal and Queen of England in the mid-seventeenth century and namesake of the borough of Queens." The statue was to become "a monument to Queen Catherine to be installed at a prominent place within the Hunters Point Redevelopment Project in Queens." See *Flack v. Friends of Queen Catherine, Inc.*, 139 F. Supp. 2d 526 (S.D.N.Y. 2001).

d. What attributes constitute the artwork? Often, sculptural works are designed for particular locations. To what extent does the spatial environment define the work and become part of the installation for purposes of VARA protection? See *Phillips v. Pembroke Real Estate, Inc.*, 459 F.3d 128 (1st Cir. 2006).

e. What constitutes a work of art of a sufficiently recognized stature to gain VARA protection? Compare *Pollara v. Seymour*, 344 F.3d 265 (2d Cir. 2003), and *Martin v. City of Indianapolis*, 192 F.3d 608 (7th Cir. 1999), with *Scott v. Dixon*, 309 F. Supp. 2d 395 (E.D.N.Y. 2004).

f. A church mural depicting a very masculine Christ met with increasing consternation by the congregation, which had the mural covered over. The artist sued under Article *6bis* of the Berne Convention but could not establish that the treaty applied to New York real property law. See *Crimi v. Rutgers Presbyterian Church*, 194 Misc. 570, 89 N.Y.S.2d 813 (1949).

g. In addition to VARA, states including California, New York, and Massachusetts have state legislation involving the protection of moral rights for authors. Some states also provide ongoing economic rights to artists such as *droit de suite* (a royalty for visual artists). See *Phillips v. Pembroke Real Estate, Inc.*, 459 F.3d 128 (1st Cir. 2006); Massachusetts Art Preservation Act, Mass. Gen. Laws ch. 231, § 85S (1984); California Art Preservation Act, Cal. Civ. Code § 987 (1979).

h. To what extent does VARA preempt the previous state statutes that provide moral rights or economic resale rights? See *Bd. of Managers of Soho Int'l Arts Condominium v. City of New York*, 2003 U.S. Dist. LEXIS 10221 (S.D.N.Y. June 17, 2003) (unreported) (reviewing N.Y. Art & Cult Affr § 14.03 (McKinney 1984)). The Court explains the standard copyright preemption standard: a "statute pre-empts a state law if two conditions are met: 1) if the work to which the rights under the state statute falls within the "subject matter" of copyright as specified in 17 U.S.C. §§ 102 and 103 and 2) if the right is the same or "equivalent" to those granted by [the state law]." *Id.* (internal citations omitted).

More recently a California district court found the California Resale Royalties Act, Cal. Civ. Code § 986 (West 2007), to be a violation of the Dormant Commerce Clause and therefore unconstitutional. *Estate of Graham v. Sotheby's Inc.*, 2012 U.S. Dist. LEXIS 77262 (C.D. Cal. May 17, 2012). The decision has sparked a controversy and will result in an appeal.

i. Another challenge to the scope of VARA involves unfinished works. In an unfortunate case involving the Massachusetts Museum of Contemporary Art, a large installation went unfinished amid claims of vague instructions, corner-cutting, and a lack of written instructions. Among the legal issues was the extent to which VARA applied to works that had yet to be completed. Reviewing the question for the first time, the First Circuit found unfinished works are covered. "Reading VARA in accordance with the definitions in section 101, it too must be read to protect unfinished, but 'fixed,' works of art that, if completed, would qualify for protection under the statute." See *Mass. Museum of Contemporary Art Found., Inc. v. Buchel*, 593 F.3d 38 (1st Cir. 2010).

j. Yet another challenge to the scope of VARA involves nontraditional media. To what extent is a park design, including its floral decoration, protected by the statute? See *Kelley v. Chi. Park Dist.*, 635 F.3d 290 (7th Cir. 2011).

k. Graffiti art has its own subculture and communal importance. In Los Angeles, the city has responded to the need for art preservation and community building with an ordinance on the subject. See L.A., Cal., Code §§ 14.4.2, 14.4.3, and 14.4.20 (all as amended), L.A., Cal., Admin. Code § 22.119, available at http://clkrep.lacity.org/onlinedocs/2011/11-0923_ord_182706.pdf. See also Eric Bjorgum, *Los Angeles Gets A New Mural Ordinance*, 36 L.A. Law. 36 (January 2014).

Problem XVII-B

Bryce has been in pre-production for a feature-length film. The director of photography hopes to shoot a location that is described in the screenplay and based on a true historical story. To shoot the location, a mural painted in 2001 would need to be covered during the shooting. Bryce has been assured by the set designer that the mural can be covered with a paint that can easily be removed. Bryce has contacted the building owners for permission to temporarily cover the mural in order to make the film. Because of the historical importance of the location and potential marketing opportunities, the building's owners would like the film to be shot, but they are concerned that the temporary covering of the mural would interfere with the artist's rights under VARA. Please advise Bryce on the obligations the mural owners have to the artist under VARA. If Bryce were to remove the image in post-production rather than by covering it, explain any VARA or other copyright issues.

C. Government Regulation of Content in the Visual Arts

National Endowment for the Arts v. Finley
524 U.S. 569 (1998)

JUSTICE O'CONNOR delivered the opinion of the Court. The National Foundation on the Arts and Humanities Act, as amended in 1990, requires the Chairperson of the National Endowment for the Arts (NEA) to ensure that "artistic excellence and artistic merit are the criteria by which [grant] applications are judged, *taking into consideration general standards of decency and respect for the diverse beliefs and values of the American public.*" 20 U.S.C. § 954(d)(1). In this case, we review the Court of Appeals' determination that § 954(d)(1), on its face, impermissibly discriminates on the basis of viewpoint and is void for vagueness under the First and Fifth Amendments. We conclude that § 954(d)(1) is facially valid, as it neither inherently interferes with First Amendment rights nor violates constitutional vagueness principles.

With the establishment of the NEA in 1965, Congress embarked on a "broadly conceived national policy of support for the ... arts in the United States," pledging federal funds to "help create and sustain not only a climate encouraging freedom of thought, imagination, and inquiry but also the material conditions facilitating the release of ... creative talent." The enabling statute vests the NEA with substantial discretion to award grants; it identifies only the broadest funding priorities, including "artistic and cultural significance, giving emphasis to American creativity and cultural diversity," "professional excellence," and the encouragement of "public knowledge, education, understanding, and appreciation of the arts."

Applications for NEA funding are initially reviewed by advisory panels composed of experts in the relevant field of the arts. Under the 1990 Amendments to the enabling statute, those panels must reflect "diverse artistic and cultural points of view" and include "wide geographic, ethnic, and minority representation," as well as "lay individuals who are knowledgeable about the arts." The panel reports to the 26-member National Council on the Arts (Council), which, in turn, advises the NEA Chairperson. The Chairperson has the ultimate authority to award grants but may not approve an application as to which the Council has made a negative recommendation.

Since 1965, the NEA has distributed over three billion dollars in grants to individuals and organizations, funding that has served as a catalyst for increased state, corporate, and foundation support for the arts. Congress has recently restricted the availability of federal funding for individual artists, confining grants primarily to qualifying organizations and state arts agencies, and constraining sub-granting. By far the largest portion of the grants distributed in fiscal year 1998 were awarded directly to state arts agencies. In the remaining categories, the most substantial grants were allocated to symphony orchestras, fine arts museums, dance theater foundations, and opera associations.

Throughout the NEA's history, only a handful of the agency's roughly 100,000 awards have generated formal complaints about misapplied funds or abuse of the public's trust. Two provocative works, however, prompted public controversy in 1989 and led to congressional revaluation of the NEA's funding priorities and efforts to increase oversight of its grant-making procedures. The Institute of Contemporary Art at the University of Pennsylvania had used $30,000 of a visual arts grant it received from the NEA to fund a 1989 retrospective of photographer Robert Mapplethorpe's work. The exhibit, entitled *The Perfect Moment*, included homoerotic photographs that several Members of Congress condemned as pornographic. Members also denounced artist Andres Serrano's work *Piss Christ*, a photograph of a crucifix immersed in urine. Serrano had been awarded a $15,000 grant from the Southeast Center for Contemporary Art, an organization that received NEA support.

When considering the NEA's appropriations for fiscal year 1990, Congress reacted to the controversy surrounding the Mapplethorpe and Serrano photographs by eliminating $45,000 from the agency's budget, the precise amount contributed to the two exhibits by NEA grant recipients. Congress also enacted an amendment providing that no NEA funds "may be used to promote, disseminate, or produce materials which in the judgment of [the NEA] may be considered obscene, including but not limited to, depictions of sadomasochism, homoeroticism, the sexual exploitation of children, or individuals engaged in sex acts and which, when taken as a whole, do not have serious literary, artistic, political, or scientific value." The NEA implemented Congress' mandate by instituting a requirement that all grantees certify in writing that they would not utilize federal funding to engage in projects inconsistent with the criteria in the 1990 appropriations bill. That certification requirement was subsequently invalidated as unconstitutionally vague by a Federal District Court, and the NEA did not appeal the decision.

In the 1990 appropriations bill, Congress also agreed to create an Independent Commission of constitutional law scholars to review the NEA's grant-making procedures and assess the possibility of more focused standards for public arts funding. The Commission's report, issued in September 1990, concluded that there is no constitutional obligation to provide arts funding, but also recommended that the NEA rescind the certification requirement and cautioned against legislation setting forth any content restrictions. Instead, the Commission suggested procedural changes to enhance the role of advisory panels and a statutory reaffirmation of "the high place the nation accords to the fostering of mutual respect for the disparate beliefs and values among us." ...

Ultimately, Congress adopted the *Williams*/Coleman Amendment, a bipartisan compromise between Members opposing any funding restrictions and those favoring some guidance to the agency. In relevant part, the Amendment became § 954(d)(1), which directs the Chairperson, in establishing procedures to judge the artistic merit of grant applications, to "take into consideration general standards of decency and respect for the diverse beliefs and values of the American public."[4]

The NEA has not promulgated any official interpretation of the provision, but in December 1990, the Council unanimously adopted a resolution to implement § 954(d)(1) merely by ensuring that the members of the advisory panels that conduct the initial review of grant applications represent geographic, ethnic, and aesthetic diversity. John Frohnmayer, then Chairperson of the NEA, also declared that he would "count on [the] procedures" ensuring diverse membership on the peer review panels to fulfill Congress' mandate.

The four individual respondents in this case, Karen Finley, John Fleck, Holly Hughes, and Tim Miller, are performance artists who applied for NEA grants before § 954(d)(1) was enacted. An advisory panel recommended approval of respondents' projects, both initially and after receiving Frohnmayer's request to reconsider three of the applications. A majority of the Council subsequently recommended disapproval, and in June 1990, the NEA informed respondents that they had been denied funding. Respondents filed suit, alleging that the NEA had violated their First Amendment rights by rejecting the

---

4. Title 20 U.S.C. § 954(d) provides in full that:

"No payment shall be made under this section except upon application therefor which is submitted to the National Endowment for the Arts in accordance with regulations issued and procedures established by the Chairperson. In establishing such regulations and procedures, the Chairperson shall ensure that—

"(1) artistic excellence and artistic merit are the criteria by which applications are judged, taking into consideration general standards of decency and respect for the diverse beliefs and values of the American public; and

"(2) applications are consistent with the purposes of this section. Such regulations and procedures shall clearly indicate that obscenity is without artistic merit, is not protected speech, and shall not be funded."

applications on political grounds, had failed to follow statutory procedures by basing the denial on criteria other than those set forth in the NEA's enabling statute, and had breached the confidentiality of their grant applications through the release of quotations to the press, in violation of the Privacy Act of 1974, 5 U.S.C. § 552(a). Respondents sought restoration of the recommended grants or reconsideration of their applications, as well as damages for the alleged Privacy Act violations. When Congress enacted § 954(d)(1), respondents, now joined by the National Association of Artists' Organizations (NAAO), amended their complaint to challenge the provision as void for vagueness and impermissibly viewpoint based.

The District Court denied the NEA's motion for judgment on the pleadings, and, after discovery, the NEA agreed to settle the individual respondents' statutory and as-applied constitutional claims by paying the artists the amount of the vetoed grants, damages, and attorney's fees.

The District Court then granted summary judgment in favor of respondents on their facial constitutional challenge to § 954(d)(1) and enjoined enforcement of the provision. The court rejected the argument that the NEA could comply with § 954(d)(1) by structuring the grant selection process to provide for diverse advisory panels. The provision, the court stated, "fails adequately to notify applicants of what is required of them or to circumscribe NEA discretion." Reasoning that "the very nature of our pluralistic society is that there are an infinite number of values and beliefs, and correlatively, there may be no national 'general standards of decency,'" the court concluded that § 954(d)(1) "cannot be given effect consistent with the Fifth Amendment's due process requirement." Drawing an analogy between arts funding and public universities, the court further ruled that the First Amendment constrains the NEA's grant-making process, and that because § 954(d)(1) "clearly reaches a substantial amount of protected speech," it is impermissibly overbroad on its face. The Government did not seek a stay of the District Court's injunction, and consequently the NEA has not applied § 954(d)(1) since June 1992. A divided panel of the Court of Appeals affirmed the District Court's ruling.... We granted certiorari and now reverse the judgment of the Court of Appeals.

Respondents raise a facial constitutional challenge to § 954(d)(1), and consequently they confront "a heavy burden" in advancing their claim. Facial invalidation "is, manifestly, strong medicine" that "has been employed by the Court sparingly and only as a last resort." To prevail, respondents must demonstrate a substantial risk that application of the provision will lead to the suppression of speech.

Respondents argue that the provision is a paradigmatic example of viewpoint discrimination because it rejects any artistic speech that either fails to respect mainstream values or offends standards of decency. The premise of respondents' claim is that § 954(d)(1) constrains the agency's ability to fund certain categories of artistic expression. The NEA, however, reads the provision as merely hortatory, and contends that it stops well short of an absolute restriction. Section 954(d)(1) adds "considerations" to the grant-making process; it does not preclude awards to projects that might be deemed "indecent" or "disrespectful," nor place conditions on grants, or even specify that those factors must be given any particular weight in reviewing an application. Indeed, the agency asserts that it has adequately implemented § 954(d)(1) merely by ensuring the representation of various backgrounds and points of view on the advisory panels that analyze grant applications.

We do not decide whether the NEA's view — that the formulation of diverse advisory panels is sufficient to comply with Congress' command — is in fact a reasonable reading of the statute. It is clear, however, that the text of § 954(d)(1) imposes no categorical requirement. The advisory language stands in sharp contrast to congressional efforts to prohibit the funding of certain classes of speech. When Congress has in fact intended to affirmatively constrain the NEA's grant-making authority, it has done so in no uncertain terms.

Furthermore, like the plain language of § 954(d), the political context surrounding the adoption of the "decency and respect" clause is inconsistent with respondents' assertion that the provision compels the NEA to deny funding on the basis of viewpoint discriminatory criteria. The legislation was a bipartisan proposal introduced as a counterweight to amendments aimed at eliminating the NEA's funding or substantially constraining its grant-making authority. The Independent Commission had cautioned Congress against the adoption of distinct viewpoint-based standards for funding, and the Commission's report suggests that "additional criteria for selection, if any, should be incorporated as part of the selection process (perhaps as part of a definition of 'artistic excellence'), rather than isolated and treated as exogenous considerations." In keeping with that recommendation, the criteria in § 954(d)(1) inform the assessment of artistic merit, but Congress declined to disallow any particular viewpoints. As the sponsors of § 954(d)(1) noted in urging rejection of the Rohrabacher Amendment, "if we start down that road of prohibiting categories of expression, categories which are indeed constitutionally protected speech, where do we end? Where one Member's aversions end, others with different sensibilities and with different values begin."; see also *id.*, at 28663 (statement of Rep. *Williams*) (arguing that the Rohrabacher Amendment would prevent the funding of Jasper Johns' flag series, "The Merchant of Venice," "Chorus Line," "Birth of a Nation," and the "Grapes of Wrath"). In contrast, before the vote on § 954(d)(1), one of its sponsors stated: "If we have done one important thing in this amendment, it is this. We have maintained the integrity of freedom of expression in the United States."

That § 954(d)(1) admonishes the NEA merely to take "decency and respect" into consideration, and that the legislation was aimed at reforming procedures rather than precluding speech, undercut respondents' argument that the provision inevitably will be utilized as a tool for invidious viewpoint discrimination. In cases where we have struck down legislation as facially unconstitutional, the dangers were both more evident and more substantial. In *R. A. V. v. St. Paul*, 505 U.S. 377 (1992), for example, we invalidated on its face a municipal ordinance that defined as a criminal offense the placement of a symbol on public or private property "'which one knows or has reasonable grounds to know arouses anger, alarm, or resentment in others on the basis of race, color, creed, religion, or gender.'" That provision set forth a clear penalty, proscribed views on particular "disfavored subjects," and suppressed "distinctive ideas, conveyed by a distinctive message."

In contrast, the "decency and respect" criteria do not silence speakers by expressly "threatening censorship of ideas." Thus, we do not perceive a realistic danger that § 954(d)(1) will compromise First Amendment values. As respondents' own arguments demonstrate, the considerations that the provision introduces, by their nature, do not engender the kind of directed viewpoint discrimination that would prompt this Court to invalidate a statute on its face. Respondents assert, for example, that "one would be hard-pressed to find two people in the United States who could agree on what the 'diverse beliefs and values of the American public' are, much less on whether a particular work of art 'respects' them"; and they claim that "'decency' is likely to mean something very different to a septuagenarian in Tuscaloosa and a teenager in Las Vegas." The NEA likewise views the considerations enumerated in § 954(d)(1) as susceptible to multiple interpretations. Accordingly, the provision does not introduce considerations that, in practice, would effectively preclude or punish the expression of particular views. Indeed, one could hardly anticipate how "decency" or "respect" would bear on grant applications in categories such as funding for symphony orchestras.

Respondents' claim that the provision is facially unconstitutional may be reduced to the argument that the criteria in §954(d)(1) are sufficiently subjective that the agency could utilize them to engage in viewpoint discrimination. Given the varied interpretations of the criteria and the vague exhortation to "take them into consideration," it seems unlikely that this provision will introduce any greater element of selectivity than the determination of "artistic excellence" itself. And we are reluctant, in any event, to invalidate legislation "on the basis of its hypothetical application to situations not before the Court." *FCC v. Pacifica Foundation*, 438 U.S. 726, 743, 57 L. Ed. 2d 1073, 98 S. Ct. 3026 (1978).

The NEA's enabling statute contemplates a number of indisputably constitutional applications for both the "decency" prong of §954(d)(1) and its reference to "respect for the diverse beliefs and values of the American public." Educational programs are central to the NEA's mission. And it is well established that "decency" is a permissible factor where "educational suitability" motivates its consideration.

Permissible applications of the mandate to consider "respect for the diverse beliefs and values of the American public" are also apparent. In setting forth the purposes of the NEA, Congress explained that "it is vital to democracy to honor and preserve its multicultural artistic heritage." The agency expressly takes diversity into account, giving special consideration to "projects and productions ... that reach, or reflect the culture of, a minority, inner city, rural, or tribal community," §954(c)(4), as well as projects that generally emphasize "cultural diversity," §954(c)(1). Respondents do not contend that the criteria in §954(d)(1) are impermissibly applied when they may be justified, as the statute contemplates, with respect to a project's intended audience.

We recognize, of course, that reference to these permissible applications would not alone be sufficient to sustain the statute against respondents' First Amendment challenge. But neither are we persuaded that, in other applications, the language of §954(d)(1) itself will give rise to the suppression of protected expression. Any content-based considerations that may be taken into account in the grant-making process are a consequence of the nature of arts funding. The NEA has limited resources and it must deny the majority of the grant applications that it receives, including many that propose "artistically excellent" projects. The agency may decide to fund particular projects for a wide variety of reasons, "such as the technical proficiency of the artist, the creativity of the work, the anticipated public interest in or appreciation of the work, the work's contemporary relevance, its educational value, its suitability for or appeal to special audiences (such as children or the disabled), its service to a rural or isolated community, or even simply that the work could increase public knowledge of an art form." As the dissent below noted, it would be "impossible to have a highly selective grant program without denying money to a large amount of constitutionally protected expression." The "very assumption" of the NEA is that grants will be awarded according to the "artistic worth of competing applications," and absolute neutrality is simply "inconceivable."

Respondent's reliance on our decision in *Rosenberger v. Rector and Visitors of Univ. of Va.*, 515 U.S. 819 (1995), is therefore misplaced. In *Rosenberger*, a public university declined to authorize disbursements from its Student Activities Fund to finance the printing of a Christian student newspaper. We held that by subsidizing the Student Activities Fund, the University had created a limited public forum, from which it impermissibly excluded all publications with religious editorial viewpoints. Although the scarcity of

NEA funding does not distinguish this case from *Rosenberger*, the competitive process according to which the grants are allocated does. In the context of arts funding, in contrast to many other subsidies, the Government does not indiscriminately "encourage a diversity of views from private speakers." The NEA's mandate is to make aesthetic judgments, and the inherently content-based "excellence" threshold for NEA support sets it apart from the subsidy at issue in *Rosenberger*—which was available to all student organizations that were "'related to the educational purpose of the University,'"—and from comparably objective decisions on allocating public benefits, such as access to a school auditorium or a municipal theater, or the second class mailing privileges available to "'all newspapers and other periodical publications.'"

It is so ordered.

CONCUR: JUSTICE SCALIA, with whom JUSTICE THOMAS joins, concurring in the judgment.

"The operation was a success, but the patient died." What such a procedure is to medicine, the Court's opinion in this case is to law. It sustains the constitutionality of 20 U.S.C. § 954(d)(1) by gutting it. The most avid congressional opponents of the provision could not have asked for more. I write separately because, unlike the Court, I think that § 954(d)(1) must be evaluated as written, rather than as distorted by the agency it was meant to control. By its terms, it establishes content- and viewpoint-based criteria upon which grant applications are to be evaluated. And that is perfectly constitutional.... One can regard [the statute] as either suggesting that decency and respect are elements of what Congress regards as artistic excellence and merit, or as suggesting that decency and respect are factors to be taken into account *in addition to* artistic excellence and merit. But either way, it is entirely, 100% clear that decency and respect are to be taken into account in evaluating applications....

This is so apparent that I am at a loss to understand what the Court has in mind (other than the gutting of the statute) when it speculates that the statute is merely "advisory." ... The statute requires the decency and respect factors to be considered in evaluating *all* applications—not, for example, just those applications relating to educational programs, *ante*, at 13, or intended for a particular audience....

Section 954(d)(1) is no more discriminatory, and no less constitutional, than virtually every other piece of funding legislation enacted by Congress. "The Government can, without violating the Constitution, selectively fund a program to encourage certain activities it believes to be in the public interest, without at the same time funding an alternative program...." *Rust v. Sullivan*, 500 U.S. 173 (1991). As we noted in *Rust*, when Congress chose to establish the National Endowment for Democracy it was not constitutionally required to fund programs encouraging competing philosophies of government—an example of funding discrimination that cuts much closer than this one to the core of *political* speech which is the primary concern of the First Amendment. It takes a particularly high degree of chutzpah for the NEA to contradict this proposition, since the agency itself discriminates—and is required by law to discriminate—in favor of artistic (as opposed to scientific, or political, or theological) expression. Not all the common folk, or even all great minds, for that matter, think that is a good idea. In 1800, when John Marshall told John Adams that a recent immigration of Frenchmen would include talented artists, "Adams denounced all Frenchmen, but most especially 'schoolmasters, painters, poets, &C.' He warned Marshall that the fine arts were like germs that infected healthy constitutions." Surely the NEA itself is nothing less than an institutionalized discrimination against that point of view. Nonetheless it is constitutional, as is the congressional determination to favor decency and respect for beliefs and values over the opposite. Because such favoritism does not "abridge" anyone's freedom of speech....

DISSENT: JUSTICE SOUTER, dissenting.

The question here is whether the italicized segment of this statute is unconstitutional on its face: "artistic excellence and artistic merit are the criteria by which applications [for grants from the National Endowment for the Arts] are judged, *taking into consideration general standards of decency and respect for the diverse beliefs and values of the American public.*" 20 U.S.C. §954(d) (emphasis added). It is.

The decency and respect proviso mandates viewpoint-based decisions in the disbursement of government subsidies, and the Government has wholly failed to explain why the statute should be afforded an exemption from the fundamental rule of the First Amendment that viewpoint discrimination in the exercise of public authority over expressive activity is unconstitutional. The Court's conclusions that the proviso is not viewpoint based, that it is not a regulation, and that the NEA may permissibly engage in viewpoint-based discrimination, are all patently mistaken. Nor may the question raised be answered in the Government's favor on the assumption that some constitutional applications of the statute are enough to satisfy the demand of facial constitutionality, leaving claims of the proviso's obvious invalidity to be dealt with later in response to challenges of specific applications of the discriminatory standards. This assumption is irreconcilable with our long standing and sensible doctrine of facial overbreadth, applicable to claims brought under the First Amendment's speech clause. I respectfully dissent....

One need do nothing more than read the text of the statute to conclude that Congress's purpose in imposing the decency and respect criteria was to prevent the funding of art that conveys an offensive message; the decency and respect provision on its face is quintessentially viewpoint based, and quotations from the Congressional Record merely confirm the obvious legislative purpose. In the words of a cosponsor of the bill that enacted the proviso, "works which deeply offend the sensibilities of significant portions of the public ought not to be supported with public funds."... In the face of such clear legislative purpose, so plainly expressed, the Court has its work cut out for it in seeking a constitutional reading of the statute....

Because "the normal definition of 'indecent'... refers to nonconformance with accepted standards of morality," restrictions turning on decency, especially those couched in terms of "general standards of decency," are quintessentially viewpoint based: they require discrimination on the basis of conformity with mainstream mores. The Government's contrary suggestion that the NEA's decency standards restrict only the "mode, form, or style" of artistic expression, not the underlying viewpoint or message, may be a tempting abstraction (and one not lacking in support). But here it suffices to realize that "form, mode, or style" are not subject to abstraction from artistic viewpoint, and to quote from an opinion just two years old: "In artistic ... settings, indecency may have strong communicative content, protesting conventional norms or giving an edge to a work by conveying otherwise inexpressible emotions.... Indecency often is inseparable from the ideas and viewpoints conveyed, or separable only with loss of truth or expressive power." *Denver Area Ed. Telecommunications Consortium, Inc. v. FCC*, 518 U.S. 727, 805 (1996) (concurrence)....

Brooklyn Inst. of Arts & Sciences v.
New York & Rudolph W. Giuliani
64 F. Supp. 2d 184 (E.D.N.Y. 1999)

The Mayor of the City of New York has decided that a number of works in the Brooklyn Museum's currently showing temporary exhibit "Sensation: Young British Artists from the Saatchi Collection" are "sick" and "disgusting" and, in particular, that one work, a painting entitled "The Holy Virgin Mary" by Chris Ofili, is offensive to Catholics and is an attack on religion. As a result, the City has withheld funds already appropriated to the Museum for operating expenses and maintenance and, in a suit filed in New York State Supreme Court two days after the Museum filed its suit in this court, seeks to eject the Museum from the City-owned land and building in which the Museum's collections have been housed for over one hundred years.

The Museum seeks a preliminary injunction barring the imposition of penalties by the Mayor and the City for the Museum's exercise of its First Amendment rights.... For the reasons that follow, defendants' motion is denied, and plaintiff's motion is granted....

Upon completion of construction of a wing of the new building, the City of Brooklyn entered into a building lease and contract (the "Contract") [in 1893] with the Institute, for a term coextensive with the Lease, to house the Institute's collections. The City of New York is the successor to the City of Brooklyn under the Lease and the Contract. The parties agree that, upon the expiration of the original term of the Lease agreement in December 1993, the Museum remained a tenant in possession of the land and the building on the same terms and conditions as contained in the Lease and Contract.... The Contract provides that "[the City] shall pay to the [Institute] each year such sum as may be necessary for the maintenance of said Museum Building, or as may be authorized by law or be apportioned or appropriated by [the City]." The Contract specifically defines "maintenance" to include: (1) repairs and alterations; (2) fuel; (3) waste removal; (4) wages of employees providing essential maintenance, custodial, security and other basic services; (5) cleaning and general care; (6) tools and supplies; and (7) insurance for the building, furniture and fixtures.

Consistent with the applicable statutes, the Lease, and the Contract, as well as with historical practices, the City's Procedures Manual specifies that public funds are provided to designated cultural institutions to help meet costs for general maintenance, security and energy, and in some instances to support education programs. City funds generally "are not used for direct curatorial or artistic services." The City also approves certain capital expenditures as part of its program "to protect and ensure the continued existence of New York City's most precious assets, its cultural institutions, for local communities, the general public and the artistic community." The City's Fiscal Year 2000 appropriation of approximately $5.7 million to the Museum specifies that the funding contributes to "maintenance, security, administration, curatorial, educational services and energy costs." The City was not asked to fund the controversial exhibit giving rise to this action. The City's Fiscal Year 2000 appropriation to the Brooklyn Children's Museum is approximately $1.6 million.

Nothing in the City's lengthy annual final report and budget request form, which each institution must supply, asks for detailed information concerning the individual works in exhibits. Instead, the form is designed to determine, among other things: the general purposes and plans of the institution; "brief descriptions" (emphasis in original) of immediate past and future programming; accomplishments and plans for educational programs for children, educators and the general public; and detailed financial information.

The Sensation Exhibit was first shown in 1997 at the Royal Academy of Art in London, where it drew record crowds for a contemporary art exhibit and generated controversy and some protest demonstrations.... Mr. Lehman's efforts to bring the Exhibit to Brooklyn continued through 1998, and plans were finalized in April 1999....

The Exhibit was scheduled to open to the public at the Museum on October 2, 1999. City officials first began raising objections to the Exhibit on September 22. On that date, Commissioner Chapin, stating that he was acting on behalf of the Mayor, advised Mr. Lehman by telephone that the City would terminate all funding to the Museum unless it canceled the Exhibit. Commissioner Chapin specifically referred to the fact that the Mayor found objectionable "The Holy Virgin Mary" by Chris Ofili. (All of the five Ofili works in the Exhibit use elephant dung together with other materials. In addition, on the painting entitled "The Holy Virgin Mary," there are small photographs of buttocks and female genitalia scattered on the background.) The Mayor explained his position publicly that day, taking particular exception to "The Holy Virgin Mary." The Mayor stated that this work "offends me" and "is sick," and he explained his decision to terminate City funding as follows:

> You don't have a right to a government subsidy to desecrate someone else's religion. And therefore we will do everything that we can to remove funding from the [Museum] until the director comes to his senses. And realizes that if you are a government subsidized enterprise then you can't do things that desecrate the most personal and deeply held views of the people in society.

The Mayor also referred to a Hirst work of two pigs in formaldehyde as "sick stuff" to be exhibited in an art museum.

The following day, the Mayor accused the Museum of violating the Lease by mounting an exhibit which was inaccessible to schoolchildren and by failing to obtain his permission to restrict access to the Exhibit, which he made clear he would not give because of his view that taxpayer-funded property should not be used to "desecrate religion" or "do things that are disgusting with regard to animals." In a letter from New York City Corporation Counsel Michael D. Hess to Mr. Lehman, dated September 23, 1999, Mr. Hess stated that "the Mayor will not approve a modification of the Contract to allow [the Museum] to restrict admission to the museum. In light of the fact that [the Museum] has already determined that it would be inappropriate for those under 17 years of age to be admitted to the exhibit without adult supervision (a determination with which the City does not disagree), [the Museum] cannot proceed with the exhibit as planned."

The Mayor and other senior City officials continued, and escalated, their attacks on the Exhibit and their threats to the Museum, vowing to cut off all funding, including construction funding, to seek to replace the Board of Trustees, to cancel the Lease, and to assume possession of the Museum building, unless the Exhibit were canceled. The Mayor asserted on September 24 that he would not "have any compunction about trying to put them out of business, meaning the board." On September 28, the Mayor publicly stated that taxpayer dollars should not "be used to support the desecration of important national or religious symbol, of any religion." A City press release that day denounced "an exhibit which besmirches religion and is an insult to the community." The press release announced that, in response to the Museum Board's formal decision that day to proceed with the Exhibit, the City would end its funding of the Museum immediately. In his deposition, Deputy Mayor Joseph Lhota acknowledged that he had earlier told the Chairman of the Museum's Board of Trustees, Robert Rubin, that all City funding to the Museum would be canceled unless the Museum agreed to remove "The Holy Virgin Mary" from the Exhibit.

In response to the City's threats, including explicit statements by senior officials that the City would withhold its monthly payment of $497,554 due on October 1, 1999, the Museum commenced this action against the City and the Mayor on September 28, 1999, pursuant to 42 U.S.C. § 1983, seeking declaratory and injunctive relief, to prevent the defendants from punishing or retaliating against the Museum for displaying the Exhibit, in violation of the Museum's rights under the First and Fourteenth Amendments, including cutting off funding, terminating the lease, seizing the building or attempting to fire the Board of Trustees. The City has in fact withheld the scheduled October payment to the Museum. Plaintiff filed an amended complaint on October 1, 1999, adding claims for damages against the defendants, and claims of violation of the Equal Protection Clause and state and local law....

THE FIRST AMENDMENT CLAIM: THE MUSEUM'S MOTION FOR A PRELIMINARY INJUNCTION

A party seeking a preliminary injunction must ordinarily demonstrate (a) irreparable harm and (b) either (1) likelihood of success on the merits or (2) sufficiently serious questions going to the merits to make them a fair ground of litigation and a balance of hardships tipping decidedly in its favor.... In any event, as will be seen, the Museum easily establishes a likelihood of success on the merits.

The Museum is suffering and will continue to suffer irreparable harm if an injunction is not granted. "The loss of First Amendment freedoms, for even minimal periods of time, unquestionably constitutes irreparable injury." Because of this, it is sometimes said that "when an injunction is sought to protect First Amendment rights, likelihood of success on the merits and irreparable harm merge into a single threshold requirement."

The City and the Mayor argue that there is no irreparable injury because the Museum has not shown that the withholding of funding prevented it from showing the Sensation Exhibit or that the loss of its operating and maintenance subsidy will force the imminent closing of the Museum. Counsel for defendants further stated at oral argument that the City's own ejectment suit cannot be a sound basis for a preliminary injunction motion because the suit has just begun and, "in the event that that particular action gets to a critical stage," the motion can be renewed. These arguments ignore the very reason that interference with First Amendment rights constitutes irreparable injury.

This is not a case involving the mere assertion of an incidental infringement of First Amendment rights insufficient to establish irreparable harm. Nor does the Museum rely on remote or speculative fears of future retaliation. The Museum has already suffered direct and purposeful penalization by the City in response to its exercise of First Amendment rights. First, the City has cut off appropriated funding. Second, the City has sued in state court to evict the Museum from the property which it has occupied for over one hundred years and in which it houses its enormous collections of ancient and modern art.... [T]he City asks the court to treat its ejectment suit as brought in good faith, that is, as brought with the goal of ejecting the Museum. It cannot on the one hand seek so serious a penalty (it could, after all, have brought only a declaratory judgment action) and on the other hand claim that no harm is imminent. For a museum of the magnitude of the Brooklyn Museum, planning for a move of one and a half million art objects would obviously be a monumental task. Given the finding of a likelihood of success on the merits of the Museum's claim of a First Amendment violation, the Museum should not have to wait until a City sheriff is at the door to seek equitable relief....

In keeping with that principle, the First Amendment bars government officials from censoring works said to be "offensive," *Texas v. Johnson*, 491 U.S. 397 (1989), "sacrilegious," *Joseph Burstyn, Inc. v. Wilson*, 343 U.S. 495 (1952), "morally improper," *Hannegan v. Esquire*, 327 U.S. 146 (1946), or even "dangerous," *Regan v. Taxation with Representation of Washington*, 461 U.S. 540, 548 (1983). "If there is a bedrock principle underlying the First Amendment, it is that the government may not prohibit the expression of an idea simply because society finds the idea itself offensive or disagreeable."

In *Hannegan*, for example, the Supreme Court held that the Postmaster General could not deny second-class postal privileges to a magazine, admittedly not containing material that was obscene and therefore illegal, because it was found by him not to be conducive to the "public good." In *Joseph Burstyn, Inc.*, the Supreme Court found the First Amendment violated by a New York statute authorizing denial of a license to motion pictures found to be "sacrilegious." ...

Similarly, in *Spence v. Washington*, 418 U.S. 405 (1974), the Supreme Court struck, on First Amendment grounds, a flag misuse statute as applied to a college student who hung an American flag with a peace symbol on it upside down out of his window. Among the grounds considered and rejected for upholding the judgment against the student, the Court noted: "that the State may have desired to protect the sensibilities of passersby" is not a basis for suppressing ideas, and that "anyone who might have been offended could easily have avoided the display." *Spence*, 418 U.S. at 412. Thus, "under our system of government there is an accommodation for the widest varieties of tastes and ideas. What is good literature, what has educational value, what is refined public information, what is good art, varies with individuals as it does from one generation to another."

The City and the Mayor acknowledge that the art being shown at the Museum and the ideas which they find that art to express are within the protections of the First and Fourteenth Amendments. Contrary to their assertions, however, although they did not physically remove the art objects from the Museum, they are not insulated from a claim that they are violating the overwhelming body of First Amendment law establishing that government cannot suppress ideas indirectly any more than it can do so directly....

In many different contexts, then, the Supreme Court has made clear that, although the government is under no obligation to provide various kinds of benefits, it may not deny them if the reason for the denial would require a choice between exercising First Amendment rights and obtaining the benefit. That is, it may not "discriminate invidiously in its subsidies in such a way as to 'aim [ ] at the suppression of dangerous ideas.'"

...

The reliance of the City and the Mayor on *National Endowment for the Arts v. Finley*, 524 U.S. 569 (1998), as support for their claim that viewpoint discrimination in arts funding is permissible, is misplaced. In *Finley*, the Supreme Court rejected a facial challenge to a provision adding "general standards of decency and respect for the diverse beliefs and values of the American public" to the "considerations" to be applied by the NEA in the awarding of grants to individual artists and arts organizations. The Court described the provision's legislative history, including Congress's rejection of language that would have prohibited awards of grants that would have the purpose or effect of denigrating particular religions, or of denigrating people on the basis of race, sex, handicap, or national origin. It noted that, ultimately, "the legislation was a bipartisan proposal introduced as a counterweight to amendments aimed at eliminating the NEA's funding or substantially constraining its grant-making authority." The Court also noted that "Congress declined to disallow any particular viewpoints," and it went on to hold the challenged provision facially constitutional upon finding that it "[did] not preclude awards to projects that might be deemed 'indecent' or 'disrespectful' nor place conditions on grants ..." and, further, because the Court did "not perceive a realistic danger" that it will be used "to effectively preclude or punish the expression of particular views." Thus, even in *Finley*, where the issue was the "considerations" that could apply in the awarding of grants, unlike here, where funding has already been appropriated for general operating expenses, the Supreme Court upheld the "decency" and "respect" considerations only by reading them, on their face, as not permitting viewpoint discrimination.

When questioned on oral argument whether the City could direct a publicly supported library to remove particular books on pain of a loss of financial support, counsel for defendants responded that the visual art in the Exhibit has a greater impact than do books. Counsel for the Museum, in reply, noted that books like *Mein Kampf* have done enormous harm, but are still protected by the First Amendment. The relative power of books and visual art is of course immaterial. The communicative power of visual art is not a basis for restricting it but rather the very reason it is protected by the First Amendment. As recently stated by the Court of Appeals for the Second Circuit, "visual art is as wide ranging in its depiction of ideas, concepts and emotions as any book, treatise, pamphlet or other writing, and is similarly entitled to full First Amendment protection." ...

The City's motion to dismiss is denied. As the Museum has established irreparable harm and a likelihood of success on its First Amendment claim, its motion for a preliminary injunction is granted.

Trebert v. City Of New Orleans

2005 U.S. Dist. LEXIS 1560 (E.D. La. Feb. 1, 2005)

Plaintiff, Marc C. Trebert, sued the City of New Orleans pursuant to 42 U.S.C. § 1983, asserting that §§ 110-121 through 110-132 of the City's Municipal Code violate his constitutional rights of free speech under the First Amendment.... Trebert takes digital photographs, prints them and colors them with pastels. The City granted Trebert a "Jackson Square A" permit dated January 6, 2004, which was to expire on December 31, 2004... "to paint and sell works of art in that area defined as 'the Jackson Square set-up area.'" "Permit A" allows its holder "to manually paint, sketch or draw on plain surfaces only in ... the Jackson Square artist set-up area." Trebert intends to make and sell art produced by digital technology, i.e., digital photographs that are colored with pastels.... On January 14, 2004, the Municipal Court temporarily enjoined Trebert "from selling [presumably within the Jackson Square A area only] any paintings, sketches or drawings produced by or with the assistance of a mechanical devices [sic] and with the use of any process used to duplicate an existing image," until February 3, 2004.

The Municipal Code provides that artists may create and sell only "original" art along the Jackson Square fence. "Original means only those works produced and for sale by the artist which have been accomplished essentially by hand and precludes any mechanical or duplicative process in whole or part." The ordinance prohibits plaintiff from selling, at his Jackson Square site [e.g. the French Quarter], digital photographs that have been printed and colored because they are not within the law's definition of "original" art. The City agreed to dismiss the criminal citation against Trebert and to refrain from enforcing the ordinance against him until the instant lawsuit is resolved....

Trebert and the City agree that the ordinance at issue is content neutral and that it regulates the time, place and manner of display and sale of the works it defines as art. They also agree that "preserving the distinctive charm, character and tout ensemble of the [French] Quarter" is a significant governmental interest....

The City has presented no evidence to sustain its burden to show that the ordinance is narrowly tailored to serve the City's significant interest in preserving the French Quarter's charm and authenticity. The City merely speculates that any less burdensome alternative would result in its interests being achieved less effectively and that "the obvious effect of lifting the restriction would be the prospect that the area surrounding Jackson Square would become one big photography studio, with cardboard images of President Clinton and faux backgrounds of French Quarter scenes."

The City also asserts that the law is narrowly tailored because "it does not prohibit duplicative processes by brush, charcoal, airbrush, finger-paint, etc." Arguably, the ordinance does prohibit such processes, inasmuch as it "precludes any mechanical or duplicative process in whole or part," and an airbrush is clearly a mechanical tool. One could also argue that an artist who churns out repetitive, albeit handmade, paintings or drawings of the same familiar French Quarter scenes for sale to tourists uses "duplicative" processes. These ambiguities in the ordinance undermine the City's argument that it is narrowly tailored to its purpose.

In *Bery*, the Second Circuit Court of Appeals invalidated the City of New York's licensing requirement for visual artists who wished to sell their works in public spaces. Despite the City's significant interest in keeping its public spaces safe and congestion-free, the court found that the law was not narrowly tailored because it effectively barred artists from selling their work on the streets. The City produced no evidence to justify such a sweeping bar on an entire category of expression. *Bery v. City of New York*, 97 F.3d 689, 697 (2d Cir. 1996)....

In contrast to these cases, the First Circuit upheld an ordinance that prohibited licensed commercial activity (including plaintiff's business of motion picture exhibition) between the hours of 1:00 a.m. and 6:00 a.m., based on the town's substantial interest in minimizing traffic, noise, litter and security problems in residential areas around the movie theater. *National Amusements, Inc. v. Town of Dedham*, 43 F.3d 731 (1st Cir. 1995). The court found that the town's avowed purposes were strongly supported by an evidentiary showing, including the records of numerous citizen complaints and the records of town meetings that led to passage of the ordinance.

The First Circuit held that the ordinance was narrowly tailored because it promoted the substantial governmental interest in preserving peace and tranquility, which could not be achieved as effectively absent the regulation, and that plaintiff had ample alternative means of reaching its intended movie-going audience during the remaining 19 hours of the day....

The City of New Orleans indisputably has a significant interest in preserving the authenticity and charm of the French Quarter. In this case, the City bears the burden to establish that its ordinance is narrowly tailored to achieve its interest. However, ... the City has produced no evidence to support its speculative assertion that any less burdensome alternative than the challenged ordinance would result in its interests being achieved less effectively. "We have never accepted mere conjecture as adequate to carry a First Amendment burden." Display of plaintiff's works does not detract from the ambiance of the French Quarter any more than electric lights do.

In the absence of any evidence submitted by the City, this court cannot find that the ordinance is narrowly tailored to serve a significant government interest. Because the City has failed to carry its burden to show that the ordinance is narrowly tailored to achieve its interest, Trebert is entitled to partial summary judgment in his favor.

Because that ruling forecloses a finding of constitutionality, the court need not address whether the ordinance leaves open to Trebert ample alternative avenues of expression. Nonetheless, for purposes of any further review of this ruling, I will analyze that prong of the constitutional test as well.

It is well established that Trebert is "entitled to a public forum for [his] expressive activities." The City argues that Trebert may sell his work from tables outside of events inside the City's Convention Center, inside the Superdome, inside arenas where concerts are held or at other events or festivals throughout the New Orleans area. Defendant contends that Trebert has failed to show that these alternative venues are inadequate. The City misconceives the evidentiary burden in this regard. It is not Trebert's burden to show that alternatives are inadequate; it is the City's burden to show that they are ample. . . .

None of the City's proposed alternative venues for Trebert's work is Jackson Square. The City has not demonstrated that events in the Convention Center, the Superdome, other arenas or festivals are as easily accessible to plaintiff and/or his intended audience as the fence area of Jackson Square, which is a unique venue for the display and sale of works like Trebert produces to passersby.

Sports events, conventions, concerts and festivals are episodic. Many sports events and concerts occur at night, as compared to plaintiff's daily, daytime access to Jackson Square. The City has not shown that Trebert could obtain access to the inside areas of the Convention Center, the Superdome, the New Orleans Arena or Kiefer UNO Lakefront Arena as simply and cheaply as he is able to obtain a one-year permit from the City for a nominal fee. . . .

Trebert [also] argues that the ordinance is unconstitutionally overbroad both on its face and as applied to him. In his motion for partial summary judgment, he asks that the court enjoin enforcement of the ordinance against him and any other person.

"[A] statute or ordinance may be considered invalid 'on its face' — either because it is unconstitutional in every conceivable application, or because it seeks to prohibit such a broad range of protected conduct that it is unconstitutionally 'overbroad.'" . . . In the instant case, Trebert has "failed to identify any significant difference between [his] claim that the ordinance is invalid on overbreadth grounds and [his] claim that it is unconstitutional when applied to [his photographically originated work]." . . .

I find that the ordinance is unconstitutional only as applied to Trebert and his activities at Jackson Square that are the subject of this lawsuit. There has been no showing that his pastel-colored, digitally initiated photographs, produced on Jackson Square, interfere with or detract from the "distinctive charm, character and tout ensemble of the [French] Quarter" or that a ban on the type of work he produces would advance protection of that interest.

This does not mean, however, that the City might not be able to show in a different case that a different type of operation than plaintiff's might be banned consistently with the First Amendment. For example, the feared prospect of a commercial photography business, featuring life-sized cardboard cutouts of presidents or other celebrities and faux backgrounds of French Quarter scenes (ironically set against the actual historic backdrop of Jackson Square) with which tourists might pose, or other similar ventures not in keeping with the unique character of Jackson Square, should they materialize, could very well be subject to prohibition under the ordinance without offending the First Amendment. In such a case, it is conceivable that the City and its lawyers might rouse themselves to develop and submit to the court evidence sufficient to bear the burden imposed by the law. In Trebert's particular case, however, they have not done so, and the ordinance unconstitutionally applies to him. Accordingly, appropriate declaratory and injunctive relief will be awarded, limited to Trebert's activities that are the subject of this lawsuit.

Notes and Questions

a. The strong support of the New York courts against Mayor Giuliani's religious outrage suggests rather unbridled control by the curators of government sponsored art exhibits. To what extent is the variation in outcome based on the independence of the museum (or its statute) and the right of the government to select which speech to adopt? Compare *Esperanza Peace and Justice Ctr. v. City of San Antonio*, 316 F. Supp. 2d 433 (W.D. Tex. 2001), with *Piarowski v. Illinois Community College Dist.*, 759 F.2d 625 (7th Cir. 1985).

b. Mayor Giuliani is not the only political figure who may be offended. The Second City, never to be outdone by New York, had its own controversy. When the Chicago Art Institute displayed a student's painting entitled "Mirth and Girth" depicting deceased former Mayor Harold Washington in a bra, g-string, stockings, and garter belt (based on a rumor he had woman's underwear on when admitted to the hospital), local officials attempted to withhold funding and to physically remove the work. See *Nelson v. Streeter*, 16 F.3d 145 (7th Cir. 1994).

c. To what extent can a jurisdiction use the power to speak for itself and to be selective in financing under *Rust v. Sullivan* and *Finley v. NEA* to choose whether or not to provide a lease for a museum? See *Cuban Museum of Arts and Culture, Inc. v. City of Miami*, 766 F. Supp. 1121 (S.D. Fla 1991).

d. Many controversies involving public museums also involve works that have a religious or anti-religious theme. To what extent may a governmental museum or government-funded organization present such art? Is religious and anti-religious art subject to the same standard? See *Lynch v. Donnelly*, 465 U.S. 668 (1984). See also *Santa Fe Indep. Sch. Dist. v. Doe*, 530 U.S. 290 (2000) (student led prayers deemed governmental speech); *O'Connor v. Washburn Univ.*, 416 F.3d 1216 (10th Cir. 2005).

e. In some cases, the municipalities wish to promote art and culture. If a city were to adopt the following ordinance, would it survive constitutional attack from those claiming that it discriminated on the basis of speech or viewpoint?

> WHEREAS, The City Council wishes to foster the production of live performances that offer theatrical, musical, or cultural enrichment to the city's residents and visitors; and

> WHEREAS, Small theaters and other small venues often promote the local production of new and creative live cultural performances, and often have the most difficulty absorbing or passing on any additional costs; and

> WHEREAS, Costs faced by those who produce live theatrical, musical, or other culturally enriching performances at smaller venues are substantial, and such performances often require governmental support since they could not otherwise flourish.

> NOW THEREFORE, the admissions fees charged for a live theatrical, live musical, or other live cultural performance shall be exempt from sales tax that take place in a space with a maximum capacity of not more than 750 people. For purposes hereof, a "live cultural performance" shall be deemed to be a live performance in any of the disciplines which are commonly regarded as part of the fine arts, such as live theater, music, opera, drama, comedy, ballet, modern or traditional dance, and book or poetry readings. This term does not include such amusements as athletic events, races, or performances conducted at adult entertainment cabarets [as defined elsewhere in the ordinance].

See *Pooh-Bah Enters. v. County of Cook*, 232 Ill. 2d 463, 467 (Ill. 2009).

Problem XVII-C

As part of Bryce's current project, Bryce has been working with a local city-owned community center to produce an exhibit of 1950s works of art that were created by local artists of the neighborhood. The board of directors for the community center was supportive of the exhibit and approved the event. Bryce also has permission to film the exhibit and possibly release a documentary about finding the works and presenting them.

Bryce now learns that the neighborhood had a much more vibrant and controversial debate during the 1950s that ended with fears from the anti-communist congressional hearings. The works Bryce has collected include both highly religious works that combine U.S. military images with religious iconography and works that depict workers chained to burning crosses. Although the approval for the exhibit had not included any approval rights over the works in the collection, word has spread regarding the works in the collection. The mayor has called the community center president and asked that the exhibit be cancelled. The city has also refused to provide Bryce a filming permit or parking permits necessary to park electrical generators for the lighting equipment that had been planned. Bryce calls you for help to stop the city and community center from frustrating the exhibit and the documentary.

D. Art Fraud & Trafficking in Art & Artifacts

United States v. An Antique Platter of Gold known as a Gold Phiale Mesomphalos C. 400 B.C.
184 F.3d 131 (2d Cir. 1999)

Michael H. Steinhardt appeals from Judge Jones's ordering of the forfeiture of a "Phiale," an antique gold platter. The district court held that false statements on the customs entry forms and the Phiale's status as stolen property under Italian law rendered its importation illegal. As such, the Phiale was subject to forfeiture.

Steinhardt contends that: (i) the false statements on the customs forms were not material under 18 U.S.C. § 542, (ii) stolen property under the National Stolen Property Act ("NSPA") does not encompass property presumed to belong to the state under Italian patrimony laws, (iii) both statutes afford him an innocent owner defense, and (iv) the forfeiture violates the Eighth Amendment. We hold that the false statements on the customs forms were material and, therefore, need not reach issue (ii). We further hold that there is no innocent owner defense and that forfeiture of the Phiale does not violate the Eighth Amendment.

At issue is a Phiale of Sicilian origin that dates from the 4th Century B.C. Its provenance since then is largely unknown, other than its possession by Vincenzo Pappalardo, a private antique collector living in Sicily, who traded it in 1980 to Vincenzo Cammarata, a Sicilian coin dealer and art collector, for art works worth about $20,000. Cammarata sold it in 1991 to William Veres, the owner of Stedron, a Zurich art dealership, for objects worth about $90,000.

Veres brought the Phiale to the attention of Robert Haber, an art dealer from New York and owner of Robert Haber & Company. In November 1991, Haber traveled to Sicily to meet with Veres and examine the Phiale. Haber informed Steinhardt, a client with whom he had engaged in 20–30 previous transactions, of the piece. Haber told Steinhardt that the Phiale was a twin to a piece in the Metropolitan Museum of Art in New York City and that a Sicilian coin dealer (presumably Cammarata) was willing to guarantee the piece's authenticity.

On December 4, 1991, Haber, acting for Steinhardt, finalized an agreement to purchase the Phiale for slightly more than $1 million—plus a 15% commission, making the total price paid by Steinhardt approximately $1.2 million. Haber and Veres also agreed to a "Terms of Sale," which stated, *inter alia*, that "if the object is confiscated or impounded by customs agents or a claim is made by any country or governmental agency whatsoever, full compensation will be made immediately to the purchaser." It further provided that a "letter is to be written by Dr. [Giacomo] Manganaro that he saw the object 15 years ago in Switz." In fact, Dr. Manganaro, a professor of Greek history and Numismatics, had examined the Phiale in 1980 in Sicily and had determined thereafter that it was authentic and of Sicilian origin.

On December 10, 1991, Haber flew from New York to Zurich, Switzerland, and then proceeded to Lugano, near the Italian border, where he took possession of the Phiale on December 12. The transfer was confirmed by a commercial invoice issued by Stedron, describing the object as "ONE GOLD BOWL—CLASSICAL … DATE—C. 450 B.C.… VALUE U.S. $250,000." The next day, Haber sent a fax to Jet Air Service, Inc. ("Jet Air"), Haber's customs broker at John F. Kennedy International Airport in New York, which included a copy of the commercial invoice. Jet Air prepared an Entry/Immediate Delivery form (Customs Form 3461) to obtain release of the Phiale prior to formal entry. This form listed the Phiale's country of origin as "CH," the code for Switzerland. In addition, Jet Air prepared an Entry Summary form (Customs Form 7501), which also listed the country of origin as "CH" and stated the Phiale's value at $250,000, as Haber's fax had indicated. Haber was listed as the importer of record.

On December 15, Haber returned to the United States from Zurich with the Phiale and later gave it to Steinhardt. Before completing the purchase, Steinhardt had the piece authenticated through a detailed examination by the Metropolitan Museum of Art. Thereafter, the Phiale was displayed in his home from 1992 until 1995.

Under Article 44 of Italy's law of June 1, 1939, an archaeological item is presumed to belong to the state unless its possessor can show private ownership prior to 1902. On February 16, 1995, the Italian government submitted a Letters Rogatory Request to the United States seeking assistance in investigating the circumstances of the Phiale's exportation and asking our government to confiscate it so that it could be returned to Italy. In November 1995, the Phiale was seized from Steinhardt pursuant to a warrant. Soon thereafter the United States filed the present *in rem* civil forfeiture action. The government claimed that forfeiture was proper under 18 U.S.C. § 545 because of false statements on the customs forms. It also claimed that forfeiture was proper under 19 U.S.C. § 1595a(c) because the Phiale was stolen property under the NSPA as a result of Article 44 of Italy's patrimony laws.

Steinhardt entered the proceeding as a claimant, and he and the government moved for summary judgment. In granting judgment for the government, the district court held that the misstatement of the country of origin was material, and, alternatively, that the Phiale was stolen property under Italian law. The court also held that an innocent owner defense was not available under either statute, and that the forfeiture did not violate the Excessive Fines Clause. This appeal followed….

Section 545 prohibits the importation of merchandise into the United States "contrary to law" and states that material imported in such a manner "shall be forfeited." 18 U.S.C.

§ 545.[5] The government claims that the importation of the Phiale was illegal because it violated 18 U.S.C. § 542, which prohibits the making of false statements in the course of importing merchandise into the United States. Steinhardt claims, however, that an element of a Section 542 violation is that such a false statement must be material and that the government has failed to show materiality in the instant case, at least for purposes of summary judgment....

Section 542 states in pertinent part:

> Whoever enters or introduces ... into the commerce of the United States any imported merchandise by means of any fraudulent or false invoice, declaration, affidavit, letter, paper, or by means of any false statement, written or verbal, ... or makes any false statement in any declaration without reasonable cause to believe the truth of such statement, or procures the making of any such false statement as to any matter material thereto without reasonable cause to believe the truth of such statement [shall be guilty of a crime].

8 U.S.C. § 542. There can be no dispute that the designation of Switzerland as the Phiale's country of origin and the listing of its value of $250,000 were false. Haber had examined the Phiale in Sicily about a month before the sale to Steinhardt, and that sale was for $1 million plus 15% commission....

The dispute pertinent to this appeal concerns the proper test for materiality. Steinhardt argues for a "but for" test of materiality, i.e., a false statement is material only if a truthful answer on a customs form would have actually prevented the item from entering the United States. The district court, however, employed a "natural tendency" test, asking whether the false statement would have a natural tendency to influence customs officials. The circuits are divided as to the proper test. The Fifth and Ninth Circuits have adopted a but for test, while the First Circuit has come down in favor of the natural tendency test. We adopt the natural tendency test.

The statutory language, caselaw, and the statutory purpose lead us to this conclusion. First, the statute prohibits importations "by means of" a false statement. Although there is overlap, this language is not synonymous with "because of," and ought not be read so narrowly. Instead, the ordinary meaning of the statutory language requires only that the false statements be an integral part of the importation process. In this case, the false statements were on custom forms and thus easily meet the by means of requirement.

Second, the Supreme Court has noted that "the most common formulation of [materiality] ... is that a concealment or misrepresentation is material if it 'has a natural tendency to influence or was capable of influencing, the decision of' the decision-making body to which it was addressed." Both the Supreme Court and this circuit have employed such a standard in numerous contexts....

Finally, the natural tendency approach is far more consistent with the purpose of the statute—to ensure truthfulness of representations made during importation—than is a

---

5. Section 545 reads, in relevant part:
Whoever fraudulently or knowingly imports or brings into the United States, any merchandise contrary to law, or receives, conceals, buys, sells, or in any manner facilitates the transportation, concealment, or sale of such merchandise after importation, knowing the same to have been imported or brought into the United States contrary to law [shall be subject to criminal penalties.] ... Merchandise introduced into the United States in violation of this section, or the value thereof, to be recovered from any person described in the first or second paragraph of this section, shall be forfeited to the United States.
18 U.S.C. § 545.

but for test. Under a but for test, lying would be more productive because the government would bear the difficult burden of proving what would have happened if a truthful statement had been made. Moreover, under such a test, liability would not attach for misstatements in cases where truthful answers would still have enabled the goods to enter the United States. Importers have incentives to lie for reasons not related to achieving actual entry of the goods—e.g., to reduce the duties payable or to obtain expeditious customs treatment. The statutory purpose would thus be frustrated by the narrow reading suggested by appellant.

We therefore hold that "a false statement is material under Section 542 if it has the potential significantly to affect the integrity or operation of the importation process as a whole, and that neither actual causation nor harm to the government need be demonstrated." For a trier of fact to determine whether a statement can significantly affect the importation process, it need ask only whether a reasonable customs official would consider the statements to be significant to the exercise of his or her official duties. This analysis is analogous to the securities context, where a statement (or omission) is material if there is a "substantial likelihood" that a reasonable investor would view it as "significantly altering the 'total mix' of information made available." Moreover, this test of materiality applies not only to the decision to admit an item but also decisions as to processing, e.g., expediting importation. With this test in mind, we turn to the misstatements on the Phiale's entry form.

Steinhardt contends that even under a natural tendency test, the misstatements are immaterial. He claims that the customs officials lacked statutory authority to seize the Phiale and that it was customs policy not to review information about the country of origin of such an object. He further argues that the statement of the Phiale's value was relevant only to the imposition of the processing fee, which was unaffected by the misstatement. Because the misstatement of the country of origin was material as a matter of law and thus proper grounds for summary judgment, we need not examine the misstatement of value.

Customs Directive No. 5230-15, regarding the detention and seizure of cultural property, fatally undermines Steinhardt's contention that listing Switzerland as the country of origin was irrelevant to the Phiale's importation. The Directive advised customs officials to determine whether property was subject to a claim of foreign ownership and to seize that property. An item's country of origin is clearly relevant to that inquiry....

The Directive provides a basis for seizing cultural property under the NSPA in the seizure provisions of 19 U.S.C. § 1595a(c). Seizure of the Phiale would clearly be authorized by this provision under *United States v. McClain*, 545 F.2d 988 (5th Cir. 1977), which held that violations of a nation's patrimony laws are covered by the NSPA. Because Steinhardt asserts that *McClain* was improperly decided, he claims that the customs officials lacked a statutory basis to seize the Phiale.

This argument, however, misperceives the test of materiality. Regardless of whether *McClain's* reasoning is ultimately followed as a proper interpretation of the NSPA, a reasonable customs official would certainly consider the fact that *McClain* supports a colorable claim to seize the Phiale as having possibly been exported in violation of Italian patrimony laws. Indeed, the Directive explicitly references the *McClain* decision and informs officials that if they are unsure of the status of a nation's patrimony laws, they should notify the Office of Enforcement. Knowing that the Phiale was from Italy would, therefore, be of critical importance....

Eighth Amendment

While Steinhardt raised an Eighth Amendment claim in the district court [that] the forfeiture violates the Excessive Fines Clause of the Eighth Amendment [in violation of

United States v. Bajakajian, 524 U.S. 321 (1998).] We disagree. [The] instant case ... bears all the "hallmarks of the traditional civil *in rem* forfeitures." First, the forfeiture here was not part of a criminal prosecution. While Section 545 is part of the criminal code, this fact alone does not render the forfeiture punitive. Although the question whether a proceeding is civil or criminal is certainly relevant, it is not dispositive. Thus, the fact that the present action is a civil *in rem* proceeding weighs against a finding that it is punitive.

Even more important to the inquiry is the nature of the statute that authorizes forfeiture. As opposed to Section 982(a), the provisions at issue in *Bajakajian*, Section 545 is a customs law, traditionally viewed as non-punitive. The Phiale is thus classic contraband, an item imported into the United States in violation of law.... It is forfeiture of the former that *Bajakajian* continues to recognize as nonpunitive and outside the scope of the Excessive Fines Clause.

We therefore affirm.

United States v. Austin
54 F.3d 394 (7th Cir. 1995)

FLAUM, *Circuit Judge*. Defendant Donald Austin was convicted and sentenced to 8 1/2 years for knowingly buying and selling counterfeit works of art. Although we uphold his conviction, the denial of his motion for a new trial, and all but one of the trial court's sentencing determinations, we remand for a reconsideration of whether Austin deserved a sentencing enhancement under the Guidelines for being an "organizer or leader."

Donald Austin owned and operated Austin Galleries, a chain of art galleries in Chicago, Detroit, and San Francisco. Austin, whose business grew from one Chicago gallery in the mid-1960s to over thirty galleries in the mid-1980s, was a "hands-on" manager who took an active interest in all facets of his business and in each of his galleries. Austin Galleries specialized in modern and contemporary artists, including Salvador Dali, Joan Miro, Pablo Picasso, and Marc Chagall, and sold mostly lithographic and serigraphic prints of their works. Although the individual galleries had prints on hand, many customers purchased prints on a "to ordered" basis; a customer would see a copy in a gallery, and order the actual print from Austin's headquarters in Palatine, Illinois.

Lithographic and serigraphic prints can be divided into three categories for the purposes of this opinion. Lithographs and serigraphs are most valuable when they are part of an "original" limited edition print, a "category 1." Art industry standards require that an original be prepared under the artist's supervision. The artist signifies his acceptance of the edition by signing and numbering them. The artist may also reserve a small percentage of the edition for his own use or that of the publisher. Called "artist's proofs," such works are identified by the designation H.C., E.A., or A.P., usually in place of the edition number. Less valuable than originals are "afters" or "category 2" prints. Afters are copies of an original work made by others with the artist's permission; these copies have nominal value in the decorative art market. Finally, there are "category 3" prints: unauthorized reproductions of an artist's work (or independent works made to look like something the artist might have created), made without the artist's involvement or approval. These works do not have an established market, and if they carry an artist's signature, they are forgeries.

Austin sold most of his art as signed original limited edition prints. His customers thought they were buying originals. The customers were wrong; most of what Austin sold were forgeries. Several of Austin's employees recalled that they never seemed to run out of any print and that there was never a time when a customer requesting a specific edition number was told that the number had been sold or was otherwise unavailable. Others noticed that a number of works they were selling were obvious forgeries and brought this to Austin's attention, to no avail. Two employees even tried removing what they thought were frauds from the walls of one gallery, but when Austin learned of this he merely became angry and ordered them to place the prints back on display.

Acting on complaints, the Federal Trade Commission ("FTC") brought suit against Austin in May, 1988. A district court placed a temporary restraining order on Austin on May 5, 1988, restricting Austin's sales of Dali, Picasso, and Chagall prints and permitting the FTC to enter Austin's galleries to inspect his prints and documents. The inspection yielded widespread evidence of forgeries among Austin's inventory and prior sales. One expert who examined 490 prints, including 387 in current inventory and 103 sold to customers, did not find a single authentic original. Records also revealed that Austin had been able to acquire prints in suspiciously large quantities, some quantities even exceeding the number in the actual edition of the print. The results of the investigation also raised concerns about the authenticity of Austin's Miro prints, and the court, after the FTC amended its complaint, added Miro's works to the list of those Austin could not sell.

Following the investigation, in April, 1990, Austin entered into a settlement agreement with the FTC. The agreement, as approved by the court, forbade Austin from making misrepresentations in the sale of artwork. Austin also agreed to surrender all of his pencil-signed Miros, Chagalls, and Picassos. Austin was allowed to sell Dalis so long as he did not represent them as authentic works of art. Additionally, the court ordered Austin to pay $625,000 into a consumer redress fund to be administered by the FTC, with the condition that if he did not pay the entire sum by January 1, 1991, or if he declared bankruptcy before that day, the amount would increase to $1.5 million. As a final part of the settlement, Austin signed a stipulation for judgment admitting the allegations of fraud contained in the complaint. The stipulation was to be filed only in the event Austin went into bankruptcy or defaulted on his payments to the FTC.

The FTC settlement failed to deter Austin. Austin did not turn over all of the Chagalls, Miros, and Picassos as required. He also attempted to sell several Chagalls to one of his art suppliers, Michael Zabrin, and to sell to another supplier, Phillip Coffaro, a "package" of Chagalls and Miros, although both men turned him down. Most significant, Austin sold nine Chagall prints to a customer, Merlin Hanson, for $50,000, with an option to repurchase within six months. Austin originally had requested only a loan from Hanson and had offered the prints as collateral, but Hanson's financial advisor had insisted on the buy-back arrangement to avoid any losses should Austin enter bankruptcy. Austin represented the prints as having a value of $70,000 wholesale and $140,000 retail. Prior to the sale, which was made eleven days after the FTC settlement, an FTC expert had informed Austin's attorney that at least one of the prints sold to Hanson was a fake.

Following these events, the government initiated criminal proceedings against Austin, and a grand jury indicted him on March 11, 1993. Counts I through VII of the indictment alleged violations of the mail and wire fraud statutes, 18 U.S.C. §§ 1341 & 1343, while Count VIII charged Austin with causing money he knew to have been taken by fraud to be transmitted in interstate commerce, 18 U.S.C. § 2314. The first five counts related to transactions prior to the FTC proceeding, while the last three concerned the Hanson sale. In the course of its investigation, the grand jury subpoenaed Austin's records for sales of Chagalls after 1988. In response, Austin did not turn over information regarding the Hanson sale; Austin testified at trial that he thought the sale was a loan and did not have to be reported.

The government, which relied heavily on the information produced by the FTC investigation, introduced at trial extensive evidence of fraud against Austin. A jury returned guilty verdicts against Austin on all counts, and the trial judge sentenced him to 102 months imprisonment to be followed by two years supervised release. The court also ordered Austin to pay into the FTC's compensation fund $505,000, which was the difference between the restitution he had already made, about $120,000, and the original sum stipulated in the FTC settlement, $625,000.

On appeal, Austin raises several challenges to his conviction. He contends that double jeopardy barred his conviction because of the earlier FTC suit and settlement and that the trial court erred in admitting much of the government's evidence....

Austin first maintains that the FTC settlement had placed him once in jeopardy for any fraud he might have perpetrated on his customers. Austin does not argue that the $625,000 he was initially required to pay into a "consumer redress fund" constituted a punishment for his actions; he admits that that sum was a remedial payment. Rather, Austin submits that when he defaulted on the $625,000 installment plan and his liability jumped to $1.5 million, the $875,000 increase constituted a punishment above and beyond his agreement to return his customers' money. This civil sanction, he suggests, placed him once in jeopardy, thereby rendering the criminal trial an unconstitutional proceeding.

Austin is correct that "punitive" civil sanctions can constitute punishment for the purposes of the double jeopardy clause. Austin is also correct that even where a civil punishment precedes a criminal trial, jeopardy may attach. Austin's argument falters, however, when he asserts that if $625,000 satisfied the FTC's remedial interests, any payment above that amount is properly categorized as "a deterrent or retribution." The FTC accepted $625,000 initially because it feared that the defendant might go into bankruptcy. The FTC's offer amounted to a discount for prompt and early payment of the total loss Austin had caused, a sum the FTC estimated to be in excess of $3.8 million. When Austin violated the terms of the settlement and the amount he owed increased, the FTC was still only holding Austin liable for an amount less than that it thought his fraud had caused. Thus, the net consequence of the FTC's actions was still remedial. Such circumstances do not implicate the Double Jeopardy Clause.

Second, Austin objects to the trial court's admission of extensive evidence relating to the FTC settlement, including the terms of the consent decree and Austin's stipulation in the settlement admitting to the allegations in the FTC's complaint. He asserts that this evidence was unfairly prejudicial because it likely led the jury to think that "the same issues had already been determined in the civil action." We review the admission of this evidence for abuse of discretion.

Austin's contentions on this point are equally unavailing. Prior to trial, the government informed Austin that it would introduce the consent decree in order to show Austin's criminal intent in subsequently violating its conditions. While Federal Rule of Evidence 408 prohibits the admission of statements made in the course of settlement to prove liability and Rule 404(b) prohibits the admission of other wrongs in order to show action in conformity therewith, both rules allow the admission of such evidence when offered for another purpose. The evidence from the civil suit served a number of alternative purposes. First, it showed that Austin was on notice when he subsequently sold other prints that those prints were forgeries. It also demonstrated Austin knew he could not sell those prints without reporting the sale to the FTC. Moreover, the facts from the FTC case both provided the background for Austin's indictment and laid the evidentiary foundation for many of the government's exhibits in the criminal proceeding. Finally, the stipulation itself constituted a direct judicial admission to the accusation of fraud in the conduct underlying the indictment. These purposes provided sufficient bases to introduce this evidence against Austin.

We also do not think that the evidence, in light of its relevance, was so "unfairly prejudicial" that the trial court should have excluded it under Fed. R. Evid. 403…. [W]e affirm Austin's conviction …

Notes and Questions

a. In *United States v. Schultz*, 333 F.3d 393 (2d Cir. 2003), the Second Circuit formally addressed the application of the National Stolen Property Act (NSPA), 18 U.S.C. § 2315, to antiquities that are not stolen from a private owner, but, rather, are excavated in violation of state law. Many countries have laws which provide for state ownership of excavated antiquities. The Court reaffirmed the position that these patrimony laws provide sufficient ownership of the property to allow for enforcement of the NSPA. See also *United States v. McClain*, 545 F.2d 988 (5th Cir. 1977).

b. Other federal statutes provide criminal sanctions, including theft of major artwork, 18 U.S.C. § 668 (to obtain by theft or fraud any object of cultural heritage from a museum); interstate or foreign shipments by carrier; state prosecutions, 18 U.S.C. § 659 (to steal or obtain by fraud anything from a conveyance, depot, or terminal, any shipment being transported in interstate or foreign commerce); fraud and swindles, 18 U.S.C. § 1341 (to cause anything to be sent through the U.S. mails in furtherance of a scheme to defraud); fraud by wire, radio, or television, 18 U.S.C. § 1343 (to cause any electronic signal to cross state lines in furtherance of a scheme to defraud); interference with commerce by threats or violence (Hobbs Act), 18 U.S.C. § 1951 (to obstruct interstate commerce by robbery, extortion, threat of violence, or actual violence); and illegal trafficking in Native American human remains and cultural items, 18 U.S.C. § 1170 (discussed below).

c. One analogy to the NSPA for intellectual property applies to the transportation and sale of bootleg records. Is there a sufficient ownership in the copyright underlying the bootleg records or the public performance of the artist to give rise to a cause of action? See *Dowling v. United States*, 473 U.S. 207 (1985).

d. The treatment of Native American sacred sites and gravesites has been one of the many troubling aspects of expropriated art and artifacts. In 1990, Congress enacted The Native American Graves Protection and Repatriation Act, codified at 25 U.S.C. §§ 3001–3013 and 18 U.S.C. § 1170. "Shorn of its excess legal verbiage, what the statute says is that it is a crime (1) to dig up, remove or damage archaeological resources on federal or Indian land; (2) to receive, transport or deal in what has been dug up or removed; or (3) to receive, transport or deal in what has been dug up or removed from private land in violation of State or local law."[6]

The bill summary provides a simple outline of the legislation:

- Clarifies the right of ownership of Indian, Alaska Native, and Native Hawaiian (Native American) human remains and artifacts, including funerary objects, religious artifacts, and objects of cultural patrimony, found on Federal or tribal lands.

- Establishes conditions for the excavation or removal of Native American human remains or cultural artifacts, including the consent of the appropriate tribe or Native American organization.

---

6. Stefan D. Cassella, *Using the Forfeiture Laws to Protect Archaeological Resources*, 41 Idaho L. Rev. 129, 135 (2004).

- Establishes notification requirements for the inadvertent discovery of Native American human remains or cultural artifacts on Federal or tribal lands.

- Establishes criminal penalties for the sale, purchase, or transport of Native American human remains or cultural artifacts without a legal right of possession.

- Directs Federal agencies and museums receiving Federal assistance to identify the geographic and tribal origins of human remains or cultural artifacts in their collections, and require the return of the remains or artifacts to the appropriate tribe or Native American organization upon request.

- Establishes a Department of Interior advisory committee to review the identification and repatriation processes for Native American human remains and cultural artifacts held by Federal agencies and federally assisted museums.

- Establishes civil penalties for museums failing to comply with requirements of this act.

e. Another difficult issue in theft and misappropriation of art and cultural artifacts stems from the atrocities of the Nazi regime during its reign through the end of World War II. Limited legal activity continues today, and new evidence provides a better historical record, if not any meaningful measure of legal relief. See *Alperin v. Vatican Bank*, 410 F.3d 532 (9th Cir. 2005).

> A group of twenty-four individuals and four organizations (the "Holocaust Survivors") claim that the Vatican Bank, known by its official title Istituto per le Opere di Religione, the Order of Friars Minor, and the Croatian Liberation Movement (Hrvatski Oslobodilacki Pokret), profited from the genocidal acts of the Croatian Ustasha political regime (the "Ustasha"), which was supported throughout World War II by Nazi forces. That profit allegedly passed through the Vatican Bank in the form of proceeds from looted assets and slave labor. The Holocaust Survivors brought suit in federal court claiming conversion, unjust enrichment, restitution, the right to an accounting, and human rights violations and violations of international law arising out of the defendants' alleged involvement with the Ustasha during and following World War II....

> The viability of the Holocaust Survivors' claims apart from the issue of the political question doctrine is not before us. Nevertheless, looking ahead, we note that the statutory grounds on which the Holocaust Survivors base their claims have, for the most part, not fared well in recent litigation. Just last term, the Supreme Court limited the [Alien Tort Statute (ATS)] in *Sosa v. Alvarez-Machain*, 542 U.S. 692 (2004) (curtailing the scope of actionable international norms under the ATS but explaining that "the door is still ajar subject to vigilant doorkeeping"); see also *Weiss v. Am. Jewish Comm.*, 335 F. Supp. 2d 469 (S.D.N.Y. 2004) (dismissing claim under the ATS for injunctive relief in connection with the construction of a Holocaust memorial in light of the Court's holding in Sosa).

> The contours of the [Foreign Sovereign Immunities Act (FSIA)] have also changed with the Supreme Court's holding in Republic of *Austria v. Altmann*, 541 U.S. 677 (2004), that the FSIA applies retroactively. See also *Abrams v. Societe Nationale des Chemins de Fer Francais*, 389 F.3d 61, 64–65 (2d Cir. 2004) (dismissing case for lack of subject matter jurisdiction because the French government's acquisition of defendant railroad company immunized it from suit under the FSIA). In *Deutsch v. Turner Corp.*, 324 F.3d 692, 719 (9th Cir. 2003), we held that a California statute on which the Holocaust Survivors' claims are based in

part, Cal. Civ. Proc. Code § 354.6, unconstitutionally intruded on the foreign affairs power of the federal government. We leave the district court to determine in the first instance to what extent the Holocaust Survivors have correctly invoked these and other jurisdictional bases.

Is the current trend against enforcement of claims for property stolen by Nazi governments consistent with the NPSA or the Native American Graves Protection and Repatriation Act? Should the provenance of stolen art or cultural artifacts be subject to a statute of limitations? Does it matter whether the work has religious significance, and if so, significance to whom?

f. Can there be an innocent art dealer in the chain of title for stolen art and artifacts? Again, does the answer change if the works are religious in nature, or if they were stolen as part of an occupational government or during the commission of human rights violations? See *Autocephalous Greek-Orthodox Church v. Goldberg & Feldman Fine Arts, Inc.*, 917 F.2d 278 (7th Cir. 1990).

g. The costs of expediting importing can be very high. Where importers listed the value of each of two works at $100.00 to simplify the import into the U.S. for a possible sale, the United States seized the works. The two Defendants *in rem* were (1) the painting *Hannibal*, by Jean-Michel Basquiat, which was purchased by the Claimant for $1 million and (2) the sculpture known as the *Togatus*, of unknown Mediterranean origin, purchased by the Claimant for $600,000. See *United States v. Painting Known As "Hannibal"*, 2010 U.S. Dist. LEXIS 50483 (S.D.N.Y. May 18, 2010).

Problem XVII-D

As Bryce has worked in the neighborhood on the feature film, art exhibit, and documentary (see Problems XVIII-B, XVIII-C), Bryce has gained the trust and respect of many of the elderly artists in the area. Alice McGreevy, one of the artists, gave Bryce a group of five oil paintings that she had made in 1952. McGreevy explained that she had sold the paintings to a collector in 1952, but then found out that the collector was planning to destroy the work out of fear that the pieces would result in his identification as a Communist sympathizer. (The collector, in fact, had attended Communist political party meetings twice in the 1930s.) McGreevy explained that she "took the artwork back" from the unnamed collector—but kept the payments.

Bryce accepted the gift, but is now worried. The exhibit and the associated publicity have generated a great deal of interest in these works. The children of the collector have contacted Bryce claiming ownership of the five works and demanding their return. McGreevy says that the family has no claim over the works, so she can dispose of them however she wants. Bryce requests your advice and guidance.

E. Museum Operations as Charitable Entities

Introduction

Nonprofit organizations are creatures of state law and federal tax law. State law governs the organizational aspects of the nonprofit entity, typically providing that the entity is a corporation organized with no shareholders and with a charitable purpose that meets the applicable state law definition. Depending on the specifics of state law, organizations can also be trusts, governmental entities, or limited liability companies. Not all nonprofit organizations are tax exempt for federal tax purposes. For example, mutual benefit organizations such as trade associations are nonprofit organizations but do not provide the members or donors a tax deduction for donations.

Charitable organizations operated exclusively for religious, charitable, scientific, public safety testing, literary, or educational purposes are exempt from federal income taxation under Internal Revenue Code, 26 U.S.C. § 501(c)(3). Donations made to those organizations may be deductible against the donor's tax liability. The organization is further limited by statute so "no part of the net earnings ... inures to the benefit of any private shareholder or individual, no substantial part of the activities ... is carrying on propaganda, or otherwise attempting, to influence legislation (except as otherwise provided in subsection (h)), and ... does not participate in, or intervene in (including the publishing or distributing of statements), any political campaign on behalf of (or in opposition to) any candidate for public office." 26 U.S.C. § 501(c)(3).

Museums and arts organizations generally qualify as tax-exempt as educational organizations. As explained in the tax exemption application, "[a] public charity has a broad base of support, while a private foundation receives its support from a small number of donors."[7] More specifically, tax-exempt organizations are those "that receive substantial support from grants, governmental units, and/or contributions from the general public." The primary test is the one-third support test, under which an organization will be deemed charitable if it "normally receive[s] more than one-third of their support from contributions, membership fees, and gross receipts from activities related to their exempt functions, and not more than one-third of their support from gross investment income and net unrelated business income."[8]

In addition to fulfilling the financial support requirements, the purpose of the organization must be charitable, as such term is generally used. Museums and cultural institutes are generally included as charitable educational institutions, assuming the other obligations are met.

> To be organized exclusively for a charitable purpose, the organization must be a corporation, community chest, fund, or foundation. A charitable trust is a fund or foundation and will qualify. However, an individual will not qualify. The articles of organization must limit the organization's purposes to exempt purposes set forth in section 501(c)(3) and must not expressly empower it to engage, other than as an insubstantial part of its activities, in activities that are not in furtherance of one or more of those purposes. This requirement may be met if the purposes stated in the articles of organization are limited in some way by reference to section 501(c)(3).

> In addition, an organization's assets must be permanently dedicated to an exempt purpose. This means that if an organization dissolves, its assets must be distributed for an exempt purpose, to the federal government, or to a state or local government for a public purpose. To establish that an organization's assets will be permanently dedicated to an exempt purpose, its articles of organization should contain a provision insuring their distribution for an exempt

---

7. *Instructions for Form 1023—Introductory Material*, IRS, http://www.irs.gov/instructions/i1023/ar01.html (last visited May 24, 2013).

8. *Id.*

purpose in the event of dissolution. Although reliance may be placed upon state law to establish permanent dedication of assets for exempt purposes, an organization's application can be processed by the IRS more rapidly if its articles of organization include a provision insuring permanent dedication of assets for exempt purposes.[9]

In addition to the charitable purpose, the organization's operation cannot result in the private inurement or financial benefit of private individuals. While reasonable salaries can be paid by the organization, transactions between the charity and its leadership are closely scrutinized and personal benefits are avoided. Similarly, income by the charity which stems from non-tax-exempt activities, such as sales of goods that do not further the organization's charitable purpose, must not grow too large or the organization may lose its tax-exempt status.

As a result, while museums generally fall within the normal range of charitable entities, galleries that sell private works of art have innumerable troubles operating in the nonprofit arena. Organizations that fill both roles also risk problems with private inurement and unrelated business income tax obligations and an income that can threaten the public support requirement of the charity.

The governance of charitable organizations must fit within both the federal obligations embedded in the tax laws and the state nonprofit corporation laws. Among these many duties are the obligation to treat the assets of the charity as a public trust and to meet the duties of care and loyalty to the entity. Similarly, the charities often serve as trustees for donations made in the form of express trusts or gifts that have trust-like fiduciary responsibilities to the donors. These obligations limit how museum boards can manage the assets under their control.

Museum of Fine Arts v. Beland
735 N.E.2d 1248 (Mass. 2000)

This is an action brought under G. L. c. 231A by the Museum of Fine Arts (MFA), seeking a declaration that the will of the late Reverend William E. Wolcott (Wolcott) does not allow the defendants to sell any of the seventeen paintings that were bequeathed to a charitable trust. The record establishes the following relevant undisputed facts. Wolcott died in 1911. In his will, executed on June 20, 1907, Wolcott bequeathed seventeen paintings, including paintings by Eugene Boudin, Camille Pissarro, and Claude Monet, to the trustees of The White Fund (trustees), a charitable trust. The provisions of the bequest read as follows:

"3. Whenever the pictures or any part of them shall come into the actual possession of the said Trustees, they shall offer the same for purposes of exhibition to the Museum of Fine Arts in the City of Boston, unless they shall determine otherwise in accordance with the discretion confirmed on them in the following paragraph:

"4. If at the time of my decease or at any subsequent time there shall exist within the present limits of the city of Lawrence a public art gallery housed in a fire-proof building and under such management as the Trustees of the White

---

9. *Oganizational Test—Internal Revenue Code Section 501(c)(3)*, IRS, Nov. 16, 2012, http://www.irs.gov/Charities-&-Non-Profits/Charitable-Organizations/Organizational-Test-Internal-Revenue-Code-Section-501(c)(3).

Fund shall approve, the said Trustees may deposit the aforesaid pictures with such art gallery for purposes of exhibition.

"5. The ownership and control of the pictures shall be vested permanently and inalienably in trust nevertheless, as aforesaid, in said Trustees of the White Fund and their successors.

"6. My purpose in making this bequest is to create and gratify a public taste for fine art, particularly among the people of the City of Lawrence. And I give to the said Trustees of the White Fund full and absolute authority in any contingency not fully provided for in the above stipulations to take such action as they judge best fitted to serve the purpose described."

In the years after Wolcott's death, the trustees came into possession of, and offered, the paintings to the MFA for exhibition. Currently, the MFA possesses all seventeen paintings, and regularly exhibits three of them. The remaining fourteen paintings are in storage, and the MFA does not plan to exhibit them in its galleries. The fourteen paintings held in storage are available, in certain circumstances, to be shown to persons interested in viewing them.

After learning that the trustees wanted to sell some or all of the paintings, the MFA brought this action in the Superior Court seeking a declaratory judgment, for purposes relevant here, that the terms of Wolcott's bequest do not permit the trustees to sell any of the paintings. The MFA moved for summary judgment, and the Attorney General, a necessary party to the litigation, filed a cross motion for partial summary judgment. The trustees filed a memorandum in support of the Attorney General's motion. A Superior Court judge allowed the MFA's motion in part, concluding that the provisions of Wolcott's bequest do not permit the trustees to sell the paintings. As to the Attorney General's claim that the primary purpose of the charitable trust created by the bequest was not being satisfied, and that the bequest should therefore be modified under the doctrines of *cy pres* or reasonable deviation, the judge concluded that (1) as to the three paintings currently exhibited, Wolcott's intent was being carried out; and (2) as to the fourteen paintings not being exhibited, a trial was necessary to decide whether the trustees should be allowed to sell the paintings through *cy pres*. She therefore denied the Attorney General's motion for partial summary judgment. Pursuant to G. L. c. 231, § 111, and Mass. R. Civ. P. 64 (a), as amended, 423 Mass. 1403 (1996), another judge in the Superior Court entered a judgment and reported the propriety of the orders to the Appeals Court. We allowed the defendants' applications for direct appellate review. We conclude that the MFA is entitled to summary judgment, that the bequest does not permit the trustees to sell any of the paintings, and that, as a consequence, a trial is not necessary. We shall direct that an appropriate declaration be entered in the case.

1. The trustees argue that, under the express terms of Wolcott's bequest, they have the complete power to sell the paintings. They maintain that this power comes into play because Wolcott's intent, "to create and gratify a public taste for fine art, particularly among the people of the City of Lawrence," is not being fulfilled in any meaningful way by the exhibition of only three paintings at the MFA. Consequently, pursuant to the "full and absolute authority" conferred on them under paragraph 6 of the bequest, the trustees conclude that they are authorized to sell the paintings. We disagree....

Paragraph 5 of the bequest states: "The ownership and control of the pictures shall be vested permanently and inalienably ... in [the] Trustees." The judge correctly interpreted the meaning of the words in this paragraph by the application of commonly accepted rules. Contrary to the trustees' assertions, the judge did not "overlook" a secondary meaning of the term "inalienable." The contention that Wolcott must have intended the word "inalienable" to be used in the bequest the same way as the word had been used in the Declaration of Independence is not persuasive. The judge properly concluded that "the phrase 'permanently and inalienably' in the will means exactly what it says — the Trustees are to have *permanent* possession and control of the paintings" (emphasis original). The bequest makes clear that the paintings may not be sold by the trustees.

The trustees read too much into the discretion conferred on them by paragraph 6 of the bequest. While the provision grants to the trustees "full and absolute authority ... to take such action as they judge best fitted," that authority is expressly limited, and the power becomes operative only in the event "any contingency [is] not fully provided for in the [earlier paragraphs or the bequest]." The record establishes that no such contingency has yet occurred. As provided in paragraph 3, the MFA has accepted the paintings and regularly exhibits three of them. Although fourteen of the paintings are normally kept in storage, the MFA has not refused to make the paintings available for exhibition, and, although not required to do so, the MFA has continued to insure and protect the paintings.

2. We reject the defendants' argument that either the doctrine of *cy pres* or the doctrine of reasonable deviation[10] should be applied to the bequest because it is impracticable or impossible to carry out its purpose. The defendants maintain that Wolcott's primary purpose was to promote fine art, particularly for the people of Lawrence. They assert this purpose is not being fulfilled because exhibition of only some of the paintings at the MFA does not benefit the people of Lawrence, and because there is little likelihood that an art gallery suitable to exhibit the paintings will be built, or can be acquired, in Lawrence.

Wolcott's expressed general charitable intent was "to create and gratify a public taste for fine art," through the auspices of the MFA, with a preference that the people of Lawrence enjoy the paintings. The inability to exhibit in Lawrence the three paintings currently on display at the MFA provides no support for the defendants' argument. Those paintings are on display in a manner that accords with the provisions of paragraph 3 of the bequest and Wolcott's general intent.

The current inability to exhibit the other fourteen paintings in Lawrence would not justify the application of *cy pres* or reasonable deviation to sell the paintings. A sale of the fourteen paintings would be the antithesis of Wolcott's intent because the sale could deprive the public of any opportunity to view them. There is information in the record suggesting that it might be possible to display some or all of the fourteen paintings at a gallery in Lawrence or at a fine arts center in nearby Andover.... The record shows that the trustees have not made reasonable efforts to explore alternative locations for exhibition. Until such efforts are made, and are shown to be futile, there is no need for further proceedings on the issue whether *cy pres* would apply to allow sale of the fourteen paintings in storage.... A judgment is to be entered declaring that the doctrines of *cy pres* and reasonable deviation do not apply, and that none of the paintings held by the trustees that are the subject of the bequest can be sold.

---

10. Under the doctrine of reasonable deviation, "the court will direct or permit the trustee of a charitable trust to deviate from a term of the trust if it appears to the court that compliance is impossible or illegal, or that owing to circumstances not known to the settlor and not anticipated by him compliance would defeat or substantially impair the accomplishment of the purposes of the trust." Restatement (Second) of Trusts § 381 (1959).

Notes and Questions

a. The donor of a work of art may lose the ability to receive a tax deduction for a charitable gift of a work of art to a museum if limitations imposed on the museum by the donor create a risk of the work's subsequent removal.

> Treas. Reg. § 1.170A-1(e) Transfers subject to a condition or power. If as of the date of a gift a transfer for charitable purposes is dependent upon the performance of some act or the happening of a precedent event in order that it might become effective, no deduction is allowable unless the possibility that the charitable transfer will not become effective is so remote as to be negligible. If an interest in property passes to, or is vested in, charity on the date of the gift and the interest would be defeated by the subsequent performance of some act or the happening of some event, the possibility of occurrence of which appears on the date of the gift to be so remote as to be negligible, the deduction is allowable.

> For example, A transfers land to a city government for as long as the land is used by the city for a public park. If on the date of the gift the city does plan to use the land for a park and the possibility that the city will not use the land for a public park is so remote as to be negligible, A is entitled to a deduction under section 170 for his charitable contribution.

Treas. Reg. § 1.170A-1(e). See also Treas. Reg. § 20.2055-2(b); Treas. Reg. § 25.2522(c)-3(b)(1) (same result).

b. Beginning in 1916, the Museum of the American Indian, Heye Foundation, developed a tremendous collection of Native American art, history, and artifacts at its initial location at 155th Street and Broadway in Manhattan. In 1989, it used *cy pres* to allow it to enter into an agreement to shift its collection to the Smithsonian as part of the National Museum of the American Indian (20 U.S.C. § 80q *et seq.* (2006)). A second *cy pres* action was brought by the Museum of the American Indian claiming that a transfer of its library collection to the Huntington Free Library was no longer appropriate, in part, because of the resources it now had pursuant to the legislation and the role of the Smithsonian. In an action by the Museum of the American Indian to recover the library collection from the Huntington Free Library under *cy pres*, what was the result? See *Bd. of Trs. of the Am. Indian, Heye Found. v. Bd. of Trs. of the Huntington Free Library and Reading Room*, 610 N.Y.S.2d 488, 493 (1994), *appeal denied*, 86 N.Y.2d 702 (1995).

c. To what extent can *cy pres* be used to accelerate a cash gift or otherwise allow the charity to determine the most efficient use of the funds? See *Museum of Fine Arts v. Beland*, 735 N.E.2d 1248 (Mass. 2000).

d. To what extent does economic efficiency take priority over the specific intent of the testator? Judge Richard A. Posner has had some thoughts on the subject:

> The dilemma of whether to enforce the testator's intent or to modify the terms of the will in accordance with changed conditions since his death is often a false one. A policy of rigid adherence to the letter of the donative instrument is likely to frustrate both the donor's purposes and the efficient use of resources.... [E]nforcement would in all likelihood be contrary to the purposes of the donor, who intended by his gift to contribute to the cure of disease, not to perpetuate useless facilities.... Since no one can foresee the future, a rational donor knows that his intentions might eventually be thwarted by unpredictable circumstances and may therefore be presumed to accept implicitly a rule permitting modifica-

tion of the terms of the bequest in the event that an unforeseen change frustrates his original intention.

Richard A. Posner, Economic Analysis of Law 556–57 (5th ed. 1998). Should the testator be presumed to be frustrated by an inability to foresee the future or by donees that prefer posthumous renegotiation?

e. Beyond the economic efficiency of trusts, there is the very practical matter of drafting the trust documents. A testator's or donor's intent can express a willingness to vary the gift as times change — if the parties draft that understanding into the trust documents. Given the ability of the donor to draft the trust and the ability of the charity to refuse gifts that do not have sufficient flexibility, what relevance do notions of efficiency have regarding the donation?

f. Another significant issue is taxable income at a tax-exempt charity. The IRS website provides a helpful introduction to the topic:

> Unrelated business income tax. Even though an organization is recognized as tax exempt, it still may be liable for tax on its unrelated business income. Unrelated business income is income from a trade or business, regularly carried on, that is not substantially related to the charitable, educational, or other purpose that is the basis of the organization's exemption. For most organizations, an activity is an unrelated business (and subject to unrelated business income tax) if it meets three requirements:
>
> 1. It is a trade or business,
>
> 2. It is regularly carried on, and
>
> 3. It is not substantially related to furthering the exempt purpose of the organization.
>
> There are, however, a number of modifications, exclusions, and exceptions to the general definition of unrelated business income.
>
> To determine if a business activity is *substantially related* requires examining the relationship between the activities that generate income and the accomplishment of the organization's exempt purpose. Trade or business is related to exempt purposes, in the statutory sense, only when the conduct of the business activities has causal relationship to achieving exempt purposes (other than through the production of income). The causal relationship must be substantial. The activities that generate the income must contribute importantly to accomplishing the organization's exempt purposes to be substantially related.

See Publication 598, Tax on Unrelated Business Income of Exempt Organizations (Rev. March 2005), available at http://www.irs.gov/pub/irs-pdf/p598.pdf. The publication provides some additional examples:

> **Artists' facilities.** An organization whose exempt purpose is to stimulate and foster public interest in the fine arts by promoting art exhibits, sponsoring cultural events, and furnishing information about fine arts leases studio apartments to artist tenants and operates a dining hall primarily for these tenants. These two activities do not contribute importantly to accomplishing the organization's exempt purpose. Therefore, they are unrelated trades or businesses.
>
> **Museum eating facilities.** An exempt art museum operates a dining room, a cafeteria, and a snack bar for use by the museum staff, employees, and visitors. Eating facilities in the museum help to attract visitors and allow them to spend

more time viewing the museum's exhibits without having to seek outside restaurants at mealtime. The eating facilities also allow the museum staff and employees to remain in the museum throughout the day. Thus, the museum's operation of the eating facilities contributes importantly to the accomplishment of its exempt purposes and is not unrelated trade or business.

Museum greeting card sales. An art museum that exhibits modern art sells greeting cards that display printed reproductions of selected works from other art collections. Each card is imprinted with the name of the artist, the title or subject matter of the work, the date or period of its creation, if known, and the museum's name. The cards contain appropriate greetings and are personalized on request.

The organization sells the cards in the shop it operates in the museum and sells them at quantity discounts to retail stores. It also sells them by mail order through a catalog that is advertised in magazines and other publications throughout the year. As a result, a large number of cards are sold at a significant profit.

The museum is exempt as an educational organization on the basis of its ownership, maintenance, and exhibition for public viewing of works of art. The sale of greeting cards with printed reproductions of artworks contributes importantly to the achievement of the museum's exempt education purposes by enhancing public awareness, interest, and appreciation of art. The cards may encourage more people to visit the museum itself to share in its educational programs. The fact that the cards are promoted and sold in a commercial manner at a profit and in competition with commercial greeting card publishers does not alter the fact that the activity is related to the museum's exempt purpose. Therefore, these sales activities are not an unrelated trade or business.

Id.

Problem XVII-E

As Bryce has worked in the neighborhood on the feature film, art exhibit, and documentary (see Problems XVIII-B, XVIII-C), Bryce has gained the trust and respect of many of the elderly artists in the area. Many of the artists want to keep their works together as a unified collection because they believe that the history of their neighborhood and the political pressures that resulted in the collection are historically important. They would like Bryce to use the documentary about the exhibit to promote funding for a permanent collection. The artists are willing to donate their works to a museum or nonprofit organization if they can be assured the collection will not be broken up or sold off in parts. Please advise Bryce on the manner in which these concerns can be alleviated. Assuming that a recipient agency can be identified and agreed upon, please draft a donative document that satisfies the concerns of the donors.

F. Bibliography and Links

Amy M. Adler, *Against Moral Rights*, 97 Calif. L. Rev. 263 (2009).

Genevieve Blake, *Expressive Merchandise and the First Amendment in Public Fora*, 34 Fordham Urb. L.J. 1049 (2007).

Sonya G. Bonneau, *Honor and Destruction: The Conflicted Object in Moral Rights Law*, 87 St. John's L. Rev. 47 (2013).

Nathan Brown, *VARA Rights Get a Second Life*, 11 J. High Tech. L. 280 (2011).

Andrea Cunning, *U.S. Policy on the Enforcement of Foreign Export Restrictions on Cultural Property & Destructive Aspects of Retention Schemes*, 26 Hous. J. Int'l L. 449 (2004).

Bert Demarsin, *Let's Not Talk about Terezin: Restitution of Nazi Era Looted Art and the Tenuousness of Public International Law*, 37 Brook. J. Int'l L. 117 (2011).

Patty Gerstenblith, *Acquisition and Deacquisition of Museum Collections and the Fiduciary Obligations of Museums to the Public*, 11 Cardozo J. Int'l & Comp. L. 409 (2003).

Steven G. Gey, *Deconceptualizing Artists' Rights*, 49 San Diego L. Rev. 37 (2012).

Jennifer Anglim Kreder, *Fighting Corruption of the Historical Record: Nazi-Looted Art Litigation*, 61 U. Kan. L. Rev. 75 (2012).

Jennifer Anglim Kreder, *The New Battleground of Museum Ethics and Holocaust-Era Claims: Technicalities Trumping Justice or Responsible Stewardship for the Public Trust?*, 88 Oregon L. Rev. 37 (2009).

Kurt G. Siehr, *Globalization and National Culture: Recent Trends toward a Liberal Exchange of Cultural Objects*, 38 Vand. J. Transnat'l L. 1067 (2005).

Ryan C. Steinman, *Taking a Mulligan: Moral Rights and the Art of Golf Course Design*, 51 IDEA 47 (2011).

Stephen K. Urice, *Between Rocks and Hard Places: Unprovenanced Antiquities and the National Stolen Property Act*, 40 N.M.L. Rev. 123 (2010).

Websites

Art and Cultural Property Law, http://www.hg.org/art.html

California Arts Council, http://www.cac.ca.gov

Federal Bureau of Investigation, Art Theft Program, http://www.fbi.gov/hq/cid/arttheft/arttheft.htm

Publication 557 (3/2005), Tax-Exempt Status for Your Organization, http://www.irs.gov/publications/p557/index.html

United States Department of State Bureau of Educational and Cultural Affairs, http://exchanges.state.gov/culprop/index.html

United Nations Educational, Scientific and Cultural Organization, www.unesco.org

Chapter XVIII

Video Games, Virtual Worlds and Social Media

A. Overview of the Industry

Origins — Video Games, Role Playing Games and Virtual Worlds[1]

Since the advent of Pong,[2] computer gamers having been searching for increasingly realistic — or at least photorealistic — experiences with their computer generated content. As the technology has allowed for ever more realistic images, sound, and even tactile response, the game experience has grown far beyond hi-score lists to become immersive, interactive environments. The "virtual environment is an interactive computer simulation which lets its participants see, hear, use, and even modify the simulated objects in the computer-generated environment."[3] ... Attributes of the genre include the ability to involve a very large number of simultaneous participants online through the Internet or other networking systems, and the ability for the participant to take on a character or role in the game. As some of these gaming environments involve millions of players, they are now coined "massively multi-player online role-playing game (MMORPG)."[4] The user-created characters in these worlds are referred to as "avatars," virtual representations of the players.

The online role-playing games trace their lineage to *Dungeons and Dragons* and the genre of role-playing games in which participants would create characters who would navigate in the fictional worlds created and managed by dungeon masters. In *Dungeons and Dragons*, the players would give themselves the attributes of wizards, warriors, trolls, elves, and similar mythic characters. The interaction of the players and their characters

1. Excerpt from Jon M. Garon, *Playing in the Virtual Arena: Avatars, Publicity and Identity Reconceptualized through Virtual Worlds and Computer Games*, 11 CHAP. L. REV. 465 (2008) (some text and footnotes omitted, other footnotes re-numbered).

2. "*Pong*, while not the first videogame, was the first coin-op arcade game and the first mainstream videogame that was available throughout the U.S. *Pong* was the impetus for the development of the videogaming industry, almost single-handedly creating both the home and the arcade videogame markets." ClassicGaming.com's Museum Atari Pong—1975–1977, http://classicgaming.gamespy.com/View.php?view=ConsoleMuseum.Detail&id=3&game=12 (last visited November 25, 2007).

3. Woodrow Barfield, *Intellectual Property Rights in Virtual Environments: Considering the Rights of Owners, Programmers and Virtual Avatars*, 39 AKRON L. REV. 649 (2006) (citation omitted).

4. *See id.* at 650.

would last in story arcs that could run for indefinite periods, and there may even be some characters still in use from 1974 when the rules were first published. Character attributes were kept on note cards and interactions mediated through polyhedral dice.

The *Dungeons and Dragons* genre moved to the online environment with games such as *World of Warcraft, The Lord of the Rings Online: Shadows of Angmar, Warhammer Online, EVE Online, Anarchy Online, RuneScape, Rappelz,* and *Shadow of Legend*. The genre also includes science fiction worlds such as the *Matrix Online* and *Star Wars Galaxies*.

Professor Erez Reuveni suggests two attributes that define the MMORPG and virtual worlds, separating them from classic computer or their Dungeons and Dragons' predecessors.[5] "Unlike traditional computer games ... virtual worlds are persistent and exist independently of any individual's presence. Virtual worlds exist in real time even after a specific player logs off, and a person's actions can permanently shape the virtual world."[6] While this is a literary distinction, the persistence and literary independence may also provide a framework for treating certain aspects of these works as distinct from novels, computer games, or motion pictures.

The persistence and literary independence of online role-playing games have spawned an entirely new genre from the fantasy worlds. In environments such as *Second Life, Moove, Active Worlds,* or *There*, the environment is a fantasy alternative to modern reality, with businesses, lounges, universities, and other brick-and-mortar equivalents. These environments are "near worlds," alternate realities set in the present with only modest changes from the world around us.

The attraction of virtual worlds comes from the technological opportunities to animate and enhance the interactions on a borderless, international landscape; the billions of dollars in revenue to be earned by the publishers and purveyors of these environments; and a growing cultural and commercial environment within each of the virtual worlds. Corporations, for example, are exploring the use of *Second Life* as a methodology and platform for employee training.[7] As communications educator Montse Anderson noted, "programs such as *Second Life* have the potential to enhance learning because they allow people to interact with each other, rather than reading a manual."[8] ...

Wikis, Blogs, Social Media — The Content of the Curatorial Audience[9]

"User-generated content can be found on wikis, blogs, Twitter feeds, YouTube, Facebook, and pirate websites, as well as in virtual worlds, reactions to news stories, reactions to others' reproductions of news stories, and ratings for products...."[10] ... In most media, however, content is generated in a range of forms, not merely the dichotomous

---

5. Erez Reuveni, *On Virtual Worlds: Copyright and Contract Law at the Dawn of the Virtual Age,* 82 Ind. L.J. 261 (2007).

6. *Id.* at 265.

7. Andrew Johnson, *Virtual training; phoenix couple launch venture to help companies use virtual world to educate, orient new employees,* The Arizona Republic, November 5, 2007 at Business 6.

8. *Id.*

9. Excerpt from Jon M. Garon, *Wiki Authorship, Social Media and the Curatorial Audience,* 1 Harv. J. Sports & Ent. L. 95 (2010) (some text and footnotes omitted, other footnotes re-numbered).

10. Debora Halbert, *Mass Culture and the Culture of the Masses: A Manifesto for User-Generated Rights,* 11 Vand. J. Ent. & Tech. L. 921, 924 (2009).

choices of commercial publisher or open source community. Journalism today, for example, reflects a range of modalities which—at one extreme—only publish the edited content created by their full-time professional staff and—at the other extreme—utilize citizen journalism with unmediated content generated from unpaid, volunteer investigators and community authors.[11]

Freelance journalists, stringers, wire copy, letters to the editor, reader comments, viewer photos, storm-watchers, twitter reports, live-from-the-scene unverified video, and similar news sources illustrate the many ways in which even so-called traditional journalism blends the content provided by full-time professionals with a wide range of other content creators. The label "user-generated content," therefore, creates an artificial dichotomy of publisher/nonpublisher content or one-to-many versus many-to-many content consumption which does not exist in practice. The authorship of distributed content reflects a continuum from the individual to the collective, from a sole scribe to a republic. If wikis represent the paradigmatic example of many-to-many collaborative authorship, the essence of individual, user-generated authorship would likely be Internet weblogs or blogs....

For this modern *audience*—an increasingly archaic characterization—sharing knowledge among friends is an important form of user-generated information. Like wikis and blogs, social media networks rely on the participation of the users to create timely, relevant content.[12] By 2007, the top three social media sites attracted over 153 million unique visitors....

Broadly speaking, Internet users value the participation in the community as more important than the content of the contribution they are making to that community. As a result, the participatory culture has a decidedly curatorial nature. A great deal of the content is not original material but postings, re-postings, commentary and conversation, making the participant a curator of the content with which he or she interacts. The curatorial audience has become an engaged participant in the creation and dissemination of content. In many ways, however, the traditional functions usurped by the curatorial audience have been the functions of the publisher and distributor more than the author. The relatively modest participation in the wikis and other forms of content creation is dwarfed by the massive participation in the social networks, video-sharing sites, and other media that modulate how content is distributed.

Nevertheless, social media's new content modalities reflect a paradigmatic shift. "The shift from a one-to-many entertainment and information infrastructure to a many-to-many infrastructure has deep consequences on many levels. It has made possible on a massive scale content such as fan fiction, mashups, music remixes, cloud computing, and collages; blogs have transformed access to, and arguably the nature of, information."[13] But the nature of the traffic strongly suggests that while all new media transformation is possible, it is content distribution where the greatest transformation is taking place. The curatorial audience has wrested control out of the distributors' hands. Wikis, blogs, and video posts now share the same characteristics of television, music, journalism, and academic publishing. All content distribution models incorporate some level of the many-

---

11. *See* Marcy Wheeler, *How Noninstitutionalized Media Change the Relationship Between the Public and Media Coverage of Trials*, 71 Law & Contemp. Probs. 135 (2008).

12. *See* Cindy Royal, User-Generated Content: How Social Networking Translates to Social Capital, Ass'n Educ. Journalism and Mass Comm. 2008 Annual Convention, available at http://www.allacademic.com/meta/p_mla_apa_research_citation/2/7/1/1/9/pages271193/p271193-1.php.

13. Daniel Gervais, *The Tangled Web of UGC: Making Copyright Sense of User-Generated Content*, 11 Vand. J. Ent. & Tech. L. 841, 842–43 (2009).

to-many modality. The curatorial audience is a participant in every aspect of content: creation, distribution, and consumption....

In addition to casual gaming, the handheld smart phones and tablet expansion of the gaming environment has come as the traditional video console manufacturers—Nintendo, Sony, and Microsoft—are increasingly relying on online interactivity for their game play and product distribution. Companies such as Gamefly, GottaPlay, and Gamerang compete with the badly ailing Blockbuster for game rentals, while Verizon provides a robust digital subscription service for PC-based gaming. The Apple App Store and the Android Marketplace provide digital distribution for the smartphone and tablet marketplace.

The impact of the social media on the gaming experience is further interconnectivity between these various aspects of interactive behavior and play. Companies will increasingly be seeking economic and legal mechanisms to use customer information to enhance their social networks, game subscriptions, and advertising revenues using the community aspects of social media and the interactive aspects of gaming to create a pervasive consumer experience. The separation between video games, virtual worlds, and social media may become less helpful than distinctions among social networks based on the demographic targets and financial models adopted by these interactive media conglomerates.

Notes and Questions

a. Video games are protected under copyright law, which afford protection of original works fixed in a tangible medium. The visual and auditory elements of video games are the proper subject matter of copyright under its protection of audiovisual works. The statute also affords video games protection as literary works under the statute, because the copyright statute recognizes the underlying computer code constituting a video game program as a literary work. Therefore, copyright protection extends to video games as expressive works, and the exclusive rights under copyright relevant to audiovisual or literary works all apply to video games. As with any work seeking copyright protection, the protection is limited to expression contained in the audiovisual or literary work, and does not encompass those elements within the video game that are essentially functional, or essentially constitute an idea. The unauthorized sale of identical or substantially similar video games will almost always warrant a finding of copyright infringement. Examples of video game infringements include *Nintendo of America, Inc. v. Brown*, 94 F.3d 652 (9th Cir. 1996) (holding the sale of identical unauthorized copies of plaintiff's video games by the defendant constituted copyright infringement); *U.S. v. O'Reilly*, 794 F.2d 613 (11th Cir. 1986) (stating that copyright infringement was sufficiently shown when even a portion of a defendant's video game was identical to another copyrighted video game); *Midway Mfg. Co. v. Dirkschneider*, 571 F. Supp. 282 (D. Neb. 1983) (finding that where three allegedly infringing video games were identical in virtually every detail to a another's video games, a *prima facie* case of copyright infringement was established by the plaintiff); *Midway Mfg. Co. v. Bandai-America, Inc.*, 546 F. Supp. 125 (D.N.J. 1982) (holding the elements of the defendant's "Packri Monster" video game were so similar to plaintiff's "Pac Man" game as to approach being identical); *Atari, Inc. v. Armenia, Ltd.*, 1981 U.S. Dist. LEXIS 16561 (N. D. Ill. Nov. 3, 1981) (holding defendant's *War of the Bugs* game was virtually identical in display, control, and arrangement to plaintiff's *Centipede* game as to constitute copyright infringement).

b. The Copyright Office has not always been friendly to registration for the simplest of games. For the plight of the video game *Breakout*, see *Atari Games Corp. v. Oman*, 979 F.2d 242 (D.C. Cir. 1992). After rejecting the copyright registration of the claim in prior district and federal courts, Judge Ruth Bader Ginsburg rejected the prior jurisprudence holding "the rejection of Breakout was unreasonable when measured against the Supreme Court's instruction that the requisite level of creativity [for copyrightability] is extremely low." *Feist Publ'n v. Rural Tel. Serv. Co.*, 499 U.S. 340, 344 (1991) (internal quotation omitted).

c. The tremendous growth of video games and interactivity has been fueled, at least in part, by technological growth of the game device controllers. Many of these disputes include patented innovation. See *Anascape, Ltd. v. Nintendo of Am., Inc.*, 2010 U.S. App. LEXIS 7529 (Fed. Cir. Apr. 13, 2010), regarding the invalidity of extending a 1996 wand patent to later innovations. As is clear from *Anascape, Ltd. v. Nintendo of Am., Inc.*, years of innovation preceded Nintendo's commercial breakthrough in 2006.

Nintendo integrated the right mix of technology, style, and content to reinvigorate the console industry in 2006 with the Wii and its wireless motion-sensing wand controller. Apple achieved similar impact in the smartphone market with its touch-screen controls and gyroscope and accelerometers movement sensors in the 2007 iPhone. Activision expanded consumer options and experience with its guitar-shaped controller for the popular Guitar Hero franchise. The popularity and importance of controller design has led to a variety of patent claims and infringement actions. For example, Gibson Guitar sparred with Activision over the Gibson's patented guitar controller. Activision had licensed Gibson's trademarks for *Guitar Hero*, but Gibson claimed the guitar-shaped game controller also infringed Gibson's patent for the controller which allowed an interactive demo mode of the company's electric guitars. See *Activision Publ'g., Inc. v. Gibson Guitar Corp.*, 2009 U.S. Dist. LEXIS 21931 (C.D. Cal. Feb. 26, 2009).

d. Does the sale of modified devices create trademark liability? A finding of infringement depends on whether the use of the trademark would produce a likelihood of confusion as to the source of the modification device. Compare *Midway Mfg. Co. v. Strohon*, 564 F. Supp. 741 (N.D. Ill. 1983) with *Sony Computer Entm't Am., Inc. v. Gamemasters*, 87 F. Supp. 2d 976 (N.D. Cal. 1999).

e. The sale of emulator devices does not raise the same trademark or copyright issues as modified devices. Emulator devices have been held to not infringe trademarks because there is no likelihood of confusion as to the source of the emulator. *Computer Entm't, Inc. v. Connectix Corp.*, 203 F.3d 596 (9th Cir. 2000).

B. Advertising and Endorsements

FTC Publishes Final Guides Governing
Endorsements, Testimonials
(10/05/2009)

Changes Affect Testimonial Advertisements, Bloggers, Celebrity Endorsements

The Federal Trade Commission … approved final revisions to the guidance it gives to advertisers on how to keep their endorsement and testimonial ads in line with the FTC Act.

The notice incorporates several changes to the FTC's Guides Concerning the Use of Endorsements and Testimonials in Advertising, which address endorsements by consumers, experts, organizations, and celebrities, as well as the disclosure of important connections between advertisers and endorsers. The Guides were last updated in 1980.

Under the revised Guides, advertisements that feature a consumer and convey his or her experience with a product or service as typical when that is not the case will be required to clearly disclose the results that consumers can generally expect. In contrast to the 1980 version of the Guides—which allowed advertisers to describe unusual results in a testimonial as long as they included a disclaimer such as "results not typical"—the revised Guides no longer contain this safe harbor.

The revised Guides also add new examples to illustrate the long standing principle that "material connections" (sometimes payments or free products) between advertisers and endorsers—connections that consumers would not expect—must be disclosed. These examples address what constitutes an endorsement when the message is conveyed by bloggers or other "word-of-mouth" marketers. The revised Guides specify that while decisions will be reached on a case-by-case basis, the post of a blogger who receives cash or in-kind payment to review a product is considered an endorsement. Thus, bloggers who make an endorsement must disclose the material connections they share with the seller of the product or service. Likewise, if a company refers in an advertisement to the findings of a research organization that conducted research sponsored by the company, the advertisement must disclose the connection between the advertiser and the research organization. And a paid endorsement—like any other advertisement—is deceptive if it makes false or misleading claims.

Celebrity endorsers also are addressed in the revised Guides. While the 1980 Guides did not explicitly state that endorsers as well as advertisers could be liable under the FTC Act for statements they make in an endorsement, the revised Guides reflect Commission case law and clearly state that both advertisers and endorsers may be liable for false or unsubstantiated claims made in an endorsement—or for failure to disclose material connections between the advertiser and endorsers. The revised Guides also make it clear that celebrities have a duty to disclose their relationships with advertisers when making endorsements outside the context of traditional ads, such as on talk shows or in social media.

The Guides are administrative interpretations of the law intended to help advertisers comply with the Federal Trade Commission Act; they are not binding law themselves. In any law enforcement action challenging the allegedly deceptive use of testimonials or endorsements, the Commission would have the burden of proving that the challenged conduct violates the FTC Act....

Title 16: PART 255—Guides Concerning Use of Endorsements and Testimonials in Advertising

Authority: 38 Stat. 717, as amended; 15 U.S.C. 41–58
Source: 74 FR 53138, Oct. 15, 2009, unless otherwise noted

§ 255.0 Purpose and definitions.

(a) The Guides in this part represent administrative interpretations of laws enforced by the Federal Trade Commission for the guidance of the public in conducting its affairs in conformity with legal requirements. Specifically, the Guides address the application of Section 5 of the FTC Act (15 U.S.C. 45) to the use of endorsements and testimonials in advertising. The Guides provide the basis for voluntary compliance with the law by advertisers and endorsers. Practices inconsistent with these Guides may result in corrective action by the Commission under Section 5 if, after investigation, the Commission has reason to believe that the practices fall within the scope of conduct declared unlawful by the statute. The Guides set forth the general principles that the Commission will use in evaluating endorsements and testimonials, together with examples illustrating the application of those principles. The Guides do not purport to cover every possible use of endorsements in advertising. Whether a particular endorsement or testimonial is deceptive will depend on the specific factual circumstances of the advertisement at issue.

(b) For purposes of this part, an endorsement means any advertising message (including verbal statements, demonstrations, or depictions of the name, signature, likeness or other identifying personal characteristics of an individual or the name or seal of an organization) that consumers are likely to believe reflects the opinions, beliefs, findings, or experiences of a party other than the sponsoring advertiser, even if the views expressed by that party are identical to those of the sponsoring advertiser. The party whose opinions, beliefs, findings, or experience the message appears to reflect will be called the endorser and may be an individual, group, or institution.

(c) The Commission intends to treat endorsements and testimonials identically in the context of its enforcement of the Federal Trade Commission Act and for purposes of this part. The term endorsements is therefore generally used hereinafter to cover both terms and situations.

(d) For purposes of this part, the term product includes any product, service, company or industry.

(e) For purposes of this part, an expert is an individual, group, or institution possessing, as a result of experience, study, or training, knowledge of a particular subject, which knowledge is superior to what ordinary individuals generally acquire.

Example 1: A film critic's review of a movie is excerpted in an advertisement. When so used, the review meets the definition of an endorsement because it is viewed by readers as a statement of the critic's own opinions and not those of the film producer, distributor, or exhibitor. Any alteration in or quotation from the text of the review that does not fairly reflect its substance would be a violation of the standards set by this part because it would distort the endorser's opinion. [See § 255.1(b).]

Example 2: A TV commercial depicts two women in a supermarket buying a laundry detergent. The women are not identified outside the context of the advertisement. One comments to the other how clean her brand makes her family's clothes, and the other then comments that she will try it because she has not been fully satisfied with her own brand. This obvious fictional dramatization of a real life situation would not be an endorsement.

Example 3: In an advertisement for a pain remedy, an announcer who is not familiar to consumers except as a spokesman for the advertising drug company praises the drug's ability to deliver fast and lasting pain relief. He purports to speak, not on the basis of his own opinions, but rather in the place of and on behalf of the drug company. The announcer's statements would not be considered an endorsement.

Example 4: A manufacturer of automobile tires hires a well-known professional automobile racing driver to deliver its advertising message in television commercials. In these commercials, the driver speaks of the smooth ride, strength, and long life of the tires. Even though the message is not expressly declared to be the personal opinion of the driver, it may nevertheless constitute an endorsement of the tires. Many consumers will recognize this individual as being primarily a racing driver and not merely a spokesperson or announcer for the advertiser. Accordingly, they may well believe the driver would not speak for an automotive product unless he actually believed in what he was saying and had personal knowledge sufficient to form that belief. Hence, they would think the advertising message reflects the driver's personal views. This attribution of the underlying views to the driver brings the advertisement within the definition of an endorsement for purposes of this part.

Example 5: A television advertisement for a particular brand of golf balls shows a prominent and well-recognized professional golfer practicing numerous drives off the tee. This would be an endorsement by the golfer even though she makes no verbal statement in the advertisement.

Example 6: An infomercial for a home fitness system is hosted by a well-known entertainer. During the infomercial, the entertainer demonstrates the machine and states it is the most effective and easy-to-use home exercise machine that she has ever tried. Even if she is reading from a script, this statement would be an endorsement, because consumers are likely to believe it reflects the entertainer's views.

Example 7: A television advertisement for a houseware store features a well-known female comedian and a well-known male baseball player engaging in light-hearted banter about products each one intends to purchase for the other. The comedian says she will buy him a Brand X, portable, high-definition television so he can finally see the strike zone. He says he will get her a Brand Y juicer so she can make juice with all the fruit and vegetables thrown at her during her performances. The comedian and baseball player are not likely to be deemed endorsers because consumers will likely realize the individuals are not expressing their own views.

Example 8: A consumer who regularly purchases a particular brand of dog food decides one day to purchase a new, more expensive brand made by the same manufacturer. She writes in her personal blog that the change in diet has made her dog's fur noticeably softer and shinier, and that in her opinion, the new food definitely is worth the extra money. This posting would not be deemed an endorsement under the Guides.

Assume that rather than purchase the dog food with her own money, the consumer gets it for free because the store routinely tracks her purchases and its computer has generated a coupon for a free trial bag of this new brand. Again, her posting would not be deemed an endorsement under the Guides.

Assume now that the consumer joins a network marketing program under which she periodically receives various products about which she can write reviews if she wants to do so. If she receives a free bag of the new dog food through this program, her positive review would be considered an endorsement under the Guides.

§ 255.1 General considerations.

(a) Endorsements must reflect the honest opinions, findings, beliefs, or experience of the endorser. Furthermore, an endorsement may not convey any express or implied representation that would be deceptive if made directly by the advertiser. [See § 255.2(a) and (b) regarding substantiation of representations conveyed by consumer endorsements.

(b) The endorsement message need not be phrased in the exact words of the endorser, unless the advertisement affirmatively so represents. However, the endorsement may not be presented out of context or reworded so as to distort in any way the endorser's opinion or experience with the product. An advertiser may use an endorsement of an expert or celebrity only so long as it has good reason to believe that the endorser continues to subscribe to the views presented. An advertiser may satisfy this obligation by securing the endorser's views at reasonable intervals where reasonableness will be determined by such factors as new information on the performance or effectiveness of the product, a material alteration in the product, changes in the performance of competitors' products, and the advertiser's contract commitments.

(c) When the advertisement represents that the endorser uses the endorsed product, the endorser must have been a bona fide user of it at the time the endorsement was given. Additionally, the advertiser may continue to run the advertisement only so long as it has good reason to believe that the endorser remains a bona fide user of the product. [See § 255.1(b) regarding the "good reason to believe" requirement.](d)Advertisers are subject to liability for false or unsubstantiated statements made through endorsements, or for failing to disclose material connections between themselves and their endorsers [see § 255.5]. Endorsers also may be liable for statements made in the course of their endorsements.

....

Example 5: A skin care products advertiser participates in a blog advertising service. The service matches up advertisers with bloggers who will promote the advertiser's products on their personal blogs. The advertiser requests that a blogger try a new body lotion and write a review of the product on her blog. Although the advertiser does not make any specific claims about the lotion's ability to cure skin conditions and the blogger does not ask the advertiser whether there is substantiation for the claim, in her review the blogger writes that the lotion cures eczema and recommends the product to her blog readers who suffer from this condition. The advertiser is subject to liability for misleading or unsubstantiated representations made through the blogger's endorsement. The blogger also is subject to liability for misleading or unsubstantiated representations made in the course of her endorsement. The blogger is also liable if she fails to disclose clearly and conspicuously that she is being paid for her services. [See § 255.5.]

In order to limit its potential liability, the advertiser should ensure that the advertising service provides guidance and training to its bloggers concerning the need to ensure that statements they make are truthful and substantiated. The advertiser should also monitor bloggers who are being paid to promote its products and take steps necessary to halt the continued publication of deceptive representations when they are discovered.

§ 255.2 Consumer endorsements.

(a) An advertisement employing endorsements by one or more consumers about the performance of an advertised product or service will be interpreted as representing that the product or service is effective for the purpose depicted in the advertisement. Therefore, the advertiser must possess and rely upon adequate substantiation, including, when appropriate, competent and reliable scientific evidence, to support such claims made through endorsements in the same manner the advertiser would be required to do if it had made the representation directly, *i.e.*, without using endorsements. Consumer endorsements themselves are not competent and reliable scientific evidence.

(b) An advertisement containing an endorsement relating the experience of one or more consumers on a central or key attribute of the product or service also will likely be interpreted as representing that the endorser's experience is representative of what consumers will generally achieve with the advertised product or service in actual, albeit variable, conditions of use. Therefore, an advertiser should possess and rely upon adequate substantiation for this representation. If the advertiser does not have substantiation that the endorser's experience is representative of what consumers will generally achieve, the advertisement should clearly and conspicuously disclose the generally expected performance in the depicted circumstances, and the advertiser must possess and rely on adequate substantiation for that representation.[14]

Nonetheless, the Commission cannot rule out the possibility that a strong disclaimer of typicality could be effective in the context of a particular advertisement. Although the Commission would have the burden of proof in a law enforcement action, the Commission notes that an advertiser possessing reliable empirical testing demonstrating that the net impression of its advertisement with such a disclaimer is non-deceptive will avoid the risk of the initiation of such an action in the first instance.

(c) Advertisements presenting endorsements by what are represented, directly or by implication, to be "actual consumers" should utilize actual consumers in both the audio and video, or clearly and conspicuously disclose that the persons in such advertisements are not actual consumers of the advertised product.

. . .

§ 255.5 Disclosure of material connections.

When there exists a connection between the endorser and the seller of the advertised product that might materially affect the weight or credibility of the endorsement (*i.e.*, the connection is not reasonably expected by the audience), such connection must be fully disclosed. For example, when an endorser who appears in a television commercial is neither represented in the advertisement as an expert nor is known to a significant portion of the viewing public, then the advertiser should clearly and conspicuously disclose either the payment or promise of compensation prior to and in exchange for the endorsement or the fact that the endorser knew or had reason to know or to believe that if the endorsement favored the advertised product some benefit, such as an appearance on television, would be extended to the endorser. Additional guidance, including guidance concerning endorsements made through other media, is provided by the examples below.

. . .

Example 2: A film star endorses a particular food product. The endorsement regards only points of taste and individual preference. This endorsement must, of course, comply with § 255.1; but regardless of whether the star's compensation for the commercial is a $1 million cash payment or a royalty for each product sold by the advertiser during the next year, no disclosure is required because such payments likely are ordinarily expected by viewers.

. . .

Example 7: A college student who has earned a reputation as a video game expert maintains a personal weblog or "blog" where he posts entries about his gaming experiences. Readers of his blog frequently seek his opinions about video game hardware and software. As it has done in the past, the manufacturer of a newly released video game system sends the student a free copy of the system and asks him to write about it on his blog. He tests the new gaming system and writes a favorable review. Because his review

---

14. The Commission tested the communication of advertisements containing testimonials that clearly and prominently disclosed either "Results not typical" or the stronger "These testimonials are based on the experiences of a few people and you are not likely to have similar results." Neither disclosure adequately reduced the communication that the experiences depicted are generally representative. Based upon this research, the Commission believes that similar disclaimers regarding the limited applicability of an endorser's experience to what consumers may generally expect to achieve are unlikely to be effective.

is disseminated via a form of consumer-generated media in which his relationship to the advertiser is not inherently obvious, readers are unlikely to know that he has received the video game system free of charge in exchange for his review of the product, and given the value of the video game system, this fact likely would materially affect the credibility they attach to his endorsement. Accordingly, the blogger should clearly and conspicuously disclose that he received the gaming system free of charge. The manufacturer should advise him at the time it provides the gaming system that this connection should be disclosed, and it should have procedures in place to try to monitor his postings for compliance.

Example 8: An online message board designated for discussions of new music download technology is frequented by MP3 player enthusiasts. They exchange information about new products, utilities, and the functionality of numerous playback devices. Unbeknownst to the message board community, an employee of a leading playback device manufacturer has been posting messages on the discussion board promoting the manufacturer's product. Knowledge of this poster's employment likely would affect the weight or credibility of her endorsement. Therefore, the poster should clearly and conspicuously disclose her relationship to the manufacturer to members and readers of the message board.

Example 9: A young man signs up to be part of a "street team" program in which points are awarded each time a team member talks to his or her friends about a particular advertiser's products. Team members can then exchange their points for prizes, such as concert tickets or electronics. These incentives would materially affect the weight or credibility of the team member's endorsements. They should be clearly and conspicuously disclosed, and the advertiser should take steps to ensure that these disclosures are being provided.

Notes and Questions

a. As highlighted in the new guidelines for endorsements and testimonials, the guides provide a form of safe harbor from a finding by the FTC that a party has committed "unfair or deceptive acts or practices" in violation of 15 U.S.C. §45. To what extent do the new guidelines shift the standards for material or deceptive practices?

b. On January 26, 2010, The Loft, a retail chain owned by Ann Taylor Stores, held an exclusive blogger preview of the clothing store's summer product line. Those invited to the event were told bloggers were in for a special treat. "Bloggers who attend will receive a special gift, and those who post coverage from the event will be entered in a mystery gift card drawing where you can win up to $500 at LOFT!" To be eligible for the gift, the blogger was required to submit posts to the company within 24 hours. At the same time, signs were posted at the event reminding bloggers of the new FTC requirements for disclosure of promotional ties. The FTC became aware of the promotion and launched an investigation. Although no action was ultimately taken, the FTC view of the new guidelines becomes more clear as seen through the letter closing the investigation.

FTC Action: Ann Taylor Stores Corp., File No. 102-3147

UNITED STATES OF AMERICA
FEDERAL TRADE COMMISSION
WASHINGTON, D.C. 20580
Division of Advertising Practices

April 20, 2010

VIA ELECTRONIC MAIL AND FEDERAL EXPRESS
Kenneth A. Plevan, Esq.
Skadden, Arps, Slate, Meagher & Flom LLP
Four Times Square
New York, NY 10036-6522

Re: Ann Taylor Stores Corp., File No. 102-3147

Dear Mr. Plevan:

As you know, the staff of the Federal Trade Commission's Division of Advertising Practices has conducted an investigation into whether your client, Ann Taylor Stores Corporation, violated Section 5 of the Federal Trade Commission Act, 15 U.S.C. § 45, in connection with providing gifts to bloggers who the company expected would post blog content about the company's LOFT division. Our inquiry focused particularly on LOFT's provision of gifts to bloggers who attended previews of LOFT's Summer 2010 collection. We were concerned that bloggers who attended a preview on January 26, 2010 failed to disclose that they received gifts for posting blog content about that event. Section 5 of the FTC Act requires the disclosure of a material connection between an advertiser and an endorser when such a relationship is not otherwise apparent from the context of the communication that contains the endorsement. Depending on the circumstances, an advertiser's provision of a gift to a blogger for posting blog content about an event could constitute a material connection that is not reasonably expected by readers of the blog.

Upon careful review of this matter, we have determined not to recommend enforcement action at this time. We considered a number of factors in reaching this decision. First, according to LOFT, the January 26, 2010 preview was the first (and, to date, only) such preview event. Second, only a very small number of bloggers posted content about the preview, and several of those bloggers disclosed that LOFT had provided them gifts at the preview.[15] Third, LOFT adopted a written policy in February 2010 stating that LOFT will not issue any gift to any blogger without first telling the blogger that the blogger must disclose the gift in his or her blog. The FTC staff expects that LOFT will both honor that written policy and take reasonable steps to monitor bloggers' compliance with the obligation to disclose gifts they receive from LOFT.

Our decision not to pursue enforcement action is not to be construed as a determination that a violation may not have occurred, just as the pendency of an investigation should not be construed as a determination that a violation has occurred. The Commission reserves the right to take such further action as the public interest may warrant....

---

15. It should be noted that LOFT posted a sign at the preview that told bloggers that they should disclose the gifts if they posted comments about the preview. It is not clear, however, how many bloggers actually saw that sign.

Problem XVIII-B

Bryce has been writing a series of "new media" reviews, including music, films, and video games. As Bryce's following has grown, Bryce has begun receiving free access to subscription media websites which allows access to material on a preview basis and to avoid the sometimes substantial fees for the games, downloads, and streams. In light of the new guidelines, advise Bryce whether disclosure of the free content is required, and if so, what method of disclosure meets the FTC guidelines.

C. Scope of First Amendment Protections

Regulation of the video game industry takes two major forms. The first is government regulations. These regulations take the form of restrictions on the sale, use, or licensing of establishments that deal in video games. Over the years, as home video game systems have become more prevalent, the focus of such government regulatory efforts have moved from arcade establishments to video game retailers. Most government regulations pertaining to video games fail due to First Amendment issues, as courts have been more willing to recognize video games as a type of expression that is to be afforded the full protection of the First Amendment, and must survive a strict scrutiny constitutional analysis to be upheld.

Second, under pressure from consumer groups, the video game industry has adopted a voluntary ratings system, where games are categorized based on their content and their appropriateness for certain consumers. Many retailers have bowed to public pressure and have adopted private regulations as to the sale of such games to minors based on this ratings scheme. Again, this system is voluntary, and does not invoke any of the constitutional issues that direct government content-based regulation present. However, state efforts to regulate video games through adoption of this voluntary regulatory scheme have failed based on due process grounds.

Brown v. Entm't Merchs. Ass'n
___ U.S. ___, 131 S. Ct. 2729 (U.S. 2011)

Justice SCALIA delivered the opinion of the Court.

We consider whether a California law imposing restrictions on violent video games comports with the First Amendment.

California Assembly Bill 1179 (2005), Cal. Civ. Code Ann. §§ 1746–1746.5 (West 2009) (Act), prohibits the sale or rental of "violent video games" to minors, and requires their packaging to be labeled "18." The Act covers games "in which the range of options available to a player includes killing, maiming, dismembering, or sexually assaulting an image of a human being, if those acts are depicted" in a manner that "[a] reasonable person, considering the game as a whole, would find appeals to a deviant or morbid interest of minors," that is "patently offensive to prevailing standards in the community as to what is suitable for minors," and that "causes the game, as a whole, to lack serious literary, artistic, political, or scientific value for minors." § 1746(d)(1)(A). Violation of the Act is punishable by a civil fine of up to $1,000. § 1746.3....

California correctly acknowledges that video games qualify for First Amendment protection. The Free Speech Clause exists principally to protect discourse on public matters, but we have long recognized that it is difficult to distinguish politics from entertainment, and dangerous to try. "Everyone is familiar with instances of propaganda through fiction. What is one man's amusement, teaches another's doctrine." *Winters v. New York*, 333 U.S. 507, 510 (1948). Like the protected books, plays, and movies that preceded them, video games communicate ideas—and even social messages—through many familiar literary devices (such as characters, dialogue, plot, and music) and through features distinctive to the medium (such as the player's interaction with the virtual world). That suffices to confer First Amendment protection. Under our Constitution, "esthetic and moral judgments about art and literature ... are for the individual to make, not for the Government to decree, even with the mandate or approval of a majority." *United States v. Playboy Entertainment Group, Inc.*, 529 U.S. 803, 818 (2000). And whatever the challenges of applying the Constitution to ever-advancing technology, "the basic principles of freedom of speech and the press, like the First Amendment's command, do not vary" when a new and different medium for communication appears. *Joseph Burstyn, Inc. v. Wilson*, 343 U.S. 495, 503 (1952).

The most basic of those principles is this: "[A]s a general matter, ... government has no power to restrict expression because of its message, its ideas, its subject matter, or its content." *Ashcroft v. American Civil Liberties Union*, 535 U.S. 564, 573 (2002) (internal quotation marks omitted). There are of course exceptions. "'From 1791 to the present,'... the First Amendment has 'permitted restrictions upon the content of speech in a few limited areas,' and has never 'include[d] a freedom to disregard these traditional limitations.' *United States v. Stevens*, 559 U.S. ___, ___, 130 S. Ct. 1577 (2010) (quoting *R. A. V. v. St. Paul*, 505 U.S. 377, 382–383 (1992)). These limited areas—such as obscenity, *Roth v. United States*, 354 U.S. 476, 483 (1957), incitement, *Brandenburg v. Ohio*, 395 U.S. 444, 447–449 (1969) *(per curiam)*, and fighting words, *Chaplinsky v. New Hampshire*, 315 U.S. 568, 572 (1942)—represent "well-defined and narrowly limited classes of speech, the prevention and punishment of which have never been thought to raise any Constitutional problem," *id.*, at 571–572.

Last Term, in *Stevens*, we held that new categories of unprotected speech may not be added to the list by a legislature that concludes certain speech is too harmful to be tolerated. *Stevens* concerned a federal statute purporting to criminalize the creation, sale, or possession of certain depictions of animal cruelty. See 18 U.S.C. § 48 (amended 2010). The statute covered depictions "in which a living animal is intentionally maimed, mutilated, tortured, wounded, or killed" if that harm to the animal was illegal where the "the creation, sale, or possession t[ook] place," § 48(c)(1). A saving clause largely borrowed from our obscenity jurisprudence, exempted depictions with "serious religious, political, scientific, educational, journalistic, historical, or artistic value," § 48(b). We held that statute to be an impermissible content-based restriction on speech. There was no American tradition of forbidding the *depiction of* animal cruelty—though States have long had laws against *committing* it.

The Government argued in *Stevens* that lack of a historical warrant did not matter; that it could create new categories of unprotected speech by applying a "simple balancing test" that weighs the value of a particular category of speech against its social costs and then punishes that category of speech if it fails the test. We emphatically rejected that "startling and dangerous" proposition. "Maybe there are some categories of speech that have been historically unprotected, but have not yet been specifically identified or discussed as such in our case law." *Id.*, at ___, 130 S. Ct. 1577, 176. But without persuasive evidence that a novel restriction on content is part of a long (if heretofore unrecognized) tradition of proscription, a legislature may not revise the "judgment [of] the American people," embodied in the First Amendment, "that the benefits of its restrictions on the Government outweigh the costs." *Id.*, at ___, 130 S. Ct. 1577, 176.

That holding controls this case. As in *Stevens*, California has tried to make violent-speech regulation look like obscenity regulation by appending a saving clause required for the latter. That does not suffice. Our cases have been clear that the obscenity exception to the First Amendment does not cover whatever a legislature finds shocking, but only depictions of "sexual conduct," *Miller, supra,* at 24.

Stevens was not the first time we have encountered and rejected a State's attempt to shoehorn speech about violence into obscenity. In *Winters*, we considered a New York criminal statute "forbid[ding] the massing of stories of bloodshed and lust in such a way as to incite to crime against the person," 333 U.S., at 514. The New York Court of Appeals upheld the provision as a law against obscenity. "[T]here can be no more precise test of written indecency or obscenity," it said, "than the continuing and changeable experience of the community as to what types of books are likely to bring about the corruption of public morals or other analogous injury to the public order." *Id.*, at 514. That is of course the same expansive view of governmental power to abridge the freedom of speech based on interest-balancing that we rejected in *Stevens*. Our opinion in *Winters*, which concluded that the New York statute failed a heightened vagueness standard applicable to restrictions upon speech entitled to First Amendment protection, made clear that violence is not part of the obscenity that the Constitution permits to be regulated. The speech reached by the statute contained "no indecency or obscenity in any sense heretofore known to the law." *Id.*, at 519.

Because speech about violence is not obscene, it is of no consequence that California's statute mimics the New York statute regulating obscenity-for-minors that we upheld in *Ginsberg v. New York*, 390 U.S. 629 (1968). That case approved a prohibition on the sale to minors of *sexual* material that would be obscene from the perspective of a child. We held that the legislature could "adjus[t] the definition of obscenity 'to social realities by permitting the appeal of this type of material to be assessed in terms of the sexual interests...' of ... minors." *Id.*, at 638. And because "obscenity is not protected expression," the New York statute could be sustained so long as the legislature's judgment that the proscribed materials were harmful to children "was not irrational." 390 U.S., at 641.

The California Act is something else entirely. It does not adjust the boundaries of an existing category of unprotected speech to ensure that a definition designed for adults is not uncritically applied to children. California does not argue that it is empowered to prohibit selling offensively violent works *to adults*—and it is wise not to, since that is but a hair's breadth from the argument rejected in *Stevens*. Instead, it wishes to create a wholly new category of content-based regulation that is permissible only for speech directed at children.

That is unprecedented and mistaken. "[M]inors are entitled to a significant measure of First Amendment protection, and only in relatively narrow and well-defined circumstances may government bar public dissemination of protected materials to them." *Erznoznik v. Jacksonville*, 422 U.S. 205, 212–213 (1975). No doubt a State possesses legitimate power to protect children from harm, but that does not include a free-floating power to restrict the ideas to which children may be exposed. "Speech that is neither obscene as to youths nor subject to some other legitimate proscription cannot be suppressed solely to protect the young from ideas or images that a legislative body thinks unsuitable for them." *Erznoznik, supra,* at 213–214.

California's argument would fare better if there were a longstanding tradition in this country of specially restricting children's access to depictions of violence, but there is none. Certainly the *books* we give children to read—or read to them when they are younger—contain no shortage of gore. Grimm's Fairy Tales, for example, are grim indeed. As her just deserts for trying to poison Snow White, the wicked queen is made to dance in red hot slippers "till she fell dead on the floor, a sad example of envy and jealousy." The Complete Brothers Grimm Fairy Tales 198 (2006 ed.). Cinderella's evil stepsisters have their eyes pecked out by doves. And Hansel and Gretel (children!) kill their captor by baking her in an oven.

High-school reading lists are full of similar fare. Homer's Odysseus blinds Polyphemus the Cyclops by grinding out his eye with a heated stake. In the Inferno, Dante and Virgil watch corrupt politicians struggle to stay submerged beneath a lake of boiling pitch, lest they be skewered by devils above the surface. And Golding's Lord of the Flies recounts how a schoolboy called Piggy is savagely murdered *by other children* while marooned on an island. W. Golding, Lord of the Flies 208–209 (1997 ed.).[16]

This is not to say that minors' consumption of violent entertainment has never encountered resistance. In the 1800s, dime novels depicting crime and "penny dreadfuls" (named for their price and content) were blamed in some quarters for juvenile delinquency. When motion pictures came along, they became the villains instead. "The days when the police looked upon dime novels as the most dangerous of textbooks in the school for crime are drawing to a close.... They say that the moving picture machine ... tends even more than did the dime novel to turn the thoughts of the easily influenced to paths which sometimes lead to prison." Moving Pictures as Helps to Crime, N. Y. Times, Feb. 21, 1909, quoted in Brief for Cato Institute, at 8. For a time, our Court did permit broad censorship of movies because of their capacity to be "used for evil," see *Mutual Film Corp. v. Industrial Comm'n of Ohio*, 236 U.S. 230, 242 (1915), but we eventually reversed course, *Joseph Burstyn, Inc.*, 343 U.S., at 502. Radio dramas were next, and then came comic books. Many in the late 1940s and early 1950s blamed comic books for fostering a "preoccupation with violence and horror" among the young, leading to a rising juvenile crime rate. But efforts to convince Congress to restrict comic books failed. And, of course, after comic books came television and music lyrics.

California claims that video games present special problems because they are "interactive," in that the player participates in the violent action on screen and determines its outcome. The latter feature is nothing new: Since at least the publication of The Adventures

---

16. Justice Alito accuses us of pronouncing that playing violent video games "is not different in 'kind'" from reading violent literature. Well of course it is different in kind, but not in a way that causes the provision and viewing of violent video games, unlike the provision and reading of books, not to be expressive activity and hence not to enjoy First Amendment protection. Reading Dante is unquestionably more cultured and intellectually edifying than playing Mortal Kombat. But these cultural and intellectual differences are not constitutional ones. Crudely violent video games, tawdry TV shows, and cheap novels and magazines are no less forms of speech than The Divine Comedy, and restrictions upon them must survive strict scrutiny—a question to which we devote our attention in Part III, *infra*. Even if we can see in them "nothing of any possible value to society...," they are as much entitled to the protection of free speech as the best of literature." Winters v. New York, 333 U.S. 507, 510 (1948).

[Justice Alito, Dissenting, stated the following:

In the view of the Court, all those concerned about the effects of violent video games—federal and state legislators, educators, social scientists, and parents—are unduly fearful, for violent video games really present no serious problem. Spending hour upon hour controlling the actions of a character who guns down scores of innocent victims is not different in "kind" from reading a description of violence in a work of literature.

The Court is sure of this; I am not. There are reasons to suspect that the experience of playing violent video games just might be very different from reading a book, listening to the radio, or watching a movie or a television show.

Id. at 180 L. Ed. 2d 708, 724 (U.S. 2011).]

OF YOU: SUGARCANE ISLAND in 1969, young readers of choose-your-own-adventure stories have been able to make decisions that determine the plot by following instructions about which page to turn to. As for the argument that video games enable participation in the violent action, that seems to us more a matter of degree than of kind. As Judge Posner has observed, all literature is interactive. "[T]he better it is, the more interactive. Literature when it is successful draws the reader into the story, makes him identify with the characters, invites him to judge them and quarrel with them, to experience their joys and sufferings as the reader's own." *American Amusement Machine Assn. v. Kendrick*, 244 F.3d 572, 577 (7th Cir. 2001) (striking down a similar restriction on violent video games).

Justice Alito has done considerable independent research to identify video games in which "the violence is astounding." "Victims are dismembered, decapitated, disemboweled, set on fire, and chopped into little pieces.... Blood gushes, splatters, and pools." Justice Alito recounts all these disgusting video games in order to disgust us—but disgust is not a valid basis for restricting expression. And the same is true of Justice Alito's description of those video games he has discovered that have a racial or ethnic motive for their violence—"'ethnic cleansing' [of] ... African Americans, Latinos, or Jews." To what end does he relate this? Does it somehow increase the "aggressiveness" that California wishes to suppress? Who knows? But it does arouse the reader's ire, and the reader's desire to put an end to this horrible message. Thus, ironically, Justice Alito's argument highlights the precise danger posed by the California Act: that the *ideas* expressed by speech—whether it be violence, or gore, or racism— and not its objective effects, may be the real reason for governmental proscription.

Because the Act imposes a restriction on the content of protected speech, it is invalid unless California can demonstrate that it passes strict scrutiny—that is, unless it is justified by a compelling government interest and is narrowly drawn to serve that interest. *R. A. V.*, 505 U.S., at 395. The State must specifically identify an "actual problem" in need of solving, *Playboy*, 529 U.S., at 822–823, and the curtailment of free speech must be actually necessary to the solution, see *R. A. V.*, *supra*, at 395. That is a demanding standard. "It is rare that a regulation restricting speech because of its content will ever be permissible." *Playboy*, *supra*, at 818.

California cannot meet that standard. At the outset, it acknowledges that it cannot show a direct causal link between violent video games and harm to minors. Rather, relying upon our decision in *Turner Broadcasting System, Inc. v. FCC*, 512 U.S. 622 (1994), the State claims that it need not produce such proof because the legislature can make a predictive judgment that such a link exists, based on competing psychological studies. But reliance on *Turner Broadcasting* is misplaced. That decision applied *intermediate scrutiny* to a content-neutral regulation. California's burden is much higher, and because it bears the risk of uncertainty, ambiguous proof will not suffice.

The State's evidence is not compelling. California relies primarily on the research of Dr. Craig Anderson and a few other research psychologists whose studies purport to show a connection between exposure to violent video games and harmful effects on children. These studies have been rejected by every court to consider them, and with good reason: They do not prove that violent video games *cause* minors to *act* aggressively (which would at least be a beginning). Instead, "[n]early all of the research is based on correlation, not evidence of causation, and most of the studies suffer from significant, admitted flaws in methodology." *Video Software Dealers Assn.* 556 F.3d at 964. They show at best some correlation between exposure to violent entertainment and minuscule real-world effects, such as children's feeling more aggressive or making louder noises in the few minutes after playing a violent game than after playing a nonviolent game.

Even taking for granted Dr. Anderson's conclusions that violent video games produce some effect on children's feelings of aggression, those effects are both small and indistinguishable from effects produced by other media. In his testimony in a similar lawsuit, Dr. Anderson admitted that the "effect sizes" of children's exposure to violent video games are "about the same" as that produced by their exposure to violence on television. And he admits that the *same* effects have been found when children watch cartoons starring Bugs Bunny or the Road Runner, or when they play video games like Sonic the Hedgehog that are rated "E" (appropriate for all ages), or even when they "vie[w] a picture of a gun."

Of course, California has (wisely) declined to restrict Saturday morning cartoons, the sale of games rated for young children, or the distribution of pictures of guns. The consequence is that its regulation is wildly underinclusive when judged against its asserted justification, which in our view is alone enough to defeat it. Underinclusiveness raises serious doubts about whether the government is in fact pursuing the interest it invokes, rather than disfavoring a particular speaker or viewpoint. Here, California has singled out the purveyors of video games for disfavored treatment — at least when compared to booksellers, cartoonists, and movie producers — and has given no persuasive reason why.

The Act is also seriously underinclusive in another respect — and a respect that renders irrelevant the contentions of the concurrence and the dissents that video games are qualitatively different from other portrayals of violence. The California Legislature is perfectly willing to leave this dangerous, mind-altering material in the hands of children so long as one parent (or even an aunt or uncle) says it's OK. And there are not even any requirements as to how this parental or avuncular relationship is to be verified; apparently the child's or putative parent's, aunt's, or uncle's say-so suffices. That is not how one addresses a serious social problem.

California claims that the Act is justified in aid of parental authority: By requiring that the purchase of violent video games can be made only by adults, the Act ensures that parents can decide what games are appropriate. At the outset, we note our doubts that punishing third parties for conveying protected speech to children *just in case* their parents disapprove of that speech is a proper governmental means of aiding parental authority. Accepting that position would largely vitiate the rule that "only in relatively narrow and well-defined circumstances may government bar public dissemination of protected materials to [minors]." *Erznoznik*, 422 U.S., at 212–213.

But leaving that aside, California cannot show that the Act's restrictions meet a substantial need of parents who wish to restrict their children's access to violent video games but cannot do so. The video-game industry has in place a voluntary rating system designed to inform consumers about the content of games. The system, implemented by the Entertainment Software Rating Board (ESRB), assigns age-specific ratings to each video game submitted: EC (Early Childhood); E (Everyone); E10+ (Everyone 10 and older); T (Teens); M (17 and older); and AO (Adults Only — 18 and older). The Video Software Dealers Association encourages retailers to prominently display information about the ESRB system in their stores; to refrain from renting or selling adults-only games to minors; and to rent or sell "M" rated games to minors only with parental consent. In 2009, the Federal Trade Commission (FTC) found that, as a result of this system, "the video game industry outpaces the movie and music industries" in "(1) restricting target-marketing of mature-rated products to children; (2) clearly and prominently disclosing rating information; and (3) restricting children's access to mature-rated products at retail." FTC, Report to Congress, Marketing Violent Entertainment to Children 30 (Dec. 2009). This system does much to ensure that minors cannot purchase seriously violent games on their own, and that parents who care about the matter can readily evaluate the games their children bring home. Filling the remaining modest gap in concerned-parents' control can hardly be a compelling state interest.

And finally, the Act's purported aid to parental authority is vastly overinclusive. Not all of the children who are forbidden to purchase violent video games on their own have parents who *care* whether they purchase violent video games. While some of the legislation's effect may indeed be in support of what some parents of the restricted children actually want, its entire effect is only in support of what the State thinks parents *ought* to want. This is not the narrow tailoring to "assisting parents" that restriction of First Amendment rights requires.

...

California's effort to regulate violent video games is the latest episode in a long series of failed attempts to censor violent entertainment for minors. While we have pointed out above that some of the evidence brought forward to support the harmfulness of video games is unpersuasive, we do not mean to demean or disparage the concerns that underlie the attempt to regulate them — concerns that may and doubtless do prompt a good deal of parental oversight. We have no business passing judgment on the view of the California Legislature that violent video games (or, for that matter, any other forms of speech) corrupt the young or harm their moral development. Our task is only to say whether or not such works constitute a "well-defined and narrowly limited clas[s] of speech, the prevention and punishment of which have never been thought to raise any Constitutional problem," *Chaplinsky*, 315 U.S., at 571–572, (the answer plainly is no); and if not, whether the regulation of such works is justified by that high degree of necessity we have described as a compelling state interest (it is not). Even where the protection of children is the object, the constitutional limits on governmental action apply.

California's legislation straddles the fence between (1) addressing a serious social problem and (2) helping concerned parents control their children. Both ends are legitimate, but when they affect First Amendment rights they must be pursued by means that are neither seriously underinclusive nor seriously overinclusive. As a means of protecting children from portrayals of violence, the legislation is seriously underinclusive, not only because it excludes portrayals other than video games, but also because it permits a parental or avuncular veto. And as a means of assisting concerned parents it is seriously over inclusive because it abridges the First Amendment rights of young people whose parents (and aunts and uncles) think violent video games are a harmless pastime. And the overbreadth in achieving one goal is not cured by the underbreadth in achieving the other. Legislation such as this, which is neither fish nor fowl, cannot survive strict scrutiny.

We affirm the judgment below....

Justice Alito, with whom The Chief Justice joins, concurring in the judgment.

The California statute that is before us in this case represents a pioneering effort to address what the state legislature and others regard as a potentially serious social problem: the effect of exceptionally violent video games on impressionable minors, who often spend countless hours immersed in the alternative worlds that these games create. Although the California statute is well intentioned, its terms are not framed with the precision that the Constitution demands, and I therefore agree with the Court that this particular law cannot be sustained.

I disagree, however, with the approach taken in the Court's opinion. In considering the application of unchanging constitutional principles to new and rapidly evolving technology, this Court should proceed with caution. We should make every effort to understand the new technology. We should take into account the possibility that developing technology may have important societal implications that will become apparent only with time. We should not jump to the conclusion that new technology is fundamentally the same as some older thing with which we are familiar. And we should not hastily dismiss the judgment of legislators, who may be in a better position than we are to assess the implications of new technology. The opinion of the Court exhibits none of this caution....

Justice Thomas, dissenting [joined by Justice Breyer]

The Court's decision today does not comport with the original public understanding of the First Amendment. The majority strikes down, as facially unconstitutional, a state law that prohibits the direct sale or rental of certain video games to minors because the law "abridg[es] the freedom of speech." U.S. Const., Amdt. 1. But I do not think the First Amendment stretches that far. The practices and beliefs of the founding generation establish that "the freedom of speech," as originally understood, does not include a right to speak to minors (or a right of minors to access speech) without going through the minors' parents or guardians. I would hold that the law at issue is not facially unconstitutional under the First Amendment, and reverse and remand for further proceedings....

As originally understood, the First Amendment's protection against laws "abridging the freedom of speech" did not extend to *all* speech....

In my view, the "practices and beliefs held by the Founders" reveal another category of excluded speech: speech to minor children bypassing their parents. *McIntyre, supra,* at 360. The historical evidence shows that the founding generation believed parents had absolute authority over their minor children and expected parents to use that authority to direct the proper development of their children. It would be absurd to suggest that such a society understood "the freedom of speech" to include a right to speak to minors (or a corresponding right of minors to access speech) without going through the minors' parents. The founding generation would not have considered it an abridgment of "the freedom of speech" to support parental authority by restricting speech that bypasses minors' parents....

Justice Breyer, dissenting.

... Applying traditional First Amendment analysis, I would uphold the statute as constitutional on its face and would consequently reject the industries' facial challenge....

In determining whether the statute is unconstitutional, I would apply both this Court's "vagueness" precedents and a strict form of First Amendment scrutiny. In doing so, the special First Amendment category I find relevant is not (as the Court claims) the category of "depictions of violence," but rather the category of "protection of children." This Court has held that the "power of the state to control the conduct of children reaches beyond the scope of its authority over adults." *Prince v. Massachusetts*, 321 U.S. 158, 170 (1944). And the "'regulatio[n] of communication addressed to [children] need not conform to the requirements of the [F]irst [A]mendment in the same way as those applicable to adults.' *Ginsberg v. New York*, 390 U.S. 629, 638, n.6 (1968) (quoting Emerson, *Toward a General Theory of the First Amendment*, 72 YALE L. J. 877, 939 (1963)).

...

E.S.S. Entm't 2000, Inc. v. Rock Star Videos, Inc.
547 F.3d 1095 (9th Cir. 2008)

We must decide whether a producer of a video game in the "Grand Theft Auto" series has a defense under the First Amendment against a claim of trademark infringement.

Rockstar Games, Inc. ("Rockstar"), a wholly owned subsidiary of Take-Two Interactive Software, Inc., manufactures and distributes the Grand Theft Auto series of video games (the "Series"), including Grand Theft Auto: San Andreas ("San Andreas" or the "Game"). The Series is known for an irreverent and sometimes crass brand of humor, gratuitous violence and sex, and overall seediness.

Each game in the Series takes place in one or more dystopic, cartoonish cities modeled after actual American urban areas. The games always include a disclaimer stating that the locations depicted are fictional. Players control the game's protagonist, trying to complete various "missions" on a video screen. The plot advances with each mission accomplished until the player, having passed through thousands of cartoon-style places along the way, wins the game.

Consistent with the tone of the Series, San Andreas allows a player to experience a version of West Coast "gangster" culture. The Game takes place in the virtual cities of "Los Santos," "San Fierro," and "Las Venturas," based on Los Angeles, San Francisco, and Las Vegas, respectively.

Los Santos, of course, mimics the look and feel of actual Los Angeles neighborhoods. Instead of "Hollywood," "Santa Monica," "Venice Beach," and "Compton," Los Santos contains "Vinewood," "Santa Maria," "Verona Beach," and "Ganton." Rockstar has populated these areas with virtual liquor stores, ammunition dealers, casinos, pawn shops, tattoo parlors, bars, and strip clubs. The brand names, business names, and other aspects of the locations have been changed to fit the irreverent "Los Santos" tone. Not especially saintly, Los Santos is complete with gangs who roam streets inhabited by prostitutes and drug pushers while random gunfire punctuates the soundtrack.

To generate their vision for Los Santos, some of the artists who drew it visited Los Angeles to take reference photographs. The artists took pictures of businesses, streets, and other places in Los Angeles that they thought evoked the San Andreas theme. They then returned home (to Scotland) to draw Los Santos, changing the images from the photographs as necessary to fit into the fictional world of Los Santos and San Andreas. According to Nikolas Taylor ("Taylor"), the Lead Map Artist for Los Santos, he and other artists did not seek to "re-creat[e] a realistic depiction of Los Angeles; rather, [they] were creating 'Los Santos,' a fictional city that lampooned the seedy underbelly of Los Angeles and the people, business and places [that] comprise it." One neighborhood in the fictional city is "East Los Santos," the Game's version of East Los Angeles. East Los Santos contains variations on the businesses and architecture of the real thing, including a virtual, cartoon-style strip club known as the "Pig Pen."

ESS Entertainment 2000, Inc. ("ESS"), operates a strip club, which features females dancing nude, on the eastern edge of downtown Los Angeles under the name Play Pen Gentlemen's Club ("Play Pen"). ESS claims that Rockstar's depiction of an East Los Santos strip club called the Pig Pen infringes its trademark and trade dress associated with the Play Pen.

The Play Pen's "logo" consists of the words "the Play Pen" (and the lower-and upper-case letters forming those words) and the phrase "Totally Nude" displayed in a publicly available font, with a silhouette of a nude female dancer inside the stem of the first "P."

Apparently, ESS has no physical master or precise template for its logo. Different artists draw the nude silhouette in Play Pen's logo anew for each representation, although any final drawing must be acceptable to Play Pen's owners. There are several different versions of the silhouette, and some advertisements and signs for the Play Pen do not contain the nude silhouettes.

Although the artists took some inspiration from their photographs of the Play Pen, it seems they used photographs of other East Los Angeles locations to design other aspects of the Pig Pen. The Pig Pen building in Los Santos, for instance, lacks certain characteristics of the Play Pen building such as a stone facade, a valet stand, large plants and gold columns around the entrance, and a six-foot black iron fence around the parking lot. The Play Pen also has a red, white, and blue pole sign near the premises, which includes a trio of nude silhouettes above the logo and a separate "Totally Nude" sign below. The Pig Pen does not.

On April 22, 2005, ESS filed the underlying trademark violation action in district court against Rockstar.... The heart of ESS's complaint is that Rockstar has used Play Pen's distinctive logo and trade dress without its authorization and has created a likelihood of confusion among consumers as to whether ESS has endorsed, or is associated with, the video depiction. In response, Rockstar moved for summary judgment on all of ESS's claims, arguing that the affirmative defenses of nominative fair use and the First Amendment protected it against liability. It also argued that its use of ESS's intellectual property did not infringe ESS's trademark by creating a "likelihood of confusion."

Although the district court rejected Rockstar's nominative fair use defense, it granted summary judgment based on the First Amendment defense. The district court did not address the merits of the trademark claim because its finding that Rockstar had a defense against liability made such analysis unnecessary. Rockstar argues that, regardless of whether it infringed ESS's trademark under the Lanham Act or related California law, it is entitled to two defenses: one under the nominative fair use doctrine and one under the First Amendment.

"Unlike a traditional fair use scenario, [nominative fair use occurs when] the defendant ... us[es] the trademarked term to describe not its own product, but the plaintiff's." *Playboy Enters., Inc. v. Welles*, 279 F.3d 796, 801 (9th Cir. 2002). The doctrine protects those who deliberately use another's trademark or trade dress "for the 'purposes of comparison, criticism[,] or point of reference.'" *Walking Mountain*, 353 F.3d at 809 (alteration omitted) (quoting *New Kids on the Block v. News Am. Publ'g, Inc.*, 971 F.2d 302, 306 (9th Cir. 1992)). In this case, however, Rockstar's use of "Pig Pen" is not "identical to the plaintiff's [Play Pen] mark." Furthermore, the district court observed that Rockstar's Lead Map Artist "testified the goal in designing the Pig Pen was ... not to comment on Play Pen *per se.*" Since Rockstar did not use the trademarked logo to describe ESS's strip club, the district court correctly held that the nominative fair use defense does not apply in this case.

Rockstar's second defense asks us to consider the intersection of trademark law and the First Amendment. The road is well traveled. We have adopted the Second Circuit's approach from *Rogers v. Grimaldi*, which "requires courts to construe the Lanham Act 'to apply to artistic works *only* where the public interest in avoiding consumer confusion *outweighs* the public interest in free expression.'" *Walking Mountain*, 353 F.3d at 807 (emphasis in original) (quoting *Rogers v. Grimaldi*, 875 F.2d 994, 999 (2d Cir. 1989)). The specific test contains two prongs. An artistic work's use of a trademark that otherwise would violate the Lanham Act is not actionable "'unless the [use of the mark] has no artistic relevance to the underlying work whatsoever, or, if it has some artistic relevance, unless [it] explicitly misleads as to the source or the content of the work.'" *Mattel, Inc. v. MCA Records, Inc.*, 296 F.3d 894, 902 (9th Cir. 2002) (quoting *Rogers*, 875 F.2d at 999). Although this test traditionally applies to uses of a trademark in the title of an artistic work, there is no principled reason why it ought not also apply to the use of a trademark in the body of the work. The parties do not dispute such an extension of the doctrine.

We first adopted the *Rogers* test in *MCA Records*, a case which is instructive for that reason. *MCA Records*, 296 F.3d at 902. In *MCA Records*, the maker of the iconic "Barbie" dolls sued MCA for trademark infringement in the title of a song the record company had released, called "Barbie Girl." The song was a commentary "about Barbie and the values ... she [supposedly] represents." *Id.* at 902. Applying *Rogers*, the court held that the First Amendment protected the record company. The first prong was straightforward. Because the song was about Barbie, "the use of Barbie in the song title clearly is relevant to the underlying work." *Id.*; See also *Walking Mountain*, 353 F.3d at 807 (holding that use of Barbie doll in photographic parody was relevant to the underlying work).

Moving to the second prong, we made an important point. "The *only* indication," we observed, "that Mattel might be associated with the song is the use of Barbie in the title; if this were enough to satisfy this prong of the *Rogers* test, it would render *Rogers* a nullity." *MCA Records*, 296 F.2d at 902 (emphasis in original). This makes good sense. After all, a trademark infringement claim presupposes a use of the mark. If that necessary element in every trademark case vitiated a First Amendment defense, the First Amendment would provide no defense at all.

Keeping *MCA Records* and related cases in mind, we now turn to the matter before us. ESS concedes that the Game is artistic and that therefore the *Rogers* test applies. However, ESS argues both that the incorporation of the Pig Pen into the Game has no artistic relevance and that it is explicitly misleading. It rests its argument on two observations: (1) the Game is not "about" ESS's Play Pen club the way that "Barbie Girl" was "about" the Barbie doll in *MCA Records*; and (2) also unlike the Barbie case, where the trademark and trade dress at issue was a cultural icon (Barbie), the Play Pen is not a cultural icon.

ESS's objections, though factually accurate, miss the point. Under *MCA Records* and the cases that followed it, only the use of a trademark with "'*no* artistic relevance to the underlying work *whatsoever*'" does not merit First Amendment protection. In other words, the level of relevance merely must be above zero. It is true that the Game is not "about" the Play Pen the way that Barbie Girl was about Barbie. But, given the low threshold the Game must surmount, that fact is hardly dispositive. It is also true that Play Pen has little cultural significance, but the same could be said about most of the individual establishments in East Los Angeles. Like most urban neighborhoods, its distinctiveness lies in its "look and feel," not in particular destinations as in a downtown or tourist district. And that neighborhood, with all that characterizes it, *is* relevant to Rockstar's artistic goal, which is to develop a cartoon-style parody of East Los Angeles. Possibly the only way, and certainly a reasonable way, to do that is to recreate a critical mass of the businesses and buildings that constitute it. In this context, we conclude that to include a strip club that is similar in look and feel to the Play Pen does indeed have at least "some artistic relevance."

ESS also argues that Rockstar's use of the Pig Pen "'explicitly misleads as to the source or the content of the work.'" This prong of the test points directly at the purpose of trademark law, namely to "avoid confusion in the marketplace by allowing a trademark owner to prevent others from duping consumers into buying a product they mistakenly believe is sponsored by the trademark owner." *Walking Mountain*, 353 F.3d at 806 (internal quotation marks and alteration omitted). The relevant question, therefore, is whether the

Game would confuse its players into thinking that the Play Pen is somehow behind the Pig Pen or that it sponsors Rockstar's product. In answering that question, we keep in mind our observation in *MCA Records* that the mere use of a trademark alone cannot suffice to make such use explicitly misleading.

Both San Andreas and the Play Pen offer a form of lowbrow entertainment; besides this general similarity, they have nothing in common. The San Andreas Game is not complementary to the Play Pen; video games and strip clubs do not go together like a horse and carriage or, perish the thought, love and marriage. Nothing indicates that the buying public would reasonably have believed that ESS produced the video game or, for that matter, that Rockstar operated a strip club. A player can enter the virtual strip club in Los Santos, but ESS has provided no evidence that the setting is anything but generic. It also seems far-fetched that someone playing San Andreas would think ESS had provided whatever expertise, support, or unique strip-club knowledge it possesses to the production of the game. After all, the Game does not revolve around running or patronizing a strip club. Whatever one can do at the Pig Pen seems quite incidental to the overall story of the Game. A reasonable consumer would not think a company that owns one strip club in East Los Angeles, which is not well known to the public at large, also produces a technologically sophisticated video game like San Andreas.

Undeterred, ESS also argues that, because players are free to ignore the storyline and spend as much time as they want at the Pig Pen, the Pig Pen can be considered a significant part of the Game, leading to confusion. But fans can spend all nine innings of a baseball game at the hot dog stand; that hardly makes Dodger Stadium a butcher's shop. In other words, the chance to attend a virtual strip club is unambiguously *not* the main selling point of the Game.

Considering all of the foregoing, we conclude that Rockstar's modification of ESS's trademark is not explicitly misleading and is thus protected by the First Amendment. Since the First Amendment defense applies equally to ESS's state law claims as to its Lanham Act claim, the district court properly dismissed the entire case on Rockstar's motion for summary judgment. Affirmed.

Dillinger, LLC v. Elec. Arts, Inc.

101 U.S.P.Q.2D (BNA) 1612 (S.D. Ind. June 16, 2011)

Plaintiff brings this action against Electronic Arts, Inc. ("EA") for allegedly using its trademarked name "Dillinger" to name weapons featured in EA's *The Godfather* video games in violation of federal and state law. Plaintiff's Complaint lists six counts, three of which (Counts I, II, and VI) have recently been dismissed. The three remaining claims (Counts III–V) arise under the Lanham Act and a common-law claim for unfair competition that is grounded in a prohibition against trademark misappropriation, which Plaintiff argues bars EA from using the Dillinger name in its games. Presently before the Court are the parties' cross-motions for summary judgment on EA's First Amendment defense to its use of the Dillinger name....

A) John Dillinger and his Connection with the Tommy Gun

Plaintiff claims to own the publicity rights of the "late depression-era bandit" John Dillinger, as well as the trademark rights in the words "John Dillinger."

John Dillinger was a legendary gentleman-bandit; according to the FBI, Dillinger was a "notorious and vicious thief"—a "lurid desperado" who "came to evoke the gangster era." Indeed, during the mid-1930s, he and his violent gang terrorized the Midwest, robbing, killing and staging jail-breaks.

In addition to his glamorous life of crime, John Dillinger is commonly associated with Thompson submachine guns, also known as "Tommy Guns," which were seized *en masse* from his hideouts by the police. Plaintiff's website thus features an iconic photograph of John Dillinger holding a Tommy Gun, and the Tommy Gun manufacturer's website itself calls the gun "Dillinger's Choice."

Depictions of John Dillinger in popular culture have reinforced his connection with the Tommy Gun over the years. In the 1995 movie *Dillinger and Capone*, Dillinger is featured alongside notorious mafioso Al Capone, and the former uses a Tommy gun throughout the film. Dillinger is also depicted using Tommy guns in films including *Dillinger* (1973) and *Public Enemies* (2009).

As EA Executive Producer Joel Wade put it, "the popular persona of John Dillinger … [became] this flashy gangster who dressed well, womanized, drove around in fast cars, and sprayed Tommy Guns."

B) The Godfather Video Games

EA is the developer and publisher of video games, including "*The Godfather*" and "*The Godfather II*" (collectively, "*Godfather games*"), which were released in 2006 and 2009 respectively.

The *Godfather* games are based on Francis Ford Coppola's film adaptations of the 1969 novel, *The Godfather* ("*Godfather* novel"), written by Mario Puzo. The novel and films portray a fictional New York mafia family, the Corleones, and in particular, the rise of Michael Corleone, who returns from World War II and ultimately replaces his father, Vito Corleone, as the leader of the Corleone family—the "Godfather." Among other things, the novel describes a fictional rivalry between Al Capone's Chicago-based syndicate and the Corleone family's New York-based operation. Both *Godfather* films include widespread use of Tommy Guns.

The *Godfather* games combine technically advanced software and creative audio-visual elements, which are constructed from thousands of video graphics, audio features, and data. Both games feature an extensive musical soundtrack, sound effects, and include new dialogue, written specifically for the game.

The first *Godfather* game, like the film, simulates the mafia world in New York during the mid-1900s. The player acts as a member of the Corleone family, guiding this so-called "in-game character" through a variety of missions predicated on the plot of the original *Godfather* film. To complete the missions, the player "intimidates, bribes, and fights his way to the top" — robbing banks, evading law enforcement, and "utilizing period-appropriate vehicles and weapons" to do so.

In the first *Godfather* game, the player may choose and use a Tommy Gun identified as the Level Three "Dillinger Tommy Gun." The "Dillinger Tommy Gun" is one of fifteen firearms in this game. It is distinguishable from other weapons based on characteristics such as a seventy-five round clip and a rapid rate of fire. The gun's label appears as a single piece of text to identify the weapon, and the words "Dillinger Tommy Gun" are not spoken by any character in the game. The "Dillinger Tommy Gun" itself does not appear in any of the *Godfather* game's advertising or promotion materials.…

John Dillinger does not appear and is not referenced in the *Godfather* movies or novel; he lived before the time period within which the games are set; and he committed crimes primarily in the Midwest, not on the East Coast. Plaintiff thus claims EA's use of the Dillinger name violates trademark law.

Although the Seventh Circuit protects video games as "literary works" under the First Amendment, Plaintiff argues that EA is not entitled to First Amendment protection of its use of the Dillinger trademark because the use of the mark has no artistic relevance to the *Godfather* games; even if it does, Plaintiff argues, the use of the name should not be protected because it "explicitly misleads players regarding the content of the games and Dillinger's approval of the mark's usage."

The parties agree that EA's First Amendment defense to Plaintiff's trademark claim is controlled by *Rogers v. Grimaldi*, 875 F.2d 994 (2nd. Cir. 1989). ("To qualify for First Amendment Protection under *Rogers v. Grimaldi* on summary judgment, EA must establish as a matter of law that its use of Dillinger was "related" in some way to the "content of the expressive work."] The *Rogers* "relatedness" test bars trademark claims unless the use of the plaintiff's likeness is "wholly unrelated to the [work] or [is] simply a disguised commercial advertisement for the sale of goods or services." To properly analyze this issue, the Court must therefore consider a two-part test: First, the Court must determine whether the use of the mark has any artistic relevance to the underlying work whatsoever; second, if the use of the trademark has some relevance, the Court must determine whether it explicitly misleads the public as to the source or content of the work. *E.S.S. Entertainment 2000, Inc. v. Rock Star Videos*, 547 F.3d 1095, 1099 (9th Cir. 2008) (citing *Rogers*, 875 F.2d at 999, 1004 (2d Cir. 1989)).

A) Does the Dillinger Name Have Any Relevance to *The Godfather* Games?

Plaintiff argues that the name "Dillinger" has no artistic relevance to the *Godfather* games because the use of the Dillinger name is not a reasonably necessary component of the games and because "[EA] does not know why it chose to use 'Dillinger' in the first place."

1. Relationship between Dillinger and the *Godfather* Games

Plaintiff argues that the use of the Dillinger name has no artistic relevance because it is "not a reasonably necessary aspect of the game[s]." More precisely, it argues, the name's use bears no relationship to the game because the mark appears nowhere in the games other than to identify the Level Three Dillinger Tommy Gun and the Modern Dillinger; because John Dillinger himself appears nowhere in the *Godfather* novel, movies, or video game storyline; and because John Dillinger was not alive during the period which any of those works was set. Because Tommy Guns are "but isolated elements in the work" with no relation to the story-line, Plaintiff maintains that EA relies on a mere "logical connection between John Dillinger and Tommy Guns," which "cannot serve as the basis for establishing a relationship under the *Rogers* test."

In support of this argument, Plaintiff attempts to distinguish this case from *E.S.S. v. Rock Star Videos*, wherein the Ninth Circuit found that the use of the name of a Los Angeles strip club had at least some artistic relevance to a video game whose goal was to "mimic the look and feel of actual Los Angeles neighborhoods." There, the game was decidedly not "about" the strip club, but since the strip club had some relation to the city of Los Angeles, the court found the use of the mark was entitled to First Amendment protection. ("[Only] the use of a trademark with no artistic relevance to the underlying work whatsoever does not merit First Amendment protection. In other words, the level of relevance merely must be above zero. It is true that the game is not 'about' the [strip club] ... but given the low threshold the game must surmount, that fact is hardly dispositive.").

Despite Plaintiff's contention to the contrary, this case is analogous to *E.S.S.* Here, it is undisputed that the *Godfather* games are not "about" Tommy Guns; the games are about a fictional world, based on the *Godfather* novel and movies, players act like criminals and mobsters who use a wide array of weapons—including Tommy Guns. Plaintiff does not dispute the relevance, or even the primacy, of Tommy Guns to the virtual world depicted in the *Godfather* games. Nor does Plaintiff dispute that the Dillinger name is closely associated with the Tommy Gun. Indeed, Plaintiff admits that there a "superficial and attenuated" link between John Dillinger and the *Godfather* video games.

As was the case in *E.S.S.*, even if the Court accepts the characterization as attenuated, such connection is enough to satisfy the *Rogers* test: The gentleman-bandit, commonly known for his public persona as a "flashy gangster who dressed well, womanized, drove around in fast cars, and sprayed Tommy Guns," has above-zero relevance to a game whose premise enables players to act like members of the mafia and spray Tommy Guns.

Plaintiff attempts to undermine this relationship by arguing that, "except for the name 'Dillinger,' [EA] chose not to include elements in its games which fell before 1940, such as John Dillinger's contemporaries (e.g., Bonnie & Clyde, Ma Barker, Machine Gun Kelly, pre-1940 Godfather movie characters and 1930s-era cars)." Neglecting to include certain elements of an era, however, quite obviously does not mean that those which are included are irrelevant.

No suggestion has been made that the *Godfather* games aim to exactly replicate the *Godfather* movies or the time-period they depict—neither the fact that Dillinger lived before the pertinent time period nor the fact that EA did not include any of Dillinger's contemporaries undermines the relevance of Dillinger's public persona to the content of the games.

It bears repeating that it is not the role of the Court to determine how meaningful the relationship between a trademark and the content of a literary work must be; consistent with *Rogers*, any connection whatsoever is enough for the Court to determine that the mark's use meets "the appropriately low threshold of minimal artistic relevance." EA has certainly shown that the "mental imagery" associated with the Dillinger name has more than zero relevance to the content of the *Godfather* games....

B) Is the Dillinger Label Explicitly Misleading as to the Source and Content of the Games?

The second element of the *Rogers* test asks the Court to determine whether the defendant's use of the plaintiff's trademark "explicitly misleads as to the source and content of the work." To be "explicitly misleading," the defendant's work must make some affirmative statement of the plaintiff's sponsorship or endorsement, beyond the mere use of plaintiff's name or other characteristic. For example, the use of "the phrase in a subtitle of 'an authorized biography' would be sufficiently explicit to be actionable, if false"; but evidence that the trademark use "might implicitly suggest that the named celebrity had endorsed the work or had a role in producing it" is "outweighed by the danger of restricting artistic expression." *Rogers*, 875 F.2d at 999–1000.

Plaintiff argues that "by using Dillinger's name in the games, EA gives the false impression that the Dillinger brand approves the association of John Dillinger's likeness with these games"; "[t]he fact that the games are based on literary and motion picture works that do not contain any reference to John Dillinger only heightens the probability of deception." In support of its claim, Plaintiff points to the fact that the "Modern Dillinger" is one of only a select few guns available through the upgrade pack for *The Godfather II*, implicitly indicating it is "arguably the most powerful gun available," and that press releases posted to EA's website list the Modern Dillinger first among all the weapons....

Plaintiff has presented no evidence that any consumer bought the *Godfather* Games because of the Dillinger name, or was otherwise confused. As was the case in *E.S.S.*, the use of the Dillinger name is "quite incidental to the overall story of the game" and "not the main selling point of the [g]ame."

Even if the Dillinger name is not a selling point of the games, Plaintiff argues, "studies show that increasing numbers of consumers believe that all marks appearing in entertainment are placed or licensed." [citing to Elizabeth Rosenblatt, *Rethinking the Parameter of Trademark Use in Entertainment*, 61 Florida L. Rev. 1011, 1032 (2009).] As an initial matter, this statement is not admissible evidence under Rule 801; but even if it were, it would not be probative as to whether the use of this particular trademark confused consumers....

Instead, in support of its position, Plaintiff attempts to analogize this case to *Parks v. La-Face Records*, 329 F.3d 437 (6th Cir. 2003), where the Sixth Circuit determined that under the *Rogers* test, the title of Outkast's hip-hop song *Rosa Parks* was not protected by the First Amendment because it had no artistic relevance whatsoever to the content of the song and because it was likely to confuse the public about the content of the work. In striking contrast to Rosa Parks, whom the court noted was an "international symbol of freedom, humanity, dignity and strength," the court deemed the Outkast song "nothing more and nothing less than a paean announcing the triumph of superior people in the entertainment business over inferior people in that business." Moreover, the court noted, "some people looking at the title *Rosa Parks* might think the song is about Rosa Parks, and for those with that false impression (as twenty-one consumer affidavits filed in this case indicate happened), the title is misleading."

In determining that the Outkast song's title was not protected by the First Amendment, the *Parks* court focused on the objective evidence of relatedness and potential for consumer confusion. And unlike *Parks*, where the plaintiff presented affidavits documenting circumstances in which the song's title led listeners to believe the song was about Rosa Parks, here Plaintiff has presented no evidence that any consumers are confused by the use of "Dillinger" in the *Godfather* games. The Court cannot simply infer that the Dillinger name confuses the public, let alone that such confusion outweighs First Amendment concerns.

In any event, Plaintiff points to no *explicit* misrepresentation — that fact alone is dispositive of this issue. All that is challenged here a single text-line used to identify one of many weapons within a visually complex video game comprised of countless artistic elements. In the face of no documented harm — or even risk of harm — whatsoever, the Court finds that there is no genuine issue of material fact regarding public confusion from the use of the Dillinger name.

Because no issue of fact exists as to whether the Dillinger name is relevant to the content of *The Godfather* Games, or as to whether the use of the name explicitly misleads consumers, the Court finds that EA is entitled to summary judgment on its First Amendment defense....

Voluntary Regulations — The Entertainment Software Rating Board (ESRB)

In response to consumer pressures to restrict certain video game sales and usage by minors, and in response to court rulings restricting the ability of governments to directly regulate such video game content, the video game industry itself developed and adopted a voluntary system of game ratings. The Entertainment Software Rating Board (ESRB) is the body responsible for the ratings system in use in the United States and Canada. The ESRB was established in 1994 by the Entertainment Software Association (ESA), and assigns content ratings to video and computer games, enforcing industry-adopted advertising guidelines as to rated games. The current ratings system consists of six ratings categories, assigned by trained ratings personnel, on the basis of sexual, violent, and other potentially objectionable content within the game.

EARLY CHILDHOOD: Titles rated EC (Early Childhood) have content that may be suitable for ages 3 and older. Contains no material that parents would find inappropriate.

EVERYONE: Titles rated E (Everyone) have content that may be suitable for ages 6 and older. Titles in this category may contain minimal cartoon, fantasy or mild violence and/or infrequent use of mild language.

EVERYONE 10+: Titles rated E10+ (Everyone 10 and older) have content that may be suitable for ages 10 and older. Titles in this category may contain more cartoon, fantasy or mild violence, mild language and/or minimal suggestive themes.

TEEN: Titles rated T (Teen) have content that may be suitable for ages 13 and older. Titles in this category may contain violence, suggestive themes, crude humor, minimal blood, simulated gambling, and/or infrequent use of strong language.

MATURE: Titles rated M (Mature) have content that may be suitable for persons ages 17 and older. Titles in this category may contain intense violence, blood and gore, sexual content and/or strong language.

ADULTS ONLY: Titles rated AO (Adults Only) have content that should only be played by persons 18 years and older. Titles in this category may include prolonged scenes of intense violence and/or graphic sexual content and nudity.

While this six-tier rating system is voluntary, the submission guidelines of the ESBA, the comprehensive membership of the ESA, and private store policies that only allow sales of rated games within their stores effectively means that virtually all games sold in the United States and Canada are rated by the ESRB.[17] The ESRB also provides advertising guidelines for publishers to adhere to, and retailers often use the ESRB ratings to implement their own voluntary policies as to sales to minors. In this way, ESRB ratings are a private matter, and do not implicate the same First Amendment issues that direct government regulations do.

Notes and Questions

a. To what extent does the determination of whether video game content is protected speech determine the rigor of the constitutional tests applied? Courts have taken three major approaches to the question over the years:

Video games per se *contain expressive or informative content:* When courts determine that video games contain expressive or informative content *per se*, courts generally apply strict scrutiny to regulations that attempt to restrict video game sales or usage. Compare *Interactive Digital Software Ass'n v. St. Louis County, Mo.*, 329 F.3d 954 (8th Cir. 2003) (determining that elements of a video games are expressive speech in the same way as other media, are to be given full First

---

17. Entertainment Software Rating Board, Frequently Asked Questions, http://www.esrb.org/ratings/faq.jsp (last visited May 27, 2010).

Amendment protection, and statutes that prohibit use, sale, or exposure to minor of certain violent or explicit video games are to be subjected to strict scrutiny analysis); *Am. Amusement Machine Ass'n v. Kendrick*, 244 F.3d 572 (7th Cir. 2001) (holding that a preliminary injunction against a municipality seeking to enforce an ordinance requiring parental content for minor to play certain classes of video games should be granted, because the ordinance would likely be struck down on free expression grounds); *Entm't Software Ass'n v. Granholm*, 404 F. Supp. 2d 978 (E.D. Mich. 2005) (striking down a state statute prohibiting minors from buying or playing violent video games, maintaining that violent depictions in such games are to be accorded full constitutional protection as expression).

Video games may contain expressive or informative content in certain circumstances: When courts take this approach to video games as protected speech, courts examine the particular content of the game in question on a case-by-case basis, sometimes finding the game to contain such speech, and sometimes finding certain games to be devoid of expression or information and more analogous to sports or board games. In *Wilson v. Midway Games, Inc.*, 198 F. Supp. 2d 167 (D. Conn. 2002), the court held that a particular work being labeled a "video game" did not necessarily mean the work has or lacks protectable expression. Instead the question is whether the particular game in question is essentially pure mechanical entertainment or whether the game does actually contain protectable expression of ideas that would afford it protection under the First Amendment.

Video games per se *do not contain expressive or informative content:* In the earlier round of cases, courts often determined that video games had no expressive or informative content and thereby applied the rational relation test to determine whether regulations are constitutionally permissible that restrict video game use or sales. Such cases include *Malden Amusement Co., Inc. v. City of Malden*, 582 F. Supp. 297 (D. Mass. 1983) (ruling that a city ordinance restricting the placement and amount of amusement machines was permissible because the activity being regulated contained no protectable expression, but was essentially mechanical entertainment); *America's Best Family Showplace Corp. v. City of New York, Dept. of Bldgs.*, 536 F. Supp. 170 (E.D.N.Y. 1982) (holding that city zoning and licensing laws related to coin-operated video games implicated no First Amendment concerns, because the activity did not consist of protectable speech); *People v. Walker*, 354 N.W.2d 312 (Mich. Ct. App. 1984) (rejecting a challenge to a local ordinance prohibiting minor presence at arcades by stating that video games were not entitled to any particular First Amendment protection as a class of entertainment); *Kaye v. Planning and Zoning Comm'n, Town of Westport*, 472 A.2d 809 (Conn. Super. Ct. 1983) (finding local regulation of video games through special permit restrictions did not violate the First Amendment, because the games did not communicate or contain any particular ideas).

b. Is there tort liability to video game producers for contributing to third party actions producing wrongful death or injury? Generally, courts have been unsympathetic to plaintiffs in cases where injured parties attempt to hold video game producers liable for third party actions, maintaining that video games enjoy protection as expression under the First Amendment. In *James v. Meow Media, Inc.*, 300 F.3d 683 (6th Cir. 2002) the court dismissed a wrongful death suit against a video game producer accused of tort liability because the plaintiff's specific complaints regarding the features of the game which allegedly contributed to the tort alleged were the expressive aspects of the game that are protected as expression under the First Amendment). See also *Wilson v. Midway Games, Inc.*, 198 F. Supp. 2d 167 (D. Conn. 2002) (holding that a video game producer could not be held liable in a wrongful death tort action for allegedly contributing to violent behavior that lead to death, because the allegations in the particular case went directly to the game's violence and interactivity, aspects of the game protected as expression under the First Amendment).

c. Some state statutes have attempted to utilize the voluntary private ratings system as a basis for government regulation of video game sales and usage. The adoption of the video game industry's own voluntary ratings system as a basis by which to classify video games and restrict use or sales to minors has been deemed unconstitutional. In *Entm't Software Ass'n v. Hatch*, 443 F. Supp. 2d 1065 (D. Minn. 2006), the court struck down a state statute criminalizing the sale of video games classified by the video game retailers' own rating system, because games are rated by a non-government body, without any supervision by the public and without any recourse for ratings decisions through official channels, effectively restricting speech by means of the government through private action. To what extent has the motion picture and music industries utilized these same voluntary standards that are incorporated into laws or ordinances?

d. Can the producer of anti-spam or other content control software block access to video games based on content or pop-up advertising? See *Zango, Inc. v. Kaspersky Lab, Inc.*, 568 F.3d 1169 (9th Cir. 2009).

Problem XVIII-C

Bryce has been collaborating with a video game publisher to produce a new interactive game for use in virtual worlds or as a stand-alone networked computer game. Based on the social life of a rock star, the game includes features for creating bands, touring, performing, and initiating bar fights. Bryce's partners also created an "adult" version that featured the sex and drugs of rock-and-roll lore. Bryce found the adult version to be highly graphic and extreme.

Bryce is concerned about the project. The parties have not specified any rating for the software prior to its creation, but Bryce is uncomfortable being associated with a graphic, adult game. Bryce is also nervous that the game can be banned from virtual world communities by the operators or lead to criminal liability. Please advise Bryce regarding the legal and business risks associated with Bryce's role on the project.

D. Publicity Rights in Video Games

Hart v. Electronic Arts, Inc.
717 F.3d 141 (2013)

In 2009, Appellant Ryan Hart ("Appellant" or "Hart") brought suit against Appellee Electronic Arts, Inc. ("Appellee" or "EA") for allegedly violating his right of publicity as recognized under New Jersey law. Specifically, Appellant's claims stemmed from Appellee's alleged use of his likeness and biographical information in its *NCAA Football* series of videogames. The District Court granted summary judgment in favor of Appellee on the ground that its use of Appellant's likeness was protected by the First Amendment. For the reasons set forth below, we will reverse the grant of summary judgment and remand the case back to the District Court for further proceedings....

Hart was a quarterback, player number 13, with the Rutgers University NCAA Men's Division I Football team for the 2002 through 2005 seasons. As a condition of participating in college-level sports, Hart was required to adhere to the National Collegiate Athletic Association's ("NCAA") amateurism rules as set out in Article 12 of the NCAA bylaws. *See, e.g.,* NCAA, *2011–12 NCAA Division I Manual* § 12.01.1 (2011) ("Only an amateur student-athlete is eligible for inter-collegiate athletics participation in a particular sport."). In relevant part, these rules state that a collegiate athlete loses his or her "amateur" status if (1) the athlete "[u]ses his or her athletics skill (directly or indirectly) for pay in any form in that sport," *id.* § 12.1.2, or (2) the athlete "[a]ccepts any remuneration or permits the use of his or her name or picture to advertise, recommend or promote directly the sale or use of a commercial product or service of any kind," *id.* § 12.5.2.1.[18] In comporting with these bylaws, Hart purportedly refrained from seizing on various commercial opportunities. On the field, Hart excelled. At 6′2″, weighing 197 pounds, and typically wearing a visor and armband on his left wrist, Hart amassed an impressive list of achievements as the Scarlet Knights' starting quarterback. . . .

Hart's participation in college football also ensured his inclusion in EA's successful *NCAA Football* videogame franchise. EA, founded in 1982, is "one of the world's leading interactive entertainment software companies," and "develops, publishes, and distributes interactive software worldwide" for consoles, cell phones, and PCs. EA's catalogue includes *NCAA Football,* the videogame series at issue in the instant case. The first edition of the game was released in 1993 as *Bill Walsh College Football.* EA subsequently changed the name first to *College Football USA* (in 1995), and then to the current *NCAA Football* (in 1997). New editions in the series are released annually, and "allow[ ] users to experience the excitement and challenge of college football" by interacting with "over 100 virtual teams and thousands of virtual players." . . .

In no small part, the *NCAA Football* franchise's success owes to its focus on realism and detail — from realistic sounds, to game mechanics, to team mascots. This focus on realism also ensures that the "over 100 virtual teams" in the game are populated by digital avatars that resemble their real-life counterparts and share their vital and biographical information. Thus, for example, in *NCAA Football 2006,* Rutgers' quarterback, player number 13, is 6′2″ tall, weighs 197 pounds and resembles Hart. Moreover, while users can change the digital avatar's appearance and most of the vital statistics (height, weight, throwing distance, etc.), certain details remain immutable: the player's home state, home town, team, and class year.

Appellant filed suit against EA in state court for, among other things, violation of his right of publicity. . . . The District Court ruled in favor of Appellee, holding that *NCAA Football* was entitled to protection under the First Amendment. . . . The matter is now before us for review.

Discussion

We begin our analysis by noting the self-evident: video games are protected as expressive speech under the First Amendment. *Brown v. Entm't Merchs. Ass'n,* ___ U.S.

---

18. The NCAA Manual also states that where a collegiate athlete's

> name or picture appears on commercial items ... or is used to promote a commercial product sold by an individual or agency without the student-athlete's knowledge or permission, the student athlete (or the institution acting on behalf of the student-athlete) is required to take steps to stop such an activity in order to retain his or her eligibility for intercollegiate athletics.

NCAA, *2011–12 NCAA Division I Manual* § 12.5.2.2 (2011).

___, 131 S.Ct. 2729, 2733, 180 L.Ed.2d 708 (2011). As the Supreme Court has noted, "video games communicate ideas—and even social messages—through many familiar literary devices (such as characters, dialogue, plot, and music) and through features distinctive to the medium (such as the player's interaction with the virtual world)." *Id.* As a result, games enjoy the full force of First Amendment protections. As with other types of expressive conduct, the protection afforded to games can be limited in situations where the right of free expression necessarily conflicts with other protected rights.

The instant case presents one such situation. Here, Appellee concedes, for purposes of the motion and appeal, that it violated Appellant's right of publicity; in essence, misappropriating his identity for commercial exploitation. However, Appellee contends that the First Amendment shields it from liability for this violation because *NCAA Football* is a protected work. To resolve the tension between the First Amendment and the right of publicity, we must balance the interests underlying the right to free expression against the interests in protecting the right of publicity. *See Zacchini v. Scripps-Howard Broad. Co.*, 433 U.S. 562, 574–75 (1977).[19]

Courts have taken varying approaches in attempting to strike a balance between the competing interests in right of publicity cases, some more appealing than others. In our discussion below, we first consider the nature of the interests we must balance and then analyze the different approaches courts have taken to resolving the tension between the First Amendment and the right of publicity.

A. The Relevant Interests at Issue

Before engaging with the different analytical schemes, we first examine the relevant interests underlying the rights of free expression and publicity.

1. Freedom of Expression

Freedom of expression is paramount in a democratic society, for "[i]t is the function of speech to free men from the bondage of irrational fears." *Whitney v. California*, 274 U.S. 357, 376 (1927) (Brandeis, J., concurring). As Justice Louis Brandeis wrote nearly a century ago:

> Those who won our independence believed that the final end of the state was to make men free to develop their faculties.... They valued liberty both as an end and as a means. They believed liberty to [be] the secret of happiness and courage to be the secret of liberty. They believed that freedom to think as you will and to speak as you think are means indispensable to the discovery and spread of political truth; that without free speech and assembly discussion would be futile; that with them, discussion affords ordinarily adequate protection against the dissemination of noxious doctrine; that the greatest menace to freedom is an inert people; that public discussion is a political duty; and that this should be a fundamental principle of the American government.

Id. at 375.

In keeping with Justice Brandeis' eloquent analysis, the great legal minds of generations past and present have recognized that free speech benefits both the individual and society....

---

19. While it is true that the right of publicity is a creature of state law and precedent, its intersection with the First Amendment presents a federal issue, and, thus, permits us to engage in the sort of balancing inquiry at issue here. *See, e.g., Zacchini*, 433 U.S. at 566–68.

The interest in safeguarding the integrity of these protections therefore weighs heavily in any balancing inquiry. Still, instances can and do arise where First Amendment protections yield in the face of competing interests. Ultimately, we must determine whether the interest in safeguarding the right of publicity overpowers the interest in safeguarding free expression.

2. The Right of Publicity

The right of publicity grew out of the right to privacy torts, specifically, from the tort of "invasion of privacy by appropriation." J. THOMAS MCCARTHY, THE RIGHTS OF PUBLICITY AND PRIVACY § 1:23 (2d ed. 2012).... However, this early conceptualization had limitations, particularly when it came to protecting the property interests of celebrities and people already in the public eye.... The first case to describe this protection as a "right of publicity" was *Haelan Labs., Inc. v. Topps Chewing Gum, Inc.,* 202 F.2d 866 (2d Cir.1953) (concerning baseball cards in gum packages). There, the Second Circuit held that "in addition to and independent of that right of privacy..., a man has a right in the publicity value of his photo graph.... This right might be called a 'right of publicity.'" *Id.* at 868. New Jersey courts, which had long recognized a "right of privacy [and] a right of property," were not far behind in voicing their support for this concept. *Ettore v. Philco Television Broad. Corp.,* 229 F.2d 481, 491 (3d Cir.1956).

In the seminal case of *Palmer v. Schonhorn Enters., Inc.,* the Superior Court of New Jersey noted that

> [p]erhaps the basic and underlying theory is that a person has the right to enjoy the fruits of his own industry free from unjustified interference. It is unfair that one should be permitted to commercialize or exploit or capitalize upon another's name, reputation or accomplishments merely because the owner's accomplishments have been highly publicized.

96 N.J.Super. 72, 232 A.2d 458, 462 (Ch.Div.1967) (citations omitted) (finding an infringement of property rights where a golfer's name was used in connection with a golf game)....

New Jersey law therefore recognizes that "[t]he right to exploit the value of [an individual's] notoriety or fame belongs to the individual with whom it is associated," for an individual's "name, likeness, and endorsement carry value and an unauthorized use harms the person both by diluting the value of the name and depriving that individual of compensation." *McFarland v. Miller,* 14 F.3d 912, 919, 923 (3d Cir.1994). As such, the goal of maintaining a right of publicity is to protect the property interest that an individual gains and enjoys in his identity through his labor and effort. Additionally, as with protections for intellectual property, the right of publicity is designed to encourage further development of this property interest.

Since neither the New Jersey courts nor our own circuit have set out a definitive methodology for balancing the tension between the First Amendment and the right of publicity, we are presented with a case of first impression. We must therefore consult the approaches of other courts in the first instance.

B. How Courts Balance the Interests

We begin our inquiry by looking at *Zacchini v. Scripps-Howard Broadcasting Co.,* the only Supreme Court case addressing the First Amendment in a right of publicity context. In this case, the Court called for a balancing test to weigh the interest underlying the First Amendment against those underpinning the right of publicity. 433 U.S. at 574–75. This decision sets the stage for our analysis of three systematized analytical frameworks that have emerged as courts struggle with finding a standardized way for performing this balancing inquiry.

1. *Zacchini* and the Need for Balance

… In setting out the interests at issue in the case, the Supreme Court noted (as we did above) that "the State's interest in permitting a 'right of publicity' is in protecting the proprietary interest of the individual in his act in part to encourage such entertainment." This aspect of the right, the Court noted, was "analogous to the goals of patent and copyright law," given that they too serve to protect the individual's ability to "reap the reward of his endeavors." In *Zacchini*, the performance was the "product of [Zacchini's] own talents and energy, the end result of much time, effort and expense." Thus much of its economic value lay "in the right of exclusive control over the publicity given to his performance." Indeed, while the Court noted that "[a]n entertainer such as petitioner usually has no objection to the widespread publication of his act as long as [he] gets the commercial benefit of such publication," the claim at issue in the *Zacchini* concerned "the strongest case for a 'right of publicity,'" because it did not involve the "appropriation of an entertainer's reputation to enhance the attractiveness of a commercial product," but instead involved "the appropriation of the very activity by which the entertainer acquired his reputation in the first place." …

In the wake of *Zacchini*, courts began applying a balancing inquiry to resolve cases where a right of publicity claim collided with First Amendment protections. While early cases approached the analysis from an ad hoc perspective, *see, e.g., Guglielmi v. Spelling-Goldberg Prods.*, 25 Cal.3d 860, 160 Cal.Rptr. 352, 603 P.2d 454 (1979) (en banc), courts eventually began developing standardized balancing frameworks. Consequently, we now turn our attention to more standardized balancing tests to see whether any of them offer a particularly compelling methodology for resolving the case at hand and similar disputes.[20]

2. The Modern Balancing Tests

Following *Zacchini*, courts began developing more systematized balancing tests for resolving conflicts between the right of publicity and the First Amendment. Of these, three tests are of particular note: the commercial-interest-based Predominant Use Test, the trademark-based *Rogers* Test, and the copyright-based Transformative Use Test. The *Rogers* and Transformative Use tests are the most well-established, while the Predominant Use Test is addressed below only because Appellant argues in favor of its adoption. We consider each test in turn, looking at its origins, scope of application, and possible limitations. For the reasons discussed below, we adopt the Transformative Use Test as being the most appropriate balancing test to be applied here.

---

20. We reject as inapplicable in this case the suggestion that those who play organized sports are not significantly damaged by appropriation of their likeness because "players are rewarded, and handsomely, too, for their participation in games and can earn additional large sums from endorsement and sponsorship arrangements." *C.B.C. Distrib. & Mktg., Inc. v. Major League Baseball Advanced Media, L.P.*, 505 F.3d 818, 824 (8th Cir.2007) (discussing Major League Baseball players); *see also, e.g., Cardtoons, L.C. v. Major League Baseball Players Ass'n*, 95 F.3d 959, 974 (10th Cir.1996) ("[T]he additional inducement for achievement produced by publicity rights are often inconsequential because most celebrities with valuable commercial identities are already handsomely compensated."). If anything, the policy considerations in this case weigh in *favor* of Appellant. As we have already noted, intercollegiate athletes are forbidden from capitalizing on their fame while in school. Moreover, the NCAA most recently estimated that "[l]ess than one in 100, or 1.6 percent, of NCAA senior football players will get drafted by a National Football League (NFL) team." NCAA, Estimated Probability of Competing in Athletics Beyond the High School Interscholastic Level, available at http://www.ncaa.org/wps/wcm/connect/public/ncaa/pdfs/2012/estimated+probability+of+competing+in +athletics+beyond+the+high+school+interscholastic+level. Despite all of his achievements, it should be noted that Ryan Hart was among the roughly ninety-nine percent who were not drafted after graduation.

a. Predominant Use Test

Appellant urges us to adopt the Predominant Use Test, which first appeared in *Doe v. TCI Cablevision*, 110 S.W.3d 363 (Mo.2003) (en banc), a case that considered a hockey player's right of publicity claim against a comic book publishing company. In *TCI*, Anthony "Tony" Twist, a hockey player, brought suit against a number of individuals and entities involved in producing and publishing the *Spawn* comic book series after the introduction of a villainous character named Anthony "Tony Twist" Twistelli.

In balancing Twist's property interests in his own name and identity against the First Amendment interests of the comic book creators, the *TCI* court rejected both the Transformative Use and *Rogers* tests, noting that they gave "too little consideration to the fact that many uses of a person's name and identity have both expressive and commercial components." The Supreme Court of Missouri considered both tests to be too rigid, noting that they operated "to preclude a cause of action whenever the use of the name and identity is in any way expressive, regardless of its commercial exploitation." The court instead applied what it called a "sort of predominant use test":

> If a product is being sold that predominantly exploits the commercial value of an individual's identity, that product should be held to violate the right of publicity and not be protected by the First Amendment, even if there is some 'expressive' content in it that might qualify as 'speech' in other circumstances. If, on the other hand, the predominant purpose of the product is to make an expressive comment on or about a celebrity, the expressive values could be given greater weight.

Id. (quoting Mark S. Lee, *Agents of Chaos: Judicial Confusion in Defining the Right of Publicity-Free Speech Interface*, 23 LOY. L.A. ENT. L. REV.V. 471, 500 (2003)). The *TCI* court considered this to be a "more balanced balancing test [particularly for] cases where speech is both expressive and commercial." After applying the test, the court ruled for Twist, holding that "the metaphorical reference to Twist, though a literary device, has very little literary value compared to its commercial value."

We decline Appellant's invitation to adopt this test. By our reading, the Predominant Use Test is subjective at best, arbitrary at worst, and in either case calls upon judges to act as both impartial jurists and discerning art critics. These two roles cannot co-exist. Indeed, Appellant suggests that pursuant to this test we must evaluate "what value [Appellee is] adding to the First Amendment expressiveness [of *NCAA Football*] by appropriating the commercially valuable likeness?" Since "[t]he game would have the exact same level of First Amendment expressiveness if [Appellee] didn't appropriate Mr. Hart's likeness," Appellant urges us to find that *NCAA Football* fails the Predominant Use Test and therefore is not shielded by the First Amendment. Such reasoning, however, leads down a dangerous and rightly-shunned road: adopting Appellant's suggested analysis would be tantamount to admitting that it is proper for courts to analyze select elements of a work to determine how much they contribute to the entire work's expressiveness. Moreover, as a necessary (and insidious) consequence, the Appellant's approach would suppose that there exists a broad range of seemingly expressive speech that has no First Amendment value.

Appellee rightly argues that the Predominant Use Test is antithetical to our First Amendment precedent, and we likewise reject the Test. We instead turn our attention to the *Rogers* Test, which was proposed by Appellee and which draws its inspiration from trademark law.

b. The *Rogers* Test

The *Rogers* Test looks to the relationship between the celebrity image and the work as a whole.[21] As the following discussion demonstrates, however, adopting this test would potentially immunize a broad swath of tortious activity. We therefore reject the *Rogers* Test as inapposite in the instant case....

Various commentators have noted that right of publicity claims—at least those that address the use of a person's name or image in an advertisement—are akin to trademark claims because in both instances courts must balance the interests in protecting the relevant property right against the interest in free expression. It is little wonder, then, that the inquiry championed by Appellee originated in a case that also focused upon alleged violations of the trademark-specific Lanham Act. *Rogers v. Grimaldi,* 875 F.2d 994 (2d Cir.1989).

In that case, Ginger Rogers brought suit against the producers and distributors of *Ginger and Fred,* a film that was alleged to infringe on Rogers' right of publicity and confuse consumers in violation of the Act. (Despite its title, the film was not about either Ginger Rogers or Fred Astaire.) In analyzing the right of publicity claim under Oregon law, the Second Circuit noted Oregon's "concern for the protection of free expression," and held that Oregon would not "permit the right of publicity to bar the use of a celebrity's name in a movie title unless the title was wholly unrelated to the movie or was simply a disguised commercial advertisement for the sale of goods or services." *Id.* at 1004 (internal quotation marks omitted). After applying this test, the *Rogers* court concluded that the right of publicity claim merited dismissal because "the title 'Ginger and Fred' is clearly related to the content of the movie and is not a disguised advertisement for the sale of goods and services or a collateral commercial product."

But while the test, as articulated in *Rogers,* arguably applied only to the use of celebrity identity in a work's title, Appellee suggests that the test can—and should—be applied more broadly....

Ultimately, we find that the *Rogers* Test does not present the proper analytical approach for cases such as the one at bar. While the Test may have a use in trademark-like right of publicity cases, it is inapposite here. We are concerned that this test is a blunt instrument, unfit for widespread application in cases that require a carefully calibrated balancing of two fundamental protections: the right of free expression and the right to control, manage, and profit from one's own identity.... [T]he right of publicity is broader and, by extension, protects a greater swath of property interests. Thus, it would be unwise for us to adopt a test that hews so closely to traditional trademark principles. Instead, we need a broader, more nuanced test, which helps balance the interests at issue in cases such as the one at bar. The final test—the Transformative Use Test—provides just such an approach.

c. The Transformative Use Test

Looking to intellectual property law for guidance on how to balance property interests against the First Amendment has merit. We need only shift our gaze away from trademark, to the broader vista of copyright law. Thus, we come to the case of *Comedy III Prods., Inc. v. Gary Saderup, Inc.,* which imported the concept of "transformative" use from copyright law into the right of publicity context. 25 Cal.4th 387 (2001). This con-

---

21. The various cases and scholarly sources refer to this test in three different ways: the Relatedness Test, the Restatement Test, and the Rogers Test. The "Relatedness" moniker should be self-explanatory even at this early point in our discussion; the propriety of the other two names will become clear shortly. For our purposes, we will refer to the test as the Rogers Test.

cept lies at the core of a test that both Appellant and Appellee agree is applicable to this case: the Transformative Use Test.

i. Genesis of the Transformative Use Test

The Transformative Use Test was first articulated by the Supreme Court of California in *Comedy III*. That case concerned an artist's production and sale of t-shirts and prints bearing a charcoal drawing of the Three Stooges. The California court determined that while "[t]he right of publicity is often invoked in the context of commercial speech," it could also apply in instances where the speech is merely expressive. *Id.*, 106 Cal.Rptr.2d 126. The court also noted, however, that when addressing expressive speech, "the very importance of celebrities in society means that the right of publicity has the potential of censoring significant expression by suppressing alternative versions of celebrity images that are iconoclastic, irreverent or otherwise attempt to redefine the celebrity's meaning." Thus, while the "the right of publicity cannot, consistent with the First Amendment, be a right to control the celebrity's image by censoring disagreeable portrayals," *id.*, the right, like copyright, nonetheless offers protection to a form of intellectual property that society deems to have social utility.

After briefly considering whether to import the "fair use" analysis from copyright, the *Comedy III* court decided that only the first fair use factor, "the purpose and character of the use," was appropriate. *Id.*, 106 Cal.Rptr.2d 126, 21 P.3d at 808. Specifically, the *Comedy III* court found persuasive the Supreme Court's holding in *Campbell v. Acuff-Rose Music, Inc.* that

> the central purpose of the inquiry into this fair use factor 'is to see ... whether the new work merely "supercede[s] the objects" of the original creation, or instead adds something new, with a further purpose or different character, altering the first with new expression, meaning, or message; it asks, in other words, whether and to what extent the new work is "*transformative.*"

Id. (emphasis added) (citing *Campbell v. Acuff-Rose Music, Inc.*, 510 U.S. 569, 579 (1994)).

Going further, the court explained that works containing "significant transformative elements" are less likely to interfere with the economic interests implicated by the right of publicity. For example, "works of parody or other distortions of the celebrity figure are not, from the celebrity fan's viewpoint, good substitutes for conventional depictions of the celebrity and therefore do not generally threaten markets for celebrity memorabilia that the right of publicity is designed to protect." *Id.* The court was also careful to emphasize that "the transformative elements or creative contributions" in a work may include — under the right circumstances — factual reporting, fictionalized portrayal, heavy-handed lampooning, and subtle social criticism. *Id.*, ("The inquiry is in a sense more quantitative than qualitative, asking whether the literal and imitative or the creative elements predominate in the work.").

Restating its newly-articulated test, the Supreme Court of California held that the balance between the right of publicity and First Amendment interests turns on

> [w]hether the celebrity likeness is one of the "raw materials" from which an original work is synthesized, or whether the depiction or imitation of the celebrity is the very sum and substance of the work in question. We ask, in other words, *whether the product containing a celebrity's likeness is so transformed that it has become primarily the defendant's own expression rather than the celebrity's likeness.* And when we use the word "expression," we mean expression of something other than the likeness of the celebrity.

Id. (emphasis added).

Applying this test, the court concluded that charcoal portraits of the Three Stooges did violate the Stooges' rights of publicity, holding that the court could "discern no significant transformative or creative contribution" and that "the marketability and economic value of [the work] derives primarily from the fame of the celebrities depicted."

ii. Application of the Transformative Use Test

Given its relative recency, few courts have applied the Transformative Use Test, and consequently there is not a significant body of case law related to its application. Nonetheless, a handful of cases bear mention as they help frame our inquiry.

In 2003, the Supreme Court of California revisited the Transformative Use Test when two musicians, Johnny and Edgar Winter, who both possessed long white hair and albino features, brought suit against a comic book company over images of two villainous half-man, half-worm creatures, both with long white hair and albino features, named Johnny and Edgar Autumn. *Winter v. DC Comics,* 30 Cal.4th 881 (2003). As the brothers' right of publicity claims necessarily implicated DC Comics' First Amendment rights, the *Winter* court looked to the Transformative Use Test. In summarizing the test, the court explained that "[a]n artist depicting a celebrity must contribute something more than a 'merely trivial' variation, [but must create] something recognizably 'his own,' in order to qualify for legal protection." *Id.*, 69 P.3d at 478 (alteration in original) (quoting *Comedy III,* 21 P.3d at 810–11). Thus, in applying the test, the *Winter* court held that

> [a]lthough the fictional characters Johnny and Edgar Autumn are less-than-subtle evocations of Johnny and Edgar Winter, the books do not depict plaintiffs literally. Instead, plaintiffs are merely part of the raw materials from which the comic books were synthesized. To the extent the drawings of the Autumn brothers resemble plaintiffs at all, they are distorted for purposes of lampoon, parody, or caricature. And the Autumn brothers are but cartoon characters — half-human and half-worm — in a larger story, which is itself quite expressive.

Id., 69 P.3d at 479. The court therefore found that "fans who want to purchase pictures of [the Winter brothers] would find the drawing of the Autumn brothers unsatisfactory as a substitute for conventional depictions." Consequently, the court rejected the brothers' claims for a right of publicity violation.

Also in 2003, the Sixth Circuit decided *ETW,* a case focusing on a photograph of Tiger Woods set among a collage of other, golf-related photographs. As we previously noted, while *ETW* mentioned both the *Rogers* case and the Restatement (Third) of Unfair Competition, the test it ultimately applied was a combination of an ad-hoc approach and the Transformative Use Test. *See ETW,* 332 F.3d at 937–38. In holding that the collage "contain[ed] significant transformative elements," *id.* at 938, the court compared it to the Three Stooges portraits from *Comedy III,* and noted that the collage "does not capitalize solely on a literal depiction of Woods." *Id.* Instead, the "work consists of a collage of images in addition to Woods's image which are combined to describe, in artistic form, a historic event in sports history and to convey a message about the significance of Woods's achievement in that event." ...

iii. The Transformative Use Test and Video Games

In mid-2006, the California Court of Appeal decided *Kirby v. Sega of America, Inc.,* 144 Cal.App.4th 47 (2006), which addressed a musician's right of publicity claim against a video game company. Specifically, the musician (Kierin Kirby) had claimed that Sega misappropriated her likeness and signature phrases for purposes of creating the character of Ulala, a reporter in the far flung future. In applying the Transformative Use Test, the court noted that not only did Kirby's signature phrases included "ooh la la" but that both she and the videogame character would often use phrases like "groove," "meow," "dee-lish," and "I won't give up." *Id.* at 613. The court also found similarities in appearance between Kirby and Ulala, based on hair style and clothing choice. *Id.* At the same time, the court held that differences between the two did exist—both in appearance and movement—and that Ulala was not a mere digital recreation of Kirby. *Id.* Thus, the court concluded that Ulala passed the Transformative Use Test, rejecting Kirby's argument that the differences between her and the character added no additional meaning or message to the work. *Id.* at 616–17 ("A work is transformative if it adds 'new expression.' That expression alone is sufficient; it need not convey any 'meaning or message.'"); *see also id.* at 617 ("[A]ny imitation of Kirby's likeness or identity in Ulala is not the sum and substance of that character.").

Several years later, in early 2011, the California courts again confronted the right of publicity as it related to video games in *No Doubt v. Activision Publishing, Inc.,* 192 Cal.App.4th 1018, 122 Cal.Rptr.3d 397 (2011). The case centered on *Band Hero,* a game that allows player to "simulate performing in a rock band in time with popular songs" by selecting digital avatars to represent them in an in-game band. *Id.* at 401. Some of the avatars were digital recreations of real-life musicians, including members of the band No Doubt. After a contract dispute broke off relations between the band and the company, No Doubt sued, claiming a violation of their rights of publicity. The California Court of Appeal applied the Transformative Use Test.

The *No Doubt* court began by noting that "in stark contrast to the 'fanciful creative characters' in *Winter* and *Kirby,*" the No Doubt avatars could not be altered by players and thus remained "at all times immutable images of the real celebrity musicians." *Id.* at 410. But this fact, by itself, did not end the court's inquiry since "even literal reproductions of celebrities can be 'transformed' into expressive works based on the context into which the celebrity image is placed." *Id.* (citing *Comedy III,* 106 Cal.Rptr.2d 126, 21 P.3d at 811). Looking to the context of the *Band Hero* game, the court found that "no matter what else occurs in the game *during the depiction of the No Doubt avatars,* the avatars perform rock songs, the same activity by which the band achieved and maintains its fame." *Id.* at 410–11 (emphasis added). The court explained:

> [T]he avatars perform [rock] songs as literal recreations of the band members. That the avatars can be manipulated to perform at fanciful venues including outer space or to sing songs the real band would object to singing, or that the avatars appear in the context of a videogame *that contains many other creative elements,* does not transform the avatars into anything other than the exact depictions of No Doubt's members doing exactly what they do as celebrities.

Id. at 411 (emphasis added). As a final step in its analysis, the court noted that Activision's use of highly realistic digital depictions of No Doubt was motivated by a desire to capitalize on the band's fan-base, "because it encourages [fans] to purchase the game so as *to perform as, or alongside, the members of No Doubt." Id.* (emphasis added). Given all this, the court concluded that Activision's use of No Doubt's likenesses did infringe on the band's rights of publicity. *Id.* at 411–12.

iv. Analysis of the Transformative Use Test

Like the Predominant Use and *Rogers* tests, the Transformative Use Test aims to balance the interest protected by the right of publicity against those interests preserved by the First Amendment. In our view, the Transformative Use Test appears to strike the best balance because it provides courts with a flexible—yet uniformly applicable—analytical framework. Specifically, the Transformative Use Test seems to excel precisely where the other two tests falter. Unlike the *Rogers* Test, the Transformative Use Test maintains a singular focus on whether the work sufficiently transforms the celebrity's identity or likeness, thereby allowing courts to account for the fact that misappropriation can occur in any market segment, including those related to the celebrity.

On the other hand, unlike the Predominant Use Test, applying the Transformative Use Test requires a more circumscribed inquiry, focusing on the specific aspects of a work that speak to whether it was merely created to exploit a celebrity's likeness. This test therefore recognizes that if First Amendment protections are to mean anything in right of publicity claims, courts must *begin* by considering the extent to which a work is the creator's own expression.

Additionally, the Transformative Use Test best comports with the cautionary language present in various right of publicity cases. Specifically, we believe that an initial focus on the creative aspects of a work helps address our own concern from *Facenda,* where we noted that "courts must circumscribe the right of publicity." *Facenda,* 542 F.3d at 1032. As our discussion below demonstrates, the Transformative Use Test effectively restricts right of publicity claims to a very narrow universe of expressive works. Moreover, we believe that the Transformative Use Test best exemplifies the methodology suggested by Justice Powell's dissent in *Zacchini:*

> Rather than begin with a quantitative analysis of the performer's behavior — is this or is this not his entire act? — we should direct initial attention to the actions of the news media: what use did the station make of the film footage? When a film is used, as here, for a routine portion of a regular news program, I would hold that the First Amendment protects the station from a "right of publicity" or "appropriation" suit, absent a strong showing by the plaintiff that the news broadcast was a subterfuge or cover for private or commercial exploitation.

Zacchini, 433 U.S. at 581 (Powell, J., dissenting). Consistent with Justice Powell's argument, the Transformative Use Test begins by asking "what use did the [defendant] make of the [celebrity identity]?" . . .

C. Application

In applying the Transformative Use Test to the instant case, we must determine whether Appellant's identity is sufficiently transformed in *NCAA Football.* As we mentioned earlier, we use the term "identity" to encompass not only Appellant's likeness, but also his biographical information. It is the combination of these two parts — which, when combined, identify the digital avatar as an in-game recreation of Appellant — that must be sufficiently transformed.

Having thus cabined our inquiry to the appropriate form of Appellant's identity, we note that — based on the combination of both the digital avatar's appearance and the biographical and identifying information — the digital avatar does closely resemble the genuine article. Not only does the digital avatar match Appellant in terms of hair color, hair style and skin tone, but the avatar's accessories mimic those worn by Appellant during his time as a Rutgers player. The information, as has already been noted, also accurately tracks Appellant's vital and biographical details. And while the inexorable march of technological progress may make some of the graphics in earlier editions of *NCAA Football* look dated or overly-computerized, we do not believe that video game graphics must reach (let alone cross) the uncanny valley to support a right of publicity claim. If we are to find some transformative element, we must look somewhere other than just the in-game digital recreation of Appellant. Cases such as *ETW* and *No Doubt,* both of which address realistic digital depictions of celebrities, point to the next step in our analysis: context.

Considering the context within which the digital avatar exists—effectively, looking at how Appellant's identity is "incorporated into and transformed by" NCAA Football,—provides little support for Appellee's arguments. The digital Ryan Hart does what the actual Ryan Hart did while at Rutgers: he plays college football, in digital recreations of college football stadiums, filled with all the trappings of a college football game. This is not transformative; the various digitized sights and sounds in the video game do not alter or transform the Appellant's identity in a significant way. *See No Doubt,* 122 Cal.Rptr.3d at 410–11 ("[N]o matter what else occurs in the game during the depiction of the No Doubt avatars, the avatars perform rock songs, the same activity by which the band achieved and maintains its fame."). Indeed, the lack of transformative context is even more pronounced here than in *No Doubt,* where members of the band could perform and sing in outer space.

Even here, however, our inquiry is not at an end. For as much as the digital representation and context evince no meaningful transformative element in *NCAA Football,* a third avatar-specific element is also present: the users' ability to alter the avatar's appearance. This distinguishing factor ensures that we cannot dispose of this case as simply as the court in *No Doubt.* Indeed, the ability for users to change the avatar accounted, in large part, for the District Court's deciding that *NCAA Football* satisfied the Transformative Use Test. We must therefore consider to what extent the ability to alter a digital avatar represents a transformative use of Appellant's identity.

At the outset, we note that the mere presence of this feature, without more, cannot satisfy the Transformative Use Test. True, interactivity is the basis upon which First Amendment protection is granted to video games in the first instance. However, the balancing test in right of publicity cases does not look to whether a particular work *loses* First Amendment protection. Rather, the balancing inquiry looks to see whether the interests protected by the right of publicity are sufficient to *surmount* the already-existing First Amendment protections. As *Zacchini* demonstrated, the right of publicity can triumph even when an essential element for First Amendment protection is present. In that case, the human cannonball act was broadcast *as part of the newscast.* To hold, therefore, that a video game should satisfy the Transformative Use Test simply because it includes a particular interactive feature would lead to improper results. Interactivity cannot be an end onto itself.

Moreover, we are wary of converting the ability to alter a digital avatar from mere feature to talisman, thereby opening the door to cynical abuse. If the mere presence of the feature were enough, video game companies could commit the most blatant acts of misappropriation only to absolve themselves by including a feature that allows users to modify the digital likenesses. We cannot accept that such an outcome would adequately balance the interests in right of publicity cases. As one amicus brief noted:

> [U]nder [Appellee's] application of the transformative test [sic], presumably no infringement would be found if individuals such as the Dalai Lama and the Pope were placed within a violent "shoot-em-up" game, so long as the game include[d] a "mechanism" by which the user could manipulate their characteristics.

With this concern in mind, therefore, we consider whether the type and extent of interactivity permitted is sufficient to transform the Appellant's likeness into the Appellee's own expression. We hold that it does not.

In *NCAA Football,* Appellee seeks to create a realistic depiction of college football for the users. Part of this realism involves generating realistic representations of the various college teams—which includes the realistic representations of the players. Like Activision in *No Doubt,* therefore, Appellee seeks to capitalize on the respective fan bases for the various teams and players. Indeed, as the District Court recognized, "it seems ludicrous to question whether video game consumers enjoy and, as a result, purchase more EA-produced video games as a result of the heightened realism associated with actual players." *Hart*, 808 F.Supp.2d at 783 (quoting James J.S. Holmes & Kanika D. Corley, *Defining Liability for Likeness of Athlete Avatars in Video Games*, L.A. Law., May 2011, at 17, 20). Moreover, the realism of the games — including the depictions and recreations of the players — appeals not just to home-team fans, but to bitter rivals as well. Games such as *NCAA Football* permit users to recreate the setting of a bitter defeat and, in effect, achieve some cathartic readjustment of history; realistic depictions of the players are a necessary element to this. That Appellant's likeness is the *default* position only serves to support our conclusion that realistic depictions of the players are the "sum and substance" of these digital facsimiles. Given that Appellant's unaltered likeness is central to the core of the game experience, we are disinclined to credit users' ability to alter the digital avatars in our application of the Transformative Use Test to this case....

In an attempt to salvage its argument, Appellee suggests that *other* creative elements of *NCAA Football,* which do not affect Appellant's digital avatar, are so numerous that the videogames should be considered transformative. We believe this to be an improper inquiry.... [W]hile we recognize the creative energies necessary for crafting the various elements of *NCAA Football* that are not tied directly to reality, we hold that they have no legal significance in our instant decision.

To hold otherwise could have deleterious consequences for the state of the law. Acts of blatant misappropriation would count for nothing so long as the larger work, on balance, contained highly creative elements in great abundance. This concern is particularly acute in the case of media that lend themselves to easy partition such as video games. It cannot be that content creators escape liability for a work that uses a celebrity's unaltered identity in one section but that contains a wholly fanciful creation in the other, larger section.

For these reasons, we hold that the broad application of the Transformative Use Test represents an inappropriate application of the standard. Consequently, we shall not credit elements of *NCAA Football* that do not, in some way, affect the use or meaning of Appellant's identity....

IV. Conclusion

We therefore hold that the *NCAA Football 2004, 2005* and *2006* games at issue in this case do not sufficiently transform Appellant's identity to escape the right of publicity claim and hold that the District Court erred in granted summary judgment in favor of Appellee....

AMBRO, Circuit Judge, dissenting.

... The Transformative Use Test gives First Amendment immunity where, in an expressive work, an individual's likeness has been creatively adapted in some way. Correctly applied, this test strikes an appropriate balance between countervailing rights — the publicity interest in protecting an individual's right to benefit financially when others use his identifiable persona for their own commercial benefit versus the First Amendment interest in insulating from liability a creator's decision to interweave real-life figures into its expressive work.

My colleagues limit effectively their transformative inquiry to Hart's identity alone, disregarding other features of the work. This approach, I believe, does not find support in the cases on which they rely. Further, my colleagues penalize EA for the realism and financial success of *NCAA Football,* a position I find difficult to reconcile with First Amendment protections traditionally afforded to true-to-life depictions of real figures and works produced for profit. Because I conclude that the Transformative Use Test protects EA's use of Hart's likeness in *NCAA Football,* I respectfully dissent....

The Transformative Use Test I support would prevent commercial exploitation of an individual's likeness where the work at issue lacks creative contribution that transforms that likeness in a meaningful way. I sympathize with the position of Hart and other similarly situated college football players, and understand why they feel it is fair to share in the significant profits produced by including their avatar likenesses into EA's commercially successful video game franchise. I nonetheless remain convinced that the creative components of *NCAA Football* contain sufficient expressive transformation to merit First Amendment protection. Thus I respectfully dissent, and would affirm the District Court's grant of summary judgment in favor of EA.

In re NCAA Student-Athlete Name & Likeness Licensing Litigation
724 F.3d 1268 (2013)

Video games are entitled to the full protections of the First Amendment, because "[l]ike the protected books, plays, and movies that preceded them, video games communicate ideas — and even social messages — through many familiar literary devices (such as characters, dialogue, plot, and music) and through features distinctive to the medium (such as the player's interaction with the virtual world)." *Brown v. Entm't Merchs. Ass'n,* ___ U.S. ___, 131 S.Ct. 2729, 2733, 180 L.Ed.2d 708 (2011). Such rights are not absolute, and states may recognize the right of publicity to a degree consistent with the First Amendment. *Zacchini v. Scripps-Howard Broad. Co.,* 433 U.S. 562, 574–75, 97 S.Ct. 2849, 53 L.Ed.2d 965 (1977). In this case, we must balance the right of publicity of a former college football player against the asserted First Amendment right of a video game developer to use his likeness in its expressive works.

The district court concluded that the game developer, Electronic Arts ("EA"), had no First Amendment defense against the right-of-publicity claims of the football player, Samuel Keller. We affirm. Under the "transformative use" test developed by the California Supreme Court, EA's use does not qualify for First Amendment protection as a matter of law because it literally recreates Keller in the very setting in which he has achieved renown. The other First Amendment defenses asserted by EA do not defeat Keller's claims either.

Samuel Keller was the starting quarterback for Arizona State University in 2005 before he transferred to the University of Nebraska, where he played during the 2007 season. EA is the producer of the *NCAA Football* series of video games, which allow users to control avatars representing college football players as those avatars participate in simulated games. In *NCAA Football,* EA seeks to replicate each school's entire team as accurately as possible....

EA's game differs from reality in that EA omits the players' names on their jerseys and assigns each player a home town that is different from the actual player's home town. However, users of the video game may upload rosters of names obtained from third parties so that the names do appear on the jerseys....

[Keller's Right of Publicity Claim]

The California Supreme Court formulated the transformative use defense in *Comedy III Productions, Inc. v. Gary Saderup, Inc.,* 25 Cal.4th 387 (2001). The defense is "a balancing test between the First Amendment and the right of publicity based on whether the work in question adds significant creative elements so as to be transformed into something more than a mere celebrity likeness or imitation." The California Supreme Court explained that "when a work contains significant transformative elements, it is not only especially worthy of First Amendment protection, but it is also less likely to interfere with the economic interest protected by the right of publicity." The court rejected the wholesale importation of the copyright "fair use" defense into right-of-publicity claims, but recognized that some aspects of that defense are "particularly pertinent."

Comedy III gives us at least five factors to consider in determining whether a work is sufficiently transformative to obtain First Amendment protection. First, if "the celebrity likeness is one of the 'raw materials' from which an original work is synthesized," it is more likely to be transformative than if "the depiction or imitation of the celebrity is the very sum and substance of the work in question." Second, the work is protected if it is "primarily the defendant's own expression"—as long as that expression is "something other than the likeness of the celebrity." This factor requires an examination of whether a likely purchaser's primary motivation is to buy a reproduction of the celebrity, or to buy the expressive work of that artist. Third, to avoid making judgments concerning "the quality of the artistic contribution," a court should conduct an inquiry "more quantitative than qualitative" and ask "whether the literal and imitative or the creative elements predominate in the work." Fourth, the California Supreme Court indicated that "a subsidiary inquiry" would be useful in close cases: whether "the marketability and economic value of the challenged work derive primarily from the fame of the celebrity depicted." Lastly, the court indicated that "when an artist's skill and talent is manifestly subordinated to the overall goal of creating a conventional portrait of a celebrity so as to commercially exploit his or her fame," the work is not transformative.

We have explained that "[o]nly if [a defendant] is entitled to the [transformative] defense *as a matter of law* can it prevail on its motion to strike," because the California Supreme Court "envisioned the application of the defense as a question of fact." *Hilton [v. Hallmark Cards, 599 F.3d 894,910 (9th Cir.2009)]*. As a result, EA "is only entitled to the defense as a matter of law if no trier of fact could reasonably conclude that the [game] [i]s not transformative."

California courts have applied the transformative use test in relevant situations in four cases. First, in *Comedy III* itself, the California Supreme Court applied the test to T-shirts and lithographs bearing a likeness of The Three Stooges and concluded that it could "discern no significant transformative or creative contribution." The court reasoned that the artist's "undeniable skill is manifestly subordinated to the overall goal of creating literal, conventional depictions of The Three Stooges so as to exploit their fame." "[W]ere we to decide that [the artist's] depictions were protected by the First Amendment," the court continued, "we cannot perceive how the right of publicity would remain a viable right other than in cases of falsified celebrity endorsements."

Second, in *Winter v. DC Comics,* the California Supreme Court applied the test to comic books containing characters Johnny and Edgar Autumn, "depicted as villainous half-worm, half-human offspring" but evoking two famous brothers, rockers Johnny and Edgar Winter. 30 Cal.4th 881, 134 Cal.Rptr.2d 634, 69 P.3d 473, 476 (2003). The court held that "the comic books are transformative and entitled to First Amendment protection." It reasoned that the comic books "are not just conventional depictions of plaintiffs but contain significant expressive content other than plaintiffs' mere likenesses." "To the extent the drawings of the Autumn brothers resemble plaintiffs at all, they are distorted for purposes of lampoon, parody, or caricature." Importantly, the court relied on the fact that the brothers "are but cartoon characters … in a larger story, which is itself quite expressive."

Third, in *Kirby v. Sega of America, Inc.,* the California Court of Appeal applied the transformative use test to a video game in which the user controls the dancing of "Ulala," a reporter from outer space allegedly based on singer Kierin Kirby, whose "'signature' lyrical expression … is 'ooh la la.'" 144 Cal.App.4th 47, 50 Cal.Rptr.3d 607, 609–10 (2006). The court held that "Ulala is more than a mere likeness or literal depiction of Kirby," pointing to Ulala's "extremely tall, slender computer-generated physique," her "hairstyle and primary costume," her dance moves, and her role as "a space-age reporter in the 25th century," all of which were "unlike any public depiction of Kirby." "As in *Winter,* Ulala is a 'fanciful, creative character' who exists in the context of a unique and expressive video game."

Finally, in *No Doubt v. Activision Publishing, Inc.,* the California Court of Appeal addressed Activision's *Band Hero* video game. 192 Cal.App.4th 1018, 122 Cal.Rptr.3d 397, 400 (2011), *petition for review denied,* 2011 Cal. LEXIS 6100 (Cal. June 8, 2011) (No. B223996). In *Band Hero,* users simulate performing in a rock band in time with popular songs. Users choose from a number of avatars, some of which represent actual rock stars, including the members of the rock band No Doubt. Activision licensed No Doubt's likeness, but allegedly exceeded the scope of the license by permitting users to manipulate the No Doubt avatars to play any song in the game, solo or with members of other bands, and even to alter the avatars' voices. The court held that No Doubt's right of publicity prevailed despite Activision's First Amendment defense because the game was not "transformative" under the *Comedy III* test. It reasoned that the video game characters were "literal recreations of the band members," doing "the same activity by which the band achieved and maintains its fame." According to the court, the fact "that the avatars appear in the context of a videogame that contains many other creative elements[ ] does not transform the avatars into anything other than exact depictions of No Doubt's members doing exactly what they do as celebrities." The court concluded that "the expressive elements of the game remain manifestly subordinated to the overall goal of creating a conventional portrait of No Doubt so as to commercially exploit its fame."

We have also had occasion to apply the transformative use test. In *Hilton v. Hallmark Cards,* we applied the test to a birthday card depicting Paris Hilton in a manner reminiscent of an episode of Hilton's reality show *The Simple Life.* 599 F.3d at 899. We observed some differences between the episode and the card, but noted that "the basic setting is the same: we see Paris Hilton, born to privilege, working as a waitress." We reasoned that "[w]hen we compare Hallmark's card to the video game in *Kirby,* which transported a 1990s singer (catchphrases and all) into the 25th century and transmogrified her into a space-age reporter, … the card falls far short of the level of new expression added in the video game." As a result, we concluded that "there is enough doubt as to whether Hallmark's card is transformative under our case law that we cannot say Hallmark is entitled to the defense as a matter of law."

With these cases in mind as guidance, we conclude that EA's use of Keller's likeness does not contain significant transformative elements such that EA is entitled to the defense as a matter of law. The facts of *No Doubt* are very similar to those here. EA is alleged to have replicated Keller's physical characteristics in *NCAA Football,* just as the members of No Doubt are realistically portrayed in *Band Hero.* Here, as in *Band Hero,* users manipulate the characters in the performance of the same activity for which they are known in real life—playing football in this case, and performing in a rock band in *Band Hero.* The context in which the activity occurs is also similarly realistic—real venues in *Band Hero* and realistic depictions of actual football stadiums in *NCAA Football.* As the district court found, Keller is represented as "what he was: the starting quarterback for Arizona State" and Nebraska, and "the game's setting is identical to where the public found [Keller] during his collegiate career: on the football field."

EA argues that the district court erred in focusing primarily on Keller's likeness and ignoring the transformative elements of the game as a whole. Judge Thomas, our dissenting colleague, suggests the same. We are unable to say that there was any error, particularly in light of *No Doubt*, which reasoned much the same as the district court in this case: "that the avatars appear in the context of a videogame that contains many other creative elements[ ] does not transform the avatars into anything other than exact depictions of No Doubt's members doing exactly what they do as celebrities." *No Doubt*, 122 Cal.Rptr.3d at 411. EA suggests that the fact that *NCAA Football* users can alter the characteristics of the avatars in the game is significant. Again, our dissenting colleague agrees. *See* Dissent at 1286–87. In *No Doubt*, the California Court of Appeal noted that *Band Hero* "d[id] not permit players to alter the No Doubt avatars in any respect." The court went on to say that the No Doubt avatars "remain at all times immutable images of the real celebrity musicians, in stark contrast to the 'fanciful, creative characters' in *Winter* and *Kirby*." *Id.* The court explained further:

> [I]t is the differences between *Kirby* and the instant case ... which are determinative. In *Kirby*, the pop singer was portrayed as an entirely new character — the space-age news reporter Ulala. In *Band Hero*, by contrast, no matter what else occurs in the game during the depiction of the No Doubt avatars, the avatars perform rock songs, the same activity by which the band achieved and maintains its fame. Moreover, the avatars perform those songs as literal recreations of the band members. That the avatars can be manipulated to perform at fanciful venues including outer space or to sing songs the real band would object to singing, or that the avatars appear in the context of a videogame that contains many other creative elements, does not transform the avatars into anything other than exact depictions of No Doubt's members doing exactly what they do as celebrities.

Id. at 410–11.

Judge Thomas says that "[t]he Court of Appeal cited character immutability as a chief factor distinguishing [*No Doubt*] from *Winter* and *Kirby*." Dissent at 1287. Though No Doubt certainly mentioned the immutability of the avatars, we do not read the California Court of Appeal's decision as turning on the inability of users to alter the avatars. The key contrast with *Winter* and *Kirby* was that in those games the public figures were transformed into "fanciful, creative characters" or "portrayed as ... entirely new character[s]." *No Doubt*, 122 Cal.Rptr.3d at 410. On this front, our case is clearly aligned with *No Doubt*, not with *Winter* and *Kirby*. We believe No Doubt offers a persuasive precedent that cannot be materially distinguished from Keller's case.

The Third Circuit came to the same conclusion in *Hart v. Electronic Arts, Inc.,* 717 F.3d 141 (3d Cir.2013). In *Hart*, EA faced a materially identical challenge under New Jersey right-of-publicity law, brought by former Rutgers quarterback Ryan Hart. Though the Third Circuit was tasked with interpreting New Jersey law, the court looked to the transformative use test developed in California. Applying the test, the court held that "the *NCAA Football* ... games at issue ... do not sufficiently transform [Hart]'s identity to escape the right of publicity claim," reversing the district court's grant of summary judgment to EA.

As we have, the Third Circuit considered the potentially transformative nature of the game as a whole, and the user's ability to alter avatar characteristics. Asserting that "the lack of transformative context is even more pronounced here than in *No Doubt*," and that "the ability to modify the avatar counts for little where the appeal of the game lies in users' ability to play as, or alongside [,] their preferred players or team," the Third Circuit agreed with us that these changes do not render the *NCAA Football* games sufficiently transformative to defeat a right-of-publicity claim.

Judge Ambro dissented in *Hart*, concluding that "the creative components of *NCAA Football* contain sufficient expressive transformation to merit First Amendment protection." But in critiquing the majority opinion, Judge Ambro disregarded *No Doubt* and *Kirby* because "they were not decided by the architect of the Transformative Use Test, the Supreme Court of California." He thus "d [id] not attempt to explain or distinguish the[se cases'] holdings except to note that [he] believe[s] *No Doubt*, which focused on individual depictions rather than the work in its entirety, was wrongly decided in light of the prior precedent in *Comedy III* and *Winter*." ... Like the majority in *Hart*, we rely substantially on *No Doubt*, and believe we are correct to do so.

Given that *NCAA Football* realistically portrays college football players in the context of college football games, the district court was correct in concluding that EA cannot prevail as a matter of law based on the transformative use defense at the anti-SLAPP stage. *Cf. Hilton*, 599 F.3d at 910–11.

EA urges us to adopt for right-of-publicity claims the broader First Amendment defense that we have previously adopted in the context of false endorsement claims under the Lanham Act: the *Rogers* test.

Rogers v. Grimaldi is a landmark Second Circuit case balancing First Amendment rights against claims under the Lanham Act. 875 F.2d 994 (2d Cir.1989). The case involved a suit brought by the famous performer Ginger Rogers against the producers and distributors of *Ginger and Fred*, a movie about two fictional Italian cabaret performers who imitated Rogers and her frequent performing partner Fred Astaire. *Id.* at 996–97. Rogers alleged both a violation of the Lanham Act for creating the false impression that she endorsed the film and infringement of her common law right of publicity. *Id.* at 997....

We first endorsed the *Rogers* test for Lanham Act claims involving artistic or expressive works in *Mattel, Inc. v. MCA Records, Inc.*, 296 F.3d 894, 902 (9th Cir.2002). We agreed that, in the context of artistic and literary titles, "[c]onsumers expect a title to communicate a message about the book or movie, but they do not expect it to identify the publisher or producer," and "adopt[ed] the *Rogers* standard as our own." *Id.* Then, in *E.S.S. Entertainment 2000, Inc. v. Rock Star Videos, Inc.*, we considered a claim by a strip club owner that video game maker Rock Star incorporated its club logo into the game's virtual depiction of East Los Angeles, violating the club's trademark right to that logo. 547 F.3d 1095, 1096–98 (9th Cir.2008). We held that Rock Star's use of the logo and trade dress was protected by the First Amendment and that it therefore could not be held liable under the Lanham Act. *Id.* at 1099–1101. In so doing, we extended the Rogers test slightly, noting that "[a]lthough this test traditionally applies to uses of a trademark in the title of an artistic work, there is no principled reason why it ought not also apply to the use of a trademark in the body of the work."

In this case, EA argues that we should extend this test, created to evaluate Lanham Act claims, to apply to right-of-publicity claims because it is "less prone to misinterpretation" and "more protective of free expression" than the transformative use defense. Although we acknowledge that there is some overlap between the transformative use test formulated by the California Supreme Court and the *Rogers* test, we disagree that the *Rogers* test should be imported wholesale for right-of-publicity claims. Our conclusion on this point is consistent with the Third Circuit's rejection of EA's identical argument in *Hart*. As the history and development of the *Rogers* test makes clear, it was designed to protect consumers from the risk of consumer confusion—the hallmark element of a Lanham Act claim.

The right of publicity, on the other hand, does not primarily seek to prevent consumer confusion. Rather, it primarily "protects a form of intellectual property [in one's person] that society deems to have some social utility." ...

California has developed two additional defenses aimed at protecting the reporting of factual information under state law. One of these defenses only applies to common law right-of-publicity claims while the other only applies to statutory right-of-publicity claims. *Montana v. San Jose Mercury News, Inc.,* 34 Cal.App.4th 790 (1995). Liability will not lie for common law right-of-publicity claims for the "publication of matters in the public interest." Similarly, liability will not lie for statutory right-of-publicity claims for the "use of a name, voice, signature, photograph, or likeness in connection with any news, public affairs, or sports broadcast or account, or any political campaign." Cal. Civ.Code § 3344(d). Although these defenses are based on First Amendment concerns, *Gill v. Hearst Publ'g Co.,* 40 Cal.2d 224, 253 P.2d 441, 443–44 (1953), they are not coextensive with the Federal Constitution, *New Kids on the Block v. News Am. Publ'g, Inc.,* 971 F.2d 302, 310 n. 10 (9th Cir.1992), and their application is thus a matter of state law.

EA argues that these defenses give it the right to "incorporate athletes' names, statistics, and other biographical information" into its expressive works, as the defenses were "designed to create 'extra breathing space' for the use of a person's name in connection with matters of public interest." Keller responds that the right of publicity yields to free use of a public figure's likeness only to the extent reasonably required to report information to the public or publish factual data, and that the defenses apply only to broadcasts or accounts of public affairs, not to EA's *NCAA Football* games, which do not contain or constitute such reporting about Keller.

California courts have generally analyzed the common law defense and the statutory defense separately, but it is clear that both defenses protect only the act of publishing or reporting.... EA is not publishing or reporting factual data. EA's video game is a means by which users can play their own virtual football games, not a means for obtaining information about real-world football games. Although EA has incorporated certain actual player information into the game (height, weight, etc.), its case is considerably weakened by its decision not to include the athletes' names along with their likenesses and statistical data. EA can hardly be considered to be "reporting" on Keller's career at Arizona State and Nebraska when it is not even using Keller's name in connection with his avatar in the game. Put simply, EA's interactive game is not a publication of facts about college football; it is a game, not a reference source. These state law defenses, therefore, do not apply.

Under California's transformative use defense, EA's use of the likenesses of college athletes like Samuel Keller in its video games is not, as a matter of law, protected by the First Amendment. We reject EA's suggestion to import the *Rogers* test into the right-of-publicity arena, and conclude that statelaw defenses for the reporting of information do not protect EA's use. AFFIRMED.

THOMAS, Circuit Judge, dissenting:

Because the creative and transformative elements of Electronic Arts' *NCAA Football* video game series predominate over the commercial use of the athletes' likenesses, the First Amendment protects EA from liability. Therefore, I respectfully dissent....

The five considerations articulated in *Comedy III,* and cited by the majority, are whether: (1) the celebrity likeness is one of the raw materials from which an original work is synthesized; (2) the work is primarily the defendant's own expression if the expression is something other than the likeness of the celebrity; (3) the literal and imitative or creative elements predominate in the work; (4) the marketability and economic value of the challenged work derives primarily from the fame of the celebrity depicted; and (5) an artist's skill and talent has been manifestly subordinated to the overall goal of creating a conventional portrait of a celebrity so as to commercially exploit the celebrity's fame. . . .

Although these considerations are often distilled as analytical factors, Justice Mosk was careful in *Comedy III* not to label them as such. Indeed, the focus of *Comedy III* is a more holistic examination of whether the transformative and creative elements of a particular work predominate over commercially based literal or imitative depictions. The distinction is critical, because excessive deconstruction of *Comedy III* can lead to misapplication of the test. And it is at this juncture that I must respectfully part ways with my colleagues in the majority.

The majority confines its inquiry to how a single athlete's likeness is represented in the video game, rather than examining the transformative and creative elements in the video game as a whole. In my view, this approach contradicts the holistic analysis required by the transformative use test. *See Hart v. Elec. Arts, Inc.,* 717 F.3d 141, 170–76 (3d Cir.2013) (Ambro, J., dissenting). The salient question is whether the entire work is transformative, and whether the transformative elements predominate, rather than whether an individual persona or image has been altered.

When EA's *NCAA Football* video game series is examined carefully, and put in proper context, I conclude that the creative and transformative elements of the games predominate over the commercial use of the likenesses of the athletes within the games. . . .

Notes and Questions

a. The saga of the NCAA litigation involving amateur players' rights of publicity continues as a class action. See *In re NCAA Student-Athlete Name & Likeness Licensing Litig.,* C 09-1967 CW, 2013 WL 5979327 (N.D. Cal. 2013) (order granting in part and denying in part, motion for class certification). Another consequence of the litigation is pressure on the NCAA to amend rules related to student athlete reimbursements and the ability of student athletes to earn income while maintaining athletic eligibility.

b. Would the *Keller* decision have the same outcome for use of players' name and likeness in television content? See *Accord Facenda v. N.F.L. Films, Inc.,* 542 F.3d 1007, 1031–32 (3d Cir. 2008) (sportscaster's breach of contract and right of publicity claims not preempted by copyright where sportscaster's contract allowed defendant to use sportscaster's voice recordings in context of sports broadcasts, not in context of television advertisements for video game). In *Dryer v. NFL,* 2010 U.S. Dist. LEXIS 24817 (D. Minn. Jan. 26, 2010), the district court has taken a much more sympathetic approach for the former players:

> Plaintiffs in this putative class action are former professional football players. They contend that Defendant National Football League ("NFL") is violating their common-law and statutory rights of publicity by using video footage from games in which they played as part of the NFL Films' promotional videos, such as the "History" series, which includes videos called "The Fabulous Fifties" and "Sensational 60s." There is no dispute that these videos are used to promote the NFL. In the course of that promotion, the NFL uses both the Plaintiffs' names and images of Plaintiffs from their playing days. . . . [F]or the purposes of this Motion ... the films at issue are commercial speech. Moreover, Plaintiffs have sufficiently established that the constitutional protection to be afforded the films may not outweigh Plaintiffs' interests in their own identities.

c. In contrast with *Dryer v. NFL*, earlier California decisions treated the somewhat promotional television content as non-commercial speech.

> Defendant Major League Baseball Properties, Inc. (MLBP), is a limited agent for each of the Clubs for certain purposes involving the use of the Clubs' trademarks. MLBP licenses the use of each Club's right to the game-related images of its current and former players. MLBP produces certain print and video publications including All-Star and World Series programs of its own.... Defendant The PHoenix Communications Group, Inc. (PHoenix), was authorized by MLBP to produce and distribute audiovisual programs containing game performances and related activities. For 13 years between 1985 and 1998, PHoenix produced certain television shows including: This Week in Baseball, Pennant Chase, and Major League Baseball Magazine, containing footage of earlier games. It also satisfied video footage requests made by third parties....

> The challenged uses involve statements of historical fact, descriptions of these facts or video depictions of them. Plaintiffs never suggest how Baseball's actions impair their economic interests. It appears equally likely that plaintiffs' marketability is enhanced by Baseball's conduct challenged here. Balancing plaintiffs' negligible economic interests against the public's enduring fascination with baseball's past, we conclude that the public interest favoring the free dissemination of information regarding baseball's history far outweighs any proprietary interests at stake. Therefore, the trial court was correct to grant summary adjudication on this cause of action.

Gionfriddo v. Major League Baseball, 94 Cal. App. 4th 400 (Cal. Dist. Ct. App. 2001)

d. The Romantics recorded "What I Like About You" in 1979. The song was used in *Guitar Hero Encore: Rocks the 80's*. Although the song was licensed for the video game, no trademark of the Romantics or publicity rights in its members were obtained. To what extent does the performance of an individual create a sufficient identity that one's publicity rights have been exploited? See *Romantics v. Activision Publ'g, Inc.*, 574 F. Supp. 2d 758 (E.D. Mich. 2008).

e. The *Hart* Court quotes from *No Doubt v. Activision, Inc.*, 192 Cal. App. 4th 1018, 122 Cal. Rptr. 3d 397 (Cal. App. 2011), regarding a finding of violation of publicity rights. To what extent would this result have changed were the case not primarily for a breach of contract?

Problem XVIII-D

As described in Problem XVIII-C, Bryce has been collaborating with a video game publisher to produce a new interactive game based on the social life of a rock star. The game includes features for creating bands, touring, performing, and initiating bar fights. In both the *Teen* and *Mature* versions of the game, it uses fictional bands and music created and recorded by Bryce.

Bryce and the other producers would like to incorporate music written by additional artists and incorporate famous bands into the game play. In particular, one of the producers believes that bands that have famously split up would be particular fun to incorporate into the game play and suggests that fair use would allow the game to use the Beach Boys, the Beatles, and other famously disbanded groups. Please identify the elements of the game that require licenses and advise Bryce the extent to which the game producers may rely on fair use for the game play.

E. Contract Issues for Consumers

Clickwrap, Shrinkwrap, TOS, and EULA

Clickwrap and shrinkwrap agreements are a method of securing an agreement with the end-user of a particular piece of software, including video games, requiring the user to comply with certain terms in using the software. Shrinkwrap agreements often take the form of a notice on the packaging of a particular software title, which puts a purchaser on notice that there are additional terms that must be complied with to use the software, terms which are usually included inside the product packaging. Browsewrap is the term used to describe such provisions when they are posted as links on a website. Typically, a website's privacy policy or copyright infringement policy are made accessible by use of a footer on the bottom of the website page. Shrinkwrap and browsewrap do not have any physical manifestation of assent.

Clickwrap agreements provide all the material terms of the contract in a page that requires the consumer to check a box or click on an "I agree" button as a condition to accessing the content of the game or website. In this way, the transaction guarantees the consumer has had access to the terms of the agreement and has manifested consent through some physical conduct. These contracts are generally referred to as "Terms of Service Agreements" (TOS) or "End User License Agreements" (EULA). Issues arising as to the enforceability of such agreements are essentially matters of contract law; therefore, the application of law and enforceability questions can vary considerably from jurisdiction to jurisdiction applying the applicable state law.

Courts have held clickwrap and shrinkwrap agreements enforceable on varied grounds. Some have found that the clickwrap or shrinkwrap agreement provided sufficient notice of additional terms that were required to use that particular piece of software. The leading case upholding clickwrap and shrinkwrap agreements is *ProCD, Inc. v. Zeidenberg*, 86 F.3d 1447 (7th. Cir. 1997), where the court found that the shrinkwrap notice on the packaging provided sufficient notice of additional terms within the package and software that required compliance for usage. In *Davidson & Assocs. v. Jung*, 422 F.3d 630 (8th Cir. 2005), the Eight Circuit upheld a TOS and EULA to stop unauthorized game reproduction as well as reverse engineering of World of Warcraft.

Beyond recognizing the existence of a contract, however, courts will also look to the substance of the transaction, as discussed in the following opinion.

Bragg v. Linden Research, Inc.
487 F. Supp. 2d 593 (E.D. Pa. 2007)

This case is about virtual property maintained on a virtual world on the Internet. Plaintiff, March Bragg, Esq., claims an ownership interest in such virtual property. Bragg contends that Defendants, the operators of the virtual world, unlawfully confiscated his virtual property and denied him access to their virtual world. Ultimately at issue in this case are the novel questions of what rights and obligations grow out of the relationship between the owner and creator of a virtual world and its resident-customers. While the property and the world where it is found are "virtual," the dispute is real. . . .

A. Second Life

The defendants in this case, Linden Research Inc. ("Linden") and its Chief Executive Officer, Philip Rosedale, operate a multiplayer role-playing game set in the virtual world[22] known as "Second Life." Participants create avatars[23] to represent themselves, and Second Life is populated by hundreds of thousands of avatars, whose interactions with one another are limited only by the human imagination. According to Plaintiff, many people "are now living large portions of their lives, forming friendships with others, building and acquiring virtual property, forming contracts, substantial business relationships and forming social organizations" in virtual worlds such as Second Life. Owning property in and having access to this virtual world is, moreover, apparently important to the plaintiff in this case.

B. Recognition of Property Rights

In November 2003, Linden announced that it would recognize participants' full intellectual property protection for the digital content they created or otherwise owned in Second Life. As a result, Second Life avatars may now buy, own, and sell virtual goods ranging "from cars to homes to slot machines."[24] Most significantly for this case, avatars may purchase "virtual land," make improvements to that land, exclude other avatars from entering onto the land, rent the land, or sell the land to other avatars for a profit. Assertedly, by recognizing virtual property rights, Linden would distinguish itself from other virtual worlds available on the Internet and thus increase participation in Second Life.

Defendant Rosedale personally joined in efforts to publicize Linden's recognition of rights to virtual property. For example, in 2003, Rosedale stated in a press release made available on Second Life's website that:

> Until now, any content created by users for persistent state worlds, such as Everquest® or Star Wars Galaxies™, has essentially become the property of the company developing and hosting the world.... We believe our new policy recognizes the fact that persistent world users are making significant contributions to building these worlds and should be able to both own the content they create and share in the value that is created. The preservation of users' property rights is a necessary step toward the emergence of genuinely real online worlds.

Press Release, Linden Lab, Linden Lab Preserves Real World Intellectual Property Rights of Users of its Second Life Online Services (Nov. 14, 2003). After this initial announcement, Rosedale continued to personally hype the ownership of virtual property on Second Life.... Rosedale even created his own avatar and held virtual town hall meetings on Second Life where he made representations about the purchase of virtual land. Bragg "attended" such meetings and relied on the representations that Rosedale made therein.

---

22. The virtual world at issue is an interactive computer simulation which lets its participants see, hear, use, and even modify the simulated objects in the computer-generated environment. *See* Woodrow Barfield, *Intellectual Property Rights in Virtual Environments: Considering the Rights of Owners, Programmers and Virtual Avatars,* 39 Akron L. Rev. 649, 649 (2006) (defining virtual world).

23. The term "avatar" derives etymologically from the Sanskrit word for crossing down or descent and was used originally to refer to the earthly incarnation of a Hindu deity. Webster's II New Riverside University Dictionary 141 (1998). Since the advent of computers, however, "avatar" is also used to refer to an Internet user's virtual representation of herself in a computer game, in an Internet chat room, or in other Internet fora. *See* Wikipedia, Definition of Avatar, *available at* http://en.wikipedia.org.

24. Although participants purchase virtual property using the virtual currency of "lindens," lindens themselves are bought and sold for real U.S. dollars. Linden maintains a currency exchange that sets an exchange rate between lindens and U.S. dollars. Third parties, including ebay.com, also provide additional currency exchanges.

C. Plaintiffs' Participation in Second Life

In 2005, Plaintiff Marc Bragg, Esq., signed up and paid Linden to participate in Second Life. Bragg claims that he was induced into "investing" in virtual land by representations made by Linden and Rosedale in press releases, interviews, and through the Second Life website. Bragg also paid Linden real money as "tax" on his land. By April 2006, Bragg had not only purchased numerous parcels of land in his Second Life, he had also digitally crafted "fireworks" that he was able to sell to other avatars for a profit. Bragg also acquired other virtual items from other avatars.

The dispute ultimately at issue in this case arose on April 30, 2006, when Bragg acquired a parcel of virtual land named "Taessot" for $ 300. Linden sent Bragg an email advising him that [Taesot] had been improperly purchased through an "exploit." Linden took Taesot away. It then froze Bragg's account, effectively confiscating all of the virtual property and currency that he maintained on his account with Second Life.

Bragg brought suit against Linden and Rosedale in the Court of Common Pleas of Chester County, Pennsylvania, on October 3, 2006.[25] Linden and Rosedale removed the case to this Court and then, within a week, moved to compel arbitration....

Defendants ... filed a motion to compel arbitration that seeks to dismiss this action and compel Bragg to submit his claims to arbitration according to the Rules of the International Chamber of Commerce ("ICC") in San Francisco.

A. *Relevant Facts*

Before a person is permitted to participate in Second Life, she must accept the Terms of Service of Second Life (the "TOS") by clicking a button indicating acceptance of the TOS. Bragg concedes that he clicked the "accept" button before accessing Second Life. Included in the TOS are a California choice of law provision, an arbitration provision, and forum selection clause. Specifically, located in the fourteenth line of the thirteenth paragraph under the heading "GENERAL PROVISIONS," and following provisions regarding the applicability of export and import laws to Second Life, the following language appears:

> Any dispute or claim arising out of or in connection with this Agreement or the performance, breach or termination thereof, shall be finally settled by binding arbitration in San Francisco, California under the Rules of Arbitration of the International Chamber of Commerce by three arbitrators appointed in accordance with said rules.... Notwithstanding the foregoing, either party may apply to any court of competent jurisdiction for injunctive relief or enforcement of this arbitration provision without breach of this arbitration provision.

...

1. Unconscionability of the Arbitration Agreement

Bragg resists enforcement of the TOS's arbitration provision on the basis that it is "both procedurally and substantively unconscionable and is itself evidence of defen-

---

25. Bragg's complaint contains counts under the Pennsylvania Unfair Trade Practices and Consumer Protection Law, 73 P.S. § 201-1, *et seq.* (Count I), the California Unfair and Deceptive Practices Act, Cal. Bus. & Prof. Code § 17200 (Count II), California Consumer Legal Remedies Act, Ca. Civ. Code § 1750, *et seq.* (Count III), fraud (Count IV), the California Civil Code § 1812.600, *et seq.* (Count V), conversion (Count VI), intentional interference with a contractual relations (Count VII), breach of contract (Count VIII), unjust enrichment (Count IX), and tortious breach of the covenant of good faith and fair dealing (Count X).

dants' scheme to deprive Plaintiff (and others) of both their money and their day in court."

Section 2 of the [Federal Arbitration Act] provides that written arbitration agreements "shall be valid, irrevocable, and enforceable, save upon such grounds as exist at law or in equity for the revocation of any contract." 9 U.S.C. §2. Thus, "generally applicable contract defenses, such as fraud, duress, or unconscionability, may be applied to invalidate arbitration agreements without contravening §2." Doctor's Assocs. v. Casarotto, 517 U.S. 681, 687, 116 S. Ct. 1652, 134 L. Ed. 2d 902 (1996) (citations omitted). When determining whether such defenses might apply to any purported agreement to arbitrate the dispute in question, "courts generally ... should apply ordinary state-law principles that govern the formation of contracts." First Options of Chicago, Inc. v. Kaplan, 514 U.S. 938, 944 (1995). Thus, the Court will apply California state law to determine whether the arbitration provision is unconscionable.

Under California law, unconscionability has both procedural and substantive components. The procedural component can be satisfied by showing (1) oppression through the existence of unequal bargaining positions or (2) surprise through hidden terms common in the context of adhesion contracts. The substantive component can be satisfied by showing overly harsh or one-sided results that "shock the conscience." The two elements operate on a sliding scale such that the more significant one is, the less significant the other need be. However, a claim of unconscionability cannot be determined merely by examining the face of the contract; there must be an inquiry into the circumstances under which the contract was executed, and the contract's purpose, and effect.

(a) Procedural Unconscionability

A contract or clause is procedurally unconscionable if it is a contract of adhesion. A contract of adhesion, in turn, is a "standardized contract, which, imposed and drafted by the party of superior bargaining strength, relegates to the subscribing party only the opportunity to adhere to the contract or reject it." Comb v. PayPal, Inc., 218 F. Supp. 2d 1165, 1172 (N.D. Cal. 2002). Under California law, "the critical factor in procedural unconscionability analysis is the manner in which the contract or the disputed clause was presented and negotiated." Nagrampa v. MailCoups, Inc., 469 F.3d 1257, 1282 (9th Cir. 2006). "When the weaker party is presented the clause and told to 'take it or leave it' without the opportunity for meaningful negotiation, oppression, and therefore procedural unconscionability, are present." Id. (internal quotation and citation omitted).

The TOS are a contract of adhesion. Linden presents the TOS on a take-it-or-leave-it basis. A potential participant can either click "assent" to the TOS, and then gain entrance to Second Life's virtual world, or refuse assent and be denied access. Linden also clearly has superior bargaining strength over Bragg. Although Bragg is an experienced attorney, who believes he is expert enough to comment on numerous industry standards and the "rights" or participants in virtual worlds, he was never presented with an opportunity to use his experience and lawyering skills to negotiate terms different from the TOS that Linden offered.

Moreover, there was no "reasonably available market alternatives [to defeat] a claim of adhesiveness." ... The procedural element of unconscionability also "focuses on ... surprise." Gutierrez v. Autowest, Inc., 114 Cal. App. 4th 77 (Ct. App. 2003) (citations omitted). In determining whether surprise exists, California courts focus not on the plaintiff's subjective reading of the contract, but rather, more objectively, on "the extent to which the supposedly agreed-upon terms of the bargain are hidden in the prolix printed form drafted by the party seeking to enforce the disputed terms." Id. In Gutierrez, the court found such surprise where an arbitration clause was "particularly inconspicuous, printed in eight-point typeface on the opposite side of the signature page of the lease." Id.

Here, although the TOS are ubiquitous throughout Second Life, Linden buried the TOS's arbitration provision in a lengthy paragraph under the benign heading "GENERAL PROVISIONS." See TOS P 13.

Comb is most instructive. In that case, the plaintiffs challenged an arbitration provision that was part of an agreement to which they had assented, in circumstances similar to this case, by clicking their assent on an online application page. The defendant, PayPal, was a large company with millions of individual online customers. The plaintiffs, with one exception, were all individual customers of PayPal. Given the small amount of the average transaction with PayPal, the fact that most PayPal customers were private individuals, and that there was a "dispute as to whether PayPal's competitors offer their services without requiring customers to enter into arbitration agreements," the court concluded that the user agreement at issue "satisfie[d] the criteria for procedural unconscionability under California law." Id. at 1172–73. Here, as in Comb, procedural unconscionability is satisfied.

(b) Substantive Unconscionability

Even if an agreement is procedurally unconscionable, "it may nonetheless be enforceable if the substantive terms are reasonable." Substantive unconscionability focuses on the one-sidedness of the contract terms. Here, a number of the TOS's elements lead the Court to conclude that Bragg has demonstrated that the TOS are substantively unconscionable.

(i) Mutuality

Under California law, substantive unconscionability has been found where an arbitration provision forces the weaker party to arbitrate claims but permits a choice of forums for the stronger party. In other words, the arbitration remedy must contain a "modicum of bilaterality." This principle has been extended to arbitration provisions that allow the stronger party a range of remedies before arbitrating a dispute, such as self-help, while relegating to the weaker party the sole remedy of arbitration.

In Comb, for example, the court found a lack of mutuality where the user agreement allowed PayPal "at its sole discretion" to restrict accounts, withhold funds, undertake its own investigation of a customer's financial records, close accounts, and procure ownership of all funds in dispute unless and until the customer is "later determined to be entitled to the funds in dispute." 218 F. Supp. 2d at 1173–74. Also significant was the fact that the user agreement was "subject to change by PayPal without prior notice (unless prior notice is required by law), by posting of the revised Agreement on the PayPal website." Id.

Here, the TOS contain many of the same elements that made the PayPal user agreement substantively unconscionable for lack of mutuality. The TOS proclaim that "Linden has the right at any time for any reason or no reason to suspend or terminate your Account, terminate this Agreement, and/or refuse any and all current or future use of the Service without notice or liability to you." TOS P 7.1. Whether or not a customer has breached the Agreement is "determined in Linden's sole discretion." Id. Linden also reserves the right to return no money at all based on mere "suspicions of fraud" or other violations of law. Id. Finally, the TOS state that "Linden may amend this Agreement ...

at any time in its sole discretion by posting the amended Agreement [on its website]." TOS P 1.2.

In effect, the TOS provide Linden with a variety of one-sided remedies to resolve disputes, while forcing its customers to arbitrate any disputes with Linden. This is precisely what occurred here. When a dispute arose, Linden exercised its option to use self-help by freezing Bragg's account, retaining funds that Linden alone determined were subject to dispute, and then telling Bragg that he could resolve the dispute by initiating a costly arbitration process. The TOS expressly authorized Linden to engage in such unilateral conduct. As in Comb, "[f]or all practical purposes, a customer may resolve disputes only after [Linden] has had control of the disputed funds for an indefinite period of time," and may only resolve those disputes by initiating arbitration. 218 F. Supp. 2d at 1175.

Linden's right to modify the arbitration clause is also significant. "The effect of [Linden's] unilateral right to modify the arbitration clause is that it could ... craft precisely the sort of asymmetrical arbitration agreement that is prohibited under California law as unconscionable. This lack of mutuality supports a finding of substantive unconscionability.

[The court then reviewed the costs and fee-splitting provisions, determining that Bragg would have to advance $3,750 to $8,625 at the outset, but the expenses could reach as high as $13,687.50. The high cost, in relation to the claim support the finding of unconscionability. Similarly, the court found the forum selection clause requiring travel to San Francisco "appears to be yet one more means by which the arbitration clause serves to shield [Linden] from liability instead of providing a neutral forum in which to arbitrate disputes." Quoting Comb.]

Arbitration before the ICC, pursuant to the TOS, must be kept confidential pursuant to the ICC rules. See ICC Rules at 33. Applying California law to an arbitration provision, the Ninth Circuit held that such confidentiality supports a finding that an arbitration clause was substantively unconscionable. The Ninth Circuit reasoned that if the company succeeds in imposing a gag order on arbitration proceedings, it places itself in a far superior legal posture by ensuring that none of its potential opponents have access to precedent while, at the same time, the company accumulates a wealth of knowledge on how to negotiate the terms of its own unilaterally crafted contract. The unavailability of arbitral decisions could also prevent potential plaintiffs from obtaining the information needed to build a case of intentional misconduct against a company....

This does not mean that confidentiality provisions in an arbitration scheme or agreement are, in every instance, per se unconscionable under California law. Here, however, taken together with other provisions of the TOS, the confidentiality provision gives rise for concern of the conscionability of the arbitration clause. Thus, the confidentiality of the arbitration scheme that Linden imposed also supports a finding that the arbitration clause is unconscionable....

(c) Conclusion

When a dispute arises in Second Life, Linden is not obligated to initiate arbitration. Rather, the TOS expressly allow Linden, at its "sole discretion" and based on mere "suspicion," to unilaterally freeze a participant's account, refuse access to the virtual and real currency contained within that account, and then confiscate the participant's virtual property and real estate. A participant wishing to resolve any dispute, on the other hand, after having forfeited its interest in Second Life, must then initiate arbitration in Linden's place of business. To initiate arbitration involves advancing fees to pay for no less than three arbitrators at a cost far greater than would be involved in litigating in the state or federal court system. Moreover, under these circumstances, the confidentiality of the proceedings helps ensure that arbitration itself is fought on an uneven field by ensuring that, through the accumulation of experience, Linden becomes an expert in litigating the terms of the TOS, while plaintiffs remain novices without the benefit of learning from past precedent.

Taken together, the lack of mutuality, the costs of arbitration, the forum selection clause, and the confidentiality provision that Linden unilaterally imposes through the TOS demonstrate that the arbitration clause is not designed to provide Second Life participants an effective means of resolving disputes with Linden. Rather, it is a one-sided means which tilts unfairly, in almost all situations, in Linden's favor. As in *Comb*, through the use of an arbitration clause, Linden "appears to be attempting to insulate itself contractually from any meaningful challenge to its alleged practices." 218 F. Supp. 2d at 1176.

The Court notes that the concerns with procedural unconscionability are somewhat mitigated by Bragg's being an experienced attorney. However, "because the unilateral modification clause renders the arbitration provision severely one-sided in the substantive dimension, even moderate procedural unconscionability renders the arbitration agreement unenforceable." *Net Global Mktg.*, 217 Fed. Appx. 598, 2007 U.S. App. LEXIS 674, at *9 (9th Cir. Jan. 9, 2007) (internal citations omitted).

Finding that the arbitration clause is procedurally and substantively unconscionable, the Court will refuse to enforce it.

Notes and Questions

a. The state court interpretation of clickwrap agreements vary. Not all have enforced the provisions, particularly of browsewrap or shrinkwrap agreements which do not include some manifestation of assent by the consumer. Compare *Snap-On Bus. Solutions Inc. v. O'Neil & Assocs.*, 2010 U.S. Dist. LEXIS 37688 (N.D. Ohio Apr. 16, 2010), with *Specht v. Netscape Communs. Corp.*, 306 F.3d 17 (2d Cir. 2002).

b. The highly popular *World of Warcraft* computer game has had difficulty protecting the game play from automated player enhancements that allow users to gain unfair advantage in the game and distort the internal gaming economies. MDY Industries, Inc. created a "bot" software program, Glider, that automated play for gamers away from their computers. Is the software client on the player's computer sufficient to constitute a technological measure that is protected by copyright? If so, then automated game programs can be barred as infringing the DMCA anti-circumvention provisions of the Copyright Act. See *MDY Indus., LLC v. Blizzard Entm't, Inc.*, 616 F. Supp. 2d 958 (D. Ariz. 2009).

c. The Copyright Act provides the exclusive source of protection for "all legal and equitable rights that are equivalent to any of the exclusive rights within the general scope of copyright...." See 17 U.S.C. § 301(a). To what extent does copyright law preempt the enforceability of clickwrap agreements? Compare *Davidson & Assocs. v. Jung*, 422 F.3d 630 (8th Cir. 2005), with *Vault v. Quaid Software Ltd.*, 847 F.2d 255, 268–70 (5th Cir. 1988).

Problem XVIII-E

As described in Problem XVIII-C, Bryce has been collaborating with a video game publisher to produce a new interactive game based on the social life of a rock star. The game includes features for creating bands, touring, performing, and initiating bar fights.

In both the *Teen* and *Mature* versions of the game, it uses fictional bands and music created and recorded by Bryce. To deal with the issues involved with the use of the game, draft an appropriate Terms of Service or End User License Agreement to protect the producers and users of the game, as well as to set forth sufficient limits on the users to allow the licensing of content necessary to create the game.

F. Bibliography and Links

Greg Lastowka, Virtual Justice — The New Laws of Online Worlds 10 (2010).

Beth A. Cianfrone & Thomas A. Baker III, *The Use of Student-Athlete Likenesses in Sport Video Games: An Application of the Right of Publicity*, 20 J. Legal Aspects of Sport 35 (2010).

Thomas F. Cotter & Irina Y. Dmitrieva, *Integrating the Right of Publicity with First Amendment and Copyright Preemption Analysis*, 33 Colum. J.L. & Arts 165 (2010).

Marc Edelman, *Closing the "Free Speech" Loophole: The Case for Protecting College Athletes' Publicity Rights in Commercial Video Games*, 65 Fla. L. Rev. 553, 554 (2013).

Joshua A.T. Fairfield, *The God Paradox*, 89 B.U.L. Rev. 1017 (2009).

William K. Ford & Raizel Liebler, *Games Are Not Coffee Mugs: Games and the Right of Publicity*, 29 Santa Clara Computer & High Tech. L.J. 1, 3 (2013).

Jon M. Garon, *Publicity Rights in Entertainment: From Second-Life to the Afterlife: Playing in the Virtual Arena: Avatars, Publicity, and Identity Reconceptualized through Virtual Worlds and Computer Games*, 11 Chap. L. Rev. 465 (2008).

James Grimmelmann, *Saving Facebook*, 94 Iowa L. Rev. 1137 (2009).

Margit Livingston, *Piggybacking on Glory*, 66 Fla. L. Rev. F. 1 (2013).

William McGeveran, *Disclosure, Endorsement, and Identity in Social Marketing*, 2009 U. Ill. L. Rev. 1105 (2009).

Salil K. Mehra, *Paradise Is a Walled Garden? Trust, Antitrust, and User Dynamism*, 18 Geo. Mason L. Rev. 889 (2011).

Raymond T. Nimmer, *Information Wars and the Challenges of Content Protection in Digital Contexts*, 13 Vand. J. Ent. & Tech. L. 825 (2011).

Lorelei Ritchie, *Reconciling Contract Doctrine with Intellectual Property Law: An Interdisciplinary Solution*, 25 Santa Clara Computer & High Tech. L.J. 105 (2008).

Elizabeth L. Rosenblatt, *Rethinking the Parameters of Trademark Use in Entertainment*, 61 Fla. L. Rev. 1011 (2009).

Robert Sprague, *Carl A. Warns, Jr. Labor & Employment Law Institute: Invasion of the Social Networks: Blurring the Line between Personal Life and the Employment Relationship*, 50 U. Louisville L. Rev. 1 (2011).

Websites

Berkman Center for Internet and Society, http://cyber.law.harvard.edu/

Electronic Frontier Foundation, http://www.eff.org/

Engadget, http://www.engadget.com/

G4, http://g4tv.com/

Game Zone, http://www.gamezone.com

Pew Research Center's Internet & American Life Project, http://www.pewinternet.org/

Wired, http://www.wired.com/

G. Epilogue

The battle over the publication of *Exposure* grew as Bryce began to write letters to the editor decrying the censorship by the subjects of the book. Bryce also maintained a website about the controversy surrounding the book that grew in popularity.

Eventually the book was published with only five of the exposés removed. Out of sheer spite, Bryce and Jesse added a very unflattering exposé of the publisher's attorney. Although the attorney had planned to sue, she found that she had assigned her copyright and publicity rights to her employer under the terms of the employee handbook she had helped author.

Bryce followed up the publication of *Exposure* with a stage musical tribute to the book and the tribulations of getting it into print. *Exposure — The Musical* is scheduled to premiere at the State Theatre and then move to an Off-Broadway venue for an indefinite run. Bryce has also arranged to cut a cast album, to film a making-of DVD, and to option the film rights to the musical.

Bryce calls you for advice. Evidently, the city council is upset because two of the photographs in the book were of nudes. To celebrate these photographs, Bryce has written a production number entitled "Warm Your Hands Before You Shoot." The city council is not amused and has told the State Theatre officials to cancel the production.

Bryce wants advice.

Seems like old times.

Index